VISIONS: THE CANADIAN HISTORY MODULES PROJECT

Pre-Confederation

Second Edition

Editorial Board:

P.E. Bryden
University of Victoria

Maureen Lux
Brock University

Daniel Samson
Brock University

Colin Coates
Glendon College, York University

Marcel Martel
York University

Lynne Marks
University of Victoria

NELSON EDUCATION

NELSON
EDUCATION

**Visions: The Canadian History Modules Project,
Pre-Confederation, Second Edition**

by P.E. Bryden, Colin M. Coates, Maureen Lux,
Lynne Marks, Marcel Martel, Daniel Samson

**Vice President, Editorial
Higher Education:**
Anne Williams

Acquisitions Editor:
Mark Grzeskowiak

Executive Marketing Manager:
Amanda Henry

Senior Developmental Editor:
Linda Sparks

**Photo Researchers/
Permissions Coordinators:**
Nicola Winstanley, Julie Pratt,
Kristiina Paul

Production Project Manager:
Christine Gilbert

Copy Editors:
Karen Rolfe, Kelli Howey,
Wendy Yano, Rodney Rawlings

Proofreader:
MPS Limited

Design Director:
Ken Phipps

Managing Designer:
Franca Amore

Interior Design:
Greg Devitt/Peggy Rhodes

Cover Design:
Martyn Schmoll

Cover Image:
From top to bottom: Portrait d'une
femme Mi'kmaq, Viscountess
Falkland Album, Library and
Archives Canada, item 2898106;
McCord Museum M4777.6; Library
and Archives Canada, Acc. No.
1983-47-21; Copyright: expired.

Compositor:
MPS Limited

**Library and Archives Canada
Cataloguing in Publication**

Visions (2015)
      Visions : the Canadian
history modules project :
pre-confederation / editorial
board: P.E. Bryden (University of
Victoria), Maureen Lux (Brock
University), Marcel Martel (York
University), Colin Coates (Glendon
College, York University), Lynne
Marks (University of Victoria),
Daniel Samson (Brock University).
— Second edition.

Includes bibliographical
references.
ISBN 978-0-17-666939-3 (pbk.)

      1. Canada—History—To
1763 (New France)—Textbooks.
2. Canada—History—1763–1867—
Textbooks. I. Coates, Colin
MacMillan, 1960–, editor II. Lux,
Maureen K. (Maureen Katherine),
1956–, editor III. Marks, Lynne
Sorrel, 1960–, editor IV. Bryden,
Penny, editor V. Martel, Marcel,
1965–, editor VI. Samson, Daniel,
1960–, editor VII. Title.

FC161.V57 2015   971.04
C2014-906651-1

ISBN-13: 978-0-17-666939-3
ISBN-10: 0-17-666939-6

TABLE OF CONTENTS

● INTRODUCTION

The past is a foreign country; they do things differently there.
—*The Go-Between*, L.P. Hartley (1953)

As editors and authors of the *Visions: The Canadian History Modules Project*, we have remained true to the key objectives of this resource, first published in 2010. Those objectives are to provide introductory Canadian history students with a solid foundation for learning how to think like a historian in the context of their introductory Canadian history course, and to allow instructors to be able to choose among a variety of teaching topics set within a common pedagogical framework that will support their students in their aim to become more sophisticated historical thinkers.

Each of the modules is designed to introduce a topic or key question that is commonly taught in introductory Canadian history classes. The short introductions set the basic context for the topic and draw attention to major historiographical themes and issues that have emerged as historians have studied it. They also attempt to show the interplay between the primary and secondary sources and illustrate how historians have used a wide variety of evidence to create their picture of the past. It is important for the students to note, however, that these introductions are merely starting points. Their job is to connect the material in the modules to the course lectures and core textbooks. A set of questions at the end of the introduction presents the framework for thinking critically about the material that follows. Each module contains a selection of primary sources from a broad range of materials, including government documents, diary entries and private letters, contemporary newspapers, and oral history interviews, as well as visual evidence in the form of maps, paintings, illustrations, and cartoons. Finally, a selection of secondary sources, the work of professional historians, foregrounds both the ways in which historians construct a narrative about the past and gives students insights into the differing ways in which evidence can be used.

The use of primary sources in conjunction with secondary sources is an essential component in the postsecondary study of history. To use an analogy, if the textbook for the course tells the overarching story of the history of Canada, the readings presented in these modules provide the rich detail that flesh out particular aspects of that story. They add the details that sensitize students to other viewpoints, other experiences, and other worldviews. If the past is indeed a foreign country, as Hartley said, then these modules are meant to give us an introduction to the tools to understand the assumptions, priorities, culture, and experience of people who lived 20 years ago or 200 years ago.

Learning to approach source material in a careful and nuanced way not only enhances students' ability to think critically, but also helps lower the barriers between the past and the present. It is important to apply these same critical approaches not only to the primary sources, but also to the secondary material. Historical actors are not the only ones influenced by the times in which they live. By showcasing different interpretations of evidence, we hope to help students realize that the past is not a set narrative, but rather that history is an argument created by historians based on how they choose and interpret the available evidence. Just as there are arguments today about issues such as climate change and how to interpret the scientific evidence for human impacts on climate, there are arguments among historians regarding a wide array of issues, from what Confederation meant to whether or not Canadians in the late nineteenth century experienced the secularization of their society.

As the *Visions: The Canadian History Modules Project* grows, we will contiue to carefully select material that meets rigorous criteria of readability, significance, and variety. We will include modules that cover a variety of approaches—social, political, environmental, religious, and so on—and a wide geographical range. Our project was conceived from the start as a living, growing database, and we have therefore had the luxury of knowing that topics we were unable to cover in earlier releases could be added as the project unfolds. Our original call to instructors using this learning resource stands—if you don't see what you need for your students, please join us!

> Mark Grzeskowiak (Acquisitions Editor, History)
> P.E. Bryden (University of Victoria)
> Colin Coates (Glendon College, York University)
> Maureen Lux (Brock University)
> Lynne Marks (University of Victoria)
> Marcel Martel (York University)
> Daniel Samson (Brock University)

v

CONTACT ZONES FROM THE SIXTEENTH TO EIGHTEENTH CENTURY

How Did Aboriginal People Perceive European Newcomers?

Colin Coates
Glendon College, York University

CONTACT ZONES FROM THE SIXTEENTH TO EIGHTEENTH CENTURY: HOW DID ABORIGINAL PEOPLE PERCEIVE EUROPEAN NEWCOMERS?

● **Introduction by Colin Coates**

3

●INTRODUCTION

Colin Coates

The encounter between Aboriginal peoples in North America and European newcomers changed the lives of people on both continents. While some aspects of this meeting were clearly very negative for Aboriginal peoples, they were not merely the passive victims of European expansion. European newcomers did not dominate Aboriginal peoples from the moment of first encounter. Rather, both groups influenced each other a great deal, and for many decades the Europeans relied on Aboriginal peoples for food and medicine. After all, the fate of the short-lived Viking settlement at L'Anse aux Meadows in northern Newfoundland around the year 1000 indicates that Europeans were not necessarily destined to flourish in the New World. By the sixteenth century, when Europeans returned to this part of the continent, they certainly enjoyed a degree of technological advantage in specific areas such as gunpowder and ships. Still, Aboriginal peoples were clearly better adapted to their terrain and climate.

Moreover, Aboriginal peoples had long experience adjusting to political and economic circumstances. The overview article by Neal Salisbury covers a variety of Aboriginal nations, showing the importance of considering the historical processes underway before the arrival of Europeans. This history of change helps us understand the nature of the contact experience. He also makes the point that the current national boundaries between Canada and the United States are irrelevant to our understanding of the early contact between Aboriginal peoples and Europeans.

One of the earliest records of the encounter of French and Aboriginal peoples is Jacques Cartier's (1491–1557) account of his voyage. But his account may not represent the first time the peoples met. When Cartier came upon Iroquoians at the Gaspé coast in 1535, they were eager to trade with him, an incident that suggests that they had established customs of trading with people who arrived on large sailing ships. Ramsay Cook's article on the extended encounter between the Iroquoians and Cartier and his men shows that not only did the French explorer "discover" North American Aboriginal society, but also the Iroquoians likewise discovered many aspects of European society. The Aboriginals, Cook argues, were not likely impressed. Likewise Cornelius Jaenen reminds us that, in this context, the French were "the other," and that it is important to try to understand Aboriginal attitudes toward the European newcomers. Aboriginal perspectives were not necessarily flattering. The material recorded by French missionary Chrestien Le Clercq (circa 1677) describes the negative Aboriginal attitudes toward many features of French society.

While Aboriginal peoples had many reasons to be wary of the newcomers, a few Europeans demonstrated some sympathy for and understanding of Aboriginal society. Indeed, Cartier and Samuel de Champlain (1567–1635) had visited other parts of the New World before coming to what is now Canada. Champlain in particular developed a broad and complex understanding of Aboriginal society. David Hackett Fisher's recent biography of Champlain argues that the French explorer developed a strikingly enlightened attitude toward Aboriginal society in New France.

In some circles, the exchanges between Aboriginal peoples and Europeans allowed for a new cultural critique to develop within European society. Europeans from the fifteenth to the eighteenth centuries undertook many voyages of exploration around the globe and saw many different societies and customs. One of the images that developed out of these encounters was the "noble savage." This personage exhibited great moral strength while living under more rudimentary conditions than most Europeans. One of the classic texts of this genre, Michel de Montaigne's famous essay, "Des Cannibales" (1580), provides a scathing comparison between contemporary French society and Aboriginal society in contemporary Brazil (at least as far as he understood it). Even though he failed to grasp many features of that Aboriginal society, de Montaigne showed how the Aboriginal peoples' moral code often surpassed that of their French contemporaries.

Another important contribution to the image of the "noble savage" is contained in the works of Baron Louis-Armand de Lom d'Ares Lahontan (1666–1715), a French military official who lived in New France in the late seventeenth century. He provided an influential account of the morality of Aboriginal life in his fictional dialogue between himself and the Iroquois leader Adario. Through this text, which contributed to changing the ways that Europeans understood Aboriginal society, Lahontan uses the literary device of portraying himself as gullible and unable to convince Adario of the virtues of French society. Adario, in contrast, provides a much more convincing account of the superiority of his way of life. Lahontan's work proved to be a significant influence on later Enlightenment thinkers in France. The Enlightenment concept of the "noble savage," while not necessarily doing justice to the complexities and subtleties of Aboriginal life in the New World, created a new image and changed European attitudes about the malleability of human nature.

The "first" encounters occurred over a long time period given the geographical expanse of the continent. The French and later the British slowly extended their reach toward the west, meeting different Aboriginal groups. Because the Rocky Mountains form such a formidable geographical barrier, relations with Aboriginal peoples on the West Coast of what is now Canada were not established until the late eighteenth century, almost 250 years after Cartier's arrival. The earliest newcomers were not always the same mix of British and French explorers. On the British Columbian coast, Russians and the Spanish arrived at the same time as the British. The excerpt from the oral history of the Squamish nation who live near present-day Vancouver deals with the arrival of the first British ship on their shore. It reminds us that "first contact" between Europeans and Aboriginal peoples occurred much later on the West Coast. In all parts of North America, as in other parts of the world, the nature of the contact experience between different peoples was complex, and it led to significant changes in the world views of both sides.

QUESTIONS

1. In the first document, what criticisms did the Mi'kmaq present about the nature of French society in the New World? Would such attitudes have influenced the likelihood of their embracing Christianity?

2. Was the encounter of Aboriginal peoples and Europeans described in "Of Laws" a positive or negative experience for the two sides? Considering that this dialogue was written in the late seventeenth century, was the nature of the cultural interaction different from that for the earlier periods discussed in this section?

3. To what extent are Adario's attitudes about the relationship between the individual and the state similar to attitudes commonly held by North Americans today? Are Adario's or Lahontan's views more "modern?"

4. Evaluate the importance of the technological advances that Europeans enjoyed over Aboriginal peoples. How does the image from Samuel de Champlain's map reflect this technological advantage?

5. Compare the attitudes toward Europeans among the Mi'kmaq in the early seventeenth century and the Squamish in the late eighteenth century? How important are the large differences in time and space?

FURTHER READINGS

Olive Dickason and David McNabb, *Canada's First Nations: A History of Founding Peoples from Earliest Times* (Toronto: Oxford University Press, 2008).

Olive Dickason, *The Myth of the Savage* (Edmonton: University of Alberta Press, 1984)

David Hackett Fisher, *Champlain's Dream* (New York: Simon & Schuster, 2009)

John S. Lutz, ed., *Myth and Memory: Stories of Indigenous–European Contact* (Vancouver: UBC Press, 2007).

Bruce Trigger, *The Children of Aataentsic: A History of the Huron People to 1660* (Montreal: McGill-Queen's University Press, 1976).

Document 1: A Micmac Responds to the French

Chrestien LeClercq

Chrestien LeClercq was a Recollect missionary, who spent twelve years among the Mi'kmaq of the Gaspé peninsula (in present-day Quebec). Having learnt their language, he provides in this excerpt their response to some features of French society.

[…] the Indians esteem their camps as much as, and even more than, they do the most superb and commodious of our houses. To this they testified one day to some of our gentlemen of Isle Percée, who, having asked me to serve them as interpreter in a visit which they wished to make to these Indians in order to make the latter understand that it would be very much more advantageous for them to live and to build in our fashion, were extremely surprised when the leading Indian, who had listened with great patience to everything I had said to him on behalf of these gentlemen, answered me in these words: "I am greatly astonished that the French have so little cleverness, as they seem to exhibit in the matter of which thou hast just told me on their behalf, in the effort to persuade us to convert our poles, our barks, and our wigwams into those houses of stone and of wood which are tall and lofty, according to their account, as these trees. Very well! But why now," continued he, "do men of five to six feet in height need houses which are sixty to eighty? For, in fact, as thou knowest very well thyself, Patriarch—do we not find in our own all the conveniences and the advantages that you have with yours, such as reposing, drinking, sleeping, eating, and amusing ourselves with our friends when we wish? This is not all," said he, addressing himself to one of our captains, "my brother, hast thou as much ingenuity and cleverness as the Indians, who carry their houses and their wigwams with them so that they may lodge wheresoever they please, independently of any seignior whatsoever? Thou art not as bold nor as stout as we, because when thou goest on a voyage thou canst not carry upon thy shoulders thy buildings and thy edifices. Therefore it is necessary that thou preparest as many lodgings as thou makest changes of residence, or else thou lodgest in a hired house which does not belong to thee. As for us, we find ourselves secure from all these inconveniences, as we can always say, more truly than thou, that we are at home everywhere, because we set up our wigwams with ease wheresoever we go, and without asking permission of anybody. Thou reproachest us, very inappropriately, that our country is a little hell in contrast with France, which thou comparest to a terrestrial paradise, inasmuch as it yields thee, so thou sayest, every kind of provision in abundance. Thou sayest of us also that we are the most miserable and most unhappy of all men, living without religion, without manners, without honour, without social order, and, in a word, without any rules, like the beasts in our woods and our forests, lacking bread, wine, and a thousand other comforts which thou hast in superfluity in Europe. Well, my brother, if thou dost not yet know the real feelings which our Indians have towards thy country and towards all thy nation, it is proper that I inform thee at once. I beg thee now to believe that, all miserable as we seem in thine eyes, we consider ourselves nevertheless much happier than thou in this, that we are very content with the little that we have; and believe also

7

Source: Chrestien LeClercq, "A Micmac Responds to the French" circa 1677, in *New Relation of Gaspesia with the customs and religion of the Gaspesian Indians*, ed. by W.F. Ganong (Toronto: Champlain Society, 1910), pp. 103–06.

once for all, I pray, that thou deceivest thyself greatly if thou thinkest to persuade us that thy country is better than ours. For if France, as thou sayest, is a little terrestrial paradise, art thou sensible to leave it? And why abandon wives, children, relatives, and friends? Why risk thy life and thy property every year, and why venture thyself with such risk, in any season whatsoever, to the storms and tempests of the sea in order to come to a strange and barbarous country which thou considerest the poorest and least fortunate of the world? Besides, since we are wholly convinced of the contrary, we scarcely take the trouble to go to France, because we fear, with good reason, lest we find little satisfaction there, seeing, in our own experience, that those who are natives thereof leave it every year in order to enrich themselves on our shores. We believe, further, that you are also incomparably poorer than we, and that you are only simple journeymen, valets, servants, and slaves, all masters and grand captains though you may appear, seeing that you glory in our old rags and in our miserable suits of beaver which can no longer be of use to us, that you find among us, in the fishery for cod which you make in these parts, the wherewithal to comfort your misery and the poverty which oppresses you. As to us, we find all our riches and all our conveniences among ourselves, without trouble and without exposing our lives to the dangers in which you find yourselves constantly through your long voyages. And, whilst feeling compassion for you in the sweetness of our repose, we wonder at the anxieties and cares which you give yourselves night and day in order to load your ship [with cod]. We see also that all your people live, as a rule, only upon cod which you catch among us. It is everlastingly nothing but cod—cod in the morning, cod at midday, cod at evening, and always cod, until things come to such a pass that if you wish some good morsels, it is at our expense; and you are obliged to have recourse to the Indians, whom you despise so much, and to beg them to go a-hunting that you may be regaled. Now tell me this one little thing, if thou hast any sense: Which of these two is the wisest and happiest—he who labours without ceasing and only obtains, and that with great trouble, enough to live on, or he who rests in comfort and finds all that he needs in the pleasure of hunting and fishing? It is true," added he, "that we have not always had the use of bread and of wine which your France produces; but, in fact, before the arrival of the French in these parts, did not the Gaspesians live much longer than now? And if we have not any longer among us any of those old men of a hundred and thirty to forty years, it is only because we are gradually adopting your manner of living, for experience is making it very plain that those of us live longest who, despising your bread, your wine, and your brandy, are content with their natural food of beaver, of moose, of waterfowl, and fish, in accord with the custom of our ancestors and of all the Gaspesian nation. Learn now, my brother, once for all, because I must open to thee my heart: there is no Indian who does not consider himself infinitely more happy and more powerful than the French." He finished his speech by the following last words, saying that an Indian could find his living everywhere, and that he could call himself the seigneur and the sovereign of his country, because he could reside there just as freely as it pleased him, with every kind of rights of hunting and fishing, without any anxiety, more content a thousand times in the woods and in his wigwam than if he were in palaces and at the tables of the greatest princes of the earth.

No matter what can be said of this reasoning, I assert, for my part, that I should consider these Indians incomparably more fortunate than ourselves, and that the life of these barbarians would even be capable of inspiring envy, if they had the instructions, the understanding, and the same means for their salvation which God has given us that we may save ourselves by preference over so many poor pagans, and as a result of His pity …

▲ Document 2: Of Laws

Baron de Lahontan

These selections show part of the fictitious dialogue between the Baron de Lahontan and the Huron chief Adario. Baron de Lahontan (1666–c. 1716) was a military officer stationed in North America in the late seventeenth century. Disaffected because of ill treatment by his superiors, he returned to Europe and wrote an account that helped create the image of the "noble savage" in European thought. While not entirely reflecting the reality of Aboriginal life or beliefs, the "noble savage" image suggested to European thinkers that humans who lived closer to a natural state enjoyed greater freedoms and lived more honourably than their European counterparts. Lahontan uses himself as a literary figure in this dialogue, and his words do not necessarily reflect his views; rather, they are used to reveal the wisdom of Adario's perspectives. The personage of Adario was patterned after the Huron chief Kondarionk (c. 1649–1701).

Note that these excerpts are from an early English-language translation of Lahontan's original French text. The spelling has been modified only slightly, and where necessary, in order to keep the flavour of the text.

Of Laws

Adario [...] let us therefore talk a little of what you call Laws; for you know that we have no such Word in our Language; tho' at the same time, I apprehend the force and importance of the Word, by virtue of the explication I had from you t'other day, together with the examples you mention'd, to make me conceive what you meant. Prithee tell me, are not Laws the same as just and reasonable Things? You say they are. Why then, to observe the Law, imports no more than to observe the measures of Reason and Justice: And at this rate you must take just and reasonable things in another sense than we do; or if you take 'em in the same sense. 'tis plain you never observe 'em.

Lahontan. These are fine Distinctions indeed, you please your self with idle Flams. Hast not thee the Sense to perceive, after twenty Years Conversation with the *French*, that what the *Hurons* call Reason is Reason among the *French*. 'Tis certain that all Men do not observe the Laws of Reason, for if they did there would be no occasion for Punishments, and those Judges thou hast seen at *Paris* and *Quebec* would be oblig'd to look out for another way of Living. But in regard that the good of the Society consists in doing Justice and following these Laws, there's a necessity of punishing the Wicked and rewarding the Good; for without that Precaution Murders, Robberies and Defamations would spread every where, and in a Word, we should be the most miserable People upon the Face of the Earth.

Adario. Nay, you are miserable enough already, and indeed I can't see how you can be more such. What sort of Men must the *Europeans* be? What Species of Creatures do they retain to? The *Europeans*, who must be forc'd to do Good, and have no other Prompter for the avoiding of Evil than the fear of Punishment. If I ask'd thee, what a Man is, thou wouldft answer me, *He's a Frenchman*, and yet I'll prove that your *Man* is rather a *Beaver*. For *Man* is not intitled to that Character upon the score of his walking upright upon two

Source: Lahontan, Baron Louis-Armand de Lom d'Ares, *New Voyages to North-America*, Vol. 2., Reuben Gold Thwaites, ed., (Chicago, IL: A.C. McClurg & Co., 1905), pp. 211 ff.

9

Legs, or of Reading and Writing, and shewing a Thousand other Instances of his Industry. I call that Creature a *Man*, that hath a natural inclination to do Good, and never entertains the thoughts of doing Evil. You see we have no Judges; and what's the reason of that? Why? We neither quarrel nor sue one another. And what's the reason that we have no Law Suits? Why? Because we are resolved neither to receive nor to know Silver. But why do we refuse admission to Silver among us? The reason is this: We are resolv'd to have no Laws, for since the World was a World our Ancestors liv'd happily without 'em. In fine, as I intimated before, the Word *Laws* does not signifie just and reasonable things as you use it, for the Rich make a Jest of 'em, and 'tis only the poor Wretches that pay any regard to 'em. But, pray, let's look into these *Laws*, or reasonable things, as you call 'em. For these Fifty Years, the Governors of *Canada* have still alledg'd that we are subject to the Laws of their great Captain. We content our selves in denying all manner of Dependance, excepting that upon the Great Spirit, as being born free and joint Brethren, who are all equally Masters: Whereas you are all Slaves to one Man. We do not put in any such Answer to you, as if the *French* depended upon us; and the reason of our silence upon that Head [topic] is, that we have no mind to Quarrel. But, pray tell me, what Authority or Right is the pretended Superiority of your great Captain grounded upon? Did we ever sell our selves to that great Captain? Were we ever in *France* to look after you? 'Tis you that came hither to find out us. Who gave you all the Countries that you now inhabit, by what Right do you possess 'em? They always belong'd to the *Algonkins* before. In earnest, my dear Brother, I'm sorry for thee from the bottom of my Soul. Take my advice, and turn *Huron;* for I see plainly a vast difference between thy Condition and mine. I am Master of my own Body, I have the absolute disposal of my self, I do what I please, I am the first and the last of my Nation, I fear no Man, and I depend only upon the Great Spirit: Whereas thy Body, as well as thy Soul, are doom'd to a dependance upon thy great Captain; thy Vice-Roy disposes of thee; thou hast not the liberty of doing what thou hast a mind to; thou'rt affraid of Robbers, false Witnesses, Assassins &c. and thou dependest upon an infinity of Persons whose Places have rais'd 'em above thee. Is it true, or not? Are these things either improbable or invisible? Ah! my dear Brother, thou seest plainly that I am in the right of it; and yet thou choosest rather to be a *French* Slave than a free *Huron*. What a fine Spark does a *Frenchman* make with his fine Laws, who taking himself to be mighty Wise is assuredly a great Fool; for as much as he continues in Slavery and a state of Dependence, while the very Brutes enjoy that adorable Liberty, and like us fear nothing but Foreign Enemies.

[....]

Adario. I'll tell thee one thing my dear Brother; I was a going one day from *Paris* to *Versailles*, and about half way, I met a Boor [peasant] that was going to be Whipt for having taken Partridges and Hares with Traps. Between *Rochel* [La Rochelle, in southwestern France, one of the main ports linking France and New France] and *Paris*, I saw another that was Condemn'd to the Gally's for having a little Bag of Salt about him. These poor Men were punish'd by your unjust Laws, for endeavouring to get Sustenance to their Families; at a time when a Million of Women were got with Child in the absence of their Husbands, when the Physicians Murder'd three fourths of the People, and the Gamesters reduc'd their Families to a Starving Condition, by losing all they had in the World; and all this with Impunity. If things go at this rate, where are your just and reasonable Laws; where are those Judges that have a Soul to be Sav'd as well as you and I? After this, you'll be ready to Brand the *Hurons* for Beasts. In earnest, we should have a fine time of it if we offer'd to punish one of our Brethren for killing a Hare or a Partridge; and a glorious sight 'twould be, to see our Wives inlarge the number of our Children, while we are ingag'd in Warlike Expeditions against our Enemies; to see Physicians Poison our Families, and Gamesters lose the Beaver Skins they've got in Hunting. In *France*, these things are look'd upon as trifles, which do not fall within the Verge of their fine Laws. Doubtless, they must needs be very blind, that are acquainted with us, and yet do not imitate our Example.

Laboutan. Very fine, my dear Friend; thou goest too fast; believe me, thy Knowledge is so confin'd, as I said before, that thy Mind can't reach beyond the appearances of things. Wouldst thou but give Ear to Reason, thou wouldst presently be sensible that we act upon good Principles, for the support of the Society. You must know, the Laws Condemn all without exception, that are guilty of the Actions you've mention'd. In the first place, they prohibit the Peasants to kill Hares or Partridges, especially in the Neighbourhood of *Paris;* by reason that an uncontroul'd liberty of Hunting, would quickly exhaust the whole Stock of those Animals. The Boors Farm the Grounds of their Landlords, who reserve to themselves the Priviledge of Hunting, as being Masters. Now, if they happen to kill Hares or Partridges, they not only rob their Masters of their Right, but fall under the Prohibition enacted by the Law: And the same is the Case of those who run Salt, by reason that the Right of Transporting it is solely lodg'd in the King. As to the Women and the Gamesters that you took notice of; you can't think sure that we'd shut 'em up in Prisons and Convents, and Condemn 'em to a perpetual Confinement. The Physicians 'twould be unjust to abuse, for of a hundred Patients they do not kill two; nay, on the contrary, they use their utmost efforts to Cure 'em. There's a necessity that Superannuated Persons, and those who are worn out, should put a Period to their Lives. And after all, tho' all of us have occasion to imploy Doctors, if 'twere prov'd that they had kill'd any Patient, either thro' Ignorance or Malice, the Law would not spare 'em no more than others.

Adario. Were these Laws observ'd, you would stand in need of a great many Prisons; but I see plainly that you do not speak all the truth, and that you're afraid of carrying the Thing farther, least my Reasons should put you to a stand. However, let's now cast our eyes upon those two Men who fled last year to *Quebec*, to avoid the being Burnt in *France*. If we look narrowly into their Crime, we'll find occasion to say, that *Europe* is pester'd with a great many foolish Laws.
[…]
Adario. The *French* in general take us for Beasts; the Jesuits Brand us for impious, foolish and ignorant Vagabonds. And to be even with you, we have the same thoughts of you; but with this difference, that *we* pity you without offering invectives. Pray hear me, my dear Brother, I speak calmly and without passion. The more I reflect up the lives of the *Europeans*, the less Wisdom and Happiness I find among 'em. These six years I have bent my thoughts upon the State of the *Europeans*: But I can't light on any thing in their Actions that is not beneath a Man; and truly I think 'tis impossible it should be otherwise, so long as you stick to the measures of *Meum* and *Tuum*. [That which belongs to me or you, i.e., private property] I affirm that what you call Silver is the Devil of Devils; the Tyrant of the *French*; the Source of all Evil; the Bane of Souls and the Slaughter-House of living Persons. To pretend to live in the Money Country, and at the same time to save one's Soul, is as great an inconsistency as for a Man to go to the bottom of a Lake to preserve his Life. This Money is the Father of Luxury, Lasciviousness, Intrigues, Tricks, Lying, Treachery, False-ness, and in a word, of all the mischief in the World. The Father sells his Children, Hus-bands expose their Wives to Sale, Wives betray their Husbands, Brethren kill one another, Friends are false, and all this proceeds from Money. Consider this, and then tell me if we are not in the right of it, in refusing to finger, or so much as to look upon that cursed Metal.

Lahontan. What! is it possible that you should always Reason so sorrily! Prithee, do but listen once in thy life time to what I am going to say. Dost not thou see, my dear Friend,

11

that the Nations of *Europe* could not live without Gold and Silver, or some such precious thing. Without that Symbol, the Gentlemen, the Priests, the Merchants, and an infinity of other Persons who have not Strength enough to labour the Earth, would die for Hunger. Upon that lay, our Kings would be no Kings: Nay, what Soldiers should we then have? Who would then Work for Kings or any body else, who would run the hazard of the Sea, who would make Arms unless 'twere for himself? Believe me, this would run us to remediless Ruine, 'twould turn *Europe* into a Chaos, and create the most dismal Confusion that Imagination it self can reach.

Adario. You fobb me off very prettily, truly, when you bring in your Gentlemen, your Merchants and your Priests. If you were Strangers to *Meum* and *Tuum*, those distinctions of Men would be sunk; a levelling equality would then take place among you as it now do's among the *Hurons.* For the first thirty years indeed, after the banishing of Interest, you would see a strange Desolation; those who are only qualify'd to eat, drink, sleep and divert themselves, would languish and die; but their Posterity would be fit for our way of living. I have set forth again and again, the qualities that make a Man inwardly such as he ought to be; particularly, Wisdom, Reason, Equity, &c. which are courted by the *Hurons.* I have made it appear that the Notion of separate Interests knocks all these Qualities in the Head, and that a Man sway'd by Interest can't be a Man of Reason. As for the outward Qualifications of a Man; he ought to be expert in Marching, Hunting, Fishing, Waging War, Ranging the Forests, Building Hutts and Canoes, Firing of Guns, Shooting of Arrows, Working Canoes: He ought to be Indefatigable, and able to live on short Commons upon occasion. In a word, he ought to know how to go about all the Exercises of the *Hurons.* Now in my way, 'tis the Person thus qualify'd that I call a *Man.* Do but consider, how many Millions there are in *Europe,* who, if they were left thirty Leagues off in the Forrests, and provided with Fusees [guns] and Arrows, would be equally at a loss, either to Hunt and maintain themselves, or to find their way out: And yet you see we traverse a hundred Leagues of Forrests without losing our way, that we kill Fowl and other Beasts with our Arrows, that we catch Fish in all the places where they are to be had; that we Dog both Men and Wild Beasts by their Footsteps, whether in Woods or in open Fields, in Summer or in Winter; that we live upon Roots when we lye before the Gates of the *Iroquese,* that we run like Hares, that we know how to use both the Axe and the Knife, and to make a great many useful things. Now since we are capable of such things, what should hinder you to do the same, when Interest is laid aside? Are not your Bodies as large, strong and brawny as ours? Are not your Artisans imploy'd in harder and more difficult Work than ours? If you liv'd after our manner, all of you would be equally Masters; your Riches would be of the same Stamp with ours, and consist in the purchasing of Glory by military Actions, and the taking of Slaves; for the more you took of them the less occasion you would have to Work: In a word, you would live as happily as we do.

Lahontan. Do you place a happy Life, in being oblig'd to lye under a pittiful Hutt of Bark, to Sleep under four sorry Coverlets of Beaver Skins, to Eat nothing but what you Boil and Roast, to be Cloath'd with Skins, to go a Beaver Hunting in the harshest Season of the Year, to run a hundred Leagues on Foot in pursuit of the *Iroquese,* thro' Marshes and thick Woods, the Trees of which are cut down so as to render 'em inaccessible! Do you think your selves happy when you venture out in little Canoes, and run the risk of being drown'd every foot in your Voyages upon the Great Lakes; when you lye upon the ground with the Heavens for your Canopy, upon approaching to the Villages of your Enemies; when you run with full Speed, both days and nights without eating or drinking, as being pursued by your Enemies; when you are sure of being reduc'd to the last extremity, if the *Coureurs de Bois* [independent French fur traders] did not out of Friendship, Charity and

Commiseration, supply you with Fire-Arms, Powder, Lead, Thread for Nets, Axes, Knives, Needles, Awls, Fishing-Hooks, Ketties, and several other Commodities?

Adario. Very fine, come, don't let's go so fast; the day is long, and we may talk one after the other at our own leisure. It seems you take all these things to be great hardships; and indeed I own they would be such to the *French*, who like Beasts, love only to eat and to drink, and have been brought up to Softness and Effeminacy. Prithee, tell me what difference there is between lying in a good Hutt, and lying in a Palace; between Sleeping under a Cover of Beaver-Skins, and Sleeping under a Quilt between two Sheets; between Eating Boil'd and Roast Meat, and feeding upon dirty Pies, Ragou's, & c. dress'd by your greasy Scullions? Are we liable to more Disorders and Sicknesses than the *French*, who are accommodated with these Palaces, Beds and Cooks? But after all, how many are there in *France* that lye upon Straw in Garrets where the Rain comes in on all hands, and that are hard put to't to find Victuals and Drink? I have been in *France*, and speak from what I have seen with my Eyes. You rally without reason, upon our Clothes made of Skins, for they are warmer, and keep out the Rain better than your Cloth; besides, they are not so ridiculously made as your Garments, which have more Stuff in their Pockets and Skirts, than in the Body of the Garment. As for our Beaver-Hunting, you take it to be a terrible thing; while it affords us all manner of pleasure and diversion; and at the same time, procures us all sorts of Commodities in exchange for the Skins. Besides, our Slaves take all the Drudgery off our hands, (if so be that you will have it to be drudgery.) You know very well that Hunting is the most agreeable Diversion we have; but the Beaver-Hunting being so very pleasant, we prefer it to all the other sorts. You say, we have a troublesome and tedious way of waging War; and indeed I must own that a *French* Man would not be able to bear it, upon the account that you are not accustom'd to such long Voyages on Foot; but these Excursions do not fatigue us in the least, and 'twere to be wish'd for the good of *Canada*, that you were possess'd of the same Talent; for if you were, the *Iroquese* would not Cut your Throats in the midst of your own Habitations, as they do now every day. You insist likewise on the risk we run in our little Canoes, as an instance of our Misery; and with reference to that Point, 'tis true that sometimes we cannot dispense with the use of Canoes, because we are Strangers to the Art of Building larger Vessels; but after all, your great Vessels are liable to be cast away as well as Canoes. 'Tis likewise true, that we lye flat upon the open ground when we approach to the Villages of our Enemies; but 'tis equally true that the Soldiers in *France* are not so well accommodated as your Men are here, and that they are oftentimes forc'd to lye in Marshes and Ditches, where they are expos'd to the Rain and Wind. You object farther, that we betake our selves to a speedy Flight; and pray what can be more natural than to flye when the number of our Enemies is triple to ours. The Fatigue indeed of running night and day without Eating and Drinking, is terrible; but we had better undergo it than become Slaves. I am apt to believe that such extremities are matter of Horrour to the *Europeans*, but we look upon 'em as in a manner, nothing. You conclude, in pretending that the *French* prevent our Misery by taking pity of us. But pray consider how our Ancestors liv'd an hundred years ago: They liv'd as well without your Commodities as we do with 'em; for instead of your Fire-Locks, Powder and Shot, they made use of Bows and Arrows, as we do to this day: They made Nets of the Thread of the Barks of Trees, Axes of Stone; Knives, Needles and Awls of Stag or Elk-Bones; and supply'd the room of Kettles with Earthen Pots. Now, since our Ancestors liv'd without these Commodities for so many Ages; I am of the Opinion, we could dispense with 'em easier than the *French* could with our Beaver Skins; for which, by a mighty piece of Friendship, they give us in exchange Fusees, that burst and Lame many of our Warriors, Axes that break in the cutting of a Shrub, Knives that turn Blunt, and lose their Edge in the cutting of a

13

Citron; Thread which is half Rotten, and so very bad that our Nets are worn out as soon as they are made; and Kettles so thin and slight, that the very weight of Water makes the Bottoms fall out. This, my dear Brother, is the answer I had to give to your Reflexions upon the Misery of the *Hurons*.

Lahontan.'Tis well; I find you would have me to believe that the *Hurons* are insensible of their Fatigue and Labour; and being bred up to Poverty and Hardships, have another notion of 'em than we have. This may do with those who have never stir'd out of their own Country, and consequently have no Idea of a better Life than their own; who having never visited our Cities and Towns, fancy that we live just as they do. But as for thee, who hast seen *France, Quebec* and *New-England*, methinks thy judgment and relish of things are too much of the Savage Strain; whilst thou prefers the Condition of the *Hurons* to that of the *Europeans*. Can there be a more agreeable and delightful Life in the World, than that of an infinity of rich Men, who want for nothing? They have fine Coaches, Stately Houses adorn'd with Rich Hangings and Magnificent Pictures, Sweet Gardens replenish'd with all sorts of Fruit, Parks Stock'd with all sorts of Animals, Horses and Hounds and good store of Money, which enables 'em to keep a Sumptuous Table, to frequent the Play-Houses, to Game freely, and to dispose handsomely of their Children. These happy Men are ador'd by their Dependants; and you have seen with your own eyes our Princes, Dukes, Marshals of *France*, Prelates, and a Mission of persons of all Stations, who want for nothing, and live like Kings, and who never call to mind that they have liv'd, till such time as Death alarms 'em.

Adario. If I had not been particularly inform'd of the State of *France*, and let into the knowledge of all the Circumstances of that People, by my Voyage to *Paris;* I might have been Blinded by the outward appearances of Felicity that you set forth: But I know that your Prince, your Duke, your Marshal, and your Prelate are far from being happy upon the Comparison with the *Hurons*, who know no other happiness than that of Liberty and Tranquility of Mind: For your great Lords hate one another in their Hearts; they forfeit their Sleep, and neglect even Eating and Drinking, in making their Court to the King, and undermining their Enemies; they offer such Violence to Nature in dissembling, disguising and bearing things, that the Torture of their Soul leaves all Expression far behind it. Is all this nothing in your way? Do you think it such a trifling matter to have fifty Serpents in your Bosom? Had not they better throw their Coaches, their Palaces and their Finery, into the River, than to spend their life time in a continued Series of Martyrdom? Were I in their place, I'd rather choose to be a *Huron* with a Naked Body and a Serene Mind. The Body is the Apartment in which the Soul is lodg'd; and what signifies it, for the Case call'd the Body, to be set off with Gold Trappings, or spread out in a Coach, or planted before a Sumptuous Table, while the Soul Galls and Tortures it? The great Lords, that you call Happy, lie expos'd to Disgrace from the King, to the detraction of a thousand sorts of Persons, to the loss of their Places, to the Contempt of their Fellow Courtiers; and in a word, their soft Life is thwarted by Ambition, Pride, Presumption and Envy. They are Slaves to their Passions, and to their King, who is the only *French* Man that can be call'd Happy, with respect to that adorable Liberty which he alone enjoys. There's a thousand of us in one Village, and you see that we love one another like Brethren; that whatever any one has is at his Neighbour's Service; that our Generals and Presidents of the Council have not more Power than any other *Huron*; that Detraction and Quarreling were never heard of among us; and in fine [in conclusion], that every one is his own Master, and do's what he pleases, without being accountable to another, or censur'd by his Neighbour. This, my dear Brother, is the difference between us and your Princes, Dukes, *&c*. And if those great Men are so Unhappy, by consequence, those of inferiour Stations must have a greater share of Trouble and perplexing Cares ....

14

▲ Document 3: How the Squamish Remember George Vancouver

The following is an account of the Squamish's first encounter with George Vancouver, as told by Squamish historian Louis Miranda (1892–1990), and presented at the Vancouver Conference on Exploration and Discovery by Chief Philip Joe in 1992. This represents an oral history passed down through the generations since 1792.

Vancouver's journal records that my ancestors who greeted him 'conducted themselves with the greatest decorum and civility.' He certainly liked the fish given and did not mind parting with a few iron tools in exchange. Vancouver took a look around the inlet and then headed into Howe Sound where an incident occurred that you may not be so familiar with, but which has been preserved in Squamish oral tradition.

As my elders tell the story, early one morning in the month called *Tim-kwis-KWAS* 'hot time,' an old man living near the mouth of the Squamish River had gone down to wash. As he raised his head, he saw an 'island' where no island had been before. The old man was alarmed and ran back to his house to wake his relatives. 'There is an island in the sound—a floating island,' he told them. The old man knew it was an island for it had skeletons of trees thrusting skyward. But it was like no island he had ever seen. Word was sent up the Squamish River for the people to come and see the mysterious floating island.

It was decided that the men would go out in their canoes to see the island. As they grew near, they saw that it wasn't a floating island at all, but a very large canoe, a strange canoe. Soon, men appeared and walked around the canoe. But what strange men they were! Every part of their body was covered except for their faces, which were white. My people scrutinized them. Finally, some of the elders came up with an explanation—these people are from the land of the dead. And they are wrapped in their burial blankets!

One of the dead people stepped forward. He had smoke coming from his mouth and it appeared that he was eating fire. The man motioned for my ancestors to go on board. They were hesitant, of course, but after much discussion, one brave young man decided that he would go, and others followed. Instantly, the dead man in the canoe extended his hand. 'Oh, he wants to play the "pulling fingers" game,' the Squamish men told one another. One man stepped forward, spit in his palm, rubbed his hands together, and thrust out his crooked finger. The fire-eating dead man shook his head no, no. 'A stronger opponent is wanted,' the Squamish decided. Another man stepped forward, spit on his hand and got ready to play the game. Again the white man shook his head, no. More Squamish men stepped forward, spit, and extended their finger, until only one man remained—a strong man from up the Squamish River. My people could see that the strangers were talking amongst themselves and we can only assume that they must have decided that this unusual behaviour was the Indian way of greeting. So the white man stepped forward to link fingers with the strong man of Squamish. The Squamish man pulled. He pulled hard. Oh, the smoke-blowing dead man hollered in pain as his finger was disconnected! Some of the Squamish had been sceptical of the strangers. Then they knew. 'Dead people don't feel pain, and this one is certainly having some!'

Fear of the strangers vanished. The Squamish looked around the strange, large canoe and when it came time to leave they climbed down into their own canoes. The white people lowered into the canoes some presents, including a barrel and a few boxes.

15

Source: Louis Miranda and Philip Joe, in Robin Fisher and Hugh J.M. Johnston, eds., *From Maps to Metaphors*, (Vancouver: UBC Press, 1993), pp. 3–5. Reprinted with permission of the Publisher from *From Maps to Metaphors: The Pacific World of George Vancouver* edited by Robin Fisher and Hugh Johnston. © University of British Columbia Press 1993. All rights reserved by the Publisher.

Back at the village the people huddled around as the men opened the treasure. When they pried the top from the barrel they were pleased to see that it contained good thick hair and face oil, much better than the deer tallow and salmon oil they had in storage. All hands dipped into the barrel and smeared it onto their faces and hair. But soon the oil began to thicken. Their hair got stiff! Their faces got thick! And they could hardly move their jaw! They ran for the water and washed it off. The gift of molasses was then emptied onto the ground.

My people had hoped that the second gift might be less trouble. Inside the box were shiny round pieces that attracted the attention of the women—who saw their value as ornaments—and the children—who thought they made fine toys. For the box of silver coins had no other value to the Squamish in 1792.

The story passed down by my ancestors tells how Vancouver provided gifts of pilot biscuits, whisky, and white flour—unfamiliar foods that they used with results that were initially comical, although history has recorded a less jovial aftermath.

Viewing the explorers' ships as 'floating islands' and the men, themselves, as 'dead people' was not a perspective unique to the Squamish. Our relatives—the Nanaimo Indians—were also visited one night by floating islands. In addition to the fire-eating habit of the strangers, they saw that their feet were wooden and made a great deal of noise when they walked! The Nanaimo people's barrel of molasses was used to mend their canoes, but it was soon found that molasses was as poor a canoe pitch as it was a hair oil.

Apparently Vancouver then sailed north, for his travels up the coast can be traced by the elders' stories of mysterious floating islands that appeared offshore, and then, just as quickly as they arrived, sailed beyond the next point.

Many of you have investigated the naming of the landscape by Vancouver and his Spanish counterparts. But perhaps you are not aware that the Squamish commemorated the historic 1792 meeting in Howe Sound by thereafter referring to the site by the Squamish name *Whul-whul-ʟᴀʏ-ton*, meaning "Whiteman place."

Indian stories and place names, like explorers' journals, are reminders of history that provide a glimpse into another era. As I hope my people's story has demonstrated, our mutual histories since 1792 have been inexorably entwined, although recalled from different perspectives.

This country, which so inspired the explorers and challenged the map makers, was the homeland of the Squamish and our neighbours the Musqueam and the Seleelwat. These beaches gave us shellfish, crabs, and eel grass. The forests and flatlands provided deer, large herds of elk, bear, and mountain goats. Food plants were harvested, and the trees supplied the wood for our houses, canoes, weapons, and ceremonial objects. The bark of red cedars was stripped to make our clothes. The inlet waters provided us with a wide variety of fish and sea mammals, and salmon returned regularly to the streams. And just as Captain Vancouver was said to have shared his molasses, biscuits, and flour, so our people shared our natural resources with those who followed in the wake of the floating islands.

▲ Document 4: Engraving Based on a Drawing by Samuel de Champlain, 1613

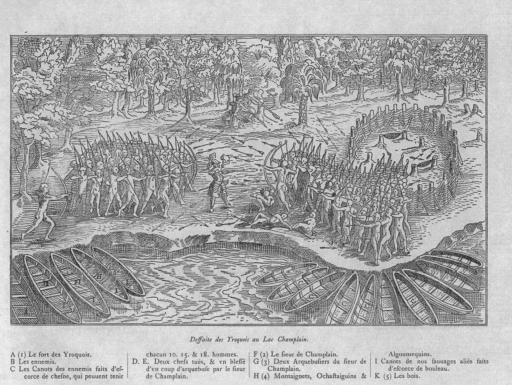

Deffaite des Yroquois au Lac Champlain.

A (1) Le fort des Yroquois.
B Les ennemis.
C Les Canots des ennemis faits d'ef-
corce de chefne, qui peuuent tenir

chacun 10. 15. & 18. hommes.
D. E. Deux chefs tués, & vn bleffé
d'vn coup d'arquebufe par le fieur
de Champlain.

F (2) Le fieur de Champlain.
G (3) Deux Arquebufiers du fieur de
Champlain.
H (4) Montaignets, Ochaftaiguins &

Algoumequins.
I Canots de nos fauuages aliés faits
d'efcorce de bouleau.
K (5) Les bois.

(1) Cette lettre manque dans le dessin. — (2) La lettre manque ; mais il est facile de reconnaître Champlain posté seul entre les combattants. — (3) Cette lettre manque dans le dessin ; mais on reconnaît aisément les deux arquebusiers sur la lisière du bois. — (4) La lettre H a été mise par inadvertance sur les canots des alliés, où il y a déjà la lettre I. — (5) Cette lettre, qui manque aussi, est facile à suppléer.

P. 344

● **This is a contemporary depiction of a battle in 1609 in which Champlain used his arquebuse to fire on his Iroquois foes. What conclusions can we draw about Aboriginal–French relations based on this image?**

Source: Deffaite des Yroquois au lac Champlain. In Champlain, Samuel de. Œuvres de Champlain / 2nd edition. Quebec : G.-É. Desbarats, 1870. Vol. 3, facing page 196. Archives of Ontario Library, 971.011 CHB http://www.archives.gov.on.ca/english/on-line-exhibits/franco-ontarian/pics/971_001_pg344_battle_520.jpg. LAC C-006780.

▲ Document 5: The Encounter Between Jacques Cartier and the Aboriginal Peoples at Stadaconé

● This image is a much later depiction of the encounter between Jacques Cartier and the Aboriginal peoples at Stadaconé (near present-day Quebec City). Quebec artist Marc-Aurèle Suzor-Côté painted this canvas in 1907. How does this image depict the encounter between the French and the Aboriginal peoples? Which group dominates the image? How well does this painting reflect the attitudes expressed in the readings for this section?

Source: http://www.mnba.qc.ca/Contenu.aspx?page=1529&langue=en. Suzor-Coté, Marc Aurèle de Foy, Jacques Cartier rencontre les Indiens à Stadaconé, 1535, Huile sur toile, 266x401 cm, Museé national des beaux-arts du Québec, Accession No. 34.12. Photographer Jean-Guy Kérouac.

■ Article 1: The Indians' Old World: Native Americans and the Coming of Europeans

Neil Salisbury

Scholars in history, anthropology, archaeology, and other disciplines have turned increasingly over the past two decades to the study of native peoples during the colonial period of North American history. The new work in Indian history has altered the way we think about the beginning of American history and about the era of European colonization. Historians now recognize that Europeans arrived, not in a virgin land, but in one that was teeming with several million people. Beyond filling in some of the vast blanks left by previous generations' overlooking of Indians, much of this scholarship makes clear that Indians are integral to the history of colonial North America.[1] In short, surveys of recent textbooks and of scholarly titles suggest that Native Americans are well on their way home to being "mainstreamed" by colonial historians.

Substantive as this reorientation is, it remains limited.[2] Beyond the problems inherent in representing Indian/non-Indian interactions during the colonial era lies the challenge of contextualizing the era itself. Despite opening chapters and lectures that survey the continent's native peoples and cultures, most historians continue to represent American history as having been set in motion by the arrival of European explorers and colonizers.[3] They have yet to recognize the existence of North American—as opposed to English or European—background for colonial history, much less to consider the implications of such a background for understanding the three centuries following Columbia's landfall. Yet a growing body of scholarship by archaeologists, linguists, and students of Native American expressive traditions recognizes 1492 not as a beginning but as a single moment in a long history utterly detached from that of Europe.[4] These findings call into question historians' synchronic maps and verbal descriptions of precontact Indians—their cultures, their communities, their ethnic and political designations and affiliations, and their relations with one another. Do these really describe enduring entities or do they represent epiphenomena of arbitrary moments in time? If the latter should prove to be the case, how will readings of Indian history in the colonial period be affected?

Far from being definitive, this article is intended as a stimulus to debate on these questions. It begins by drawing on recent work in archaeology, where most of the relevant scholarship has originated, to suggest one way of thinking about pre-Columbian North America in historical terms.[5] The essay then looks at developments in several areas of the continent during the centuries preceding the arrival of Europeans and in early phases of the colonial period. The purpose is to show how certain patterns and processes originating before the beginnings of contact continued to shape the continent's history thereafter and how an understanding of the colonial period requires an understanding of its American background as well as of its European context.[6]

In a formidable critique of European and Euro-American thinking about native North Americans, Robert F. Berkhofer, Jr., demonstrates that the idea of "Indians" as a single, discrete people was an invention of Columbus and his European contemporaries that has been perpetuated into our own time without foundation in historical, cultural, or ethnographic reality. On the contrary, Berkhofer asserts,

> The first residents of the Americas were by modern estimates divided into at least two thousand cultures and more societies, practiced a multiplicity of customs and lifestyles, held an enormous variety of values and beliefs, spoke numerous languages mutually unintelligible to the many speakers, and did not conceive of themselves as a single people—if they knew about each other at all.[7]

While there is literal truth in portions of Berkhofer's statement, his implication that Indians inhabited thousands of tiny, isolated communities in ignorance of one another flies in the face of a substantial body of archaeological and linguistic scholarship on North America and of a wealth of relevant anthropological literature on nonstate polities, nonmarket economies,

Source: Neil Salisbury, "The Indians' Old World: Native Americans and the Coming of Europeans" *The William and Mary Quarterly*, Third Series, Vol. 53, No. 3 (July 1996): 435–58. Reprinted with permission.

19

and noninstitutionalized religions. To be sure, indigenous North Americans exhibited a remarkable range of languages, economies, political systems, beliefs, and material cultures. But this range was less the result of their isolation from one another than of the widely varying natural and social environments with which Indians had interacted over millennia. What recent scholars of precolonial North America have found even more striking, given this diversity, is the extent to which native peoples' histories intersected one another.

At the heart of these intersections was exchange. By exchange is meant not only the trading of material goods but also exchanges across community lines of marriage partners, resources, labor, ideas, techniques, and religious practices. Longer-distance exchanges frequently crossed cultural and linguistic boundaries as well and ranged from casual encounters to widespread alliances and networks that were economic, political, and religious. For both individuals and communities, exchanges sealed social and political relationships. Rather than accumulate material wealth endlessly, those who acquired it gave it away, thereby earning prestige and placing obligations on others to reciprocate appropriately. And as we shall see, many goods were not given away to others in this world but were buried with individuals to accompany them to another.[8]

Archaeologists have found evidence of ongoing exchange relations among even the earliest known Paleo-Indian inhabitants of North America. Ten thousand years before Columbus, in the wake of the last Ice Age, bands of two or three dozen persons regularly traveled hundreds of miles to hunt and trade with one another at favored campsites such as Lindenmeier in northern Colorado, dating to ca. 8800 B.C. At the Lindenmeier site, differences in the flaking and shaping of stone points distinguished regular occupants in two parts of the camp, and the obsidian each used came from about 350 miles north and south of Lindenmeier, respectively.[9] Evidence from a wide range of settlement sites makes clear that, as the postglacial warming trend continued, so-called Archaic peoples in much of the continent developed wider ranges of food sources, more sedentary settlement patterns, and larger populations. They also expanded their exchanges with one another and conducted them over greater distances. Highly valued materials such as Great Lakes copper,

Rocky Mountain obsidian, and marine shells from the Gulf and Atlantic coasts have been found in substantial quantities at sites hundreds and even thousands of miles from their points of origin. In many cases, goods fashioned from these materials were buried with human beings, indicating both their religious significance and, by their uneven distribution, their role as markers of social or political rank.[10]

While the Archaic pattern of autonomous bands persisted in most of North America until the arrival of Europeans, the complexity of exchange relationships in some parts of the continent produced the earliest evidence of concentrated political power. This was especially so for peoples who, after the first century A.D., developed food economies that permitted them to inhabit permanent, year-round villages. In California, for example, competition among communities for coveted acorn groves generated sharply defined political territories and elevated the role of chiefs who oversaw trade, diplomacy, and warfare for clusters of villages. Similar competition for prime fishing and trading locations strengthened the authority of certain village chiefs on the Northwest Coast.[11] Exchange rather than competition for resources appears to have driven centralization in the Ohio and Illinois valleys. There the Hopewell peoples imported copper, mica, shell, and other raw materials over vast distances to their village centers, where specialists fashioned them into intricately crafted ornaments, tools, and other objects. They deposited massive quantities of these goods with the dead in large mounds and exported more to communities scattered throughout the Mississippi Valley. Hopewell burials differentiate between commoners and elites by the quantity and quality of grave goods accompanying each.[12] In the Southwest, meanwhile, a culture known as Hohokam emerged in the Gila River and Salt River valleys among some of the first societies based primarily on agriculture. Hohokam peoples lived in permanent villages and maintained elaborate irrigation systems that enabled them to harvest two crops per year.[13]

By the twelfth century, agricultural production had spread over much of the Eastern Woodlands as well as to more of the Southwest. In both regions, even more complex societies were emerging to dominate widespread exchange networks. In the Mississippi Valley and the Southeast, the sudden primacy of maize horticulture is marked archaeologically in a variety of ways—food remains, pollen profiles, studies of human bone (showing that maize accounted for 50 percent of people's diets), and in material culture by a proliferation of chert hoes, shell-tempered pottery for storing and cooking, and pits for storing surplus crops. These developments were accompanied by the rise of what archaeologists term "Mississippian" societies, consisting of fortified political and ceremonial centers and outlying villages. The centers were built around open plazas featuring platform burial mounds, temples, and elaborate residences for elite families. Evidence from burials makes clear the wide social gulf that separated commoners from elites. Whereas the former were buried in simple graves with a few personal possessions, the latter were interred in the temples or plazas along with many more, and more elaborate, goods such as copper ornaments, massive sheets of shell, and ceremonial weapons. Skeletal evidence indicates that elites ate more meat, were taller, performed less strenuous physical activity, and were less prone to illness and accident than commoners.[14] Although most archaeologists' conclusions are informed at least in part by models developed by political anthropologists, they also draw heavily from Spanish and French observations of some of the last Mississippian societies. These observations confirm that political leaders, or chiefs, from elite families mobilized labor, collected tribute, redistributed agricultural surpluses, coordinated trade, diplomacy, and military activity, and were worshipped as deities.[15]

The largest, most complex Mississippian center was Cahokia, located not far from the confluence of the Mississippi and Missouri rivers, near modern East St. Louis, Illinois, in the rich floodplain known as American Bottoms. By the twelfth century, Cahokia probably numbered 20,000 people and contained over 120 mounds within a five-square-mile area. One key to Cahokia's rise was its combination of rich soil and nearby wooded uplands, enabling inhabitants to produce surplus crops while providing an abundance and diversity of wild food sources along with ample supplies of wood for fuel and construction. A second key was its location, affording access to the great river systems of the North American interior.[16]

Cahokia had the most elaborate social structure yet seen in North America. Laborers used stone and wooden spades to dig soil from "borrow pits" (at least nineteen have been identified by archaeologists),

which they carried in wooden buckets to mounds and palisades often more than half a mile away. The volume and concentration of craft activity in shell, copper, clay, and other materials, both local and imported, suggests that specialized artisans provided the material foundation for Cahokia's exchange ties with other peoples. Although most Cahokians were buried in mass graves outside the palisades, their rulers were given special treatment. At a prominent location in Mound 72, the largest of Cahokia's platform mounds, a man had been buried atop a platform of shell beads. Accompanying him were several group burials: fifty young women, aged 18 to 23, four men, and three men and three women, all encased in uncommonly large amounts of exotic materials. As with the Natchez Indians observed by the French in Louisiana, Cahokians appear to have sacrificed individuals to accompany their leaders in the afterlife. Cahokia was surrounded by nine smaller mound centers and several dozen villages from which it obtained much of its food and through which it conducted its waterborne commerce with other Mississippian centers in the Midwest and Southeast.[17]

[...] Given the archaeological record, North American "prehistory" can hardly be characterized as a multiplicity of discrete microhistories. Fundamental to the social and economic patterns of even the earliest Paleo-Indian bands were exchanges that linked peoples across geographic, cultural, and linguistic boundaries. The effects of these links are apparent in the spread of raw materials and finished goods, of beliefs and ceremonies, and of techniques for food production and for manufacturing. By the twelfth century, some exchange networks had become highly formalized and centralized. Exchange constitutes an important key to conceptualizing American history before Columbus.

Although it departs from our familiar image of North American Indians, the historical pattern sketched so far is recognizable in the way it portrays societies "progressing" from small, egalitarian, autonomous communities to larger, more hierarchical, and centralized political aggregations with more complex economies. The image is likewise subverted when we examine the three centuries immediately preceding the arrival of Europeans. In both American Bottoms and the San Juan River basin [in present-day New Mexico], where twelfth-century populations were most concentrated, agriculture most productive, exchange most varied and voluminous, and political systems most complex and extensive, there were scarcely any inhabitants by the end of the fifteenth century. What happened and why?

Cahokia and other Mississippian societies in the Upper Midwest peaked during the late twelfth and early thirteenth centuries. Data from soil traces indicate that even then laborers were fortifying Cahokia's major earthworks against attack. At the same time, archaeologists surmise, Cahokia was headed toward an ecological crisis: expanded settlement, accompanied by especially hot dry summers, exhausted the soil, depleted the supply of timber for building and fuel, and reduced the habitat of the game that supplemented their diet. By the end of the fourteenth century, Cahokia's inhabitants had dispersed over the surrounding countryside into small farming villages.[18]

Cahokia's abandonment reverberated among other Mississippian societies in the Midwest. Fortified centers on the Mississippi River from the Arkansas River northward and on the Ohio River appear to have been strengthened by influxes of people from nearby villages but then abandoned, and signs from burials indicate a period of chronic, deadly warfare in the Upper Midwest. One archaeologist refers to the middle Mississippi Valley and environs during the fifteenth century as "the vacant quarter." A combination of ecological pressures and upheavals within the alliance that linked them appears to have doomed Cahokia and other midwestern Mississippian centers, leading the inhabitants to transform themselves into the village dwellers of the surrounding prairies and plains observed by French explorers three centuries later.[19]

The upheavals may even have extended beyond the range of direct Mississippian influence to affect Iroquois and Hurons and other Iroquoian speakers of the lower Great Lakes region. These people had been moving from dispersed, riverside settlements to fortified, bluff-top villages over the course of several centuries; the process appears to have intensified in the fourteenth century, when it also led to the formation of the Iroquois and Huron confederacies. The Hurons developed fruitful relations with hunter-gatherers to the north, with whom they exchanged agricultural produce for meat and skins, and Iroquois ties with outsiders appear to have diminished except for small-scale interactions with coastal peoples to the south and east. Across the Northeast, political life was characterized by violence and other manifestations

of intense competition. Whether the upheavals in exchange ties occasioned by the collapse of Cahokia were directly linked to the formation of the Iroquois and Huron confederacies, as Dena Dincauze and Robert Hasenstab have suggested for the Iroquois, or were simply part of a larger process generated by the advent of farming and consequent demographic and political changes, the repercussions were still evident when Europeans began to frequent the region during the sixteenth century.[20]

[...] Combinations of continuity and change, persistence and adaptability, arose from concrete historical experiences rather than a timeless tradition. The remainder of this article indicates some of the ways that both the deeply rooted imperatives of reciprocity and exchange and the recent legacies of competition and upheaval informed North American history as Europeans began to make their presence felt.

Discussion of the transition from pre- to post-contact times must begin with the sixteenth century, when Indians and Europeans met and interacted in a variety of settings. When not slighting the era altogether, historians have viewed it as one of discovery or exploration, citing the achievements of notable Europeans in either anticipating or failing to anticipate the successful colonial enterprises of the seventeenth century. Recently, however, a number of scholars have been integrating information from European accounts with the findings of archaeologists to produce a much fuller picture of this critical period in North American history.

[...] In the Northeast, [...] Iroquoian-speaking villagers on the Mississippian periphery and Archaic hunter-gatherers still further removed from developments in the interior met Europeans of several nationalities. At the outset of the century, Spanish and Portuguese explorers enslaved several dozen Micmacs and other Indians from the Nova Scotia-Gulf of St. Lawrence area. Three French expeditions to the St. Lawrence itself in the 1530s and the 1540s followed the Spanish pattern by alienating most Indians encountered and ending in futility. Even as these hostile contacts were taking place, fishermen, whalers, and other Europeans who visited the area regularly had begun trading with natives. As early as the 1520s, Abenakis on the coast of Maine and Micmacs were trading the furs of beavers and other animals for European goods of metal and glass. By the 1540s, specialized fur traders, mostly French, frequented the coast as far south as the Chesapeake; by the 1550s or soon thereafter, French traders rendezvoused regularly with Indians along the shores of upper New England, the Maritimes, and Quebec and at Tadoussac on the St. Lawrence.[21]

What induced Indians to go out of their way to trap beaver and trade the skins for glass beads, mirrors, copper kettles, and other goods? Throughout North America since Paleo-Indian times, exchange in the Northeast was the means by which people maintained and extended their social, cultural, and spiritual horizons as well as acquired items considered supernaturally powerful. Members of some coastal Indian groups later recalled how the first Europeans they saw, with their facial hair and strange clothes and traveling in their strange boats, seemed like supernatural figures. Although soon disabused of such notions, these Indians and many more inland placed special value on the glass beads and other trinkets offered by the newcomers. Recent scholarship on Indians' motives in this earliest stage of the trade indicates that they regarded such objects as the equivalents of the quartz, mica, shell, and other sacred substances that had formed the heart of long-distance exchange in North America for millennia and that they regarded as sources of physical and spiritual well-being, on earth and in the afterlife. Indians initially altered and wore many of the utilitarian goods they received, such as iron axe heads and copper pots, rather than use them for their intended purposes. Moreover, even though the new objects might pass through many hands, they more often than not ended up in graves, presumably for their possessors to use in the afterlife. Finally, the archaeological findings make clear that shell and native copper predominated over the new objects in sixteenth-century exchanges, indicating that European trade did not suddenly trigger a massive craving for the objects themselves. While northeastern Indians recognized Europeans as different from themselves, they interacted with them and their materials in ways that were consistent with their own customs and beliefs.[22]

By the late sixteenth century, the effects of European trade began to overlap with the effects of earlier upheavals in the northeastern interior. Sometime between Jacques Cartier's final departure in 1543 and Samuel de Champlain's arrival in 1603, the Iroquoian-speaking inhabitants of Hochelaga and Stadacona (modern Montreal and Quebec City) abandoned their communities. The communities were crushed militarily, and the survivors dispersed among both Iroquois and Hurons. Whether the perpetrators of these dispersals were Iroquois or Huron is a point of controversy, but either way the St. Lawrence communities appear to have been casualties of the rivalry, at least a century old, between the two confederations as each sought to position itself vis-à-vis the French. The effect, if not the cause, of the dispersals was the Iroquois practice of attacking antagonists who denied them direct access to trade goods; this is consistent with Iroquois actions during the preceding two centuries and the century that followed.[23]

The sudden availability of many more European goods, the absorption of many refugees from the St. Lawrence, and the heightening of tensions with the Iroquois help to explain the movement of most outlying Huron communities to what is now the Simcoe County area of Ontario during the 1580s. This geographic concentration strengthened their confederacy and gave it the form it had when allied with New France during the first half of the seventeenth century.[24] Having formerly existed at the outer margins of the arena of exchange centered in Cahokia, the Hurons and Iroquois now faced a new sources of goods and power to the east.[25]

The diverse native societies encountered by Europeans as they began to settle North America permanently during the seventeenth century were not static isolates lying outside the ebb and flow of human history. Rather, they were products of a complex set of historical forces, both local and wide-ranging, both deeply rooted and of recent origin. Although their lives and worldviews were shaped by long-standing traditions of reciprocity and spiritual power, the people in these communities were also accustomed—contrary to popular myths about inflexible Indians—to economic and political flux and to absorbing new peoples (both allies and antagonists), objects, and ideas, including those originating in Europe. Such combinations of tradition and innovation continued to shape Indians' relations with Europeans, even as the latter's visits became permanent.

The establishment of lasting European colonies, beginning with New Mexico in 1598, began a phase in the continent's history that eventually resulted in the displacement of Indians to the economic, political, and cultural margins of a new order. But during the interim natives and colonizers entered into numerous

23

relationships in which they exchanged material goods and often supported one another diplomatically or militarily against common enemies. These relations combined native and European modes of exchange. While much of the scholarly literature emphasizes the subordination and dependence of Indians in these circumstances, Indians as much as Europeans dictated the form and content of their early exchanges and alliances. Much of the protocol and ritual surrounding such intercultural contacts was rooted in indigenous kinship obligations and gift exchanges, and Indian consumers exhibited decided preferences for European commodities that satisfied social, spiritual, and aesthetic values. Similarly, Indians' long-range motives and strategies in their alliances with Europeans were frequently rooted in older patterns of alliance and rivalry with regional neighbors.[26] Such continuities can be glimpsed through a brief consideration of the early colonial-era histories of the Five Nations Iroquois in the Northeast [...]

Post-Mississippian and sixteenth-century patterns of antagonism between the Iroquois and their neighbors to the north and west persisted, albeit under altered circumstances, during the seventeenth century when France established its colony on the St. Lawrence and allied itself with Hurons and other Indians. France aimed to extract maximum profits from the fur trade, and it immediately recognized the Iroquois as the major threat to that goal. In response, the Iroquois turned to the Dutch in New Netherland for guns and other trade goods while raiding New France's Indian allies for the thicker northern pelts that brought higher prices than those in their own country (which they exhausted by midcentury) and for captives to replace those from their own ranks who had died from epidemics or in wars. During the 1640s, the Iroquois replaced raids with full-scale military assaults (the so-called Beaver Wars) on Iroquoian-speaking communities in the lower Great Lakes, absorbing most of the survivors as refugees or captives. All the while, the Iroquois elaborated a vision of their confederation, which had brought harmony within their own ranks, as bringing peace to all people of the region. For the remainder of the century, the Five Nations fought a gruelling and costly series of wars against the French and their Indian allies in order to gain access to the pelts and French goods circulating in lands to the north and west.[27]

Meanwhile, the Iroquois were also adapting to the growing presence of English colonists along the Atlantic seaboard. After the English supplanted the Dutch in New York in 1664, Iroquois diplomats established relations with the proprietary governor, Sir Edmund Andros, in a treaty known as the Covenant Chain. The Covenant Chain was an elaboration of the Iroquois' earlier treaty arrangement with the Dutch, but whereas the Iroquois had termed the Dutch relationship a chain of iron, they referred to the one with the English as a chain of silver. The shift in metaphors was appropriate, for what had been strictly an economic connection was now a political one in which the Iroquois acquired power over other New York Indians. After 1677, the Covenant Chain was expanded to include several English colonies, most notably Massachusetts and Maryland, along with those colonies' subject Indians. The upshot of these arrangements was that the Iroquois cooperated with their colonial partners in subduing and removing subject Indians who impeded settler expansion. The Mohawks in particular played a vital role in the New England colonies' suppression of the Indian uprising known as King Philip's War and in moving the Susquehannocks away from the expanding frontier of settlement in the Chesapeake after Bacon's Rebellion.

For the Iroquois, such a policy helped expand their "Tree of Peace" among Indians while providing them with buffers against settler encroachment around their homelands. The major drawback in the arrangement proved to be the weakness of English military assistance against the French. This inadequacy, and the consequent suffering experience by the Iroquois during two decades of war after 1680, finally drove the Five Nations to make peace with the French and their Indian allies in the Grand Settlement of 1701. Together, the Grand Settlement and Covenant Chain provided the Iroquois with the peace and security, the access to trade goods, and the dominant role among northeastern Indians they had long sought.[28] That these arrangements in the long run served to reinforce rather than deter English encroachment on Iroquois lands and autonomy should not obscure their pre-European roots and their importance in shaping colonial history in the Northeast.

[...] As significant as is the divide separating pre- and post-Columbian North American history, it is not the stark gap suggested by the distinction between prehistory and history. For varying periods of time after their arrival in North America, Europeans adapted to the social and political environments they found, including the fluctuating ties of reciprocity and interdependence as well as rivalry, that characterized those environments. They had little choice but to enter in and participate if they wished to sustain their presence. Eventually, one route to success proved to be their ability to insert themselves as regional powers in new networks of exchange and alliance that arose to supplant those of the Mississippians, Anasazis, and others.

To assert such continuities does not minimize the radical transformations entailed in Europeans' colonization of the continent and its indigenous peoples. Arising in Cahokia's wake, new centers at Montreal, Fort Orange/Albany, Charleston, and elsewhere permanently altered the primary patterns of exchange in eastern North America. The riverine system that channelled exchange in the interior of the continent gave way to one in which growing quantities of goods arrived from, and were directed to, coastal peripheries and ultimately Europe.[29] [...] More generally, European colonizers brought a complex of demographic and ecological advantages, most notably epidemic disease and their own immunity to them, that utterly devastated Indian communities;[30] ideologies and beliefs in their cultural and spiritual superiority to native people and their entitlement to natives' lands;[31] and economic, political, and military systems organized for the engrossment of Indian lands and the subordination or suppression of Indian peoples.[32]

Europeans were anything but uniformly successful in realizing their goals, but the combination of demographic ecological advantages and imperial intentions, along with the Anglo-Iroquois Covenant Chain, enabled land-hungry colonists from New England to the Chesapeake to break entirely free of ties of dependence on Indians before the end of the seventeenth century. Their successes proved to be only the beginning of a new phase of Indian-European relations. By the mid-eighteenth century, the rapid expansion of land-based settlement in the English colonies had sundered older ties of exchange and alliance linking natives and colonizers nearly everywhere east of the Appalachians, driving many Indians west and reducing those who remained to a scattering of politically powerless enclaves in which Indian identities were nurtured in isolation.[33] Meanwhile, the colonizers threatened to extend this new mode of Indian relations across the Appalachians. An old world, rooted in indigenous exchange, was giving way to one in which Native Americans had no certain place.

NOTES

1. See James Axtell, "A North American Perspective for Colonial History," *History Teacher*, 12 (1978–1979), 549–62. The beginning of this shift was signaled by Gary B. Nash, *Red, White, and Black* (Englewood Cliffs, N. J., 1973), and Francis Jennings, *The Invasion of America: Indians, Colonialism, and the Cant of Conquest* (Chapel Hill, 1975).

2. See James H. Merrell, "Some Thoughts on Colonial Historians and American Indians," *William and Mary Quarterly [WMQ]*, 3d Ser., 46 (1989), 108–10, and Daniel K. Richter, "Whose Indian History?" ibid., 50 (1993), 381–82.

3. See Frederick E. Hoxie, *The Indians Versus the Textbooks: Is There Any Way Out?* (Chicago, 1984); Hoxie, "The Problems of Indian History," *Social Science Journal*, 25 (1988), 389–99.

4. A volume that draws on all these approaches is Alvin M. Josephy, Jr., ed., *America in 1492: The World of the Indian Peoples Before the Arrival of Columbus* (New York, 1992). The best surveys of North American archaeology are Brian M. Fagan, *Ancient North America: The Archaeology of a Continent* (New York, 1991), and Stuart J. Fiedel, *Prehistory of the Americas*, 2d ed. (Cambridge, 1992). On languages see Harold E. Driver, *Indians of North America*, 2d ed. (Chicago, 1969), and Joseph H. Greenberg, *Language in the Americas* (Stanford, Calif., 1987), esp. chap. 2. Two especially interesting examples of work that utilizes oral traditions as historical sources to supplement "prehistoric" archaeology are Roger C. Echo-Hawk, "Kara Katit Pakutu: Exploring the Origins of Native America in Anthropology and Oral Traditions" (M.A. thesis, University of Colorado, 1994), and Donald Bahr et al., *the Short, Swift Time of Gods on Earth: The Hohokam Chronicles* (Berkeley, Calif., 1994).

5. On archaeology as a foundation for Indian history see Bruce G. Trigger, "Archaeology and the Image of the American Indian," *American Antiquity*, 45 (1980), 662–76, and "American Archaeology as

Native History: A Review Essay," *WMQ*, 3d Ser., 40 (1983), 413–52. Among works that incorporate archaeology into historical narratives, the most exemplary by anthropologists are Trigger, *The Children of Aataensic: A History of the Huron People to 1660* (Montreal, 1976), and Kathleen J. Bragdon, *Native People of Southern New England, 1500–1650* (Norman, Okla., 1996), and by historians, Daniel K. Richter, *The Ordeal of the Longhouse: The People of the Iroquois League in the Era of European Colonization* (Chapel Hill, 1992). The most thorough argument for the role of indigenous contexts in shaping post-Columbian American history is Francis Jennings, *The Founders of America: How the Indians Discovered the Land, Pioneered in It, and Created Great Classical Civilization; How They Were Plunged into a Dark Age by Invasion and Conquest; and How They Are Reviving* (New York, 1993). But Jennings argues for a pervasive "Mexican influence" in North America by the 15th century A.D. and makes several other inferences that are highly speculative at best. Lynda Norene Shaffer, *Native Americans before 1492: The Moundbuilding Centers of the Eastern Woodlands* (Armonk, N. Y., 1992), is a useful overview by a historian whose interest is world, rather than American, history.

6. The need for an understanding of its West African contexts is equally critical but outside the scope of this article and its author's expertise. For a beginning in this direction see John Thornton, *Africa and Africans in the Making of the Atlantic World, 1400–1680* (Cambridge, 1992), and the review of that volume by Ira Berlin in *WMQ*, 3d Ser., 51 (1994), 544–47.

7. Robert F. Berkhofer, Jr., *The White Man's Indian: Images of the American Indian from Columbus to the Present* (New York, 1978), 3.

8. The basic contribution to the vast literature on gift exchange economies are Marcel Mauss, *The Gift: Forms and Functions of Exchange in Archaic Societies*, trans. Ian Cunnison (London, 1954); Karl Polanyi, *The Great Transformation* (New York, 1944), chap. 4; Marshall Sahlins, *Stone Age Economics* (Chicago, 1972); and George Dalton, "The Impact of Colonization on Aboriginal Economics in Stateless Societies," in Dalton, ed., *Research in Economic Anthropology: An Annual Compilation of Research* (Greenwich, Conn., 1978), 1:131–84. On North America see William A. Turnbaugh, "Wide-Area Connections in Native North

America," *American Indian Culture and Research Journal*, 1:4 (1976), 22–28.

9. Edwin S. Wilmsen, *Lindenmeier: A Pleistocene Hunting Society* (New York, 1974); Turnbaugh, "Wide-Area Connections in Native North America," 23–24.

10. Fiedel, *Prehistory of the Americas*, chap, 4; Turnbaugh, "Wide-Area Connections in Native North America," 24–25; Jesse D. Jennings, "Epilogue," in Jennings, ed., *Ancient Native Americans* (San Francisco, 1978), 651; Barbara Bender, "Emergent Tribal Formations in the American Midcontinent," *American Antiquity*, 50 (1985), 52–62; Lynn Ceci, "Tracing Wampum's Origins: Shell Bead Evidence from Archaeological Sites in Western and Coastal New York," in Charles F. Hayes et al., eds., *Proceedings of the 1986 Shell Bead Conference: Selected Papers*, Rochester Museum and Science Center, Research Records No. 20 (Rochester, N. Y., 1989), 65–67.

11. Fiedel, *Prehistory of the Americas*, 133–43.

12. Joseph R. Caldwell, "Interaction Spheres in Prehistory," in Caldwell and Robert L. Hall, eds., *Hopewellian Studies*, Illinois State Museum, Scientific Papers, 12 (Springfield, 1964), 133–43; David S. Brose and N'omi Greber, eds., *Hopewell Archaeology: The Chillicothe Conference* (Kent, Ohio, 1979); Fiedel, *Prehistory of the Americas*, 240–51.

13. Linda S. Cordell, *Prehistory of the Southwest* (Orlando, Fla., 1984), 207–11; Fiedel, *Prehistory of the Americas*, 209–12.

14. Fiedel, *Prehistory of the Americas*, 251–60; Dan F. Morse and Phyllis S. Morse, *Archaeology of the Central Mississippi Valley* (New York, 1983), chaps. 10–11; Bruce D. Smith, "The Archaeology of the Southeastern United States: From Dalton to de Soto, 10,500–500 P.P.," *Advances in World Archaeology*, 5 (1986), 53–63; Vincas P. Steponaitis, "Prehistoric Archaeology in the Southeastern United States, 1970–1985," *Annual Review of Anthropology*, 15 (1986), 387–93.

15. The successful integration of archaeology, history, and theory as well as the range of approaches possible with these as foundations can be seen by surveying the relevant essays in Charles Hudson and Carmen Chaves Tesser, eds., *The Forgotten Centuries: Indians and Europeans in the American South, 1521–1704* (Athens, Ga., 1994). See also Chester B. De Pratter, "Late Prehistoric and Early Historic Chiefdoms in the Southeastern United States" (Ph. D. diss., University of Georgia, 1983);

Charles Hudson et al., "Coosa: A Chiefdom in the Sixteenth-Century Southeastern United States," *American Antiquity*, 50 (1985), 723–37; David G. Anderson, *The Savannah River Chiefdoms: Political Change in the Late Prehistoric Southeast* (Tuscaloosa, Ala., 1994). The most recent theoretical discussion is Randolph J. Widmer, "The Structure of Southeastern Chiefdoms," in Hudson and Tesser, eds., *Forgotten Centuries*, 125–55.

16. Melvin L. Fowler, "A Pre-Columbian Urban Center on the Mississippi," *Scientific American*, 233 (August 1975), 92–101; William R. Iseminger, "Cahokia: A Mississippian Metropolis," *Historic Illinois*, 2:6 (April 1980), 1–4.

17. Archaeologists disagree as to the complexity and power of Cahokia, but see Patricia J. O'Brien, "Urbanism, Cahokia, and Middle Mississippian," *Archaeology*, 25 (1972), 188–97; Fowler, "Pre-Columbian Urban Center on the Mississippi"; Iseminger, "Cahokia"; Fowler, *The Cahokie Atlas: A Historical Atlas of Cahokia Archaeology*, Studies in Illinois Archaeology, 6 (Springfield, 1989); George R. Milner, "The Late Prehistoric Cahokia Cultural System of the Mississippi River Valley: Foundations, Florescence, Fragmentation," *Journal of World Prehistory*, 4 (1990), 1–43; Thomas E. Emerson and R. Barry Lewis, eds., *Cahokia and the Hinterlands: Middle Mississippian Cultures of the Midwest* (Urbana, 1991). For European accounts of the Natchez and other Mississippians who sacrificed individuals when a paramount chief died see DePratter, "Late Prehistoric and Early Historic Chiefdoms," 64–77.

18. Fowler, "Pre-Columbian Urban Center," 8–11; Iseminger, "Cahokia"; Milner, "Late Prehistoric Cahokia Cultural System," 30–33.

19. Dena F. Dincauze and Robert J. Hasenstab, "Explaining the Iroquois: Tribalization on a prehistoric Periphery," in *Comparative Studies in the Development of Complex Societies*, 3 (Southampton, Eng., 1986), 5, 7–8; George R. Milner et al., "Warfare in Late Prehistoric West-Central Illinois," *American Antiquity*, 65 (1991), 581–603; Morse and Morse, *Archaeology*, chap. 12; Stephen Williams, "The Vacant Quarter and Other Late Events in the Lower Valley," in David H. Dye and Cheryl Anne Cox, eds., *Towns and Temples along the Mississippi* (Tuscaloosa, 1990), 170–80.

20. James A. Tuck, *Onondaga Iroquois Prehistory: A Study in Settlement Archaeology* (Syracuse, N. Y., 1971), chaps. 2–4; James W. Bradley, *Evolution of the Onondaga Iroquois: Accommodating Change, 1500–1655* (Syracuse, N. Y., 1987), 14–34 passim; Trigger, *Children of Aataentsic*, 1:119–76 passim; Trigger, *Natives and Newcomers: Canada's "Heroic Age" Reconsidered* (Kingston, Ont., 1985), 38–110 passim; Dean R. Snow, *The Archaeology of New England* (New York, 1980), 307–19 passim; Dincauze and Hasenstab, "Explaining the Iroquois." One influential version of the oral account of the Iroquois Confederacy's founding confirms that it occurred against a backdrop of violence among the Five Nations Iroquois and their common enmity with the Hurons; see William N. Fenton. ed., *Parker on the Iroquois*, (Syracuse, N. Y., 1968), bk. 3, pp. 14–29.

21. Neal Salisbury, *Manitou and Providence: Indians, Europeans, and the Making of New England, 1500–1643* (New York, 1982), 51–56; Trigger, *Natives and Newcomers*, 118–44.

22. Christopher L. Miller and George R. Hammell, "A New Perspective on Indian-White Contact: Cultural Symbols and Colonial Trade," *Journal of American History [JAH]*, 73 (1986), 311–28; Trigger, *Natives and Newcomers*, 125–27; Bradley, *Evolution*, chap. 21 Calvin Martin, "The Four Lives of a Micmac Copper Pot," *Ethnohistory*, 22 (1975), 111–33; James Axtell, "At the Water's Edge: Trading in the Sixteenth Century," in Axtell, *After Columbus: Essays in the Ethnohistory of Colonial North America* (New York, 1988), 144–81; Trigger, "Early Native North American Responses to European Contact: Romantic versus Rationalistic Interpretations," *JAH*, 77 (1991), 1195–1215. Compare the barbed Delaware-Mahican tradition of early relations with the Dutch recorded by John Heckewelder in his *An Account of the History, Manners, and Customs of the Indian Nations, Who Once Inhabited Pennsylvania and the Neighbouring States* (Philadelphia, 1819), 71–75.

23. Trigger, *Natives and Newcomers*, 144–48.

24. Ibid., 157–61.

25. See Dincauze and Haasenstab, "Explaining the Iroquois."

26. See, for example, Kenneth E. Kidd, "The Cloth Trade and the Indians of the Northeast during the Seventeenth and Eighteenth Centuries," in Royal Ontario Museum, *Art and Archaeology Annual* (1961), 48–56; Wilcomb E. Washburn, "Symbol,

Utility, and Aesthetics in the Indian Fur Trade," *Minnesota History*, 40 (1966), 198–202; Donald J. Bladeslee, "The Calumet Ceremony and the Origin of Fur Trade Rituals," *Western Canadian Journal of Anthropology*, 7, No. 2 (1977), 78–88; Bruce M. White, "Give Us a Little Milk: The Social and Cultural Meanings of Gift Giving in the Lake Superior Fur Trade," *Minnesota History*, 48 (1982), 60–71, and "A Skilled Game of Exchange: Ojibway Fur Trade Protocol," ibid., 50 (1987), 229–40; Francis Jennings et al., eds., *The History and Culture of Iroquois Diplomacy: An Interdisciplinary Guide to the Treaties of the Six Nations and Their League* (Syracuse, N.Y. 1985), chaps. 1, 4–7; Richard White, *The Middle Ground: Indians, Empires, and Republics, 1650–1815* (Cambridge, 1991), chaps. 2–4 passim.

27. Richter, *Ordeal of the Longhouse*, 30–104.

28. Pennsylvania joined the Covenant Chain early in the 18th century; Francis Jennings, *The Ambiguous Iroquois Empire: The Covenant Chain Confederation of Indian Tribes with English Colonies from Its Beginnings to the Lancaster Treaty of 1744* (New York, 1984), chap. 8; Richter, *Ordeal of the Longhouse*, 105–213 passim.

29. Shaffer, *Native Americans before 1492*, esp. 10–11, 94–96.

30. Alfred W. Crosby, *Ecological Imperialism: The Biological Expansion of Europe, 900–1900* (Cambridge, 1986).

31. Roy Harvey Pearce, *The Savages of America: A Study of the Indian and the Idea of Civilization* (Baltimore, 1953); Richard Slotkin, *Regeneration through Violence: The Mythology of the American Frontier, 1600–1800* (Middletown, Conn., 1973); Berkhofer, *White Man's Indian*.

32. Jennings, *Invasion of America*, pt. 1.

33. For summaries of these developments see Salisbury, "The History of Native Americans from before the Arrival of the Europeans and Africans until the American Civil War," in Stanley L. Engerman and Robert E. Gallman, eds., *The Cambridge Economic History of the United States*, vol. 1: *The Colonial Era* (Cambridge, 1996), chap. 1, and "Native People and European Settlers in Eastern North America, 1600–1783," in *The Cambridge History of the Native Peoples of the Americas*, vol. 1: North America, ed. Trigger and Washburn (Cambridge, 1996).

Article 2: Donnacona Discovers Europe: Rereading Jacques Cartier's *Voyages*

Ramsay Cook

Jacques Cartier's *Voyages* is the most informative and reliable French description of the northern coast and the St Lawrence region of North America written in the sixteenth century. The report that the Florentine navigator Giovanni Verrazzano composed for the French king, Francis I, describing the 1524. voyage along the coast from the Carolinas to Cape Breton, captures both the changing topography and the different groups of people who lived on the Atlantic seaboard. But it lacks detail and depth. André Thevet,

cosmographer to Francis I, wrote two works about 'France antartique' during the second half of the century—though he may never have travelled to the St Lawrence area. His works, *Les Singularitez de la France antartique* (1556) and *La Cosmographie universelle* (1575), relied heavily on Cartier, with whom he was acquainted. He provides some fascinating details not found elsewhere—his description of the snowshoe for example—but his reliability is problematic. If Verrazzano approximated Montaigne's 'plain simple fellow' who did not 'construct false theories,' then Thevet exemplified the 'men of intelligence' who could not 'refrain from altering the facts a little' in order to substantiate their interpretation.[1]

Cartier's observations are frequently detailed and include an impressive range of information about the geography, natural history, and ethnography from Funk Island to the Amerindian settlement at Hochelaga at the foot of the mountain he named Mount Royal. The *Voyages*, for over 450 years, have provided almost the only documentation for the beginning of European contact with this region. They reveal a man with both the virtues of an honest

Source: From Cook, R. *The Voyages of Jacques Cartier*, 1993, ix–x, xviii–xli. © 1993, University of Toronto Press. Reprinted with permission of the publisher.

observer and the assumptions and preoccupations of a shrewd Breton navigator. Since he interpreted what he saw, he 'never presents things just as they are' and, especially in his discussion of his relations with the people who lived along the St Lawrence, he 'could twist and disguise [facts] to conform to [his] point of view.' Like all historical documents, Cartier's *Voyages* can be both informative and misleading.[2] [...]

The critical test of Cartier's representation of what he saw in eastern North America is [...] his ethnology. For Cartier was, unwittingly Canada's first ethnologist, an activity practiced long before its invention as a science.[3] Cartier's *Voyages* can usefully be put to the test of a successful ethnographer set by Clifford Geertz: 'Ethnographers need to convince us … not merely that they themselves have truly been there, but … had we been there we should have seen what they saw, felt what they felt, concluded what they concluded.'[4] Historians, from Marc Lescarbot in the seventeenth century to Samuel Eliot Morison and Marcel Trudel in the twentieth, have given Cartier almost uniformly high marks by that standard.[5] Cartier's descriptions of the native people he met carry conviction. But the question may fairly be posed: is it necessary to *conclude* what Cartier concluded, even if his description bears the mark of authenticity? That question can best be approached by focusing on the well-known story of Cartier's troubled relationship with Donnacona, 'the lord of Canada,' and his two sons Dom Agaya and Taignoagny, always remembering that all the evidence about that relationship is provided by Cartier, a judge on his own case.[6]

Can that same evidence be used to discover the voices and motives of Cartier's protagonists, to tease out a dialogue where too often only a single voice has been heard in the past? It is worth attempting, even if the results must be tentative, even conjectural, since it must be constructed from limited, often obscure, clues.[7] Moreover, it is important to realize that, in attempting to reconstruct the Cartier-Donnacona dialogue, the problem of language and communication is enormous. Naturally, on Cartier's first trip, the language barrier was total and native speech was almost always described as a 'harangue' or a 'sermon.'[8] Yet in his account of his contacts with the local inhabitants he confidently describes actions, motives, and relationships as though communication had been fairly straightforward. But was it? For example, he describes the relationship among Donnacona, Dom

Agaya, and Taignoagny as that of a 'father' and his 'sons.' How did Cartier know? The vocabulary compiled on the first voyage does not contain these words. On his second voyage he had, part of the time, the assistance of the two men he had carried off to France. How much French had they learned? How faithfully did they translate their own language that had developed in the North American context into an imperfectly understood European tongue? Many European concepts, as the missionaries would later discover, had no local equivalents.[9] The opposite was almost certainly true: the lack of European words for important Amerindian concepts. The more extensive vocabulary gathered during the second voyage still amounts to little more than a tourist's elementary phrase book: numbers, body parts, food, basic questions and commands. Writing of European accounts of contact with native people, Stephen Greenblatt remarks: 'The Europeans and the interpreters themselves translated such fragments as they understood or thought they understood into a coherent story, and they came to believe quite easily that the story was what they actually heard. There could be, and apparently were, murderous results.'[10] The *Voyages* certainly present a fairly coherent story of the Cartier-Donnaconna relationship. The more that relationship is examined, however, the more obvious it becomes that it was based on a dialogue of incomprehension, a dialogue in which Donnacona's actions were made to speak in European words. It ended, if not in murder, then certainly in tragedy.

IV

Cartier arrived in eastern North America already somewhat familiar with the character of its inhabitants.[11] That doubtless explains the matter-of-fact tone to his description of the scattered groups his expedition came across along the coast of Labrador. In 'the land God gave to Cain' he found a 'wild and savage folk' who painted themselves 'with certain tan colours'—Boethuk hunting seal. Before long he realized that these North American people were not all alike: they spoke different languages, practised contrasting lifestyles, and, he eventually realized, warred against one another. From first contact he feared them or at least doubted their trustworthiness, especially if he was outnumbered. He would retain that suspicion and fear even after numerous experiences of welcoming hospitality, though he would tell

King Francis I of 'their kindness and peacefulness'. When forty or fifty canoe-loads of Micmac in the Bay de Chaleur signalled a desire to trade with a French party in one longboat, Cartier 'did not care to trust to their signs.' When they persisted, he drove them off with gunfire. French security and potential dominance was established.

This meeting also suggests that Cartier and his party may not have been the first Europeans whom the local native people had met. They wanted to trade and showed no fear. In fact, by 1534, trade between Europeans—Bretons, Basques, English, and other people who lived and fished on the Atlantic seaboard—had a history of several decades, possibly beginning before Columbus.[12] Cartier provides the first detailed description of the ceremonials surrounding trade when the people he had previously driven off returned on 7 July, 'making signs to us that they had come to barter.' Cartier had brought well-chosen trade goods: 'knives, and other iron goods, and a red cap to give their chief.' The first exchange was brisk, the natives leaving stripped even of the furs that covered their bodies. Three days later, amid ceremonial gift exchanges, dancing and singing, business resumed. The young women hung back, suggesting earlier experiences with European sailors. Cartier watched these events with a careful eye, concluding that 'we perceived that they are a people who would be easy to convert'. This was not an immediate goal, but rather a thought for the future. It was an indication that from the outset the French were fishers of men as well as 'explorers,' and that Cartier saw no reason to accept these 'savages' on their own terms.

At Gaspé Harbour, later in July, Cartier made his first contact with members of the native community to which his future in Canada would be inextricably tied. These were people from Stadacona—Laurentian Iroquoians—making their annual fishing expedition to the east coast. Cartier's reports are the only record of these people who 'disappeared,' probably as a result of warfare and perhaps disease, by the end of the century.[13] His first impression of the Stadaconans is important because it illustrates Cartier's powers of observation again, and also provides a clear insight into his use of the term 'sauvaiges.' He wrote: 'This people may well be called savage; for they are the sorriest folk there can be in the world, and the whole lot of them had not anything above the value of five sous, their canoes and fishingnets excepted. They go

quite naked, except for a small skin, with which they cover their privy parts, and for a few old skins which they throw over their shoulders. They are not at all of the same race or language as the first we met. They have their heads shaved all around in circles, except for a tuft on the top of the head, which they leave long like a horse's tail. This they do up upon their heads and tie in a knot with leather thongs. They have no other dwelling but their canoes, which they turn upside down and sleep on the ground underneath. They eat their meat almost raw; only warming it a little on the coals; and the same with their fish [...] They never eat anything that has a taste of salt in it. They are wonderful thieves and steal everything they can carry off'.

For Cartier the word 'sauvaiges' was interchangeable with 'gens,' 'personnes,' 'peuple,' 'hommes du pays,' 'hommes,' 'femmes'—he never used 'Indiens.' This usage suggests that Cartier accepted the Amerindians as human, like himself—a matter much disputed in the aftermath of Columbus's initial encounter with the people in America.[14] That impression is supported by Cartier's belief that the inhabitants of the St Lawrence region could be converted to Christianity; had they not been 'men,' that potential would have been denied. But still they were 'savages,' which apparently meant poverty stricken, lacking in worldly possessions and civic institutions, bereft of religion and culture. (They certainly fulfilled Montaigne's definition: 'we all call barbarous anything that is contrary to our own habits'!)[15] Because of their 'savage,' 'wild' state, their lack of culture, Cartier believed that native people could easily be 'dompter': subdued, subjugated, tamed,[16] or as Biggar says, 'moulded.' Consequently, while native people were accepted as 'human,' they were only potential, not actual, equals of the Europeans. Only if the 'savage' characteristics that made them different were 'tamed' or 'moulded' could they become actual equals. Different *and* equal was inconceivable.[17] Finally, since these Laurentian people were 'savages' without culture, religion, or government, Cartier, like those European explorers who had preceded him, saw no reason to ask permission to explore and eventually settle their lands.

Nothing better emphasizes Cartier's assumptions about his rights—and Donnacona's reaction—than the drama that was acted out on 24 July 1534 at the entrance to Gaspé Harbour. There Cartier presided over the raising of a thirty-foot wooden cross to which was fixed a coat-of-arms bearing the fleurs-de-lys and a board on which was emblazoned the words: 'VIVE LE ROI DE FRANCE.' In the presence of Donnacona's people, the French 'knelt down with our hands joined, worshipping it before them; and made signs to them, looking up and pointing towards heaven, that by means of this we had our redemption, at which they showed many marks of admiration, at the same time turning and looking at the cross'.

Any 'marks of admiration' Cartier thought he detected were soon erased by a vigorous act of protest by native leaders. Cartier's account of this reaction demonstrates that what was viewed as an arbitrary European intrusion into eastern North America was not passively accepted. The protest was led by the person Cartier identified as 'the leader' and 'three of his sons and his brother.' Even the language barrier did not prevent Cartier from understanding—or thinking he understood—the meaning of the demonstration: 'pointing to the cross he [the leader] made us a long harangue, making the sign of the cross with two of his fingers; and then he pointed to the land all around about, as if he wished to say that all this region belonged to him, and that we ought not to have set up this cross without his permission'.

Neither the action of the French, in raising the cross, nor the reaction of the native people is totally unambiguous. Cross-raising, beginning with Columbus, had already become something of a tradition in the Americas. It contained both religious and political symbolism. Cartier had previously raised at least one cross—an undecorated one at St Servan's Harbour in June—and he would raise others later. Some of these crosses were raised unceremoniously and doubtless were intended to function as 'a landmark and guidepost into the harbour'. Though Cartier explained the Gaspé cross that way, its bold symbols of church and state, and the accompanying ceremony, surely represented something more. If it was not an explicit legal claim, recognizable in international law, to French possession of this territory, it was surely at least what Trudel calls 'une affirmation solennelle des droits de la France sur cette terre.'[18] This was not an anonymous directional sign; it distinctly affirmed the French presence. It is also worth emphasizing that in introducing the account of his second voyage, Cartier related his exploration both to the protection and promotion of Catholicism

against the threat of 'wicked Lutherans, apostates, and imitators of Mahomet' and to 'these lands of yours,' 'your possessions,' and 'those lands and territories of yours'. If, then, the crosses were merely traffic signals, they should at least be described as *French* traffic signals.

And what of the native people's protest? Cartier's interpretation of it as a rejection of the French right to act without permission can be seen, at the least, as a sign of a guilty conscience. Certainly he knew that no European sovereign would accept such an act on his or her territory. But did a North American 'leader,' especially one whose home territory was somewhere up the St Lawrence, have the same sense of sovereign or proprietary rights? Was the chief claiming the Gaspé harbour area as his people's fishing and hunting territory? It seems altogether likely. What is beyond doubt is that a protest did take place, a protest Cartier suspected was an expression of territorial jurisdiction. Moreover, Cartier acted quickly and deceptively to quell the protest.

When the chief—we later learn this was Donnacona[19]—completed his 'harangue,' a sailor offered him an axe in exchange for the black bear skin he was wearing. Responding to the offer of barter, Donnacona's party moved closer to the French ship only to have their canoe boarded and themselves taken prisoner, though Cartier did not use that term. On the second voyage he did, however, refer to them as 'captured' and 'seized'. Once on board they were cajoled—'made to eat and drink and be of good cheer' (was the drink alcoholic?)—into accepting the sign-post explanation. Cartier then announced that he intended to release only three of the prisoners—compensated with hatchets and knives. The other two, now decked out in shirts, ribbons, and red caps, would be taken 'away with us and afterwards would bring them back again to that harbour'. Since no destination was announced, it seems entirely unlikely that the two young men, or their father, understood this to mean an Atlantic crossing and a nine-month stay in France. Cartier made the final departure seem amicable, and perhaps it appeared that way to Donnacona's people who, if they understood what was taking place, probably recognized that resistance was hopeless. Cartier admitted that 'we did not understand the parting harangues,' and there is equally no reason to believe that Donnacona understood what Cartier had tried to tell him. At best the day ended

31

in mutual misunderstanding—hardly the basis for an 'alliance.'[20]

In acting as he did—and the action seemed premeditated—Cartier followed an established European precedent. Europeans assumed a right to 'explore' new-found lands and to set up traffic crosses, indicating at least an intention to return and perhaps even staking a claim to possession. So, too, kidnapping native people began with Columbus, and Cartier may even have committed similar actions on earlier voyages to Brazil. Since at the time of the seizure of the natives Cartier had not determined whether to continue his explorations or to return to France before winter, his initial intention may have been simply to make use of the men as short-term guides. More plausible, however, is the view that Cartier planned to take the captives back to St Malo as concrete evidence of 'discovery' and to provide them with language training. With the aid of interpreters and go-betweens, the further penetration of North America, leading to the much sought after route to Asia—Cartier's primary goal—would be expedited. Or so Cartier doubtless hoped.

Exactly how Dom Agaya and Taignoagny, as the young men are identified in the account of the second voyage, spent their time between their arrival in St Malo on 5 September 1534 and their departure for home on 19 May 1535 is unrecorded. Nor is there any direct evidence revealing their reactions to their unexpected discovery of Europe. The harrowing experiences of an eighteenth-century Chinese visitor named John Hu, a man similarly untutored in French language and customs, offer some clues to the complexity of cultural contact: he was driven to such unpredictable behaviour that he was confined to the asylum at Charenton pondering the question, 'Why am I locked up?'[21] The two North Americans survived somewhat better, even though they must often have asked similar questions. They doubtless witnessed many strange and wonderful sights. Yet it seems unlikely that either the standard of living of ordinary Frenchmen—housing, food, or medical care—or the political and religious life of a country wracked with religious strife won their enthusiastic approval.[22] Perhaps they concluded, as Jean de Léry did after returning to France from Brazil, that 'one need not go beyond one's own country, nor as far as America, to see [...] monstrous and prodigious things.'[23]

By the time of their return home, they spoke some French, though the level of fluency cannot have been very high. They had learned to dress in the French manner. They may have calculated, and filed for future use, the comparative values of French trade goods, a knowledge that would earn them the epithet of 'rogues'. They had not been baptized, though they had observed that ceremony and other Catholic rites. To Cartier they may have seemed at least partly 'moulded' or 'tamed,' though he would continue to call them 'sauvaiges.' He apparently believed they were ready and willing to work for him. It was not yet in their interest to disabuse him of that notion. That could wait until they were safely back in Stadacona. Then their actions and attitudes would reveal that they had no wish to go on their foreign travels again.

V

During the winter of 1534–5, Dom Agaya and Taignoagny provided Cartier with much useful information about eastern North America. The French navigator certainly wanted to know whether a route to Asia could be found by continuing westward from the mouth of the St Lawrence. Perhaps they encouraged his hopes that a route existed. What he obviously did learn from them was that their home was far inland, up an enormous river at Stadacona, beyond a rich region known as the Saguenay. It was there that they wished to be returned, not to the Gaspé as their father had been promised. Consequently it was from knowledge gained from the two native men, and as a result of their directions, that Cartier was able to attain his principal geographical achievement: 'he was,' Marcel Trudel noted, 'the first to make a survey of the coasts of the St Lawrence [...] and, what is most to his credit, in 1535, he discovered the St Lawrence River.'[24] In fact, Cartier himself described what happened somewhat more accurately. On Friday, 13 August 1535, sailing from southwestern Anticosti, 'it was told us by the two savages whom we had captured on our first voyage, that this cape formed part of the land on the south which was an island; and that to the south of it lay the route from Honguedo where we had seized them [...] and that two days journey from this cape and island began the kingdom of the Saguenay, on the north shore as one made one's way towards this Canada'. Four days later, when Cartier was in some doubt about the route, 'the two savages assured us that this was the way to the mouth of the great river of Hochelaga [St Lawrence] and the route towards Canada [...] and that one could make one's way so far up the river that they had never heard of anyone reaching the head of it'. Cartier and his crew were the first known Europeans to be guided along the St Lawrence to Stadacona. They then insisted that the guide service be continued further up to Hochelaga. That demand resulted in a crisis in the hitherto satisfactory relationship with Dom Agaya, Taignoagny, and their father.

Not surprisingly, the return of the captives to their people in the Stadacona region was an occasion for great joy. At first the local inhabitants were cautious, even fearful, but once the returning men had identified themselves, the ceremonies and gift exchanges began. On 8 September, near the Ile d'Orléans, 'the lord of Canada' arrived alongside and began a 'harangue,' 'moving his body and his limbs in a marvellous manner as is their custom when showing joy and contentment.' Had Cartier interpreted the body language correctly? At this happy reunion, Cartier reported that the sons informed their father 'what they had seen in France, and the good treatment meted out to them there.' Donnacona expressed his gratitude with warm embraces for the French leader. Bread and wine were shared before the returning travellers departed with their father.

It was not until a week later, during which Dom Agaya and his brother had ample time to discuss their travels in more detail with their father, that Cartier met with them again. He was now impatient to move on, but he detected a marked, disturbing change in the mood of his former companions. Sailing towards Stadacona, Cartier met a large party of native people. 'All came over towards our ships,' he noted, 'except the two men we had brought with us [...] who were altogether changed in their attitude and goodwill, and refused to come on board our ships, although many times begged to do so. At this we began somewhat to distrust them.' Cartier's attitude was obviously changing, too. Nevertheless he believed they were willing to guide him to Hochelaga, a place of whose existence they had apparently informed him.

During the next five days, until Cartier pushed on up-river without his guides, the issue of the continuing service of Dom Agaya and Taignoagny resulted in an almost total break in relations between the Stadaconans and the St Malouins. The issue in dispute was simple. Cartier believed that his interpreters had promised to continue on with him to Hochelaga. Donnacona and his sons (Taignoagny more consistently, it would seem, than his brother) either did not want the French to continue westward at all or at least not without first making some binding commitment or alliance with the Stadaconans. If it is true, as some have concluded, that Donnacona hoped to prevent Cartier from making contact with other native groups so that Stadacona could control trade between the French and the hinterland, or that Donnacona hoped to enlist French military aid against the Hochelagans, there is nothing in Cartier's account to support these speculations.[25] Nor is it fair to accept Cartier's claim that on their return to Stadacona, Dom Agaya and Taignoagny began to 'intrigue' against him.[26] They had, after all, painfully concrete reasons for distrusting Cartier, and legitimate grounds for looking to their own interests in the face of French incursions into their territory. To judge these confusing events—which make it plain that the language barrier had not been effectively breeched—solely from Cartier's perspective implicitly denies the legitimacy of Donnacona's stance. Yet what Cartier viewed as 'treachery,' from Donnacona's point of view was a perfectly reasonable insistence that foreign visitors conduct themselves with due respect for the wishes and customs of their hosts. This is not to argue that the actions of the Stadaconans were so straightforward that Cartier was simply obtuse in failing to understand them. It does have to be remembered that the account of these events is Cartier's and therefore reflects his confusion and suspicion; it does not necessarily represent faithfully the intentions of the other actors whose behaviour may have had a logic of its own. A tentative analysis of a series of events that left Cartier impatient, suspicious, and frightened helps to reveal this logic.

On 16 September Taignoagny informed Cartier that Donnacona was 'annoyed' by the Frenchman's decision to visit Hochelaga and that he would not accompany him. Taignoagny then rejected Cartier's offer of a present—a bribe—in return for disobeying his father. The following day Donnacona appeared, and a ceremony—though Cartier may not have recognized it as such—took place in which the chief presented Cartier with a girl about twelve years old, said to be Donnacona's niece, and two younger boys, one of whom was said to be Taignoagny's brother, though these relationships seem confused. Cartier first understood these gifts as an attempt to convince him to forgo his Hochelaga trip—an apparent bribe. He refused that condition and was then told that the gifts were offered out of friendship and 'in sign of alliance'. Cartier attributed these conflicting stories to Taignoagny, 'as well by this as by other bad turns we had seen him do [...] was a worthless fellow, who was intent upon nothing but treason and malice'. He ignored or disbelieved, or failed to understand, the meaning of a 'sign of alliance.'

It is possible that in order to cement an alliance with the French, Donnacona was proposing a reciprocal gift, an exchange of persons? Cartier was familiar with gift-giving, for he had engaged in it since his first arrival in North America. But he probably did not understand its ceremonial implications in North American native societies, especially that such ceremonies could include the exchange of people.[27] This interpretation is perhaps borne out by the fact that after the Stadaconans failed in what, from Cartier's account, seemed to be a clumsy attempt to invoke the aid of their divinity to frighten the French away from the western trip, a new proposal was advanced. 'Taignoagny and Dom Agaya told the Captain that Donnacona was unwilling that either of them should accompany him to Hochelaga unless he [Cartier] should leave a hostage behind on shore with Donnacona'. It is, of course, possible that Donnacona suspected another kidnapping and wanted a hostage. Alternatively, this proposal may have been a misunderstood attempt to explain the reciprocal nature of the gift-exchange treaty ceremony.

Cartier summarily rejected this new proposal, for he had now completely lost confidence in his former interpreters. He would go without them, sweeping Donnacona's objections aside. But the questions remain: Did Cartier misinterpret Donnacona's objections and the proposal he made? Had Donnacona merely been asking Cartier to complete the reciprocal action that had begun when Cartier accepted the children who had been offered as a 'sign of alliance'? If an alliance had been offered and rejected, was it not quite natural for Donnacona's people to suspect that the French expedition to Hochelaga might have results that would be detrimental to the interests of Stadacona? 'In these primitive and archaic societies'— one might prefer the term stateless societies—Marcel

Mauss wrote in his *Essai sur le don*, 'there is no middle path. There is either complete trust or mistrust. One lays down one's arms, renounces magic and gives everything away, from casual hospitality to one's daughter or one's property. It was in such conditions that men, despite themselves, learnt to renounce what was theirs and made contracts to give and repay.'[28] Cartier had first refused to lay down arms ('to carry them … was the custom in France'; had then insisted that their magic, not his, should be renounced ('their god Cudouagny was a mere fool [...] Jesus would keep them safe'; and finally had refused the reciprocal gift that would have sealed an alliance, even when the lord of Canada's own niece and son were offered to him. Where complete trust might have been established, mistrust, on both sides, resulted.

Unable to understand the framework in which the Stadaconans acted, Cartier was reduced to denunciation, charging his lost allies with ill-will and treason. But the problem was a much deeper one. Cartier had taken Dom Agaya and Taignoagny to France to train them as interpreters so they could act as go-betweens, easing him along his way. On their return to the St Lawrence region armed with their new language skills, they were to act in his interests and aid him in achieving his objectives. In a sense, he expected them to act as Frenchmen. What he failed to comprehend, or accept, was that after a brief nine months of total immersion, Dom Agaya and Taignoagny remained pretty much as they had always been: St Lawrence Iroquoians. Once reunited with their own people, they reverted completely to their own identities and refused to collaborate unconditionally with their former captors.[29] When Cartier learned that what had appeared to be friendship in France had disappeared—a friendship he thought had been affirmed by the welcome he received on his first arrival at Stadacona—he could only explain it by character defects in the native people. They were unreliable, untrustworthy, treacherous rogues—a typical European conclusion.[30] Yet the behaviour that Cartier condemned as 'treason'—a word implying that loyalty was owed to the French— was, by Donnacona's logic, a rejection of that very idea, a rejection of French mastery. The first act of resistance had taken place at Gaspé Harbour. The struggle over Cartier's trip to Hochelaga was but another action in the same drama. Everything was now in place for the dénouement.

VI

Cartier's Hochelaga trip, as he recorded it, stands in marked contrast to the gathering atmosphere of mistrust and confused signals between the French and the Stadaconans. That contrast is seen in the first contact he made with native people up the river: 'they come towards our boats in as friendly and familiar manner as if we had been natives of the country'. Further along Cartier felt the same easy relationship, and at one point allowed a powerful man to carry him ashore 'as if he had been a six-year-old child'. There were gift exchanges; one local leader presented Cartier with 'two of his children,' though only the girl, who was eight or nine, was accepted. The culmination of this almost royal progress came at Hochelaga. As the French approached the village on 2 October they were greeted by 'more than a thousand persons, men, women and children, who gave us as good a welcome as ever father gave to his son [...] They brought us quantities of fish, and of their bread [...] throwing so much of it into our longboats that it seemed to rain bread'.

Cartier accepted this treatment as perfectly natural, perhaps even to be expected from people whom he may have assumed were familiar with Europeans. But what he interpreted as signs of familiarity were quite likely just the opposite, as he may gradually have realized. In fact, the character of the reception the French received at Hochelaga bore the marks of a first contact, one in which the native people mistook the French, marshalled in their armour and speaking a strange language, for something other than ordinary men. Women repeatedly brought their children to be touched, and the women showed none of the shyness evident in those earlier trading sessions when their men kept them at a distance. The next day, within the pallisaded village, a remarkable ceremony took place, one in which Cartier found himself in the role of shaman or healer—and accepted his unexpected casting. Cartier and his men were ushered to the centre of the town square and seated on elaborately woven mats. Soon they were joined by the village's leader, carried in on the shoulders of nine or ten strong men. When he took his seat on a deerskin near Cartier, it became obvious that he was severely paralysed and that he expected to be 'cured and healed' by his visitor. Cartier, taking his cue, 'set about rubbing his arms and legs with his hands. Thereupon this *Agouhanna*

took the band of cloth he was wearing as a crown and presented it to the Captain.' Then the sick, the lame, the blind, and the aged were brought forward for Cartier to 'lay his hands upon them, so that one would have thought Christ had come down to earth to heal them.' Cartier performed his appointed role in the only style he knew, 'making the sign of the cross over the poor sick people, praying God to give them knowledge of our holy faith'. So convincing was his interpretation that the local women tried to prevent the French from leaving by offering large quantities of food. Cartier rejected it for it was unsalted, though he was probably anxious to depart before being called for an encore.

Whether Cartier exaggerated these events of the early days of October 1535, and what exactly they meant to the St Lawrence Iroquoians, can only be guessed at. Certainly they were unlike any other ceremony recorded in the *Voyages*. It was obviously not an occasion for commerce, though some gifts were distributed by the French, for the Hochelagans showed none of the frenzied desire to exchange furs for European goods that was displayed at earlier meetings. Instead, the ritual performed in the village square bore the signs of some prophecy being fulfilled with the arrival of otherworldly healers.[31] Cartier's quick intelligence apparently allowed him to interpret the signals accurately. Perhaps it was the realization that his healing powers were at best untested that led to his hasty departure on the following day 'for fear of any misadventure'. Even the almost worshipful reception of the Hochelagans had not removed Cartier's distrust of the St Lawrence Iroquoians.

The French undoubtedly contrasted the respectful reception they had received at Hochelaga with what they interpreted as the cagey manoeuvring of Donnacona and his sons. Now they set out to return to Stadacona, convinced there was gold and silver to be found somewhere in the region and apparently under the impression that 'the Canadians and some eight or nine other peoples are subjects' of the Hochelagans. Perhaps this belief stiffened Cartier's determination to deal with Donnacona's people more firmly and, if necessary, harshly. The western trip had done nothing to dispel his suspicion that even the friendliest of gesture on the part of the leaders a Stadacona only masked treacherous intentions.

35

VII

Cartier's peremptory departure for Hochelaga on 19 September doubtless left the Stadaconans displeased, suspicious, and perhaps even hostile. When the French party returned a week later they found that the men they had left behind had built themselves a fort 'with artillery pointing every way'. Obviously relations had deteriorated further. Still Donnacona issued an almost immediate invitation to visit Stadacona—something Cartier had not done before going to Hochelaga, which may have been another cause for Donnacona's earlier unease. On visiting Stadacona, Cartier received a warm and formal welcome. He attached no particular significance to a display of scalps that Donnacona explained had been harvested during a war with the 'Toudamans,' though this may have been a request for French assistance.

During this period Cartier began closer observation of local customs, and concluded that the St Lawrence Iroquoians had 'no belief in God that amounts to anything.' He attempted to inform them about Christianity, but when Donnacona and his sons rounded up the whole village for baptism 'an excuse was made to them': there were no priests to conduct the ceremony and there was no consecrated oil. Whether this was the whole truth is unclear. Cartier had told Donnacona earlier that he had consulted his 'priests' before going to Hochelaga, at the time when an attempt had been made to prevent Cartier's departure by an appeal to the local god. Moreover, a mass was 'said and sung' some months later. If the priests had not died in the interim—and that is possible—then Cartier prevaricated on one of these occasions. It is significant that Cartier refused baptism for two reasons: 'we did not know their real intention and state of mind and had no one to explain to them our faith'. Yet the incident further convinced him that conversion would be easy.

Still, Cartier continued to distrust the Stadaconans, especially his two former guides after they urged their fellows to bargain for better prices. Both on his trip to Hochelaga and after returning, the French had been encouraged by some native people to beware of Dom Agaya and his brother. After a number of small incidents had heightened Cartier's apprehensions, and 'fearing that they should attempt some treasonable design,' he reinforced the fort and ordered a round-the-clock watch, thus provoking annoyance and puzzlement among Donnacona's

followers. Yet by the time winter had set in—and it was a terrible winter—relations had apparently been restored to 'as friendly a manner as before'.

December brought disaster in the shape of a scurvy epidemic, the best-known incident in Cartier's career. Disease was the scourge of sixteenth-century Europeans even more than for pre-contact North American people. In France disease was widespread, often epidemic, and cures were few. In March 1535, prior to Cartier's second trip, an 'epidemic and plague' broke out in St Malo and was perhaps carried up the St Lawrence. Europeans had, however, developed immunities, complete or partial, to a large number of communicable diseases, which meant they were no longer fatal. But European pathogens were largely unknown in America, making measles, small pox, tuberculosis, influenza, and other common diseases deadly. The cures—herbal and spiritual—that North Americans successfully applied to their own illnesses were impotent against the European biological invasion that silently accompanied Columbus.[32] Of course, Europeans could contact unexpected health problems in North America, too.

According to Cartier's account, the 'pestilence' that struck in December broke out first among the people of Stadacona and, despite efforts at quarantine, the French were soon infected. Since Cartier's graphic description of the disease makes it certain it was scurvy caused by a vitamin C deficiency, the suspicion of contagion was unfounded. Moreover, since the native people had an effective cure for scurvy, Cartier's assumption that both communities were suffering from the same illness may be questioned, especially when he reported 'more than fifty deaths' at Stadacona. Perhaps the native people had contracted a French imported virus. That the French brought diseases with them is documented by Cartier's observation that the scurvy remedy that was eventually used 'cured all of the diseases they had ever had. And some of the sailors who had been suffering for five or six years from the French pox [la grande vérole] were by the medicine cured completely'. What this disease really was—syphilis or small pox or something else—is impossible to say. But micro-organisms certainly entered the St Lawrence region with the French, likely began infecting the inhabitants by the early winter of 1535, and may even have played a part in the eventual disappearance of the St Lawrence Iroquoians.[33] Of course, native people suffered from vitamin C deficiencies, too; it is the reported fifty fatalities that suggests scepticism about Cartier's diagnosis.

What is incontestable is that while the scurvy raged through the French camp, afflicting all but three or four and killing twenty-five of the 110 members of the company, Cartier's fears and suspicions—his 'great dread' of the Stadaconans—grew. Utterly convinced that the native people bore the French ill will, Cartier resorted to a series of ruses to disguise the weakness of his stricken contingent from them—instead of asking for assistance. When, for example, a party led by Donnacona set off for the annual winter hunt and did not return exactly when expected, Cartier concluded that 'a large force to attack us' was being assembled. Nor were those suspicions and fears erased by the most obvious sign of Iroquoian good will imaginable in the circumstances. Dom Agaya, who had apparently himself suffered severely from a scurvy-like disease, not only prescribed the cure he had used but even ordered two women to gather the 'Annedda' (white cedar) branches for him.[34] It was not Cartier 'skillfully questioning'[35] Dom Agaya that is noteworthy in this episode, but rather the young Iroquois' quick, willing response to the plight of his one-time kidnappers. That Cartier was blind to this generosity is perhaps seen in his enthusiastic thanks to God, rather than to Dom Agaya, for the miraculous cure.

What even more obviously reveals Cartier's almost paranoid suspicion of the Stadaconans is the evidence that Dom Agaya's gift of the cure did nothing to undermine the 'dread' that Donnacona was plotting an attack on the French. When the headman returned from his trip, accompanied by a large number of hunters, and showed some signs that Cartier interpreted as secretiveness and caution, those fears were heightened. When Cartier learned that 'a leader of that region named Agona' was somehow a problem for Donnacona, he made no offer of support to the old man and his sons or to draw any connection between this problem and Donnacona's mysterious movements. Instead Cartier, 'on being informed of the large number of people at Stadacona, though un-aware of their purpose, yet determined to outwit them, and to seize their leader [Donnacona], Taignoagny, Dom Agaya, and the headmen. And moreover he had quite made up his mind to take Donnacona to France, that he might relate and tell to the king all he had seen in the west of the wonders of the world'. If Cartier believed

that by removing Donnacona's party he could place Agona in power and thus establish French control of the St Lawrence region through a puppet, there is nothing in his account that even hints at such 'a plan for a revolution.'[36]

Every effort was now focused on drawing Donnacona and his supporters into a trap. When the Stadaconans, perhaps suspecting foul play, proved reluctant prey, Cartier took this as a further sign of 'knavishness'. That the Stadaconans had the uneasy feeling that the French were planning a trip for them was revealed by Taignoagny's expression of relief when Cartier assured him that the king had 'forbidden him to carry off to France any man or woman, but only two or three boys to learn the language'. Taignoagny, the supposed scheming rogue, naïvely swallowed this blatant lie and promised to bring his father to the French fort the next day.

That day, 3 May, was Holy Cross Day, an appropriate occasion for a repetition of the events that had taken place at Gaspé Harbour two years earlier. First a cross raising, at a location where a traffic marker was hardly needed. Its Latin letters read: FRANCIS-CVSPRIMVS, DEI GRATIA, FRANCORVM REX, REGNAT.' Perhaps recalling the earlier ceremony, Donnacona was nervous and reluctant to enter the fort 'to eat and drink as usual'. Cartier became impatient with the cat-and-mouse game: he ordered his men to seize the chief, his two sons, and two others. A desperate attempt by Taignoagny to pull his father back came too late. Once the five 'had been captured and the rest had all disappeared, Donnacona and his companions were placed in safe custody'. They were prisoners.

Donnacona's followers, fully aware of the deadly fire power of the French canon, probably concluded that any attempt to free their leader would result in disaster. One apparent threat was made, but Cartier ordered Donnacona brought on deck to calm his people with the promise that within 'ten or twelve moons' he would return to his homeland. Ceremonies followed on this and subsequent days when Cartier was presented with large quantities of *esnoguy* or wampum, 'the most valuable articles they possess in this world; for they attach more value to it than to gold or silver'. These gestures were surely not made in homage to the French explorer who had deceived them but rather as a pathetic attempt to purchase a guaranteed return passage for their chief and his companions. Cartier generously repeated his promise, for what it was worth, and on 6 May 1536 his ships and their human cargo sailed away.

Cartier probably intended to return to Stadacona the next year, but King Francis was preoccupied by a war with Spain. The return journey was delayed for more than three years. None of the ten native people—the five captives plus five others who were 'gifts'—ever returned to Canada. All but one woman died before Cartier set out again, and she remained in France. She might have brought some embarrassing news had she returned. Before he died, Donnacona had been to court, apparently performing as Cartier had hoped. According to Thevet, he died 'a good Christian, speaking French.'[37] The fate of his companions is unrecorded except that, in all, three were baptized, whether voluntarily, or *in articulo mortis,* is unknown.[38] Probably the diseases that Dom Agaya and Taignoagny had escaped on their first trip now took their toll. Four years was a long time to be away from home. The 'slips of trees and the seeds of the rarest [plants] of Canada' that Cartier presented to Francis I were planted in the garden at Fontainebleau.[39] The 'lord of Canada' and his companions were presumably interred in humbler ground.

When the navigator of St Malo finally reappeared before Stadacona on 23 August 1541, he offered a self-serving account of the fate of the men, girls, and boys he had so callously transported to France. When he met with Agona who, he noted, 'was appointed king there by Donnacona,' Cartier told him that 'Donnacona was dead in France, and that his body rested in the earth, and that the rest stayed there as great Lords, and were married, and would not return back into their country.' The French leader was satisfied that the lie had been carried off convincingly, especially since Agona was now the unchallenged 'Lord and Governor of the Country'.

The third voyage, of which the record is so fragmentary, proved a complete fiasco. The settlement Cartier had been sent to help establish—leadership now rested with Sieur de Roberval—was short-lived. In the spring of 1542 the St Lawrence Iroquoians turned against him. Even Agona, whose loyalty the French so confidently believed had been bought by Donnacona's demise, apparently joined the opposition. Cartier, hoping a fistful of 'Canadian diamonds' would justify his desertion of Roberval, decided to flee.[40] Did he ever suspect that the St Lawrence Iroquoians had finally realized the true fate of Donnacona and the others?

Cartier's failure, for that is what it was, resulted from his ethnology, his attempt to understand the people who lived along the St Lawrence River. His description of them was careful and often perceptive. He leaves the impression of having truly 'been there.' But his judgment, and therefore his representation, of these people was mortally flawed. They existed only in European terms, never in their own, their *alterité* unrecognized because it was unaccepted. Though Cartier successfully mapped the St Lawrence, he misidentified the St Lawrence Iroquoians, who remained as mysterious as the *adhothuys* [belugas] and 'seahorses' [walruses] who played near the mouth of the Saguenay River. For Cartier, a flawed ethnology brought only failure; for Donnacona's people it proved fatal.

VIII

The *Voyages of Jacques Cartier* document the French discovery of the St Lawrence valley. They contain unique geographical, biological, and ethnological descriptions, but they also recount something else. Their pages record the St Lawrence Iroquoians' discovery of France, a country of overdressed and often underfed people, where men grew hair on their faces and did women's work in the fields. Women in France were said to be sexually voracious, babies consigned to wet nurses, and children subjected to harsh discipline. Most families lived huddled together while a few idle men enjoyed extensive estates, hunting and fishing for sport. Theirs was a religion of churches, priests, and preachers warring over dogma. From French ports sailed creaking ships filled with self-confident adventurers and sharp traders who carried arms, ignorant of local customs. These suspicious, scheming intruders brought unknown illnesses, frightened native women, told lies, and shamelessly kidnapped even those who helped them. The French, Donnacona's people might have concluded, 'are wonderful thieves and steal everything they can carry off.'

NOTES

1. Laurence C. Wroth, *The Voyages of Giovanni de Verrazzano,* 1524–28 (New Haven and London: Yale University Press 1970), Roger Schlesinger

and Arthur P. Stabler, eds., *André Thevet's North America: A Sixteenth-Century View* (Kingston and Montreal: McGill-Queen's University Press 1986). See also Frank Lestringant, *Le Huguenot et le Sauvage* (Paris: Aux Amateurs de Livres 1990).

2. The Montaigne quotations are from 'On Cannibals' in Michel Montaigne, *Essays* (London: Penguin Books 1958), 108.

3. Numa Broc, *La géographie de la Renaissance* 1420–1620 (Paris: Bibliothèque nationale 1980), where it is said of Renaissance explorers that 'par essence et par vocation, ils seront plus ethnologues que géographes' (80), Margaret Hogden, *Early Anthropology in the Sixteenth and Seventeenth Centuries* (Philadelphia: University of Pennsylvania Press 1964). Michèle Duchet in her *Anthropologie et histoire au siècle des lumières* (Paris: François Maspero 1971), argues that early travelers were not anthropologists in the modern sense because they failed to give up their civilized status 'to become participant-observers' (15). This is an elevated view of modern anthropologists, whose 'science' is effectively questioned in James Clifford, *The Predicament of Culture* (Cambridge, Mass.: Harvard University Press 1988), and by Clifford Geertz in *Work and Lives: The Anthropologist as Author* (Stanford: Stanford University Press 1988).

4. Geertz, *Work*, 16

5. Bruce Trigger's *The Children of Aataentsic: A History of the Huron People to 1660,* 2 vols. (Montreal and London: McGill-Queen's University Press 1976), I, 177–208, and Olive P. Dickason's *The Myth of the Savage* (Edmonton: University of Alberta Press 1984), 163–71, adopt a more sceptical approach to Cartier's evidence.

6. For a reconstruction of Amerindian views of European contact, based on sixteenth-century accounts and anthropological work, see Nathan Wachtel, *The Vision of the Vanquished: The Spanish Conquest of Peru through Indian Eyes 1530–1570* (New York: Barnes and Noble 1977). These rich sources are lacking for the sixteenth century in Canada. See Georges Sioui, *Pour une autohistoire amérindienne* (Québec: Les Presses de l'Université Laval 1989). For a brilliant discussion of the problems of documentation for nonliterate cultures see Inga Clendinnen, *Aztecs: An Interpretation* (Cambridge: Cambridge University Press 1991), 277–94. For an interpretation from an Amer-

indian perspective see Bernard Assiniw, *Histoire des Indiens du Haut et du Bas Canada* (Montréal: Leméac 1974).

7. On the 'conjectural model' and the use of clues see Carlo Ginzburg,' Morelli, Freud and Sherlock Holmes: Clues and the Scientific Method.' *History Workshop* 9 (spring 1980): 5–36.

8. Cartier used several terms, including 'harangue' (26), 'sermon' (57), and 'prédication et preschement' (54), all suggesting a hortatory tone, a characteristic of formal Amerindian speech.

9. James Axtell, *The Invasion Within* (New York and Oxford: Oxford University Press 1985), 81–3

10. Stephen.J. Greenblatt, *Learning to Curse: Essays m Early Modern Culture* (New York and London: Routledge 1990), 27; see also Stephen Greenblatt, *Marvellous Possessions: The Wonder of the New World* (Chicago: University of Chicago Press 1991), 86–118. For valuable insights into the problem of communications see Lois M. Feister, 'Linguistic Communication between the Dutch and the Indians in New Netherlands, 1609–94,' *Ethno-history* 20, 1 (winter 1973): 25–38, David Murray, *Forked Tongues Speech: Writing and Representation in North American Indian Texts* (London: Pinter Publishers 1991), 1–48, and Robin Ridington, 'Cultures in Conflict: The Problem of Discourse,' in his *Little Bit Knowing Something* (Vancouver: Douglas and McIntyre 1990), 186–205. Charles Darwin's chapter on the Fuegians, in *The Voyages of the Beagle* (New York: Dutton 1977), is an interesting example of the way sixteenth-century attitudes to aboriginal peoples survived into the nineteenth century, though Darwin did recognize that 'wherever the European has trod, death seems to pursue the aboriginal' (418). Of particular interest is his comment on the problem of communication: 'Although all three could speak and understand, it was singularly difficult to obtain much information from them, concerning the habits of their countrymen: this was partly owing to their apparent difficulty in understanding the simplest alternative. Everyone accustomed to very young children knows how seldom one can get an answer even to so simple a question as whether a thing is black or white, the idea of black or white seems alternately to fill their minds. So it is with these Fuegians, and hence it was generally impossible to find out, by cross-questioning, whether one had rightly understood anything

39

which they had asserted' (198). Inga Glendinnen, '"Fierce and Unnatural Cruelty": Cortés and the Conquest of Mexico,' *Representations* 33 (winter 1991): 65–100

11. Michel Mollat, *Les explorateurs du XIIIe au XVIe siècles: Premiers regards sur des mondes nouveaux* (Paris: J.C. Lattès 1984), 184–5

12. David Beers Quinn, *England and the Discovery of America 1481–1620* (New York: Oxford University Press 1974), chap. 1, and James Axtell, 'At the Water's Edge: Trading in the Sixteenth Century,' in his *After Columbus* (New York: Oxford University Press 1988), 144–81; John Dickenson, 'Les précurseurs de Jacques Cartier,' in Fernand Braudel, *Le monde de Jacques Cartier* (Montreal: Libre-Expression 1984), 127–48

13. Bruce G. Trigger, ed., *Handbook of North American Indians, vol. 15: Northeast* (Washington: Smithsonian Institution 1978), 357–61

14. Anthony Pagden, *The Fall of Natural Man: The American Indian and the Origins of Comparative Anthropology* (Cambridge: Cambridge University Press 1986)

15. François-Marc Gagnon and Denise Petel, *Hommes effarables et bestes sauvaiges* (Montreal: Boréal, 1986), 91–115; Kupperman, *Settling*, 197–40; Montaigne, *Essays,* 108

16. *Cassell's Concise French-English French Dictionary* (New York: Macmillan 1968), 121

17. Tzvetan Todorov, *The Conquest of America* (New York: Harper and Row 1984), 42

18. Marcel Trudel, *Histoire de la Nouvelle-France: Les vaines tentatives* (Montréal: Fides 1963), 82; Brian Slattery, 'French Claims in North America, 1500–54,' *Canadian Historical Review* 59, 2 (June 1978): 139–69, argues convincingly that this act did not represent: a legally recognizable claim, but in dismissing the symbolism he is, I think, too literal. Moreover, he underplays the importance of Cartier's remarks in the introduction to the Second *Voyage.* See also Olive P. Dickason, 'Concepts of Sovereignty at a Time of First Contacts,' in L.C. Green and Olive P. Dickason, *The Law of Nations and the New World* (Edmonton: University of Alberta Press 1989), 232, Cartier's action followed the precedent already set by Columbus on 12 October 1492, when he met his first group 'naked people.' In his brilliant *Columbus* (Oxford and New York: Oxford University Press 1991), Felipe Fernandez-Armesto writes: 'This was

not just a description, but a classification. A late fifteenth century reader would have understood that Columbus was confronting "natural men," not citizens of a civil society possessed of legitimate political institutions of their own. The registering of this perception thus prepared the way for the next step, the ritual appropriation of sovereignty to the Castilian monarchs, with a royal banner streaming and a scribe to record the act of possession'. (82). For a fuller exposition of this argument see the same author's *Before Columbus: Exploration and Colonization from the Mediterranean to the Atlantic 1229–1492* (London: Macmìllan 1987), 223–45.

19. Marcel Trudel, 'Donnacona,' *Dictionary of Canadian Biography* (DCB), I, (Toronto: University of Toronto Press 1966), 275–6. This biography, based on the only existing documentation, Cartier's *Voyages,* accepts unquestioningly Cartier's evaluation of Donnacona's actions.

20. Trudel, 'Cartier,' *DCB,* I, 167. There is no documentation for the claim that an 'alliance' was made. Nor is there any evidence that 'Cartier also stated that he wished to take two of Donnacona's sons to France for the winter.' Trigger, *Children,* 182

21. Jonathan Spence, *The Question of Hu* (New York: Knopf 1988), 126. Another suggestive source is Shusaku Endo's stories in *foreign studies* (Seven Oaks, England: Sceptre 1990).

22. Robert Mandrou, *Introduction to Modern France 1500-1640: An Essay in Historical Psychology* (London: Edward Arnold 1975), passim

23. Jean de Léry, *History of a Voyage to the Land of Brazil, Otherwise Called America* (Berkeley, Los Angeles, Oxford: University of California Press 1990), 133

24. Trudel, 'Cartier,' 171, though earlier Trudel gives some credit to the guides. See also Samuel Eliot Morison, *The European Discovery of America: The Northern Voyages A.D. 500–1600* (New York: Oxford University Press 1971), 395–423.

25. Trudel, 'Cartier,' 167; Trigger, *Children,* 187–8

26. Trudel, *Histoire,* 110; Cornelius Jaenen, *Friend and Foe: Aspects of French-Amerindian Cultural Contact in the Sixteenth and Seventeenth Centuries* (Toronto: McClelland and Stewart 1973), 13

27. See Marshall Sahlins, 'The Spirit of the Gift,' in his *Stone Age Economics* (Chicago: Aldine 1972), 149–84, and also a brilliant application of this idea in Peter Hulme, 'John Smith and Pocahontas,' in his

Colonial Encounters: Europe and the Native Carib-bean 1492–1797 (London and New York: Methuen 1986), 147–52.

28. Marcel Mauss, *The Gift: Forms and Functions of Exchange* in *Archaic Societies* (London: Cohen and West 1954), 80; Trigger, *Children*, 187–90

29. Marie-Christine Gomez-Géraud, 'Taignoagny et Dom Agaya: Portrait de deux truchements,' in Alain Parent, *La renaissance et le nouveau monde* (Québec: Musée de Québec 1984), 52–4. This is perhaps the only article on Cartier that attempts to understand the viewpoint of Donnacona's sons.

30. Hulme, *Colonial, 163*; Karen O. Kupperman, 'English Perceptions of Treachery, 1583–1640: The Case of the American Savages,' *Historical Journal 20, 2* (1977): 263–87

31. George R. Hamell, 'Strawberries, Floating Islands, and Rabbit Captains: Mythical Realities and European Contact in the Northeast during the Sixteenth and Seventeenth Centuries,' *Journal of Canadian Studies* 21, 4 (winter 1986–7). 72–4; Christopher L. Miller and George R. Hamell, 'A New Perspective on Indian-White Contact: Cultural Symbols of Colonial Trade,' *Journal of American History* 73, 2 (Sept. 1986): 311–28. Bruce Trigger, in 'Early Native North American Responses to European Contact: Romantic versus Rationalistic Interpretations,' *Journal of American History* 77, 4 (March 1991): 1195–1215, criticizes the 'cultural' interpretation of

early contact, though he admits that it may apply to first contacts. His position seems unnecessarily rigid.

32. H.P. Biggar, ed., *A Collection of Documents relating to Jacques Cartier and the Sieur de Roberval* (Ottawa: Public Archives of Canada 1930), 51; Alfred W. Crosby, Jr, *The Columbian Exchange: Biological and Cultural Consequences of* 1492 (Westport, Conn: Greenwood Press 1972).

33. Bruce G. Trigger and James E. Pendergast, 'The Saint Laurence Iroquoians,' in Bruce G. Trigger, ed., *Handbook of North American Indians,* vol. 15: *Northwest* (Washington, DC: Smithsonian Institute 1978), 36. On syphilis see Crosby, *Columbian,* 122–64, and Claude Quétel, *History of Syphilis* (Baltimore: Johns Hopkins University Press 1990), chap. 1.

34. Jacques Rousseau, 'L'Annedda et l'arbre de vie,' *Revue d'histoire de l'Amérique française:* 7, 2 (Sept. 1954): 171–201

35. Trudel, 'Cartier,' 168

36. Ibid., Trudel, *Histoire*, 110–12

37. Schlesinger and Stabler, eds., *Thevet*, 9; Ch.-A. Julien, *Les voyages de découvertes et les premiers établissements XVe–XVIe siècles* (Paris: PUF 1948), 138–9

38. Trudel, 'Donnacona,' 276

39. Schlesinger and Stabler, eds., *Thevet*, 83

40. Trudel, *Histoire*, 142–68

■ Article 3: The *Other* in Early Canada

Cornelius J. Jaenen

[This article deals with] [...] the image of the "other" at the time of New France, inspired to a certain extent by the magisterial works of Nathan Wachtel, *The Vision of the Vanquished: the Spanish conquest of Peru through Indian eyes, 1530–1570*, trans. by Ben and Siân Reynolds (New York: Barnes and Noble, 1977), Jean Meyer, *Les Européens et les autres* (Paris: Colin, 1975) and Tzvetan Todorov, *The Conquest of America: the question of the other*, trans. by Richard

Howard (New York: Harper & Row, 1984) among others. I believe that the issue of the complex relations between oneself and the "other", between identity and alterity exists in all time periods. Nonetheless, I distance myself from those who admire these great historians because I do not conceive of the "other" as being Amerindian, aboriginal, indigenous, seen either as a "cannibalistic and brutish beast" or as a "good man of nature" at the first stage of human history. These historians based their views on texts like the celebrated passage in the *Histoire naturelle* (1761) of Buffon, the naturalist, one of the most widely read works of 18th-century literature:

> The American [Indian], it is true, is little less in stature than other men, yet that is not sufficient to form an exception to the general remark—that all animated nature is

Source: Cornelius J. Jaenen, "L'autre' en Nouvelle France/ The 'Other' in Early Canada", Historical Papers (Vol. 24, 1989), pp. 1–12 with portions translated from the French. Reprinted with permission from the Canadian Historical Association.

comparatively diminutive in the new continent. In the [Indian] the organs of generation are small and feeble; he has no hair, no beard, no ardour for the female [...] possessed of less sensibility [sensitivity], yet he is more timid and dastardly; he has no vivacity, no activity of soul [...] he will remain for days together in a state of stupid inactivity.[1]

From this scientific tract, the transition is easy to the polemic work written by Corneille de Pauw, *Recherches philosophiques*, who declared that plants, animals, men and, I presume, even European institutions transplanted to America lost their vigour and strength. From this point, he concluded:

So far we have only considered the peoples of the Americas from their physical attributes, which being essentially tainted, have occasioned the loss of moral faculties: degeneration affects their senses and their organs: their soul has lost in proportion to their body. Nature, having taken everything away from one hemisphere of the globe to give it to another, placed in the Americas only children, who have not yet become men. When the Europeans arrived in the West Indies, in the fifteenth century, not a single American knew how to read or write; there is still today not a single American who knows how to reason.[2]

The polemic served to justify colonization since the Swiss jurist Emmerich de Vattel, the great authority in international law, could conclude that "the people of Europe, too closely pent up at home, finding land of which the [Indians] stood in no particular need, and of which they made no actual and constant use, were lawfully entitled to take possession of it, and settle it with colonies [...]" Still, [the eighteenth-century French philosopher] Diderot could not stop himself from asking if his compatriots would support the same argument in the circumstance whereby Amerindians "brought by chance to your coasts [...] would write in the sand of your shores or on the bark of your trees: 'This land belongs to us!'"[3]

This 18th-century Eurocentrism is hardly surprising to historians, as we are used to making the intellectual effort to place ourselves in the context of the past in which we are interested. But what worries me a little, is perhaps that we ourselves—am I wrong here?— may be too often Eurocentric as well. Is it not true that we always are content with the idea that the "other" in the Americas is always the Amerindian, in the Congo, the Congolese, or in India, the Tamil? The first inhabitants of this vast continent were clearly the Amerindians. Am I wrong, consequently, in formulating the thesis that the "other" on this continent, was and still is the European, whether Viking, Breton or Basque!

As for New France, it seems to me that the French—the *newcomers* of [historical anthropologist] Bruce Trigger and the *virtuous settlers* of [nationalist historian] Lionel Groulx—are the true "others". These "others" appear in a number of guises, from the fisher from St Malo who ravished aboriginal women, the *coureur de bois* rapidly assimilated to indigenous values, to the *Black Robes*, the great Christian shamans, capable of solving droughts and dangerous floods or of avoiding the negative consequences of smallpox. What I want to sketch is the great variety of images, or stereotypes of the "other"—the invader who came from beyond the Atlantic in search of gold, precious stones, a maritime passage, land to cut timber or to grow crops, that is with motives largely incomprehensible to the first inhabitants of this world that would be baptized "the New World."

The European, in this case the French, was perceived by Amerindians, at least by Algonquian and Iroquoian peoples, according to different aspects of his culture and beliefs, as both strangers and strange. In the first place, his physical appearance provided little reassurance. Of course, they appeared to be creatures that resembled the Amerindians, but this meant little in itself, because the moose and the beaver also shared the spirit of life, possessed an intelligence adapted to their environment, and were worthy of respect as "persons", that is in European terms as "persons other than humans." Brother Sagard, Recollect missionary to the Huron, related, "And in this connection I must relate that a savage one day seeing a Frenchman with a beard turned to his companions and said as if in wonder and amazement, 'O, what an ugly man! Is it possible that any woman would look favourably on such a man [...]'"[4]

Was there a link between the physical appearance of this European "other" and his intelligence? The Nipissings were clear on this point, according to Sagard:

It happened that after the interpreter of the Epicerinys had spent two years among them they, thinking they were paying him a compliment, said to him: Well, now that you are beginning to speak our language well, if you had no beard you would have almost as much intelligence as such and such a people, naming one that they considered much less intelligent than themselves, and the French still less intelligent than that people. Thus these good folk judge us to be very unintelligent by comparison with themselves, and at every moment and on the slightest occasion they say to you *Téondion* or *Tescaondion*, that is to say 'You have no sense'; *Atache*, 'ill balanced.'[5]

The missionary Louis Hennepin informs us that certain Amerindians of the *pays d'en haut* [the Upper Country], "added, that we had all Tails like Beasts, that the European Women have but one Pap in the middle of the Breast, and bear five or six Children at a time [...]"[6] This representation of the "other" is worthy of the image of the man of the woods, the *wildeman*, and the world of monsters left to us by the folklore of the Middle Ages.

In fact, in comparison to Amerindians, the French appeared puny, weak and skinny. They had "legs of wool" when it was necessary to traverse the great Canadian forests and "brains of rabbits" as far as the *petite guerre* ["guerilla" warfare tactics] was concerned. This "other" was generally weak in spirit, vain, boasting, boisterous, quarrelsome and, worst of all, without courage and lacking honesty. This was the stereotype of the colonizing Frenchman. Even Amerindian children believed themselves superiors in intelligence to the missionaries, "so good a conceit have they of themselves and so little esteem for others," according to a Recollect father.[7] [The Algonquin chief] Iroquet's band refused to take a young interpreter that Champlain wished to impose on them,[8] and whom they found too weak and inexperienced, "fearing that harm might come to the youth, who was not accustomed to their manner of life, which is in all respects hard, and that if any accident befell him the French would be their enemies."[9]

Can the intelligence—or rather the Frenchman's lack of intelligence—be seen in his material culture? Our historiography has always depicted the primitive "savage" confronting superior European technologies and science. But we should perhaps ask ourselves if the Amerindian found the firearms, the wagons, European clothing, and so on, superior to his own possessions. It is true that in the early 16th century, Gonneville provided important evidence of the first contacts between French and Amerindians and the reactions of the latter: "They were completely amazed by [the] size of the ship, the artillery, the mirrors, and other things that they saw on the ship, and especially by writing that was sent from the ship to the crewmen who were in the villages. These men did what had been asked of them, although the Indians could not explain to themselves how the paper could talk."[10]

However, some twenty years later, Verrazzano remarked that they were not impressed by all the Europeans' products. He tells us:

> They did not esteem the silk, gold or other cloths, and did not wish to receive them. The same was true of metals like iron and steel. Again and again they declared that they had no admiration for the arms which we showed them. They did not want any from us and were only interested in their mechanisms. They even did not wish to receive mirrors: after they looked at themselves in the mirrors, they returned them to us, laughing.[11]

We know that fifty years later, Breton and Norman fishers exchanged knives, combs, needles and bronze pots for beaver and moose hides, a trade that is often qualified as being of unequal value. But I believe that we would do well to ask ourselves how Amerindians perceived these exchanges. If it really involved an unequal exchange, in what ways did they perceive the inequality? Who was fooled? Here is an example which illustrates well the problem: "you [Frenchmen] are also incomparably poorer than we, and [...] you are only simple journeymen, valets, servants, and slaves, all masters and grand captains though you may appear, seeing that you glory in our old rags and in our miserable suits of beaver which can no longer be of use to us."[12]

In answer to Recollect missionaries who wished to make the Amerindians into French people by making them believe that from all points of view the lifestyle of Europeans was superior to their own, a chief of Ile Percée replied that he was astonished that the French had "so little cleverness." Why, for instance, construct houses "which are tall and lofty [...] as these trees [for] men of five to six feet in height, [why do they] need houses which are sixty to eighty?" He continued, "my brother, hast thou as much ingenuity and cleverness as the Indians, who carry their houses and their wigwams with them so that they may lodge wheresoever they please, independently of any seignior whatsoever? [...] [W]e can always say, more truly than thou, that we are at home everywhere [...]"[13] "The other" in this case did not enjoy the liberty which characterized the life of Amerindians. The Frenchman was always, it seems, enslaved to a master, a superior, whether it was an authoritarian head of family, a priest, a seigneur, an officer, a magistrate, a governor, or a king.

How did Amerindians perceive the society that "the other" transplanted to American territory? First of all, it was hierarchical, therefore fundamentally based upon inequalities in all areas, favouring a small class of privileged people, in contrast to the Amerindian society generally lauded for their equality and their fraternity. It was possible to find "the other" authoritarian, intolerant and close-minded. French society focused on profits, often to the point of lacking charity and compassion for one's neighbour. I return to our Gaspesian chief who expressed so clearly his people's sentiments.

> Well, my brother, if thou dost not yet know the real feelings which our Indians have towards thy country and towards all thy nation, it is proper that I inform thee at once. I beg thee now to believe that, all miserable as we seem in thine eyes, we consider ourselves nevertheless much happier than thou in this, that we are very content with the little that we have; and believe also once for all, I pray, that thou deceivest thyself greatly if thou thinkest to persuade us that thy country is better than ours. For if France, as thou sayest, is a little terrestrial paradise, art thou sensible to leave it?[14]

If the French were so attached to their inferior lifestyle, it was their choice, but it was not necessary to impose it in America. "*Aoti Chabaya,* [they say] That is the [Indian] way of doing things. You can have your way and we will have ours; every one values his own wares."[15]

The "other's" diet was also disliked: the salted dishes, the bread that tasted of wood ash and the wine which resembled bitter absinthe.

> We see also that all your people live, as a rule, only upon cod which you catch among us. It is everlastingly nothing but cod—cod in the morning, cod at midday, cod at evening, and always cod, until things come to such a pass that if you wish some good morsels, it is at our expense; and you are obliged to have recourse to the Indians, whom you despise so much, and to beg them to go a-hunting that you may be regaled. Now tell me this one little thing, if thou hast any sense: Which of these two is the wisest and happiest?[16]

In sum, almost all aspects of life and culture of the European "other" had little attraction for the Amerindians because, among them, individual autonomy and responsibility were the dominant values. The individual recognized no master and was never the subject of coercion. In a culture which held in high regard liberty, they also valued generosity and collective commitment. The conclusion of all these comparisons, according to Chief Gachradodow, in 1744, was a condemnation of European colonization.

> The World at the first was made on the other Side of the Great Water different from what it is on this Side, as may be known from the different Colours of our Skin, and of our Flesh, and that which you call Justice may not be so amongst us; you have your Laws and Customs, and so have we. The Great King might send you over to conquer the *Indians*, but it looks to us that God did not approve of it; if he had, he would not have placed the Sea where it is, as the Limits between us and you.[17]

In few realms is the Amerindian vision of the European intruder and of the worth of his own culture better demonstrated than in the responses to evangelization, to the efforts of French missionaries to francisize and christianize the Natives in a context which confused the kingdom of God with the kingdom of France. In responding to missionary intrusion the Native peoples were also responding to a variety of economic, social, and political values and assumptions. The Jesuits, for example, have been praised by some historians for their principle of accommodation to foreign cultures, their cultural relativism. Nevertheless, in the Canadian missions they still worked towards altering to some extent the structures of what they perceived to be a primitive society, to introduce new domestic values, agricultural techniques, a more serviceable political system, formal schooling, and so forth. Amerindian reactions, therefore, were not simply to a new theology or belief system but also to a radically different social organization in which this theology and belief system were embedded. Missionaries, as I have said elsewhere, were aggressive purveyors of a new and supposedly superior way of life, whose purpose was to remake individuals and whole societies in the image of their ideal. The Amerindians dealt with this challenge in a variety of ways and in so doing reveal to us their vision, their perception of this "other being" so intent on converting and transforming them, as well as their view of the culture and beliefs he represented.

It has often been stated that the Amerindians, in general, were attracted by the liturgy and sacraments and were convinced by the preaching of the missionaries. Those who became what some evangelizers called "people of prayer" saw virtues in Catholicism, to be sure, but it is from their point of view that any assessment must be made. Wampum was used in the public confessions that preceded festivals, funeral rites were ended by the interment of the dead "near whom they took good care to bury a sufficient quantity of provisions," in battle a crusader-like cry was raised to the Master of Life, and Christian prayers on crucial occasions could be accompanied by offerings of tobacco and salutations to the sun. Amerindians were able to assimilate the other's religion to their own spiritual concepts. God and devil might emerge from such a fusion with the same appelation, Jesus as the Sun, and the Holy Spirit as Thunder. Some Innu hunters were delighted Jesus had appeared in a dream to promise a successful hunt. They could not understand why their missionary was upset when they recounted how Jesus expected tobacco in return for His intercession. Was He not the Supreme Shaman? Could they not enlist His aid as did their French brothers in their daily problems? Father Biard had acknowledged that "they accept baptism as a sort of sacred pledge of friendship and alliance with the French." Was the desire of some to convert any less sincere because it seemed to afford access to greater spiritual power, to useful trade and military relations, to possible protection from disease and famine, and to revitalization of one's own spiritual heritage?[18]

Of such Native converts Luc-François Nau was able to write: "I know a great number who serve God as faithfully as is observed in the best regulated religious communities."[19] On the other hand, Corneille de Pauw seriously doubted that, from an objective and detached point of view, this interpretation of conversion was accurate. He quoted from an inquiry into Native beliefs made after the British conquest, therefore a presumably anti-Catholic report: "Several were questioned on the articles of faith which were absolutely unknown to them, although these dogmas had been preached in their country for two centuries. Others had a very uniform notion of the story of Christ. They answered that he was a shaman, French by origin; that the English had hanged him in London; that his mother was French; and that Pontious Pilatous had been a lieutenant in the service of Great Britain."[20] De Pauw attributed this travesty of sacred history more to Native assimilation of the other's religion than to missionary intrigues.

All Amerindian cultures shared an ability to entertain and give assent to a variety of views, even if they were contrary to their better judgement, in what has been called institutionalized hospitality.[21] Sister Duplessis de Ste. Hélène reported that "the greatest number listen to the mysteries which are preached as to a fairy tale" and these left few impressions. The abbé Gaulin believed that they were "sufficiently enlightened to formulate an infinity of difficulties concerning all our mysteries." Did not the soldiers and *coureurs de bois* tell them that "it is the work of a black robe to preach, but one must not be concerned by what he says." So the Baron de Lahontan observed that they listened "to all the Jesuits preached without ever contradicting them, contenting themselves with scoffing between sermons." He explained their viewpoint as he understood it:

> When they preach the incarnation of Jesus Christ to them, they reply that is admirable;

when they ask them do they wish to become Christians, they answer that it is laudable, that is to say they will think about it. And if we Europeans exhort them to come in crowds to church to hear the word of God, they say it is reasonable, that is to say they will come; but in the end it is only to obtain a pipeful of tobacco that they approach the holy place; or else to mock our Fathers, as I have said already, for they have such fortunate memories that I am acquainted with more than ten of them who know Holy Writ by heart.[22]

This value placed on deference and detachment was interpreted by the missionaries as dissimulation, which they traced back to their supposedly faulty permissive child-rearing practices: "Dissimulation, which is natural to those Savages, and a certain spirit of acquiesence, in which the children of that country are brought up, make them assent to all that is told them; and prevent them from ever showing any opposition to the sentiments of others, even though they may know what is said to them is not true."[23] Louis Hennepin, true to his own independence of mind, saw this tolerant indifference as part of their conscious antipathy to aggression. He wrote:

Notwithstanding that seeming Approbation, they believe what they please and no more; and therefore 'tis impossible to know when they are really persuaded of those things you have mentioned to them, which I take to be one of the greatest Obstructions to their Conversion; For their Civility hindering them from making any Observation or contradict what is said unto them, they seem to approve of it, though perhaps they laugh at it in private, or else never bestow a Moment to reflect upon it, such being their indifference for a future Life.[24]

The Sorbonne theologians eventually advised the colonial bishop to warn against baptizing those who made their profession of faith "only because they do not wish to contradict the Missionary."[25]

Another response was the assertion of a dichotomous universe, with a present and a hereafter designed for themselves, and separate ones for the "others." The western tribes told Jean-Pierre Aulneau that they "were not made for that religion." Just as there were two paths on earth so there were separate places for the souls of the departed. The Catholic concept of the hereafter was challenged: "This [...] 'tis like all the rest of your fine lies, all the souls, among our people at least, go to the same place; two of our souls came back once and told us all I have said."[26] On another occasion another missionary was interrupted with the same argument: "It's well for those of your Country: but we do not go to heaven after Death. We go only to the Country of Souls, whither our People go to hunt fat Beasts, where they live in greater Tranquility [....]"[27] An Innu shaman said, "Thy God has not come to our country and that is why we do not believe in him; make me see him and I will believe in him." When Paul Le Jeune countered such a statement with the assertion that Jesus Christ had not gone to Europe either, it only brought the noncommittal, "I have nothing to say against all this, for I have not been taught anything to the contrary."[28]

It was commonly believed that the missionaries possessed peculiar spiritual powers. When employed for ends that served their bands and tribes, they were perceived as powerful intercessors. When their intrusion was accompanied by epidemics, famine, or disastrous defeat at the hands of enemies, however, a cause-effect relationship was postulated. So, smallpox and Iroquois assaults on the Huron confederacy brought charges of witchcraft to bear against the missionaries. As a correspondent noted, "They were on the dock as criminals in a council of natives. The fires were lit closer to each other than usual, and they seemed to be so only because of them, for they were esteemed guilty of witchcraft, and of having poisoned the air which caused the pestilence throughout the country."[29] The same charges were not made against the traders, however. A young fisherman reported a visitation dream in which it was revealed to him by louskeha, "the true Jesus," that it was "the strangers who alone are the cause of it; they now travel two by two through the country, with the design of spreading the disease everywhere."[30]

I underscore the fact that there was great tolerance for the religion of the "other," but witchcraft was one of the few crimes in their society punishable by death. One of the first missionaries to come to Canada had opined that "no one must come here in the hope of suffering martyrdom [...] for we are not in a country where the natives put Christians to death on account of their religion."[31] He added that, quite to the contrary, they "leave every one to his own belief." The martyrs, in most cases, were victims of intertribal war.

I believe that the views of Amerindian women deserve attention. They believed that their persons and their social roles were the objects of a two-fold attack on the part of the missionaries—first as women, and secondly as natives. Among the nomadic bands the proscription of polygamy, if adhered to, would have greatly increased a woman's workload. Among the sedentary agricultural tribes the women, especially the "grandmothers" as the Jesuits called the matrons, refused to give up their children to be educated at Quebec. The men as hunters, traders, and warriors might be more amenable to conversion as a means of consolidating their relationship with the French, but the women saw few immediate advantages. What right had the missionary to undermine a woman's authority in the clan, or to assign a man to women's agricultural work? More than one matron drove the converted son-in-law from the longhouse. The men who were appointed "prayer captains" by the missionaries on one reserve exclaimed: "It is you women who [...] are the cause of all our misfortunes. It is you who keep the demons among us. You do not urge to be baptized; you are lazy about going to prayers; when you pass before the cross you never salute it; you wish to be independent. Now know that you will have to obey your husbands and our prayer captains. [. . .]"[32]

This introduction of so-called Christian discipline was deeply resented by many women. At Sillery a runaway wife was returned chained by one foot to her husband. Another woman was beaten by her "young Christian" husband; they were reprimanded but, the *Relations* specify, "especially the woman, who was more guilty than her husband." When a priest suggested that the disobedient had a fire "kindled in the other world" to torment them, women replied "in a deriding way," that, if so, then "the Mountains of the other World must consist of the Ashes of souls." One boldly asserted on another occasion: "I do not recognize any sins."[33]

We can understand why a missionary in the upper country complained that there were "no persons more attached to silly customs, or more obstinate in their error, than the old women, who will not even lend an ear to our instructions."[34] Were they not protecting their culture and traditional belief system? This sometimes required some unusual action. It was a woman who alerted the Huron council to the Jesuit peril: "Do you not see that when they move their lips, what they call prayers, those are so many spells that come forth from their mouths? It is the same when they read in their books. [...] If they are not promptly put to death, they will complete their ruin of the country, so there will remain neither small nor great."[35]

Finally, it might be objected that the missionaries in New France were not without success. Indeed, as I have said, there were conversions at various levels of understanding and for various motives. There were even a few who renounced their identity and heritage to join the "others," saying "I am French." Chief Garakontié of the Onondaga, for example, was derided by traditionalists because "he was no longer a man, that he had become French, that the Black Gowns had turned his head." Even so, the vision of the "other" may not have been what Europeans expected. The Innu are reported to have said their own mass in the absence of missionaries. The Micmacs, we are told, "have often been seen dabbling with, and affecting to perform the office and functions of missionary, even to hearing confessions. [...]" Even more disturbing was the knowledge that Micmac women had taken on a spiritual role in the "new religion" which was not denied them in their traditional religion. "These in usurping the quality and name of *religieuses* [nuns] say certain prayers in their own fashion, and affect a manner of living more reserved than that of the commonalty of Natives, who allow themselves to be dazzled by the glamour of a false and ridiculous devotion." Not only did women dare to take on a role the clergy disapproved of but they were also generally honoured for doing so: "They look upon these women as extraordinary persons, whom they believe to hold converse, to speak familiarly, and to hold communication with the sun, which they have all adored as their divinity." One woman in particular was honoured among the Abenakis. She was 114 years old, and said her prayers on unstrung beads of a rosary which she gave out as relics saying they had fallen from heaven into her hands.[36]

The vision of the "other" in the religious domain was conditioned by the fact that French

47

and Amerindian cultures confronted each other as entities and that, by that fact, the conversion of individuals demanded much more than a superficial revision of personal convictions. Nonetheless, converts and non-converts seem to have been in agreement on one point: the "other" had a lifestyle and beliefs that were appropriate for him, but these should only be adopted after serious reflection. It is true that I have especially used missionaries' writings to show the vision that Amerindians could have of the "other" come from France, but I remind you of a sentence from Montesquieu: "It is necessary for them to tell the truth when they have no interest in hiding it in order to be believed when they wished to lie."

NOTES

1. *Buffon's Natural History containing a Theory of the Earth, [....] from the French*, vol. VII (London, T. Gillet, 1807), p. 39.

2. Corneille de Pauw, *Recherches philosophiques sur les Américains*, London, 1770, t. II, p. 153 (translated by editor).

3. Emmerich de Vattel, *The Law of Nations or the Principles of Natural Law*, quoted in Walter B. Scaife, "The Development of International Law as to Newly Discovered Territory", *Papers of the American Historical Association*, 4, 3 (July 1890), p. 275. Diderot, quoted in Yves Bénot, *Diderot: De L'athéisme à l'anticolonialisme*, (Paris; Maspero, 1970), p. 197 (translated by editor).

4. George M. Wrong, ed., *Sagard's Long Journey to the Country of the Hurons* (Toronto: Champlain Society, 1939), p. 137.

5. Ibid., p. 138.

6. Louis Hennepin, *A New Discovery of a Vast Country in America* (Chicago, 1903), vol. 2, p. 84.

7. Wrong, ed., *Sagard's Long Journey*, p. 138.

8. Marc Lescarbot, *The History of New France*, trans. by W. L. Grant (Toronto: Champlain Society, 1914), vol. III, p. 21–22.

9. Ibid., p. 22.

10. "Le Voyage de Paulmier de Gonneville à Brésil (1503–5)" in Ch. A. Julien, *Jacques Cartier: Voyages au Canada. Avec les relations des voyages en Amérique de Gonneville, Verrazano et Roberval*, (Paris, 1981), p. 53 (translated by editor).

11. "Le voyage de Giovanni Da Verrazono à la Francesca (1534)", ibid., pp. 89–90 (translated by editor).

12. William F. Ganong, ed., Chrestien Le Clercq, *New Relations of Gaspesia with the Customs and Religion of the Gaspesian Indians* (Toronto: Champlain Society, 1910), p. 105.

13. Ibid., pp. 103–04.

14. Ibid., p. 104.

15. R. G. Thwaites, *The Jesuit Relations and Allied Documents*, (New York, 1959), vol. 3, p. 121.

16. Ganong, ed., Le Clercq, *New Relation of Gaspesia*, p. 105.

17. *The Treaty held with the Indians of the Six Nations*, (Williamsburg, 1744), p. 42.

18. W.I. Kip, ed., *The Early Jesuit Missions in North America* (New York, 1846), 166–67; Library and Archives Canada, MG 17, A 7-1, Vol 4, No. 1, "Relation d'une expédition contre les Renards," p. 2658; Thwaites, *Jesuit Relations*, 4:201; 5:223; 8:27–37; 9:213; 11:259. See also James Axtell, *After Columbus* (New York, 1988), Chap. 7.

19. *Rapport de l'Archiviste de la Province de Québec pour 1926–27* (Québec, 1927), 313.

20. De Pauw, *Recherches philosophiques*, 161–62.

21. Calvin Martin, *Keepers of the Game* (Berkeley, 1975), 153.

22. NA, MG 3, Series T, Carton 77, pp. 27, 104; *ibid.*, Series K. Carton 1232, No. 4, p. 112; Baron de Lahontan, *Mémoires de l'Amérique septentrionale* (Baltimore, 1931), 107.

23. Thwaites, *Jesuit Relations*, 52:203.

24. Louis Hennepin, *A New Discovery of a Vast Country in America* (London, 1698), 2:70.

25. Mgr. H. Têtu and Abbé C.-O. Casgrain, eds., *Mandements, lettres pastorales et circulaires des évêques de Québec* (Québec, 1887), 1:447.

26. François du Creux, *The History of Canada or New France* (Toronto, 1951), 1:119.

27. Hennepin, *A New Discovery*, 577.

28. Thwaites, *Jesuit Relations*, 7:101; 11:157.

29. Dom Guy Oury, *Marie de l'Incarnation, Ursuline (1599–1672). Correspondance* (Solesmes, 1971), Lettre XXX, 67–68.

30. Thwaites, *Jesuit Relations*, 20:27–29.

31. Joseph LeCaron, *Au Roy sur la Nouvelle-France* (Paris, 1626), n.p.

32. Thwaites, *Jesuit Relations*, 28:105–07.

33. *Ibid.*, 18:155 and 23:111.

34. *Ibid.*, 54:143.

35. Oury, *Marie de l'Incarnation*, Lettre L, 117–18.

36. LeClercq, *New Relation*, 229–30.

WOMEN AND THE CHURCH
IN NEW FRANCE

Elizabeth Jane Errington
Queen's University
Royal Military College

WOMEN AND THE CHURCH IN NEW FRANCE

51

● INTRODUCTION

Elizabeth Jane Errington

When the young widow Marie de l'Incarnation, set out from France in 1639, to establish a "seminary for Indian girls" in the new colony in North America, she explained to one of her brothers that "the infinite blessings of the King of Heaven … has been pleased to choose me to go there to live." She knew the voyage was dangerous, and she was going to a place "where God is almost unknown." Moreover, she did not expect to return home. "But all this is nothing," she wrote. "[L]ife and death are alike to me, and I make this sacrifice of myself more willingly than anything I have done in my life."

Marie de l'Incarnation was one of the first of hundreds of women religious who went to New France in the seventeenth and the first half of the eighteenth centuries. They were part of the international mission to counter the heretical teachings of the Reformation and to convert the peoples of the New World to Catholicism. While the Jesuits established missions in remote First Nations communities, religious women served God by opening schools for French and Aboriginal girls and establishing hospitals and places of refuge for those with no other means of care. During a time in which the Church was an instrument of imperial French policy, Marie de l'Incarnation and her colleagues were, in many ways, agents of the state. Yet, as her letters attest, for Marie de l'Incarnation and other women religious, their faith was an inseparable part of who they were. The same was true for a number of Aboriginal women, like Kateri (Catherine) Tekakwitha, who came to embrace the Catholic teachings.

The articles here explore different but complementary aspects of the relationships of women and the church in New France. At first glance, Kateri Tekakwitha and Mother St. Claude de la Croix could not have been more different. One was a young Mohawk girl who died at the end of the seventeenth century. The other was a French noblewoman who ran one of the largest institutions for the poor in New France and had the ear of colonial officials, and after 1759, British officers. Both women were, however, devout Catholics; they were also public figures who were well known in their communities, and in the larger imperial world. Moreover, the status and reputation of these women rested, in part, on how their belief in God directed their lives (and their deaths).

Religious women in Quebec in the seventeenth and eighteenth century have been very fruitful subjects for women's and social historians. Although New France was a patriarchal society and all women were legally subordinate to their fathers or husbands or if, a nun, to church authorities, as Jan Noel illustrates in her seminal article "Les Femmes favorisées," the gender imbalance in the colony (there were far fewer women than men) resulted in all women often assuming roles that were traditionally male. Certainly, this was the case for many women religious, such as Marie de l'Incarnation and other Ursulines, or the Hospitallers of Hôtel-Dieu in Quebec or others who lived and worked "outside" the traditional structures of family life. Religious orders seemed to be a quintessential "women's world," one that offered residents a sense of community, structure, support, and a degree of freedom than was unavailable to other women in the colony. Moreover, a number of scholars have argued that by coming to the New World, women like Marie de l'Incarnation gained greater freedom and independence than they could have enjoyed at home in France.

But Marie de l'Incarnation's letters home indicate that she had no interest in creating a new world for herself. And the convent may have been a women's world, but it was, as Terrence Crowley and others have concluded, a world in which distinctions of class and status were maintained and often jealously guarded. Although all the women were equal in the eyes of God, some were more equal than others. Most convents in the colony were led by women of noble birth. Officially, they were subject to the authority of male church officials and other government authorities; Mother Superiors were not loath, however, to assert their position and their faith to further the interests of their community. Moreover, they and their well-born sisters also had to manage the day-to-day affairs of the convent, and authority over the many others who lived there. After all, a life of contemplation and public work required women who were willing to undertake the necessary menial tasks (cooking, cleaning etc.) to maintain the community. What those who were members of what were called the "converse" sisters thought of this is still largely unknown. Many were nonetheless attracted to the life and they served God by serving their sister associates.

A number of scholars have questioned, however, whether Aboriginal women benefitted from their association with the Church and were really attracted to its teachings. Until quite recently, historians have assumed that Christianity was an agent of oppression of Aboriginal peoples. In their zeal to convert and "civilize" the Aboriginal population, French missionaries denigrated traditional practices and, it is argued, successfully destroyed much of the cultural fabric of Aboriginal societies. To some scholars, it was clear that the impact of this on Aboriginal women was particularly devastating. In *Chain Her by One Foot*, Karen Anderson noted, for example, that French missionaries were appalled by the power that Montagnais and Huron matrons had in their communities and disconcerted by women's resistance to the Christian message. The Jesuits were determined, however, and went to often extraordinary lengths to convince "les sauvages" of the errors of their ways. But embracing Christianity meant rejecting traditional social and cultural structures and adopting Western ideas of the nuclear, patriarchal family. Anderson and others have concluded that as missionary efforts became more "successful," Aboriginal women lost their traditional roles and the respect and influence they had had within their communities.

A number of ethnohistorians (those scholars who examine relations between Aboriginals and Europeans by considering the cultural assumptions of all sides of encounters) have begun to challenge such sweeping interpretations. Many First Nations were vibrant, strong and dynamic communities when the Jesuits arrived. Instead of being victims of the missionaries, scholars have concluded that many Aboriginals, including Aboriginal women, incorporated the Christian message into their own traditional ways of thinking and believing. In addition, many point out that how this occurred varied, depending on any number of factors, including the nature of the relationship between a particular First Nation community and the white society.

The debates about the relationship between women and the Church in New France, and the role that race, culture, and gender expectations had on these relationships often rest on quite differing readings of the same evidence. Both social and religious historians have found *The Jesuit Relations* and personal letters from individuals like Marie de l'Incarnation invaluable sources; they cannot be taken at face value, however. Their authors were, in part, writing to gain continued support from home, so it was in their best interest to highlight their many successes. And what they considered a success was understood within their own and their readers' view of the primacy of Christianity, the concern about upholding the values of "civilized" society, and the inability of converts to be both Christian and Aboriginal. But when read "against the grain" and with an understanding of Aboriginal culture and spirituality, these sources can reveal how both native converts and resisters understood their world and this new way of thinking.

53

QUESTIONS

1. What cultural, social and personal factors might have encouraged both Kateri Tekakwitha and nuns like Mother St. Claude de la Croix be attracted to life as a Christian convert or nun?

2. Nancy Shoemaker is writing what is often called "revisionist" history. How can her conclusions differ so fundamentally from earlier understandings of the impact of Christianity on First Nations society and culture? What sources does Shoemaker use? What are their strengths and their limitations?

3. What does Noel mean by a clientage system? How did women such as Madame de St. Claude use this system to her advantage?

4. What values did Marie de L'Incarnation and other women and men religious want to instill in their Aboriginal charges and why?

5. How did the Jesuits' and nuns' own understanding of appropriate gender roles influence how they judged Aboriginal peoples?

FURTHER READINGS

Karen Anderson, *Chain Her by One Foot: The Subjugation of Native Women in Seventeenth Century New France* (New York: Routledge, 1991).

Terrence A. Crowley, "Women, Religion, and Freedom in New France" in Larry D. Eldridge, ed., *Women & Freedom in Early America* (New York: New York University Press, 1997).

Natalie Zemon Davis, "Iroquois Women, European Women" in Peter C. Mancall and James H. Merrill, eds., *American Encounters: Natives and Newcomers from European Contact to Indian Removal, 1500–1850* (New York: Routledge, 2000).

Dominique Deslandres, "In the Shadow of the Cloister: Representations of Female Holiness in New France" in Allan Greer and Jodi Bilinkoff, eds., *Colonial Saints: Discovering the Holy in the Americas* (New York: Routledge, 2003).

Carol Devens, Countering Colonization: Native American Women and Great Lakes Mission, 1630–1900 (Berkeley: University of California Press, 1992).

Allan Greer, *Mohawk Saint: Catherine Tekakwitha and the Jesuits* (New York: Oxford University Press, 2005).

Cornelius J. Jaenen, *The Role of the Church in New France* (Ottawa: Canadian Historical Association, 1985).

Jan Noel, "New France: Les Femmes favorisées" in Veronica Strong-Boag and Anita Fellman, eds., *Rethinking Canada: The Promise of Women's History* (Toronto: Copp Clark, 1986).

Jan Noel, *The Women of New France* (Ottawa: Canadian Historical Association, 1998).

Elizabeth Rapley, *The Dévotes: Women and Church in Seventeenth Century France* (Montreal: McGill-Queen's University Press, 1990).

Patricia Simpson, *Marguerite Bourgeoys and Montreal*, 1640–1665 (Montreal & Kingston: McGill-Queen's University Press, 1997).

Susan Sleeper-Smith, "Fur and Female Kin Networks: The World of Marie Madeleine Reaume L'archeveque Chevalier," in Jo-Anne Fiske, Susan Sleeper-Smith, and William Wicken, eds., *New Faces of the Fur Trade: Selected Papers of the Seventh North American Fur Trade Conference, Halifax, Nova Scotia, 1995* (East Lansing: Michigan State University Press, 1998).

▲ Document 1: Excerpts from Father Paul LeJeune "On the Hopes of Converting This People," 1636

In 1636, Father Paul LeJeune, Superior of the Jesuit Mission in New France explained to his superiors and readers of The Jesuit Relations *how he and his colleagues hoped to continue their good work among the First Nations peoples. One of the ways was to establish a hospital in the colony that would provide succour to ill and dying Indians. And as the following excerpt from* The Jesuit Relations *illustrates, the Jesuits also believed that teaching and converting Native children, particularly young girls, could be key their success.*

…, the Hospital that we are encouraged to hope for, will have, we believe, powerful results. It is certain that all the sick Savages will come to die there. For to be sick among these Barbarians, and to have already one foot in the grave, is one and the same thing; of this they are very well aware. Hence, I know none among them who do not prefer in sickness the poorest house of the French to the richest Cabin of the Savages. When they find themselves in comfortable beds, well fed, well lodged, well cared-for, do you doubt that this miracle of charity will win their hearts? We are very impatient indeed to see this wonder. But I beg those good sisters who are to have the care of them, not to cross over the sea until their House is in such a condition that they can exercise their duties. Simply to be here, is not all; they must accomplish something; otherwise, it would be far better to be in France. As soon as buildings are erected, we shall send for them; We see clearly that their Hospital will fill the Seminaries with boys and girls; for the children of those who die there, will belong to them. I will say still more,— that, in succoring the fathers and mothers, it will be necessary to feed and clothe the children; it is precisely this that is requisite, that they may be instructed. Would to God that they were already charged with fifty little girls as boarders; they would soon have some brave Ursulines here, who would take these children, and would leave the sisters to their sick, who will give them enough to do; and thus both, in exercising the practical virtues, will have something to keep them busy here. And then they must have a good income, to feed and maintain persons who will use more clothes in one year than others would in three. In short, let them bear in mind that they are leaving France, a Country full of comfort and politeness, to come to a Country of rudeness and barbarism.

…, we have done so much for these poor unbelievers, that they have given us some of their daughters, which seems to me an act of God. These little girls, brought up as Christians and then married to Frenchmen, or baptized Savages, will draw as many children from their Nation as we shall desire. All will lie in our succoring them, in giving them a dowry, in helping them to get married, which I do not think they will fail to secure; God is too good and too powerful. These children are being kept at the house of sieur Hebout [Hubou], who married the widow of the late Monsieur Hebert, first resident of Kébec. He has one of them himself, whom he feeds and supports. Sieur Olivier Ie Tardif keeps another of them in the same house, whom the Savages have given him; he pays her board, as we do that of the others who are in the same lodging. These little girls are dressed in the French fashion; they care no more for the Savages than if they did not belong to their Nation. Nevertheless, in order to wean them from their native customs, and to give them an opportunity of learning the French language, virtue, and manners, that they may

Source: Excerpts from Father Paul LeJeune, "On the Hopes of Converting This People," 1836. *Jesuit Relations*, Vol. 9, p. 99, 101, 103, 105, 107.

after-wards assist their countrywomen, we have decided to send two or three to France, to have them kept and taught in the house of the Hospital Nuns, whom it is desired to bring over into New France … [I]t seems to me that the glory of our Lord requires that they be taught in the house of the Sisters who will bring them back in such way as shall be prescribed to them. It does not seem best to separate them, lest they lose the knowledge of their own language. Oh, if we could only send a certain one who is to remain in the house of which I have spoken, what comfort I could give those who would get her! This child has nothing savage about her except her appearance and color; her sweetness, her docility, her modesty, her obedience, would cause her to pass for a young well-born French girl, fully susceptible of education. Her father gave her to us only for two years, on condition that she should not go to France. Ah, how I fear that this child will escape us! I pray God to give her so strong a desire to continue with the French, that her parents will never be able to take her away…

I consider it very probable that, if we had a good building in Kébec, we would get more children through the very same means by which we despaired of getting them. We have always thought that the excessive love the Savages bear their children would prevent our obtaining them. It will be through this very means that they will become our pupils; for, by having a few settled ones, who will attract and retain the others, the parents, who do not know what it is to refuse their children, will let them come without opposition. And, as they will be permitted during the first few years to have a great deal of liberty, they will become so accustomed to our food and our clothes, that they will have a horror of the Savages and their filth. We have seen this exemplified in all the children brought up among our French. They get so well acquainted with each other in their childish plays, that they do not look at the Savages except to flee from them, or make sport of them. Our great difficulty is to get a building, and to find the means with which to support these children. … Experience shows us that it must be established where the bulk of the French population is, to attract the little Savages by the French children. … What a blessing from God if we can write next year that instruction is being given in New France in three or four languages. I hope, if we succeed in getting a lodging, to see three classes at Kébec,— the first, of little French children, of whom there will be perhaps twenty or thirty Pupils; the second, of Hurons; the third, of Montagnés. We can have the latter all winter. But I confidently expect that they will continue right on, after once having tasted the sweetness of a life that is not always crying hunger, as do these Barbarians. …

These are some of our reasons for hoping that in the course of time we shall make something out of our wandering Savages. I say nothing of the sedentary ones, like the Hurons and other Tribes who live in villages and cultivate the land. If we have a grain of hope for the former, who are fickle and wandering, we have a pound, so to speak, for the latter, who live clustered together.

▲ Document 2: Excerpts from Marie de L'Incarnation to a Lady of Rank, 3 September 1640 and Marie to her Son, 9 August 1668

From the time of her arrival until shortly before her death in 1672, Marie de L'Incarnation described her life in the colony in letters she wrote to her son, to friends, and to her patron. A skilled administrator and teacher, Marie de l'Incarnation was a mystic and a keen observer of the world around her. The letters, which convey her devotion and fervent spiritual life, have been an invaluable source for social and religious historians.

PART A—TO A LADY OF RANK

Quebec, 3 September 1640

Madame:

Your letter had brought me a consolation I cannot express or sufficiently acknowledge. Even had your occupations prevented you from writing to me or mishaps of the sea deprived me of so precious a letter, I should not have failed to send you news of this dear country until the *Relation* shall give you more ample ones.

We have every reason then, Madame, to praise the Father of mercies for those he has so abundantly poured upon our Savages since, not content with having themselves baptized, they are beginning to become settled and to clear the land in order to establish themselves. It seems that the fervour of the primitive Church has descended to New France and that it illuminates the hearts of our good converts, so that if France will give them a little help towards building themselves small lodges in the village that has been commenced at Sillery, in a short time a much further progress will be seen. …

There is talk of giving us two girls of this nation and two Algonkins, these in additions to the eighteen that have filled our seminary, not to speak of the day-girls that come here continually. I assure you, Madame, that in France it will be hard to believe the benedictions God continually pours upon our little seminary. I shall give you a few particulars so as to acquaint you with our consolation.

The first Savage seminarian that was given to us, Marie Negabamat by name, was so used to running in the woods that we lost all hope of keeping her in the seminary. The Reverend Father Le Jeune, who had persuaded her Father [Noël Negabamat] to give her to us, sent two older Christian girls with her. These remained with her for some time in order to settle her, but to no avail, for she fled into the woods four days later, after tearing a dress we had given her to pieces. Her father, who is an excellent Christian and lives like a saint, ordered her to return to the seminary, which she did. She had not been here two days when there was a wonderful change. She seemed no longer to be herself, so disposed was she to prayer and the practices of Christian piety, so that today she is an example to the girls of Quebec, although they are all very well brought-up. As soon as she has committed a fault, she comes to ask pardon on her knees and she does the penances she is given

Source: Excerpts from Marie de L'Incarnation to a Lady of Rank, 3 September 1640. *Word from New France: The Selected Letters of Marie De L'Incarnation*, Joyce Marshall, trans and ed., (Toronto: Oxford University Press, 1967), 70–77. b) Marie de L'Incarnation to Her Son, 9 August 1668, Ibid., 333–337.

with incredible submissiveness and amiability. In a word, it is impossible to look at her without being touched by devotion, so marked is her face by innocence and inner grace.

At the same time we were given a big girl of seventeen years whose name is Marie Amiskouevan. One could not see anything more tractable, more innocent, or more candid even than this girl, for we have never surprised her in a lie, which is a great virtue among the Savages. If her companions accuse her, she never excuses herself. She is so ardent in praying to God that it is never necessary to advise her to do so; she even leads the others, and it seems as if she were their mother, so much charity has she towards them. She has great intelligence for retaining what is taught her, especially the mysteries of our holy Faith, which makes us hope she will do great good when she returns to the Savages. She is sought in marriage by a Frenchman, but it is intended to give her to a man of her own nation because of the example it is hoped she will give the other Savages. If God would give someone in France the devoutness to help her build a little house, this would undoubtedly be a work of very great merit. This girl has helped us greatly in the study of her tongue because she speaks French well. In a word, she wins everyone's heart by her great sweetness and her fine qualities. ...

It would take me too long to speak to you separately of them all but I shall tell you in general that these girls love us more than they love their parents, showing no desire to accompany them, which is most extraordinary in the Savages. They model themselves upon us as much as their age and their condition can permit. When we make our spiritual exercises, they keep a continual silence. They dare not even raise their eyes or look at us, thinking that this would interrupt us. But when we are finished, I could not express the caresses they give us, a thing they never do with their natural mothers. ...

It is a singular consolation to us to deprive ourselves of all that is most necessary in order to win souls to Jesus Christ, and we would prefer to lack everything rather than leave our girls in the unbearable filth they bring from their cabins. When they are given to us, they are naked as worms and must be washed from head to foot because of the grease their parents rub all over their bodies; and whatever diligence we use and however often their linen and clothing is changed, we cannot rid them for a long time of the vermin caused by this abundance of grease. A Sister employs part of each day at this. It is an office that everyone eagerly covets. Whoever obtains it considers herself rich in such a happy lot and those that are deprived of it consider themselves undeserving of it and dwell in humility. Madame our foundress performed this service almost all year; today it is Mother Marie de Saint-Joseph that enjoys this good fortune.

Besides the Savage women and girls, whom we receive in the house, the men visit us in the parlour, where we try to give them the same charity we do their women, and it is a very sensible consolation to us to take bread from our mouths to give it to these poor people, in order to inspire them with love for Our Lord and for his holy Faith.

But after all it is a very special providence of this great God that we are able to have girls after the great number of them that died last year. This malady, which is smallpox, being universal among the Savages, it spread to our seminary, which in a very few days resembled a hospital. All our girls suffered this malady three times and four of them died from it. ...

The Savages that are not Christians hold the delusion that it is baptism, instruction, and dwelling among the French that was the cause of this mortality, which made us believe we would not be given any more girls and that those we had would be taken from us. God's providence provided so benevolently against this that the Savages themselves begged us to take their daughters, so that if we had food and clothing we would be able to admit a very great number, though we are exceedingly pressed for buildings. ...

For all lodgings we have only two small rooms, which serve us as kitchen, refectory, retreat, classroom, parlour, and choir. We have had a little church built of wood, which is pleasing for its poverty. There is a little sacristy at the end in which sleeps a young man who is in the service of Madame de la Peltrie. He serves us as extern and provides us with all our necessities. No-one would believe the expenses we incur in this little house, though it is so poor that we see the stars shining through the ceiling at night and we can scarcely keep a candle alight because of the wind.

I shall tell you how we are able to hold so many people in so small a place. The ends of the rooms are divided into alcoves made of pine-boards. One bed is close to the floor and the other is as if on the roof of the first, so that one must climb up to it by a ladder. Despite all this we consider ourselves happier than if we were in the best-appointed monastery in France. It seems to me that we are too well-off for Canada where I myself expected to have for all lodging only a cabin made of bark.

My sisters say to me sometime, "If we have trouble in Canada, it is from not having any and from not suffering enough". We rejoice when we are given nothing so we can be poor in all things.

In consequence, Madame, are we not the happiest and most fortunate of the earth? I cannot express the happiness in my soul. Bless for me the Author of such great mercies towards so unworthy a creature. It seems that our good Master Jesus takes pleasure in our deprivations. We had requested workmen from France to build us lodgings in the place we had chosen near the Savages. We have not been sent a single one, our affairs not permitting it, and we have even been told that we cannot live, maintain seminarians, and build. So here we will be for a long time to come in our little alcoves if divine Goodness does not assist us in ways it alone can know. Madame our foundress is full of goodwill towards us and of the desire to build us lodgings, but her kinsmen do not permit her to act in accordance with her zeal. …

PART B—TO HER SON

Quebec, 9 August 1668

My very dear son:

Here is the reply to your third letter. I thank you as much as I possibly can for the holy and precious relic you have sent me; it will be kept in a beautiful reliquary from which we removed the relics to place them in the alter of our church when its consecration was held. You have obliged me by sending me the attestations, because the relic is to be exposed to the public. When I saw this holy relic, my heart was moved by devotion and I thanked this great saint for honouring this country with his venerable remains. I thank you once again, my very dear son. …

I wrote to you by all the ways, but as my letters may perish, I shall repeat here what I have said elsewhere about our employment, since you desire that I should discuss it with you.

Firstly, we have seven choir religious employed every day in the instruction of the French girls, not including two lay sisters who are for the day-girls. The Savage girls lodge and eat with the French girls, but it is necessary to have a special mistress for their instruction, and sometimes more, depending upon how many we have. I have just refused seven Algonkin seminarians to my great regret because we lack food, the officers having taken it all away for the King's troops, who were short. Never since we have been in Canada have we refused a single seminarian, despite our poverty, and the necessity of refusing these has caused me a very sensible mortification; but I had to submit and humble myself in our helplessness, which has even obliged us to return a few French girls to their parents. We are limited to sixteen French girls and three Savages, of whom two are Iroquios and one a captive to whom it is desired that we should teach the French tongue. I do not speak of the poor, who are in very great number and with whom we must share what we have left. But let us return to our boarding pupils.

Great care is taken in this country with the instruction of the French girls, and I can assure you that if there were no Ursulines they would be in continual danger for their salvation. The reason is that there are a great many men, and a father and mother who would not miss Mass on a feast-day or a Sunday are quite willing to leave their children at home with several men to watch over them. If there are girls, whatever age they may be, they are in evident danger, and experience shows they must be put in a place of safety.

In a word, all I can say is that the girls in this country are for the most part more learned in several dangerous matters than those of France. Thirty girls give us more work in the boarding-school than sixty would in France. The day-girls give us a great deal also, but we do not watch over their habits as if they were confined. These girls are docile, they have good sense, and they are firm in the good when they know it, but as some of them are only boarders for a little time, the mistresses must apply themselves strenuously to their education and must sometimes teach them in a single year reading, writing, calculating, the prayers, Christian habits, and all a girl should know.

Some of them are left with us by their parents till they are of an age to be provided, either for the world or for religion. We have eight, both professed and novices, who did not wish to return to the world and do very well, having been reared in great innocence, and we have others that do not wish to return to their parents since they feel comfortable in God's house. ...

In the case of Savage girls, we take them at all ages. It will happen that a Savage, either Christian or pagan, wishes to carry off a girl of his nation and keep her contrary to God's law; she is given to us, and we instruct her and watch over her till the Reverend Fathers come to take her away. Others are here only as birds of passage and remain with us only until they are sad, a thing the Savage nature cannot suffer; the moment they become sad, their parents take them away lest they die. We leave them free on this point, for we are more likely to win them over in this way than by keeping them by force or entreaties. There are still others that go off by some whim or caprice; like squirrels, they climb our palisade, which is high as a wall, and go to run in the woods.

Some persevere and we bring them up to be French; we then arrange their marriages and they do very well. One [Marie-Madeleine Chrestienne] was given to Monsieur [Pierre] Boucher, who has since been Governor of Trois-Rivières. Others return to their Savage kinsmen; they speak French well and are skilled at reading and writing.

Such are the fruits of our little labour, of which I wished to give you some particulars as a reply to the rumours you say are put about that the Ursulines are useless in this country and that the *Relations* do not speak of their accomplishing anything. ...

My very dear son, what we accomplish in this new Church is seen by God and not by men; our enclosure covers all, and it is difficult to speak of what one does not see. It is quite otherwise with the Hospitalière Mothers; the hospital being open and the good done there seen by everyone, their exemplary charities can be rightly praised. But ultimately they and we await recompense for our services from the One that penetrates into the most hidden places and sees as clearly in the shadows as in the light; that is sufficient for us.

▲ Document 3: Catherine Tekakouita Iroquoise du Saut S. Louis de Montréal en Canada morte en odeur de Saintete

"Catherine Tekakouita Iroquoise du Saut S. Louis de Montréal en Canada morte en odeur de Saintete". This image of Kateri Tekakwitha (who was baptized Catherine) first appeared in the early eighteenth century, more than 100 years after her death. For European readers of *The Jesuit Relations*, Catherine's story exemplified the success of French missionaries to Christianize and to "civilize" the peoples of North America. Kateri Tekakwitha continues to inspire many today; in October 2012, she became the first Aboriginal American woman to be elevated to sainthood. How did this illustration materially assist in constructing Catherine, "the saint?" How does this picture of Catherine also depict the twin missions of the Jesuits—to convert and to civilize?

Source: Claude-Charles Bacqueville de La Potherie, *Histoire de l'Amerique septentrionale*, Vol 1. (Paris: Jean-Luc Nion and Francois Didot, 1722) (from Library and Archives of Canada, Illustrations from Rare Book).

▲ Document 4: "St. Marguerite Bourgeoys"

● **"St. Marguerite Bourgeoys," by Sister St. Renne, 1904, from Centre Marguerite Bourgeoys, Montréal. Marguerite Bourgeoys arrived in New France in 1653 and opened her first school in 1658. She was not a member of one of the cloistered orders that had already established themselves in the colony. Here, as she had done at home, she was determined to devote her life to God by working in the secular world. Many in the Church found this disconcerting, but in the end, after almost 40 years of lobbying, she convinced the church hierarchy to recognize what is often called "the third way"—being in the world but not of it as a wife and mother—and authorized the formation of a non-cloistered spiritual community, the Congregation de Notre Dame. Looking at this painting closely, what did painter Sister St. Renne's painting of St. Marguerite Bourgeoys assume about her subject?**

Source: Portrait of Marguerite Bourgeoys, attributed to Pierre Le Ber, oil, 62.3 × 49.5 cm. In 1700. Archives of the Sisters of the Congregation of Notre-Dame, Montreal.

▲ Document 5: A View of the Orphan's or Ursuline Nunnery from the Ramparts

"A View of the Orphan's or Ursuline Nunnery from the Ramparts," 1761, by Richard Short. As is apparent in this print, drawn in 1761 just after the fall of New France to the British, the Ursuline nunnery (at the centre of the picture) was one of the most imposing buildings in the community. This reflected not only the importance of the Church to the residents of New France, but also was a testament to the influence of women religious.

Source: "A View of the Orphan's or Ursuline Nunnery from the Ramparts", 1761, by Richard Short. Library and Archives Canada, Acc. No. 1970-188-14. W.H. Coverdale Collection of Canadiana.

▪ Article 1: Kateri Tekakwitha's Tortuous Path to Sainthood

Nancy Shoemaker

Kateri Tekakwitha died at Kahnawake in 1680 in the odour of sanctity (a sweet odour filled the room). Pilgrims from all over New France journeyed to her tomb to ask her to intercede with God on their behalf. In 1683, Tekakwitha's divine intervention saved several Jesuits from certain death when a windstorm caused the mission church at Kahnawake to collapse around them.[1] Ten years later, André Merlot's "inflammation of the eyes" healed after he made a novena to Tekakwitha, rubbing his eyes with a solution of water, earth from Tekakwitha's grave, and ashes from her clothing.[2] Colombière, canon of the Cathedral of Quebec, testified in 1696 that his appeal to Tekakwitha relieved him of "a slow fever, against which all remedies had been tried in vain, and of a diarrhea, which even ipecacuana could not cure."[3] The Roman Catholic Church acknowledged Tekakwitha's holiness by declaring her venerable in 1943. In 1980, Tekakwitha was beatified. Perhaps soon, Tekakwitha will pass the next and final step of canonization and be recognized as a saint. She is the only Native American to rise so far in the saintly canon of the Catholic Church.[4]

Kateri Tekakwitha appears in most historical accounts of missionization in New France except, oddly enough, those that deal explicitly with women and missionization.[5] The now classic research of Eleanor Leacock and two recent books on women and missionization, one written by Karen Anderson and the other by Carol Devens, do not mention Tekakwitha.[6] More surprising is that the historical literature on Native women and religion in New France ignores the Iroquois, even though there is a voluminous literature debating the power of Iroquois women before and after European contact.[7] Leacock

Source: Nancy Shoemaker, "Kateri Tekakwitha's Tortuous Path to Sainthood," in *Negotiators of Change: Historical Perspectives on Native American Women* (New York: Routledge, 1995). Reprinted in *Rethinking Canada: The Promise of Women's History*, 4th ed., edited by Veronica Strong-Boag, Mona Gleason, and Adele Perry (Don Mills, Ont.: Oxford University Press, 2002), 15–13. Reproduced with permission of ROUTLEDGE in the format Republish in a book via Copyright Clearance Center.

and Devens confirmed their studies to the Montagnais (an Algonquin-speaking tribe), while Anderson's research focused on the Montagnais and Huron, who were culturally and linguistically related to the Iroquois but often at war with them.

Tekakwitha's experience does contradict the usual argument that missionaries forced Native people to adopt patriarchy along with Christianity and that missionization helped to devalue women's role in Native societies. The usual narrative of missionization's impact on Native women in New France describes how epidemic disease and progressively deeper involvement in the fur trade created an economic imbalance and a crisis of faith within Native communities; the Jesuits' persistent vilifying of Native customs, especially marriage customs, eventually led missionized Indians to abandon the old ways and accept the basic tenets of Christianity and Western culture.

The choicest pieces of evidence used to support the argument that Native people in New France ultimately conformed to missionary preachings and Western patriarchy come from a 1640 Jesuit account of the Montagnais mission at Sillery, which was recovering from a severe smallpox epidemic. One particular incident figures prominently in the arguments of Leacock, Anderson, and Devens. Several Montagnais women complained to the Jesuits that the men had brought them to a council to reprimand them:

> "It is you women," they [the men] said to us [the women], "who are the cause of all our misfortunes—it is you who keep the demons among us. You do not urge to be baptized; you must not be satisfied to ask this favor only once from the Fathers, you must importune them. You are lazy about going to prayers; when you pass before the cross, you never salute it; you wish to be independent. Now know that you will obey your husbands."[8]

Leacock and Anderson gave this as evidence of missionized Indian men dominating women. Devens used this example to show that Native women resisted Christianity, partly because of its patriarchal implications. However, Devens' argument is weakened by her own discussion of how some women eagerly embraced Christianity.

These arguments presume a linear, assimilationist model of change and seem to come from a Western narrative tradition that depicts people as one thing, and after a crisis of some sort, they become another thing. However, it seems more likely that historical change is constantly in motion, perhaps moving in many different directions at once. Crisis may not lead automatically to permanent change but instead may simply be the moment in time when competing interests clash in a visible and tangible way. Smallpox made 1640 an especially stressful year in this Montagnais village, and men and women may have become embattled as they sought to reassert some control over their lives. Montagnais men were probably not successfully dominating women, but they may have been trying to and may have tried using the symbols of Christianity to do so. Some women may have in similar moments called upon the symbols of Christianity to assert their own identity and authority within the Native community.

This narrative of a decline into patriarchy appeals to those of us with historical hindsight; however, even though we may view Christianity as part of a patriarchal, Western tradition that assisted in the conquest of America, Native people may have interpreted it differently. First, Roman Catholicism, especially in the way the Jesuit missionaries presented it, paralleled Iroquois religious beliefs, allowing certain aspects of Christianity to be easily incorporated. Second, Roman Catholicism, perhaps more than any other Christian religion, employs feminine imagery, such as the Virgin Mary and women saints, which could be co-opted by women as symbols of power. And third, while scholars of missionization in New France have emphasized Jesuit efforts to enforce monogamous, lifelong marriages on Native converts as crucial to women's disempowerment, they have ignored the Jesuits' even more profound admiration of women who refused to marry, a novel idea when introduced to the Iroquois and one that some women may have appreciated as an alternative to their prescribed role within Iroquois society. The Jesuits preached patriarchy, but also brought to the Iroquois a toolkit of symbols, stories, and rituals that portrayed women as powerful or that gave women access to power. Just as Native people transformed Europeans' material toolkit of guns, blankets, and glass heads to suit their own needs, Iroquois women and men may have sometimes adopted, sometimes rejected, but continually worked to transform the spiritual and symbolic toolkit of Christianity to meet the needs of the moment.

The Jesuit compulsion to missionize in the Americas was partly the product of a religious revival that swept through elite circles in France in the early 1600s.[9] Jesuits first arrived at the French colonial settlement of Quebec in 1625. After briefly losing the colony to an alliance of English colonists and the disaffected French Protestants known as Huguenots, France re-established Quebec in 1632, and within the year the Jesuits arrived again, this time to set up permanent missions. At first, the Jesuits concentrated their missions among the Hurons, Montagnais, and Algonquins. They made several attempts to missionize the Iroquois but did not survive long in any of the Iroquois villages. However, some Iroquois, many of them Huron or Algonquin war captives who had been adopted into Iroquois families, left their villages to form Christian communities. One of the largest and most successful of these "praying towns" was Kahnawake. ...

According to Tekakwitha's two hagiographers, the Jesuits Pierre Cholenec and Claude Chauchetière, Tekakwitha was one of the many Mohawks who sought refuge at Kahnawake.[10] She was born in 1656 at Gandaouague (now Auriesville, New York) near present-day Albany. Her mother was an Algonquin who had been missionized by the Jesuits at Trois-Rivières, and her father was Mohawk and a "heathen." When Tekakwitha was about four years old, a smallpox epidemic killed her immediate family and left Tekakwitha disfigured and with weak eyes that could not bear bright light. She was raised by her aunts and by an uncle who was considered one of the most powerful men in the village as well as a vehement opponent of Christianity.

As a young girl, Tekakwitha did what all Iroquois girls did. (However, she was also "gentle, patient, chaste, innocent, and behaved like a well-bred French child."[11]) She helped gather firewood, worked in the cornfields, and became skilled at various decorative crafts. And although she later "looked back upon it as a great sin" requiring "a severe penance," she arrayed herself in typical Iroquois finery and engaged in other vanities.[12] When Tekakwitha reached marriageable age, her relatives began pressuring her to marry. At one point, they even arranged a marriage, but when the intended bridegroom came into the longhouse and seated himself next to Tekakwitha, by which custom the arranged marriage was revealed to her, she "left the lodge and hid in the fields."[13]

Tekakwitha first encountered the Jesuits as a young girl when Fathers Frémin, Bruyas, and Pierron stayed in her uncle's lodge while arranging to establish missions among the five Iroquois Nations. It was not until several years later, however, that Tekakwitha received her first instruction in Christianity. Jacques de Lamberville, then Jesuit missionary to the Mohawk, visited Tekakwitha's lodge and found her eager to hear more, or at least she was one of the few Iroquois he could get to listen. (Her eye problems and other ailments often kept her confined to the longhouse while other women went to work in the cornfields.) He baptized her in 1676 and gave her the Christian name of Catherine.[14] Harassed by the non-Christian majority, Tekakwitha fled to Kahnawake about a year and a half later, arriving shortly after the village had relocated from La Prairie to Sault St Louis.

While at Kahnawake, Tekakwitha's enthusiasm for Christianity became more intense. She moved in with her adopted sister and faithfully learned Christian prayers and the lives of the saints from Anastasia, "one of the most fervent Christians in the place" and the matrilineal head of the family in that longhouse.[15] Her first year there, she went on the winter hunt as was the custom for residents of Kahnawake, but could not bear being deprived of Mass, the Eucharist, and daily prayer. She built her own shrine, a cross, in the woods and prayed to it, but would have preferred to be back in the village. The next winter, she refused to go on the hunt, which meant that she also chose to go without meat for the entire winter.

Once again, Tekakwitha's relatives, including Anastasia, pressured her to marry. They even solicited Cholenec's assistance in convincing Tekakwitha of the importance of marriage. At first Cholenec took the side of the relatives, for he knew that in Iroquois society women were dependent on men for clothing (provided through the hunt and later through the fur trade), and that, without a husband to contribute meat and hides to the longhouse, Tekakwitha was not helping herself or her longhouse family. But Tekakwitha insisted that she could "have no other spouse but Jesus Christ." Finally persuaded that she was "inspired by the Holy Spirit," Cholenec changed sides in the family dispute and began to defend Tekakwitha's decision to remain unmarried.[16]

Meanwhile, Tekakwitha had formed a close friendship with another young woman, Marie Therese. They dedicated themselves to each other, to Christianity, and to leading lives modelled after that of the nuns in Quebec and Montreal. Cholenec ascribed their knowledge of the nuns to Tekakwitha, and said that she had for herself seen how the hospital nuns in Montreal lived and had learned of their vows of chastity and penitential practices.[17] However, Chauchetiére credited a third young woman, Marie Skarichions, with suggesting to Tekakwitha and Marie Therese that they model themselves after the nuns.[18] Skarichions was from Lorette, a community similar to Kahnawake but located near Quebec, and she had once been cared for there by the Sisters de la Hospitalière.

These three women determined to form their own association, in which they dedicated themselves to virginity and helped each other in their self-mortifications. Tekakwitha's penances were many and varied. She walked barefoot in ice and snow, burned her feet "with a hot brand, very much in the same way that the Indians mark their slaves [war captives]," put coals and burning cinders between her toes, whipped her friends and was whipped by them in secret meetings in the woods, fasted, mixed ashes in her food, and slept for three nights on a bed of thorns after hearing the life story of Saint Louis de Gozague.[19] Tekakwitha's self-mortifications eventually took their toll, and she became ill— so ill that Cholenec, making an exception for her, had to bring all his ritual equipment to her lodge to perform the last rites. She died at age 24 on 17 April 1680.

This narrative of Tekakwitha's life needs to be interpreted from two different perspectives. First, there is the issue of Tekakwitha as a Jesuit construction. Why did they think she might be a saint? How did their own culture shape the narrative of Tekakwitha's life story? Second, what was she really doing? Was she forsaking traditional Iroquois beliefs to become Christian or did her actions make sense within an Iroquois cultural framework?

Undeniably, Tekakwitha was to some extent a Jesuit construction.[20] If you were to strip this narrative of its occasional Iroquois element—the longhouse, women in the cornfields, the winter hunt—it could have taken place in fourteenth-century bourgeois Siena. Her life story follows the hackneyed plot line typical of women's hagiographies, especially that of Saint Catherine of Siena, except that Tekakwitha did not live long enough to become an adviser to popes and kings.[21] First, there are the unrelenting relatives who try to force Tekakwitha into marriage, purportedly for her own sake but primarily for the economic advantage of the family as a whole. Then, there is her complete devotion to Christian ritual: persistent prayers, a particular emotional intensity expressed for the Holy Eucharist, and her feelings of desperation and longing when deprived of the ritual experience. And finally, like other women who by the seventeenth century had been recognized as saints or likely saints, Tekakwitha's reputation for holiness was based entirely on her dedication to virginity and her proclivity for abusing her own body. Because Tekakwitha's life story follows an established hagiographical model, it could be that Cholenec and Chauchetière fictionalized their narratives to make her life fit the model. However, it is more likely that they thought she might be a saint because her life fit the model so well.

There were other potential saints among the Indians at Kahnawake. There was, for instance, Catherine Gandeacteua, the founder of the Native village at La Prairie. The Jesuits praised her effusively, but according to the other model typical for women saints. Instead of being a self-mortifying virgin, Gandeactcua, "like Saint Anne," impoverished herself through her charity to others. She died before the village moved to the Sault, and so her body was buried at La Prairie. When the Native village moved, the Indians and French colonists at La Prairie vied for who should possess her corpse.[22] The Indians probably planned to rebury Gandeacteua's body near the new village. The French at La Prairie, however, must have thought Gandeacteua had virtues worthy of a saint, for they wanted the body, "the relics," presumably so they could have access to her intercessory powers with God. It was the custom in Europe to pray for a saint's intercession at the tomb or to the more portable relics (the saint's bones, clothes, dirt from near the tomb, whatever had physically been the saint or been touched by the saint).[23] French colonists were probably suffering from saint-deprivation, for there were as yet no saints' tombs in New France and most of the more easily transported relics were still in Europe. In this unusual colonial

struggle, the French won and Gandeacteua's body remained at La Prairie.

There were even more saintly possibilities among Tekakwitha's peers at Kahnawake. She was merely one of many to join a penitential fervour that raged through the village in the late 1670s and early 1680s. According to Chauchetière,

> The first who began made her first attempt about Christmas in the year 1676 [the year before Tekakwitha arrived at Kahnawake], when she divested herself of her clothing, and exposed herself to the air at the foot of a large Cross that stands beside our Cemetery. She did so at a time when the snow was falling, although she was pregnant; and the snow that fell upon her back caused her so much suffering that she nearly died from it—as well as her child, whom the cold chilled in its mother's womb. It was her own idea to do this—to do penance for her sins, she said.[24]

Chauchetière then described how four of her friends, all women, followed her example but invented other, more elaborate forms of penance. Tekakwitha learned about penance from other Indians at Kahnawake and did not initiate the practice.[25]

Moreover, penitential practices seem to have reached their peak after Tekakwitha's death. Chauchetière gave the clearest account of this development in his short history of the Mission at the Sault. After referring to how, in 1680, the "mission gave to paradise a treasure which had been sent to it two years before, to wit, the blessed soul of Catherine Tegakwita, who died on the 17th of april," Chauchetière recounted the events that transpired later that years:

> The demon [the devil], who saw the glorious success of this mission, used another kind of battery. Transfiguring himself as an angel of light, he urged on the devotion of some persons who wished to imitate Catherine, or to do severe penance for their sins. He drove them even into excess—in order, no doubt, to render christianity hateful even at the start; or in order to impose upon the girls and women of this mission, whose discretion has never equaled that of Catherine, whom they tried to imitate. There were Savage women who threw themselves under the ice, in the midst of

winter. One had her daughter dipped into it, who was only six years old—for the purpose, she said, of teaching her penance in good season. The mother stood there on account of her past sins; she kept her innocent daughter there on account of her sins to come, which this child would perhaps commit when grown up. Savages, both men and women, covered themselves with blood by disciplinary stripes with iron, with rods, with thorns, with nettles; they fasted rigorously, passing the entire day without eating—and what the savages eat during half the year is not sufficient to keep a man alive. These fasting women toiled strenuously all day—in summer, working in the fields; in winter, cutting wood. These austerities were almost continual. They mingled ashes in their portion of Sagamité; they put glowing coals between their toes, where the fire burned a hole in the flesh; they went bare-legged to make a long procession in the snows; they all disfigured themselves by cutting off their hair, in order not to be sought in marriage…. But the Holy Ghost soon intervened in this matter, enlightening all these person[s], and regulated their conduct without diminishing their fervor.[26]

For the Jesuits, who knew that one saint was rare and ten or twenty completely implausible, the only way to explain this was to distinguish Tekakwitha's self-mortifications as inspired by God and everyone else's as inspired by the devil.

Despite their attempts to isolate Tekakwitha as especially holy, the Jesuit accounts show that the entire village of Kahnawake—both men and women, but especially the women—were taking Christianity to an extreme. The Jesuits frequently mentioned having to intervene to "regulate" penitential practices, and as Chauchetière admitted, "The Savage women sometimes propound to us doubts in spiritual matters, as difficult as those that might be advanced by the most cultured persons in France."[27] The Christian Indians at Kahnawake were inventive and self-motivated, exhibiting an independence and intensity which frightened the Jesuits because they risked being unable to control it. But still, from the Jesuits' perspective, Tekakwitha and the other Indians at Kahnawake were behaving in ways that were comprehensible as Christian.

However, the historical literature on missionization in New France has shown how Christian Indians created a syncretic religion, a new religion that melded traditional Native beliefs and Christian rituals.[28] The Jesuits assisted the syncretic process in their accommodationist approach to Native cultures. Similarities between Christianity and Iroquois religious beliefs, which the Jesuits rarely admitted to, also made syncretism possible.

The Jesuits' previous missionizing experiences and their scholarly emphasis led them to develop a somewhat sly missionary philosophy. They learned the Native language and world-view in order to package Christianity in a conceptual framework that was familiar to the people they were attempting to missionize. In China, the Jesuits had first tried to ease into Chinese society by looking and acting like Buddhist monks. They then switched to the more comfortable role of scholar and began to dress and act like the Chinese literati.[29] In New France, the Jesuits retained their usual style of dress (which is why the Indians called them "'Black Robes") but slid into the only social category that approximated what they were: shamans. And even though the Jesuits saw themselves as superior to the Native "conjurors," they did act just like shamans. They performed wondrous miracles by foretelling eclipses.[30] They interpreted "visions," while railing against Native shamans who interpreted "dreams."[31] To cure people, they had their own set of mysterious and powerful rituals, such as bleeding, songs, and prayers, and strange ritual implements.[32] Since they feared backsliders and usually only baptized adults who were on the verge of death, they were often perceived as either incompetent shamans or shamans who used their powers for evil purposes.[33] But in any case, the Indians were able to view them as people who had access to special powers.

These special powers were most observable in the new rituals which the Jesuits introduced to the Indians. Tangible manifestations of Christianity proved to be more important than theology in assisting the missionizing effort. Visual images and stories about people, either Bible stories or saints' lives, were the most efficacious missionary tools. Chauchetière was especially proud of his collection of religious paintings and drawings, some of which he drew himself or copied from other works. His depiction of "the pains of hell" was "very effective among the savages." The mission church at Kahnawake also had on display "paintings of the four ends of man, along with the moral paintings of M. le Nobletz," and eventually after Tekakwitha's death, a series of paintings by Chauchetière depicting events in her life.[34]

Although the Jesuits shied away from attempting to explain the abstract principles of Christainity, which could not easily be translated into Native languages anyhow, there were conceptual similarities between Iroquois religious beliefs and seventeenth-century Catholicism which also furthered missionization. Christian stories, from Adam and Eve to the birth of Jesus Christ, are similar to the Iroquois origin story, which even has an Immaculate Conception.[35] The Holy Family—the somewhat distant and unimportant Joseph; the powerful and virtuous Virgin Mary; her mother, Saint Anne; and the son, Jesus Christ—was structurally more like the matrilineal Iroquois family than the patriarchal nuclear family of Western culture.[36] And the rosary, a string of beads with spiritual significance, resembled Iroquois wampum—belts and necklaces made of shell beads, which had spiritual and political meaning.[37] Indeed, many of the actions of Christianized Indians, which the Jesuits proudly recorded and took credit for, conformed to the cultural norms of traditional Iroquois society. Gandeacteua's Christian virtues—her generosity, especially in giving food and clothing to the poor, and her complete disavowal of all her personal possessions when she heard, mistakenly, that her husband had died—were more than virtues among the Iroquois: they were established customs.[38]

In emphasizing the syncretism of Christianity at Kahnawake, however, I do not want to belittle the significance of becoming Christian as people at the time perceived it. Christian Indians did see themselves as different, and non-Christian Indians ascribed a distinct identity to Christian Indians, even if they lived within the same village and spoke the same language. Also, even though the Indians at Kahnawake maintained many of their traditional beliefs and customs, they agreed to conform to some Jesuit demands, such as their prohibition of divorce.[39] For an Iroquois in the seventeenth century, becoming Christian and choosing to live near the Jesuits would have been a difficult decision, for the Iroquois rightly associated Christian missions with the French, who were, except for brief interludes, their enemies. The tensions arising from such a decision reached their peak in the early 1680s, when the Iroquois at Kahnawake reluctantly joined the French in a war against the main body of Iroquois to their south.[40]

Also, despite the conceptual similarities between Iroquois beliefs and Christianity, those who converted to Christianity do seem to have been already marginal within their communities. As Daniel Richter has observed, many of the residents at Kahnawake were former war captives who had been adopted into Iroquois families.[41] This might also explain the prominence of women in the mission accounts of Kahnawake. Since female war captives were more likely than men to be adopted permanently into the tribe, many Iroquois women had a dual ethnic identity. Tekakwitha's marginality came from two directions: her mother and her disfigurement from smallpox. The Mohawks in Tekakwitha's original village thought of her as an Algonquin, suggesting that her mother, although presumably formally adopted as Iroquois, still strongly identified as Algonquin or was strongly identified by others as Algonquin.[42] According to her hagiographers, Tekakwitha was also self-conscious about her weak eyes and her smallpox scars. Unlike other Iroquois women, she always tried to keep her face covered with her blanket. Supposedly, some of her fellow villagers ridiculed her and said, after she died, "that God had taken her because men did not want her."[43]

The marginality of Tekakwitha and adopted Iroquois women might explain why they, and not others, chose Christianity, but it does not explain what they saw in Christianity. In Tekakwitha's case, there seem to have been three conceptual similarities between Iroquois beliefs and seventeenth-century Catholicism which make her actions comprehensible from both the Iroquois and Jesuit cultural perspectives. First, the Iroquois Requickening ceremony and the Christian ceremony of baptism, though conducted through different kinds of rituals, achieved the same end of renewal through imitation. Second, the Iroquois and the Jesuits employed voluntary societies as an additional level of social organization beyond the family and the political council. Voluntary societies served as an avenue by which individual women and men could acquire prestige, authority, and kin-like bonds within the larger community. And third, Iroquois and Jesuit beliefs about the body, the soul, and power were similar enough to allow for a syncretic adoption of self-denial and self-mortification as spiritually and physically empowering acts.

Undeniably, the Jesuits favoured men in their daily administration of the mission. If given the choice, the Jesuits would have preferred to have more male converts, especially men of influence, than female converts. The Jesuits also granted men

69

more authority and prestige by giving them roles as assistants in church services and by making them "dogiques" (Native catechists). However, women turned Christianity to their advantage and incorporated the ritual of baptism, Christian societies, virginity, and penance as means to establishing a firmer place for themselves in a changing Iroquois society.

First, the Christian ritual of baptism resembled an Iroquois Requickening ceremony. In both ceremonies, someone assumed the name and the metaphorical identity of an important person who had died. In both ceremonies, water played a purifying role. The Jesuits sprinkled holy water to mark the baptismal moment, whereas the Iroquois drank "water-of-pity" to signify the transition to a new identity. Among the Iroquois, names of important people were passed on within clans. Individuals from later generations assumed these names and were expected to live up to them by imitating the person who had died and by fulfilling the obligations that went along with the name. For instance, when the Jesuit Lafitau arrived as a missionary at Kahnawake in 1712, the Iroquois requickened him in the pace of Father Bruyas.[44] Although men and women could be renamed and "requickened," the ceremony was also held as part of the Condolence ceremony, the raising up of a new chief, and therefore was in its most prestigious manifestation held as a ceremony for men.[45]

The Jesuits introduced the Iroquois to new images of women in their stories of the Virgin Mary and women saints, and then provided the ritual, baptism which encouraged imitation of these seemingly powerful women. When Tekakwitha was baptized, "The spirit of Saint Katherine of Sienna and of other saints of this name was revived in her."[46] She was at the same time requickened as Saint Catherine of Siena, a women whom the Jesuits featured prominently in their stories and devotions. Tekakwitha probably was deliberately modelling herself after her namesake. She would have heard the story of Saint Catherine's life many times—the fasting and penitential practices, her refusal to marry and her marriage to Jesus Christ in a vision, and her later role as an adviser to male political leaders. Tekakwitha and the other women at Kahnawake may have sensed the underlying patriarchy of the Jesuit mission, but also heard the Jesuits talk of powerful women, like Saint Catherine of Siena, and were urged to imitate them.

Second, the women at Kahnawake used the model of the Christian society to enhance their collective role as the women of the village. One such Christian association was the Confraternity of the Holy Family, an organization of men and women which the Jesuits established at Kahnawake to bind the most devoted Christians together.[47] Women appear to have been among the most active participants in this organization. Perhaps the Jesuits' use of the Holy Family as the model for this society's devotions inspired its members to assume a matrilineal organization for determining members' relationships, mutual obligations, and decision-making powers.

The Jesuits viewed the Confraternity of the Holy Family as a successful operation but expressed some doubts about the indigenous Christian organizations sprouting at Kahnawake. For example, Tekakwitha and her two friends attempted to form a nunnery. They planned to leave the village and set up a separate community of Christian women on Heron Island, until Father Frémin talked them out of it.[48]

... However, "confraternities" were fundamental, well-established components of Iroquois village life. Iroquois women used similar "confraternities" to organize their work and acknowledge women's achievements.[49] The Iroquois also had healing societies, like the False–Faces, which possessed a specialized knowledge and their own healing rituals.[50] The women at Kahnawake added to this familiar kind of social institution the newly introduced Christian example of the nunnery, of which several existed in New France. In Quebec in 1639, the Ursulines arrived to start a mission school for Indian girls, and the Sisters de la Hospitalière opened a hospital. Later, Montreal also had some hospital sisters.[51] Although the Catholic Church restricted the authority of women's religious orders by making them ultimately subject to a male director, the women at Kahnawake were more likely to be aware of how these women, because of their unusual lifestyle and their healing activities, appeared to be powerful and respected members of French colonial society. As their husbands became the Jesuits' "dogiques," women may have refashioned their work-oriented organization after the Christian model to reassert a traditional balance of power, which the Jesuits were disrupting by appointing men to positions of power and high status. The women's dedication to penance, and the envy among the men which this inspired, further suggests that both men and women at Kahnawake came to view penance as an empowering ritual.

Iroquois and Jesuit philosophies about the relationship between the body, the soul, and power illuminate why Tekakwitha and the other residents of Kahnawake accepted the Christian ideals of virginity and penance. In Catholic and Iroquois religious traditions, there was an ambivalence about the connection between the body and the soul. Both belief systems characterized the soul as a separate entity from the body, but elaborate funerary rites and the homage paid to soulless corpses show that they were reluctant to disavow all connections between the soul and the body. In Catholic theology, the soul left the body upon death and, in the case of saints and other holy people, resided in heaven. The Iroquois believed the soul left the body at death and lived an afterlife that would be like life on earth, but better.[52] The Iroquois also believed that the soul left living bodies while they were asleep. Dreamers made trips to this other world and brought back important messages needing interpretation. Shamans' skills included diagnosing these dreams so that they could be acted upon for the good of the individual and the community.[53] Although Iroquois dream interpretation was from the Jesuit point of view one of the most despicable and pagan aspects of Iroquois culture, in the Catholic tradition holy people also bridged these two worlds. In their lifetime, they might have visions which connected them to the Virgin Mary or Jesus Christ, and after their death, they became the intercessors for others.

Saints functioned like guardian spirits, which in Iroquois culture were not people who had died but instead were animals or some other being that was part of the natural world.[54] In Iroquois tradition, a token (which might be a feather, a pebble, or a piece of oddly shaped wood) was the physical key to the spiritual world, just as Catholics prayed to the saint's physical remains, to a relic, or at the tomb to reach guardian angles and saints.[55] Since the Iroquois believed everything in nature had a soul (unlike Christians, who believed only people did), their range of possible guardian spirits was broader. However, the idea of appealing to a guardian spirit for miraculous cures, for success in hunting and warfare, for love and happiness, or for special powers was part of both religions. Among the Iroquois, everyone and everything had some power, or "orenda," but some had more than

others.[56] This power could be called upon by appeals to guardian spirits, and could be used for either good or bad. The Jesuits believed that only a few were graced with divine power. And even though they had earthly authority as administrators of Christianity, few Jesuits were also graced with divine authority, as martyrs or as people who exhibited such extreme devotion to Christian ideals that they had to be saints.

Within the Christian tradition, it was difficult for women to acquire authority on earth, but mystical experiences and Christian virtue carried to extremes produced saints. Self–mortification, virginity, and especially fasting appear in most hagiographies but especially dominate in the stories of women saints' lives. … By fasting, making a vow of chastity, and engaging in penitential self-abuse, Catherine of Siena and other women saints revealed that they were among the select few graced with divine authority. As in the case of Catherine of Siena, a woman saint's divine authority could bring her some earthly authority as well, authority over her own life as well as over the lives of others. Saint Catherine of Siena's marriage to Jesus Christ in a vision partly explained why she could not marry on earth and also gave her the authority to tell kings and popes what to do.

In Iroquois society, one could similarly acquire power by controlling one's own body through fasting and sexual abstinence. Although lifelong celibacy struck the Iroquois as odd, virginity and sexual abstinence were conceived of as sources of power.[57] Virgins had certain ceremonial roles, and Iroquois legends told of there having once been a society of virgins.[58] The Iroquois viewed sexual abstinence as an avenue to physical and spiritual strength and as essential to men's preparations for war and the hunt. Fasting and tests of physical endurance also could be used as a means to acquire power. The Iroquois coming of age ritual for young men and women was a vision quest.[59] They went into the woods by themselves, fasted, and hoped to receive a vision or token from a guardian spirit. Those with especially powerful visions might become shamans (professional healers and visionaries).[60] Since some Indian residents at Kahnawake accused Tekakwitha of being a "sorceress," apparently the same acts that inspired the Jesuits to think of her as holy also gave her access to "orenda."[61]

Bell and Bynum revealed how virginity and fasting had a special meaning for women saints in medieval Europe. In contrast, among the Iroquois,

71

virginity and fasting seem to have been equally available to men and women as sources of individual empowerment. Still, Bell's and Bynum's analyses of the relationship between food and control can shed light on why the Iroquois had a more democratic understanding of who could acquire "orenda" and how. Although Iroquois women controlled the distribution of food, both men and women made important complementary contributions to food production. Women grew corn, and men hunted meat. Moreover, both men and women equally shared in their fear of starvation during winter. Iroquois rituals—many of which involved fasting, feasting, or cannibalism—all show an obsession with food, which may have been a cultural expression of daily anxieties about an uncertain supply of food in the future.

Virginity and fasting resonated with Iroquois traditions. Penance was an entirely new ritual, but one that paralleled Iroquois ritual torture of war captives. The Iroquois adopted all war captives into the place of deceased clan members, and clans then chose whether the adoptee would live or die in the spirit of their namesake. Those consigned to die in the place of a mourned relative were put through a lengthy and painful series of tortures, after which parts of their bodies might be eaten. If the captive had died an especially brave death, he (usually it was a he) was more likely to be eaten because his body parts were seen as possessing that strength and courage. Through ritual torture, war captives became the repositories for violent emotions; by directing anxiety, stress, and grief for dead relatives outward, the Iroquois kept peace among themselves.[62]

Although the Jesuits condemned Iroquois torture, they recognized awkward similarities between Iroquois cannibalism and the Eucharist. The Eucharist is a metaphoric ritual in which participants eat the body of Christ and drink his blood, a reference to the theological notion that Christ sacrificed himself so that others might live. Fearing that the Iroquois might think they condoned cannibalism, the Jesuits translated the Eucharist to mean a feast and did not tell the Iroquois about its sacrificial connotations.[63] If it had not been so uncomfortably reminiscent of Iroquois ritual cannibalism, the Eucharist might have been a useful missionizing tool with which the Jesuits could have offered the Iroquois a ritual to replace the torture of war captives.

However, David Blanchard has argued that the Indians at Kahnawake replaced the ritual torture of war captives with ritual self-torture. They called their penitential practices "hotouongannandi," which Chauchetière translated to mean "public penance."[64] According to Blanchard, a better translation of the term would be "they are making magic," suggesting that the Iroquois saw penitential practices as a ritual source of power. Blanchard emphasizes the importance of this ritual in helping the Iroquois, as in their dreams, to leave the world on earth and visit "the sky world."[65] It is also important to emphasize, however, that they used visits to "the sky world" to control and improve life on earth.

The Indians at Kahnawake probably saw penance as a powerful healing and prophylactic ritual. Since the penitential practices at Kahnawake began at about the same time as a 1678 smallpox epidemic, which ebbed quickly and caused little damage, penitents at Kahnawake may even have viewed penance as an especially effective ritual to counter new diseases like smallpox.[66] The rise of penitential practices in Europe, evident in such movements as the Flagellants, which emerged after the Bubonic Plague, suggests that Christians in fourteenth-century Europe also thought that self-induced abuse of the body was a means to control the uncontrollable.[67] Also, the Iroquois at Kahnawake may have viewed penance as a prophylactic ritual to prevent torture and death at the hands of one's enemies. The Jesuits deliberately drew analogies between Christian hell and the torture of war captives practised by northeastern Indians, and promised that Christian devotion would save one from an eternity in hell.[68]

In conclusion, the Iroquois who adopted Christianity did so for reasons that made sense within an Iroquois cultural framework. Certain Christian rituals fit easily into traditional Iroquois beliefs, while the new ritual practices, like penance, offered a special power lacking in traditional Iroquois rituals. Whereas the Jesuits emphasized the importance of Christian ritual in determining one's place in the afterlife, Tekakwitha and other Christian Iroquois had new and pressing needs for empowering rituals to control the increasingly uncertain, earthly present. Smallpox, increased warfare, alcohol, and the economic and political assaults on traditional gender roles did create a growing sense of crisis Iroquois communities. To deal with that crisis and control their changing world, many Iroquois women and men turned to Christianity. However, they did not become Christian in the way the Jesuits intended, instead, they transformed Christianity into an Iroquois religion.

During one particular moment of crisis, at Kahnawake in the 1670s and 1680s, Iroquois women and men struggled to reshape the Jesuits' preaching into something meaningful to them. Part of the struggle had to do with the patriarchal structure of Christianity. The Jesuits supported male authority in the village by promoting men as administers of Christianity and church activities. Women responded by using Christian symbols to assert their authority and identity within the community. Through a syncretic transformation of the ritual of baptism, the Christian society, virginity, and self-mortification, Tekskwitha appeared holy and Christian to the Jesuits while pursuing status and a firmer sense of her own identity within Iroquois society. The Jesuits tried to implement patriarchy at their missions, but they also brought the symbols, imagery, and rituals women needed to subvert patriarchy.

NOTES

The author thanks Deborah Sommer and Louis Dupont for their help with this article.

1. Claude Chauchetière, "Annual Narrative of the Mission of the Sault, from Its Foundation Until the Year 1686," in *The Jesuit Relations and Allied Documents: Travels and Explorations of the Jesuit Missionaries in New France, 1610–1791 (JR)*, ed. Reuben Gold Thwaites (NY; Pageant, 1959), 63: 229; Pierre Cholenec more elaborately tells how Tekakwitha appeared to Chauchetière in a vision and prophesied the destruction of the church in "The Life of Katharine Tegakoüita, First Iroquois Virgin" (1696), Document X, in *The Positio of the Historical Section of the Sacred Congregation of Rites on the Introduction of the Cause for Beatification and Canonization and on the Virtues of the Servant of God Katharine Tekakwitha, the Lily of the Mohawks*, ed. Robert E. Holland (NY: Fordham University Press, 1940), 312.

2. Peter Rémy to Father Cholenec, 12 March 1696, Document IX, in *The Positio*, 227.

3. Colombière is quoted in "Letter from Father Cholenec, Missionary of the Society of Jesus, to Father Augustin Le Blanc of the Same Society, Procurator of Missions in Canada," in *The Early*

Jesuit Missions in North America: Compiled and Translated from the Letters of the French Jesuits, with Notes, ed. William Ingraham Kip (Albany: Joel Munsell, 1873), 115.

4. "'Lily of the Mohawks,'" *Newsweek* 12 (1 August 1938), 27–8; "The Long Road to Sainthood," *Time* 116 (7 July 1980), 42–3. ... [She was sanctified in 2012.]

5. James Axtell, *The Invasion Within: The Contest of Cultures in Colonial North America* (NY: Oxford University Press, 1985), 23–127; Cornelius J. Jaenen, *Friend and Foe: Aspects of French–Amerindian Cultural Contact in the Sixteenth and Seventeenth Centuries* (NY: Columbia University Press, 1976); Daniel K. Richter, *The Ordeal of the Longhouse: The People of the Iroquois League in the Era of European Colonization* (Chapel Hill: University of North Carolina Press, 1992), 105–32.

6. Eleanor Burke Leacock, "Montagnais Women and the Jesuit Program for Colonization," *Myths of Male Dominance: Collected Articles on Women Cross-Culturally* (NY: Monthly Review Press, 1981), 43–62; Karen Anderson, *Chain Her By One Foot: The Subjugation of Women in Seventeenth-Century New France* (NY: Routledge, 1991); Carol Devens, *Countering Colonization: Native American Women and Great Lakes Missions, 1630–1900* (Berkeley: University of California Press, 1992), 7–30. An exception is Natalie Zemon Davis' article "Iroquois Women, European Women," which argues that Christianity may have given Indian women in New France access to a public voice denied them in traditional Iroquois oratory. This article is in *Women, 'Race' and Writing in the Early Modern Period*, eds. Margo Hendricks and Patricia Parker (NY: Routledge, 1994), 243–58, 350–61.

7. W. G. Spittal, *Iroquois Women: An Anthology* (Ohsweken, ON: Iroqrafts, 1990).

8. *JR* 18 (1640), 105–7; Leacock, 52; Anderson, 219; Devens, 7.

9. W. J. Eccles, *France in America* (NY: Harper and Row, 1972); Cornelius J. Jaenen, *The Role of the Church in New France* (Toronto: McGraw-Hill Ryerson, 1976); J. H. Kennedy, *Jesuit and Savage in New France* (New Haven: Yale University Press, 1950).

10. The historical documents on Tekakwitha are conveniently available in *The Positio*, the compendium of materials used by the Vatican to determine whether she was worthy of Veneration. Cholenes,

73

who headed the mission at Caughnawaga during Tekakwitha's stay there, wrote at least four versions of her life, which are usually but not entirely consistent. The 1696 "Life" (Document X in *The Positio*) is the most elaborate in describing Tekakwitha's virtues, trials, and posthumous miracles. Document XII, which also appears in Kip, is Cholenec's 1715 letter to Augustin Le Blanc and is a more straightforward account. Chauchetière's "The Life of the Good Katharine Tegakoüita, Now Known as the Holy Savage," probably first drafted in 1685 and revised or amended in 1695, is Document VIII in *The Positio*. Cholenec, Chauchetière, and Frémin (who apparently chose not to write a life of Tekakwitha) were the Jesuits stationed at Kahnawake during the time Tekakwitha lived there.

11. Chauchetière, *The Positio*, 121.
12. Cholenec, in Kip, 83.
13. Chauchetière, *The Positio*, 125.
14. Catharine, Katharine, Katherine, Catherine, Kateri ("gadeli" as it is pronounced among the Mohawks), and Katerei all appear in the records; Kateri seems to be the more accepted contemporary term.
15. Cholenec, in Kip, 95.
16. Cholenec, in Kip, 105.
17. Cholenec, in Kip, 108.
18. Chauchetière, *The Positio*, 175.
19. Cholenec, in Kip, 111; Cholenec, *The Positio*, 295.
20. K. I. Koppedrayer, "The Making of the first Iroquois Virgin: Early Jesuit Biographies of the Blessed Kateri Tekakwitha," *Ethnohistory* 40 (1993): 277–306.
21. Rudolph M. Bell, *Holy Anorexia* (Chicago: University of Chicago Press, 1985); Caroline Walker Bynum, *Holy Feast and Holy Fast: The Religious Significance of Food to Medieval Women* (Berkeley: University of California Press, 1987); Donald Weinstein and Rudolph M. Bell, *Saints and Society: The Two Worlds of Western Christendom, 1000–1700* (Chicago: University of Chicago Press, 1982).
22. Chauchetière, *The Positio*, 161, 165.
23. Peter Brown, *The Cult of the Saints: Its Rise and Function in Latin Christianity* (Chicago: University of Chicago Press, 1981).
24. Chauchetière, *JR* 62 (1682), 175.
25. Cholenec, in Kip, 98–9.
26. Chauchetière, *JR* 63 (1686), 215–19; also see Cholenec, in Kip, 106–8.
27. Chauchetière, *JR* 62 (1682), 187.

28. See Axtell; Jaenen, *Friend and Foe*; David Blanchard, "… To the Other Side of the Sky: Catholicism at Kahnawake, 1667–1700," *Anthropologica* XXIV (1982), 77–102. Also see Henry Warner Bowden's discussion of the Hurons and the Jesuits in *American Indians and Christian Missions: Studies in Cultural Conflict* (Chicago: University of Chicago Press, 1981), 59–95.
29. Jacques Gernet, *China and the Christian Impact: A Conflict of Cultures* (NY: Cambridge University Press, 1985); Charles E. Ronan and Bonne B. C. Oh, *East Meets West: The Jesuits in China, 1582–1773* (Chicago: Loyola University Press, 1988).
30. *JR* 58 (1673–74), 181–3 , *JR* 62 (1683), 199.
31. *JR* 60 (1675), 61–3.
32. Le Jeune's 1634 *Relation* of his mission among the Montagnais, in *JR* 7, shows in great detail how Jesuits deliberately competed with shamans to prove their superior access to supernatural authority.
33. *JR* 6 (1634), 139; *JR* 58 (1673–74), 191, 219–21; *JR* 61 (1679), 229.
34. Chauchetière, *The Positio*, 115–16, 146. See also *JR* 5 (1633), 257–9. François-Marc Gagnon, *La Conversion Par L'Image: Un Aspect de la Mission des Jésuites Auprès des Indiéns du Canada au XVIIe Siècle* (Montréal: Les Éditions Bellarmin, 1975).
35. Hazel W. Hertzberg, *The Great Tree and the Longhouse: The Culture of the Iroquois* (NY: Macmillan, 1966); J. N. B. Hewitt, "Iroquoian Cosmology," Part Two, *Annual Report,* Bureau of American Ethnology, 1925–1926 (Washington, DC: 1928), 465.
36. For example, see Pamela Sheingorn, "The Holy Kinship: The Ascendancy of Matriliny in Sacred Genealogy of the Fifteenth Century," *Thought* 64 (1989), 268–86. Also, for a fascinating discussion of how the Jesuits responded to Iroquoian matrilineality and their won need for a patriarchal authority structure to justify their role as "fathers", see John Steckley, "The Warrior and the Lineage: Jesuit Use of Iroquoian Images to Communicate Christianity," *Ethnohistory* 39 (1992), 478–509.
37. *JR* 58 (1673–74), 185–9; Blanchard's "… To the Other Side of the Sky" discusses the rosary-wampum syncretism at length.
38. Chauchetière, *The Positio*, 162.
39. *JR* 58 (1672–73), 77.
40. Daniel K. Richter, "Iroquois versus Iroquois: Jesuit Mission and Christianity in Village Politics, 1642–1686," *Ethnohistory* 32 (1985), 1–16.

74

41. Richter, *The Ordeal of the Longhouse*, 124–8.

42. Cholenec, in Kip, 87.

43. Chauchetière, *The Positio*, 123.

44. Lafitau, Volume II, 240; Volume 1, xxxi; J. N. B. Hewitt, "The Requickening Address of the Condolence Council," ed. William N. Fenton, *Journal of the Washington Academy of Sciences* 34 (1944), 65–85.

45. Lafitau, Volume 1, 71, JR 60 (1675), 37.

46. Chauchetière, *The Positio*, 169, 137.

47. *JR* 58 (1672–73), 77; Cholenec, *JR* 60 (1677), 281.

48. Chauchetière, *The Positio*, 176.

49. Arthur C. Parker, "Secret Medicine Societies of the Seneca," *American Anthropologist*, n.s., vol. 11 (1909), 161–85; Lafitau, Volume II, 54–5.

50. William N. Fenton, *The False Faces of the Iroquois* (Norman: University of Oklahoma Press, 1987).

51. Joyce Marshall, ed., *Word from New France: The Selected Letters of Marie De L'Incarnation* (Toronto: Oxford University Press, 1967).

52. Lafitau, Volume II, 230–1, 237–8; for a comparison of Huron (Iroquoian) and Christian conceptions of the soul, see *JR* 7 (1635), 293; *JR* 10 (1636), 287. Also see John Steckley's linguistic analysis of these concepts in Huron in "Brébeuf's Presentation of Catholicism in the Huron Language: A Descriptive Overview," *Revue de l'Université d'Ottawa/University of Ottawa Quarterly* 48 (1978), 93–115.

53. Lafitau, Volume I, 231–4; *JR* 54 (1669–70), 65–73; Anthony F. C. Wallace, "Dreams and the Wishes of the Soul: A Type of Psychoanalytic Theory among the Seventeenth Century Iroquois," *American Anthropologist* 60 (1958), 234–48.

54. Lafitau, Volume I, 230.

55. Lafitau, Volume I, 236, 243; "Narrative of a Journey into the Mohawk and Oneida Country, 1634–1635," in *Narratives of New Netherland, 1609–1664*, ed. J. Franklin Jameson (NY: Charles Scribner's Sons, 1909), 137–62.

56. J. N. B Hewitt, "Orenda and a Definition of Religion," *American Anthropologist*, n.s., 4 (1902), 33–46; Hope L. Isaacs, "*Orenda* and the Concept of Power among the Tonawanda Senecas," in *The Anthropology of Power: Ethnographic Studies from Asia, Oceania, and the New World*, eds. Raymond D. Fogelson and Richard N. Adams (NY: Academic Press, 1977), 167–84.

57. Lafitau, Volume I, 218. Also see Marina Warner, *Alone of All Her Sex: The Myth and Cult of the Virgin Mary* (NY: Alfred A. Knopf, 1976), 48–9, for a discussion of how the Christian ideal of virginity has roots in classical beliefs about virginity as a magic source of power.

58. Lafitau, Volume I, 129–30.

59. Lafitau, Volume I, 217.

60. Lafitau Volume I, 230–40.

61. Chauchetière, *The Positio*, 208.

62. Lafitau, Volume II, 148–72; *JR* 54 (1669–70), 25–35; Daniel K. Richter, "War and Culture: The Iroquois Experience," *William and Mary Quarterly* 40 (1983), 528–59; Thomas S. Abler and Michael H. Logan, "The Florescence and Demise of Iroquoian Cannibalism: Human Sacrifice and Malinowski's Hypothesis," *Man in the Northeast* 35 (1988), 1–26.

63. See Jaenen, *Friend and Foe*, 145; Steckley, "Brébeuf's Presentation of Catholicism in the Huron Language," 113.

64. Chauchetière, *JR* 64 (1695), 125.

65. Blanchard, 97.

66. Chauchetière, *JR* 63 (1686), 205.

67. Philip Ziegler, *The Black Death* (NY: John Day Company, 1969), 86–98; also see Andrew E. Barnes, "Religious Anxiety and Devotional Change in the Sixteenth Century French Penitential Confraternities," *Sixteenth Century Journal* 19 (1988), 389–406, which is about a resurgence of penance during the crisis of the Protestant Reformation and simultaneous with Catholic-Huguenot violence.

68. See Axtell's discussion of the Jesuits' conflating hell and torture as a way to attract converts, in *The Invasion Within*, 114–15; Steckley, in "The Warrior and the Lineage," shows how the Jesuits described hell as worse than the ritual torture practised by northeastern tribes.

75

Article 2: Caste and Clientage in an Eighteenth-Century Quebec Convent

Jan Noel

Captain John Knox was with General James Wolfe's British forces when they made the fateful capture of Quebec in September 1759. Knox was sent to guard the big Hôpital Général outside the town walls and to insure that this institution gave no help to French forces still lurking in the neighbourhood. The captain had a peculiar relationship with a nun who held the office of Superior that year, Mother St Claude de la Croix. On the one hand, he admired the institution she led. It provided identical care to both French and English wounded. Most of the nuns were young and fair. The wards were clean and airy, and each patient had a curtained bed. Knox observed that "when our poor fellows were ill, and [transferred here] … from their own odious regimental hospitals … they were … rendered inexpressibly happy."[1] Mother St Claude had personally cared for a young British captain, and she wept when he died. Knox experienced her hospitality first hand when she invited him to a private room to join her for English tea served from a silver pot, treating him to two hours of agreeable conversation at a time when French officers in the Hôpital were shunning him.[2] On the other hand, Knox also perceived the courteous nun as a treacherous schemer, trying to demoralize the British officers under her care. "Madame de St. Claude," he wrote, "is reputed the industrious inventress of … many … groundless rumours" of the defeat of Amherst's invading army and other British losses. Knox said he was credibly informed that the British commander, General James Murray, had written her a letter of reproach, chiding her that "it is his opinion a woman who had shut herself up in a convent and retired from the world, has no right to intermeddle with what passes in it."[3] Knox said Murray taunted Mother St Claude that "if she is tired of living out of the world, and will change her habit for that of a man, she being of a proper stature, his Excellency will inroll [sic] her as a grenadier."[4]

Source: Jan Noel, "Caste and Clientage in an Eighteenth-Century Quebec Convent," *Canadian Historical Review* 81, no. 1 (September 2001): 465–90. Reprinted with permission from University of Toronto Press (www.utpjournals.com).

These glimpses of Mother St Claude as the colony was falling to the British, as well as a handful of remarks relating to her in convent annals, colonial correspondence, and family documents, supply only scant knowledge of this figure. But the information we possess is consistent with her position in one of the leading noble families of New France. Her story speaks for many, because a large number of sisters had an elite background.[5] Though they were fiercely loyal to France, they possessed skills that would help convents avert disaster when conquered by a Protestant nation.

Nuns' powers were real. Jo Ann MacNamara entitled her history of nuns *Sisters in Arms* because "they have always been in the forefront of religion's battles. They shared the prejudices, the will to domination … sisters have been united in a long war not only against the enemies of their religion, but also against the misogynist elements within that religion."[6] Canadian historian Terrence Crowley wrote that "the prominent role played by Roman Catholic women in French colonial life contrasted sharply with the situation in British possessions to the south … The freedoms that religious life afforded … allowed them to make a vital contribution to colonial development."[7] Marguerite Jean, who made a detailed study of the conflicts between bishops and convents in New France, concluded that several of the latter successfully resisted the "intransigent wills" of bishops to alter their rules or their mission.[8] What was the source of such authority? An examination of New France's ranked society, with its highly privileged Second Estate, can help answer the question.[9]

It is enlightening to compare the two phases of Mother St Claude's life. As a child she lived in the Norman-style Château de Ramezay, with its four chimneys and massive stone walls, the estate from which her father governed the town between 1704 and 1724. The second phase began when she entered the novitiate of the Hôpital Général de Québec at the age of nineteen. The more one observes her convent surroundings, the more they appear to match the chateau culture into which she was born. In both convent and chateau, a woman could be economically and politically active without loss of caste.[10] Authority sprang not from gender but from noble status and the attendant command of people and resources. Writers on *ancien régime* clienteles point out spousal connections and discuss the occasional woman as an active agent. Even nuns, who receive little mention in the literature on clientage, would seem to be candidates for inclusion, for the convent cases that began to come before French Parliaments in the eighteenth century required protectors in addition to legal counsel. This article contributes to scholarship on clienteles by showing how the system penetrated the walls of convents.[11]

To include a cloister in the political process is consistent with a new school of writing about Renaissance and *ancien régime* government. It acknowledges that the formal, abstract state, based on an ideal of impersonal public service, is a modern construction. Unofficial groups, noble and clerical factions, and family connections have sometimes been viewed as private, illegitimate interferences with proper government. Historians now conceive them as the very essence of the pre-modern state, which did not, Julius Kirchner asserts, acquire "its celebrated modern impersonality" until the eighteenth century.[12] There is, according to Giorgio Chittolini, "a growing conviction that a history of the state conceived as a history of public structures of governance, tidily planned institutions, hierarchies of power, and actions of magistrates and officials cannot adequately describe the … dynamics" at work. A state functioning in the name of abstract sovereignty and public interest above any "private" purposes and forces, Chittolini observes, "simply did not exist."[13]

Government can be conceived as a vast constellation of groups, large and small, using noble patrons to advance their interests in ruling circles. Colonial historian Peter Moogk believes that, in New France, real power lay with "high appointees from France who each built up a following from members of different families," to the extent that one official exclaimed, "be a relative or a friend of one of the members of high society and your fortune is made!"[14] Still, clientage systems connected "high society" to the populace. Colonial clientage, S. J. R. Noel observes, constituted a broad strand of government "woven into the total fabric of the community," with an effectiveness "all the greater because it was not exclusively political."[15] Even in the continental absolutist state, clientage systems offered a flexibility that created areas of "choice and voluntarism in French political life."[16] One example of such flexibility was the bargaining power convents possessed, regardless of their exclusion from formal political structures.

It should be noted at the outset that analyzing a colonial convent's place in noble clientage systems can only partially explain the influence of convents in New France. Indeed, there were several respected convents that had few nobles in their ranks, although all had some. Another article could, with equal pertinence, analyze spiritual sources of convent authority. As in early New England, the colony's highly religious orgins offered a certain latitude to saints of both sexes,[17] and the heroic piety of mystics such as Marie de l'Incarnation carried respect. It is also important to recognize that the religious and the secular were thoroughly intertwined, that even the most combative or power-seeking nun likely believed successful appeal to the Crown would allow her better to serve God and his people. In soliciting the Crown she was not appealing to a "secular" ruler, but one viewed in Christian doctrine as upholding a divine covenant with the ruled. However, this study leaves aside religious dimensions of the sisters' work to concentrate on their politics. It examines the noble status so many nuns possessed, and the way it opened doors for them. This analysis of convent authority centres on two interrelated concepts, caste and clientage.

NOBLES AND "CASTE"

To be a noble, according to Lorraine Gadoury's study of the 181 noble families of New France, one needed to meet three minimum requirements. First, there had to be documentary proof, such as registered letters of nobility, marriage certificates, or other documents identifying ancestors by noble titles such as *écuyer* (esquire) or *chevalier* (knight). Documents prove that Mother St Claude's family was noble as far back as 1532; they had a coat of arms and passed muster with the intendant of Paris that they "issued from noble race."[18] Particularly before 1760 the term "race" was frequently used to denote the *ancien régime* nobility. Guy Chaussinand-Nogaret identified the belief in eighteenth century France that nobility conferred "superiorité séminale … l'affirmation d'une excellence biologiquement transmise."[19] In contrast to bourgeois honour, which accrued to the individual, noble honour attached to the lineage. Nobles were seen as a race apart, with separate rules, laws, and customs that made them almost a caste. Along with written pedigree, there were two other criteria of nobility that called for distinctive behaviour. The requirement to "live nobly" meant that nobles had to avoid manual labour. They could not have commerce as a vocation, though it might be an avocation, subordinate to administrative or military duties.[20] Avoiding toil and money grubbing distinguished the noble from the *villein*, or vile person, the commoner. The other behavioural requirement was to "servir le Roi," to serve the king in some capacity such as bearing arms, performing ceremonial duties, or civil or church administration. Sending generation after generation of its sons into the military, the nobility in New France comprised a group whom historians William Eccles and Dale Miquelon likened to a hereditary caste.[21] Its founding pool of 181 nobles intermarried to the extent that, within a few generations, they were nearly all related.

The family life of Mother St Claude illustrates what noble performance entailed. Born in 1697, she was baptized Marie-Charlotte de Ramezay. Her home had orchards, gardens, and fields that stretched down to the St Lawrence. Her father claimed that their house was "unquestionably the most beautiful in Canada."[22] Inside, visitors found the typical features of Canadian chateaux: coats of arms, tapestries, gold-framed mirrors, and handsome furniture. Chateaux also offered the rare sight—in a colony where most were illiterate—of a few books and a writing desk.[23] This was a life of privilege.

The people who assembled there were distinct in their dress and even in the way they moved. Their attire included powdered wigs, floral brocades, velvet and lace garments, and silk stockings that nobles of both sexes wore by prerogative. Another trademark, more difficult to usurp, was their physical grace, developed from childhood. Little French nobles learned how to bow precisely the appropriate degree to persons of varying rank. Youths learned to ride and dance with style. On the day she replaced her ornate gowns with the plain black and-white habit of the Augustinian nuns, Marie-Charlotte de Ramezay would not shed that noble demeanour, that almost physical sense of superiority.[24]

NOBLES AND CLIENTAGE

Patron–client relationships were usually based on face-to-face contact and reciprocal exchanges. Often they involved material benefits such as land or employment in return for loyalty. A person could be both client to someone higher and patron to those below. Typically these were voluntary, vertical alliances between people of unequal status. The language of both master–servant and affectionate friendship was used. The bonds were often emotional, and were frequently strengthened by kin or marriage ties. Patron–client bonds existed over a period of time, involving informal and ongoing bargaining and negotiation.[25]

Sometimes patron–client relations were not face to face, but mediated by brokers. In France, brokers used various kinds of patronage to attach provincial nobles and institutions, particularly those in the peripheral provinces, to the throne.[26] Since weather and distance severed communications between colony and mother country for seven months each year, the governor, intendant, and bishop often had to make their own decisions while awaiting court instructions, and the court, in turn, relied heavily on their advice. They all played the broker's role. …

In a colony where bishops were often absent, the Crown controlled basic aspects of colonial convent life such as dowries, number of recruits, and decisions about expansion. Convents needed to find powerful friends, to use their status and connections to ingratiate themselves with governing officials. Though this article focuses on activities in Quebec City, the Hôpital Général was clearly part of a chain that extended upward, for it had a procurer at Versailles. In return, the nuns offered the reciprocal loyalty and service at the heart of the patron–client relationship. They were agents of state social control. They housed beggars, prostitutes, and the insane as well as the elderly and disabled. During epidemics they served as a quarantine station for soldiers and sailors from the king's ships. They also performed other services for their patrons, such as accepting as postulants or boarders protegées of the governor, intendant, and minister of marine. This was indeed a reciprocal arrangement, with nuns providing loyal service in exchange for protection by the mighty in Quebec and at Versailles.

Such practices came naturally to the noblesse. Certainly in the home where Mother St Claude was born, building clienteles had always been part of everyday family life. In order "to display the wealth that promised generosity to his clients … a great noble needed to maintain a large household."[27] As best he could, her father pursued that strategy. He purchased the modest office of governor of Trois-Rivières and proceeded to build a splendid estate to host dignitaries who passed through the village. A French aristocrat's style was to be constantly on show, "forever courting the public opinion ... [of other nobles] so that they may pronounce him worthy."[28] Claude de Ramezay won Governor Frontenac's accolade as "a real gentleman."[29] Promotion to the Montreal post and the building of the famous chateau followed. The governor's modest salary meant he was soon imploring the Crown for subsidies, the governorship requiring "much expense to sustain ... with honour."[30]

To consolidate their position, the family opened their chateau to frequent visits from Madame de Ramezay's powerful kin, the governor's military cronies, and all kinds of official visitors to Montreal. Beds of assorted sizes were typically scattered about in most of the inter-connecting rooms, even the kitchens and vestibules. In those days servants often slept beside their masters. Truly private space was reduced to the space inside the bedcurtains when they were closed.

Seeking Crown patronage to finance their sociable lifestyle was typical of the colonial noblesse. La Potherie wrote that Canada was a poor country, heavily dependent on Crown gratifications. Lobbying was essential. Officials received petition after petition — and doubtless any number of verbal requests—from Canadian nobles unable to support their families. When Claude de Ramezay died in 1724 Governor Vaudreuil commented that he had served "with honour ... and lived very comfortably, having always spent more than his salary, which is the reason he has left only a very small estate to his widow and children."[31] Fortunately his survivors were well connected. Noble youths frequently went to other households to build such connections, and Marie-Charlotte and her sisters had been packed off, as young as the age of five, to the elite Ursuline Convent school in Quebec City, where they met other noble girls and their families. The widow and one of the daughters took over the seigneurial sawmilling operation, and Madame de Ramezay penned the supplications.[32] The colonial officials, who doubtless had savoured the hospitality of her banquets and dances, seconded her appeals. She secured a pension for herself and her daughters, forgiveness of family debts, and a captaincy for her son Nicolas-Roch.

NOBLES AND CROWN SERVICE

Despite their privileges, the nobility did not exist merely to decorate the earth. They served the Crown, often at the cost of their lives. In an underpopulated colony surrounded by enemies, the nobles were expected to lead the defense. The king encouraged this role by awarding the coveted St Louis Cross to officers for outstanding service. Canadian officers were noted for valour and willingness to campaign.[33] They shed their blood for their king not only at Lake Champlain and Labrador but also under the boiling sun in Senegal and Pondicherri. Wives, mothers, even nuns of these warrior families discussed military strategy.[34] Marie-Charlotte's brothers, father, brothers-in-law, cousins, and nephews were all military officers, becoming ensigns as early as the age of six. All four of her brothers served, three dying young. Her brother Roch survived and served for four decades.

The women of the military caste also heard the call to serve the king. They might participate by accompanying the intendant as part of his retinue when he travelled. A few wielded political power directly. Elisabeth de Vaudreuil, wife of an early eighteenth-century governor, ingratiated herself with patrons and clients at Versailles so effectively that Quebec officials complained she controlled all the colonial appointments.[35] It is not surprising that ladies from governing families knew something about statecraft, since the family home in those days was also the seat of government, and constant hosting was a requirement of office. Contemporary terminology recognized the familiar responsibility, terming official wives "La Gouvernante" and "L'Intendante." Certainly, Marie-Charlotte and her siblings grew up in the public eye. According to a family story, she and her sister Catherine expressed surprise at seeing their mother setting off pale and tired early one morning for a regimental review. While admitting that this life took its toll, Madame de Ramezay admonished her daughters: "What would people think of us, if we refused to associate with his Majesty's officers, with high-ranking citizens?" Their response was that their mother had "more cares than pleasures ... permit your daughters to embrace a state which never offers such vexations."[36] In the meantime, even the children served the Crown, joining their parents to review troops that day. Continuing this tradition of public service, three of the daughters later offered to nurse the town's sick during a smallpox epidemic. By that time their sister Marie-Charlotte had already entered the convent.

THE CONVENT AND CASTE

Marie-Charlotte chose the Hôpital Général, an institution founded by the aristocratic Bishop Saint-Vallier, who had been a chaplain at Louis XIV's court. The bishop actively recruited noblewomen to his order. He helped pay their dowries and encouraged them to assume convent administration. Hôpital Général historian Micheline D'Allaire calculated that 37–46 percent of the nuns were noble. By Gadoury's stricter definition, some 22 per cent were noble.[37] Either proportion is high, for only about 3 per cent of the colonial population held this status. Because the elite nuns occupied the more visible positions, visitors perceived nobles as the majority. Charlevoix (1720) wrote that "most are girls of rank," Kalm (1749) stated that "most of them are noble," and Pascau du Plessis (1756) identified them as "all girls of rank."[38]

Despite its purpose to serve the poor, the Hôpital must have conjured up memories of home for Mother St Claude. Visiting the colony in 1720, French historian Charleviox pronounced the Hôpital Général "the most beautiful house in Canada."[39] It overlooked meadows, woods, and a meandering river. As in the Château de Ramezay, private space was scant and public space, grand. The nuns slept in small, unheated cells, struggling to keep warm in blue-curtained beds. The communal rooms were warm and handsome. The church in particular was magnificently adorned, just as Marie-Charlotte's home had been. There were gold and silver fixtures, oak wainscotting, large portraits and landscapes, and fine tapestries. Like the de Ramezays, the nuns put on a fine show. When Swedish botanist Pehr Kalm visited, a large flock of nuns showed him around. They presented a banquet with dishes "as numerous and various as on the tables of great men," and Mother St Claude was described as "the daughter of a Governor ... [having] a very grand air."[40]

The nuns also duplicated another aspect of the chatelaine's lifestyle: they commanded a multitude. Noble nuns usually held the highest administrative offices. Between 1700 and the colony's end in 1760, the mother superiors were noble more than two-thirds of the time.[41] Nobles often supervised wards, novices, and finances.[42] When Marie-Charlotte de Ramezay became Mother St Claude, she held a number of offices, including that of superior for six years; as depositary, she directed finances for twenty-six.[43]

Inside the convent, Marie-Charlotte encountered the same sharply drawn hierarchies she had known at the Château. Choir nuns and converse sisters inhabited the same convent, but different worlds. Even if they were adolescents, choir nuns were addressed as "mother." Choir nuns passed much of their day in prayer, meditation, and song, though they spent some time in the wards and teaching the poor.[44] The converses, in contrast, were typically illiterate daughters of the working class. Their dowries were much lower. While sisters wore shoes, they wore clogs. Their bed linen was coarse. Required to be healthy, robust, and docile, converses took care of the barnyard and did the heavy work in the garden, laundry, and stable. These "Cinderellas of the convents" could not sing in the choir or vote in convent elections. They came to community meetings only to confess their faults.[45]

Choir nuns directed not only the converses but the numerous inhabitants of the institution and its three seigneuries. There were as many as thirteen domestic servants. Hundreds of *habitant* farmers paid dues and homage to their convent seigneuresses. Choir nuns, including Mother St Claude, personally crossed the river to inspect their St Vallier seigneurie. While there, they performed a function typical of dignitaries: they became godparents to new babies, who were then named after them. They also employed carpenters and builders, harvest crews, and male nurses. Though the nuns may have felt deference towards the resident bishop and convalescent military officers, most of their clients were in a subordinate position, outranked by the religious and also dependent upon them.[46]

With all this help, the Hôpital carried out the noble mandate to serve the Crown. The institution was founded, as were a number of hôpitaux généraux in France, in the seventeenth century to deal with a growing number of beggars, prostitutes, petty criminals, and vagabonds. The Quebec Hôpital usually housed some fifty inmates.[47] An hôpital was not a hospital; rather, it combined the functions of workhouse and hospice. Nonetheless, in times when the regular hospital (the Hôtel-Dieu) was full or incapacitated, the Hôpital also served the sick.

It filled this role in wartime, and during epidemics in 1756–7, when ten nuns lost their lives caring for stricken soldiers and sailors.[48] The Crown compensated the nuns for these services. Like other faithful clients of the Crown, they continued to serve even when the pay failed to arrive.

The nuns' wealth, like that of the military *noblesse* in general, was based on various sources of income and a good deal of womanly enterprise. Besides Crown and seigneurial revenues, they had two kinds of paying pensioners. Aging women and men often lodged there and some paid through service. One pensioner crossed the river each spring to the St Vallier seigneurie to collect rents for the convent;[49] and a widow whose husband had died at the Hôpital offered to serve as *soeur tauriére* (gatekeeper) for life. The nuns also acquired a group of young pensioners when they opened a school in 1725. Noting the lack of milling available for local *habitants*, the nuns erected a huge windmill that became a major source of revenue.[50] Sisters, inmates, or servants busied themselves with farming, dairy, and poultry, churning, preserving, baking, and hunting to supply the table, as well as weaving, sewing, and shoemaking. The nuns ran a pharmacy and performed such feminine arts as filigree embroidery and artificial flower making. Other income came from those who admired the sisters' work. Donations arrived from couples without heirs and from court fines levied on petty offenders. Alms of all kinds arrived in such quantity that they rivalled seigneurial earnings as the largest source of revenue.[51]

The income came from solid service to various clients and patrons. The Hôpital school was renowned;[52] the quality of care in the spotless wards won consistent praise. Women young and old came to count on the Hôpital to house them in widowhood or in wartime.[53] The St Vallier seigneurie was well developed, its windmill serving the government and the farmers for miles around. The operation would become even more vital as both a field hospital and a refugee centre in the French regime's final days. The sisters' varied activities were termed "indispensable service" by the Crown brokers above them and were much used by the local inhabitants.

THE CONVENT AND CLIENTAGE

It took some time for the nuns to master the art of securing protectors. Bishop St-Vallier's initial decision to found the Hôpital and to staff it with Augustinian nuns from the Hôtel-Dieu was done much against the will of the order, which did not wish to see its forces spread too thin. The bishop overpowered the opposition. He employed the emotionalism that so often characterized patron–client relations, he visited the Hôpital-Dieu and wept to soften their hearts. They cried too, but did not budge. He proceeded to the French court, and there he won his cause. Once the Hôpital was established, the bishop became its powerful protector.

The nuns' powers were put to the test when St Vallier died in 1727. Infighting among various clerical and lay leaders brought one faction to the doors of the Hôpital, where his body lay. Fearful that his request to be buried at his Hôpital would be countermanded by the other faction, which preferred the cathedral, Mother Superior Geneviève Duchesnay, a noblewoman, permitted the visitors to hold an impromptu midnight service. The poor held the candles, the mass was sung, and the bishop duly buried. When the rival faction discovered this deception, they denied the Hôpital chaplain the right to administer sacraments to the nuns and proceeded to replace Mother Duchesnay as superior.[54] The majority of the sisters rebelled and continued to obey her.

Part of an imbroglio between high officials, this episode was also the first of a series of brushes with ecclesiastics who seem to have detested the nuns. The Quebec sisters were making decisions ordinarily made by men, for Hôpitaux in France were administered by laymen. The clerics seem to have been repelled by the independence of the sisters. In 1730 Bishop Dosquet would accuse them of "bad conduct" and an abusive "spirit of independence and liberty," as he asked the minister to reduce their numbers.[55]

The nuns responded to the coup against Mother Duchesnay by soliciting patrons. In the face of ecclesiastical hostility they could turn to secular rulers, for colonial bishops faced more state control than French ones did.[56] The nuns wrote directly to the colonial minister with their version of events. Mother Duchesnay, in the master–servant language of patronage, "took the liberty to write to your Lordship to supplicate very respectfully the honour of your protection," hoping he would apply his "penetrating mind" to their problem. She noted, in the affectionate language of patronage, of how the minister's kinsman, Governor Charles Beauharnois, like "a good father full of charity," had come and restored peace to the convent.[57] Yet she also enclosed, and endorsed as "simple and truthful," the memoir of Sister Agnes.

Sister Agnes, in her office of convent secretary, signed her note "on behalf of the whole community." She claimed that Governor Beauharnois had himself divided their community, forcing on false pretenses some of the younger or more timid nuns to bow to authority.[58] The governor was evidently a frequent visitor, and he convinced some of the more impressionable sisters only "after a thousand entreaties." But Sister Agnes reiterated firmly, twice, that, on behalf of the convent in general, sentiments were ever the same for retention of their chaplain and their rights.[59] The letter shows that in seeking help from the authorities, the nuns were not altogether beholden to them. Particular care was needed, since the governor initially sided with the faction hostile to the Mother Superior. Still, Governor Beauharnois proved to be a friend. He protested against the arbitrary condemnation of Mother Duchesnay and used his authority to have the interdiction lifted.

A second imbroglio occurred when Mother Duchesnay died in 1730. The bishop's representative was determined to break the rule of the proud noblewomen at the head of the Hôpital.[60] He arbitrarily appointed a non-noble nun as the superior. This act violated the order's constitution, which called for election by secret ballot. Mother St Claude and seven others retired to their cells during this illegal procedure, taking care first to disable the convent bell.[61]

After inspecting the convent's constitution, Governor Beauharnois ... and Intendant Hocquart ... both agreed with the nuns. They asked the minister to call for a new election. They added that vexations (*tracasseries*) were common in convents. They insisted that the nuns generally conducted themselves appropriately. ... The Crown did not go so far as to remove the appointee, but Mother Duchesnay's younger sister was elected superior in 1732, and for the rest of the time until the Conquest the superior was always a noblewoman. Nor was there further complaint of ecclesiastics interfering in elections.[62] From 1732 onward, according to D'Allaire, the Crown looked with favour on the convent.[63]

... Patron–client linkages were generally face to face, making them hard for historians to trace. We know there was an unusual amount of visiting by governors and their wives, along with their retinues of officers and friends. This familiarity violated cloister to the extent that both St Vallier and his successor, Bishop Dosquet, appealed to the court to stop the outrage.[64] The nuns even went to dinner parties at the chateaux of the governor and the intendant.[65] In the decade in which the colony fell, both the appalled Bishop Briand and the delighted novelist Frances Brooke agreed that the nuns were very worldly. Brooke characterized their conversation as so polite and animated that one forgot the nun and saw only the lady of distinction. The austere Briand fumed: "What is one to think of the introduction of the abuse of having one's own money at her disposition [this applying to Mother St. Claude] ... buying her own food ... liquors ... clothes?"[66] He went on to accuse the nuns of talking indiscreetly about sexual scandals, rising late, neglecting prayers and rules of silence, and being libertine in recreation time. These ladies were not letting the veil interfere with the art of cultivating friends in high places, dining and conversing in the style to which they had been born.

What the bishop saw as sin, others saw as accomplishment. Mother St Claude's service as depositary (financial officer) during wartime was lauded in the convent annals. While her vocation made her "humble, modest and devoted," she was also "obliged by her employment to have daily dealings with people of all ranks, she showed herself, by the nobility of her manners and the delicacy of her behaviour, always worthy of her high birth."[67] True to family form, she distinguished herself as superior by launching a building program.

Along with links to the polite world of colonial government, the nuns also had the reliable network of kin to reinforce their position. Unlike priests, nuns were typically Canadian born. With many relatives in the town's shops and warehouses, Legislative Council seats, and government posts, reciprocal patron–client relationships blossomed. Supplies were purchased and donations arrived from families such as the Soumandes, Hazeurs, and de la Chesnayes, who were related to the superiors.[68] Loans were extended or forgiven, and lands were swapped for services. Officials contributed to dowries for needy noble postulants, while nuns educated officials' daughters and cared for their widows. They taught their own nieces (many of whom also took the veil) and boarded their elderly relatives. Amid so many kin, graduates, and friends, the Hôpital was well fixed to weather what storms might come.

THE FALL OF QUEBEC

The storm that arose in 1759 was one of the most devastating imaginable. Having weathered three years of battle, New France was in an exhausted condition. That year, British-American forces were converging along the invasion routes into the colony. In midsummer, General James Wolfe's army, well supported by the British Navy, sailed up the St Lawrence, ensconced itself on shore opposite Quebec City, and began shelling. One young noble, Mother Sainte-Elizabeth Adhémar de Lantagnac, set up a field hospital right at the scene of skirmish where, having a sword held to her throat, "seemed to inspire her with fresh zeal."[69] Wolfe studied ways to lay siege to the well-fortified city on its lofty cliff. Meanwhile his forces ravaged nearby settlements and continued bombarding the town until most of its buildings were in ruins.

During this siege, the Hôpital Général's suburban location was a godsend. Kin and towns people came pouring into the building with their belongings. Both the Ursuline and Hôtel-Dieu nuns also fled their crumbling convents and came streaming over the fields, carrying their bedding. Soon every attic, hall, barn, and outbuilding was crammed with refugees, patients, inmates, and nuns. Buildings designed for 120 people would house 800.[70]

On the fateful night of 12 September, Wolfe's troops slipped past French sentries and crept up a path leading to the Plains of Abraham. From their windows the sisters, who customarily rose at four, were among the first to learn of the landing. Taken by surprise, Montcalm rushed out to meet them, without even waiting for nearby reinforcements. One of history's most famous battles was over in less than half an hour, as French forces broke ranks and ran back into the walled town. The nuns watched in horror from their windows. After the battle, hundreds of French wounded were carried to the Hôpital.[71]

That night the nuns were frightened by the loud knock of a British officer at the door. Upon entering, he declared himself their protector. The nuns had already woven the victors into their network. From the time Wolfe sailed up the river, they had accepted the British wounded who had been captured in various skirmishes.[72] Mother St Claude personally cared for the British officer David Ochterloney and wept when he died. In gratitude for her services, General Wolfe declared that should fortune of arms favour the British side, he would extend his protection to her and to the Hôpital.[73]

When the regrouped French forces returned to fight a second battle at nearby Ste-Foy in April 1760, the boom of cannons shook the Hôpital. The nuns saw brothers, fathers, uncles, and nephews fall and be carried in, nearly 500 men in all. The annalist described the scene: "It requires another pen than mine to paint the horrors [we saw] ... the cries of the dying and the sorrows of the watchers. Those moments required a force above nature to bear it without dying. We had in our infirmaries seventy-two officers; thirty-three died. One saw nothing but severed arms and legs."[74]

The sense of caste prevailed even in the face of death. The sisters did not separate patients by nationality but by rank, quartering French and British officers in one wing together. This proximity caused some embarrassment, but the officers attempted the courtesy expected of gentlemen.[75] Mother St Claude, who was superior from 1756 to 1759, was imbued with the same sense of courtesy. ... She took pains to entertain the British officers within her walls, personally hosting Captain Knox. Scarcely a week after her brother, town commander Nicholas-Roch de Ramezay, yielded the starving place to the British, Mother St Claude sent the British officer Monckton some preserves the nuns had made. They were, she wrote, "eager to present their respects to his Excellency, to express their deep appreciation for his protection, wishing him health.[76] Writing to a nun in France, she expressed fear that "all the world" would shun them. Mother St. Claude's concern to maintain connections and supporters had been developed from the time of her childhood at the chateau, and it served her well. The French regime came to a close with the capitulation of Montreal in September 1760. Fortunately for the nuns, it fell into the hands of gentlemanly British officers with a similar sense of honour and of clientage.

Despite sisterly solicitude towards the foe, it is impossible to read the annals of any of the town's three convents without discerning their passionate attachment to the French cause. The nuns chronicled battle after battle, the Ursulines even including

83

dispatches sent to them by General Montcalm himself. The Hôpital, where a full 40 percent of the choir sisters were daughters of St Louis Cross holders,[77] was no less patriotic. The nuns vigorously protested thefts by the British guard, but accepted with equanimity times when French forces purloined the cattle and grain needed to feed Hôpital patients. They maintained secret communications with General Lévis and helped recovered soldiers rejoin French lines.[78] If Mother St Claude spread false rumours of French victories, it was in keeping with the obvious patriotism of the nuns.

With good connections, the Hôpital weathered the change of empires. For a while its survival was in doubt. It was the hardest hit of any of the colony's seven convents, experiencing deep losses when French bills of exchange were redeemed at a fraction of their face value. The sisters were also stunned when the king, for the first time, refused to repay the expenses they had incurred as a military hospital in the final years of the war. To meet their debts they were forced to sell their most valuable seigneurie, St Vallier. The new governor of Quebec, James Murray, wrote that the nuns belonged to the best families in Canada, those families being their principal source of subsistence, but that the nobility in general was now plunged into distress.[79]

At this juncture the friendship of the English rulers was crucial. Forgiving any white lies the nuns may have told, Governor Murray donated flour and lard to the Hôpital and paid the expenses of the British patients. After the war, he lobbied both the French and the English governments to make financial concessions to the indebted Hôpital.[80] The British government stepped into the role formerly occupied by France, providing annual grants in return for care of the infirm and the insane. Between 1800 and 1823, these grants amounted to about 20,000 British pounds.[81]

Outside the walls, a new gender order was emerging in the Western world. Segregation by sex would gradually become almost as stringent as the old segregation by rank that preceded it. The revolutionary decades that followed the Conquest were hard on chatelaines, court favourites, and powerful women in general. As women outside the convents faced increasing constraints, the Hôpital Général and other convents continued to provide a range of occupations and administrative positions for talented and strong-minded individuals whom convent annals identify as *femmes fortes*. When the elderly Mother St. Claude died in 1767 after a lingering illness, she could rest secure. Neither Victorian prejudices nor twentieth century secularization would succeed in stifling her order of nuns, who to this day work and worship in the ancient convent. …

CONCLUSION

When the Seven Years' War broke out in 1756 the sisters at the Hôpital Général de Quebec, like their brothers on the battlefields, gave their all to the cause, and many died in the line of duty. Nobles that they were, they conducted themselves in ways that answered both the call of honour and the imperatives of a clientage system. Their mastery of that system is suggested by the triple role history has assigned to Mother St Claude: tearful nurse to dying British officers, lady of high breeding serving them tea, and secret agent working on behalf of the French. Whether her rumoured role as French agent is accurate or apocryphal, it is undeniable that she and her sisters supported their own brothers who fought beneath their convent windows. They housed hundreds of French refugees and calmly let French forces pillage their supplies. All the while they cultivated the esteem of the British command, who would soon rule Quebec. When their brothers faced ridicule and exile, the nuns stayed in a colony that continued to appreciate them.

What is the significance of presenting caste and clientage as a source of the nuns' authority? It bolstered the ability of convents to survive the change of empires. Travellers to New France, and the gentlemanly army officers who ruled after the Conquest, repeatedly expressed their admiration for the gentility and generosity of the nuns. Even relatively weak or unskilled convent administrators could rely on a well-developed system, one honed during a variety of imbroglios with ecclesiastics during the French regime. Though none of the other convents had as many nobles as did the Hôpital Général, the five large, long-established ones in Montreal and Quebec all had at least 14 per cent of their recruits from this class.[82] They too could benefit from whatever networks these nuns could command, and they adjusted successfully during a period when both male officers and male clergy faced plummeting numbers and morale.[83]

This study also supports scholarly views of clientage as a pervasive form of power lying outside regular political channels. Here we see that it can be particularly helpful in explaining the control elite women sometimes exerted. Convents with large complements of nobles are one case of interests and societal forces joining clienteles to achieve a certain flexibility and independence within the absolutist state. An ingrained code of honour made even nobles within cloisters desire to serve the Crown—and Crown administrators desire to serve them. This situation is, indeed, "a transformed public/private dialectic ... a state organisation in which institutions appear more minutely engaged and more fully interactive, deriving from their role a more compelling legitimacy and a greater authority."[84] Authority flowed through Crown brokers to numerous community-based institutions such as the Hôpital Général de Quebec. The Hôpital had hundreds of ties to the local populace, and it had aristocrats at the top who parlayed with governors and ministers. ... Mother St Claude and other brides of Christ did not shed the persona of proud and well-connected elites when they knelt to take their vows. That attribute equipped them well for battles with ecclesiastical factions and domineering bishops. Those were workaday problems, and things grew considerably worse when British forces took the town. More than ever, Mother St Claude and her sisters needed the self-confidence of the blue-blood, and skill in the noble art of making connections. Through war, pestilence, and the death of an empire, caste and clientage served them well.

NOTES

I would like to acknowledge the *CHR* editors and reviewers, and the inspiration of the late Professor William J. Eccles.

1. Captain John Knox, *An Historical Journal of the Campaign in North America for the Years 1757, 1758, 1759 and 1760*, ed. A. G. Doughty (Toronto: Champlain Society 1914), 2: 213. The chief primary documents for this article are the official colonial correspondence at the National Archives of Canada (NA), MG 1 series C11A, and also MG 18, H54, the Ramezay Family Papers. Also invaluable are the annals of the Hôpital Général, much of them printed verbatim in the nineteenth-century edition of [Helena O'Reilly], *Monseigneur de Saint-Vallier et l'Hôpital général de Québec* (Quebec: C. Darveau,

1882). My thanks to soeur Juliette Cloutier, the archivist of the Hôpital Général who supplied me with documents relating specifically to Mother St Claude de la Croix. Micheline D'Allaire's *L'Hôpital-général de Québec, 1692–1764* (Montreal: Fides 1977) is the definitive history, based on exhaustive combing and sophisticated qualitative and quantitative analysis of the seventeenth- and eighteenth-century records in the Hôpital archives. Unless otherwise attributed, most details on Hôpital possessions, procedures, and personnel are drawn from D'Allaire's book.

2. Knox, *Historical Journal*, 2: 237.

3. Ibid., 368.

4. Ibid. This story is repeated, with additional details of Mother St Claude's rumours, in [O'Reilly], *Mgr de Saint-Vallier*, 393–4. Doughty notes in Knox's *Journal* that Murray's subsequent goodwill to the Hôpital made him "unwilling to believe that Murray had any knowledge of the letter attributed to him by the author. Possibly it was mere gossip circulated in the camp." *Historical Journal*, Knox, 367–8 note. D'Allaire, however, accepted the story as true in her biography of Mother St Claude for the *Dictionary of Canadian Biography*, vol. 3 (Toronto: University of Toronto Press 1974), 544. ...

5. Religious vocations were related to caste. Nobility passed down from father to son, but daughters would lose noble status if they married non-nobles. Unfortunately there were not enough noble grooms to go around. Eighteen per cent of noblewomen entered religion, compared with 6 per cent of noblemen. ...

6. Jo Ann Kay McNamara, *Sisters in Arms: Catholic Nuns through Two Millennia* (Cambridge: Harvard University Press 1996), ix–x.

7. Terrence Crowley, "Women, Religion and Freedom in New France," in Larry Eldridge, ed., *Women and Freedom in Early America* (New York: New York University Press 1997), 110–11.

8. Marguerite Jean, *Évolution des communautés religieuses de femmes au Canada de 1639 à nos jours* (Montreal: Fides 1977), 199.

9. On the ranked society, see Dale Miquelon, *New France, 1701–1744, "A Supplement to Europe"* (Toronto: McClelland & Stewart 1987), 228ff, and Peter Moogk, *La Nouvelle France: The Making of French Canada* (East Lansing: University of Michigan Press 2000), chaps. 6–7. On the "caste system,"

see William Eccles, "The Social, Economic and Political Significance of the Military Establishment in New France," in Eccles, *Essays on New France* (Toronto: Oxford 1987), 115–16.

10. Laywomen's activities are signalled in Guy Frégault, "Politique et politiciens," in his *Le XVIIIe siècle canadien* (Montreal: Éditions HMH 1968), 159–241. They are the focus of Anka Muhlstein's *La femme soleil: Les femmes et le pouvoir* (Paris: Denoel/Gonthier 1976); of Sharon Kettering, "The Patronage Power of Early Modern French Noblewomen," *Historical Journal* 32 (1989), 817–41; and Sara Chapman, "Patronage as Family Economy: The Role of Women in the Patron–Client Network of the Phélypeaux de Pontchartrain Family, 1670–1715," *French Historical Studies* 24, 1 (2001): 9 ff. See also my "Women of the New France Noblesse," in Eldridge, *Women and Freedom*, 26–43.

11. On convents and parlements, see Mita Choudhury, "Despotic Habits: The Critique of Power and Its Abuses in an Eighteenth Century Convents," *French Historical Studies* 12, 1 (2000): 35, 50. On the powers of Tridentine Mother Superiors, see Olwen Hufton, *The Prospect before Her* (London: Fontana 1997), 370 ff.

12. Julius Kirchner, "'Introduction: The State Is Back In," *Journal of Modern History* 67 (supplement) (Dec. 1995): 1.

13. Giorgio Chittolini, "The 'Private,' the 'Public,' the State," *Journal of Modern History* 67 (supplement) (Dec. 1995): 42–3. Well before this wave of writing on the modern state, John Bosher drew attention to the phenomenon in New France. Bosher, "Government and Private Interests in New France," *Canadian Public Administration,* 10 (1967), 244–57.

14. Moogk. *La Nouvelle France: The Making of French Canada*, 184.

15. S. J. R. Noel, *Patrons, Clients, Brokers: Ontario Society and Politics, 1791–1896* (Toronto: University of Toronto Press 1990), 14.

16. Sharon Kettering, *Patrons Brokers and Clients in Seventeenth-Century France* (Oxford: Oxford University Press 1986), 11.

17. Elaine Forman Crane, *Ebb Tide in New England: Women, Seaports and Social Change, 1630–1800* (Boston: Northeastern University Press 1998), 62–97. ... On Catholic latitude as it related to saintliness, see Dominique Deslandres, "La saintété à l'ombre des cloîtres: Quelques observations sur les

représéntations de la sainteté feminine en Nouvelle-France," paper presented at the conference Colonial Saints: Hagiography and the Cult of Saints in the Americas, 1500–1800, University College, University of Toronto, May 2000.

18. Ramezay Family Papers, Documents 1709ff, 1 June 1701, Jean Phélypeaux to Claude Ramezay, Certification of Nobility.

19. Guy Chaussinand-Nogaret, *La noblesse au XVIIIe siècle* (Paris: Hachette 1976), 53, 70. These racial notions are also discussed in Jonathan Dewald, *Aristocratic Experience and the Origins of Modern Culture: France, 1570–1715* (Berkeley: University of California Press 1993), 127, 206. Pride in lineage was seen in the tendency of noble nuns to select the name of a parent as a name in religion. Mother St Claude assumed her father's first name.

20. Lorraine Gadoury, *La noblesse de Nouvelle-France: families et alliances* (Lasalle, QC; Hurtubise HMH 1991), 15–20, 25 n38.

21. Eccles, "Significance of the Military," 115–16; Miquelon, *New France*, 240, 242.

22. *Dictionary of Canadian Biography* 2: 546.

23. See for example, the inventory of the Château St Louis in *Rapport de l'archivist de la Province de Québec, 1922–3 [RAPQ]* (Quebec: Archives nationales du Québec 1924). Other works casting light on aristocratic material culture include the catalogue *Château Ramezay* (Montreal: Société d'archéologie et de numismatique 1984); Yves Landry, dir., *Pour le Christ et le roi: La vie au temps des premiers Montréalais* (Montreal: Libre expression 1992); Ernest Gagnon, *Le Fort et le Château Saint-Louis* (Quebec 1895); John Hare et al., *Histoire de la ville de Quebec* (Montreal: Boréal 1987); and Monique Eleb-Vidal with Anne Debarre-Bianchard, *Architectures de la vie privée: maisons et mentalités, XVIIe-XIXe siècles* (Bruxelles: Archives d'architecture moderne 1995).

24. The significance of physical grace is discussed in M. Motley, *Becoming a French Aristocrat* (New Jersey: Princeton University Press 1990), 57–8, 140–9. La Potherie noted, as did many other observers, that Canadian elites were passionately fond of dancing. A contemporary indication of the rigid social segregation of the military noblesse is that, in Quebec City, this group was reported to have attended dinner parties separate from those of administrators and bourgeoisie. C.-C. Le Roy de Bacqueville

de la Potherie, *Histoire de l'Amérique septentrionale* (Paris: Nyon 1753), 1: 278–9.

25. Kettering, *Patrons, Brokers, and Clients,* 38. She fills out her definition on pages 3–15.

26. Ibid., 9. Noel, *Patrons, Clients, Brokers,* 71, notes the importance of brokers in the pioneer province of Upper Canada in integrating local leaders to the centre.

27. Kettering, *Patrons, Brokers, and Clients,* 34.

28. J. Péristiany makes this point in *Honour and Shame: The Values of Mediterranean Society* (London: Weidenfeld 1965), 11.

29. P.-G. *Roy. La Famille de Ramezay* (Levis: Np, 1910), 7.

30. NA, MG 1, C11A, vol. 22, 12 Oct. 1705, Ramezay to the Minister.

31. Ibid., Vaudreuil and Beauhamois to Maurepas, 2 Oct. 1724; *Dictionary of Canadian Biography,* 2: 548; V. Morin, "Les Ramezay et leur Château," *Cahiers des dix,* 3 (1938), 43. For La Potherie's comment, see *RAPQ* 1926–/, 111–31.

32. See, for example, NA, MG 1 C11A, vol. 50, Mme de Ramezay à Maurepas, 8 Oct. 1728. With regard to boarding school, future estate manager Louise de Ramezay was sent to the Ursulines at the age of five.

33. Louis Franquet, *Voyages et mémoires sur le Canada* (Montreal: Éditions Élysee 1974), 56; La Potherie, *Histoire,* 1: 366–8. See also Eccles, "Military Establishment."

34. Mother St Claude informed nuns in France about colonial military strategy, including the size of the forces and the strengths of various forts. Her letter is printed in [O'Reilly], *Mgr Saint-Vallier* 331–3. Madame de Vaudreuil informed the colonial minister on the different strategies and equipment needed for summer and winter raids in the colony. General Montcalm chastised the wife of second Governor Vaudreuil for interfering in military councils.

35. Ruette d'Auteuil, "Memoire sur l'état présent du Canada," *RAPQ,* 1922–3, 50. The *Dictionary of Canadian Biography* 2: 301–2 contains an excellent compilation of sources on Madame Vaudreuil.

36. Abbé François Daniel, *Histoire des grandes familles françaises du Canada* (Montreal: Senécal 1867), 438–40.

37. D'Allaire, *L'Hôpital-général,* 93, 114, and her *Les dots des religieuses au Canada français, 1639–1800* (Montreal: Hurtubise HMH 1986), 167. D'Allaire's time frames vary. Her 37.2 per cent figure applies to the period 1693–1800, while her 45.9 per cent figure appears to relate to 1700–60. Is it possible that Gadoury, in *La noblesse,* 68, based her lower 22 per cent figure on converses and choir nuns, and D'Allaire on the latter alone?

38. P.F.X. De Charlevoix, *Histoire et description général de la Nouvelle-France* (Paris: Nyon 1744), 3: 78; Peter Kalm, *The America of 1750* (New York: Wilson-Erickson 1937), 454–5; P.-G.-Roy, *La ville de Québec sous le régime français* (Quebec 1930), 2: 265. See also Ruette d'Auteuil, "Mémoire sur l'état de la Vouvelle-France," *RAPQ,* 1923–4, 6.

39. De Charlevoix, *Histoire et description* 3: 77–8: "C'est la plus belle Maison du Canada, & elle ne depareroit point nos plus grandes villes de France." On the Hôpital building, see also Kalm, *The America of 1750,* 454–5; Roy, *La ville de Québec sous le régime français,* 2: 265; d'Auteuil, "Mémoire sur l'état de la Nouvelle-France," 6; Knox, *Historical Journal,* 2: 214–15; [O'Reilly], *Mgr Saint-Vallier,* 331.

40. Kalm, *Travels* 2: 455. They also had stables, various carraiges and sleighs and both large and small boats. D'Allaire, *L'Hôpital-général,* 160ff.

41. For sketches of the superiors, see Joseph Trudelle, *Les jubilés et les églises et chapelles de la ville et de la banlieu de Québec, 1608–1901* (Quebec: Le Soleil 1904) 116–19.

42. The Juchereau Duchesnays are an example. They were drawn from a line of warriors so illustrious that one writer remarked that their history resembled a novel, and they included many women who took the veil. Mother Geneviève de St Augustine ruled as superior for a decade. Her younger sister Mother Marie-Joseph de l'Enfant-Jesus became her assistant superior at the age of twenty-one. She ruled for nearly twenty years as superior, and for another twenty in such offices as hospital director, depositary, and *discrète*. Their niece, Mother Marie-Catherine de St Ignace, wrote the annals. P.-G. Roy, *La famille Juchereau Duchesnay* (Lévis: Np, 1903), 1: 178–86, 221.

43. *Dictionary of Canadian Biography,* 3: 544.

44. D'Allaire, *L'Hôpital-général,* 168–9, has a fascinating hour-by-hour description of their routine, which brings out the spiritual side of their existence—a subject deserving fuller study.

45. There was one exception: converses were allowed to vote on whether the community confessor's term

87

should be extended. Ibid., 152–3. "Cinderellas of the convents" is Miquelon's phrase.

46. [O'Reilly], *Mgr Saint-Vallier*, 253, discusses godparenting. D'Allaire, *L'Hôpital-général*, 120–1, lists the population of domestics, pensioners, and ecclesiastics.

47. This estimate is based on D'Allaire's figures, *L'Hôpital-général*, 120–2. Mother St Joseph claimed in 1716 that they cared for more than sixty, a figure higher than any on D'Allaire's chart. NA, MG 1, C11A, vol. 36, Mother St Joseph to Conseil de la Marine, 12 and 14 Nov 1716. For an introduction to the literature and the controversies regarding hôpitaux and poor relief in Europe, see M. H. D. van Leeuwen, "Logic of Charity: Poor Relief in Preindustrial Europe," *Journal of Interdisciplinary History*, 24, 4 (1994): 589–613.

48. [O'Reilly]. *Mgr Saint-Vallier*, 327–32.

49. D'Allaire, *L'Hôpital-général*, 19, 128.

50. NA, MG 1, C11A, vol. 29, 137. Mother Superior to Pontchartrain, 1708. D'Allaire discusses revenue in *L'Hôpital-général*, 39–49.

51. For the couple without heirs, see P.-G. Roy, *Le Vieux Québec* (Quebec: Np, 1922), 109. On alms, see D'Allaire, *L'Hôpital-général*, 41.

52. P.-G. Roy, La Ville de Québec sous le régime français (Quebec: Redempti Paradis 1930), 1: 528.

53. D'Allaire attributes the upsurge of postulants in the 1750s to the desire for a safe haven in wartime, a theory also expressed by Bishop Briand. See also Crowley, "Women, Religion and Freedom," 121.

54. On ecclesiastical infighting and its negative effect on convents, see Henri Tetu, *Les évêques de Québec* (Quebec: N. Hardy 1889), 175–6. On the burial controversy, see also Miquelon, *New France*, 253–4, and Dale Standen, "Politics, Patronage and the Imperial Interest: Charles Beauharnois's Disputes with Gilles Hocquart," *Canadian Historical Review* 60, 1: (1979): 19–40.

55. NA, MG 1, C11A, Dosquet to Maurepas, 16 Oct. 1730. He also requested that they be returned to the control of the Hôtel Dieu.

56. D'Allaire, *L'Hôpital-général*, 135. Fortunately for the convent, its letters patent required concurrence of governor and intendant with the bishop on major changes. On the relatively large powers of the state, see Jean, *Évolution des communautés religieuses*, 201–2, 208. Guy Frégault elucidates the complex

relations between church and state in *Le XVIIIe siècle canadien*, 86–158.

57. NA, MG 1, C11A, vol. 50, Geneviève St Augustin Superière à Votre Grandeur, 4 Oct. 1728.

58. The false pretenses were that legal proceedings might be taken against the party that had offended them, and that they would be shunned.

59. NA, MG 1, C11A, Soeur Agnes to the Minister, 19 Oct. 1728.

60. Ibid., vol. 54, Beauharnois and Hocquart to the Minister, 15 Jan. and 3 and 6 Oct. 1731. D'Allaire too identifies a spirit of independence as the nuns' foremost trait. *L'Hôpital-général*, 173.

61. This information comes from a letter from the Quebec Hôpital which survived in the Augustinian archives at Rennes, cited in D'Allaire, *L'Hôpital-général*, 176.

62. Jean, *Evolution des communautés réligieuses*, 199, 295, provides the context showing various cases where nuns sometimes won, sometimes lost, disputes with ecclesiastics. In this case the nuns seem to have lost the battle but won the war.

63. D'Allaire, *L'Hôpital-général*, 135. For supportive letters from governor and intendant, see NA, MG 1, C11A, vol. 57, 1 Oct. 1732, and vol. 107, 26 Oct. 1735 and 6 Oct. 1736.

64. Letters from both ecclesiastics are printed in A. Gossolin, *Mgr de Saint-Vallier et son temps* (Evreux Imprimerie de l'Eure 1898) 97–102. Governor Philippe Rigaud de Vaudreuil and his wife expressed great affection for the Hôpital's first superior, and Madame de Vaudreuil even brought French medicines to her bedside.

65. NA, MG 1, C11A, vol. 56, Dosquet to Maurepas, 4 Sept. 1731.

66. She was one of two Hôpital nuns reporting personal funds (215 *livres* in paper money) in 1762. Trudel, L'Église canadienne, 2: 307. Trudel also quotes Brooke's letter (302). Briand's 1766 letter (now at the Archives of the Archdiocese of Quebec) is cited, and partially reproduced, in D'Allaire, *L'Hôpital-général*, 184–5.

67. [O'Reilly], *Mgr Saint-Vallier*, 393.

68. On links with the Soumandes, Duchesnays, and Hazeurs, see D'Allaire, *L'Hôpital-général*, 18, 28, 49, 95, as well as her other study, Micheline D'Allaire, *Les dots des religieuses au Canada français, 1639–1800* (Montreal: Hurtubise HMH 1986), 23–4, and [O'Reilly],

Mgr Saint-Vallier, 370n. The Levasseur family supplied sculptors, craftsmen and craftswomen, postulants and pensioners. R. Traquair and G. A. Neilson, "The Architecture of the Hôpital-Général—Quebec," *Journal of the Royal Architectural Institute of Canada* 7, 2 (1931), 69. Trudel notes Conquest-era loans from kin such as Mme Boishebert (Mother St Claude's sister) and M. de Lanaudière.

69. P.-G. Roy, *La famille Adhémar de Lantagnac* (Levis: Np, 1908), 21.

70. See D'Allaire, *L'Hôpital-général*, 32ff, and [O'Reilly], *Mgr Saint-Vallier*, 350ff.

71. A month later the Hôpital cemetery was full of French dead, and 183 battle victims were still being cared for by the nuns. See H. R. Casgrain, ed., *Lettres de divers particuliers au Chevalier de Lévis* (Quebec: Demers 1895), 16–17.

72. Mother Saint-Henri unbound and hid a British officer about to be tortured by one of France's native allies. [O'Reilly], *Mgr Saint-Vallier*, 615.

73. A. Doughty and G. W. Parmelee, *The Siege of Quebec and the Battle of the Plains of Abraham* (Quebec: Dussault and Proulx 1901), 2: 164.

74. [O'Reilly], *Mgr Saint-Vallier*, 360.

75. Another nice example of the gentlemanly ethos was General Murray's volunteering to supply the French officers, encamped some distance from the town, with their customary coffee, sugar, wine, and liquors. This hospitality eased the dilemmas of the officer Malartic, in charge at the Hôpital, of needing to buy from the British "sans témoigner beaucoup d'empressement ni avoir l'air d'un acheteur, ce qui ne convient pas à un officier de garde." Casgrain, ed., *Lettres de divers particuliers*, 220–2.

76. The French original is quoted in Trudel, *L'Église canadienne*, 2: 312. Mother St Claude's letter to France also expressed concern that there would be no new postulants. D'Allaire, *L'Hôpital-général*, 132.

77. Trudel, L'Église *canadienne*, 2: 202. The order with the next highest proportion, 6.7 per cent, was the Ursulines.

78. [O'Reilly], *Mgr Saint-Vallier*, 355–8.

79. A. Shortt and A. Doughty, eds., *Documents relating to the Constitutional History of Canada* (Ottawa: King's Printer 1914), 2: 54

80. It is indicative of the elite mindset of the time that Murray informed the British government that nothing would be more popular with the inhabitants of the colony than assisting the Hôpital since the nuns came from the best Canadian families. NA, MG 1, series Q, 2: 367.

81. *Journal of the Legislative Council of Lower Canada,* 1824, Appendix 1, "Report of the Special Committee for Insane, Foundlings, Sick and Infirm Poor," 2–3.

82. Gadoury, *La noblesse*, 68, gives the figures: Quebec Ursulines, 20.7 per cent, Quebec Hôtel-Dieu, 17.2 per cent, Quebec Hôpital-Général, 22.4 per cent. In Montreal, the Hôtel-Dieu had 19 per cent and Congrégation de Notre Dame, 14.6 per cent.

83. Trudel, *L'Église canadienne*, 1: 76ff, documents the difficulties among both parish priests and members of orders. On the declining noblesse, see Murray's remark above and Gadoury's figures, *La noblesse*, 156. From a peak of 3.5 per cent of the Canadian population in 1695–1704, nobles declined steadily. They were 1.3 per cent of the population in 1754 and 0.8 per cent in 1764. In absolute terms their numbers dropped from 809 in 1745–9 to 474 in 1765.

84. Chittolini, "The 'Private,', the 'Public,' and the State," 53.

ON THE EDGE OF EMPIRES

Acadians and Mi'kmaq in the Eighteenth Century

Daniel Samson
Brock University

⬤ ON THE EDGE OF EMPIRES: ACADIANS AND MI'KMAQ IN THE EIGHTEENTH CENTURY

⬤ **Introduction by Daniel Samson**

● INTRODUCTION

Daniel Samson

When most of us think about the past, we imagine a simpler world. We populate our imagined historical landscapes with hardy farmer-settlers, virtuous women, and adventurous men. Such visions also often include a fairly simple understanding of ethnic and national identity: in the New World, there were British people, French people, and Aboriginal peoples, and they struggled for supremacy. In some places, this view reasonably approximated what was on the ground. Certainly, for example, if we were to read a Boston newspaper in the 1740s, there would be much talk of how "we" (Britons) were fighting "them" (French and Aboriginals). But the reality was often much more complex, especially away from the major centres of the colonies, where warfare and frontier-like conditions frequently overturned lives and communities, rewriting the rules by which lives were lived.

This was especially so in smaller borderland colonies such as Acadia that lay between the major imperial centres. From the 1650s to the 1750s, Acadians spent much of their time attempting to negotiate a safe existence between their larger neighbours, neighbours who often fought their wars in those very locations. Acadia, of course, was a French colony, but its place as a strategic battleground meant that its people quickly learned that their own best interests and those of their parent country were not always the same. Traditional accounts tell the story as a contest between the British and the French (with some attention to the French allies, the Mi'kmaq). But a closer examination shows that this was true only at the larger levels of imperial struggles. We see Acadians (only some of whom seem to have regarded themselves as being French subjects): New Englanders (some of whom had good trade relations with the Acadians, some of whom advocated a scorched-earth policy against their "Romish" neighbours); Mi'kmaq (some of whom had intermarried with Acadians, most of whom had converted to Catholicism, many of whom would actively support the French in wars against the British, and most of whom jealously protected their continued independence); French colonial officials (only some of whom seemed committed to running an efficient regime, and who very often distrusted the Acadians more than the New Englanders); and British colonial officials (most of whom saw in Nova Scotia a way to advance their careers, and thus to get to some better colonial post). And that's only scratching the surface: Before the final conquest of Acadia in 1710, Acadian men married Mi'kmaq women (some of these families remained more closely tied to the Acadian settlements, while some remained more tied to the Mi'kmaq villages); after the conquest, British soldiers (most of whom were militiamen from New England) married Acadian women (who were then ex-communicated from the Church, and might later find themselves under siege by people who were once neighbours). In Acadia/Nova Scotia, identity was a messy issue.

Confused? You should be. It was confusing, and it was no less confusing for those on the ground. Not only were Acadia's ethnic and political identities fluid, but also was control of its government: Port Royal, the capital of Acadia, changed hands seven times between 1630 and 1710. Acadians might have been French Catholics, but they lived under British rule for 60 years in the century between 1654 and 1755. In this situation, where one's governors changed almost with the seasons, the most pressing issue was where one's interests lay—that is, which side you were on (or were thought to be on!). As control passed back and forth, as British, French, New England, Canadian, and Mi'kmaq (not to mention occasional Mohawk and Abenaki) warriors assaulted its peoples and possessions, most Acadians came to agree that the best way forward was to be neutral.

Most people know only one thing about the history of the Acadians: that they were expelled from modern-day Nova Scotia in 1755. This one act, today often described as an early example of what we now call ethnic cleansing (the forced relocation of one group conquered by another), seems compelled to carry the weight of all Acadian history. Indeed, a lively debate exists on the causes of the expulsion. Some writers maintain that this was a ruthless crime committed by the British empire on a weak and helpless people, some that it was unfortunate but a military necessity, some that it was the Acadians' own fault for refusing to take the unqualified oath of their conquest. The blame game may be fun for some, but too often it ignores the larger story. Blame falls typically on the British for being cruel (or at best as being too blind to the consequences of their actions), to the French for using their former citizens as pawns in a larger game, to the New Englanders for being fanatically anti-Catholic and anti-Indian, or on the Acadians themselves for stubbornly refusing to face the facts and not taking the oath of allegiance. But when historians have looked closer, they have seen that all these characterizations, while true to some extent, miss the day-to-day complexities and changes that marked life on the ground for all these people. When we look at the decades prior to the expulsion, rather than focusing on that moment, we see ever-shifting terrain, miscommunications, misunderstanding, inconsistent policies, shifting alliances, and yet still some emerging patterns and consistencies that make clear that ethnic and political identities were of necessity by no means constant.

Most readings centre on *le grand dérangement*—the expulsions of 1755–58—but here we'll try to focus not on that moment but on its context: on the social and political history of Acadia before 1755. Francis Parkman, one of the most famous American historians ever, emphasizes the place of religion and more particularly of the Roman Catholic priests who he feels manipulated the Acadians. Another American historian, Geoffrey Plank, also sees manipulation, though this time on the part of the New England colonial officials. But his analysis of the Acadians is quite different than Parkman's. John Mack Farragher, a historian at Yale University, nicely illustrates how, in 1745, the majority of Acadians adhered to the promise of neutrality despite being pushed by both sides. Naomi Griffiths, the author of what is by far the most important book on the Acadians—*From Migrant to Acadian* (2004)—offers us a sense of the many facets of Acadian identity. The sum is complex. We should get a sense of a diverse and determined people being buffeted by many different circumstances and of the difficulties such complexity offers the historians of *Acadie*. While the available evidence is small, Griffiths outlines the close cultural and familial ties between Acadian and Mi'kmaq peoples. Yet, as William Wicken illustrates, those ties were subject to changing pressures. This work reminds us that for these peoples histories were linked but evolved differently.

QUESTIONS

1. What factors shaped Acadians' political worldviews?
2. Why did the Acadians show such mixed support for France?
3. Were they loyal? Is that the right question?
4. Today, people speak of *la nation acadienne*. Can we see a nation emerging in the eighteenth century? If not, what did it lack? If so, what were its defining characteristics?
5. Three of our four historians (Parkman, Plank, and Farragher) are Americans. Explain the interest of American historians in the history of Acadia.

FURTHER READINGS

John Bartlet Brebner, *New England's Outpost: Acadia before the Conquest of Canada* (New York, Columbia University Press, 1927).

Naomi F.S. Griffiths, *From Migrant to Acadian: A North American Border People, 1604–1755* (Kingston and Montreal, McGill-Queen's University Press, 2005).

John Reid et al, eds., *The "Conquest" of Acadia, 1710: Imperial, Colonial, and Aboriginal Constructions* (Toronto, University of Toronto Press, 2004).

A Note on Geography: Following the players in this story is messy enough, but the claims on who lived where changed over the course of the story as well. The maps in our images section make clear some of the troubles here, but a few basics are still in order: from 1604 to 1710, Acadia was all of the present-day Maritime provinces and much of northern Maine (although, practically, most of the people lived in what is now southwestern Nova Scotia). In 1710, New England forces captured Port Royal (again!), and for the first time the subsequent treaty (Treaty of Utrecht, 1713) did not return it to the French. However, the treaty did return the islands in the Gulf of St. Lawrence: Ile Royale (Cape Breton), and Ile St. Jean (Prince Edward Island). The French claimed that the treaty offered them more, but they were unable to enforce their claims. French imperial officials urged Acadians to relocate to these islands, though few were willing to give up their now well-established farms. Thus, from 1710 until their expulsion 45 years later, most Acadians lived in British territory. Yet, as some of our readings make clear, real British power extended little beyond the walls of Annapolis Royal. Indeed, whatever was indicated by maps drawn in London or Paris, the Mi'kmaq remained the effective power throughout most of the mainland. Not until the conclusion of the Seven Years War would France be removed from America, and thus only after 1763 could the British claim control over all of what was once Acadia.

▲ Document 1: A British Map of Acadia, 1732

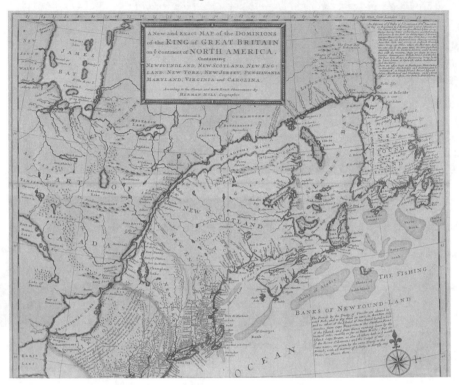

● Maps were information, but also propaganda tools. This British map emphasized complete British control of the mainland, allowing French control of Ile St. Jean, Ile Royale, and Anticosti (green). In the world according to this map all the Acadians on the mainland were under British rule. If the French claims we see elsewhere seem excessive, note here Britain's claim that it controls the southern shore of the St. Lawrence River. Who was the audience for this map? What features stand out as different from a modern-day map? Do these help us to better understand the larger struggle?

Source: Herman Moll, "A new and exact map of the Dominions of the King of Great Britain on ye continent of North America Containing Newfoundland, New Scotland, New England, New York, New Jersey, Pensilvania, Maryland, Virginia and Carolina." London, 1732 [1715]. (Wikipedia commons). Courtesy of the John Carter Brown Library at Brown University.

▲ Document 2: A French Map of Acadia, ca. 1745

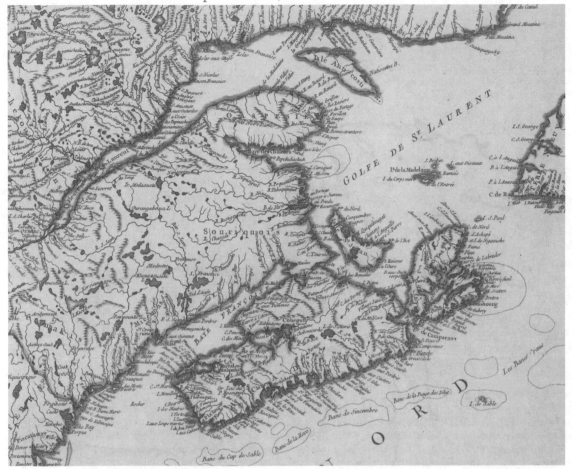

This French map notes a quite different interpretation of the terms of the Treaty of Utrecht, one that limited British control to Annapolis Royal (the British renamed Port Royal; note the small red circle around the town), and the southern and eastern shores of what is now mainland Nova Scotia (ending in the east at Canso). Indeed, here, the French claimed all of what is now the southern coast of New Brunswick and Maine (the assertion being that in Utrecht they gave up Acadia, but these territories were in Canada, an assertion that certainly seemed to contradict past practices). Under the terms indicated here, most Acadians remained under French control. Practically, this did not matter much to the Acadians, or to the French, but it offered an angle in negotiating with the British and coercing the Acadians to stay true to their mother country; however, it did not stop the British from building small forts at Minas (Fort Edward) and Beaubassin (Fort Cumberland). We might also note that this French map has a much greater number of references to Aboriginal peoples (Souriquois, Micmacs, Abenakis) and place names (Tatamagouche, Casquembec, Niganiche), a point that reflects not only greater French awareness of these people and places but perhaps also a greater acknowledgement of their continued control of territory. Why would the French argue for this interpretation of Acadia's limits?

Source: Detail from "Carte des pays connus sous le nom de Canada, dans laquelle sont distinguées les possessions françoises, & angl? Dédiée et présentée à Monseigneur le comte D'Argenson, pour le le Département de la guerre, par le Sr. Robert de Vaugondy fils, géographe ordinaire du roi". Maps and Charts of North America and the West Indies, 1750–1789, 15. American Memory, Geography and Map Division, Library of Congress. G3400 1753.R6 Vault.

▲ Document 3: A New French Map of Acadia, 1751

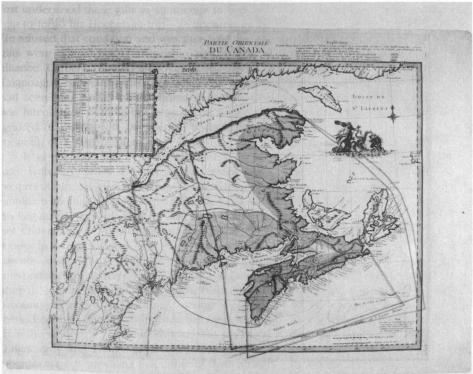

This French map illustrates a French interpretation of a British proposal from 1751. The white areas (modern-day Cape Breton and Prince Edward Island) Britain did not dispute; the green area France argued was all that Britain controlled; the red area (which includes about a third of mainland Nova Scotia) was claimed by both. Originally engraved by British mapmaker Thomas Jefferys, this version was overdrawn by French mapmaker Georges Louis Le Rouge in 1755. Why were maps so important in these debates? What do these different versions tell us about our use of such maps to understand the past?

Source: James W. MacNutt Collection of Historic Maps, Prince Edward Island Museum and Heritage Foundation, Number HF.96.1.13. Not to be reproduced without permission.

▲ Document 4: An Illustration from *Evangeline*

● Illustration by F.O.C Darley, from an 1897 edition of Longfellow's, *Evangeline*. The point is often made that no one influenced the popular view of Acadians and the deportation more than Longfellow. But it should be added that illustrations such as these, printed and reprinted numerous times well into the 20th century, were almost as powerful. This depiction of village life prior to the expulsion shows an imagined view of peaceful, simple country-folk at play after their hard day of work in the fields. As much influenced by anti-modern anxieties about modern urban life in industrializing North America, such views helped readers imagine the innocence of these stalwart peasants before being cruelly uprooted by British "Redcoats". Playing up innocence was central to Longfellow's rendering of the tragedy as a crime committed on helpless people by the world's most powerful empire. Similarly, Longfellow, an American patriot, downplayed the fact that most of those "Redcoats" were New England militiamen.

Source: Henry Wadsworth Longfellow. *Evangeline: A Tale of Acadie.* Boston: Houghton, Mifflin and Company, 1892. Collection Musée acadien de L'Université de Moncton.

▲ Document 5: Declaration Sent to the French Acadians, 1717

[Copy of the Declaration sent to the French Acadians for Signature enclosed in the fore-going Letter to the Secretary of State and War.]

Wee the french Inhabitants whose names are under written now dwelling in Annapolis Royal and the adjacent parts of Nova Scotia or Lacadie formerly subjects to the late french King who by the Peace concluded att Utrecht did by *articles therein deliver up the whole country of Nova Scotia and Lacadie to the late Queen of Great Britain, wee doe hereby for the aforesaid reason and for the protection of us and our Familys that shall reside in Annapolis Royall or the adjacent parts of Nova Scotia or Lacadie, now in possession of his most sacred Majesty George, by the Grace of God King of Great Britain, and doe declare that we acknowledge him to be the Sole King of the said Country and of Nova Scotia and Lacadie and all the Islands depending thereon and we likewise doe declare and most solemnly swear before God to own him as our Sovereign King and to obey him as his true and Lawfull subjects in Witness whereof we sett our hands in the Presence of John Doucett his Majesty's Lieut. Governor of Annapolis Royal this day ____of ____   in the year of Our Lord 1717.

Source: Copy of the Declaration sent to the French Acadians for Signature, 1717 in Thomas B. Akins, ed., *Selections from the Public Documents of the Province of Nova Scotia* (Halifax, Charles Annand, 1869), 14–15.

▲ Document 6: The Acadians' Reply, 1717

Copy of the answer to the above Declaration, sent to the Secretary of State.

[Translated from the French.]

We the undersigned inhabitants of Acadie, according to the orders which the Lieutenant Governor has been pleased to cause to be published on the part of King George viz. that we have fully to declare ourselves regarding the oath of fidelity which is demanded of us in the said orders, humbly entreat Mr. John Doucette our Governor, to be pleased to consider, that we constitute but a small number of the inhabitants.

We therefore respectfully request him to assemble the deputies of the other colonies of Minas, Beaubassin and Cobequid, with ourselves, in order that we may answer the demands that have been made on us, as we are instructed that they are now made for the last time.

For the present, we can only answer, that we shall be ready to carry into effect the demand proposed to us, as soon as his Majesty shall have done us the favor of providing some means of sheltering us from the savage tribes, who are always ready to do all kinds of mischief, proofs of which have been afforded on many occasions since the peace, they having killed and robbed several persons, as well English as French. Wherefore we pray his Excellency to consider this, and to represent to his Majesty the condition in which we are.

That unless we are protected from these savages, we cannot take the oath demanded of us without exposing ourselves to have our throats cut in our houses at any time, which they have already threatened to do.

In case other means cannot be found, we are ready to take an oath, that we will take up arms neither against his Britannic Majesty, nor against France, nor against any of their subjects or allies.

Such, Sir, is the final opinion which the inhabitants take the liberty of presenting to your Excellency, as they are not able to act otherwise at present.

Signed by all the inhabitants in this neighborhood.

NOTES

*The 12th article of the treaty, made at Utrecht between Anne, the Queen of Great Britain, and Louis the 14th, King of France, is as follows:

"The most Christian King shall cause to be delivered to the Queen of Great Britain, on the same day on which the ratifications of this treaty shall be exchanged, solemn and authentic letters or instruments, by virtue whereof it shall appear that the island of St. Christopher is to be possessed hereafter by British subjects only; likewise that all Nova Scotia or Acadie, comprehended within its ancient boundaries; as also the city of Port Royal, now called Annapolis Royal, and all other things in these parts which depend on the said lands and Islands, together with the dominion, property and possession of the said islands, lands and places, and all right whatever by treaties, or any other way attained, which the most Christian King, the Crown of France, or any the subjects thereof, have hitherto had to the said islands, lands and places, and to the inhabitants of the same, are yielded and made over to the Queen of Great Britain, and to her crown for ever; as the most Christian King doth now yield and made overall the said premises, and that in such ample manner and

Source: Thomas B. Atkins, ed., *Selections from the Public Documents of the Province of Nova Scotia* (Halifax, Charles Annand, 1869).

101

form that the subjects of the most Christian King shall hereafter be excluded from all kind of fishing in the seas, bays, and other places on the coasts of Nova Scotia, that is to say, on those coasts which lie towards the East, within thirty leagues, beginning from the island commonly called Sable, inclusively, and thence stretching along towards the South West."

14th Article.—"It is expressly provided that in all the said places and colonies to be yielded and restored by the most Christian King in pursuance of this treaty, the subjects of the said King may have liberty to remove themselves, within a year to any other place, as they shall think fit, together with all their movable effects. But those who are willing to remain there, and to be subject to the Kingdom of Great Britain, are to enjoy the free exercise of their religion according to the usage of the Church of Rome as far as the laws of Great Britain do allow the same."

Treaty signed 11 April 1713.

(31 March, Old style.)

LETTER OF QUEEN ANNE

Anne R.

Trusty and well beloved, we greet you well. Whereas our good brother, the most Christian King, hath, at our desire, released from imprisonment on board his galleys, such of his subjects as were detained there on account of their professing the Protestant religion. We being willing to show by some mark of our favour towards his subjects how kind we take his compliance therein, have therefore thought fit hereby to signify our will and pleasure to you, that you permit such of them as have any lands or tenements in the places under our government in Accadie and Newfoundland, that have been or are to be yielded to us by virtue of the late treaty of peace, and are willing to continue our subjects, to retain and enjoy their said lands and tenements without any molestation, as fully and freely as other our subjects do or may possess their lands or estates, or to sell the same, if they shall rather choose to remove elsewhere. And for so doing, this shall be your warrant, and so we bid you heartily farewell. Given at our court at Kensington, the 23rd day of June, 1713, and in the 12th year of our reign.

By her majesty's command,

(Signed) DARTMOUTH,

Superscribed,

To our trusty and well beloved Francis Nicholson, esquire, governor of our province of Nova Scotia or Accadia, and general and commander-in-chief of our forces, in our said province and in Newfoundland in America.

▲ Document 7: "Our French Inhabitants"

Govr. Mascarene to____ ____
ANNAPOLIS ROYALL, Decr. 1744.
SIR,—

I promised you the Sequel of the French attempts upon us and of our transactions here, which is as follows—

As soon as the French and Indians had left our River the Deputies of the Inhabitants came before me in Council and represented the dread they had been kept under by the French Commander, producing his written orders threatening with Death those who should disobey; They assur'd me however that notwithstanding the entreaties and threats of Monsr. Duvivier, none of the Inhabitants could be persuaded to take up Arms and Joyn the Enemy. They were dismissed with some checks for their remissness in their past, and exhortations towards their future conduct. A few days after came Deputies from Manis, who testified also their having withstood the same entreaties and threats and produc'd the same threatening orders concerning provisions and other assistance requir'd from them, as also a representation made by them to Mons. Durivier, on his offering to keep one hundred and fifty men with officers at that Place, by which they dissuaded him from it and oblig'd him to leave them, and to go to Chignicto. The Missionaries also writt to me and made their Conduct appear to have been on this occasion farr better than could have been expected from them.

The Deputies from Manis were no sooner dispatch't, than I was acquainted early in the morning by one of the french Inhabitants that he had been that night taken out of his bed by a party of french and carry'd in the Bassin on board a Shipp, which he suppos'd to be of fourty or fifty guns having in company a Brigantine of about twenty with Officers and Soldiers, which came in the evening before, and took two of our Vessels with Stores for the Garrison from Boston, which enter'd the Bassin the same tide after them. I call'd the Officers together and acquainted them with the information, without telling the way I had it, nor the latter part relating to our two Vessells being taken, and order'd every one to their charge according to the Disposition I had made for our Deffence.

The French Commander of this Sea armament finding their land force gone did not think themselves strong enough to attack us, tho' a Sloop which as I hear'd, had three mortars, some canon and other warlike Stores came in the next day. After staying three days without doing any thing else than taking wood and water they all departed with their two prizes and once more left us free of Enemies. I was in no small concern for fear one of the Vessells taken by them should be freighted with the Provisions I expected from the Contractor for the Garrison; but I was taken out of my pain four days after the Departure of the French, by the arrival of the Massachusetts Galley, Brigantino and Sloop; convoying a Schooner loaded with our Provisions. The tryall between them and the French if they had Stay'd would have been hard, as the Ennemy had a much superior Force, tho' I am sure their Commander could neither in conduct or Courage have equall'd ours. They had notice att Boston of the French sea Armament, butt not a just notion of their Force. Governor Shirley who has so vigorously imploy'd himself for our relief and to whose indefatiguable endeavours this Place in a great measure owes it preservation, had sent this Armament not only to Convey our Provisions; butt also to assist in the means of driving the French wholly out of this Province, judging, on what I wrote to his Excellency, that they might

Source: Excerpt from Governor Paul Mascarene's Report on the conduct of "our French Inhabitants" and "their Clanns of Indians", 1745, in Thomas B. Akins, ed., *Selections from the Public Documents of the Province of Nova Scotia* (Halifax, Charles Annand, 1869), 147-9.

take their winter Quarters att Manis. As by this time I was certain they had remov'd from that Place and gone to Chignicto, it was thought advisable considering the lateness of the Season (November) and the difficulty of navigation for such Shipping in the part of the Bay, to postpone the Expedition, and in the meantime to send a Small Shalloup with my letter to the Inhabitants thereby to know their temper and the situation of the Ennemy, whilst the Shipping Stay'd in our basin to give countenance to my proceedings. Before they left us I had the satisfaction to acquaint the Commander Captain Tyng, that I had certain information the French were gone from that Place back to Lewisbourg, and a few days after the Deputies of Chignicto came with a very Submissive letter, representing their case pretty near in the same manner as those of Manis, having resisted the entreaties and threats Monsr. Duvivier made them to oblige them to take up arms, and having by their Representations contributed to make him and his party depart from them.

Thus were the French with their Clanns of Indians oblig'd to leave us att last for this year after making three several attempts in which tho' their measures had been well conserted att first, yet were baffled att last; for we have heard since that the men of Warr mention'd by Monsr. Duvivier had every thing ready to come to reduce us, butt that on some intelligence of an English Squadron bound to these Northern parts they drop't their Enterprise and sent the Shipping above mention'd.

To the Breaking the French measures; the timely Succours receiv'd from the Governor of Massachusetts, and our French Inhabitants refusing to take up arms against us, we owe our preservation. The first had prepar'd such a Force as in the opinion of all, considering the ill condition of this Fort, we should not have been able to resist: By the second our men were eas'd in the constant Duty the many ruious places in our Ramparts requir'd to attend: and if the Inhabitants had taken up arms they might have brought three or four thousand men against us who would have kept us still on harder Duty, and by keeping the Enemy for a longer time about us, made it impracticable to repair our Breaches or to get our firewood and other things of absolute necessity.

Another concern of no small importance and under which I still labour, is my being oblig'd to supply with the Provisions laid in for the five Companys, all the Auxiliaries and other additional People for whom Provisions are not laid in store, such as Artificers belonging to the office of ordnance and others. These have found means since to supply themselves tho' what has been advanc'd to some of them is not yet made good to the Stores, by the misfortune happen'd to the Vessell which brought it being one of the two taken in our Bassin by the French Shipping. As for the Auxiliaries they came victuall'd only for three months so that from the first of October most have had provisions from our Stores and all the rest att different periods since. As the Government of Massachusetts, who have otherwise been att a great Expense for our Relief, may not think themselves oblig'd to answer this, nor clothing which it is absolutely necessary to provide for their men; I may find myself oblig'd to engage in that Expence, and to answer it give Bills on the Treasury. I hope in that case the Governor and you will not be wanting in representing the absolute necessity which forces me to such a step.

The Company of Indians or wood Rangers come last from Boston have prov'd of great service to this Place, they fell soon after their arrival on a family of Indians, kill'd some and scatter'd the rest and by their excursions they have kept off the Indian Ennemy who in small partys rov'd continually about us, which hindred the Inhabitants from supplying of us with fire wood, materials and other necessarys we wanted. As our regular Troops are not us'd to that way of annoying the Enemy, it would be a great advantage to this Place if such a Company could be establish'd here in time of Warr, and therefore I desire the Governor may Joyn his Sollicitation to what may be represented from hence and from the Government of Massachusetts for the Establishment of such a Company for the service of this Province.

▲ Document 8: Report on the Nature and State of the Province [Nova Scotia], ca. 1752

APPENDICES

For the better explanation of the following Sheets I believe it will be necessary to take some Notice of the Nature and State of the Province before the late Scheme for Peopling and establishing of it, which will shew what has been since done and the steps wh. have been taken to carry the Scheme into execution.

Before Mr. Cornwallis's Arrival in this vast Titular Dominion of ours, we had only one slight Fortress (this excepted) We had not an English Inhabitant nor a Rood of Land in our Possession throughout the whole Country, and this Little Fortress was rather to keep up our right to the Bay of Fundy than any other influence it could have on the rest of the Province—This is our talkd of Annapolis Royal, which is not strong by Nature or Improvement, however otherwise the last may stand in the Board of Ordinances Accounts. (at this time it had Six weak Company's of the Governors (then Phillips's Regimt. & an Independent Company of a hundred Rangers.[)]

Here there was no Trade, nor scarcely any Ships seen, except their annual Ones, that came like Spanish Galleons in the Season, with salt Beef and cloathing for the Troops, and Ordinance Stores—They had no communication, nor usefull Intercourse with the Indians and their Valuable Trade in Furrs and Sables was entirely engrossed by the French tho' they acknowledged themselves under our Government seldom paid further respect to it, than sometimes a Deputy to the Lieutenant governor who had scarce Power to raise a Tax or demand their Service.

These People were in the quiet Possession of the most fertile and cleard parts of the Country, particularly between Chebucto and Chegnecto likewise about the River Minas sharing everything in common with the Indians I have heard their Numbers computed at twenty thousand Souls, I believe them little short of it, and they are a laborious contented, healthy and Tempreate People who live chiefly on Corn, Milk and Roots, and are the truest Picture of the first Tenders of Flocks.

When the late French War broke out [1741–48] the Governor of Canada who knew the weakness as well as consequence of Annapolis set on Foot an Expedition against it wherein the Indians of the Province and those of Quebeck joynd—most of our French Subject encouraged, or at least wished well to it, some actually did joyn them, but as this Enterprize entirely depended on a Squadron commanded by Monsieur De Anville[1] from France which meeting with Misfortune luckily prevented their Success and they raised their Siege of three Months it might be rather calld a Blockade as they made no regular Approaches to it. However they were much more successful in another Expedition under Monsieur Le Corne who surprised and butchered Colonel Noble with five hundred new England Men.[2] These Accounts you may have formerly read in the English News Papers.

The Troops from Canada had now received Orders to continue in the Province accordingly they tooke Possession of the best Parts of it settling themselves at St. Johns and Chegonecto where they established a kind of military Government to which most of

Source: Anon., report on the "Nature and State of the Province [Nova Scotia]" ca.1752, reprinted in *The Northcliffe Collection,* PAC, 1926, pp. 68–76.

the others submitted except those of Annapolis—and as they encreased in Strength they diminished in Loyalty and Affection to us.

Besides French there are the Aborigines or Native Indians of the Country, or as the French call them Les Savages, these may be about Two or three thousand in all, who are divided into several little Tribes, of which these four are the principal

1. St. Johns Indians
2. Mick Macks Indians
3. Cape Sable Indians and
4. Bay Verte or Cape Breton Indians

The Mick Macks Tribe are the most numerous Tribe and possess most of the clear Country from the River St. Croix by Minas, Pisquaid, & Copequaid to Chegnecto, which last is their principal Settlement.

The St. Johns are not the most numerous Tribe, but are deemed most civilized and brave of their Tribes, they inhabit along the River St. Johns from whence they are calld, and which lyes opposite to Annapolis in the back part of Canada.

The Cape Sable Indians are likewise nam'd so, from that point of the Country about which they reside and whose contiguity to Halifax may make them troublesome Neighbours. These are rather a Branch of the Mickmacks, than a separate Tribe.

The Bay Verte or Cape Breton Indians live mostly along the Coasts on these Parts, but are frequently through the Province after their Game and particularly come to trade at Chgenicto which is only eighteen miles from Bay Verte, or as We call it Green Bay.

These Indians are dispersed through the whole Province, and live chiefly on fishing in Summer, and hunting in Winter,—From this manner of Life, they are an active hardy People, capable of Fatigue, Hunger, and Cold and know perfectly the use of Arms. And tho' their Number nor their Valour may not make them a formidable Enemy, their little Wood Skirmishing, and bush fighting will always make them a very troublesome one.

They have no Skill nor Inclination to Husbandry nor Craft but truck for these with the French for Sables and Furrs, who likewise supply them with Rum, Brandy, Arms and Amunition. of all which they are very fond and much addicted to. They generally go naked, except a sort of Blanket girt about them, and paint most furiously in War.

These Indians mingle and even sometimes intermarry among the French, and then they become tolerably civilized. They are bred up the most simple bigoted Papists, and in all the Cruelty and Ignorance of the most implicit Believers. For this Purpose they have always their Missioners amongst them either sent by the Bishop of Canada or immediately from France; and these keep them in the true belief, that the Service of God and the Grand Monarque are one and the same thing.

The Chief amongst these Priests is Monsieur De Luther, with whom you will be tolerably well acquainted in the Course of this Journal.—He has (I am told) a very Good Pension from the Court of France and serves them very faithfully for it.

This Deluther is the Master of their Wills and Guide to their Consciences. He manages their Trade in Peace and their Arms in War, supplys their Wants and grants Indulgence to their Barbarities—It is He who Arms and sends them thro'. the Province fixing a Price for the murderd or taken. For this purpose regular Remittances are made him from Canada and Lewisburgh. He punctually pays them for every scalp they bring into Him. The scalp (you must know) is the Forepart of the Head raising the Skin from the Forehead to the Crown Hair and all wisely considering, they might kill more than they cou'd conveniently bring in, He prudently contrivd this safe and easy Method no ways liable to Fraud or mistake, as our Hair and Compenxions differ from Le Savage.—

This Holy Man, or as He styles himself Preter Missionaire lives in the midst of them at Chignecto, among the French Regular Troops that are there. His Influence & Authority are great amongst them as His Services are so considerable to the Court of France.

This was the State of the Country when Mr. Cornwallis came to this Province.

On His first Arrival and settling, the Indians came peacibly down, and lived near us. And it is certain, they suspected nothing more from us than the Establishing a Fishing Town and fortifying the little Island to secure it. Had they known our Intentions and declared War, they coud have raisd infinite Difficulties at our first landing and Hutting, besides retarding our Settlement in so advanced and rigorous a Season, they might probably have frighted away many of our New England Traders, who since delivering up of Lewisburgh were not in Humour to follow Fresh Conquests.

To Strengthen so necessary and Beneficial A Peace, the Governor sent a Deputation by Capt. Howe, with a Sloop of War and Presents for the Indians up the River St. Johns. And He concluded a very regular Peace with them. He likewise obliged the French Canada Troops that were there to strike their Flag and retire from it.—The Indians agreeing to return and Trade with us at Halifax and supply us with Fish, Deer, Game &c.

When the Indians were returned they found the Face of things much alterd. they now begin to Open their Eyes and saw clearly that something more than a fishing Town was intended along the Coast—Colonel Warburtons Regiment was arrived from Lewisburgh, and Ranging Companies completed. from New England, and the Town already formd with Regularity and Strength: they saw the French Peasants were cutting a Road thro.' the great Wood to the clear Country of Minas and Pisquaid by the Governours Order and Payment.

They likewise saw a Tolerable Fort erecting at the Head of the Bason of Chebucto for a Communication to this Road. besides they knew the Governour had orderd another to be begun at Minas, and had drawn a Detachment of His Regiment from Annapolis for that purpose, They now began to meet the ranging Companies reconoitring thro.' the Country. Add to all this that they heard the Governour had taken four armd Sloops into the Service of the Province to carry Provisions and stores to the several Forts up the Country. and which were indeed further designd, in case of War to cruize in the Bay of Fundy, and land and Cover any of our Rambling Parties.

All these Matters quickly gave the Alarum and dreadful Apprehensions for the Loss of their Country which soon hurried them into the Designs, they afterwards follwd—happy had it been for us—if they had taken these measures earlier, or they had put them into execution sooner, for then Hobsons Regiment might have been detained for the Service of the Province which was just arrived with Warburtons from Lewisburgh and then in the Harbour. How far His Excellency might have Authority to have done so, or have thought it necessary at a Time of Peace with both French and Indians, I will not take upon me to determine—but this We have been fully convinced of since—That Double that number of Troops, would not have been superfluous, for thoroughly reducing and securly Establishing the Province.—

The French were not Idle Spectators of our growing greatness, and plainly saw, We were resolvd to be Masters of all the Country that rightfully belong'd to us, The Governors of Cape Breton and Canada were very well apprized of the Consequences of such formidable Neighbours to Lewisburgh and Quebeck and indeed to the whole French Interest in General thro.' North America, they therefore thought it their Duty to prevent it at the Expence of a little Money and the Breach of a little Faith.

107

Accordingly under pretence that the Boundaries were not yet settled by the two Courts at Home, they send Orders to their Troops to remain at Chignecto, and Others to return to St. Johns, with Orders to keep possession of them in the Name of the King their Master and likewise they gave private Instructions to all our French Subjects at Annapolis Minas & Pisquaid immediately to quit the Country and retire to them many of whom had already done so, and others were preparing to follow them.—

Monsieur De Luther must likewise assist on his part. He calls together all His Indians, and lays before them our Preparations for War. and our Incursions thro.' their Country— And tells them We are come to destroy their Trade, their Religion and themselves, and that We are seizing all their fishing and Hunting Places for that purpose—Then to encourage them to break with us. He sets forth the mighty Protection the French will give them, and puts them in mind of what they have already done, and what they themselves may easily do, and declares that the French only waited for Letters from Europe to joyn immediately in the War. Most part of this was found in an intercepted Letter to the Governor of Canada by a little smuggling vessel that was seizd in the Bay of Fundy.

And now having sufficiently provided them with Arms and Ammunition and insured them the Rewards of Heaven in the next World and Money for Scalps in this, He sets forth with his Tribes—fair La Sainte Guerre.—

Now all at once the Indians disappear from about Halifax, and soon after they send us a formal Declaration of War, in French and Indian. a Copy of which you may have seen in the Papers. And very soon they began to let us feel the want of their assistance and the inconveniency of their War.

In a very short Time they fall upon the little Fishing Town of Dartmouth, killing and Scalping some of their People, soon after a considerable Party lay in Ambuscade in the Woods for a Company of Rangers, and attack them between Halifax and Pisquaid on the Banks of the River St. Croix, killd some and wounded the Captain with a few others. soon after they beset and in a manner besieged the little Fort of Minas for above three Weeks. At which Time they took an Officer and all his Party killing his Centrys who fired on them. Now there was no stiring from the Forts without a good Convoy and no working near Halifax without covering Parties. They almost shut up the Communication between Annapolis and the other parts of the Province. or renderd it very Dangerous and Uncertain by stopping the Courriers and even Provision became very Dear, as the Indians not only made War upon us but frighted the French Peasantry from bringing any of us.

These Tidings were very acceptable to the French Troops who took care to furnish them with Arms, and Amunition and pay them for the Scalps, Encouraging and Sheltering them on their return to St. Johns and Chegnecto which last Place they now held so indisputably their own that they took the Lieutenant of one of our Sloops of War Prisoner for coming a Shore there without their Leave or Consent.

NOTES

1. This was an expedition comprising, it was said, nearly half the French navy with 3,150 veteran soldiers, which sailed from Rochelle on June 20, 1747 under the command of the Duc d'Anville with the object of retaking Louisburg, capturing Annapolis, and harrying the towns and settlements of New England. Disaster attended the expedition throughout. A great storm off Sable Island destroyed several of the ships, and pestilence which broke out wrought havoc among the crews and troops. When the remainder of the fleet reached Halifax d'Anville died, and a few days later the

Vice-Admiral committed suicide. M. La Jonquière, afterwards governor of Canada, succeeded to the command, and he took the fleet to Annapolis. But ill-luck still pursued them. Off Cape Sable a storm dispersed the ships, and only two of them entered the Annapolis Basin. Here they found two British war vessels, and retired. The remnant returned to France, two-thirds of the troops having been lost.

2. Colonel Arthur Noble, who occupied Grand Pré with about 500 men from Massachusetts, was surprised on July 22, 1747, by a party of Canadians and Acadians, who had come over from Chignecto, and was completely defeated. Colonel Nobel and some 70 others were killed, and 38 wounded and 69 taken prisoners. These are the English figures; the French account nearly doubled the number of killed and wounded, and put the number of prisoners at 54. The English proposed terms of capitulation, which were accepted, and under the terms the troops to the number of about 350 retired to Annapolis.

Article 1: Montcalm and Wolfe

Francis Parkman

Louis Joseph Lo Loutre, vicar-general of Acadia and missionary to the Micmacs, was the most conspicuous person in the province, and more than any other man was answerable for the miseries that overwhelmed it. The sheep of which he was the shepherd dwelt, at a day's journey from Halifax, by the banks of the River Shubenacadie, in small cabins of logs, mixed with wigwams of birch-bark. They were not a docile flock; and to manage them needed address, energy, and money,—with all of which the missionary was provided. He fed their traditional dislike of the English, and fanned their fanaticism, born of the villanous counterfeit of Christianity which he and his predecessors had imposed on them. Thus he contrived to use them on the one hand to murder the English, and on the other to terrify the Acadians; yet not without cost to the French Government; for they had learned the value of money, and, except when their blood was up, were slow to take scalps without pay. Le Loutre was a man of boundless egotism, a violent spirit of domination, an intense hatred of the English, and a fanaticism that stopped at nothing. Towards the Acadians he was a despot; and this simple and superstitious people, extremely susceptible to the influence of their priests, trembled before him. He was scarcely less masterful in his dealings with the Acadian clergy; and, aided by his quality of the Bishop's vicar-general, he dragooned even the unwilling into aiding his schemes.

But the movement most alarming to the French was the English occupation of Beaubassin,—an act perfectly lawful in itself, since, without reasonable doubt, the place was within the limits of Acadia, and therefore on English ground.[1] Beaubassin was a considerable settlement on the isthmus that joins the Acadian peninsula to the mainland. Northwest of the settlement lay a wide marsh, through which ran a stream called the Missaguash, some two miles beyond which rose a hill called Beauséjour. On and near this hill were stationed the troops and Canadians sent under Boishébert and La Corne to watch the English frontier. This French force excited disaffection among the Acadians through all the neighboring districts, and

constantly helped them to emigrate. Cornwallis therefore resolved to send an English force to the spot; and accordingly, towards the end of April, 1750, Major Lawrence landed at Beaubassin with four hundred men. News of their approach had come before them, and Le Loutre was here with his Micmacs, mixed with some Acadians whom he had persuaded or bullied to join him. Resolved that the people of Beaubassin should not live under English influence, he now with his own hand set fire to the parish church, while his white and red adherents burned the houses of the inhabitants, and thus compelled them to cross to the French side of the river.[2] This was the first forcible removal of the Acadians. It was as premature as it was violent; since Lawrence, being threatened by La Corne, whose force was several times greater than his own, presently reimbarked. In the following September he returned with seventeen small vessels and about seven hundred men, and again attempted to land on the strand of Beaubassin. La Jonquière says that he could only be resisted indirectly, because he was on the English side of the river. This indirect resistance was undertaken by Le Loutre, who had thrown up a breastwork along the shore and manned it with his Indians and his painted and be-feathered Acadians. Nevertheless the English landed, and, with some loss, drove out the defenders. Le Loutre himself seems not to have been among them; but they kept up for a time a helter-skelter fight, encouraged by two other missionaries, Germain and Lalerne, who were near being caught by the English.[3] Lawrence quickly routed them, took possession of the cemetery, and prepared to fortify himself. The village of Beaubassin, consisting, it is said, of a hundred and forty houses, had been burned in the spring; but there were still in the neighborhood, on the English side, many hamlets and farms, with barns full of grain and hay. Le Loutre's Indians now threatened to plunder and kill the inhabitants if they did not take arms against the English. Few complied, and the greater part fled to the woods.[4] On this the Indians and their Acadian allies set the houses and barns on fire, and laid waste the whole district, leaving the inhabitants no choice but to seek food and shelter with the French.[5]

How the homeless Acadians from Beaubassin lived through the winter is not very clear. They probably found shelter at Chipody and its neighborhood, where there were thriving settlements of their countrymen. Le Loutre, fearing that they would

---

Source: Francis Parkman, *Montcalm and Wolfe*, (Boston, Little Brown, 1884), pp. 113–17, 120–22.

return to their lands and submit to the English, sent some of them to Isle St. Jean. "They refused to go," says a French writer; "but he compelled them at last, by threatening to make the Indians pillage them, carry off their wives and children, and even kill them before their eyes. Nevertheless he kept about him such as were most submissive to his will."[6] In the spring after the English occupied Beaubassin, La Jonquière issued a strange proclamation. It commanded all Acadians to take forthwith an oath of fidelity to the King of France, and to enroll themselves in the French militia, on pain of being treated as rebels.[7] Three years after, Lawrence, who then governed the province, proclaimed in his turn that all Acadians who had at any time sworn fidelity to the King of England, and who would be found in arms against him, would be treated as criminals.[8] Thus were these unfortunates ground between the upper and nether millstones. Le Loutre replied to this proclamation of Lawrence by a letter in which he outdid himself. He declared that any of the inhabitants who had crossed to the French side of the line, and who should presume to return to the English, would be treated as enemies by his Micmacs; and in the name of these, his Indian adherents, he demanded that the entire eastern half of the Acadian peninsula, including the ground on which Fort Lawrence stood, should be at once made over to their sole use and sovereign ownership,[9]—"which being read and considered," says the record of the Halifax Council, "the contents appeared too insolent and absurd to be answered."

The number of Acadians who had crossed the line and were collected about Beauséjour was now large. Their countrymen of Chipody began to find them a burden, and they lived chiefly on Government rations. Le Loutre had obtained fifty thousand livres from the Court in order to dike in, for their use, the fertile marshes of Memeramcook; but the relief was distant, and the misery pressing. They complained that they had been lured over the line by false assurances, and they applied secretly to the English authorities to learn if they would be allowed to return to their homes. The answer was that they might do so with full enjoyment of religion and property, if they would take a simple oath of fidelity and loyalty to the King of Great Britain, qualified by an oral intimation that they would not be required for the present to bear arms.[10] When Le Loutre heard this, he mounted the pulpit, broke into fierce invectives, threatened the terrified people with excommunication, and preached himself into a state of exhaustion.[11] The military commandant at Beauséjour used gentler means of prevention; and the Acadians, unused for generations to think or act for themselves, remained restless, but indecisive, waiting till fate should settle for them the question, under which king?

[...]

By the treaty of Utrecht, Acadian belonged to England; but what was Acadia? According to the English commissioners, it comprised not only the peninsula now called Nova Scotia, but all the immense tract of land between the River St. Lawrence on the north, the Gulf of the same name on the east, the Atlantic on the south, and New England on the west.[12] The French commissioners, on their part, maintained that the name Acadia belonged of right only to about a twentieth part of this territory, and that it did not even cover the whole of the Acadian peninsula, but only its southern coast, with an adjoining belt of barren wilderness. When the French owned Acadia, they gave it boundaries as comprehensive as those claimed for it by the English commissioners; now that it belonged to a rival, they cut it down to a paring of its former self. The denial that Acadia included the whole peninsula was dictated by the need of a winter communication between Quebec and Cape Breton, which was possible only with the eastern portions in French hands. So new was this denial that even La Galissonière himself, the foremost in making it, had declared without reservation two years before that Acadia was the entire peninsula.[13]

NOTES

1. La Jonquière himself admits that he thought so. "Cette partie le étant, à ce que je crois, dépendante de l'Acadie." La Jonquière ou Ministre, 3 Oct. 1750.
2. It has been erroneously stated that Beaubassin was burned by its own inhabitants. "Laloutre, ayant vu que les Acadiens ne paroissoient pas fort presses d'abandonner leurs biens, avoit lui-même mis le feu à l'Église, et l'avoit fait mettre aux maisons des habitants par quelques-une de ceux qu'il avoit gagnés," etc. Mémoires sur le Canada, 1749–1760. "Les sauvages y mirent le feu." Précis des Faits, 85. "Les savauges mirent le feu aux maisons." Prévost au Ministre, 22 Juillet, 1750.
3. La Vallière, Journal de ce qui s'est passé à Chenitou [Chignecto] et autres parties des Frontière de l'Acadie, 1750–1751. La Vallière was an officer on the spot.

111

4. Prévost au Ministre, 25 Sept. 1750.

5. "Les sauvages et Accadiens mirent le feu dans toutes les maisons et granges, pleines de bled et de fourrages, ce qui a cause une grande disetto." La Vallière, ut supra.

6. Mémoires sur le Canada, 1749–1760.

7. Ordonnance du 12 Avril, 1751.

8. Écrit donné aux Habitants réfugiés à Beausour 10 Août, 1754.

9. Copie de la Lettre de M. l'Abbé Le Loutre, Prétre Missionnaire des Sauvages de l'Accadie, à M. Lawrence à Halifax, 26 Août, 1754. There is a translation in Public Documents of Nova Scotia.

10. Public Documents of Nova Scotia, 205, 209.

11. Compare Mémoires, 1749–1760, and Public Documents of Nova Scotia, 229, 230.

12. The commission of De Monts, in 1603, defines Acadia as extending from the fortieth to the forty-sixth degrees of latitude, — that is, from central New Brunswick to southern Pennsylvania. Neither party cared to produce the document.

13. "L'Acadie suivant nes anciennues limites est la presquisle borne par son isthme." La Galissonnière au Ministre, 25 Juillet, 1749. The English commissioners were, of course, ignorant of this admission.

Article 2: An Unsettled Conquest

Geoffrey Plank

After 1745 political developments in Britain helped recast the terms of the debate surrounding the Acadians. In 1746, in the aftermath of an uprising in Scotland on behalf of the Stuart claimant to the throne, the British government debated a series of measures designed to pacify broad stretches of the Scottish Highlands and culturally assimilate the Highlanders. Ideas originally developed as a solution for perceived problems in Scotland were considered as policy options for the Acadians. Perhaps the most important idea that reached America in this way was a proposal to move suspect populations within the British Empire. Before the pacification of the Highlands, those who had proposed moving the Acadians imagined that they would be expelled altogether from the British colonies (as the New Englanders sent the French colonists from Ile Royale to France in 1745). But from 1746 forward, under the influence of proposals developed in the Scottish context, the debate shifted as policymakers considered forced migrations designed to incorporate the Acadians into the communal life of British North America.

In the years following the outbreak of the War of the Austrian Succession, events far from Nova Scotia had profound effects on the lives of the peoples of

Source: Geoffrey Plank, *An Unsettled Conquest: The British Campaign Against the Peoples of Acadia* (Philadelphia, University of Pennsylvania Press, 2001), pp. 108–115. Reprinted with permission of the University of Pennsylvania Press.

the province. This chapter highlights the influence of groups who came to the colony from elsewhere in the British and French Empires. It begins with the decision of the French colonial administrators on Ile Royale to attack the British fishery at Canso, and proceeds with an analysis of the military response of the New Englanders and the impact of the imperial war on the lives of the Mi'kmaq and the Acadians.

When the French colonial authorities began the large-scale settlement of Ile Royale in 1714, they had hoped that the island colony would attract most, if not all, of the Mi'kmaq and the Acadians. The French succeeded in convincing some Acadian families to move, though fewer than they expected. Similarly, Ile Royale attracted fewer Mi'kmaq than the French would have preferred, and many of those who went only visited. Nonetheless, even without a wholesale migration of Mi'kmaq and Acadians from Nova Scotia, the French colony on Ile Royale prospered. By the early 1740s, Louisbourg alone had nearly two thousand inhabitants; three-quarters were civilians, including the families of soldiers, fishermen, colonial officials, merchants, artisans, and laborers. The island as a whole had a population approaching five thousand.[1]

Though the French could not entice all the Mi'kmaq or Acadians to move to Ile Royale, various French missionaries and colonial officials remained interested in the affairs of the peoples of Nova Scotia. They continued to think of the Acadians as compatriots, and they thought of the Mi'kmaq as a client people, dependent on the French for pastoral care, trade, and a measure of political direction. As early as 1734, Joseph Saint-Ovide de Brouillan, the governor of Ile Royale, made tentative plans to retake Nova Scotia in the event of a war.[2] His advisors assured him that all of the Acadians and most of the Mi'kmaq would greet the French forces as liberators. Subsequent administrators continued to hold similar views.[3] The outbreak of the War of the Austrian Succession presented the colony's officials with an apparent opportunity to bring the Mi'kmaq and the Acadians back within the borders of the French Empire. Instead of asking them to move, the French would try to shift the boundary and drive Britain's colonial administration away.

The French attack on Canso was intended as a first step toward recapturing all of Nova Scotia. There were several reasons for striking the fishing settlement first. Driving the British from Canso foreclosed any possibility that the island could be used as a base for privateers. The French also hoped to cripple the British fishery in the North Atlantic and thereby acquire a larger share of the world market in fish. Canso seemed vulnerable, and since some of the British settlers there had well-furnished homes the possibility of plunder made it easier for the French to recruit volunteer troops in Louisbourg. Furthermore, many of the Mi'kmaq continued to resent the British presence on the Atlantic coast, and thus the attack on Canso helped secure a wartime Franco-Mi'kmaq alliance.[4]

The decision to start with an attack on the fishing settlement appears in retrospect to have been a strategic mistake, however, because it had the effect of bringing New Englanders into the conflict from the moment the fighting began.[5] Though they had lost Canso, New England's fishermen and privateers could reach the waters off Nova Scotia from other bases, and the Atlantic fishing banks soon became a battle zone, as New Englanders sought retaliation against the French, and the French responded in kind. In a matter of months hundreds of fishing vessels were taken or destroyed.[6] Within Massachusetts, fishermen supported Governor William Shirley's decision to reinforce the garrison of Annapolis Royal, and fishermen were among the earliest proponents of his project to seize Ile Royale.[7]

More than anyone else it was Shirley who defined and directed New England's response to the renewal of conflict in the maritime region. In many ways he personified an increasingly dominant, cosmopolitan outlook among active members of New England's political elite.[8] He was an English-born lawyer who had trained in London; he had lived in Massachusetts only since 1731, and remained equally at ease on both sides of the Atlantic Ocean. Shirley secured the Massachusetts governorship in 1741 with the help of his patron, Secretary of State Thomas Hollis-Pelham, the duke of Newcastle, and he entered office at a time when Massachusetts was badly divided. Economic disruptions associated with the war with Spain, political struggles over the emission of paper money, and religious upheavals associated with revivalism had combined to divide the colonial population into a complex set of mutually antagonistic groups.[9] Shirley never gained the support of all the colonists, but, as several historians have shown, his military ventures gave him the patronage power he needed to secure political support from the competing factions and govern Massachusetts effectively.[10] Self-interested merchants and office-seekers supported Shirley and his campaign against the French, as did a broad cross-section of the colonial public, including evangelical preachers, conservative Congregationalists and Anglicans, fishermen, and young men eager to advance their prospects through military service and the acquisition of land. The New England churches abandoned their earlier reticence and endorsed Shirley's actions.[11] It helped that the French and the Mi'kmaq appeared to be the aggressors.

The early reports of combat appearing in the Massachusetts newspapers emphasized the participation of Mi'kmaq warriors and presented them in the worst possible light. In June 1744 a correspondent to the *Boston Gazette* indicated that the Mi'kmaq who took part in the attack of Canso had pleaded with the French for permission to slaughter the English-speaking residents of the town and that the French had struggled to restrain them.[12] Similar stories were repeated often during the war and served to convince many New Englanders that the Mi'kmaq were innately irrational and violent.[13]

Such beliefs had long circulated in Massachusetts, and they inspired the New England colonists during the War of the Austrian Succession to adopt a stance toward the Mi'kmaq similar to the one they had adopted in their previous wars. But in 1744 and 1745 the colonists were mobilized for war in the maritime region on an unprecedented scale.

On October 20, 1744 the government of Massachusetts officially declared war on the Mi'kmaq.[14] Five days later the Massachusetts General Court

113

offered a bounty of £100 (provincial currency) for the scalp of any adult male member of the Mi'kmaq nation. For the scalps of women and children, the legislature offered £50.[15] Similar rewards were available for Mi'kmaq prisoners taken alive. Recognizing that it would be difficult to identify scalps by tribe, on November 2 Shirley announced that he would grant a reward for any "Indian" killed or captured east of the St. Croix River, regardless of his or her language group. By necessity he made an exception for native warriors serving under the Anglo-American military command.[16]

There is no record of Jean-Baptiste Cope's activities during the war, but the mission near his home on the Shubenacadie River became a center of Mi'kmaq resistance. The resident missionary at the Shubenacadie mission, Jean-Louis Le Loutre, served as the principal intermediary between the French forces and the Mi'kmaq on peninsular Nova Scotia. It was Le Loutre who informed the Mi'kmaq in the interior of Nova Scotia of the plan to strike at Canso, and, acting on the advice of the governor of Louisbourg, he also sent them directions to lay siege to Annapolis Royal in the weeks immediately after that attack. Le Loutre accompanied Mi'kmaq warriors to the British colonial capital and played an active role as an advisor to the Mi'kmaq in the first three years of the war.[17] Pierre Maillard, another missionary working among the Mi'kmaq, also traveled with the bands on the peninsula of Nova Scotia and at Ile Royale. He provided advice and delivered speeches aimed at strengthening the warriors' discipline and resolve.[18] After disease struck the Mi'kmaq in 1746, the missionaries told them that the British had deliberately infected them by distributing contaminated cloth.[19]

Le Loutre and Maillard may have argued more strenuously than necessary, because the scalp-bounty policy, by itself, was enough to foreclose easy reconciliation between the Mi'kmaq bands and the British. At least among those living within the traditional bands, almost all of the Mi'kmaq supported the war effort. They were fighting not just for land but for survival, and men, women, and children overcame severe hardships to keep the warriors afield. The choices facing the Mi'kmaq bands seemed simple; Mi'kmaq-speakers who lived away from their ancestral bands among the Acadians, and the descendents of such individuals, had more complicated decisions to make.

On January 4, 1745 a group of Acadian deputies from eastern Nova Scotia brought a petition to the provincial council. They had heard about the new scalp-bounty policy and feared for the safety of some of their neighbors. The Acadians, they said, had "a great number of mulattoes amongst them who had taken the oath and who were allied to the greatest families."[20] The delegates asked the council to rule whether people of mixed ancestry were liable to be scalped. The council deliberated on the matter and decided that persons with Mi'kmaq ancestry who lived in the Acadian villages would not be subject to the bounty policy. Paul Mascarene, the acting governor at the time, explained the decision.

> In regard to the notion the inhabitants had amongst them that all who had any Indian blood in them would be treated as enemies, it was a very great mistake, since if that had been the design of the New England armed vessels it might very well be supposed that the inhabitants of this river, many of whom have Indian blood in them, and some even who live within the reach of the cannon, would not be suffered to live peaceably as they do.[21]

The petitions from the Acadian deputies revealed the difficulty of applying a racially based policy in Nova Scotia. Ancestry did not always determine how a person lived, or what community he or she belonged to. Nor did biology necessarily dictate anyone's political stance. The council's statement to the Acadian deputies was intended to reassure them, though it did not contain any clear standards for determining a person's vulnerability under the scalp-bounty program. At best, the councilmen had suggested that ancestry by itself did not define the risk. Farmers, herders, merchants, and fishermen who spoke French, lived in Acadian villages, and conformed to European customs would be exempted from the bounty policy. But the ruling left an important question unanswered concerning how thorough a person's integration into the Acadian community would have to be to gain an exemption. The vagueness of the ruling promoted the government's interest in an important respect: the ambiguity of national categories made it imperative for many Acadians, particularly those with family ties to the Mi'kmaq,

114

to stay away from their Algonkian neighbors if they wanted to avoid reclassification. But the question raised by the deputies would not go away. Officials in Nova Scotia struggled to define the boundaries between the Mi'kmaq and the Acadian communities for the next eleven years.

After their seizure of Louisbourg, the New Englanders transported the French-speaking population of Ile Royale to France.[22] That decision inspired a brief debate within the provincial council of Nova Scotia over the possibility of similarly expelling the Acadians, though the option was ultimately rejected as impractical.[23] Proponents of deportation argued that the Acadians had not taken valid oaths of allegiance and that their refusal to contemplate military service undermined the credibility of their professed loyalty to Britain. The councilmen also cited the Acadians' recent behavior. Those who favored removing them argued that they had helped supply the French army and Mi'kmaq warriors and refused to sell provisions to the British except at exorbitant prices. The Acadians had seemed slow to inform the British about French and Mi'kmaq military preparations, and the councilmen assumed that they provided the French and the Mi'kmaq useful intelligence. Along with providing information and logistical support, the Acadians behaved in ways that boosted enemy morale. According to a report of the provincial council, when Mi'kmaq warriors and French soldiers first laid siege to Annapolis Royal, Acadian "men, women and children frequented the enemy's quarters at their mass, prayers, dancing and all other ordinary occasions."[24]

As the debate over expelling the Acadians made clear, the outbreak of armed hostilities increased the political ramifications of many aspects of the Acadians' lives. When Acadian merchants and farmers raised the price of food, the men in the garrison interpreted the action as a show of support for the king of France. When Acadian women danced with French soldiers, provincial councilmen took it as evidence of sedition. In part because their daily behavior came under scrutiny, many Acadians who had formerly worked closely with the provincial government fled Annapolis Royal when the fighting began.[25] Prudent Robichaud, for example, disappeared.[26]

Acadian men and women reacted to the pressures of living in wartime in various ways, and it is difficult to generalize about their behavior. A few young men left their homes and went to fight alongside Mi'kmaq warriors.[27] Others hired themselves out as civilian workers for the British army.[28] At least one merchant who had formerly traded with the British garrisons offered his services to the French military and spent the war ferrying men and equipment to French-controlled regions at the eastern end of the Bay of Fundy.[29] At the other extreme, Jacques Maurice Vigneau responded to the news of New England's capture of Louisbourg by volunteering his services to the council at Annapolis Royal. In 1746 he began carrying men, provisions, orders, and intelligence from the provincial capital across the isthmus of Chignecto and on by sea to British-controlled Louisbourg.[30]

If there was anything "typical" about the Acadians' pattern of behavior, it was that almost none of them could hold a consistent political stance. Vigneau, for example, had earlier played host to a commander of the French army. French soldiers had occupied his village, and he had little choice but to allow the officer to stay in his family's home. But according to French accounts Vigneau had been more than accommodating. He gave the commander information and advice, and made his ship available when the French decided to attack Annapolis Royal.[31] The British may not have known about Vigneau's earlier behavior when they gave him their business in 1746, but they would have had difficulty finding any merchant in Beaubassin who had refused to offer services to the French during the military occupation. Later in the war, when the French military returned, Vigneau and his family would again offer the commanding officer assistance.[32]

By 1746 the policy debates surrounding the Acadians had changed. Early in the conflict, Shirley and various members of Nova Scotia's provincial council had contemplated mass deportations or large-scale retributive raids, especially against the Acadian villagers at the eastern end of the Bay of Fundy, who seemed to have given the most assistance to the French and their native allies.[33] In 1745, writing to his commander on Ile Royale, Shirley had wistfully complained, "It grieves me much that I have it not in my power to send a part of 500 men forthwith to Menis [Menas] and burn Grand Pré, their chief town, and open all their sluices, and lay their country waste."[34] But by the winter of 1746 Shirley had shifted his efforts and began to seek ways to gain the Acadians' cooperation and ultimately win their hearts.

115

Several factors contributed to this change in thinking. In the previous summer a French fleet sent to recapture Louisbourg foundered on the Atlantic coast of Nova Scotia, and from that time forward the British military position seemed more secure, particularly at Annapolis Royal. Disease had swept through the Mi'kmaq community, killing hundreds and weakening the military power of the survivors.[35] Equally important, the New Englanders within the garrison at Annapolis Royal gradually changed their outlook toward the Acadians. Given more time to interact with the villagers outside the context of an immediate military crisis, they began to believe that they could gain the Acadians' friendship. The soldiers depended on Acadian farmers and merchants for food and firewood, and the social environment encouraged the men to seek the company of Acadians outside the context of trade.

In the first year of the war relations between the garrison and the community had deteriorated. Most of the Acadians in Annapolis Royal had shunned the English-speakers in their village when French or Mi'kmaq forces were in the area. In any event there were fewer English-speakers in the French-speaking village; most of the married officers and soldiers at Annapolis Royal had sent their wives and children to Boston for protection, and the departure of their families helped cut the men off from the Acadian community, at least temporarily.[36] Over time new bonds were formed, however, and by the last two years of the war, official British discussions of the Acadians returned repeatedly to the issue of intermarriage between the soldiers and Acadian women.[37]

Overcoming significant cultural obstacles, by 1747 a few New England soldiers managed to court and marry Acadian women in Annapolis Royal.[38] According to reports that reached Shirley, the women who married the New England men were punished with excommunication from the Catholic Church. Shirley complained bitterly about the church's reaction. Though he hoped that the women would leave the church eventually, he knew that church-imposed sanctions would humiliate them and isolate them from their neighbors; excommunication was a strong deterrent to intermarriage. Shirley objected not only for the sake of the soldiers and their spouses, but also because he believed that the church's policy deterred British settlement in Nova Scotia. Almost certainly exaggerating the influence of the policy, he claimed that it "has had so general an effect as to prevent the settlement of any one English family within the province."[39]

When Shirley referred to "English" families, he meant families in which the husband spoke English. This is evident, not only in the context of his concern over the marital fortunes of the soldiers, but also in light of long-term proposals he was developing to promote marriages between Acadian women and English-speaking settlers in Nova Scotia. Intermarriage became a central feature of Shirley's project to transform the Acadians culturally. He wanted to convert them to Protestantism, teach them English, and make them loyal British subjects. As part of that program, he wanted to change the composition of the Acadians' families by encouraging soldiers to settle permanently in Nova Scotia and providing Acadian women with incentives to marry English-speakers and Protestants. He also wanted to force the Acadian women to send their children to English-language schools so that their descendants would become, as he succinctly put it, "English Protestants."[40]

Shirley advanced this plan in response to the experiences of the soldiers at Annapolis Royal. Though only a few marriages had taken place between the men of the garrison and Acadian women, he saw those unions as a model for social development in the entire colony. In 1747 Shirley began designing a project to intermingle soldiers and Acadians throughout the eastern Bay of Fundy region, to facilitate integration and gradual assimilation. Annapolis Royal gave him inspiration, but he was also responding to contemporary events in Britain, where the ministry was engaged in a similarly forceful effort at cultural assimilation.

NOTES

1. Moore, "The Other Louisbourg"; McNeill, *Atlantic Empires of France and Spain,* 20–24.
2. McNeill, *Atlantic Empires of France and Spain,* 84.
3. See Rawlyk, *Yankees at Louisbourg,* 6.
4. Ibid., 2–4.
5. For accounts of the attack, see Flemming, *The Canso Islands,* 45; William Shirley to Newcastle, July 7, 1744, in Lincoln, ed., *Correspondence of William Shirley,* 1: 133; McLennan, *Louisbourg,* 111; Mascarene to Philipps, June 9, 1744, Add. Mss. 19,071, doc. 45; *Boston Postboy,* June 11, 1744.

6. For accounts of New England vessels taken, see *Boston Evening Post,* June 11, June 25, 1744; *Boston Newsletter,* September 20, 1744; *South Carolina Gazette,* July 4, 1744. For New England's attacks on the French fishery, see *Boston Evening Post,* September 24, October 22, November 26, 1744; *Boston Gazette,* August 21, 1744; *Boston Newsletter,* August 16, September 20, September 27, October 25, 1744; *Boston Postboy,* September 24, October 22, 1744; *New York Gazette,* October 1, 1744; Douglass, *Summary,* 1:339.

7. See Hamilton, "The Itinerarium," 261. See also Rawlyk, *Yankees at Louisbourg,* 37, 38; Schutz, *William Shirley,* 90. It was a fisherman who first alerted Boston of the attack on Canso, but the printer of the *Boston Evening Post* chose not to publish the story because it was "looked upon as fishermen's news." Only after a merchant confirmed the report was it placed in the paper. *Boston Evening Post,* May 28, 1744. For the reaction of the legislature, see *Journals of the House of Representatives of Massachusetts* 21: 8–11, 29, 42; *Boston Postboy,* June 4, 1744; *Boston Newsletter,* June 14, 1744.

8. See Schutz, *William Shirley.*

9. Ibid., 23–44; Remer, "Old Lights and New Money."

10. See, for example, Schutz, *William Shirley,* 80–103; Bailyn, *Origins of American Politics,* 116–17; but see Pencak, *War, Politics, and Revolution,* 115–47.

11. Hatch, "Origins of Civil Millennialism in America."

12. *Boston Gazette,* June 26, 1744.

13. See, for example, *Boston Newsletter,* June 6, 1745; *Boston Evening Post,* July 29, 1745.

14. *Boston Evening Post,* October 22, 1744.

15. *Journals of the House of Representatives of Massachusetts* 21: 99, 106–7; *Boston Evening Post,* November 5, 1744.

16. *Boston Evening Post,* November 11, 1744; using a contemporary term, Shirley called the St. Croix the Passamaquodi River.

17. Rogers, "Abbé Le Loutre"; Jean-Louis Le Loutre, "Autobiography," translated by John Clarence Webster, in Webster, ed., *Career of the Abbé Le Loutre,* 33–50, 35; See also Rawlyk, *Yankees at Louisbourg,* 7–11.

18. Pierre Maillard, "Lettre," in Casgrain, *Les Soirées canadiennes,* 289–426, 322–28; Webster, *Career of the Abbé Le Loutre,* 10.

19. "Motifs des sauvages mickmaques et marichites des continuer la guerre contre les Anglois depuis la dernière paix," in De Beaumont, *Les Derniers jours,* 248–53, 251.

20. This is the only use of the word "mulatto" I have seen in connection with Nova Scotia in the first half of the eighteenth century.

21. Council minutes, January 4, 1745, in Fergusson, *Minutes,* 55–56.

22. Steele, "Surrendering Rites," 152–53; *Boston Evening Post,* July 15, July 22, August 5, September 2, October 21, 1745; *Boston Postboy,* July 22, September 9, September 30, 1745; *Boston Newsletter,* September 12, 1745.

23. Mascarene to Shirley, December 7, 1745, CO 217/39, doc. 316, PRO; Shirley to Newcastle, December 23, 1745, RG1, vol. 13, doc. 21, PANS; Shirley to Newcastle, February 11, 1746, RG1, vol. 13A, doc. 5, PANS; see Moody, "A Just and Disinterested Man," 334–42.

24. "State of the Province of Nova Scotia," November 8, 1745, CO 217/39, doc. 320, PRO.

25. For accounts of the general wartime migration to French-controlled territory, see Clark, *Acadia,* 278, 285, 291; Roy, "Settlement and Population Growth," 151–52; Jean Daigle, "Acadia from 1604 to 1763," 36.

26. There is no record of Robichaud's whereabouts after 1744, but several members of his family moved to the isthmus of Chignecto and present-day New Brunswick, regions that were controlled by the French during the war. Raymond, *River St. John,* 86, 94, 117; Mascarene to Frances Belleisle Robishau, October 13, 1744, in Akins, *Selections,* 136; Robichaud, *Les Robichaud,* 153–54. According to Donat Robichaud, who recorded the Robichaud family's history in the 1960s, the elder Prudent was still alive in 1756 and boarded the ship *Pembroke* for transportation south. The *Pembroke* left Annapolis Royal in late January or early February 1756, bound for North Carolina, but the 226 Acadian prisoners onboard took control of the ship, ran it aground in the mouth of the St. John River, and burned it. The Acadians were greeted on the banks of the river by Mi'kmaq or Wuastukwiuk warriors, who guided them to Québec. Prudent Robichaud, according to the family history, died on the trail and never reached New France. The newspaper accounts of this incident indicate that the *Pembroke* embarked from Chignecto, but Lawrence's letter states that it left Annapolis Royal, and

117

he probably had better intelligence than the newspaper writers did. None of the documents cited above, other than the Robichaud family history, mention Prudent Robichaud by name. See Abstract of Dispatches from Canada, in O'Callaghan, *Documents,* 10: 427; Claude Godfrey Coquard to his brother, 1757, in O'Callaghan, *Documents,* 10: 528; Charles Lawrence to Shirley, February 18, 1756, in Akins, *Selections,* 297; *Boston Evening Post,* March 15, 1756; *Pennsylvania Gazette,* March 18, 1756; Knox, *Journal,* 1: 115.

27. Report of Jean Luc de La Corne, September 28, 1747, RG1, vol. 3, doc 89, PANS; Statement of Honore Gautrol, December 13, 1749, in Akins, *Selections,* 177; *Boston Evening Post,* January 15, 1750; Salusbury, *Expeditions of Honour,* 76; Edward Cornwallis to Board of Trade, March 19, 1750, CO 217/9, doc. 188, PRO.

28. Mascarene to Philipps, June 9, 1744, Add. Mss. 19,071, doc. 45; Mascarene to Secretary of State, June 15, 1748, CO 217/40, doc. 22, PRO; Mascarene to Gorham, August 6, 1748, Add. Mss. 19,071, doc. 119; Mascarene to ?, September 29, 1749, Add. Mss. 19,071, doc. 99.

29. Mascarene to Shirley, spring 1745, in Gaudet, "Acadian Genealogy and Notes," 38; Council minutes, May 2–4, 1745, in Fergusson, *Minutes,* 68–70; Council minutes, November 14, 1746, in Fergusson, *Minutes,* 94; Shirley to Newcastle, May 22, 1746, in Lincoln, *Correspondence of William Shirley,* 1: 150; see also O'Callaghan, *Documents,* 10: 155; "Relation d'une expédition faite sur les anglois dans le pays de l'Acadie, le 11 fevrier 1747, par un détachement de canadiens," in Casgrain, *Collection,* 2: 10-16, 15; "Journal de la compagne du détachement de Canada à l'Acadie et aux mines, en 1746–47" in Casgrain, *Collection,* 2: 16–75, 47, 51–52. For evidence of the merchant's earlier cooperation with the government, see Mascarene to William Douglass, July 1740 and August 20, 1741, Mascarene Family Papers; Casgrain, *Pèlegrinage,* 519; Council minutes, August 17, 1736, in MacMechan, *Minutes,* 361–62.

30. Proclamation of the provincial council of Nova Scotia, May 19, 1746, RG1, vol. 21, doc. 81, PANS.

31. Pothier, *Course à L'Accadie,* 70–71, 73, 87–88, 139; Instructions for François Dupont Duvivier, MFM 12082, French Records, Acadia 1711–88, reel 8, 100, PANS; "Ordre et instruction de Duquesnel pour Duvivier, 1744," in Pothier, *Course à L'Accadie,* 159.

32. "Journal de la campagne," 1746–47, in Casgrain, *Collection,* 2: 16–75, 28.

33. See Mascarene to Deputies of Mines, Pisiquid and River Canard, October 13, 1744, in Akins, *Selections,* 137; Shirley to Board of Trade, October 16, 1744, in Lincoln, *Correspondence of William Shirley,* 1:150; Shirley to Newcastle, October 16, 1744, RG1, vol. 12, doc 37, PANS.

34. Shirley to Pepperell, May 25, 1745, in *Collections of the Massachusetts Historical Society* 6th ser. 10 (1899): 219.

35. "Journal de la campagne," 1746–47, in Casgrain, *Collection,* 2: 16–75, 44, 48; *Boston Evening Post,* December 1, 1746; see also *Boston Evening Post,* November 3, November 17, 1746; Wicken, "Encounters," 184–205. For a vivid description of the epidemic, see "Journal," July 25, 1748–September 14, 1748, AC, F3, vol. 50, doc. 447, NAC.

36. *Boston Evening Post,* May 28, 1744.

37. See, for example, Shirley to Newcastle, October 20, 1747, RG1, vol. 13A, doc. 32, PANS; Shirley to Newcastle, November 21, 1746, RG1, vol. 13, doc. 33, PANS; Charles Knowles and Shirley to Newcastle, April 28, 1747, RG1, vol. 13A, doc. 25, PANS; Shirley to Newcastle, July 8, 1747, RG1, vol. 13A, doc. 27, PANS.

38. See "Journal de la campagne," 1746–47, in Casgrain, *Collection,* 2: 16–75, 48.

39. Shirley to Newcastle, October 20, 1747, RG1, vol. 13A, doc. 32, PANS.

40. Shirley to Newcastle, November 21, 1746, RG1, vol. 13, doc. 33, PANS; Knowles and Shirley to Newcastle, April 28, 1747, RG1, vol. 13A, doc. 25, PANS; Shirley to Newcastle, July 8, 1747, RG1, vol. 13A, doc. 27, PANS.

■ Article 3: A Great and Noble Scheme

John Mack Farragher

[British Governor] Mascarene assumed office with a clear view of the task before him, one based on three decades of experience in l'Acadie. British interests in the region, he argued, were best advanced by encouraging the Acadians to be good subjects and emphasizing to them the advantages of British rule. In the short run, that offered the best prospect of dissuading them from supporting the French, and over time they might even become loyal British subjects. Mascarene had not always taken this position. Twenty years before, he had argued for the removal of the Acadians and the recruitment of Protestant settlers. He had been a skeptic about their pledge of neutrality when they took the oath of allegiance in 1730, and had proposed his own scheme of settling Huguenots at Chignecto. But over the subsequent decade he had gradually become convinced that the vast majority wished "to live at peace and in submission to the King." Eventually he came around to the position advocated by his predecessors Thomas Caulfeild and Lawrence Armstrong, which Mascarene summarized as making the inhabitants "sensible of the advantage and ease they enjoy under the British Government, Whereby to wean them from their old masters," although he recognized that "to do this effectually, a considerable time will be required." This policy would require the active participation of Acadians in civil society, and Mascarene committed himself to recruiting responsible deputies and utilizing them to the limits of their capacity. "Must try to get the inhabitants to choose for Deputies men of good sense," he reminded himself soon after his selection as council president. "Upright men of property, having the good of the community at heart, and sensible to the duty to which they are bound by their oath of allegiance."[1]

The armed conflict Mascarene feared began in 1744. For three years France had been allied with Spain and Prussia in an invasion of Austria's central European dominions. Great Britain supported Austria

Source: John Mack Farragher, *A Great and Noble Scheme: The Tragic Story of the Expulsion of the Acadians from their American Homeland* (New York, Norton, 2005), pp. 211–23. Copyright © 2005 by John Mack Faragher. Used by permission of W. W. Norton & Company, Inc.

and was at war with Spain. Neither Britain nor France wanted war, but it became impossible to avoid. Pressed by Spain, France declared war on Great Britain on 15 March 1744, and Britain responded with its own declaration three weeks later. During what Europeans knew as the War of the Austrian Succession (which British North Americans called King George's War) the maritime region would be the most important colonial theater. The news of war arrived at Louisbourg on 3 May, and French governor Jean-Baptiste-Louis Le Prévost Duquesnel—who had replaced Saint-Ovide—immediately ordered Captain François Dupont Duvivier, adjutant of the garrison, to organize an assault on the British outpost at Canso. Duvivier saw the war as the opportunity to win back the province lost thirty years before. With 350 *troupes de la marine* he sailed into Canso harbor with a small fleet of vessels on 13 May and announced his presence by hurling a salvo toward the British blockhouse. The small garrison surrendered without resistance, and after burning the buildings at the site, Duvivier carried the British soldiers back to Louisbourg in good cheer. More ominous was the attack by Mi'kmaq on a New England fishing vessel anchored in the harbor. Fired up by the recent kidnapping of one of their chiefs and his family by a privateer sailing out of Massachusetts, native fighters overwhelmed the vessel and killed nearly the entire crew.[2]

Mascarene learned of the attacks within days. He knew an assault on Fort Anne soon would follow and he considered his prospects "dismal." The 50th Regiment was seriously understrength. "I had but one hundred [men]," he later wrote, "twenty or thirty whereof were utter Invalides, [and] of ten or a dozen of Officers not above two or three who had ever seen a gunn fir'd in anger, and who for the most part were tainted by Republican principles"—that is to say, they were New Englanders, accustomed to electing their own officers. The fort itself was in terrible condition. Built by the French more than thirty years before, it had not been substantially improved by the British and was "mouldering away," as Mascarene put it. There were no bomb-proof casements or shelters for protection during a siege, and according to an official report prepared for the British Board of Ordnance, the palisade was "of no use in the world but to keep the cattle out of the ditch." By contrast, Louisbourg was one of the most heavily fortified places in all North America, and its garrison numbered some eighteen

119

hundred men and officers. Moreover, a French census of 1739 counted six hundred Mi̇kmaw fighters available for service. Mascarene had regularly appealed to London for additional men and the resources to reinforce Fort Anne, but there had been no reply to his request. "Without some assistance of a Sea force, an augmentation of the Garrison, or a good healthy and lively recruit, it cannot be expected that the place when attacked can hold out long," he wrote.[3]

[Massachusetts Governor William] Shirley responded eagerly to Mascarene's call for help in late May 1744. In contrast to the Board of Trade, he believed the maritime region was the key to success in the struggle with France for supremacy in North America. The loss of l'Acadie, he feared, would directly threaten the security of Massachusetts and New England. He instructed John Henry Bastide, the colony's chief military engineer, to organize a force of several dozen workers and proceed immediately to Annapolis Royal to assist in the repair and refortification of Fort Anne.

As Bastide and his work crews set to strengthening the decrepit fortifications, Mascarene received a visit from the Annapolis deputies. They pledged their loyalty and offered assistance, but also reiterated their position of strict neutrality—they would bear arms for neither side. "It is certain we can never force them to take up arms against the French," Mascarene reported to the Board of Trade after the meeting, "but if I can succeed in what I have labour'd for these four years past, that is to wean them so far from the French as to prevent their joining with or assisting them and hinder by their means the Indians about us giving us any disturbance here, it will make it more difficult for the French of Cape Breton to attack us." All through the month of June and into the second week of July the Acadians of the *banlieu* brought timbers, hauled stone, and labored on the fortifications alongside the workmen from Massachusetts.[4]

On 11 July the deputies reported to Mascarene that three hundred Mékmaq and Maliseets were on their way from Minas and would soon attack. The inhabitants working on the fort immediately left, and all the Acadians of the *banlieu* swiftly barricaded themselves in their homes. Although the assault force included no French or Canadien troops, it had been assembled on the orders of Governor Duquesnel of Ile Royale by Pierre Maillard, the missionary who for the previous decade had lived and worked among the Mi̇kmaq, learning their language and gaining considerable influence in their councils. The assault came the following morning. The attackers killed two soldiers tending their gardens outside the fort, and hiding themselves behind fences and barns, took potshots at the defenders whenever they took the chance of looking over the ramparts. But aside from torching the abandoned English *faubourg* and indiscriminately slaughtering the livestock of the inhabitants, the Mi̇kmaq were unable to do any serious damage. The affair came to an end with the arrival on 15 July of vessels from Boston with Shirley's two companies. The next morning, the Mi̇kmaq and Maliseets were gone.[5]

Within hours the Acadians returned to the fort with fresh provisions and supplies. Mascarene was pleased. They had kept faithful to their promise of neutrality, he reported, "and no ways join'd with the Enemy, who has kill'd most of their cattle." Native fighters had targeted the farms of Acadians known as friends of the British. A few days later two deputies arrived from Minas with a letter signed by the leading inhabitants there, pledging to do their best to prevent livestock from being driven to Louisbourg to supply the French garrison. Mascarene was appreciative, and he wrote sympathetically to Shirley of the Acadians' plight: "The French inhabitants are certainly in a very perilous Situation, those who pretend to be their Friends and old Masters having let loose a parcel of Banditti to plunder them, whilst on the other hand they see themselves threatened with ruin and destruction if they fail in their allegiance to the British government."[6]

The native army retreated to Minas, where in late August 1744 it was joined by Captain Duvivier with a company of fifty French troops from Louisbourg. The great-grandson of Charles de La Tour and an Acadian by birth, François Dupont Duvivier had great expectations of support from his countrymen. Since the British conquest in 1710, he wrote in a *mémoire*, the inhabitants had "preserved the hope of returning to their allegiance to the king." So strong was their zeal that "with one hundred men only from the garrison of Louisbourg, and a certain quantity of arms and ammunition to distribute to the inhabitants, the Sieru Duvivier puts his head on the line [*s'engagerait sur sa tête*] to make the conquest of this part of North America." This was the plan Governor

Duquesnel approved. Duvivier was to foment an uprising among the Acadians, and with a combined force of inhabitants and natives was to march on Annapolis Royal, where he would be met by two French warships carrying siege guns and additional troops. The fort would be taken, the British expelled, and l'Acadie returned to France.[7]

Duvivier was to be bitterly disappointed. Although a number of Acadians assisted the French— the merchant Joseph-Nicholas Gautier, related to Duvivier by marriage, offered Bélair, his *haute rivière* estate, as French headquarters, and transported Duvivier's men and equipment in his schooners— the overwhelming majority did not. The Acadians of Minas and the *haute rivière* did not greet him as a liberator. Duvivier, who had planned to live off the country, was forced to requisition the supplies he needed. The inhabitants resisted by hiding their stores, and in frustration Duvivier issued draconian commands, ordering them to furnish horses, cattle, grain, tools, and boats under penalty of severe punishment. He required the deputies to swear loyalty to the French king, threatening that those who refused would be "left to the discretion of *les sauvages* to be punished by death." The Acadians obeyed reluctantly and bitterly, and not one of them agreed to shoulder arms. On the morning of 8 September, when Duvivier arrayed his forces before Fort Anne, there were no Acadians among them.[8]

The French vessels with the siege guns had not yet arrived, so Duvivier could do little more than the natives had done several weeks earlier, pinning down the British with small-arms fire. The stand-off continued until 26 September, when the sails of two vessels were sighted entering the basin. To Duvivier's disappointment and Mascarene's great relief they proved to be an armed brigantine and a sloop from Boston, carrying a company of seventy Abenakis of the Pigwacket band, who had hired on as mercenaries to fight under the command of Captain John Gorham of Maine. A few days later Gorham led his native rangers in a surprise attack on the Míkmaw encampment, killing women and children and mutilating their bodies. Demoralized by this assault, the Míkmaq retreated, and the following day, 5 October, Duvivier withdrew as well. The French vessels finally arrived three weeks later, but beat a quick retreat when their commander learned Duvivier had already gone.[9]

The French, Míkmaq, and Maliseets arrived at Minas totally bereft of provisions, and Duvivier sent them out to forage what they could from the inhabitants. The Acadians were outraged and the Minas deputies, "in the name of their communities," pleaded with him to desist. "We hope," they petitioned, "that you will not plunge both ourselves and our families into a state of total loss, and that this consideration will cause you to withdraw your *sauvages* and troops from our districts. We live under a mild and tranquil government, and we have good reason to be faithful to it. We hope, therefore, that you will have the goodness not to separate us from it; and that you will grant us the favour not to plunge us into utter misery." This remarkable statement amounted to an all but explicit ratification of Mascarene's policy. Three days later Duvivier pulled out of Minas and returned to Louisbourg.[10]

When some time afterward Captain Duvivier was charged with leading an incompetent campaign, he defended himself by producing a copy of that petition, lamenting that the Acadians had "observed the neutrality they had promised." He blamed the priests. Abbé Desenclaves at Annapolis Royal had "fully informed the English governor of all he could learn of the French plans and exhorted his parishioners to remain faithful to the King of England," Duvivier testified, and Chauvreulx at Pisiquid had "pronounced excommunications against those of his parishioners who took arms in favor of the French." Lieutenant-Governor Mascarene reported much the same thing. The conduct of the parish priests, he wrote Shirley, had been "farr better than could have been expected." Indeed, the Catholic clergy in l'Acadie maintained this position throughout the war, despite considerable pressure from Québec. Mascarene's policy of *rapprochement* had paid off.[11]

Soon after Duvivier's departure the Acadians deputies detailed for Mascarene the oppression they had suffered under French occupation. According to Louis Robichaud, the son of Prudent Robichaud and an Annapolis deputy, he and his family "ran the risk of our lives" by providing intelligence of French movements to the British. Native fighters had plundered their household goods and livestock and he had suffered a bad beating because of his loyalties. "They assur'd me," Mascarene reported to Shirley, "that notwithstanding the entreaties and threats of M.

Duvivier, none of the inhabitants could be persuaded to take up Arms and Joyn the Enemy." But Shirley received a contradictory report from John Henry Bastide, his military engineer, who wrote from Annapolis Royal criticizing the wavering loyalty of the inhabitants, arguing that only the vigorous use of military power would keep them in "proper awe and attachment to the Garrison," and suggesting that Shirley order the Massachusetts troops to seize Acadian hostages in order "to deter the inhabitants from taking arms."[12]

Shirley considered this an excellent idea. In the last days of October he ordered Captain Edward Tyng, of the Massachusetts militia, to fit out several vessels for an assault on the Acadians of the upper bay. The purpose of the expedition, Shirley informed the Board of Trade, was "to take satisfaction of such of the French Inhabitants as have already revolted from their allegiance and join'd the French Enemy, by destroying and burning their Settlements and taking them prisoners, and to take hostages from among them, who have not yet revolted to be deliver'd to the Garrison as pledges for the fidelity of the Country." Shirley simultaneously declared war on the Abenakis, Maliseets, and Míkmaq, setting a bounty of £100 on the scalps of males, £50 for those of women and children. Because Acadians and Míkmaq were interrelated, it amounted to placing a price on the heads of inhabitants as well.[13]

Concerned that four years of patient work was about to be wrecked, Lieutenant-Governor Mascarene sent a friendly but forceful warning to the Acadian deputies. While he was much pleased that most of them had remained true to the allegiance they owed the king, he knew there were men among them who had supported the French, and unless those rebels surrendered themselves immediately, he feared the whole community would suffer the consequences of an attack by the forces of Massachusetts. "Those who have done their duty, and for whom we have great consideration," he wrote, "must unavoidably share in the trouble that military people bring with them, and which I should like to prevent as much as possible." The Acadians were granted a temporary respite by fortuitous storms in the Bay of Fundy that prevented Captain Tyng from sailing north. In late December, however, after reporting to the council that a great body of native fighters had assembled at Minas and Chignecto, "supported by the assistance

of the French inhabitants," Captain Gorham began planning another assault by his much-feared Abenaki rangers.[14]

In January 1745 the deputies of Minas wrote to Mascarene, pledging their loyalty and promising to deliver to Annapolis Royal the inhabitants who had supported the French. In turn they appealed for Mascarene's protection from the New Englanders, who were planning "to destroy all the inhabitants that had any Indian blood in them and scalp them." Since they counted "a great number of mulattoes amongst them who had taken the Oath and who were allied to the greatest families, it had Caused a terrible Alarm which made many put themselves on their Guard being very much frighten'd." Mascarene could only offer his assurance that the bounty had not been intended to include Acadians of mixed ancestry. If that had been the policy, he wrote, "the inhabitants of this river, many of whom have Indian blood in them, and some even who live within reach of the cannon, would not be suffered to live peaceably as they do." As it happened, bad weather once again postponed the planned expedition. But Mascarene's words were cold comfort. For the duration of the war the Acadians remained under constant threat from bounty hunters.[15]

Shortly thereafter the deputies of Minas and Chegnecto delivered to Annapolis Royal a number of inhabitants suspected of supporting the French, and they were subjected to questioning by the council. Typical was the interrogation of Louis-Amand Bugeaud, a merchant trader of Grand Pré. Bugeaud was evasive in his answers, at first claiming the French had confiscated his vessel, then admitting he had transported arms from Beaubassin to Minas, although contending he had been forced do so at gunpoint. At first he denied, then acknowledged, an eyewitness report—which could only have come from another Acadian—that he had been "dancing and making merry in Company with the Enemy." On one point, however, he was clear and insistent: "I did not bear weapons against this Government." Witnesses provided corroboration of his denial, testifying that they had seen a French officer command Gugeaud to arm himself, and heard Bugeaud respond that he would not touch any weapons— *"ne toucherait aucun armes."* It was a consistent feature of the testimony of all the Acadians the council questioned. While they may have consorted with the enemy and provided them with succor, they had done all they could to avoid violating the pledge not to bear arms. In fact, with the exception of Joseph-Nicholas Gautier, a collaborator whom Mascarene ordered arrested, the council uncovered no evidence that any Acadian had willingly violated the neutrality agreement. "The French inhabitants have in general behav'd well," Mascarene wrote Shirley after completing the investigation, "tho' it can not be surprising the Enemy has creatures amongst them."[16]

NOTES

1. Mascarene to Board of Trade, n.d. [c. April 1740], Brymner: 93; Mascarene to Newcastle, 1 Dec 1743, Akins: 129; Mascarene, certificate issued to certain Acadians, 1 July 1741, and Mascarene, notes, 27 May 1740, MacMechan (1900): 241, 243–44.

2. Murdoch 2:27; Maillard: 62–70.

3. Mascarene to King Gould, 9 June 1744, Mascarene to William Shirley, April 1748, and James Wilbault, "Defenses of Annapolis," n.d. [c. 1740], Moody: 195, 204; Mascarene to Colonel Ladeuze, n.d. [11 November 1752], Casgrain (1888–90) 2:82.

4. Mascarene to King Gould, 2 June 1744 [13 June 1744 ns], Moody: 301; Mascarene to Board of trade, 9 June 1744 [20 June 1744 ns], Casgrain (1888–90) 2:80.

5. Mascarene to Board of Trade, 20 September 1744, and Mascarene to Shirley, n.d. [c. December 1744], Akins: 131–32, 141–49. Most accounts of this attack claim it was led by the missionary Louise-Joseph Le Loutre. But according to his own statement, in which he made no disavowal of his other military activities, Le Loutre claimed he first became involved in the fighting in 1745; see Webster (1933): 10, 35

6. Mascarene to Shirley, 28 July 1744, Richard 1:207–08.

7. Casgrain (1888) 520; François Dupont Duvivier, *mémoire,* 1735, Murdoch 1:508–11.

8. Duvivier, orders to the Acadians of Minsa, Pisiquid, Canard, and Cobequid, 27 August 1744, Akins: 134–36; Duvivier, order to René Leblanc, 22 September 1744, Fergusson: 63. In general, see Fergusson: 62–67 *passim.*

9. Maillard: 62–70; Rawlyk: 122–24.

10. Casgrain (1897): 376–77; Acadians of Grand Pré, Canard, Pisquid, and Cobequid to Michael de Gannes de Falaise, 10 October 1744, and de Gannes to Bourg, 13 October 1744, Akins: 134–36.

11. Duvivier quoted in Casgrain (1897):375; Duvivier to Maurepas, n.d., Griffiths (1969):58–60; Mascarene to Shirley, n.d. [c. December 1744], and Mascarene to Shirley, 6 April 1748, Akins:141–49, 159–60.

12. Louis Robichaud to Shirley, 10 September 1756, Gaudet Appendix I, 197–98; Mascarene to Shirley, n.d. [c. December 1744], Akins: 141–49; John Henry Bastide to Shirley, 3 October 1744, Moody: 248.

13. Shirley to Board of Trade, 16 October 1744, Shirley 1:150; Murdoch 2:50.

14. Mascarene to Deputies of Minas, 13 October 1744, Akins: 137–38; Council Minutes, 8 December 1744, Fergusson: 51.

15. Council Minutes, 4 January 1745, Akins: 153–55.

16. Casgrain (1888):520; Council Minutes, 26 January 1745, Fergusson: 61–63; Mascarene to Shirley, 15 March 1745, Akins: 150–51.

■ Article 4: Mating and Marriage in Early Acadia

Naomi F.S. Griffiths

The simplest place to begin the analysis of Acadian marriage patterns in the seventeenth century is what John Demos has called the inescapable groundwork of family history, that of demography. Even a cursory analysis reveals that fertility and child mortality rates for the colony were very different from those of much of contemporary Europe. A separate sheet attached to the census, headed 'A summary of the families' of Acadia notes that there were 63 households in Port Royal, made up of 63 men, as many women plus five widows and 227 children. In the body of the census one can only discover some 59 households. As to the rest of the colony, there were recorded 11 people at Pobomkou, 3 at Cap Neigre, 6 civilians and 25 soldiers at Pentagouet, 13 people at Mouskadabouet and 1 soul at Saint-Pierre. In a study which used not only this census but later ones made in the 1680s and the early 1700s it was calculated that women married on the average three to four years younger than in contemporary France.[1] Families which were not disrupted by the death of one or other partner before the woman reached the onset of menopause were large. Women marrying before age 20 had on the average 10.5 children, those marrying between 20 and 24 had nine children and those marrying between 25 and 29 had 7.5 children.[2] Approximately 20 percent of women married before their twenties, and another 20 percent or so before they were 25. Infant mortality was remarkably low compared to contemporary France.[3] Hynes' figure show that three-quarters of the children born at Port Royal during the period she studied, 1671–1730, reached adulthood.[4] In 1672, the Acadian population was young. There were twenty-two little-ones recorded, including 5 week old twins, who were less than a year old as Molin made his enquiry.

Who were these people and where did they originate? What was their heritage of custom and tradition that would structure their social relationships?

Source: Naomi F.S. Griffiths, "Mating and Marriage in Early Acadia," *Culture, Theory and Critique*, Vol. 35, Issue 1, 1992, pp. 116–127 (excerpts). Reprinted by permission of Taylor & Francis Group, http://www.informaworld.com

A crucial analysis which helps to answer some of these questions was published thirty years ago by a French scholar, Geneviève Massignon. Her purpose was a linguistic enquiry and she hoped to trace the roots of Acadian linguistic patterns. To do this she made an extensive enquiry in French archives as to baptismal records and other documents relating to Acadian families. She discovered that about twenty of the seventy or so families named in 1671 could be traced to a series of small villages in Vienne, near Loudun.[5] She followed the records of some families from French village to Acadian settlement. There was the Brin family, for example, whose first two children were baptized in France and who appear with a family of five children in the 1671 census in Port Royal. The names and ages of the first two children reported in the census match the data of French baptismal records.

Massignon was able to demonstrate that a number of families were linked by marriage to one another before they left France for Acadia, noting kin lines between thirteen of the twenty.[6] In fact, if one traces links through in-laws, the in-law of one's in-law (!), the community of Port Royal becomes a web of relations.

What would have been some of the ideas and attitudes they brought with them? Turning first to the group from Vienne, some of the names of families such as the Leblanc can be traced as tenants of the particular estate of the man responsible for recruiting blocks of colonists, but no baptismal or marriage records can be found for them.[7] This part of France very definitely had a strong, although not predominant Huguenot population at this time. It is my belief that the Leblancs were indeed adherents of the Reform, in other words, Huguenots. This would account for the absence of Catholic church records when there are records for paying dues to the land-owners.[8] The Melansons were definitely noted as having forsworn the Protestant faith before marriage to women already in Acadia.[9]

What all this suggests, given the fact that we know that early expeditions to Acadia were definitely composed of both Huguenots and Catholics, is that Acadian Christianity was not overly rigid. It has also to be borne in mind that from 1654 when Acadia was controlled by Crowne and Temple out of Boston until 1670 when it was restored to France, it was a colony almost continuously without priests. Any family with children where the oldest was 16 or

124

less in 1671 probably had their marriage publicly recognized without the benefit of Catholic clergy. This applied to more than half the community. Finally, given the attitude of three of the households questioned towards the priest making the census—that of the Melansons, already noted but a similar attitude was displayed by the Robichauds and the Lanous—there is an absence of any overwhelming respect for the clerical hierarchy.

The severe morality that one can discern in the reports by Jesuit and Recollet missionaries from Acadia, did not find its pattern in Acadian practices. Unlike the new colonists along the St. Lawrence, none of the Acadians in the seventeenth century chose celibacy and a religious life. Marriage was entered into young. Child-bearing did not seem to be lethal to the mother and the families were, in some sense, spaced. Gysa Hynes has shown that the average interval was 28.55 months; in the large families, those of 7–10 children, a little shorter: 24 months. Death rates are such as to rule out famine or epidemic.

In fact, to broach that most dangerous ground of all in family history, what Demos has described as the problems of 'emotional experience or more simply "affect"',[10] Acadian home life was pleasant. The position of women was not obviously subordinate and the way in which widows ran their own families and households does not suggest their subservience to their children. The example of Barbe Baiolet, the widow of a man who contributed money to the settlement of the colony, was that of a vigorous lady of 63 who, since she had children on both sides of the Atlantic, travelled about the world to ensure that all her family remembered her.[11] There is no evidence to suggest that the Acadians were particularly concerned with having priests always present, and there is quite a lot of evidence from later years that shows they were happy enough with an intermittent appearance among them of clerics.[12]

Acadian family life was lived in a healthy, mixed economy, comprising farming, fishing, hunting, forest work, and fur-trading. Women had a place as effective partners and were regarded as such.[13] There is insufficient detail from the census to decide quite what 'house-hold' or 'family' meant for the people of Port Royal in 1671 but there is at least enough evidence to show that most people lived in quarters shared among a fair number. Obviously some households were three generational, while others held just parents and children. In Port Royal, families shared households and lived as physically close neighbours to four or five other households.[14] It should not be thought of as an 'earthly Paradise'. By the sixteen eighties a neat little charge of witch-craft was hatched in the colony, arising from jealousy over the growth of a flock of chickens.[15] But the growth of early Acadia was the development of a community that was fortunate in its lack of the tragedies of the Apocalypse, famine, plagues and warfare.

Further, the Acadians would find support throughout the community as well as through kin. Part of this would arise naturally from the importance of communal activity during the early years of settlement. House and barn building, tree clearing, ditch digging and dyke building, are all activities that proceed better through group action than by individual self-help. To turn to the ideas of those who consider family something to be seen above all as a 'function', of 'cost' and 'benefit' and of 'fit' to the society, the Acadian family can be seen as an archetype indeed of what has been described as 'the family of pre-modern times'.[16] It was indeed what Demos has described as 'a hive of instrumental activity; of production (e.g. the "family farm"), of schooling, of worship, of medical practice, and of care for all sorts of "dependents" (orphans, elderly people, the insane even criminals)'.[17]

But the strength of the Acadian colony was not built in isolation from the Micmac society. The establishment of a successful Acadian community owed a very great deal to the aid given by the Micmac. The relationship of European and Micmac was very different from the relationships along the St. Lawrence between European and Iroquois. Not only was there no continuous warfare between newcomer and native in Acadia but there was inter-marriage, according to the rites of the newcomers, between the two peoples.

Evidence here relates both to the generality of the practice and to specific examples. As early as 1611, the Jesuits were commenting that men sent out to establish a colony of France had sought a different life among the Micmac: 'la plupart se marient à des sauvagesses, et passèrent le reste de leurs jours avec les sauvages adoptant leur manière de vie'.[18] Since five years later there were clerical complaints of the licentious habits of various Frenchmen, living

125

in marriage without the benefit of a priestly blessing, the admittance in this document of the relationships [having] had a certain legitimacy in Jesuit eyes [is] interesting. This recognition by the Jesuits that marriages existed between Frenchmen and Micmac is particularly interesting because within five years, Recollets were complaining about sinful cohabitation of Frenchmen with Micmac.[19]

At this time the population of New France was perhaps some 3,000 people of European descent. By 1671 Acadia's Euroamerican population was around 600 and in a community of some seventy households there were at least five where the legitimate wife was Micmac.

Further, the strength of this link was reinforced by marriages between European and Micmac according to Micmac rite which were lived among the Micmac. The evidence that we have, from the diaries of such explorers and settlers as Champlain and Denys,[20] as well as the reports of the Jesuits,[21] builds a picture of rite and social custom in Micmac marriage. The Micmac were hunter-gatherers and, while they came together in gatherings of two hundred or more in spring and summer, spent a fair part of the year separated into small groups. Tradition names seven distinct districts within the Micmac territories. Custom required that the groom, usually a man in his twenties, spend about two years in the tent of his prospective father-in-law. During this time sexual relations between the intending partners were forbidden. The actual marriage, the public recognition of the union, was a matter celebrated by several days feasting, long speeches of advice to the couple from parents and elders of the group and by the shaman. If, in later years, the couple wished to separate, matters were not difficult to arrange.[22] Matters of property and children were not matters that were settled entirely on the power of one sex over the other. Since the woman drew the man to her family, she would not be left destitute with no blood relation support. Further, illegitimate children were considered a sign of fertility rather than of shame. The social demand on the family was for the unit to be capable of self-support whenever possible as well as of aid to others in emergencies. Within this context, the relationship of individuals was subject to all the realities of human affection.[23]

What is interesting about the evolution of the relationship between European men and Micmac women, however, is the significant presence of Micmac women within the Acadian communities. It has been often observed that the appearance of European women within a colony frequently led to an emergence of racism. Yet Micmac women seem to have been assimilated within the Acadian communities without difficulty and their offspring do not seem to have been discriminated against as marriage partners.

While marriage between European men and Micmac women was obviously beneficial for the Acadians, it was much less obviously positive for the Micmac men. The immediate results of the early expeditions to settle Acadia was a challenge to Micmac males. The percentage of marriages by Catholic rite to other forms of union between Frenchmen and Micmac women is impossible to estimate but there is no doubt that the latter were much more common. The children of such unions followed the mother and became part of her society. But whether the relationship was lived briefly or at length, whether offspring were assimilated within the new or the old society, the impact on the Micmac was profound.

The shock for the Micmac family system did not come primarily from the arrival of new males and the establishment of new kin lines. After all the possibility of marriage between Micmac and other groups of people such as Ojibwa, Ottawa and Algonquins north of the Great Lakes had always existed.[24] What was completely revolutionary was that at the same time as new marriage partners, there came radical new attitudes about sexuality as a whole as well as new precepts about the proper regulation of marriage and divorce. Further, the transmission of many of the new ideas came in contradictory context: missionaries, celibate men of austere and exemplary conduct, preached a new relation and instilled a new sense of sin about the whole range of sexual conduct, inculcating a strong fear of damnation. As well the actions of others from Europe, particularly the itinerant, the traders and fishermen presented a different vision of the new morality.

The early years of Acadian history forced the Micmac to respond to a cumulative impact of the new: the continuing and growing commerce bringing new technology as well as different goods, the spread of new religion, the presence of strangers living in alien ways within their lands, the shock of epidemic disease. When he wrote his land-mark study *The*

Conflict of European and Eastern Algonquin Cultures for his doctorate in the 1930s,[25] Bailey saw only that these developments had wrought a devastation and produced a desperation of life. He considered that 'the imposition of alien sex mores, involving in some cases the subordination of free contracting parties to external control and in others the segregation of the sexes in convent institutions[26] resulted in a loss of the will to live.'[27] His study dealt as much with the eastern Algonquins as with the Micmac. There is no doubt that the situation of the Micmac was somewhat less disastrous even if the alteration in their lives was quite as profound.[28]

One of the factors that mitigated, if only minimally, the situation for the Micmacs was the process of Acadian development during the first three-quarters of the century. The growth of this society posed problems for the Micmac but it also offered a balance both to the fervent teachings of the missionaries and to the behaviour patterns of the itinerant Frenchmen.

The community built by the Acadians by 1671 was one which had as its dominant characteristic the foundation of a society, not only for the living but for the next generations. However brutal the life in the early European settlements in North America, it was a life that offered more to those who were at the lower levels of society than did the life of Europe. As Cole Harris wrote, North America gave people the 'the opportunity to bypass both the confining grid of custom and power that dominated European property and the vagaries of chance that, at the personal level, usually turned on relative life spans.'[29] This did not mean a rejection of all the migrant had known. As Harris goes on to say: 'Those of European descent in North America at the end of the seventeenth century spoke European languages and practiced countless European ways while living in societies without precise European equivalents.'[30] In the final analysis, those who crossed the Atlantic East to West would find, again in Harris's words: 'the context had drastically altered … and the nature of New World societies cannot be deduced from an understanding of Old World ideas.'[31]

Those who built the Acadian society arrived with a variety of different heritages, a dissimilarity of tradition as much as a resemblance of customs. They would find that they possessed a number of solutions to the political and social problems that they faced. The settlers were to a very large extent left alone by external authority. The supervision of the metropolitan authorities, whether by the church or the royal government, indeed of any group from France, was much less than of the settlements along the St. Lawrence. Any attempt at a seigneurial system was broken, not only by the interregnum of British rule 1654–1670 but also by the fighting between d'Aulnay and La tour. There was no dominant impact of the structures of the Catholic church, as opposed to the survival of Christian belief, in these early years.

In considering these parts of Acadian history, one has few reflective philosophical musings of the actual people who lived them to enlighten the imagination. One can only attempt to assign motivation through the assessment of what is known about what actually was created. In the first seventy years of the seventeenth century, a small group of Europeans established themselves as neighbours to the Micmac. Events so developed that the very divergent societies did not attempt to kill off one another—in fact fighting was internecine, both for the Acadians and for the Micmac.

Part of the circumstances which mitigated against bloodshed was the way in which the family was established in the Acadian community. At least some of the barriers which would allow both to believe the other alien beyond endurance were not there. From the Micmac the Acadians learnt the best ways to build a canoe and efficient ways to hunt and fish. The Micmac women who married Acadian men taught the newcomers a great deal about plants that would be good to eat,[32] as well those useful for medical purposes. Scurvy ceased to be a problem for the Acadians after the winter of 1606. The full story of what one might call 'medieval' Acadian history has yet to be told but one can at least assert that the beginnings saw the emergence of customs of tolerance which would continue for at least another seventy years before the impact of a world-wide struggle had these neighbours at one another's throats.

NOTES

1. Gysa Hunes, 'Some Aspects of the Demography of Port Royal, 1650–1755', *Acadiensis Reader* vol. I: *Atlantic Canada Before Confederation* (Fredericton, N. B. 1985), p. 22.
2. Hynes, 'Port Royal', p. 22.
3. Goubert's comments on the France of Louis XIV bear repeating: 'In 1969 the average expectancy of

life [in France] is something over 70 years. In 1661 it was probably under twenty-five … Out of every hundred children born, twenty-five died before they were one year old, another twenty-five never reached twenty and a further twenty-five perished between the ages of twenty-five and forty-five'. *Louis XIV and Twenty Million Frenchmen* (New York, 1966), p. 212.

4. Hynes, 'Port Royal', pp. 18–19.

5. Massignon, *Les Parlers français,* vol. I, p. 36.

6. Massignon, *Les Parlers français,* vol. I, p. 37.

7. Governor Charles d'Aulnay is a person in question and it is his seigniory in France, inherited through his mother that provided the large group of inter-related colonists. Massignon: *Les Parlers français,* Vol. I, pp. 34–35.

8. On the question of rents and baptismal records, see Massignon, *Les Parlers français,* vol. I, p. 43, and p. 38. The possibility of Huguenot descent does not occur to Massignon.

9. This from the memoirs of their descendants, cited Massignon, *Les Parlers français,* vol. I, p. 48. The question of whether they remained after the Scottish attempt at settlement 1628–33, or came later is a matter of dispute. See memoir of Lamothe-Cadillac, 1685: Archives Nationales, Acadie C 11 D, X.

10. John Demos, *Past, Present and Personal: The Family and the Life Course in American History* (New York, 1986), p. 15.

11. A. D. Charente-Maritime, Minutes Teuleuron: La Rochelle, contracts for passage on board ship.

12. In particular see the records of the episcopal visit, that of the Vicar General Saint-Vallier, 1686. *Mandements, letters pastorals et circulaires des evéques de Québec* (Quebec, 1887), and the visit, a year earlier of an Intendant from Quebec, Demeulle in 1685: account published in full in *Acadiensis Nova,* I, pp 1–124.

13. On this see particularly Michael Miterauer and Reinhard Sieder, *The European Family: Patriarchy to Partnership from the Middle Ages to the Present* (Chicago, 1983), pp. 53ff, where it is argued that the roles of wife and husband in such an economy are fully inter-dependent, to such an extent that remarriage is necessary for the economy of the unit on the death of either partner.

14. A. H. Clark, *Acadia: The Geography of Early Nova Scotia* (Wisconsin, 1968), p. 122: figure 5.3, 'Port Royal Basin and Valley: Population 1671–1710'.

15. See documents about same published in Rameau de St. Père, *Une colonie féodale en Amerique: L'Acadie (1604–1881)* (Paris and Montreal, 1889), vol. II, pp. 304–7.

16. See particularly *Household and Family in Past Time,* edited by Peter Laslett (Cambridge, 1974), and *Family History at the Cross-roads,* edited by Tamara Hareven and Andrejs Plakans (Princeton, 1987).

17. Demos, *Past Present and Personal,* p. 17.

18. J. A. Maureault, *Histoire des Abenakis depuis 1605 jusqu'à nos jours* (Soel, 1888), p. 84.

19. Candide de Nantes, *Pages glorieuses* (Montreal, 1927), pp. 309ff.

20. See the Champlain Society editions of their works, as well as the work of Lescarbot.

21. In particular, Baird. As well as the Thwaites edition of his reports, see also the edition in Lucien Campeau, *La première mission d'Acadie,* (1602–1616) (Laval, 1967).

22. This paragraph based upon Bock, 'Micmac', p. 114.

23. About which, perhaps, the 13th century poem of Lady Horikara says it all: 'How can one e'er be sure/if true love will endure? My thoughts this morning are/as tangled as my hair', in *Anthology of World Poetry,* edited by Mark van Doren (London, 1929), p. 29.

24. A. G. Bailey, *Conflict of European … and Algonquin cultures.* pp. 113–14.

25. First published in 1937, reissued in a second edition in 1969 by the University of Toronto Press. Recently deemed by Bruce Trigger a work remarkable for its originality and clarity, *Native and Newcomers,* pp. 164–5.

26. It is often forgotten that Acadia had its own institution which paralleled the work of Marie de l'Incarnation of the St. Lawrence. This was the work of Madame Brice between 1644 and 1652. She was in charge of some 30 girls at Port Royal during her stay there. *DCB,* vol. I, p. 129.

27. Bailey, *Conflict of European … and Eastern Algoquin,* p. 115.

28. The most sensitive published analyses of what is happening here are: Calvin Martin, *Keepers of the Game: Indian-Animal Relationships and the Fur Trade* (Berdeley, 1978), Part One: 'An Ecological Interpretation of European Contact with the Micmac', pp. 27–68; and James Axtell, *The European and the Indian: Essays in the Ethnohistory of*

Colonial North America (Oxford, 1981), Section 3: 'The Invasion Within: The Contest of Cultures in Colonial North America', pp. 39–86.

29. Cole Harris, 'European Beginnings in the North-West Atlantic: A Comprehensive View', in *Seventeenth-Century New England,* edited by D.D. Hall and D.G. Allen (Boston, 1984). Report of a

conference held by the Colonial Society of Massachusetts, 18–19 June 1982, pp. 119–52.

30. Cole Harris, 'European Beginnings' p. 120.
31. Cole Harris, 'European Beginnings', p. 122.
32. The absorption of words in Acadian speech about various flora, words Massignon asserted, have a Micmac root is interesting evidence for this.

■ Article 5: Re-examining Mi'kmaq-Acadian Relations, 1635–1755

William Wicken

During the years immediately after 1632, a close trading relationship had developed between individual Acadian and Mi'kmaq families. Though evidence is lacking, it is likely that some of these links were strengthened through intermarriage and maintained despite the declining importance of the fur trade during the seventeenth century.[1] Communication was also enhanced by the recognition by both peoples that they shared a common spiritual world. The Mi'kmaq might have understood Catholicism differently from the way the Acadians did, but the two groups could nonetheless attend mass and observe other rituals side by side. These economic, social, and cultural ties, created during the early seventeenth century, made possible a peaceful co-occupation of adjoining lands. Eventually, however, Acadian expansion and the escalation of French-English rivalry would undermine the prospects for continuing amicable relations. Before analysing the separate effects of these two developments, we turn first to the population of both communities.

The Mi'kmaq inhabited a broad geographical area that encompassed the present-day provinces of Nova Scotia and Prince Edward Island, southern Newfoundland, the eastern coast of New Brunswick, the Gaspé, Saint-Pierre and Miquelon, and the Magdelaine Islands. In the Bay of Fundy region, where the principal Acadian population was concentrated, Mi'kmaq villages were located at Baye Sainte-Marie,

Source: W.C. Wicken, "Re-examining Mi'kmaq-Acadian Relations" in S. Departie et al., eds., *Habitants et Marchands, Twenty Years Later: Reading the History of Seventeenth-and-Eighteenth-Century Canada,* (Montreal: McGill-Queen's University Press, 1998), pp. 95–109. Printed with permission from the publisher.

Port Royal, Minas, Piziquit, Cobequid, and Chignecto. While it is impossible to make definitive statements about population growth in these communities between 1635 and 1755, it can be said that European-borne diseases such as smallpox, measles, and scarlet fever periodically took their toll on the Mi'kmaq as they had on other aboriginal societies.[2] Recurring hostilities with New England between 1689 and 1760 also slowed population growth. Though village size cannot be known for certain, war and Acadian expansion clearly precipitated migration from favoured fishing sites. Census data from 1722 show relatively low numbers of people living at Minas, Port Royal, and Chignecto[3] compared with the totals collected between 1706 and 1708, suggesting either recent depopulation or the inability of the missionary priest, Abbé Gaulin, to obtain a reasonable account of the actual population.[4] Despite this, we might say that during the eighteenth century village size varied from a minimum of forty people to more than a hundred.

In the Bay of Fundy region, Mi'kmaq families depended upon a variety of resources.[5] During the warm-weather months running from mid-March to the autumn, they mainly fished the abundant marine life that swarmed through the rivers and estuaries of the Bay of Fundy.[6] Fish were deboned, smoked, and stored for later consumption. During May, garden crops were planted close to fishing sites, to be harvested during the autumn fish runs. In winter, villages broke up into smaller hunting groups, composed of three to five families, to hunt for moose, caribou, beaver, and other terrestrial animals.

Substantially more statistical information is available regarding the Acadians who had settled near Port Royal in 1635. Between 1671 and 1755, their population multiplied almost thirty times, averaging an annual growth rate of 3.75 per cent.[7] Rapid growth was possible because Acadian women married young and natural restraints upon the population such as disease, infant and child mortality, and harvest failures were minimal.[8] Thus, what had begun as a relatively small population of one hundred in 1635 grew to approximately fifteen thousand by 1755, principally through natural increase.

The Acadians were a prosperous people who exploited marshland areas both to grow crops and to feed livestock. Like farmers elsewhere, their lives were governed by the annual cycle of planting and harvesting.[9] In April and May, fields of hay, wheat, oats, rye, and barley were sown and garden crops such as carrots, turnips, cabbage, and onions were planted. Apple and cherry trees, which had been imported from France in the seventeenth century, were cultivated, while in the surrounding countryside cranberries, blueberries, and gooseberries grew wild and were picked by women and children during the late summer. In summer, hay was harvested and sheep were shorn,[10] and as autumn drew nearer and the growing season came to a close, wheat and oats were also harvested, the men moving back and forth across the fields, cutting the stocks of grain. As fodder was often scarce during the winter, as much as 30–40 per cent of the cattle might be slaughtered, the meat drawn into quarters, salted, and either sold or stored for the coming months.[11] Women and the older girls worked hard preserving vegetables and fruits, while the men and boys spent most of their days in the forested areas of the farm, cutting down trees for firewood. Occasionally they forsook the forest and fished for salmon or eels, which teemed in the surrounding rivers during the autumn.

Initially concentrated near Port Royal, Acadian settlements began in the late seventeenth century to emerge in fertile lands bordering on the Bay of Fundy, at Chignecto in 1671, Minas in 1682, Cobequid in 1697, and Piziquit in 1703. Those settling in new areas were at first outnumbered by Mi'kmaq residents. In 1686, for example, the Acadian Minas population totalled 58 people, while the neighbouring Mi'kmaq village probably reached 100 or more. But by 1703, the Acadian population had mushroomed to 507, roughly two and a half times the size of the Mi'kmaq communities living near the Cornwallis and Piziquit rivers. Similarly, 245 Acadians lived at Chignecto in 1703, compared to roughly half as many Mi'kmaq residents.[12] Thirty years later, the population imbalance between the two communities had grown even greater. In 1737, for example, census data show 2,113 Acadians inhabiting lands between the Canard

River and Grand Pré and another 1,816 occupying lands adjacent to Chignecto.[13] The Mi'kmaq population inhabiting the Nova Scotian mainland and Unimaki[14] also grew, from 838 in 1722 to approximately 1,158 in 1735.[15] Though these figures likely under-represented the actual population, statements by sakamows (headmen or chiefs) during the 1730s suggest that the population expanded between 1725 and the mid-1730s.[16] Nonetheless, the Mi'kmaq clearly did not experience growth rates similar to the Acadians, particularly during the eighteenth century, when war precipitated migration away from favoured fishing sites. Had the growth rates been more comparable, Acadian expansion into new farmland prior to the 1740s would surely have generated more than the two or three reports of altercations that survive in the official records.[17]

The effects of opposed economic lifestyles and of an increasing population imbalance became more apparent as the eighteenth century progressed. Because community exploitation of local resources diverged, conflicts erupted over the Acadians' use of land and the Mi'kmaq's use of livestock owned by the colonists. As imperial rivalry intensified, French Catholic priests intervened to resolve such disputes, recognizing that an alliance with the Mi'kmaq would promote France's strategic interests in the region. Expanding the missionary presence in Mi'kmaq society, however, had the effect of furthering social distances between the Mi'kmaq and the Acadians by removing the necessity for the two communities to come together for religious services.

If open conflict with the increasingly numerous Acadians appears to have been rare prior to the 1740s, the Mi'kmaq nonetheless attempted to exert some political control over lands lying adjacent to the Bay of Fundy.[18] In the early eighteenth century, episodic reports from officials, traders, and fishermen refer to Mi'kmaq complaints concerning European encroachments upon their lands. Such complaints hint that the Mi'kmaq believed in the need to maintain jurisdiction over their lands and to enforce proprietary rights. In 1720, for instance, a group of sakamows informed the governor of Île Royale, Joseph de Saint-Ovide, that he must "learn from us that we have lived on this earth that you trample with your feet and upon which you walk, before even the trees that you see began to grow, it is ours and never can we be removed from it, nor can we be made to abandon it."[19] That same year, Peter Nunquadden, a sakamow of the Minas Mi'kmaq, was quoted as demanding that the New England trader John Alden pay him fifty livres "for liberty to trade, saying this Country was theirs and every English Trader should pay Tribute to them."[20] Permission was also required to build or settle on Mi'kmaq lands, as the Acadian René Le Blanc discovered after he was commissioned by the English government to build a blockhouse near Minas during the early summer of 1732. Jacques, son of Winaguadesh from the Piziquit River, told Le Blanc that he "was King of that Country," and he forbade Le Blanc from building there.[21] Indeed, records suggest that Acadians did not establish new settlements without the consent of neighbouring Mi'kmaq people. In November of 1724 the governor of Île Royale wrote that five or six Acadian families living below the Chebenacadie River were inhabiting land that had been given to them by the Mi'kmaq.[22] Similar ideas were expressed in 1740 by Major Paul Mascarene, then president of the Nova Scotia Executive Council, who reported that Acadians who wanted to acquire new landholdings, but who did not have the approval of the British government to do so, settled on lands that they said had been purchased from the Mi'kmaq.[23]

Agreements to occupy adjoining lands were only possible because Mi'kmaq and Acadians followed different economic cycles and because, initially, population densities were low. As farmers, Acadians did not at first interfere with Mi'kmaq fishing and hunting. Co-occupation therefore was possible so long as fish and animal populations remained stable and harvests did not fail. Acadian population growth, however, would jeopardize the Mi'kmaq's access to the region's marine and terrestrial resources. As a non-agricultural people, the Mi'kmaq moved freely through their territory in a seasonal cycle that encompassed a broad geographical area, fishing along river systems and hunting in the interior for moose and caribou. For each individual, survival as well as personal prestige was dependent upon maintaining a harmonious relationship with the animal spirits. Failure to observe the sacred rituals thought necessary to maintain harmony could have catastrophic consequences.[24] Thus, their association with the land differed markedly from that of Acadians, whose attention was focused upon a relatively small and confined land area.[25] For French and English settlers, life was rooted firmly in cultivated land and did not routinely extend to the forests that surrounded agricultural communities. For much of the seventeenth and eighteenth centuries, forests were feared, deplored as obstacles to European expansionism, and linked in the minds of the French and the English alike with dark, uncontrolled emotions, chaos, and savagery.[26] In contrast, colonial officials and missionaries extolled the neat, orderly world of the farm, occupied year round by inhabitants who in the process of tending their crops, enclosing their fields, and maintaining their buildings were adding materially to the wealth of the colony and ultimately to that of its benefactors, the European monarchies. Hard-working settlers, in turn, might be rewarded by the gain of additional land, held for an older son or some other family member. Thus, as the Acadian population grew, so did the size and number of its farms: for example, in 1686, there were but 671 arpents under cultivation; by 1688, 896 arpents, and five years later, 1,300 arpents.[27] By 1748–50, dyked marshlands had increased to approximately 12,600 acres throughout the Bay of Fundy area, including 3,000 acres at Port Royal, 4,000 at Minas, 2,500 at Piziquit and Cobequid, and another 3,000 within the Chignecto region. And as Acadian cultivated order thus beat back fearsome wilderness, Mi'kmaq were excluded from ever greater spaces in the landscape.[28]

Acadian farming practices also forced the Mi'kmaq to redefine how land could be used and what rights accrued to individuals who occupied it.[29] Unlike the Mi'kmaq, the Acadians dramatically altered the landscape, building dykes and destroying marshlands that had long been habitats for waterfowl and other animal life. The Acadians also claimed exclusive proprietary rights over farm animals. To the Mi'kmaq, people occupying specific territories were custodians of the land, preserving its faunal and floral life for the collectivity. Others could use resources found within the territory, particularly if they were in need. As was also true of New England's relations with aboriginal peoples,[30] conflicts emerged between Acadian and Mi'kmaq communities regarding rights to unfettered livestock. During the 1750s, Abbé Maillard, a missionary who lived among the Mi'kmaq between 1735 and 1761, recounted a conversation with some Unimaki Mi'kmaq regarding what should be done with livestock that had wandered far from the French settlements.

My Father, [a Mi'kmaq man said] we found livestock more than three leagues from the french settlements; we look upon them as lost and gone astray forever in the woods; isn't it better that we kill them to profit from their flesh, and from their hides, rather than to leave them lost? I [Maillard] then replied: When I will know that it is not yourselves that have chased them [the cattle] to this distance in the woods, I will then know to invite you to take hold of them. If you take it upon yourselves to do this before the answer that I had told you to wait for, M. the Governor will be informed of it, and entry into the Church will be refused to you until you have brought me in money, [or] in goods that which the livestock was known to be worth.[31]

During the eighteenth century, such customary practices became increasingly strained for two reasons. First, Acadian development increased both the number of farms and the overall size of the livestock population. Furthermore, warfare between Great Britain and France inhibited Mi'kmaq use of traditional fishing sites, leading to migrations into the interior and hence to a greater reliance upon terrestrial mammals, which in turn tempted individual Mi'kmaq families to kill Acadian livestock for food. Prior to 1749, however, such dislocations in village subsistence patterns had been temporary. Following proclamations of peace, as in 1713, 1725, and 1748, fishing sites were reoccupied.[32] However, with the establishment of English settlements at Halifax in 1749 and at Lunenberg in 1753, reoccupation of eastern coastal sites became more tenuous, forcing communities either to move laterally along the coastline or to move into the interior, along the Piziquit and Shubenacadie rivers. The participation of Jean-Baptiste Cope, identified as a sakamow from Shubenacadie, in the negotiation of a treaty of peace and friendship in 1752 with the British suggests such migrations: traditionally inhabitants of the eastern coast, the Cope family appears thus to have migrated to a position of prominence in Shubenacadie by the early 1750s.[33]

Tensions arising from different concepts of property were accentuated as expanding Acadian settlements widened physical and social distances between Acadians and local Mi'kmaq communities. That social distances grew is suggested by the registers kept for the parishes of Chignecto between 1681 and 1686 and of Grand Pré between 1709 and 1749. Though records for Chignecto are sporadic, they show that during the early years of its settlement,

thirty-four Mi'kmaq were baptized by the local parish priest, Claude Moireau, with godparents selected from prominent Acadian members of the community, particularly Michel Le Neuf, a one-time governor of Acadia, who had been granted a seigneury in the region in 1676. During the following century only four Mi'kmaq were baptized.[34] For Minas, parish registers extant only for the period 1709 to 1748 do not record any baptisms, marriages, or burials among the local Mi'kmaq population.[35] A different situation prevailed at Port Royal, where registers are extant from 1702 to 1755. As Fort Anne became the centrepoint for British-Mi'kmaq discussions, particularly after 1725, some Mi'kmaq families converged on Port Royal, accompanying prominent individuals involved in the meetings. Consequently, thirty-one births, marriages, and deaths are recorded between 1722 and 1735, twenty-eight of them occurring after 1725. No similar acts appear in the registers between 1735 and 1755. While not conclusive, the registers do suggest that as settlement increased, contacts between Acadians and surrounding Mi'kmaq populations became scarcer.

The lack of social interaction discouraged intermarriage between the two communities. During the early years of the fur trade and immediately after a settlement was established by Isaac de Razilly at La Hève in 1632, some Europeans had married Mi'kmaq women. However, when the Acadians migrated to the Annapolis Basin in 1635, these couples remained behind, some living separately from Mi'kmaq villages and acting as intermediaries in the fur trade.[36] Officially sanctioned marriages between members of the two communities, however, would have been extremely rare after 1635. This is demonstrated by an examination of both census records and parish registers made of the Acadian population. The 1671, 1678, 1686, and 1693 Acadian censuses show that only one aboriginal woman was the wife of an Acadian and lived in an agricultural community.[37] Significantly, she was Abenaki and probably had agricultural skills. Though parish registers are not available for these communities for most of the seventeenth century, both the 1671 and the 1686 censuses provide the maiden name of each married woman and widow, which with the one exception are of European origin. While the registers kept by missionaries living among the Mi'kmaq, such as those of the Abbés Gaulin, Courtin, Maillard, and Le Loutre, have not survived, parish registers from the Acadian settlements at Port Royal, Chignecto, and Minas do exist. These list the parents' names for and the place of residence of the bride and groom, but do not record Mi'kmaq-Acadian marriages.[38]

Social tensions between Mi'kmaq and Acadian communities along the Bay of Fundy worsened as a result of the English conquest of Port Royal in 1710. That year was an important watershed in Mi'kmaq-Acadian relations, as from that point until the Acadian expulsion of 1755 British officials attempted to coerce Acadians into becoming loyal subjects of the Crown. Though unsuccessful in establishing complete authority, colonial officials did enlist Acadians in various tasks that placed them in conflict with the Mi'kmaq. Repairing the fortifications at Annapolis Royal, conveying information to British officials, serving as pilots in British vessels, and acting as intermediaries with the Mi'kmaq, Acadians were manoeuvred into playing a duplicitous role in their relations with their native neighbours.[39] Not surprisingly, long-standing tensions between the two communities erupted under the pressures of heightened Anglo-French rivalry during the 1740s and 1750s.

The two communities perceived the British conquest of Port Royal in different terms. While many Acadians resented the English presence, they nevertheless hoped to maintain the peace, since trade with New England was an important component of their economy. As Acadian farming progressed, exports of grain and livestock to colonial American markets replaced the fur trade, now in decline, which had financed the earliest years of French settlement. Mi'kmaq communities, however, viewed the English presence with alarm. By the 1720s sakamows began to fear a recurrence within their own territories of the perfidy they had witnessed further westward, where settlement had eventually precipitated a northward migration of many Abenaki villages.[40] These misgivings increased with an English reluctance to enter into a relationship that involved an annual exchange of gifts.[41] Though the British signed a treaty of peace and friendship with the Mi'kmaq in June 1726, the agreement did little to assuage the community's concerns regarding ultimate British interests. Indeed, as events in the post-1726 period suggest, both parties to the treaty understood it differently. While the British ostensibly thought the Mi'kmaq had agreed to become "subjects" of the Crown, the Mi'kmaq believed that they had merely agreed to become allies of the king.[42]

The failure to arrive at a mutual understanding of their relationship in the post-1710 period led to a series of conflicts that disrupted the Acadian economy. On several occasions between 1714 and 1737, Mi'kmaq villagers attacked British merchant vessels trading in the Minas Basin. In some cases, confrontations between Acadians and Mi'kmaq ensued. At Chignecto in 1714, Richibouctou people pillaged a French trader's vessel sailing from Boston. When local Acadians tried to intervene, the Mi'kmaq threatened to burn "their houses and livestock if they opposed them in their design, as was their custom to do."[43] In a similar incident at Minas in July of 1724, thirty Mi'kmaq from the Saint John River and forty to fifty from Chebenacadie and the eastern coast stopped Acadians from trading with two English vessels.[44] In 1734 three Acadians journeyed from Port Royal to Minas to ask the Mi'kmaq to stop their opposition to the establishment of an English post at Minas. Though some listened favourably to their entreaty, two sakamows chased the Acadians away, threatening to "break their heads" if they ever returned.[45]

The pillaging of New England trading vessels by the Mi'kmaq interrupted the flow of goods into Nova Scotia and increased their cost, as traders attempted to compensate themselves for actual or expected losses. Moreover, English colonial officials forced the Acadians to reimburse New Englanders for goods lost and it is likely that the bulk of the reimbursement funds were contributed by the more prosperous members of the community, including local merchants.[46] Conflict between the Mi'kmaq and New England also necessitated more armed vessels along the eastern coast to protect English fishermen, which made trading with Louisbourg a more hazardous and costly enterprise. In September 1724 Nicolas Gauthier of Port Royal was returning from Île Royale when he was stopped near Cap Sable by a sloop commanded by Joseph Marjory, who had been commissioned by the Massachusetts government to protect the fishery. According to Gauthier, Marjory demanded that a hogshead of wine and a quarter cask of brandy be given to him, a "request" with which Gauthier grudgingly complied.[47] Some Acadian vessels were seized and confiscated. For example, an Acadian by the name of Pellerin, travelling to Louisbourg with a boatload of cattle, had his vessel seized by the commander of the English garrison at Canceau, Major Cosby, who subsequently used it to patrol the Fronsac Passage.[48]

Anxious that peace be maintained in the region, Acadian merchants at times assumed an intermediary role between Mi'kmaq sakamows and British officials. On several occasions, Acadian traders ransomed English soldiers and civilians held prisoner by the Mi'kmaq. In 1724 Pierre Le Blanc purchased the freedom of an Englishman captured by the Mi'kmaq near Canceau, while on at least two occasions, in 1745 and 1753, Jacques Vigneaux (*dit* Maurice) bought or tried to buy that of English civilians held prisoner from the Mi'kmaq.[49] All of these prisoners were subsequently returned to English authorities.

Acadians understood the dangers of not aligning themselves with the Mi'kmaq. Those, like Joseph Brossard, who were summoned by the Nova Scotia Executive Council in 1724 to explain why they had not provided information regarding Mi'kmaq plans to attack Port Royal, replied that if they had done so, their families would have been destroyed.[50] Colonial officials, however, offered the Acadians little choice but to assist in attempting to extend the English's jurisdiction over Acadia. Initially, this included forcing residents to repair the garrison's fortifications and to serve as interpreters in discussions with the Mi'kmaq and Maliseet. In April of 1714 Claude Melançon of Port Royal and Jean Landry of Minas accompanied an expedition headed by Pierre Capon, a representative of the English government. Together they visited Acadian and Mi'kmaq inhabitants at Minas, Chignecto, and the Saint John River, whom Capon invited to swear allegiance to the English Crown. Similarly, in the same year Pierre Arceneau of Chignecto visited Mi'kmaq villages along the eastern coasts of Nova Scotia and New Brunswick, inviting the people to Port Royal to treat with the English.[51] In effect, English recruitment of Acadians as intermediaries with the Mi'kmaq was yet another sign of diverging interests.

Despite the willingness of some prominent Acadian merchants, such as Nicolas Gauthier, to align themselves with French imperial interests, most Acadians sought a solution that would secure their families and their farms from the vicissitudes of war. Farms were not movable, and as the heirs of more than 120 years of settlement, the Acadians would have faced the prospect of dislocation with terror.

While war had periodically affected them, particularly between 1689 and 1713, the Acadians had never been exposed to the full force of imperial armies trudging through their lands. Rather, hostilities had been occasional affairs, resulting in few casualties and only limited damage to homesteads and farms. The British conquest of Port Royal in 1710, the settlement of Halifax in 1749, and the establishment of Fort Lawrence in 1750 along the Missiquash River near the Acadian settlements at Beaubassin introduced a new and far more dangerous element into the Acadian and Mi'kmaq worlds. Virtually ignored by both Great Britain and France for most of the seventeenth century and the first half of the eighteenth, the Acadians were culturally and physically unprepared to confront the imperial war that was to erupt in their midst. While Mi'kmaq communities viewed war with similar distaste, their economy, being more flexible, insulated women, children, and elders from injury.

Conclusions stemming from this examination of Mi'kmaq-Acadian relations, though tentative, illustrate a final, broader theme in the history of New France. Just as settlement in that colony varied from English settlement along the eastern seaboard, so different patterns emerged in colonial relations with aboriginal peoples. In the British colonies, aboriginal communities relied heavily on farming and adapted with difficulty to the steady but massive immigration onto their lands. French settlement in Acadia and Canada, on the other hand, proceeded more slowly and in areas where aboriginal peoples were engaged in fishing, hunting, and gathering. A relatively long period of adjustment ensued,[52] during the earliest years of which individual contacts between aboriginal people and French traders and farmers developed. Such contacts, in turn, helped forge French-aboriginal alliances in the late seventeenth century. Over time, however, the very economic differences that had made accommodation possible between the colonists and the Algonkian hunting and gathering societies contributed to increased cultural and social distances between them, inhibiting consistent communication. As a result, personal trading and kinship relations were slowly but irrevocably undermined. As the French-speaking population swelled during the eighteenth century, these tensions spilled over into the political sphere, where discussions between French colonial officials and their erstwhile aboriginal allies exacerbated misunderstandings and suspicions.

134

By the time war once again danced through the North American landscape in the early 1750s, a new political conjuncture in French-Algonkian relations had emerged, limiting France's ability to parry the final (and fatal) British thrust.

NOTES

1. Wicken, "Encounters with Tall Sails and Tall Tales: Mi'kmaq Society, 1500–1760" (Ph D dissertation, McGill University, 1994).

2. On the Mi'kmaq, the major research in this respect has been done by Virginia Miller; see her "Aboriginal Micmac Population: A Review of the Evidence," *Ethnohistory* 23 (1976): 117–29. See also Ralph Pastore, "Native History in the Atlantic Region during the Colonial Period," *Acadiensis* 20, no. 1 (autumn 1990): 208–11; and Wicken," Encounters with Tall Sails," 184–204.

3. AC, c11B 6:77r, "Recensement des Sauvages dans l'isle Royalle et de la peninsule de l'acadie," 27 December 1722.

4. Chicago, Newberry Library, William Ayers Collection, "Recensement general fait au mois de Novembre mil Sept cent huit de tous les Sauvages de l'Acadie."

5. On Mi'kmaq economic patterns, see Patricia Nietfeld, "Determinants of Aboriginal Micmac Political Structure" (Ph D dissertation, University of New Mexico, 1981), 306–84.

6. Pierre Biard, "Relation of 1616," in Reuben Thwaites, ed., *Jesuit Relations and Allied Documents*. 73 vols. (Cleveland: Burrow Brothers, 1896), 3:79–81; Marc Lescarbot, *History of New France*, vol. 3, trans. W.L. Grant (Toronto: Champlain Society, 1914), 236; and Nicolas Denys, *Description and Natural History of the Coasts of North America (Acadia)*, ed. William F. Ganong (Toronto: Champlain Society, 1908), 124.

7. Jacques Houdaille, "Quelques aspects de la démographie ancienne de l'Acadie," *Population* 3 (1980): 582; and Raymond Roy, "La Croissance démographique en Acadie de 1671 à 1763" (MA Thesis, Université de Montréal, 1975), 58.

8. Gisa Hynes, "Some Aspects of the Demography of Port Royal, 1650–1755," *Acadiensis* 3 (1973): 8–9, 17. Among Acadian women living at Port Royal between 1725 and 1739, the average age at first marriage was 21. For the period between 1703 and 1755, Jacques Houdaille has calculated that the average age at

which women first married was 20.4. (Houdaille, "Quelques aspects de la démographie," 585, 593).

9. Much of the following description relies on Andrew Hill Clark, *Acadia: The Geography of Early Nova Scotia to 1760* (Madison: University of Wisconsin Press, 1968).

10. AC, c11D 2:19, "Relation de l'acadie envoyée par le Sr. Perrot," 9 August 1686.

11. Clark, *Acadia,* 167–9.

12. AC, G1 466 28, "Recensement de l'Acadie," 1703.

13. Clark, *Acadia,* 208, 210.

14. "Unimaki" is a Mi'kmaq term to describe the territory they inhabited on Cape Breton Island, on Saint-Pierre and Miquelon, as well as in southern Newfoundland.

15. AC, c11B 6:77r, "Recensement des Sauvages dans l'isle Royalle et de la peninsule de l'acadie," 27 December 1722; 1735: AC, G1 466: doc. 71. The 1735 census provides only the number of men capable of bearing arms. The figure of 1,158 has been calculated through reference to the 1722 census, which shows that 31.6 per cent of the population is composed of men thirteen years of age and older.

16. See for instance, AC, c11B 11:255V, Saint-Ovide au ministre, 14 November 1732; AC, c11B 21:77, de Forant au ministre, 14 November 1739; AC, c11B 22:38v, MM. de Bourville et Bigot au ministre, 17 October 1740.

17. This new farmland was located along the Chebenacadie River, on the eastern coast of Nova Scotia, Epikoitik (Prince Edward Island), and the Petitcodiac and Wulstukw (Saint John) Rivers (Clark, *Acadia,* 201–24).

18. Nietfeld, "Determinants," 325–48.

19. NA, MG 18, F29, "Discours curieux des sauvages du Canada par M. de Saint-Ovide gouverneur de l'Île royale au sujet des mouvements du Gouverneur Anglois de l'Acadie avec les réponses que les sauvages y ont faites" [1720–22].

20. PRO, CO 217 4:151r, "Memorial of John Alden," 14 September 1720.

21. Archibald MacMechan, ed., *Original Minutes of His Majesty's Council at Annapolis Royal, 1720–1739* (Halifax: Public Archives of Nova Scotia, 1908), 239.

22. AC, c11B 7:29v, Saint-Ovide au ministre, 24 November 1724.

23. PRO, CO 217 8:77, Mascarene to Board of Trade, 16 August 1740.

135

24. On similar patterns in other aboriginal societies, see Fred Myers, "Burning the Truck and Holding the Country: Property, Time and the Negotiation Identity among Pintupi Aborigines," in Tim Ingold, David Riches, and James Woodburn, eds, *Hunters and Gatherers, vol. 2: Property, Power and Ideology* (New York and Oxford: Berg Publishers, 1988), 65–70; and Keith Basso, "Stalking with Stories: Names, Places and Moral Narratives among the Western Apache," in *Proceedings: The American Ethnological Society,* ed. Edward M. Bruner (Washington: American Ethnological Society, 1983), 48–9.

25. For an account of the ways in which aboriginal peoples and Europeans living in New England differed in their treatment of the land, see William Cronon, *Changes in the Land: Indians, Colonists and the Ecology of New England* (New York: Hill and Wang, 1983), 34–81.

26. Keith Thomas, *Man and the Natural World: Changing Attitudes in England, 1500–1800* (London: Allen and Lane, 1983), 193–5; and D.G. Charlton, *New Images of the Natural in France* (Cambridge: Cambridge University Press, 1984), 42.

27. Clark, *Acadia,* 163–4; and AC, G1 466: doc. 10, "Recensement de l'Acadie," 1686.

28. Clark, *Acadia,* Table 6.11,236.

29. Over the last two decades, scholars have turned to the ecological consequences of European colonization. Samples of the earliest works include Cronon, *Changes;* Alfred Crosby, *Ecological Imperialism: The Biological Expansion of Europe, 900–1900* (New York: Cambridge University Press, 1986); Richard White, *Land Use, Environment and Social Change: The Shaping of Island County, Washington* (Washington: University of Washington Press, 1980).

30. Cronon, *Changes,* 129–30.

31. "Lettre de M. l'abbé Maillard sur les missions de l'Acadie et particulièrement sur les missions micmaques à Madame de Drucourt," in *Les Soirées Canadiennes* (1863), 366–67 [author's translation].

32. Abbé Gaulin's 1722 aggregate census of the Mi'kmaq population hints at the possible effects of war: for villages located within the vicinity of both Minas and Port Royal, Gaulin noted that they did not have a fixed point of residence, AC, c11B 6:77r, "Recensement des Sauvages dans l'isle Royalle et de la peninsule de l'acadie," 27 December 1722.

33. *Treaty or Articles of Peace and Friendship renewed, between His Excellency Peregrine Thomas Hopson Esq.... and Major jean Baptiste Cope ...* (Halifax: printed by John Bushell, Printer to the Government, 1753).

34. Parish registers for Chignecto (Beaubassin) exist only for the years 1681 to 1686, 1712 to 1723, 1732 to 1735, and 1740 to 1748. PANS, Churches: Acadian French Records (transcripts).

35. PANS, Church: Acadian French Records, Registres des baptêmes, mariages et sépultures, Grand Pré, 1709–48 (transcripts).

36. François-Edmé Rameau de Saint-Père, *Une colonie féodale en Amérique L'Acadie (1604–1881),* vol. 1 (Paris: E. Pion, Nourrit et cie., 1889), 153.

37. "Familles établies à L'Acadie, 1671," 3. Bona Arsenault states that Anne Ouestuorouest was Abenaki. Bona Arsenault, *Histoire et généalogie des Acadiens,* vol. 2 (Montreal: Leméac, 1978), 673.

38. Parish registers clearly indicate the ethnic origin of each individual. Thus, the Mi'kmaq appear as "sauvage de ..." followed by their usual place of residence.

39. AC, c112A 35:110r–111r, 121v, 122r, Bégon au ministre, 25 octobre 1715; British Museum, Add. Mss. 19071, Paul Mascarene to secretary of war, 2 July 1744, 48r; and PANS, RG 1, 25: doc. 28, Mascarene to Richard Collins, 9 August 1746.

40. On Abenaki dislocation, see David Lyn Ghere, "Abenaki Factionalism, Emigration and Social Continuity: Indian Society in Northern New England, 1725 to 1765" (Ph D dissertation, University of Maine, 1988), 158–234.

41. PRO, CO 217 2:194r, John Doucett to Board of Trade, 10 February 1718.

42. "Indian Explanation of the Treaty of Casco Bay, 1727," in *Dawnland Encounters: Indians and Europeans in Northern New England,* ed. Colin G. Calloway (Hanover and London: University Press of New England, 1991), 115–18; and William C. Wicken, "The Mi'kmaq and Wuastukwiuk Treaties," *University of New Brunswick Law Journal* 43 (1994) 242-53.

43. AC, c11A 35:120v, Bégon au ministre, 25 octobre 1715.

44. MacMechan, ed., *Original Minutes,* 58.

45. AC, c11B 15:3v, Conseil de la Marine, Saint-Ovide au ministre, 1 décembre 1734·

46. MacMechan, ed., *Original Minutes,* 31.

47. MSA, 63:416, "Declaration of Joseph Marjory," 18 Decembre 1724.

48. AC, c11D 9:65r Felix Pain, "Extrait des nouvelles de l'acadie," [1724].

49. AC, c11D 9:65, "Extraits des nouvelles de l'Acadie raportée par le père félix missionaire Récollets de l'acadie," [1724]; and *The Journal of Captain William Pote, Jr. During his Captivity in the French and Indian War from May, 1745, to August, 1747* (New York: Dodd, Mead and Company, 1896), 49.

50. MacMechan, ed., *Original Minutes,* 71.

51. AC, c11A 35:110–111, 121v, 122, Bégon au ministre, 25 octobre 1715.

52. Jaenen, *Friend and Foe,* 194.

THE FOURTEENTH COLONY

Nova Scotia and the American Revolution

Daniel Samson
Brock University

THE FOURTEENTH COLONY: NOVA SCOTIA AND THE AMERICAN REVOLUTION

● **Introduction by Daniel Samson**

▲ **Primary Sources**   **page 143**

■ **Secondary Sources**   **page 154**

● INTRODUCTION

Daniel Samson

The American Revolution made Canada. We don't often acknowledge this point (surely we made ourselves!), but prior to 1783 "we" were the British-conquered and -occupied former French colonies of Acadia and Canada. After the revolution, these colonies of conquest became the remnant of British North America and eventually Canada. A century of heavily mythologized, Loyalist ideals would influence how we understood that history. In Loyalist eyes—and hence in our eyes too—that tale would come to have a certain natural inevitability about it. "They" were bad radicals, bent on the destruction of British liberties; "we" were good Tories, determined to preserve all that was valuable in what was then the world's greatest empire. Americans, too, saw their struggle through their own eyes: the product of slow grinding pressure exerted by an increasing oppressive colonial state on 13 fiercely independent colonies.

But of course there weren't 13 colonies; there were 15. The 13 old British settler colonies, and the two recently conquered French colonies. One of these, Canada, had a population of 30,000 French-speaking, Roman Catholics. While some of the American Revolutionaries saw these occupied peasants as natural allies—surely they must hate the British as much as we do!—decades of warfare between New England and New France meant there was little trust or goodwill. Even the idealists in the revolutionary camp knew that there would be little enthusiasm for yet another war. Indeed, why would the *les canadiennes* trust the same Yankees who less than 15 years earlier had cried for the removal of the popish threat to Protestant security?

The other colony, however, was different. It, too, was an occupied French colony, but one in which the majority French population—*les acadiennes*—had been forcibly removed 20 years earlier. In the meantime, Britain had begun to resettle the area with a mixture of New Englanders and "foreign protestants" (mostly Swiss and German). By 1775, on the eve of the revolution, Nova Scotia had a population of more than 10,000, two-thirds of whom came from the very heartland of revolutionary New England. The lives of these transplanted New Englanders were quite different from the lives of those who remained behind; life in a young colony—building farms, establishing communities—brought with it very different concerns. Yet many of the former New Englanders (or, as historian J. B. Brebner referred to them, the "Nova Scotia Yankees") also had concerns about the direction of colonial policy, particularly how British officials in Halifax seemed determined to deny them the local township-style government they had had in New England. While cultural distrust may have held back *les canadiennes*, Nova Scotia was in many ways an extension of New England, populated by the same peoples and sharing many of the same concerns. In places like Maugerville [near modern-day Fredericton, New Brunswick], and Cumberland [near modern-day Amherst, Nova Scotia], they rallied to the defence of liberty and property. Compelled to navigate aboriginal, British, and community pressures, historian Ernest Clarke shows us how some Nova Scotians attempted to forge a revolutionary course.

Most, however, did not. Thus, a number of historians have sought to answer a simple question: Why did the Nova Scotia Yankees not join the revolution? Why did so few raise muskets to their shoulders in defence of liberty? John Bartlett Brebner's classic account from the 1930s argues that the Nova Scotia Yankees either attempted to pursue a deliberate policy of neutrality—as had the Acadians before them—or were simply apathetic. Turning their attention to the religious and cultural world of the settlers themselves, George Rawlyk

141

and Gordon Stewart offer a more positive sense that the settlers were consumed not by a revolutionary political ideology but by a New England–style evangelical revival. But what made the Nova Scotians' responses so different? Did they not believe in democracy? In liberty? Were they monarchists? Cowards? Were they wary of the powerful presence of the British military—especially the commanding presence of the Royal Navy, much of it parked in Halifax harbour—and its capacity to enforce calm? Or were the "Planters," as the settlers called themselves, just as wary of the still-threatening presence of the Mi'kmaq? John Reid reminds us that although the Aboriginal peoples of Nova Scotia were no longer the major threat they had been during their alliance with the French, they retained the capacity to raid villages, harass shipping, and generally wreak havoc in the lives of settlers remote from the protection of British troops. Finally, Elizabeth Mancke draws our attention to the structures of local government. Her fascinating comparison of Liverpool (Nova Scotia) and Machias (Maine), both settlements established by Massachusetts interests in the 1760s, forged very different paths when Revolution broke out in 1776. Whether the Nova Scotia Yankees were reaching an accord with their Aboriginal fellows or with their God, or simply trying to stay out of the fray, historians offer us several ways to understand this decisive turning point in Canadian history.

If Nova Scotia did not join the revolution, most of its people were nonetheless affected by it. Jutting out into the Atlantic, the southern part of the peninsula was far closer to Boston than it was to Quebec or London. Its settlements were still young, poorly developed, and interspersed with Mi'kmaq bands. And, in an age before databases and electronic passports, spies moved easily in and out of communities. Our documents offer some insight into the different interests of various peoples in Nova Scotia. Loyalists, such as the Liverpool, N.S. merchant Simeon Perkins, lived in a time of great uncertainty and a place where public politics faced the practical issues of economic survival. Aboriginal peoples, some with historical enmities to the British in New England, suddenly had to take sides in a fratricidal war. Others, such as the Yankee settlers in Maugerville, fully aligned themselves with the rebellion, declaring their willingness to die for liberty and property.

QUESTIONS

1. Do you think revolution was viable in Nova Scotia?
2. What prompted the Nova Scotia rebels to join the revolution? What factors determined their actions? Their inaction?
3. Compare the explanations of the historians. How do they arrive at such different views?
4. What was the role of the Mi'kmaq? Do the documents allow us to see their role? How did the other players assess the Mi'kmaq role?

FURTHER READINGS

J. M. Bumsted, "1763–1783: Resettlement and Rebellion," *The Atlantic Region to Confederation: A History*, eds. P. A. Buckner and John G. Reid (Toronto: University of Toronto Press, 1994), pp. 156–83.

Elizabeth Mancke, "The American Revolution in Canada," Jack P. Greene and J. R. Pole, eds. *A Companion to the American Revolution* (Malden, MA: Blackwell, 2004), pp. 503–510.

Hilda Neatby, *Quebec, 1760–1791* (Toronto: McClelland & Stewart, 1966).

George Rawlyk, *Nova Scotia's Massachusetts: A Study of Massachusetts–Nova Scotia Relations, 1630–1784* (Kingston and Montreal: McGill-Queen's University Press, 1973).

▲ Document 1: Nova Scotia Petition

Robert Hanson Harrison to George Washington

To the President of Congress

Cambridge, March 27, 1776.

I beg leave to transmit you the Copy of a Petition from the Inhabitants of Nova Scotia, brought me by Jonathan Eddy Esquire mentioned therein, who is now here with an Accadian. From this it appears, they are in a distressed situation, and from Mr. Eddy's account, are exceedingly apprehensive that they will be reduced to the disagreeable alternative of taking up Arms and Joining our Enemies, or to flee their Country, unless they can be protected against their Insults and Oppressions—he says that their Committees think many salutary and valuable consequences would be derived from five or 600 Men being sent there, as it would not only quiet the Minds of the People from the anxiety and uneasiness they are now filled with and enable them to take a part in behalf of the Colonies, but be the means of preventing the Indians (of which there are a good many) from taking the side of Government, and the Ministerial Troops from getting such Supplies of Provisions from thence as they have done.

How far these good purposes would be answered, if such a force were sent, as they ask for, is impossible to determine, in the present uncertain State of things.

For if the Army from Boston is going to Halifax, as reported by them before their departure, that or a much more considerable force would be of no avail. If not and they possess the friendly disposition to our Cause, suggested in the Petition and declared by Mr. Eddy; It might be of great service, unless another body of Troops should be sent there by Administration too powerful for them to oppose. It being a matter of some Importance, I Judged It prudent to lay it before Congress, for their consideration, and requesting their directions upon the Subject, shall only If they determine to adopt it desire that they will prescribe the Number to be sent and Whether It is to be from the Regiments which will be left here I shall wait their decision and whatever it is, will endeavour to have it carried into execution. I have the Honor etc.[1]

Source: "To the President of Congress" (Robert Hanson Harrison to Washington, Cambridge, MA, March 27, 1776), in John C. Fitzpatrick, ed., *The Writings of George Washington*, from the original manuscript source, 1745–1799. Vol. 4 October 1775–April 1776 (Washington, DC: U.S. Government Printing Office, 1931–33), pp. 434–5, 436–8.

[1]In the writing of Robert Hanson Harrison.

▲Document 2: Anonymous Letter to the *Nova Scotia Gazette,* 1776

The Demagogues, which raised this disturbance, are a motely [sic] crew of hungry lawyers, men of broken fortunes, young persons eager to push themselves in the world, others, gentlemen of opulence, vain & blustering—Amongst this medley there are several of good party, and great reading, with withal little versed in the complicated interests, and springs, which move the great political world, because untutored in the Courts of Europe, where alone that science is required—These could not preceiving the growing importance, as they call it, of Amercia, and what she might one day arrive to; so far indeed they judged with propriety, if they could only give time, and leave her to herself; but the greatness of the object dazzled the eyes of their undersanding; and they began to think Empire, without considering the infant state of their country, how much of it is in want of every requisite for war, what a might nation they have to contend with, & that the untied interest of every other nation in Europe likewise forbids their being anything more than dependent colonies—However, as if envying their prosperity, they hastened to bring on the great and glorious day, which would hail them masters of a quarter of the globe; and set up claims which, they thought, would either place them in that eveated station or in one more suitable to their present condition viz. To make the Mother Country drudge and slave to support, and protect them, for yet a while longer, without contributing a farther towards that expence that they should think proper; afterwards how soon they could no longer bear the thoughts of dependence, and that they should emancipate themselves (which indeed this mode would soon enable them to do) to dispute the expediency of the purposes for which their aids were to be applied, offer only a trifling sum, taking that opportunity of declaring their independence and maintain it too.

The menaces of the Americans to run to arms, their violent proceedings in the first stage of the insurrection, they levying troops, which every where belongs to the executive branch, so notoriously [...] their collecting warlike weapons [...] were all such strong acts of rebellion as no government could put up with it, it destroyed the merits of their cause, were it otherwise good: for resisting legal authority in that manner, however warrantable when oppression is intolerable, is yet a nice affair, and can only be justified when tyranny is well ascertained, generally felt, and after the milder methods of redress have been effectually tried; which the impartial world is satisfied was by no means the case [...]

Had they acted in a moderate, dutiful, and justifiable manner, like subjects averse to break with their Sovereign, like men, who even in their own cause wished only for material justice, and not actuated by any indirect views but by the force of principles, they protested; there is no doubt but whatever appeared to them harsh and dangerous, in the claims of Great Britain, would have departed from, and matters settled on the basis of indulgence to the Colonies, and justice to the Mother Country. But His Majesty's Paternal voice was bar'd access to his beloved subject; He could not treat with them, but thro' the false and villainous medium of the proud demagogues, who paid no regard to the truth, to loyalty, to peace or justice

Source: *Nova Scotia Gazetter* and the *Weekly Chronicle* (Halifax) 10 September, 1776.

▲ Document 3: Resolutions of the Inhabitants of Maugerville, May 1776

F. Kidder, ed.

1st. *Resolved*, That we can see no shadow of justice in that extensive claim of the *British* Parliament, viz: the right of making laws binding on the Colonies in all cases whatsoever. This system, if once established, we conceive, hath a direct tendency to sap the foundation not only of liberty, that dearest of names, but of property, that best of subjects.

2dly. *Resolved*, That as tyranny ought to be resisted in its first appearances, we are convinced that the United Provinces are just in their proceedings in this regard.

3dly. *Resolved*, That it is our minds and desire to submit ourselves to the Government of the *Massachusetts Bay*, and that we are ready, with our lives and fortunes, to share with them the event of our present struggle for liberty, however *God* in his Providence may order it.

4thly. *Resolved*, That a Committee be chosen, to consist of twelve men, who shall immediately make application to the *Massachusetts* Congress or General Assembly for relief; and that said Committee, or the major part of them, shall conduct all matters, civil or military, in this County, till further regulation be made.

5thly. *Resolved*, That we, and each of us, will most strictly adhere to all such measures as our said Committee, or the major part of them, from time to time prescribe for our conduct; and that we will support and defend them in this matter at the expense of our lives and fortunes, if called thereto.

6thly. *Resolved*, That we will immediately put ourselves in the best posture of defence in our power. That to this end, we will prevent all unnecessary use of Gunpowder, or other Ammunition in our custody.

7thly. *Resolved*, That if any of us shall hereafter know of any person or persons that shall, by any ways or means, endeavour to prevent or counteract this our design, we will immediately give notice thereof to the Committee, that proper measures may be taken for our safety.

8thly. *Resolved*, That we, and each of us, will pay our proportion of all such sums of money as may be necessary for carrying these matters into execution; and finally, that we will share in, and submit to, the event of this undertaking, however it may terminate, to the true performance of all which we bind and obligate ourselves firmly each to the other, on penalty of being esteemed enemies and traitors to our country, and submitting ourselves to popular resentment.

145

Source: "Resolutions of the Inhabitants of Maugerville (May 1776)" in F. Kidder, ed., *Military Operations in Eastern Maine and Nova Scotia During the Revolution* (Albany, NY: J. Munsell, 1867), pp. 54–55.

▲ Document 4: The Mi'kmaq Decline America's Invitation to Join the Revolution

Coquen, 19 September 1776

Friends Brothers & Countrymen

In the spring of the Year we received with Joy and Gladness, a very kind Letter from our Friend & Brother His Ex'y George Washington.

What he said therein gave us great satisfaction and Determinded we were to Continue in that Friendship, with the same faith as he professed towards us and to Keep the chain bright as Ever.

A few days ago an alarm was spread among us that another paper was to come, to require us to take up the hatchet.

We met thereupon, and found that some of our Young men had been with you in the Character of Chiefs and made a Treaty to go to war, Contrary to our Desire, and as we understand from them not being rightly understood.

Our situation and Circumstances being such at present, Our naturaal inclination being Peace, only accustomed to hunt for the subsistence of our family, We could not Comply with the Terms – Our numbers being not sufficient among other objections. And as it was not done by our authority & Consent of the Difft Tribes we are necessitated to return it.

Still depending upon the promise of our Brother Washington, and relying upon the friendship of all our Brothers & friends your way we hope & trust no offence in sending it back.

And protesting at the same time that the Chain of Friendship is still subsisting between us on our side & that we hope for ever—A further Account of our situation will in our Name be Delivered our brothers & Countrymen by John Allan Esq Bearer of this—Our love and friendship be with you all

We are
Your Friends & Brothers

Joseph Sapsarough Chief of Miramichi
Jean Baptist Alymph Chief of Rechiboutou [Richibucto]
Augustin Michel of Rechiboutou
Thomas Athanage Chief of Chediac and Cocaga [Shediac and Cocaigne]
Jerome Athanage of Chediac
Baptist Arguimon Chief of Chiguenictou [Chignecto]
Charles Aleria of Cape Sable

Source: American Intelligence, Nova Scotia Events, John Allen, September 1780, George Washington Papers at the Library of Congress, 1741–1799: Series 4. General Correspondence, 1697–1799. Washington, United States Government, Government Printing Office.

▲ Document 5: Detail of Southwestern Nova Scotia

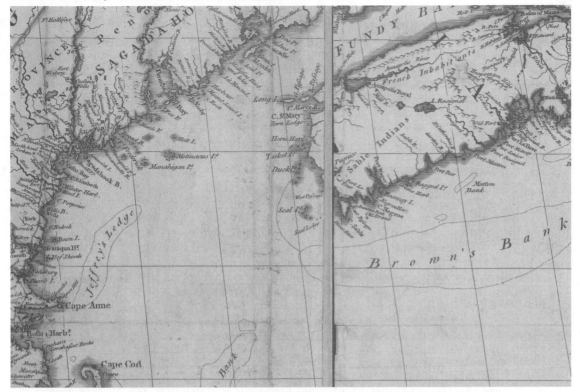

● **A little bit of geography goes a long way. How does this map help us to understand Nova Scotia's place in the revolution? Does it allow us to see features a modern map might not?**

Source: John Mitchell, *A Map of the British and French Dominions* (London: Jefferys and Faden, 1755 [1757 edition]).

▲ Document 6: The Diary of Simeon Perkins, 1776

Perkins, like most of the early settlers of Liverpool, was born in New England. He arrived in Nova Scotia in 1762 just after the expulsion of the Acadians and the end of the Seven Years War. As both a merchant whose business interests lay in New England and a member of the provincial government, Perkins found that the revolution sometimes pitted his political loyalties against his economic interests—and indeed sometimes his fiercely independent (but not revolutionary) town against the equally fierce loyalty of the capital. How does Perkins allow us to see the forces of revolutionary politics at work in his town? How did he (and his fellow townspeople) navigate the different interests that emerged?

The location of Liverpool is not on the Mitchell map (Document 5), but it's in the same harbour the French called Port Rossignol.

Wednesday, Oct. 12th,—Mrs. Lewin is very sick. Herman Kenney, Esq., arrives from Barrington, and brought £17.2. 14 worth of fish and other articles. Amounting to £10. 15. ll. collected from the county rates for the gaol. He says that Jonathan Pinkham, Esq.,[1] and a number of families moved from Barrington to Kennecbunk.

Thursday, Oct. 13th,—Benjamin Harrington and John McKay got into Pudding Pan [East Berlin], with boat damaged. William Cheever is married to Rebecca Holmes.

[...]

Sunday, Oct. 16th,—Capt. Martin sails for Salem. Capt. Dean ships one, a Capt. Sterling, and two seamen out of our fishermen.

Tuesday, Oct. 18th,—The wife of John Lewin dies towards morning. I go partridge hunting in the afternoon with Nichols, Capt. Christopher, and Capt. Snow. No success. At evening we meet the candidates for militia officers, to see if they will accept commissions, on the terms of paying for them a certain fee to the Secretary's officer. The majority of them refused.

[...]

Thursday, Oct. 20th,—I, with Capt. William Dean, and Capt. Christopher talk of chartering the schr. Peggy, to load pickled fish for New York. Codfish are plentiful, so that the boats load at Moose Harbour.

[...]

Saturday, Oct. 29th,—Capt. Banajah Collins arrives from Connecticut.

Source: Harold A. Innis, ed., *The Diary of Simeon Perkins*, Vol. 1: *1766–1780* with an introduction and notes by Harold A. Innis (Toronto: Champlain Society, 1948), pp. 84–5, 93–99 [October–November 1775 and June–August 1776], pp. 84–85, 93–99.

Sunday, Oct. 30th,—Cold and windy. A brigt from Gibraltar, Capt. Grady or Grandy, of Marblehead, arrives, a 60 days passage. Reports the war between the Russians and Turks on again, that France and Spain are about to assist the Turks. Nathaniel Godfrey is here from Boston. He brings last Monday's papers containing news from the Grand American Congress. One Capt. Hatch is here from the Magdalene Islands. He belongs to Cape Cod. Tuesday, Nov. 1st,—Capt. Joseph Freeman sails in the schr. Polly for barrels, bread, etc.

Wednesday, Nov. 2d,—Working on the highways. A vessel from Halifax brings news that the Assembly made an Act to lay a duty on molasses, and sugar, from the Colonies, and to allow West India rum to be imported duty free.[2]
[...]
Thursday, March 16th,—Windy. Sit again upon the Cheever and Godfrey case, and get award ready at 3 p.m. I have a bad headache all this morning and this afternoon. This morning Capt. Elisha Hopkins arrives from Hampton, in Virginia, with corn. I have a letter from Capt. Dean who says that the Virginians on the Straight adhere to the resolutions of the Congress, and he had difficulty in getting liberty to trade.

Monday, March 20th,—I go on board the schr. Liberty, Capt. Benajah Collins, for Salem. I give my powers and orders to Stevenson. Blowing hard. Wind S.E., and put back. Sail the next day, and arrive at Marblehead, Friday, March 24th, in good health. Kept minutes in my pocket book until my arrival at Liverpool again, on May 28th, at 10 p.m.
[...]
Friday, June 2d,—Brig. Liberty, Capt. Cole, sails for Maryland. Capt. David Smith, and Capt. Joseph Barss sail for Halifax. Schr. Lucy, Capt. Harriss, sails. Capt. David Bray, of Boston, from Quebec, goes with him. He left his vessel, a snow, here, the crew refusing to go because of the press at New England.

Saturday, June 3d,—a schr. Capt. Shirtliff, from Plymouth, with Mr. White, a merchant on board, and also owner, arrives, bound to Halifax to register his vessel.

Monday, June 5th,—A ship arrives from Sheepscot, Capt. Christopher Williamson, of White-haven, loaded with salt from Lisbon, some cordage, iron anchors, and sail cloth. He wants a load of square timber. He was [?] liberty to unload at Sheepscot, for which reason his merchant there came on board, with his wife and family, and are now here. His name is Abiel Wood, from Middleborough.
[...]
Saturday, June 10th,—Ship Christian is now in the river. I take out salt from my brig, and put it in the store. A topsail schr. arrives from Falmouth, England, one Boden, master. The vessel is owned by Capt. Foster, of Marblehead, who was lately in this Province. He says the City of London is about to petition the King in behalf of America.

Sunday, June 11th,—Capt. Williamson, and Capt. Martin dine with me. A sloop from Sheep-scot River, Capt. Hall arrives. He speaks of an action on one of the islands near Boston. 200 Regulars killed and a few of the Provincialists wounded.[3] They took a number of horses and cattle. To-night a fight among the seamen of several vessels here. With the assistance of others I made peace.

Wednesday, June 14th,—Busy hauling oak timber. An extra Sessions of the Peace for appointing Tavern Keepers.

[...]

Tuesday, June 20th,—this day begin to unload [?] the ship Christian, Capt. Christopher Williamson, White Haven, with oak and pine timber, for Glasgow. Begin to-day the foundation for the Meeting House.

Thursday, June 22d,—Capt. Jabez Cobb arrives from Machias and reports a disturbance. The inhabitants took one of the King's ships,[4] killed the captain, and one Robert Avery, of Norwich, being forced to stand the deck, on board of her, was killed by a ball in the head. [...]

Tuesday, June 27th,—Capt. White, Plymouth, arrives from Boston with an officer and sergeant on board. he brings news of an engagement between the King's troops and the Provincialists at Bunker Hill, Charlestown, and that Charlestown is burnt to ashes. The action commenced in the Provincials intrenchments by fire of the "Somerset" man of war, and then landed 1800 troops, under the guns, and with a reenforcement of 900 men, attacked the trenches, driving out the Provincials, who retreated one mile, and then retrenched. Brigadier Putnam was wounded in the heel by the rebound of a cannon ball. The Provincials lost in killed, 300, the King's troops, 140.[5]

Wednesday, June 28th,—Capt. Martin's schr. arrives from Nfld., bringing Capt. John Cobb and his crew, he having sold his vessel. I interviewed Capt. White, and an officer who is called Capt. McDonald. He tells me the engagement was on Saturday the 17th. That 360 Provincials were buried on Monday, and 38 afterwards. That Doctor Warren is among the dead. That Brigadier Putnam had his leg broken, his servant captured, made prisoner, and now dead. General Gage issued a proclamation dated June 15th,[6] offering His Majesty's pardon to those who lay down their arms, except Samuel Adams and John Hancock.

Saturday, July 1st,—Lay the sills of the Meeting House. Three carpenters arrive from Boston, working about a place for fish.

Monday, July 3d,—An election during the afternoon for a member of Assembly for the town. Thomas Cochran was chosen.[7] He gets 28 votes. Ephraim Dean gets 22 votes.

Tuesday, July 4th,—Pleasant day. We raise the Meeting House, 50 ft. long, 42 ft. wide. Finish the whole in one day. No accidents. Capt. Thomas Davis arrived from Plymouth Sunday night, bringing Capt. David Bray, Capt. William Freeman, Jabez Gorham, Joseph Trible, and wife, and Catherine Doggett. They bring news of the late battle between the King's troops and Provincials. The reports of numbers killed differ essentially. [...]

Monday, July 10th,—The master appears and wants the prosecution stopped. Hunter is discharged, he paying the costs, 10/6 and 2/ fine for swearing. The Justices and Magistrates meet to consult about the time and manner of swearing the people that may come from different parts of America, agreeable to the Governor's proclamation we appoint July 29th, at nine a.m.[8] [...]

Thursday, July 13th,—Moved my barn from Birch Point, to set it near my dwelling house. Settle the schr. Betsey's accounts, and conclude to load out Capt. William Dean's schr. for the West Indies. Ephraim Dean, Robert Stevenson, Nathaniel Freeman, John Cobb, and me have 1/5 each, with £500 cargo.

150

Friday, July 14th,—Raise my barn and sow turnips. Have a letter from the Secretary to the Justices, with a Proclamation requiring us to take special care that there be no opposition to the Government.[9]

[...]

Wednesday, July 19th,—The Proprietors meeting and day appointed for administering the oath of allegiance, abjuration, and supremacy, which was done to thirteen persons lately arrived from New England, in persuance of orders from His Excellency, the Governor.

Thursday, July 20th,—Fill up the ground before the Meeting House. A number of the Proprietors last evening, of the new Meeting House,[10] conclude to have a belfry and steeple, upon the top of the House.

Wednesday, July 26th,—I conclude the writing of the sloop Betsey. A topsail schr. from Halifax, Capt. Moore and lady, come to take passage by Capt. Williamson to Great Britain. News comes that we have been represented to the Government as a lawless and rebellious people, and the plan is laid to annex this town to Lunenburg, and to remove the Courts to Yarmouth.

Thursday, July 27th,—Bartlett Bradford is married to the widow Hannah Dean.
Friday, July 28th,—Ship Christian, Capt. Christopher Williamson, sails for Glasgow. The sloop Betsey, with Abiel Wood and wife, sail for Pownalborough.

Sunday, July 30th,—Pleasant day. Full meeting. The Governor's proclamation,[11] forbidding all intercourse with New England rebels, was read.

Monday, July 31st,—An auction of some lands at Herring Cove, I took by execution from Nathan Nickerson. I bid them off for Joseph Verge, at 15.10. The remainder of the pews in the Meeting House are sold, also some land belonging to the estates of Bruce Stuart and Ward Tupper. I bought a 30 acre lot, Letter A, No. 8. for £4.5. John Thomas from Plymouth brings newspapers.

[...]

Friday, Aug. 25th,—Capt. Bradford comes in three weeks from fishing. About 200 qtls. Capt. Ford from Newfoundland, with 215 bbls salmon. A sloop arrives from Nantucket with 130 bushels of corn, and onions. One of the Jebaco boats [small, two-man fishing boats] that makes fish here, arrived, the other, was taken by one of the King's vessels. I agree for 40 bushels of corn.

Saturday, Aug. 26th,—I can only raise cash to pay for 32 bushels of corn, from Capt. Buddington. The people who bid pews in the Meeting House are not making punctual payments.

Sunday, Aug. 27th,—The Jebaco boat was released and arrives with one man less, who was detained by the King's vessel, Abraham Caldwell, by name.

Wednesday, Aug. 30th,—Foggy and rainy since Sunday. Two schooners came into the harbor firing, which alarmed the people. One was from Jamaica with sugar, and molasses, the other from Salem, consigned to William Pitts. Thomas Prince [?] boat arrives from fishing. Hine comes in her. He went to Halifax to enter and register the schr. Lynn, in a Malagash boat, and was cast-a-way at Prospect.

NOTES

1. His property was confiscated as a result of the revolution. See Crowell, *A history of Barrington Township and vicinity*, p. 546.
2. See H. A. Innis, *The Cod Fisheries* (New Haven, 1940), p. 207. See a study of early provincial taxation (*Bulletin of the Public Archives of Nova Scotia*, 1937).
3. The fight on Noddle's Island,—apparently only two regulars were killed. See Allen French, *The first year of the American Revolution* (Boston 1934), pp. 190 f4.
4. The *Margaretta*,—the difficulties began on June 22. "The first sea fight of the American Revolution." See *ibid.*, pp. 360–1.
5. French estimates 140 provincials killed and 226 of the King's troops.
6. June 12.
7. See Brebner, *The neutral Yankees*, pp. 271–2.
8. A proclamation of June 22 direct it that state oaths be sworn before magistrates following an order-in-council of May 6. See Beamish Murdoch, *A History of Nova Scotia or Acadia* (Halifax, 1866), 14, p. 546.
9. Proclamation of July 5, *Ibid.*, vol. ii, p. 548.
10. This became known as "old Zion."
11. July 5.

▲ Document 7: A Spy's Map of Defences at Halifax, September 25, 1780

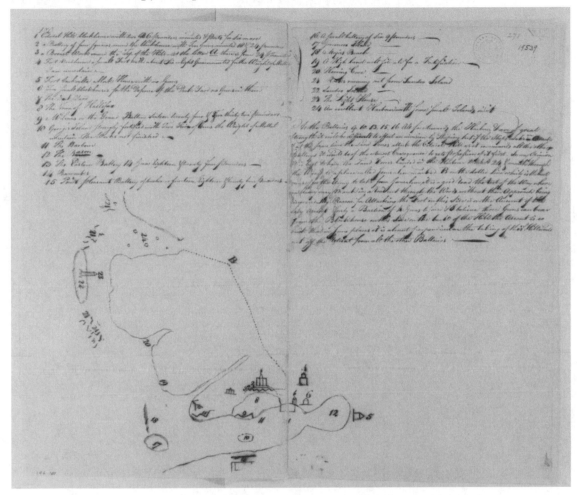

● **What might this map have told the revolutionary army? What might this map tell us?**

Source: American Intelligence, 25 September 1780, "Sketch of Halifax, Nova Scotia, with notes," George Washington Papers, Library of Congress, 1741–99: Series 4. General Correspondence. Image 637, Library of Congress, Manuscript Division.

◼ Article 1: The Siege of Fort Cumberland

Ernest Clarke

July 1776. A political watershed for thirteen of Britain's North American colonies was reached during the first week of July 1776.[1] For Britain's colony around the Bay of Fundy a turning point of sorts was also in the works. A new regime of a distinctly loyalist hue was inaugurated in Cumberland on Monday 1 July, with due commissioning of two Yorkshire settlers, William Black Sr and Christopher Harper, as justices of the peace.[2] It was hoped in Halifax that these appointments in conjunction with the new garrison would strengthen the government's administrative grip beyond the capital, improve law and order, pacify the people, and restore the "precarious" real estate market.[3] Civic calm and political stability were the qualities esteemed by the Nova Scotia government, not the political radicalism of the Continental Congress. While the remarkable event of independence occurred in America, Black and Harper began to help Goreham restore order to Cumberland, It became clear that the garrison, no matter how slovenly clothed and desertion-prone, impressed "luke warm" loyalists, a point conceded by John Allan who found the people no longer interested in political argument. The population was determined to remain quiet "on any terms." If the new regime had a calming effect on the general populace, it appeared to sanction a backlash against patriots. "The Friends to America became new objects of Vengeance,"[4] explained Allan, himself being one such object.

The Declaration of Independence was announced in Philadelphia on Thursday 4 July. This unilateral action by the united colonies cut final ties with England and excluded Nova Scotia. While political dissent was triumphant in America, it was cause for persecution in Nova Scotia. Seen through patriot eyes, Nova Scotia had a military government and an arbitrary one at that. Magistrates came in for scurrilous criticism. To Josiah Throop they were "chiefly old broken subalterns, sergeants or drum[mer]s used to condemning, Kicking, caning and flogging, and never easy!" The enthusiasm with which the recent appointees tackled their jobs led some to suppose that Arbuthnot "gave unlimited discretionary Commissions" to his magistrates. Black, Harper, and other appointees were seen as tools of the government sent among the people to spy on them. There were instances, it was said, of settlers being arrested "by these Creatures" on suspicion alone, "never examined," and confined at the fort "to be abused and insulted by the Soldiers." They were arrested simply for "being Suspected to be friendly to the United States." By the "Arbitrary Order" of a magistrate one settler was sent on board a warship in Cumberland Basin; others were put in gaol in irons at the magistrate's pleasure, "without even the Ceremony of an Accusation!" Asked Throop rhetorically: "did the States Ever Serve Torys so?"[5]

Of course "Torys" in the new United States suffered more than "Rebels" in Nova Scotia; it was in America that the civil war raged and the military crisis mounted even as independence was declared. Considering the emergency and acting on a plan proposed by George Washington on 4 July, Congress agreed to incite the Native nations against Nova Scotia. The decision was taken for tactical reasons and Washington could not have been aware of the plan John Allan had recently sent to Massachusetts, a plan that also proposed to employ Native people. "At a crisis like the present," rationalized Washington, when Britain was waging war "with unexampled severity" and in the course of which "have excited Slaves and Savages to Arms against us," he felt that Americans were "impelled by Necessity [...] to call to our Aid so many of the St. Johns [Maliseet], Nova Scotia [Micmac] and Penobscot Indians as I might judge necessary." From the information he had, the prospect for recruiting a regiment of Nora Scotia Natives seemed bright; "it ought to be done," urged George Washington on that first Independence Day.[6]

Washington's scheme was to raise a regiment of Native people from the Penobscot, Passamaquoddy, Maliseet, and Micmac nations to serve "for two or three years," be provisioned by Congress, and put on continental army pay although, added the parsimonious general, "Having professed a strong Inclination to take part with us [...] It is probable they may be engaged for less pay." The Native regiment would be of "infinite service in annoying and harassing" the enemy, thought Washington. It was widely presumed that they favoured America and Washington likely

Source: Ernest Clark, *The Siege of Fort Cumberland*, pp. 56–66, McGill-Queen's University Press 1995. Reprinted with permission.

read the newspapers which had reported recently that the Maliseets were "highly incensed against the ministerial party and are determined at all Hazards to join the Americans." He foresaw full recruitment. "I have been told [...] perhaps five or six hundred or more," would join up he informed Congress and Massachusetts, the state to which Congress deferred "in this business," and asked to negotiate the international treaty that would set the eastern Native nations on the warpath.[7] Washington was not alone in supposing that the Native peoples could be bought cheaply. Nova Scotians also assumed that Native allegiance was an easy bargain. John Cort, the Miramichi merchant, expressed the general view when he said of the Native people that "with a few trifling presents and fair words, they might be made very serviceable subjects."[8] Chronic indifference to Native rights and studious neglect of their needs were interrupted by the revolution and in the summer of 1776 both sides courted the Native peoples with words that were as frivolous as their presents were trifling.

Less than a week after declaring itself independent the United States hosted an international conference and authorized the signing of one of its first treaties. Negotiations with the Micmac and Maliseet nations were held in the Watertown meeting house by the Massachusetts State Council at the request of Washington and with the approval of Congress. Having been conveyed from Machias to Salem in Francis Shaw's sloop, the ten Native delegates "rode hither in Carriages" to Boston and were already there when Washington's final instructions arrived.[9] It was cloudy on 10 July but the mood was festive because news of the Independence Declaration had just reached town. At one o'clock a crowd gathered on the Town House steps to hear the Declaration read and "an Huzza ensued." Toasts were given by President James Bowdoin in the Council Chamber where wine, crackers, and cheese were "set for all the Company."[10] After the ceremony, Bowdoin chaired the preliminary meeting with the ten delegates in the Council Chamber, while outside in the street the celebration continued with a raging bonfire fuelled by the king's arms from Faneuil Hall, the crown and mitre from King's Chapel, and any other combustible royal symbols that could be found. The royal coat of arms was nowhere to be seen as Edward Winslow had rescued it in March.[11] The meeting adjourned after formal introductions and more toasts were made

before the Native delegates retired for "refreshments" with Francis Shaw who had "ordered good Lodgings and entertainment" for his international guests.[12]

The delegation had not come to Boston to sign a treaty and lacked the authority to do so. The most senior of the ten was Ambroise St Aubin of Aukpaque on the St John River, a secondary chief of the Maliseets. The Micmacs of Cocagne were represented only by two "Young men," John Baptiste and Matua, in New England to seek supplies and bring good wishes to Washington.[13] But the Americans were not dissuaded by St Aubin's admission that "it's not in our power to answer now for the whole of our Tribes," and formal negotiations began two days later at Watertown. The State Board and House of Representatives sat in joint session across the table from St Aubin's delegation. French was the official language of the sessions.

Native demands were simply stated: "We want a truckhouse and a Priest." The priest had to be French because "we shall not hear any prayers that come from England." As for trade, they expected "proper Goods for our Furs and Skins and we want them up the St. John River." The Americans were not sure they could find a French priest and could hardly operate a trading post in Nova Scotia. Machias would have to do for the time being and they could only pay "for your skins and furs the same price they will fetch in Boston." The Americans pursued Washington's request to make military allies of the Native peoples. "It was strongly urged upon them to join with us in the war." The sessions lasted a week. Hospitality was lavish and Congress paid the bill. Eventually, St Aubin agreed Native people would "join in the War on your side. You may depend upon it [...] We will not break our Words. We will not Lie!" He was also heard to say: "we will engage in the War [...] We love Boston!"[14]

"Would your Warriors form a Body in conjunction with a number of our people?" asked the Americans, getting down to specifics. "Yes," was St Aubin's reply. In an effort to strenghten the commitment the chief was asked in a later session if "you are hearty to enter into the War with us?" He replied, "yes we are" and he shook hands with Bowdoin. It was only after tallying the numbers of those capable of bearing arms in the widely scattered Native villages that it became evident only a fraction of the force envisaged by Washington might be available and only at a fraction of the speed. St Aubin admitted "it is not in our power to tell how many Men we can raise; we will git as many as we can."[15] Even using Bowdoin's generous estímate, the Native nations "could furnish about 120 men" only, and they "could not engage to come till next Spring." Under pressure St Aubin "promised to return early in the Fall with about 30 of their Tribe" and four delegates actually offered to go at once to join Washington. By any measure, these results fell far short of Washington's request "to engage [...] five or Six hundred Men [...] and have them marched with all possible expedition to join the Army here." The Americans were just as equivocal in meeting Native demands. When pressed on the trade issue, for example, they responded in generalities, promising to supply the Penobscot truckmaster with "a further Quantity" of goods to meet the "Necessaries and Conveniences of Life."[16]

The document signed on 19 July was "a Treaty of Alliance and Friendship." In Bowdoin's mind it satisfied Washington's request. He had urged the Native peoples to join the war, "and accordingly they have engaged to do it, and have signed a Treaty for that purpose." The delegation supposed their people would enjoy enhanced trade with the United States. Both sides portrayed the treaty as a great achievement but it remained that the Americans struck a deal with an unauthorized delegation which, like the American team, offered up considerably less than hoped for by the opposite side. Also, the Penobscots, the nearest Native nation to Boston, were not included in the treaty; Bowdoin intended to meet with them shortly to bind them to the same terms. Perhaps in recognition of the treaty's weakness, "the Council thought it best" to send agents home with the delegates "to procure" with "utmost expedition" the number of Native soldiers Washington wanted. If these agents were effective, the treaty might yet serve to generate a Native uprising in Nova Scotia as desired by George Washington and John Allan.[17]

The Native peoples also intended to advance their interests under the treaty. At Machias, the truckmaster was already under pressure, being forced to pay a higher-than-Boston rate for beaver pelts "to hinder them from trading with Nova Scotia." Some Native people refused to pay their bills and subjected the truckmaster to "many insults." Their position was clear: either the Americans would supply them or they would "rely on the assistance of Nova Scotia."[18] It was a position they used in reverse with the Nova Scotians and which doubled their supplies.

Second Chief Ambroise St Aubin returned to the mid-summer heat of Aukpaque a few miles upriver from Maugerville on the St John River with a treaty he believed gave the Maliseets favoured trading status with the Americans. This nation appeared to be drifting into the American camp and Nova Scotia was doing nothing about it. The overture made to the Micmacs spearheaded by Goreham and Bennett may have been late, but it was more forward-looking than the disregard of the Maliseets. This was a serious lapse. In some respects they were strategically more important than the Micmacs: they were less dependent on Halifax, generally more belligerent and closer to the war-path, and their territory lay closer to Massachusetts. It seemed likely in the summer of 1776 that this nation, bound now by treaty to New England, would join forces with Barker's patriots who had applied to join Massachusetts.

Barker's patriots, who had already sent one loyalist family to gaol in New England, were ready in July to transport a second one. Charles Jadis had been "a prisoner" in Maugerville since May, his wife and five children were "proscribed" and a penalty was placed on anyone giving them supplies. The family suffered many hardships and Charles was pressured to join the rebellion. When he resisted, the patriots sent for their Machias friends to come and "take him and a few others" to New England. Faced with the real prospect of following John Anderson into American captivity, Jadis decided to make a pretence of co-operating with the patriots in an attempt to escape their grasp. A note was "sent to the Committee to inform them he was ready to join in any Enterprise or Service they would appoint him to," using his military skills on the side of the patriots, as the Committee-of-Safety wanted. A delighted Barker informed the Americans of his committee's success in recruiting a veteran army officer (who also had naval experience) to the cause. Captain Jadis was welcomed by the patriots and, by gaining their confidence, he was able to observe their organizational structure and become privy to their plans for the overthrow of the government.[19]

The local patriot organization was a loose structure centred in Cumberland, Cobequid, and Maugerville, with minor centres in Pictou and Passamaquoddy. The centres were linked with Machias but agents of the Maugerville group generally maintained contact beyond there to Boston and to

Washington's headquarters. Militant Native groups were linked in Maugerville and Cumberland. Various plans for adding the Nova Scotia stripe to the American flag were advanced that summer with most conceived in Cumberland, the political centre of the network, where John Allan and others operated in the shadow of the fort, having now to "meet in a private manner." Results of these meetings, including plans and rumours of plans, were circulated through the network and to Machias by patriot agents.[20]

The many plans for the reduction of Nova Scotia differed only in detail. Invariably they relied on American invasion, a Native uprising, and the commissioning of local officers to lead a patriot army that was expected to grow considerably in Nova Scotia. The plan to which Jadis became privy foresaw an army of 6,000 Americans and Nova Scotians with an auxiliary force of 300 Native people. The plans never varied in strategy: Fort Cumberland was the first objective ("which must have fallen an easy conquest," admitted Jadis) after which the army would advance on the capital. The Native members would have already infiltrated Halifax under the guise of having deserted the Americans. The capital would fall and then the whole province would fall. Jacob Barker and the Maugerville committee explained this fantastic plan to Charles Jadis. In command of the army with the rank of major-general would be none other than Jadis himself.

"As soon as he was in possession of these Facts," Jadis devised "the means of his escape." Anyone leaving the St John River valley needed Barker's permission and a plausible excuse was demanded. Jadis found one: "the ill-state of health he was then in (owing to his late hard treatment) proved a very plausible [...] pretext." He asked to go to New England "for the recovery of his health" and "gave out" that he intended to join George Washington. This story was believed and, "As soon as he had obtained the Pass" and after "some delay and great distress," the Jadis family "escap'd in the night time."[21] Making his way to the river mouth, Jadis "committed himself and family, then six in number, to the mercies of Providence and the Dangers of the Sea in a small Birch Bark Canoe and crossed the Bay of Fundy." To brave these waters in a canoe took courage and faith. On the far side the family "was providentially taken up at the Mouth of the Gut of Annapolis by the *Viper* Sloop-of-War" and delivered safely to Annapolis Royal.[22]

The plight of Anderson and Jadis demonstrated the power of the Maugerville committee, but it did not have absolute power. Sunbury's member of the Assembly, James Simonds, and others of the trading cartel of Simonds, Hazen, and White remained at large in the valley and neutral in politics. To be publicly neutral in Sunbury that summer was an act of defiance, but even when pressed these loyalists avoided being drawn out. Chairperson Barker singled out James Simonds, his partner James White, and Jarvis Saye who had "not thought proper to fall in with" Committee of Safety mandates; "neither have you declared against them," pointed out the committee clerk, Israel Perley, hopefully. "This conduct of yours gives uneasiness to many of the Inhabitants" and, he might have added, reflected poorly on the authority of the committee. In June Perley had requested that the three make "an explicit Declaration of your sentiments." He foresaw a preference for neutrality "but this will not be a satisfactory answer." Simonds, White, and Saye did not respond. In July, when Simonds "was up River," he was questioned closely by the committee. Still he refused to cooperate. Fumbling for compromise, committee members suggested Simonds "leave some tiling privately with the Committee expressing his Sentiments"; even this "he declined," adding obliquely "that he could be of more service to the People, not to Do it."[23]

Retreating still further from their initial position, the Committee-of-Safety asked Simonds to guarantee that he would not inform Halifax of their treasonous act of "Entering into an alliance with the People of New England." This also "he refused," causing some members to complain "that they could not Esteem such a man their friend, nor a friend to the Cause," nor could they have dealings with him. Simonds dared to clarify that "if he Did Do Such a thing" as they requested, he would have to write "that he was compelled to do it which," he added cleverly, "would be Rather against the People."[24] By standing up to the committee, Simonds, White, and Saye revealed its weakness. As strong as local patriots were in July they dared not deal with all loyalists as decisively as they had with the unfortunate Charles Jadis. Sunbury loyalists were weak and lived under the double shadow of Machias and Aukpaque.

By July the centre of patriot activity in Nova Scotia had shifted from Cumberland to Sunbury County. Although Barker was not in total control and

St Aubin had still not won over Chief Tomah, these patriot leaders enjoyed far more freedom of action than their counterparts in Cumberland. The events that signalled this shift were the Maugerville declaration of rebellion in May, the arrival of the Royal Fencibles in Cumberland in June, and the return of St Aubin to Aukpaque in July. Another sign was the return of Perley and Kimball from Boston with arms and ammunition "for the use of their constituents." They delivered a barrel of gunpowder, 250 weight of lead, and a stand of small arms.[25] Political inspiration still issued from the Cumberland zealots, but the avenue for action and the fountainhead of rumour was the St John River valley.

The most persistent rumour in Halifax that July was of an attack by Maliseets and New England patriots along the lines of the plan known to Charles Jadis. "It has often been reported," wrote an officer of this rumour; "we are daily alarmed," wrote another. The number of patriots was estimated as high as 2,000 and Goreham heard they "are within three days march of his Post."[26] Even more extreme versions of this rumour circulated. The alarm was due in part to news of the formal contacts between the Maliseets and the Americans that reached Halifax in July. That news pointed to an alliance of Native peoples, Americans, and local patriots. [Governor] Arbuthnot heard that Eddy was back in Nova Scotia "with power" from New England "to try to corrupt the St. John's Indians."[27] In the end, Council concluded that the rumour of an attack was false. It was false (or at least premature), but it was not groundless. The rumour supported Jadis's contention that a plan existed, and the march from the St John River to the Petitcodiac, the direction of the attack, would be made easier by the road Samuel Rogers was in fact cutting through the woods. The rumour mistook a plan of attack for an actual attack; the plan was real as Jadis well knew and tentative steps were under way to implement it, but there was no current danger.

Jonathan Eddy was in the province as Arbuthnot had heard, but his freedom was circumscribed by Goreham's patrols and restricted by the warrant for his arrest. The situation was intolerable in Cumberland for patriots; they dared not assemble except on the most urgent business and only in secret. Many ceased political activity. The new magistrates were so diligent that it seemed a matter of time before accused patriots must surrender or flee the isthnus.

"We were drove to our wits end," explained one patriot. William How had already fled because of his altercation with the deputy sheriff in March and Eddy decided to leave in July, no more than a month after his return. He was forced into exile but he went also on official business: he set out to make a final bid to obtain American help for local rebellion. "Eddy was to return to the Honourable Congress," announced Samuel Rogers and "we found means to send off Mr. Eddy," added Josiah Throop, a member of the committee.[28]

Eddy's second mission to America was prompted by the news that Allan's letter had not reached Boston. It was "thrown overboard" in St John Harbour when a warship challenged the vessel carrying it.[29] Lost was the invasion plan with its idea of using Natives (so much like the plan of George Washington); it was now up to Eddy to carry the message directly to Congress. He and his family left near the end of the month with some optimism that the Native peoples, Acadians, and New Englanders in Nova Scotia were ready for action if only he could bring back American help. Left behind were Allan and Rogers, the former carrying on in closely watched Cumberland and the latter beyond the Petitcodiac, chopping a line through a vast forest alive with black flies and stifling in the July heat. They laboured under difficulties that were purely local. The focus of irritation had shifted away from Halifax where a more adroit administration managed affairs. Unlike the antagonistic Legge, the new chief executive avoided issues that might promote dissent in the outsettlements. Arbuthnot was not one to stay out of sight; he was planning a public relations offensive that would carry his loyalist message directly to the people.

With the fleet gone and the Assembly prorogued, Arbuthnot felt freer than he had in months. Now in a more relaxed mood, he decided on a remarkable initiative—a tour of Nova Scotia outsettlements. The idea was pure Arbuthnot, a genuine effort to meet the people by one who genuinely enjoyed pressing the flesh. Nothing less characteristic of Governor Legge could be imagined. Arbuthnot's affability, however, was edged in cleverness, even cunning, and the tour would be no idle walkabout but a calculated scheme for the encouragement of loyalty pursuant to his official instructions. These were similar to Legge's instructions but light years separated the former governor's methods from those of the jovial commodore.

Arbuthnot would stress informality and visit districts never seen by a governor. Justice Isaac Deschamps would go with him and also Michael Francklin who was for most Haligonians the acknowledged outsettlement expert.

Into the wilderness behind Citadel Hill and across the centre of the Nova Scotia peninsula rode the Halifax delegation led by the chief executive himself. To a sailor like Arbuthnot the forested, hilly interior was an exotic place, sultry in the mid-July heat and lacking the salt air he was used to. His interest in North American fauna was indulged. The wildcats that roamed those woods especially took his fancy; a live one would make a perfect Christmas present for his London patron, the Earl of Sandwich.[30] Arbuthnot and Deschamps were joined by Francklin in Windsor and together they circulated through the townships of Horton and Cornwallis. Arbuthnot reviewed the militia in each community by meeting the volunteers and conversing with their officers. He got to know the magistrates and "bettermost people by dining together." The commodore was a memorable host. Robustly overweight, with a prodigious appetite, sturdy drinking habits, and a string of stories (of the crude, nautical variety), the red-faced, cheery, "blustering tar" regaled his guests nightly through the Annapolis Valley. "It seemed to have a good effect," Arbuthnot observed as when officers were asked for their opinions "they unanimously expressed much loyalty, zeal and satisfaction." Not a little of the good effect resulted from the contagious optimism and nightly good humour of their chief executive.[31]

NOTES

1. A resolution for independence was introduced in Congress on 7 June and was approved by Congress in committee on 1 July, it was signed by President John Hancock on 4 July 1776. Copies of the declaration of independence were sent to various state and colonial assemblies the next day. Nova Scotia's copy arrived in Halifax about mid-August but only a portion of it was published in the local *Gazette*.

2. Bulkeley to Harper and Black, 1 July 1776, Claim of Christopher Harper, NA AO 13, Bundle 92. Also Commission Book, PANS RG 1, Vol. 168.

3. McDonald to Ogilvie, 24 April 1776, McDonald Letterbook, 266–8 McDonald was responding to an enquiry about property owned by John Huston, one-time resident of Cumberland. "I don't think

it advisable to Lay out money immediately," he warned, but offered to look after the enquirer's interest until the political troubles were past and to consult William Allan about its value. Like any good real estate agent, McDonald exuded optimism: "The affairs in America Must be settled Sometime or another," and he added philosophically, "Land cannot be carried away." Another agent would speculate on land for his client only "when the present storm subsides," see Morris to Desbarres, 27 November 1776, PANS Desbarres Papers, Series 5, vol. 3. William Allan was concerned enough in July to go to Cumberland "immediately to secure his Property," see Morris to Legge, 12 July 1776, *The Earl of Dartmouth Papers*, 708.

4. Allan to Massachusetts Council, 19 February 1777, PANS MG 100, vol. 129.

5. Throop to Massachusetts Council, 29 May 1777, MA Vol. 142, 66–77.

6. Washington to Massachusetts Council, 11 July 1776, and same to Congress, 4 July 1776, John C. Fitzpatrick, ed., The *Writings of George Washington from the Original Manuscript sources 1745–1799*, vol. 5, (Washington: Government Printing Office), 261–2, 220–1. Maugerville Committee to Massachusetts Council, 21 May 1776, AA 5, Vol. 1, 706.

7. Washington to Massachusetts Council, 11 July 1776, and same to Congress, 4 July 1776, *Writings of Washington* 5, 261–2, 220–1. JCC, July 1776, 527. The Maliseet news item in *American Gazette*, 19 June 1776.

8. Memorial of John Cort, 8 April 1777, CO 217, vol. 27, 298.

9. Record of a Conference of the St John and Micmac Native peoples with the Americans, 10 to 17 July 1776, James P. Baxter, *Documentary History of the State of Maine* 24 (Portland: LeFavor-Tower Co. 1910), 165–93.

10. Diary of Caleb Gannett, 1776–77, Houghton Library, Harvard, MS AM 516.3. This portion of the diary is published, see Maurice W. Armstrong, "The Diary of Caleb Gannett for the Year 1776," *The William and Mary Quarterly* 3 (1946), 117–22.

11. Ibid. This royal artifact, which hung in the Massachusetts Council Chamber, now hangs in Trinity Church, Saint John, New Brunswick. For another account of the celebrations in Boston, including the bonfire of royal artifacts, see Edward M. Griffin, *Old Brick Charles Chauncey of Boston 1705–1787*

159

(Minneapolis: University of Minnesota Press 1980), 162.

12. Conference Record, July 1776, Baxter, *History of Maine* 24:165–93.

13. Micmac Chiefs to Massachusetts Council, 19 September 1776, Kidder, *Military Operations,* 57–8.

14. Conference Record, July 1776, Baxter, *History of Maine* 24:165–93.

15. Ibid.

16. Bowdoin to Washington, 30 July 1776, Baxter, *History of Maine* 14:361–2. Washington to Massachusetts Council, 11 July 1776, *Writings of Washington* 5, 261–2.

17. Bowdoin to Washington, 30 July 1776, Baxter, *History of Maine* XIV: 361–2. Regarding Shaw's part, see Massachusetts Council to Captain Lambert, 27 July 1776, NDAR 5, 1238.

18. Smith to Massachusetts Council, 22 June 1776, AA 5, Vol. 1, 703.

19. Jadis to Treasury, 30 March 1787, PRO T1/664, and Claim of Charles Jadis, 24 October 1776, NA AO 13.

20. Allan to Massachusetts Council, 19 February 1777, PANS MG 100, Vol. 129.

21. Jadis to Treasury, 30 March 1787, PRO T1/664, and Claim of Charles Jadis, 24 October 1776, NA AO 13.

22. Ibid. See the certificate of the *Viper's* Captain Samuel Graves, 19 September 1785, PRO T1/664.

23. Jacob Barker to James Simonds, James White And Jarvas Say, 20 June 1776, and appendix dated 24 September 1776, MA Vol. 181, 248–9.

24. Ibid.

25. *Massachusetts Resolves,* 26 June 1776, No. 89, 468, mfm at MA.

26. The July rumour of an attack on Nova Scotia was amply mentioned: Executive Council Minutes, 29 June 1776, PANS RG 1, Vol. 212; McDonald to Small, early July 1776, McDonald Letterbook, 278; Massey to Germain, 5 July 1776, NA MG 11, Vol. 96, 82–6; Arbuthnot to Germain, 8 July 1776. NA MG 11, Vol. 96, 92–7; Gibbons to Legge, 8 July 1776, The Earl of Dartmouth Papers, 3922–5; and Feilding to Denbigh, 10 July 1776, Marion Balderston and David Syrett, eds., *The Lost War, Letters from British Officers during the American Revolution* (Horizon Press: New York 1975), 90–2.

27. Arbuthnot to Germain, 8 July 1776, NA MG 11, Vol. 96, 92–7.

28. Rogers Extracts, PCC 41, Vol. 8; Throop to Massachusetts Council, 29 May 1777, MA Vol. 142, 66–77.

29. Allan to Massachusetts Council, 21 November 1776, Kidder, *Military Operations,* 166–79.

30. For the lieutenant-governor's presents to the earl, see Arbuthnot to Sandwich, 11 October 1777, *Sandwich Papers* 1:304–6.

31. Arbuthnot to Germain, 15 August 1776, dar 12, 183–4. See also Arbuthnot to Germain, 8 July 1776, na mg, Vol. 96, 92–7.

◼ Article 2: The Neutral Yankees of Nova Scotia

John Bartlet Brebner

There was not even a sense of solidarity in Nova Scotia. Settlements were scattered at intervals along the edges of a long, narrow peninsula whose rough surface defied the road makers. The unpredictable sea was the road between settlements. There were long stretches of uninhabited forest along the shores all the way from Cans to Annapolis Basin.
[...]
Perhaps, then the principal clue to Nova Scotian behaviour in this, as in many other problematical situations, lies in her insulation from the rest of North America. The northeastward trend of the coast, the Appalachian uplands of Maine and New Brunswick, and the deep invasion of the Bay of Fundy, push her outward toward Newfoundland and Europe from the main body of North America. Nova Scotia has always had to contemplate the possibility that she may be in North America but not of it, and this mould of circumstances has pressed with varying weight on some generations of Nova Scotians to modify their traditional loyalties and inclinations. France and England, New France and New England, tried to exploit her during the seventeenth century without accepting the responsibility for continuous reinforcement and aid to the inhabitants. In 1710 New England and Old found it imperative to conquer her, but again their support was an intermittent and barely adequate counter to the efforts of France and New France. Her people of that day, the Acadians, had made the land support and increase them, but they were mere pawns in international politics. Small wonder, then, that their one persistent aim from 1710

to 1755, when it sealed their fates, was to be, and to be generally accepted as, neutrals—"the neutral French." Small wonder, too, that after a brief flurry of conflicting aims in 1775, Nova Scotians a bare fifteen years out of New England naturally and almost inevitably, when confronted by the Revolution, made the same plea.

All in all, both external and domestic circumstances operated to dilute very considerably in Nova Scotia the clash of opinion which prevailed elsewhere. It is now generally believed that in most of the thirteen rebellious American Colonies the majority of the population was passive, but that the radicals formed the larger of the two active minorities and thereby involved their communities. As events proved, the majority in Nova Scotia was also passive, and neither minority was able to rouse its members beyond individual acts or minor joint enterprises for or against Government.

With the probable exception of Halifax, the available evidence demonstrates the quite natural refusal of most Nova Scotians to risk becoming involved in fratricidal strife with the rebellious Colonies. Inevitably this attitude was interpreted by the official loyalists as being synonymous with treason to Great Britain and with the desire actively to assist the rebels. The resident officials of a colony who had vigorously represented it to be ultra-loyal were loath to allow this embarrassing belief to reach London, but such persons as Legge, Gibbons,* and various naval or military officers felt no such compunctions. Yet it is permissible to doubt the many assertions that Nova Scotians' sympathy with the revolutionaries was so great that only their own weaknesses prevented them from joining the American Revolution. In all parts of the Province, outside of Halifax, there were a few men who did participate in the Revolution by emigrating or by conspiring at home to aid the rebels and overthrow British authority. They appear to have been distinctly more numerous and more active than the similarly scattered minority who had the courage actively to assist Great Britain. But both groups were negligible as compared with the mass of Nova Scotians, whose former affiliations and present environment put them in the paradoxical position of being positive only in a negative action. They refused to fight their blood brothers, even, as we shall see, to the point of failing in their professed willingness to

Source: John Bartlet Brebner, *The Neutral Yankees of Nova Scotia: A Marginal Colony During the Revolutionary Years* (Toronto: McClelland and Stewart, 1969 [1937]), pp. 261–2, 274–6, 289–90, 292–3, and 309–10.

*Francis Legge was the lieutenant-governor of Nova Scotia until being recalled in 1776, largely because of his incompetence. Richard Gibbons, an ally of Legge, was a Halifax-born merchant and politician; he later became solicitor-general and attorney-general.

defend their homes against them. They felt incapable, even when they were willing, of taking overt action to destroy British control. They were desperately concerned by the interruption in their economic intercourse with New England. The Nova Scotian settlers were weak and exposed, and knowing this, like the Acadians whom they had supplanted, asked that the belligerents treat them as neutrals.

The question naturally arises as to what the Colonists in open rebellion thought and did about the sincere, if naive, desire of Nova Scotians to be neutral and at the same time to maintain a life line of trade between the contestants, as the Acadians had done before them and as Nova Scotians and New Englanders were to do in the War of 1812. They made no secret of what they thought. John Adam's growling comment that Nova Scotians were "a set of fugitives and vagabonds who are also kept in fear by a fleet and an army" was an angry man's epitome of what less laconic speakers and writers delighted to amplify and embroider to relieve their disappointment and hate.[1] The revolutionaries were equally blunt in action. Almost before the war was formally opened they began to seize the "neutral" trading vessels which were sustaining their enemies, and to announce the imminent conquest of Nova Scotia. Two important considerations gradually modified these intentions notably: first, the genuine, occasionally vital, economic relationship which made New England political leaders consent to subterfuges for maintaining trade with Nova Scotia if Nova Scotians would trade in foreign, as well as in domestic, products; and second, the obstacles, material, diplomatic, and strategic, to an American conquest.

The Cape Sable shore presented the economic situation most comprehensively, for that region had been closely affiliated with Massachusetts for a century and a half and had never made more than the barest acknowledgments of Halifax rule.[2] Moreover, a special situation existed there because of the substantial investment in commerce and credit near Yarmouth and Barrington of the Honourable James Pitt, of Boston. His son John was managing his father's affairs in Boston at the beginning of the Revolution and in June, 1775, his son William was sent to Nova Scotia to try to repatriate the family capital in the form of goods or to carry on vestiges of the family business, while James and John lobbied for their interest at the Legislature.[3] Massachusetts gradually

became aware of and accustomed to the desirability of this sort of contraband trade with the region and issued special orders to privateers in general to spare that shore.

Speedily it became evident that Nova Scotians were as willing to trade with Massachusetts as with the British forces, even when they had to evade the British Navy stationed on their shores. From Weymouth to Roseway there grew up an uneasy and occasionally interrupted intercourse with Massachusetts, carried on by the Acadian and Nova Scotian skippers to whom its continuance was vital, and supplemented by feeding operations which ran down from the Bay of Fundy and from the South Shore. The starting point was to secure from the Massachusetts General Court a pass permitting the holder to return to the fold in New England with his family, his effects, and his realizable capital in the form of goods. If time could be spared or if the risks justified it, an export permit to some port held by the British was also secured from the Nova Scotian authorities. Using these to hold off privateers and inquisitive naval officers while fishing and trading, the Nova Scotian collected fish, lumber and wood products, salt, manufactured goods, and fugitive or shipwrecked American privateersmen at various centres along the shore. He then slipped across to New England, repatriated the prisoners, and asked permission to sell his cargo in order to buy provisions. This was usually granted, and the round began all over again.[4]

While Halifax pretty well threw up its hands over the possibility of controlling the Cape Sable shore, it did make occasional efforts to keep the South Shore in line from Chester and Lunenburg southwestward. Liverpool was quite properly the subject of constant suspicion.[5] The substantial, venturesome leaders there trimmed their sails as best they could to the squally, changeable winds, now closing their eyes to contraband trade, now suffering from privateers, and now privateering themselves.[6] At the end of February, 1776, for instance, the *Senegal* came in and the master called on Perkins "for a warrant to search Wm Freeman's store, my store, and Robert Stevenson's store for molasses, and cocoa nuts, landed by Capt. Nowell, which I granted. They accordingly searched and found in all the stores mentioned. They went on board at evening, the marines and sailors, many of them drunk. The officers behaved very civilly, and invited myself and Capt. Freenman to dine with them at Mrs. Doggett's." [7]

Trade went on, usually through Yarmouth or Barrington, but sometimes even with Boston directly; and hard cash circulated as seldom before when one side desperately needed some commodity like salt or flour which the other could provide. When captures took place, it was sometimes possible to give personal ransoming and the confiscation and sale of vessel and cargo enough of the colour of a straight commercial transaction to reduce losses a little. Some neighbouring places, such as Port Mouton and Ragged Islands (Lockeport), were so American in sympathy as periodically to serve as advance bases for American privateers and for the disposal of their captures. Gradually, however, as the policy of the revolutionary Colonies became more single and as revolutionary confidence grew, this early exciting and adventurous prosperity in the outports was reduced to meagre proportions and ultimately was largely replaced for Nova Scotians by the sheer agony of hanging on for the end.

During 1775 and 1776, the very years when profits were most substantial, Nova Scotians and revolutionaries also explored the possibilities of another very natural course of action—an attack which should bring the Province under the control of Congress. There were men in Nova Scotia and easternmost Massachusetts (Maine), like the Green Mountain Boys of Vermont, for example, who were ready and anxious to strike the blow. The Rev. James Lyon, from among the New Hampshire Ulstermen of the Cobequid region; John Allan, a substantial farmer among the New Englanders near Fort Cumberland, who had come to Nova Scotia from Scotland in 1749 as a boy of three and had married into their ranks;[8] Josiah Throop[9] and Jonathan Eddy,[10] of the same region; the Rev. Seth Noble of Maugerville; and less-conspicuous others here and there in the Province either emigrated to the centres of rebellion or sent memorials urging speedy action, while by committees and meetings they prepared the ground at home.[11]

Lyon made his residence at Machias, a fishing and lumbering settlement on the Maine coast just across the interprovincial boundary, where he found the sort of human material that Ethan Allen used to capture Ticonderoga and where he formed and presided over the local "Committee of Safety."[12] As early as June 11–12, 1775, this group seized two sloops (and their armed schooner escort) which were loading lumber for Boston. They then turned naturally to arming small vessels to break up the provision trade from the Fundy settlements to the British forces and thus initiated an enterprise which gradually was converted from these moderately successful defensive operations to raids on Nova Scotia's almost defenceless settlements and one formal invasion of the Province.[13]

They took the offensive in August, 1775, under Stephen Smith's leadership, by a neatly executed attack on the mouth of the St John, where they burned Fort Frederick, captured its four defenders, and went off home with a Boston provision ship as a prize. They did not yet venture to consolidate with the St. John River settlers, or to hold their conquest at the mouth of the river, but they let it be known that Annapolis would be next.[14] The inhabitants of Passamaquoddy and of the St. John Valley, lying near to Machias, seeing the light, asked Congress to admit them to association in the Revolution.[15]

To Lyon, at Machias, to Allan and Eddy, of Cumberland, to Alexander McNutt, of Roseway, after he had decided that the Americans were winning, and to the Nova Scotians whose appeals they presented, the great objective was to secure the backing of General Washington and Congress for a systematic conquest, or failing them, the active support of the Massachusetts General Court. These efforts in the course of seven years produced a mountain of eloquent and lengthy memorials and of discouraging or begrudging replies which it is not necessary to repeat here, for the controlling circumstances, as corroborated by the events, can be indicated much more briefly.[16]

The Machias plan,[17] as presented to Washington in August, 1775, proposed the assembly of one thousand men and a fleet of four armed vessels and eight transports to proceed to the heart of Nova Scotia, at Windsor, to capture the Tories there, and to use it as a rallying place for a general uprising and advance for the destruction of Halifax. This scheme, if risky, was well conceived as an isolated raid of the Ticonderoga type, but Washington looked farther ahead. He wrote to the Committee of the Massachusetts Legislature, from Cambridge, on August 11, 1775, that, while he applauded the spirit and zeal of the promoters, be thought "such an Enterprize inconsistent

163

with the General Principal upon which the Colonies have proceeded," since defence, not conquest, was their objective.[18] He then put his finger on the fatal flaw in the proposal for the side which had no navy.

It might, perhaps, be easy, with the Force proposed to make an Incurrence into the Province and overawe those of the Inhabitants who are Inimical to our cause; and, for a short time prevent the Supplying the Enemy with Provisions; but the same Force must Continue to produce any lasting Effects. As to the furnishing Vessels of Force, you, Gentn, will anticipate me, in pointing out our Weakness and the Enemy's Strength at Sea. There would be great Danger that, with the best preparation we could make, they would fall an easy prey either to the Men of War on that Station, or some who would be detach'd from Boston [...] our Situation as to Ammunition absolutely forbids our sending a single ounce out of the Camp at present.

While there were temporary alterations in the situation and while to New Englanders in particular Nova Scotia was in itself desirable for the sake of the fisheries,[19] the simple strategic consideration singled out by Washington proved to be sufficient for the salvation of Nova Scotia from American conquest.

On November 10, 1775, Congress responded to the embarrassing solicitations from Nova Scotians for an attack by resolving to send two spies to view the Province, to sound out the people and to report to Washington, and by authorizing him "in case he should judge it practicable and expedient" to dispatch a raiding, instead of an occupying, force for the destruction or removal of war materials. Washington sent off Aaron Willard and Moses Child, but they did not get beyond their own frontier at Campobello because of their fears of Legge's precautions against strangers. Their hearsay report was almost worthless, and anyway "Washington had already decided that he could not possibly spare any troops from his meagre force at Cambridge. He shifted the responsibility back to Congress, recommending them to raise men "in the Eastern parts of this Government."[20]

During the spring of 1776 Washington, Congress, and the Massachusetts Legislature were abundantly solicited for aid by emissaries or petitions from Machias, the River St. John, Cumberland, the Cobequid region, and Yarmouth. Washington was not enthusiastic, fearing that even by a raiding expedition "the Innocent and Guilty will be involved in one common Ruin." Congress was more than busy with the thwarted Canadian campaign. The British evacuation of Boston meant that a reinforced Halifax could not be stripped and despoiled by any small raiding force. Yet Washington admitted that he was much impressed by the solid qualities of Jonathan Eddy and his Acadian companion, Isaiah Beaudreau, the emissaries from Cumberland, and by their proposal to capture the Isthmus of Chignecto, thereby safeguarding the revolutionaries from Indian troubles on their right flank, reducing the supply service for the British forces, and creating an American base for Nova Scotian sympathizers. He could do nothing himself but was willing to be instructed by Congress. That body felt reduced by adverse circumstances to the defensive again and in concert with the General could entertain no action more ambitious than authorizing and urging Massachusetts to win over the St. John River Indians as a defence against attacks from Indians in the British interest. Moreover, by the late summer of 1776 there seemed to be a distinct possibility of an alliance with. France, which involved instructions to the negotiators that the French should be bound not to invade or take possession of "Labrador, New Britain, Nova Scotia, Acadia, Canada, Florida [...] not of the islands of Newfoundland, Cape Breton, St. John's, Anticosti, nor of any other islands lying near to the said continent in the seas, or in any gulph, bay or river."[21] It would be better, if it proved necessary, to make terms with the British about the fisheries than to see France ensconced again with the advantages wrested from her (after generations of effort) only thirteen years before. In 1776 Nova Scotia presented too complicated a problem for an immediate, comprehensive solution.

[...]

In the lives of most Nova Scotians the last six years of the Revolution were the woeful period when privateering raids on their homes or on their property at sea not only made it uncertain from one day to another whether a man was solvent or ruined but even whether he and his family would have enough to eat. The more daring and ingenious carried on the trade exchange with New England for the duration of the Revolution; but the uncertainties of that

164

contraband were endless, and those engaged in it had to be on constant watch against the warders of both sides and, when caught, had to rely on their wits, on a choice from their credentials, and on the tolerance or stupidity of their captors. The Nova Scotians who ventured to sea or attracted at home the attention of the raiders might disappear for months, sometimes forever, while their families and friends tried to pick up here and there from the gossip of the ports some inkling of their fate. A port such as Yarmouth or Barrington was a sort of information centre where men of both sides pooled their knowledge of captives and wanderers for one another's benefit and for the folk at home. Cargoes, as well as men, also disappeared, even very bulky cheap commodities such as lumber, fish, and hay. If the captor could not spare a prize crew to sail his spoils home, he was likely to scuttle, wreck, or burn the vessel and its contents and turn loose its owners and crew in small boats or on the roadless shore. In Nova Scotia during the Revolution new paths were made by mariners and escaped prisoners from place to place along or even across the Peninsula.

No substantial Nova Scotian settlement except Halifax seems to have escaped completely from land raids by American privateers. These were supposed by their commissions not to operate above the high-water mark, but such niceties were too much to expect.
[...]
It was natural that the South Shore villages suffered more than those inside the Bay of Fundy and the Minas Basin, and two of the more substantial ports, Liverpool and Lunenburg, probably provided the most dramatic episodes.[21]

Liverpool afforded a sequential development of events and policies which was both natural and revealing. Simeon Perkins began by making an honest, if vain, attempt not only to maintain a predominantly loyalist attitude in the town where he was a natural leader, but to organize the townsmen in their own defence.[22] As we have seen, he was not above contraband trade, but that was in the best pre-Revolutionary mercantile tradition. After a number of early losses in ventures on shares, he had been relying during 1776 on his schooner *Betsey*, which could run down to Ragged Islands or Yarmouth and sell her cargoes for hard cash without questions asked as to ultimate destination. Liverpool had not

yet suffered direct attack, although Port Medway was swept clean in late September. Perkins thereupon put fifteen of the militia on duty and scaled the two guns set up at the Point. Traitors in his own camp foiled him almost at his door-step on October 16, 1776.

> They say that a whale boat, sent from a Marblehead schooner, one Craw, took my schooner Betsey out of this river. They report that this boat stopped down the harbour in the daytime, and some of the people came by land, and were on my wharf and other parts of the town.

He sent off a vain expedition to recapture her, offering one-third of the cargo as reward.
[...]
On September 28, 1777, privateersmen again came right into town, took a schooner from Perkins' wharf and towed her down the river, and the two boats got away clear in a good breeze before a muster of the people would or could stop them. That night Collier arrived with the *Rainbow* and a brig, heard the tale, and did nothing except cheat Perkins on the price of fat ox. Next April a privateer sloop came right into harbour to loot Tinkham's store and vessel, the sentry, Robert Branham (who had helped land Tinkham's goods), having turned traitor. The same month a richly laden French vessel the *Duc de Choiseul*, was chased into Liverpool harbour, where she ran aground and capsized. While her cargo was being salvaged, two privateers turned up, looted the town of all the salvage they could seize quickly and departed under some fire from shore, towing a captured sloop. When Liverpool fell under suspicion for collusion in disposing of the salvaged pigs of tin, cases of arms, and so on, the discouraged leading men of the town decided that they would henceforth keep a guard by subscription, muster the militia only at alarms, treat with privateers, and not molest them unless they landed or took vessels out of the river.
[...]
Clearly no summary phrase can be adequate to explain the behaviour of so unintegrated a province. Pensioned Halifax might be another New York for loyalism, but, like New York, she was separated from the rest of her Province by more than geographical factors. Her habitual subservience to London, given explicit outward form by commitments made in the

165

campaign against Legge, had been crystallized by war prosperity, by the presence of the navy and the army, and by the stories of the Loyalist refugees. Opposition at the capital was driven underground. Against this stand the sympathizers with rebellion among the outlying population could make no headway because their friends in the rebellious Colonies had no navy and because they themselves could not assemble from the scattered settlements an effective force for unassisted revolt. Neither the "Boston Massacre" of March, 1770, nor the blood shed at Lexington five years later, could arouse the general body of New Englanders in Nova Scotia to solidarity or to emulation of the efforts of those who were somewhat similarly placed in New Hampshire and Georgia. This apathy can be attributed to poverty about as much as to the topographical barriers between the settlements. Economically Nova Scotia could neither stand alone nor maintain an effective alliance with New England. She could not even afford to be properly represented in her own Assembly. In her dependence, she completed her gradual progress out of New England's orbit into Great Britain's. The general North American tide of migration had turned west. New England, having received what she thought she wanted most at the peace settlement in the St. Croix boundary and in access to the North Atlantic fisheries, released her already weakend grip. To use a generalization so broad as to be almost meaningless without corroborative detail, Nova Scotia had insulated and neutralized the New England migrants so thoroughly that as Nova Scotians they had henceforth to look eastward to London for direction and help rather than southwestward to Boston as they had done in the past.

NOTES

1. For example, sec pp. 147n., 264n, 298n.
2. Peole's *Annals of Yarmouth and Barrington in the Revolutionary War* (Yarmouth, 1899) contains very effective matching of Massachusetts records with those of the Cape Sables shore to demonstrate clearly both the economic relationship and the techniques of its operations.
3. James, senior, died Jan. 25, 1776.
4. Both sides used the process for military and naval intelligence, but the advantage was naturally with New England. See the two letters by See the two letters by Stephen Parker, of Yarmouth, to George Washington, Jan. 15 and 16, 1776, *Collections*, Maine Hist. Sec., XIV (1910), 322-26; and other illustrations, ibid., 343, 346, 350. Machias, for instance, traded wheat for hay with "New england people only, who appeared real friends to the welfare of America. "Halifax sent down a detachment of troops to Yarmouth and warned the magistrates to assist them "that the Troops may not be oblig'd to obtain what is necessary by Compulsion," Dec. 4, 1778, *P.A.N.S.*, 136, 268. Perhaps the most striking example of the trade relation is that John Allan, who was raising the Indians of the Maine border to attack Nova Scotia, complained to the Massachusetts authorities of the high cost and poor quality of trade goods received and pointed out that if he were allowed "to procure and Assortment from Nova Scotia, his money would have gone many Gates farther and have purchased much better goods; Aug. 4. 1778, *Collections*, Maine Hist. Soc., XVI (1910). 49.
5. See Council Sept. 19. 1775. *N.S. B*16, 179.
6. Perkins's *Diary, passim*. Perkins was discreet, but the barest Liverpool chronicle could not be other than revealing.
7. Tavern, see above, p. 155n. The officers were spending their anticipated prize money. The local collector of customs. William John-stone, bestirred himself too late and the Navy would not allow him his tardy confiscations; see *Diary*, Feb. 29, March 7, 1776. The whole episode was probably a sequel to the seizure and examination at Halifax of Perkins's correspondence, which he reports Feb. 9, 1776. See another example, Dec 14, 1778.
8. Member of Assembly for Cumberland Township, vice Jonathan Eddy, Oct. 30, 1775.
9. Member of Assembly for Cumberland County, 1765-70, origin unknown He took the militia protest to Halifax.
10. Member of Assembly for Cumberland Township 1770-75, from Norton (now Mansfield), Massachusetts.
11. The presence of the Yorkshiremen al the end of the Bay of Fandy created a local split not unlike the division in other colonies. Sec *N.S. A95*, 108 and 112. Professor W. B. Kerr, who has investigated this situation in some detail, has allowed me to read and use his unpublished essays on Allan. See his "The American Invasion of Nova Scotia, 1776-7," *Canadian Defence Quarterly*. XIII, 433 (July, 1936).

12. The principal rebels' names as of June, 1775, including Captain Stephen Smith (delegate to Congress) and he notable Jeremiah and William O'Brian, will be found in the deposition concerning their attack on the armed schooner *Margaret, N.S. A94*, 77-91. The most comprehensive account of this border warfare is in F. Kidder, *Military Operations in Eastern Maine and Nova Scotia dating the Revolution* (Albany, 1867), Which is supplemented from the Nova Scotian side by D. C Harvey, "Machias and the Invasion of Nova Scotia," *C.H.A.R.,* 1932, pp. 17-28, and by Professor Kcrr's published and unpublished papers.

13. The *N.S.A. series*. Vols. 93-102, and *B series,* Vols. 16-18, seldom omit an incident in the actual warfare, see *P.A.C.R.,* 1894 where they ate very fully calendared. Only special or obscure individual citations will be made hereafter.

14. "*the people* at Mechias declar'd, that they only waited untill the Hay and Corn in Nova Scotia, ware cut down & collected and then they would come and carry it off."—Deposition of William Shey, Ang. 16. 1775, *M.S. B*16, 149.

15. "In May, 1776, the Reverend Seth Noble and others organized the Mangerville settlers in the American interest and petitioned Massachusetts for union and protection.

16. "Xidder and Kerr have used the Massachusetts materials most extensively. Harvey quotes substantial portions from Massachusetts transcripts. The more important documents will be found as follows: Force, *op. cit.*, fourth series, III, 90, 1183, IV, 460, 1149, 1182, V, 522, 935, fifth series, I, 703, III, 909, J, C. Fitzpatrick, ed., *The Writings of George Washington from the orginal Manuscript Sources. 1745-1799* (10v., Washington, 1933-35). III, 414, IV, 99, 111, 112, 152, 292, 331, 437, 457, V, 3, 220, 261, 403, VI, 391, 434–36. VIII, 481, 486, IX, 193; W. C. Ford. ed., *Journals of the Continental Congress* (33v., Washington. 1904–26), I, 102, II, S4, III, 316, 343, 348, 401, 413, IV, 155, 307. V, 527, VI, 1055, VII, 18, 30, 38, 73. 313, XI, 498, 518, XII, 1039, XIII, 242, 428, XIV, 924, 959 XXIII, 471; *Secret Journals of the Acts and Proceedings of Congress* (4v., Boston. 1820–21), I, 34, 47, 51, 52, 98, 110. II, 11, 39, 123, 133–35, 219; B. C. Burnett. ed., *Letters of Members of the Continental Congress* (Tv., Washington, 1921–34), III, 237, 476, IV, 60, 103, 142, 144, 164, 185, 246, 251, 254, 352; *P.A.N.S. 364* (Transcripts from Mass.); *N.S.H.S.* II, 11–16, (Halifax, 1881); Massachusetts Historical Society, *Collection,* LLX, 269, 436, LXIV, 235, LXV, 62, 64, 81, 275; Maine Historical Society, *Collections*, first series, III, 179, V. 440, second series, I, 389–400

17. Known as Colonel Thompson's plan.

18. Washington was much embarrassed by the unauthorized raid on the Island of St. John and removal of the principal officers, Writings, IV, 152.

19. Samuel Adams never tired of arguing that Nova Scotia and Canada must be conceded to the United Colonies for this reason.

20. "If it is attempted, it must be by people from the country." Writings, IV, 292–93.

21. Secret, Journals, II, 11 and 39.

22. The raid on Annapolis and Granville of late August, 1781, was their nearest rival. See W. A. Calnek and A. W. Savary, *History of the County of Annapolis* (Toronto, 1897), 163–64.

23. *Diary, passim.*

■ Article 3: A People Highly Favoured of God

Gordon Stewart and George Rawlyk

During the war years a powerful leader of public opinion emerged in the Yankee out-settlements of Nova Scotia. Henry Alline became the popular leader of a major religious revival that, by the end of the war, had spread through most of the colony. The fact that Alline achieved such extensive popularity indicated the strong influence that religious values still exerted on the Nova Scotia Yankees at the height of the American political and military struggle against Britain. The Yankees in Nova Scotia turned to a religious rather than a political figure in their search for guidance on the many distressing problems produced by the war.

[...]

Alline's view of the world in which he lived was determined in its overall structure by his belief that the world was in its latter ages and heading rapidly towards the Judgement Day. Such a belief was common enough among American evangelicals in the middle of the eighteenth century. But Alline imbued it with a special urgency and derived from it various conclusions about the contemporary state of man that distinguished his interpretation of the course of history from evangelicals in, for instance, New England. The basic premise from which Alline worked was that this was a "dying world" which had not long to survive before God would demand a final reckoning as he wound up the redemptive process. Various signs convinced Alline of the imminence of the end of the world. In marked contrast to the spiritual harmony that had, according to Alline, existed in paradise, he emphasized that "now there is Separations, Wars and disorders." The war and its attendant disorders were depicted as dire signs of the impending day of doom. "This world," he reiterated on another occasion, is "under so many disorders, darkness and sin." Alline accepted that wars and disorder in human affairs

Source: Gordon Stewart and George Rawlyk, *A People Highly Favoured of God: The Nova Scotia Yankees and the American Revolution* (Toronto: Macmillan, 1968), pp. 153, 157–9, 163–4, 174–5, and 178. Reprinted with permission from Gordon Stewart.

were not unique to this period, for these evils had existed since the first appearance of man on earth, but he believed that these convulsions in the world had reached an unprecedented, and, therefore, significant, intensity. In his long treatise written sometime before 1782 Alline made no effort to conceal his fear of an imminent judgement. "O the Midnight Darkness," he exclaimed, "that now overspreads the World [...] the Day of Grace is over and the World undone."

[...]

It was not unusual to regard the times as sinful but Alline's conclusion that New England was partly responsible for such alarming signs among men became the basis upon which the Nova Scotia Yankees discerned a radically different pattern in current events than that perceived by their former friends and relatives in New England. To the American patriots it was axiomatic that "an unjust war had been commenced against" the colonies. The view that the war had begun as an unprovoked attack by Britain on the Colonists enabled the Americans to justify their resort to arms. Sylvanus Conant, of the First Church in Middleborough, took pains, in 1777, to explain that "as for the bloody contest between Great Britain and these United States, it is our opinion, upon careful enquiry, that we are not aggressors in the quarrel." Such reasoning permitted Americans to overcome any feelings of guilt they may have had about going to war against another Protestant power. The British administration appeared "to have many of the features and most of the temper and character of the image of the beast which the apostle represents." As the war with Britain commenced a whole body of evangelical literature emerged to persuade the American people that they were fighting in a just and noble cause.

Like many New England preachers, Alline was certain that the war between Britain and America, two Protestant nations, was a sign that Christian history had reached a critical juncture.

[...]

Alline urged the people to take note of the omens. With a tremendous explosion of feeling, and yet with characteristically tight control of his delivery, Alline recited the signs of the times:

> The Great Men and Kings of the Earth grown proud and lofty; all Manner of Debauchery spreading like a Flood; Stage

Plays, Balls and Masquerades received as an Indulgence from Heaven; [...] while the Heralds of the Gospel, if any hold forth the Truth, are accounted as mad men and Enthusiasts; Libraries glutted with Tragedies, Comedies, Romances, Novels and other profane histories [...]; cursing, swearing and blaspheming, not only the language of Troops and Mariners but also of Towns and Countries and received as expressions of Politeness; Drunkenness a Common Amusement accounted neither Sin or Disgrace; the Rich exalted, the Poor trampled in the Dust; Signs and Wonders seen in the Earth, Air and Water; Wars and Rumours of War, yea, the most inhuman Wars spreading Desolation thro' the world like a Flood; and these most alarming Prodigies [...] as little regarded as the Shadows of Evening.

The people in the out-settlements of Nova Scotia were, according to Alline, surrounded by a world crisis of unparalleled severity.

[...]

From such reasoning Alline was able to explain to the people the significance of the revival that was taking place throughout their townships. In a world sinking into general disorder their colony was to fulfill an exemplary role. The revival was producing visible saints who were forming purified churches and in the midst of world chaos these people were maintaining a firm centre of order. They would be in the vanguard of God's cause and ensure continued Christian progress. In order to convince followers of the validity of attaching such significance to the revival, Alline had to demonstrate that converts were appearing in large numbers in Nova Scotia and that they were a dramatic example to the outside world that God's cause was being led by his chosen people.

[...]

This was the dramatic message Alline delivered to the out-settlements of Nova Scotia during the seven years of the revolutionary war. These people were to perform an exemplary and salutary role in a world sinking into general disorder. The effects of the war had confused the Nova Scotia Yankees and had introduced a pervasive feeling of insecurity into their lives. Yet Alline, by drawing an even gloomier picture of life in New England and elsewhere, reassured people on his travels throughout the colony that Nova Scotia had actually been spared from the rampant disorder of the times. Surely then, the inhabitants had "cause to love much, for you are blest in basket and in store in time and eternity." The war, along with other indicators, was a sign that God was "about to expell that hellish darkness from the poor blinded world, and has already delivered most of his people in this part of the vinyard." The Nova Scotia Yankees were "a people highly favoured of God."

[...]

The Yankees responded to this religious ideology much more spontaneously, and in far larger numbers, than they had to the revolutionary ideology in 1775 and 1776. The evangelical religious values popularized by Alline were, compared with the political rhetoric of the American Revolution, reassuringly familiar to them. Lagging several years behind the American Patriots in terms of political understanding they could not easily commit themselves to the revolutionary war against Britain. But they could understand the ideology of the revival because this was merely an exploitation and elaboration of values they had held throughout the pre-revolutionary decade. The Nova Scotia Yankees did not participate in the American Revolution but by means of the religious movement led by Alline they experienced a revolution of their own. During the revival they demonstrated that they could function independently as a society with distinct attitudes, values and goals. At the very moment they revealed their New England background, by appropriating New England's traditional "sense of mission," they had declared their independence of New England.

169

■ Article 4: *Pax Britannica* or *Pax Indigena?*

John G. Reid

[...] Planters [in Nova Scotia] who arrived in the expectation that tensions with Aboriginal inhabitants had been laid to rest would soon find out otherwise. Treaty-making continued apace until the summer of 1761, when an elaborate signing ceremony at the Governor's Farm in Halifax—attended by Mi'kmaq chiefs from the Miramichi, Shediac, Pokemouche, and Cape Breton—brought the acting governor, Jonathan Belcher, to declare that "a covenant of peace" now existed.[1] Like any covenant, however, this one had two sides. Time would tell that peace would prevail to a remarkable degree over the ensuring two decades. However, it was neither an easy peace nor one that was passively sustained by Aboriginal leaders, who proved ready and willing to use the threat of coercion to reinforce their interpretation of a treaty relationship that, in their estimation, precluded undue Planter encroachments. Apprehension of the application of Mi'kmaq and Wulstukwiuk force thereupon became a central theme of the Planter experience during the 1760s, and a central concern of successive governors of Nova Scotia.

As late as the summer of 1759, a year after the fall of Louisbourg, the ability of Aboriginal forces to inflict damage on British settlements and outposts had been graphically demonstrated. In April of that year, Governor Lawrence had reported to London on raids taking place at Lunenburg and on the Isthmus of Chignecto. Although he hoped to be able "to cover the inhabitants against these mortifying and very discouraging incursions upon them," by September he was forced to admit that matters had become even worse as a result of Aboriginal raids on land and the sea-borne activities of armed Acadian fugitives.[2] Not only did these circumstances

lead to the postponement of the first Planter migrations for a year,[3] but also Lawrence ensured that initial Planter settlements were planned with defence in mind. In Horton, Cornwallis, and Falmouth townships, reported his successor Jonathan Belcher, "Pallisadoed Forts were erected in each [...] by order of the late Governor, with room sufficient to receive all the Inhabitants, who were formed into a Militia to join what Troops could be spar'd to oppose any attempts that might be formed against them."[4] Even so, and even after the treaty-making process was well under way, there were serious doubts about whether the protection would be adequate. The surveyor Charles Morris wrote to the Nova Scotia council from Pisiquid in June 1760 that "the want of a sufficient number of Troops at this Juncture where so many Settlements are carrying on, is not a little discouraging to the new Settlers. I am in hopes no accident will happen to make a greater number necessary."[5]

[...]

Jonathan Belcher, acting as governor after Lawrence's death in late 1760, was acutely aware of these imperatives. To the council and assembly of Nova Scotia in March 1762, Belcher praised the role of favourable trade terms in consolidating the treaty relationship, and urged that "every reasonable Method ought to be pursued for preserving this Peace inviolate, and fixing their Affections and Attachments from the Sense and experience of Protection, Integrity and Friendship."[6] Six weeks later, he turned his attention to the land question, issuing a proclamation that reserved for the use of Aboriginal inhabitants, pending confirmation or otherwise by the Crown, lands adjoining the entire coastline from Musquodoboit to the Bay of Chaleur. Justifying the proclamation to the Board of Trade, Belcher made it clear that it stemmed from "the Pretensions of the Indians" and from his recognition that Aboriginal discontent could have "disagreeable consequences in the present Situation of Affairs."[7] [...] Even though the concessions specifically made in the Nova Scotia proclamation were too extensive to be received favourably in London, they offer persuasive testimony on the crucial importance attached by Belcher in the spring of 1762 to the placation of Aboriginal interests.

The summer of 1762 brought more direct evidence to bear, as perceived Aboriginal threats brought desertions from Planter settlements and disaffection in the militia. ... Planters from the King's

Source: John G. Reid, "*Pax Britannica* or *Pax Indigena*? Planter Nova Scotia (1760–1782) and Competing Strategies of Pacification," *Canadian Historical Review* (85:4) (December 2004): pp. 679–688. © 2004 University of Toronto Press Incorporated. Reprinted by permission of University of Toronto Press, www.utpjournals.com

County settlements of Horton, Cornwallis, Falmouth, and Newport protested the removal of their militia for duties at Fort Edward and Fort Sackville at a time when "a Considerable Body of Indians were assembled together menacing the Inhabitants with Destruction," and the Halifax council of war responded by allowing the King's County men to return home, "but to hold Themselves in Readiness to March hither at a Moments Warning."[8] By August, both Belcher and the council of war were taking note of desertions from the King's County settlements. Belcher also reported to General Jeffery Amherst that by that time the threat had been extended to Halifax, where in his view the nearby assembly of an Aboriginal force estimated at 600 strong, along with the presence in the town of several hundred captive male Acadians of military age, "should make the people in the New Settlements fear the fate of this Town [Halifax], and their own."[9]

The crisis of 1762 ended as suddenly as it had begun. By early September, Belcher believed the threat had subsided and credited "the Measures … taken for checking and dispersing the Indians."[10] The question remains whether Aboriginal forces had ever intended more than a show of force. [...] The vulnerability of the settlers and the continuing insecurity of the British presence had, however, been clearly demonstrated.

[...]

In mid-1768, as British troops began to leave Halifax to meet the revolutionary crisis in New England, the Nova Scotia council expressed concern about the weakening of military outposts in the region, notably Fort Cumberland.[11] When Campbell arrived back in Nova Scotia in September after travels in England and New England, he wasted no time in writing to senior imperial administrators to warn that troop withdrawals would provide "cause of most uneasy Allarmes for the safety of the yet thinly Inhabited Settlements in the Interior parts of the province," and that Nova Scotia was an "infant struggling Province" and vulnerable to Aboriginal attack.[12] Some six weeks later, he reported further to the colonial secretary, Lord Hillsborough, that "I have daily advices from [...] [the interior settlements] which seem to confirm my apprehensions are not groundless." Campbell then went on to set out the military balance of power succinctly: "the outposts of this Province fixt, as a Shelter and retreat for the Inhabitants settled upon

the Frontiers, left destitute of Garrisons, to protect them, may be either destroyed or possessed by the Savages, a very small Number of which, would be able at this juncture to bring fire and Destruction to the very entrance of this Town [Halifax]."[13]

By early 1769, Campbell was still reaffirming to Hillsborough the vulnerability of Nova Scotia. "They are daily coming in here," he wrote of the Mi'kmaq, "and demanding provisions in such terms, as indicates their being sensible of the weak State of the Interior parts of the Province, deprived of all Military protection."[14] Yet it was noteworthy that what the governor was describing was not an attack but a request for supplies. No doubt, to judge from Campbell's description, it was made as a request that could not reasonably—or, from a British standpoint, safely be refused.

[...]

Aboriginal–British relationships had become less troubled as the pace of Planter settlement had slackened. A report reaching London in 1773 declared, even though with some over-simplification, that "the Indians [...] since the French have been expell'd from the neighbourhood of this Province [...] have become quiet and at present are well disposed."[15] A year later, the Yorkshire travellers John Robinson and Thomas Rispin portrayed the Aboriginal population of the region as "very expert in hunting, and excellent marksmen with the gun," but to the settlers "friendly, harmless, well-behaved."[16] In effect, the Planters—from being the provacateurs of the 1760s—had become the new Acadians of the 1770s. The number of non-Aboriginals in the region remained, even at the end of that decade, many fewer than on the eve of the Acadian deportation. Although population figures for this period are necessarily estimates based on imperfect sources, Julian Gwyn has put the population of mainland Nova Scotia (including the modern New Brunswick) at 18,000 in early 1755, including Acadians, British and British-sponsored, and Aboriginal inhabitants. The corresponding figure for 1781 was 14,000.[17] As a number of scholars have observed, the rural settlements of Planter Nova Scotia were scattered and lacked effective interconnecting routes.[18] Furthermore, Planter incursions into cleared uplands had been limited in scope, and Planter marshland agriculture retained many affinities in technique with the old Acadian forms of cultivation.[19] Thus, insofar as the Planter migration had represented a coordinated, military-inspired intervention into Aboriginal territory, and one that had intended substantial environmental change in selected locations, it had met with no greater success than had the British efforts of the 1750s. Despite the persistence of occasional tensions between settlers and Aboriginal inhabitants,[20] and of debates among Aboriginal leaders during the mid-1770s over the merits of support for the revolutionaries,[21] the Halifax regime had settled into a pattern that made it only the latest of the many imperial intrusions that the Aboriginal nations had been able to domesticate since the early seventeenth century.

The Loyalist migration, beginning in 1782, was different. Most importantly, the Loyalists arrived with crude force of numbers. At least 30,000 Loyalist refugees flooded into Nova Scotia. [...] Although they met Aboriginal resistance in some areas, ranging from Antigonish to Fredericton, this was a migration that was fully capable of filling in the valleys and the interstices of the region.[22] The Loyalists did not lack for military support, either from the forces deployed to Nova Scotia for the purpose or from the presence among the settlers of disbanded Loyalist troops.[23] Yet the primary force of their transformative effect was environmental. No longer were either lack of settlement or an enforceable treaty relationship containing forces. Instead, the chief constraint now was simply the limited quantity of productive agricultural land in the region. Even this was insufficient to prevent substantial encroachment on Aboriginal lands, and the severing of Aboriginal communication routes by settlement. Although in places some versions of the hunting-gathering-fishing economy were able to persist for a time, the Aboriginal nations now faced a defensive struggle that had little likelihood of success in the foreseeable future. [...]

In this context, the older questions about Planter settlement re-emerge in a newer context. Or, rather, the two traditional questions—why the Planters did not give substantial support to the American revolution, and what made the Planters distinct from the Loyalists—coalesce into the same question. What were the characteristics of the Planter Nova Scotia that distinguished it and its colonists from the rebelling colonies and from those of their inhabitants who were protagonists on one side or the other? The overarching answer to the question, however, can best be approached by posing a newer one that can be and should be applied by historians to any and all areas of early modern northeastern North America: What were the prevailing balances between Aboriginal, imperial, and colonial interests? In Planter Nova Scotia, the simple reality was (though the implications were far from simple) that the relationship between colonists and the imperial state was not a significant *remise en question*.* More urgent was the relationship between colonists and Aboriginal neighbours. [...]

As for the settlers themselves, the crucial historiographical flaw in so much of the analysis that flowed from the work of Brebner and his successors was that it posited a symmetrical choice for the Planters—they could be revolutionaries, they could be Loyalists, or they could avoid the choice altogether by being apathetic. In reality, however, the symmetry was absent. Active Loyalism was indeed an option, but even that choice would not excuse the Planters from their more urgent involvement in working through the relationship between the state and the aboriginal nations as embodied in the treaties and lived out in the region every day.

NOTES

1. Record of Governor's Farm Ceremony, 25 June 1761, fols. 277–83, C0217/18. PRO.
2. Lawrence to Board of Trade, 20 April, 20 Sept. 1759, fols. 317–18, 322, C0217/16, PRO.
3. Minutes of Nova Scotia Council, 16 July 1759, 88–90, vol. 188, RG1, NSARM.
4. Belcher to Board of Trade, 12 Dec. 1760, fol. 81, C0217/18, PRO.
5. Minutes of Nova Scotia Council, 5 June 1760, 149, vol. 188, RG1, NSARM. Morris's letter, recorded in the minutes, was written on 1 June 1760.
6. Belcher to Council and Assembly, 23 Mar. 1762, fol. 31, C0217/19, PRO.
7. Proclamation, 4 May 1762, fols. 27–8, C0217/19, PRO; Belcher to Board of Trade, 2 July 1762, fols. 22–3, C0217/19, PRO.
8. Petition of King's County Inhabitants [July 1762], no. 10, Brown Transcripts. vol. 284, RG1, NSARM; Minutes of Council of War, 21 July 1762, 11–12, vol. 188A, RG1, NSARM.
9. Minutes of Council of War, 11 Aug. 1762, 18–19, vol. 188A, RG1, NSARM; Belcher to Amherst, 12 Aug. 1762, fols. 103–4, C0217/43, PRO.

*A matter of constant questioning.

10. Belcher to Board of Trade, 7 Sept. 1762, fols. 70–9, C0217/19, PRO.

11. Minutes of Nova Scotia Council, 11 July 1768, 104–5, vol. 189, RG1, NSARM.

12. Campbell to Lord Hillsborough, 12 Sept. 1768, fols. 245–6, C0217/45, PRO; Campbell to Lord Barrington, 12 Sept. 1768, fol. 251, C0217/45, PRO. See also Francis A. Coghlan, "Lord William Campbell," in *Dictionary of Canadian Biography*, eds. George W. Brown et al. (Toronto: University of Toronto Press, 1966–) 4:131–2.

13. Campbell to Lord Hillsborough, 25 Oct. 1768, fols. 272–3, C0217/45, PRO.

14. Campbell to Lord Hillsborough, 13 Jan. 1769, fol. 112, C0217/25, PRO.

15. Report of the Present State and Condition of His Majesty's Province of Nova Scotia, 1773, fols. 19–20, C0217/50, PRO.

16. John Robinson and Thomas Rispin, *Journey through Nova-Scotia Containing a Particular Account of the Country and Its Inhabitants* (1774: repr., Sackville, NB: Ralph Pickard Bell Library, Mount Allison University, 1981), 27.

17. Julian Gwyn, *Excessive Expectations: Maritime Commerce and the Economic Development of Nova Scotia, 1740–1870* (Kingston and Montreal: McGill-Queen's University Press, 1998).

18. M. W. Armstrong, "Neutrality and Religion in the Revolutionary Nova Scotia," *New England Quarterly* 19 (1946), 50; Graeme Wynn, "Late 18th Century Agriculture on the Bay of Fundy Marshlands," *Acadiensis* 8, no. 2 (Spring 1979) 88. See also Campbell to Lord Shelburne, 27 Feb., 21 May 1767, 293–5, fols. 167, C0217/44, PRO.

19. Alan R. MacNeil, "The Acadian Legacy and Agricultural Development in Nova Scotia, 1760–1861," in *Farm, Factory and Fortune: New Studies in the Economic History of the Maritime Provinces*, ed. Kris Inwood (Fredericton: Acadiensis Press, 1993).

20. See L.F.S. Upton, *Micmacs and Colonists: Indian–White Relations in the Maritimes, 1713–1867* (Vancouver: UBC Press, 1979), 68–71.

21. Ibid., 72–8; Stephen Augustine, "*Lsipogtog*, 'River of Fire': A Historical Analysis" (Report to the Big Cove Band, 2003), 5–6; Ernest Clarke, *The Siege of Fort Cumberland 1776: An Episode in the American Revolution* (Montreal and Kingston: McGill-Queen's University Press, 1995), 73–5, 82–3. My thanks to Stephen Augustine for permission to cite his unpublished report.

22. L.F.S. Upton, *Micmacs and Colonists: Indian–White Relations in the Maritimes, 1713–1867* (Vancouver: University of British Columbia Press, 1979), 82–3; W.S. MacNutt, *New Brunswick: A History, 1784–1867* (Toronto: Macmillan, 1963), 78.

23. See Robert S. Allen, ed., *The Loyal Americans: The Military Role of the Loyalist Provincial Corps and Their Settlements in British North America, 1775–1784* (Ottawa: National Museum of Man/National Museums of Canada, 1983), passim.

173

■ Article 5: The Fault Lines of Empire: Political Differentiation in Massachusetts and Nova Scotia, ca. 1760–1830

Elizabeth Mancke

The Liverpool-Machias comparison prompts us to turn to an assessment of political geography rather than physical geography for an answer to why two similarly remote communities had different responses to the imperial crisis. Both were communities on the margins of political systems and the salient questions relate to their orientation to a political center, the location of the center, the strength of the connection between a center and its peripheries, and the strength of any periphery, Indeed, one of the signal historical problems of the early modern British Empire is to explain how a peripheral area could create a centripetal dynamic of its own, in particular how thirteen North American colonies became strong enough to risk challenging and severing their connection to the imperial center.[1] Machias and Liverpool, and more generally eastern Maine and Nova Scotia, were politically weak and therefore drawn toward the centers of larger systems, but in ways that had less to do with the physical geography than with the political geography of the British Atlantic world as it had evolved over the seventeenth and eighteenth centuries. Quite simply, geographic remoteness is an insufficient explanation for complex political arrangements that had emerged over the previous 200 years. More significant and provocative is why similar communities were oriented toward different political centers in the Atlantic world. [...]

In 1760 Yankees arrived in Nova Scotia thinking that they would have the same rights and privileges they had enjoyed in New England and acted accordingly. The Liverpool proprietors petitioned Charles Morris, the provincial surveyor, to issue a warrant

for them to call a meeting to choose "a moderator, a clerk, and a committee to manage their affairs,"[2] He issued the warrant and they met, but before long they, and settlers throughout Nova Scotia, discovered that the promise of "Government [...] constituted like those of the neighbouring colonies" did not extend to township affairs and that British officials in Halifax and London would not sanction the endeavors of settlers to replicate civic life as they had known it in New England."[3] Rather, local affairs were to be governed through the Courts of Sessions with magistrates appointed by the governor. Committees of settlers appointed by the executive council were to distribute land in the townships.

Nova Scotia's governor and council closely monitored settlement rates in the new townships, quite unlike colonial governments in New England, which were generally lax in enforcing the terms of grants. In 1761, the summer after the first settlers arrived in Nova Scotia, the council appointed proprietors' committees to admit new grantee-settlers in the places of those grantees who had moved to the province, and instructed the committees on how much land to give each category of people. Farmers with families of seven or more members were to receive one and a half shares, or 750 acres. Farmers with families of six or fewer members were to receive one share. Single farmers under twenty-one years of age were to receive a half-share. The committee for Liverpool had permission to admit fishermen, carpenters, "and other Professions belonging to the Sea," Then in March 1762 Jonathan Belcher, the lieutenant governor, issued a proclamation announcing vacancies in Sackville, Amherst, Granville, Yarmouth, Barrington, Onslow, New Dublin, and Chester townships arising out of the "failure in the Grantees of performance of required Conditions of Settling with their Families within Limited time."[4] The combination of the appointment of proprietors' committees and the gubernatorial invitation for people to join some townships elicited petitions of protest from throughout Nova Scotia. Settlers from the Minas Basin remonstrated that they had been "wholly deprived of those Rights and Priviledges," that they had known in New England and had been led to believe they would enjoy in Nova Scotia, including the right to control membership in the proprietorships.[5] Liverpool's residents protested that "as free men [...] born in a Country of Liberty in a Land that belongs to the

174

Crown of England," they had the "right of authority vested in ourselves [...] to nominate and appoint men among us to be our Committee and do Other Offices that the Town may Want"[6]

The response from Halifax to the memorials and protests was at best equivocal. In Nova Scotia the divergence from New England practices of. Local government became entangled with both provincial and imperial politics. In 1759, when Nova Scotia's settlements were still concentrated around Halifax and Lunenburg, the newly-convened assembly attempted to pass a law allowing for the establishment of a municipal government for Halifax. After sparring with the council, which balked at granting municipal privileges, the assembly crafted a bill entitled "Act for Preventing Trespasses," which provided for town officers to be appointed by the grand jury of the Court of Sessions during its annual fall meeting. Such was the extent of local government for Halifax. In 1763, the council, in response to Yankee settlers who protested the absence of the believed-to-have-been-promised New England–style town government, initiated a bill to provide for it Modifications by the assembly meant that its final form achieved little more than had the March 1759 "An Act for Preventing Trespasses" with the grand juries of the Courts of Sessions remaining in control of appointing town officers. The token concession made to advocates of town government was to allow for annual town meetings to set the poor rate and to elect assessors to collect it. In 1765 the system of local government received its last fine-tuning for many decades when an act established that the grand juries in the Courts of Sessions would nominate town officers and the justices would appoint them from the nominees.[7]

Even had the assembly and council reached a consensus on establishing town government and proprietors' rights, the Crown would probably have disallowed any legislation. In 1761 the assembly passed and the council approved "An Act to enable Proprietors to divide their lands held in common," but the Crown disallowed it, If proprietorships were disallowed, a form of corporation that had even more limited powers and lifespan than town governments, then the Crown probably would have disallowed legislation on local government had the council and assembly been able to agree on the powers to be delegated to localities. As well, such legislation would have conflicted with a four-decade-old metropolitan policy to establish local governments in Nova Scotia on a Virginia model of county government, and not a New England model of town government.[8]

Although the Board of Trade was active in proscribing or disallowing what it knew it did not want in Nora Scotia, it was less directive in determining what it would consider permissible. The disallowance of the proprietors' act left settlers without a good legal mechanism to divide the land until the council appointed committees, which in turn elicited protests about the violation of settler rights. Nevertheless, Liverpool's residents learned that if they did not unduly provoke officials in Halifax they could modify, if not ignore, many of their directives and thereby achieve considerable local autonomy. Liverpool's residents gave a broader definition to title proprietors' committee than Halifax had intended, and used it to distribute land, to add new settlers at their discretion, to elect men for numerous tasks, and to set aside public lands. In 1784 they submitted a disingenuous proprietors' report to Halifax indicating that all the land is the township had been distributed, but over two-thirds of that distribution was on paper only, and for two centuries (until 1978) the proprietors' committee (later called trustees) continued to oversee the allocation, of the undivided land.[9] Nothing in Nova Scotia's statutes or executive orders sanctioned most of the committee's actions, but Halifax first turned a blind eye to its activity, and then in die nineteenth century used it for land management issues because It served a useful function.

Liverpool settlers at once drew on their New England heritage for remedies to the institutional weaknesses they experienced in Nova Scotia and yet remained mindful of potential constraints from Halifax. Settlers in Horton assumed similar powers for the distribution of land; albeit without the longevity of Liverpool's committee.[10] It is important to note, however, in each township settlers made adjustments based on local needs, their prior experience, and the degree of oversight from Halifax. The agricultural townships with their valuable land seem to have received more scrutiny from Halifax than did the South Shore fishing villages with their poor rock ground. In October 1766 the provincial secretary, Richard Bulkeley, informed the justices of the peace in Londonderry that the committee in that township which had taken upon itself the distribution of the

175

undivided lands was illegal. He further stated that "it is a very Extraordinary proceeding to choose persons for the division of the lands after fitt persons had been appointed by the Government for that purpose, who had they been Negligent in their business would have been removed and others have been appointed."[11] Sitting in Halifax, Bulkeley could think the actions of the Londonderry committee were extraordinary, but the records of Liverpool and Horton show that what it did was quite ordinary in many townships.

Land distribution in Liverpool and Horton reflected the New England practice of proprietorial control, but in Nova Scotia the behavior did not produce the same political and social results as it did in New England. Proprietors in Nova Scotia had no legal corporate rights, so to distribute lands as a group was to act beyond statute law, but proprietors in both townships did it, thereby making possible the sale of township lands. Recent grantees were not to sell land without a license from Halifax, but they nevertheless engaged in a lively, and unlicensed, land trade.[12] Jonathan Belcher, a prolific writer of proclamations, issued one in 1763 prohibiting the sale of land after learning "that many Grantees had alien'd their property and had afterward by Concealment obtained Rights in Other Counties in Manifest abuse of the Special trust Confidence and Liberality of Government in the Respective Grants."[13] Proclamations notwithstanding, neither Belcher nor his successors actively prosecuted these grant violations, partly because they had little interest in doing so. Belcher's warning, however, did make the settlers wary because the possibility remained that the government might step in. Unlike New England proprietors who divided land with the assurance of both custom and statute law behind them, proprietors in Nova Scotia divided their land outside the statute law, using a set of customs that officials in Halifax and London found in principle to be threatening and undesirable.

Settlers in Nova Scotia also found themselves caught between New England practice and Nova Scotia policy on the issue of church support. In New England, most churches were supported through a town assessment for the minister's rate, which all townspeople had to pay unless they were members of an officially recognized dissenting church. In Nova Scotia, the absence of town government made it illegal to tax, whether for religion, roads, or schools,

although many settlements raised a minister's rate in their early years, Liverpool's proprietors levied one for four years, then for a brief while the "freeholders" in townshipwide meetings voted, assessed, and collected ministerial taxes. In the late 1770s another form of assessment applied until the time the Reverend Israel Cheever stepped down as the Congregational minister in the town in 1782, which Simeon Perkins referred to in his diary, although neither the proprietors' nor the freeholders' records mention it. Presumably the church and congregation collected a minister's rate, but they had no corporate rights to levy a tax on their members. For twenty years the people of Liverpool had persisted in following a modified version of the New England practice of public support of religion, even when it had no basis in statute law. There is no evidence that the government tried to stop the practice of ministerial assessments, and eventually religious dissent and the lack of town government proved effective prosecutors against them. The important point, however, is that as New Englanders reconstructed their lives in Nova Scotia, they borrowed heavily from their cultural background, all the while recognizing that it might be in conflict with official policy if not the law. And in most instances, the provincial government did little or nothing.[14]

Communication between Halifax and outlying communities over the application of metropolitan and provincial policy fell into some discernible patterns. For the most part Halifax dismissively acknowledged the early protests from townships over the appointment of proprietors' committees or the absence of town government. By the mid-1760s, people in the townships settled by New Englanders largely ceased submitting remonstrances to Halifax, just when colonists in the older colonies began their protests of new metropolitan policy. Not all was quiet, however, in the townships. In Liverpool "Some Publick Marks of discontent were Shewn" upon news of the Stamp Act.[15] When word of its repeal reached the town on June 3, 1766 the people celebrated. Perkins recorded a

> Day of rejoicing over the repeal of the Stamp Act. Cannon at Point Laurence fired, colours flown on shipping. In the evening the Company marched to the home of Major Doggett, and were entertained. People made a bon-fire out of the old house of

Capt. Mayhew, a settler here, and continued all night, and part of next, carousing.[16]

This display of discontent, however, was isolated, remained within Liverpool, was not extended to other townships, and was not expressed to officials in Halifax. By the time Parliament repealed the Stamp Act in 1766, communication between townships and Halifax over political rights had been curtailed, thus creating a deceptive silence in the government records that masked continuing local adaptations and developments. By the mid-1760s, Nova Scotia's Yankees had learned that their protests to Halifax elicited little or no response, or if the assembly or council acted in favor of the settlers through legislation or executive orders, the king was likely to veto them. Settlers also learned that if they kept quiet and did not create disturbances they had considerable local control, most of which Halifax tolerated.

Halifax did not indiscriminately tolerate local developments. Colonial governors threatened prosecution if towns called local meetings to discuss colonial or imperial affairs. In 1774 Governor Legge banned meetings to "Disturb the Peace and promote illegal confederacies, combinations, public disorders and the highest contempt to Government." After the Revolution Governor John Wentworth removed justices in Hants and Annapolis counties who organized meetings to protest the dismissal of Naval Officer William Cottnam Tonge.[17] The message was quite clear. In the management of local affairs the government might tolerate, although not guide or sanction, the development of particularistic local institutions, but those local developments were not to be exported or used to agitate against the provincial or imperial governments. Indeed, the governor and council seemed to have issued just enough rebukes to keep the settlers on their guard, but not enough to stop their local adaptations. For the most part, Halifax lacked the coercive power to stop them, although it could make their lives awkward. The assembly and council, for their part, were not in a position to provide the institutional mechanisms to handle local needs. In the gap between prohibitions and absences, localities accommodated themselves as necessity and their customs dictated.

By the time fighting broke out in 1775, Yankees in Liverpool had considerable experience in dealing with undesirable metropolitan policy. Their political education in the colony emphasized reticence toward colonial officials and an inward turning as a way to achieve local autonomy. For over a decade and without clear markers and signals Nova Scotia's Yankees devised local compromises and accommodations that allowed them to reestablish their lives in another colony without inviting government censure. Their behavior served local needs, but would not be auspicious for participating in any organized political action beyond the boundaries of a township and certainly not for organizing a colonywide resistance, which would have been necessary for Nova Scotia to be the fourteenth united state. In suppressing town government without viable alternatives among a people zealous of their local rights, the British had eliminated the institutional mechanisms, and by turn the political behavior, for initiating communications among settlements. One town could not solicit the aid of another town, the assembly could not organize towns, and responding institutions, such as town governments, did not officially exist. The local autonomy that Nova Scotia's Yankees had learned could be theirs would have been jeopardized had people tried to link towns in common action.

In the short run, British authorities had created, partly by design and partly by default, a political system that could not organize itself to challenge metropolitan governance. [...]

Machias, and the other downeast settlements in Maine, contrast sharply with the inward turning localism of Nova Scotian settlements. The Machias grant, the thirteenth between the Penobscot and St. Croix Rivers, finally received the governor's signature in 1700, after three readings in the General Court, but the Crown approved neither it nor the earlier grants of twelve other townships. The lack of royal approbation jeopardized the viability of the thirteen grants and forestalled the establishment of governmental institutions in the region, especially incorporated towns.

The weakness of local government in the Territory of Sagadahoc, like that in Nova Scotia, came from changes in metropolitan policy, but the remedies varied enormously. In Nova Scotia, settlers confronted the implementation of a forty-year-old metropolitan plan to establish the colony without replicating the perceived republican vices of the New England colonies, especially locally vested rights such as town government. In the Territory

177

of Sagadahoc Yankees encountered a variation of the same plan, played out in a decades-old contest between Whitehall and Boston over the control of settlement in the area.[18] To thwart the authority of the Massachusetts government, the Board of Trade blocked the approval of grants and with them the establishment of town governments.

Unlike the situation in Nova Scotia, the settlers in eastern Maine could not even establish clear title to their land. As well, all of eastern Maine was one enormous county, far larger than some colonies. The Massachusetts government could not divide it and create a new county because of the conflict between Whitehall and Boston over jurisdiction in the region. The judicial system in the easterly reaches of Maine was therefore virtually nonexistent, which was not the case in Nova Scotia. Beneath these similarities and differences, it can be said that people in both Liverpool and Machias, and in Nova Scotia and eastern Maine, were dissatisfied with the lack of local, and particularly town, government. But the relationships of the settlements to the larger political world forced people in both areas to respond to these deficits in local government in quite different ways.

The unwillingness of the king to approve the township grants in the Territory of Sagadahoc within the eighteen months allowed by the General Court disrupted the lives of the people who had settled or planned to settle. To bid for more time and to safeguard the security of their investments the grantees applied to the General Court to extend the time limit to receive royal approval. This situation especially affected the first twelve townships granted in 1762. On June 10 and 11, 1765, the proprietors from Townships Four, Five, and Six (now Steuben, Addison, and Harrington) held separate meetings in Falmouth (now Portland), Maine, to vote to request that the General Court extend the time limit for obtaining royal approbation for their grants. Then in a single petition to the General Court, the grantees of all three townships asked the assembly to renew their grants and to give them the right to sell the shares of those proprietors who had not paid their portion of expenses.[19] These people worked together in their negotiations with Boston, and to get three groups meeting within one day of each other meant that prior organization had taken place. In 1767 and 1768, the grantees from the various townships again worked in concert to petition for a time extension.[20] This synchronization of

effort among townships, which largely disappeared in Nova Scotia, would prove important to organizing the resistance and revolutionary movement.

Until 1769 Machias was without justices of the peace. In the fall of that year merchant Stephen Parker of Machias wrote to Governor Hutchinson complaining that the absence of any authority had encouraged "licentious" behavior among the inhabitants. As well, the lack of civil authority made merchants wary of supplying Parker, thereby making the provisioning of Machias extremely difficult.[21] Shortly thereafter, Governor Hutchinson appointed Jonathan Longfellow a justice of the peace. In the fall on 1770 four men attacked him and "beat and bruised him to such a degree, that he … [was] incapable of going about his business." As the sole magistrate in Machias he could not charge them with an attack on himself. The nearest appointed magistrate able to hand the case was location in Gouldsboro, some twenty leagues (about sixty miles) down the coast, and according to Longfellow, that magistrate had gone to Boston for the winter. In a memorial in support of Longfellow's report, the people of Machias reasoned that the best way to resolve the problem was to appoint another justice of the peace. Hutchinson responded by appointing a deputy sheriff and a second justice of the peace in Machias.[22]

The lack of justices of the peace also frustrated people in Township Four who reported to the General Court that "neither Law nor Gospel [is] embraced among us every one doing what's right in his own eyes and a great spirit of mobbing and Rioting prevails, Cursing, Swearing, fighting, threatening, Stealing, pulling down Houses and the like as we cant sleep at nights without fear." Without corroborating evidence it is impossible to know if the settlement was as riotous as portrayed, or whether settlers used hyperbolic rhetoric to convince Governor Hutchinson "to interpose in this affair to redress our Grievances" and appoint a justice of the peace, the closest then being either twenty miles to the west in Gouldsboro or over twenty miles to the east in Machias. They recommended Captain Wilmot Wass, a settler from Martha's Vineyard, but added that they would not object should the governor choose a different person.[23]

Hutchinson also commissioned a committee of three from the General Court to travel to eastern Maine and make a report on the status of law and order in the thirteen townships without confirmed grants, in particular Machias, and to assess the damage to the king's woods.[24] The committee recommended that to assure "as much peace and good order at Machias as in the other twelve granted Towns" the existing authority should be strengthened. As an immediate measure they swore in one resident Mr. Sinkler as deputy sheriff, explaining in their report that it "was absolutely necessary, especially as there neither was nor could be a Constable in that place, it not being Incorporated." They also noted that the only jail in the county was over seventy leagues away by water, making it difficult to use for purposes of maintaining law and order, and in winter when the harbors were frozen it was inaccessible. They recommended that the governor use his powers to establish a temporary civil jail at Fort Pownall, about thirty-six leagues from Machias, but he seemingly did not do so.[25]

Under pressure from settlers and the Massachusetts General Court, Hutchinson signed the Machias grant and appointed justices of the peace. His actions were taken against the policy of his superiors on the Board of Trade. But, as he tried to explain to Lord Hillsborough, the General Court would not prosecute the settlers as trespassers and with upwards of 1,500 settlers in the thirteen contested townships some form of governance had to be provided or the people would form their own government much as the regulators had done in the Carolinas. Hutchinson's action in appointing justices of the peace, however, gave sanction to the settlers and reinforced their tie to Boston.[26]

[...]

Unlike the Nova Scotia townships where the petitions and memorials for redress of grievances virtually creased after 1765, in Maine they continued throughout the war.

By 1775 the people of Machias and Liverpool had evolved significantly different attitudes about how their respective localities fit into the larger political world. In Machias, the people actively sought the help of the provincial government in Boston, which guided local developments. Through petitions and memorials the people communicated their needs and Boston usually responded favorably. When the Board of Trade blocked confirmation of the grants the General Court and the governor responded with interim measures to allow the people to organize their public lives in familiar ways that could later be merged into the customary institutions of town and county government. In Liverpool the petitions and memorials for the establishment of New England–style local government ceased soon after the settlers arrived in Nova Scotia. The absence of town government and proprietorships and a weak county government created a vacuum at the local level in which developed mutations of New England institutions, and which were efficacious given the peoples' cultural predispositions and local needs, but were at variance with British policy and extralegal, if not illegal. In eastern Maine people avoided local innovation if given centrally guided accommodation. These differences in the way localities communicated with other units of government created very different environments in which people responded to political issues. It is not surprising, therefore, that when armed conflict broke out, people in Nova Scotia townships responded by defending isolated township interests, while those in eastern Maine townships worked in concert with each other, with the provincial government in Boston, and with the Continental Congress to defend the common interests of their polities.

The channels of communication between the Massachusetts government and the towns, and among towns, were critical in developing a resistance movement to the British. The rights of towns to hold meetings at their discretion, to communicate among themselves as legally incorporated entities, and of assembly members to urge action upon the towns were critical to the revolutionaries' efforts. As the resistance movement grew, associations of revolutionaries throughout the colonies utilized existing political institutions, which in New England often meant the town meeting.[27] Indeed the New England town meetings were well suited to forging united opposition to British policy, and other colonies tried to imitate them with large public meetings.[28] Despite being unincorporated, settlements in eastern Maine used customary inter-town patterns of communication to link themselves into the political system. In Nova Scotia comparable channels of communication and networking never developed or were discouraged and suppressed. The weak or passive response of New Englanders in Nova Scotia to the Revolution resulted from their political isolation, not their geographic isolation.

During the Revolution most Nova Scotian Yankees assumed a position of nonengagement that protected their local autonomy. Militarily active loyalism would have conceded too much to the legitimacy of British metropolitan policy. In the townships, accommodation, to that policy had involved too much quiet defiance for people to support it suddenly. But their means of accommodation depended on quiescent forms of local adaptation that precluded the development of systems of organization that were needed to sustain rebel activity. Their position was not one of neutrality, nor did it reflect confusion about their choices in Nova Scotia. They had essentially evolved a new political culture of idiosyncratic localism and loyalty to the Empire. They did not openly endorse British policy, but from their local bases neither did they resist it. The metropolitan government had achieved its immediate needs. The prohibition of New England town government in Nova Scotia eliminated competing levels of political authority and allegiance from which people could threaten the Empire, By the outbreak of armed conflict in 1775 there was politically little in Nova Scotia that stood between the town and the empire.

This difference in the political behavior of people in the two areas is nicely illustrated in the issue of neutrality in both Nova Scotia and eastern Maine. From Yarmouth, Nova Scotia, came an oft-quoted 1775 petition for neutral status, and that scholars have used to argue the case for colonywide neutrality. In eastern Maine there was a movement for neutrality in 1781 during the time that the British were occupying Castine on Penobscol Bay. Beyond the difference in timing there was a more profound difference in the method of requesting neutrality that shows how the political culture of the two areas had diverged in the years after 1760.[29]

The Yarmouth petition for neutral status came shortly after Governor Francis Legge tried to call out the colony's militia units to defend Halifax, which as governor he could do.[30] Throughout the colony militia units refused to muster, those that mustered had no men who would volunteer to go to Halifax, and men refused officers' commissions. The people in Yarmouth also responded to the military confusion with a request for neutral status stating,

> We were almost all of us born in New England, we have Fathers, Brothers & Sisters in that country, divided betwixt natural affection to our nearest relations, and good Faith and Friendship to our King and Country, we want to know, if we may be permitted at this time to live in a peaceable State, as we look on that to be the only situation in which we with our Wives and Children, can be in any tolerable degree safe.

The Governor and Council were unequivocally against the idea. They responded to the Yarmouth memorialists

> that the request & proposition of the Memorialists, cou'd neither be receiv'd or Admitted a Neutrality being utterly Absurd and inconsistent with the duty of Subjects, who are always bound by the Laws to take Arms in defence of Government and oppose and Repel all Hostile Attempts and Invasions, that the duty they owe as Subjects cannot be dispensed with.

Duty or not, most Nova Scotian men refused to do service in Halifax. There is no evidence that people in Yarmouth joined with any other towns to request neutrality, and there were no similar pleas for neutrality from other settlements. The only concerted action taken against the militia call-up was in the Assembly where representatives from the outports fiercely debated the passage of new militia laws.[31]

The movement for neutrality in eastern Maine came after the British had occupied Bagaduce (Castine) at the head of the Penobscot Bay. The General Court in Boston responded to the occupation by asking Brigadier General Peleg Wadsworth to plan a strategy of defense for Lincoln County. He placed all settlements in the county within firing range of an armed vessel under martial law for six months. To residents of islands in the Penobscot Bay he extended neutral status, thereby preempting British compulsion to have them swear oaths of allegiance to the Crown. He indicated that all other settlements in Lincoln County would continue to support the revolutionary cause, which left them subject to British harassment and pressure to take oaths of loyalty. Many also feared that the British Navy would revive its campaign to destroy the seacoast towns in eastern Maine, which British raids on the homes of prominent men only reinforced.[32]

The movement for neutrality began in Gouldsboro under the leadership of Francis Shaw, a magistrate, merchant, and major in the militia. He, according to the reports out of Machias, planned the move in consultation with Nathan Jones a fellow merchant in Gouldsboro, and Captain William Nickells of Narraguagus. Apparently Shaw worked first through the committees of safety in Gouldsboro, Narraguagus, and Frenchmen's Bay, which agreed to his plan to ask the General Court to declare the region between the Penobscot and the St. Croix Rivers neutral. He then sent a letter to Stephen Jones of Machias asking him to support the proposal there, a draft of which he included in the letter. He also sent letters to the committees of safety at Chandler's River and Pleasant River. Jones showed Shaw's letter and draft petition entitled "Representation of the Inhabitants of all the Tract of Land, lying & being on & between the Rivers Penobscot & St Croix inclusive," to the Machias committee of safety which promptly called a meeting of the inhabitants to discuss it.[33] The people of Machias voted unanimously to oppose any plan for neutrality and to work to defeat it in all other settlements as far west as Frenchmen's Bay. They agreed to write to the governor and General Court disavowing all support of the plan, and passed resolutions censuring the behavior of Shaw "who hath made it evident that he hath his private Interest at heart, more than the good of his Country," an opinion supported by the Pleasant River committee of safety. When it heard of the plan it stated that "not one Person here has coveted to be Neutors at Present Neither do we Desire to be so Sneeking as Leave our Friends at the Westerd to Beat the Bush & we to catchh the Hare."[34]

What the actions of both the Frenchmen's Bay and Machias people show is that they believed that they did not live in isolated communities that could negotiate their own arrangements with the Massachusetts government or with the British in Penobscot Bay. Even if one settlement was the author of a movement, it nonetheless endeavored to persuade other settlements of its position. The process worked two ways. Francis Shaw of Gouldsboro attempted to organize the settlements to support his proposal of neutrality, and the people of Machias worked to defeat it. The networking among towns was an important part of New England political culture, prominently manifested in the Revolution with the committees of correspondence and committees of

safety. Even in areas where settlements were not incorporated the practice of seeking widespread support was still employed. In Nova Scotia the British had not been able to suppress the local orientation of New England political life, and local institutions and power structures emerged without central approval. But to maintain that local autonomy the Yankees had to sacrifice the communication among towns that in New England served to temper excessive localism and to knit the towns into a larger political system. The single petition from Yarmouth is a reflection of political, not geographic, isolation.

The meaning of neutrality in Yarmouth and eastern Maine also differed fundamentally. Yarmouth residents wrote their petition on December 8, 1775, in response to the governor's call for men and almost seven months before the signing of the Declaration on Independence. Given this timing, the request only refers to not fighting against the rebels, many of whom were friends, family, and former neighbors, and not to any considered political position with a meaning at odds with the British Empire. Despite the governor's response that the request was "utterly Absurd and inconsistent with the duty of Subjects," precedents existed for British American colonists to refuse to participate in military service, especially in actions against fellow civilians, and yet still claim to be loyal. Colonists had done it during the Seven Years' War and again during the Stamp Act crisis. The request for neutrality from Yarmouth was issue-oriented rather than systemically oriented. They could ask to be treated as neutrals in the decision to bear arms against the rebels without declaring themselves to be disloyal to the Crown or Empire. Issue-oriented neutrality (or nonengagement) and loyalty were not mutually exclusive.

Only with the signing of the Declaration of Independence did a middle ground emerge in English-speaking North America that was beyond the pale of the British Empire. The eastern Maine movement for neutrality carried the implication that militarily and politically a middle ground had emerged, if only temporarily, between the British and Americans. Indeed Shaw used revolutionary ideology to argue that the people of Maine had a right to declare themselves neutral. He claimed that they had "Repeatedly Petition'd the former Government of Massachusetts [...] for Protection & Support, as that Government did the Kingdom of Great Britain, for Redress of

Grievances." Despite the petitions Massachusetts had, Shaw asserted, "Refused or Neglected to give Protection to use the said Inhabitants in Return for our Allegiance." In the absence of that protection and "Compressed between Two Potent contending Powers" the people had a right to ask to be treated as neutrals.[35] This was a very different interpretation of neutrality than that asked by the people in Yarmouth and one that acknowledged a position between Britain and the United States. Indeed some Anglo-Americans fully exploited the position, most notably those in Vermont.[36]

The possibility of a neutral position in Anglo-America came about because of an extreme polarization in positions between colonial Americans and British officialdom. For the people in Machias that polarization made them vilify Francis Shaw and his associates after they attempted to gain neutral status for the area between the Penobscot and the St. Croix Rivers. In their letter to the Massachusetts General Court, they described the plan for neutrality "as the sycophantic production of a few disiging Men, rather than the genuine feelings & sentiments of a faith full & brave People."[37] The Declaration of Independence may have created the possibility of a middle ground in Anglo-America, but in some areas the ideological positions had become so contrary that a neutral one was largely untenable, although Shaw's neutrality movement carried the implication that militarily and politically there was a middle ground between the British and the Americans. Nova Scotians did not entertain this position and throughout the war continued to see themselves within the pale of the empire and the war as a civil rather than an international conflict.

The ideological polarization in some parts of Anglo-America also created new meanings for loyalism and patriotism, definitions that no longer represented ranges on a spectrum of sentiment but rather quite circumscribed points. In Nova Scotia most people continued to use a definition of loyalty that was defined not in the heat of the revolution, but by the range of loyal behavior that had been acceptable in more peaceable times. Thus the "Loyalists", those people in the thirteen revolting colonies who supported the empire and who fled to Nova Scotia, New Brunswick, and Canada after the war, were an American creation. While the remaining parts of the British Empire absorbed those Loyalists and those Loyalists tried to apply their definition of loyalty to all British subjects in North America, it is not a definition that can be widely applied and used to assess the positions and attitudes of all the people who remained loyal at the time of the Revolution.[38] To judge the behavior of Nova Scotians during the war, a British definition of loyalty encompassing more than the time of the Revolution must be used. Thus, if one asks whether Nova Scotians' behavior, despite complaints of governors, fitted within a British definition of loyalty, then the answer is yes. But if one asks, were Nova Scotians Patriots or Loyalists—which is an inherently American question—then the answer is no, but one has asked a question that is inappropriate to Nova Scotia. For most Nova Scotians, one could be both loyal to the Crown and Empire and militarily not engaged. For Patriots and Loyalists in the thirteen rebelling colonies, military action and allegiance were increasingly linked, whereas in Nova Scotian minds they remained distinct. As tensions heightened in the 1770s it would have an impact on how the settlements responded to the bearing of arms.

NOTES

1. For essays exploring this problem for all the European empires in the America, see Daniels and Kennedy, eds., *Negotiated Empires*. For revolution in the British Atlantic see Eliga H. Gould, "Revolution and Counter-Revolution," in *The British Mantle World,* 1500-1800, eas., David Armitage and Michael J. Brad dick (Basingstoke, UK and New York: Palgrave, 2002), 196–213.
2. Liverpool Proprietors' Records, NSARM, MG 4, Vol. 77:2–4.
3. Proclamation, 11 January 1759, NSARM, RG 1, Vol 188. No. 39–44.
4. Proclamation, NSARM, RG 1, Vol 165, p. 213;. J.S. Martell, "Pre–Loyalist Settlements around the Minas Basin," (M.A. thesis, Dalhousie University. 1933), 122.
5. Proclamation, 25 March 1762. NSAKM, RG 1, Vol. 165: 213; Memorial from Peleg Coffin, et al., 8 July 1762, NSARM, RG 1, Vol. 211: 25–25I; Stewart and Rawlyk. *'A People Highly Favoured of God',* 19–20.
6. Council Minutes, 15 August 1761. NSARM, RG 1, Vol. 188: 263–264; Memorial from Peleg Coffin, et al, 8 July 1762. NSAKM, RG 1, Vol. 211:250–251.

7. Brenner. *The* Neutral *Yankees,* 111–217; J. Murray Beck, *The Government of Nova Scotia* (Toronto: University of Toronto Press, 1957), 134–135; Harvey, "The Struggle for the New England Form of Township Government," 15–23.

8. Mancke, "Imperial Transitions," 183–185.

9. See Chapter 3 for an analysis of land distribution in Liverpool and Machias.

10. McNabb "Land and Families in Horton Township, N.S., 1760–1830," 22–41.

11. Richard Bulkeley to Richard Upham, David Archibald, & John McKean, Esqrs., Londonderry, 29 October 1766, NSARM, RG 1, Vol. 136, No. 96.

12. McNabb," Land and Families in Horton Township, N.S., 1760–1830," 47–56.

13. Proclamation, 25 March 1763, NSARM, RG 1, Vol. 165, No. 260.

14. Liverpool Proprietors' Records, 28 August. 1761; 8 October 1762; 1 December 1763:29 May I764; NSARM, MG 4, Vol. 77; Perkins's Diary 1:4 June 1777; 1:26 February 1773; 1:3 March 1778; 2:12 March 1781; 2:5 February 1782.

15. Brebner, *Neutral Yankees,* 157.

16. *Perkins's Diary,* 1:3 June 1766: Governor to the Board of Trade. 19 September 1765, NSARM, RG 1, Vol. 37.

17. Quoted in Beck, *The Government of Nova Scotia,* 136. See also Margaret Ells, "Governor Wentworth's Patronage," *Collection of the Nova Scoria Historical Society* 25 (1942): 49–73.

18. Williamson, *The History of the State of Maine,* 2:359-360.

19. Minutes of Meetings, *DHMe,* 13:412-413; Petition, *DHMe,* 13:413-414.

20. Petition of Samuel Doane and Mathew Thorton, 28 January 1767, *DHMe,* 13:20-21; Petition of Nathan Jones and Others, 28 January 1767, *DHMe,* 13:21-22; Resolves of the House of Representatives, 5 February 1767, *DHMe,* 13:23; Petition of David Bean and Others, May 1768, *DHMe,* 13:83; Resolve of the House of Representatives, 28 June 1768. 13:83-84.

21. Letter, Stephen Parker to Thomas Hutchinson, 11 November 1769, CMaA, Vol. 25:339-340.

22. "Jonathan Longfellow's Memorial to Governor Hutchinson." 8 November 1770 and "Memorial of the Inhabitants of Machias," 9 November 1770, *DHMe,* 14:112-115; Jones, "Historical Account of Machias," 49; Letter, Hutchinson to Lord Hillsborough, 30 November 1770, CMaA, 27:59-60; Letter, Hutchinson to Lord Hillsborough, July 1771, CMaA, 27:196; Letter, Hutchinson to Jonathan Longfellow, 17 December 1770, CMaA, 27:79; Letter from Hutchinson to Col. Goldthwaite, 9 May 1771, CMaA, 27:162-163.

23. "Petition to Govr. Hutchinson by Inhabitants of the Fifth Township," n.d., *DHMe,* 14:92-93.

24. Order by Thomas Hutchinson to William Brattle, James Bowdoin, and Thomas Hubbard, 26 July 1771, CMaA, Vol. 279:23.

25. Report of Commissioners, 12 September 1771, *DHMe,* 14:137-139; Letter from Thomas Goldthwaite to Hutchinson, 12 October 1772, CMaA, Vol. 25:540-541.

26. Hutchinson's Message to the House of Representatives, 19 June 1771, *DHMe,* 14:132-34; Hutchinson to Hillsborough, 15 July 1772, CMaA, Vol. 27:363. See also Hutchinson's Speech, 1770, *DHMe,* 13:103-106.

27. Richard D. Brown, *Revolutionary Politics in Massachusetts: The Boston Committee of Correspondence and the Towns, 1772–1774* (Cambridge, MA Harvard University Pres, 1970).

28. Pauline Maier, *From Resistance to Revolution Colonial Radicals and the Development of American Opposition to Britain, 1765–1776* (New York, Knopf, 1973) 117–118.

29. Cf. the fallowing discussion of issues of neutrality in Nova Scotia and Mime with Brebner, *The Neutral Yankees* Stewart and Rawlyk, *'A People Highly Favoured of God*; Leamon, *Revolution Downcast,* 131–134; Clarke, He *Siege of Fort Cumberland,* xi, 16; and Donald Desserod, "Nova Scotia and the American Revolution: A Study of Neutrality and Moderation in the Eighteenth Century," in Margaret Conrad, ed., *Making Adjustments change and community in Planter Nova Scotia, 1759–1800* (Fredericton, NB: Acadiensis University Press, 1991), 89–112.

30. Labaree, ed. *Royal Instructions,* 117–8, 392

31. Brebner, *Neutral Yankees* 308–310; Letter from Richard Bulkeley, Provincial Secretary to Justices of the Peace in Yarmouth December 1775, NSARM, RG 1, Vol. 136:231; James D. Snowdon, "Footprints in the Marsh Mud: Politics and Land Settlement in the Township of Sackville, 1760–1800" (M–A. thesis, University of Not Brunswick, 1974), 94.

32. Proclamation of Martial Law, 18 April 1780, *DHMe.* 18:222–224: Martial Law Proclaimed Lincoln County

183

by John Allan, 26 June 1780, ibid., 18:333–335. See also James S. Leamon, The Search for Security: Maine after Penobscot,[12] *Maine Historical Society Quarterly* 21, 3 (1982): 119–L53.

33. The documents to piece this *story* together can be found in the *Documentary History of Maine,* They are: Letter of the Chairman of the Committee of Correspondence, Pleasant River, 9 April 1781, 19:191; Machias Committee of Correspondence to the Governor Hancock, 11 April 1781,19:193; Memorial of the Inhabitants of Machias to the Governor Hancock, 1781,19:225–228; Letter of Francis Shaw to Stephen Jones, 17 March 1781, 19:235–236; Minutes of the Meeting of the Inhabitants of Machias, 29 March 1781, 19: 236–238; Letter of the Madras Committee of Correspondence to Governor Hancock:, April 1781,19:238–241; Deposition of Jonas Farnsworth, 11 April 1781,19:241–243; Copy of the Representation written by Francis Shaw, 17 March 1781, 19:243–246; Letter of Francis Shaw to the Governor and Council, 3 May 1781,19:246–249.

34. Letter of the Pleasant River Committee of Correspondence, 9 April 1781, *DHMe,* 19:191.

35. Copy of Representation of the Inhabitants of all the Tract of Land, lying & being on & between the Rivers Penobscott & St. Croix inclusive, by Francis Shaw, *DHMe*, 19:243-246.

36. Bellesiles, *Revolutionary Outlaws*, passim.

37. Memorial of the Inhabitants of Machias, 29 April 1781, *DHMe*, 19:228.

38. MacKinnon, *This Unfriendly Soil*, 67-88; J.M. Bumsted, *Understanding the Loyalists*, (Sackville, NB. Centre for Canadian Studies. Mount Allison University, 1986), 39-49.

184

THE REBELLIONS OF 1837-8 IN LOWER AND UPPER CANADA

Why Did People Take Up Arms Against the Government?

Colin Coates
Glendon College, York University

THE REBELLIONS OF 1837–8 IN LOWER AND UPPER CANADA
Introduction by Colin Coates

INTRODUCTION

Colin Coates

As a historical event, the Rebellions of 1837–1838 make Canadians nervous. Even if Canadians usually underestimate the role of violence in the country's history, it is indeed rare for its citizens to flirt with the prospect of civil war. The Rebellions of 1837–1838 were one of the few instances when violence defined Canadian political differences, and substantial groups of people contested the very legitimacy of the government.

Nonetheless, many Canadians choose to emphasize the brevity of the rebellious enthusiasm and the clearly disorganized nature of the uprising against British imperial rule, particularly in Upper Canada (Ontario) but also in Lower Canada (Quebec). Without a doubt, the uprising in Lower Canada was a larger and deadlier affair. In Lower Canada, political cleavages built on social and cultural divisions between English-speaking elites and the French-speaking peasantry. The events in Upper Canada were linked thematically and chronologically but were not exacerbated by the powerful hostilities apparent in the St. Lawrence Valley.

The Rebellions occurred in two phases. After years of building political tensions and a concerted attempt on the part of the governors in Quebec City and Toronto to curb all opposition, rebellious groups launched attacks in the early winter of 1837, a time of the year when, in theory, the British would not be able to reinforce the local troops. But the local soldiers alongside pro-government volunteers contained the rebellions, and additional troops undertook the arduous winter journey from the Maritime colonies overland to the St. Lawrence Valley. The Lower Canadian rebels achieved success in the battle at St. Denis and forced the British troops to withdraw, but they lost the bloody battles at St. Charles and St. Eustace.

On the basis of faulty information about the success of the Patriote rebels in Lower Canada, radicals in Upper Canada launched a disordered uprising in Toronto and western Ontario. These were quickly controlled by loyal troops, and the leaders escaped to the United States. In the case of Lower Canada, the first phase in 1837 cleared away the more moderate leadership. Politicians such as Louis-Joseph Papineau fled to the United States, and others took over the leadership role. The following year, the rebellion entered a more radical phase, with Robert Nelson issuing a "Declaration of Independence of Lower Canada." Hoping for support from American sympathizers, the Iroquois near Montreal, and Patriote followers in the colony, the rebels launched a second series of attacks in 1838, which were quickly suppressed.

Similar attacks from across the border between Upper Canada and New York failed to inspire the larger uprising that the rebels were anticipating. The British authorities reasserted their authority, and the rebellions were over. Some rebel leaders in both colonies were hanged as an example, while others were deported to the Bahamas or Australia.

The popular view of the Rebellions is determined in large part by their failure. Yet part of the task of the historian is to recognize the uncertainty of historical events. At the time of the Rebellions, one could not predict the outcome. There was unquestionably a good deal of public sympathy for the rebel position, particularly in Lower Canada, at the same time that many supported the government in place.

The following documents illustrate some of the issues that led to the outbreak of hostilities and capture the contingency of the events. At the same time, the sources show how participants attempted to ascribe historical meaning to the events: the work of a disorganized mob, a reflection of the French Revolution of 1789 (still within the historical memory of people living), or a battle of principles about the importance of local political sovereignty. We should keep in mind the size of the largest towns in Lower and Upper Canada (Montreal at about 27,000 in 1832 and Toronto—recently renamed from York— about 10,000 in 1837). Although important trading centres, the towns were still relatively small. Many of the rebellious activities occurred in the countryside, where the density of population was, of course, even smaller. Consequently, such political turmoil pitted neighbour against neighbour, as people chose which side to support.

Historians have proposed a number of broad causes for the Rebellions (including political unrest in Britain and in the United States, economic difficulties throughout North America in 1837, shifts in the class structures of the colonies, and the increasing penetration of the capitalist economy into the countryside). The articles in this module examine some of the causes of the Rebellions in the two colonies. Allan Greer evaluates the importance of ethnic tensions in Lower Canada, and Colin Reid and Robert Stagg summarize the range of economic, political and social issues that contributed to the uprising.

At the time of the outbreak of armed conflict, individuals had to make choices about whether they would support the rebels or the government, or try to remain neutral. Many of the rebels in both Lower and Upper Canada were land-owning farmers with families to support. Why did they risk their freedom, their lives, and their livelihoods? Limited by the sources that have survived, historians often grapple with the difficult issue of assessing the motivations of people in the past. People may choose to take particular actions for a wide variety of reasons, some of which they are either unaware or which they may choose not to articulate in their own accounts. By looking at the Rebellions, we can see individuals faced with a confusing and complicated series of events in which they had to make difficult decisions about which side they should support.

QUESTIONS

1. From the point of view of the rebels, was the choice of rebellion logical? How can political manifestos allow us to understand the motivations of the rebels?
2. Can evidence from loyalists, such as the painting and diary entry by Jane Ellice, permit us to make sound conclusions about the rebels' actions?
3. How do we weigh evidence produced close to the event itself against documents produced some weeks or months after the events, when people knew the outcome of the rebellions?
4. How important is the form of a particular document (i.e., what are the differences between a diary entry, courtroom testimony, an appeal for clemency, a political manifesto)?
5. To what extent do the primary sources support the interpretations of the Rebellions by Allan Greer and Colin Read and Ronald J. Stagg?

FURTHER READINGS

Jean-Paul Bernard, *The Rebellions of 1837 and 1838 in Lower Canada* (Ottawa: Canadian Historical Association, 1996), Vol. 55.

Allan Greer, "1837–38: Rebellion Reconsidered." *Canadian Historical Review* 76, 1 (1995): 1–18.

Allan Greer, *The Patriots and the People: The Rebellions of 1837 in Rural Lower Canada* (Toronto: University of Toronto Press, 1993).

Colin Read, *The Rebellion of 1837 in Upper Canada* (Ottawa: Canadian Historical Association, 1988), Vol. 46.

Colin Read, *The Rising in Western Upper Canada, 1837–8: The Duncombe Revolt and After* (Toronto: University of Toronto Press, 1982).

Colin Read and Ronald J. Stagg, eds., *The Rebellions of 1837 in Upper Canada* (Don Mills, ON: Oxford University Press, 1985).

Primary Sources (Lower Canada)

▲ Document 1: Adresse des Fils de la liberté de Montréal aux jeunes gens des colonies de l'Amérique du Nord [Address of the Sons of Liberty of Montreal to the young people of the colonies of North America], October 4th, 1837

This political manifesto was issued before the outbreak of hostilities. Why is the appeal made to men only? What concerns do the signatories express about the nature of imperial rule in Lower Canada? Does the document reflect a typical understanding of the role of government today? Note that the Legislative Council was not an elected body, but it had the right to initiate or disallow legislation (rather like Canada's Senate today). The Executive Council was also appointed, and it served a similar role to the cabinet today.

Brothers:

[…] We maintain that governments are created for the common good and can only rightfully exist with the consent of the governed, and that whatever artificial change may occur in human affairs, an elected government remains nevertheless an inherent right of the people. Since this principle cannot be surrendered, one always has the right to demand it and put it into practice.

[…] The authority of a motherland over a colony can only exist as long as it pleases the colonists who live there; because it was established and populated by these colonists, this country belongs to them by right, and consequently can be separated from any foreign connection whenever the disadvantages, resulting from an executive power located at a distance and which ceases to be in harmony with a local legislature, make such a step necessary to its inhabitants, in order to protect their lives and their freedom or to achieve prosperity.

By taking the title of *Fils de la liberté* [Sons of Liberty], the association of the young people of Montreal by no means intends to make it a private cabal, a secret junta, but rather a democratic body full of strength, which will comprise all the youth whose love of the fatherland renders them sensitive to the interests of their country, whatever their faith, their origin or that of their ancestors.

[…] After seventy years of English domination, we are brought to see our country in a state of misery when compared to the flourishing republics which have had the wisdom to throw off the yoke of monarchy. We see the emigrants of the same classes coming from the other side of the sea, who are miserable on our soil, but content the moment they join the great democratic family, and every day we have the sad experience that it is only to the noxious actions of the colonial government that we must attribute all our suffering […].

[…] A legion of officers appointed without the approval of the people, to whom they are largely opposed and never responsible, who hold their public charge at the pleasure

Source: Adresse des Fils de la liberté de Montréal aux jeunes gens des colonies de l'Amérique du Nord, October 4th, 1837. (Ottawa: Institut canadien de microreproductions historiques, 1983). Translated by editor.

191

of an irresponsible Executive, now holds authority over us with their salaries that are enormously disproportionate to both our means and to the services they render, such that these positions appear to be created rather for family interests or personal ambition, than to benefit the people or to satisfy their needs.

Trial by jury, which we had been taught to see as the guarantee of our freedoms, has now become a vain illusion, an instrument of despotism, since the sheriffs, creatures of the executive, on whom they depend daily for their continuation in a position to which enormous emoluments are attached, have the freedom to choose and summon such juries as they wish, and consequently can become the judges of the people in political actions launched against them by their oppressors.

Properties of an immense value, given by a wise and far-sighted government or by individuals distinguished by their generosity, to the late order of the Jesuits[1] and dedicated by them solely for the benefit of education, had been diverted from such a worthy goal, to be used as instruments of corruption and to throw money at useless and almost always reprehensible officials, while the children of the province who are deprived of the funds intended for their instruction, have grown up without being able to take advantage of this benefit, and then see themselves being criticized for their lack of education.

Our public lands, defended in two consecutive wars [i.e. the invasion of American rebels in 1775 and the War of 1812] by the bravery of the inhabitants of the country, later developed by opening communication routes accomplished at the cost of great exertion, and by settlements stretching as far as the wilderness, have been sold or given, despite our protests, to a company of speculators, living on the other side of the Atlantic, or divided amongst parasitic officials, who for personal motives leagued together in a faction to support a corrupt government, enemy of the people's rights and opposed to their desires, while our fathers, our relatives, our brother colonists experience only refusals, or are unable to acquire these uncultivated lands to establish themselves.

[…] Trade regulations for this colony, adopted by a foreign parliament are currently operating against our consent. Therefore, we find ourselves limited to specific outlets and deprived of the means to extend our trade to all the ports of the world at a time when the markets of Great Britain are not as advantageous to the disposal of our products; this results in the impotence and inertia of our commercial enterprises.

The representation of the country has become a remarkable object of mockery. A corrupt executive has constantly worked to make our House of Assembly an instrument for imposing slavery upon its members; and seeing that it did not succeed in its vile project; it has made the Assembly impotent through frequent prorogations or dissolutions, or by refusing assent to laws essential to the people even when these had been passed unanimously by the members.

A Legislative Council whose members are chosen by an authority that is ignorant of the affairs of the colony, and which resides 3,000 miles away, and which mainly comprises people who have no sympathy for the country, still currently exists as a sort of an impotent screen between the governors and the governed, always ready to nullify all attempts at useful legislation. An Executive Council appointed in the same way, whose influence has poisoned the heart of each successive governor, still remains intact, protecting the accumulation of government offices [i.e., by the same person] and all the abuses which are found in each government department. A governor as ignorant as his predecessors, and who has followed the example of each one of them, has become an official partisan and leads the governmental machine for the advantage of the few, little concerned with the interests of the majority, or is even determined to be an obstacle to those desires.

Our grievances have been faithfully and on several occasions submitted to the King and the Parliament of Great Britain, in resolutions passed by our local meetings and our representatives in the Assembly, and in the humble petitions of all the nation. We have expressed our remonstrances with all the power of the arguments, and with all the moral strength of the truth. No remedy was put forward, and finally, when the tyranny of those who are invested with power in the province has increased at an unbearable level because of the impunity which is assured them, an ungrateful motherland takes advantage of a time of general peace, to force us to close our eyes and approve our own humiliation, by threatening to seize our public revenues by force, thus defying natural rights, and all the principles of law, of politics and justice.

Given that the current state of the humiliation of our country is the result of three-quarters of a century of warm devotion to our connection with England, and of our mislaid confidence in British honour, we would show ourselves as criminals and born for slavery if we limited our resistance to mere protests. The perfidious projects of the British authorities have broken all the bonds of sympathy with a motherland who reveals her insensitivity. A separation has started between the two parts, and it will never be possible to cement this union again, and in fact, the separation will continue with a growing vigour, until one of those unexpected and unforeseen events, which we sometimes have witnessed in our current times, provides us with a favourable occasion to take our place among the independent sovereignties of the Americas. We have let two superb occasions slip by: let us be prepared for a third. A destiny full of glory is reserved for the youth of these colonies. Our ancestors spent a long career of humiliations fighting daily against all the phases of despotism. After their deaths, they bequeathed us a heritage, which they worked hard to expand at the cost of all the sacrifices that patriotism imposed on them. We are entrusted with the duty to pursue their sublime projects, and to liberate, in our own time, our beloved homeland from any human authority other than a dauntless democracy rooted in its soil.

[...] Consequently, we, the officers and members of the association of the *Fils de la liberté* in Montreal, in our own name, as well as the names of those we represent, solemnly commit ourselves to our maltreated homeland, and to each one of us, to devote all our energy, and to keep ourselves ready to act, according to what the circumstances may require, in order to obtain for this province:

- a reformed system of government, based upon the principle of election;
- an executive government responsible [to the people];
- control by the representative branch of the legislature of all public incomes from all sources;
- the repeal of all the laws and charters passed by a foreign authority which encroach on the rights of the people and its representatives and especially those which pertain to property and the tenure of lands belonging either to the public or to individuals;
- an improved system for the sale of public lands, so that those who desire to settle can do it with the least amount of fees possible;
- the end of the possibility of holding multiple offices and the irresponsibility of public officers,
- and a strict equality before the law for all classes without distinction of origin, language or religion.

Confident in Providence and strengthened by our rights we invite, through this declaration, all the *young people* of these provinces to form associations in their respective

localities, for the purpose of obtaining a just, inexpensive and responsible government, and ensuring the safety, the defence and the extension of our common liberties.
Montréal, October 4th, 1837

NOTE

1. The Jesuit order was suppressed by the Pope between 1773 and 1814. As they owned a great deal of land in the St Lawrence Valley, the use of the moneys from that land became a major political issue in the 19th century. French-Canadian politicians claimed that the revenues from the land should be used to support educational institutions.

▲ Document 2: Declaration of Independence of Lower Canada, 1838

*During the more radical phase of the Rebellions, Patriote leaders, now based across
the border in the United States, wanted to stage an invasion of Lower Canada. In
a meeting of rebel leaders in Vermont in early 1838, Montreal-born Robert Nelson
was selected as president of the future independent state. In February, the rebels
distributed copies of this Declaration of Independence. How revolutionary is the
political system envisioned in this manifesto? What economic and social implications does the manifesto contain?*

DECLARATION

WHEREAS, the solemn covenant made with the people of Lower Canada [...] hath been
continually violated by the British Government, and our rights usurped; and, whereas our
humble petitions, addresses, protests, and remonstrances against this injurious and uncon-
stitutional interference have been made in vain, that the British Government hath disposed
of our revenue without the constitutional consent of the local Legislature, pillaged our
treasury, arrested great numbers of our citizens, and committed them to prison, distributed
through the country a mercenary army, whose presence is accompanied by consternation
and alarm, whose track is red with the blood of our people, who have laid our villages in
ashes, profaned our Temples, and spread terror and waste through the land: And whereas
we can no longer suffer the repeated violations of our dearest rights, and patiently support
the multiplied outrages and cruelties of the Government of Lower Canada, WE, in the name
of the PEOPLE OF LOWER CANADA, acknowledging the decrees of a Divine Providence,
which permits us to put down a Government, which hath abused the object and intention
for which it was created, and to make choice of that form of Government which shall reestablish the empire of justice, assure domestic tranquillity, provide for common defence,
promote general good, and secure to us and our posterity the advantages of civil and
religious liberty,

SOLEMNLY DECLARE;

1. That from this day forward, the PEOPLE OF LOWER CANADA are absolved from all
   allegiance to Great Britain, and that the political connexion between that power and
   Lower Canada, is now dissolved.
2. That a REPUBLICAN form of Government is best suited to Lower Canada, which is
   this day declared to be A REPUBLIC.
3. That under the Free Government of Lower Canada, all persons shall enjoy the same
   rights; the Indians shall no longer be under any civil disqualification, but shall enjoy
   the same rights as all other citizens in Lower Canada.
4. That all union between Church and State is hereby declared to be DISSOLVED, and
   every person shall be at liberty freely to exercise such religion or belief as shall be
   dictated to him by his conscience.
5. That the Feudal or Seignorial tenure of land is hereby abolished, as completely as if
   such tenure had never existed in Canada.
6. That each and every person who shall bear arms, or otherwise furnish assistance to
   the people of Canada, in this contest for emancipation, shall be, and is discharged

195

Source: *Report of the State Trials, Before a General Court Martial Held at Montreal in 1838-1839*
(Montreal: Armour and Ramsay, 1839) Volume II, pp. 562-564.

from all dues or obligations, real or supposed, for arrearages in virtue of Seignorial rights, heretofore existing.

7. That the *Douaire Coutumier* is for the future abolished and prohibited.

8. That imprisonment for debt shall no longer exist, except in such cases of fraud as shall be specified in an Act to be passed hereafter by the Legislature of Lower Canada for this purpose.

9. That sentence of Death shall no longer be passed nor executed, except in cases of murder.

10. That all mortgages on landed estates shall be special, and to be valid, shall be enregistered in offices to be erected for this purpose, by an Act of the Legislature of Lower Canada.

11. That the liberty and freedom of the press shall exist in all public matters and affairs.

12. Source: Declaration of Independence of Lower Canada, 1838.

13. That TRIAL BY JURY is guaranteed to the people of Lower Canada in its most extended and liberal sense, in all criminal suits, and in civil suits, above a sum to be fixed by the Legislature of the State of LOWER CANADA.

14. That as General and public Education is necessary and due by the Government to the people, an act to provide for the same shall be passed as soon as the circumstances of the country will permit.

15. That to secure the elective franchise, all elections shall be had BY BALLOT.

16. That with the least possible delay, the people shall choose Delegates, according to the present division of the country, into Counties, Towns, and Boroughs, who shall constitute a Convention or Legislative Body, to establish a Constitution, according to the wants of the country, and in conformity with the disposition of this Declaration, subject to be modified according to the will of the people.

17. That every male person, of the age of twenty-one years and upwards, shall have the right of voting, as herein provided, and for the election of the aforesaid delegates.

18. That all *Crown Lands*, also, such as are called *Clergy Reserves*, and such as are nominally in possession of a certain Company of Land holders, in England, called the "British North American Land Company," are of right the property of the State of Lower Canada, except such portions of the aforesaid lands as may be in possession of persons who hold the same in good faith, and to whom titles shall be secured and granted, by virtue of a law which shall be enacted to legalize the possession of, and afford a title for such untitled lots of land in the Townships as are under cultivation or improvement.

19. That the French and English languages shall be used in all public affairs.

And for the fulfilment of this Declaration, and for the support of the Patriotic cause in which we are now engaged, with a firm reliance on the protection of the Almighty, and justice of our conduct, WE, by these presents solemnly pledge to each other our lives, our fortunes, and our most sacred honour.

By order of the Provisional Government,

ROBERT NELSON,

President.

[February 28, 1838]

▲Document 3: Jane Ellice's Watercolour Portrait of the "Rebels at Beauharnois"

● Katherine Jane Balfour was the aristocratic wife of Edward Ellice junior. Ellice served as the private secretary to John Lampton, Lord Durham, sent in 1838 to investigate the Lower Canadian rebellions of the previous winter. She and her husband were visiting the Ellice seigneury of Beauharnois, near Montreal, in November 1838, when a second uprising began. An accomplished painter, she later depicted the rebel attack on the seigneurial manor. How does Jane Ellice represent the rebels?

Source: Library and Archives Canada/C013392.

▲ Document 4: The Diary of Jane Ellice

Jane Ellice also kept a diary of her trip to Lower Canada. She recorded her memories of the rebel attack in the following passages. How closely does this diary entry reflect her visual depiction of the rebels in Lower Canada? The reference here to Robespierre is telling. Who was Robespierre, and why did Ellice make this comparison? How important was Ellice's social class in her interpretation of the events? How important was her gender?

November 4 (1838)

We laughed at our fears & declared we would go to sleep but we had not been in bed five minutes before a long, loud, horrid yell close to the house made us start up. The house was surrounded on all sides, Guns going off in all directions, striking the hours, breaking the windows on every side so that Edward put Tina & I between two doors, to be out of the way of shot, while he pulled on a scanty supply of clothes. He then drag'ed us down stairs after him, just as we jumped out of bed without even slippers on our feet, and pushed us thro' the trap door into the cellar, the firing & yelling increasing every moment. Oh! How my heart sank within me when he left us there & went to join in the mêlée above, and my fears pictured all sorts of horrible things to my imagination. Presently all the maids joined us, most of them crying & screaming in spite of all we could say to keep them quiet. Poor Georgine was wounded above the Eyes. She ran to the window when the firing commenced & it was only a mercy she was not killed. As it is she fears she will lose the sight of that eye.

Several of the farm people came down to the cellar to hide some half dozen loaded muskets which they feared would fall into the hands of the Rebels.

I thought it was a foolish plan as they would be sure to find them. There we sat quaking for what seemed to me an interminable time. The cellar was damp & very cold & all covered with broken bottles, so that I cannot conceive how we escaped having our feet cut to pieces, as we had nothing on our feet. At last we saw a man come down, creeping down the ladder, in the Canadian dress, his *longue Carabine* pointed at us. Both Tina & I thought he has going to fire at us. She threw herself into my arms saying *"Oh Janie!"* & I felt as if they were the last words I should ever hear. We both called out *"Que voulez vous – qui êtes vous?"* ["What do you want—who are you?"] but still he continued creeping on without answering. I think we must have died of fright if he had not just then turned his face towards our lantern & discovered himself to be *Scott*, the farmer, come to hide his Gun.

At last we were told that all was quiet & no one wounded except Mr. Brown who was shot in the hand, but nothing serious. Edward was unhurt, which I had hardly dared to hope. However He & Mr. Brown were both prisoners, as well as every other British person in the village and they were taken instantly away, (it was about two o'clock in the morning, *raining in torrents* & bitterly cold), leaving Tina & I seated *en chemise de nuit* & robe de Chambre [in night shirt and night robe], in the midst of five or six of the most ruffian looking men I ever saw (except in my *dreams* of *Robespierre*) and without a single being to give us either advice or assistance.

No sooner were the prisoners taken away then in rushed about *30 more* rebels calling for arms & saying they were sure we had some concealed, as Edward had given up his own *rifles* & desired all the arms to be given up. I assured them there were none but they were determined to search for themselves; some running upstairs, others into the

Source: *The Diary of Jane Ellice*, ed. by Patricia Godsell (Oberon Press, 1975), pp. 132–139.

cellar, from whence we soon heard a yell of triumph occasioned by finding the *Muskets* which very foolishly had not been given up. They came up looking very angry, one man declaring that he would kill everything that opposed him that he had already *"mis vôtre gros chien en poudre,"* ["destroyed your big dog,"] and he looked as if very little would make him do the same to us. They then proceeded to make a second examination of the house, turning everything topsy turvy. They found Edward's little *dress sword* and another yell announced they had made the discovery of a gun and sword of Mr. Brown's under the mattress of an uninhabited bedroom. Who hid them there we know not.

After about an hour we were allowed to go upstairs. Georgine was very sick & unable to assist us; the Cook the same & the two other girls too much frightened to be of any use. Tina & I dressed each other & commenced bundling all the things we most cared about into a box, that we might be ready to start if we had an opportunity. All that Edward had time to say was *"Get to Montreal if you can* in the Steam Boat, Canoe or any how."

We had about 3, & at one time 500, *armed patriots* round the house & we took our station behind a curtain at the window to watch for the arrival of the *Henry Brougham* steamer. It was just beginning to be light when we saw its smoking chimney. The pier was covered with men concealed behind logs of wood, & as soon as it touched they sprang on deck, took possession of it and took some screws out of the machinery to prevent its being possible to use it. All the passengers were taken prisoners. All hope of making our escape in the Steamer being at an end, we turned out thoughts to the bark Canoe. We sent to one of the rebel *Captains* and asked leave to go away, as we thought they could not have any object in keeping females prisoners. He was very Civil and said they would hold a Council of War & let me know the result in a quarter of an hour. We watched from the windows and saw them go and poke their swords & pikes thro' the little Canoe, thus cutting off our only means of escape. He then came back to tell us we might go when we liked if we had any conveyance of our own & was sorry he had none of his own to offer us.

By this time they had broken in to the Store room, *dairy* [and] larder and had taken every thing that was eatable & drinkable. They were throwing the sugar about and all had blocks of Maple Sugar which they were devouring. Several *100* lbs. disappeared in a moment. Fortunately we were not hungry, for nothing eatable was to be found in the house except the remnant of a small loaf which Prewet had secured for our breakfast. At last they commenced the Attack I so much dreaded upon the Cellar and drank without any discretion of every thing they could find, Symptoms of which we very soon saw in their boisterous conduct on the Green, quarelling with each other, some fighting, others dancing, some swearing & firing at marks or throwing stones at the window.

We had bribed a man to go to Monsr. Quintal, the Priest, to ask him to come to us, and he answered he could not be with us till 12 o'clock. In the mean time the Scene around us became every moment worse & worse; troops of men coming thro' our rooms, every now & then turning over the beds, drawers, &c., hunting for arms, *powder*, & calling for more wine.

Prewet said he was obliged to hide himself as they wanted to kill him, and had held a pistol at his breast while they made him give up the keys of the cellar & *draw* the cherry brandy we had made to take *home*. As a proof how good it was, they were the only bottles they did not break the necks of for fear of losing a drop.

Scott, the farmer, with one of the ploughmen, came creeping into our room without their shoes for fear of being heard; as pale as death, trembling in every joint, groaning & crying like a child. In place of saying any thing to comfort us, he told us we should none of us be alive in the morning; that most of the men were *"quite mad* from drink" and that they were drinking *Brandy* in bottles full. We heard them *screaming* down stairs &

shouting for more *arms*, more wine, & there we sat, watch in hand, counting the minutes till *12* o'clock. How long that half hour appeared.

Twelve o'clock came, but *no Priest*. Scott, our only comforter, crept back to say he knew the *"popish priest"* better than we did, and "he's afraid *to come*. Na—na—we'll none of us *live to see the morning; & they've threatened* some of *our lives already*." He went away again to hide himself & left us, as before, watching the hour. Just then one of the Captains, followed by several men, *all* quite tipsy, came into the room where we were sitting, with all the doors open, in the middle of boxes & *confusion* of all description. He walked straight to us: "N'ayez pas peur, Madame, nous ne voulons pas vous faire du mal; ne craignez rien." ["Have no fear, Madame, we don't want to hurt you; don't worry."] He held a great horse pistol in his hand, the mouth of which was almost touching me, & he was so drunk that I was afraid he would make it go off by mistake. I asked him if it was loaded: *"Oui, oui, pour le sûre, mais ne craignez rien."* ["Yes, yes, of course, but don't worry."]

(One man said to us "Tenez, mesdames; sauvez vous si vous pouvez, car je ne réponds de rien cette nuit—tout le monde est ivre et tout le monde est maître.") ["Look, my ladies, save yourselves if you can, because I can't promise anything this night—everyone is drunk and every one thinks he is in charge."]

Tina & I mustered all our courage & sd. we were quite sure they would not hurt two *defenceless* females who were quite alone & in their power, but that if they went on drinking they might frighten us without meaning it. I was in a horrid fright all the time I was speaking & was thankful when they all staggered out of the room. Tina behaved *beautifully*, and tho' many, many times that day I wished she had never left Scotland, I don't know what I should have done without her—*quite alone*. Oh! It would have been dreadful.

As it was, we were the greatest comfort to each other, tho' we scarcely spoke a word, but we both looked forward to the *night* with despair. I shudder to think of all the horrible things that passed thro' my mind. The only man of ours left in the house was *Prewet*, and even had he been allowed to come to our room, what could he have done against 300 armed men—all drunk. Georgine was on her bed, very sick, and the only hope was to put our trust in God. And we both did so.

In the afternoon Mrs. Brown & her little girl came to us to ask our *advice*. She knew not where to go & was told that the village was to be burnt that night. She was crying very much, & so much frightened & agitated she scarcely knew what she was doing & talked of flying into the woods with her child. How different from poor Tina, who, tho' pale as death & trembling like an Aspen leaf, was quite composed. We decided that if the Priest came to us we should try & return with him to his *presbytère* at the top of the hill. We sat watching his house from the window with the greatest anxiety; the *hubbub* down stairs increasing every moment. At last we saw him leave his house; go into the Church & then come down the hill to the Seigniory house.

He evidently did not know what to advise: "Il faut *'Manger,' 'parler;'* ne rien craindre." ["You must 'eat,' 'speak;' don't worry."] But we could do neither. At last he got permission for us to go to his house. They got a wagon for us & went away leaving us to follow, which he thought more prudent than to accompany us.

The hall was full of people & the front of the house crowded. I spoke to one or two with a trembling heart and the most smiling face I could *put on*.

It was raining in torrents and the roads one mass of mud. How thankful I was when we arrived in safety under the roof of the Curé. We did not undress but laid down like watch dogs, listening to every sound & looking at our watches. How slowly the hours passed. We had great difficulty in keeping a light with a few ends of candles we had collected.

200

▲ Document 5: Testimony from the Court Martial of Some of the Lower Canada Rebels

These documents are transcriptions of court documents during the treason trials of some of the rebels who attacked the seigneurial manor at Beauharnois in 1838. How similar are these discussions of the events to Jane Ellice's diary entries? How do the rebels account for their participation in this uprising? Why did Brien wish to insist upon his civility? How important was the faulty intelligence about other military activities in the colony?

LAWRENCE GEORGE BROWN, of Beauharnois, Esquire, being called into Court, and the charge read to him, he is duly sworn, and states as follows: —

On Sunday morning, the fourth of November last, at about the hour of half-past one, some person knocked at the door of my house, in the village of Beauharnois. I went to see who it was, and found an individual of the name of Normand, and another of the name of Bean. I enquired what they wanted? They informed me that the Canadians had risen in rebellion on the south side of the Chateauguay, and had taken John M'Donald prisoner, and that they were making all the British population prisoners down the road. I first doubted their intelligence, but afterwards believed it, and requested them not to make a noise to alarm the people of the village.

I went up to the scigniory house, where Mr. Ellice and the ladies of his family were, and on my way, crossing from the seigniory farm-yard, I met Toussaint Rochon, the prisoner before the Court, followed by two other persons whom I did not know. I did not see any arms about him. I communicated to Mr. Ellice the intelligence which I had received; I put on my sword, which was in the house, and called up the rest of the family, and sent two persons to rouse the British population.

On leaving the house, I met John Bryson, and proceeded to the house of John Ross; at the corner of Ross's house, I found ten or twelve of the volunteers, under my command, under arms. My attention was directed by John Ross, who was Captain of volunteers, to an orchard where we saw a number of men armed; Captain Ross and myself approached these men, upon which they presented their fire-arms at our breasts. I told them not to fire. On looking round, I discovered my groom, Robert Fenny, a prisoner with them. We ordered the volunteers to advance, upon which the rebel party immediately dispersed, with the exception of one, who fell upon his knees and begged for mercy. He was taken to Ross's house, and bound. I do not know his name.

On advancing further, the volunteers took another prisoner, whose name I do not know, and brought him to Ross's house, and bound him. The volunteers soon after returned, and I formed them in front of Ross's house; immediately after, I was informed that a large number of armed men, amounting from one hundred and fifty to two hundred men, were assembled on the height near the Catholic Church.

I am Lieutenant Colonel of the Beauharnois Loyal Volunteers. I said to Captain Ross that we must march up, and endeavour to cover the seigniory house. We accordingly advanced, and I formed the men, at the farm yard gate, close by the office attached to the seigniory house. I had hardly joined, them, when a body of men rushed down from the

Source: *Report of the State Trials, Before a General Court Martial Held at Montreal in 1838–1839* (Montreal: Armour and Ramsay, 1839) Vol. I, pp. 295–301.

height, of which I have spoken, upon us, with a tremendous yell, and a discharge of, I should think, at least seventy or eighty fire arms. I received a shot in the thumb. A man of the name of Scott, a farm steward, declared that his clothes were perforated with balls, as did also Captain Ross. A number of balls passed through the windows of the office, and the clapboarding of another house was very much cut up. I desired the volunteers to return the fire, which they did. My men amounted to about ten or twelve in number, and on discovering that the numbers opposed to us were very great, I considered it useless to risque the lives of my men, and ordered them to retire into the seigniory house, which we did.

On entering the inner kitchen, I found Mr. Ellice putting the females of the family into the cellar for protection from the shots, of which several had passed through the house. I told Mr. Ellice that their numbers were so great, that it was useless resisting, and that I had better go and say to them that we surrendered, and claim protection for the females. This I did in company with Captain Ross. In the meantime the rebels had surrounded the house. Some were armed with guns, and others with pikes. After surrendering, we asked who were the leaders? Upon which Joseph Dumouchelle and Jean Baptiste Henri Brien, two of the prisoners before the Court, came forward as the leaders. I claimed protection at their hands for the ladies and females of the house, who were in a state of great apprehension. Upon which both of them, and particularly Brien, declared that no injury would be done to persons or property.

I thereupon asked what they meant by such conduct, whereupon a considerable number of voices, perhaps, ten, twelve, or twenty, proceeding from some of the party who had withdrawn into a shed, called out, "We have suffered long enough—we want no more of the present Government—the Canadians must have their rights." Brien, apparently apprehensive that his party would commit themselves, told them to hold their tongues, for that they had not come there to speak but to act.

Brien said to me, they understood that we had a large depot of arms and ammunition there, viz: three hundred stand of arms, three pieces of cannon, and a large quantity of gunpowder, which I must deliver up immediately. I stated that the muskets were in the hands of the volunteers, whom they saw—that we had no cannon, although there was a small quantity of gunpowder. Some of them said, they would not take my word for this, and demanded my keys. I told my farm-steward, Scott, to get the keys and a light, and that I would accompany them in the search. I went with them to the stable to search in the first instance, whereupon a large number of the party rushed in, when the prisoner, Brien, desired them to keep back, saying that two or three were sufficient. I mention this, to show the complete command which Brien had over the party.

One of the prisoners, Joseph Dumouchelle, declared that if I would be candid with them, and show them where the arms and powder were, they would not search. I replied, that I had told them what was correct, and that what we had would be delivered. Joseph Dumouchelle replied, they had been informed by one of my own people, that three hundred stand of arms were concealed in the sheepfold; whereupon we proceeded, with a considerable number of the rebel party, through the piggery, to the sheepfold. They pulled up some of the planks, and found nothing. I had several Canadians in my employment at that time. I then desired my man, Scott, to declare where the powder was concealed, and to deliver it up. The powder was then given up. It was so dark in the barn where it was, that I could not recognize any of the individuals there. On leaving the barn, and proceeding through the shed, to the house, one of the party, whom I did not know, opened my cloak, and took from me my scabbard and sword belt, saying that I did not want it. My sword had some time before been knocked out of my hand.

Shortly after, I met Brien, who said he must make us prisoners, and that we must get ready for marching. Brien consented that we should go in a carriage, and I ordered my groom to get the waggon ready. Brien then appared to be in haste, urging us very much, and declaring that they had other business to do, and ordered two double carts to be turned out for the guard, who were to accompany us, which was done. I asked permission to go and see my family before I went, and get some necessary articles; to which he consented. I accordingly went, with four guards, armed with guns and sent by him. On reaching my house, I desired the guard not to enter, as their appearance would very much alarm Mrs. Brown. One of the guard said they must go in and search the house for arms, whereupon another person (not of the guard) called out, "we have searched already, and found one gun." One of my guards then said to me, "Gentlemen like you generally have pistols." I replied, "I will be candid with you; I have two in my pocket." I pulled them out, and gave one to one of them and the other to another. I returned to the yard of the seigniory house, and Mr. Ellice got into the waggon there; I also got into the waggon; my servant, Robert Fenny, drove, and Dr. Brien was seated by his side.

During a short detention, we thought we heard firing, and Brien said that there were six thousand American troops entering the province, and that three battles were going on at that time—one at Chambly, one on the River Richelieu, and one at Laprairie—that the affair might be considered decided, for that the whole province had risen in arms—that a large body of Canadians had gone up the River Chateauguay, to disarm the British inhabitants.

We asked what was to be our destination? He said he could not exactly say, but the immediate intention was, to take us somewhere to the frontier, where was a great meeting of the chiefs. He enquired for Colonel Campbell, who commands the volunteers of Beauharnois District; he expected to find the Colonel in the village, but he had gone to Huntingdon. We were then joined by several other prisoners, viz: Captain Ross, John Bryson, and Mr. David Normand. These are all I recollect. We left the village between four and five on the morning of the fourth, and proceeded to Chateauguay village, where we arrived about seven o'clock, and found a large body of armed men, about one hundred in number, collected. They took us to a small tavern, kept by a person whose name, I understand, was Duquette. We remained at this house until about three o'clock, when we were removed to a house of a better description, kept by one of the name of Mallette. Brien put us in charge of one Moyse Dalton [...]

At Brien's request, I sent him in my waggon to a place called the "Stone Tavern," which is the last I saw of him. We were detained prisoners from that day until the following Saturday, the tenth of November.

Question from the Judge Advocate—Look at the prisoners before the Court, and declare whether, on the fourth of November last, or at any other time up to the tenth, you saw any of the prisoners before the Court; if yes, declare when, and where, and how they were engaged?

Answer—I saw the prisoner Dr. Brien, as I have stated above. I saw Ignace Gabriel Chevrefils among the armed party who surrounded the house, when I went out from the seigniory house to declare that we had surrendered; I cannot swear that he was armed; my impression is that he was. Joseph Dumouchelle I have already spoken of; he was not armed, as I saw, but he was a leader. Louis Dumouchelle, I saw in the farm-yard of the seigniory house, with the armed party; he was not armed, that I saw; he appeared to be actively engaged. I saw Toussaint Rochon, as I have stated before, and I also saw him in the yard of the seigniory house, with the armed party; I cannot say he was armed; I cannot state precisely what part he took, but I believe he was in the barn when the powder was given up. Jean Laberge I saw standing with Chevrefils in the yard, with the armed party; he seemed to be taking an active part; I cannot say that he was armed. The party had grounded their arms, and it was too dark to perceive distinctly who had arms and who had not. François Xavier Touchette I saw taking an active part amongst the armed men; I cannot say whether or not he was armed; he was also in the yard of the seigniory house. All these men I saw at Beauharnois, in the parish of St. Clement.

Q. from the same—From all that you heard and observed, what did you understand to be the intention and object of these men?

A.—A complete rebellion—the subversion of the Government, and taking possession of the country, and establishing another Government.

Q. from the same—Do the prisoners you have already spoken of reside in the village of Beauharnois, or in the neighbourhood?

A.—The prisoner, Rochon, lives in the village of Beauharnois; Brien, Chevrefils, Joseph Dumouchelle, Prieur, Laberge, Touchette, and Wattier dit Lanoie, reside at from eight to ten miles from Beauharnois; Louis Dumouchelle lives about four miles and a half from Beauharnois; and Guyette, about two miles from Beauharnois—all in the province of Lower Canada. Beauharnois is about twenty-five miles from the province line.

Q. from the prisoner Brien—Was it not after we had left Beauharnois, and proceeded a considerable distance towards Chateauguay, that I enquired after Colonel Campbell?

A.—I think it was after we left Beauharnois; but I cannot exactly say where it was asked—I rather think it was just after we had left the village.

Q. from the same—Did you mean to say, that I ordered carts to be turned out for the guards; did I not request you or Mr. Ellice to provide the guards with vehicles?

A.—Brien asked civilly for the carts; others came up rudely and said, "If you think we are going to walk after you, you are mistaken—we must have carts."

Q. from the same—Did I not behave towards you, and the other prisoners, with as much humanity and kindness, as the unfortunate enterprise I had embarked in would allow of?

A.—His conduct was very civil.

Q. from the Court—Are the prisoners before the Court, tenants or *censitaires* to the seignior of Beauharnois, and is St. Martine in the seigniory?

A.—The whole of them, except Dr. Brien, Chevalier De Lorimier, and Prieur, are *censitaires* of the seigniory of Beauharnois, and St. Martine is in the seigniory of which I am agent.

▲ Document 6: Address of Touchette, Rochon, Goyette, Chevrefils, and Laberge

What are the key arguments these prisoners make in favour of clemency? Does this formal request for clemency inform us about their motivations for becoming involved in the Rebellion?

Gentlemen of the Court:

The brief interval allowed us to prepare our defence, coupled with the indisposition of one of our Counsel, has deprived us of the advantage of fully discussing the evidence produced before you, which may affect us, either to incriminate or to justify.

But the high character of our Judges, and the indulgence extended towards us during our trial, warrant us to expect that every circumstanstance [sic] developed in the course of the tedious, and to us anxious, investigation, which may tend, in the slightest degree, to militate in our favour will have its due weight upon your deliberations.

As brave men, you must regard with an eye of generous compassion, the humble and unfortunate individuals who stand before you, charged with the greatest political crime, although, from their ignorance, wholly unconscious of the criminal character of the acts which have been imputed to them. We know that ignorance is no excuse for crime, before the human tribunal; but we feel confident, that though you may be convinced we participated in the late insurrectionary movements, which we so deeply deplore, you will, nevertheless, deem us worthy to be recommended to the clemency of our gracious Queen, whose noblest prerogative consists in the power of tempering with mercy the severity of the law towards those, who, though convicted, may yet be considered as victims, rather than criminals. Peaceable as we were in our habits—reproachless in our characters— unconscious of the plots previously formed against the Government—though found guilty, if we may be, of a momentary error, we will not, assuredly, after all our sufferings—not only in the loss of liberty and property, but in the persons we hold most dear, our house- less wives and starving children—we will not, assuredly, be condemned to a more severe punishment than a continuation of the painful imprisonment we have already endured.

Source: *Report of the State Trials, Before a General Court Martial Held at Montreal in 1838–1839* (Montreal: Armour and Ramsay, 1839) Vol. II, Appendix G, pp. 358–359.

205

Primary Sources (Upper Canada)

▲ Document 7: W L Mackenzie on Resistance to Oppression, *Constitution*, Toronto, 22 November 1837

Scottish-born William Lyon Mackenzie emerged as an important political figure in Upper Canada in the 1830s. Publisher of the Toronto newspaper, Constitution, he galvanized opposition to the colonial elite that governed the colony. In 1837, as political turmoil was increasing in British North America, he published this political manifesto in his newspaper. How effective is the use of the concept of "slavery" in Mackenzie's explanation of the political problems of the colony?

Look and deeply consider!!!
    PEOPLE OF UPPER CANADA [...]
I again say, whatever may have been the grievances complained of hitherto by the Lower Canadians, or how unjust or unfounded soever they may have been, is not now to be considered by us. The question is—Are the British Government right or are the Lower Canadians—the one in taking the taxes of the People against their will, and the last in opposing like freemen this gross aggression by a tyrannizing Executive? Behold the oppressors!! in order to enslave a free people encamp soldiers all over their country!! O! Englishmen of Canada and Upper Canadians, have you no brotherly sympathy for the Lower Canadians? Will you calmly and coldly see them put down by military force? No methinks not, I tell you if they are put down by soldiers you will be so too! If the British Kingdom can tax the People of Lower Canada against their will, they will do so with you when you dare to be free. I tell you, your lot will be like theirs—their fate will be yours!!
    [...]
Oh, men of Upper Canada, would you murder a free people! [Governor Bond] Head has sent down his troops, next he will try and send you down to put down your countrymen. Before you do so pause, and consider the world has its eyes on you—history will mark your conduct—beware lest they condemn. Oh who would not have it said of him that, as an Upper Canadian, he died in the cause of freedom ! To die fighting for freedom is truly glorious. Who would live and die a slave?

A FRIEND TO DEMOCRACRY

Source: Colin Read and Ronald J. Stagg, eds., *The Rebellion of 1837 in Upper Canada: A Collection of Documents* (Ottawa: Carleton University Press, 1985), pp. 105–106. Reprinted with permission from McGill-Queen's University Press.

▲ Document 8: John Powell's Account of Events, Toronto, 14 February 1838

John Powell was an elected alderman in Toronto in 1837, and partly on the strength of his information about the Rebellion, he was later elected mayor of the city. Samuel Lount was one of the key rebel leaders, and was later hanged for his role in the Rebellions. What does Powell's evidence indicate about the level of organisation among the rebels in Toronto?

On Monday Evening, December 4th, about 9 o'clock, when engaged at the City Hall in swearing in special constables and distributing arms, I found, from the number of magistrates present, I could be of more service in taking charge of several volunteers, who had assembled to patrole on horseback the approaches to the city during the night, for the purpose of reconnoitering the body of rebels said to be assembling, and more particularly those who were reported to be in arms on Yonge Street, Mr. A. McDonell offered to accompany me, as I had determined to take the Yonge Street road myself. Just as I had made my arrangements, Captain Fitzgibbon, Mr. Brock, and Mr. Bellingham, rode up to the Hall. Captain Fitzgibbon told me of his intention to go out, and I said we would accompany him; Mr. McDonell went home for his horse, intending to meet me on Yonge Street, and I rode with Captain Fitzgibbon to the foot of Yonge Street, where I left him to go to my own house for arms. When I loaded my gun, I found I had no caps; so abandoned the idea of taking it, and proceeded to overtake the party, having only two small pistols lent me by the high bailiff, as I left the Hall.

I went alone as far as the Sheriff's hill (about a mile from the city,) where I met Captain Fitzgibbon returning alone; he said Brock and Bellingham have gone on. I came back with him as far as the toll gate, where we met McDonell coming to join us. Captain Fitzgibbon then said all was quiet up the street, and he would return to town. Mr. McDonell and myself agreed we would proceed up the street to overtake Brock and Bellingham.

We were going leisurely along, when, at the rise of the Blue Hill four persons on horseback met us; we thought they were our friends; but as we approached, Mackenzie himself advanced and ordered us to halt; the others immediately surrounded us. Mackenzie was armed with a large horse pistol, the rest had rifles. Mackenzie then told us that we were his prisoners; I demanded by what authority? He replied, he would let us know his authority soon! Anderson (one of them) said, their authority was their rifles! Mackenzie asked us many questions as to the force in town? what guard at the Governor's? and whether we expected an attack that night? To all these questions I returned for answer, He might go to town and find out. This appeared to engage him very much, and he ordered Anderson and Sheppard to march us to the rear and *"Hurry on the men."* Anderson took charge of me; Sheppard of McDonell. I went first; McDonell was about ten yards in the rear. Anderson was very abusive towards the Governor, and said he let "Bond Head know something before long." I asked him of what he had to complain, and reasoned with him on the impropriety of their conduct; he replied, "They had borne tyranny and oppression too long, and were now determined to have a government of their own." From all I could gather from him, I found the rebels were on their march to town, for the purpose of

Source: Colin Read and Ronald J. Stagg, eds., *The Rebellion of 1837 in Upper Canada: A Collection of Documents* (Ottawa: Carleton University Press, 1985), pp. 136–139. Reprinted with permission from McGill-Queen's University Press.

207

surprising it, and that they (the four persons who took us prisoners) were the "advanced guard." Opposite Mr. Howard's gate a person on horseback met us; Anderson ordered him to halt, and asked him who he was? he replied, "Thomson" I immediately said, "Mr. Thomson, I claim your protection; I am a prisoner." The person recognized my voice, and said, "Powell, the rebels have shot poor Colonel Moodie, and are coming on to town." He then put spurs to his horse and succeeded in passing them; they turned round to fire, but were prevented by our both being between them and Brooke, who was the person we met.

Upon this intelligence, I made up my mind, and determined to make my escape at any hazard, as I felt confident the salvation of the town depended upon correct information being given at once. I made several attempts to fall back; but Anderson, who had me, threatened if I attempted to escape, he would "drive a ball through me." I went on as far as Mr. Heath's Gate, when I suddenly drew my pistol and fired, not being more than two feet from him; he fell and I instantly set off full speed down the street; McDonell did so likewise; Sheppard followed, and fired; the ball passed between us. McDonell was far in the advance; I shouted to him to ride hard and give the alarm as my horse would not keep up.

At the Sheriff's Hill we were again met by McKenzie [sic] and the other persons. Mackenzie rode after me and presenting his pistol at my head, ordered me to stop. I turned on my horse and snapped my remaining pistol in his face; the pistol must have touched him, I was so near; his horse either took fright, or he could not stop him, and he got some little distance in front of me. I drew up suddenly at Dr. Baldwin's road, galloped up about twenty yards, and then jumped off my horse and ran through the woods. I heard them pursue me, lay down behind a log, for a few minutes, (a person on horseback was within ten yards of the place where I lay.) I then ran down through the College fields and avenue, keeping near the fence.

I went immediately to Government House, and after some little difficulty saw the Governor in bed. I related to him in a few words what had passed; he seemed to doubt whether I could be certain as to Mackenzie, but at last appeared to take the alarm. From Government House I proceeded to the City Hall.

McDonell was re-captured at the Toll Gate, and neither Brooke nor any other person arrived in town until the bells were ringing.

Lount has told several persons that the death of Anderson alone prevented their coming in that night.

▲ Document 9: Petition of John A. Tidey to Sir F.B. Head, London Gaol, 8 March 1838

John Tidey was a merchant, farmer and deputy provincial surveyor in Sodom, Norwich Township (near Woodstock, ON). Compare Tidey's request for clemency to that of the Lower Canadian rebels.

Humbly Sheweth:

That your Petitioner in the beginning of December last while your Petitioner was assisting Mr. Wallace in Norwich—a Lad presented himself at the Store door with an open letter dictated to one of the Magistrates, the letter was handed into the Store and read by Wallace before those present, Stating that McKenzie with resistless numbers hemmed in Toronto—and other matters—The Boy after thus shewing the Letter took it to its destination.—About the middle of the afternoon of the same day Charles Duncomb himself came forward—a considerable party had now got together at his rendevous [sic]—he called me and several others aside and in his usual specious and insinuating manner—pretending love and confidence (when he possessed no honor himself) told us that Warrants were out for himself and for three or four of the leading Reformers in each and every Township through the Country—That the Governor was intending to inflict such vengence upon the Land as was never heard of.—This communication alarmed and tearified [sic] all those who heard him, and a general meeting was called for the next day (8 or 9 December) to take the matter into consideration—Accordingly next day at a very large Meeting a Body of men for the defence of Norwich was organized—no other particular tendency that Body at first appeared to have.—A few days after, a deputation from the Malcolms came in—after which the Report was that the men should shortly be marched down to Scotland [in Brant County], which was the place of the Rendevous.—

In looking back upon those proceedings—it is impossible for me or any person to tell what I did in the business—Like the restless frightened persons about me I did and said many things which cannot now be recalled and for which I must at present content myself by expressing my unfeigned sorrow—[…]

Source: Colin Read and Ronald J. Stagg, eds., *The Rebellion of 1837 in Upper Canada: A Collection of Documents* (Ottawa: Carleton University Press, 1985), pp. 197–198. Reprinted with permission from McGill-Queen's University Press.

209

▲ Document 10: Rebellion Box of Martin Switzer

May vengence draw the sword in wra[...]
And justice smile to see it done
And smite the traitors for the death
Of Matthews Lount and Anderson

Source: 972.33.2.A: Prisoner's Box made by Martin Switzer; Canada; circa 1838. Mackenzie House Collection, City of Toronto, accession number 1960.1526.26.

While imprisoned under accusation of treason, many supporters of the rebels in Upper Canada carved intricate boxes (called subsequently "Rebellion boxes"), often with political verses or messages. Irish-born Martin Switzer (1778-1852) was jailed for his actions during the Rebellions of 1837. He was released in September 1838 having promised to keep the peace for three years. He quickly joined his wife and family, who had already left for Illinois. What do the verses on these boxes tell us about Switzer's political views?

May vengence [sic] draw the sword in wrat[h]
And justice smile to see it done
And smite the traitors for the death

Of Matthews Lount and Anderson
***
Let Canada mourn, for her liberties weep
By the ravage of tyrany [sic] torn
May the true sons of freedom in peace never sleep
Till their banners in triumph are borne.
***
G[rea]t. Genius of liberty fair art thy f[orm]
How oft have I sought thine embrace
Imprisoned maltreated in political storm

By a wicked tyranical [sic] race
***
There is a land of pure delight
Where truth and justice reigns
Their institutions all aright
To crush the tyrant chains

211

◼ Article 1 (Lower Canada): Two Nations Warring

By Allan Greer

I expected to find a contest between a government and a people: I found two nations warring in the bosom of a single state: I found a struggle, not of principles, but of races; and I perceived that it would be idle to attempt any amelioration of laws or institutions until we could first succeed in terminating the deadly animosity that now separates the inhabitants of Lower Canada into the hostile divisions of French and English.

Lord Durham[1]

Robert Hall was a farmer of British origin who lived in the predominantly French-Canadian parish of Ste Scholastique, north of Montreal. In late June and early July of 1837 he and other English speakers in the county of Two Mountains began to suffer various forms of ill treatment at the hands of their francophone neighbours. Several families fled to the city, Hall's among them, and there he found a magistrate and swore out the following deposition.

I have lived with my family in the said parish of Ste Scholastique for two years past. I have always lived on the best terms with my neighbours the Canadians but since political meetings have been held in that, and the adjoining parishes of St Benoit and others the Canadians have ceased to have any communication with the inhabitants of English extraction.

After certain committees were organized and appointed in his parish depredations were committed almost nightly on the said English inhabitants as also some

Source: Allan Greer, *The Patriots and the People: The Rebellion of 1837 in Rural Lower Canada* (Toronto: University of Toronto Press, 1993), Chapter 6, pp. 153–188, abridged. © University of Toronto Press Inc. Reprinted with permission of the publisher.

Scotch inhabitants and on the Canadians who do not belong to the patriote party. On the night of the twenty eighth June last the door of his house was broken open by that party and one of the windows of his house smashed to pieces with stones. One of the stones about five pounds in weight fell very near to some of my infant children who slept on a bunk on the floor. Part of my fences were thrown down and destroyed and my corn field laid open to the cattle in which I found several heads of cattle the ensuing morning. My horses manes and tails were shaved and so disfigured as to be almost unfit for use, so much so that when I travel with them I am universally laughed at.[2]

The English minority of the region was boycotted quite thoroughly. A St Benoit blacksmith, Donald McColl, suddenly found he had no more customers; only two French Canadians patronized him in a month and both found their horses minus mane and tail the next day. He hired a local carter to drive him to the next village and the poor carter's horse was similarly shaved. McColl's father was a small-scale entrepreneur, but after June no French Canadians could work for him or sell him ashes for his potash works without suffering threats and vandalism.[3] To all appearances the campaign to defend the liberty of Lower Canada had already degenerated into a series of ugly attacks on members of a cultural minority.

Was the conflict in Lower Canada fundamentally ethnic (or, to follow nineteenth-century usage, 'racial'), as Lord Durham and a host of commentators before and after him have argued? Was a fight that seemed to be over democracy and national independence actually a tribal conflict of English and French in which the two sides took up contradictory political positions as a means of justifying more primitive impulses to strife? Difficulties arise the moment one begins considering these questions seriously, since Lord Durham's catchy formula is based on a series of false dichotomies. Why must a conflict be *either* 'of principles' *or* 'of races'? Can it not be both? And if a government is of one nationality and the bulk of the people it rules of another, as was the case in Lower Canada, surely any contest between the two will inevitably take on a 'racial' coloration. Lord Durham's reductionist analysis is based on the assumption that different nations cannot live peacefully 'in the bosom of a single state,' and so any confrontation pitting English against French would have to arise from their cultural differences. This was a comforting doctrine for a liberal representative of the crown who might have had some qualms about reimposing imperial rule on a defeated population had he not been assured that popular opposition was based on mere national prejudice. Canadian historians have also tended to find this interpretation congenial, since it lends credence to the view that 1837–8 saw no revolutionary crisis with fundamental political issues at stake; the Rebellion was simply one more instance, like the imperial wars of the seventeenth and eighteenth centuries or the conscription crises of the twentieth century, when relations between English and French took a violent turn.

One response to the Durham interpretation is to deny the reality of French-English conflict in the Rebellion by pointing to the many anglophones, including prominent leaders like O'Callaghan and the Nelson brothers, who rallied to the Patriot cause, and to the francophones who supported the government. The insurrection was 'really' a class struggle, say some, not an ethnic conflict.[4] This is just another false dichotomy and one that flies in the face of the empirical evidence. The ethnic polarization was by no means perfect, but French and English speakers certainly did tend to line up on opposite sides in 1837. One needs only to glance at the lists of rebel prisoners and 'Loyal Volunteers' to notice the overwhelming prevalence of French names on the first and of British names on the second. Moreover, the geography of rebellion seems to support the notion that the mutual irritation of the two linguistic groups played a part in the conflict; [...] most of the action occurred in the section of the province (cities excepted) where the French and the English had the greatest contact. One might go further and note that, even within the turbulent District of Montreal, in localities where immigrant settlements adjoined French-Canadian communities, such as Beauharnois, L'Acadie, and Two Mountains counties, some of the most serious fighting in 1837–8 took place. Indeed, Robert Hall's county of Two Mountains was the area where the revolutionary process developed most rapidly and went the furthest. [...]

THE JULY TROUBLES

The events of 1837 began here on a festive note. The Two Mountains anti-coercion meeting, held at Ste Scholastique on 1 June, was a splendid event carefully staged by the middle-class leaders—Scott, Girouard, Dr Luc Masson, Emery Féré, and others—of the county's Patriot movement. 'The Great Meeting of the Men of the North,' as the *Vindicator* called it, followed a format pioneered at St Ours. There was a triumphant procession from St Benoit, through the heart of radical Two Mountains, to the assembly site in front of the rectory at Ste Scholastique. All along the way the houses were decorated with flags and banners and the air rang with 'patriotic national songs, and repeated bursts of fervent cheers for Papineau, the Assembly and the honest Patriots of this and the neighbouring Colonies.'[5] The meeting itself featured a long address delivered by Papineau himself as well as speeches in both French and English by lesser luminaries. Finally a series of resolutions was presented to the acclamation of the crowd. Following the precedent established during protest campaigns earlier in the decade, a 'permanent committee' was set up, with representatives from each parish in the county, to coordinate future activities and to correspond with Patriots in other parts of the province. All these proceedings, exciting as they may have been for one section of the population, were most disturbing to the Constitutionalists of Two Mountains, and when extra-legal actions began a few weeks later, the latter had little doubt that the 1 June meeting and the sinister committee established then were to blame.

It was at this time that the ostracism of the 100 or so English-speaking families of St Eustache, St Benoit, and Ste Scholastique began in earnest. Stones were thrown and fences toppled, and, as Robert Hall reported in his deposition quoted above, manes were shaved and property damaged. These depredations must have been annoying, even terrifying, for the human victims, but it was the horses of Two Mountains that bore the brunt of patriot hostility. A common form of ritual aggression in this county during the troubles of 1837, the cropping of manes and tails was comparatively rare in other parts of the province.[6] It seems to have been regarded more as an indignity than an injury. Robert Hall says he was 'universally laughed at'; other accounts of Two

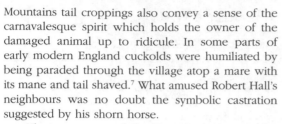

Mountains tail croppings also convey a sense of the carnavalesque spirit which holds the owner of the damaged animal up to ridicule. In some parts of early modern England cuckolds were humiliated by being paraded through the village atop a mare with its mane and tail shaved.[7] What amused Robert Hall's neighbours was no doubt the symbolic castration suggested by his shorn horse.

There was more to the Two Mountains troubles than mockery and ostracism. Crops were damaged, windows broken. Young men gathered at a country tavern in Ste Scholastique and threw stones at the carriages of passing Constitutionalists.[8] Individuals known to be hostile to the patriots were threatened, most commonly with having their houses and barns burned. Throughout the crisis of 1837–8 there were numerous threats of arson, and they were reported in various parts of Lower Canada. It was the obvious menace, perfectly calculated to chill the hearts of people who lived with their families and all their valuable possessions in wooden houses situated on relatively isolated farmsteads. What could be easier than to put the torch to a barn, and how could even the most vigilant foil a determined incendiary? Fire was indeed a favoured weapon in popular struggles in many other parts of the world, and yet there were very few cases of buildings' actually being burned in Lower Canada; or, to be more exact, there were very few until after the patriots had been defeated and the 'forces of order' had gained the upper hand. The patriots may have been restrained simply because the mere threat of arson was all the terror that was required.

It was certainly enough to keep John Oswald, a St Eustache farmer, up at night. About 11 p.m. on the night of 7 July, he later recounted, 'being then watching his property being kept in continual fear of its being damaged through reports and menaces, heard loud screamings towards Belle rivière occasioned by a mob, and that screaming was used by said mob at every old country man's house and canadian loyalists, hourrahing for Papineau and the Patriots; said mob crossed the river, and directed their steps towards a barn belonging to Messire Paquin curate of St Eustache which barn was that night demolished, the screaming continuing for some time when at that barn.' The destruction on this occasion was not as great as it sounds, because the barn was under construction and only half built. No doubt it presented too tempting a target for the 'mob' to

resist. It was unprotected, since the owner lived far away in the village. Moreover, it was likely being built to receive tithe grain, which could hardly have endeared it to these Catholic cultivators. Finally—and this seems to have been decisive—Curé Paquin was a notorious Constitutionalist; recently he had begun using the pulpit, as he had in 1834, to speak out against the patriot movement. 'That was good for a chouayen priest,' one of the party later declared, using a popular term meaning 'traitor' or 'coward' but reserved in 1837 for anti-Patriot French Canadians.[9]

The destruction of the barn was an isolated event, but the 'screaming mob' that John Oswald heard, seems to have been one of several that disturbed the peace of Two Mountains county about that time. Groups of men up to 100 strong went out at night wearing red toques, their faces blackened, and roamed the villages and the rangs [i.e., countryside] shouting patriot slogans and making as much ruckus as possible. The disguises, the nocturnal setting, and the noise all recall in a vague way the custom of the charivari, and, like a charivari, these demonstrations required some organization. A country store-cum-tavern in Ste Scholastique seems to have been the meeting place. Michel Rochon, a tanner and no friend of Papineau, happened to come there on business one day, and the proprietor asked him if he was a patriot. There were several men present and all of them seemed interested in his response; the tanner gave a prudent, rather than a strictly accurate, answer. 'Good,' replied the merchant, "I'll show you your night clothes,' and he produced a 'red cap decorated with paper' and carbon to blacken his face. Rochon went with the band that night and shouted himself hoarse, but after that he stayed home. A troop passed his house the next night and he heard someone yell, 'Rochon, you may be sleeping quietly with your wife, but if you were a *chouaguen*, you wouldn't be left in peace.'[10] Clearly the purpose of these midnight expeditions was to intimidate the hostile and the wavering. The actions were scarcely bloody; in fact, except for pulling down the frame of a barn, the 'screaming mob' committed almost no action at all. Yet there was a tangible menace of violence. The charivari form, combining a spectacle of symbolic aggression with actual restraint, was therefore wonderfully appropriate.

The marauders did cross the line dividing ritual violence from the real thing one night when they fired shots through the windows of two houses, one of them belonging to Captain Eustache Cheval of St Eustache. A senior habitant close to sixty years of age, Cheval happened to have conveyed his farm by a notarized deed of gift to one of his sons only a month before the attack, and so we have some record of his material circumstance in 1837.[11] His 117-arpent farm, with house, barn, equipment, and livestock, can be described only as typical of the period. Though he was no longer, strictly speaking, a land-owner as of May, his deed of 'gift' was loaded down with so many restrictions that it made his son a virtual tenant-farmer, if not a hired hand, for the rest of Eustache's life. None of these circumstances would have set Cheval apart economically from most other habitants of his age, but his militia commission and his political leanings did. Cheval had originally gained his militia commission during the election campaign of 1827 as a reward for supporting his seigneur and lieutenant-colonel, and he was well known in the area as a creature of the St Eustache Dumont clique.

A decade of standing up for an unpopular cause may have toughened Cheval. Certainly he was not easily intimidated; when he was warned in advance that his property would be a target of patriot ire, he prepared for resistance, gathering four friends to help guard his home. In the middle of the night prowlers were spotted by the stable, but Cheval managed to chase them away. Later, however, a shot crashed through the window and a little girl was cut by the broken glass.[12] Eustace Cheval was sure that the intention was to assassinate him, which is probably what the attackers wished him to think. Actually, this incident seems to be consistent with the larger campaign of restrained terror; it was simply the extreme case where a more dramatic threat seemed necessary to deal with an opponent more determined than most.

What then was the point of these threats and this harassment? Who wished to frighten whom and why? Among those named in the depositions as taking an active role in the July campaigns were three 'yeomen' (i.e., habitants), three labourers, and one tanner.[13] There is no mention of the prominent middle-class politicians of the area. Only the Major brothers, small merchants of Ste Scholastique, qualify marginally as bourgeois, and they do seem to have played a leading role. More so than the actions of later stages of the crisis of 1837, this was a wholly plebeian campaign, and one carried out by the peasantry, including a disproportionate number of presumably poor labourers.

But were these people acting under the orders or at the instigation of the Patriot 'high command'? Many victims of the campaign of harassment noted that the troubles began soon after the Ste Scholastique meeting. Papineau and the other speakers certainly used every rhetorical device to rouse the patriotic indignation of their massive audience, but the accounts of the speeches give no indication that they advocated violent measures. Far from fanning the flames of national hostility, the resolutions passed on that June afternoon called for understanding and reconciliation.

> We therefore fervently implore all the inhabitants of the Province of every creed, origin and language, to be united for their common defence; to sacrifice their prejudices for the honor and safety of the country, and to help each other, for the purpose of obtaining a wise and protecting Government, which, in re-establishing harmony amongst us, would, at the same time, cause agriculture, commerce, and our national industry to flourish, and we on our part assure of our fraternity and of our confidence our fellow subjects of British origin who superior as well to the cajoleries as to the antipathies of power, have united with us in our just demands, that we never entertained, but on the contrary that we have always reproved, the unfortunate national distinctions which our common enemies have sought, and still wickedly seek, to foment amongst us.[14]

When violence was later reported in Two Mountains, the radical papers of Montreal seemed quite embarrassed by the commotion and did their best to ignore it. Meanwhile, dozens of protest meetings were being held all across Lower Canada, and none of them was followed by disturbances. What was so special about Two Mountains county that political mobilization there should lead to bitter civil conflict?

Surely the peculiar balance of patriot and Constitutionalist forces was what distinguished Two Mountains from other rural counties. A substantial section of the county was hostile to the Patriots and

215

had given proof in 1834 of its willingness to resort to violence. Three years later, by June 1837, it was clear that the province was on the verge of a much more serious crisis. Papineau might talk vaguely of a great revolution in distant future, but the people of southern Two Mountains must have been more keenly aware of the dangerous reactions such rhetoric was likely to provoke both from the government and from their Constitutionalist neighbours. We cannot hope to understand the actions of these people unless we appreciate the danger to which the anti-colonial mobilization exposed them. Hence the more rapid preparations for action, the noisy bravado to reassure the committed and intimidate the hostile. Hence also the punitive reaction against figures such as Curé Paquin who were identified with the larger threat. If the flags, the slogans, and the speeches of the Ste Scholastique meeting gave voice to the hopes of the patriots of Two Mountains, the attacks on Robert Hall and Eustache Cheval expressed their fears.

Alongside the rather 'paranoid' dimensions of these incidents, there is also a more rational sense to the campaign of 'persecution.' All the testimony indicates that the immediate and expressed purpose of the intimidation and harassment was to force people to change their political allegiance. 'Join the Patriot party,' was the demand put to dissidents; otherwise, 'there will be trouble.'[15] No one seems to have been asked to change his language, religion, or customs: only his politics. In some cases men were asked to sign a free trade petition to the United States Congress that was being circulated throughout Lower Canada. But surely a few additional signatures— which could always be forged in any case—did not justify all the commotion and scare tactics. Clearly the petition itself was less important than the public gesture of support for the patriots implied by the act of signing. The real purpose of intimidation was, first, to get the timid, the wavering, the opportunistic to commit themselves to the patriotic cause. People like Michel Rochon were likely to side with the stronger party at any given time; pressuring him to take part in charivaris made him an accessory and therefore less likely to help the government forces (although Rochon did in fact inform on the patriots). The second purpose of intimidation was to identify the staunch and determined opponents of the movement. When Robert Hall refused, in spite of strong

pressure, to make even a symbolic gesture of solidarity, he showed himself to be altogether different from those who held back out of timidity or a lack of civic spirit. He was not a negligent citizen: he was an enemy. There was political logic then to the actions of the marauders; it could in fact be called a terrorist logic, though that seems a rather strong term to attach to such restrained coercion. Both brutal political rationality and fear-inspired outbursts can be discerned in the July troubles, and both can be traced to the special situation in which Two Mountains patriots found themselves in the summer of 1837.

Of course the irony is that the disturbances only hastened the outside reactions that the radicals dreaded. Rumours spread that the tough Orangemen of the Gore had promised to come to the aid of the beleaguered anglophones of the south. And every frightened Constitutionalist who swore out a deposition in the city made armed intervention of the state more likely. As allies and witnesses on the side of the threatening outside forces, anti-patriots in St Eustache, St Benoit, and Ste Scholastique seemed all the more threatening. Toussaint Cheval, a Ste Scholastique labourer and no doubt suspect because he was related to the notorious Eustache, was one of those who fell afoul of his neighbours. On the evening of 10 July four men whom he apparently knew well stormed into his house and began shouting accusations to the effect 'that he had been to the River du Chêne [St Eustache village] to sign up to get troops.' Shaking his fist under poor Toussaint's nose, Isidore Lauzon denounced him for 'swearing a deposition against us.' In fact, since Cheval's name does not appear in the surviving depositions sworn before that date, the specific charge was probably unfounded. But Isidore Lauzon had no access to certain information on that point. All he knew was that a punitive expedition was rumoured to be on its way and that Toussaint Cheval, because of something he said or did, appeared to be blameable. 'You've put our head in a noose,' he continued, 'you cannot live among us any more. You can pack up and leave right now.' Cheval took seriously this sentence of banishment and the threat that lay behind it; without delay he left for Upper Canada and stayed there for weeks. Returning at last to the parish, he had to hide out in the woods for a day and a night before he ascertained that the alarm had passed and it was safe to return to his family.[16]

The noisy promenades, the stone-throwing, the shots, the horse mutilation, and the fence-breaking, combined with rumours and threats of much worse horrors, made a vivid impression on the little Constitutionalist contingent of St Eustache, St Benoit, and Ste Scholastique. By mid-July, even though no one had been hurt, these people were well and truly terrified.[17] News of the events was then spreading through the province as the Tory press of Montreal published lurid accounts of the 'anarchy' in the northern countryside. The government, still hoping to defuse the large political crisis, was placed in a difficult position. Clearly the law had been broken repeatedly, and the local delegates of the state either were themselves involved in the actions or were completely powerless to oppose them. Something had to be done if the government was to appease Constitutionalist extremists and maintain its own sovereignty in the region. The solicitor-general therefore decided to offer a reward for information that would identify those who had shot at Cheval. At the same time, he ordered the arrest of four men already named in depositions sworn by Robert Hall and the others.

On the morning of 13 July, with the Montreal garrison on the alert, a party led by the high constable left the city on its way to St Eustache. This officer (whose duties normally involved organizing the night watchmen of Montreal) had warrants to arrest four men on charges of 'conspiracy,' and he was accompanied by two bailiffs, a carter, and two other private citizens.[18] They must have formed a curious and highly conspicuous procession, bumping along the dusty roads in their five calèches, looking for all the world like the legal officials who came to serve warrants of execution when a farm was seized for debt.

Another pair of bailiffs had ridden out separately from Montreal charged with distributing posters offering, in the name of the governor, a reward of £100 for information in the Eustache Cheval case.[19] Arriving at the village of St Benoit, they went straight to a tavern owned by a man named Coursolle. When they tried to post the proclamation, however, the innkeeper stopped them, unimpressed by their announcement that they were acting under orders from the attorney-general. Coursolle proclaimed 'that the Attorney-General was filthy damned trash [sacré crasseux] and so is the governor,' before he went to get help. Dr Masson, a local Patriot leader, arrived

with other neighbours and took charge. He told the bailiffs their lives would be in danger if they put up their posters in the village and added, in a remark that nicely expressed current local notions of criminality and legitimate authority, that he would like to offer £100 for the governor's head. But the conversation was cut short when a man galloped up to announce the arrival at Côte St Joseph of a larger party that had come to take prisoners. Everyone rushed off in pursuit. One man was heard to suggest that the high constable should be stripped naked and tied up at the top of the mountain and left to be eaten by the mosquitoes.

Meanwhile, the high constable's expedition was also running into difficulty.[20] When it landed at St Eustache, inquiries were made to locate the four men named in the warrants, but of course no one would say where they lived. According to Patriot accounts, the officers attempted to intimidate the population by saying that they were being followed by a force of soldiers and artillery.[21] The scare tactics may have been effective, since they did manage to locate one of the accused, François Labelle, at his farm three leagues back from the river in the parish of St Eustache. Labelle tried to run away, but he was soon captured. As they were securing the prisoner, the captors noticed Labelle's wife running to the neighbours for help. Other residents were going from house to house, and soon a crowd had gathered around, armed with sticks and farm implements. The lawmen brandished guns to keep the people at bay and hurried off towards the ferry almost ten kilometres away. All along the way angry crowds gathered by the roadside, menacing the constables and shouting encouragement to the prisoner. Hopes were lodged with the party of militia men now speeding to the rescue from St Benoit. The band of would-be rescuers, according to one report, was made up of about fifty men armed with sickles, axes, and pitchforks,[22] but they did not arrive at St Eustache in time to bring this agricultural weaponry into play.

The law officers narrowly beat them to the river crossing and turning their guns on the ferryman, forced him to take them over to Ile Jésus. The St Benoit contingent came galloping up to the shore just in time to see their quarry in mid-stream, rowing furiously towards the opposite shore in the only available boat. A few pot-shots were fired, but there was no question of pushing the pursuit any further.

217

The urban authorities may have taken one prisoner, but the patriots of Two Mountains had been successful in driving them away, along with the placard-posting bailiffs, before they could accomplish their mission. Now they had every reason to fear retaliation from the military expedition promised by the high constable. Accordingly, the force from St Benoit divided into parties of four or five men each and scattered to hide and ambush any troops that might arrive. They stayed in the woods all night, but no invasion materialized.[23]

The fear of military intervention was vivid in Two Mountains, and with good reason. Under the circumstances, the high constable's threats seemed only too plausible, especially in view of the troop movements currently taking place in the province. The government was moving units from Quebec City up to Montreal, and the first contingents of reinforcements from Nova Scotia began to arrive in the capital on 11 July.[24] Two hundred soldiers had in fact been placed on the alert on the day of the constables' foray, but they were never dispatched to Two Mountains. The authorities were too worried about troubles in Montreal itself, and they kept the troops standing by in case urban patriots tried to force the release of François Labelle.

In the wake of the events of 13 July both parties seemed to draw back from the brink of armed conflict. The government, wishing neither to press matters to a showdown nor to let an open challenge to its authority go unanswered, sent the deputy sheriff to serve the three remaining warrants two days later. This legal officer seems to have travelled north without an armed escort and to have carried out his mission with considerable tact. Some of the Patriot leaders of St Benoit, including the tavern-keeper Coursolles and the radical priest Etienne Chartier, claimed they cooperated with the deputy sheriff in securing the surrender of one of the delinquents.[25] It might be more correct to say that the deputy sheriff cooperated with the Patriots, because some sort of unofficial peace treaty seems to have been negotiated, the terms of which allowed the official barely to save face while protecting the accused from any serious punishment. In the end, one of the three men named in the warrants was persuaded to appear, but in St Benoit, not in Montreal. Rather than face criminal charges, he had only to post a bond for good behaviour, which he did before a Patriot justice of the peace, effectively ensuring that the bond would remain a dead letter.

Lower Canada's attorney-general, Charles Ogden, came up to Montreal about this time and gave his approval to the policy of conciliation.[26] Without a regular police force, Ogden shrewdly pointed out, the government had few options. It would be very risky to send in a military expedition. Armed resistance seemed likely and, even if the regular soldiers proved stronger, which seemed certain, would they succeed in arresting the men named in the warrants? If it was not entirely successful, said Ogden, an army intervention would have the most disastrous effects. Moreover, even if arrests could be made, would the accused men be convicted in a court of law? This result, too, seemed uncertain given the impossibility of gathering good evidence in such a case. (Of course the attorney-general was quite right on this point: the Montreal grand jury eventually threw out the case against François Labelle in early September.) All he could suggest was that the governor try to enlist the aid of the Catholic clergy. Thus the local crisis of legitimacy was left unresolved. In the five months following the ill-fated expedition of 13 July there were no further attempts to assert government authority in the patriot sections of Two Mountains.

And what of the ethnic dimension of Two Mountains' troubled summer? Were the attacks on English-speaking settlers simply the expression of some primitive French-Canadian xenophobia, as the Tory press would have it? The Montreal *Gazette* thundered:

> Is it to be permitted for one moment that men of the Old Country shall be insulted and menaced, their properties ruined and destroyed, and themselves and their little ones driven from their homes in this land, to which they are entitled as much as any 'enfant du sol' that vegetates around them, simply because they do not choose to relinquish the laws, the language, and the institutions of their forefathers, or to link themselves to a FRENCH faction, whose sole end and aim is to deprive them of every vestige of nationality—to tinker them into FRENCHMEN?[27]

Suspicion of the 'other' was no doubt a reality on both sides of the linguistic divide in Two Mountains, but it is hardly the key to the aggressive acts of June and July 1837. The persecution of 'men of the Old Country' was not the culmination of years of ethnic hatred; rather it was something quite unprecedented, as the victims themselves recognized. Echoing the words of Robert Hall, Duncan McColl declared that he and his family had lived in St Benoit for eighteen years, 'in the greatest peace and harmony with our Canadian neigh-bours until the time when a certain political meeting took place at Saint Scholastique […] about a month ago.'[28] Note also that the two most serious attacks were directed against Curé Paquin and Captain Cheval, both French Canadians associated with the Dumont connec-tion of St Eustache. Moreover, several of the region's Patriot leaders were English speakers: William Henry Scott, to take the most prominent example, or, at a second level of leadership, John Hawley, a Yankee wool carder, was most active in the cause. The Irish parish of St Columban was in fact notorious as a hot-bed of radicalism.

The lines of conflict then were fundamentally political and incidentally ethnic. It was those who opted for Britain rather than Canada and who defied the hegemony of the Patriot movement who made themselves the target of popular ire in the southern parishes of Two Mountains. 'Join us or suffer the consequences,' was the brutal message of the stone-throwers and mane-shavers. Certainly this was coer-cive politics, but it was hardly racist.

FRENCH AND ENGLISH AT WAR

As the struggle between the Patriot movement and the government developed into outright war, the ethnic polarization in Two Mountains and elsewhere in the province became more pronounced and more bitter. The two sides girded for battle, leaving less and less room for polite inquiries. In the confusion and uncer-tainties of civil strife actors on both the government and the rebel sides had to be able to distinguish enemies—actual and potential—from friends. Lives often depended on a rapid assessment. Experience taught that French Canadians were likely to rally to the patriot colours, while English speakers generally gravitated to the opposite side. It was only natural, therefore, that in emergency situations people acted as though language was a clear boundary between friend and foe. The inevitable injustices that ensued served of course to embitter the atmosphere and deepen the national cleavage.

During the risings of 1837 and 1838 the first act of the insurgents in many parts of Lower Canada was to send expeditions against local anglophones. One of these originated in St Jérôme, a French-Canadian parish situated near the ragged linguistic boundary of the Two Mountains region. When news of the initial skirmishes of November 1837 reached St Jérôme, it seemed clear that the crisis was nearing its long-awaited military climax. That being the case, the attention of local patriots would normally be focused on Montreal, the main enemy stronghold in the western half of Lower Canada. Yet it was not south towards Montreal, but north in the direction of a less distant source of danger that the people of St Jérôme first turned. New Paisley, just up the river from St Jérôme, was settled by Scottish immigrants only in the 1820s; with a population of 191 at the time of the 1831 census, it was numerically much weaker than its neighbour. As far as I can tell, there was no history of conflict between the two commun-ities. St Jérôme and New Paisley seem to have gone their separate ways without paying much attention to one another. Three St Jérôme men who were later arrested and interrogated referred variously to the settlers as 'les irlandais,' 'les anglais,' and 'les habi-tants d'outre-mer,' ['Irish', 'English', and 'farmers from overseas'] indicating how little they knew their Scot-tish neighbours![29] The question local patriots had to ask themselves as the Lower Canadian crisis came to a head was how would the immigrants behave in the ultimate conflict? A largely unknown but apparently inoffensive settlement, New Paisley nevertheless took on an ominous character for the patriots, because its position to the rear of St Jérôme made it the potential source of a blow from behind.

Accordingly, on 20 November an armed party set off northward from St Jérôme under the leader-ship of Jérôme Longpré, a thirty-nine-year-old habi-tant.[30] Previously, a St Jérôme blacksmith had been to New Paisley, ostensibly on business but in fact to find out how many settlers possessed firearms. Meanwhile the St Jérôme militia was ordered to turn out on Monday, 20 November; no doubt the arrange-ments were made on the day before when everyone had assembled for church services. Pressure was brought to bear on any men who appeared reluc-tant to participate. A local merchant and innkeeper named William Scott, for example, made himself very unpopular by his staunch refusal to join the expedition. 'Too bad for the English if the Canadians win,' Longpré warned him, 'and you more than the others.'[31] Most men were glad to take part, however, and some 2–300 congregated on the appointed day with whatever guns they could procure and marched off to New Paisley. As they approached the Scottish settlement, a party of New Paisley men advanced to meet them. James Rennie, a local leader in Paisley, reports that the intruders began by asking what the people of New Paisley intended to do in the current crisis.[32] Remain in peace and quiet was the answer. But that is impossible, retorted the St Jérôme spokesman, for the war has now begun. (This was perfectly true; before long a company of Loyal Volunteers was formed in New Paisley, armed by the government and under the command of James Rennie.) The interpreter from St Jérôme explained to Rennie that 'Most of the Scotch won't go to fight [and so] they must give up their arms—for we mean to go and attack Montreal and we cannot get our people (meaning the Canadians) away leaving you all armed behind their settlements.' The demand then was that New Paisley give up its guns, and since Rennie and his followers were so badly outnumbered, they had no choice but to comply. The announcement of the surrender was greeted with 'great hallooing' from the St Jérôme men. They went from house to house and collected thirty-one firearms.[33] No further aggression was committed against New Paisley, even though the Scottish settlement was now completely at the mercy of the St Jérôme patriots.

Though thirty-one rusty muskets hardly constituted a major addition to the patriot armoury, the expedition was nevertheless deemed a success. It had effectively neutralized a potential opponent, and perhaps more importantly, it had demonstrated that the habitants of St Jérôme were capable of concerted action when required. Returning to St Jérôme, about twenty-five of the militia men stopped at William Scott's tavern for a drink to mark their victory. 'Treat us to free drinks, you,' shouted Jérôme Longpré, waving his sword through the air. 'We really won; we have had a good march.' Needless to say, the drinks were on the house. The Constitutionalist innkeeper reported that his unwelcome guests had insulted and abused him for having stayed at home instead of going with them to New Paisley. Victory celebration, punitive visitation, and warning for the future (not to mention armed robbery), this little party served

many purposes. And why was William Scott singled out for victimization? In sorting out this question we must consider, not only the hostile talk about 'les anglais,' but also the fact that his neighbours wanted Scott to join them, to accept the responsibilities of a full-fledged resident of the parish of St Jérôme. As far as they were concerned, the community itself was in real danger and therefore refusal to march against New Paisley implied indifference—or something worse—towards St Jérôme as well as 'the nation.'

New Paisley did have its revenge. Thousands of enraged anglo-Canadians rushed to take up arms against the patriots, and although they played only a minor role in the military engagements of the Rebellion, these Volunteers proved to be zealous rebel-hunters in the ensuing pacification campaigns. The 'Loyal Volunteers Corps' quickly became an anglo-phone preserve. Even though many French Canadians remained attached to the government, an English officer was appalled to find that 'not more than 100 out of the 10,000' provincial Volunteers were French Canadians.[34] Thus the atmosphere was particularly bitter when a second revolt broke out in November 1838 and the national polarization became even more pronounced. Bands of patriots began in most localities by disarming or arresting the English-speaking men in their midst (frequently members of the hated Volunteer Corps). David M'Clennaghan later recalled a conversation with one of his captors: 'I asked him what he meant by taking the arms from the old country people? and he replied, "We want the arms from the old country people, that they may not come behind us when we go to face the soldiers."'[35] As in 1837, attacks against immigrants were mainly motivated by elementary considerations of military security, although no doubt revenge also played a part.

The second rising was mastered even more easily than the first, but nevertheless it unleashed a francophobic outburst even more ferocious that those of the past. When Olivier Gagnez of Lacolle went to join the Volunteers preparing to repel a rebel invasion from Vermont, the captain told him (through an interpreter), 'that he would not take those who did not speak English.' Instead, he placed poor Gagnez in jail for two days![36] The military occupation of regions involved in the insurrection gave wide scope for brutal bigots such as a Volunteer sergeant named Harrison, who, without provocation, pistol-whipped an habitant near Napierville. Called to account, he declared that such behaviour was 'not only proper but indispensable in dealing with the French Canadians.' His commander let the matter drop.[37] The Harrison case is extreme, but it does express a view, widely held at the time in 'loyal' anglophone circles, that anyone who spoke French was politically suspect. Even a civilized and humane man like Lieutenant-Colonel W.C. Chandler had difficulty when ordered in 1839 to purge his Nicolet militia battalion of officers whose loyalty might be questioned. 'The local populations, comprised, as they are principally of French Canadians; for although there does exist amongst them many well disposed individuals, the question is, how to discriminate, in these times.'[38]

'How to discriminate': that was precisely the problem that faced both patriots and Constitutionalists in those troubled times, when political conflict over the shape of the Lower Canadian state reached a revolutionary crisis, and language and national origin often came to serve as rough and ready indicators of political allegiance. The armed conflict served only to accelerate the process of national polarization, so that by the time Lord Durham visited Canada in 1838, hatred between English and French was at an all-time high. Who can blame him for assuming that virulent 'racial' hostility was a fundamental fact of Lower Canadian public life and for concluding, quite erroneously, that the revolutionary upheaval was the product of national animosity?

NOTES

1. C.P. Lucas, ed., *Lord Durham's Report on the Affairs of British North America*, 3 vols (Oxford: Clarendon 1912), 2:16

2. Archives nationales du Québec [ANQ], 1837, no. 607, deposition of Robert Hall, 15 July 1837

3. Ibid., no. 836, deposition of Duncan McCall, 11 July 1837

4. Daniel Salée, 'Les insurrections de 1837-1838 au Québec: remarques critiques et théoriques en marge de l'historiographie,' *Canadian Review of Studies in Nationlism* 13 (Spring 1986): 13–29

5. *Vindicator*, 6 June 1837

6. ANQ, 1837, no. 659, déposition d'Eustache Cheval, 4 July 1837; ibid., no 3446, W.K. McCord to T.M.C. Murdock, 27 April 1840; Hardy, 'l'essor du protestantisme,' 180; *Le Populaire*, 29 September 1837. Perhaps animal mutilation was a practice the local habitants picked up from the Irish immigrants who lived in their midst; for we know that the mutilation of livestock, often in quite gruesome forms, was a favoured punishment directed against landlords and others who broke community norms in the Irish countryside. On the other hard, there is evidence of mane and tail cropping in rural French Canada from before the conquest. George Rudé, *Protest and Punishment: The Story of the Social and Political Protestors transported to Australia 1788–1868* (Oxford: Oxford UP 1978), 149–52; Louise Dechêne, personal communication

7. Martin Ingram, 'Ridings, Rough Music and the "Reform of Popular Culture" in Early Modern England,' *Past and Present*, 105 (November 1984): 87

8. National Archives of Canada [NA], Lower Canada Civil Secretary, 515: 265, George Gillanders to S. Walcott, 23 July 1837

9. ANQ, 1837, no. 789, deposition of John Oswald, 15 July 1837; ibid., no. 816, déposition de Toussaint Cheval, 10 July 1837

10. Ibid., no. 815, déposition de Michel Rochon, 8 July 1837 (author's translation)

11. ANQ (Montreal), gr., J.-L. de Bellefeuille, donation entre vifs par Eustache Cheval et son épouse à Frs-Xavier Cheval leur fils, 29 May 1837

12. ANQ, 1837, no. 659, déposition d'Eustache Cheval, 4 July 1837

13. Ibid., passim.

14. *Vindicator*, 6 June 1837

15. ANQ, 1837, no. 834, deposition of Duncan McColl, 6 July 1837; cf. ibid., no. 833, deposition of Alexander McColl, 6 July 1837; ibid., no. 835, deposition of William Starke, 6 July 1837; LAC, Lower Canada Civil Secretary, 514: 132, F.E. Globensky to D. Daly, 11 July 1837 (author's translation)

16. ANQ, 1837, no. 610, déposition de Toussaint Cheval, 6 September 1837 (author's translation)

17. NA, Lower Canada Civil Secretary, 514: 90, petition of several inhabitants of St Eustache to Governor Gosford, 9 July 1837

18. ANQ, 1837, no. 669, déposition d'André-Henri Baron, 14 July 1837; ibid, no. 837, affidavit de Joseph Aymond et François Poitra, 14 July 1837; ibid., no. 838, affidavit of Benjamin Delisle, 14 July 1837; ibid., no. 839, affidavit d'Amable Loiselle, 14 July 1837

19. Ibid., no. 669, déposition d'André-Henri Baron, 14 July 1837

20. Ibid., no. 837, affidavit de Joseph Aymond, 14 July 1837; ibid., no. 838, affidavit of Benjamin Delisle, 14 July 1837; ibid., no. 839, affidavit d'Amable Loiselle, 14 July 1837

21. *La Minerve*, 27 July 1837

22. *Le Populaire*, 14 July 1837

23. ANQ, 1837, no. 607, deposition of Robert Hall, 15 July 1837

24. *Le Populaire*, 14 July 1837

25. Ibid., 19 July 1837; Archives du diocèse de St Jérôme, Chartier to Lartigue, St Benoit, 18 July 1837

26. NA, Lower Canada Civil Secretary, 515: 186–9; Ogden to Gosford, 17 July 1837

27. *Gazette*, 21 September 1837

28. ANQ, 1837, no. 836, deposition of Duncan McColl, 11 July 1837

29. Ibid., no. 572, examen volontaire de Jean Latour, 14 February 1838; ibid., no. 574, déposition de Jean-Baptiste Renaud, 31 January 1838; ibid., no. 577, examen volontaire de François Pillon, 14 February 1838

30. Ibid., no. 643, examen volontaire de Laurent Longpré, 14 February 1838

31. Ibid., no. 571, deposition of William Scott, 1 February 1838 (author's translation)

32. Ibid., no. 633, deposition of James Rennie, 5 February 1838

33. Ibid., no. 702, examen volontaire de Jérôme Longpré, 14 February 1838

34. Quoted in Elinor Senior, *Redcoats and Patriots: the Rebellion in Lower Canada 1837–38* (Ottawa: Canada's Wings 1985), 109

35. *Report of the State Trials, Before a General Court Martial Held at Montreal in 1838–1839: Exhibiting a Complete History of the Late Rebellion in Lower Canada*, 2 vols (Montreal: Armour and Ramsay 1839), 2: 162

36. ANQ, 1837, no. 1145, examen volontaire d'Olivier Gagnez, 22 November 1838

37. NA, Lower Canada Stipendiary Magistrates, vol. 2, Gugy to Goldie, 25 March 1839

38. NA, Lower Canada, Adjutant General, vol. 51, Chandler to Young, 17 June 1839

222

■ Article 2 (Upper Canada): The Causes of the Rebellion

By Colin Read and Ronald J. Stagg

Angry men in homespun clothing debating at public meetings; neighbour fighting neighbour over their right to disagree; tired farmers slogging down a muddy December road, a wagon load of assorted rifles, fowling pieces, pikes, axes, and pitchforks accompanying their dogged march; a lone steamboat sailing a frigid winter lake bearing a motley cargo of gentlemen, storekeepers, and more farmers, all determined to stop the advance of the group that came by road; the thump of a trapdoor pitching two men to their deaths at the end of a rope; men fleeing by land and water, cold, tired, and frightened. These are

Source: Colin Read and Ronald J. Stagg, eds., *The Rebellion of 1837 in Upper Canada: A Collection of Documents* (Ottawa: Carleton University Press, 1985), pp. xix–xxxv. McGill-Queen's University Press, 1985. Reprinted with permission.

just a few impressions of the uprisings of 1837 in the colony of Upper Canada, uprisings of which much has been written but much remains unknown.

The Upper Canadian rebellions have left behind a curious legacy. The uprising in the London District, often called the Duncombe Rebellion after its chief character, has been largely ignored in accounts of the troubles of 1837. [...]

The Home District outbreak, variously called the Mackenzie Rebellion, the Yonge Street Rebellion or, rather grandly, the Upper Canadian Rebellion, has not been well served by historians either. [...]

The grievances which underlay the rebellions were of long duration, their roots entangled in the provisions of the Constitutional Act of 1791 which had created Upper Canada's political framework. The provisions of the act had been governed by the British desire to prevent a second revolt against imperial rule in North America. The lesson of the American Revolution learned by Secretary of State William Grenville and others was that they must retard in their fledgling colony "the growth of a republican or independent spirit."[1] This was to be done by checking closely the influence in the colony's government of those inhabitants of little education and wealth, who, it was thought, could easily be led astray by men of liberal ideas. The voice of the common man might be heard in the Assembly but it was to have limited strength.[2] As a curb on the power of the people an appointed upper house, the Legislative Council, and a lieutenant-governor, appointed by and responsible to the British government, had also to approve legislation. As well, an Executive Council, technically only an advisory body to the lieutenant-governor but in actuality a body which heavily influenced executive policy, could impede the popular will as expressed by the Assembly.

Since members of the Executive Council tended also to be appointed to the Legislative Council and the lieutenant-governor had a remarkably similar philosophical outlook to that of many of the executive councillors, the upper strata of the colonial government more often than not acted as a unit. Local officials throughout the colony—sheriffs, district clerks and treasurers, justices of the peace and so on—were appointed by the executive from the more affluent conservative segment of colonial society, and in many if not most cases men with outlooks similar to those of the executive councillors and lieutenant-governors were chosen. With real power at the local level residing in these men, especially with the justices of the peace, instead of with locally elected officials, the voice of the common man was muted indeed. The small group of men who wielded so much power at the provincial capital became known as the Family Compact, but small family compacts emerged across the colony occupying most the official positions in the local areas, often having social and economic ties to the central elite.

In the very early life of the colony its oligarchic form of government worked reasonably well, for the province's settlers were less concerned with politics than they were with wresting a living from their new land. Then as population swelled political strife developed. Before the War of 1812 such strife was limited, revolving as it did about a few prominent personalities who were dissatisfied with their positions in the colony. After the war political tensions heightened as colonial officials, convinced that American aggression was a symptom of mob rule or democracy and doubly frightened by the apparent extent of disloyal conduct among Upper Canadians during the war, determined to control the menace by denying American immigrants land and the right to hold political office.

The Alien Question, as it became known, caused consternation among a large proportion of the population. The British government's interpretation of the executive's actions, if carried to its logical conclusion, would have deprived many long-established settlers of their rights as British citizens. By the time the Colonial Office imposed a compromise solution in 1826, alliances had formed in opposition to the executive's policies which, though often shifting or ephemeral, provided organizational precedents for future action. In the mid-1820s a whole series of issues, most of which involved questions of education, religion, land development, and internal improvements, arose and brought men together in a more cohesive group, the Reform Movement, which disagreed with the Family Compact's attempts to impose its values and priorities on the society.

Striving as they were to create a conservative British society with as many safeguards against popular democracy as possible, the oligarchy offended not only those who felt the people could be trusted to make political decisions but also those who objected to the Compact's interpretation of Britishness and loyalty. Religious questions offer an example. Until 1831, when the Assembly finally altered the policy, only magistrates and ministers of the established faiths, those denominations which were state churches in other countries, the Church of England, Church of Scotland, and Roman Catholic Church, were allowed to perform marriages. The other denominations were deemed too dominated by their American parent churches to be trustworthy. Attacks on the loyalty of what was probably the largest religious sect in Upper Canada, the Methodists, by the Compact's religious leader and one of its chief spokesmen, John Strachan, only exacerbated the situation.

Religious tensions were compounded by the Compact's reserves policy. The Constitutional Act and a later proclamation had established clergy and crown reserves totalling two-sevenths of the surveyed lands of the province. Spread out as they were across the colony, these reserves angered many, because few people would rent or later buy the lots while land was available very cheaply in much of the province. Without settlement the reserve lands were not developed and thus local communications in

223

many areas were made difficult. But, beyond this, the clergy reserves gave the Church of England a privileged position. Interpreting the ambiguous wording of the Constitutional Act to mean that the Church of England was the established church in the province, and believing that an established church was needed to assist in providing stability by checking the base nature of the common man, the Compact insisted that all revenues from the reserves belonged to this denomination alone.

Though the British government admitted in 1820 the possibility of the Church of Scotland's sharing in the reserve revenues, the Kirk continued to be excluded from them, as were other non-Anglican denominations. Unlike the Kirk, however, most of the latter were voluntarist, believing that no church should receive state aid. Instead the money from the reserves should be used for education and internal improvements.

By the late 1820s the Family Compact was accused of sins as diverse as trying to force education into a mould created by the Church of England and failing to develop roads within the colony. It was seen as too closely allied with major business concerns such as the Bank of Upper Canada, the Welland Canal Company, and the Canada Company, the last of which had taken over the sale of crown reserves and of considerable undistributed crown lands in 1826, in return for an annual payment to the executive. Numerous other contentious issues, major and minor, caused hostility against the Compact among certain segments of the population and, together, all the issues suggested to them the necessity of change. In 1828 the province's electorate returned a majority of reformers to the Assembly.

Winning one election did not guarantee reform victory. In 1830 the tories turned the reformers out in the election and gained control of the House. In many ways they represented as diverse a collection of individuals and views as did the reformers. A minority were outright Family Compact supporters, while others advocated many of the same practical reforms as their opponents. They did not, however, call for constitutional reforms to break the power of the Compact, as increasingly the reform movement did; and, whatever may have divided them internally, they shared a common loyalty to the British crown. To the men in the Legislative and Executive Councils this was the key. Though the members of the Compact might be frustrated at times by the tory Assembly's actions, at least that Assembly could be counted on not to try to alter the British system of colonial government.

To Compact members, certain segments of the reform group appeared to be courting disaster. The Baldwins, Robert and his father William Warren, might advocate responsible government and the handing over of power to the Assembly, but other reformers, with William Lyon Mackenzie in the lead, openly flirted with American-style democracy as the answer to Upper Canada's problems. The political liability of this latter position was that both those who advocated it and the reform movement as a whole could be branded as disloyal to the monarch and to the mother country. The Compact and many other tories were not above doing this, even though the Baldwin solution was well within the sphere of British political discussion.

Though in the 1830s the reform movement often appeared united because of its policy of not criticizing its own members even when there were disagreements of principle, it was in fact composed of diverse factions and led by many men, of whom Robert Baldwin, John Rolph, Marshall Spring Bidwell, and William Lyon Mackenzie were the most notable. On the other hand, the tories, or "constitutionalists" as they preferred being called, though divided on questions of change, were united in their opposition to disloyalty. They had considerable public appeal and in the 1830s were able to compete on reasonably equal terms with the reformers at the polls. They took the election of 1830, but then the electorate, obviously dissatisfied with their glacial approach to reform and angered over the continued expulsion of William Lyon Mackenzie from the Assembly, which he continually criticized, returned the reformers in 1834. Mackenzie, hoping to strike a mortal blow at the Compact and its supporter the lieutenant-governor, set up a committee of the Assembly to investigate grievances and abuses of power. Its report, largely Mackenzie's own work, was a compendium of reform grievances, but its intemperate tone and emphasis on concerns not shared by all reform members embarrassed many of his colleagues. Nevertheless it had important results, helping persuade the British government to remove Sir John Colborne, the lieutenant-governor, and to appoint someone it believed more acceptable.

In January of 1836, [...] Upper Canada received its new governor, a rather improbable one, in the person of Sir Francis Bond Head. A sometime adventurer and more recently senior poor law commissioner in Kent, he had no political experience or finesse and soon collided violently with the reform majority in the Assembly. At first Head tried conciliation, in the hopes of heading off demands for constitutional reform. In February he admitted Robert Baldwin and John Rolph to his Executive Council, the very body that Baldwin wanted to make responsible to the people, through the Assembly. The accommodation was short-lived. Baldwin, who had been reluctant to enter the Council, soon tired of the position in which he found himself: while the Council might tender the governor advice, the latter could ignore it, as Head was wont to do. He persuaded the five remaining councillors to present Head with a document, dated 4 March, insisting that they be given greater influence in the affairs of state. Head refused publicly and insisted that the six join in withdrawing the document. When all did not, he installed six new councillors, all tories. Battle was then joined in earnest.

The reform-dominated Assembly established a select committee to investigate the affair. The committee reported in April that responsible government had already been incorporated into Upper Canada's constitution! To secure Head's recognition of this, it advised the House to stop the supplies [i.e., to withhold approval of spending]. The Assembly agreed. Head retaliated by refusing to grant contingency funds and by withholding assent from money bills already passed. In May he informed the electors of Toronto that he was not the instigator of "the stoppage of … Supplies [that] has caused a general stagnation of business, which will probably end in the ruin of many of the inhabitants of this city". He then dissolved the Assembly, denounced his opponents as disloyal in terms which made many Compact statements seem mild, and accused them of conspiring with external enemies, obviously Americans. He challenged those enemies. *"Let them come if they dare!"* In the ensuing election he was not above making public denunciations of the "republican" reformers. All this was extraordinary but highly effective conduct.

Head having made the issue of the election one of loyalty to the crown, tories of every stripe mustered behind him. Some re-established the defunct British Constitutional Society, originally founded in York in 1832 to preserve the British tie. Particularly in western Upper Canada this body busily solicited support for "constitutional candidates." Clerics of the Church of England, Church of Scotland, and Roman Catholic Church also actively joined the cause of loyalty. The Catholic bishop, Alexander Macdonell, actually enjoined his priests to secure results favourable to the lieutenant-governor.[3]

More damning for the reform cause was the attitude of the largest Methodist faction, the Canadian Wesleyan Methodist Church, which was the product of an 1833 merger of the major Canadian body with the smaller British Wesleyan Methodist one. To this union, the British Methodists brought with them a small government grant for Indian missions. Many reform votes had traditionally come from Methodists, but William Lyon Mackenzie had alienated large numbers by attacking the leadership of the denomination for accepting government money in defiance of their voluntarist principles and for their generally conservative political and social views. In fact, his campaign degenerated to a large degree into a personal vendetta against that youthful but formidable figure, the Reverend Egerton Ryerson. Not surprisingly, many "Ryersonian" Methodists turned to the "constitutional" cause.

Also working for Head was that host of government functionaries who could, in quiet ways, do so much to influence the course of an election. Land patents, which conferred the right to vote, were made available to sympathetic voters in several areas. For example, officials of the Crown Lands Office agreed to a request from the tory candidate in the town of London, Mahlon Burwell, that they give several applicants from London their land patents, to qualify them as voters. To oblige Burwell, those involved had to date at least one patent improperly, but this helped influence an election where but thirty-eight votes were cast, thirty-one of them for Burwell.[4] Other official intervention saw returning officers discounting the votes of reformers by insisting on proof of citizenship from men well known to them and local officials arranging for sympathetic voters to be treated to free liquor. Just how widespread these practices were is impossible to assess, but reformers were convinced they were widespread indeed, far more so than in any previous election. This electoral fraud and the unprecedented intervention of the lieutenant-governor largely explained, they felt, the defeat they had suffered.

From the reform standpoint the election was a catastrophe. More than twice as many tories as reformers were elected. Many prominent reformers, Bidwell, Robert Baldwin, and Mackenzie among them, were defeated. Mackenzie gathered evidence of corruption to present to the assembly but illness prevented him from submitting the material within the time limit for contesting election results. An unsympathetic Assembly refused to extend the deadline.[5] Dr. Charles Duncombe, a successful reform candidate in Oxford County, did Mackenzie one better. He took his convictions and his charges to England in a petition to the House of Commons. Duncombe claimed that he had "been deputed by the Reformers" of the province to apprise the Commons of widespread electoral fraud, when he had been sent, in actual fact, by just some of the Toronto reformers. If his backing was small, his charges were many. The instances of corruption cited in the petition, "encouraged by the Lieutenant-Governor and public functionaries in every part of the Province," had, he claimed, "overwhelmed" "the real Electors."

While the petition did reach the House of Commons, Duncombe was unsuccessful in his bid to present it to the colonial secretary, Lord Glenelg. The latter, importuned by Head,[6] refused to see the infuriated reformer. A co-traveller with Duncombe, Robert Baldwin, also had cause to be displeased, for he discovered while in Britain that a vengeful Upper Canadian government was seeking out its enemies and had dismissed a variety of reformers from their posts. Among these was his father, who lost his District and Surrogate Court judgeships.

For the reformers, grievance seemed to pile upon grievance, and little remedy appeared available to them within the existing system. This was underlined in January of 1837 when an Assembly committee, controlled and directed by tories, reported that it had investigated Duncombe's petition and its majority had concluded that all of the doctor's charges were without foundation. While a reading of the report and of Duncombe's petition shows that some charges were laid to rest, others not dealt with convincingly, and still others not addressed at all, this mattered little to the crushed reformers. Clearly the whole report was a tory device to hide tory sins.

From the reform perspective the end of 1836 and the early months of 1837 brought forth a whole catalogue of Family Compact and tory iniquities. Some of them were old and some were new but all emphasized the forces ranged against social and political change. The report, largely Mackenzie's work, of a committee appointed by the old Assembly to inquire into the Welland Canal Company affair charged that the officers of this government-subsidized body had committed serious defalcations of funds and had abused their power of granting contracts. It was learned that Sir John Colborne, just before leaving office, had endowed fifty-seven rectories of the Church of England. Increasingly, establishment churches and the Wesleyan Methodists were seen as being in the pockets of government. The anti-Catholic, pro-monarchy Orange Order was also denounced as a government tool because of its support of constitutional candidates in the election, although it had never previously taken a public anti-reform stand. The Canada Company, the Bank of Upper Canada, and all the old enemies were still active, while a deepening economic crisis gripped the province.

In 1836 much of the western world had been afflicted by a tightening of credit following hard on the heels of a long period of economic expansion in both Great Britain and the United States. By early 1837, with the international economy in confusion, money was in short supply in Upper Canada. The provincial banks responded by asking the provincial government for the right to suspend specie payments, as had been done elsewhere in British North America, in order to prevent a run on their reserves by citizens fearing for the security of their deposits and by those who distrusted the value of paper currency. Before the Bank of Upper Canada received such permission, it was reduced to having its friends and supporters clog the bank all day to make withdrawals, which were quietly returned to the vaults by night.[7] This shortage of cash was felt in all aspects of the province's affairs, not just by men like Mackenzie who believed banks conspired against the public good.

Agricultural problems also took their toll. The crop yields had been at best uneven.[8] Consequently, in 1837 foodstuffs were in short supply and prices rose all through the spring and summer. With the populace eagerly awaiting the new crop, that also

226

proved deficient. Well-established farmers with crops to sell probably suffered little economic hardship from the short-falls in the harvests, benefiting as they did from higher prices. But those who had to buy those crops—townsfolk, newer farmers, and those in areas particularly hard hit by crop failures—suffered. Food shortages provided another economic concern; to many reformers, deficient crops, the bank crisis, and rising interest rates were all interconnected, flowing inevitably from Compact policies.

For Mackenzie, if not for all reformers, the final straw seems to have been Lord John Russell's "Ten Resolutions" of March 1837, which allowed government by executive decree in Lower Canada. If the British government could treat one province this way, reasoned Mackenzie, then it was certain to treat Upper Canada similarly. It was no longer possible to hope, as reformers previously had, for aid from the mother country.[9] After their defeat at the hands of the lieutenant-governor and after seeing the actions the new Assembly took in 1837 to prolong its life beyond the expected death of the king, leading reformers such as Robert Baldwin and Marshall Spring Bidwell had withdrawn from politics. A vacuum existed in the reform leadership which radicals such as Mackenzie, eager to try new solutions, could fill.

These radicals decided that the British government would have to be pressured to make changes through extra-parliamentary action. In October of 1836 a group of reformers, seeking to organize such action and desiring to revitalize the reform movement, had created the City of Toronto Political Union. Upper Canada was no stranger to political unions, the device having been used following the example set in Britain at the time of the great Reform Bill in the early 1830s. It was an excellent way to express frustrations that could no longer be vented through the assembly. More than this, it was a way of demonstrating what the radicals felt were the legitimate desires of the people for reform.

In the summer of 1837, Mackenzie, who had recently begun to discuss the possibility of rebellion in his newspaper the *Constitution* and had pointed out the similarities between the grievances of Upper Canada and those that led to the American Declaration of Independence, suggested that the province's reformers create a pyramidal structure of political unions. These could, he observed, "be easily transferred ... to military purposes," but would not be. At the end of July he was instrumental in having the Toronto Political Union publish an address calling for an end to political corruption and unrepresentative government, the creation of a network of political unions, a boycott of imported goods, the formation of a close working relationship with reformers from Lower Canada, and the establishment of a joint convention of the two provinces to discuss their common afflictions.

The Toronto declaration brought swift results. Reform newspapers across the province reprinted it, and reformers in many locales followed the example of those in the capital. Unions sprang up in the Home District, then elsewhere. Beginning in August, Mackenzie, as agent and corresponding secretary of the "Committee of Vigilance" created by the Toronto meeting, scheduled fifteen meetings to organize unions throughout the Home District.[10] Of these, two were broken up by gangs of Orangemen, although one was later held in a private home, and two, to be held Peel County, centre of Orange strength in the District, were never convened. At three more, the reformers found themselves outvoted by tory supporters and were forced to meet separately to pass their resolutions.

It is hard to argue that the meetings which were held were intended as the prelude to rebellion. Only three of the Home District meetings passed resolutions which could be interpreted as calls to use force to achieve change, and the meeting which issued the most blatant statement, that at Whitby, was not attended by any of those later associated with the leadership of the Toronto rising.[11] On the other hand, the Lloydtown meeting, held in the centre of one of the most disaffected areas and attended by Mackenzie and others who drafted beforehand many of the resolutions passed at those meetings, resolved that "the resistance we contemplate is not that of physical force, much may be done without blood."[12] Essentially, those at the meetings were trying to demonstrate their resolution to have reform, not their resolution to seize it by force of arms.

In the months to come reformers in other centres—Brockville, Belleville, and Hamilton, for example—established political unions. Among the most ardent supporters of the movement were the reformers in the London District. Its three southern countries, Norfolk, Oxford, and Middlesex, had in 1836 bucked the provincial trend by returning

227

only reformers to the Assembly. Also, the district had the leading reform journal west of Hamilton, the St. Thomas *Liberal*. In 1837 this was edited by thirty-nine-year-old John Talbot, son of a prominent London Township pioneer and a distant relative of that irascible and unregenerate tory, Colonel Thomas Talbot. The latter, who had been involved in organizing the settling of no less than twenty-seven townships,[13] thought himself entitled to exercise paternal authority over the settlers. Despite his best efforts, the reformers in the west, or Liberals as they styled themselves, had grown from strength to strength. Many, among them John Talbot, welcomed the call to unionize.

The meetings in the London District went very much as had those in the Home. Some, such as those at Sodom in Norwich Township[14] and at Sparta in Yarmouth,[15] endorsed the principles of the Toronto reformers. Others, such as the Richmond meeting, in Bayham, resulted in a set-to with tory forces. The outcome of the riot was disputed by the two sides, but it was clear, the Liberals were a force to be reckoned with in the District. This was proved beyond a doubt by the Westminster meeting of 6 October, when over one thousand reformers swarmed onto the field,[16] pushing out local tories who had met to condemn those who spread sedition in Upper and Lower Canada.

The tories became very alarmed at this display of strength and at a public meeting on 21 October requested government assistance. Head replied with assurances that the laws of the province would be upheld by "the vigilance of the Magistracy & the loyalty of" the people. In fact, he had already demonstrated such confidence in the citizens of the colony by readily complying with the request of Sir John Colborne, now stationed in Lower Canada as lieutenant-general commanding the forces, to send as many men as possible from the British regiment in the province, the 24th, to aid the Lower Canadian authorities.[17] By early November the province was denuded of troops.

Although the move to organize unions was winding up in the Home District by early fall, it continued in the London District and was spreading to other districts. In early November, Charles Duncombe began to take part in this work. Since his return from England he had maintained a low profile, perhaps because of the shock and subsequent grief at finding

that his teenage son, Charles, had died during his absence. Now he was ready for action. He spoke with "eloquence and spirit."[18] To a correspondent he explained, "it is high time for the reformers to be up and doing" for "the time has come when are to decide whether we will be bondsmen or slaves."

The meetings spread into the farthest corners of the district, one being held in the Huron Tract on 10 November. In November also, the organizational activity spread to the Gore District, with meetings at Hamilton and Guelph. To the south, in the Niagara District, the reformers of the Short Hills, back of St. Catharines, held their meeting in early December.[19] Scattered about the province were other unions. In total, however, the number organized probably did not exceed two score.

Writers such as William Lyon Mackenzie have given an inflated idea of the extent of the political union movement. Building on this, Charles Lindsey and those who have followed his line of thought have suggested that a great many political unions were created, with the intention of organizing the members for rebellion. As proof of this, the military "trainings" held in the Home District at the time of the formation of the unions are cited as being the next step in the organization. But Mackenzie reported only one training prior to October, in the Home District, and none at all were held in the London District. Although some Hamilton men decided to purchase rifles, and others at Wellington Square determined to form a rifle company,[20] the Gore District saw such actions only a short time before the outbreak, and these seemed to be no part of a coherent and widespread plan.

Everywhere, the union meetings were merely attempts to show the strong resolve of the people to have reform. As Mackenzie put it in the *Constitution* of 13 September, the unions' purpose was "Agitation! agitation! agitation!" to convince the government that it did not have the support of the people, thereby bringing about change. The culmination of all of this activity was to be the great convention of citizens which the Toronto reformers had suggested in their declaration of July. This would prove even to the imperial authorities the necessity of reform.

Why is it widely believed that the organization of political unions was the first link in a chain leading to rebellion? Certainly Lindsey's work had a great deal to do with creating this belief, as does the human desire to see neat linear progressions. When no positive evidence exists to support such a progression, it must be substantiated by circumstantial means. Thus Mackenzie's publication of a draft constitution for Upper Canada on 16 November has been held to show that a revolutionary plot was well under way. Such historical assumptions, based on no concrete evidence, can create serious distortions. It is highly unlikely that Mackenzie's constitution was part of a longstanding and widespread plot. All of the men who acted as leaders in the Toronto rising who later commented on it insisted that they knew nothing of a rising until shortly before the rebellion took place.[21] Far from being a widespread conspiracy, the uprising at Toronto was uniquely the creation of a frustrated William Lyon Mackenzie.

Only one piece of evidence exists to suggest an organized effort at rebellion, the correspondence of John G. Parker, a wealthy American-born Hamilton merchant and radical reformer. He and a handful of cohorts in and about Hamilton diligently worked for rebellion. In his letters to acquaintances in the province and in Lower Canada he was eager to spur on the faint-hearted, to give the impression that all was ready for rebellion. He informed one correspondent, "Upper Canada is at this time in a great excitement and should Lower Canada revolutionize, Upper Canada would follow at once and join the States.... The country is already well organized by the formation of Political Unions."[22] Parker was arrested in early December and his correspondence seized. Authorities reading it then and those perusing it since have found it easy to believe that the course of rebellion had long been charted. Yet Parker was not plotting with any of those who later organized the uprisings. No other seized correspondence or other correspondence that has survived from the period suggests there was any organization. To use this isolated evidence as proof of a general movement is to make a general case from an exceptional one.

[...] [Those who rebelled clearly had undertaken little planning.] In October of 1837 Mackenzie swore he had not written "a line in politics to any person" in the London District "for months past."[23] Neither did he correspond frequently with reformers elsewhere; nor did his colleagues. They had no deeply laid plans for rebellion, and hence were not in constant contact with each other [...].

What existed then in Upper Canada in the summer and early fall of 1837 was a movement of extra-parliamentary protest by the more radical elements of the reform movement. Even the military trainings that were held appear to have been just more emphatic demonstrations of determination than the political unions were. No attempt was made to arm the trainees, and the men who later led the Toronto rising claimed afterwards that they did not know while the trainings were going on that there was to be a rising. No doubt there were many frustrated individuals, but only in November and December would an attempt be made to direct this frustration to armed action against the government.

NOTES

1. Gerald M. Craig, *Upper Canada: The Formative Years, 1784–1841* (Toronto, 1963) p. 15.
2. The existence of a property franchise for the Assembly helped limit somewhat the influence of the common man there.
3. John Alexander Macdonell, *A Sketch of the Life of the Honourable and Right Reverend Alexander Macdonell*...(Alexandria, 1890), pp. 38–9.
4. National Archives (UK), microfilm in Archives of Ontario, CO42, v. 440, p. 97, "Extracts from the Poll-Books..."
5. Charles Lindsey, *The Life and Times of William Lyon Mackenzie...*, I (Toronto, 1862), p. 382.
6. Sir Francis Bond Head, *A Narrative, with Notes by William Lyon Mackenzie*, edited by S. F. Wise (Toronto, 1969), pp. 61–2.
7. Lindsey, *The Life and Times of William Lyon Mackenzie*, II, p. 34.
8. *United Secession Magazine*, VI (April 1838), p. 211, extract of a letter from Rev. Wm. Proudfoot, London, 1 Jan. 1838.
9. R. J. Stagg, "The Yonge Street Rebellion of 1873: An Examination of the Social Background and a Reassessment of the Events" (Ph.D. thesis, University of Toronto, 1976), pp.31–2.
10. *Constitution* (Toronto), 2 Aug. 1837, 13 Sept. 1837.
11. *Patriot* (Toronto), 11 Oct. 1837.
12. *Constitution*, 9 Aug. 1837.
13. *Appendix to the Journals of the House of Assembly of Upper Canada*, Second Session, Twelfth Parliament, 1836, v. 1, no. 22, p. 24.
14. *Constitution*, 13 Sept. 1837.
15. See *Liberal*, ibid., 27 Sept. 1837.

16. *Gazette* (London), ibid., 18 Oct. 1873

17. Library and Archives Canada [LAC], RG7 G16A, Lieutenant-Governor's Internal Letter Books, v. 2, p. 2, Head to Colborne, 17 Oct. 1837.

18. *Constitution*, 15 Nov. 1837.

19. LAC, RG 9 I B1, Adjutant General's Office, Correspondence, v. 29, Lincoln file, Deposition of Solomon Camp, 26 Feb. 1838.

20. Ibid., RG5 A1, Upper Canada Sundries, v. 185, p. 103594, Deposition of John S. McCollom, 29 Dec. 1837.

21. Stagg, "The Yonge Street Rebellion of 1837," p. 53, n. 32.

22. National Archives (UK), CO 42, v. 467, p. 13, John G. Parker to J. Williams, Hamilton, 1 Dec. 1837.

23. *Constitution*, 18 Oct. 1837.

UNFREEDOM IN EARLY CANADA

Race, Empire, and Slavery

Jarett Henderson
Mount Royal University

UNFREEDOM IN EARLY CANADA: RACE, EMPIRE, AND SLAVERY

● INTRODUCTION

Jarett Henderson

In 1858, just months before his death, Jacques Viger, a former Patriot and Mayor of Montreal, was again practising his habit of collecting matters of history.[1] This time, and in connection with the Historical Society of Montreal, Viger was cataloguing whatever documents he could that archived the long history of unfreedom in Canada. *De L'esclavage en Canada / The Slave in Canada,* published just months after Viger's death, contained the documents of colonial and imperial administrators, both French and British: government ordinances, court transcripts, and notorial records.[2] These are the sources that archive the purchase, regulation, and manumission of *Panis* (Aboriginal) and Black slaves in early Canada. For Viger's contemporaries, his work was noteworthy because it contradicted the nationalist argument made by François-Xavier Garneau in his *Histoire du Canada.* Canada, Garneau wrote in 1860, "happily escaped the terrible curse of Negro slavery."[3] Rather *L'esclavage en Canada* illustrates that both Black and Indigenous people lived lives of unfreedom in, and along, the empire of the St. Lawrence. This module introduces you to the varied and often ignored history of slavery in northeastern North America. In what follows you will interrogate the social and political complexities of race, slavery, and empire on the Indigenous lands that were becoming early Canada.

Generations before white French colonizers arrived in the "New World," Indigenous people across the continent, through a diverse system of knowing, ordered their societies by ascribing various meanings to different human bodies. On the northwestern coast of North America, for example, Leland Donald has explored the nuanced social and economic histories of Indigenous slavery.[4] Closer to the St. Lawrence, and throughout the region that French colonizers termed the *Pays d'en Haut,* Brett Rushforth explores the complicated ways that the Huron, Ottawa, Iroquois, Sioux, Illinois, and Fox nations understood human bondage. Through a methodology that draws from archeology, history, ritual, and linguistics, Rushforth traces how central Algonquian and Siouan peoples spoke about slavery. His chapter reproduced here draws upon the French dictionaries created and used by Jesuit missionaries to learn Indigenous languages. These sources reveal that Indigenous people often used metaphors of domestication and mastery and compared their captives to dogs and other domesticated animals. Anishinaabe-speakers, for example, called their slaves *awakaan,* which meant captive, dog, or animals kept as pets. Rushforth has found that Indigenous slavery—often a diplomatic act of exchanging "a little flesh"—was central to the maintenance of Indigenous and Indigenous–French alliances in the fledgling outposts that constituted New France.[5]

As New France sputtered into existence, Indigenous understandings of human unfreedom encountered French imperial understandings of enslavement. The images of an Indigenous slave halter and French iron shackles reproduced here vividly expose the similarities and differences between unfreedom in these cultures. As Robin Winks illustrates, over the seventeenth and eighteenth centuries, missionaries, merchants, and government officials increasingly worked to ensure that French imperial understandings of slavery took hold in a colony marked by settler–Aboriginal violence, an exhaustingly slow rate of population growth, and a frigid reputation.[6] Missionaries struggled to remedy this situation by instructing the *sauvage* in the teachings of Christianity. In 1698, Father Hennepin published, for European audiences, accounts of his travels through the *Pays d'en Haut*, his mission work, and his capture; these were tales that would have simultaneously intrigued

234

and worried his contemporaries. *A New Discovery of a Vast Country in North America* recounted how Hennepin and his two French servants were captured by Sioux warriors on 20 April 1680. Hennepin's vivid account appears to have been insufficient at capturing the exigency of Indigenous slavery, for he also included a horrific image that fused all that he knew, and likely had heard about Indigenous slavery, into an image that depicted "The Cruelty of the Savage Iroquois."[7]

As missionaries like Hennepin worked and travelled among Indigenous nations, white French colonizers from fur traders to merchants through to government and church officials increasingly purchased both Black and Indigenous peoples, fusing Indigenous and French imperial understandings of slavery.[8] In 1685, the French Empire established, for the first time, the legal and social distinctions between masters and slaves through the *Code Noir*. Though historians continue to debate the extent to which the *Code* applied to the unfree peoples of northeastern North America, it nonetheless marked a significant shift in how ideas of race and freedom were mobilized in the French Empire to order its peoples.[9] Regardless of the *Code's* application in New France, it nonetheless regulated nearly every aspect of the master–slave relationship and would come to have important repercussions for *Panis* and Black slaves, free Indigenes and Blacks, and white colonizers in early Canada. So much so that 50 years later it had become necessary for French imperial administrators to sanction an ordnance for the local colonial context of New France. In April 1709, Jacques Radout rendered an ordinance on the subject of "the Negroes and the Indians called Panis." Radout's ordinance, reproduced here, established that Indigenous slaves in New France were to be treated and regulated "like Negros in the Islands."[10] It is yet a further indication of the wider imperial context that shaped the institution of slavery as it struggled to take hold in early Canada.

As was true of the Indigenous peoples who practised forms of human unfreedom prior to, and after, contact, no two sites of France's Empire in northern North American yielded the same experience of slavery. Exciting projects such as the *Great Unsolved Mysteries in Canadian History—Torture and the Truth: Angelique and the Burning of Montreal* and Afu Cooper's *The Hanging of Angelique* have brought to light the history of Angelique, a Black domestic slave whose act of resistance led to not only the burning of significant portions of eighteenth-century Montreal, but also a trial that culminated with the burning of her body.[11] Kenneth Donovan explores the interactions that slaves had with the families for whom they worked in Louisbourg, on Île Royale. As a central node in the French Empire's expansive trade network that included both sugar and slaves, this case study illustrates the differing conditions of domestic enslavement that *Panis* and Black slaves experienced in this cosmopolitan imperial outpost.[12]

Though slaves were often vulnerable, sometimes abused, and purchased for a variety of social and sexual purposes, the mixing of Indigenous and French systems of enslavement did offer pathways to freedom. Long before the abolitionist campaigns of the late-eighteenth century, female slaves who lived in the *Pays d'en Haut* and married French settlers were often freed by their new husbands. Other slaves could be manumitted by verbal agreement or by purchasing their own freedom. Running away, of course, was also an option and a tactic slaves frequently employed.[13] As the rising number of manumitted slaves increased in the first decades of the eighteenth century, it became necessary for French colonial administrators to establish a uniform system to distinguish free from slave. On 1 September 1736, Giles Hocquart issued the ordinance, reproduced here, which made it necessary that for a slave to be freed, by either gift or purchase, a notary must record his or her manumission and register it with the royal registry office. This decision indicates, Winks argues, that slavery had grown to

235

such an extent that it required both records and regulation.[14] When the Indigenous territories that constituted New France were transferred to the British in 1763, the Articles of Capitulation that Viger chose to archive in 1858 indicate that both white French and British imperial administrators were careful to make concessions for slave owners.[15] The institution of slavery would continue in Quebec, Britain's newest imperial territory to the century's end, as the notorial records documenting the purchase and subsequent manumission of "a certain Negro boy or lad called Rubin" indicate.[16] Early Canada remained a place where contrasting and competing ideas of human unfreedom, both Indigenous and European operated, creating a colonial order that revolved around the complex intersection of empire, race, and slavery.

QUESTIONS

1. How did Indigenous societies in the Great Lakes region speak of unfreedom/captivity? What role did Indigenous captives have in Indigenous societies?
2. How do the two tools of enslavement pictured here differ? How are they similar? Can you speculate as to the effect of the confluence of French and Indigenous slavery in early Canada?
3. How does Hennepin represent Indigenous enslavement and captivity? Why do you think he depicted this history in such a fashion? In what ways is Hennepin helpful for understanding the history of unfreedom in early Canada? Can you identify any problems with his depictions of Indigenous enslavement and captivity?
4. What did the *Code Noir* regulate? Do you think this had any effect on how colonists in early Canada understood the connection between race and freedom? Why or why not?
5. Why do you think imperial administrators felt they needed to regulate slavery in New France in 1709? How can we gauge the success of their efforts? What types of information do the records of notaries teach us about unfreedom in early Canada? How can we use these documents to make historical inferences about the institution of slavery in eighteenth-century northeastern North America?
6. What types of work did slaves perform in early Canada? How convinced were you by Donovan's argument? Would you characterize slavery in New France as a "benign" form of slavery as some historians have? Why or why not?

FURTHER READINGS

Cooper, Afua. "Acts of Resistance: Black Men and Women Engage Slavery in Upper Canada, 1793–1803." *Ontario History* 99, no. 1 (Spring 2007): 5–17.

Donovan, Kenneth. "Slaves in Île Royale," *French Colonial History* 5 (2004): 25–42.

Harris, Jennifer. "Black Life in a Nineteenth Century New Brunswick Town," *Journal of Canadian Studies* 46, no. 1 (Winter 2012): 138–66.

Lee, Maureen Elgersman. *Unyielding Spirits: Black Women and Slavery in Early Canada and Jamaica.* New York: Garland Publishing, 1999.

Rushforth, Brett. *Bonds of Alliance: Indigenous and Atlantic Slaveries in New France.* Chapel Hill, NC, University of North Carolina Press, 2012.

Sapoznik, Karlee. "Where the Historiography Falls Short: La Vérendrye through the Lens of Gender, Race and Slavery in Early French Canada, 1731–1749." *Manitoba History,* no. 62 (Winter 2009): 22–32.

Vidal, Cécile, and Emily Clark. "Famille et Esclavage à la nouvelle-orléans sous le régime français, 1699–1769." *Annales De Demographie Historique,* no. 2 (Novembre 2011): 99–126.

Whitfield, Harvey Amani. "The Struggle Over Slavery in the Maritime Colonies," *Acadiensis* XLI, no. 2 (Summer/Autumn 2012): 17–44.

Winks, Robin W. *The Blacks in Canada: A History*. Second Edition. Montreal-Kingston: McGill-Queen's Press, 1997.

NOTES

1. Bettina Bradbury, *Wife to Widow: Lives, Laws, and Politics in Nineteenth-Century Montreal,* (Vancouver: UBC Press, 2011).

2. Jacques Viger, Louis Hippolyte Lafontaine, Eds., *De l'esclavage en Canada,* (Montréal: Société historique de Montréal, 1859).

3. François–Xavier Garneau, *History of Canada: From the Time of Its Discovery to Till the Union Year*, Trans, Andrew Bell, (Montreal: John Lovel, 1860), 95.

4. Leland Donald, *Aboriginal Slavery on the Northwest Coast of North America,* (Berkeley, CA: University of California Press, 1997).

5. Brett Rushforth, *Bonds of Alliance: Indigenous and Atlantic Slaveries in New France,* (Chapel Hill, NC: University of North Carolina Press, 2012).

6. Allan Greer, *The People of New France,* (Toronto: UTP, 1997).

7. Father Louis Hennepin, *A New Discovery of a Vast Country in America,* Edited by Reuben Gold Thwaites, (Chicago: A. C. McClurg and Company, 1903).

8. Karlee Sapoznik, "Where the Historiography Falls Short: La Vérendrye through the Lens of Gender, Race and Slavery in Early French Canada, 1731–1749," *Manitoba History* 62 (Winter 2009) and Marcel Trudel avec Micheline D'Allaire, *Deux siècles d'esclavage au Québec,* (Montreal: Éditions Hurtubise, 2004). See also the recent exhibitition on Slavery in New France at the Grand Bibliothèque in Montreal, Canada. Unfortunatley, as of yet, no publication has resulted from this exhibit.

9. *Le code noir, ou Recueil des règlements rendus jusqu'à présent: Concernant le gouvernement, l'administration de la justice, la police, la discipline & le commerce des Nègres dans les colonies françaises,* (Paris: Chez L.F. Prault, imprimeur du Roi, quai des Augustins, à l'Immortalité, 1788).

10. "Ordinance Rendered on the Subject of the Negroes and the Indians Called Panis," Bibliothèque et Archives nationales du Québec, Centre de Québec, Ordonnance des Intendants, E1, S1, P509, Raudot, Jacques, Ordinance Relative to Slavery in Canada, April, 13, 1709.

11. *Great Unsolved Mysteries in Canadian History: Torture and the Truth,* www.canadian mysteries.ca and Afua Cooper, *The Hanging of Angelique,* (Toronto: Harper Collins, 2006).

12. Kenneth Donovan, "Slaves in Île Royale, 1713–1758," *French Colonial History,* Volume 5 (2004): 25–42.

13. Maureen G. Elgersmanm, "Slavery in Early Canada," in *Unyielding Spirits: Black Women and Slavery in Early Canada and Jamaica,* (New York, Garland Pub: 1999).

14. Robin Winks, *Blacks in Canada: A History,* Second Edition (Montreal-Kingston: McGill-Queen's University Press, 2000).

15. Viger, *De l'esclavage en Canada,* (1859).

16. *Rapport de L'Archiviste de la Province de Québec pour 1921–22,* (Quebec: Louis-Amable Proulx, Imprimeur de Sa Majesté Le Roi, 1922).

▲ Document 1: Aboriginal Slave Halter

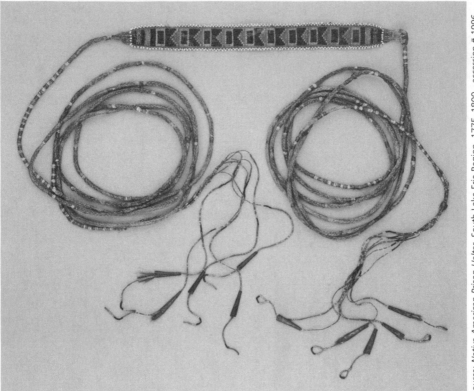

Source: *Native American Prison Halter, South Lake Erie Region, 1775–1800, accession # 1996–816, image # DS1996–914. The Colonial Williamsburg Foundation. Museum Purchase.*

● Because of their delicate nature, few indigenous halters like this one have survived. Yet they were common across north america in the seventeenth and eighteenth centuries. Jesuits identified these tools of enslavement as bridles or harnesses, while algonquians around the great lakes called them "sacant8tagane."

▲ Document 2: French Iron Shackles

Source: © Chicago History Museum/The Bridgeman Art Library

239

● To be in irons was to be a slave. Though very different from the Aboriginal Slave Halter in Document 1, both of these tools were symbols of unfreedom. What was their physical purpose? What social or cultural messages did they imply?

▲ Document 3: "The Cruelty of the Savage Iroquois"

Source: From "The Cruelty of the Savage Iroquois," in Father Louis Hennepin, *A New Discovery of A Vast Country in America*, Edited by Reuben Gold Thwaites, Chicago: A. C. McClurg and Company, 1903.

● This image, from Father Hennepin's *A New Discovery of a Vast Country*, was designed to depict the "cruelty" of the "savage" Iroquois. After reading Hennepin's account that follows in Document 4, what do you realize about this image? How can we use this image to understand how captives/slaves were viewed by Iroquoian society?

▲ Document 4: Father Hennepin's Writing on Indigenous Slavery

On 11 April 1680, Louis Hennepin, a Recollect missionary and his two French servants were captured by a war party of Sioux Indians. Hennepin, who was eventually adopted by Chief Aquipaguetin, was held captive for eight months among the Sioux. Although not an account of his transition to life in captivity, the excerpt below chronicles Hennepin's interpretation of the cultural, social, and political aspects of enslavement in Iroquoian society.

There are no Savages in all the Northern America but what are very cruel to their Enemies. We are astonished at the Cruelties which the Neroes, the Dioclessans, and the Maximins inflicted upon the Christians, and have their Names in Detestation and Horror; but the Inhumanity of the Iroquois towards the Nations they make Slaves goes beyond theirs.

When the Iroquois have killed a Man, they tear off the Skin of his Skull, and carry it home with them as a certain Mark of their Victory. When they take a Slave, they tie him, and make him run after them; if he is unable to follow them, they stick their Hatchet into his Head, and there leave him, after they have torn off Skin and Hair together. They don't spare sucking Infants: If the Slave can march after them, they tie him every Night to a piece of Wood made in the form of a St. Andrew's Cross, and leave him exposed to be stung by the Mosquitoes and other Flies, in Summer-time, and use him as cruelly as may be.

Sometimes they fix four Pegs into the Ground, to which they Fasten their Slaves by the Feet and Hands, and so leave them all Night long upon the Ground in the sharpest Weather. I omit a hundred other Sufferings, which these miserable Wretches undergo in the daytime. When they are near their Villages, they set up loud Cries, whereby their Nation knows that their Warriors are returned with Slaves. Then the Men and Women put on their best Apparel, and go to the entrance of the Village to receive them; there they make a lane for the Slaves to pass through them. But 'tis a lamentable Reception for these poor People: The Rabble fall upon them like Dogs or Wolves upon their Prey, and begin to torment them, whilst the Warriors march on in File, mightily puffed up with their own Exploits.

Some kick the Slaves, some cudgel them, some cut them with Knives, some tear off their Ears, cut off their Noses or Lips, insomuch that most of them die in this pompous Entry. Those that resist against these rude Treatments are reserved for exemplary Punishment. Sometimes they save some, but very rarely. When the Warriors are entered into their Cabins, the Ancients assemble themselves to hear the relation of what passed in the War.

If the Father of a Savage Woman has been killed, they give her a Slave for him, and 'tis free for that Woman either to put him to Death, or save him alive. When they burn them, this is their manner; They bind the Slave to a Post by the Hands and Feet, then they heat red-hot Musket-barrels, Hatchets, and other Iron Instruments, and apply them red-hot from head to foot, all over their Body; they tear off their Nails, and pluck out their Teeth; they cut Collops of flesh out of their Backs, and often flay their Skin off from their Skull: After all this they throw hot Ashes upon their Wounds, cut out their Tongues, and treat them as cruelly as they can devise. If they don't die under all these Torments, they make them run and follow them, laying them on with Sticks. It is reported, that once a Slave ran so well,

241

Source: "The Cruelty of the Savage Iroquois," in Father Louis Hennepin, *A New Discovery of a Vast Country in America,* Edited by Reuben Gold Thwaites, Chicago: A. C. McClurg and Company, 1903. Republished by Toronto: Coles Publishing Company, 1974, 507–12. Link: http://archive.org/stream/anewdiscoveryav00paltgoog#page/n176/mode/2up

that he saved himself in the Woods, and could not be caught again. It is probable he died there for want of Succour. But what is more surprising is that the Slaves sing in the midst of their Torments, which frets their Executioners exceedingly.

An Iroquois told us, that there was one Slave whom they tormented cruelly; but he told them, You have no Ingenuity, you don't know how to torment your Prisoners, you are mere Blockheads; if I had you in my Circumstances, I'd use you after another manner: but whilst he ran on so boldly, a Savage Woman gets a little Iron Spit heated red-hot, and runs it into his Yard: this made him roar; but he told the Woman, You are cunning, you understand something, this is the Course you should take with us.

When the Slave, which they burn, is dead, they eat him; and before his Death they make their Children drink some of his Blood, to render them cruel and inhumane. Those that they give their Lives to, live with them, and serve them like Slaves: But in length of time they recover their Liberty, and are looked upon as if they were of their own Nation.

The Savages of the Louisiana that dwell along the River Mississippi, and are situated seven or eight hundred Leagues beyond the Iroquois, as the Issati and Nadouessans, among who I was a Slave, are no less brave than the Iroquois; they make all the Nations round them tremble, tho' they have nothing but Bows, Arrows, and Maces. They run swifter than the Iroquois and make excellent Soldiers; but they are not so cruel: they don't eat the Flesh of their Enemies; they are content to burn them only. Once having taken a Huron, who eat human Flesh as the Iroquois, they cut off pieces of Flesh from his own Body, and said to him; You that love Man's Flesh, eat of your own, to let your Nation know, who now live among the Iroquois, that we detest and abominate your Barbarities; for these People are like hungry Dogs that devour any sort of Meat.

The Iroquois are the only Savages of North America that eat human Flesh; and yet they don't do but in cases extraordinary, when they are resolved to exterminate a whole Nation. They don't eat human Flesh to satisfy their Appetites; 'tis to signify to the Iroquois Nation, that they ought to fight without ever submitting to their Enemies; that they ought rather to eat them than leave any of them alive: They eat it to animate their Warriors; for they always march out of their five Cantons the day after, to fight with their Enemies; for the Rendezvous for next day is always given notice of by these Feasts of human Flesh.

… I don't describe these five Cantons of the Iroquois here, I only treat of their Barbarity and Cruelty, and add, that they have subdued a very large Country since within these fifty Years; that they have extended their Territories, and multiplied their Nation by the Destruction of other People, the Remainder of whom they have made Slaves, to increase the number of their Troops.

▲ Document 5: The *Code Noir* (1685)

The Code Noir *was first issued in 1685. It legalized slavery in the French Atlantic Empire, while detailing the duties and conditions of slaves as well as the responsibilities that masters had to their property.*

II. All slaves in our said province will be baptized and instructed in the Catholic, Apostolic, and Roman religion. We order those inhabitants who purchase newly arrived Negroes to inform the Governor and Intendant of the said islands within a week at the latest or face a discretionary fine …

III. We forbid any public exercise of any religion other than the Catholic, Apostolic, and Roman; we wish that any offenders be punished as rebels and disobedient to our orders. We prohibit all congregations for this end, declare them illicit and seditious, and subject to the same penalty, which will be levied, even against masters who allow or tolerate them among their slaves.

IV. No overseers will be given charge of Negroes who do not profess the Catholic, Apostolic, and Roman religion …

VI. We charge all our subjects, whatever their status and condition, to observe Sundays and holidays that are kept by our subjects of the Catholic, Apostolic, and Roman religion. We forbid them to work or to make their slaves work on these days from the hour of midnight until the other midnight, either in agriculture, the manufacture of sugar or all other works, on pain of fine and discretionary punishment of the masters and confiscation of the sugar, and of the said slaves who will be caught by our officers in their work.

VII. Equally we forbid the holding of Negro markets and all other markets the said days on similar pains, including confiscation of the merchandise that will be found then at the market and discretionary fine against the merchants.

IX. The free men who will have one or several children from their concubinage with their slaves, together with the masters who permitted this, will each be condemned to a fine of two thousand pounds of sugar; and if they are the masters of the slave by whom they have had the said children, we wish that beyond the fine, they be deprived of the slave and the children, and that she and they be confiscated for the profit of the [royal] hospital, without ever being manumitted. …

XI. We forbid priests to officiate the marriages of slaves unless they can show the consent of their masters. We also forbid masters to use any means to constrain their slaves to marry [them] against their will.

XII. The children who will be born of marriage between slaves will be slaves and will belong to the master of the women slaves, and not to those of their husband, if the husband and the wife have different masters.

XIII. We wish that if a slave husband has married a free woman, the children, both male and girls, will follow the condition of their mother and be free like her, in spite of the servitude of their father; and that if the father is free and the mother enslaved, the children will be slaves the same.

XV. We forbid slaves to carry any weapon, or large sticks, on penalty of the whip and of confiscation of the weapon to the profit of those who seizes them; with the exception of those sent to hunt by their master or who carry their ticket or known mark.

243

Source: *Le code noir, ou Recueil des règlements rendus jusqu'à présent: Concernant le gouvernement, l'administration de la justice, la police, la discipline & le commerce des Négres dans les colonies françaises,* (Paris: Chez L.F. Prault, imprimeur du Roi, quai des Augustins, à l'Immortalité, 1788): 28–58. Link: http://archive.org/details/lecodenoirourecu00fran

XVI. We also forbid slaves belonging to different masters to gather together in the day or night on pretexts such as a wedding or otherwise, whether on their master's property or elsewhere, and still less in the main roads or faraway places, on pain of corporal punishment, which will not be less than the whip and the fleur-de-lis and which in cases of frequent violations and other aggravating circumstances can be punished with death …

XIX. We forbid slaves to expose for sale, at the market or to carry to private houses for sale any kind of commodity, even fruits, vegetables, firewood, herbs for their food and animals of their manufacture without express permission of their masters by a ticket or by known marks, on pain of confiscation of the things thus sold, without restitution of the price by their masters, and of a fine of six livres tournois to their profit for the buyers.

XXII. Each week masters will have to furnish to their slaves ten years old and older for their nourishment two and a half jars in the measure of the land, of cassava flour, or three cassavas weighing at least two-and-a-half pounds each or equivalent things, with two pounds of salted beef or three pounds of fish or other things in proportion, and to children after they are weaned to the age of 10 years half of the above supplies.

XXVI. Those slaves who are not fed, clothed and supported by the masters according to these orders will notify our attorney and give him their statements, based on which and even as a matter of course, if the information comes to him from elsewhere, the masters will be prosecuted by him and without cost, which we want to be observed for the cries and barbarous and inhumane treatments of masters towards their slaves.

XXX. Slaves will not be invested with offices or commissions having any public function, nor act as agents for any other than their masters in acting or administering any trade or judgment in loss or witnesses, either in civil or criminal matters; and in cases where they will be heard as witnesses, their dispositions will only serve as memorandum to aid the judges in the investigation, without being the source of any presumption, conjecture or proof.

XXXIII. A slave who strikes his master or the wife of his master, his mistress, or their children to bring blood, or in the face will be punished with death.

LV. Masters twenty years old will be able to manumit their slaves by all [legal] deeds or by cause of death, without being required to provide the reason for this manumission, neither will they need the permission of parents, provided that they are minors twenty-five years of age.

LVIII. We command manumitted slaves to retain a particular respect for their former masters, their widows and their children; such that the insult that they will have done be punished more severely that if it had been done to another person: we declare them however free and absolved of any other burdens, services and rights that their former masters would like to claim, as much on their persons as on their possessions and estates as patrons.

LIX. We grant to manumitted slaves the same rights, privileges and liberties enjoyed by persons born free; desiring that they merit this acquired liberty and that it produce in them, both for their persons and for their property, the same effects that the good fortune of natural liberty causes in our other subjects.

Document 6: Like Negroes of the Islands

This 1709 ordinance archives the confluence of local concern and imperial policy in the rules guiding the practice of slavery in the French settlements of northern North America. In making comparisons to French imperial slavery in the Caribbean, this ordinance, issued in Quebec City, established the legal precedent that made Panis slaves akin to Negro slaves on the French islands: full chattel slavery had come to New France.

April 13, 1709

Ordinance rendered on the subject of the Negroes and the Indians called Panis

It is well known how this colony would benefit were its inhabitants able to securely purchase the Indians called Panis, whose country is far distant from this one, and who can only be obtained from Indians who capture them in their territory and sell them to the English of Carolina, and who have at times sold them to the people of this country, who at times find themselves cheated out of the considerable sums that they must pay for them because of the notions of liberty inspired in them by those who did not purchase them, which means that they almost always abandon their masters under the pretext that there are no slaves in France, which is not necessarily true for the colonies attached to it, since in the islands of this continent all the Negroes bought by the inhabitants are always regarded as such, and as all colonies must be considered on the same footing, and as the people of the Panis nation are needed by the inhabitants of this county for agriculture and other enterprises that might be undertaken, like Negroes in the Islands, and as these bonds are very important to this colony, it is necessarily to ensure ownership to those who have purchased or will purchase them.

We, according to His Majesty's good pleasure, ordain that all the Panis and Negroes who have been purchased, or who shall be purchased hereafter, shall be fully owned as property by those who have purchased them and be known as their slaves; we forbid the said Panis and Negroes from abandoning their masters and order a 50 livres fine against anyone who corrupts them. We order that the present ordinance be read and published in the customary locations in the towns of Quebec, TroisRivières, and Montreal, and that it be registered by the notaries of these jurisdictions, under the diligence of our sub-delegates, done and given at our resident at Quebec the 13 of April 1709,

[Signed] Raudot

Read and published at the church in lower town after seven o'clock and at the door of the parish church of Quebec after high mass the 21st of April 1709 by me, court bailiff in the jurisdiction of Quebec and resident of Rue. St. Pierre, [Signed] Congnet

245

Source: "Ordinance Rendered on the Subject of the Negroes and the Indians Called Panis," Bibliothèque et Archives nationales du Québec, Centre de Québec, Ordonnance des Intendants, E1, S1, P509, Raudot, Jacques, Ordinance Relative to Slavery in Canada, April, 13, 1709. http://pistard.banq.qc.ca/unite_chercheurs/description_fonds?p_anqsid=20120716124331702&p_centre=03Q&p_classe=E&p_fonds=1&p_numunide=806897

 Document 7: Purchasing People

Historians of early Canada owe much to the work, and registers, of public nota-
ries. What do we learn about slave owners from these documents? What details are
we provided about the lives of slaves in the colony?

I. THE SALE OF FIVE NEGROES BY CHARLES RHÉAUMÉ, TO LOUIS CUREUX DE SAINT-GERMAIN (25 SEPTEMBER 1743).

Before the undersigned Royal Notary, at the Provostship of Quebec, therein Residing, and the witnesses named below, was present Mr. Charles Rhéaumé merchant usually Residing on The Seigneury of the Isle of Jesus near the City of Montreal and presently in this city, who has sold, with a guarantee against all problems and hindrances whatsoever, to Mr. Loüis Cureuxdit St Germain, bourgeois of this city, who accepts the acquisition for himself and his assignees, five Negro slaves, two men and three women and girls, whom the said purchaser has seen currently at the house of the widow Madame Cachelievre. The said vendor promises to deliver them shortly to the said purchaser for the sum of three thousand livres, which the said purchaser, promises to pay to the said seller, upon the delivery of the said slaves.

Thus it was &c, obliging, &c. done and passed in Quebec, at the Office of the said notary, on the morning of the twenty-fifth of September seventeen hundred forty-three, in the presence of Mr Loüis Lambert and Mr. Nicolas Bellevüe, witnesses residing at Québec, who along with the said Mr. Rhéaumé and the notary did sign, the said Mr. St Germain having declared to not know how to write or sign as requested, following a reading done of it.

[SIGNED] L. LAMBERT
[SIGNED] BELLEVÜE
[SIGNED] C RHÉAUMÉ
[SIGNED] PINGUET

Source: *Rapport de L'Archiviste de la Province de Québec pour 1921–22,* (Quebec: Louis-Amable Proulx, Imprimeur de Sa Majesté Le Roi, 1922): 113. http://archive.org/details/rapportdelarchiv02arch

II. SALE OF A PANIS NAMED FANCHON, AGED ABOUT TEN OR ELEVEN YEARS, NON-BAPTIZED, BY JACQUES-FRANCOIS DAGUILLE, A MERCHANT OF MONTREAL, TO MATHIEU-THÊODOZE DE VITRÉ, SHIP CAPTAIN (4 NOVEMBER 1751)

In attendance were, Mr. Jacques-François Daguille, Merchant of Montreal, currently in this city to voluntarily sell to Mr. Mathieu-Théodoze de Vitré, a ship captain, the terms presented deemed acceptable, a Panis named Fanchon, who is not yet baptized, aged about ten or eleven. Mr. [Daguille] willingly made the sale, subject to the price and sum of four hundred pounds, which was paid by Mr. de Vitré, who happily accepted the sum. Whereby, the above mentioned seller, Mr. Daguille, agrees that Mr. de Vitré is able to enjoy

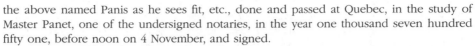
the above named Panis as he sees fit, etc., done and passed at Quebec, in the study of Master Panet, one of the undersigned notaries, in the year one thousand seven hundred fifty one, before noon on 4 November, and signed.

DAGUILLE
DENYS VITRE
BAROLET
PANET

Source: *Rapport de L'Archiviste de la Province de Québec pour 1921–22,* (Quebec: Louis-Amable Proulx, Imprimeur de Sa Majesté Le Roi, 1922): 118. Link: http://archive.org/details/rapportdelarchiv02arch

III. SALE OF A NEGRO NAMED RUBIN, BY DENNIS DALY, TAVERN KEEP OF QUEBEC, TO JOHN YOUNG, MERCHANT, ALSO OF QUEBEC (15 AUGUST 1795)

Before the Public Notaries for the City of Québec and Province of Lower Canada here unto subscribing Personally came and appeared Mr. Dennis Daly of the city of Quebec, tavern keeper, and John Young, of the said city of Quebec, Esquire, merchant, when the said Dennis Daly of his own free will and accord acknowledged and declared that for, and in consideration of the sum of seventy pounds Halifax currency to him the said Dennis Daly satisfied and paid by the said John Young Esquire the Receipt whereof is by the said Dennis Daly hereby acknowledged was bargained and sold and by these presents doth bargain and sell unto the said John Young Esquire a certain Negro boy or lad called Rubin. To have and to hold the Negro lad named Rubin unto the said John Young Esquire his heirs, executors, administrators and assigns from henceforth and forever, which said Negro lad was purchased and acquired by him the said Dennis Daly from John Cobham, of the city of Quebec, as appears by deed of sale bearing date the sixth day of September in the year of Our Lord one thousand seven hundred and eighty six delivered up to the said John Young Esquire at the execution hereof.

The said Dennis Daly hereby covenanting, promising and agreeing for himself, his executors, curators or administrators, to guarantee, warrant and defend this present sale against all claims and demands whatsoever of him, the said Dennis Daly, or all and every person or persons whatsoever. Thus done and passed at Québec in the office of Charles Stewart this fifteenth day of August in the year of Our Lord one thousand seven hundred and ninety five the said Dennis Daly having hereunto set his hand and the said John Young as testifying his acceptance to this minute deposited in the office of the said Charles Stewart the same having been first read over.

DENNIS DALY
JOHN YOUNG
A. DUMAS
CHAS. STEWART

Source: *Rapport de L'Archiviste de la Province de Québec pour 1921–22,* (Quebec: Louis-Amable Proulx, Imprimeur de Sa Majesté Le Roi, 1922): 122. Link: http://archive.org/details/rapportdelarchiv02arch

▲ Document 8: Freedom before Abolition

In the years before the abolition of slavery, a slave depended on the humanity of their master if they were to become free. In 1736, it became necessary to establish a legal framework for manumission (the process of becoming legally free) as numerous slaves had sought freedom by running away from their masters. Laws were created to curtail this; the Code Noir *addressed this "problem" directly. Running away, however, was not the only path to freedom. As this notary record from 1797 indicates, some owners willfully emancipated their slaves. Can you speculate as to why Rubin's master decided to free him only two years after he had purchased Rubin?*

I. ORDINANCE BY GILLES HOCQUART RELATIVE TO THE LIBERATION OF SLAVES [1 SEPTEMBER 1736]

1 September 1736
Ordinance Concerning the Liberation of Slaves
Gilles Hocquart

Upon having been informed that a number of Individuals in This Colony have liberated their Slaves with no more formality than verbally granting them their freedom, And it being necessary to determine the Status of Slaves that may be liberated hereafter, We after having conferred with M. le Marquis de Beauharnois, Governor and lieutenant general for the king in this Colony, Ordain that in the future all individuals in this Country, regardless of their status, who wish to liberate their Slaves will be required to do so according to an act signed by Notaries for which minutes will be kept, And which will be Recorded at the registry of the closest Jurisdiction Royale; we Declare that all other liberations not concluded according to the above form will be Null and Void, and the present ordinance will be read and published in the customary manner, and recorded in the Registries of the Royal Jurisdictions of Québec, Montréal, and TroisRivières. Mandated, etc, done at Quebec on the first of September 1736.

[Signed] Hocquart

Source: Archives nationales du Québec, Centre de Québec, Registre des Commissions et Ordonnances rendues par monsieur Hocquart Intendant de justice, police et finances en la Nouvelle france, E1, S1, P2855, Hocquart, Gilles, Ordinance relative to the liberation of slaves, September 1, 1736, fol. 99.

II. THE EMANCIPATION OF A NEGRO LAD NAMED RUBIN, AGE EIGHTEENTH YEARS, BY JOHN YOUNG, MERCHANT OF QUEBEC (8 JUNE 1797)

Before the public notaries, personally appeared, John Young, Esquire of the city of Québec, merchant, who freely and voluntarily declared that whereas by deed of sale passed before Charles Stewart Esquire and his fellow notaries bearing date at Quebec the fifteenth day of August which was in the year of Our Lord one thousand seven hundred and ninety five, he, the said John Young, for the sum of seventy pounds currency, being the consideration expressed in the said deed, did purchase and acquire from Mr. Dennis Daly, of the said city of Québec, tavern-keeper, a certain Negro lad, named Rubin, about the age of eighteen and, whereas he, the said John Young, being desirous of emancipating the said Negro lad Rubin, and as an encouragement to honesty and assiduity in the said lad, Rubin, declared in the presence of Charles Stewart, one of the subscribing notaries, that if he, the said Rubin, should faithfully serve him, his executors or assigns for and during the term of seven years from the date hereof at the end and expiration of that time he would give him his free and full liberty and in the meantime he would give maintain and cloth him in a decent manner suited to one in his station.

The above declaration however is made upon this express condition that if he, the said Rubin, shall at any time during the said term of seven years to be computed from the date of these presents get drunk absent himself without leave or neglect the business of the said John Young Esq. his master he shall forfeit his title to his liberty anything herein contained to the contrary notwithstanding. But on the other hand if he shall will and truly perform his duty and in all things demean and behave himself as a good and faithful servant he may at the end of the said term of seven years demand of the said John Young his free liberty to which he shall be entitled by virtue of these presents. And further on condition of his good behaviour he shall be allowed monthly as pocket money the sum of two shillings and six pence per month.

Thus done and passed at Quebec aforesaid the eight day of June one thousand seven hundred and ninety seven this minute having been first duly read to and subscribed by the said John Young and explained to the said Rubin who engaged to fulfill the condition of this agreement and accepted with gratitude the generous offer made him by John Young Esq. his master in the presence of the said subscribing notaries these presents remaining of record in the office of the above named Charles Stewart.

JOHN YOUNG
RUBIN X [his mark] YOUNG
A. DUMAS
CHS. STEWART

Source: *Rapport de L'Archiviste de la Province de Québec pour 1921–22,* (Quebec: Louis-Amable Proulx, Imprimeur de Sa Majesté Le Roi, 1922): 123. Link: http://archive.org/details/rapportdelarchiv02arch

Article 1: I Make Him My Dog /My Slave

Brett Rushforth

On April 12, 1680, a Belgian monk-turned-missionary named Louis Hennepin tinkered with a canoe on the banks of the Mississippi River. As two French servants boiled a wild turkey for his lunch, Hennepin surveyed the strange and beautiful country before him. His party had traveled the Mississippi for eleven days without incident, but, as he awaited his meal, Hennepin "suddenly perceived ... fifty bark canoes, conducted by 120 Indians, entirely nude, who descended this river with great speed." Hennepin called out to them, twisting his tongue around rudimentary Algonquian to assure the Indians of his good intentions. "Misti-gouche," he cried, using the Algonquians' name for his people to identify himself and his servants as their friends. As Siouan speakers, the approaching war party did not understand his words. But, unfortunately for Hennepin, they got the message: these bearded foreigners were allies of the Algonquian-speaking peoples of the Mississippi Valley, the very peoples the Sioux had to attack.[1]

Hennepin and his party quickly realized the danger and scrambled to evade an impending assault. Ditching the turkey in the brush, the servants ran to the canoe, joining Hennepin in a hasty retreat. Within seconds, Sioux canoes surrounded them. Raising ceremonial war cries, the attackers boarded Hennepin's canoe and took him captive. "We offered no resistance," Hennepin later recalled, "because we were only three against so great a number." Now using signs because he "did not know a word of their language," Hennepin tried to urge the Sioux on to their original target, but to no avail. Next he offered bribes, first tobacco from Martinique, then two wild turkeys they had saved for dinner. This pleased his captors, and their demeanor seemed to soften, but by nightfall Hennepin and the Frenchmen still feared for their lives. The servants resolved to die fighting like men, but Hennepin was more resigned to his fate, whispering a vow that he would "allow them to kill me without resistance in order to imitate the Savior, who gave himself voluntarily into the hands of his executioners."[2]

Rather than dying a martyr, Hennepin lived the next eight months as a captive among the Sioux. For nineteen days he and his companions were forced to row their overburdened canoe against the Mississippi's strong current. Reaching the northern edges of navigable waters, the Sioux destroyed Hennepin's canoe to prevent his escape and then marched the prisoners over half-frozen marshlands toward their villages. The prisoners faced daily threats to their lives, enduring "hunger, thirst, and a thousand outrages ... marching day and night without pause." When Hennepin's hunger and fatigue caused him to lag, his captors set fire to the meadows only behind him, forcing him to push ahead. In short, according to Hennepin, "The insults that these barbarians committed against us during our journey are beyond all imagining."[3]

When they reached the Sioux villages, the prisoners faced another wave of humiliating assaults. They were stripped naked, their bodies were painted, and they were forced to sing and dance as they drummed a rattling gourd. The warriors stood the prisoners in front of tall stakes, set in the ground and surrounded by straw and wood, erected to burn incoming captives. Then they began to negotiate Hennepin's fate. A few urged good treatment to curry favor with the French, but their voices were overwhelmed by those arguing for his execution. They began to torture him but were cut short when an influential war chief named Aquipaguetin stepped forward and claimed the priest as a replacement for his son, who had fallen at the hands of Hennepin's allies. In Aquipaguetin's charge Hennepin entered the chief's village, injured and demoralized but glad to be alive.[4]

As he made the transition to life in captivity, Hennepin found it difficult to make sense of his position in Sioux society or even to find the right word to define it. His captors themselves said that "they considered [him] a slave that their warriors had captured in their enemies' territory." Yet, because of his ceremonial adoption as Aquipaguetin's son, he expected a level of independence and respect he never achieved. He was beaten. He faced repeated

Source: Brett Rushforth, *Bonds of Alliance: Indigenous and Atlantic Slaveries in New France*, (Chapel Hill: University of North Carolina Press, 2012): 35–51; 70–71. Published for the Omohundro Institute of Early American History and Culture. Copyright © 2012 by the University of North Carolina Press. Used by permission of the publisher. www.uncpress.unc.edu

death threats. He performed forced labor, farming with Aquipaguetin's wives and children on a nearby island. And he was under almost constant surveillance: "The more I hid myself, the more I had Indians after me … for they never stopped watching me." But it was hunger that troubled him the most. To keep him weak and dependent, Hennepin's newly adopted kin fed him only five or six meals a week, giving him just enough wild oats and fish eggs to keep him alive. "I would have been very content had they given me something to eat, as they did their children," he remembered. "But they hid [their food] from me … conserving what little fish they had to feed their children." Despite the metaphorical kinship conferred by his adoption, he and his captors understood the difference between real and fictive sons. "They thus preferred the lives of their children to mine," a distinction that even Hennepin admitted was only reasonable. If the priest could not fully grasp his experience as a Mississippi Valley captive, he was eager for it to end: "It must be said that it is a sweet and pleasant thing to come out of slavery."[5]

The Indians who would engage in a century-long slave trade with French colonists brought their own complex and evolving practice of slavery to the colonial encounter. The act of enslavement dominated and defined Natives' thinking about slavery far more than the long-term status of those they enslaved. Indigenous slaves lived under a wide range of conditions, some dehumanizing and others nearly familial, and a particular slaves's place in the community could change over time. But all of them had to pass through the ritualized system of enslavement designed to strip them of former identities and forcibly integrate them into the capturing village. In war dances and diplomatic ceremonies, through the binding and marking of bodies, and with a sophisticated language of dominion and ridicule, the Native peoples of the Pays d'en Haut articulated an elaborate idiom of slavery as a form of human domestication that reduced enemy captives to the status of dogs and other domesticated animals. Simultaneously expressing and seeking power, enslavement involved a series of scripted acts of physical and psychological dominion designed, in the words of several Algonquian and Siouan languages, to tame and domesticate captured enemies. In so doing, captors harnessed the enemy's power to serve the needs of their own people.

Although slaves were defined by their place in Native war culture, they also labored in agriculture and performed other useful tasks. For men, this work often violated gender norms, as they were compelled to perform traditionally female tasks like hoeing in the fields or carrying baggage on hunting expeditions. Female slaves often became subordinate wives, adding their reproductive and domestic labor to the households that incorporated them. Full of possibilities for social integration, enslaved women's work also carried many dangers, including the potential for sexual violence that seems to have been a hazard unique to their slave status. Some of enslaved individuals' most important labor was performed in the area of diplomacy. As both agents and objects of intercultural relations, indigenous slaves mediated between the violent impulses that led to their enslavement and the alliance building that their bodies facilitated as symbols of generosity. As a regionally and temporally specific system of human bondage, Algonquian and Siouan slavery differed in important ways not only from European chattel slavery but also from other forms of Indian captivity in North America.

NIT'AOUAKARA—I MAKE HIM MY DOG / MY SLAVE

"This reception is very cruel; some tear out the prisoners' nails, others cut off their fingers or ears; still others load them with blows from clubs."

–Sébastien Rale, Jesuit, 1723

Indians of the Pays d'en Haut expressed their relationship to slaves through metaphors of domestication and mastery, comparing captives to dogs and other domesticated animals. More than a simple insult, the metaphorical domestication of enemy captives represented an elaborate cultural idiom that shaped the practice and defined the meaning of indigenous slavery. To shame and intimidate their enemies, Algonquians and Siouans treated their prisoners with great disrespect through symbolic acts of humiliation designed to strip them of their former identities and incorporate them as subordinate domestics. Beginning with demeaning abuse on the journey home, continuing through acts of torture as captives were received into the village, and culminating in ceremonial killing or forced incorporation, Indians designed their rituals of enslavement to demonstrate their mastery over weaker enemies

251

and to secure the allegiance and passivity of those they would keep alive as slaves.

Anishinaabe-speakers called their slaves *awakaan*, which meant "captive," "dog," or "animals kept as pets." The earliest French lexicon of central Algonquian languages, recorded between 1672 and 1674 by Jesuit Father Louis Nicolas, included *aouakan*, meaning "slave or prisoner of war," as one of eight essential nouns for missionaries to know to effectively teach western Indians. After living among the Anishinaabes of Michilimackinac and Sault Sainte Marie, Lahontan composed his own dictionary of essential Anishinaabe terms, listing *Ouackan* for "slave."[6]

The most-advanced French linguist of Anishinaabemowin in the seventeenth century was Louis André, a Jesuit trained in Latin linguistics and later a linguistics professor at Quebec's Jesuit college. Living in several Native villages and working closely with Ottawa informants, he conducted a fourteen-year study of their language and produced an eight-hundred-page manuscript dictionary and phrase book designed to teach other missionaries the language. André recorded dozens of Anishinaabe terms and phrases relating to slavery, most of which expressed the metaphor of slaves as domestic animals. André wrote that the verb to enslave (*nit'aouakara*), for example, literally meant to make someone a dog. Often rendered in the first person possessive, it described enslavement as an act of animal domestication: to say "I make him my slave" was to say "I make him my dog." One of the most intriguing variations of this verb was translated by another Jesuit among the Ottawas as "I make him my plaything, my slave." Rendered in the diminutive form, it could be translated more literally as "I make him my little dog/puppy."[7]

The act of domestication—turning enemies into dogs—began even before the warriors left their village for the raid. Raids originated in communal, and quite often contested, discussions of issues ranging from the need for retaliation to preemptive raids designed to weaken a threatening enemy. Among the Illinois, elder male relatives of anyone killed by an outsider could call a council and demand revenge. "If my strength and my courage equalled yours, I believe that I would go to avenge a relative as brave and as good as he was," one Illinois elder said in a late-seventeenth-century war council. "But being as feeble as I am, I cannot do better than address myself

to you," the young warriors. He persuaded them to fight by appealing to their sense of collective revenge and individual masculine honor.[8]

Louis Hennepin witnessed similar negotiations among the eastern Sioux, seeing for himself the beginning of a process that had led to his own enslavement. The warrior or family initiating the raid sent invitations around the village, and sometimes to neighboring villages, to join in a war feast. Accepting this invitation meant accepting the call to war. Those who wished to join the war party gathered at the home of the one who invited them, singing their warrior songs as they arrived. In these songs, Sioux men recounted their deeds of bravery and recalled the captives they had taken, vowing similar success on this raid: "I am going to War, I will revenge the Death of such a Kinsman, I will slay, I will burn, I will bring away Slaves, I will eat Men." A feast and dance followed, called by the Sioux *šunkahlowanpi*—literally "ceremonial song of the dog"—described by later Sioux informants as "a parade with singing made by those who are on the point of going to war."[9]

Eating men and taking slaves expressed the central theme of the *šunkahlowanpi* and other war feasts in the Pays d'en Haut. As Pierre-François-Xavier de Charlevoix explained, warriors "say also in direct Words, that they are going to *eat a Nation;* to signify that they will make a cruel War against it; and it seldom happens otherwise." The metaphorical equation of eating men and taking slaves found its physical expression in the ritual consumption of dog meat, which was the centerpiece of the warriors' feast that preceded the raid. "This feast is one of dog's flesh," explained Nicolas Perrot of the rite among the Anishinaabes, "which [among them] is ranked as the principal and most esteemed of all viands. ... Feasts of this sort are usually made only on the occasion of a war, or of other enterprises in which they engage when on expeditions against their enemies." The practice was so entrenched in the Pays d'en Haut that one colonial official concluded, "The feast of dogs is the true war feast among all the savages." Dog feasts sometimes continued into the journey toward an enemy's territory, and evidence suggests that war parties sometimes killed and ate enemy dogs as sign of power over them.[10]

When captured, slave raiders could find their own logic turned disastrously against them. An Ottawa war chief named Sinagos, who had a reputation as a brutal slaver, conducted a raid in Sioux territory in the early 1670s "putting the men to flight and carrying away the women and children whom they found there." Those who escaped the raid gathered reinforcements who pursued and captured Sinagos and the surviving captives. Recognizing his prominence, the Sioux decided to make an example of him rather than kill or enslave him. "They made him go to a repast," wrote Nicolas Perrot, "and cutting pieces of flesh from his thighs and all other parts of his body, broiled these and gave them to him to eat—informing Sinagos that, as he had eaten so much human flesh and shown himself so greedy for it, he might now satiate himself upon it by eating his own."[11]

Because Indians imagined enslavement as the violent consumption of flesh, they compared freeing captives to vomiting: a violent release of the flesh they had eaten. When a Fox war chief entertained a French delegation in the 1680s, he offered his French guest some venison. When the Frenchman refused on the grounds that he was unhappy with Fox slave raids against French-allied Indians, the Fox man called for four captives, whom he released to his French guest. "Here is how reasonable the Fox can be ... he vomits up the meat that he had intended to eat ... even as it is between his teeth he spits it out, he asks you to return it to where he captured it." Jacques Gravier recorded an expression for releasing captives among the Illinois: "nisicarintama8a ac8i8ssemahi. je done la vie a cinq prisoniers," I give life to five prisoners. The Algonquian verb means "to vomit."[12]

Carrying mental images drawn from this rich verbal and ceremonial milieu, warriors began their journey to enemy territory seeking slaves to domesticate. In the indigenous war culture of the Pays d'en Haut, taking captives took precedence over killing enemies and especially over territorial conquest, which was extremely rare. "When a Savage returns to his own country laden with many scalps, he is received with great honor," wrote Sébastien Rale, "but he is at the height of his glory when he takes prisoners and brings them home alive." Such feats of bravery, Rale explained, allowed a warrior to be considered "truly a man." "They are so eager for this glory that we see them undertake journeys of four hundred leagues through the midst of forests in order to capture a slave."[13]

Once warriors carried captives a safe distance away from a raided village, they bound them tightly by the hands and neck with a halter. Keeping the captives' legs free except when they slept, the captors "immediately tie their hands and compel them to run on before at full speed, fearing that they may be pursued ... by the companions of those whom they are taking away." Louis Hennepin explained the danger of slowing the captors down. "When they have taken a slave, they garrote him and make him run," he wrote shortly after his own release from slavery among the Sioux. "If he cannot keep up they strike him on the head ... and scalp him. "This was a second wave of sorting strong captives from those who might become an immediate liability or a long-term drain on local resources. The old and infirm were rarely taken from the village, and the necessity of running, bound, for long stretches with little food ensured another level of fitness for surviving slaves"[14]

Led along by a leash, captives faced physical and verbal abuse during their long march to the captors' village. An Illinois warrior might refer to a slave he had captured as *ninessacanta*, "my slave, the one whom I bring," a phrase drawn from the root word "to beat, batter, bludgeon" and occasionally, "to beat to death." Louis Hennepin found his repeated beatings more terrifying than debilitating, enhancing his captors' arbirary power by making him fear constantly for his life. Indeed, the march northward to the Sioux villages was so disorienting for Hennepin that he lost all sense of place and distance, sketching on his return to Europe a map of the Upper Mississippi Valley that stretched it hundreds of miles north of its headwaters. Copied by several subsequent cartographers, Hennepins's bewilderment registered in European cartography long after his release from captivity.[15]

As the returning warriors neared their village, the war chief signaled their arrival with a series of high-pitched cries, one for each captive in the party. In some accounts, individual warriors also cried out once for each of the captives they had taken, "As soon as he arrives, all the people of the village meet together, and range themselves on both sides of the way where the prisoners must pass," wrote Sébastien Rale. "This reception is very cruel: some tear out the prisoners' nails, others cut off their fingers or ears: still others load them with blows from clubs." Among the most degrading of the gauntlet's many torments was the participation of women and children, whose taunts fell with special poignancy on captured male warriors. Like the ceremonies that initiated the slave raid, the

253

logic of subordination required that captives' incorporation into village society be a public affair involving all segments of Native society.[16]

Those disfigured by the gauntlet bore permanent marks of their status as a captive enemy, especially when such wounds occurred in conspicuous locations like the face or hands. Maiming the hands also served another purpose: preventing escape or rebellion. Describing a similar strategy used by the Iroquois, one Jesuit observed. "They began by cutting off a thumb of each [captive], to make them unable to unbind themselves." According to one account, Algonquians adopted this practice to avenge those captured by their Iroquois enemies. The resulting scarring and disfiguration were considered "the marks of their captivity," which remained with living captives long after the trauma of initiation had passed.[17]

Strategic slave marking registered in the Algonquian languages of the Pays d'en Haut. The Anishinaabes used a phrase that Louis André translated as "I cut a young slave to mark him. "The Illinois had a whole family of expressions dealing with personal marking of slave bodies, all drived from the root word *isc8*, meaning "mark of imperfection/defect." These included *isc8chita*, "someone who has a cropped ear"; *isc8chipag8ta*, "bitten on the ear, ear removed with the teeth"; *nitisc8ic8rep8a*. "I crop his nose with my teeth." Other Indians of the Pays d'en Haut marked men in an especially painful way, using "red-hot javelins, with which they pierced the most sensitive parts of his body." Even these physical markers of slavery narrated the act of enslavement as domestication, emphasizing the very personal power exercised over these enemies by capturing warriors. Like enslavement itself, biting the tip from a captive's nose or ear was at once an alienating and terribly intimate act of dominion.[18]

Cropping the nose of the wild thunderer tamed him and transferred his significant power to the dominating village. Consistent with the intent of enslavement generally, this rite expressed the prowess of the captor while appropriating the power of the captive. Perhaps this is why enemy warriors percieved as especially threatening were made to "suffer according to their Merits." Those who cried out during torture were considered less potent and thus less worthy of an honorable death. "When a victim does not die like a brave man," according to Charlevoix, "he receives his death's wound from a woman or from children; he is unworthy, say they, to die by the hands of men."

Even in death male captives faced the prospect of emasculation from their enemies.[19]

After being beaten and marked, slaves were undressed and forced to sing (in some cases the singing began before entering the village). This was the final metaphorical act of stripping slaves' former identities from them, preparing them for death or the forced integration that would follow. At least one Algonquian language made explicit the connection between the humiliation of stripping and slavery: Illinois-speakers used the phrase *nilci8i-nakiha arena*, which meant both "I lift up his loin cloth" and "I treat him like a slave."[20]

Once the initial tortures subsided, another round of sorting divided captives marked for death from those who would stay alive as slaves. Among the Illinois, male heads of household "assemble and decide what they will do with the prisoner who has been given to them, and whether they wish to give him his life." Hennepin came to understand that his fate had been decided in the same way among the Sioux. "When the warriors have entered their lodges, all the elders assemble to hear the account of all that has happened in the war, then they dispose of the slaves. If the father of an Indian woman was killed by their enemies, they give [her] a slave in his place, and the woman is free to give him life or have him killed." "The Anishinaabes did much the same, granting life to some and subjecting others to a slow and painful death. Although the particular reasons for sparing individual captives varied from family to family and village to village, captives could be kept alive to augment population growth, to replace a dead relative or to facilitate alliances through trade. Once the captive had been granted life, he or she was washed, clothed, and given a new name, often that of the deceased he or she was intended to replace. One Illinois word describing the decision to grant life to a captive derives from the word meaning "to cure or heal."[21]

Captives marked to die were forced to sing what the French described as "chansons de mort," or death songs, according to Pierre Deliette, " to afford entertainment to their executioners." François de Montigny witnessed the spectacle when a Winnebago war party passed by an Illinois village "in triumph" with two Missouri slaves, "who were forced to sing their death songs, which is a custom among all the Indians." Called *kikit8inaki8a*, meaning "slave songs," by the Illinois, captives were forced to sing at the entrance of each household that had lost a family member to the captive's people, allowing grieving kin a chance at violent (or at least verbal) catharsis. Condemned slaves were handed a special staff and forced to march from cabin to cabin as they sang. At ten to twelve feet long, the staff was wrapped in feathers to signify the captors otherworldly power over the slave. It must have also become a physical burden to captives who had to carry it around the village for hours. The staff was eventually planted in the ground to become torture stake, where condemned slaves spent their final hours enduring a slow, smoldering death.[22]

Captors spared women and children more often than men. In addition to targeting the male warriors for revenge killings, this strategy maximized the demographic benefits of slavery, as increasing the number of adult males in a village would do little to change its reproductive capacity. During times of high mortality due to disease or warfare, female captives often represented the best hope for rapidly restoring lost population. Especially in the frequently polygynous societies of the Pays d'en Haut, female captives integrated smoothly into present social structures as second or third wives of prominent men. Children were especially prized because of the relative ease with which they assimilated into the capturing society, learning new languages and customs much more quickly than older captives. This selection process left a surplus of male captives, who were often traded outside the village. Welcomed communally, slaves were controlled individually. The warrior who captured each slave exercised mastery over the person as a private possession, and any family wishing to kill or adopt a slave would have to negotiate terms with the original master. This process could lead to conflict among the captors as the ultimate future of each slave became a matter of group deliberation.[23]

Of the many possible fates facing a captive who survived the rituals of domestication, the most familiar to modern readers is a captive's adoption into a household to take the place of the dead. If it was not the most common outcome, it was certainly the status that French observers recognized most readily. "When there is any dead man to be resuscitated, that is to say, if any one of their warriors has been killed, and they think it a duty to replace him in his cabin," wrote Sébastien Rale, "they give to this cabin one of their prisoners, who takes the place of the deceased; and

this is what they call 'resuscitating the dead'." In times of peace this role was played by other members of the same village, who took the place of prominent villagers who had died, thereby assuming their full identity and status. Nicolas Perrot insisted that among the ottawas a dead person of high status was sometimes replaced by another resident of the village, "and they regard themselves as united to this family, as much as if they were actually kindred." But because the adoptee "must be of the same rank" as the dead, captives were rarely chosen to replace influential men and women.[24]

What captive adoption meant in Native societies is elusive at best. French law and culture granted an adopted father an essentially proprietary authority over the adopted child, and this shaped what French observers meant to convey with the notion of captive "adoption," never intended by French authors to indicate the creation of true kinship. Even captives themselves, like Louis Hennepin, found their relationship with adopted relatives hard to comprehend, not familial in any sense that they recognized yet still expressed as kinship. When it came to difficult choices, as it did with Sioux food supplies, Hennepin acknowledged that his adopted kin favored their actual relatives over the fictive kinship created by his ceremonial adoption. Transcending the limits of European observations and filling in their silences, indigenous languages provide a glimpse of how Indians themselves understood the category of kinship created by captive adoption. Their own metaphors suggest meanings much more complex than colonists understood.[25]

Kinship terminology was conspicuously absent from Algonquian idioms describing adopted captives. Rather than using the common verb *nintoohsimaa*, "I have him as a father," for example, Illinois captives identified their master by the household where they stayed. Only two recorded kinship terms applied to adopted captives or slaves. The first was an expression used by families who wanted to kill a slave from a returning war party. They would say to the warrior who captured the slave, *nita8embima*, a unique word from meaning "that is my relative," which was said only "by the executioner to whoever brings a slave" to the village. Rather than indicating actual kinship, the term condemned the captive to death in memory of the dead relative. The Jesuit Thierry Beschefer recorded the presence of a second kinship term in 1683, specifically used to demean adoptees. Using a different form of the word *son*, captors signified "a submission of which They make use to command us, as They do the Slaves whom they have adopted." According to a French trader, among the Anishinaabes adopted captives "never lie in their Masters Huts," another mark of distinction from the household's actual kin similar to the exclusion experienced by Hennepin among the Sioux. The master was, in the words of Pierre Chaumonot, a "feigned parent," or fictive kin.[26]

Adopted slaves, then, were bound to a household of fictive kin, occupying the physical and metaphorical place of a child but constantly aware that they were not actual relatives. Slaves' history and the terminology used to describe them equated them more with the family's domestic animals than with their children. And because they had no actual kin but were attached to a household at the master's pleasure, they were bound to the family at a single point rather than through the multiple lines created by kinship. Like dogs, their linguistic equivalents, adopted slaves were thus part of the household but never really part of the family.

The presence of fictive kinship bonds created by slaves' ritual adoption followed a pattern of linking family and slavery in a wide range of historical slave systems. The expression of mastery in familial terms—what sociologists of slavery call "quasi-filial" kinship—pervaded slaveries from ancient Rome to the antebellum southern United States, Indeed, the English word *family* derives from the Latin *famulus*, meaning household slave. Across vast cultural differences, masters have imagined themselves fathers, but they have always understood the difference between their slaves and their biological family. This was especially evident in the particular language of kinship used by those adopting slaves in the Pays d'en Haut, where they made careful distinctions between real and fictive sons, between actual kin and those forced to take their place in the household.[27]

The French did not find in the Pays d'en Haut a benign system of captivity that they would transform into slavery. The Siouan and Algonquian peoples there had an elaborate and often brutal war culture centered on a form of slavery, built on different assumptions and employed for different reasons than the plantation slavery developing in the contemporary Atlantic. Focused on the act of enslavement rather than the production of commodities, indigenous slavery was at its heart a system of symbolic dominion, appropriating the power and productivity of enemies and facilitating the creation of friendships built on shared animosity toward the captive's people. The intensely personal violence experienced during the first few months could be brutal and often deadly, but those who survived and weathered the storm of insults that followed found themselves in a system with many well-worn pathways out of slavery. These paths were often difficult to take, they were not available to everyone, and the prevalence of diplomatic slave trading served as a constant reminder of slaves' marginal and precarious position. And it goes without saying that, given the choice, no one would have sought enslavement, no matter what the outcome. But, if only in the next generation, slaves could at least hope to rise to full acceptance by the society that enslaved them, becoming identified with a people they once considered less than fully human.

Slavery in the Pays d'en Haut simultaneously disrupted and facilitated the broader political economy of trade and intermarriage that linked peoples and places throughout the region and beyond. Among allies, the sharing of enslaved enemies cemented alliances and created the bonds of fictive kinship that linked the region's peoples to one another across ethnic and linguistic lines. Among enemies, enslavement provided outlets for violent expressions of enmity that stopped short of total destruction and provided mechanisms of repopulation and enhanced productivity. As in all historical contexts, enslaved individuals in the Pays d'en Haut were agents as well as objects, responding to the trauma and alienation of slavery with creative adaptation to their new surroundings. French colonizers would bring their own evolving notions of slavery to the colonial encounter, which began a century-long conversation that would transform the vocabularies and structures of slavery in both the Pays d'en Haut and the French Atlantic world.

NOTES

1. "J'apperçus tout d'un coup … cinquante Canots d'ecorce conduits par six vingt Sauvages tous nuds, qui décendoient d'une fort grande vitesse sur ce Fleuve." Louis Hennepin, *Nouvelle découverte d'un très grand pays situé dans l'Amérique, entre le Nouveau Mexique et la mer glaciale* (Utrecht, 1697), 314–315. Catherine Broué discusses problems with Hennepin's credibility, concluding that the 1697 edition is largely reliable and highly valuable. Broué, "En filigrane des récits du Pére Louis

Hennepin: 'trous noirs' de l'exploration louisianaise, 1679–1681," *Revue d'histoire de l'Amérique française*, LIII (1999–2000), 339–366. For the negative view, see Jean Delanglez, *Hennepin's Description of Louisiana: A Critical Essay* (Chicago, 1941). Perhaps the foremost authority on seventeenth- and eighteenth-century Sioux history and culture, Raymond J. DeMallie concludes that Hennepin's writings, if evaluated carefully, "present valuable ethnographic detail" about the eastern Sioux. DeMallie, "The Sioux at the Time of European Contact: An Ethnohistorical Problem," in Sergei A. Kan and Pauline Turner Strong, eds., *New Perspectives on Native North America: Cultures, Histories, and Representations* (Lincoln, Nebr., 2006), 243.

Throughout this study I use the term "Sioux" rather than the recently fashionable "Dakota" because the latter term excludes those Sioux who are Lakota or Nakota and because "Sioux" is a much more widely recognized term among Anglophone readers. French sources from the seventeenth and eighteenth centuries do not allow a clear distinction between various Sioux bands, so the broader term also better reflects the historical record. Several modern tribal organizations in the United States use "Sioux" in their official names, but none uses "Dakota" except to designate their location. See Raymond J. DeMallie, "Sioux until 1850," in *Handbook*, XIII, *Plains*, part 2, 718; and, for a different perspective, Gary Clayton Anderson, *Kinsmen of Another Kind: Dazlota-White Relations in the Upper Mississippi Valley, 1650–1862* (Lincoln, Nebr., 1984).

2. "Nous ne faisons aucune resistance, parce que nous n'étions que trois contre un si grand nombre," 316: "Je ne savois pas un mot de leur langue," 320; "J'avois resolu de me laisser tuer sans resistance afin d'imiter le Sauveur, qui s'étoit remis volontairement entre les mains de ses bourreaux," 319: Hennepin. *Nouvelle découverte*.

3. "Le faim, la soif, et mille outrages ... marché jour et nuit sans delai," 342: "Les Insultes, que ces Barbares nous firent pendant nôtre route, sont au dessus de toute imagination," 322: Hennepin, *Nouvelle découverte*.

4. Ibid., 355.

5. "Elles me consideroient comme un Esclave, que leurs Guerriers avoient fait dans le pays de leurs Ennemis," 362; "plus je m'enchois, plus j'avois de Sanvages à ma suite ... car ils ne me quittoient point de veuë. 320–321; "J' aurois esté fort content, s'ils m'eussent

donné à manger, comme à leurs enfans. Mais ils se cachoient de moy ... conservoient le peu de poisson, qu'elles avoient, pour en nourrir leurs enfans. ... Elles préféroient done la vie de leurs enfans à la mienne. En quoy il est certain, qu'elles avoient raison," 362; "Il Paul avoüer. qu'il est bien doux et bien agreeable de sortir de l'Esclavage," 463: Hennepin, *Nouvelle découverte* For mistreatment and labor, see Louis Hennepin, *Description de la Louisiane, nouvellement découverte au Sud'Ouest de la Nouvelle France* (Paris. 1683), 246; Hennepin, *A New Discovery of a Vast Country in America, Extending above Four Thousand Miles, between New France and New Mexico* (London, 1698) (Wing H1451), I log. William Henry Foster similarly argues that the power of Native women to control slaves "came not from physicality but from the hearth." Foster. *The Captor's Narrative: Catholic Women and Their Puritan Men on the Early American Frontier* (Ithaca, N.Y., 2003), 9.

6. John D. Nichols and Earl Nyholm, *A Concise Dictionary of Minnesota Ojibwe* (Minneapolis, Minn., 1995), 14; Frederic Baraga, *A Dictionary of the Otchipwe Language, Explained in English* (Cincinnati, Ohio, 1853), 49–50, 453; C. Douglas Ellis, *Âtalôhkâna nêsta tipâcimôwina: Cree Legends and Narratives from the West Coast of James Bay* (Winnipeg, 1995), 55, 85, 159, 449. Although there are many variant spellings of *awakaan*, I use Nichols and Nyholm's version as the most recent standardization of the orthography. For Nicolas, see Diane Daviault, ed., *L'algonquin au XVIIe siècle: une édition critique, analysée et commentée de la grammaire algonquine du Père Louis Nicolas* (Sainte-Foy, Que., 1994), 5, 34, 106–107; [Louis-Armand de Lom d'Arce], Baron de Lahontan, *Voyages du Bon de Lahontan dans l'Amérique Seplentrionale* (Amsterdam, 1705), II, 321. Jonathan Carver echoed Lahontan's spelling in his own word list more than sixty years later; "Esclave, Ouackan." See Carver, *Voyage dans les parties intérievres de l'Amérique Septentrionale pendant les années 1766, 1767, et 1768* (Yverdon. Switzerland, 1784), 312.

Linguists tend to distinguish between words historically recorded forms and their standardized spellings by placing those words quoted from historical sources in quotation marks and placing standardized non-English words in italics. I break from that convention, here—by generally italicizing all Algonquian words—for two reasons. First, because the MiamiIllinois language lost most of its native speakers quite early, it has relatively few standardized words, and none of the Algonquian languages has standardized forms for much of the seventeenth-century vocabularies I discuss here. Second, the large number of Algonquian words in the text would make the use of quotation marks cumbersome, interfering with the narrative rather than clarifying its meaning. Algonquian words quoted from historical sources are spelled as they were recorded in the original manuscript or printed text.

7. "Je le fais esclave": André, "Preceptes, phrases, et mots de la langue algonquine outaouaise," s.v. "esclave," "J'en fais mon joiiet, mon esclave": Pierre Du Jaunay, "Dictionarium gallico-outaouakum, "MS, 1748, copy in Smithsonian Institution Anthropology Library, s. v. "esclave." Du Jaunay also confirms Andre's translation of *nit'aouakara:* "nit'a8akan. mon [ésclave] nit'a8akara. Je le fais esclave."

8. Pierre Deliette, "Memoir of De Gannes [Deliette] concerning the Illinois Country," in Theodore Calvin Pease and Raymond C. Werner, ed. and trans., *The French Foundations, 1680–1693*, Collections of the Illinois State Historical Library, XXIII (Springfield, Ill., 1934), 377 (hereafter cited as Deliette, "Memoir").

9. Hennepin, *New Discovery*, II. 72: Eugene Buechel and Paul Manhart, *Lakota Dictionary: Lakota-English/ English-Lakota* (Lincoln, Nebr., 2002), 191, 291.

10. Charlevoix, *Letters to the Dutchess of Lesdiguieres,* 131 ("*eat a nation*"); Perrot, *Memoir,* in Blair, ed. and trans., *Indian Tribes,* 53–54 ("most esteemed"); Antoine Denis Roudot, "Memoir concerning the Different Indian Nations of North America," in W. Vernon Kinietz ed., *The Indians of the Western Great Lakes, 1615–1760* (Ann Arbor, Mich., 1940), 403 ("true war feast"); Henri Joutel, *The La Salle Expedition to Texas: The Journal of Henri Joutel, 1684–1687*, ed. William C. Foster, trans. Johanna S. Warren (Austin, Tex., 1998), 119.

11. Perrot, *Memoir,* in Blair ed, and trans., *Indian Tribes,* 189, 190.

12. "Le Chef prenant la parole dit, voici en quoi I Outagamis peut etre raisonnable ... il vomit la viande qu'il a eû dessein de manger ... et l'ayant entre ses dents il la crache, il te prie de la remettre eû il l'a prise." Bacqueville de La Potherie. *Histoire de l'Amérique Septentrionale*. II 214; Gravier and Largillier, "Dictionnaire illinois–français." 527 ("to vomit").

13. Raudot, "Memoir," in Kinietz,ed.. *Indians of the Western Great Lakes*, 355–356. For the Rale quote. see *Jesuit Relation*. LXVII. 171–173.

14. "Quand ils ont pris un esclave. ils le garotttent [sic] et le font courir; s'il ne peut les suivre. ils luy donnent un coup de hache à la teste et le laissent après lay avoir enlevè la peruque ou cheveleure": Hennepin. *Déscription de la Louisiane*, 63. *Jesuit Relations*. LXVL, 275 ("tie their hands").

15. Gravier and Largillier, "Dictionnaire illinois-français." 28, 340. The first map influenced by Hennepin's information was a 1681 Paris map titled *Carle de la Nouvelle France*, which could have been drawn only from Hennepin because of its placement of the "Issati," or Sioux villages. Derek Hayes, *American Discovered: A Historical Atlas of North American Exploration* (Vancouver, 2004), map 92. Hennepin's own map, first published in his 1689 *Description de la Louisiane,* was reprinted several times into the early eighteenth century, including in his *Nouvelle decouverte* (1697 and subsequent editions).

16. *Jesuit Relations,* LXVII, 173. Rale speculated that the Illinois adopted these cruelties only after their similar treatment as captives of the Iroquois: "It was the Iroquois who invented this frightful manner of death, and it is only by the law of retaliation that the Illinois, in their turn, treat these Iroquois prisoners with an equal cruelty," See *Jesuit Relations*, LXVII, 173–175. This statement should be assessed cautiously, however, as the French frequently minimized the violence of their allies and exaggerated that of the Iroquois. See, for example, a report from 1660 that describes French-allied Indians' tearing out fingernails, cutting off fingers, and burning hands and feet at Quebec, dismissed by another Jesuit as "merely the game and diversion of children" (*Jesuit Relations*, XLVI, 85-101, esp. 93). "Tout le Village assiste à cette derniere Ceremonie" (Bacqueville de La Potherie. *Histoire de l'Amérique Septentrionale*. II, 26). For a description of the gauntlet among eastern Algonquians, see James Axtell, "The White Indians of Colonial America," *WMQ*. 3d Ser., XXXII (1975), 70—71. For the Iroquois, see Daniel K. Richter, "War and Culture: The Iroquois Experience," *WMQ*. 3d Ser., XL (1983), 557.

17. *Jesuit Relations*, L. 39 ("cutting off a thumb"). XLV, 257 ("marks"). For the best descriprion of Iroquoian disfiguration, see Roland Viau, *Enfants du néant et mangeurs d'âmes: guerre, culture, et société en Iroquoisie ancienne* (Montreal, 1997), 172–186; William A. Starna and Ralph Watkins, "Northern Iroquoian Slavery," *Ethnohistory*, XXXVIII (1991), 43–45. For additional eaxmples from the Pays d'en Haut, see *Jesuit Relations*, XLVIII, 85–101, LXVIII,

171–175. For hand mutilation, see also Gravier and Largillier, "Dictionnaire illinois-francais," 176.

18. "Je coupe un jeu[n] esclave pour marquer": Andre, "Preceptes, phrases, et mots de la langue algonquine outaouaise," s.v. "marquer." "Qui a l'oreille coupèe": "mordu a l'oreolle, oreille emportee avec les dents": "je luy coupe le nès avec le dents": Gravier and Largillier. Dictionnaire illinois-francais," 111. 176, *Jesuit Relations*, XLVIII, 99 ("red-hot javelins").

19. For the long-nosed god and thunderers, see James R. Duncan, "Of Masks and Myths." *Midcontinental Journal of Archaeology*, XXV (2000), 1–26. Hennepin. *New Discovery*. L. 186 ("according to their Merits"). P. de Charlevoix, *Journal of a Voyage to North-America* (London, 1761), II. 107.

20. "Je luy oste son brayet, la traite en esclave": Gravier and Largillier, "Dictionnaire illinois-français." 209.

21. Deliette, "Memoir," 384 ("assemble and decide"). "Quand les guerriers sont entrés dans leurs cabannes, tous les anciens s'assemblent pour entendre la relation de tout ce qui s'est passé en guerre, ensuitte ils disposent des Esclaves. Si le pere d' une femme Sauvage a esté tué par leurs ennemis, ils luy donnent un Esclave à la place, et il est libre à cette femme de luy donner la vie ou de le faire mourir." Hennepin, *Description de la Louisiane*, 65–66, For post-torture healing and naming, see Bacqueville de La Potherie, "History of the Savage Peoples Who Are Allies of New France," in Blair, ed. and trans., *Indian Tribes*, II, 36–43; Daniel K. Richter, *Ordeal of the Longhouse: The Peoples of the Iroquois League in the Era of European Colonization* (Chapel Hill, N.C., 1992), 59–74; Viau, *Enfants du néunt,* 137–160. For "nimpelakiihaa," see Antoine-Robert Le Boullenger. "Dictionnaire français-illinois." MS, ca, 1720s, John Carter Brown Library, Brown University, Providence R.I.; Daryl Baldwin personal communication.

22. Deliette, "Memoir," 383 ("chansons de mort"); *Jesuit Relations*.XLV.183 ("entertainment") "En triomphe… ces pauvres prisonniers qu' on obligeoit de chanter leur chanson de mort, qui est une maniere qu' ont tous les sauvages": the Illinois demanded the slaves release because they were Missouris, "comme ayant toujours este amis" (as they had always been friends"): frangois de Montigny, "Lettre de M. de Montigny sur les missions du Mississippi." Aug. 25, 1699, 1–2, ASQ.SME (text nt clear), For the torture staff, see Deliette, "Memoir"383–384: Gravier and largillier "Dictionnaire Illinois-franeais, 373."

23. Richter, *Ordeal of the Longhouse,* esp. 67–68; Gordon M. Sayre, *Les Sauvages Américains: Representations of Native Americans in French and English Colonial Literature* (Chapel Hill, N.C., 1997), 248–304. For Illinois social structure, see Susan Sleeper-Smith, *Indian Women and French Men: Rethinking Cultural Encounter in the Western Great Lakes* (Amherst, Mass., 2001), esp 1–37, where she indicates the importance of women to integrating outsides into Illinois kin structures. For a similar captive selection process among the Indians of the Southwest, see James F. Brooks. *Captives and Cousias: Slavery, Kinship and Community in the Southwest Borderlands* (Chapel Hill, N.C., 2002), esp. 1–40.

24. *Jesuit Relations,* LXVII, 173 ("resuseitating"): Perrot, *Memoir* in Blair. ed. and trans., *Indian Tribes*. 1, 84 ("same rank") 85 ("actually kindred").

25. Kristin Elizabeth Gager, *Blood Ties and Fictive Ties: Adoption and Family Life in Early Modern France* (Princeton, N.J., 1996); Hennepin, *Nouvelle découecrle,* 362. Compare this to Perrot's report that Anishinaabe wives could turn to their extended kin when they needed protection or redress. Perrot, *Memoir,* in Blair, ed. and trans., *Indian Tribes,* 1, 64–65.

26. "Cest mon parent, dit le boureau a qui conque amene un esclave": Gravier and Largillier, "Dictionnaire illinois–français," 36. For Illinois kinship terms, see David J. Costa, "The Kinship Terminology of the Miami-Illinois Language," *Anthropological Linguistics,* XLI (1999), 28–53: *Jesuit Relations,* LXII, 213 ("to command us"). Pierre Deliette confirmed Beschefer's sense that calling adoptees "son" was a mark of disrespect. See Deliette, "Memoir," 363. For "never lie in their Masters Huts," see Lahontan, *New Voyages,* II, 37. For "feigned parent," see *Jesuit Relations*. XVIII, 29.

27. Orlando Patterson, *Slavery and Social Death: A Comparative Study* (Cambridge, 1982), 62–65; *Oxford English Dictionary*. s.v. "family." In 1376, the French political philosopher Jean Bodin wrote. "For the very name of a Familie came of *Famulus* and *Famulativ,* for that it had in it a great number of Slaves: and so of the greatest part of them that are in subjection in the Familie, men call all the whole household a Familie: or else for that there was no greater means to gather wealth than by slaves and servants, which the Latines call *Famuli,* the auntients not without cause have called this multitude of Slaves and servants a Familie." Bodin. The Six Bookes of Commonweule. ed. Kenneth Douglas McRae (Cambridge. Mass., 1962), 32.

259

Article 2: Slavery in New France

Robin Winks

Slavery was given its legal foundation in New France between 1689 and 1709, and had the timing been different, the institution might well have taken a firmer hold than it did. Prior to 1663 New France had been a seigneury of the Compagnie des Cent-Associés, administered by the company with an eye to quick profits from the fur trade and fitfully aided by the Society of Jesus as a mission colony. Colonization had been subordinated, and economic rather than social ends had shaped the conventional wisdom of the time. The fur trade required no skilled labor; it required no gang labor either. A full-blown slave system had not been needed, and although the Indians enslaved many of their captives, on occasion selling a *pani* to work as a field hand or as a domestic servant for the French, there had been no economic base upon which slavery could profitably be built and little demand for either slave or *engagé* ("indentured") labor.

When New France was transferred from company to royal control in 1663, this conventional wisdom was broken temporarily and Louis XIV set about building a new colony. Upon the wilderness he imposed an effective form of administration, with a governor who was responsible for external affairs and the military and an intendant who was to maintain law and order, to provide a secure financial basis for the colony and to take charge of internal development. The following year the Coutume de Paris was introduced by a newly created Conseil Souverain, thus bringing local laws into conformity with those of the metropole. Jean-Baptiste Colbert, the Minister of the Marine, encouraged intermarriage between French and Indians so that a new people of one blood might emerge, with their loyalties and their future pinned to the revitalized colony. And for five years Jean Talon, "The Great Intendant," labored to diversify the economy of New France.

Under Talon and his immediate successors the colony was a projection into the New World of a growing, centralized society near the height of its power. Religious orthodoxy was mandatory after the revocation of the Edict of Nantes in 1685. A local militia began training in Montreal. Talon brought in purebred livestock, tested seed grain, encouraged the development of industry, investigated the fisheries, tapped the filling reservoir of skilled workers, and endeavored to begin trade with the French West Indies. More seigniories were granted, and in order to increase population the state brought in *filles de roi*, gave dowries to the needy and grants to those who went forth and multiplied, and forced bachelors into marriage. Careful censuses were taken to measure the colony's growth in manpower, to gauge the proper use of the skilled immigrants, and to forecast possibilities for new industries and new channels of trade.

During this period of imaginative and expansive thinking, slavery appeared to be one means of increasing manpower. In 1677 Jean-Baptiste de Lagny, Sieur des Bringandières, obtained royal permission to exploit the mines of New France. He soon found that there was too much to do and too few to do it: the fisheries, the mines, and agriculture all offered potential wealth too great for only nine thousand colonists to tap. Consequently, sometime in 1688 apparently, he communicated his conviction to the governor, Jacques-René de Brisay, Marquis de Denonville, who in turn and together with the intendant, Jean Bochart de Champigny, that year appealed to France for Negro slaves. "Workers and servants are so rare and extraordinarily expensive," they wrote, "… as to ruin all those who attempt to be enterprising. We believe that the best means to remedy this is to have Negro slaves here. The Attorney General of the Council, who is in Paris, assures us that if His Majesty agrees to this proposition, some of the principal inhabitants will have some [slaves] bought for them in the Islands as vessels arrive from Guinée, and he will do so as well."[1]

Denonville was an aggressive governor who already had shown little regard for other races and who was determined to build the economy of New France, at least in some measure, along the lines laid down by Talon. Two years earlier he had sought diligently for two Negro slaves who had escaped from New York, and in 1687 he had seized forty Iroquois whom he had invited to a peace conference and had shipped them to France as slaves. Now he was in the midst of a war precipitated by his duplicity. By the end of the year

Source: Robin Winks, "Slavery in New France, 1628–1760" in *Blacks in Canada: A History*, Second Edition, (Montreal-Kingston: McGill-Queen's University Press, 2007): 3–9.

he was to be defeated and, in 1689, recalled by Louis XIV. In 1685 the *Code Noir* had been promulgated for the West Indies, and Denonville reasoned that the *Code*, as well as the slaves, might be brought from the islands to help solve New France's chronic shortage of unskilled labor. In this wish he was helped by the Attorney General, Charles-François-Marie Ruette d'Auteuil, who early in 1689 sent a memorandum to the King in which he argued that slavery would be profitable for New France, since even the expense of clothing the slaves might be turned to advantage; the Negroes could, as the Algonquins did, wear dry beaver skins which, through use, would become *castor gras* of doubled value.[2]

Whether moved by a vision of more productive mines or of prime pelts from black backs, Louis XIV assented on May 1, 1689.[3] In doing so, he rather carelessly limited his remarks to the importation of Negro slaves to help with agriculture, and he cautioned that since these expensive purchases would be coming from a radically different climate, the entire project might well fail should the sudden contrast in environment prove too much for the Negroes. Almost immediately thereafter, the outbreak of King William's War, and Denonville's recall, virtually nullified the royal assent. The King gave a second authorization in 1701,[4] four years after the Treaty of Ryswick. Queen Anne's War, or the War of the Spanish Succession, broke out during the following year, however, once again making sea routes dangerous and transport scarce. Thereafter, the colony was left to its own devices for obtaining slaves, and when, in 1704, Paris declared that colonies existed solely to serve the mother country and should not compete for industry, commerce, or population, New France reverted to an economy based in part upon the declining fur trade, effectively ending any likely need for a large number of slaves.

Nonetheless, slavery continued to grow slowly, for domestic servants and field hands were wanted by the wealthier families, and local authorities tried to give to it a more secure legal base when they could. The word *esclave* itself had not been used in the civil registers of New France before 1694,[5] but thereafter it became increasingly common. Clearly, confusion as to the formal status of the slave and how to give him his freedom lay back of the final step by which slavery acquired its tenuous footing in New France. On April 13, 1709, the intendant, Jacques Raudot, disturbed by the presence of a number of Indians who,

despite the widespread assumption that they were slaves by law, were claiming to be free men, read a lengthy *ordonnance*[6] in which he declared that "all the *panis and Negroes who have been purchased and who will be purchased, shall be the property of those who have purchased them* and will be their *slaves.*" Anyone who induced a slave to run away from his master was to be fined fifty livres.[7]

But if Raudot were to provide an official statement in support of slavery, official action also was necessary to ensure that those *panis* and Negroes whom their masters genuinely wished to set free might enjoy that freedom. Between 1706 and 1736 the number of slaves who had been given their freedom—or claimed they had—increased rapidly, leading to confusion (especially among the unchristianized who shared the same or similar names) about who was slave and who was free. Accordingly, in the latter year the intendant, Gilles Hocquart, issued a new *ordonnance* that provided for a uniform means of manumission. Verbal agreements were no longer sufficient: to free a slave by gift or by purchase, the owner or purchaser was to obtain a notary's certificate, and all such transactions were to be registered immediately with a royal registry office. Previous manumissions were valid, but none could depart from this procedure after the first of September. Clearly, slavery had grown sufficiently to require records as well as regulation; equally clearly, there was a body of opinion that wished to extend freedom to the slaves, since we may presume that Hocquart's *ordonnance* was in response to a petition, although the initiative may have come not from owners but from freed Negroes and *panis*.[8]

The status of slaves in New France also was regulated by the *Code Noir*, which though never proclaimed in the colony[9] appears to have been used as customary law. There were, in fact, two codes: the first, of 1685, was limited specifically to the West Indies; a revised code of 1724 applied to the new colony of Louisiana as well. The second code did not depart from the first in any significant way except to forbid intermarriage. The original *Code* was drafted to protect the white man from forms of slave violence: theft, revolt, and escape. Since slaves were not numerous in New France, little attention was given to specific regulations covering such eventualities until a specific case arose, which then was dealt with on its merits and within the spirit of the code. Because gang

261

labor was virtually impossible, and since most Negro slaves in particular were domestic servants, less attention needed to be given to safeguards—either for owner or for slave—with respect to clothing, housing, and working conditions. The memory of Colbert and Talon appears to have lingered, for no steps were taken to prevent intermarriage in New France, and if a white man took a Negro slave wife, she was freed by the act of marriage, Further, by the Coutume de Paris, Negro slaves were chattels (*meubles*), and as personal property they were not attached to the land as serfs but solely to their owners.

Hocquart issued his ordinance partially because, as he said, slaves were deserting their masters almost daily under the mistaken belief that there could be no slavery in France or in her dominions. There had been slaves in France, in fact, from early in the seventeenth century. Slavery, it was true, never had been expressly recognized in France: in 1571, when a cargo of Negroes was landed at Bordeaux for sale, the *parlement* ordered their release because slavery did not exist there; and in 1691 the Minister of the Marine declared that Negroes who were brought into the country would be free upon arrival. But his order did not touch upon the legality of slavery in the colonies. In any case, regulations of this sort were seldom enforced, and slaves did serve government officials, ship captains, soldiers, and planters throughout the century. That de facto slavery existed is proven by the suits for freedom undertaken in the eighteenth century.[10]

King and colony were by no means in agreement about slavery, adding to the confusion created by having one set of regulations in France, another—the *Code Noir*—in the Antilles, and a third for New France. A concert of opinion between governor and intendant in 1688 and 1701 had elicited formal approvals of slavery from the King, but by 1716 such a bond of opinion was broken. In October the intendant, Michel Bégon, repeated Champigny's plea: as there were only twenty thousand inhabitants in New France, he wrote, labor was expensive and scarce. If the colony were encouraged to enter into the slave trade, local industry, agriculture, and commerce would improve much as they had in the English colonies to the south. Boston supported a thriving economy partially on slaves, and in New York the land was cultivated by Negroes so that white energies could be directed to trade. In New France, the intendant suggested, Negroes could till the soil,

fish for cod, saw timber, build ships, and exploit the iron mines "out of which the King and the colony could derive the greatest advantages" if there were but workers to develop them.

Apparently Bégon anticipated the major objection at its source, for the governor, Philippe de Rigaud, Marquis de Vaudreuil, later wrote in the margin of Bégon's *mémoire* that the climate was too cold and the expense of clothing slaves too great. In prior refutation Bégon pointed out that the climate of Boston and New York was not markedly different and that those Negroes already in New France were in good health. Further, the expense need not be lasting, for the free trade in beaver skins, fresh letters of exchange, and the normal royal funds spent on the colony would provide sufficient revenue. Since in 1716 the slave-trading monopolies enjoyed by the Compagnie de Guinée and the Compagnie du Sénégal were broken by opening the trade to the Guinea Coast to all, Bégon may also have hoped to create in New France a small center for building slave ships. In this he would have been frustrated, however, for the King required that vessels engaged in the Guinea trade should be fitted out exclusively at Bordeaux, Nantes, Rochelle, or Rouen.[11]

Although persistent, without Vaudreuil's support Bégon could accomplish very little. In 1720, one month after the Compagnie des Indes was given a new monopoly over the Guinea trade, Bégon asked the King to send Negroes to work in the hemp market, and he forwarded a memorial in which the inhabitants of New France undertook to buy one hundred and one Negroes from the company at six hundred livres each. In June 1721, the Navy Board informed Bégon that it would have the company carry a cargo of Africans to Quebec, but no action appears to have been taken after the Board learned that the Negroes of Sénégal, who might be sent, were worth one thousand livres each in the West Indies.[12]

Other evidence that the intendants, and on occasion the governors, wished to push slavery while the King was reluctant to do so may be found in the circumstances of Hocquart's *ordonnance* in 1736. The intendant apparently had wished to be more sweeping than his statement reveals, for the King told both him and the governor, Charles, Marquis de Beauharnois, that he did not approve of their proposal to decide on the status of *panis* and other slaves by an explicit law, and it was he who ordered that the colony's judges should be content to follow the custom that considered *panis* to be slaves until those masters who wished to do so granted them freedom by notarial deed.[13] Any move to advance the assumption that all Negroes were slaves—as was occurring for Negroes in the English colonies at this time—and thus to formalize their condition along purely racial lines, was thereby blocked.

NOTES

1. On Lagny, see Benjamin Sulte, "L'eselavage en Canada," *La revue Canadienne,* n.s., *8* (1911), 318, who gives more prominence to Lagny's letter than do other authors. Extracts from the letters of Denonville and Champigny, dated August 10, October 31, and November 6, 1688, are printed in [Jacques Viger and Louis Hippolyte Lafontaine, eds.], "De l'esclavage en Canada," in La Société Historique de Montréal, *Mémoires et documents relatifs à l'histoire du Canada I* (1859), 1–2, The translation is my own. Francis Parkman, while engaged in research for *The Old Regime in Canada* (1874) and *A Half-Century of Conflict* (1892), had extracts copied from these and other pertinent documents; the copies are in the Parkman Papers in the MHS. Viger kept his notes in books that he called *Ma Saberdache,* from which he quotes: When Viger died in 1858, Lafontaine carried the work forward. Lafontaine's copies of the documents are in the PAC., Lafontaine Papers, *14,* file 64, fols. 5552–65; the originals are in the Laval University library.

2. Viger and Lafontaine, "L'esclavage," pp. 2–3; Trudel, pp. 20–21; Parkman Papers, *25,* 294, on d'Auteuil; A. Judd Northrup, "Slavery in New York: A Historical Sketch," *83d Annual Report 1900,* New York State Library, Appendix 6: *State Library Bulletin History No. 4* (Albany), pp. 258–59, 275.

3. Several brief summaries of slavery erroneously state that it was authorized in New France by the rescript of 1688, a mistake apparently perpetuated from Hubert Neilson, "Slavery in Old Canada Before and After the Conquest," *Transactions of the Literary and Historical Society of Quebec,* ser. 2, no. 26 (1906), p. 21. It was Louis's reply of 1689 that legalized slavery.

4. Archives de la Province de Québec, Quebec, Ordres du Roi, ser. B, 22: King to Louis Hector de Callière, governor of New France, and to Champigny, May 31, 1701. On October 5, the governor and intendant reported that they permitted colonists to hold Negro slaves (Parkman Papers, 6, 238).

5. Trudel, p. 315.

6. Presumably Raudot acted upon a petition or remonstrance from slave-owners, for an *ordonnance* normally arose from a petition addressed to the King or to his representative.

7. Printed in Viger and Lafontaine, pp. 4–5.

8. *Arrêts et Règlements du Conseil Supérieur de Québec, et Ordonnances et Jugements des intendants du Canada* (Quebec, 1955), p. 371.

9. There is some disagreement on this point. William Renwick Riddell, in "Le Code Noir," *JNH, 10* (1925), 321, n. 1, feels there is "no sufficient ground" for doubting that the code was applied to New France, but the only evidence he gives is dubious. While Neilson ("Slavery in Old Canada," p. 26) asserts that, since the code of 1685 was incorporated in the Coutume de Paris, which received royal sanction as being applicable to all colonies in the New World, it did apply, he appears to confuse the code itself with the Coutume's regulation concerning *meubles.* Trudel (pp. 27, 163, 213, 316) points out that he could find no evidence that the code was promulgated formally.

10. On slavery and attitudes toward slavery in France, see Gaston Martin, *Histoire de l'esclavage dans les colonies françaises* (Paris, 1948); Paul Trayer, *Etude historique sur la condition légale des esclaves dans les colonies françaises* (Paris, 1887); Charles de la Roncière, *Nègres et négriers,* 9th ed. (Paris, 1933); and Shelby T. Mc. Cloy, *The Negro in France* (Lexington, Ky., 1961), especially pp. 5–6, 12–14, 22–51, Hilda M. Neatby, *The Administration of Justice under the Quebec Act* (Minneapolis, 1937), pp. 9–11, discusses the validity of the Coulume de Paris in New France.

11. *Collection de manuscrits contenant lettres, mémoires et autres documents historiques relatifs à la Nouvelle-France …* (Quebec, 1884), *3,* 21.

12. See Ordres du Roi, *44,* fols. 3, 528 1/2; *47,* fol. 1242. These are summarized by Edouard Richard in *Report concerning Canadian Archives for the Year 1904* (Ottawa, 1905), App. K. 21, 28, 54. See also Joseph-Noël Fauteux, *Essai sur l'industrie au Canada sous le régime française,* (Quebec, 1927), *1,* 476–77.

13. Ordres du Roi. *63,* fol. 642 1/2, as printed by Richard in *Canadian Archives Report 1904,* p. 211.

Article 3: Slaves in Île Royale, 1713–1758

Kenneth Donovan

Charles, an 18-year-old black slave, produced much of the food consumed in his owner's household in 1733. Charles was the property of Pierre Benoist, an ensign in the garrison at Louisbourg, who lived with his family in block two of the town. By 1733, Pierre and his wife, Anne Levron, residents of the town since 1722, had two daughters, 15-year-old Anne and eight-year-old Marie Anne. Maintaining the Benoist household was a full-time job for Charles. The court-yard of the property had a garden measuring 34 by 45 feet, and three animal sheds housing two goats, a sow, 30 hens and roosters, eight ducks, and six turkeys. In addition, Benoist had a half share of an ox and a heifer. Besides their backyard garden, the Benoists had another 900-square-foot garden in nearby block 22 of the town. When not planting, weeding, harvesting the vegetables, or feeding the livestock, Charles was kept busy cutting kindling and keeping the stoves and fireplaces supplied with wood. By December 1733 the Benoists had ten cords of wood in their backyard. A prized member of the household, Charles was valued at 512 *livres* in 1733.[1]

At least 266 individuals like Charles were enslaved in Île Royale from 1713 to 1758, with 232 or 87.2 percent of them in Louisbourg. Recent scholarship on the slave trade has emphasized how slaves in communities such as Île Royale were part of "Atlantic history," and as such, slaves circulated like ambulant property throughout the Atlantic basin, connecting communities around the Atlantic word.[2] Yet, in spite of the thematic unity, the new scholarship has also highlighted the heterogeneous nature of the slave experience. "No one slavery, no unitary slave trade, no single black experience existed," wrote Philip D. Morgan.[3] The lives of slaves who came to Île Royale reinforced Morgan's contention of "no single black experience," since their work and situation were shaped by the unique history and culture of the island.

Most of the 266 slaves in Île Royale, with different backgrounds but a common experience as slaves,

spoke French and had similar occupations.[4] This paper asserts that Île Royale slaves, although designated as property, were by no means passive. The majority of slaves in Île Royale—246 or 92.4 percent—were domestics, performing work to support the functioning of households; they became servants, nursemaids, gardeners, and did most of the daily chores. Only 19 slaves—one fisherman, two cabin boys, 15 sailors, and one executioner—worked outside the household.[5] This paper shows that the increase of slaves in Île Royale followed the growth of the general population, especially the number of families and children. Slaves removed the burden of heavy domestic work and thus, in effect, supported French women in bearing more children than they otherwise would have done: during the years 1722 to 1758 there were 2,200 children born in Louisbourg.[6] Female slaves helped to rear these children. Much of the literature on slaves to date has shown little concern for the humanity or individual behavior of slaves and the relations between the enslaved and their masters.[7] This paper discusses how individuals, both slave and free, interacted with each other within a French and New France context. By focusing on the lives of 23 slaves (14 women 9 men), the paper provides evidence of the importance of slave work to the success and comfort of households and family life in Île Royale.[8]

With the end of the War of the Spanish Succession in 1713, the French were forced to leave Newfoundland and move to Île Royale. By 1714 there were more than three hundred refugees at Louisbourg, including Georges, a black slave who had been purchased by Pastour de Costbelle, the governor of the colony, prior to leaving Newfoundland.[9] George appears to have been the first enslaved African in Île Royale. The nature of the African slave trade ensured that slaves such as George had been separated from their families, their communities, and their heritage: slavery, as Orlando Patterson has observed, entailed "social death," the loss of all recognition of previous marks of identity.[10] The slaves of Île Royale, like most slaves, were not literate, and they were not named or counted as persons in most of the numerous censuses that were conducted on the island. The slaves had no names except those given by their masters, and even then 25 of the 266 slaves in this study had to be recorded as "anonymous."[11] Nor did Île Royale slaves leaves narratives or other significant traces of their identity. Nevertheless, it is possible to

---

Source: Kenneth Donovan, "Slaves in Île Royale," *French Colonial History,* Volume 5 (2004): 25–42. Adapted with permission by the French Colonial History Society.

study their lives by examining a variety of sources such as records of birth, marriage, and death; lists of returning settlers (1749); contracts of sale; court proceedings; ship departures and arrivals; military enlistment rolls; official correspondence; diaries; and newspapers. Relying on a cumulative methodology, the lives of the 266 slaves have been reconstructed from a mass of disparate primary materials.

The first slave in Île Royale came with Governor Pastour de Costbelle, but it was another eleven years before slaves in significant numbers began to appear on the island. In 1724 there were four slaves in Louisbourg out of a total civilian population of 894. By 1726 there were only three slaves in the colony; but over the next eight years, there was a dramatic increase in the slave population. There were 28 slaves in Louisbourg by 1734 (2.4 percent of the town's population); in 1737 there were 50 slaves (3.3 percent of the population). During the same period (1734–1737) the number of children had grown from 394 to 664, an increase of 40.6 percent. Over the same period, Louisbourg families purchased 22 slaves, an increase of 44 percent in three years. And the trend continued. Over a period of 33 years (1724–1757), there was a steady advance in the number of slaves as the population of Louisbourg and Île Royale increased. By 1752 there were 63 slaves in the town, and five years later, in 1757, that number had more than doubled to 125 slaves, representing 3.1 percent of Louisbourg's estimated civilian population of 4,000. With slaves representing a maximum of slightly more than three percent of Louisbourg's people, they composed a small fraction of the society. Thus, Île Royale was a society *with* slaves, not a "slave society" dominated by the ramifications of slaveholding. Although the remaining records can provide only a glimpse of the world of the slaves in eighteenth-century Louisbourg, they demonstrate that in spite of their relatively small numbers, black and *panis* slaves were in demand throughout the colony's history, and that they contributed significantly to its sustainability.

There was a constant shortage of labor in Île Royale, but there was apparently little inclination to purchase slaves to do most of the labor that produced saleable commodities. As the capital and commercial center of the colony, Louisbourg had an economy that depended on the fishery, the military, and trade.[12] By 1718 Île Royale was producing and exporting 150,000 *quintals* (7.5 million kilos)

of dried codfish per year. (One *quintal* equals approximately 50 kilograms). Île Royale cod production in the first half of the eighteenth century accounted for one-third of all the cod caught by the French in North American waters; but free and indentured men, not slaves, operated the fishery. Only one slave is known to have participated in the Île Royale fishery: George, "the Black," a slave of fishing proprietor Marie Anne Peré, who was paid as a member of fishing crews.[13]

Louisbourg started out as a simple base for the cod fishery, but as the town prospered and also took a major role in the re-export of Caribbean sugar products, Louisbourg developed into one of the most important ports in New France. By 1734 the town was basically completed. Fishing properties—most with landing stages, drying platforms, and a few buildings—surrounded the harbor. At the same time, Louisbourg became the main French military stronghold in the Atlantic region. As a fortress, Louisbourg resembled a European fortified town: it was enclosed by walls, and had batteries and outer works. By the 1730s more than 150 ships were sailing into Louisbourg, making it one busiest seaports in North America. Besides its economic and commercial importance, Louisbourg was the capital and administrative center of Île Royale.

Louisbourg's stratified society was dominated by senior colonial officials, military officers, and successful merchants: categories that were not mutually exclusive. Down the social scale, petty marchants, innkeepers, and artisans served garrison, port, and fishery. By the 1740s Louisbourg's full-time population ranged from 2,500 to 3,000. Each summer, Breton, Norman, and Basque migrant fisherman swelled the population. In Louisbourg's newly formed society, people tended to change occupations more readily than in France, but because almost all manufactures were imported, their occupational choice was narrow. As in small French towns of the day, people of different status lived side by side.[14] Slaves were part of the local society, and yet they were cosmopolitan as well. They were multilingual and came from the West Indies, Africa, India, France, Canada, and the British-American colonies.[15]

Slaveholding in Île Royale was part of a broader phenomenon that began in the sixteenth century when the first slaves were brought from Africa to America; but slaveholding was not significant in terms of numbers. The French enslaved the first

265

blacks in Canada as early as 1608. By 1759, the end of French regime, there were 3,604 slaves in Canada—1,132 of whom were black.[16] The majority of the slaves in New France—69 percent—were not African but *panis,* a term derived from the Caddoan tribes of the Great Plains. The *panis* included slaves from more than 20 aboriginal societies such as the Fox, Sioux, Iowa, Kansa, Chickasaw, Blackfoot, and Comanche. The French name *panis* had become a generic term for "aboriginal slaves" by 1750.[17] During the period from 1713 to 1758, Île Royale, which had a smaller population than the communities along the St. Lawrence, included some 266 slaves: 144 males, 97 females, and 25 whose gender could not be determined. Unlike Canada, where the majority of the slaves were *panis*, most of the slaves in Île Royale—90.9 percent (242 out of 266)—were blacks, reflecting the colony's close trade links with the French West Indies. There were, however, at least 24 *panis* enslaved in Île Royale.

Official French policy toward slavery was established in 1685 with the adoption of the Black Code (*Code Noir*) for the West Indies, which was reissued, with minor revisions, in 1724. In principle, the 60 articles of the Black Code offered some protection to slaves, for it "insisted on the basic humanity of the slave: each was to be instructed, baptized, and ministered unto as a Christian, families were to be recognized, and freed slaves were to receive the rights of common citizens—in theory the African could aspire to become a Frenchman."[18] Slave owners were forbidden to have children by concubinage with their slaves, and those who broke the law were subject to a fine of two thousand pounds of sugar. Various articles of the code also obliged masters to provide minimum weekly quantities of food to all slaves ten years old or over, and forbade them from substituting *guildive* (sugar-cane brandy) for edibles. Slave owners were also required to provide each slave with two suits of clothing or four ells of cloth per year. Finally, masters had to take care of slaves in their old age. Even in slave societies of the West Indies, however, a wide gap yawned between the theory expressed in the code and the practice of slave owners; the Black Code was never even registered in Île Royale and Canada, although it was observed to the extent that slaves were to be baptized, and adults were not to work on Sundays and holy days of obligation.[19]

The overwhelming majority of slaves in Île Royale engaged in some sort of domestic service, and there was a rough division of labor by gender. The men, such as Charles, worked outdoors. They tended gardens, fed animals, cleaned stables, carried water, cut firewood, mowed hay, picked berries, gathered seaweed, shoveled snow, and ran errands. Thus, for those who could afford it, purchasing a slave not only brought higher status but also significantly improved living conditions. Slaves were highly valued because they could do most of the daily chores, especially the heavy and demanding work. Since they had considerable work experience, mature slaves such as François *dit* Jasmin could take on even more responsibility. Born in the French West Indies in 1688, François was a slave of Elie and Simone Thesson *dit* La Floury. Though the Floury family had an extensive fishing and mercantile operation, with two schooners and six shallops, and hired upwards of 80 fishermen each spring, they also owned farm animals, meadowland along the road to the Mira River, and farm and fishing property in Little Bras d'Or and at Scatary Island. François doubtless helped with the farm chores; besides feeding and caring for three cows and two horses, he had to cut hay, churn butter, and attend to numerous other duties associated with a fishing and mercantile property.[20]

Whereas François looked after the outdoor chores, an unnamed New England slave woman assisted Simone Floury with the household, which included nine girls and two boys. Enslaved women performed a wide range of household duties, from looking after children to cleaning clothes, scrubbing floors, preparing meals, and washing dishes. A similar role was intended for Rosalie, a 14-year-old female purchased by Andre Carrerot and his wife Marie for 550 *livres* in June 1736. At the time of purchase, the Carrerots had five children ranging in age from two to ten years, and Marie Carrerot was expecting her sixth child. Rosalie became a live-in nanny and servant in the Carrerot home. Rosalie was considered to be an adult. Besides looking after the children, she had numerous household chores, since the Carrerots lived in a large two-story, half-timbered house on rue Toulouse in block 2 of the town. If Rosalie did not have the necessary household skills, that posed little difficulty, since the law permitted the Carrerots to train Rosalie in the manner that suited their lifestyle. The sale agreement noted that Jean

Gouin transferred to "Carrerot any right of ownership of the said Negress, to be disposed of as he sees fit, in accordance with the usual practice in like cases."[21] The Carrerots eventually had 11 children, and Rosalie worked hard to help raise the children and maintain the household.

Slaves like Rosalie were much sought after in communities such as Louisbourg and Halifax, and slaves were traded between the ports after Halifax was founded in 1749, even though it was a British colony. By 1750 there were 14 enslaved black people in Halifax.[22] The types of slaves being sold there were clearly comparable to those employed in Île Royale. In September 1751 when the schooner *Success* arrived in Halifax, having made its second voyage from Antigua that summer, it brought "9 negro men, the property of Captain Bloss."[23] The following year, Joshua Mauger, a Halifax merchant who had commercial dealings in Louisbourg, offered six additional slaves for sale, including one female and five males. Promoting the domestic skills of the female slave, Mauger described her as "a very likely Negro Wench, of about thirty five years of Age." She was "Creole born," he noted, adding that she had been "brought up in a Gentleman's Family, and [was] capable of doing all sorts of Work belonging thereto, as Needlework of all sorts, and in the best manner; also Washing, Ironing, Cookery, and every other Thing that can be expected from such a slave."[24]

Slave women in Île Royale practiced similar skills and specific occupations in Louisbourg households. Maria, for instance, was a chambermaid in the home of Jean Laborde, the treasurer of the colony during the 1750s. She was one of six slaves in this large household, which included another woman who worked as a servant, Adelaise; Cezar and Thomas, also domestic servants; while Polidor was the personal servant of Sebastien, Laborde's son. Touissant was the cook for the household, in which six slaves looked after five people: Laborde, his wife, a son, a daughter, and a nephew.[25] Since Laborde was one of the leading colonial officials and therefore was obliged to entertain in the town's highest social circles, many of the slaves in the Laborde household were called upon to perform their tasks in a relatively public way. By the late 1750s Laborde, whose property and holdings were valued at quarter of a million *livres*, could easily afford six slaves and host lavish dinner parties and social events.[26] As testimony to his

vast wealth, Laborde purchased an additional slave for 805 *livres* at a Louisbourg auction in November 1756. The unnamed slave was one of 13 crewmembers aboard the Newport schooner *New Brunswick* that had been captured off Île Royale after returning from the Newfoundland Grand Banks with a cargo of whale oil.[27] Laborde thus had seven slaves, including one from New England.

Numerous other skilled slaves lived in Île Royale. Among them were Dauphine (the cook) and Anne Honiche Nanon, a servant in the home of Nicolas Larcher.[28] An African native, Anne, who was born in 1734, helped to run Larcher's household affairs. Although a bachelor, Larcher, like Andre Carrerot, was also a member of the Superior Council and a wealthy merchant who lived in a large house outside Louisbourg's walls.[29]

Dauphine, Touissant, and Anne Honiche might have known another cook, Marie Marguerite Rose, a slave also skilled in food preparation. A native of Guinea in West Africa, Marie Marguerite helped to prepare the meals in the home of Louisbourg officer Jean Loppinot and his wife Magdelaine. Purchased in 1736, Marie Marguerite worked as a slave in the Loppinot household for 19 years and helped to raise their 12 children (plus her own) until she was freed in 1755. Upon obtaining her freedom, Marie Marguerite married Jean Baptiste Laurent, a Mi'kmaq, and opened a tavern in Louisbourg. Although illiterate, Marguerite had a cookbook entitled *Le Cuisinier Royal* among her goods when she died two years later. Documents suggest that she did not learn to read and write after her marriage, so she may have kept the cookbook as a prized gift from her mistress. Marie also had an extensive wardrobe of used clothing, some of which she may have received used from her former owner.

The inventory of Marie Marguerite Rose's estate, drawn up in 1757, revealed that she had an even broader range of household skills. A capable tavernkeeper, Marie was also a seamstress who could knit, dye and iron clothes, as well as make her own soap. Since Marie died suddenly in August 1757, the inventory recorded some of her projects in progress at the time of her death, including "a pair of woollen stockings, half made, along with two balls of wool of the same colour." In addition, she had "a ball of white wool and another of brown" and "three small balls of cotton." Apparently, Marie was also making her husband a shirt, since there was a new

267

man's shirt "having only one sleeve, the other being attached with a pin." Marie may have valued blue-hued clothing,[30] as she had "a little blue starch" in her chest for dyeing clothes. Marie also collected remnants of numerous fabrics that she intended to reuse in order to make different types of clothing, along with five balls of her own home-made soap to wash the clothes, and a laundry iron to ensure that they were neatly pressed. Nor did Marie confine herself to the interior of her home. A skilled gardener with her own shovel, she had vegetables in her garden that brought 40 *livres*, 15 *sols* when her effects were sold, making them the most valuable item in her entire estate. She also had "a barrel in which there were some raspberries," together with six pounds of sugar that was doubtless to be used for making preserves.[31]

In one instance, there is more evidence about what a personal servant might be expected to do. Catharine Congo, a slave of Louisbourg merchant Bernard Detcheverry and his wife Jeanne, was one of 14 people seated at Captain Gerard Jaulery's table on the ship *Le Comte de Maurepas* when it departed Bayonne for Louisbourg on 30 May 1749 with 83 passengers, 69 of whom received ordinary rations. Catharine Congo and her owners were entitled to extra rations and special treatment at the captain's table for a passage fee of 62 *livres*, 10 *sols* per person.[32] Self-interest on the part of the Detcheverrys probably played a role in Catharine's seating arrangement, since it was only at the captain's table that she could cater to her owner's wishes.

Of the slaves like Catharine Congo and Marie Marguerite Rose whose birthplace are known, 13 were natives of French West Africa, 25 were from the French West Indies, nine were from Canda, nine from British North America, and 33 people were born in Île Royale.[33] The majority of the remaining 186 slaves in Île Royale were doubtless from the French West Indies also; it is likely that only a small percentage were born in Africa. Much the same patterns held for black slaves in British North America during the eighteenth century. Unlike Île Royale or New France, the data for the origins of New England slaves is more conclusive. Most slaves in the British northern colonies such as Pennsylvania, New Jersey, New York, Connecticut, Rhode Island, Massachusetts, and New Hampshire were born in the British West Indies or were purchased in the southern colonies of North America. The merchants of these British colonies, like their counterparts in Île Royale, did not participate in the international slave trade, but took orders or requests for slaves from merchants or others who often had connections with the Caribbean islands.[34] Northern merchants also sold one or two slaves with a West Indies or North American cargo, solely on a speculative basis. Thus, well-known Boston merchant Peter Faneuil, who traded with Louisbourg throughout the 1730s and 1740s, occasionally sent black slaves as part of cargoes of foodstuffs—including the ship, which was to be sold as well. In July 1737 Faneuil insructed Thomas Kilby, his agent at Canso, Nova Scotia, to sell a sloop at Louisbourg, as well as its cargo of bread, flour, pork, and beef. Included among the shipment were "Two young negro men which if you can get a good price for pray dispose of them." If the price was not suitable, the slaves were to be returned to Boston.[35] On another occasion, 27 April 1753, Captain James Spellen of New York sold Jean, an 11–year-old slave, in Louisbourg. Spellen was a regular trader between New York, Louisbourg, and Halifax.[36]

Only ten slaves, however, came to Île Royale via the British North American colonies. The majority of slaves, such as Marie Flore, arrived in Île Royale from the French West Indies. A native of Martinique, Marie Flore was a one-year-old child when she debarked at Louisbourg in 1741 with her owner, ship captain Pierre Boullot. Boullot had made 13 voyages from Martinique to Louisbourg from 1737 to 1751. Settling in Louisbourg in 1753, Boullot married Jeanne Richard, a Louisbourg native, two years previously, and during the 1750s they had six children.[37] Marie Flore, like Rosalie in the Carrerot household, became a nanny and servant in the Boullot family, and eventually gave birth to a son, Denis. Marie Flore, who was 12 years old in 1753, was likely Boullot's daughter. Describing her in 1762, Boullot noted that "he kept a creole from Martinique at his home for approximately 20 years.[38] The Boullots also had an unnamed slave who was merely described as a "carib," and another "*negresse*" as well.[39]

With the constant demand of feeding, changing diapers, washing, and caring for six young children, Marie Flore, the "*negresse*," and the "carib" assumed responsibility for the household and the outdoor chores of the Boullot family. Similarly, two slaves who were contemporaries of Marie Flore—Louise, an 18-year-old slave, and her fellow worker, Cezar—undertook the same tasks in the home of Louis La Groix. Like Boullot, La Groix married a Louisbourg native, Magdelaine Morin, in 1753 and settled in Louisbourg. A native of Quebec, La Groix was a ship captain and merchant who had been trading from Quebec to Louisbourg to the French West Indies since the 1730s. La Groix purchased Louise and Cezar just prior to his marriage. Within three years of their wedding, the La Groixs had three children. Unfortunately, Louise died on 24 May 1755, when her mistress was five months pregnant with her second child. Another slave, Marie Anne—who would in turn have her own child, Jeanne Joseph, in 1758—soon replaced Louise.

The birth of Jeanne Joseph, as well as the death of Louise, was recorded in Louisbourg's parish records. In most Roman Catholic colonies, the church's response to slavery was driven not so much by a humanitarian concern about the plight of slaves in colonial society as by a religious conviction that slaves had souls to save and therefore represented potential converts. Accordingly, the church maintained that the moral and spiritual nature of the slave was more significant than the slave's temporary servile status.[40] One hundred and twenty-three black and aboriginal slaves appear in the Île Royale parish records: 80 baptisms, five weddings, 18 burials, 11 witnesses, and nine mothers of babies.

Even though many of the 80 baptized slaves were adults who hailed from the French West Indies, where according to the stipulations of the Black Code, slaves "were to be baptized" and "masters were to instruct their slaves in the Catholic religion, on pain of a discretionary fine," they had not been baptized before their arrival in Louisburg.[41] As elsewhere in New France, slaves were baptized more readily in Île Royale because there were no powerful interests—primarily slave owners and plantation managers—who opposed religious instruction of the slaves.[42] But in some cases, such baptisms occurred only on their deathbeds, after years of service in their masters' households. Some slaves were never baptized in Louisbourg. Anne Honiche Nanon was only baptized in 1759 after she and her owner had returned to France.[43] Moreover, the baptismal ceremony might have been a demeaning experience for slaves. Young children of the owners often served as godparents at most baptisms, as they also did for newborn French infants. This practice may have served to create a formal bond between child and nurse, but we know nothing of what the slave thought of it.

No matter what their particular situation, slaves in Île Royale were forced to adapt to a life they did not choose and could not control. And yet the evidence reveals that these slaves were individuals, with particular life and work skills, who established identities for themselves individually and a significant presence in Île Royale as a group. Male slaves such as Charles, François *dit* Jasmin, Cezar, Thomas, and Polidor were crucial workers in the daily exploitation of the local properties of Louisbourg because they cut wood, carried water, cut hay, milked the cows, fed the chickens, and weeded the gardens. A shortage of workers in Île Royale ensured that slaves' labor was highly valued, especially among growing families, and thus the number of slaves increased as the general population expanded. Over 92 percent of Île Royale slaves were domestics. Slaves such as Touissant, Dauphine, and Anne Honiche Nonon were skilled cooks who prepared meals for prominent members of the Superior Council. Maria was a chambermaid and Adelaise a servant; another servant, Catharine Congo, received special treatment while traveling with her master's family from Europe. Female slaves such as Rosalie, Marie Marguerite Rose, Catharine Françoise, Marie Flore, Louise and Marie Anne were especially highly prized because they helped to rear children as well as to maintain their masters' households. Clearly the work they did supported the demographic expansion of Louisbourg, thereby contributing to the success of the settlement in a fundamental way.

Slaves in Louisbourg did not remain socially dead. They formed relationships with the families for whom they worked and the children they likely nursed. They also formed relationships with each other. Few in numbers, the slaves in Île Royale would have known each other, and may even have collaborated on work in this small society where a few slaves together did not constitute a threat. Dauphine, Touissant, and Anne Honiche, for example, were cooks for three prominent members of the Superior Council, and they may have shared recipes and collaborated on preparing special meals for official gatherings. There is evidence that slaves also gathered on their own account, on occasions such as slave weddings and baptisms; at least five slaves were allowed

269

to marry. Most important, the enslaved people of this society became parents, since nine enslaved women are listed in the records as mothers. The humanity of these enslaved people becomes apparent because they were individuals with their own story to tell; they were part of an evolving African-French colonial culture. Although Île Royale was a small colony, the world of the slaves was even smaller since they were not permitted to work in the large-scale exploitation of the fishery for commodity production, or on the construction of the fortifications. Instead, they provided support for the domestic and personal aspects of life, and thus they were integrated tightly into the life of the town.

NOTES

This paper was first presented at the 27th Annual Meeting of the French Colonial Historical Society, East Lansing and Detroit, Michigan, 2001. I want to thank the anonymous reviewers for their comments, and Robert DuPlessis, the former editor, and Patricia Galloway, the current editor, for their insightful criticisms of this article.

1. Inventory after death of Anne Levron at the request of Pierre Benoist, her husband, 19 December 1733, Centre des Archives d'Outre-mer, Aix-en-Provence, France [hereafter CAOM], G 2, vol. 182, fols. 986–1009. See also Brenda Dunn, "The Private Properties of Block 2," unpublished manuscript, Fortress of Louisbourg Library, National Historic Site of Canada 1978 [revised], 78–85.

2. In a recent work, Robert Harms uses the voyage of the French ship *Diligent* in 1731–32 to link the communities or "worlds" of the French slave trade in the eighteenth century. Harms's "worlds" include France, West Africa, and Martinique, as well as some offshore islands. See Robert W. Harms, *The Diligent: A Voyage through the Worlds of the Slave Trade* (New York: Basic Books, 2002).

3. Philip D. Morgan, "African and American Atlantic Worlds," preface to a special issue on African and American Atlantic Worlds, *William and Mary Quarterly* 56, no. 2 (April 1999), 241–42. In the same issue, see Robin Law and Kristin Mann, "West Africa in the Atlantic Community: The Case of the Slave Coast," 307–34. On studying "Atlantic history," see Bernard Bailyn, "The Idea of Atlantic History," *Itinerario* 20, no. 1 (1996): 38–44. On the African contribution to Atlantic history, see John Thorton, *Africa and Africans in the Making of the Atlantic World, 1400–1680* (Cambridge: Cambridge University Press, 1992).

4. The colony of Île Royale included the islands of Île Royale (Cape Breton) and Île St. Jean (Prince Edward Island). The French used the names Île Royale and "Cap Breton" interchangeably. I have compiled a nominal list of 216 slaves found in the Île Royale documentation. See Kenneth Donovan, "A Nominal List of Slaves and Their Owners in Île Royale, 1713–1760," *Nova Scotia Historical Review* 16, no. 1 (June 1996): 151–62. The list includes the name, age, and origin of the slaves, if available, together with the date of their arrival in the colony. The names and occupations of the owners are also part of the data. Since 1996, I have identified an additional 197 slaves for the years 1713–1810 for a total of 413 people. See Kenneth Donovan, "Slavery in Cape Breton, 1713–1810," unpublished manuscript, Fortress of Louisbourg, National Historic Site of Canada. The list comprises 266 slaves during the French regime, 1713–1758.

5. Donovan, "Slavery in Cape Breton, 1713–1810," lists the occupations of all 266 slaves in Île Royale.

6. A. J. B. Johnston, *Religion in Life at Louisbourg, 1713–1758* (Kingston: McGill-Queen's University Press, 1984), 113.

7. Philip D. Morgan, *Slave Counterpoint: Black Culture in the Eighteenth-Century Chesapeake and Low-country* (Chapel Hill: University of North Carolina Press, 1998), xxii.

8. On family life, see Kenneth Donovan, "Communities and Families: Family Life and Living Conditions in Eighteenth-Century Louisbourg," in Eric Krause, Carol Corbin, and William O'Shea, eds., *Aspects of Louisbourg: Essays on the History of an Eighteenth-Century French Community in North America* (Sydney, Nova Scotia: University College of Cape Breton Press, Louisbourg Institute, 1995), 117–49; A. J. B. Johnston, *Control and Order in French Colonial Louisbourg, 1713–1758* (East Lansing: Michigan State University Press, 2001), 223–42.

9. Purchase of the slave Georges, account of Governor Costebelle with George De Lasson and Michel Daccarette, 1711–1713, CAOM, G 2, vol. 178, fols. 18–23.

10. See Orlando Patterson, *Slavery and Social Death: A Comparative Study* (Cambridge, Mass.: Harvard University Press, 1982).

11. Donovan, "Slavery in Cape Breton, 1713–1810."

12. Louisbourg's permanent civilian population was 633 in 1720; 813 in 1724; 1,463 in 1737; and 2,690 in 1752. These figures do not include totals for the garrison, fishermen, or other transients who were in the colony on a seasonal basis. By the late 1750s Île Royale's population, including soldiers, approached 10,000 people. See A. J. B. Johnston, "The Population of Eighteenth-Century Louisbourg," *Nova Scotia Historical Review* 11, no. 2 (December 1991), 75–86.

13. CAOM, 1735, G 2, vol. 194, dossier 80. George was a slave of Marie Peré, a widow of fishing proprietor Antoine Peré. Included among the debts owed to Madame peré was a list of her fishermen who owed for supplies. Georges, "the Black," owed 70 *livres*.

14. Kenneth Donovan, "Île Royale, Eighteenth Century," in R. Cole Harris, ed., *Historical Atlas of Canada: From the Beginning to 1800*, vol. 1 (Toronto: University of Toronto Press, 1987), plate 24; Kenneth Donovan, "Tattered Clothes and Powdered Wigs: Case Studies of the Poor and Well-to-Do in Eighteenth-Century Louisbourg," in Kenneth Donovan, ed., *Cape Breton at 200: Historical Essays in Honour of the Island's Bicentennial* (Sydney, Nova Scotia: University College of Cape Breton Press, 1985), 2–3.

15. Kenneth Donovan, "Slaves and their Owners in Île Royale, 1713–1760," *Acadiensis* 25, no.1 (1995), 3–32.

16. Robin W. Winks, *The Blacks in Canada: A History* (Montreal: McGill-Queen's University Press, 1971), 9; Marcel Trudel, *Dictionnaire des esclaves et de leurs propriétaires au Canada francais* (Quèbec: presses de l'Université Laval, 1990), xiii-xxviii. See also Marcel Trudel, *L'Esclavage au Canada français: Histoire et conditions de l'esclavage* (Quèbec: Presses de l'Université Laval, 1960), 20–21.

17. Brett Rushforth, "Savage Bonds: Indian Slavery and Alliance in New France." Ph.D. diss., University of California-Davis, 2003; Cornelius J. Jaenen, *Friend and Foe: Aspects of French-Amerindian Cultural Contact in the Sixteenth and Seventeenth Centuries* (New York: Columbia University Press, 1976), 138; Dale Miquelon, *New France, 1701–1744: A Supplement to Europe* (Toronto: McClelland and Stewart, 1987), 238–39; Trudel, L'Esclavage au Canada, 60–64; J. R. Miller, *Skyscrapers Hide the Heavens: A History of Indian-White Relations in Canada* (Toronto: University of Toronto Press, 1989), 45; James Cleland Hamilton. "The Panis: An Historical Outline of Canadian Indian Slavery in the Eighteenth Century." *Proceedings of the Canadian Institute* (February 1897), 19–27.

18. D.W. Meinig, *The Shaping of America*, (New Haven: Yale University Press, 1986), 171. For a contemporary description of the Black Code, see Le Romain, "Negroes," in *Encyclopedia, Selections: Diderot, d'Alembert, and a Society of Men of Letters*, translated with an introduction by Nelly S. Hoyt and Thomas Cassirer (Indianapolis: Bobbs-Merrill, 1965), 258–73. The Black Code has been printed in Mederic Louis Elie Moreau de Saint-Mèry, ed., *Loix et constitutions des colonies francoises* (Paris, 1784–1790). A complete version is available in *Le Code Noir, au Recueil des Reglemens* (Basse-Terre, Gaudeloupe, 1980), 446.

19. Cornelius J. Jaenen, *The Role of the Church in New France* (Toronto: University of Toronto Press, 1976), 152.

20. Inventory of the estate of Elie Thesson *dit* La Floury, 22 March 1741, CAOM, G 2, vol. 197, dossier 143. By 22 March 1741, there were 448 pounds of butter in the La Floury storehouse, together with three sickles. For background on the La Floury family and business operations, see Kenneth Donovan, "Property of Elie Thesson dit La Floury," unpublished paper, Fortress of Louisbourg Library, Louisbourg National Historic Site of Canada, 1992.

21. Sale of the slave Rosalie, 19 June 1736, CAOM, G 3, 2039–1, pièce 168.

22. James W. St. G. Walker, *The Black Loyalists: The Search for a Promised Land in Nova Scotia and Sierra Leone, 1783–1870* (New York, 1976), 41.

23. The Naval Office Shipping Lists for Nova Scotia, 1730–1820, in the Public Record Office, London, 1981, p. 132. The *Success*, a thirty-ton schooner under Captain Mathew Milbourn, had a three-man crew. Registered in Antigua on 18 April 1750, the *Success* was owned by Charles Hay and Company. Microfilm copy consulted from Memorial University, St. John's, Newfoundland.

24. *Halifax Gazette* (Halifax). 30 May 1752. For some of Mauger's trading activities at Louisbourg, see the sale of the cargo of the schooner *Speedwell*, with Joshua Mauger as the supplier of the cargo, Louisbourg, 8 May to 14 August 1751 , AC, C11B, vol. 30, fols. 123–34.

271

25. Louisbourg residents debarking at La Rochelle, 28 April 1759, AC, C11B, vol. 38, fol. 268.

26. T. A. Crowley, "Government and Interests: French Colonial Administration at Louisbourg 1713–1758," Ph.D. diss., Duke University, 1975, 298; J. F. Bosher, "Jean Laborde," *Dictionary of Canadian Biography* 4:421.

27. Sale of a slave from the schooner *New Brunswick*, Louisbourg. 12 November 1756, no. 19, B, 6112, A.C.M. The complete court case includes documents numbered from 14 to 34.

28. Louisbourg residents debarking at La Rochelle, 28 April 1759, AC, C11B, vol. 38, fol. 267.

29. Declaration by Nicolas Larcher that Anne Honiche Nanon was his slave in Louisbourg, 5 April 1762, Admiralty of France, 4th register, AC, F 1B4, fol. 16. For details on Larcher, see Christopher Moore, "Nicolas Larcher," *Dictionary of Canadian Biography* 4:438–39; Nicolas Larcher, AC, E256, Dossiers Personnels, Archives de la Marine.

30. Robert Louis Stein, *The French Slave Trade in the Eighteenth Century: An Old Regime Business* (Madison: University of Wisconsin Press, 1979), 71–72.

31. Inventory and sale of the estate of Marie Marguerite Rose, CAOM, G2, vol. 212, dossier 552, 27 August 1757.

32. List of people at the Captain's table on the ship *Le Comte de Maurepas*, Bayonne, 30 May 1749, AC, F5 B. No folio number given.

33. See Donovan, "Slavery in Cape Breton, 1713–1810."

34. Ira Berlin, *Many Thousands Gone: The First Two Centuries of Slavery in North America* (Cambridge, Mass.: Harvard University Press, 1998), 47.

35. Peter Faneuil to Thomas Kilby, Boston, 20 June 1737, Faneuil Letter Book, Baker Library, Harvard University, Boston.

36. Captain James Spellen of New York sold the slave Jean in Louisbourg on 27 April 1753, and was also trading in Halifax during 1753. Sale of the slave Jean, 27 April 1753, CAOM, G 3, 2047–2, no. 74. For Spellen in Halifax, see the *Halifax Gazette* (Halifax), 10 November 1753.

37. The six children included Anne Louise, Charles Pierre, Marguerite Louise, Jean Pierre, Bertrand Joseph, and Josephine Louise. For the children of Pierre Boullot and Jeanne Magdelaine Richard, see the family reconstitution file at Fortress Louisbourg National Historic Site, and Louisbourg residents debarking at La Rochelle, 28 April 1759, AC, C11B, vol. 38, fol. 271.

38. Declaration of Pierre Boullot, 23 June 1762, Archives Departmentales, St. Servan, Brittany, Ile and Valine, 9B8, fol. 99.

39. Louisbourg residents debarking at La Rochelle, 28 April 1759, AC, CIIB, vol. 38, fol. 271. For details regarding Boullot's voyages from Martinique to Louisbourg, see AC, C7, 41, Dossiers Personnels, Archives de la Marine. For the death of Marie Flore's son Denis on 25 September 1760 in France, see Registre Paroissial St Jean des Champs, Normandy; for a declaration by Pierre Boullot that he had the slave Marie Flore for 20 years, see registers of the admiralty of St Malo, 23 June 1762, cited in research note, Madame Michèle Godret to A. J. B. Johnston, Paris, 4 March 1997. This letter and note is on file at the Fortress of Louisbourg archives.

40. Jaenen, *The Role of the Church*, 151–53; Winks, *The Blacks in Canada*, 12. See also Marcel Trudel, "L'Attitude de l'église Catholique vis-à-vis l'esclavage au Canada français," *Canadian Historical Association Report* (1961); "The Attitude of the Roman Catholic Church toward the Negro during Slavery," in W. D. Weatherford, *American Churches and the Negro* (Boston, 1957); Mary Veronica Miceli, "The Influence of the Roman Catholic Church on Slavery in Colonial Louisiana under French Domination, 1718–1763," Ph.D. diss., Tulane University, 1979. More recent scholarship has challenged the role of all Christian churches, citing an "African spiritual holocaust" in which the psychological balm of Christianity helped to control slaves. See Jon F. Sensbach, "Charting a Course in Early African-American History," *William and Mary Quarterly* 50, no. 2 (April 1993): 401; Norrece T. Jones, *Born a Child of Freedom, Yet a Slave: Mechanisms of Slave Control and Strategies of Resistance in Antebellum South Carolina* (Middletown, Conn.: Wesleyan University Press, 1990); Peter Kolchin, *Unfree Labor: American Slavery and Russian Serfdom* (Cambridge, Mass.: Belknap Press of Harvard University Press, 1987); and Jon Butler, *Awash in a Sea of Faith: Christianizing the American People* (Cambridge, Mass.: Harvard University Press, 1990).

41. Le Romain, "Negroes," 270. See also E. V. Goveia, *The West Indian Slave Laws of the Eighteenth Century* (Barbados, 1970), 39.

42. Many plantation managers opposed religious instruction of the slaves in the West Indies. The French Catholic Church in the sugar islands

during the eighteenth century was also a pale imitation of the church in France. See Robert Forster, "Slavery in Virginia and Saint-Domingue in the Late Eighteenth Century," in Philip Boucher, ed., *Proceedings of the Thirteenth and Fourteenth Meetings of the French Colonial Historical Society* (Lanham, Md.: University Press of America, 1990), 9; Eugene D. Genovese, *Roll, Jordan, Roll: The World the Slaves Made* (New York: Pantheon Books, 1974), 174; C. L. R. James, *The Black Jacobins: Toussaint L'Ouverture and the San Domingo Revolution* (London: Secker and Warburg, 1938); Alfred Metraux, *Voodoo in Haiti, trans.* H. Charteris (New York: Schocken Books, 1972); A. Gisler, *L'Esclavage aux Antilles françaises (XVIIe–XIXe siècle): Contribution au problème de l'esclavage* (Paris: Karthala, 1981).

43. For the baptism of Anne Honiche Nanon, see the declaration by Nicolas Larcher that he had his slave baptized at St Méry in 1759, in extracts from the registers, 1760 to 1777, AC, F1B4, fol. 16.

273

WORLDS OF WORK

Pre-Industrial Work, 1860–1880

Daniel Samson
Brock University

WORLDS OF WORK: PRE-INDUSTRIAL WORK, 1860–1880

Introduction by Daniel Samson

INTRODUCTION

Daniel Samson

When most people think about history they think of wars and revolutions—the big stuff, with lots of blood, and a certain amount of glory. They don't often think about work. This is odd because it's what most people spend most of their lives engaged in, and from which we derive most of our ability to live and much of our public sense of identity, and where we find many of our best friendships and relationships. This is true today, but it was even more true for eighteenth- and nineteenth-century immigrants, many of whom arrived in the colonies with nothing but their labouring bodies. We also tend to think of immigrants as settlers—as arriving, getting a land grant, clearing the land, and setting up a farm. For many, this was in fact the case. But for just as many—and in some periods more—arrival was followed by a search for the employment that might provide the money they would need to set up that farm, or even to pay rent as a tenant. Indeed, many established farms were economically marginal operations that required the men to spend months away at waged work, which in turn left the work of the farm to the wife and children. This work was usually unskilled—labouring jobs in lumber camps, canal and other forms of construction, or farm labour. For some, this was a transitional phase—a way to get the cash to start the farm or the small workshop—but for many others it was all they would ever obtain. And even for those who successfully established farms, few would establish themselves so well that they could provide for the many sons and daughters that nineteenth-century families produced. Many in the next generation found themselves working in lumber camps, mines, or the farms and homes of their more prosperous neighbours.

The nineteenth century was also a time of significant change in work. Britain was "the workshop of the world," and led the changes that we now call the Industrial Revolution. Whereas up until the late eighteenth and early nineteenth centuries most people worked on farms, this was changing as cities grew and industrial production began to transform where things were produced, how, and by whom. In the past, articles such as fabrics, shoes, tools, and food were produced either in the home or in small local workshops. The advent of new technologies and the new forms of factory production increasingly meant that artisans stopped working for themselves and began working for others in factories. Agricultural production was also changing dramatically, much of it fuelled by mechanization and the consolidation of many smaller farms into larger ones. More machinery and bigger farms meant fewer people were needed in the country. In short, over the course of the nineteenth century, the basic structures of society changed dramatically: people who once lived on a farm in the country, produced for themselves, and achieved a modest independence now lived in a city, worked in a factory, produced for other people, and had become completely dependent on wages and a prosperous industrial economy. In the colonial period, this transformation was not yet complete (indeed, it's still not totally complete today—ask a farmer!), and most people still lived in that older framework. But signs of change were evident.

In this period before those changes, the world of work was remarkably diverse. Because the factory system was not yet established, most goods that were produced in the colonial economy were either staple products (timber, fish, minerals, farm produce), fairly uncomplicated manufactured products such as rope or shoes, or fine-skilled but technologically straightforward goods such as furniture or wooden sailing ships. For most people, at least part of their work entailed some form of labour on a farm. For others, especially

277

in urban centres, skilled work, based in the ancient traditions of apprentices, journeymen, and masters, still prevailed. Opportunities for women were very much restricted, mostly owing to social conventions that frowned on women engaging in the public (masculine) sphere of work. Much of the waged work that was available required little more than a strong body to cut down trees, to paddle a canoe, or to haul nets. All these jobs required skills—a knack, we might say, that allowed the workers to be very good at their jobs, but only the older urban skilled trades had craft guilds that formally taught (and protected) the traditional skills of the Old World. Similarly, and also largely in the cities, opportunities for female employment grew, too, especially in domestic work and education. The growth of a prosperous middle class throughout colonial society meant that there were opportunities to work in wealthier people's homes. Increasingly, too, small artisanal producers expanded their operations, so that, rather than taking apprentices into their homes and businesses, they hired workers. There were many opportunities for work, in a wide range of areas, and these areas themselves were changing.

Sources are one of the major challenges facing the historian of work. While many skilled workers were literate, most unskilled workers weren't, and the result is that our sources tend to be written not by the workers themselves but by their employers and supervisors. And yet even these sources can tell us a lot about class relations, at least from one side of that class divide. The men who journeyed north with Franklin's expedition up the Coppermine River in 1819 were a mixed crew of British officers, French Canadian voyageurs, and Aboriginal guides. While we seldom hear the latter groups' voices, we certainly get a sense of their masters' views of the workers, and even catch occasional glimpses of the servants' views of their masters. Similarly, the newspaper account of the opening of the railway in Albion Mines, Nova Scotia, in 1839 offers us a window not only on the celebration of a technological marvel of the day, but also on how that celebration incorporated the class dynamics of an industrial community. Here, as part of a celebration, relations between masters and servants were quite good, although we can certainly sense elements of conflict. But quite often these relations could break down into strikes, and occasionally even riots. Events in Upper Canada on the still under construction Welland Canal descended into disorder several times in the 1840s, and the letters reproduced here illustrate not only the economic conflicts of early class societies, but also their religious and ethnic dimensions.

Historians have tried to understand the world of work, how it influenced colonial society, how it changed, how these changes affected people's lives, and how they reflected the broader changes of an industrializing world. While work itself was rarely discussed by historians before the 1960s, assumptions about the daily activities of colonial settlers lay underneath the surface. The conventional wisdom went something like this: Most farmers were neither rich nor poor, and all were more or less equal; the *voyageurs* were a group of hardy and colourful men who lived lives of adventure and daring; the advance of the factory system showed Canadians' ingenuity and sense of progress. These positions are in some ways true. But so too is it true that while many farms were expanding and investing in agricultural machinery, many other farms were unable to provide a future for their children, or even to survive; so too is it true that the dangers of the fur trade were many, and the "adventures" often ended in death in the North, and mourning mothers in the East; and so too is it true that the factory system ended many skilled workers' hopes for a respectable and independent future. The historians we read here offer us some sense of that complexity. Very little had changed for the work of the French Canadian *voyageurs* and Aboriginal guides described by Carolyn Podruchny. Their work was extremely dangerous, but their various *rendezvous* also allowed the traders and labourers to make their own world. Women's work, surveyed here by Elizabeth Jane Errington, was much less expansive, but even in their smaller confines women could find their own place. Rusty Bittermann tackles one of the great myths of colonial society—the independence offered by life on the land—and challenges us to think about what this means for our broader understanding of colonial society, and for life on the land today. Finally, T.W. Acheson shows us the important place of the craft traditions in Saint John business and politics, though an importance that was changing. In the city and on the frontier, in the home and across the countryside, work set the pattern for most people's lives.

QUESTIONS

1. What drew people to the different worlds of work that we see in this chapter? What was Franklin paying the Dene for?
2. How vulnerable were workers in the nineteenth century?
3. How independent were workers' actions? Did they, as historians like to say, make their own worlds?
4. How did ethnicity affect one's place in the world of work? Were women restricted in their worlds?
5. How do these historians understand the place of work in nineteenth-century society? Do you see differences that go beyond their choices of subjects? Do they understand work differently?

FURTHER READINGS

Edith Burley, *Servants of the Honourable Company: Work, Discipline, and Conflicts in the Hudson's Bay Company, 1770–1879* (Toronto, Oxford University Press, 1997).

Marjorie Cohen, *Women's Work, Markets and Economic Development in Nineteenth-Century Ontario* (Toronto: University of Toronto Press 1988).

Paul Craven, ed., *Labouring Lives: Work and Workers in Nineteenth-Century Ontario* (Toronto, University of Toronto Press, 1995).

Bryan Palmer, *Working-Class Experience: Rethinking the History of Canadian Labour, 1800–1991,* 2nd edition (Toronto, McClelland & Stewart, 1992).

Graeme Wynn, *Timber Colony: A Historical Geography of Early Nineteenth Century New Brunswick* (Toronto: University of Toronto Press 1981).

279

▲ Document 1: Chinese Miners Washing Gold

280

William G. R. Hind, *Chinese Miners Washing Gold*, 1862. "Move west young man!" was the cry heard throughout North America as eastern farmlands overflowed and gold was discovered in California in 1849. But many of those young men had moved east, from China. By 1871, almost 5 percent of British Columbians were Chinese immigrants. Miners and adventurers came to California, but many moved north as that rush declined and another emerged in the Yukon and British Columbia in the 1860s. Is there anything unusual about these workers?

Source: McCord Museum, Montreal, M609.

▲ Document 2: Images of Voyageurs

William G. R. Hind, *Resting on the Portage*, 1863.

281

Source: Library and Archives Canada, C-013980.

▲ Document 3: Shooting the Rapids

● Frances Anne Hopkins, *Shooting the Rapids*, 1879. The long days, sustained hard work, danger, and equally often the sheer boredom of work in the fur trade meant that adventurous representations such as Anne Frances Hopkins' were much less realistic than Hind's unexciting but probably more realistic depiction of fur-trader guides from 1862. While their work was challenging and often dangerous, it was also simply uneventful. These artists both travelled through the west in the 1860s, but offered us very different views of the life of the voyageur. Hopkins's image is much better known than Hind's. Why? How do such representations affect our understanding of fur-trade society?

Source: Library and Archives Canada, C-002774 K.

▲ Document 4: British Naval Officers, *Canadian Voyageurs*, and Chipewyan (Dene) Travel North

NARRATIVE OF A JOURNEY
to the shores of the
POLAR SEA,
in
THE YEARS 1819-20-21-22.
by
JOHN FRANKLIN, Capt. R.N., F.R.S., M.W.S.,
and commander of the expedition.

1820, July 18. EARLY this morning the stores were distributed to the three canoes. Our stock of provision unfortunately did not amount to more than sufficient for one day's consumption, exclusive of two barrels of flour, three cases of preserved meats, some chocolate, arrow-root, and portable soup, which we had brought from England, and intended to reserve for our journey to the coast the next season. Seventy pounds of moose meat and a little barley were all that Mr. Smith was enabled to give us. It was gratifying, however, to perceive that this scarcity of food did not depress the spirits of our Canadian companions, who cheerfully loaded their canoes, and embarked in high glee after they had received the customary dram. At noon we bade farewell to our kind friend Mr. Smith. The crews commenced a lively paddling song on quitting the shore, which was continued until we had lost sight of the houses.

[....]

The wind and swell having subsided in the afternoon, we re-embarked and steered towards the western point of the Big-Island of Mackenzie [...] We coasted along the eastern side of the bay, its western shore being always visible, but the canoes were exposed to the hazard of being broken by the numerous sunken rocks, which were scattered in our track. We encamped for the night on a rocky island, and by eight A.M. on the following morning, arrived at Fort Providence, which is situated twenty-one miles from the entrance of the bay. The post is exclusively occupied by the North-West Company, the Hudson's Bay Company having no settlement to the northward of Great Slave Lake. We found Mr. Wentzel and our interpreter Jean Baptiste Adam here, with one of the Indian guides: but the chief of the tribe and his hunters were encamped with their families, some miles from the fort, in a good situation for fishing. Our arrival was announced to him by a fire on the top of a hill, and before night a messenger came to communicate his intention of seeing us next morning. The customary present, of tobacco and some other articles, was immediately sent to him.

[....]

I endeavoured to explain the objects of our mission in a manner best calculated to ensure his exertions in our service. With this view, I told him that we were sent out by the greatest chief in the world, who was the sovereign also of the trading companies in the country; that he was the friend of peace, and had the interest of every nation at heart. Having learned that his children in the north, were much in want of articles of merchandize, in consequence of the extreme length and difficulty of the present route; he had sent us to search for a passage by the sea, which if found, would enable large vessels to

Source: Sir John Franklin, *Narrative of a Journey to the Shores of the Polar Sea, in the Years 1819-20-21-22* (London, J. Murray, 1824), 301-2, 312-3, 316-8, 321-2, 323-5, 334-5, 338-40, 341-3, 344-6, and 347-51.

transport great quantities of goods more easily to their lands. That we had not come for the purpose of traffic, but solely to make discoveries for their benefit, as well as that of every other people. That we had been directed to inquire into the nature of all the productions of the countries we might pass through, and particularly respecting their inhabitants. That we desired the assistance of the Indians in guiding us, and providing us with food; finally, that we were most positively enjoined by the great chief to recommend that hostilities should cease throughout this country; and especially between the Indians and the Esquimaux, whom he considered his children, in common with other natives; [...] on his return he and his party should be remunerated with cloth, ammunition, tobacco, and some useful iron materials, besides having their debts to North-West Company discharged.

The chief, whose name is Akaitcho or Big-foot, replied by a renewal of his assurances, that he and his party would attend us to the end of our journey, and that they would do their utmost to provide us with the means of subsistence. He admitted that his tribe had made war upon the Esquimaux, but said they were now desirous of peace, and unanimous in their opinion as to the necessity of all who accompanied us abstaining from every act of enmity against that nation. He added, however, that the Esquimaux were very treacherous, and therefore recommended that we should advance towards them with caution.

As the water was unusually high this season, the Indian guides recommended our going by a shorter route to the Copper-Mine River than that they had first proposed to Mr. Wentzel, and they assigned as a reason for the change, that the rein-deer would be sooner found upon this track. They then drew a chart of the proposed route on the floor with charcoal, exhibiting a chain of twenty-five small lakes extending towards the north, about one half of them connected by a river which flows into Slave Lake, near Fort Providence.

[....]

We presented to the chief, the two guides, and the seven hunters, who had engaged to accompany us, some cloth, blankets, tobacco, knives, daggers, besides other useful iron materials, and a gun to each; also a keg of very weak spirits and water, which they kept until the evening, as they had to try their gun before dark, and make the necessary preparations for commencing the journey on the morrow. They, however, did not leave us so soon, as the chief was desirous of being present, with his party, at the dance, which was given in the evening to our Canadian voyagers. They were highly entertained by the vivacity and agility displayed by our companions in their singing and dancing: and especially by their imitating the gestures of a Canadian, who placed himself in the most ludicrous postures; and, whenever this was done, the gravity of the chief gave way to violent bursts of laughter. In return of the gratification Akaitcho had enjoyed, he desired his young men to exhibit the Dog-Rib Indian dance; and immediately they ranged themselves in a circle, and, keeping their legs widely separated, began to jump simultaneously sideways; their bodies were bent, their hands placed on their hips, and they uttered forcibly the interjection *tsa* at each jump. Devoid as were their attitudes of grace, and their music of harmony, we were much amused by the novelty of the exhibition.

August 1.—This morning the Indians set out, intending to wait for us at the mouth of the Yellow-Knife River. We engaged another Canadian voyager at this place, and the Expedition then consisted of twenty-eight persons, including the officers, and the wives of three of our voyagers, who were brought for the purpose of making shoes and clothes for the men at the winter establishment; there were also three children, belonging to two of these women˙.

[....]

August 8.—During this day we crossed five portages, passing over a very bad road. The men were quite exhausted with fatigue by five P.M., when we were obliged to encamp on the borders of the fifth lake, in which the fishing nets were set. We began this evening to issue some portable soup and arrow-root, which our companions relished very much; but this food is too unsubstantial to support their vigour under their daily exhausting labour, and we could not furnish them with a sufficient quantity even of this to satisfy their desires. We commenced our labours on the next day in a very wet uncomfortable state, as it had rained through the night until four A.M. The fifth grassy lake was crossed, and four others, with their intervening portages, and we returned to the river by a portage of one thousand four hundred and fifteen paces.

The chief having told us that this was a good lake for fishing, we determined on halting for a day or two to recruit our men, of whom three were lame, and several others had swelled legs. The chief himself went forward to look after the hunters, and promised to make a fire as a signal if they had killed any rein-deer. All the Indians had left us in the course of yesterday and to-day to seek these animals, except the guide Keskarrah.

[....]

August 13.—We caught twenty fish this morning, but they were small, and furnished but a scanty breakfast for the party. Whilst this meal was preparing, our Canadian voyagers, who had been for some days past murmuring at their meagre diet, and striving to get the whole of our little provision to consume at once, broke out into open discontent, and several of them threatened they would not proceed forward unless more food was given to them. This conduct was the more unpardonable, as they saw we were rapidly approaching the fires of the hunters, and that provision might soon be expected. I, therefore, felt the duty incumbent on me to address them in the strongest manner on the danger of insubordination, and to assure them of my determination to inflict the heaviest punishment on any that should persist in their refusal to go on, or in any other way attempt to retard the Expedition. I considered this decisive step necessary, having learned from the gentlemen, most intimately acquainted with the character of the Canadian voyagers, that they invariably try how far they can impose upon every new master, and that they will continue to be disobedient and intractable if they once gain any ascendency over him. I must admit, however, that the present hardships of our companions were of a kind which few could support without murmuring, and no one could witness without a sincere pity for their sufferings.

After this discussion we went forward until sunset. In the course of the day we crossed seven lakes and as many portages. Just as we had encamped we were delighted to see four of the hunters arrive with the flesh of two rein-deer. This seasonable supply, though only sufficient for this evening's and the next day's consumption, instantly revived the spirits of our companions, and they immediately forget all their cares. As we did not, after this period, experience any deficiency of food during this journey, they worked extremely well, and never again reflected upon us they had done before, for rashly bringing them into an inhospitable country, where the means of subsistence could not be procured.

After starting we first crossed the Orkney Lake, then a portage which brought us to Sandy Lake, and here we missed one of our barrels of powder, which the steersman of the canoe then recollected had been left the day before. He and two other men were sent back to search for it, in the small canoe. The rest of the party proceeded to the portage on the north side of the Grizzle-Bear Lake, where the hunters had made a deposit of meat, and there encamped to await their return, which happened at nine P.M., with the powder. We perceived from the direction of this lake, that considerable labour would have been spared if we had continued our course yesterday instead of striking off at the guide's suggestion, as the bottom of this lake cannot be far separated from either Hunter's Lake or the one to the westward of it. The chief and all the Indians went off to hunt, accompanied by Pierre St. Germain, the interpreter. They returned at night, bringing some meat, and reported that they had put the carcases of several rein-deer *en cache*. These were sent for early next

285

© 2015 Nelson Education Ltd.

morning, and as the weather was unusually warm, the thermometer, at noon, being 77°, we remained stationary all day, that the women might prepare the meat for keeping, by stripping the flesh from the bones and drying it in the sun over a slow fire. The hunters were again successful, and by the evening we had collected the carcases of seventeen deer. As this was a sufficient store to service us until we arrived at Winter Lake, the chief proposed that he and his hunters should proceed to that place and collect some provision against our arrival. He also requested that we would allow him to be absent ten days to provide his family with clothing, as the skin of the rein-deer is unfit for that purpose after the month of September. We could not refuse to grant such a reasonable request, but caused St. Germain to accompany him, that his absence might not exceed the appointed time. [...]

August 19.—Embarking at seven next morning, we paddled to the western extremity of the lake, and there found a small river, which flows out of it to the S.W. To avoid as strong rapid at its commencement, we made a portage, and then crossed to the north bank of the river, where the Indians recommended that the winter establishment should be erected, and we soon found that the situation they had chosen possessed all the advantages we could desire. The trees were numerous, and of a far greater size than we had supposed them to be in a distant view, some of the pines being thirty or forty feet high, and two feet in diameter at the root.

The united length of the portages we had crossed, since leaving Fort Providence, is twenty-one statute miles and a half; and as our men had to traverse each portage four times, with a load of one hundred and eighty pounds, and return three times light, they walked in the whole upwards of one hundred and fifty miles. The total length of our voyage from Chipewyan is five hundred and fifty-three miles.

A heavy rain, on the 23d, prevented the men from working, either at the building, or going for meat; but on the next day the weather was fine, and they renewed their labours. The thermometer, that day did not rise higher than 42°, and it fell to 31° before midnight. On the morning of the 25th, we were surprised by some early symptoms of the approach of winter; the small pools were frozen over, and a flock of geese passed to the southward. Akaitcho arrived with his party, and we were greatly disappointed at finding they had stored up only fifteen rein-deer for us. St. Germain informed us, that having heard of the death of the chief's brother-in-law, they had spent several day in bewailing his loss, instead of hunting. We learned also, that the decease of this man had caused another party of the tribe, who had been sent by Mr. Wentzel to prepare provision for us on the banks of the Copper-Mine River, to remove to the shores of the Great Bear Lake, distant from our proposed route. Mortifying as these circumstances were, they produced less painful sensations than we experienced in the evening, by the refusal of Akaitcho to accompany us in the proposed descent of the Copper-Mine River. When Mr. Wentzel, by my direction, communicated to him my intention of proceeding at once on that service, he desired a conference with me upon the subject, which being immediately granted, he began, by stating, that the very attempt would be rash and dangerous as the weather was cold, the leaves were falling, some geese had passed to the southward, and the winter would shortly set in; and that, as he considered the lives of all who went on such a journey would be forfeited, he neither would go himself, nor permit his hunters to accompany us. He said there was no wood within eleven days' march, during which time we could not have any fire, as the moss, which the Indians use in their summer excursions, would be too wet for burning, in consequence of the recent rains; that we should be forty days in descending the Copper-Mine River, six of which would be expended in getting to its banks, and that we might be blocked up by the ice in the next moon; and during the whole journey the party must experience great suffering for a want of food, as the rein-deer had already left the river.

He was now reminded that these statements were very different from the account be had given, both at Fort Providence and on the route hither; and that, up to this moment, we had been encouraged by his conversation to expect that the party might descend the Copper-Mine River, accompanied by the Indians. He replied, that at the former place he had been unacquainted with our slow mode of travelling, and that the alteration in his opinion arose from the advance of winter.

We now informed him that we were provided with instruments by which we could ascertain the state of the air and water, and that we did not imagine the winter to be so near as he supposed; however, we promised to return on discovering the first change in the season. He was also told that all the baggage being left behind, our canoes, would now, of course, travel infinitely more expeditiously than any thing he had hitherto witnessed. Akaitcho appeared to feel hurt, that we should continue to press the matter further, and answered with some warmth: "Well, I have said every thing I can urge, to dissuade you from going on this service, on which, it seems, you wish to sacrifice your own lives, as well as the Indians who might attend you: however, if after all I have said, you are determined to go, some of my young men shall join the party, because it shall not be said that we permitted you to die alone after having brought you hither; but from the moment they embark in the canoes, I and my relatives shall lament them as dead."

*The following is the list of the officers and men who composed the Expedition on its departure from Fort Providence:

John Franklin, Lieutenant of the Royal Navy and Commander.
John Richardson, M.D., Surgeon of the Royal Navy.
Mr. George Back, of the Royal Navy, Admiralty Midshipman.
Mr. Robert Hood, of the Royal Navy, Admiralty Midshipman.
Mr. Frederick Wentzel, Clerk to the North-West Company.
John Hepburn, English seaman.

Canadian Voyagers.

Joseph Peltier,	Gabriel Beauparlant,
Matthew Pelonquin, dit Crèdit,	Vincenza Fontano,
Solomon Belanger,	Registe Vaillant,
Joseph Benoit,	Jean Baptiste Parent,
Joseph Gagné,	Jean Baptiste Belanger,
Pierre Dumas,	Jean Baptiste Belleau,
Joseph Forcier,	Emanuel Cournoyée,
Igance Perrault,	Michel Teroahauté, an Iroquois.
Francois Samandré.	
Pierre St. Germain,	Chipewyan Bois Brulés.

287

▲ Document 5: Agricultural and Domestic Wages

Emigrants Wages in Upper Canada, Distress, &c.

In the recent discussions which have taken place on the condition of emigrants arriving from the Mother Country, many of whom, it must be confessed, are in a state of great wretchedness, the rate of wages has been estimated for both Provinces. In this Province, it is, perhaps, a more difficult matter to fix a standard that in Upper Canada, because few of the inhabitants of French origin have more land than they can cultivate with the aid of their families, and, therefore, they rarely employ hired servants, except in hay time and harvest. In Upper Canada, it is much more common to hire agricultural labourers, and there the rates of wages may be more easily ascertained. We are enabled, on good authority, to state, that in the Newcastle District, in that Province, where the Hon. Peter Robinson is at present engaged in locating settlers, the following were the general prices paid during the past month:

Carpenters, 7s. 6d. per diem | without board
Masons ... ditto ... |

Labourers, by the day, 2s. 6d. to 3s. and found in board. By the month, 40s. to 60s. and boarded, and the same rate is paid to those who engage by the year.

Women servants, living in the family, earn from 15s. to 20s. per month.

It is stated, that the tailors and shoemakers find ready employment in that District; and that a brickmaker, having a little capital to commence with, would find an advantageous opening. Thus, there is encouragement in that quarter, at least, for a portion of the strangers who have arrived this year in our harbour.

A society has been set on foot in Montreal, for the Relief of Destitute Emigrants: the following is the third of a series of resolutions, adopted at the meeting, and really, after all, with temporary shelter, except in cases of sickness, (and that is otherwise provided for,) it is the only relief which Emigrants require.

> "That it be an instruction to this Committee, to confine their labours chiefly to the object of forwarding destitute Emigrants to those parts of Upper and Lower Canada, in which they may be most likely to obtain labour and lands". [...]

> "Notice. As the public hospitals of this city have been found insufficient to afford medical assistance to the encreasing [sic] number of Emigrants arriving daily, and threatening the city with contagious diseases—the undersigned Medical Practitioners, in conformity with the request made by the Emigrant Society, established to relieve the distress of the destitute emigrants, have associated themselves to conduct a Dispensary, to be connected with the building about to be erected, on the plains of St. Anne, where indigent emigrants may obtain, *gratis*, advice and

Source: "Agricultural and Domestic Wages," *Quebec Mercury*, 28th June, 1831.

medicine every day from 7 a.m. to 8 a.m. upon the recommendation of one of the Committee of said society, signed by

Dr. Stephenson, Dr. Demers, Dr. Vallee".

This is a point to which we have for some time contemplated calling to the public attention. [...]

There is certainly much distress amongst those who remain in the cities, but there is certainly, not a small portion of the emigrants, who, so long as they can subsist by exciting sympathy and extracting alms from the more wealthy, will not make an exertion to gain a livelihood by a more active, but certain operation. From circumstances which have recently come to our knowledge, we are inclined to think that much of this distress arises from an unwillingness on the part of the emigrants to open their eyes to their actual situation, to be convinced that they must submit consequences of the temporary glut of labor the arrival of such unexampled numbers has occasioned, and to take such wages as are going. Two instances have been mentioned to us, from sources every way entitled to credit, where emigrants have refused employment, not because the wages tendered to them were insufficient for their support, but because they not such as they *expected* to obtain. [...]

But although there is a redundance of labor in the immediate neighbourhood of the cities and along the banks of the St. Lawrence, the rate of wages, we have above given, in Upper Canada, shews that labor is not there a superabundant commodity, and there is a demand for it in the Eastern Townships. [...]

We have no wish to discourage any benevolent plan for the relief of emigrants; on the contrary, we shall always feel happy in promoting any thing which may tend to their permanent welfare, but of this we feel certain, that so long as those who are hale and able to work, so long will there be a burthensome list ready to avail themselves of the charitable feelings of the community; and therefore, in administering assistance great caution and discrimination are necessary, or the public will be duped by a set of people who had rather stoop to beg than earn a livelihood by honest labour.

289

▲ Document 6: Workers, Managers, and Townspeople Celebrate the Dawning Age of Railroads

> *The first railway built in Nova Scotia (and the second in British North America) had its first public run in September 1839. The railway connected the growing industrial town of Albion Mines with the shipping facilities at nearby New Glasgow. While we should be careful in thinking about the future it signaled (something the participants could not have imagined), it was clearly an important day marked by a very enthusiastic celebration. What is the significance of the carefully ordered parade? What do the parade and the later feast tell us about the nature of class and gender in an early industrial town? The General Mining Association was a British-financed mining company that dominated the coalfields of Nova Scotia from 1827 into the 1870s.*

One of the most novel and imposing spectacles ever witnessed in this portion of the world took place on Thursday last on the premises of the General Mining Association. [...]

The event [...] was the running of the locomotive carriages for the first time on the completion of the new Rail Road. [...]

The prediction of an unusual demonstration of feeling was amply verified on the morning of the 19th [September]. At 6 o'clock our little town presented a scene of bustle and agitation, which at that time is rarely exhibited by its peaceful inhabitants. On the arrival of the steamer *Pocohontas* at about half past 6 o'clock, every street and alley was crowded with the votaries of enjoyment making their way in the direction of the boat, and bound for Mount Rundell [the large and by the standards of the day quite luxurious home of the manager of the company] on a pilgrimage of pleasure.

The scene of embarkation was one of great excitement and interest. [...] Half an hour after the tolling of the bell, the note of preparation for the steamer wending her way, having on board upwards of 300 souls, commencing, we have no hesitation in stating as great a portrait of grace and beauty as were ever simultaneously on her deck before. The Albion Steamer, which the agents of the Association had also politely dispatched for the gratuitous accommodation of the Volunteer Artillery Company, arrived some time after the other; they picked up a few choice spirits who were unprepared to be sent in the first boat. These, however, did not long maintain undisturbed possession of the quarter deck—in a short time she was crowded to over-flowing. [...] The tedium of the passage up the river, occasioned by a head wind and a rapid tide against us, was beguiled by a succession of lively and plaintive airs—among which, the "Caledonian Rant", "We'll gang away to yon home" and "The Campbells are coming" may be stated as the most exhilarating and happiest specimens of the musician's art. Our arrival at the New Glasgow bridge was announced by a volley of artillery. [...]

The procession started at McKay's Hotel at 11 o'clock, a.m., and moved off in the following order:

Source: "Albion Mines Locomotive Steam Engine Celebration," *Mechanic and Farmer* (Pictou, Nova Scotia) 25 September 1839.

FIRST

100 horses, mounted by their respective drivers—Horses and men decorated, carrying flags.

Device 1st flag—a large Crown in the centre; a Rose, Shamrock, Thistle, and Mayflower in the corners.

Motto—Long life to Queen Victoria.

Device 2nd flag—2 horses with 2 wagons, each loaded with coal, coming out of the pit bottom, meeting 2 Colliers going to their work, with picks under their arms.

Motto—Success to the Coal Trade; as the Old Cock Crows, the young one learn.

Device 3rd flag—Blue, Red, and White Silk flag.

SECOND

Enginemen with Flag.

Device—A Steam Engine—Pit Frame etc, drawing coal [much like a steam-driven conveyor belt which lifted the coal out of the shaft].

Motto—   Long may the Company flourish
And their servants rejoice;
May Steam Navigation never fail
To burn our Coal and send us sale.

FOURTH

Colliers, carrying two Flags.

Device 1st Flag—2 Colliers in the Board [in the mine] at their work, and a horse appearing from behind the Coal, coming out with a Skip load of coal.

Motto—   Though shrouded in darkness, yet from us proceed
A thing that is useful and all persons need.

Device 2nd Flag—A Locomotive engine at one end, a winding engine at the other; in the centre is 2 Colliers meeting, one going from the other to his work.

Motto—   United we stand, when divided we fall,
Unanimous as brethren.

FIFTH

The Freemasons, with Flags and Bagpipes.

SIXTH

The Foundrymen and Blacksmiths, with a Flag.

Device—Archimedes on one side, and Watt on the other.

Motto—   Ours and for us.

SEVENTH

Bricklayers and Stonemasons, with Flag.

Device—Tools of their Trade.

Motto—   Success to the Locomotive Engines, and all the Trades belonging to the Albion Mines.

EIGHTH

Carpenters, with a Flag.
Device—Square and Compass, &c.
Motto—   The Albion Mines and Joseph Smith, Esq.

NINTH

Bagpipes.

TENTH

Artillery, with Flags and Band.

ELEVENTH

Visitors on horseback.

The procession returned to the Rail Road station at 1 o'clock, when a salute was fired by the Artillery. The most important part of the ceremony, the running of the Locomotives, was to take place at 2 o'clock, p.m., the intervening time was spent in examining their construction, and admiring these most astonishing monuments of human ingenuity. They are universally allowed by competent judges to be engines of superior manufacture, and the various parts of their machinery are in the highest state of polish and repair. The Locomotives are three in number, and are called the Hercules, the John Buddle, and the Sampson [sic]. [Hercules and Samson were obvious choices for the names of these powerful machines. John Buddle was an important British mining engineer who had business connections with the GMA.]

On this occasion the first two only were called into active service. For though the false Delieah [variant spelling of Delilah, the biblical seductress who was said to have shorn Samson's hair, thus depriving him of his strength] would labour in vain to sap the physical energy of the modern Samson, especially when he has his steam up, yet the others were quite sufficient to discharge the duty, and the great antagonist of the Philistines is kept as a *corps de reserve* to be called into requisition on any pressing emergency.

At the appointed hour the carriages were cleared of the vulgar throng with which they were crowded, and instantly filled with those to whom the gentlemen of the Association had sent tickets of admission. In a few minutes both trains were in motion—the Hercules taking the lead having a train of 35 carriages, containing upwards of 700 souls. The John Buddle with an equal number of carriages and passengers followed in hot pursuit—by Jove it was a splendid sight to see those noble efforts of human mechanism, at the magic touch of the Engineers "walking it off like a thing of life", at a rapidity varying from 10 to 20 miles per hour and each having a tail infinitely longer than that sported by Dan O'Connel [sic] [a reference to Daniel O'Connell who led the fight for Catholic emancipation in Ireland], the representative of all of Ireland!!!

After running two trips in the Locomotive, all workmen again formed in procession and marched to four tables which were spread out for them opposite the office of the establishment, at which not less than 750 individuals partook of a repast. "There was none of your humbugging of French Sauces" but about 1200 lbs. of Beef and Mutton, 6 hhds. [a now antiquated English unit of measure; typically, it was a wooden barrel, the size of which varied (depending on time, locality, and what was being measured) but approximately 60 gallons (250 *l*)] of Ale, with bread and vegetables in abundance, with the other substantial of life, formed the principal items of the Bill of Fare, provided by the generosity of the Commissary General. The masticating apparatus of those seated at the table was speedily in operation, and were it possible that the appetite of the votaries of Epicurus could renew its virginity at every additional supply, we feel confident that the zest with which the *bon vivants* of the Albion Mines relished the good things of this life, could not, even under these circumstances, have been surpassed.

After drinking the health of the Queen, the prosperity of the General Mining Association, and long life and happiness to its Agents, they departed from the tables in the most perfect regularity and order. The Freemasons and Artillery partook of a lunch in one of the new houses, which they washed down with Brandy and water.

In the evening, a dinner was given by Mr. Smith [Joseph Smith, the manager of the Albion Mines] at which 150 persons were sumptuously entertained. On entering the Engine House, which was converted into a Saloon for the occasion, the effect produced on the mind was pleasing in the extreme. At the north end of the room, above the head of the President, the Ensign, and the Union Jack were seen in juxtaposition with the Star Spangled Banner of Republican America, indicative, we presume, of the friendly relations at present subsisting between these two mighty Empires. Two tables, capable of containing 200 persons, were spread on each side of the building. A small table made to cross the others was erected at the northern extremity of the hall, behind which, on an elevation of about two feet, stood the President's Chair. Richard Brown, esq. [The Association's senior manager in Nova Scotia], ("That Prince of Good Fellows") discharged the duty of President, assisted as Croupier by Joseph Smith, Esq., whose gentlemanly conduct during the course of the evening evinced in his anxiety to anticipate the desires of his guests, formed the theme of universal commendation. On the right and left of the President were seated the Hon. William Lawson, and Mssrs. Dickson, Holmes, Hatton, and Archibald, Members of the House of Assembly, and a number of the Clergy and Magistrates of the County. On the removal of the cloth, two carriages, each containing five decanters of wine, traversed both tables, on a *Rail Road*. This device had a capital effect, and its discovery elected a burst of applause from the guests, that shook the tenement to its foundation. In a moment after, away went the *vinous locomotives*, and the votaries of Silenus [a friend and teacher of Dionysus, the god of wine] propitiated the rosy divinity in copious libations of Champagne.

At about 9 o'clock, the scene of festivity was much enlivened by the unexpected appearance of the Ladies, who, at an earlier hour, had been entertained by Mrs. Smith at Mount Rundell [the home of the manager].

Their *entrée* into banqueting hall was greeted by nine deafening acclamations. The standing toasts were cast aside, and "Ladies, Heaven's last best gift to man", given by the President, which was drank with all the honors. The President called upon the individual who had last presented an offering on Hymen's altar, but none forthcoming, one of the fraternity who delight "to roam in bachelor meditation fancy free" discharged this duty in a highly effective manner. After remaining about a quarter of an hour, the Ladies made a precipitate retreat and the Lords of Creation were "left alone in their glory"; during their stay, however, they were much gratified and amused, and the visions of happiness which danced through their mind appeared equally delightful with those "which maidens dream of when they muse on love".

At about 10 o'clock, the President left the Chair, and the guests much gratified with the amusements of the day, departed in quest of accommodation for the night. During the course of the evening, several appropriate speeches were delivered, which, together with the toasts, our limits prevent us from inserting.

293

▲ Document 7: Correspondence on Strikes at the Welland Canal, Upper Canada, in 1845

THE "GREAT
SWIVEL LINK":
CANADA'S
WELLAND CANAL
TORONTO
THE CHAMPLAIN SOCIETY
2001

Thomas A. Begly to W.B. Robinson
21 September 1842
[NAC, RG 11, Vol. 116 *Letterbook 1838–1842*, #1227]

Mr. Killaly desires me to say that about fifty soldiers are to be permanently stationed at St. Catharines, the same number at Thorold, and the barracks at Broad Creek should be made for seventy five, comfortable dry &c and should be ready as soon as possible. For the Officers he has settled with the Military authorities to make them the usual weekly allowance for lodging. The Officers at Broad Creek Mr. Killaly does not well know what is to be done with but leaves that altogether to you. Mr. Killaly desires me to say that no inducements whatever are being held out to Connaught or other men going over to your work. [...]

Contractors to Magistrates of Niagara District
19 December 1842
[NAC, RG 11, Vol. 65-7, p.9]

We the undersigned Contractors upon the Welland Canal, do most respectfully recommend to the Magistrates of the Niagara District in Special Session assembled to withhold from all applicants Licences for Taverns and Groceries, at the Quarries and the vicinity of the operations upon this Canal, with the exception of those now authorised.

In offering this suggestion, we have in view the quiet and orderly prosecution to this Great Public Work in which we are intimately concerned, and the best interests of the labourers themselves.[1]

Samuel Power to William H. Merritt [Mayor of St. Catharines]
4 January 1843
[AO, F662, MS 74, *Merritt Papers*, Package 15]

[...] my prediction has been fulfilled, and the work suspended between the Junction and Marshville. The army being useless without a magistrate, I had recourse to Mr. Church, and found a willing ally in Mr. McDonagh the R.C. clergyman, who accompanied me to a party of the idlers. They promised to resume work tomorrow. I shall be in Marshville early and hope to see their pledge fulfilled. I also sent Bonnalie for Capt. Farrell, J.P. My reason for mentioning this is to shew the necessity for a resident Magistrate. Mr. Robinsons efforts would I fear be worse than useless as if his purpose were known of appointing his political partisans constables, the riots would occur more frequently, and assume a more

Source: Roberta M. Styran and Robert R. Taylor, The *"Great Swivel Link": Canada's Welland Canal* (Toronto, The Champlain Society, 2001). Reprinted with permission from The Champlain Society.

serious aspect, from the long cherished feelings of hostility existing between the Irish laborers, and the lower class of Orangemen, who it seems are Mr. R's especial favorites. I cordially detest ultra politics of every description, and hope that the laborers may not be unnecessarily exasperated by placing them beneath the surveillance of those whom they view as their old tyrants. While speaking on this subject, I should call your attention to the colored troops, who were <u>not</u> sent to Broad Creek until the sickly season had passed. The Baron de Rottenburg considers them most unsuitable for the duty which they now discharge. It is only by the most rigid discipline that the laborers can be governed but let us not necessarily provoke them. [...]

Hamilton H. Killaly to Rev. William P. McDonagh
7 January 1843
[NAC, RG 11, Vol. 117, *Letterbook 1842–1844*, #1679]

Upon being apprised of the intention of Government to dispense with the services of the Baron de Rottenburgh,[2] I represented to Council the necessity of securing, as far as possible, peace & order along the line of the works on the Welland Canal, which object I consider would be materially forwarded by their authorizing me to avail myself of the influence, which I know you to possess over the laborers, from your profession, from being from the same country with much the greater number of them, and from your being able to address them in their native language.

I have received directions for making this arrangement, and I have, therefore, to entreat that you will not lose a moment in going through the works generally, & exert all your authority, religious & moral, in repressing insubordination, & all tendency to outrage. I need not point out to you the several forcible points, which can be urged to induce them to conduct themselves peaceably. I think it necessary to mention but two matters, first wholly to discountenance the sale & use of spirits on the works, and secondly to represent to them that, <u>most unquestionably</u>, upon any riot of a serious nature occurring, the Government will stop the work wholly for a season and exonerate the Contractors from their obligations so far as time is concerned [...]

Power to Begly
25 August 1843
[NAC, RG 43, Vol. 2097, *Letterbook 1842–1843*, #2671]

[...] I shall now reply to the principal points adverted to in your letter [of the 21st][3] [...]

When the lake fever was raging at Broad Creek to such an extent, that at one time 800 persons were ill and 4 deaths occurred daily. [...]

My monthly reports even monthly descriptions of the frauds of the contractors, and consequent riots among the men, until I became wearied with reiterating the same tale, it may also be recollected that the impossibility of conducting the work under the old form of contract, when in such hands led me to suggest the clauses in the present contracts for the protection of the laborer ... after mature reflection I am convinced that if I should ever again be so unfortunate, as to be placed under similar circumstances in contracts with men strangers to every principle of honesty, and honor, regard to justice & prudence alone must compel me to pursue precisely the same course, and I am certain that the Board on reconsidering all the circumstances of the case will withdraw their censure, which I cannot help feeling was most undeserved. [...]

In opposition to the assertion the additional force consisted of <u>one man</u>, you have the solemn affirmation of Mr. Bonnalie, that he at once placed <u>35 men</u> on the work, and he must from time to time have placed much greater numbers, for I visited the work every week, and almost on every occasion directed him to increase the force on neglected parts but in addition to this his evidence affords a clear proof that the entire force consisting of several hundreds was placed upon the work by my direct orders acting on the part of the Board. [...]

The 3rd point adverted to by the Board is "my countenancing sub-contracting"!! an arrangement against which I have ever protested and prevent which I introduced a clause into the contract. [...]

David Thorburn to D. Daly[4]
10 January 1844
[NAC, RG11, Vol. 68-5 pp. 34–43]

From the riots and disturbances that have recently taken place on the line of the Welland Canal, I have deemed it to be my duty to give you for the information of the Governor General an outline of the proceedings and apparent exciting causes to riot and uneasiness by the labourers as well as the position of matters in general for the prevention of like recurrence. I have therefore the honor to state that for some time past the labourers have shown a disposition to be troublesome and to keep them in check has engaged the attention of Mr. Power the chief Engineer and the Constabulary or Police force, principally under the direction of Messrs MacFarlane and Hobson, J.P.s of the Township of Thorold; these gentlemen are the two Councillors for that Township and have at my request since I left for the Legislature, had a constant care for the preservation of the Peace especially from Thorold Mountain to the upper parts of the works; Mr. Bonnalie the Head Officer of the Police knew this and received from them every aid, instruction, countenance and direction. His general arrangements for the preservation of the Peace could not have been better with his officers, few in number considering the extent of canal from Thorold to Dunnville, Broad Creek and Port Colborne, and the distant stone quarries from the canal in all not less than fifty miles for intelligence has been transmitted to the paper quarter with the least possible delay upon the appearance of an outbreak. Thus giving confidence to the inhabitants of their vigilance and of that of the Civil and Military authorities who have at all times cordially cooperated for the keeping and promoting of order. [...]

Indeed there is no disquiet can occur on any part of the line without the knowledge of the Police. Such being the preventative position on the slightest outbreak steps are soon taken to put it down and to prevent a further extention of it. Indeed had such not been our well regulated position, the result of recent outbreaks must have ended in the loss of human life for an organized system exists amongst the labourers, they are armed with all and every kind of weapon, consisting of guns, pistols, swords, pikes or poles, pitch forks, scythes, &c, &c. They are determined to do evil when they think that by doing so will answer some end consonant with their views which hath no bounds their affrays or riots are against each other or against their contractors as yet in every instance their plans have been promptly met and put down with the destruction of some shanties, cooking utensils &c &c and often broken heads which generally takes place at the commencement of their rows, when uneasiness takes place on any of the works the firing of guns and blowing of horns throughout the night on such works is the sure presage of trouble. Some of the constables have had beatings and one of them, Mr. Wheeler, late a Lieut. of the 5th Bat., incorporated Militia, received from one of them by a gun shot, a ball in his hip and I am sorry to say it there remains for it is too deep seated to be extracted, his health is recovering.

One of the most alarming Riots that has yet been upon the works began at Stone Bridge within one mile of Lake Erie on Monday the 25th Decr. (Christmas Day) caused by the fighting of two drunken men in one of the shantys. Like wild fire the evil spirit ran throughout every work on the whole line when the Cork and Connaught party immediately were roused in the worst character every part of the works were stopped. [...] The Cork men began it, in several instances bodies of four, five and six hundred of them (every one of the men in arms) were met and dispersed, their women & children flew from their shanties for safety, and took refuge where ever they found a door whether it was a stable, barn, dwelling house or even a church, and many of them fled to the woods. The Stone Bridge riot had just commenced when Mr. Bonnalie arrived there when he quelled it, at that place, for the moment with two of his officers, aided by the Contractors, their foremen and some of the well disposed inhabitants and secured a few of the ring leaders as prisoners. Early the following day Mr. McFarland and Capt. Macdonald with a detachment of twenty five of the Coloured Incorporated Militia arrived from Port Robinson by wagon and just in time to prevent a nasty conflict, as a large body of Connaughts came to avenge the wrongs done by the Corkmen to some of their more immediate kindred the preceding day. Mr. Power got there late in the evening and on the following morning I arrived in company with two additional Magistrates. [...]

The first moving cause that excites the trouble is the want of work, if not employed they are devising schemes to procure it, such as driving away the party who are fewest in number who are not of their County. The Corkmen began the Christmas affray, but there is no visible difference with them for either when an opportunity offers will drive off the other.

Another cause is when the wages do not suit, they combine and stop from working indeed the well disposed are compelled to go with the majority for in such cases a patrolling band with bludgeons drive off the workers. The Priest says that Secret Societys exist amongst them binding them by oaths to be faithful to each other. One is called the Hibernian and another the Shamerick Society and that he is unable to break them up.[5]

Some time in Novr. the Contractors by common consent throughout the line dropt the doctor's wages to 2/6 Cy. per day, about the same time provisions advanced particularly potatoes and butchers meat the former of which commodities to 2/6 Cy per bushel, at same time the inclemency of the weather prevented constant work, the combination of such circumstances made their case a hard one particularly for men of families some of whom not able to procure a sufficiency of food even of potatoes, so situated schemes for relief are readily listened to, but unfortunately they too generally rely for assistance through some unlawful proceeding thus adding misery to misery when caught out punished for so doing. The Chief Engineer informs me that the men upon the line will number five thousand and their women and children as many more in all ten thousand people, and that over three thousand cannot find employment, the work does not require more than that number of men [...] seven thousand who earn nothing and those who are employed can put in but little work for a month at this season of the year. I am glad to report that the Contractors are now paying 3/1½ Cy per day. I have not heard of any outbreak among them since the end of the last month, peace and order now reign and I fondly hope will continue not only from the advance of their wages but more particular that their plots and schemes have been promptly met and at once put down and some of their ring leaders are undergoing the sentence of the law while others have been bound over to keep the peace. All those things are quickly known through their Societys.

Mr. Merritt and Mr. Power have desired that I take the general supervision for the preservation of the Peace along the line to which request I have consented, from my general knowledge of the people and of all authorities residing near or in the neighbourhood of the works, occasional visits and from an active correspondence [...][6]

Power to Begly
20 December 1844
[NAC, RG 43, Vol. 2248, *Letterbook 1844–1846*, #5995]

I have been requested by Dr. Campbell to state that during the last two years he has been engaged in attending the laborers employed on the upper part of the line of the Welland Canal & the subordinate servants of the Board stationed in that unhealthy region. That the latter have been unable to pay him in consequence of the very low rate of salaries received by them & that the former were unwilling to remunerate him because they erroneously supposed that he was paid by the Govt. Dr. Campbell has thus sustained a considerable loss & the public have derived great benefit from his services as the attention of a Physician supposed to be in the employment of the Board has doubtless tended to prevent the more frequent occurrence of riots. Under these circumstances I must take the liberty of advising the Board to grant Dr. Campbell's very moderate request that he should receive the same remuneration as one of the Police Officers, his pay to commence from the 1st May last. I can with propriety recommend this measure feeling assured that Dr. Campbell could materially assist Mr. McDonagh in preserving the peace.[7]

Robert Holmes and Dilly Coleman[8] To Merritt
11 April 1845
[AO, F662, MS 74, *Merritt Papers*, Package 15]

From the frequent depredation committed in the village of Port Robinson and its environs Mr. Coleman and myself take the Liberty of addressing a few lines to you upon the subject, the Troops (I mean the Colored Core) were stationed for the Protection of the Inhabitants, along the line of canal but instead of their being a protection they have certainly become a Public Nuisance and are looked upon in that light by the respectable portion of the Inhabitants generally. As we are informed a good deal of pilfering has been committed upon said Inhabitants of said village and Neighbourhood and we want to further add, the Church has been robbed [...] and this morning a most glaring robbery has been committed upon Jesse D. Lacy, Merchant of this place [...] and on passing one of the sentinels he spoke to him making enquiry no doubt if any thing had been discovered by him whilst on duty. Mr. Lacy informed me that Mr. Roberts one of the officers belonging to the Colored Core threatened to report Mr. Lacy for daring to speak to the sentinel to Capt. McDonnell. This morning Mr. McFarland found pasted up near his office an advertisement threatening to burn the premises of Duncan McFarland Esqr, Dilly Coleman [...] and myself, should we dare to enforce the law against certain individuals for selling spiritous liquors without a Licence. We strongly suspect that from certain language used by Capt. McDonnell towards D. McFarland on the previous enquiry that he is the author of the advertisement. I can assure you that such a state of things are not very desirable in this place and the sooner the Troops are removed from this place for the comfort of the Inhabitants the better. We therefore hope that you will use your influence with the Government to get the same removed as we should like a Company of the Rifles instead of the present Company stationed here, and indeed we should much rather be without any troops than to continue the present ones. Mr. McFarland and myself have a good deal of difficulty to contend with as Magistrates sometimes in keeping quiet the labourers upon the Public Works, but I can assure you, that many obstacles are thrown in our way by those from whom we expected assistance to maintain the Dignity of Laws. Should I meet with such Treatment at the hands of Capt. McDonald as I have upon a former occasion I shall feel it my duty, at once to report him to his Excellency as he has conducted himself to me when on the discharge of my duty as a Magistrate, was quite unbecoming any man much less a gentleman holding the situation which he holds in Her Majesty's Service.

NOTES

1. The petition is dated at Thorold and was signed by eight contractors or their representatives.

2. Baron George Frederick de Rottenburg (1807–1894) was probably born in England, a son of Baron Francis (Franz) de Rottenburg, who had served with distinction in the British army in the War of 1812. The son apparently followed his father in a military Career, serving in the Militia in Canada West.

3. Power had written to Begly earlier, urging the need to get on with the proposed work on the Welland. The delay was occasioned by the Board of Works' hesitation concerning the precise instrctions to be given regarding the attempt to achieve the Lake Erie level for the Canal. On 1 August, he had said that "however easy it may be for those, who are at a distance, to speculate on the propriety of delaying the work until precise instructions may arrive, it is very different for me surrounded by men infuriated by hunger, to persist in a course which must drive them to despair ..." On the 6th, he pleaded "If the Board will consent to my original design the work can be immediately commenced &c all danger bloodshed & tumult prevented ..." (*ibid*, #2519).

4. Sir Dominick Daly (1798–1868) was an original member of the Board of Works, 1841–46. He refused to serve on the government-appointed Board of Management for the Welland Canal. He was Provincial Secretary at this time.

5. The "Shamerick" Society is probably a spelling variant of "Shamrock." According to Dr. Donald H. Akeson, of Queen's University History Department, "Shamrock" societies were common among first generation immigrants and were probably mutual benefit societies (personal communication 13 August 1998).

6. On 17 January, Thorburn again reported to Daly, describing further violence (NAC, RG 11, Vol. 68–5, Part 1, pp. 49–51).

7. Despite Power's urging, the Board's response was negative. Begly referred Power to a previous communication, nothing that, since this was question "upon which the Executive Government have already determined not to interfere, "the Board could not grant the request (NAC, RG 11, Vol. 118, *Letterbook 1844–1845*, #5397).

8. This letter was marked "Confidential." Holmes was a J.P. and one of the Magistrates involved in the peace-keeping efforts in 1844. In the 1860s and '70s, Coleman was at various times a farmer, grocer, and proprieter [sic] of the Mansion House.

299

■ Article 1: Making the Voyageur World

Carolyn Podruchny

Voyageurs had much more leisure time during the winter months spent at interior posts than they did during the canoe journeys of the summers. Yet here they also had more time to feel homesick and anxious in the midst of a foreign world. Much of their play was reminiscent of French Canada, such as celebrating annual holidays, drinking, and holding balls; these festivities helped voyageurs create a sense of home away from home. Voyageurs also had the time to create new connections, form new families, and solidify a distinctive society in the Northwest. Their celebrations helped them create new memories and new traditions rooted in their new locations.

An annual schedule of holiday celebrations accompanied the yearly round of labor, which was especially important to the men living at isolated posts, away from their families and friends. Men often journeyed from outlying posts to congregate at larger central forts to celebrate the holidays and gladly risked the dangers and discomfort of winter travel, even a week of walking with snowshoes, to avoid spending a holiday alone.[1] Holidays helped to mark the passage of time and provided structure during the long, dreary, and often lonely months at the interior posts. Coming together to celebrate at specific times helped to generate camaraderie and fellow feeling with one another, their masters, and Aboriginal peoples.

Christmas and New Year were the most popular holidays for the fur traders and were rarely forgotten or ignored. Other holidays that were sometimes celebrated included All Saint's Day on November 1, St. Andrew's Day on November 30, and Easter in early April.[2] Similar celebrations occurred at HBC posts.[3] The occasional mention of celebrations occurred on Palm Sunday, the king's birthday (June 4, George III), and Epiphany, or "Little Christmas" (January 6).[4] Men seemed willing to commemorate any day, regardless of its origins or significance to them, because

Source: Reprinted from *Making the Voyageur World: Travelers and Traders in the North American Fur Trade* by Carolyn Podruchny by permission of the University of Nebraska Press. © 2006 by the Board of Regents of the University of Nebraksa, pp. 174–7, 181, 192–4, and 196–9.

it served as an excuse for a celebration and drams from the bourgeois. Commemorating St. Andrew, the patron saint of Scotland, and observing the birthday of George III, king of Great Britain, were probably holidays introduced by the Scottish and English bourgeois and clerks, while Christmas, New Year's, All Saint's Day, and Easter would have been common celebrations in French Canada.[5] George Landmann noted that in late eighteenth-century Montreal, New Year's Day was "a day of extraordinary festivity, which was extended to the two or three following days. Amongst the Canadians it was [...] the fashion for everybody to visit everybody during one of the three first days of the year, when a glass of noyeau or other liquor was, with a piece of biscuit or cake, presented to the visitor, which, after a hard day's work in calling at some twenty or thirty houses, frequently terminated in sending a number of very respectable people home in a staggering condition toward the close of the day."[6] Feasting, drinking, and levees, or paying courtesy calls on masters (particularly on New Year's Day), were characteristic of celebrations in fur trade society.

The holiday celebrations seemed to follow a formula. Specific rituals and ceremonies, giving the day a sense of orderly formality and tradition, were followed by chaotic parties, where wild abandon and heavy drinking predominated. Alexander Henry the Younger complained on New Year's Day in 1803 that he was plagued with ceremonies and men and women drinking and fighting "pell mell."[7]

During most holiday celebrations at fur trade posts, men generally did not have to work.[8] During the Christmas and New Year's holidays, voyageurs and bourgeois frequently arranged to visit other posts or invited visitors to their post for the day or for the entire holiday season.[9] Many men tried to organize their work schedules so they would not miss any of the festivities. In December 1818 at Tête au Brochet, George Nelson was frustrated by one of his voyageurs named Welles. Nelson had sent Welles to Falle de Perdix on December 23, but Welles returned to the post on December 30, claiming that the snow and ice prevented him from reaching his destination. Nelson suspected that this was a lie and that Welles really wanted to be back at the post for the New Year's celebrations.[10] Men of different companies sometimes put aside their different allegiances to celebrate together. During the Christmas holidays in 1805, XYC employees celebrated with their NWC neighbors at Lac La Pluie,[11] Frequently Aboriginal people came to the posts to participate in the festivities, which helped the traders solidify trading ties and foster goodwill with them.[12] Donald McKay noted that it was customary for Aboriginal people to arrive at the post on all feast days.[13] Voyageurs sometimes visited Aboriginal lodges as part of the day's celebrations.[14] Those Aboriginal people who were closely involved with provisioning and fur trading, such as the "homeguard," celebrated with the traders.

The day's festivities on Christmas and New Year's usually began early in the morning. Voyageurs ceremoniously called on their bourgeois or clerk to formally wish him well and pay their respects.[15] The early morning firing of muskets or cannons usually woke the masters.[16] In 1793 Alexander Mackenzie wrote. "On the first day of January, my people, in conformity to the usual custom, awoke me at the break of day with the discharge of fire-arms, with which they congratulated the appearance of the new year. In return, they were treated with plenty of spirits, and when there is any flour, cakes are always added to the regales, which was the case, on the present occasion,"[17] Like the firing of muskets when a brigade arrived at a post, this salute was a symbolic welcome and a formal honoring of the holiday.

After the firing of muskets, all the residents of the fort gathered together in a general meeting where the bourgeois or clerk would provide regales or gifts to the voyageurs. Depending on the wealth of the post, regales could be as little as a single dram or as much as great quantities of alcohol, especially if there was a shortage of food.[18] At the beginning of 1802, Daniel Harmon gave his men a dram in the morning and then enough rum to drink throughout the course of the day, to help distract them from the scarcity of meat.[19] In an effort to secure more alcohol for the day's festivities, men would go to great lengths to salute their bourgeois or any passing visitor or dignitary, in hopes of gaining a treat.[20] Regales on New Year's seemed to be slightly more generous than those at Christmas, as men were frequently given tobacco in addition to drams.[21] At wealthier posts the men's regales included food, usually specialty items that were hard to procure, such as flour and sugar, though the regale could include meat and grease.[22]

Holding a formal ball was an importation from French Canada, but the dancing and music were culturally distinctive. The "old fiddle and Indian drum" symbolized the mixing of European and Aboriginal forms.[23] Dancing was not restricted to holidays but continued throughout the seasons at fur trade posts. Having dances or "balls" was a fairly common occurrence both at the Great Lakes posts and in the interior.[24] Either fiddlers or singers provided the music. Fast and spirited dancing predominated. The descriptions of the "lively reels" of country dances reflected a rough and tumble joie de vivre that was characteristic of many voyageurs' activities. Balls at Grand Portage during the rendezvous, however, were genteel affairs for the benefit of the bourgeois, with music from the bagpipe, violin, flute, and fife.[25] Yet even at these balls, "country music" combined musical forms from Canada, Scotland, England, and Aboriginal peoples. Dances were often held to celebrate specific events, such as the coalition of the XYC and the NWC in 1804, but the most common occasions were weddings and to honor visitors to the post.[26] Men from different companies frequently attended each others' dances.[27] Sometimes dances were held for no particular reasons other than to have fun and enliven the monotony of post life, especially during the long winters.[28]

The social life and play of voyageurs at the interior posts reveals an interesting tension between old and new social practices. Voyageurs preserved social traditions from French Canada to create a sense of home in the pays d'en haut, which could be overwhelming in its strangeness. Celebrating annual holidays, drinking, and dancing reminded voyageurs of their lives in rural French Canada and allowed them to continue to be part of that social world. Yet the circumstances of the fur trade led to the emergence of new behaviors. Contests and trickery became important because they bolstered the heightened masculinity of the male-dominated workplace, which valued toughness and strength, and the liminal social spaces of canoe journeys and post life. Men made every effort to demonstrate their strength, endurance, and good humor, especially in the face of hardship and privation. They were influenced by the cultural practices they observed among Aboriginal peoples, and imitating Aboriginal peoples became a way of increasing symbolic capital.

How did the liminal position of voyageurs working in the fur trade affect their relationships with one another? How did the men work out the social conventions of their new cultural locations? How were their friendships with fellow voyagers different from their friendships with men in French Canada? These questions are difficult to answer. The dearth of work on male friendships among habitants makes comparisons especially challenging. A significant drawback in assessing the shape and nature of voyageur friendships is that their lives are mainly visible in the writings of their bourgeois and clerks, who were probably not aware of many of the relationships among their men, and would have little reason to record them in their letters and journals unless the behavior directly affected fur trade work. The documentary record contains descriptions of extremes in behavior, situations that were remarkable or abnormal, and conduct that hindered the workings of the trade. Despite these daunting drawbacks, it is possible to trace the outlines of voyageur camaraderie. In friendships between the men we can see expressions of a voyageur social order, such as an emphasis on good humor, generosity, rowdiness, and strength. In a culture where money and material possessions had limited significance, the quest for a strong reputation became more important.

Politeness was a social convention brought from French Canada. Traveling through the Canadas in the early nineteenth century, John Lambert noted that French Canadians were generally "good-humoured, peaceable, and friendly" and remarkably civil to one another and to strangers. People bowed to each other as they passed on the streets, and men sometimes even kissed each other on the cheek.[29] Similarly writers remarked on the good humor and affection that voyageurs showed to one another and even to their masters. Ross Cox marveled that the men referred to each other as *mon frère* (my brother) or *mon cousin* without being related and that they made up pet names for their bourgeois.[30] Bestowing kinship names on one another may have been a practice borrowed from Aboriginal peoples, who frequently adopted outsiders or assigned them kinship designations to incorporate them into their social order.

Yet civility among voyageurs was often described as "rough," and verbal exchanges were described as the "coarse & familiar language of brother voyageurs."[31] Swearing or blasphemy was not restricted to expressions of anger but was common in many different contexts. Expressions of profanity usually had to do with religious imagery, such as *sacré* (sacred), *mon Dieu* (my God), and *baptême* (baptism), which probably eased tension and poked fun at serious situations.[32] Masters' characterizations of voyageur familiarity and camaraderie as "rough" may reflect the bourgeois' desire to be "civilized."[33] Peter Moogk asserts that verbal and physical abuse among "the lower orders" in New France was commonplace, but it did not mean that habitants were particularly vulgar or wanton people. Bakhtin notes that billingsgate, or curses, oaths, and popular blazons, figured prominently in folk humor in early modern Europe. Abusive language was a mark of familiarity and friendship.[34] The "rough" civility may have found a particularly exaggerated expression in the pays d'en haut. Because the men worked in harsh and dangerous conditions, they wanted to be especially jovial and rowdy to demonstrate their lack of fear and their great strength in living amidst adversity. Rediker suggests that at sea "rough talk" was a way for sailors to express an opposition to "polite" bourgeois customs and their ideals of gentility, moderation, refinement, and industry. He asserts that "rough speech" was a transgressive means to deal with shipboard isolation and incarceration.[35] Likewise rough talk among voyageurs was probably a verbal cue for a distinct masculine identity.

Despite the "rough talk" social conventions among voyageurs stressed charity and generosity, especially in the face of hardship. Voyageurs could demonstrate that they were tough and strong enough to be kind in a brutal environment. If the difficulty of life in the fur trade sometimes caused men to be harsh and cruel to one another, much of this ill will could be expressed in the frequent and usually organized "sport" fighting. The tension between a desire for equality and the centrality of social ordering influenced relationships among men in both good and bad ways. Voyageurs worked very closely together and relied on one another for survival. Their often deep friendships, however, were threatened by the transience of the job.

How deep did friendships among men develop? Did the homosocial environment, especially on canoe journeys, lead to the development of homosexuality as a normative expression of affection? Did sex between men become a common voyageur pastime? How would this affect the ideal of masculinity central to voyageur culture? Some scholars have argued that masculinity or gendered identities cannot be separated from sexuality and that heterosexuality is often a key part of working men's masculine identity.[36] This construction of masculinity becomes especially problematic in homosocial working environments when men do not have access to women for erotic pleasure. The situation of the voyageurs is historically unusual: they often worked in all-male environments, yet they had access to women of a "savage race." Was heterosexuality constructed in the same way when the sexual "other" was also the racial "other"?

The bourgeois and the clerks portrayed voyageurs as heterosexual and were conspicuously silent on homosexual practices. Masters may have consciously chosen to overlook the occurrence of homosexuality, considering it an unmentionable deviance. The silence may also indicate an ignorance of homosexual practice among voyageurs and Aboriginal men. Or homosexuality may not have existed as a social option for voyageurs who had easy access to Aboriginal women for sex. In any case, the silence demands close scrutiny.

Many all-male sojourners, most notably sailors, have a documented history of practicing sodomy, although it remains a clouded issue.[37] Without being essentialist about the nature of erotic desire, one is not unreasonable to assume that voyageurs sometimes had sexual feelings for each other or participated in sexual acts together. If sexuality is understood to be situational, then men working together in isolated groups probably developed sexual and emotional relationships with one another.[38] The voyageurs who transported goods and furs on the arduous route between Montreal and Lake Superior worked in isolated settings and had limited contact with Aboriginal peoples. These men, however, worked in the trade only during the summer months and returned to their French Canadian parishes, where not only homosexuality but any kind of nonmarital sexual practice was prohibited.[39] Is it possible that in the isolation and freedom of their summer jobs they experimented with different kinds of sexual pleasure? Or were they simply too tired to be interested in sex? Voyageurs who worked in the interior were often cooped up in trading posts, far away from the regulative forces of the Catholic Church and the scrutiny of social peers, and they had the time and leisure to pursue erotic pleasure. Here one might expect to find significant

emotional and possibly sexual bonding. The difficulty of fur trade work and the great risks in canoeing and portaging often created intense bonds of friendship and trust between men.[40] One clue to homosocial practice in the interior may lie in the patterns and rates of marriages between voyageurs and Aboriginal women.

Documentation on sodomy in early modern settings has been found mainly in legal records. I have found no prosecutions for voyageur buggery, or sodomy, in French Canadian courts. The Montreal traders did not impose rigid military discipline on their workers as did the HBC, and thus voyageurs were less socially regulated and freer than HBC laborers.[41] Edith Burley has found a few prosecutions for sodomy among the Orkney men working at HBC posts, but she asserts that "officers appear to have had little interest in the regulation of their men's sexuality and were probably content to overlook their improprieties as long as they did not interfere with the company's business."[42] Was the same true for the Montreal bourgeois? Many violations of contracts and other crimes were not formally punished because legal systems did not exist in the interior. Perhaps because the bourgeois knew they could neither prosecute buggery nor prevent it, they turned a blind eye to it. The silence regarding sodomy in bourgeois writings may reflect that the practice was considered deviant, amoral, illegal, and possibly unimaginable. If sexual contact between voyageurs and masters occurred, it would have been silenced by masters, who did not wish to be incriminated.

Masters may have chosen to overlook sexual relations between voyageurs and Aboriginal men so that they would not threaten trading alliances or create enemies. A substantial group of scholars have explored homosexuality among Aboriginal societies in the cultural form of berdaches.[43] Berdaches occupied "third sex" roles and were sometimes called "two-spirited people." They were most often people who played opposite or both male and female roles and held significant spiritual power, and they often became culture heroes. Although berdaches represented many different configurations of gender roles and sexual practices in different Aboriginal cultures, their widespread presence may indicate that sexuality was not dichotomous in many Aboriginal societies and that there was space for the expression of homosexual desire. Some scholars suggest that berdaches represented forms of "institutionalized" homosexuality. It is possible that the presence of berdaches indicates that homosexuality was permissible in some Aboriginal societies and thus permissible among voyageurs and some Aboriginal men.

It is difficult to know the extent to which the intense physicality of voyageur culture, the worship of masculine qualities of strength and physical endurance, and the scarcity of women enabled experimentation at a sexual level. If such relations among self-identified heterosexual men occurred in this liminal setting, like other forms of play they probably fortified friendships, and increased a sense of collectivity among voyageurs. At the same time, competition over partners and rejected advances probably created tensions and facilitated cultural divisions.

Because voyageurs lived between worlds, they found opportunities to transcend social restrictions learned at their homes in French Canada. In the process of trying out or "playing at" new ways of living, they could reinvent or refashion themselves. The play of voyageurs was influenced by customs brought from French Canada, by new practices learned from Aboriginal societies, and by the everyday life of the fur trade workplace. The working environment especially encouraged new "experimental" behavior because voyageurs were constantly traveling and thus isolated from established communities. Voyageurs' penchant for trickery and play became a tool for carving out the contours of their workspace. Play also became a social space where voyageurs could assert their particular ideal of manhood and where they could appropriate the behavior of Aboriginal peoples in order to be successful voyageurs. By providing a space for voyageurs to test new forms of social behavior, play strengthened voyageurs' social bonds with one another and encouraged camaraderie and a unified identity. At the same time, play became a vehicle through which voyageurs distinguished categories among themselves and deepened occupational fissures determined mainly by job status. It thus had a simultaneously homogenizing and diversifying effect on the voyageurs' world.

NOTES

1. Lefroy, *In Search of the Magnetic North*, Lefroy to Isabella, Lake Athabasca, Christmas Day, 1843, 84.
2. For examples of All Saint's Day, see LAC, MG19 CI, vol. 12, November 1, 1804, 25; MRB, MC, C.28, November 1, 1807, 12; and Keith, *North of Athabasca*, 316. For examples of St. Andrew's Day, see OA, reel MS65, Donald McKay, Journal from January to December 1799, November 30, 1799, 43 (my pagination); and MRB, MC, C.24, Sunday, November 30, 1800, 6. For examples of celebrating Easter, see LAO MG19 CI, vol. 1, April 8, 1798, 53; LAC, MG19 CI, vol. 14, April 12, 1800, 23; and OA, MU 842, April 11, 1819, 43.
3. Morton, "Chief Trader Joseph McGillivray"; and Payne, *Most Respectable Place*, 65, 87–92.
4. For an example of celebrating Palm Sunday, see OA, MU 842, April 4, 1819, 42. For examples of celebrating the King's birthday, see TBR, S13, George Nelson's journal, April 1, 1810–May 1, 1811, June 4, 1810, 11 (my pagination); and Landmann, *Adventures and Recollections*, 2:167–68. For and example of celebrating Epiphany, see Henry (the Younger), *New Light*, January 6, 1810 1:165.
5. For comments on New Year's celebrations as a French Canadian custom, see Harmon, *Sixteen Years*, January 2, 1801, 41; see also Grenon, *Us et coutumes du Québec*, 153–68; Lamontagne, *L'hiver dans la culture québécoise*, 101–3; and Provencher, *Les Quatre Saisons*, 449–57, 463–70.
6. Landmann, *Adventures and Recollections*, 1:239–40.
7. Henry (the Younger), *New Light*, January 1, 1803, 1:207.
8. OA, reel MS65, Donald McKay, Journal from January 1805 to June 1806, December 25, 1805, 47 (my pagination); TBR, S13, George Nelson's journal, November 3, 1807–August 31, 1808, December 25, 1807, 14; November 1, 1807, 7; and Henry (the Younger), *New Light*, November 1, 1810, 2:660.
9. OA, reel MS65, Donald McKay, journal from January to December 1799, December 24, 1799, 46 (my pagination); TBR, S13, George Nelson's journal, November 3, 1807–August 31, 1808, December 25, 1807, 14; George Nelson's journal, April 1, 1810–May 1, 1811, December 23, 1810, 39 (my pagination).
10. OA, MU 842 December 23 and 30, 1818, 22–23.
11. Faries, "Diary," December 25–28, 1804 and January 1, 1805, 223–24.
12. Henry (the Younger), *New Light*, January, 1, 1801, 1:162–63; and Harmon, *Sixteen Years*, January 1, 1811 and 1812, 136, 147–48.
13. OA, reel MS65, Donald McKay, Journal from August 1800 to April 1801, December 25, 1800, 17.

14. LAC, MG19 CI, vol. l2, January 1, 1805, 35.

15. LAC, MG19 CI, vol. 14 January 1, 1800, 9; Faries, "Diary," January 1, 1805, 224; LAC, MG19 CI, vol. 8, January 1, 1805, 37; and Keith, *North of Athabasca*, 197.

16. MRB, MC, C.13, January 1, 1800, 11 (my pagination); Henry (the Younger), *New Light*, January 1, 1801 and 1802, 1:162, 192; TBR, S13, George Nelson's journal, November 30, 1815–January 13, 1816, Monday, December 25, 1815, 91; George Nelson's journal and reminiscences, 84; and Franchère, *Journal of a Voyage*, 107–8.

17. Mackenzie, *Voyages from Montreal*, January 1, 1793, 252. On other comments of the long- standing custom, see MRB, MC, C.28, January 1, 1808, 20; Keith, *North of Athabasca*, 326; and Franklin, *Narrative of a Journey*, January 1, 1802, 53.

18. For drams, see LAC, MG19 CI, vol. 1, November 1 and December 25, 1797, 17, 27; MRB, MC, C.24 December 25, 1800, 13; LAC, MG19 CI vol. 6 December 25, 1800, 72; vol. 8 December 25, 1804, 34; and MRB, MC, C.28, December 25, 1807, 20; see also Keith, *North of Athabasca*, 122, 196, 325. For large quantities of alcohol, see LAC, MG19 CI, vol. 67, December 25, 1798, 23; MRB, MC, C.13, December 25, 1799, 10 (my pagination); Harmon, *Sixteen Years*, December 25, 1801,52; and LAC, MG19 CI, vol. 12 November 1 and December 25, 1804, 25, 34.

19. Harmon, *Sixteen Years*, January 1, 1802, 53.

20. TBR, S13, George Nelson's journal, November 30, 1815–January 13, 1816, December 25, 1815, 91.

21. MRB, MC, C.7, January 1, 1794 and 1795, 6, 23; OA, MG19 CI, vol. 1, January 1, 1798, 29; LAC, MG19, CI, vol. 7, January 1, 1799, 24; and vol. 12, January 1, 1805 35.

22. Mackenzie, *Voyages from Montreal*, January 1, 1793, 252, Henry (the Younger), *New Light*, December 25, 1800, 1:161; LAC, MG19 CI, vol. 9, January 1, 1806, 21; Cox, *Adventures on the Columbia River*, 305–6; and MRB, MC, C.8, January 1, 1806, 10.

23. See also Van Kirk, "Many *Tender Ties*," 126–29.

24. For examples of balls at Great Lakes posts, see Pond, "Narrative," Mackinaw, 47; and OA, MU 1146, Frederick Goedike, Batchiwenon, to George Gordon, Michipicoten, February 11, 1812, 1–3. For examples of balls at interior posts, see TBR, S13, George Nelson's Journal, November 3, 1807–August 31, 1808, Fort Alexandria, June 18, 1808, 42; and Ross, *Adventures of the First Settlers*, Spokane House, summer 1812, 212.

25. Harmon, *Sixteen Years*, Grand Portage, July 4, 1800, 22.

26. TBR, S13, George Nelson's coded journal, June 28 1821 29; Henry (the Younger), *New Light*, September 6, 1810, 2:626; and Faries, "Diary," December 16, 1804, February 24, March 31, April 28, May 12 and 17, 1805, 222, 230, 234–35, 238, 240–41.

27. For an example of NWC and HBC men dancing together at Fort George, see McGillivray, *Journal*, March 22, 1795, 66. For an example of NWC and XYC men dancing together, see Faries, "Diary," January 11 1805, 224–25. For an example of NWC, XYC, and HBC men dancing together at Rivière Souris, Fort Assiniboine, see Harmon, *Sixteen Years*, May 27, 1805, 89–90.

28. Henry (the Younger), *New Light*, January 27, 1810, 2:584.

29. Lambert, *Travels* through *Canada*, 1:173.

30. Cox, *Adventures on the Columbia River*, 306. Also see Ross, *Fur Hunters*, 1:304.

31. TBR, S13, George Nelson's journal "No. 5," 30 (my sequential pagination)/214 (Nelson's pagination).

32. For a few examples see TBR, S13, George Nelson's diary of events, June 18, 1822; Nelson, *My First Years*, 35–36; and Cox, *Adventures on the Columbia River*, 167.

33. See Podruchny, "Festivities, Fortitude and Fraternalism," for a discussion of bourgeois efforts to reconcile what they perceived as "rough" and "gentle" forms of masculinity.

34. Moogk, "Thieving Buggers"; and Bakhtin, *Rabelais and His World*, 5, 16–17.

35. Rediker, *Between the* Devil, 166.

36. Maynard, "Rough Work"; and Blye, "Hegemonic Heterosexual Masculinity."

37. Gilbert, "Buggery and the British Navy"; Maynard, "Making Waves"; T. D. Moodie, "Migrancy and Male Sexuality"; and Chauncey, "Christian Brotherhood."

38. Maynard, "Rough Work," 169.

39. Gagnon, *Plaisir d'Amour*, 12–23.

40. Ross, *Fur Hunters*, 1:303–4.

41. Brown, *Strangers* in Blood, 87–88.

42. Burley, *Servants of the Honourable Company*, 129–30.

43. Harriet Whitehead, "The Bow and the Burden Strap." For a critique of Whitehead's imposition of a two-gender model on Aboriginal societies, see Roscoe, "How to Become a Berdache." See also Williams, *Spirit and the Flesh*. On lesbianism see Allen, "Lesbians in American Indian Cultures."

■ Article 2: Wives and Mothers, School Mistresses and Scullery Maids

Elizabeth Jane Errington

By 1833, the capital of Upper Canada had become a bustling market town. Although many of York's approximately 9,000 residents continued to depend directly on the government for their livelihood, a growing proportion of the local population relied on the retail, manufacturing, or service trades to earn a living. William Ware, for example, sold spirits, wines, and groceries; William Cormack and Co. was a wholesale and dry goods firm. When Anna Jameson arrived in York in 1836, she could purchase supplies at Donald Ross's retail shop on King St. If she did not want to go to the Market House for fresh produce, she could go to Holmes and Co., which was located on Yonge St. The 1833 *York Directory* included twenty-two such retail and wholesale businesses in the community; it also listed dozens of small specialty shops, numerous inns, taverns, hotels, and many small manufacturing establishments.[1]

Almost hidden among the growing number of retail outlets were Mrs Owen's boarding-house, Mrs Bell's candle and soap factory, and the York Hotel, owned and operated by Mrs Jane Jordan.[2] Though many women were probably aware that Mrs Claris' millinery and dressmaking shop had a new supply of the "latest fashions" in August 1833,[3] probably only a few frequented Mrs Shaw's millinery business, which she ran out of her home. Despite the diminutive size of their businesses, these, and many other women were a vital part of the local economy. Like many of their male neighbours, they provided goods and services that residents of this government town needed.

The eclectic commercial scene that was characteristic of York in the 1830s was also apparent in other colonial towns and villages. Small communities such as Cobourg, Picton, and Peterborough supported a butcher, a baker, and a candlestick maker, as well as a number of general stores. An increasing

number of towns and villages, including, of course, Kingston and Niagara, also had at least one millinery and mantuamaking shop [a mantua is an Italian-styled gown, fashionable in the eighteenth and nineteenth centuries] and a school for young ladies. And it was not unusual for one of the local boarding-houses, inns, and hotels to be owned by a woman.

In the pre-industrial economy of Upper Canada, women were frequently involved in the marketplace. Although women were "by definition basically domestic,"[4] this did not preclude them from assuming economic as well as familial responsibilities. Many colonial wives were, by necessity, actively involved in the economic affairs of their husbands.[5] Just as Mary O'Brien, Fanny Hutton, Susanna Moodie, and other farm wives helped their husbands plant and harvest, urban women too assisted their husbands in their shops and at their crafts. As was the custom in Europe in the eighteenth century, some artisans' wives "prepared or finished material on which [their] husbands worked."[6] Others cooked and served guests of family inns. When their husbands were ill or away, wives became their "representatives" and even their "surrogates." As Laurel Ulrich has noted, "female responsibility [...] was [...] very broad [...] the role of housewife and the role of deputy husband were two sides of the same coin."[7]

For many women, working beside and with their husbands, fathers, or brothers was not always enough to sustain the family, however. Particularly in Upper Canada's towns and villages, families were units of consumption as well as of production and the family economy was a wage economy.[8] Households depended increasingly on cash to buy goods and services that they did not or could not produce themselves. Women together with the children were often obliged to find waged work to supplement the family income.

In the premodern world, "any task was suitable" for a woman" as long as it furthered the good of the family" and if she was married, it "was accepted by her husband."[9] A woman's opportunity to earn a wage in Upper Canada was determined by a number of factors, including her age, her marital status, her skill, and her available capital. Women were also restricted in their choice of work by where they lived. (Only in urban areas was there sufficient custom actually to set up a dress shop or open a girls' school.) Wage-earning women were also influenced

---

Source: Elizabeth Jane Errington, "Beyond the Bounds of Domesticity", *Wives and Mothers, School Mistresses and Scullery Maids: Working Women in Upper Canada, 1790–1840* (Kingston and Montreal, McGill-Queen's University Press, 1995), pp. 185–88. Reprinted with permission.

by colonial assumptions about what type of work was appropriate for persons of their sex. Women were not admitted to most crafts. Married women could not own property; legally, they could not hire employees.

As in rural areas, "domestic service was probably the most common waged employment" open to women living in town.[10] To meet the vagaries of seasonal unemployment or those fluctuations in market demand that inevitably affected the income of the family business, married women often sewed, took in washing, became a char, took in a few lodgers, or marketed other "homemaking" skill on a part-time basis.[11] Usually considered unskilled labourers, such women received minuscule wages for their work and coped with often appalling working conditions. Yet a wife's ability to earn even a little money was indispensable to ensuring an adequate family wage.[12]

Though domestic service was the most prevalent type of women's waged work, it was by no means the only one. Many widows who were left "solely responsible for maintaining the family" tried to continue with the family business. With the help of their children, they managed family farms, village stores, or their late husbands' craft shops. In some and perhaps most instances, the death of a husband meant "the destruction of the family economy," however. A number of widows were forced into service, others opened their homes to boarders. After 1820, a growing number of widowed women entered, or often re-entered, one of the "female trades."[13]

Particularly in the second generation of colonial development, a number of women—widowed, single, and married—opened schools for girls, dressshops, and millinery and mantuamaking establishments. Some of these women were recent immigrants who had come to Upper Canada to take advantage of expanding business opportunities and perhaps to escape some of the social and economic strictures that were emerging at home.[14] They were well aware that the chatelaine of the big house needed appropriate clothing, and that Upper Canadian mothers wanted proper schooling for their daughters. Either alone or with female relatives or colleagues, such women opened businesses that consciously catered to these demands.

Nevertheless, relatively few women had the financial resources, skills, and personal confidence necessary to embark on what was inevitably a risky enterprise.[15] The majority of Upper Canadian women were not independent merchants, shopkeepers, or craftswomen who sold their skills in the open marketplace; they were wives and mothers whose primary responsibility remained "the well being of [...] husband and children."[16] Even so, many urban labouring-class women took part in "the common commerce of life" at some time in their lives.[17]

Evidence of women's varied market activities is, for the most part, available only indirectly. Most women who were homemakers for hire, assistants in their husbands' businesses, or small independent tradeswomen were part of the "hidden economy" of Upper Canada.[18] They relied on their local reputation or on contacts made on the street or at the market to gain work. Many of them were undoubtedly part of an informal economy of barter and exchange. However, a growing number of women did sometimes place notices in local newspapers advertising their business. It is these notices, together with brief references in gentlewomen's diaries and aside comments printed in local newspapers that allow us to begin to piece together the world of wage-earning women in Upper Canada's towns and villages.

307

NOTES

1. George Walton, *York Commercial Directory and Street Guide and Register*, 1833–34 (York: Thomas Dalton 1834).
2. *The Patriot*, 8 December 1833; *British American Journal*, 25 February 1834; *The Patriot*, 24 April 1840.
3. *The Patriot*, 2 August 1833. This establishment was also listed in the Directory.
4. Ulrich, *Good Wives*, 36.
5. Ibid., 49. As Tilly and Scott note in *Women, Work, and Family*, 48, a woman in a pre-industrial society "was her husband's indispensable partner." See also the work of Cohen, *Women's Work, Markets, and Economic Development*; Ryan, *The Cradle of the Middle Class*, particularly her discussion of frontier women; Stansell, *City of Women*; Norton, *Liberty's Daughters*; Rule, *The Labouring Classes*; for the later period, Bradbury, *Working Families*.
6. Tilly and Scott, *Women, Work and Family*, 48. See also Sally Alexander, "Women's Work in Nineteenth-Century London," in Mitchell and Oakely, eds., *The Rights and Wrongs of Women*, 59–111, 64–5.
7. Ulrich, *Good Wives*, 50, 37, 47. This, of course, was most graphically illustrated during the American

Revolution. See Norton, *Liberty's Daughters*, Chapter 7; Potter-MacKinnon, *While the Women Only Wept*.

8. Tilly and Scott, *Women, Work, and Family*, 19. See also Bradbury, *Working Families*, Chapter 5.

9. Ulrich, *Good Wives*, 37–8.

10. Stansell, *City of Women*, 12. See also Alexander, "Women's Work," 97–9.

11. See John's "Introduction" to *Unequal Opportunities*.

12. In the pre-industrial world of Upper Canada, as in Montreal in a later period, no one assumed that the male head of the household would, or perhaps indeed even should be able to support his family on one wage: Bradbury, *Working Families*, 13–16. The assumption that the head of the household should be the sole "breadwinner" is quite modern. And although it is to some degree a product of the

nineteenth-century middle-class ideology that has been examined so eloquently by Davidoff and Hall, *Family Fortunes* as in so many aspects of this, the rhetoric enunciated by the few did not, nor was it expected to be lived by the many.

13. Tilly and Scott, *Women, Work and Family*, 51, 53, 47.

14. Hammerton, *Emigrant Women*.

15. Ulrich, *Good Wives*, 48.

16. Alexander, "Women's Work," 77.

17. Ulrich, *Good Wives*, 48.

18. Rule, *The Labouring Classes*, 13. See also McCalla, *Planting the Province*, 113, who notes that though women were involved in considerable "productive" work, it "was not captured by standard statistics." Alexander, "Women's Work," 72, found a similar situation in London, England during this period.

■ Article 3: Farm Households and Wage Labour in the Northeastern Maritimes in the Early 19th Century

Rusty Bittermann

One of the most enduring mythologies of rural life in the temperate regions of North America has centred on the freedom resulting from easy access to land. In the New World unlike the Old, the story goes, land was plentiful, free from the encumbrances of a feudal past, and common folk might gain unimpeded access to its abundance and carve an independent niche for themselves. In the 18th and 19th centuries, the mythology was fostered by the effusions of travel accounts and emigrant manuals as well as by the writings of immigrants themselves. Since then it has been broadly sustained in North American historiography.

That the image of the independent yeoman was to a certain degree a reflection of a reality experienced by some rural residents in the Maritimes is indisputable. The opportunities for acquiring an

independent rural livelihood were relatively greater in British North America than they were in the Old World. Many transformed these possibilities into reality and achieved a "propertied independence."[1] Those who enjoyed such circumstances, however, were but one component of a larger farming population. And many who came to enjoy a modicum of yeomanly independence only experienced this condition during a fraction of their lives. Like any pervasive mythology, the image of the independent yeoman is partly rooted in a reality. Problems arise, though, when a fragment of the rural experience becomes a characterization of the whole. It is not my intention here to consider how this mythology developed, or to unravel the various strands of peasant dream, liberal ideology, and social critique that have sustained it. Rather, I want to examine what it has obscured, indeed tends to deny: the importance of wage labour to farmfolk in the northeastern Maritimes in the first half of the 19th century.[2] The survey which follows underlines the significance of wages to the farm population and highlights the profile of farm dwellers within the larger labour force.

For many, the quality of land resources available—particularly when coupled with a poverty that diverted labour and capital away from farm improvements and toward the needs of basic sustenance—precluded ever escaping the necessity of engaging in extensive wage work.[3] As the Crown surveyor in Baddeck, D. B. McNab, noted in 1857, there were "hundreds" of farms in this region of Cape Breton

Source: Rusty Bittermann, "Farm Households and Wage Labour in the Northeastern Maritimes in the Early 19th Century," *Labour/Le Travail* 31 (1993), No. 31, pp. 13–45. Reprinted with permission.

where ten, twenty, or thirty years after initial settlement their occupants remained heavily reliant on off-farm employment in order to "eke out the means of a scanty subsistence."[4] In general, he contended, such settlers occupied the difficult hill lands, the backlands, of the Island and tended to be squatters rather than freeholders. The Land Commissioners taking evidence on Prince Edward Island in 1860 heard similar testimony concerning areas of Prince Edward Island, often predominantly occupied by squatters, where few settlers successfully managed to derive the bulk of their livelihood from the soil.[5]

While some households made ends meet by combining wage work with the sale of selected farm "surpluses," often enough exchanging costly foods like butter and meat for cheaper breadstuffs and fish, there were others which appear to have been exclusively, or almost exclusively, reliant on the sale of labour to meet the costs of household goods and food and to procure seed and animal provisions. The ledger books of the North Sydney trader, John Beamish Moore,[6] for instance, reveal a number of backland households whose occupants had nothing but labour to sell during the years of their dealings with him.[7] During the period 1853 to 1860, the members of Angus Link's household paid for their supplies of oatmeal, barley flour, and oats through a combination of Angus's own labour and that of his wife and daughter.[8] So, too, did the Angus McDonald household pay its debts through Angus's own labour and that of his sons and daughter.[9] The debts of the Murduch Ferguson household as well were repaid entirely by Murdoch's labour and that of a female member of the household.[10] Moore's account book reveals something of the seasonality of the pressures on these backland households as well. Between 1853 and 1861, the accounts of those identified as backlanders in his books reveal recurrent debts for hay, barley flour, and oatmeal needed in April and May to replenish exhausted winter supplies, and seed grain (barley and oats) needed in May and June to permit planting another season's crop. Merchant ledgers reveal only a fragment of these patterns. Wealthier members of rural communities as well often took on the role, and assumed the benefits, of acting as provisioners and sources of credit to poorer households through the months of greatest scarcity. It appears to have been particularly common for those acting as road commissioners to sell provisions on credit

during the winter and to retain the road-work returns due to these households the following summer.[11]

Backlanders such as these, though possessing or occupying considerable acreages, were yet compelled by necessity to participate extensively in labour markets near and far in order to make up for the great inadequacies of their farm returns. They were, as the Crown surveyor in Baddeck, D.B. McNab, noted, the New World equivalent of Great Britain's day labourers: they "represent[ed] this class."[12] Quantitative analysis of census data from Middle River in Cape Breton and from Hardwood Hill in Pictou County suggests that in the third quarter of the 19th century, somewhere between a quarter and a third of the households in these agricultural districts of northeastern Nova Scotia needed to earn $100 or more in off-farm income in order to secure a minimal livelihood.[13] At the common agricultural wage rate of roughly 80 cents per day, this would be the equivalent of 125 or more working days.[14] Viewed in another fashion, given an average family food requirement of roughly $200, these farms at best probably derived only half their food needs from their own resources.[15] Data from Middle River confirms as well D.B. McNab's assertion that reliance on off-farm sources of income most often occurred among those who occupied rough hill lands: 84 per cent of the households with negative net farm incomes estimated to be greater than $100 in 1860–61 were those of backlanders.[16] Physical constraints necessitated much of the pattern of adaptation that McNab and others described.

Besides new settlers requiring an income during their years of farm establishment and backlanders grappling with chronic resource problems, analysis of the Middle River census returns indicates yet another stream of rural peoples being propelled into participation in the work force in the mid-19th century and beyond. Estimates of the relationship between farm resources and household needs reveal three basic household categories. At one end of the spectrum there were households, primarily those of backlanders, where farm returns were chronically and substantially short of household subsistence needs—households that of necessity had to look for income beyond the farm across the full course of the family life cycle. On the other extreme there was a significant minority of households, the commercial core of the valley's agricultural economy, where farm production was well in excess of household

309

subsistence needs and the returns from farm product sales were sufficient to permit substantial reinvestments in agriculture and in other pursuits. Members of such households had the option of working for themselves with their own resources or working for others. Wedged between these two strata were families whose condition more closely approximated the image of household self-sufficiency permeating so much of the literature on the rural Maritimes—farms on which the value of production roughly matched current needs. Although they possessed sufficient resources to derive a livelihood from the land, it is clear though, from the census and probate returns, that the resources of many of these households were not expanding at a rate sufficient to permit all their offspring to begin life in similar circumstances. Demographic growth was forcing, and would force, many individuals from an emerging generation within these middle strata households into participation in the labour force.[17]

Throughout the early 19th century, then, substantial numbers of the members of farm households situated in the northeastern Maritimes—new settlers, backlanders (along with others whose farm resources were chronically insufficient for household needs), and some of the offspring of middle-strata households—necessarily had to maintain a significant and regular involvement in the labour force despite the fact that they had access to extensive tracts of land. Added to the ranks of these workers of necessity were many who were drawn for one reason or another by the opportunities afforded by off-farm work, people who might move in and out of the workforce at will alternately deriving a living from farm resources or choosing to participate in the labour force.

Wage work in the timber trade and the shipbuilding industry—agriculture's great rivals for labour in the first half of the 19th century—was, in general, quite different from that in agriculture. This was male employment, and much of the work in these industries was concentrated at sites at some distance from the farms from which many came. Such employment was often for extended periods of time, for woods work was available from late fall until spring, and shipbuilding, when the market dictated, might be conducted on a year-round basis.[18] There were, of course, considerable variations in the nature of the work experience in woods work and shipbuilding.

Some of the employment available within these industries was local and organized in small, perhaps primarily family-based, crews. Hired hands might be added to cluster of brothers cutting logs for the winter or be employed casually in one of the many lesser shipyards turning out modest numbers of smaller vessels. Employment with small local operations where one might return home on a daily basis aided the integration of wage work with farm work. The Irish who settled on the backlands of Lot 29 in southwestern Queen's County, Prince Edward Island, for instance, and who worked in W.W. Lord's timber and shipbuilding operations, were said to have been able to clear their lands and hoe their crops "in spare time."[19] Looking back on his Cape Breton childhood, Aeneas McCharles recalled that his father combined working on his farm in the Baddeck Valley with carpentry work at the shipyards four miles away in the port of Baddeck.[20] Labour in these pursuits, however, was also being organized by capitalists operating on a much larger scale, who relied upon recruiting labourers from beyond the immediate locality of their operations. Entrepreneurs like the Archibalds in Cape Breton and the Popes, Macdonalds, and Cambridges on Prince Edward Island hired scores of men of work at their shipyards, sawmills, and woods operations. So too did their counterparts elsewhere in the region who, even before steam vessels and rail transportation eased the burdens of travel, were drawing labourers from the farms of northern Nova Scotia and Prince Edward Island to work in their operations. By the 1820s and 1830s, farmers in significant numbers were traveling back and forth between the timber camps and shipyards of the Miramichi and their homes in northern Nova Scotia and Prince Edward Island.[21]

Many of those working in these operations were likely to spend part of their lives as bunkhouse men, living at the worksite and labouring on a regular schedule for extended periods of time.[22] In both logging and boatbuilding, wages might be paid partly in kind—shipyards tended to be organized around a truck store—and differentially paid in accordance with a division of labour along skill lines.[23] Farmers and farmers' sons working in the large shipyards shared their workspace with greater numbers than did those in woods camps, and were engaged in work that required more complex forms of organization.[24] The experience of work in the shipbuilding yards that produced large vessels was, as Richard Rice has argued, that of a large, complexly-orchestrated manufactory.

Clearly as the nature of off-farm work varied, so too the ways in which it was integrated into the household economy differed. Daily work close at hand, such as on a neighbouring farm or for a local merchant, permitted, at least in theory, a good deal of flexibility. That farmers and merchants alike required casual labour and employed adults and children, both males and females, meant that various household members might move back and forth between work on the home farm and wage employment. John Beamish Moore's ledger from North Sydney in the 1850s, for instance, shows that the backlander Archy McDonald's household earned wages alternately from Archy's work, that of "his boys," and that of "the girl."[25] The accounts of other backlanders on Moore's ledger show a similar heterogeneity in the composition of household labour made available to the merchant for wages. The same pattern of varying daily movement of different members of the same household in and out of the local agricultural labour force is apparent in the MacNutt farm ledger as men and children, male and female, appear in varying numbers from day to day. One day a father and a couple of sons might be on the pay-roll, another day perhaps only the sons or only the daughters would be employed. There is no way to know whether the pattern was set by demand or by supply, or to discern how in fact those who momentarily disappear from the day book deployed their labour, but clearly local work afforded the possibility of a varied and shifting household response to the needs of the home farm. Local contract work and putting-out work offered similar flexibility. A man who had been hired to mow a field, dig a cellar, or clear land might, particularly if the work was close at hand, exercise some discretion in choosing his hours of employment and integrating such work into other tasks concerning his own resources. As well, he might flexibly use the labour of other members of his household to complete the task. Such would also be the case with the farmer/tailors contracted to sew trousers or for shirtmaking, or the farm women employed by the piece for spinning, weaving, or knitting.

Other employments permitted less flexibility. Some types of work—such as that in shipbuilding, the timber industry, employment with the American fishing fleet, or the construction trades—provided employment almost exclusively for adult males and often entailed working at a considerable distance from one's residence. In homes where the male head engaged in such work, women often were left to manage household and farm for extended periods. Seeking lodgings at a farm house on the Cape Breton-side of the Strait of Canso in the summer of 1831, David Stewart, a Prince Edward Island landlord, and his traveling companion Richard Smith of the General Mining Association, discovered that the man of the farm "was gone to Miramichi to cut lumber."[26] Only Mrs. MacPherson and her two children were home. At midcentury, the Crown surveyor in Baddeck, D.B. McNab, reported that there were "hundreds" of farms located on poorer lands in his region of the Island where the men of the household traveled to "distant parts of the province or to the United States" each summer and left the maintenance of the farm to "their wives and children."[27] With the boom in railway construction and coal mining in the third quarter of the 19th century, a local observer noted that Cape Breton farmers and their sons "by hundreds, nay, thousands, [were] leaving their farms to the women, and seeking employment at the colleries and railways."[28] Some, such as a Highlander born on Lewis residing in Middle River who planted his crop of oats and potatoes and then traveled on foot to Halifax to work on the railway each year, appear to have regularized their patterns of distant wage work so that they synchronized with the seasonal rounds of farming. Come harvest time, the Lewis man would be back in Middle River.[29] In other households the distant wage work of males was made possible because females and children assumed a full array of farm tasks.[30]

Other farm-based workers in the northeast Maritimes, of course, may have resigned themselves to the necessity of perpetually maintaining the dual commitments of self-employment and working for others, or may indeed have embraced wage work never seeking to attain a degree of choice over their involvement in the labour marker.[31] Given the sporadic and uneven nature of the demand for labour in the region in the early 19th century, life without the fall-back of an agricultural holding could be precarious.[32] Rather than working so that they might farm, some, no doubt, farmed so that they might live to work. For many, however, access to the soil held out the hope of achieving control over their time and their labour, and persistence in straddling two worlds constituted a way of resisting the imperatives and dependence of wage work.[33]

We need to look more closely at the transformation of these dreams, which had been closely associated with the myth of the independent yeoman, and at changes in the strategies adopted by working people. Few still maintain that true independence is to be gained by eschewing wage work for agricultural pursuits and by struggling to gain a toehold on the soil. The goal of a "propertied independence" that was embedded in the mythology and once held such an important position in the aspirations of working people of the North Atlantic world has long since lost its lustre. And though many rural residents in the region continue to engage in seasonal work at near and distant job sites, fewer and fewer rely on farming as a means to survive periods when they are not engaged in wage work.[34] Surely these will be key themes for those who would write the environmental history of the region. The decline of the belief that the labourer's salvation was to be found on the land and the decline of agriculture as a safety net have profoundly affected our perception of the significance of arable soil, and of land more generally. For increasing numbers, even of rural residents, it is no longer a matter of importance.

NOTES

1. The phrase is drawn from Daniel Vickers' superb analysis of the ideal and some of its implications. Daniel Vickers, "Competency and Competition: Economic Culture in Early America," *William and Mary Quarterly*, 3rd Series, 47:1 (1990), 3–29.

2. The mythology is often incongruously juxtaposed with another reality. Neil MacNeil, for instance, even as he extols the independence Washabuckers achieved on the land, tells of the regular flow of labour southward and of his grandfather's difficult experiences commuting on foot between Washabuckt and a job many miles north in industrial Cape Breton.

3. In his study of farm-making in Upper Canada in this period, Norman Ball notes the presence of immigrants trapped by similar cycles of poverty there. Norman Rodger Ball, "The Technology of Settlement and Land Clearing in Upper Canada Prior to 1840," PhD dissertation, University of Toronto, 1979, 30–2.

4. D. B. McNab to Uniacke, 3 January 1857, Nova Scotia House of Assembly, *Journals*, 1857, app. 71, 421.

5. Ian Ross Robertson, ed., *The Prince Edward Island Land Commission of 1860* (Fredericton, 1988), 136.

6. A number of John Moores lived in and about North Sydney in the mid-19th century. Stephen Hornsby treats this account book as being that of John *Belcher* Moore. The Public Archives of Nova Scotia, though, stand by their description of it as being that of John *Beamish* Moore. Stephen J. Hornsby, *Nineteenth-Century Cape Breton: A Historical Geography*, 72, 138–9; private correspondence with J.B. Cahill, 26 October 1992.

7. These backlanders may have been selling farm products elsewhere, perhaps closer at hand, but the fact that they routinely purchased bulky items, such as 1/2 barrels of flour and bushels of grain from Moore without ever selling farm goods seems to suggest that they had little or nothing to sell.

8. John Beamish Moore Account Book, 1848–67, 14, Micro Biography, PANS.

9. *Ibid.*, 22.

10. *Ibid.*, 23.

11. *Spirit of the Times* (Sydney), 19 July 1842, 347; Captain W. Moorsom, *Letters From Nova Scotia*, 288.

12. Nova Scotia House of Assembly, *Journals*, 1857, Appendix No. 72, 421.

13. Rusty Bittermann, Robert H. Mackinnon, and Graeme Wynn, "Of Inequality and Interdependence in the Nova Scotian Countryside, 1850–1870," *Canadian Historical Review*, (forthcoming March 1993).

14. The estimate of an average agricultural wage for Nova Scotia is drawn from Julian Gwyn, "Golden Age or Bronze Moment? Wealth and Poverty in Nova Scotia: the 1850s and 1860s," *Canadian Papers in Rural History*, 8 (1992), 195–230.

15. Charles H. Farnham, "Cape Breton Folk," *Harpers New Monthly Magazine* (1886), reprinted in *Acadiensis*, 8:2 (Spring 1979), 100. These estimates are considered in detail in Bittermann, MacKinnon, and Wynn, "Of Inequality and Interdependence in the Nova Scotian Countryside," and Rusty Bittermann, "Middle River; The Social Structure of Agriculture in a Nineteenth-Century Cape Breton Community," MA dissertation, University of New Brunswick, 1987, app. IV.

16. Rusty Bittermann, "Economic Stratification and Agrarian Settlement: Middle River in the Early

Nineteenth Century," in Kenneth Donovan, ed., *The Island: New Perspectives on Cape Breton History 1713–1975*, 86–7.

17. *Ibid.*; Rusty Bittermann, "Middle River: The Social Structure of Agriculture in a Nineteenth-Century Cape Breton Community," 157–9.

18. A.R.M. Lower, *The North American Assault on the Canadian Forest: A History of the Lumber Trade Between Canada and the United States* (Toronto 1938), 32–3; Graeme Wynn, *Timber Colony*, 54; Richard Rice, "Shipbuilding in British America, 1787–1890: An Introductory Study" PhD dissertation, University of Liverpool, 1977, 178–81.

19. Mary Brehaut, ed., *Pioneers on the Island* (Charlottetown 1959), 58. On the local organization of farm-based labour for Prince Edward Island's shipyards see too Basil Greenhill and Ann Giffard. *Westcountrymen in Prince Edward's Isle* (Toronto 1967), 56–76; Malcolm MacQueen, *Skye Pioneers and "The Island"* (Winnipeg 1929), 26.

20. Aeneas McCharles, *Bemocked of Destiny: The Actual Struggles and Experiences of a Canadian Pioneer and the Recollections of a Lifetime* (Toronto 1980), 10–1.

21. *Prince Edward Island Register*, 20 October 1825, 3; John MacGregor, *Historical and Descriptive Sketches of the Maritime Colonies of British America* (London 1828), 168: David Stewart's Journal, 31, PAPEI, 3209/28; *Royal Gazette*, 30 May 1837, 3. See too the *Royal Gazette* 26 June 1838, 3, on the theft of £35—a season's wages—from a lumberman returning from the Miramichi woods to his residence in West River, Pictou County.

22. Abraham Gesner, *The Industrial Resources of Nova Scotia* (Halifax 1849), 215–7; Graeme Wynn, *The Timber Colony*, 62; Arthur R.M. Lower, *Great Britain's Woodyard: British America and the Timber Trade, 1763–1867* (Montreal 1973), 189–96. On shipyard/bunkhouse deaths due to drunkeness and violence see the *Prince Edward Island Register*, 25 September 1824, 3; *Prince Edward Island Register*, 27 February 1827, 3.

23. Richard Rice, "Shipbuilding in British America, 1787–1890: An Introductory Study," PhD dissertation, University of Liverpool, 1977, 171, 186–92. The labour contracts from the 1840s entered in Joseph Dingwell's ledger indicate that he paid most of his labourers half in cash and half in "trade." Joseph Dingwell Ledger, Ms. 3554/1, PAPEI. Capt Moorsom's account of labour relations on the waterfront in Liverpool in the summer of 1828, suggests the reasons for Dingwell's clear indications of the mode of payment in his contracts. There were, he noted, "two scales of value, the "cash price," and the "goods price," and "the various gradation thereof distinctly marked in all transactions between employers and labourers." Moorsom reported a rate of exchange in favor of cash at a ratio of 3 to 4. Captain W. Moorsom, *Letters From Nova Scotia; Comprising Sketches of a Young Country*, 292. For information on Joseph Pope's shipyard and truck store see John Mollison, "Prince County," in D.A. Mackinnon and A.B. Warburton, eds., *Past and Present of Prince Edward Island* (Charlottetown 1906), 86. Lemuel and Artemas Cambridge offered their ship carpenters the choice of employment by the month or payment "by the seam." *Prince Edward Island Register*, 23 May 1826, 3.

24. According to Dougald Henry (b.1817) the modest shipbuilding operation run by the Bells of Stanley River Prince Edward Island employed 30 or more men in the yards. Working days, he relates, began at six with a break for breakfast at 8. For Dougald Henry's account of shipyard life as compiled by Dr. Hedley Ross, see Mary Brehaut, ed., *Pioneers on the Island*, 47.

25. John Beamish Moore Account Book, 1848–67, 22.

26. David Stewart's Journal, 31, PAPEI, 3209/28.

27. Nova Scotia House of Assembly, *Journals*, 1857, Appendix No. 72. 421.

28. *Journal of Agriculture for Nova Scotia*, July 1871, 652.

29. Francis MacGregor, "Days that I Remember," January 1962, Mg. 12, vol. 71, 31, Beaton Institute, Sydney, Nova Scotia.

30. These different patterns of domestic life in poorer households no doubt underwrote the perception that backland women were particularly able workers. Backland girls, notes Margaret MacPhail's character John Campbell, made the best marriage partners as "They can work outside and in and keeps a fellow warm in bed. What else would you want!" Margaret MacPhail, *Loch Bras d'Or* (Windsor, Nova Scotia 1970), 84, 65.

31. Many emigrants had experience with similar work patterns before they migrated. See Barbara M. Kerr, "Irish Seasonal Migration to Great Britain, 1800–38," *Irish Historical Studies*, 3 (1942–3), 365–80;

313

A.J. Youngson, *After the Forty-Five: The Economic Impact on the Scottish Highlands* (Edinburgh 1973), 182–4; T.M. Devine, "Temporary Migration and the Scottish Highlands in the Nineteenth Century," *Economic History Review*, 32(1979), 344–59; William Howatson, "The Scottish Hairst and Seasonal Labour 1600–1870," *Scottish Studies*, 26 (1982), 13–36; E.J.T. Collins, "Migrant Labour in British Agriculture in the Nineteenth Century," *Economic History Review*, 29 (1976), 38–59, As Maritimers moved on, some carried these patterns of work to new locales. See Aeneas McCharles. Bemocked of Destiny, 28; Neil Robinson, *Lion of Scotland* (Auckland 1952, 1974), 28, 80, 99.

32. Judith Fingard, "A Winter's Tale: The Seasonal Contours of Pre-Industrial Poverty in British North America, 1815–1860," *Historical Papers*, (1974),

65–94; D.B. MacNab to Uniacke, 3 January 1857, Nova Scotia House of Assembly, *Journals*, 1857, app. 71, 421.

33. On the significance of agrarian strategies to working-class struggles in Great Britain and the United States in this period see Malcolm Chase, *'The People's Farm:' English Radical Agrarianism, 1775–1850* (Oxford 1988); Sean Wilentz, *Chants Democratic: New York City and the Rise of the American Working Class*, 1788–1850 (New York 1984), 164–216, 335–43; Paul Conkin, *Prophets of Prosperity: America's First Political Economists* (Bloomington 1980), 22–58.

34. The terms of eligibility for unemployment benefits have played a role here in forcing some to choose between a state-based or land-based safety net and/or to define themselves as workers rather than farmers.

Article 4: Saint John: The Making of a Colonial Urban Community

T.W. Acheson

If merchants and merchant leaders were able to dominate the community agenda, particularly before 1840, the opposition to this domination came not from the manual labourers dependent on their system but from the producers' interest. That interest bound together a number of status groups, ranging from apprentice artisans to shopkeepers to established small manufacturers, led by a petite bourgeoisie of small masters. It is an interest that Michael Katz described as a class in his early work on mid-nineteenth-century Hamilton; in his later study of Hamilton and Buffalo he argued that the journeymen and masters were members of competing classes.[1] Other historians have been more tentative in judgment. All agree that an artisanal interest existed in the eighteenth century and that it was gradually eroded in the face of nineteenth-century industrialism. In her study of nineteenth-century Newark, Susan Hirsch argues that artisan deference to the merchant élite

Source: T.W. Acheson, *Saint John: The Making of a Colonial Urban Community* (Toronto, University of Toronto Press, 1984), pp. 67, 68–71, and 73–77. © 2006 University of Toronto Press. Reprinted with permission of the publisher.

had waned by the time of the American Revolution and that a significant artisanal system in which most journeymen were able to become masters by the time they were forty flourished until at least 1830. A similar community of interest among Kingston artisans is described by Bryan Palmer.[2] British studies suggest that even in the late nineteenth century the aristocracy of labour and a petite bourgeoisie of small proprietors remained closely linked.[3] The experience of the artisan group in Saint John demonstrates that it was not just an economic interest but a politically self-conscious social group.

Artisans composed nearly half the original Loyalist freemen of 1785.[4] Throughout the first half of the nineteenth century they rather consistently composed about a third of freeman admissions, a proportion confirmed by the 1851 Census. Comprising a wide variety of occupations and wide range of incomes, the artisans were always a powerful interest and on a number of important issues they did act as a class. By mid-century they perceived themselves, and were perceived by observers of the scene, as the 'bone and sinew' of the community. In terms of economic function, artisans were distinguished from those of higher and lower status in one important way: other groups were concerned with the provision of services, but craftsmen produced all the goods made in the city apart from the simple mechanical process of sawing deals.

In no way did the early city so faithfully reflect the late medieval origins of its institutions as in the means through which the townspeople organized themselves for the production of goods. Production was equated to craft and each craft was structured around a trade, which in turn was organized on the traditional triad of apprentice/journeyman/master. The importance accorded the trades was reflected in the city's constitution, which attempted to restrict both the franchise and the benefit of the trade to those who had served a satisfactory apprenticeship under a master who was a freeman of the city. The apprenticeship process was central to the trades system.[5] Not only did it provide a critical form of educational and skills development, but it instilled the pride, confidence, and sense of apartness that distinguished the training of professionals. This formation of the artisan usually began in early adolescence when the youth was bound over by his parents to a master craftsman. The standard indenture of apprenticeship was a legal document formally assented to by a magistrate binding the young man to a life of servitude in his master's household for a period of from four to eight years. *The Courier* editor, Henry Chubb, 'voluntarily and of his own free will,' was bound to a master printer for seven years at the age of fifteen. The contract, borrowed from traditional English models, provided that the master should teach the art, trade, and mystery of a printer and provide board, lodging, washing, and a new suit of clothing for his apprentice. In return Chubb was required to serve faithfully, keep his master's secrets and commands, neither to damage nor waste his master's goods. He was further forbidden to commit fornication, contract matrimony, play at cards or dice, buy or sell goods without his master's permission, or frequent taverns or theatres.[6]

The control that masters were given over their charges was an attractive feature to civic authorities since it played an important role in the maintenance of order and good discipline among a large segment of the city's male population during the sometimes difficult passage from adolescence to manhood. The exercise of this authority by the masters was encouraged by Common Council, which placed responsibility for the public misdemeanours of apprentices clearly on the shoulders of the masters.[7] The rigorous control was frequently not appreciated by the prentices, and the search for fugitives became a regular feature of the daily press before 1850. By 1817, Henry Chubb, now Master Chubb, was beset by problems with his own apprentice, 'Peter James Wade, 16, smart but a drunkard,' who had fled his master's service.[8] Chubb offered 5*s*. for the return of the apprentice and £5 for information leading to the conviction of those harbouring him. The complaint was not uncommon, but as the law made the harbouring of a fugitive apprentice a hazardous undertaking, most fled the city.[9] As late as 1841, Sam Wilson was arrested for absconding from his master, the sailmaker and assistant alderman Robert Ray, and sentenced to two months at hard labour for assaulting the city marshal who made the arrest.[10]

Despite these commotions, and restrictions, the apprentice system had a good deal to offer young men.[11] In the short run, there was promise of a skill and a paid series of night courses. In the long run, there was a respectable status, admission to the freedom of the city, and the possibility of becoming a master with ownership of a shop.[12] Among a number of Loyalist families, the artisan's status became a tradition that engendered a native tradeocracy comprising an intricate pattern of fathers, sons, grandsons, nephews, uncles, and cousins. Many young second-generation natives could combine a respectable trade with their father's freehold and shop, a sure guarantee of becoming both master and burgher. The Bustins, the Hardings, and the Olives provide characteristic examples of the great trades families of the city. Fifteen Bustins, sixteen Hardings, and sixteen Olives were admitted as freemen between 1785 and 1858. The Bustin clan included five carpenters, four butchers, three harness makers, two masons; the Olives, six ship carpenters, three carpenters, two ship wrights, and a joiner; the Hardings, four tanners, two shoe-makers, and a blacksmith.[13]

Only toward mid-century did the ranks of this tradeocracy begin to break as young third-generation members began to move toward commerce and the professions. The Hardings were particularly successful in this: three became medical doctors, two were merchants, and one entered the law. This mid-century shift out of the trades on the part of young natives is confirmed by the 1851 Census. A sample of 732 east-side households reveals 23 apprentices almost equally divided between natives and Irish arrivals in the 1840s. By contrast the ranks of the young merchants' clerks expanded rapidly in the 1840s and by

1851 their members rivalled those of the apprentice artisans. More than two-thirds of the clerks were natives. Confirmation of the trend out of the crafts, particularly on the part of young natives, is found in the late 1850s in the complaints of *The Courier* editor who bewailed the abandonment of the crafts by young men of artisan families and scolded their parents—particularly their mothers—for denying the dignity of manual work and for placing a premium on any occupation that permitted its occupant to wear a white collar.[14] The decline of the crafts among native families was probably a reaction against the admission of Irish tradesmen who depressed the wages and reduced the importance of the status of artisans. The native-Irish tension was reflected in the matching of masters and apprentices. Native masters accepted only native apprentices, a fact which meant that almost all journeymen boat and coach builders would be natives while the shoemaking trade was given over to the Irish.[15] The native preferences doubtless reflected a traditional pattern of fathers apprenticing their sons to friends and acquaintances in the fathers' craft or in other similar crafts.

The purpose of the apprentice system was to train an exclusive body of skilled workers dedicated to the craft and determined to restrict its practice to those of like formation. The journeymen craftsmen constituted a broad and influential cross-section of the city's population. Together with the masters, they comprised about 35 per cent of the freemen and 35 per cent of all employed males in the city.[16] Thus they easily formed the largest electoral group in the city, outnumbering all commercial freemen by a ratio of two to one.

In 1851, more than three of every four artisans were family heads living in tenements or freeholds of their own. A very small number—about one in fourteen—were single men living with their parents and the remainder—about one in six—were lodgers, one-third of whom lived with employers. Although all were legally required to be freemen to practise their trade, only about two out of five of those in the sample did so. Virtually every master was a freeman but journeymen, particularly in the lesser trades, frequently failed to acquire their freedom. The proportion of freeman rose to half among the native tradesmen, fell to two in five among the Irish, and to little more than one in five among the other groups. It was remarkably low among those of English,

American, Nova Scotian, and Islander origins—doubtless indicating a view toward a temporary residence in the city on the part of members of these groups.

The traditional and emerging trades structures were both plainly visible in 1851. A significant number of master artisans, particularly in the footwear and clothing trades, maintained households that contained both their journeymen and their apprentices. At the other extreme, some individual firms had grown so large that the enterprises might more accurately be described as small factories. Most notable among these were the iron foundries. The Portland blacksmith James Harris had expanded his operations to include a block of buildings employing more than seventy men and boys. Within the city Thomas Barlow employed another sixty-five, and the city's other founders employed comparable numbers. The wage spread between the blacksmith and the foundry-engineers in the metals trades was no greater than that between the small master cabinetmakers employing a few journeymen in their shops and a leading furniture maker like J. W. Lawrence, who employed sixteen men and boys in making furniture to the value of £2250.[17]

Expanding local markets brought about a rapid change in the structure of the traditional trades. Master tradesmen responded to these opportunities in a variety of ways. Immigration produced large numbers of shoe-makers and tailors. These trades required only limited capital—in some cases artisans even owned their own tools—and the result was a profusion of small shops and small masters.[18] By contrast, those trades permitting the application of steam-generated energy tended to remain concentrated in the hands of relatively few masters who added to their shops and employed an increasingly sophisticated technology.[19] Thus, while the shoemaking shops increased in number, offering numerous opportunities for ambitious young tradesmen to possess their own shops, the tanneries were concentrated in the hands of a few masters who came to employ more men in a more structured fashion and to play increasingly important roles in the life of the city. Daniel Ansley, who entered the trade as freeman tanner in 1809 at the age of eighteen and became a leading master tanner, finally classified himself as a merchant in the 1851 Census. Already possessing substantial shops in the early 1830s, four of the tanners greatly increased their capacity after 1840 by the installation of steam engines.[20]

316

The same development occurred in the flour trade. Grist-mill owners had constructed sixteen plants by 1840, each costing between £3000 and £5000 and each capable of grinding between 7000 and 12,000 barrels annually.[21] The most important elements in the city's industrial activities were the sawmills and iron and brass foundries, which became increasingly capital intensive as steam engines largely replaced water-driven mills.

The principal masters of that trade provide a useful insight into the successful trades leadership of the city. James Harris came from Annapolis as a young man and began to practise his blacksmith's craft. He gradually added machine, pattern, and fitting shops to his blacksmith's enterprise. In 1831 he added a blast furnace. Over the next few years a stove shop, a car shop, and a rolling mill completed the New Brunswick Foundry. His partner was a Scottish machinist, Thomas Allen, who completed his apprenticeship in Glasgow and settled in Saint John in 1825. Allen's son Thomas apprenticed as a machinist in his father's foundry, and a second son, Robert, became a moulder through the same process; a third son, Harris, studied as a brass founder. All three came to be owners of Saint John foundries by the early 1860s.[22] The Saint John Foundry was established in 1825 by Robert Foulis (a Scottish scientist and inventor and graduate in medicine of Aberdeen University) and was later taken over by a Fredericton merchant, T.C. Everitt, and two Saint John men, John Camber, a blacksmith, and James Wood, a machinist. George Fleming established the Phoenix Foundry in 1835. Fleming had served as a machinist's apprentice at the Dumferline Foundry in Scotland and then had worked as a journeyman in Glasgow, Cork, Pictou, Saint John, Boston, and Baltimore. His partners included a local carpenter, Thomas Barlow, an iron moulder, John Stewart, and later a long-time clerk with the firm, Thomas Humbert.[23] The city's ten iron and brass foundries in 1860 were thus distinguished by their Scottish and native ownership, by their structure as multiple partnerships that enabled them to bring together the necessary capital resources, and by the size of their producing units.

The foundries were the largest producing units in the city by the end of the colonial period. Three hundred journeymen and apprentices worked in them in 1850;[24] by 1873 the New Brunswick Foundry alone possessed a work-force of 300. The foundries were clearly operating on the factory system. In these, as in the bakery, carriage and cabinet making, tanning, and milling trades, the application of steam power and new technology to create a more efficient system of production was well under way by 1840. The founders, of course, were using steam power before 1830. Barzilia Ansley first brought steam power to a tannery in 1838. Thomas Rankine, a product of a Scottish bakers apprenticeship, introduced hand machinery to his business in 1844 and steam power eight years later. G.F. Thompson did the same in the paint trade in 1850. Four years later, Joseph and George Lawrence introduced steam power to the furniture-making firm their father had established in 1817. That same year Jeremiah Harrison applied steam to the carriage-making trade.[25]

The application of newer techniques to the traditional trades and the consequent growth of the firms between 1830 and 1860 certainly led to the growth of a group of prosperous masters having less and less in common with their journeymen and, conversely, limited the opportunities for those journeymen to acquire their own shops.[26] Yet the effect of this should not be overplayed. The growth of larger producing units was a slow process and in most firms involved a master artisan who had been a long-time resident of the city. Most important, apart from the iron foundries and a few sawmills, none of the producing units before 1850 could be described as factories in the sense that they employed more than twenty-five people in a plant powered by steam engines or water paddles. Most Saint John artisans in 1851 worked either in artisans' shops employing no more than five people or in the shipyards.[27] Moreover, the trades represented as much a social as an economic status. James Harris, Daniel Ansley, and the baker Stephen Humbert might become prominent, prosperous burghers, might even hold the Queen's Commission of the Peace with the right to style themselves 'Esquire.' Yet they remained artisans, married the daughters of artisans, and expressed the attitudes and biases of artisans, were perceived as tradesmen by their social superiors, and supported the interests of artisans. Throughout the colonial period—despite the changing structure and work relationships within some trades—that ethos remained a powerful source of identification binding most elements of the trades into a common interest.

This is not to suggest that loyalty to that interest was not sometimes divided or that elements of the

317

interest did not war among themselves. The masters' use of the law to enforce obedience upon the apprentices has already been mentioned. Richard Rice has demonstrated the presence of Friendly Societies of carpenters, joiners, cabinet-makers, and painters as early as 1837, but no evidence that any of them took action against the masters.[28] Confrontations between masters and journeymen, usually over rates of pay or slow payment, occasionally occurred. As early as 1830 the journeymen tailors of the city threatened to withhold their labour until the masters agreed to make payment of wages within three days of the completion of their work and to charge no more than 12*s.* board each week. No further evidence of confrontation occurred until 1841 when a mechanic wrote to the smiths and moulders of the city in the columns of *The News* calling for a one-hour reduction in the workday.[29] In 1856 journeymen printers at *The Courier* withdrew their services because their employer had taken an extra apprentice into the office.[30] Significantly, although Eugene Forsey has provided evidence of a ship carpenters organization, there is no evidence of any confrontations in the shipyards of Saint John.[31]

But incidents of this nature, although indicating an underlying tension within the interest, were relatively few. More important, they were short-lived and left few permanent scars. For the deeply alienated journeyman, Boston lay near and emigration provided a final solution when insoluble problems arose. By contrast, the activities of masters and journeymen, whether working alone or in concert with other groups within the city, revealed something closely resembling a genuine class consciousness.

NOTES

1. See M.B. Katz, *The People of Hamilton, Canada West* (Cambridge, Mass. 1975), 27, 311, and with M.J. Doucet and M.J. Stern, *The Social Organization of Early Industrial Capitalism* (Cambridge, Mass. 1982), ch. 1. In his second work, Katz argues that all nineteenth-century urban societies were divided into a business class and a working class and these corresponded to those who owned the means of production and those who sold their labour in return for money. Membership in the class, then, has nothing to do with class consciousness or class awareness; one is a member of a class because of one's relationship to the means of production. It is difficult to quarrel with any objective statement of classification. However, Katz destroys the objectivity of his model by insisting that the business class contains not only 'those individuals who owned the means of production' but also 'those whose interests and aspirations identified them with the owners' (p. 44). Using this definition Katz assigns entire categories of men to the business class: all professionals and even the meanest clerk or school teacher become a capitalist. It is not improbable that a majority of members of the business class did not own the means of production unless it is defined in terms of skills or hand tools. Leaving aside the question of how the historian measures the aspirations of each member of a society—a concept that, in any event, seems very akin to class consciousness—why does Katz assume that no artisan or labourer possessed any aspiration to become a proprietor or at least to better his material lot in life? And if that possibility is admitted, is it possible to assign artisans en masse to the working class?

2. Susan Hirsch, *Roots of the American Working Class: The Industrialization of Crafts in Newark 1800–1860* (Philadelphia 1978), 8, 11, 12, 41; Bryan Palmer, 'Kingston Mechanics and the Rise of the Penitentiary, 1833–1836,' *Histoire Sociale/Social History* (May 1980):7–32.

3. See, for example, Robert Gray, *The Labour Aristocracy in Victorian Edinburgh*.

4. Freemen's roll of the city of Saint John 1785–1862, NBM.

5. A point made by Hirsch in her study of Newark. Palmer, however, sees it as an exploitative arrangement after 1800. See Hirsch, Roots, 6, and Bryan A. Palmer, *Working–Class Experience: The Rise and Reconstitution of Canadian Labour 1800–1980* (Toronto 1983), 28–9.

6. Indenture of Henry Chubb, Chubb Family Papers, NBM.

7. See, for example, the firecracker ordinance of 1819 that provided a 20s. fine against the master of the offender (*City Gazette*, 11 August 1819).

8. *The Courier*, 15 January 1817.

9. See, for example, *The Courier*, 18 January, 25 September, and 15 November 1817.

10. Ibid., 12 June 1843.

11. Despite Katz's contention that few nineteenth-century journeymen became masters, Bruce Laurie

has demonstrated that over half the Methodist and Presbyterian journeymen in 1830 were masters or small retailers by 1850. Hirsch found that most Newark artisans over the age of forty were masters. See Bruce Laurie, *The Working People of Philadelphia 1850–1880* (Philadelphia 1980), 48.

12. See the Mechanics Institute School in *The Courier*, 28 December 1839 and the petition of Peter Cougle for release from his apprenticeship after 3 years, 9 months of service with H. Littlehale, a house joiner. Common Council supplementary papers, vol. 4, 30 June 1842, PANB.

13. These examples are drawn from the Roll of Freeman.

14. *The Courier*, 28 October 1858.

15. These data are drawn from the 1851 Census manuscript sample.

16. On the relative strength of the artisan group in other British North American cities see Palmer, *Working-Class Experience*, 31, and Katz, *The People of Hamilton*, 70.

17. Saint John 1851 Census manuscript, Kings Ward, 238, PANB.

18. As was the case in Newark. See Hirsch, 'Roots', 8.

19. Ibid., ch 2.

20. RLE/834, pe. 91; RLE/845, pe, 208; PANB.

21. RLE/828, pe. 42, 43; RLE/840, pe. 122; RLE/850, 418; *The Chronicle*, 22 March 1839.

22. *St. John and Its Business: A History of St. John* (Saint John 1875), 124, 128–9.

23. Ibid., 125–6.

24. RLE/851, pe. 412, PANB.

25. *St. John and Its Business*, 101, 103, 105, 137.

26. This is what Katz assumed in his work on Hamilton and Buffalo. Crossick, too, has reservations about the closeness of small masters and men in mid-nineteenth-century Birmingham. Hirsch, however, found that small masters in Newark paid fairer wages and kept their firms operating longer in times of adversity than did larger operations. See Crossick, 'Urban Society and the Petite Bourgeoisie,' 322, and Hirsch, *Roots*, 89–90.

27. A useful comparison and discussion of work place forms is found in Bruce Laurie, *Working People of Philadelphia 1800–1850* (Philadelphia 1980), ch. 1.

28. J.R. Rice, 'A History of Organized Labour in Saint John, N.B., 1815–1890' (MA thesis, University of New Brunswick 1968), ch. 1. Rice suggests that collective action by shipwrights and carpenters may have begun in 1799, but it is probable that the principal shipwrights' who composed the organization were the masters, not the journeymen. The earliest active unions were among shop clerks, the semi-skilled and unskilled sawyers, and ship labourers. The first documented instance of artisans taking action against masters occurred in 1864 when the caulkers struck for several months. (ch. ii).

29. *The Courier*, 29 May 1830. Tailors were usually paid half in board and half in cash; *The News*, 17 May 1841.

30. *The Courier*, 20 December 1856.

31. Eugene Forsey found evidence of organizations among sawyers, ship carpenters, carpenters and joiners, tailors, and cabinet-makers between 1835 and 1849. Yet there is no indication of any activity directed against their employers. See Forsey, *The Trade Unions in Canada* (Toronto 1982), 9–10.

319

THE MÉTIS AND RED RIVER SOCIETY

Change, Adaptation, and Resistance—1830s to 1870s

Maureen Lux
Brock University

THE MÉTIS AND RED RIVER SOCIETY: CHANGE, ADAPTATION, AND RESISTANCE—1830s TO 1870s

Introduction by Maureen Lux

● INTRODUCTION

Maureen Lux

In August 1830 George Simpson, governor of the Hudson's Bay Company (HBC), returned to Red River from Scotland, accompanied by his new bride (who also happened to be his cousin), Frances Simpson. Although she would leave after a few short years, Mrs. Simpson's arrival presaged fundamental changes to fur trade society. Her presence as one of the first white women at Red River reinforced emerging distinctions of race and class. As one trader remarked upon her arrival, "things are not on the same footing as formerly."[1]

The Red River settlement sat at the forks of the Red and Assiniboine rivers (the heart of modern-day Winnipeg), which had long been an important transportation route and meeting place for the Cree, Saulteaux, Assiniboine, and later French-Canadians, English, Scots and Métis.[2] It was the hub of the Montreal-based North West Company's (NWC) fur trade transportation network and the centre of pemmican production that provisioned the canoe brigades en route to the farthest reaches of the Athabasca country. Fierce and often violent competition between the HBC and the NWC, so destructive to traders and their Aboriginal clients, was even more disastrous for company profits. As a result, in 1821 the rival companies merged while retaining the HBC name. By the time Mrs. Simpson arrived at Red River it was home to traders and their families arriving from outlying posts where, since the merger, their services were no longer needed; to farmers working their long river lots, who also engaged in annual buffalo hunts; and to Métis buffalo hunters and traders who engaged in the increasingly lucrative buffalo hide trade and who, by the 1840s, successfully challenged the HBC monopoly on trade.

As historian Sylvia Van Kirk argues in "The Impact of White Women on Fur Trade Society," Aboriginal social and cultural norms heavily influenced fur trade society. *Marriage à la façon du pays,* or marriage in the country manner, was only the most obvious. Mrs. Simpson's arrival was symbolic of larger changes taking hold of fur trade society; ideas of race, class, and respectability that were swirling throughout the British Empire arrived in the West as well. Newly arrived Protestant missionaries took a dim view of fur trade marriages, however stable and loving, characterizing them as sinful and pagan. Christianity and permanent settlement, not Aboriginal and Métis mores and culture based in the hunt, should define Red River society. And although Mrs. Simpson's stay was brief, the new notions that increasingly divided society along racial lines remained.

Economic change too defined the middle decades of the nineteenth-century West. In "Dispossession or Adaptation," historian Gerhard Ens examines changes in the economic pursuits of the Red River Métis. Ens revises the interpretations of an earlier generation of scholars who characterized the Métis as both culturally and economically "primitive" and thus unable to adapt to change. He also argues that Métis westward movement in the decades surrounding the 1869–70 Red River resistance was primarily motivated by the increasingly profitable buffalo-robe trade, and not necessarily in response to the social and political changes at Red River. While Ens's interpretation tends to discount the racism and duplicitous dealings of the incoming Canadians, he does allow that the Métis actively pursued their own interests and were not merely victims of a changing economic, political, and social world.

Norbert Welsh's life, recounted in his remarkable memoir *The Last Buffalo Hunter,* spanned some of these profound changes in the prairie West. Born in 1845 at Red River, Welsh went out to work at the tender age of eight. His father, an HBC employee, died

323

when Welsh was an infant, so his Métis mother worked their small plot on the Assiniboine River and sold moccasins and coats to support her seven children. As a trader Welsh migrated westward with the disappearing buffalo herds, trading with Aboriginal hunters and wintering with other mixed-blood families on the prairies. Not an educated man by academic standards, Welsh spoke seven languages—French, Cree, Sioux, Blackfoot, Assiniboine, Stoney, and English. In 1931 Mary Weekes, a budding writer, quite by chance met the blind 86-year-old Welsh while she was holidaying in cottage country in the Qu'Appelle Valley east of Regina and convinced him to tell his life story. One of the few surviving oral accounts of the period, Welsh's extraordinary life story was originally published in 1939, and reprinted in 1994. Welsh's story tends to support Ens's conclusions that economic opportunity enticed some Métis from Red River.

Red River society was increasingly stratified by the 1850s with HBC officers at the top, wealthier merchants in the middle, and the Métis cartmen and boatmen at the bottom. With the arrival of a small but noisy group of Canadian expansionists calling themselves the Canadian Party, led by John Christian Schultz, agitation for Canadian annexation of Red River and points west began in earnest. Utilizing the language of racial superiority, the expansionists argued that as white Anglo-Saxons, the pinnacle of "civilization," they should control the wealth and resources of the West. Métis and Aboriginal people, as "primitives," were incapable of developing what was increasingly seen as a settlement frontier. Canada—or rather Ontario—was looking West and saw its future, indeed the future of the British Empire itself, in the development of the West for settlement and investment. Alexander Morris, an Ontario lawyer, Conservative politician, and ardent expansionist, published his 1858 lectures as *Nova Britannia*. Confederation and westward expansion would lift Canada into national greatness and at the same time add another jewel to the British Empire. For many like Morris, to be a Canadian nationalist was to be an imperialist. But his description of the West as "unoccupied" foreshadowed the clumsy efforts of the Canadian government to annex the West, which prompted the 1869–1870 Red River Resistance.

In 1869 the newly formed Canadian government purchased Rupert's Land, or the Hudson's Bay Company lands, in what was surely one of the world's greatest real estate transactions: nearly four million square kilometres or about 40 percent of the modern nation for £300,000, but also 5 percent of all the land. Unfortunately the annexation was pursued like a business deal. No one bothered to consult the nearly 12,000 Métis and Aboriginal people at Red River whose homeland had just been sold! Rumours spread about the new government's intentions when the arriving Canadians associated themselves with the racist and condescending Canadian Party at Red River. As historian Gerald Friesen explains in "The Métis and the Red River Settlement," a group of French-speaking Métis led by Louis Riel first organized the resistance in October 1869 by forcing surveyors from their lands; next, they refused entry to the incoming Lieutenant-Governor William McDougall; and on 2 November they occupied Upper Fort Garry, the administrative and economic centre of the settlement. And not a shot had been fired. As head of the provisional government, Riel demanded the right to negotiate Red River's entry into Confederation and pressed for provincial status, responsible government, bilingual institutions, and guarantees of land titles. The *Manitoba Act* of 1870 embodied most of the Métis demands. But the dream of Confederation, a western colony for settlement and investment controlled by Ottawa, would not be lost in the negotiations. While the *Manitoba Act* created the tiny "postage stamp" province of Manitoba, it also created the vast North-West Territories. Canada finally acquired the colony it desired.

In the aftermath of the Resistance, which the Métis at Red River suffered at the hands of Colonel Wolseley's undisciplined troops, which arrived at Red River in 1870. Moreover, the government seemed unable or unwilling to make good on its promise of 1.4 million acres of land for the Métis. Many left Red River to join family and friends in established communities farther west at Batoche on the banks of the Saskatchewan River—where, 15 years later, Riel would lead another resistance but with a much more tragic end.

NOTES

1. Quoted in Sylvia Van Kirk, "The Impact of White Women on Fur Trade Society."
2. *Métis* refers to the offspring of marriages between Europeans and Aboriginal women. The Métis, in particular those of French and Aboriginal ancestry, lived throughout the West, but Red River was the centre of settlement where they pursued a mixed economy of agriculture and buffalo hunting. They had, by the mid-nineteenth century, developed a distinct and unique society, neither French nor Aboriginal, calling themselves the New Nation. Generally, Métis or mixed-blood children of Aboriginal and English ancestry (often the children of HBC officers), raised and educated in their father's cultural and religious tradition, did not develop as a separate society.

QUESTIONS

1. In current debates about marriage, it is often stated that a Christian notion of lifelong marriage is "normal" and "traditional." But it is clear that different forms of marriage were widespread in the west. How and why was marriage *à la façon du pays* supplanted?
2. Norbert Welsh's memoir *The Last Buffalo Hunter* is a recollection of events long past. What are the strengths of this kind of historical source? What are the weaknesses?
3. How did changing notions of race and class arrive at Red River? Does economic change affect social change?
4. Gerhard Ens maintains that the Métis were not so much pushed from Red River, but that economic 'adaptation' drew them west. What sources does he use to prove his point? What sources does he leave out? Are you convinced by his argument?
5. Alexander Morris' 1858 lecture saw the Hudson's Bay Company as the only obstacle to western expansion. Why were the people at Red River not consulted?
6. Why did Riel and his supporters at Red River resist the Canadian plans for their homeland?

FURTHER READINGS

Brown, Jennifer S. H. *Strangers in Blood: Fur Trade Company Families in Indian Country*. Vancouver: University of British Columbia Press, 1980.

Bumsted, J. M. *Louis Riel v. Canada: The Making of a Rebel*. Winnipeg: Great Plains Publications, 2001.

Cater, Sarah. *Aboriginal People and the Colonizers of Western Canada to 1900*. Toronto: University of Toronto Press, 1999.

Ens, Gerhard. *Homeland to Hinterland: The Changing Worlds of the Red River Métis in the Nineteenth Century*. Toronto: University of Toronto Press, 1996.

Van Kirk, Sylvia. *Many Tender Ties: Women in Fur-Trade Society, 1670–1870*. Winnipeg: Watson & Dwyer, 1999, reprint 1980.

▲ Document 1: The Last Buffalo Hunter

Norbert Welsh

Chapter 1: My First Buffalo Hunt

At eighteen years of age I joined a trading party and left St. Boniface to go west, buffalo hunting. I was hired to a man called Joseph MacKay, who had ten Red River carts and fifteen horses in his outfit. MacKay got his goods from an Englishman named Bannatyne, a big merchant at that time at Fort Garry.

We packed everything in those ten carts and left Fort Garry [Red River] on September 10, 1862. On our first day we came to place called St. François Xavier, eighteen miles from Fort Garry, coming west. This was MacKay's headquarters; he was staying with his father-in-law, Pierre Poitras. We spent two days here, fixing up things for the trip; then we hitched up and travelled as far as Portage-la-Prairie, forty-two miles from St. François Xavier.

We generally travelled all day without stopping, except for two hours at noon to rest and to feed our horses. When we were in a settlement we bought fresh meat, but on the prairie we ate pemmican—buffalo steak pounded with fat—and dried buffalo meat. The two women in the party did the cooking. They made fine bannocks by mixing flour, water, and baking powder together, and cooking it in frying pans before an open fire. We carried butter in jars, and, of course, we had plenty of tea and sugar. Sometimes we could get potatoes at the Hudson's Bay Company's posts.

There were in our party Trader MacKay, his wife and little boy, MacKay's brother-in-law and his wife, and myself. We went on to MacKay's headquarters at Big Stone Lake, near Victoria Mission[1]—this was north-east of Edmonton—and put up there for the winter. It took us nearly thirty days to make the trip.

MacKay's supplies consisted of tobacco, tea, sugar, powder, shot, small bullets, Hudson's Bay blankets, all kinds of prints and cottons, vermilion (lots of vermilion), axes, butcher knives, files, copper kettles, guns, and—the main thing—alcohol, lots and lots of alcohol.

We were now across the river on the south side of the north branch of the Saskatchewan. We were travelling southwest in the direction of the Rockies. We hitched up our horses. We had now about twenty-five carts in the brigade, a man to each cart. We travelled for two days, but saw no sign of buffalo. We were getting anxious as we hadn't much grub with us. But just then one of our scouts, who had started out very early in the morning on the lookout for buffalo, sighted a cow which he shot and skinned; the carcass he brought back to camp on his horse before we were up.

We soon dressed. Each man was given a piece of buffalo meat, which he cooked for his breakfast. We made a big feast. The buffalo scout said that as this had been a lone buffalo, he had shot it. Had he seen a herd, he would not have fired. A shot would have started a stampede.

The next day we came across the buffalo herd, a small one, and each man that had a buffalo horse—that is, a fast runner, one that can run a half mile a minute—got on its back and chased buffalo. There were fifty or sixty in the herd, and out of these we killed forty-five. We used single and double-barrelled guns, and loaded our guns as we rode. We skinned the buffalo, cut up the meat and packed it in our carts. I was delighted, as this was my first buffalo hunt.

Source: Mary Weekes, *The Last Buffalo Hunter*, (Saskatoon: Fifth House, 1994). First published 1939.

The next morning we started back home. We had enough meat for the winter. It was now two or three weeks since we had left our headquarters at Big Stone Lake. It was the beginning of November and very cold.

Chapter Two: My First Trading Trip

That winter my boss sent me out on a trading trip. He fitted up two dog trains, four dogs on each train, and gave me an outfit of goods worth two hundred and fifty dollars, some dried meat, and pemmican. I had my dogs well harnessed, plenty of bells on them and ribbons flying all over. These dogs were of common breed—we could not get Eskimo dogs—but they were strong. Each dog could pull four hundred pounds and race with it. I had a young Indian driving one team. We went very fast over the plains. Sometimes we would ride on the sleigh, and sometimes we would run beside or behind it.

We took in trade, at that time, buffalo robes, and all kinds of furs, fox, wolf, beaver, otter, badger, and skunk.

When I wanted to buy a robe from an Indian I examined it, and I turned it over. If it was a good one, I told the Indian that it was, and that I would give him *pee-ack-wap-sh*. That meant in Cree about a dollar for a good buffalo robe. If it was not a good one, I would not pay that much.

For one buffalo robe valued at a dollar and a quarter, we gave in trade one pound of tea, which cost twenty-five cents at Fort Garry, and half a pound of sugar which cost five cents.

In trading with the Indians, we sold our tea for a dollar a pound, sugar for fifty cents a pound, and one big plug of T and B tobacco for a dollar. This tobacco cost, in Fort Garry, eighty cents a pound, and there were four plugs to the pound.

Any kind of print or cotton measured to the extension of the arms, approximately two yards, and which cost ten cents a yard, we sold for a dollar a yard. For powder, one pint (two little tin dippers-full made a pound) that cost forty cents a pound by the keg, we got a dollar a pound. Bullets that cost two dollars and a half for a twenty-five pound sack, we sold at the rate of ten for fifty cents.

We had different sizes of Hudson's Bay copper kettles. If an Indian wanted a kettle, we would ask what size, and how many gallons. The gallon size was priced at a dollar and a half, the two gallon size at three dollars, and so on. Vermilion was expensive. We would take a knife, dip it into the tin of vermilion, and what we could hold on the tip of it was worth twenty-five cents. (Later, when I traded for myself, I kept a teaspoon in my vermilion box and gave a teaspoonful for twenty-five cents.) A pound of vermilion cost eighty cents wholesale. Butcher knives cost two dollars and a half a dozen. We sold the large ones for two dollars each, the smaller ones for a dollar and seventy-five cents, and so on down.

South of what is now Edmonton, we came to a big camp of Indians. They saw us coming, and one of the headmen came out to meet us. He invited us to trade in the camp, which was Poundmaker's.

I did not know much about the Indians at that time, but MacKay had told me, "When you get to an Indian camp, they will give you a tent for yourself always. The first thing you do is to give them a little tea, sugar, and tobacco. Then they will make tea, smoke, visit, and tell each other that they ought to trade with you."

I followed this advice. Soon the Indians began to come toward us, the headmen, the women, and the children. They drank tea. They brought their furs. We began to trade.

That was not a very good year for robes as the buffalo were beginning to get scarce, but all the same I made a good trade. I think I must have taken out of that camp twenty-two

327

buffalo robes. I also took ten wolf skins—not coyote but regular prairie wolf—five red foxes, and some dried meat and pemmican. The furs alone were valued at three hundred dollars. My boss had given me an outfit worth two hundred and fifty dollars, but I tell you it did not take much goods to total that amount in those days. The prices of goods were high, and the prices for the furs were low.

I spent two days trading in Poundmaker's camp. Poundmaker's own tent was very large. It was conical in shape, and took sixteen buffalo hides to cover it. The buffalo skins were well tanned, and well decorated with stripes, figures, and animals. There were seven people in his family, and they all lived in this tent.

[…]

There were about sixty tents, or lodges, in Poundmaker's whole camp. The Indians were mixed. There were some Crees, a few Assiniboines, but very few, and a few Chipewyans. The Indians were always mixed in those big camps. Poundmaker himself was a Cree, but he had a little mixed blood. There were two tribes, the Crees who had pure blood, and the Little Crees, who had mixed blood. Poundmaker was slightly related to me by one of my grandfathers, André Trottier, on my deceased wife's side.

Poundmaker was very quiet. He never visited the other tents of his camp unless he was invited. He did not come to trade himself. I did business with his headmen, who called me *Wa-ka-kootchick*, which meant "Turned-Up-Nose." Poundmaker was a man of good judgment. He was well liked by his men, and that was everything. They had confidence in him, and were contented.

[…]

We started about the last of August, 1863, and travelled to the Saskatchewan country, to a place called Round Plains (now Dundurn) along the south branch of the Saskatchewan River.

We got there quite late, about the last of October, so we decided to make this place our headquarters for the season. […]

One day, after we had been there for two or three days, an Indian galloped up to my tent. He rode a fine horse. He was well painted with vermilion, and finely dressed in buckskins. His saddle was well decorated with beads.

I spoke to him in Cree, asking where he had come from, and what he wanted. He shook his head and answered in Assiniboine that he did not understand Cree. We then talked in Assiniboine. He told me that he and his band of ten tents were going to camp on the top of the hill. In these ten tents there would be between forty and fifty Indians. It was the Chief of the band that I was talking to, but I did not know it.

I found out by further questioning that his name was Hoo-hoo-sish, or Little Owl. I asked him what he wanted. He replied that he wanted to trade, and wanted to know if I were a trader. I replied that I was, and asked him what he needed. He wanted tea, sugar, tobacco, prints, blankets, and lots of things, alcohol as well, he answered. He said that he had many furs to sell. I told him that I would trade with him. He said that he would tell his people, and he went back to this tents.

[…]

Chapter Three: Alcohol—The Stuff of Trade

It was now winter and I had to cross the river to find out what my men, who were hunting buffalo, were doing. The hunting-camp was quite a distance from the river. It consisted of fifty or sixty lodges. The Chief of the camp was One Arrow[1] (Kah-payuk-wah-skoonum). He told me that I had come in good time to see the Indians run a band of buffalo into a pound. We went to examine the pound, for I had never seen one before. It was in a bluff.

I saw what work the hunters had put in. They had shut in a good half acre with trees, and around this they had built, out of poplar logs, a wall about four feet thick. This wall was very solid. I noticed a big poplar tree standing in the centre of the corral. I asked the Chief why they had left this tree. It was for the good Manitou, he said, who would induce the buffalo to come. They would put offerings on the tree, and in the morning there would be a big herd.

Night came. The Chief and an Indian went from tent to tent collecting tobacco, tea, and sugar to give to the scout. He was a fast rider who was going out to ride all night, and to locate and herd the buffalo in the direction of the pound. This man was an expert at herding buffalo. After the scout had gone, the Chief invited me to get a gun, and to be ready to join in the buffalo hunt the next day.

Morning came. We had no watches, but we could tell time fairly accurately. It was about eight or nine o'clock when the buffalo were sighted. On the road, which spread out for a mile from the pound, men and women were placed a quarter of a mile apart to jump up and scare, or lump, the buffalo as they were driven into the pound. The pound was soon full, and there must have been a thousand buffalo outside of it.

I was standing on top of the fence looking on as the buffalo came in. I found it droll that the first buffalo that entered the pound went round and round the centre tree in a circle like the sun, and each buffalo that was driven in afterward did the same thing. Now the pound was so crowded that the buffalo could not move. We started to shoot. We had guns, bows and arrows, and butcher-knives. When we got through there were one hundred and seventy dead buffalo in the pound. The buffalo were shared. My men got twelve.

I made several trips that winter to Indian camps. I got a lot of furs. I had brought this year from Fort Garry, two forty-gallon kegs of pure alcohol. I never took goods with alcohol when I went out on trading trips, because when the Indians got drunk they wanted the goods for nothing. So, on one trip I took alcohol, and on the next, goods.

One night on my return from a trading trip it came to my mind what a bad deal I had made with Tait—the agreement to sell so much alcohol to the Indians. Right there I decided to make the alcohol stronger; that is, dilute it one to two, instead of one to three. I did this. Ho! My Indians discovered the change at once, and wanted to know why the alcohol was more intoxicating. The second barrel was stronger than the first, I told them. To this they said, "Oh! Oh! We understand."

My idea was to get rid of the alcohol as quickly as possible. My conscience was telling me that I was selling too much water. I got rid of the alcohol. My conscience was eased and I felt better. Now I had nothing but the goods to trade and that didn't take long. Spring arrived. About the middle of April a big thaw came. We packed our furs and buffalo robes, and got our carts ready to start for Fort Garry.

All the fur-traders started together. We were a big company, about one hundred and fifty carts, and thirty families. It took us four days to travel from Round Plain to Devil's Lake (now Watrous). We camped beside the big bush that was there at that time.

We were a very jolly group. We sang as we travelled. Someone would start singing the songs of the trail, and soon the whole crowd would be singing. We sang *Les Adieu* and *Le Braconnier*, and many other songs.

I must have taken in on that trip four thousand dollars worth of furs. We reached Fort Garry on the 25th day of May, 1864. When I came to settle up with Robert Tait, he claimed

329

that I was short sixty dollars. He took this amount out of my pay of two hundred and fifty dollars for managing his fur trading trip. I had not made a mistake about his character.

Chapter Five: A Winter Hunt

A few weeks later we started on a winter hunt, just the men. A party of ten started out on our buffalo runners. A blinding blizzard came on. It was about forty below zero, but we kept on. I shot ten buffalo. Then we had to skin the buffalo in the blizzard. We were on the open plain, and had no shelter, but we were not cold. We were no weaklings, we men of the old brigades! I had a man helping me. The first cow we skinned, we cut her open, and to pieces. Then I cut a hole in the tripe. The manure was hot, and whenever our hands got cold, we would run and put them in the manure, and they would get as warm as fire.

At night when we got back to camp (there were three tents of us) my uncle, Charles Trottier, said he would go and find out how many buffalo the other fellows had killed. In our little brigade of fifteen men—five had joined our party since we left home—we had shot eighty buffalo, skinned them, and brought hides and carcasses back to camp. Next morning we packed our meat and hides into jumpers and returned to our headquarters.

On a second hunt that winter, a lot of us, twenty or thirty men, crossed the river. We travelled for two days, but saw no sign of buffalo. Our rations were getting low. Our chief, *Ak-a-pow*,[1] Gabriel Dumont's father, called a meeting. He asked us what we thought we should do. There was no sign of buffalo and we were nearly out of fresh meat. One man got up and asked Dumont to propose what we should do.

Dumont appointed four men to get up early in the morning and go scouting for buffalo. One was named to go to the east—more north than east; one to the south-east; one to the south-west; and the other to the north-west. I was named the first, and directed to go to the south-west. That would be in the direction of where Calgary is now, but on the west side of the south branch of the Saskatchewan River.

Dumont told me to go south-west to the forks of the Red Deer River,[2] and south branch of the Saskatchewan. If I hadn't seen buffalo before that, I would see there a big hill which I was to climb to get a good view of the country. Gabriel Dumont was appointed to go north-east. Baptiste Parenteau was sent south-east. He also had to climb a hill. Another fellow, Joseph Azure, was sent north-west.

We got up early in the morning and started off. I had a fine big horse. He could gallop all day. I tied a little lunch to my saddle and rode away. I galloped until I thought, by the sun, that it was dinner time. We could tell time almost exactly by standing and facing the sun. If we could step the length of our shadow it was twelve o'clock. The Indians and traders measured time this way.

I could see buffalo all over. There were thousands and thousands of them travelling in the direction in which I had seen the bull. There was not one herd, but many. Our Chief decided that we would have breakfast before we did anything. He went from tent to tent and gathered up all the food. We had a good breakfast, and by ten o'clock were ready to chase the buffalo.

Two or three men took a herd. That afternoon twenty-five men shot three hundred buffalo. Buffalo never came very close to camp. They would smell us, bunch together, and move away. They seldom came nearer than two or three miles.

The next day we went after the buffalo again and killed four hundred. All around us, as far as we could see, the plains were black with buffalo. The prairie seemed to be moving.

There was one thing that I did not like about that hunt. I saw hundreds of buffalo, during that week, slaughtered for their hides. The whole carcass was left to rot on the plains. One time I saw three fine fat buffalo cows lying dead, side by side. I jumped off my horse, cut out their tongues, tied them to my saddle, and took them home. Buffalo tongue was very choice.

There were many bands of hunters on the plains beside ours. In all my years of buffalo hunting, I never destroyed buffalo for their pelts alone. I always took the whole carcass, except the head, home.

My wife had once said that since we were going to make a living hunting buffalo, she did not want me to kill more than we could dry and pack. She told me that if I brought in an extra hide without the carcass, she would not dress it. One day my brother-in-law and I were travelling on the prairie, and we sighted a little herd of buffalo. I let fly and killed a cow. We skinned it, and took a little of the fattest part of the animal. When we reached our tent, I threw the hide and saddle down. My wife smiled, and lightly kicked the hide away. She meant what she said. I gave the hide to my mother-in-law.

After the second day of this particular hunt there were a great many buffalo shot for their hides. Too many. But I can say that very few of the hunters in our brigade wanted to kill buffalo just for the hides

We camped there for a week. We had a hundred people in our brigade, and they were all loaded—the carts followed the hunters. It took us four days to get home. All around us the buffalo travelled. When we got back to Round Plain, we found the buffalo there, too. We had a good time that winter. Plenty of buffalo.

The Yankees shot more buffalo for their hides than all the Indian and half-breed hunters put together. The Indians knew better. They did not want to see the buffalo gone forever. Parties of Yankees used to come up to the North-West to shoot for sport. They would sit on a hill and shoot. Once Buffalo Bill came on a shooting trip, and shot five hundred buffalo—just for fun.

Colonel Cody was known as "Buffalo Bill," because he contracted with the Kansas Pacific Railway to supply its laborers with buffalo meat. In eighteen months he killed four thousand two hundred and eighty buffalo. In 1883 he organized the "Wild West Show," an exhibition designed to represent life on the frontier.

[…]

NOTES

Chapter 1

1. Author's Note: The Hudson's Bay Company had a post at Victoria Settlement on the North Saskatchewan River about 70 miles below Edmonton. It was established about 1870.

Chapter 3

1. One Arrow (Kah-payuk-wah-skoonm) was one of signers of the Forts Carlton and Pitt Treaty in 1876. Spotted Calf, the adopted mother of Almighty-Voice, was a daughter of One Arrow.

Chapter 5

1. In his Journal, Alexander Henry, the explorer and fur-trader, mentions a Gabriel Dumont, who was at Rocky Mountain House with him in 1810–1811. (See Henry's Journal—Ed. Elliott Coues—p. 634.) The North West Company's posts extended south into what is now American Territory. Dumont probably accompanied Henry on his trip to the Mandan Indians, prior to his visit to Rocky Mountain House.
2. Red Deer River empties into Red Deer Lake about 35 miles east of Hudson's Bay Junction. The old trader was very clear in his statement that these men travelled on courses 90 degrees from each other.

▲ Document 2: Excerpts from Nova Britannia: Or Our New Canadian Dominion Foreshadowed

Alexander Morris

Alexander Morris was sworn in as the second lieutenant-governor of Manitoba and the North-West Territories in 1872. As a representative of the Canadian government Morris negotiated many of the Numbered Treaties in the 1870s.

Lecture 1: Rupert's Land

Above us, again, is that vast expanse claimed by the Hudson's Bay adventurers, which will yet, and possibly soon, be inhabited by a large population, comprising as it does, 3,060,000 square miles.

This great country cannot much longer remain unoccupied; and if we do not proceed to settle it the Americans will appropriate it, as they did Oregon. Without entering into the question of the alleged vices in the charter by which that powerful company holds its possessions, and the mode of adjudicating thereon, there are certain practical measures which should be at once adopted. A means of communication by road and water, for summer and winter use, should be opened between Lake Superior and the Red River settlement; and that settlement should be placed under the jurisdiction of Canada, with power to this province to colonize the territory.[1] This power should at once be given, and will doubtless be conceded on application. This obtained, and a settlement of 7,000 souls added to our population as a centre of operations, steps can be taken for obtaining more accurate information as to the nature of the immense tract of territory, of which a large part once belonged to the Hundred Partners of Old France, and which, though believed to be the property of Canada, is now held by the Hudson's Bay Company. The great valley of the Saskatchewan should form the subject of immediate attention. Enough is known to satisfy us that in the territory commonly known as the Hudson's Bay Territory there is a vast region well adapted for becoming the residence of a large population. Once the Red River settlement is opened to our commerce, a wide field extends before our enterprise; and those who recollect or have otherwise become familiar with the struggles, forty years ago, of the settlers in Western Canada, and the painful, toilsome warfare with which they conquered that rising portion of the Province from the wilderness, will regard the task of colonization as a comparatively light one.

Imperial as well as colonial interests urgently demand the opening up of that vast stretch of rich agricultural territory of which the Red River "holds the key." Apart from the arable areas on the highway between Canada and the Red River, that settlement forms a nucleus round which will gather a dense population scattered over those vast prairies, covered with the rankest luxuriance of vegetation, and holding out to settlers rich inducements to go in and possess the land. Should such a "Paradise of fertility" as this remain longer locked up? Will the gathering of a few peltries compensate for the withdrawal of such a region from the industry of our race? Assuredly not. The knell of arbitrary rule has been rung.

333

Source: The Hon. Alexander Morris, P.C., D.C.L., Late Lieutenant-Governor of Manitoba, the North-West Territories and Keewatin. Excerpts from *Nova Britannia: or Our New Canadian Dominion Foreshadowed*. Published by Hunter Rose and Company, 1884.

It will suffice to express my confident belief that Canada has only to express in firm but respectful tones her demands as to that vast territory, and these will be cheerfully acceded to by Great Britain. Those demands should be ripely considered, and so matured as to evince, not a mere grasping thirst of territorial aggrandizement, but a large-spirited and comprehensive appreciation of the requirements of the country, and a proper sense of the responsibilities to be assumed in regard to the well-being of the native and other inhabitants, and the due development of the resources of the territory. In such a spirit our statesmen will I trust be found acting. The position of our Province, too, is to be weighed. To a large portion of the territory we have an indubitable legal claim; to another portion the Crown of Britain would be entitled; but all that is adapted for settlement should be placed under the jurisdiction of representative government, and any further extension of the rights of the Company to trade in the more northerly regions should be subjected to the approval or control of colonial authorities.[2] The subject is not without its difficulties; but, I doubt not, these can all be satisfactorily overcome, and the interests of the whole Empire imperiously demand their prompt and satisfactory adjustment.

Our Northern rising nationality has an ample field before it—a brilliant future in the distance. To occupy that field—to attain to that future in all its grandeur —the people of British North America must take high views of their plain and manifest responsibilities. They must evince an adequate appreciation of their duties, and must possess a thorough knowledge of the advantages which they possess, and of the vast resources which Providence has placed at their disposal, in order that they may advance steadily toward that high position among the nations which they may yet attain—in order that they may enter upon the full fruition of that rich inheritance of civil and religious liberty, and of high social and political privileges, which is their birthright as an offshoot of the three united nations who compose the British people.

It is, then, under the influence of such trains of thought, and with such objects in view, that I ask you to-night to travel with me up the Ottawa Valley, and over the trail of the enterprising adventurers of the old Canadian North-West Company, and, taking our stand there, judge for ourselves, like the Israelitish spies, of the character of that section of a future great empire, which has for a century past been claimed as the domain of a company of merchants—the vast preserve which has been so carefully guarded from the encroachments of modern civilization, and which is popularly known as the HUDSON'S BAY TERRITORIES.[3]

NOTES

1. Rupert's Land, as the reader is aware, now forms part of the Dominion, and one portion of it (including Red River settlement) has been erected into the Province of Manitoba, with a Local Legislature, and with representation in the general Parliament at Ottawa. The other recommendations in the text have also become realities. The Dawson Route was but the precursor of the C.P.R.

2. The negotiations which finally led to the absorption of the North-West by the Dominion proved the soundness of the lecturer's views as propounded in the text. Indeed the entire history of the surrender of the Territory by the Hudson's Bay Company to the Imperial Government, and of the subsequent acquisition thereof by the Dominion, forms a striking commentary upon these passages in the lecture.

3. It seems almost unnecessary to remind the reader that since 1870 the Hudson's Bay Territories have been part and parcel of the Dominion.

334

▲ Document 3: Métis Couple, Red River, MB

Photography would have been a relatively new technology in Red River in 1870, and likely only available to the comparatively wealthy. What does this portrait of a Métis couple at Red River and the family portrait below tell you about their social class? Why might they want their portraits taken? How does their engagement with 'modern' technology contrast with Canadian views of the Métis as 'primitive'?

Source: Glenbow Archives, NA-4405-15

335

▲ Document 4: Mrs. Nellie Isbister and Daughter, Red River, MB

Mrs. Nellie Isbister and Daughter, Red River, MB.

Source: Glenbow Archives, NA-4405-4

▲ Document 5: Ox and Red River Cart, MB

● Norbert Welsh would have used Red River carts like this (often several carts in a train) to transport trade goods to the West and return with them heavily loaded with buffalo robes and furs. The Red River cart was designed for western conditions and constructed without the use of metal or nails allowing repairs to be performed on the trail. The wooden carts and their loads could also be easily floated across rivers.

Source: Glenbow Archives, NA-249-21

336

▲ Document 6: St. Andrew's Anglican Church, Red River, MB

● St. Andrew's Anglican Church, Red River (1858). How did changing ideas about race, class, and 'respectable' church marriage lay the foundation for the Red River Resistance?

Source: Glenbow Archives, NA-325-6

▲ Document 7: Thomas Scott

Thos. Scott.
Murdered by *Riel on 4 March*
TON,
YONGE STREET.
TORONTO

● The execution of Ontarian Thomas Scott by Riel's troops in March 1870 created a martyr for the Canadian cause. Who might have created this particular image of Scott? Why?

Source: Glenbow Archives, NA-576-1

© 2015 Nelson Education Ltd.

■ Article 1: The Impact of White Women on Fur Trade Society

Sylvia Van Kirk

During the early period of the fur trade, the white man in penetrating the wilds of Western Canada, faced a situation in which, for practical purposes, the social norms of European civilization were no longer operable. Since colonization was not envisaged, no white women accompanied the fur traders. Family units which would have reflected, in however rough a state, their former domestic life were impossible. Instead, the traders were forced to come to terms with an alien, nomadic culture; their livelihood depended upon the very existence of the Indian whose way of life gave him distinct advantages in coping with the wilderness environment. In this light, the Indian woman played an important role as a liaison between the two cultures. Trained as she was in the skills necessary for survival, a native woman, while filling the role of wife and mother left void by the absence of white women, was uniquely qualified to help the white trader adapt to the exigencies of life in Rupert's Land.

The men of the Montreal-based North West Company, who had inherited the framework and traditions of the French colonial fur trade, had always appreciated the economic advantages to be gained by forming alliances with Indian women. Besides helping to secure the trade of her tribe or band, the Indian woman did much to familiarize the Nor'wester with Indian life and, in teaching him the native tongue, greatly contributed to his effectiveness as a trader. In contrast, the London Committee, the remote ruling body of the Hudson's Bay Company, had early forbidden any dealings between its servants and Indian women on the grounds that the expense which would accrue from their support plus the possible danger of affronting Indian sensibilities outweighed any advantages to be derived. In practice, this regulation proved difficult to enforce. Although it prevented the practice of taking Indian wives from

Source: Sylvia Van Kirk, "The Impact of White Women on Fur Trade Society," in Susan Mann Trofimenkoff and Alison Prentice, eds. *The Neglected Majority: Essays in Canadian Women's History*. Toronto: McClelland & Stewart, 1977. Reprinted with permission from Sylvia Van Kirk.

becoming widespread within the lower ranks of the English company, keeping an Indian woman became the prerogative of an officer in charge of a post.[1]

When forced into open competition with the Nor'Westers in the late decades of the 18th century, the Hudson's Bay Company was compelled to modify its policy towards Indian women. In attempting to recruit the highly-prized French-Canadian voyageur into its service, the Company was made aware that the right to have an Indian helpmate was not one which the Canadian would relinquish lightly,[2] and this attitude influenced its own men. In 1802, the council at York Factory appealed to the London Committee, stressing that their Indian women were in fact "your Honors Servants" and played an important economic role in the struggle against the rival concern:

> [...] they clean and put into a state of preservation all Beavr. And Otter skins brought by the Indians undried and in bad Condition. They prepare Line for Snow shoes and knit them also without which your Honors servants could not give efficient opposition to the Canadian traders they make Leather shoes for the men who are obliged to travel about in search of Indians and furs and are useful in a variety of other instances [...][3]

By the time of the union of the two companies in 1821, taking a native woman for a wife was a widespread social practice, known as marriage *à la façon du pays*. Although it might involve the payment of a bride price, a country marriage was an informal arrangement whereby a couple agreed to cohabit for an unspecified length of time. It derived from the Indian concept of marriage and was but one example of the extent to which the social mores and customs of the Indians influenced the norms of fur trade society. As the explorer Sir John Franklin remarked, the white man seemed "to find it easier to descend to the Indian customs, and modes of thinking, particularly with respect to women, than to attempt to raise the Indians to theirs."[4] The first missionaries, who arrived relatively late in Rupert's Land, were horrified by what they considered to be the Europeans' uncivilized treatment of their Indian wives.[5] Such usage, however, reflected the position of women in Indian society. Partly through economic necessity, they were subjected to an endless round of domestic drudgery, even to the extent of being reduced to beasts of burden. The excuse was advanced that if the white man displayed tender feelings towards his wife, the Indian, to whom such notions were foreign would despise him.[6] It is likely, however, that within the fur trade post, European conventions did tend to ameliorate the Indian woman's lot, particularly in the higher ranks of the service where she would have shared in her husband's privileges.

Although, there were occasions (especially during the drunken days of the trade war) when Indian women were abused by the traders, in general, an unwritten code of honour developed marriage *à la façon du pays* was considered to be as binding as any church ceremony in the Indian Country. There were many examples of a lasting and honorable relationship developing between the white trader and his Indian helpmate. The domestic pleasures of family life undoubtedly did much to reconcile the European to the isolated and monotonous life of a fur trade post.[7]

The greatest social problem occurred when the trader retired from Rupert's Land. It became customary to forsake one's Indian family for it proved extremely difficult for the wife in particular to make the transition to "civilised" living whether in Great Britain or the Canadas.[8] In the early days of the fur trade, when widowed or abandoned, an Indian wife with her children had been welcomed back into her tribe. This became increasingly rare as the structure of Indian society crumbled through the effects of European contact. It was also not feasible for the half-breed woman, who knew little of the life outside the fur trade post, and from whose growing ranks many wives were chosen in the early decades of the 19th century. A practice which was dubbed "turning off" arose, by which the retiring husband endeavoured to assure that his spouse was placed under the protection of or became the country wife of another fur trader. Such had been the fate of the kind-hearted washerwoman Betsey, who when Letitia Hargrave encountered her at York Factory in 1840 was not sure whether her last protector had been her fourth or fifth husband.[9] Although it was fairly common for fathers to bequeath some money for the maintenance of their country-born children, they were not legally compelled to do so. As a result, during the decades immediately preceding the union of the two

companies, the number of deserted women and children being maintained at the expense of the posts, especially those of the North West Company, reached alarming proportions. In an attempt to reduce this heavy economic burden, the North West proprietors ruled as early as 1806 that in future its servants were to choose only half-breed women as wives. They also contemplated the creation of a settlement in the Rainy Lake area where their superannuated servants, particularly the French-Canadian voyageurs, could retire with their Indian families.[10]

The whole question was pushed into the background by the struggle for the control of the fur trade, but when the Hudson's Bay Company absorbed its rival in 1821, the London Committee recognized that steps must be taken to solve this pressing social problem if only for reasons of economy and security.

> We understand that there are an immense number of Women and Children supported at the different Trading Posts, some belonging to men still in the Service and others who have been left by the Fathers unprotected and a burden on the Trade. It becomes […] a serious consideration how these People are to be disposed of. […][11]

Philanthropic considerations also influenced Company policy at this time, mainly through the efforts of Benjamin Harrison, a prominent member of the Committee and an associate of the Clapham Sect. He played an important part in developing a plan for the settlement of these families in the fledgling colony of Red River which had been founded in the previous decade by the idealistic Lord Selkirk. A Catholic mission already existed to minister to the large French-Canadian sector and several Anglican clergymen were sent out under Company auspices who, with the help of the Church Missionary Society, were to establish a school for orphan children.[12] In a marked change of policy, the London Committee also encouraged those servants who did not wish to retire in Rupert's Land to take their families with them provided they possessed sufficient means for their support.[13]

[…]

The Hudson's Bay Company gave official status to marriage *à la façon du pays* by the introduction

339

of a marriage contract which emphasized the husband's economic responsibilities. Although there is some variation in the actual format of the certificates which survive in the Company's records, usually both parties signed or made their mark on a document which declared that the woman was recognized as one's legal wife.[14] In retrospect power over Rupert's Land, these contracts can be seen as an early form of civil marriage. The prerogative of the Church in this sphere, however, was acknowledged by the proviso that the couple would undertake to be married by a clergyman at the first possible opportunity.[15]

The Company's first chaplain, the Rev. John West, considered this to be one of his most pressing duties upon his arrival in the Indian Country in the fall of 1820; "the institution of marriage", he proclaimed, along with "the security of property" were "the fundamental laws" of any civilized society.[16] When he left Rupert's Land three years later, the worthy parson had performed a total of sixty-five marriages, among them those of several prominent settlers in Red River, former Company officers who had continued to live with their Indian wives *à la façon du pays*. His success was greeted with approbation by Nicholas Garry, a visiting member of the London Committee, who considered the practices of the Indian Country most demoralizing:

> [...] Mr. West has done much good in persuading these Gentlemen to marry [...] thus introducing more proper Feelings and preventing that Debasement of Mind which must, at last, have rooted out every honorable and right Feeling. Perhaps nothing shows Debasement of Mind so much as their having lived themselves in an unmarried state, giving up their Daughters to live the same Life as their Mothers, and this Feeling, or rather its Justification, had become general all over the Country. [...] [17]

Clearly the moral code of the fur trade society was in a state of confusion. It was the missionaries themselves who emphasized the concept of "living in sin", for many fur traders, and certainly the Indians, considered a country marriage to be a legal and honorable union. While officially the Company was attempting to introduce accepted Christian standards into fur trade life, as can be seen in a list of regulations designed to effect "the civilization and moral improvement" of the families attached to the various posts,[18] it is difficult to estimate the actual success of these measures. Although the social and religious conventions of European society were undoubtedly taking hold in the basically agrarian settlement of Red River, the old norms of fur trade society persisted, especially in isolated areas. In 1825 George Simpson, the Governor of the Northern Department, advised that any missionary appointed to the Columbia District across the Rockies would be wise to let the custom of the country alone:

> [...] he ought to understand in the outset that nearly all the Gentlemen & Servants have Families altho' Marriage ceremonies are unknown in the Country and that it would be all in vain to attempt breaking through this uncivilized custom.[19]

When Simpson was appointed Governor of the vast territories of the Northern Department in 1821, he had had only one year of experience in the Indian Country as a trader in opposition to the Nor'Westers on Lake Athabasca. He soon proved himself a capable administrator, and his hard-headed, often pragmatic approach to business is reflected in his official views on the position of Indian women in fur trade society.

Simpson's journal of his winter in Athabasca reveals his appreciation of the valuable economic role played by Indian women in the functioning of the fur trade. Besides performing such routine tasks as making moccasins and collecting wattappe for sewing the birch-bark canoes, they were essential as interpreters. In enumerating the reasons for the strong position of the Nor'Westers at Fort Chipewyan, Simpson declared:

> ... their Women are faithful to their cause and good Interpreters whereas we have but one in the Fort that can talk Chipewyan ...[20]

This one was the crafty Madam Lamallice, the wife of the brigade guide, who was not only adept at hoarding provisions but even managed to carry on a private trade. Simpson, concerned that this couple, who possessed much influence over the Indians, might desert to the rival concern, was forced to wink at these misdemeanors and urged the disgruntled

340

post commander to humor them with flattery and a few extra rations.[21]

In making plans to extend the Company's trade into the remote areas of New Caledonia and McKenzie's River, formerly the preserve of the North West Company, the Governor emphasized the value of marriage alliances. Early in the spring of 1821, he engaged the French-Canadian Pering [Perrin] to help establish a depot on Great Slave Lake primarily because his wife was "extensively connected amongst the Yellow Knife and Chipewyan tribes in that quarter . . . and will be enabled to remove any prejudice that our Opponents may have instilled on their minds against us."[22] Viewing the Committee's policy of discouraging liaisons with Indian women as detrimental to the Company's expansion, he recommended that in New Caledonia the Gentlemen should form connections with the principal families immediately upon their arrival as "the best security we can have of the goodwill of the Natives."[23]

During his rapid tours of the posts in the early 1820s, however, Simpson became increasingly aware of the problems caused by the large numbers of women and children being supported in established areas, and he favoured the Committee's proposed economic reforms.[24] A major source of inefficiency and expense was the practice of allowing families, particularly those of the officers, to accompany the brigades on the long summer journey to and from the main depot at York Factory. Simpson's low opinion of one Chief Factor, John Clarke, was confirmed when Clarke abandoned some of the goods destined for Athabasca en route to make a light canoe for the better accommodation of his half-breed wife and her servant—an extravagance which Simpson estimated had cost the Company five hundred pounds.[25] After his visit to the Columbia in 1824–25, the Governor further decried the extent to which family considerations hindered the expedition of business:

> … We must really put a stop to the practise of Gentlemen bringing their Women & Children from the East to the West side of the Mountains, it is attended with much expense and inconvenience on the Voyage, business itself must give way to domestick considerations, the Gentlemen become drones and are not disposable in short the evil is more serious than I am well able to describe.[26]

The following year, the annual session of the Council passed a resolution stating that Gentlemen appointed to the two districts across the Rockies were not to encumber themselves with families.

Although Indian women were relegated by custom to an inferior status, the ladies of the country appear to have exerted a surprising influence over their fur-trader husbands. Simpson was appalled by the widespread power of these "pettycoat politicians", whose interests he suspected even affected the decisions of top-ranking officers.[27] In expressing his dissatisfaction with Chief Factor James Bird's management of the Company's business at Red River, he lamented, "I find that every matter however triffling or important is discussed wh. his Copper Colld. Mate before decided on and from her it finds its way all over the Colony."[28] Likewise, he described Mrs. McDonald, the country wife of the officer in charge at Fort Qu'Appelle, as "a stout good looking Dame not master p. Force but through persuasion & cunning [...]"[29] In the Columbia District, the Governor claimed, two out of the three Chief Traders were completely under the control of their women. They frequently neglected business in their jealous attempts to "guard against certain innocent indiscretions which these frail brown ones are so apt to indulge in."[30]

If the irregularities in the workings of the trade caused by native families disturbed Simpson, he was even more adamant that the Indian Country was no place for a white women. In a private letter to Committee member Andrew Colvile, he expressed concern that the example of three of the Company's officers in taking wives from among the Red River settlers in the early 1820's might establish a trend which he considered most undesirable:

> [...] it not only frustrates the intentions of the Company and executors, in respect to the Colony, but is a clog on the gentlemen who take them [...] native women are a serious incumbrance but with women from the civilized world, it is quite impossible the gentlemen can do their duty.[31]

In light of his own subsequent experience, Simpson could perhaps have shown a little compassion for the marital difficulties of some of his contemporaries. His extraordinary private correspondence with his close friend Chief Factor John George

McTavish reveals a Simpson curiously different from the person his official pronouncements would lead one to expect. For a novice, he adapted with ease to the social conventions of Rupert's Land, succumbing as readily as any Nor'Wester to the charms of the ladies of the country.

Sometime during his first winter, possibly at Oxford House, Simpson was attracted to a damsel called Betsey Sinclair, a daughter of the late Chief Factor William Sinclair and his native wife Nahovway.[32] Although she accompanied him to York Factory in the fall of 1821, the newly-appointed Governor soon found her presence bothersome. He left Betsey at York when he embarked on a tour of inland posts in December and shortly afterward instructed McTavish then in charge of the Factory, to see that she was "forwarded" in the spring to the Rock Depot where her brother-in-law Thomas Bunn was stationed.[33] Simpson's rather cavalier references to this woman as "my japan helpmate" or "my article" suggest that he himself may never have thought of her as a country wife in the true sense. That many of his contemporaries considered her as such is revealed by an entry in the York Fort Journal dated 10 February 1822 which reads: "Mrs. Simpson was delivered of a Daughter."[34] Although the Governor was at York when this infant was christened Maria by the Rev. John West on August 27,[35] he was still determined to avoid the encumbrance of a family. The proposal to place Betsey under the care of Thomas Bunn had been abandoned, but Simpson departed in early September for an extensive tour of the Athabasca and Peace River districts, leaving it to McTavish to settle the matter expeditiously:

> My Family concerns I leave entirely to your kind management, if you can dispose of the Lady it will be satisfactory as she is an unnecessary and expensive appendage, I see no fun in keeping a woman without enjoying her charms which my present rambling Life does not enable me to do. [...][36]

He needlessly expressed concern for her virtue. Not long after his departure, Betsey Sinclair became the country wife of the clerk Robert Miles, a high-minded Englishman, who had spent the winter of 1820–21 with Simpson in the Athabasca country. The match was celebrated in the customary fashion by a dance and supper where liquid cheer flowed freely, and the couple were reported to be very happy.[37]

Despite protestations that he was too busy to be bothered by domestic considerations, the Governor seems to have found time to indulge his inclination during his tours of the Company's domains. In fact, he confided to McTavish that he suspected his amours were gaining him a notorious reputation.[38] Although the identities of the recipients of his favours remain obscure, it is known that in 1823 a son named James Keith Simpson was born.[39]

Simpson, however, appears to have made a distinction between the behaviour he considered appropriate in that motley outpost of civilization, the Red River Colony, and the behaviour acceptable in the rest of the Indian Country. While wintering at Fort Garry in 1823–24, he apparently held aloof from romantic entanglements, describing himself as one of the most "exemplary Batchelors" in the settlement.[40] Furthermore, in spite of his country romances, the intention of returning to England to marry seems to have been in the back of the Governor's mind during this period.[41] Who the object of his affection was is not known, although it is established that Simpson had another daughter in Scotland called Maria, born before he left for Rupert's Land.[42] He was cautioned by his mentor Andrew Colvile against taking any hasty action, however:

> A wife I fear would be an embarrassment to you until the business gets into more complete order & until the necessity of those distant journies is over & if it be delayed one or two years you will be able to accumulate something before the expense of a family comes upon you.

Simpson acquiesced and set off in the fall of 1824 on his tour across the Rockies to the Columbia. While at Fort George, he was at pains to prevent himself from being drawn into the system of marriage alliances which had helped to secure the loyalty of the powerful Chinook nation, especially the great Chief Concomely. It was considered most prestigious among the "aristocracy" of this highly-complex tribe to claim a fur trader for a son-in-law. A most assiduous social-climber was an influential personage known as "Lady Calpo", who on more than one occasion had warned the fort of impending treachery. She proved a valuable source of information for Simpson, but he found himself in a delicate situation when this old dame, in order to reaffirm her rank, endeavoured to secure him as a husband for her carefully-raised daughter.

> I have therefore a difficult card to play being equally desirous to keep clear of the Daughter and continue on good terms with the Mother and by management I hope to succeed in both altho' her ladyship is most pressing & persevering ....[43]

Simpson seems to have succumbed somewhat, however, for if the Chinooks expressed sorrow at his departure in the spring, "the fair princess 'Chowie'", he suspected, was not the least grieved.[44]

When Simpson returned to Red River to wind up business prior to sailing for England, he found a situation which likely made him reconsider the feasibility of bringing a European wife to Rupert's Land. The new governor of the settlement, Capt. R. P. Pelly, now felt compelled to return to England owing to the ill health of his wife, who only two short years before had accompanied her husband out to Red River. This was a great disappointment to Simpson as he had hoped Pelly would be able to effect some order and stability in the chaotic affairs of the colony. While every effort had been made to ensure the material comfort of the family, Simpson himself had noted that "Mrs. Pelly appears to be a delicate woman and does not yet seem quite at home among us."[45] When he sailed from York Factory in September 1825, the Governor was accompanied by Capt. Pelly and his ailing wife. While it is unknown how he settled any romantic attachments he may have had in Great Britain, Pelly's unhappy example undoubtedly contributed to the fact that Simpson returned to Rupert's Land still a bachelor, apparently prepared to resume former arrangements *à la façon du pays*.

Contrary to the assertions of several authors, it is only now that Margaret Taylor, the half-breed daughter of George Taylor, a former sloop master at York, appears in the Governor's life. She was definitely not the mother of either Maria or James Keith Simpson. When Simpson first became attached to her is uncertain, but she was probably introduced to him by her brother Thomas Taylor, the Governor's

personal servant during these years. As was his practice when embarking on an extensive tour, Simpson left this woman at York in the fall of 1826 under the surveillance of his friend McTavish, to whom he wrote in a jocular, if rather crude fashion:

> Pray keep an Eye on the commodity and if she bring forth anything in the proper time & of the right color let them be taken care of but if any thing be amiss let the whole be bundled about their business ....[46]

The lady does not seem to have warranted his suspicion, and in the spring of 1827, a son was born, named George after his father.[47] Simpson honoured his responsibility for the support of his family at York, allowing Margaret the enjoyment of special rations such as tea and sugar and even providing financial assistance for her widowed mother.[48]

In his brief biography of Simpson, A. S. Morton stated that domestic concerns played no part in the Governor's life at this time, but such is not the case.[49] Although she is never mentioned in the official journals, Simpson's private correspondence reveals that Margaret Taylor accompanied him when he left York in July 1828 on another cross-country voyage, this time to New Caledonia. At first she was so unwell that he was afraid he might have to leave her in Athabasca, but she recovered and proved herself a valued companion for Simpson rapidly found his two associates Dr. Hamlyn and Chief Trader "Archy" McDonald rather tiresome. "The commodity," he confided to McTavish, "has been a great consolation to me."[50] By this time, Simpson himself seems to have regarded Margaret Taylor as his wife according to the custom of the country. While returning in the spring, he speaks of her affectionately as "my fair one" and although disgruntled at the conduct of her brother Thomas, acknowledges him as a brother-in-law.[51] Simpson, however, was now preparing for another trip to England via the Canadas. On his way east, he left Margaret, now far advanced in her second pregnancy, at Bas de la Rivière under the care of the Chief Factor John Stuart, whose country wife was her sister Mary Taylor. There, at the end of August 1829, Margaret gave birth to another boy, later christened John McKenzie Simpson.[52]

John Stuart's letters to the Governor during his absence provide a touching picture of Simpson's

343

country wife and her little ones. Young Geordy and his baby brother were thriving; "I never saw finer or for their age more promising Children," claimed Stuart. His praise of their quiet and good-natured mother was also unstinted: "[…] in her comportment she is both decent and modest far beyond anything I could expect—or ever witnessed in any of her countrywomen."[53] Old Widow Taylor was living with the family at Bas de la Rivière, and Stuart credited her with instilling such commendable habits of cleanliness and industry in her daughters. He emphasized that Margaret was counting the days until Simpson's return:

> A little ago when at supper I was telling Geordy that in two months and ten days he would see his father. [His mother] smiled and remarked to her sister that seventy days was a long time and [she] wished it was over.[54]

It must have been a grievous shock, therefore, when the Governor did return to Rupert's Land in May 1830—a lovely young English bride at his side! There can be little doubt that John Stuart had not the slightest intimation that Simpson intended taking a wife in England. His obsequious attempts to curry favour are much in evidence,[55] and he unquestionably described Simpson's country family in such glowing terms because he thought that was what the Governor wanted to hear.

It is extremely difficult to pinpoint the time or cause of Simpson's change of heart. In a letter dated March 1828, his cousin Aemileus Simpson advised the Governor, then contemplating retirement in Rupert's Land, that this was not likely to be a happy course of action.

> […] rather look for some amiable companion in the civilized world with which to conclude your days in the true comforts of a domestic life.[56]

Whatever his private feelings for Margaret Taylor, Simpson may have decided that her background and lack of education made her unsuitable for the role of "first lady" of Rupert's Land. Furthermore, his reasoning appears to have been influenced by the experience and council of his close friend John George McTavish, who in the winter of 1829–30 was also on furlough in Great Britain searching for a wife.[57]

Before becoming a Chief Factor in the Hudson's Bay Company in 1821, J. G. McTavish, the son of a Scottish chieftain, had had a long and distinguished career as a Nor'Wester. During his early days at Moose Factory, though in opposition, he formed a union with one of the daughters of Thomas Thomas, the governor of the English company's establishment. It appears to have been a particularly unhappy relationship: the woman was driven to infanticide and McTavish subsequently renounced his connection with her.[58] It should be noted that infanticide was not unknown in Indian society in times of famine or great hardship. In the case of the women of the fur traders it was perhaps symptomatic of their fear of being abandoned for it usually occurred when the husband was on furlough.

Around 1813 sometime after this unfortunate episode, McTavish took another country wife, young Nancy McKenzie, otherwise known as Matooskie, the daughter of a prominent Nor'Wester Roderic McKenzie and an Indian woman. She was to live with him for seventeen years and bear him a lively family of at least six daughters of whom McTavish seems to have been very fond. In the late 1820's, however, there are signs of a growing estrangement between himself and their mother; McTavish confided to Simpson that he contemplated packing Nancy off to Red River where her uncle, Donald McKenzie, was now governor.[59] Although his wife may have feared the outcome of such a long separation, the fact that McTavish took their young daughter Anne with him when he sailed for England in September 1829 must have been reassuring.[60]

The glimpses of the two friends' quest for a "tender exotic" in Britain reveal that the rough and ready society of the fur trade left its gentlemen ill at ease in the intricacies of genteel courtship. Simpson wrote encouragingly to McTavish who was in Scotland:

> I see you are something like myself shy with the fair, we should not be so much so with the Browns […] muster courage "a faint heart never won a fair Lady."

Simpson was, in fact, very ill during his sojourn in England, the years of strenuous travelling having caught up with him, but he queried jauntily, "Let me know if you have any fair cousin or acquaintance likely to suit an invalid like me [...]"[61] McTavish had little time to offer assistance. A few weeks later Simpson wrote ecstatically, "Would you believe it? I am in Love."[62] The middle-aged, hard-hearted Governor had fallen completely under the spell of his eighteen-year-old cousin Frances Simpson, who had been but a child when he had first started his career as a clerk in her father's firm. At first it was decided that the wedding should await Simpson's return from America in the fall of 1830, but the prospect of such a separation prompted him to persuade her parents to give their immediate consent.[63] The couple were united on February 24 and embarked on a short honeymoon to Tunbridge Wells.

McTavish, in the meantime, had not met with such immediate success. An attempt to secure the affection of a "Miss B." failed, but by February, the old Nor'Wester was able to report, much to Simpson's delight, that he too was to be wed—to a Miss Catherine Turner, daughter of the late Keith Turner of Turnerhall, Aberdeenshire.[64] They were married in February 22 in Edinburgh, their honeymoon being no more than a hasty journey to London to join the Simpsons prior to sailing for North America. Simpson, who appreciated how much the ladies would value each others' company, took pains to ensure their comfort on the voyage, reserving the sole use of the Ladies' Cabin for their party.

Although Frances Simpson was undoubtedly a very pretty and cultivated young lady, her sheltered upbringing and delicate constitution made her an unlikely candidate for the role of Governor's lady in the inhospitable wilds of Rupert's Land. Her diary of the voyage to the Indian Country reveals that parting from the close family circle of Grove House was almost more than she could bear:

> I can scarcely trust myself to think of the pang which shot thro' my heart, on taking the last "Farewell" of my beloved Father, who was equally overcome at the first parting from any of his children—suffice it to say, that this was to me a moment of bitter sorrow [...][65]

Shortly after the ship sailed from Liverpool on March 10, the young woman succumbed to a violent attack of sea-sickness; she was so ill that Simpson was prepared to bribe the Captain to put her ashore in Ireland, but stormy weather foiled the attempted landing. Fortunately, over the course of the voyage her health improved. The party spent several pleasant days in New York and then proceeded overland to Montreal, where the ladies divided their time between sight-seeing and being entertained by fashionable society.

Before embarking at Lachine for the canoe trip to the interior, however, an incident occurred which threw the contrasting mores of fur trade society and middle-class gentility into sharp focus. McTavish's open affection and continuing responsibility for his eldest daughters made it inevitable that his new wife would learn of their existence. In fact, his thirteen-year-old daughter Mary was at school near Montreal. One evening after dinner, the Governors' servant threw open the door and announced "Miss Mactavish" to the assembled company:

> [McTavish] rose & took her up to his wife, who got stupid, but shook hands with the Miss who was very pretty & mighty impudent . . . [Mrs. McTavish] got white & red & at last rose & left the room, all the party looking very uncomfortable except [her husband] & the girl. [Mrs. Simpson] followed & found her in a violent fit of crying, she said she knew the child was to have been home that night, but thought she would have been spared such a public introduction.[66]

Simpson seems to have endeavoured to spare his wife similar indignities. Letitia Hargrave, in recounting this episode in 1840, commented wryly that "Mrs. Simpson evidently has no idea that she has more encumbrances than Mrs. Mactavish, altho' she did say that she was always terrified to look about her in case of seeing something disagreeable."[67] (This may help to explain Simpson's relative neglect of his mixed-blood children in later years. There is no evidence that they, unlike many of the children of Company officers, were ever sent overseas or to Canada to be educated, and all were excluded from Simpson's final will of 1860.)[68]

[...] But if the European women left much to be desired, the ladies of the country were now definitely

345

personae non gratae. This self-enforced exclusiveness of the Governor had unfortunate repercussions. Those Company officers who had mixed-blood wives were much insulted when Simpson indicated that their society was no longer acceptable. No one felt this slight more acutely than Chief Factor Colin Robertson, a proud Scotsman who had had a long if somewhat erratic career in the service of both companies. Robertson had earned Simpson's dislike partly because his genuine concern for the betterment of his half-breed wife Theresa Chalifoux and their family had often resulted in extravagance and a neglect of business. The old Chief Factor intended to take his country family with him when he retired from Rupert's Land, but his attempt to introduce his wife to the society of Mrs. Simpson when passing through Red River met with a scathing rebuff from the Governor:

> ... Robertson brought his bit of Brown wt. him to the Settlement this Spring in hopes that She would pick up a few English manners before visiting the civilized World. . . . I told him distinctly that the thing was impossible which mortified him exceedingly.[69]

At Moose Factory, McTavish had similarly ruffled feelings by refusing to countenance certain of the officers' wives. Even Simpson expressed concern lest McTavish go too far in alienating Chief Factor Joseph Beioley whose capacities he rated highly, although the Governor fully sympathized with his friend that it was the height of impertinence for Beioley to expect that "his bit of circulating copper" should have the society of Mrs. McTavish.[70] The mixed-blood, though Anglicized families of former company officers, such as that of George Gladman at Moose, were highly incensed at such treatment as they considered themselves among the upper crust of fur trade society. Simpson, however, encouraged McTavish to keep these people in their place:

> I ... understand that the other Ladies at Moose are violent and indignant at being kept at such a distance, likewise their husbands, the Young Gladmans particularly.... The greater distance at which they are kept the better.[71]

Only two half-breed women had been allowed to come within a dozen yards of Mrs. Simpson, he informed McTavish, and these in a purely menial capacity.[72] The extent to which the Governor found himself avoided caused him to muse: "They do not even venture within gun Shot of me now—I have seen the time when they were not so shy."[73]

By this time, the responsibilities of married life weighed heavily on the Governor for Frances Simpson, like Mrs. Pelly before her, proved unequal to the rigours of frontier life. Despite constant medical care, her health deteriorated rapidly as her first pregnancy advanced. Simpson, who now appears the most attentive of husbands, was distraught at the necessity of leaving her during the summer of 1831 to attend the annual council at York Factory.[74] His speedy dispatch of company business was not this time motivated simply by a desire for efficiency, and he hurried back to Red River in time for the birth of a son, which his wife barely survived. During the winter, Simpson was much heartened by the steady, if slow progress of both mother and child. The christening of George Geddes Simpson in January 1832 was a considerable social event in the colony. But his happiness was short-lived; the sudden death of the little boy a few months later plunged his parents into the depths of despair.[75]

Domestic tribulations had, in fact, brought the Governor to the low point of his career: his own health was breaking down, he confessed himself little interested in business, detested most of his associates, and was only prevented from retiring from the fur trade by the loss of a large sum of money.[76] His vision of a comfortable family life in Red River now shattered, Simpson had to accept that his wife, who was desperately in need of skilled medical attention, could no longer remain in Rupert's Land:

> She has no Society, no Friend, no Relative here but myself, she cannot move wt. me on my different Journeys and I cannot leave her in the hands of Strangers [...] some of them very unfeeling [...][77]

He, therefore, took Frances home via Canada in the summer of 1833, and she never returned to the Indian Country. Simpson's subsequent efforts to divide his time between his family in England and the superintendence of the fur trade in Western Canada tended to hamper his effectiveness as Governor.[78]

346

Perhaps it was Catherine McTavish's Scottish constitution which enabled her to withstand the harsh climate of Hudson Bay because she appears to have adapted with less difficulty to life at Moose Factory. A kind, sensible woman, "tho' not handsome",[79] she reconciled herself to McTavish's former arrangements. She presented the old fur trader with two more little girls and for a time had the care of four of her stepdaughters.[80] McTavish himself was suffering badly from gout, and Simpson, ever solicitous of his friend's welfare, sought a more amenable situation for the family. Thus in 1835, McTavish moved to the Lake of Two Mountains, a post about one hundred miles from the Chats on the Ottawa River where he had invested in a farm. The Governor declared it the ideal solution:

> Here your Family could be reared and Educated cheaply while Mrs. McTavish & yourself could enjoy the comforts of civilized society in a moderate degree as the country is becoming closely settled all about you, a Steam Vessel plies regularly to your Door & there is a Church within 3 or 4 Miles of it.[81]

Although neither Mrs. Simpson nor Mrs. McTavish remained for long in the Indian Country, their coming contributed to the decline in the position of native women in fur trade society. The implication was apparent that in more established areas, particularly at Red River, a country wife was no longer acceptable. In considering possible successors to McKenzie for the governorship of the colony, Simpson initially discounted the highly-competent Alexander Christie because he had an Indian family *à la façon du pays*.[82]

It now became fashionable for a Company officer to have a European wife. As Hargrave unfeelingly observed, "this influx of white faces has cast a still deeper shade over the faces of our Brunettes in the eyes of many."[83] When Chief Factor James McMillan brought his Scottish wife out to Red River in the fall of 1831, one old fur trader, commenting on this "novelty of getting H Bay stocked with European Ladys", conjectured that several others would avail themselves of their furlough "with no other view than that of getting Spliced to some fair Belinda & return with her" to the Indian Country.[84] Even some of those who had strongly professed a

sense of duty to their country wives succumbed. Simpson commented wryly on Chief Factor William Connolly's marriage to his wealthy cousin in Montreal in 1832:

> You would have heard of Connolly's Marriage—he was one of those who considered it a most unnatural proceeding "to desert the Mother of his children" and marry another; this is all very fine, very sentimental and very kindhearted 3000 Miles from the Civilized World but is lost sight of even by Friend Connolly where a proper opportunity offers.[85]

The coming of white women to the Indian Country brought into disrepute the indigenous social customs of the fur trade. Marriage *à la façon du pays* was now no longer acceptable, especially with the presence of missionaries intolerant of any deviation. The presence of white women underlined the perceived cultural shortcomings of mixed-blood wives, particularly in more settled areas where their native skills were no longer required. European ladies themselves, by zealously guarding what they considered to be their intrinsically superior status, actively fostered an increasing stratification of fur trade society. The arrival of the white woman can be seen as symbolic of a new era: the old fur trade order was gradually giving way to agrarian settlement which was unquestioningly equated with civilization.

NOTES

1. Glyndwr Williams, ed., *Andrew Graham's Observations on Hudson's Bay 1767–91* (London: Hudson's Bay Record Society (hereafter referred to as HBRS), 1969), p. 248.

2. Hudson's Bay Company Archives (hereafter referred to as HBC), B22/a/6, Brandon House, f. 8d, Nov. 13, 1798: "[. . .] Jollycoeur the Canadian wanted an old Woman to keep [...] he says every Frenchman has a woman & why should we stop him."

3. HBC, B239/b/79, York Factory, fos. 40d.-41, as quoted in Alice M. Johnson, ed., *Saskatchewan Journals and Correspondence, 1795–1802* (London: HBRS, 1967).

4. John Franklin, *Narrative of a Journey to the Shore of the Polar Sea in the Years 1819-20-21-22* (London: 1824). p. 101.

347

5. John West, *The Substance of a Journal during a residence at the Red River Colony*. [...] (London 1827), p. 16: "They do not admit them as their companions, nor do they allow them to eat at their tables, but degrade them *merely* as slaves to their arbitrary inclination [...]" See also pp. 53–54.

6. Franklin, *Narrative*, p. 106.

7. G. P. de T. Glazebrook, ed., *The Hargrave Correspondence, 1821-43* (Toronto: Champlain Society, 1938), p. 381, Jas. Douglas to Jas Hargrave, Fort Vancouver, 24 March 1842: "There is indeed no living with comfort in this country until a person has forgot the great world and has his tastes and character formed on the current standard of the stage [...] To any other being [...] the vapid monotony of an inland trading Post, would be perfectly unsufferable, while habit makes it familiar to us, softened as it is by the many tender ties, which find a way to the heart."

8. John Siveright in his letters to James Hargrave as published in the Hargrave Corres. frequently observed that Indian traders who retired with their families to farms in the Canadas were rarely successful. He cited the case of Alexander Stewart's wife who died soon after her arrival in Montreal.

9. Margaret A. Macleod, ed., *The Letters of Letitia Hargrave* (Toronto: Champlain Society, 1947), p. 72, To Mary Mactavish, York, 1 Sept. 1840.

10. W. Kaye Lamb, ed., *Sixteen years in the Indian Country: The Journal of Daniel Williams Harmon* (Toronto: 1957), pp. 5-6. See also W.S. Wallace, ed., *Documents relating to the North West Company* (Toronto: Champlain Society, 1934), p. 211.

11. E.E. Rich, ed., *Minutes of Council of the Northern Department of Rupert's Land 1821-31* (London: HBRS, 1940) pp. 33-34.

12. Rich, *Minutes of Council,* pp. 33-34. See also HBC, B235/z/3, f. 545 for a circular outlining the proposals for the establishment of a boarding school for female children, natives of the Indian Country. A similar institution for boys was not actually established until the 1830's.

13. Rich, *Minutes of Council,* pp. 94-95. See also p. 382, Simpson to Gov. & Committee, York, 1 Sept. 1822: "Messrs. Donald Sutherland and James Kirkness have this season requested permission to take their Families to Europe, which I was induced to comply with being aware that they had the means of providing for them so as to prevent their becoming a burden on the Company, and some labourers are in like manner permitted to take their children home."

14. Quite a number of these contracts are to be found in the miscellaneous file (z) under the heading of the various posts, i.e., B239/z/l, f. 32d.

15. HBC, B49/z/1, B156/z/1, f. 96.

16. West, *Journal*, p. 26.

17. Nicholas Garry, *Diary of* [...] (Ottawa: TRSC, Ser. 2, vol. 6, 1900), p. 137.

18. Rich, *Minutes of Council,* pp. 60-61. There is evidence that Chief Factor James Keith drew up these rules during the winter of 1822-23 at Severn. See HBC, B198/e/6, fos. 5d-6.

19. Frederick Merk, ed., *Fur Trade and Empire: George Simpson's Journal*. [...] (Cambridge, Mass.: 1931), p. 108.

20. E.E. Rich, ed., *Simpson's Athabaska Journal and Report* (London: HBRS, 1938) p. 231.

21. HBC, B39/a/16, Ft. Chipewyan, Simpson to Wm. Brown, 17 Oct. 1820, et al.

22. Rich, *Athabaska Journal*, p. 264, Simpson to Jn. Clarke, Isle a la Crosse, 9 Feb. 1821.

23. Rich, *Athabaska Journal*, pp. 392, 395–96.

24. HBC, D3/3, f. 35, 7 March 1822, Brandon House: ". . . no less than 87 people including women & children which is a very serious drawback." B239/c/1, f. 91, Simpson to McTavish, Isle â la Crosse, 12 Nov. 1822: "the Deptmt. is dreadfully overloaded with Families no less than 102 women & children & no less than three births since my arrival here . . ."

25. Rich, *Athabaska Journal*, pp. 23-4.

26. Merk, *Fur Trade*, p. 131.

27. Merk, *Fur Trade,* pp. 11-12: ". . . they are nearly all *Family Men.*"

28. HBC, D3/3, 1821-22, f. 52.

29. D3/3, f. 34

30. Merk, *Fur Trade*, pp. 58, 131–32. These two Chief Traders were John McLeod, whose wife was a daughter of J.P. Pruden, and John Warren Dease. There is other evidence that jealousy often caused the men to shirk their duty, see B39/a/22, Ft. Chipewyan, f. 42.

31. HBC, Copy No. 160a, Selkirk Correspondence, f. 1157c, Simpson to Colvile, York, 11 Aug. 1824. These three men were Donald Ross, Clerk, who took Mary MacBeath, daughter of a Selkirk settler, in 1820, John Clarke, Chief Factor, who took a Swiss girl Mary Ann Traitley in 1822; and Robert

McVicar, Chief Trader, who took Christy MacBeath at Norway House in 1824. Since there is no record of any of these marriages in the Red River Register of Marriages, it is likely that, initially at least, they were after the fashion of the country.

32. This is a good example of a lasting marriage *"la façon du pays"*. William Sinclair, an Orkneyman who served in the Hudson's Bay Company from 1792-1818, spent most of his career at Oxford House which he built in 1798. Little is known about the origin of his wife Nahovway, by whom he had eleven children, but she may have been a daughter of Moses Norton. See Dennis Bayley, *A Londoner in Rupert's Land: Thomas Bunn of the Hudson's Bay Company* (Chichester, Eng.: 1969) and D. Geneva Lent, *West of the Mountains: James Sinclair and the Hudson's Bay Company* (Seattle: 1963) for details of the Sinclair family.

33. HBC, B239/c/1, York Inward Corres., f. 60, Geo. Simpson to J.G. McTavish, Rock Depot, 14 Dec. 1821; same to same, f. 71, 25 Jan 1822 and f. 83, 4 June 1822.

34. HBC, B239/a/130, York Factory, f. 38d. This is a curious entry for it has been crossed out by someone at a later date. However A.S. Morton in his biography of Simpson is wrong in stating that this child was born in October 1821 for he confused this Maria with another natural daughter also called Maria who was born in Britain before Simpson ever came to Rupert's Land. Simpson received the news that this daughter was to be married to one Donald McTavish of Inverness in 1833 (B135/c/2, f. 110, Simpson to McTavish, 1 July 1833) and if she was then sixteen, as Morton states, she must have been born in 1817. Furthermore, there is no evidence that Simpson ever sent Betsey Sinclair's child to Scotland to be educated; she appears to have been at Mrs. Cockran's school for girls in Red River in 1830 (b4/b/1. f. 5v, J, Stuart to Simpson, 1 Feb. 1830) and in the fall of 1837 she married the botanist Robert Wallace at Fort Edmonton (*Hargrave Corres.*, p. 274, J. Rowland to Hargrave, Edmonton, 31 Dec. 1838). That this daughter was not a child of Margaret Taylor's as Morton states is conclusively proved in a letter from Robert Miles to Edward Ermatinger dated 8 Aug. 1839 (HBC Copy No. 23, fos. 304-305) which tells of Betsey Sinclair's grief on learning that her first daughter Maria had been drowned at the Dalles on the Columbia River in the fall of 1838.

35. HBC, E4/la, Red River Register of Baptisms, f. 39.

36. B239/c/l, f. 92, Simpson to McTavish, Isle à la Crosse, 12 Nov. 1822.

37. HBC, B235/c/1, Winnipeg, fos. 3d-4, Geo. Barnston to Jas. Hargrave, York, 1 Feb. 1823. This country marriage was a long and happy one. Betsey bore Miles at least eight children and retired with him to Upper Canada. I have found no evidence to support the suggestion of two writers (Lent, pp. 30-31 and Bayley, p. 46) that Betsey Sinclair was left out of her father's will because of her loose behaviour. Whatever the reason, her actions seem no worse than that of other young ladies growing up in the Indian Country.

38. B239/c/1, f. 92, Simpson to McTavish, Red River, 4 June 1822, f. 83.

39. Macleod, *Letitia's Letters*, p. 205, n. 1. The tombstone of James Keith Simpson records that he died on 28 Dec. 1901 at the age of 78. He is reputed to have had a very sickly childhood but eventually entered the company's service in the mid-1840's. He was definitely not a son by Margaret Taylor as Morton claims. Macleod suggests his mother may have been the "country wife" of Chief Factor James Keith; Keith does indeed seem to have had some interest in this child for he bequeathed him the sum of five pounds for the purchase of books in his will of 1836 (HBC, A36/8, f. 58). During this period Simpson may also have had a liaison with Jane Klyne, who later became the wife of Chief Factor Archibald MacDonald. She was the half-breed daughter of a former Nor'Wester Michael Klyne who was stationed at Great Slave Lake in 1822-23. See *Letitia's Letters*, p. 213: "[...] poor Mrs. MacDonald was an Indian wife of the Govr's [...]"

40. B239/c/1, Simpson to McTavish, Red River, 7 Jan, 1824, f. 136. See also f. 127: Simpson refused to allow Capt. Matthey, one of the leaders of the de Meuron segment of the population, to introduce his wife to the English wife of the Colony's governor R. P. Pelly because Mrs. Matthey was not his legal wife and she had been guilty of some indiscreet amours.

41. HBC Copy No. 112, vol. 2, fos. 638-39, Simpson to A. Colvile, York, 16 Aug. 1822: ". . . I should certainly wish to get Home for a Season if my inclination continues to lead the same way . . . "

42. In his biography *Sir George Simpson*, A. S. Morton places much emphasis on a Miss Eleanor Pooler who is kindly remembered in Simpson's letters to

349

her father Richard Pooler (se pp. 124, 161). One can only speculate, however; perhaps he intended to make an honest woman out of the mother of Maria, his Scottish-born daughter.

43. Merk, *Fur Trade*, pp. 104-05.

44. Merk, *Fur Trade*, p. 122

45. HBC Copy No. 160a, f. 1112, Simpson to Colvile, York, 8 Sept. 1823.

46. B239/c/1, f. 283, S. to McT., Norway House, 28 Aug. 1826.

47. HBC, B239/a/136, York Factory, f. 111d. For the date 11 Feb. 1827, there has been added the tiny postscript /G.S. Born/ with a curious comment by Robert Miles "say 11th March". This may well establish the date of the birth of Margaret's son, christened George Stewart; Simpson's letter to McTavish of 15 Sept. 1827 confirms that a son had been born.

48. B239/c/1, f. 346, Memo. for J. G. McTavish.

49. Arthur S. Morton, *Sir George Simpson: Overseas Governor of the Hudson's Bay Company* (Toronto: 1944) p. 162. There may also have been another woman in Simpson's life at this time, maintained at his headquarters at Lachine established in 1826—See HBC, D5/3, Aemileus Simpson to Geo. Simpson, Ft. Vancouver, 20 March 1828: ". . . I do not think it improves the arrangements of your domestic economy to have a mistress attached to your Establishment—rather have her Elsewhere."

50. B239/c/1, f. 366, Simpson to McTavish, Stuart's Lake, 22 Sept. 1828.

51. B239/c/2, F. 10, S. to McT., Saskatchewan River, 10 May 1829.

52. HBC, B4/b/1, fos. 2d-3, Jn. Stuart to Simpson, Bas de la Rivière, 1 Feb. 1830. This son was baptized by the Rev. Wm. Cockran at Red River on 26 Dec. 1830 (E4/la, f. 80).

53. B4/b/1, same to same, 1 Feb. 1830, fos. 2d-3.

54. B4/b/1, same to same, 20 March, f. 7.

55. B4/b/1, Jn. Stuart to Simpson, Norway House, 8 Aug. 1825, f. 18: " [...] permit me my heartfelt acknowledgements for the many Kindness [es] and marks of friendship manifested towards me on various occasions [...] before I can cease to be grateful I must cease to be myself. [...]" See also same to same, 1 Feb. 1830, fos. 2d, 6d.

56. D5/3. AEmileus Simpson to Geo. Simpson, Fort Vancouver, 20 March 1828.

57. B135/c/2, f. 76, Simpson to McTavish, Red River, 3 Jan. 1832: Simpson indulging in mutual congratulation on their choice of wives— "Now my good friend, we are in great measure indebted to each other for all this happiness, our mutual Friendship having been one of the "primitive" causes thereof . . ."

58. Macleod, *Letitia's Letters*, p. 83. This country wife of McTavish was reputed to have smothered two children, one while he was on his way to England. See also HBC, John Stuart Papers, Stuart to McTavish, Bas de la Rivière, 16 Aug. 1830—Stuart reminds McTavish that it was at Moose "you abandoned the first of your Wives."

59. B135/c/2, f. 50, Simpson to McTavish, 10 July 1830. Donald McKenzie was the brother of Nancy's father Roderic McKenzie who had retired in the early 1800's to Terrebonne in Lower Canada.

60. Macleod, *Letitia's Letters*, p. 84, To Mrs. Dugald McTavish, York, 1 Dec. 1840.

61. B135/c/2, fos. 33d-34, *Simpson* to McTavish, London, 5 Dec. 1829.

62. B135/c/2, f. 35d, same to same, 26 Dec. 1829.

63. B135/c/2, f. 42, same to same, 12 Jan. 1830.

64. Morton, *Simpson*, p. 164.

65. HBC, D6/4, p. 2.

66. Macleod, *Letitia's Letters*, To Mrs. Dugald McTavish, Gravesend, 21 May 1840, pp. 34-36.

67. Macleod, *Letitia's Letters*, p. 36.

68. What little education his sons did receive was at various schools in the Indian Country (D5/9, f. 236) and this undoubtedly contributed to their lack of advancement in the Company's service. Simpson also demanded a standard of conduct, particularly from his son George, which made little allowance for the boy's background or the insecurity of his childhood (D5/10, f. 50). Although a small bequest was made to his sons George, John and James in a draft will of 1841 (D6/1, fos 1-11), the Scottish-born Maria, now widowed and living in Upper Canada, was the only natural child to be remembered in his final will. Even she seems to have suffered his neglect, (see D5/9, fos. 260-61, Maria McTavish to Geo. Simpson, 22 Nov. 1843: ". . .Certain you must not be ashamed at countenancing me a little everyone knows I am your acknowledged daughter. . . .")

69. B135/c/2, f. 73, same to same, York, 15 Aug. 1831.

70. B135/c/2, f. 78, same to same, Red River, 3 Jan. 1832.

71. B135/c/2, f. 74, same to same, York, 15 Aug. 1831.

72. One of these women was Nancy Leblanc who nursed Mrs. Simpson's infant during her illness. Mrs. Simpson unflatteringly described her as "a complete savage, with a coarse blue sort of woolen gown without shape & a blanket fastened round her neck." (*Letitia's Letters,* To Mrs. Dugald McTavish, Gravesend, 20 May 1840, p. 36).

73. B135/c/2, f. 74d, Simpson to McTavish, York, 15 Aug. 1831.

74. B135/c/2, f. 70, same to same, York, 7 July 1831.

75. B135/c/2, f. 83, same to same, Red River, 1 May 1832.

76. B135/c/2, f. 85, same to same, York, 19 July 1832.

77. B135/c/2, f. 83, same to same, Red River, 1 May 1832.

78. Angus Cameron, for example, was happy to learn that the Governor intended to bring his family out to Lachine: "he will be more conveniently situated to superintend his various important duties than by going backwards and forwards to England every

year." (*Hargrave Corres.*, Angus Cameron to Hargrave, Temiscamingue, 25 April 1843, p. 434.)

79. PAC. MG19 A21(1), vol. 3, p. 813, Ed. Smith to Hargrave, Norway House, 8 July 1834.

80. Macleod, *Letitia's Letters*, p. 84, To Mrs. Dugald McTavish, 1 Dec. 1840.

81. B135/c/2, f. 115, Simpson to McTavish, London, 10 Jan. 1834.

82. PAC, MG19 A21(1), vol. 21, Hargrave to Charles Ross, York, 1 Dec. 1830.

83. B135/c/2, f. 106, Simpson to McTavish, Michipicoten, 29 June 1833. Alexander Christie did eventually become the Governor of Red River. He appears to have been devoted to his country family, his wife being Anne, the daughter of Thomas Thomas.

84. Glazebrook, *Hargrave Corres.*, p. 66, Cuthbert Cumming to Hargrave, St. Maurice, 1 March 1831.

85. B135/c/2, f. 96, Simpson to McTavish, Red River, 2 Dec. 1832.

▪ Article 2: Dispossession or Adaptation? Migration and Persistence of the Red River Métis, 1835–1890

Gerhard Ens

The scholarly debate about the migration and dispersal of the Métis[1] of Red River has generally focussed on some concept of the immutable nature of "Métis society," and has concentrated on the period after 1870. Those who argue that the Métis were essentially a "primitive people" saw the Métis exodus from Manitoba as a self-imposed exile, a return to primitivism. More recently, scholars have rejected this civilization-savagery dichotomy and argued that the Métis of Red River were a settled people with strong attachments to the land. In this view the Métis dispersal was, in effect, a forced dispossession by the Canadian government and aggressive capitalism. While these views have some validity, both

oversimplify the causes of Métis emigration from Red River, and do not examine the role of the changing nature of the Métis economy in Red River. Specifically they do not analyze the bases of migration and persistence of the Métis in Red River previous to 1870. An examination of this earlier period not only provides a more comprehensive explanation of the dispersal of the Métis, but accounts for the variability in the Métis experience at Red River.

Both G.F.G. Stanley and Marcel Giraud, whose works appeared in the 1930s and 1940s, saw the Métis as a primitive people doomed by the advance of the agricultural frontier. Unequipped to deal with the new economic order, they were submerged by the land rush after 1870.[2] G.F.G. Stanley's early work on the Métis was, in fact, much coloured by the increased impoverishment of the Métis in the 1930s, which he saw as leading inexorably to their eventual disappearance.[3] Stanley insisted that the troubles in the North-West (in both 1869 and 1885) were not primarily racial or religious, but normal frontier problems—the clash between primitive and civilized peoples. This view led Stanley to characterize Métis society as "static" and the Métis themselves as "indolent," "improvident," and unable to adjust.[4] Migration was the only alternative to racial absorption by an unfamiliar aggressive civilization

Source: Gerhard Ens, "Dispossession or Adaptation? Migration and Persistence of the Red River Métis, 1835–1890,"*Journal of the Canadian Historical Association*, Vol. 23, No. 1, pp. 120–144. Reprinted with permission from the Canadian History Association.

that flowed into Manitoba after 1870. While Marcel Giraud's classic study of the Métis presented a much more comprehensive view of Métis society, it adopted Stanley's cultural-conflict thesis in which the Métis were doomed by the advance of agricultural settlement. Maltreated, pushed aside, and unable to adjust, the Métis left Red River for the north and west where they attempted to rebuild their traditional life.[5]

This view of Métis emigration from Red River has been disputed by D.N. Sprague, a historian retained by the Métis Federation of Manitoba to undertake research into Métis land claims. In a series of articles and in a published collection of quantitative data relating to the Red River Métis, Sprague has argued that the actions of the Canadian government, preceding and following the Resistance of 1869–70, and the promulgation of the Manitoba Act, represented a deliberate attempt on the part of Prime Minister Macdonald and Ontario to appropriate Red River from the Métis, legally or illegally.[6] Elsewhere, Sprague has argued that by 1870 the Métis of Red River were committed settlers, not primitive, nomadic hunters as Giraud and Stanley had claimed. Their subsequent migration to the North-West was to recover a livelihood denied them in Manitoba.[7]

Métis emigration from Red River, in fact, was tied very closely to the changes in their political economy from the 1830s to 1890. Métis persistence in, and migration from, Red River went through a number of stages of which the period after 1870 was only one, albeit the most dramatic. Until at least 1875, this emigration of Red River Métis was a response to attractive new economic activities that emerged in the fur trade after 1850. With the opening of new fur markets the Métis increasingly combined different types of economic activity in the same household: petty-commodity production, trading activities, and temporary wage labour. In effect, some Métis communities abandoned agriculture and increasingly specialized in the fur trade as new roles were opened to them. Migration was part of the relocation of labour consequent on this reorganization of the Métis family economy following the expansion of the capitalistic fur trade. Accordingly, the dispersal of the Red River Métis between 1850 and 1875 should not be seen primarily as the self-inflicted exile of a "primitive" people nor the forced dispossession by the Canadian government. Rather, it should be seen as an adaptive, innovative response to new economic opportunities.

Only this broader economic view of the dispersal of the Red River Métis can make sense of the differential rate of migration, not only between the various Métis communities, but also within these communities at Red River. This is not to deny the fact that there were push factors involved in the Métis emigration after 1870—in particular the hostility of the incoming Ontario settlers.

The main sources for this study of persistence and migration were three sets of quantitative records: the Red River censuses of 1835, 1849, and 1870,[8] the North-West half breed scrip applications,[9] and the land records of the department of the Interior and Winnipeg Land Titles Office. The "Half-Breed Scrip" commissions of 1885–86 accepted claims from those Métis who had left Red River prior to 15 July 1870. These applications for claims thus provide an indication of emigration from Red River for the period previous to 1870. These applications, allowed by other scrip commissions up until 1906, gave the age and date of migration from Red River, home parish, and successive destinations. A more detailed analysis of persistence and migration has been carried out on the two Métis parishes of St. Andrew's and St. François Xavier, using the Red River censuses of 1835, 1849, 1870, and 1881. This has also been supplemented by a lot-by-lot analysis of the alienation of Métis land in these two parishes after 1870, along with a 10 per cent sample of the lots in the remaining parishes.[10]

To understand the transition that occurred in the economy of the Red River Métis in the period after the 1840s, and the effect this had on Métis emigration, some reference must be made to the Métis economy previous to the 1840s. By 1835 the various Métis communities of Red River had established a functioning way of life whose primary constituents were semiautonomous village communities and cultures. Their subsistence household economy was based on the buffalo hunt, small-scale cultivation, and seasonal labour for the Hudson's Bay Company (HBC). It was, in effect, a "specialized" peasant economy whose primary aims were to secure the needs of the family rather than to make a profit. This society would have conformed to A.V. Chayanov's concept of a peasant society, which posits a balance between subsistence needs and a substantive distaste for manual labour determining the intensity of cultivation and size of the net product.[11] While produce from the buffalo hunt and farm was exchanged in Red River for other goods, and while the Métis were engaged in other activities such as occasional wage labour, the family remained the main unit of production in an essentially noncapitalistic mode of production. Given the level of local technology at the time and the absence of any real market, this was a rational course of action.[12]

In the period before 1849, these peasant communities exhibited a strong geographic stability or persistence. Of the ninety-four families in St. Andrew's in 1835, 80 per cent were still persistent in 1849.[13] In St. François Xavier 66 per cent of the ninety-seven families were still persistent in 1849. Those family heads who did migrate were generally younger and had smaller families and fewer resources. The limited qualitative evidence related to emigration from Red River before 1849 confirms this. In the 1830s and 1840s there was a small but steady trickle of emigrants to the USA from all communities in the settlement,[14] along with the movement of Hudson's Bay Company servants and officers to other posts in the northwest. The one large movement consisted of the trek of twenty families to Columbia under the direction of James Sinclair. This migration had been organized by the HBC to counteract the projected American movement of settlers into Oregon.[15] The impact of these migrations on the colony was, however, minimal.

Instead it was changes in the political economy of the Red River Métis in the 1840s, changes that integrated the colony into the wider world, which produced large upheavals. These changes were tied to the increasing Métis involvement in a new capitalistic fur trade, especially the emerging buffalo-robe trade. This resurgence of Métis involvement in the fur trade did not signal a return to "primitivism" or "nomadism," but the penetration of an early form of capitalism into the Métis family economy—that is, the increasingly close association between household production of furs and robes based on the family economy on the one hand, and the capitalist organization of the trade and marketing of these products on the other. In the context of Red River these developments emerged with the breakup of the Hudson's Bay Company monopoly and the establishment of a new market for furs in the 1840s. Increasing Métis involvement in this new capitalistic fur trade, especially the emerging buffalo-robe trade,

took place within the context of the Métis family economy. Involvement in this new "rural industry"[16] led to an abandonment of agriculture by a segment of Métis, and was an important impetus to emigration from Red River.

An important stimulus to this new capitalistic fur trade was the establishment in 1844 of a trading post at Pembina, seventy miles south of Red River in the American territory. This had the effect of bringing the American market to the front door of the Red River Colony.[17] Not only did this post create an alternative market, it became source of supplies and capital that transformed the Métis economy of the region and precipitated an outburst of trading in furs throughout the Red River district. Especially important was the expansion of the buffalo-robe trade in the 1840s and 1850s. Buffalo robes had become an important and valuable trade item in the Upper Missouri in the late 1830s as the beaver trade waned[18] and, in the Red River Colony, the price received for buffalo robes increased in the 1840s and 1850s. Buffalo robes had long been used by traders and Indians as blankets and for packing furs, but their increasing value in the eastern market made them a prime trade item in the late 1830s and 1840s.[19]

An indication of the extent and expansion of this trade can be gleaned from the increase in the number of carts travelling annually to St. Paul. In 1844 only six carts are recorded as making the journey to St. Paul,[20] by 1855 four hundred carts,[21] by 1858, eight hundred carts,[22] and by 1869, twenty-five hundred carts were carrying furs and goods to St. Paul.[23] Fur sales in St. Paul, on the other hand, rose from $1,400 in 1844 to $40,000 in 1853, to $182,491 in 1857, and an average of over $215,000 annually in the following eight years.[24] The majority of these furs shipped to St. Paul from Red River were buffalo robes[25] and, by the late 1850s and early 1860s, St. Paul fur houses were sending "runners" to Red River to buy up buffalo robes in large quantities.[26] Norman Kittson, who had precipitated this new trade in the region by opening a post just south of the Canada/USA border at Pembina, was reported returning to Mendotta in 1857 with over four thousand buffalo robes.[27] In 1862 the settlement newspaper, the *Nor'wester,* commented that "the great business in this country is at present the trade in furs [...] Farming, shop-keeping, and all other vocations whatsoever, dwindle to the merest nothing when compared, in point of profits, with this

353

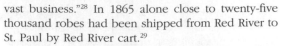
vast business."[28] In 1865 alone close to twenty-five thousand robes had been shipped from Red River to St. Paul by Red River cart.[29]

Increasingly the Métis took advantage of these opportunities, and became involved in commodity production for market (furs, particularly buffalo robes) rather than for home consumption. Rather than being sold to the Hudson's Bay Company, their surplus was increasingly appropriated by merchant traders, many of whom were Métis themselves. Participation in this new trade cut across community and ethnic boundaries as both English and French Métis responded to the opportunities. The most important component of this new fur trade, and the greatest impetus to wintering on the plains and hence abandoning agriculture, was the growing Métis involvement in the buffalo-robe trade. With its intensive labour demands, and the imperative for hunters and their families to winter near the buffalo herds as they drew ever further away from the Red River settlement, this trade significantly altered the geographic mobility of those Métis families who participated in it. The demands this trade, or household industry, placed on Métis families would draw them away from Red River in increasing numbers. As the demands for robes increased and as the herds moved further from the settlement, the practice of Métis families wintering near the herds became increasingly common. By 1856 Governor Simpson reported that the phenomenon of wintering villages had become widespread.[30]

The point to be stressed here is that the buffalo-robe trade became a household industry for those Métis families involved in it. In securing the buffalo robes and hides hunting groups developed a considerable organization with a clearly defined division of labour. Some engaged only in riding and shooting, others in skinning, while still others followed up to stretch and tan the skins and robes.[31] There was, in fact, a good deal of intensive labour involved in producing a buffalo robe for market, and this had a significant effect on the Métis family formation. The Métis family became, in effect, a household factory in the production of buffalo robes, necessitating long absences from the colony and thus making it impossible to continue cultivation of their family river lots.

A further stimulus to the transformation of the Métis economy in the 1840s was the succession of bad crop years, which failed to produce enough even for subsistence. In the five-year period 1844 to 1848, only 1845 produced a harvest sufficient to feed the colony.[32]

Faced with a limited market for grain and a succession of bad crop years, it is small wonder that a large number of Métis abandoned agriculture and concentrated on the fur trade for which there was now an expanding market. Even without bad crop years, Governor Simpson commented, "the want of market [for wheat] [...] has prevented any agriculturalist from expanding their farms and increasing their livestock beyond the requisite quantity to meet the demands of the Company and their own absolute wants."[34]

By the time the 1849 census was taken in Red River, it was clear that some Métis families were abandoning agriculture completely. While the total area under cultivation increased, from 3504 acres in 1835 to 6392 acres in 1849, some communities showed a decrease in cultivated acres despite the fact that their population had almost doubled. The connection between the new trading opportunities and the decline of agriculture was observed by the *Nor'wester* in discussing the decline of sheep farming in the settlement. Introduced in 1830, the number of sheep in the colony rose to a peak of 4222 in 1846, declined to 3096 in 1849, and to 2245 in 1856, and totalled even less by 1860. The reason for this decline, the *Nor'wester* noted, had to do with the increase in dogs in the settlement and this, in turn, was related to the increase in plains trading. "About the year 1848 parties commenced their excursion out of the settlement to trade with the Indian, and were of course accompanied by dogs. As the traffic and the dogs increased the sheep diminished. They were attacked and destroyed by the dogs."[35]

The brief sketch of the Métis economy between 1835 and 1870 makes it clear that by the 1830s the Métis communities in Red River combined subsistence agriculture and hunting to secure the needs of the family rather than to make a profit. Differences in cultivation between communities began to become apparent in the late 1840s as some Métis abandoned agriculture to pursue new economic opportunities in the emerging capitalistic fur trade, especially the buffalo-robe trade. This transition was more evident in St. François Xavier than in St. Andrew's, which continued to rely on peasant agriculture to a much greater degree. With the growing importance of the robe trade in the 1860s, Métis families in Red River were increasingly forced to make a decision between subsistence agriculture or the hivernement existence which went with the trade.[36] Hivernants (literally winterers) were those Métis who spent the winter on the plains to be nearer the buffalo herds. The best or "prime" buffalo robes were those taken from the animals in the winter when the hair was thickest. As the buffalo withdrew further from Red River it was thus necessary to winter on the plains. These Métis lived in temporary camps ranging from a few families to large encampments replete with a resident priest. Most Métis families did not have the capital required to remain in Red River and still continue in the buffalo-robe trade. The wealthier Métis, on the other hand, could outfit relatives or employees to visit these camps and trade for buffalo robes.

From the information given in North-West scrip applications, it is possible to see that permanent emigration from Red River began to increase in the 1850s,[37] and that the parishes experiencing the greatest emigration were St. François Xavier, St. Andrew's, Portage la Prairie, and St. Boniface (see Table 2 [...]). This timing corresponds very closely with reports of when hivernement camps were becoming more permanent.[38]

That these emigrants were responding to the exigencies of the buffalo-robe trade can be tested by examining the association between the number of migrants leaving Red River[39] and the rising buffalo-robe prices between 1847 and 1869 [which] shows a positive linear relationship between the two variables[;] the .67 correlation coefficient calculated from this data indicates a significant positive correlation between rising buffalo-robe prices and Métis emigration from Red River.[40] The destination of the individual migrants identified in the scrip applications further reinforces the association between the robe trade and Métis emigration. The majority of those leaving Portage went to Victoria, a settlement of English Métis buffalo hunters, while those from St. Andrew's left for both Victoria and the Saskatchewan Forks area. Those leaving St. François Xavier and St. Boniface, the two French Métis parishes which had the highest number of emigrants, left for the hivernement sites of Qu'Appelle, Wood Mountain, Saskatchewan Forks, Lac la Biche, Cypress Hills, and the Fort Edmonton area.[41] In 1864 the *Nor'wester* reported that twenty-five French Métis families were leaving Red River for Lac la Biche. While they were taking their stock and farm implements, the main purpose of the migration, the correspondent noted,

355

◉ TABLE 1

Population and Cultivation in St. Andrew's and St. François Xavier 1835 to 1870[33]

	ST. ANDREW'S				ST. FRANÇOIS XAVIER			
	1835	1849	1856	1870	1835	1849	1856	1870
Total Population	547	1068	1207	1456	506	911	1101	1857
Number of Single Adults	3	10	—	44	5	4	178	24
Number of Families	94	187	214	287	97	165	6.18	334
Average Family Size	5.78	5.66	5.64	4.91	5.16	5.49	—	5.47
Percentage of Métis Family Heads	53.6	68	—	75.1	74.5	82	5.82	91.2
Total Cultivated Acres	566	1368	1646	2002	594	527	3.26	1335
Average Cultivation / Family	6.02	7.3	7.7	6.97	6.12	3.19	0.53	3.99
Average Cultivation / Person	1.03	1.28	1.4	1.37	1.17	0.58	0.53	0.72
Cultivation / European Family	4.04	10.6	—	10.35	4.62	5.1	—	18.8
Cultivation / Métis Family	7.93	5.2	—	8.8	9.34	9.34	—	3.8

was to bring them near the buffalo, the pursuit of which would engross much more of their time than agriculture.[42]

The Red River-based buffalo hunt was by this time on its last legs with no more than one hundred and fifty carts participating in 1866.[43] The herds were now too far away, and to continue in the buffalo-robe trade necessitated migration. In the autumn of 1869 alone, forty families left St. François Xavier and Pembina to winter at Wood Mountain, and many never returned.[44] Large numbers of Métis from St. François Xavier also returned to the region of Battle-ford in the fall of 1869 because of the large buffalo herds there in past years.[45] In order to find large herds by the late 1860s it would have been necessary to travel five hundred miles from Red River.[46] While large hunts continued to take place, these no longer originated from Red River.

[…]

Writing to John A. Macdonald in 1871 Lieutenant-Governor Archibald warned that the French Métis were very excited,

> not so much, I believe by the dread about their land allotment as by the persistent ill-usage of such of them as have ventured from time to time into Winnipeg from the disbanded volunteers and newcomers who fill the town. Many of them actually have been so beaten and outraged that they feel as if they were living in a state of slavery. They say that the bitter hatred of these people is a yoke so intolerable that they would gladly escape it by any sacrifice.[47]

In 1872 Father André reported that the French-speaking Métis wintering near Carlton held with an invincible repugnance any thought of settling in Red River again. Too many changes, at odds with their customs and morals, had taken place in both social and political realms.[48] The arrival of the Wolseley Expedition in 1870, in fact, instituted a reign of terror in the settlement. Intent on avenging the death of Thomas Scott, the Ontario volunteers acted in defiance of all law and authority and established virtual mob rule in Winnipeg in 1871–72. It was not safe for a French Métis to be seen near Fort Garry, the location of the land office, and those who did venture into Winnipeg risked life and limb.[49]

TABLE 2

Métis Migration From Red River Before 1870

Parish	Number	Percentage
St. Peters	23	3.8
St. Andrew's	38	6.3
Portage	63	10.4
St. Pauls	7	1.1
St Johns	5	0.8
Ft. Garry-Winnipeg	25	4.1
St. Boniface	76	12.5
St. Norbert	22	3.6
St. Vital	15	2.5
St. Charles	4	0.7
St. James	4	0.7
High Bluff	2	0.3
Poplar Point	3	0.5
St. François Xavier	187	30.9
Scratching River	1	0.2
Kildonan	3	0.5
Ste. Agathe	2	0.3
Baie St. Paul	20	3.3
Headingly	1	0.2
Unknown	105	17.3
TOTAL	606	100.0

Source: Scrip Records.

Father Kavanagh, the parish priest of St. François Xavier, who himself was almost killed by Protestant extremists on his way to Winnipeg, also complained that while the Métis of his parish had designated the lands promised them in the Manitoba Act, this had scarcely stopped the Orangemen from Ontario from occupying the same land. In the face of this infringement on what they took to be their land, Kavanagh reported that some Métis had begun to defend themselves, but most were abandoning the struggle and, in growing arrogance and resignation, were leaving for the plains. Many were, in fact, offering to sell their lands to the same Protestants: "Selon toute apparence nous sommes donc enveloppés et engloutis par le *protestanisme* et *l'orangisme*. C'est si visible maintenant, que ces personnes influentes dont j'ai parlé plus haut, en conviennent; mais il est bien tard!!!"[50] While these land issues were also problems for the English Métis of St. Andrew's,[51] the language and religion they shared with the newcomers made the issue of contiguous reserves less important, and the conflict over land less bitter.

An analysis of the alienation of river lots in the parishes of St. François Xavier and St. Andrew's, and a sample of the other parishes between 1870 and 1890 bears out the timing of this exodus. In both parishes and in Red River generally, the alienation of river lots[52] peaked in the periods 1872–75 and 1880–82 [ ]. The first period coincided with the delays and frustrations over the granting of Métis lands, but it also represented a continuation of the exodus, which had begun previous to 1870, of those Métis involved in the buffalo robe trade. This early glut of river-lot sales would seem to contradict Mailhot and Sprague's assertion that 90 per cent of those Métis found in the 1870 census were still in the settlement in 1875. According to Mailhot and Sprague this high percentage indicated that the Métis were indeed "persistent settlers," that their exodus after this time was due to government lawlessness, and that the land surveyors were part of a conspiracy to overlook most Métis while recording a few.[53] The evidence, however, does not support Sprague's argument.

[…]

Those Red River Métis who held onto their lots in this period generally did so until 1880, when the real-estate boom in Winnipeg and surrounding area made river lots prime real estate. Sales in this period might well be seen as taking advantage of a financial opportunity, allowing Métis a cash stake to reestablish themselves on larger farms elsewhere. The upsurge of emigration in this period also coincided with the loss of political power by the Métis in Manitoba. The connection between the loss of political power and emigration is perfectly illustrated in the person of Louis Schmidt. On losing his seat in the legislature in the 1878 election in St. François Xavier, Schmidt packed his bags and moved to Batoche.[54]

An examination of the destination of those who left after 1870 illustrates how the two peaks of emigrations (the early 1870s and the period around 1880) differed. While there is no consistent time-specific quantitative data that can be used to analyze the destination of migrants, individual references in parish files and other sources give some indication. Of those leaving in the early 1870s, many left for Métis wintering sites, in effect continuing their involvement in the buffalo trade. Pascal Breland, writing to Alexander Morris in 1873, noted that there were a great many Métis wintering at Wood Mountain. Of the four leaders he mentioned, two were St. François Xavier Métis who had been enumerated in 1870: Pierre Boyer, a landless Métis, and Pierre Poitras, who owned lot 41 and would sell it in 1874.[55] Similarly, François Swain left S. François Xavier with his parents in 1872 to move to Cypress Hills, while John Pritchard Mckay and his son sold lot 214 to the Catholic church in 1872 to winter on the plains.[56] Le Métis also reported that large numbers of Red River Métis had settled in the vicinity of Wood Mountain and near Carlton in the early 1870s.[57] This type of migration, while more impelled than before 1870, could still be characterized as adaptive to the trading economy of the early seventies.

Those who sold their lots later (1879–90) had already made the decision to farm. Their exodus after 1878 reflected the difficulty of commercial grain farming on narrow river lots. The problem was especially acute in cases where a head of family died without specifying a sole heir. In all cases encountered of this type, the heirs decided to sell the lot instead of subdividing it, moving elsewhere to farm.[58] Lists of claimants for "Halfbreed Scrip" in the settlements of St. Louis de Langevin, Batoche, and Duck Lake in the mid-1880s read like the parish rolls of St. François Xavier.[59] In 1882–83 alone twenty families, many of them from St. François Xavier, moved to Batoche from Red River.[60] Not all who left the parish lots in the late 1870s and 1880s went to the North-West, however. Many simply sold their lots to homestead and settled in areas of Manitoba where it was possible to live with kin and friends. Some from St. François Xavier moved to St. Eustache, St. Rose du

357

Lac, or Ste. Anne, while a number of families from St. Andrew's moved sixty miles north to the community of Grand Marais on Lake Winnipeg.[61] A new settlement also arose ten miles east of St. Andrew's on Cook's Creek. According to James Settee this settlement was started in 1871 and comprised fifty adults by 1872.[62] Probably the largest offshoot community of St. François Xavier in Manitoba was the Métis settlement at Rivière aux Ilets de Bois, south of the Assiniboine. By the 1880s, Father Kavanagh was making regular trips to the mission (St. Daniel) to minister to the approximately thirty Métis families residing there.[63] Families such as the Emonds, Delormes, Lillies, Prudens, and Gagnons sold their parish lots and bought larger farms here (the majority of Métis settled on township 7, range 5 W).[64]

A final determinant affecting the persistence and migration of the Métis of Red River, and one which explains, to some extent, the differential rates within communities after 1870, is that of class. While difficult to define and document in the social flux of Red River in the 1860s and 1870s, it was none the less observable. The one study that has dealt with this issue in the context of the Métis dispersal from Red River is Nicole St-Onge's work on the dissolution of the Red River Métis community of Pointe à Grouette (Ste. Agathe).[65] St-Onge sees the emergence of two distinct Métis groups separated by the late 1860s on economic and occupational lines; on the one hand were the trading and farming elite, and on the other the poorer bison hunters. In her analysis the richer traders and farmers were able to hold onto their land much longer than the poorer buffalo hunters, who had largely sold out and left the community by 1876. The fact that Métis speculators were involved in the buying out of their kinsmen suggests to St-Onge that the dispersal of the Métis was related to class rather than ethnicity.[66]

This pattern corresponds roughly to what occurred in St. François Xavier. Increasing involvement in the buffalo-robe trade after 1850 also fragmented Métis communities on socio-economic lines, and this explains a good deal of the differing rates of migration within communities. Those Métis families who were involved at the production end of the buffalo-robe trade had less land and fewer cultivated acres, and were generally the first to emigrate. The destination of these migrants was, in most cases, Métis wintering sites in the North-West. Continued involvement in the buffalo-robe trade for merchant traders, on the other hand, was not as dislocating. Not involved in the production end of the industry, this bourgeoisie could afford to stay in the settlement outfitting younger sons and relatives to undertake trading missions and, at the same time, maintain their river lot farms. Many of these wealthy Métis families remained in Manitoba through the 1880s, and became prominent in provincial politics.

J. Daignault, arriving in St. François Xavier in the 1870s from Quebec, observed that the parish was divided on socio-economic and geographic lines. While all got along with each other, there were distinct lines. Those Métis who lived in the Pigeon Lake community to the west of the church[67] were closely tied to the buffalo-robe trade as hunters, and held to traditional cultural practices. They were known as the "Purs." By contrast those Métis living to the east and south of the river and involved in the buffalo-robe trade as merchant traders and farmers were identified as living in "Petit Canada." These Métis made a show of imitating the French Canadians in their customs and dress.[68] The third group mentioned by Daignault was the emerging group of French Canadians from Quebec, who were starting to displace the Métis in the parish.

An analysis of the persistence of these two identifiable Métis classes corresponds to the pattern identified earlier, and the chronology of emigration identified by St-Onge. Of the nine landowning families resident at Pigeon Lake in 1870, only five retained their land after 1875, and only three past 1880. Those identified by Daignault as residing in "Petit Canada" all retained their land beyond 1881. My analysis differs from that of St-Onge in the emphasis placed on the actions of the federal government. Agreeing with Sprague, she argues that the poorer Métis hunters "left because of changes in the Manitoba Act which they were unable to circumvent." Incapable of establishing their improvements, and unable effectively to challenge adverse decisions related to their claims as the more affluent Métis were able to, "they sold, abandoned, or were swindled out of their claims for small amounts of money."[69] This theory, however, is not proven and little evidence is presented. St-Onge does show that the poorer Métis left first, but nowhere establishes that the motivation or the cause for their leaving was their inability to establish their claims. A closer examination of this

358

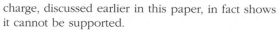
charge, discussed earlier in this paper, in fact shows it cannot be supported.

In my analysis the decision to migrate was more a function of the changing Métis family economy and its involvement in the buffalo-robe trade. Increasing Métis involvement in this trade after 1850 necessitated an occupational specialization for those families involved and a consequent abandonment of agriculture. When the exigencies of the trade forced a permanent hivernement existence, emigration was the result. This emigration began well before Manitoba's entry into Confederation and continued to the mid-1870s when the buffalo-robe market collapsed. If there was an element of coercion in the Métis exodus from Red River, it was the intolerant actions and behaviour of the incoming Protestant settlers from Ontario.

Métis migration from Manitoba after the mid-1870s had other causes. Those who had retained their land to 1880 had, in fact, made the decision to farm rather than concentrate on the robe trade. The spate of river-lot sales, and the exodus from the Métis parishes in the early 1880s, were in response to high land prices during the real-estate boom of 1880–82. These sales gave the Métis a cash stake to reestablish larger farms elsewhere. By the late 1870s and early 1880s, there was a growing recognition of the limitations of the narrow river lots for commercial grain farming, and those Métis who wished to continue farming combined with occasional wage labour and freighting could best do this farther west. Those leaving in this period left to homestead in other areas of the province, or to join the growing Métis farming communities in the North-West.

NOTES

1. The term Métis, for the purposes of this paper, includes both the historical métis who arose in the St. Lawrence-Great Lakes trading system, who chose to see themselves in various collectivities distinct from their Indian neighbours and the "white" community, and those individuals of mixed Indian and European ancestry who arose in the Hudson Bay trading system who held similar views as to their relations with Indians and whites.

2. G.F.G. Stanley, *The Birth of Western Canada: A History of the Riel Rebellions* (Toronto, 1961). Marcel Giraud, *Le Métis Canadien: Son rôle dans l'histoire de provinces de l'Ouest*, 2 vols. (Paris, 1945).

3. G.F.G. Stanley, "The Métis and the Conflict of Culture in Western Canada." *Canadian Historical Review* 28 (1947).

4. Stanley, *The Birth of Western Canada*, 8, 18.

5. Giraud, *Le Métis Canadien*, 2: 1134.

6. D.N. Sprague, "Government Lawlessness in the Administration of Manitoba Land Claims, 1870–1887," *Manitoba Law Journal* 10: 4 (1980): "The Manitoba Land Question 1870–1882," *Journal of Canadian Studies* 15: 3 (1980); D.N. Sprague and R.P. Frye, *The Genealogy of the First Métis Nation: The Development and Dispersal of the Red River Settlement 1820–1900* (Winnipeg, 1983).

7. P.R. Mailhot and D.N. Sprague, "Persistent Settlers: The Dispersal and Resettlement of the Red River Métis, 1870–1885," *Canadian Ethnic Studies* 17: 2 (1985).

8. Manitoba. Public Archives (PAM), Nominal Censuses of the Red River Settlement.

9. Canada. National Archives (NA), RG 15, North-West Half Breed Scrip Applications.

10. The information for this lot-by-lot analysis comes from the Abstract Book of the Winnipeg Land Titles office which recorded the first sales of these parish lots after 1870. Also used were the parish lot files (PAM, RG17 D2), which were files kept by the department of Interior on each river lot, pertaining to the ownership and patenting of parish land. Some files are missing from the set found in the PAM. These were files retained by the department of the Interior when the records were transferred to Manitoba in 1930. These missing files are now located in the Manitoba Act Files, NA, RG15, vol. 140–68.

11. A.V. Chayanov, *The Theory of Peasant Society*, ed. Daniel Thorner, Basile Kerblay, and R.E.F. Smith (Homewood, Ill., 1966).

12. While the HBC purchased pemmican, dried meat, and agricultural produce from the settlers of Red River at an early date, the annual demand was fairly constant while the population in Red River increased rapidly. John Elgin Foster, "The Country-Born in the Red River Settlement, 1820–1850." PhD diss., University of Alberta, 1973, 219.

13. Censuses of this period listed only the head of the family along with the number of adults and children in the family. A family was considered persistent if the head of the family listed in the 1835 census reappeared in the 1849 census. In those cases where it could be shown that the head of

359

the family had died in the intervening years, and the family was present and listed under another name in the 1849 census, the family was still considered persistent. This required cross-referencing the census returns with the parish registers.

14. Foster, "The Country-Born." 219n.

15. George Gladman to James Hargrave (Fort Garry) 3 June 1843, as cited in *The Hargrave Correspondence, 1821–43*, ed. G.P. de T. Glazebrook (Toronto, 1938), 348.

16. As Irene Spry has written, the buffalo hunt "was, in fact, the basis of the first great industry in Western Canada." Irene Spry. "The 'Private Adventurers' of Rupert's Land," in *The Developing West: Essays on Canadian History in Honor of Lewis H. Thomas*, ed. John E. Foster (Edmonton, 1983), 54.

17. Alvin Charles Glueck, "The Struggle for the British Northwest: A Study in Canadian-American Relations," PhD diss., University of Minnesota, 1953, 27.

18. Erwin N. Thompson, *Fort Union Trading Post: Fur Trade Empire on the Upper Missouri* (Medora, N.D., 1986), 34–35.

19. These robes consisted of buffalo skins tanned on one side with hair on the other. In 1843 George Simpson, writing to the governors of the Hudson's Bay Company, commented that the Indians in the Saskatchewan District were paying more attention than usual to the preparation of buffalo robes, and that there was a large trade in these robes for which there was now a demand in both Canada and the United States. The Hudson's Bay Company, he added, intended to encourage this trade to the utmost extent of the company's ability to transport the robes. Hudson's Bay Company Archives (HBCA), D4/62, fo. 11–14, Simpson to governors. 21 June 1843.

20. Hattie Listenfeldt, "The Hudson's Bay Company and the Red River Trade," *Collections of the State Historical Society of North Dakota* 4 (1913).

21. HBCA, D4/75, George Simpson to governor and committee, 29 June 1855.

22. CMS Records, Incoming Correspondence, Letter Book VI, p. 368 (reel 6), Rev. Kirkby to the secretaries, 2 August 1858.

23. G.F.G. Stanley, *Louis Riel* (Toronto, 1963), 37.

24. *Nor'wester,* 31 January 1866; "To Red River and Beyond." *Harpers* (February 1861): 309–10.

25. *Nor'wester*, 14 May 1860, 15 June 1861, 31 January 1866.

26. *Nor'wester*, 14 June 1860.

27. William John Peterson, *Steamboating on the Upper Mississippi* (Iowa City, 1968), 164.

28. *Nor'wester*, 1 September 1862.

29. *Nor'wester*, 31 January 1866.

30. HBCA, D4/76A, Simpson to governors and committee, 26 June 1856.

31. Merrill Burlingame, "The Buffalo in Trade and Commerce," *North Dakota Historical Quarterly* 3:4 (1929): 287.

32. CMS Records, Incoming Correspondence, Letter Book IV, pp. 196–97, 213, 387, Smithurst to secretary, 18 November 1846; Wm. Cockran to secretary, 5 August 1847; Rev. James to secretary, 2 August 1848. PAM, Donald Ross Papers, MGI, D20, File 161, Alexander Ross to Donald Ross, 9 August 1847.

33. Except for 1856, this information has been reconstructed from the nominal censuses of the Red River settlement. The 1856 figures come from the tabulated census.

34. HBCA, D4/68, Simpson's report of 1847, p. 264.

35. "Sheep Farming in Red River," *Nor'wester*, 14 May 1860.

36. The literature on the hivernement experience is not large but is growing. The best contemporary description is found in the letters and writings of Father Decorby located in the Provincial Archives of Alberta. The best historical study to date is R.F. Beal, J.E. Foster, and Louise Zuk, "The Métis Hivernement Settlement at Buffalo Lake, 1872–77," report prepared for the Alberta Department of Culture, Historic Sites and Provincial Museums Division (April 1987).

37. These North-West scrip applications should not be regarded as a comprehensive record of all migration from Red River. For example, those Métis who migrated to the United States and never returned to Canada, would obviously never have applied for scrip. Further, since scrip claims were only made after 1885, over fifteen years after the event they recorded, migration from Red River was probably under-reported in all periods but probably more so in the 1830s and 1840s due to the death of Métis individuals. Despite these shortcomings, scrip records are useful in determining the general trends of emigration from Red River.

38. These hivernement camps, consisting of merchants and hunting families, ranged in size from a few families to upwards of two hundred. Some known hivernement sites included Turtle Mountain, Qu'Appelle River, Wood Mountain, Touchwood Hills, Cypress

Hills, Souris River, Petite Ville, Buffalo Lake, Lac Ste. Anne, La Coulée Chapelle, Lac la Vieille, Coulées des Cheminées, St. Laurent, and Prairie Ronde.

39. These are the individual migrants identified in the scrip applications.

40. To calculate this correlation coefficient using simple linear regression, robe prices at year N were paired with migrants in year N+1 since price information cannot affect market behavior before it can become known. The coefficient may be said to measure how closely the correlation approaches a linear functional relationship. A coefficient value equivalent to unity denotes a perfect functional relationship and all the points representing paired values of x and y would fall on the regression line representing this relationship. Correlation coefficients are expressed in values ranging between –1 and +1. The nearer a value is to either of these extremes, the better is the correlation between the two variables. If the value is positive then the correlation is direct; as the independent variable increases, so does the dependent variable. If the value is negative, the correlation is inverse.

41. North-West Half-Breed Scrip Applications.

42. *Nor'Wester*, 21 June 1864.

43. [*sic*]

44. *Henri Létourneau Raconte* (Winnipeg, 1980), 44.

45. Giraud, *Le Métis Canadien*, 821–22.

46. F.G. Roe, *The North American Buffalo* (Toronto 1951), 396.

47. A. G. Archibald to Macdonald, 9 October 1871, reprinted in *Journals of the House of Commons of the Dominion of Canada,* 37 Vic. (1874), vol. VIII, "Report of the Select Committee on the Causes of the Difficulties in the North-West Territories in 1869–70." Appendix (No. 6).

48. *Le Métis*, 3 avril 1872.

49. There were, in fact, a number of deaths and scores of attacks and beatings attributed to the soldiers in Winnipeg. This reign of terror has been painstakingly documented by Allen Ronaghan, "The Archibald Administration in Manitoba, 1870–72." PhD diss., University of Manitoba, 1987, 417–21, 500–05, 596–607.

50. Archives of the Archdiocese of Saint Boniface (AASB), Fonds Taché, T9222-9224, Kavanagh to Taché, 14 août 1871.

51. There were numerous articles and reports of meetings about the land question in the English Métis parishes in the *Manitoban* in the early 1870s.

52. For the purposes of this analysis of persistence and migration, the alienation of a lot was defined as the passage of the river lot out of the family. Thus a sale of a lot by an older parent to a son was not considered an alienation. Likewise a sale to a daughter, son-in-law, or wife was also not considered an alienation.

53. Mailhot and Sprague, "Persistent Settlers," 5.

54. PAM, Louis Schmidt Memoirs.

55. PAM, Morris Papers, Pascal Breland to Lt. Governor Morris, 10 May 1873.

56. PAM, St. François Xavier Parish Files; *Henri Létourneau Raconte*, 36.

57. *Le Métis*, letter of Father Lestanc. 23 janvier 1877; letter of Father André, 3 avril 1872.

58. This information is found in the parish files located in the PAM. These files recorded the alienation of these lots and often enclosed wills where they had a bearing on the transmission of the lot.

59. *Detailed Report upon All Claims to Land and Right to Participate in the North-West Half-Breed Grant by Settlers along the South Saskatchewan and Vicinity West of Range 26 W 2nd Meridian* (Ottawa, 1886).

60. Diane Payment, *Batoche, 1870–1910* (Saint Boniface, 1983), 24.

61. PAM, Parish Files: PAM, interview of Elsie Bear by Nicole St-Onge, 16 May 1985.

62. CMS Records, C. 1/0, I.C. reel 26, J. Settee to CMS, 9 December 1872.

63. AASB, Fonds Taché, T23724-23725, Kavanagh to Taché, 22 avril 1880.

64. Crown Lands Branch, Patent Diagrams: *The Rural Municipality of Dufferin, 1880–1980* (Rural Municipality of Dufferin, 1980).

65. Nicole J.M. St-Onge, "The Dissolution of a Métis Community: Pointe à Grouette, 1860–1885." *Studies in Political Economy* 18 (Autumn 1985).

66. Ibid., 157–62.

67. The body of water known as Pigeon Lake was situated on river lots 122 to 129. This was the former bed of the Assiniboine River, which through the natural process of erosion had relocated itself further south. Lots here were subdivided a good deal more than in the rest of the parish, and consequently had smaller acreages.

68. J. Daignault, "Mes Souvenirs," *Les Cloches de Saint-Boniface* (février 1945): 28.

69. St-Onge, "The Dissolution of a Métis Community," 162.

361

■ Article 3: The Métis and the Red River Settlement

Gerald Friesen

The Métis resistance led by Riel was a movement not of the entire French-speaking community, let alone of all Red River. As in any political event, the resistance won and lost adherents throughout its life of ten months. The alignment of factions is thus uncertain. Riel was opposed by the Canadian annexationists associated with John Christian Schultz and by the recent Ontario settlers west of Winnipeg on the Assiniboine River. He was opposed also by the Indians of the 'Lower Settlement' where Schultz and British patriotism were strong. Riel was supported with varying degrees of enthusiasm by the Roman Catholic clergy, the Americans, and many of the French-speaking Métis. And some of the French and many of the English-speaking settlers—Métis, Scot, Orkney, Canadian—were in the middle, ready to move from side to side depending on the issue and the circumstance. The heart of the resistance lay with the men mobilized by Riel—the cartmen and boatmen who wintered in the settlement and were quite prepared to serve as an army in a good cause.

The resistance took shape slowly and deliberately between June and October 1869. Several public meetings and numerous gatherings at church doors on Sundays addressed the issue of the transfer, but, despite rumours of Canadian annexation and uncertainty about the consequences, no decision was reached on a course of action. Then, on 11 October, as the Canadian survey party reached the Métis river lots near St. Vital, Louis Riel and a few followers rode up from the river to join the owner of the farm, André Nault, in challenging the right of the Canadian government to cross their lands or, more important, to conduct any survey in the northwest. It was a considered political act, symbolic of the Métis determination to stand up for their rights. As the survey party withdrew to safer tasks in accordance with their instructions, the Métis began to organize in earnest.

Source: Gerald Friesen, "The Métis and the Red River Settlement," in *The Canadian Prairies: A History*. Toronto: University of Toronto Press, 1987, pp. 119–128. © University of Toronto Press, Inc. 1987. Reprinted with permission of the publisher.

Within two weeks they had created a National Committee, administered oaths of loyalty to their members, erected a barrier across the main trail to the United States—the site has been called La Barrière ever since—and begun to police the highway and the plains stretching to the west in order to control access to the settlement. They now had to prevent William McDougall, member of the federal cabinet, noted Canadian annexationist, and the man nominated to be first lieutenant-governor of the North-West Territories, from taking up his commission. McDougall ignored the first message requiring him to remain in American territory, but the armed party of Métis horsemen that confronted him on 2 November was more convincing. He retired across the border to Pembina, never to return and never to fulfil his task. As in the challenge to the survey, so in the opposition to McDougall's entry, the Métis had made it apparent that they would not only assert their concerns but also prevent annexation to Canada until they had won recognition of their rights.

These opening skirmishes were doubtless illegal, but they were not violent and did not involve property. However Riel could not stop at symbolic acts. He lived in a land where guns and violence were well-known and where an Indian rising or a Canadian-Métis skirmish was quite possible. Again he showed the decisiveness that was his mark. On 2 November, he sent several hundred Métis to the tree-covered south banks of the Assiniboine from where, in groups of three and four, they crossed to Upper Fort Garry. Without a shot being fired, the Métis soldiers seized the strongest bastion in the settlement, including cannon, small arms, and considerable stores of pemmican (sufficient to feed an army for the winter) and thereby established the military dominance that would sustain them for the duration of the resistance. An illegal violation of company property rights but a brilliant stroke of tactics, the seizure of the fort was the single most important act in the Métis campaign. Winter was fast approaching, and with it protection from outside intervention for at least six months. Henceforth, Riel negotiated from a position of military strength.

His great task was to create common cause with all groups in the settlement in order to present a united front to the Canadian government. To that end, he called a convention of twelve English- and twelve French-speaking parish representatives for

16 November. Riel proposed to that convention that they form a provisional government to replace the moribund Hudson's Bay Company administration. While this and other possibilities were being debated and the leaders of the settlement's various factions were jockeying for power, William McDougall made his last appearance on the western stage.

McDougall had been languishing at Pembina for a month, observing the construction of a log cabin—his own—and awaiting advice from Ottawa on his next step. He had been told to do nothing until he heard that the transfer had actually occurred, but because the mails required two weeks for delivery he was not abreast of events and therefore assumed that the original date for the transfer, 1 December, remained unchanged. Moreover, he assumed, wrongly as it happened, that the government of the Hudson's Bay Company expired at the transfer and that he must be in a position to inaugurate Canadian authority. Having received no new instructions, he crossed the border on the night of 30 November and read a proclamation to the wind and the stars announcing the transfer and the commencement of his rule. He was wrong. Prime Minister John A Macdonald, having learned of the Métis resistance and of McDougall's forced sojourn at Pembina, had wired London in late November to postpone the transfer on the grounds that Canada was entitled to peaceable possession. Thus, the rule of the Hudson's Bay Company remained intact and McDougall's proclamation was void.

Riel was still regarded as a law-breaker by many in Red River because he had seized the fort. However, he had refused to challenge the sovereignty of the crown, and so most residents did not view him as a rebel. Then came the news of McDougall's proclamation and the circulation of McDougall's commission to John S. Dennis to put down those in arms against constituted authority. At this point, the community moved to the brink of armed conflict. The Canadian loyalists moved to the area of Lower Fort Garry, twenty miles north of Riel's base and in a site equally defensible as a military redoubt. Armed deadlock would have resulted had there not been a Canadian government shipment of pork in Schultz's house in the village of Winnipeg within gunshot of Riel's troops. Though guarded by Schultz and fifty men, and fully sufficient to sustain the Canadian loyalist army throughout the winter, the pork had

not been removed to the safer ground of the Lower Fort. Riel seized the initiative once again and on 7 December compelled the surrender of the house, pork, and garrison. This was a significant blow to his opponents.

Even more important as a factor in defusing opposition among the English-speaking settlers was the relative moderation of Riel's political program. The convention of twenty-four had received McDougall's proclamation on 1 December and, of course, believed it to be valid. It had also heard a list of rights prepared in haste by the French members which seemed a reasonable declaration. But the delegates had been unable to agree on their next move. The English wished to permit the queen's representative (as he was thought to be), McDougall, to enter the territory; Riel was adamant that he should not, for fear that he would rally the Canadian loyalists and destroy his plans for a united negotiating stance. The convention then dissolved, and Riel went forward with his French Métis supporters alone.

On 8 December, the day after his raid on Schultz's house, Riel proclaimed the establishment of a provisional government. In the accompanying declaration, often described as the Declaration of Métis Independence because of its obvious similarity to the American document of 1776, he and his adviser, Father Dugas, argued that the Hudson's Bay Company had ceased to provide effective government and that its transfer of the northwest to another authority without the consent of northwest inhabitants violated the 'rights of man'; therefore 'the law of nations' supported the Métis right to proclaim a provisional government. This new government was prepared, however, to treat with Canada on terms of union. The document, W.L. Morton concluded, 'is no more than an assertion of the right of the Métis to negotiate the terms on which Canadian authority would be established in the North-West.'[1] Riel thereby won the silent sympathy, if not the political support, of the English-speaking settlers. That sympathy, coupled with the military blow to the Canadian forces in the battle over government pork and the intervention of several Protestant ministers who dispersed the loyalist military force, was sufficient to maintain Riel's control over Red River. In the mean time, McDougall had been defeated. In mid-December, he collected his belongings and headed across the plains for St Paul and, eventually, Canada.

363

Riel was now in command of Red River and it had become the turn of Prime Minister Macdonald to find a means of commencing negotiations. His first tactic, six months late in conception, was to dispatch two commissioners to explain that Canadian intentions were honourable. His second was to prepare for a military expedition in the summer of 1870. His third was to re-establish Hudson's Bay Company rule through Donald A. Smith, chief factor in charge of company affairs in North America, who was made a special commissioner and asked to buy off the insurgents or otherwise break Riel's hold over the colony. The two innocent commissioners, Thibault and de Salaberry, were powerless. The armed force was to come into play only later. But Smith initiated a new phase in the resistance.

Shrewd, cool, and decisive, Donald A. Smith was a match for Riel. He had the power of the Hudson's Bay Company at his disposal at a time when the tripmen usually required credit to get through the winter, and he had Macdonald's commission in reserve. His goal was to negotiate the transfer with the people of Red River, whereas Riel wished that Canada deal only with his provisional government. Smith forced Riel to convoke an extraordinary general meeting of the entire settlement at Upper Fort Garry on 19 and 20 January 1870. There, with settlement notables standing on the gallery of the mess hall, and over a thousand people below them in the courtyard, and despite the −20° (Fahrenheit) cold, Smith assured the settlers of liberal treatment by the Canadian government. For reasons that have never been explained, he did not press his advantage by reading his proclamation and thereby making continuation of the provisional government a rebellious act; instead, perhaps because the compromise had been arranged in advance, he acquiesced in Riel's call for a new representative convention, the so-called convention of forty, to consider his proposals.

Once more Riel was in command, and Smith, whatever his hopes for the new assembly, had lost. The result was a second convention, a second list of rights, and an agreement to send delegates to Ottawa to negotiate terms of entry into Confederation. Riel did not secure the convention's repudiation of the Canadian bargain with the Hudson's Bay Company or its approval of provincial as opposed to territorial status. But he did win its approval for the establishment of an interim provisional government,

representative of the entire settlement, with himself as president. It was the culmination of the campaign he had begun the previous October to create a united settlement. By 10 February, when the convention ended, Riel seemed to have won his way.

The crisis of the following week set in train the events that led to Riel's downfall. Canadian loyalists, including members of the Canadian survey party and men who had escaped or been released from Fort Garry after the capture of Schultz's house in December, apparently decided to attempt to release the remaining prisoners in the fort. They met with Schultz and others in the lower settlement and then, probably because Riel was fulfilling a promise to the convention by releasing the prisoners, decided to disband. Unfortunately, Riel had already decided to meet them in combat. His armed horsemen surrounded their opponents in deep snow just as they passed the village of Winnipeg on their return home and imprisoned them in the fort. Capt. C.A. Boulton, leader of the group, was sentenced to be shot as an example to the rest and perhaps, too, as an example to the Canadian government. But this threat passed; Boulton's sentence was commuted, the new provisional government was elected, and the settlement seemed still to be awaiting peaceful annexation to Canada.

Two individuals who had been involved in this latest military fiasco were now brought to the fore and, almost alone, destroyed the settlement's unity. John Christian Schultz had escaped arrest in the loyalist 'march' and had set out for Duluth, Minnesota, across country, smouldering with resentment. He was headed for Ontario where he planned to launch a crusade to save the northwest from the French Catholic Métis. Thomas Scott, a twenty-eight-year-old labourer from Ontario, had been captured for the second time in two months and soon managed to make himself the most hated man in the barracks. His dysentery and his contempt for the Métis irritated his captors beyond endurance. When the guards almost shot him on the spot, the Métis leaders, perhaps including Riel but certainly Ambroise Lepine, ordered that Scott be given a military courtmartial. He was sentenced to death. In the early morning of 4 March, a still incredulous Scott was led into the sunshine behind the fort and cut down by a firing squad. Riel may have believed that the execution was necessary to pacify the Métis guard. He may have wished to hasten the completion of the transfer by impressing his opponents with the depth of his resolve. But the 'murder' of Scott was a fatal error because it created a political martyr. John Christian Schultz arrived in Ontario to discover that the bullets that had executed Thomas Scott provided ample ammunition to ensure the conquest of Riel and the Métis.

The resistance had run its course by April 1870. Only two interrelated issues had to be settled. The first was the negotiation between the Red River delegates and the Canadian government of the terms of entry into Confederation, including, of course, the question of an amnesty for those who had participated in the event. The second was the means by which authority over the territory would be transferred from President Riel and his still-unrecognized provisional government to the new lieutenant-governor and the Canadian state. Failure to reach appropriate agreement on these matters was to render futile all Riel's efforts in the preceding year.

The Red River delegates left for Ottawa at the end of March with a third list of rights as a basis for negotiation. This list owed much to the work of the convention of forty but was not identical to its so-called second list of rights. The important changes, inserted secretly at the insistence of Riel, it would appear, called for the admission of the northwest as a province rather than a territory, for a bilingual lieutenant-governor, and for a general amnesty covering all acts and all participants in the resistance. The third 'secret' list was supplemented by yet another, or fourth list, probably at the instigation of Bishop Taché, who had returned to Red River just before the delegates departed. In this final list, the delegates were instructed to seek the establishment of denominational schools and the creation of an upper house, or senate, as well as an assembly, following the Quebec model. These were significant departures from the will of the community as expressed in the convention of forty and caused much disagreement— were never approved, in fact—when presented to the legislative council of the provisional government in early May. But the lack of Red River support for these lists was not known in Ottawa, where the delegates arrived in April. There, the three Red River men discovered that the agitation over the death of Thomas Scott was still growing. Only after two of the three had passed an unpleasant sojourn in jail were they permitted to carry out their assignment by meeting representatives of the federal cabinet and negotiating the terms of transfer.

The new province of Manitoba was created by the Manitoba Act, which received royal assent on 12 May and came into effect when proclaimed on 15 July 1870. It embodied most of the rights demanded by the Métis, including responsible government and provincial status, bilingual institutions, denominational schools, and guarantees of land titles and of federal respect for Indian title. But in several crucial matters the negotiators failed. The related issues of provincial status, control of lands, and Métis land rights were handled skilfully by Macdonald. He created not a province of the North-west, but a tiny self-governing province of Manitoba—approximately one hundred miles square—and a vast unit called the North-West Territories, administered from Ottawa. In both jurisdictions, the federal government retained control of public land and natural resources, the only area in the country where this was to be the case. As W.L. Morton commented, 'Thus was Riel's demand for provincehood at once granted and made almost a mockery.'[2] To the English- and French-speaking Métis, Macdonald granted security of tenure within accustomed plots of land, for whatever that was worth, and he reserved 1.4 million acres to be allotted to their unmarried children. But he had not granted great blocks of land intact, as the Métis and Bishop Taché probably desired, and thus had not created a buffer and a preserve for the maintenance of Métis culture. And, despite the pointed demands of one of the negotiators, Father Ritchot, an amnesty had not been granted in writing. Despite these considerable failures, the demands of the colony had been heard and an agreement quite unlike the federal government's original intentions had been won. Even with the considerable omissions, and assuming that the amnesty issue would be resolved satisfactorily, it was an acceptable deal. The results were greeted with relief in Red River and accepted without dissent by the provisional government.

The question of what would happen to the provisional government still remained. In December, when casting about for a means of handling the resistance, Macdonald had set plans under way for a military expedition to Red River. The reason for such a military adventure had long since ceased to exist, but Col Garnet Wolseley had set off in the spring

365

none the less, with the 60th Rifles, symbol of British concern for the farthest marches of the empire, and volunteers, chiefly from the Ontario militia, to reinforce Canadian authority. The expedition was a product of political necessity—a challenge to American annexationists and a sop to Ontario nationalists for the death of Scott. As might have been predicted, it was a punitive expedition, despite Wolseley's declaration that his was 'a mission of peace.' Wolseley himself explained privately to his wife: 'Hope Riel will have bolted, for although I should like to hang him to the highest tree in the place, I have such a horror of rebels and vermin of his kidney, that my treatment of him might not be approved by the civil powers.'[3] Riel, uncertain about the nature of Wolseley's commission, could rely only on the word of his advisers, Father Ritchot and Bishop Taché. They, in turn, could only trust their most powerful acquaintance in the federal cabinet, George-Étienne Cartier. In telling Riel that an amnesty was certain, Ritchot and Taché were transmitting the assurances they had received in Ottawa. But Macdonald would not sustain Cartier's promise. Given the political storm over Scott's death, the Canadian government refused to grant such an amnesty, and the imperial government, to which Ottawa handed the matter, was not yet prepared to act. Riel had no way of knowing these problems. He had considered resistance to the Manitoba Act because of the absence of an amnesty and had continued to drill Métis troops in May and early June, but when the pressures of the season— the annual employment on the hunt and the cart and boat brigades—forced a decision, he had accepted the word of his advisers and permitted the dispersal of his men. For the rest of the summer he was isolated, a president of a rudimentary government with, as of 15 July, no authority and little apparent support.

Bishop Taché perceived the difficulty of the Métis, particularly of Riel, and rushed to Ottawa in July in a vain attempt to hasten the departure of the newly appointed lieutenant-governor, Adams Archibald, in order that the civil authority might be securely installed before Wolseley and the military arrived. Taché failed, and the Wolseley expedition reached the settlement a week in advance of the governor. The timing was important if only as a symbol because, instead of a peaceful transfer of power from Riel to Archibald and an implicit reconciliation of contending forces, the settlement was suddenly turned into an armed camp.

The imperial troops moved upstream through the lower settlement in purposeful fashion, landed in a rainstorm on Point Douglas, where they immediately assumed battle formation, and advanced toward the Upper Fort as if expecting an armed encounter. Riel was warned of their impending arrival and fled across the river to St Boniface leaving, it was said, his breakfast unfinished on the table. He travelled south to the Métis settlement of St Joseph, (now Walhalla) in American territory, to begin an exile that never really ended until his death fifteen years later. English-speaking troops invested the settlement, asserting the authority of Canada. More important, they asserted the determination of Ontario to remake the west in its own image.

The events of 1869–70 had great significance for the new Canadian state. They culminated in the transfer of the northwest to Canada rather than to Minnesota and thus ensured that a continent-wide nation would be established. They also reinforced the principle at the heart of Confederation by extending an essential part of the 1867 compromise—'a dual culture in political union'—to the first new province of the dominion. Because it contributed to the creation of a tiny Manitoba and to federal control of public lands, the resistance helped to establish the western 'bias'—the theme of western regional dissatisfaction and grievance—that has been an important aspect of Confederation from that day to the present.[4] But one must always return to the French- and English-speaking Métis, for Red River was overwhelmingly their settlement. Riel had given the Métis a voice and a program, it is certain, but he had not solved their political problems. He had won a temporary victory on land tenure and, in the 1.4-million-acre grant, a potential buffer against Canadian encroachment. He had created a political and institutional framework in which the Métis could assert their rights, especially in the regulations concerning the assembly, language, and schools. But Riel himself had been driven into exile. And his victories could easily be overturned. The Métis had made their presence felt by means of the resistance and had defended their right to an equal start in the incoming order, but they could neither hold back the tide of newcomers nor guarantee the integrity of their community. Their ability to command political and economic power would determine how they fared in the new order.

NOTES

1. Morton, *Alexander Begg's Red River Journal and Other Papers Relative to the Red River Resistance of 1869–70* (Toronto 1956) 76.
2. Morton *Manitoba: A History* first pub 1957 (Toronto 1967) 141; the purposes of the federal government are discussed in D.J. Hall '"The Spirit of Confederation": Ralph Heintzman, Professor Creighton, and the Bicultural Compact Theory' *Journal of Canadian Studies* 9 no 4 (1974) 24–43
3. Morton *Begg's Journal* 144
4. W.L. Morton 'The Bias of Prairie Politics' *Transactions of the Royal Society of Canada* series 111 49 (1955) 57–66.

SCHOOLS, PRISONS, AND ASYLUMS IN MID-NINETEENTH CENTURY BRITISH NORTH AMERICA

What Did Institutional Reforms Have in Common?

Colin Coates
Glendon College, York University

SCHOOLS, PRISONS, AND ASYLUMS IN MID–NINETEENTH CENTURY BRITISH NORTH AMERICA: WHAT DID INSTITUTIONAL REFORMS HAVE IN COMMON?

Introduction by Colin Coates

● INTRODUCTION

Colin Coates

Schools, penitentiaries, and insane asylums are different types of state-run institutions that together reflected and created new relationships between individuals and the state. In the areas that became parts of Canada in 1867, these institutions all took shape during the middle decades of the century. Colonial governments followed the lead of other jurisdictions, such as Massachusetts and of course Great Britain. Elites placed great stock in the new institutions. The imposing buildings were signs of "progress," fine displays of the appropriate use of government revenue to effect societal change. Government officials and politicians pointed proudly to the substantial investments made in these institutions, a gauge of the promise of the country.

In recent years, historians have seen the middle decades of the nineteenth century as a key period of "state formation." Of course, Confederation itself was a clear sign of the state-formation process. But the previous decades had seen major growth in the responsibilities and capacities of the colonial state, as well as increases in the number of institutions required to oversee these new roles. Asylums, prisons, schools, and hospitals were the most obvious of these new institutions. Yet we should also note the dramatically expanded role played by the state in developing infrastructure, most notably the construction of railways and canals. Taken together, these were massively expensive undertakings, requiring the state not only to raise new revenues through taxation and tariffs, but also to assemble bureaucracies to oversee their operation and to collect and administer the taxes to build them. By mid-century, colonial governments that had once prided themselves on their inexpensive operations were running major budgets and assuming significant debts.

In the 1840s and 1850s, politicians and bureaucrats were faced with huge waves of immigration, and they felt the need to address the arrival of thousands of relatively poor people in British North America. The school system offered the opportunity to form the young minds of children, the penitentiary promised a punishment regime to reform the individual criminal, and the asylum represented a means to restore the sanity of the misguided. In each case, the institutions aimed at reforming the individual. Surveillance and self-regulation were the means to effect these changes, a significant shift from the earlier reliance on physical punishment. As was the case in the countries of western Europe and the United States, British North American proponents of institutional reform in the nineteenth century believed that the publicly funded schools, prisons, and asylums constituted a break with past techniques and methods. The document written by Gordon McCall Theall, who left British North America for a distinguished career in South Africa, reflects on an older form of schooling in the 1840s and reveals the physical punishment and rote learning that he expected had disappeared from schools in subsequent decades. Reformers recommended moving away from physical punishment and restraint as a way of dealing with undesirable behaviour to focusing instead on the attitudes of the individual. They thus intended to provide a more just treatment encouraging the individual to become a productive member of society. However, Charles Duncombe's report on penitentiaries in the United States submitted to the legislature of Upper Canada in 1836 contains some recommendations on reforms of punishment techniques that may not appear so benign today.

Furthermore, there was often a discrepancy between the stated goals of such institutions and the ways in which they were managed and experienced. Many of the institutions cost a great deal of money, not only to build but also to staff. The relatively limited taxation base of the British North American colonies meant that the institutions often lacked the funds that would have been necessary to meet the goals of their founders. The article by Daniel Francis conveys this point in looking at the insane asylums in New Brunswick and Nova Scotia.

The institutions represented an important shift in the relationship between individuals and the state. Through inspectors, the government-funded schools demanded certain types of behaviour from youth and their families, insisting, for instance, that the young attend school rather than help out with farm work. In his article, Robert Lanning discusses the role of school inspectors in Nova Scotia from the 1850s to the 1870s. Many members of the public remained distrustful of taxation, and some protested the use of public funds for such projects. Therefore, while the magnificent asylum buildings might prove venues for public tours in nineteenth-century Canada West/Ontario, as Janet Miron's article points out, and as Susanna Moodie's chapter illustrates, the public was often less enthusiastic about having to expend government funds. Others feared the intrusion of these institutions into their lives. The expansion of the schooling system in Canada East/Quebec in the 1840s, for instance, led in some districts near the town of Trois-Rivières to what some at the time called the "Candlesnuffers' War." Local elites and farmers greeted school inspectors and tax collectors with a great deal of hostility, recognizing how their activities infringed upon the rural autonomy previously enjoyed. The proponents of the new schools claimed that those who defended local concerns were trying to snuff out the candle of learning. Robert Harris's famous painting of the meeting between the local school trustees and the new female schoolteacher in a small rural schoolhouse on Prince Edward Island conveys some of the complexity of the relations between the state-appointed educator and local citizens.

State intervention in individual lives had different implications in Quebec than it did in other jurisdictions. In Quebec, the majority of the population was French speaking and Catholic, while English-speaking Protestants dominated much of the political life. This period saw the beginning of a long-lasting issue in Canadian public life, the question of whether schooling should respect denominational boundaries. In Quebec, many institutions did not develop from state funds, but rather were offered by the Catholic Church and, indeed, until recently, education remained divided along denominational lines.

The story of institutional development in the middle decades of the nineteenth century is rather mixed. Reform-minded leaders attempted to influence behaviour through creating new large-scale institutions and channelling taxes to such projects. Although they saw a clear break with the past, in some cases their proposals were less innovative, at least in retrospect, than they may have appeared at the time. Meanwhile, they faced important limitations on what they could achieve: individuals resisted elements of the reforms and a limited tax base restricted what could be done. Even today, citizens and politicians continue to debate self-consciously "humanitarian" perspectives on societal problems and the significant expenditures that are involved in such processes.

QUESTIONS

1. According to Charles Duncombe, what is the purpose of the penitentiary or prison? Is punishment or reform the main purpose? What methods would ensure that the prisoner became more docile?
2. What assumptions underlie the school system as conveyed in Rev. Egerton Ryerson's report? What was the goal of mass education, according to Rev. Ryerson?
3. Compare the reasons for and methods of controlling the populations of Upper Canada (Ontario) as outlined in the proposals by Charles Duncombe and Rev. Egerton Ryerson. Which groups of people did the proposed reforms aim to control?

4. In what ways do the goals of Rev. Egerton Ryerson's school system differ from the type of school experience that Gordon McCall Theal had had in Nova Scotia in the 1840s?

5. Compare the exterior view of the Ontario provincial asylum as depicted in Susanna Moodie's account and William James Thomson's painting and the interior observations as recounted by Moodie. Did the exterior and interior perspectives match?

FURTHER READINGS

Axelrod, Paul, *The Promise of Schooling: Education in Canada, 1800–1914* (Toronto: University of Toronto Press, 1997).

Curtis, Bruce, *Building the Educational State: Canada West, 1836–1871* (London: The Althouse Press, 1988).

Nelson, Wendie, "'Rage against the Dying of the Light': Interpreting the Guerre des Éteignoirs" *Canadian Historical Review* 81, 4 (December 2000): 551–581.

Oliver, Peter N., *'Terror to Evil-doers': Prisons and Punishments in Nineteenth-Century Ontario* (Toronto: University of Toronto Press, 1998).

Shortt, S.E.D., *Victorian Lunacy: Richard M. Bucke and the Practice of Late Nineteenth-Century Psychiatry* (Cambridge: Cambridge University Press, 1986).

▲ Document 1: Report of the Commissioners on the Subject of Prisons, Penitentiaries, etc., etc. etc.

Charles Duncombe

Charles Duncombe was a doctor and political figure in Upper Canada. In 1837, he would become involved in the Rebellion against the government. The year previously he presented a report to the colonial legislative on his investigation into penal practices in various parts of the United States.

The great object of the institution of civil government, is to advance the prosperity, and to increase the happiness of its subjects. The agents of the government, become, in this point of view, the fathers of the people; and it may surely be ranked among the duties incident to this paternal care, not only that those who are guilty of crime should receive the chastisement due to their offences; but that no pains should be spared to remove the causes of offence, and to diminish, as far as possible, the sources of temptation and corruption. This obligation applies with peculiar force to the case of juvenile offenders; a class whose increasing numbers, and deplorable situation loudly calls for more effective interposition, and the benevolent interference of the legislature.

Every person that frequents the streets of this city [Toronto] must be forcibly struck with the ragged and uncleanly appearance, the vile language, and the idle and miserable habits of numbers of children, most of whom are of an age suitable for schools, or for some useful employment. The parents of these children, are, in all probability, too poor, or too degenerate to provide them with clothing fit for them to be seen in at school; and know not where to place them in order that they may find employment, or be better cared for. Accustomed, in many instances, to witness at home nothing in the way of example, but what is degrading; early taught to observe intemperance, and to hear obscene and profane language without disgust; obliged to beg, and even encouraged to acts of dishonesty to satisfy the wants induced by the indolence of their parents—what can be expected, but that such children will in due time, become responsible to the laws for crimes, which have thus, in a manner, been forced upon them?—Can it be consistent with real justice that delinquents of this character should be consigned to the infamy and severity of punishments, which must inevitably tend to perfect the work of degradation, to sink them still deeper in corruption, to deprive them of their remaining sensibility to the shame of exposure, and establish them in all the hardihood of daring and desperate villainy? Is it possible that a christian community can lend its sanction to such a process, without any effort to rescue and to save?

If the agents of our municipal government stand towards the community in the moral light of guardians of virtue; if they may be justly regarded as the political fathers of the unprotected, does not every feeling of justice urge upon them the principle, of considering these juvenile culprits as falling under their special guardianship, and claiming from them the right which every child may demand of its parent, of being well instructed in the nature of its duties, before it is punished for the breach of their observance? Ought not every one who has a just sense of the reciprocal obligations of parents and children to lend his aid to the administrators of the law, in rescuing those pitiable victims of neglect and

Source: *Journal of the House of Assembly of Upper Canada* (1836), Appendix 71, pp. 4–5.

wretchedness, from the melancholy fate which almost inevitably results from an apprenticeship in our common prisons?

It is well worth the attention of the legislature to devise some means by which criminals may be speedily brought to trial after arrest; and while imprisoned for crimes in the common gaols of the different districts of the province that they should be classed so that the unfortunate debtor and the highly culpable criminal, should have no communication with each other—Nor would I, if it were possible to do otherwise, allow criminals to have any communication among themselves during their confinement previously to or after trial: and when sentence of condemnation to hard labor had been passed upon them, I would advise that the punishment should be carried into effect in the manner least likely to debase the human mind, and the most calculated to produce the *reformation* of the convict. I would still treat him as an accountable being, both to God and to society. His treatment should be just and consistent and as lenient as his situation would admit of. He should be taught to feel, that upon himself still, to a certain extent, depended his future prospects in life wherever the term of sentence admitted of a rational prospect of a return to society; and even where that was not the case, he should be brought to acknowledge that much of his present comfort or misery must as a matter of course, depend upon himself,—and where he had no hope of enjoyment from society beyond the walls of the prison, he should be directed to look for happiness from within his own bosom *here*, and the hope of future blessedness hereafter. He would then become a better man as a convict—enjoy more comfort in confinement, and be likelier, in consequence, to be liberated.

The flogging in penitentiaries is highly reprehensible. Fear should not be the only incentive to action—convicts should feel a respect for themselves; for the good opinion of the keepers; and even of their fellows.

In the penitentiary at Frankfort in Kentucky, I witnessed a new mode of punishment, that of *suspended animation*—which appeared to me to be better adapted to penitentiary punishment than any thing I had before seen; for while it instantly subdued the most turbulent and obstinate spirits, it neither debased the mind, nor left it in that sour, unhappy and degraded state; the usual concomitant of corporal punishment.

This suspended animation was inflicted in the easiest and quietest manner possible; without much loss of time, or danger to the health, or injury of the convict,—and from the short experience of this institution upon man, and from comparisons long since made upon the brute creation, it is admitted to be one of the most potent subduers of the malevolent animal passions ever had recourse to. It is thus produced:—

The convict is placed in an easy chair resembling the tranquilizing chair, used in Lunatic asylums.—The convict, sitting, apparently, at perfect ease, has his feet, legs, body, and arms, safely secured, a box (or spout) with a box at one end of it is brought up behind his chair. The spout stands upon three legs, and just high enough from the floor to place the body of the convict on a horizontal line with it, when his easy chair resting upon a broad bottom, shall be inclined backwards so as to admit his head into one end of it. The side and partition next the top of his head are a little higher than the top of his nose as he lies on his back with his head in the box. In that position the collar is put down about his neck and secured. The partition at the top of his head does not rest on the bottom of the box by one inch; so that the water poured in will run out and be conducted into a large pot or tub placed under the lower end of the spout to receive the water. The keeper then takes a bucket of water and fills the box until it covers the convict's face and mouth entirely, and thereby suspends animation as long as may seem necessary to subdue his passions, and on allowing him to breathe he has invariably become a reformed man; with his turbulent passions quite subdued. He pursues his work in the penitentiary without any of that morose and unhappy feeling which so often succeeds the flogging, and other usual corporal punishment that only restrains the convict by fear from the repetition of the offence. Fear debases, never ennobles the mind, and therefore should be had recourse to as seldom as possible, as a mode of punishment in any system of improvement. In our civil or political institutions teach children from their infancy *to govern themselves*: early accustom them to the exercise of the *moral* and *intellectual* faculties, thereby giving those organs of the mind an ascendency over the malevolent animal passions and propensities. Let all our literary civil and political institutions be so conducted, that the organs of benevolence, veneration, conscientiousness and hope may predominate. Thus shall we most effectually and permanently promote the peace, prosperity, welfare and good government of this province.

All which is respectfully submitted

Charles Duncombe, Acting Commissioner for obtaining certain information etc. etc.

▲ Document 2: Excerpt, "Part I of the Report on a System of Public Elementary Education for Upper Canada"

Rev. Egerton Ryerson

Egerton Ryerson was the key figure in developing the educational system of Upper Canada. He patterned the school system after that available in Ireland, but in this report he compared educational practices in many European jurisdictions and in the United States.

Part I Of The Report On A System Of Public Elementary Instruction For Upper Canada.

[...] What [is] meant by Education

By Education, I mean not the mere acquisition of certain arts, or of certain branches of knowledge, but that instruction and discipline which qualify and dispose the subjects of it for their appropriate duties and employments of life, as Christians, as persons of business and also as members of the civil community in which they live.

Basis and Extent of the System

The basis of an Educational structure adapted to this end should be as broad as the population of the country; and its loftiest elevation should equal the highest demands of the learned professions, adapting its gradition [sic] of schools to the wants of the several classes of the community, and to their respective employments or profession, the one rising above the other—the one conducting the other; yet each complete in itself for the degree of education it imparts; a character of uniformity as to fundamental principles pervading the whole; the whole based upon the principles of Christianity, and uniting the combined influence and support of the Government and the people.

The branches of knowledge which it is essential that all should understand, should be provided for all, and taught to all; should be brought within the reach of the most needy, and forced upon the attention of the most careless. The knowledge required for the scientific pursuit of mechanics, agriculture and commerce, must needs be provided to an extent corresponding with the demand, and the exigencies of the country; while to a more limited extent are needed facilities for acquiring the higher education of the learned professions.

Comparative Neglect of Elementary Education

Now, to a professional education, and to the education of the more wealthy classes, no objection has been made, nor even indifference manifested. On the contrary, for these classes of society, less needing the assistance of the Government and having less claims upon its benevolent consideration than the laboring and producing classes of the population, have liberal provision been made, and able Professors employed, whilst Schools

Source: J. George Hodgins, ed., *Documentary history of education in Upper Canada, from the passing of the Constitutional Act of 1791, to the close of Rev. Dr. Ryerson's administration of the Education Department in 1876,* Vol. 6 (Toronto: Warwick Bro's & Rutter, 1899): 142–146.

377

of Industry have been altogether overlooked, and primary Instruction has scarcely been reduced to a system; and the education of the bulk of the population has been left to the annual liberality of Parliament. Nay, even objections have been made to the education of the laboring classes of the people; and it may be advisable to show, at the outset, that the establishment of a thorough system of primary and industrial education, commensurate with the population of the country, as contemplated by the Government, and as is here proposed, is justified by considerations of economy as well as of patriotism and humanity.

First, such a system of general education amongst the people is the most effectual preventative of pauperism, and its natural companions, misery and crime.

General Education a Preventive of Pauperism

To a young and growing country, and the retreat of so many poor from other countries, this consideration is of the greatest importance. The gangrene of pauperism in either cities or states is almost incurable. It may be said in some sort to be hereditary as well as infectious,—both to perpetuate and propagate itself,—to weaken the body politic at its very heart,—and to multiply wretchedness and vice.

What Statistics of Pauperism Prove

Now, the Statistical Reports of pauperism and crime in different countries, furnish indubitable proof that ignorance is the fruitful source of idleness, intemperance and improvidence, and these the fosterparent of pauperism and crime. The history of every country in Europe may be appealed to in proof and illustration of the fact,—apart from the operation of extraneous local and temporary circumstances,—that pauperism and crime prevail in proportion to the absence of education amongst the labouring classes, and that in proportion to the existence and prevalence of education amongst those classes, is the absence of pauperism and its legitimate offspring. [...]

System of Education should be universal

1. The first feature then of our Provincial system of Public Instruction, should be *universality*; and that in respect to the poorest classes of society. It is the poor indeed that need the assistance of the Government, and they are proper subjects of their special solicitude and care; the rich can take care of themselves. The elementary education of the whole people must therefore be an essential element in the Legislative and Administrative policy of an enlightened and beneficent Government.

Should be practical

2. Nor is it less important to the efficiency of such a system, that it should be *practical*, than that it should be universal. The mere acquisition or even the general diffusion of knowledge without the requisite qualitites to apply that knowledge in the best manner, does not merit the name of education. Much knowledge may be imparted and acquired without any addition whatever to the capacity for the business of life. There are not wanting numerous examples of persons having excelled, even in the higher departments of knowledge, who are utterly incompetent to the most simple, as well as the most important, affairs of every day life. [...]

▲ Document 3: Schooldays, Schooldays … Cocagne Academy in the 1840s

Gordon McCall Theal

These reminscences were published in 1894 after Theal, having emigrated to South Africa, returned to Canada for a visit. He describes his childhood experiences at his local school. This excerpt provides an example of the punishment regime that humanitarians were attempting to reform.

[...] Let us look first at the Cocaigne Academy, a good specimen of a Canadian public school—regarded as of the first class—in the olden time. The building, erected by public subscription, stood close to the shore, at one end of the long wooden bridge that spanned the river at its mouth, so as to be in a central position. All the classes were taught in one large room, which was warmed in winter by an immense stove in the centre, round which the desks were ranged. The principal was the reverend Alfred Horatio Weeks, a clergyman of the church of England, and the assistant, or usher as he was termed, was Mr. David Miller, a layman. The government did not contribute anything to the support of the institution, which was maintained entirely by school fees and by subscriptions guaranteed in case the fees fell short. The hours of attendance were from 9 to 4, with an hour for lunch, except on Saturdays, when the school closed at 1. The holidays were about half as long as those at present given. The discipline was cruelly severe. The reverend principal was conscientious, and as he really believed that to spare the rod was to spoil the child, he tried to do his duty regardless of his muscles.

I asked my old classmate if he remembered the punishment inflicted on a particular occasion upon several boys for what would now be regarded as a very trifling fault. I have need to, he replied, and baring one of his wrists he showed me a large mark which he has borne ever since as the result of it.

Yet the reverend principal was not naturally a cruel man. He was a very strict disciplinarian, but he could say kind words and act generously enough outside the schoolhouse. He made me a present of a pair of skates once, so, in spite of the drubbings I received, I have a warm place in my memory for him. He was still living, though at a very advanced age, a widower, and childless, when I was in Canada, but I had not time to visit the part of the province where he was then residing, and shortly after my return to London I received intelligence of his death.

The school being a place of terror, it was a natural result that no one went to it of his own free will. If a boy did not know his lessons, he would argue he might as well play truant for the day, as the punishment for the one offence would be no worse than for the other. And there was frequently a strong temptation to play truant, even when a boy could repeat his home task, but knew he would likely be belaboured for something else. In the spring time a habitant was making maple sugar only half-a-dozen miles up the river, and it would be so nice to help carry the little bark dishes of sap from the trees to the boiler, and get a block when it was taken from the mould. Or later the wild strawberries—the delicious wild strawberries of Canada—were ripening in some warm locality, and each boy

379

Source: Gordon McCall Theal, "Schooldays, Schooldays ... Cocagne Academy in the 1840s" *Acadiensis: Journal of the History of the Atlantic Region,* Vol. 5, 2 (1976): 134–147 (Excerpted). Reprinted with permission.

thought he would like to be the first to eat them. And then as the season advanced there were the wild raspberries and the blueberries in the newly burnt clearings on the border of the forest, and later still the hazel nuts on the Island, all powerful magnets for schoolboys dreading the reverend principal's cane. Or a report would pass round that the fishing was particularly good in a certain stream, or that a big wolf had been trapped by somebody, or a schooner was to be launched, or in winter the river and the harbour would be one great sheet of ice inviting races on skates; with these on one side and the rod on the other, the pupils of the Cocaigne Academy often turned away from the path that led to knowledge.

One day—it was the 3rd of November 1847—four boys were standing on the bridge watching great clouds of wahwahs [wild geese] and wild ducks of other kinds that were on the wing from the north towards warmer latitudes, knowing by instinct that winter was approaching. The oldest of the four had a gun, but somehow the flocks all took a course that led away from the bridge, and he had no chance of testing his skill. A light canoe was fastened to one of the piers, so, tired of waiting, three of the boys jumped in, and with two of them paddling and the other holding the gun in readiness, shot out into the harbour to a spot that the birds were passing over. The chance came, but the gun recoiled, and with even so slight a shock the canoe turned over. The water was so cold that to swim very far was impossible. One of the boys who clung to the canoe was saved, the corpse of the one who had the gun was found that night just where the accident took place, and the body of the other was recovered nearer the shore. The effect of this sudden death of two of the brightest boys in the school was felt long afterwards.

One day there was a violent storm. The north-west wind in its fury swept over the Strait, and piled the water in Cocaigne harbour higher than had ever been known before. The moon was full, and under ordinary circumstances the tide line would have been within a few feet of the schoolhouse, but now the water surrounded the lonely building, great waves came rolling in before the gusts to dash against the outer wall of wood, and soon the place was a wreck, to the intense delight of every boy that saw it. But our mutual congratulations were soon over. A gentleman who lived close to the other end of the bridge, and who had a number of sons, offered a wing of his house, and in a few days the school was opened again.

I have yet to describe the method of teaching, and to enumerate the subjects taught. The usher took spelling, reading, geography, arithmetic, what was called philosophy, and once a week French. Only once a week was there a lesson in one of the principal languages of the country, and then it was bare reading without any explanation whatever. The geography lessons were home tasks, and were nothing more than the repetition by each boy of a certain quantity of matter in a book. It was really a test of memory, and nothing else. The philosophy meant answering by rote a series of questions from a long catechism, and for practical value may be classed with the geography. The arithmetic was better, and as this was Mr. Miller's strong point, we really got some explanation of rules and were helped forward in our work.

The principal took the Latin and Greek languages, history, and penmanship. His own handwriting was remarkably good, almost like copperplate, and he laid down the sensible rule that the test of writing was the ability of any one whatever to read it without hesitation or difficulty. He used to set a copy for us to follow, and then warm with his cane the hands of those whose performance was not to his satisfaction. The history taught was that of Greece, Rome, and England, but we learnt little more than lists of events and names of rulers. Of the life of the Greek people, of the effects of Roman institutions upon modern nations, and of everything in fact that would be really useful for us to know, we remained ignorant. The great movements of our own times, the stirring events of modern Europe and America, even past occurrences in Canada, were utterly ignored. We could repeat the legend of Romulus, and could remember the name of Miltiades, but we never heard in school of Frederick the Great or of George Washington, except indirectly as their actions affected England. A knowledge of the Latin and Greek languages was, in the opinion of the principal, the first and highest object of a schoolboy's life, and consequently a very large portion of time was taken up with those studies. I went to the Cocagne Academy from an infant school, where English grammar was beyond the capacity of the pupils, and the day I entered it I had a copy of the Eton Latin grammar put into my hands, with a long home task marked off in it. Thereafter two hours every day I stood before the principal declining Latin nouns and adjectives and conjugating verbs, without ever a word of explanation or comparison with the structure of English speech, with no help or guidance whatever but the rod when a mistake was made. So it went on, through the Delectus, and the Commentaries of Caesar and the Lives of Cornelius Nepos and the Aeneid of Virgil, all dull rote, with no life and no real teaching in it at all, so that I believe unless a boy had an extraordinary natural inclination for Latin lore, his training at this school would forever have repelled him from it. Mathematics were not taught at all, and if I had not at a later date had the advantage of a course of lessons in this branch of knowledge from an Irishman named O'Donnell—an eccentric but very estimable man—of algebra and geometry I should have remained absolutely ignorant.

The institution which I have been describing was a fair specimen of a public school in Canada half a century ago. The system of instruction was then generally held to be good, and the severe discipline was regarded as scriptural and correct. No parent dreamed of complaining about it. There was but one exception that I know of the Grammar School of St. John, of which Dr. James Paterson was the principal, under whose guidance many boys were trained who have made their mark in Canada. It was my good fortune to attend this school for some time after leaving the Cocagne Academy, and to Dr. Paterson more than to any other teacher I owe what little knowledge I had when I entered upon the duties of active life … His idea of a school was that it should be a place of preparation for a boy to educate himself, the teacher could only lay a foundation, the pupil must build upon it; but he took care to lay the foundation strong and well, and he pointed out the way in which the edifice should be raised. He devoted more time to Latin than to all other subjects put together—it was the custom of the day.—but the Aeneid in his hands was a thing of life and beauty to his pupils. A single lesson from him on the use of globes was worth more than all the geography ever taught at Cocaigne. He pointed out too the good for admiration, and cast scorn upon the mean and bad, till every boy felt an enthusiasm to do what was right. He worked by attraction, not by fear, and I never knew of a case of truancy from his school. But, as I said before, the Grammar School of St. John was exceptional in its system, and I think just on that account many people looked somewhat askance upon it; the other institution, which I described first, represents the ideas of education at that time.

▲ Document 4: Robert Harris, *A Meeting of the School Trustees,* 1885 (National Gallery of Canada)

● Robert Harris (1849–1919) was a well-known Canadian painter, most famous perhaps for his depiction of the Fathers of Confederation. This painting illustrates the disagreement between a young female teacher in Prince Edward Island and the school trustees, ostensibly over the introduction of new teaching methods. What message does this painting attempt to convey? What are the gender dynamics of the painting? How does the artist use light to underline the point he is making?

Source: Harris, Robert, *A Meeting of the School Trustees,* 1885. National Gallery of Canada, Ottawa. Photo © National Gallery of Canada.

▲ Document 5: Visit to the Toronto Asylum

Susanna Moodie

As Janet Miron's article suggests, tourists often visited asylums in nineteenth-century Ontario. Susanna Moodie, one of the most celebrated authors of British North America, describes her visit to the Toronto Queen Street asylum in her 1853 book, Life in the Clearings versus the Bush. *What access did Moodie and her family have to the inmates? Why did she visit the asylum? What did she learn in doing so?*

Our next visit was to the Lunatic Asylum. The building is of white brick,—a material not very common in Canada, but used largely in Toronto, where stone has to be brought from a considerable distance, there being no quarries in the neighbourhood. Brick has not the substantial, august appearance that stone gives to a large building, and it is more liable to injury from the severe frosts of winter in this climate. The asylum is a spacious edifice, surrounded by extensive grounds for the cultivation of fruits and vegetables. These are principally worked by the male patients, who are in a state of convalescence, while it affords them ample room for air and exercise.

A large gang of these unfortunates were taking their daily promenade, when our [horse-drawn] cab stopped at the entrance gate. They gazed upon us with an eager air of childish curiosity, as we alighted from our conveyance, and entered the building.

We were received very politely by one of the gentlemen belonging to the establishment, who proceeded to show us over the place.

Ascending a broad flight of steps, as clean as it was possible for human hands to make them, we came to a long wide gallery, separated at either end by large folding-doors, the upper part of which were of glass; those to the right opening into the ward set apart for male patients, who were so far harmless that they were allowed the free use of their limbs, and could be spoken to without any danger to the visitors. The female lunatics inhabited the ward to the left, and to these we first directed our attention.

The long hall into which their work-rooms and sleeping apartments opened was lofty, well lighted, well aired, and exquisitely clean; so were the persons of the women, who were walking to and fro, laughing and chatting very sociably together. Others were sewing and quilting in rooms set apart for that purpose. There was no appearance of wretchedness or misery in this ward; nothing that associated with it the terrible idea of madness I had been wont to entertain—for these poor creatures looked healthy and cheerful, nay, almost happy, as if they had given the world and all its cares the go-by. There was one thin, eccentric looking woman in middle life, who came forward to receive us with an air of great dignity; she gave us her hand in a most condescending manner, and smiled most graciously when the gentleman who was with us inquired after her *majesty's* health. She fancies herself Victoria, and in order to humour her conceit, she is allowed to wear a cap of many colours, with tinsel ornaments. This person, who is from the lowest class, certainly enjoys her imaginary dignity in a much greater degree than any crowned monarch, and is perhaps far prouder of her fool's cap than our gracious sovereign is of her imperial diadem.

The madwomen round her appeared to consider her assumption of royalty as a very good joke, for the homage they rendered her was quizzical in the extreme.

Source: Susanna Moodie, *Life in the Clearings versus the Bush* (London: Richard Bentley, 1853), pp. 299–308.

There are times when these people seem to have a vague consciousness of their situation; when gleams of sense break in upon them, and whisper the awful truth to their minds. Such moments must form the drops of bitterness in the poisoned cup of life, which a mysterious Providence has presented to their lips. While I was looking sadly from face to face, as these benighted creatures flitted round me, a tall stout woman exclaimed in a loud voice—

"That's Mrs. M——, of Belleville! God bless her! Many a good quarter dollar I've got from her;" and, running up to me, she flung her arms about my neck, and kissed me most vehemently.

I did not at first recognise her; and, though I submitted with a good grace to the mad hug she gave me, I am afraid that I trembled not a little in her grasp. She was the wife of a cooper, who lived opposite to us during the first two years we resided in Belleville; and I used to buy from her all the milk I needed for the children.

She was always a strange eccentric creature when sane—if, indeed, she ever had enjoyed the right use of her senses; and, in spite of the joy she manifested at the unexpected sight of me, I remember her once threatening to break my head with an old hoop, when I endeavoured to save her little girl from a frightful flagellation from the same instrument [...]

She is at present an incurable but harmless maniac; and, in spite of the instance of cruelty [...] towards her little girl, now, during the dark period of her mind's eclipse, gleams of maternal love struggled like glimpses of sunshine through a stormy cloud, and she inquired of me earnestly, pathetically, nay, even tenderly, for her children. Alas, poor maniac! How could I tell her that the girl she had chastised so undeservedly had died in early womanhood, and her son, a fine young man of twenty, had committed suicide, and flung himself off the bridge into the Moira river only a few months before. Her insanity saved her from the knowledge of events, which might have distracted a firmer brain. She seemed hardly satisfied with my evasive answers, and looked doubtingly and cunningly at me, as if some demon had whispered to her the awful truth.

It was singular that this woman should recognise me after so many years [...]

Another stout, fair-haired matron, with good features and a very pleasant face, insisted on shaking hands with us all round. Judging from her round, sonsy [cheerful], rosy face, you never could have imagined her to have been mad. When we spoke in admiration of the extreme neatness and cleanness of the large sleeping apartment, she said very quietly—

"Ah, you would not wonder at that could you see all the water-witches at night cleaning it." Then she turned to me, and whispered very confidentially in my ear, "Are you mad? You see these people; they are all mad—as mad as March hares. Don't come here if you can help it. It's all very well at first, and it looks very clean and comfortable; but when the doors are once shut, you can't get out—no, not if you ask it upon your knees." She then retreated, nodding significantly.

Leaving this ward, we visited the one which contained the male lunatics.

They appeared far more gloomy and reserved than the women we had left.

One young man, who used to travel the country with jewellery, and who had often been at our house, recognised us in a moment; but he did not come forward like Mrs.—— to greet us, but ran into a corner, and, turning to the wall, covered his face with his hands until we had passed on. Here was at least a consciousness of his unfortunate situation, that was very painful to witness. A gentlemanly man in the prime of life, who had once practised the law in Toronto, and was a person of some consequence, still retained the dress and manners belonging to his class. He had gone to the same school with my son-in-law, and he greeted him in the most hearty and affectionate manner, throwing his arm about his shoulder, and talking of his affairs in the most confidential manner. His mental aberration was only displayed in a few harmless remarks, such as telling us that this large house was his, that it had been built with his money, and that it was very hard he was kept a prisoner in his own dwelling; that he was worth millions; and that people were trying to cheat him of all his money, but that if once he could get out, he would punish them all. He then directed my son-in-law to bring up some law books that he named, on the morrow, and he would give him a dozen suits against the parties from whom he had received so many injuries […]

There were two boys among these men who, in spite of their lunacy, had an eye to business, and begged pathetically for coppers, though of what use they could be to them in that place I cannot imagine. I saw no girls under twelve years of age. There were several boys who appeared scarcely in their teens.

Mounting another flight of snowy stairs, we came to the wards above those we had just inspected. These were occupied by patients that were not in a state to allow visitors a nearer inspection than observing them through the glass doors. By standing upon a short flight of broad steps that led down to their ward, we were able to do this with perfect security. The hands of all these women were secured in mufflers; some were dancing, others running to and fro at full speed, clapping their hands, and laughing and shouting with the most boisterous merriment. How dreadful is the laugh of madness! how sorrowful the expressions of their diabolical mirth! tears and lamentations would have been less shocking, for it would have seemed more natural. […].

385

▲ Document 6: William James Thomson, Untitled Painting of the Provincial Asylum, Toronto, 1890

● **This image demonstrates the size and grandeur of the Provincial Asylum in Toronto. How does the landscaping indicate the public nature of this building? What is the purpose of a painting such as this?**

Source: William James Thomson, untitled painting of the Provincial Asylum (opened 1850), Toronto. Ink and watercolour on paper, 1890. Collection of the Centre for Addiction and Mental Health (CAMH), Toronto. Courtesy CAMH Archives. An ink and sketch version originally appeared as an illustration in the *Toronto Globe*, 5 April 1890.

■ Article 1: The Development of the Lunatic Asylum in the Maritime Provinces

Daniel Francis

Late in the year 1835 some two dozen reputed lunatics who had been imprisoned in the county gaol in Saint John were removed first to the city's almshouse and then, early the next year, to the basement of a small, wooden building on Leinster Street. This building, constructed originally as a cholera hospital but as of February 1836 housing fourteen lunatics in its depths and as many sick paupers upstairs, was Canada's first mental institution. It would be another twelve years before New Brunswick had a permanent treatment center and another twenty-three years before its sister province of Nova Scotia had one.[1] Yet this little hospital, inadequate as it was, represented an important change in the treatment of the insane in the Maritimes. At last it was being recognized that the most important thing about the mentally ill was that they were mentally ill, not poor or violent or criminal, and that they required a specific kind of supervision in a specific kind of institution. It had not always been so.

The first law regarding the insane in the two colonies was a 1759 statute establishing a workhouse in Halifax. No special accommodation was provided for insane paupers in the building who were lumped indiscriminately with "all disorderly and idle persons, and such who shall be found begging, or practising any unlawful games, or pretending to fortune telling, common drunkards, persons of lewd behaviour, vagabonds, runaways, stubborn servants and children, and persons who notoriously misspend their time to the neglect and prejudice of their own and their family's support". Special consideration was given only to the retarded and lunatics who were physically incapable of labouring. Others were to be put to work alongside their fellow inmates and with them to be whipped "moderately" upon entering the workhouse and strenuously if they proved "stubborn

or idle".[2] In 1774 a second statute, entitled "An Act for Punishing Rogues, Vagabonds, and other Idle and Disorderly Persons", provided that persons "furiously mad and dangerous to be permitted to go abroad" should be "safely locked up in some secure place".[3] In New Brunswick an 1824 statute directed dangerous lunatics to be "kept safely locked up in some secure place" and if necessary chained, a practice which was already being followed.[4] Lunatics who fell afoul of the law were thus placed in conditions which could only aggravate their illness and then expected to behave normally or suffer for it.

Yet the insane certainly were not actively persecuted. If they caused no problems and could look after themselves, they were left to wander at will. Those who were either wealthy themselves or had wealthy relations were usually packed off to a private madhouse in the United States or Britain. Far from seeking out inmates for the prisons and poorhouses, the authorities hoped a mentally ill person's family would assume the responsibility of caring for him at home. But since many of the insane were quite understandably paupers, those who could not support themselves or rely on their families were placed in almshouses or workhouses. From their beginnings the two colonies adopted the British poor law system which was based on the administrative principle that each town or parish had to support its own poor by a compulsory assessment of the inhabitants.[5] While able-bodied unemployed were either gaoled for being "idle and disorderly persons" or set to work by an Overseer of the Poor, some kind of accommodation was found for the infirm poor, often in private homes or in buildings rented for the purpose. A major drawback to this system of relief was that many communities did not have the resources to care for their poor and as a result the practice of auctioning off paupers developed.[6] Overseers of the Poor were authorized to pay local residents to take paupers into their homes and support them for a year. The price was arrived at by a process of down-bidding at a public auction. The person willing to take the pauper for the least amount of money won his or her services. Originally the practice was regulated but gradually controls were relaxed and the system became one of brutal abuse. Paupers became a kind of slave labour in the backwoods of the provinces and people began to use the auctions as a means of making an income and as a source

Source: Daniel Francis, "The Development of the Lunatic Asylum in the Maritime Provinces," *Acadiensis: Journal of the History of the Atlantic Region*, Vol. 6, 2 (1977): 23–38. Reprinted with permission.

387

of subsidized labour. Clearly, many of the victims of the auction block, at least before asylums were built, would have been paupers suffering from mild forms of mental illness.

In Nova Scotia the mentally ill first were provided for in the Halifax Poor's Asylum in 1812. It was originally intended that they be confined apart from the healthy paupers but as the institution became overcrowded this distinction was not enforced. In 1832 a legislative committee touring the poorhouse reported that "every room from the cellar to the garret is filled to excess" and told of one room with eighteen beds which nightly held forty-seven persons.[7] The committee urged the erection of a hospital but did not consider a separate lunatic asylum necessary. It was not really until Hugh Bell became mayor of Halifax in 1844 that an energetic movement for the establishment of an asylum began. Bell had arrived in the colony from Ireland in 1782 at the age of two years and had been in turn a journalist, a Methodist preacher, a successful brewer and a politician. He was sixty-four when, apparently influenced by a term as commissioner of the Poor's Asylum, he undertook to persuade the government to build an asylum.[8] His first move was to pledge his own salary as mayor to a special asylum fund. Next, he organized public meetings to gather similar private pledges, hoping to force the government's hand. Bell's campaign was supported by a number of wealthy Haligonians and endorsed by at least two Halifax newspapers, the *Novascotian* and the *Times,* but the scheme did not seem to capture the imagination of the populace. As the *Times* reluctantly reported. Bell's activities "do not appear to be well seconded".[9] In 1845, prompted by an abortive suggestion from New Brunswick that it, Nova Scotia and Prince Edward Island build a joint asylum, a commission was established with Bell as the chairman to investigate the possibility of establishing an asylum in Nova Scotia. The Bell Commission enthusiastically endorsed the project the next year but no action was taken and in 1848 another legislative committee argued that "it would be improper at this time to recommend any appropriation of the public monies which would require so great an expenditure".[10] Early in 1850 Dorothea Dix, the American psychiatric reformer, delivered an impassioned plea to the legislature on behalf of the mentally ill but she failed to prompt any action and not until 1852 did "an Act for Founding a Lunatic

Asylum" pass the Assembly and not until January 1859 were the first patients admitted.[11]

A number of factors may have contributed to this delay. During the 1840s, when Hugh Bell was trying to get government backing for an asylum, the assembly was preoccupied with the noisy struggle for political power between James Johnston's faction and the "Liberals" led by Joseph Howe. Another explanation, the one advanced at the time, was that other demands were being made on the provincial treasury.[12] For the first half of the century the hospital annexed to the Halifax Poor's Asylum was the only public hospital in the city. During the typhus epidemic in 1847 this facility was woefully overcrowded and the local medical community began to petition the government for a new hospital. In 1849 a legislative committee conducted an investigation into the matter which resulted in funds being allotted. Since at the same time the assembly was financing the construction of a new prison, the legislators apparently felt justified in putting off the asylum recommended by the 1846 commission. Furthermore, in the early 1850s railway fever absorbed the attention and the revenues of the province. "Provincial finances were completely compromised by railway legislation and there was a powerful aversion to new taxation for any other purpose".[13]

Agitation for the reform of treatment of the mentally ill began earlier in New Brunswick than in its neighbouring colony, perhaps because in the former the social dislocation associated with higher rates of immigration made the plight of the insane more evident and more urgent. The movement was led by a medical man, Dr. George Peters. Peters had been born in Saint John in 1811 but had been exposed to more advanced ideas about insanity during his years as a medical student in Edinburgh.[14] In the 1830s he was the visiting medical officer at the Saint John almshouse and county gaol and it was the degraded condition in which he found the insane incarcerated in these institutions which prompted him to petition the assembly for the provision of an asylum. In the gaol Peters was horrified to find that warders were making no attempt to separate the mentally ill from other criminals and he discovered many lunatics under heavy restraint, "some of them perfectly naked and in a state of filth"[15] At the Almshouse Peters found similarly inadequate conditions. This institution had been built in 1819 to house sixty persons.[16]

In 1836 it held one hundred and forty paupers, forty of whom required medical treatment and were kept in a makeshift two-room infirmary big enough to handle eight people comfortably.[17] Sick patients overflowed these two rooms into the section of the almshouse reserved for the mentally ill. It was this situation which provoked Peters into seeking permission from the government to move the insane from the almshouse to the basement of the cholera hospital. Unfortunately, the situation did not improve. Lunatics were able to mingle freely with the sick paupers who were being treated in the upper stories of the hospital and the building was too crowded to allow Peters to practice any kind of treatment. The temporary asylum was really just an extension of the almshouse; as Peters himself described it, it was "essentially a pauper institution".[18]

At the same time as the temporary asylum was opening in 1836, the justices of the peace in Saint John County, alarmed at the growing number of mentally disturbed inmates in the gaols, petitioned the assembly to establish a more permanent asylum.[19] A legislative committee was appointed with instructions to gather information from the United States and Europe about the treatment of the insane and to plan a permanent facility. Although this committee reported in December of that year, it was a decade before the assembly was convinced of the inadequacy of the temporary building and appropriated funds that allowed construction of the new asylum to begin.[20] It is not difficult to account for this reluctance to commit provincial funds to the asylum project. While it is true that between 1838 and 1841 the newly acquired control over the revenues from the crown lands swelled the provincial coffers, the decentralized manner in which these funds were dispensed meant that provincial projects did not always receive financial support. As MacNutt has pointed out, the individual assemblyman had control over how and where government money was spent in his constituency.[21] Control of the purse strings was crucial to him because by deploying the money skillfully he could ensure electoral support. He might be reluctant, therefore, to surrender any portion of his patronage money to projects of a more general purpose. Yet the parochialism of legislators should not be exaggerated. The late 1830s and early 1840s were years of heavy immigration and economic crisis in the colony and the assembly was faced

with a variety of immediate needs. In response, it undertook in the years between 1834 and 1847 four major welfare measures aside from the asylum.[22] In 1834 a cholera hospital was opened in Saint John; in 1836 funds were authorized for the construction of a county gaol in the city and a house of correction; in 1838 a new alms-house-workhouse-infirmary complex was approved; and in 1847 the Emigrant Orphan Asylum opened its doors in Saint John. Proponents of a mental asylum had to vie with all these different interests for a share of the public funds and were actually at a disadvantage since gaols and poorhouses could if necessary double as mental institutions.

The Maritime mental institutions which eventually were established in the 1840s and 1850s were designed to accommodate a specific treatment technique known as moral treatment. A few simple drugs, both tranquillizers and purgatives, were administered to control behaviour; assorted bathing techniques were advised for manic or depressed patients; and blood-letting had not entirely been discredited. But moral treatment, or the humane method, was the principal therapeutic technique. It was to the nineteenth century what psychoanalysis became to our own. Moral treatment had its origins in the last decade of the eighteenth century in Europe where it developed out of the practical experiences of Philippe Pinel in France and William Tuke in England. Pinel (1745–1826) attained legendary stature in the history of psychiatry by being the first to strike the chains from the insane and free them from confinement in dungeons, first at the Hopital de Bicêtre in Paris in 1793 and two years later at the Saltpetrière, a hospital for women. His major work, *A Treatise on Insanity,* was published in an English translation in 1806 and his theories were known in the Maritimes as he was referred to approvingly in the New Brunswick report of 1836. Tuke (1732–1822), an English tea merchant and Quaker, pioneered moral treatment in the York Retreat for the Insane which he founded in 1792. His grandson, Samuel Tuke, wrote *Description of the Retreat* in 1813, which was published in the United States the following year and became a standard text for reformers throughout the English-speaking world. Really not treatment in a medical sense at all, the moral method employed compassion and lenience within a strictly controlled environment in an attempt to coax the mind back to sanity. The intention was

389

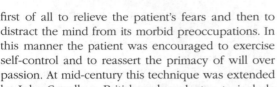

first of all to relieve the patient's fears and then to distract the mind from its morbid preoccupations. In this manner the patient was encouraged to exercise self-control and to reassert the primacy of will over passion. At mid-century this technique was extended by John Conolly, a British asylum doctor, to include the complete abolition of all mechanical and physical restraints.

The principles of moral treatment were carried into the Maritimes by reform-minded laymen such as Hugh Bell and more importantly by doctors who had been educated in Europe or the United States. At the beginning of the century most Maritime medical men were trained as apprentices but by the 1830s a number were being educated at universities in Great Britain and this was certainly true of the doctors who became medical superintendents at the new asylums and the main exponents of moral treatment in the two colonies.[23] George Peters, the original superintendent of the New Brunswick institution, and his successor John Waddell, superintendent for twenty-seven years, both received their degrees from Scottish universities affiliated with mental hospitals where modern treatment techniques were employed. James DeWolf, the first superintendent of Mount Hope, likewise was a graduate of Edinburgh University. Later in the century aspiring doctors began to attend American medical schools; for example, James Steeves, Waddell's successor, studied in Pennsylvania and New York.[24] Even when these early alienists were not formally trained in the United States, their annual reports indicate that they kept a close watch on developments there and frequently toured the more famous American institutions where moral treatment was practiced. While the broad principles of moral treatment were endorsed by all the asylum superintendents, there were differences in the way these principles were applied. This was especially true of the elimination of physical restraints. In New Brunswick Waddell early on rejected the "indiscriminate and frequent use" of mechanical restraints but argued that sometimes they had to be applied for the good of the patient and this moderate position was adopted by his successors.[25] In Nova Scotia, on the other hand, there were quite radical differences of opinion at different points in time. Dr. DeWolf invoked Conolly and endorsed "the total disuse of mechanical restraint" whereas his successor, Dr. A. P. Reid, defended physical restraints as a form of discipline.[26] Despite these differences of

emphasis, however, medical personnel at the Maritime asylums shared a perception of themselves as practitioners of moral treatment.

Moral treatment enjoyed such unequivocal allegiance because it was believed to be effective. The decades of the 1840s and 1850s were a period of unbridled optimism regarding the curability of mental illness. "It is the decided opinion of most persons who have investigated the subject," the New Brunswick commissioners reported in 1836, "that insanity is on the increase. But at the same time it is consolatory to observe, that the disease is not now considered of so formidable a nature as it used to be. because it is found easily to yield to judicious treatment timely applied."[27] In the United States optimism reached a high point in the period 1830–1850 and it is not surprising that the same is true of the Maritime colonies since they looked across the border for proof that their asylums would be successful.[28] The Bell Commission, for example, reported recovery rates of 82½ per cent and 86½ per cent respectively at the Worcester Asylum in Massachusetts and Boston's McLean Asylum and concluded confidently that "Wherever an Asylum is established, there the numbers of Insane in proportion to the population begin to diminish".[29] An important qualification invariably made was that a lunatic was curable primarily in the very early stages of his illness, usually in the first three months. If madness could be detected at the outset and the afflicted person removed from his home to an asylum before temporary symptoms became permanent illness, then cure was virtually assured. If not, if family or friends hesitated before bringing the mentally ill to the asylum, then doctors promised nothing. In fact, they hinted at the worst. When John Waddell stated categorically that "No insane man recovers at home" he was speaking for all his colleagues.[30] Insanity demanded moral treatment and moral treatment demanded the asylum.

A clear idea of the aim of moral treatment is best obtained by examining how it was intended to be implemented in the new, Maritime asylums. Practitioners began with the building itself. The ideal location was on a height of land commanding a scenic view, right at the edge of civilization. Such a site offered the insane the scenery which was expected to soothe their frenzies and divert their attention. Advocates of moral treatment had great faith in the remedial influence nature exerted over the deranged mind: "[…] the sounds caused by rushing water is the music of nature, and is always in harmony with, and soothing in its effects on, the nervous organism".[31] Diversion was also a rationale for building the asylum on the edge of a city, remote enough so that the insane were insulated from the excitement of urban life but close enough so that they had "constant proofs that they are in a world of hope, and among beings who are engaged in the every day business of life."[32] These asylums were not built on secluded sites far from the centers of population. On the contrary, as examples of the charitable character of the populace, they were trophies to be displayed.

The physical appearance of the institution was an important aspect of moral treatment. As in all things, the emphasis was on symmetry and good taste, what came to be called "moral architecture".

> As it is found that the external appearance, as well as the internal economy of the Hospital for the Insane, exert an important moral influence … it is a principle now generally recognized and acted on, that good taste and a regard for comfort, should characterize all the arrangements both external and internal, as calculated to induce self-respect and a disposition to self-control.[33]

As important as the countenance of the asylum was the arrangement of its buildings. Within the Maritime asylums certain classes of patients were to be isolated from each other. For example, patients were segregated by sex and special accommodation was provided for "frantics" whose violent behaviour might disturb the other inmates. Another criterion for separating patients was social class. In part the rationale for this practice was economic. Asylum administrators hoped to attract wealthy patients whose fees would contribute to the upkeep of the institutions. It was thought necessary to offer this class of patient comfortable surroundings and assurances that it would not be subjected to the unsettling manners and morals of lower class lunatics.[34] This reasoning also betrays a therapeutic rationale. Patients had to be insulated from all that was offensive to them and which might cause them to retreat into their derangement. Segregation by class was one of the practices asylum personnel anticipated would make Maritime institutions superior to their American counterparts

in which conditions were distressingly democratic.[35] As it turned out, however, overcrowding and lack of funds kept asylums in Nova Scotia and New Brunswick from achieving a rigorous separation of social classes. It was a recurring complaint throughout the century that the indiscriminate mixing of classes was diverting wealthier patients to foreign institutions, thereby losing local asylums desperately needed funds.[36]

As for the organization of time within the asylum, moral treatment combined three elements—work, play and worship. The most important of this trinity was work, physical labour within the asylum itself or in the gardens surrounding the institutions. Useful employment was intended to have a variety of effects, not the least of which was to defray the expenses of maintaining the institution. More importantly, labour had therapeutic value, if for no other reason than it exhausted the patients, improving their sleeping habits and their physical health. Like the scenery, physical work, by forcing the patient to concentrate on something other than himself, diverted his attention from his sickness, theoretically weakening the irrational forces in their struggle with the will. Since many of the insane seemed to suffer from excess energy which made their behaviour frenzied and unpredictable, regular labour was intended to divert and give vent to some of this energy in a more useful and healthy way. But perhaps the most important influence labour was expected to have on the insane was its moral influence. If a patient was to rejoin society as a productive member, then he or she had to be taught independence, industry and self-respect. Useful employment was as much a way of instilling moral values as it was of healing broken minds.[37] But work could not occupy all the time nor all the patients in an asylum. It was anticipated that upper class inmates, who apparently did not require the moral lessons of useful employment, would be exempt from physical labour. For them, and for the lower classes in their spare time, instructive recreation had to be provided. As well, regular religious observances were scheduled, though for reasons more behavioural than spiritual. Religion was useful as another distraction and the services, because of their communal nature, were considered excellent opportunities for practicing decorum and restraint.[38]

The final element of moral treatment, and one which circumscribed all the others, was isolation.

While it was considered healthy that the mentally ill be aware of, and to some degree witness to, the daily life of society beyond the asylum walls, it was also considered crucial that the individual patient be removed from the immediate social surroundings which had been witness to his fall from reason.

> The first and most important step is to remove the patient from his own home and from all the objects which he has been accustomed to see. His false notions and harassing impressions are associated in his mind with the objects exposed to his senses during the approach of his disease. His relations have become to him stale and uninteresting, and afterwards cause of angry irritation. […] The most favourable situation is a retirement, where the patient will be surrounded by objects which have a composing influence.[39]

The mind, once shattered, needed a quiet place, a kind of laboratory, in which it could be carefully reconstructed. Throughout the century medical men repeatedly warned the public that the insane could not be treated at home, that they had to be surrendered up to the asylum if they were not to become forever incurable.

When all these elements were combined, the result was a self-enclosed, rightly organized institution, the aim of which was the reformation of its inmates' behaviour into socially conventional patterns. Perhaps the most revealing statement about moral treatment can be found in the Nova Scotia report of 1846—"without system there cannot be success".[40] The asylum was a system. Everything from its location to the table manners of its inmates was interrelated to transform behaviour. In charge of this process was the medical superintendent, "the very light and life of the Institution", who was expected not to practice medicine but to attract the confidence, the obedience and the emulation of his charges.[41] The system ignored causes because the understanding of them was rudimentary.[42] Instead, doctors concentrated on symptoms—the hallucination, the frenzy, the melancholy—and tried to eliminate them by reinforcing the patient's self-control. This was the moral system and it flowered in a brand new institution, the asylum.

At the same time as the new Maritime asylums were opening their doors, a noticeable change occurred in the attitude of the law to the incarceration of the insane. Prior to this time statutes had illustrated a reluctance on the part of the lawmakers to take responsibility for the care of the mentally ill. However, as the asylum began to be emphasized as the only proper place for treatment, legislators became much more aggressive in their attitude toward the insane. In New Brunswick the original bylaws governing the new asylum restricted inmates to "lunatics proper" and refused admission to all but exceptional cases of idiocy and delerium tremens.[43] This changed in 1852 when "An Act to Amend the Law Relating to Lunatics and Insane Persons" provided that "any person furiously mad or so far disordered in his reason as to be dangerous when at large" was to be taken forcibly to the asylum and incarcerated there on the orders of two Justices of the Peace.[44] No doctor need be consulted and the superintendent of the asylum could not refuse a patient. Seven years later the law was changed to ensure that no one was admitted to the provincial asylum without first being certified by a doctor but the asylum's superintendent still had no right to refuse admittance to anyone so certified, be they senile, retarded or epileptic.[45] The legal emphasis was on making it as easy as possible to get the mentally ill into the asylum. In Nova Scotia the situation was similar. Prompted by four murders committed within a year, all by men who were subsequently found to be insane, the legislature passed a law which allowed two Justices of the Peace to hold in custody any person who "seemed" to be insane and "seemed" to have "a purpose of committing some crime".[46] If found to be mentally disturbed by a doctor, the individual was held either in gaol or in the poorhouse, or in the asylum when it opened four years later. The Nova Scotia asylum superintendents had more discretionary power than their New Brunswick counterparts. From the beginning the Nova Scotia asylum at Mount Hope was governed by a law which allowed recent and acute cases of insanity to be given preference over more chronic cases.[47] This meant that when the institution became crowded, which it very soon did, mental defectives and cases of long-term illness were refused admittance. While at no time were persons ever legally committed to the Nova Scotia asylum without certification by a physician, there was a perceptible shift in the legal attitude. An 1858 statute, "An Act For the Management of the Hospital for the Insane", provided for the incarceration of any person who could be proven to be "by reason of insanity, unsafe to be at large or suffering any unnecessary duress or hardship".[48] By 1872 the law made no reference to public or personal safety. It merely stated that "any lunatic being at large may be apprehended".[49]

Unhappily, the medico-legal campaign to institutionalize the mentally ill had an effect quite opposite to that intended by reformers and medical men. To be effective, moral treatment required a small number of patients, all of whom were in the acute stage of their illness, and a large staff to work with them. What happened, however, was that the asylums were immediately and continuously overcrowded, especially with what were considered chronic incurable cases, and had neither the staff nor the facilities to be anything more than places of confinement. The heady optimism of mid-century evaporated into exasperation, and sometimes plain brutality, as asylums proved unable to fulfill their role as successful treatment centers.

The New Brunswick asylum opened in December 1848 and in his report for the following year the medical superintendent, John Waddell, was already asking that the institution be enlarged.[50] When completed, it was intended to handle 180 patients in a complex of three buildings, but these were not finally built until 1864, at which time the daily average of patients at the asylum was 194.[51] Demands for expansion continued but it was not really until 1885, when a farm annex capable of handling 150 of the more long-term cases was built, that a satisfactory patient population was achieved.[52] New Brunswick now had facilities for 320 acute cases and almost half that many chronics and complaints about overcrowding were seldom heard. In Nova Scotia the Mount Hope Asylum was also constantly overcrowded from its opening in 1859 until the commencement in 1886 of the county asylum system. The county institutions were meant to accommodate "harmless insane, idiotic persons, and epileptic persons who are insane but who have not manifested symptoms of violent insanity".[53] By 1897 there were fifteen of them throughout Nova Scotia.[54] Crowded conditions at the asylums made the successful treatment of patients almost impossible and cure rates never approximated the heady forecasts of eighty and ninety per cent. By 1882 Dr. A. P. Reid was admitting that at Mount Hope only about ten per cent of the four hundred patients had much hope of regaining their mental health.[55] In 1891 the superintendent of the New Brunswick institution admitted that "Out of four hundred and forty-two patients, only sixteen were expected to be restored to mental health".[56] That is barely more than three per cent. The asylum had become a place of confinement for hundreds of mentally ill people who were given next to no hope of recovery.

Not only were the asylums hopelessly overcrowded, they were also poorly staffed. At first, the superintendent was the only medically qualified staff member. Later in the century he was given an assistant. It was the intention of both asylums that these doctors make daily visits to all the patients but evidence given at a number of enquiries suggests that these duties were frequently neglected. Daily care of asylum inmates devolved upon a small number of attendants who had no training and often, because of overwork, or simple meanness, no sympathy. Since turnover in these jobs was rapid and steady, the insane seldom even had the benefit of experienced care. Given these conditions, it is not surprising to find that there were a number of publicized incidents of attendants abusing patients. In New Brunswick, just a year after the asylum opened, two attendants were dismissed for what was delicately called "gross misconduct".[57] A short while after Mount Hope opened in Nova Scotia the institution's steward, Amos Black, was dismissed by a committee of investigation, apparently for having sexual relations with a number of the patients. In any event Black and DeWolf, the superintendent, were frequently at odds, the committee terming the situation at the asylum a "civil war" between the two men with the patients neglected as a result.[58] Five years after the Black incident, the bruised, lice-ridden corpse of Richard Hurley became the center of a controversy about the standard of care at the asylum. During the twenty-four-year-old Hurley's six-month stay at Mount Hope no members of his family were permitted to visit him until the day the father was summoned to take the consumptive body of his son home to die. A committee investigating the incident concluded that parts of the asylum were indeed overcrowded and filthy, although it declared that there was "no evidence to fix any blame on either Dr. DeWolf or any of the attendants".[59]

393

While unqualified attendants were undoubtedly the cause of some abuse, the biggest problem in the asylums was lack of space. In 1877 Dr. James Steeves, superintendent of the New Brunswick hospital from 1876 to 1896, travelled to Fredericton to try and convince the legislature to finance an addition to the building. There were 284 patients in an institution built to accommodate only two hundred, Steeves told the Saint John *Daily Telegraph,* and one hundred of these did not have the separate rooms they required for proper treatment. "The evils involved in this simple fact are such as could not well be described in our columns," wrote the interviewer, "for the details would be offensive and even shocking".[60] In Nova Scotia the "offensive" details of overcrowding were described publicly, as a result of an investigation into conditions at the asylum in May, 1877.[61] It was established that because of crowding, patients were being neglected, wards were filthy and no treatment was being carried out. Kate Cameron, an attendant at Mount Hope for four years, told the committee that she had once seen a female patient stripped, bound and left unattended in a room with no bed and no heat, simply because she had torn her clothes. It was December and the woman froze to death but no inquest was held into the incident.[62] Michael Meagher, another attendant, told the following story:

A patient named Graham was in the dark room (solitary confinement) while I was at the Hospital. It was in the Winter time. The glass was broken, and the rain came in and wet the floor. Graham was lying on the floor on a mattress. The room was in a very dirty condition. There was straw on the floor, and human excrements. I saw the snow not melted on the floor. We put the food in over the door sometimes. The doctor would occasionally enquire how he was. [...] He never went to see him. A man put in the dark room was entirely neglected. Graham was subject to fits: he might have died without assistance during the night: he was left entirely to his own resources after locking him up. Graham was a powerful, muscular man. It was the practise of the attendants to give as little food as possible to patients in that state to reduce their

strength: just enough food to sustain them. The doctors never enquired into the quantity of food given them. Graham was in the dark room from one to three weeks. The room was bitterly cold; it was hardly fit for a dog: it was not fit for a human being.[63]

These abuses at Mount Hope may have been aggravated by Superintendent DeWolf, an arrogant man with whom most of his employees found it difficult to work. But the fact that both the New Brunswick and Prince Edward Island asylums were also, in different degrees, found to be inadequate institutions, suggests that Mount Hope was not the exception but the rule.[64]

The evidence indicates that the Maritime asylum failed to live up to its founders' expectations. Instead of a place of treatment it had become a place of confinement Good intentions were one thing, but lack of adequate space and facilities meant inevitably that the emphasis at the asylums was on custody, not treatment. Organization became paramount as the logistics of caring for hundreds of mentally ill inmates became complicated and costly. Behaviour was subordinated to a rigidly controlled pattern of daily institutional life. The county asylums built in Nova Scotia after 1885 epitomized this trend. The regulations for one of these institutions warned that "any inmate guilty of drunkenness, disobedience, obscenity, disorderly conduct, profane or indecorous language, theft, waste or who shall absent himself or herself from the premises without the permission of the Superintendent or who shall injure or deface any part of the house or furniture therein, or who shall commit waste or destruction of any kind in regard to property connected with the Asylum shall be subject to merited punishment".[65] "Merited punishment" included solitary confinement on a diet of bread and water for up to twenty-four hours. All activity at these institutions—getting up in the morning, eating meals, taking exercise, going to bed at night—was done en masse and regulated by the sounding of bells. Given the intolerable conditions of the asylum, the humane aspect of moral treatment had been sacrificed to the requirements of the system. The Maritime asylum had become more a jail than a hospital.

NOTES

1. Prince Edward Island is not considered in this article because not until very late in the period

under discussion was a hospital for the mentally ill constructed on the Island. An asylum was opened near Charlottetown in 1847 but it doubled as a house of industry and in construction resembled a workhouse more than a hospital. This building, chronically overcrowded and underfinanced and poorly lit and ventilated, remained the only facility for the mentally ill until 1879 when the first proper hospital built for the purpose was opened. See R. N. Stalwick, "A History of Asylum Administration in Canada Before Confederation" (unpublished Ph.D. thesis. University of London, 1967), pp. 89 *passim;* Henry Hard, ed., *The Institutional Care of the Insane in the United States and Canada* (Baltimore 1917), vol. 4, pp. 203 *passim.* When the term Maritime is used in the article, therefore, it is meant to refer to New Brunswick and Nova Scotia only.

2. *Statutes of Nova Scotia,* 32 Geo 11, c.1.

3. *Ibid.,* 10 Geo III. c.5.

4. *Consolidated Statutes of New Brunswick,* 5 Geo IV. c.9.

5. For the following discussion of poor relief I am indebted to Brereton Greenhous,. "Paupers and Poorhouses: The Development of Poor Relief in Early New Brunswick", *Social History,* I (April. 1968), pp. 103–26, and James Whalen, "New Brunswick Poor Law Policy in the Nineteenth Century" (M.A. thesis. University of New Brunswick. 1968), part of which was published in *Acadiensis,* II (I).

6. See Greenhous, *op.cit.,* and Grace Aiton, "The Selling of Paupers by Public Auction in Sussex Parish". *Collections of the New Brunswick Historical Society,* 16 (1961). pp. 93–110.

7. Nova Scotia. Legislative Assembly, *Journals,* 1832. App. 49 [hereafter references to Assembly journals in the Maritimes will be to *JLA*].

8. Henry Hurd. *op. cit.,* p. 549.

9. *Novascotian.* 25 November 1844 and *Times.* 5 November, 22 December 1844.

10. Nova Scotia, *JLA.* 1846. App. 32; *JLA.* 1848. App. 54.

11. Nova Scotia. *JLA,* 1850. App. 72.

12. *Novascotian,* 23 March 1846.

13. W. S. MacNutt *The Atlantic Provinces* (Toronto, 1965), p. 261.

14. Hurd, *op.cit.,* p. 584.

15. George Peters to Executive Council, 28 November 1836, New Brunswick, Records of the Executive Council, Health and Sickness, vol. 2, Provincial Archives of New Brunswick [hereafter PANB].

16. Whalen. *op.cit.,* p. 55.

17. *New Brunswick Courier* (Saint John), 24 December 1836.

18. George Peters to Executive Council, 3 May 1845, New Brunswick, Executive Council Pupers, vol. 118, p. 1442, PANB.

19. Hurd, *op.cit.,* p. 37.

20. Report of the Commissioners, December 1836, New Brunswick, *JLA.* 1836–7. App. 3.

21. W. S. MacNutt. *New Brunswick* (Toronto, 1963), pp. 258–9.

22. Whalen, *op.cit.*

23. See K. A. Mackenzie, "Nineteenth Century Physicians in Nova Scotia". *Collections of the Nova Scotia Historical Society.* 31 (1957). pp. 119–20 and J. W. Lawrence, "The Medical Men of St. John in its First Half Century". *Collections of the New Brunswick Historical Society.* 1 (1897), pp. 273–305.

24. Hurd. *op.cit.,* pp. 561, 584, 591, 595.

25. Report from the Medical Superintendent of the Provincial Lunatic Asylum, New Brunswick. *JLA,* 1851. App.

26. Report of the Medical Superintendent of the Nova Scotia Hospital for the Insane, Nova Scotia, *JLA.* 1872. App. 20: 1881. App. 3A.

27. New Brunswick, *JLA.* 1836–7. App. 3.

28. See Norman Dain. *Concepts of Insanity in the United States, 1789–1865* (New Brunswick, N.J., 1964), p. 114.

29. Nova Scotia, *JLA,* 1846. App. 32.

30. Report of the Medical Superintendent, New Brunswick, *JLA,* 1849. App.

31. Report of the Medical Superintendent, New Brunswick, *JLA,* 1875. App. 6.

32. Report of the Commissioners, New Brunswick, *JLA,* 1836–7. App. 3.

33. Nova Scotia, *JLA,* 1846. App. 32.

34. Report of the Commissioners, New Brunswick, *JLA,* 1836–7. App. 3.

35. Report of the Medical Superintendent, New Brunswick, *JLA,* 1849. App.

36. See, for example, New Brunswick, *JLA,* 1850, 1851. App. and Nova Scotia, *JLA,* I860. App.; 1874. App. 6.

37. See Report of the Commissioners, New Brunswick. *JLA,* 1836–7. App. 3 and Nova Scotia, *JLA,* 1846. App. 32.

38. Report of the Commissioners, New Brunswick. *JLA,* 1836–7. App. 3.

39. *Ibid.*

40. Nova Scotia. *JLA,* 1846. App. 32.

41. *Ibid.*

42. For a detailed discussion of contemporary theories of insanity and its causes see my thesis, "That Prison on the Hill; The Historical Origins of the Lunatic Asylum in the Maritime Provinces" (unpublished M.A. thesis, Carleton University. 1975).

43. Correspondence, Reports and Returns, New Brunswick, Records of the Executive Council, vol. 118, Lunatic Asylum, 1843–57, pp. 1540–6, PANB.

44. Report of the Medical Superintendent, New Brunswick. *JLA.* 1854. App.

45. *Consolidated Statutes of New Brunswick, 1903,* vol. 1, c. 101.

46. *Nova Scotian,* 1 January 1855; *Statutes of Nova Scotia,* 1855, c. 34. ser. 1–6.

47. Nova Scotia, *JLA,* 1859. App. 10.

48. *Statutes of Nova Scotia,* 1858. c. 38.

49. *Ibid.,* 1872. c. 3.

50. Report from the Medical Superintendent, New Brunswick, *JLA,* 1850. App.

51. *Ibid.,* 1865. App. 14.

52. *Ibid.,* 1886. App.

53. *Statutes of Nova Scotia,* 1886, c 44.

54. Report of the Medical Superintendent. Nova Scotia, *JLA,* 1899. App. 3A.

55. *Ibid.,* 1883. App. 3A.

56. Report from the Medical Superintendent, New Brunswick. *JLA,* 1891. App.

57. *Morning News* (Saint John), 7 December 1849.

58. Nova Scotia, *JLA,* 1861. App. 6; *Novascotian,* 28 May 1860.

59. Report of Committee on Humane Institutions, Nova Scotia, *JLA.* 1867. App. 38.

60. *Daily Telegraph.* 28 August 1877.

61. Report of Commission to investigate the condition and general management of the Provincial Hospital for the Insane, Nova *Scotia, JLA,* 1878. App. 10.

62. Nova Scotia. *Supplementary Evidence as to the Management of the Hospital for the Insane* (Halifax. 1872).

63. *Ibid.*

64. In 1874 a Grand Jury visited the Prince Edward Island asylum and reported that they "find it difficult to ask your Lordships to believe that an institution, so conducted, would be allowed to exist in a civilized community. In a cell below the ground, about six feet by seven feet, they found a young woman, entirely naked, beneath some broken, dirty straw. The stench was unbearable. There were pools of urine on the floor, evidently the accumulation of many days, as there were gallons of it". The superintendent of the institution was apparently "an ordinary labourer" and the Jury concluded that "the whole Asylum is one state of filth". (Grand Jury Presentment on the state of the Asylum. P.E.I., *JLA,* 1875. App. G).

65. *Bylaws,* Cumberland County Hospital for the Insane, 1895, Public Archives of Nova Scotia.

■ Article 2: "Open to the Public": Touring Ontario Asylums in the Nineteenth Century

Janet Miron

In the 1880s E. Katharine Bates embarked on a transatlantic tour of North America, visiting such cities as Montreal, New York, Boston, Philadelphia, and Washington. While in Toronto for a few days, she included in her sightseeing itinerary the law courts of Osgoode Hall, the University of Toronto, Rosedale Park, and the insane asylum on Queen Street.[1] A few years earlier, Thomas Dick, a young farmer living outside the city, came to Toronto for a visit on the occasion of the national exhibition and chose to spend his time seeing not only the Central Prison but the asylum grounds as well.[2] The visits by Bates and Dick to Toronto's asylum were part of an extremely popular pastime in Ontario in the nineteenth century, whereby large numbers of people poured into the asylums hoping to inspect both the buildings and the people confined within them.[3]

Historians have tended to dismiss visitors such as Bates and Dick as cruel voyeurs who were drawn to mental institutions in search of cheap thrills and excitement, and as irritating intruders who greatly vexed institutional officials.[4] However, when the aims of these visitors, their experiences on their tours, and

Source: James E. Moran and David Wright, eds., *Mental Health and Canadian Society: Historical Perspectives* (Montreal: McGill-Queen's University Press, 2006), pp. 19–20, 21, 22–26, 30–32, 34–42. Reprinted with permission.

the attitudes of asylum employees towards them are critically analyzed, institutional tourism becomes a complex phenomenon that represented more than a mere "shameful" or "degrading spectacle."[5] Indeed, the practice embodies invaluable information for the historian and helps to illuminate both the relationship between asylums and their broader community and popular attitudes towards the insane. In particular, the discourse surrounding visitors demonstrates that many asylum superintendents and government inspectors believed the public had the potential to influence both the success of the asylum and the treatment of mental illness. Moreover, it suggests that an array of motives lay behind people's decisions to visit a hospital for the mentally ill. While not all alienists shared the views of visitors and not all visitors were propelled by the same considerations, the debates that arose and the records left behind by officials and visitors provide important insights into the role these institutions served in the nineteenth century, the influence the public had upon their functionings, and the relationships that were forged with the communities beyond the asylum's walls. [...]

It is the thousands of casual observers with which this chapter primarily is concerned. When we explore asylums through the eyes of such individuals, it becomes clear that nineteenth-century Canadians and tourists from abroad were not mere passive receptacles of the ideologies espoused by those in the medical profession but, instead, were active participants in the effort to understand and study what was deemed to be aberrant behaviour. [...]

Proponents Of Visiting

Most superintendents and government inspectors did not believe that asylums could be easily isolated from greater society; nor did many of them actually desire complete segregation. Instead, a number of administrators strove to foster close ties with the communities beyond their walls, arguing that such relationships were beneficial for a variety of reasons. Moreover, many recognized that the public was crucial to these institutions in a number of ways and that perceptions of and attitudes towards asylums were as dependent on "official" discourse as they were on the laity's experiences while passing through them. As state-run institutions relied on government funding, public approval was essential for asylums, and inevitably, this dependence led asylum officials to embark on campaigns to bolster popular support through the practice of visiting.

Many officials perceived visiting as an important part of the process of social legitimization and believed that the practice was the best means by which public confidence could be gained. These officials were aware of the public's growing fascination with asylums, evinced by the fact that the reports of superintendents, government inspectors, and commissioners were regularly reprinted in the popular press and that the recommendations, criticisms, and impressions of "professional" visitors or prominent reformers commonly appeared in newspapers as well. However, officials were also cognizant of the prejudice towards asylums that pervaded society and undermined the view of their institutions as curative. Indeed, much of the printed information available to the general populace painted a grim picture of institutions for the mentally ill. In the nineteenth century, "shocking" tales of conditions inside asylums appeared regularly in newspapers, sparking concern over the treatment of the institutionalized and fostering suspicion about the buildings that housed them. Until the latter half of the nineteenth century, medical practitioners affiliated with either hospitals or asylums were treated with skepticism by a populace that was not oblivious to the highly publicized grave-robbings committed by some of their peers or the autopsies performed on unwilling subjects.[6] In the mid-1850s, for example, the Toronto Asylum was plagued with many charges of abuse and corruption. A number of employees claimed that the steward had impregnated a female patient, while one former attendant, James Magar, charged that he had "known the bodies of the dead to be dissected for the information of Doctors not connected with the Asylum, and their brains kept after the body was interred."[7] Such scandals easily led to the image of the doctor who sacrificed patients in the pursuit of medical knowledge and helped to foster suspicion of all medical establishments.

Moreover, there were other, more flagrant reasons as to why people feared institutionalization in a medical establishment. Because of their unsanitary conditions and the fact that few people left them healed, hospitals were not perceived as therapeutic institutions. Instead, they were seen as places where the most unfortunate went to die and thus were avoided by all except for the very poor.[8] This view of hospitals imbued attitudes towards asylums. Even as late as the 1860s, Wolfred Nelson, inspector of asylums and prisons for the Province of Canada, remarked that "very erroneous views are generally entertained in regard to Asylums" and that they were often viewed with "distrust and alarm."[9] Consequently, institutional officials hoped to dispel negative publicity by advocating that people view their asylums first-hand and see for themselves the progress that had been made in them.

As a means of gaining society's confidence and alleviating skepticism, superintendents and other government officials encouraged visiting in their annual reports, which were reprinted in local papers. The early annual reports of the Provincial Lunatic Asylum at Toronto repeatedly emphasized that the institution was open to visitors from 12 o'clock until 3 and that it was "as open to the public as is compatible with the welfare of the patients and the duties of their attendants."[10] Such promotion was apparently effective since, in 1850, 1,400 visitors reportedly passed through the asylum during that year alone.[11] Even three decades later, in 1880, officials in the province could still be found encouraging the practice in newspapers, including Richard Maurice Bucke, superintendent of the London Asylum, who wrote a letter to the London *Free Press* publicizing that "the Asylum is always open to inspection by the whole public."[12]

As a way of alleviating social stigma, institutional tourism represented an excellent opportunity to educate the broader society on the causes and contemporary treatment of insanity. In their annual reports, officials often referred to the impressions of visitors, thereby highlighting the importance that was granted to public opinion. The chairman for the Provincial Lunatic Asylum in Toronto reported in 1852. that "Large numbers of visitors have … from time to time, been attended through the building, and these have witnessed the condition of the apartments, the appearance and happiness of the patients, the kindly, but effective discipline, which prevails amongst the afflicted and their attendants. The result has been, so far as is known, a universal satisfaction to visitors, many of whom had been acquainted with similar Institutions in Europe, or the United States."[13] Moreover, many believed that the successful treatment of insanity was dependent upon early committal to an asylum and that the longer loved ones waited, the less likelihood of a cure being achieved. Thus, as Wolfred Nelson pointed out, the "attainment

of successful results" was contingent upon the community's "countenance and good opinion."[14]

Mistrust or suspicion was not the only problem with which asylum officials had to contend while negotiating their relationship with the public. As the nineteenth century progressed, asylum expenditure grew, and superintendents were increasingly pressured to justify their efficacy in treating insanity. According to historian S.E.D. Shortt, asylums in Ontario consumed almost 16.5 per cent of the provincial budget in the 1870s, a share that stabilized at more than 19 per cent in the late 1880s. In 1893 this represented twice the combined expenditure on penal institutions, general hospitals, houses of refuge, and orphanages.[15] As James Moran has noted, the "difficulty in raising funds to construct and maintain the province's public asylums" was a persistent problem.[16] As heads of costly institutions, not only were superintendents compelled to highlight their success rates to portray the therapeutic treatments of their institutions as effective, but they also became even more aware of their need for public support.

The dependence of institutions on public funds made many feel particularly vulnerable and pressured to appease taxpayers, thereby placing asylum superintendents in a difficult situation: at what cost did their efforts to win public support through the practice of visiting endanger the mental improvement of patients? While refusing (at least in theory) to open the doors of the Toronto Asylum to the masses, Superintendent Daniel Clark admitted, much to his chagrin, that many people felt they had a right to tour asylums. "It is a public Institution," he lamented, "and it is the privilege of the British subject, if he should happen to be 'a free and independent elector' to look upon an Asylum to the support of which he has contributed his mite of taxes, as a huge menagerie, erected for the purpose of gratifying his morbid curiosity."[17] Although some may have been opposed to the practice, few institutions could afford to, or had the power to, keep the public out entirely. As the superintendent of the Maiden Lunatic Asylum explained, "Public opinion is all powerful; and by its help only we can carry into practise the most enlightened principles of management; and by the spread of enlightened principles, only, can we hope for that liberal pecuniary support from the Parliament, which is absolutely essential to the welfare of our asylums."[18] [...]

VISITORS TO ASYLUMS

[...] By the mid-nineteenth century, visiting was far from an uncommon or marginal pastime: thousands of urban and rural dwellers alike flocked to asylums annually. In fact, as the century progressed, the activity became so popular that institutions were frequently overwhelmed on holidays, by the "crush and confusion resulting from so many persons being admitted."[19] Thus, while harsh criticism of visiting was voiced and administrators complained of troublesome visitors, few could actually enforce a closed-door policy, and there do not appear to have been any publicly funded asylums in Ontario that could keep the public out entirely. Even if officials were opposed to asylum tourism, they usually had to tolerate the public's presence, and while Clark was officially against sightseers, the practice continued at the Toronto Asylum well into the late nineteenth century, as it did at all other public asylums in Ontario.[20]

Although historians have tended to agree with the attitudes expressed by Clark, the records left by visitors suggest that their motives and experiences were diverse and defy being reduced to voyeurism. Like many other Victorian pursuits, visiting was undeniably rooted in a fascination with those considered deviant and related to the desire to observe or witness the unfamiliar. It was part of the broader "spectacularization" of modern life in the nineteenth century, where "reality seemed to be experienced as a show—an object to be looked at rather than experienced in an unmediated form."[21] However, this phenomenon should not inevitably lead one to conclude that all visitors were merely interested in catching a peep show of the insane. Many visitors certainly treated asylum as human menageries where patients were spectacles to be gawked at and regarded these institutions as entertainment venues that differed little from the circuses and "freak" shows that frequently appeared in their towns and cities. At the same time, although asylum tourism was for many an opportunity to engage in sheer voyeurism, the incentives behind this practice were complex and illuminate the ideological currents and contradictions pervading Victorian culture. Voyeurism was inherent in visiting, yet for a large number of people, institutional tours were a source of self-improvement, "scientific" education, and community pride. Moreover, while its ramifications or effectiveness may be questioned, visiting nevertheless fostered greater exchange and dialogue between the public and the institutionalized and thereby served as an important means through which notions regarding the insane were constructed and defined at the lay level. Thus, by analyzing asylums not as mere physical structures but as tourist sites where popular representations of the "mad" were formed, we can understand these institutions as virtual civic monuments closely connected to the world beyond their walls.

Both Clark and Bucke tended to see all visitors as a homogeneous group, respectively as either voyeurs or responsible citizens. However, those who engaged in asylum tourism were not only guided by an array of incentives but were also from a wide range of social and cultural backgrounds that transcended the lines of gender, class, ethnicity, and age. Local farmers, female leisure travellers, and male bankers visited insane asylums, and children of all ages were exposed to their interiors. As one man remarked on his tour through the Toronto Asylum, "There was a party consisting of a Lady, Gentleman, and a little Girl going over the establishment, and, as I entered I enjoined them."[22] Visitors lived in the communities connected to these institutions or travelled from other regions and countries, some as far away as Mexico, England, and Germany. In terms of sheer numbers alone, the visitors who recorded their experiences were predominantly of a privileged social stature. Reflecting the cultural and political context of the nineteenth century, the majority of records that exist today were written by white, middle-class males, but, while particular voices dominate the written sources, such individuals did not exercise a complete monopoly over asylum tourism. The fact that many accounts were recorded by a wide range of people who did not fit a particular socio-economic profile is significant, and it thereby provides a more nuanced understanding of community attitudes towards asylums. In addition, while the predominant voice in travel narratives might be middle-class and male, since it was not uncommon for visitors to comment upon members of their tour group, their observations often shed light on the experiences of others. [...]

VISITORS' MOTIVES

The public enthusiastically responded to the promotion of asylum tourism and sought to see both the interiors of these institutions and their inhabitants for a variety of reasons that often transcended spectatorship. But this is not to imply that visitors can simply be divided between voyeurs and the well-intentioned, as all who entered into these institutions were voyeurs to a certain degree. Visitors often presented themselves as urban reformers investigating the conditions of institutions, yet, as Judith Walkowitz has argued, "the 'zeal for reform' was often accompanied by 'a prolonged, fascinated gaze' from the bourgeoisie."[23] In order to comment upon the approaches employed in asylums, visitors had to study the institutionalized, but as the power dynamic between these two groups was unequal in that the institutionalized had not made an active "choice" to be viewed by the public, patients were spectacles because of the very nature of such interactions.[24] At the same time, in spite of the fact that there was always a certain power imbalance inherent in these interactions, some visitors were much more inclined than others to view institutional tours as pure amusement and folly. For such individuals, visiting seems to have represented an alluring form of transgression, an opportunity to cross over into the nether world of "abnormal" society and to be risqué by watching, and in many cases ridiculing, the confined.

Visitors mocked patients, taunted them with tobacco, provoked outbursts, and delighted in being able to watch them without necessarily being seen themselves. While some defenders claimed that visiting served an important educational function, others believed these institutions merely offered free, "real-life" amusement. Although the nineteenth century has been characterized as a period in which treatment of the insane was reformed and, in many ways, humanized, a large number of individuals at the lay level continued to perceive asylums as little more than human menageries, in which visiting was an opportunity to gaze at the confined.

The tendency to regard custodial institutions for their entertainment value paralleled many other aspects of nineteenth-century culture. Indeed, the headline for one newspaper article reads like a circus playbill: "The Unsound of Mind. How They are Kept at the London Asylum. A Trip Through the Corridors and Rooms. The Eccentricities of the Patients. Exciting Experiences, Sad Scenes and Amusing Incidents."[25] Until the latter half of the nineteenth century, public executions, "freak" shows, and medical exhibitions encouraged both treatment of the body

as an object to be displayed and the perception that the mental and physical suffering of others could constitute a source of amusement. As Vanessa Schwartz has illustrated in her wonderful monograph *Spectacular Realities,* even in death the body was displayed for the purpose of public consumption and popular entertainment. The morgue visiting she documents in Paris was not as common in Ontario, but the popularity of public executions in Canada is a similar phenomenon that certainly attests to the continent's fascination with the human spectacle. For example, when a man sentenced to be hanged committed suicide, city officials in Toronto displayed his body to the public in the morgue in order to appease the thousands who had hoped to witness his execution.[26] Similarly, society's obsession with the physical suffering of others was highlighted in Montreal when tickets to see the last rites being given to a condemned murderer were sold to the public by the sheriff and thousands gathered to watch his hanging.[27] Alongside such popular practices as public executions, visiting can clearly be seen as one element in a rather impressive roster of nineteenth-century voyeuristic, and at times sadistic, pastimes.

Generalizations about the insane were frequently made by voyeuristic visitors, who tended to relay what they perceived as "humorous" anecdotes of female hysterics and childlike men. One journalist, on his tour of the Toronto Asylum under Dr Scott, described the patients he or she saw: the "religious mad … who will bore you on some knotty point," those "truly pitiable objects" who were suffering from melancholy, with their "downcast head and look," and others with "much vivacity of manners, loquaciousness of speech, and fondness for narrative." The writer also portrayed one individual who "strutted about attired most ludicrously, fancying herself a Queen."[28] Such visitors saw institutions for the mentally ill primarily as sources of entertainment, and presented the insane as parodies, as characters who could easily have stepped out of a Hogarth print. One popular writer, Susanna Moodie, toured the Toronto Asylum with her daughter and son-in-law, entering areas where "strangers have seldom nerve enough to visit," and proudly relayed her sensationalist impressions and experiences to an undoubtedly dazzled audience.[29]

In spite of the efforts of many asylum superintendents, onlookers motivated by a "perverse" curiosity generally were not prevented from passing through their institutions. As was discussed above, many did struggle with the ways in which such visitors could be kept out. At the same time, though, others were untroubled by the potential presence of visitors who were unsympathetic to the plight of the incarcerated. Dr Sippi, who served as bursar at the London Asylum from 1893 to 1897, complained that the thousands who came through the institution were motivated merely by "idle" and harmful curiosity. However, Bucke refused to stem the flow of tourists, and throughout his career he remained adamant that visitors be allowed into the asylum.[30] Similarly, prior to Daniel Clark's superintendence, the Toronto Asylum was well known amongst many not necessarily for its treatment of the mentally ill but for its receptivity to strangers. After providing a lengthy and rather lurid portrait of the patients in the asylum, one journalist claimed of the superintendent: "Dr. Scott appears to be very attentive to visitors, and gives all information in his power that the most prying could desire." In this institution, the author noted, people could acquire intimate details of patients from asylum personnel, in spite of the fact that some of the lunatics treated visitors "as if they were intruding."[31] Scott may have been oblivious to his visitor's insensitivity, but he clearly was not uncomfortable with members of the "prying" public touring his institution.

As all historians who enjoy peeking into the lives of earlier generations are professional voyeurs in a sense, it is not surprising that the basest of visitors' motives have captured the attention of scholars. However, when visitor narratives are critically examined and situated within their broader cultural context, it becomes apparent that a number of factors stimulated institutional tourism and that focusing on spectatorship obscures the complexities of the practice. In particular, the growing number of people who flocked to asylums in the nineteenth century was related to the socio-economic environment. Urbanization, immigration, and industrialization are traditionally seen as the benchmarks of the nineteenth century, and along with these changes arose an increased anxiety amongst many.[32] Consequently, those who toured asylums often did so in search of a sense of stability and security and as a means of negotiating or mediating the changing urban landscape of the time. In addition, the nineteenth century was an era of reform, a period in which approaches to insanity were being transformed. Moral therapy,

as advocated by Philippe Pinel of the Bicêtre in the late eighteenth century and by William Tuke of the Quakers' York Retreat for the insane in the nineteenth, infiltrated the programs of Ontario asylums. As a result, many people wanted to see first-hand the "progress" that had been made in the sphere of health care reform. One journalist in the London *Free Press* highlighted the importance of visiting in this regard and wrote, "Knowing that a great moral and social problem was being worked out at the Asylum, in the success of which humanity's best instincts are interested, to visit it was part of our programme."[33]

In the accounts written by members of the public, there is a strong sense that they believed themselves to be conducting inspections on their tours of asylums. The majority of visitors critiqued the cleanliness and efficiency of institutions, the appearances of patients, and the approaches of superintendents, and also expressed their approval or disappointment with the institution. Consequently, their judgments resonate throughout their writings: "[We] saw nothing to complain of, but on the contrary, plenty to admire" and "beautifully clean and well kept" were typical evaluations of institutions made by visitors.[34] One visitor to the London Asylum noted, "A look through the building is always instructive and while the demented state of the inmates cannot but excite pity, the visitor will be pleased to see the manner in which the unfortunates are cared for."[35] Another visitor to the Toronto Asylum for the annual Christmas feast remarked, "The terrors associated with lunatic asylums made many conceive of them only as abodes of unmitigated wretchedness. The cell, the whip, the strait-jacket, the filth, the food flung to the poor creatures as if they were dogs, are the prevalent notions connected with them; but here we found an Elysium in comparison with those we have read of, and those we have known. The insane were wont to be governed by the law of brutality; now it is the law of kindness, and the influence of it was fully perceived here on Friday last."[36]

Visitors thus frequently claimed that misconceptions were rectified by visits to asylums and that by seeing such institutions and the people inside them, they could understand new approaches to mental illness. Officials of institutions themselves encouraged people to play a role as unofficial visitors, and annual reports frequently referred to the impressions of casual visitors, thereby granting legitimacy to the efforts made by the public.[37] For example, many superintendents

101

believed the public could gain a better understanding of both insanity and contemporary therapeutic practices merely through custodial tourism and observation. One official in the United States expressed great faith in the people's potential to be astute visitors, and his views were undoubtedly shared by many of his Canadian counterparts. He wrote: "The public, generally, have wrong impressions in relation to the inmates of a Lunatic Asylum. They suppose them to be either idiots, or completely mad, and in both cases incapable of appreciating kindness. If this was true, moral treatment certainly would prove of little avail. But one visit to a well conducted Institution of this kind would be sufficient to correct this error."[38] Moreover, if any lay visitor was an "untrained observer" unsure of how to evaluate custodial institutions, he or she could always consult John S. Billings and Henry M. Kurd's *Suggestions to Hospital and Asylum Visitors* to "learn how to critically inspect [asylums] with a reasonable chance of seeing what is wrong and learning how to value what is praiseworthy," and to learn *"what* to see and *how* to see it."[39]

Even if some Canadians feared that insanity was increasing in the nineteenth century, most looked upon the institutions established to deal with this problem not as shameful or demonstrative of social degeneration, but instead, as symbols of progress. As visitor narratives illustrate, asylums were prominent sources of civic pride. Fairs, exhibitions, and holidays—events that are often associated with enhanced expressions of community pride—were particularly popular days for visiting. The London Asylum, for example, drew over 1,700 visitors in just three days during the fall fair in 1877,[40] and it was invariably described as one of the most beautiful spots around London.[41] This sense of civic pride is further evinced by the fact that residents drew the attention of visitors to their asylums, seeing them as important sites of interest and as community landmarks. Hosts and guides often insisted that travellers tour their institutions (occasionally to the chagrin of the tourist), and one newspaper reporter noted that "the average Londoner never fails to ask you with a conscious pride, 'Have you been out to the Asylum yet?' And if you reply in the negative," the author further noted, "you are told, with no little *empressment,* 'You must go!'"[42] Another writer further propounded, "Such institutions, which are amongst the last results of civilization, are an honour to the country which founds and maintains them; they are a credit and

ought to be the pride of the PEOPLE to whose wise liberality their existence is due."[43]

In addition to civic boosterism, asylum tourism represented an educational opportunity for many visitors, and in this regard, the incentives behind institutional tourism were inextricably tied to the nineteenth-century impulse towards self-education and self-improvement. John C. Burnham has examined nineteenth-century popular interest in science in relation to the rise of the commercial museum in the United States and has made a number of arguments that are relevant to the phenomenon of institutional tourism.[44] In many ways, asylums constituted living museums that encouraged the diffusion of knowledge through tourism and observation, and even Clark, the staunch opponent of visitors to the Toronto Asylum, supported tours by "professional men having scientific objects in view."[45] Visiting encouraged the public to examine the institutionalized and thus reason with the "experts" about the causes of mental disease, and as one visitor remarked, "a look through the [London Asylum] building is always instructive."[46] Although this particular visitor was touring the Kingston Penitentiary, his belief that information could be obtained "with the evidence of our own eyes"[47] was undoubtedly shared by many asylum visitors as well.

Since education in the nineteenth century was guided by faith in empiricism and the notion that knowledge could be acquired through observation, many people viewed asylums as sites where "scientific" knowledge could be learned. By simply touring the Toronto Asylum and seeing the patients, for example, one writer felt that visitors were given "an idea of the peculiar but lamentable circumstances that conspired to create insanity,"[48] and many felt their tours had enhanced their knowledge of medical practices. After visiting asylums, people often remarked on how the experience contrasted with prevalent assumptions or popular belief, and one writer commented that the most effective way to establish an understanding of asylum management "was to present to their own eyes, to let them see for themselves what had been done, and how it had been done."[49] Embedded as they were in the nineteenth-century culture of looking or visual display, it is clear that when many visitors described different forms of insanity or the impact that institutionalization had on humans, they were expressing a belief in their right to participate alongside other "experts" in current debates, as well as the idea that seeing or observing could foster understanding.

For those interested in contemporary approaches to deviant behaviour, visiting furthermore represented a "safe" opportunity that allowed for the study of the insane in person. One visitor to the Toronto Asylum remarked that the patients were "under such good management [...] even a stranger or a child would be unmolested by the worst of them."[50] Visitors often spoke directly to patients, inquiring into the conditions of the respective institution and the causes behind their mental illness, and frequently recorded their conversations with them.[51] Nevertheless, although the desire to better comprehend the mentally ill permeated the writings of asylum visitors, this was not necessarily accompanied by a desire to *freely* mix with them. Through asylum tourism, the public could get close to those deemed mad, yet still maintain a clear boundary between "normal" and "other." Consequently, many who would have felt threatened had they met the institutionalized in the public realm felt comforted by the fact that, in many ways, institutional tours were orchestrated affairs which were not without certain restrictions and parameters. While many sought to understand the plight of the mentally ill, "sane" citizens could feel unthreatened in the controlled context of visiting and could be assured that employees would intervene if the institutionalized became unruly. Asylum attendants stepped in when necessary, barred windows and doors often separated the institutionalized from visitors, and violent cases were frequently restrained or removed from their presence altogether. The lines could become somewhat blurred at asylum social events such as dances, lectures, or athletic games, yet there was always a clear demarcation between the institutionalized and the visitor.

For many visitors, engaging themselves with the work being done for those suffering from mental illness was closely linked to the ideals surrounding philanthropic pursuits and the notion of "Christian duty." Special events at asylums often attracted members of the public, and the writings surrounding such occasions as concerts, fairs, or dances suggest that citizens were expected to attend as part of their civic duty. However, while events such as sports games were open to all, other events such as dances or holiday parties could be more exclusive affairs in which the invited guests were usually of a certain socio-economic profile (generally, prominent members of the middle class), and the moral obligation in attending such social functions was even more prominent. At the Toronto Asylum in 1847, Superintendent Telfer believed that interaction between asylum patients and the outside world was conducive to the welfare of the former, and he accordingly secured by invitation "the attendance of some of the citizens and their families, whom it was reasonable to conceive, would, each and all, be anxious, so far as in them lie, to aid in a work which promised a wide field, not only for 'the good Samaritan,' but for many good Samaritans."[52] While perhaps attending out of a sense of obligation, one newspaper reporter described the London Asylum Ball as a charitable event that was nevertheless enjoyable to all: "One of the most pleasant events in connection with the routine of Asylum life is the annual ball. For years it has been looked forward to with pleasant anticipation by not only the members of the staff and attendants but many in the city, who have either participated in its festivities, and they desired to be present again, or, having heard of its usually pleasant character, were anxious to be among the fortunate invited." [53] Moreover, a number of visitors speculated that such social events had salutary effects on all participants by revealing the efficacy of kind, gentle treatment, and that they could even transform those who had been drawn to asylums out of "morbid curiosity" and generate compassion and empathy for those afflicted with mental illness.[54] Indeed, whereas many initially thought the lunatic ball to be held in Toronto in 1847 was a "strange and cruel hoax," they found that not only was the evening enjoyed by patients and visitors alike, but that they themselves had broadened their knowledge of insanity and its treatment by interacting with the people in the asylum.[55]

The motives behind institutional tourism reveal that not every "free" member of society would experience his or her visit to an asylum in the same way. For some, spending their leisure time visiting was an opportunity to ridicule the suffering of the confined; for others, it was a means to improve oneself, the confined, or society at large. Nevertheless, whether it was for amusement, education, or reform, the practice reveals a society that privileged the visual and upheld the value of the spectacle in a variety of different contexts and for a variety of different purposes. More importantly, the phenomenon of visiting demonstrates that a substantial number of people in nineteenth-century Ontario sought a closer relationship to the asylums around them and actively endeavoured to better understand the people housed within them, thereby rendering these institutions important and familiar sights in the urban landscape.

Many people in the nineteenth century were fascinated by the growing number of asylums found in Ontario and felt compelled to spend their leisure time inspecting them. Individuals embarked on tours that took them through the corridors, rooms, arid grounds of asylums, allowing them not only to view the conditions the incarcerated experienced but to observe the patients themselves. The public not only read about asylums in contemporary newspapers, periodicals, and fiction, but they also toured and inspected these institutions themselves. Their interiors, therapeutic practices, and inmates were described, analyzed, and recorded in letters, diaries, and articles by people who were not members of the medical elite but who simply believed that asylums represented something remarkable in society. Asylums were important sites that were visited by thousands of people and, in contrast to traditional interpretations, were deeply embedded within the broader culture of the nineteenth century.

The popularity of visiting was maintained throughout the century, and even those superintendents who strongly opposed the practice found it very difficult to entirely exclude casual visitors and to disregard the advantages that institutional tourism offered. Some superintendents wanted to keep casual visitors out of their establishments and sought to bar their entry, yet sightseers continued to be a presence in asylums in spite of these employees' wishes. Visiting did not entirely dissolve boundaries, but its pervasiveness reveals that the asylum walls were frequently penetrated by those on the outside, and that the desire of some superintendents to remove the mentally ill from all contact with the "free" world did not automatically materialize into practice. Officials of institutions could voice their opposition to the practice, but the efforts to abolish visiting usually did not amount to more than being able to set certain parameters, such as restricting the hours in which the institution could be seen by the public. The thousands of people who toured Ontario's asylums reveal that these institutions were not as isolated from society as many have thought, and it is these moments of interchange that allow us to better understand popular perceptions of the insane and the asylum, as well as the impact the general public had upon the development of these institutions. While attitudes of both the public and asylum officials varied, the practice of visiting nevertheless illustrates that the relationship between asylums and the larger community beyond their walls was at times characterized by interaction and fluidity, rather than unilateral segregation and alienation.

NOTES

1. E. Katharine Bates, *A Year in the Great Republic* (London: Ward and Downey, 1887).

2. Archives of Ontario, MU 840 1-D-4, Diary of Thomas Dick (1867-1905).

3. The terms "insane" and "lunatic asylum" are used in this article as part of the lexicon surrounding mental illness in the nineteenth century. Their usage is not meant to be disrespectful of those suffering from mental illness in any way.

4. This article stems from a broader study. See my "'As in a Menagerie': The Custodial Institution as Spectacle in the Nineteenth Century" (PhD dissertation, York University, 2004).

5. Jennifer A. Crets, "'Well Worth the Visitor's While': Sightseeing in St. Louis, 1865-1910," *Gateway Heritage* 20, no. 3 (Winter 1999-2000): 18; Patricia Allderidge, "Bedlam: Fact or Fantasy?" in W.F. Bynum, Roy Porter, and Michael Shepherd, eds., *The Anatomy of Madness: Essays in the History of Psychiatry,* vol. 2, (London and New York: Tavistock Publications, 1985), 24. Similarly, many historians have provided only cursory references to visitors. See, for example, Pamela Michael, *Care and Treatment of the Mentally Ill in North Wales,* 1800-2000 (Cardiff: University of Wales Press, 2003), 88.

6. See, for example, R.D. Gidney and W.P.J. Millar, "'Beyond the Measure of the Golden Rule': The Contribution of the Poor to Medical Science in Ontario," *Ontario History* 86 (1994): 219-35.

7. "Report of the Medical Superintendent of the Provincial Lunatic Asylum at Toronto," *Journals of the Legislative Assembly* (1856), appendix OO.

8. On public views of North American hospitals, see: Judith Walzer Leavitt, "Politics and Public Health: Smallpox in Milwaukee, 1894-1895," in Judith Walzer Leavitt and Ronald L. Numbers, eds., *Sickness and Health in America: Readings in the History of Medicine and Public Health,* 2nd ed. (Madison:

University of Wisconsin Press, 1985), 374. Only in the early twentieth century, with technological and therapeutic changes, would hospitals be transformed into "respectable" and curative institutions used by the middle class. See, for example, Charles Rosenberg, "Community and Communities: The Evolution of the American Hospital," in Diana Elizabeth Long and Janet Golden, eds., *The American General Hospital: Communities and Social Contexts* (Ithaca: Cornell University Press, 1989), 3-17; and Joel Howell, *Technology in the Hospital: Transforming Patient Care in the Early Twentieth Century* (Baltimore: Johns Hopkins University Press, 1995).

9. "Separate Report of Wolfred Nelson for 1861," in *Second Annual Report of the Board of Inspectors of Asylums, Prisons, &c 1861,* Canada (Province), *Sessional Papers,* no. 19 (1862).

10. "Report of the Medical Superintendent of the Provincial Lunatic Asylum at Toronto," *Journals of the Legislative Assembly of the Province of Canada* (1852), appendix J.

11. "Report of C. Widmer, Chairman," *Journals of the Legislative Assembly for the Province of Canada* (1851), appendix J; ibid. (1850), appendix C.

12. London *Free Press,* 8 June 1880.

13. "Report of C. Widmer, Chairman," *Journals of the Legislative Assembly for the Province of Canada* (1852), appendix J.

14. "Report of the Inspector of Asylums and Prisons for the Province of Canada," *Sessional Papers,* no. 19 (1862).

15. S.E.D. Shortt, *Victorian Lunacy: Richard M. Bucke and the Practice of Late Nineteenth-Century Psychiatry* (Cambridge: Cambridge University Press 1986), 26.

16. James E. Moran, *Committed to the State Asylum: Insanity and Society in Nineteenth-Century Quebec and Ontario* (Montreal: McGill-Queen's University Press 2002), 49.

17. "Report of the Medical Superintendent of the Asylum for the Insane, Toronto, for the Year Ending 30th September, 1876," Appendix to "Report of Inspector of Asylums, Prisons, and Public Charities for the Year Ending 30th September, 1876," in Ontario, *Sessional Papers,* 1877, ix, part I, no. 2 (Toronto: Hunter, Rose, & Co., 1877): 208.

18. "Report of the Medical Superintendent of the Maiden Lunatic Asylum," appendix to "Report of Inspector of Asylums, Prisons, and Public Charities

for the Twelve Months Ending 30th September, 1869," Ontario, *Sessional Papers,* 1869, ii, no. 4 (Toronto: Hunter, Rose & Co., 1869): 60.

19. Archives of Ontario, MS 717, Journal of the Superintendent for the Kingston Asylum, 21 September 1882, 157-8.

20. For example, E. Katharine Bates claimed to have toured the Toronto Asylum with Clark, whom she described as "most kind and good-natured" and relying chiefly on "moral control." See Bates, *A Year in the Great Republic,* 26-7

21. Vanessa Schwartz, *Spectacular Realities: Early Mass Culture in Fin-de-Siècle Paris* (Berkeley: University of California Press 1998), 11.

22. Archives of Ontario, John Symons Family Papers, F 786-2.-0-1, box 2, Manuscript book of travels through the United States and Canada West (1852).

23. Judith Walkowitz, *City of Dreadful Delight: Narratives of Sexual Danger in Late-Victorian London* (Chicago: University of Chicago Press 1992), 16.

24. However, this is not to say that the institutionalized passively allowed themselves to be gawked at. Rather, as my dissertation argues, the insane often actively resisted being treated as compliant exhibits and used the presence of strangers to their own benefit.

25. London *Free Press,* 22 November 1880.

26. Toronto Reference Library, Mickle Family Diary, S 27, William Mickle to father, February 1864.

27. Montreal *Pilot,* 1 May 1845.

28. *Bathurst Courier,* 16 August 1850.

29. Susanna Moodie, *Life in the Clearings Versus the Bush* (1853), reprint (Toronto: McClelland and Stewart, 1989), 272.

30. University of Western Ontario Archives, Diary of Dr Charles Sippi, bursar of the London Insane Asylum, 20 September 1893, 20 September 1894.

31. *Bathurst Courier,* 16 August 1850.

32. Pioneering works that correlate the rise of the asylum with social anxiety are David J. Rothman, *The Discovery of the Asylum: Social Order and Disorder in the New Republic* rev. 2nd ed. (Boston: Little, Brown, and Co. 1971), and Michael Katz, Michael J. Doucet, and Mark J. Stern, *The Social Organization of Early Industrial Capitalism* (Cambridge and London: Harvard University Press, 1982).

33. London *Free Press,* c. end of June 1878.

34. *British Whig,* 12 April 1848; Bates, *A Year in the Great Republic,* 26.

405

35. *London Advertiser,* 1 July 1880.

36. *British Colonist,* 29 December 1846.

37. For example, one annual report for the Toronto Asylum stated, "It has been the desire of the Directors to have the Asylum as open to the public as is compatible with the welfare of the patients and the duties of their attendants. Large numbers of visitors have therefore, from time to time, been attended through the building, and these have witnessed the condition of the apartments, the appearance and happiness of the patients, the tender, but effective discipline, which prevails amongst the afflicted and their attendants. The result has been, so far as is known, a universal satisfaction to visitors." See "Report of C. Widmer, Chairman," *Journals of the Legislative Assembly for the Province of Canada* (1852), appendix J.

38. *Annual Report of the Alms House Commissioners, Comprising Reports from the Several Departments Embraced in the Institution* (New York, 1848), 62.

39. John. S. Billings and Henry M. Hurd, *Suggestions to Hospital and Asylum Visitors,* intro. S. Weir Mitchell (Philadelphia, 1895), 5-6.

40. University of Western Ontario Archives, E 16, Black Box 3; R.M. Bucke, Medical Superintendent's Journal.

41. See, for example, *London Advertiser,* 1 July 1880.

42. London *Free Press,* c. end of June 1878.

43. *Sarnia Canadian,* 24 July 1878.

44. John C. Burnham, *How Superstition Won and Science Lost* (New Brunswick, NJ: Rutgers University Press, 1987).

45. "Report of the Medical Superintendent of the Asylum for the Insane, Toronto, for the Year Ending 30th September, 1876," 208.

46. *London Advertiser,* 1 July 1880.

47. *British Whig,* 12 April 1848.

48. *Bathurst Courier,* 16 August 1850.

49. *London Free Press,* 9 June 1898.

50. *Bathurst Courier,* 16 August 1850.

51. For example, see John MacGregor, *Our Brothers and Cousins: A Summer Tour in Canada and the States* (London: Seeley, Jackson and Halliday 1859); and George Moore, *Journal of a Voyage across the Atlantic* (London: Printed for Private Circulation, 1845).

52. *British Colonist,* 8 January 1847.

53. *London Free Press,* 21 January 1881. This particular ball was deemed "the greatest assemblage in the history of the institution" and attracted 125 people from the city.

54. *British Colonist,* 8 January 1847; see also Toronto *Globe,* 9 January 1847.

55. *Toronto Examiner,* 13 January 1847; see also *British Colonist,* 29 December 1846.

Article 3: Awakening a Demand for Schooling: Educational Inspection's Impact on Rural Nova Scotia, 1855–74

Robert Lanning

Nova Scotia's Education Act of 1864 was central to the province's public schooling. Voters had often petitioned governments for wider access to schooling; educators and politicians had come to expect a free school system; and earlier legislation had improved educational provision. But the Act of 1864 had greater uniformity of purpose and was far more advanced administratively than any of a dozen earlier attempts.

The resulting school system was to be centrally organized and managed. State funding was increased, and financial support of schools through local taxation encouraged by offering bonuses to compliant communities. Classification and examination of pupils were regularized, and the Executive Council given authority to oversee matters as the Council of Public Instruction. Crucially, the Act also established a system of inspection[1] through a locally-based inspectorate—a system for producing the knowledge and attitudes necessary for compliant citizenship and social progress.

As early as 1851, William Dawson, the first Superintendent of Education,[2] suggested clerks of each county's Board of School Commissioners might conveniently and cheaply combine their duties with school inspection. Inspection would have a two-fold

Source: Robert Lanning, "Awakening a Demand for Schooling: Educational Inspection's Impact on Rural Noval Scotia, 1855-74," © *Historical Studies in Education/Revue d'histoire de l'éducation* 12, nos. 1&2 (Spring & Fall, 2000): 129–142. Reprinted with permission.

purpose.[3] First, it would be "of great service in stimulating teachers, trustees and people" who had yet to appreciate the value of schooling for their children and its necessity for social progress. In 1854 Dawson's successor, Alexander Forrester,[4] stressed "stimulation" as one of the few tools at the disposal of superintendents to create an appetite for education:

> The primary business of the school is not so much to impart knowledge as to awaken a demand for it, to furnish the means of meeting that demand. If there is no felt want of a thing, no effort will be put forth to get it.[5]

Inspection's second purpose was "collecting educational information" with which the system could be evaluated. Information gathering was haphazard for most of the period between 1851 and 1864. Both Dawson and Forrester in turn made annual tours of the province, which in 1854 was divided into eastern and western districts each assigned one inspector. (Few inspection reports survive beyond the summary comments and data contained in Forrester's Annual Reports.)

A rationale for an inspectorate in a public system of education is suggested in Bruce Curtis's *True Government by Choice Men?* Examining intellectual, political, and administrative preconditions for common schooling and inspection in Canada West, Curtis shows how core interests of the middle class, growing in size and substance, and deriving local power from the political centre, were diffused and supervised by school inspectors. Curtis characterizes inspection as the "development of connections between central authorities and local sites that centred upon knowledge/power relations."[6] The first corps of inspectors in Canada West exercised a certain moral and ideological imperative in its work of information gathering, evaluation of the knowledge-producing and disciplinary functions of schooling, and overseeing relations between social classes. Curtis had earlier forged a convincing argument against the "voluntarist" model of educational reform in Canada and the United States which saw mass schooling as a triumph of local over central (state) interests, and saw inspectors as benevolent overseers. Curtis argued mass schooling was in fact a well-organized political incursion of dominant cultural interests upon the everyday lives of agricultural families, on the children of an embryonic industrial labour force, and on the offspring of the commercial middle class.[7] In what follows I have used Curtis's analysis of Canada West to make sense of Nova Scotia's early history of education and inspection.

Education in Nova Scotia was a distinctly rural activity. Census data for 1861 show 87% of the province's population (330,857 in total) lived on farms or in towns of less than 3000 people; two-thirds of the population lived outside villages (defined as a minimum population of 2000). The political and commercial centre of Halifax, with more than 25,000 people, was the only city in the province that exceeded 5000. Nova Scotia's economy was based in agriculture and natural resources. In 1861, more than half of the labour force were farmers (43%) or farm labourers (10.5%), and through most of the 19th century agriculture grew in importance in the provincial economy. The 1854 Reciprocity Treaty with the United States and the boost in trade during the American Civil War contributed to consolidation and expansion of the agricultural sector. The growth of industry and shipping encouraged migration from rural areas, and contributed to the 18% growth of Halifax between 1861 and 1871—almost equivalent to the population increase for the entire province. Between these census dates the rural proportion of the population remained virtually unchanged (though the agricultural sector declined by about 10%). During the same period, the commercial sector increased significantly, and the comparatively small proportions of the industrial and professional occupations doubled.[8]

Securing a financial base for schooling meant overcoming rural poverty and general doubt of the value of schooling. One task for an agency of inspection was to convince the public that education was vital to economic and cultural progress. But efforts by locally-based inspectors inevitably disrupted familiar rural cultural patterns and generated spontaneous resistance to schooling. The additional function of inspection, then, was to *manage* disruption, challenging the rooted values of agricultural families in the name of the "common interest" of progress.

As represented by inspectors and their superintendents, middle and upper class interests had a future-oriented, enterprising outlook—one that viewed individual success and national progress as integrally related, especially in the new features of industrial and commercial economy. Class values

407

required stabilizing and reproductive social forces under the authority of economically powerful and culturally authoritative groups. The forms of communication at their disposal were crucial in securing their interests since they transmitted the formative goals of dominant social interests into new areas of social life[9]—even if these interests were described as "common" to all Nova Scotians. A major instrument of communication during Forrester's tenure, the *Journal of Education and Agriculture*, treated educational and agricultural intelligence as linked activities. [...]

Toward the Development of Mass Schooling in Nova Scotia

The Nova Scotia legislation of 1808 was the first to encourage school construction and hiring of teachers through a combination of freehold tax assessments and periodically increased government grants. The state tried other forms of encouragement in Education Acts up to the Act of 1866, which finally established compulsory, tax-supported free schools and eliminated education by subscription. Generalized resistance to assessment delayed full systematization of schooling.

Most of the Acts increased numbers of school buildings, teachers, and pupils. The intention was to increase availability of schooling generally, but those who had money benefited most. As in jurisdictions such as Upper Canada/Canada West, dominant classes only slowly saw the necessity of schooling as a means of political socialization.[10][...]

Reluctance to support taxation did not mean complete lack of interest in education. Petitions from hundreds of people around the province to the House of Assembly throughout the 1850s to the mid-60s demanded that schooling be more widely available—without "excessive" financial burden.[11]

During his tenure as Superintendent of Education and Head of the Normal School in Truro, Forrester repeatedly called for province-wide assessment and a system of inspection. Before the Act of 1864, he issued a ten-point appeal to the public outlining the rationale and value of a school system funded through universal taxation, and distributed petitions around the province to gather support. Taxation would equalize access to schooling for all, regardless of property. "This principle," he argued, "is in consonance with the purest equity, and the strictest justice;" and compatible "with the true principles and ends of civil government."[12] Taxation would increase the number of schools and teachers, and universally improve the quality of education. Forrester repeatedly cited the success of Egerton Ryerson in founding such a system in Canada West. Like Ryerson, he saw such legislative measures as "just taxation" producing more than administrative benefits. A school system founded on that basis "will tend to diffuse a spirit of unity and mutual affection among the inhabitants," linking "every man to his fellow men in the obligation of the common interests."[13] Ironically, by the time the Education Act of 1866 entrenched universal assessment, Forrester, arguably the most dynamic force in the establishment of mass schooling in the province, was no longer Superintendent of Education, holding only the position of Normal School principal.

Forrester knew the value of inspection and annually so reminded his political masters. His vision of inspection, put into practice by his successors, was a centrally-organized and managed body of state agents taking educational ideas into the field and reshaping everyday life to conform to the new social institution throughout the province. But in 1857 he "despair[ed] of ever being able to make out an accurate and full tabular statement of all educational statistics, without the appointment of a well-equipped staff" of inspectors. For example, the quality of official knowledge was limited by incomplete reports from trustees. Inspectors could solve this problem by organizing meetings of teachers and parents to press for "harmony" and "uniformity of action."[14] Reporting on a number of visits in 1859, he wrote that the "grand desideratum to give full effect to these visitations is a thorough system of local inspectorship."[15]

The Education Act of 1864 assigned one inspector to each of the 18 counties in the province and a committee of school commissioners to Halifax.[16] Forrester argued in his Report of 1859 that inspectors should be men of "superior Scholarship, and educational enthusiasm, and of considerable practical experience."[17] Thomas Harding Rand,[18] who succeeded Forrester, complained there were not enough qualified men to choose from, but managed to appoint thirteen "classical scholars" and five "good English scholars."[19] Among the 46 men who served as inspectors from 1864 to 1874, eleven were clergy, four members of the bar, and two medical doctors. Inspectors' reports show many others were men with teaching experience, some educational careerists.

Inspection was not a position that men of higher education or professional qualifications held for long periods of time. The average term was about four years. Only two who served in this first decade remained inspectors in 1874. It was a time-consuming and burdensome occupation. Inspectors spent 4 to 5 hours travelling to each school and back, spending only an hour to a half-day actually in the school. As the system developed their workloads increased. In 1865 there were 854 schools in 18 counties; in 1874 the same number of inspectors evaluated 1491 schools—a 75% increase.[20] Each inspector had also to act as clerk to the county Board of School Commissioners, to serve on committees to revise school boundaries and on examination committees, and to lecture on educational subjects in each school section. In 1866 (the earliest year for which complete figures are available), remuneration was based on a percentage of the average of teachers' salaries in each county,[21] plus $1.50 for each semi-annual visit to a school. Thus the average annual salary of inspectors for 1866 was about $422, a little more than one-third the salary ($1200) of the Superintendent of Education. By 1874, the average salary among inspectors had increased to $658.

Taxation as Cultural Conflict

The state's imposition of financial obligation to support schools was a sustained assault on the preservationist attitude of the rural population. Partial assessment in the 1864 Act was intended by the government leader, Charles Tupper, to "render that system as gradually acceptable to the people as it is possible."[22] After the House of Assembly began debating revisions to the Education Act to include compulsory taxation, the demands of petitioners for education changed. In December 1864, for example, 359 residents of King's county signed a request for repeal of the legislation. Such taxation, they wrote, was "at variance with the wishes of your petitioners and in its details, expensive, ridiculous and in many instances oppressive. [...]"[23] Their poor economic situation would be made worse by the Act.

Legislative requirements for education finance provided a convenient avenue by which political and cultural groups encroached upon rural life. Rural resistance to taxation was thus a barometer of rural values and of rural commitment to general progress and improvement. Although government grants to

school sections increased by a third in 1865,[24] the legislation required each section raise an additional amount equal to two-thirds of their grant. Any money required for buying, leasing or building a school house "shall be levied on the real and personal property [...] of the residents."[25] The amount of money raised locally could positively or negatively affect physical facilities, quantity of the educational apparatus purchased for the school, and calibre of teachers hired. Teachers, school buildings, and apparatus—all were perennial sources of inspectoral complaint.

Inspectors' evaluations of local commitment to education were based on an assessment of the quality of education in these areas. In a clear presentation of cultural differences over the value of education, J.B. Calkin, inspector for King's County, scolded parents whose attempts at "improvement" he considered self-serving. Some parents, he wrote,

> will do more to improve their stock, their grains and their roots, than to elevate the tone of society around them; take more interest in the architecture of a stable than of a school house, more pride in a well-groomed horse than a well-educated son.[26]

There is no evidence the state used the courts to enforce assessment legislation. A slower means of "awakening demand"—pressure applied by inspectors—was more desirable and enduring. Inspectors not only policed conformity to law, but evaluated "backward" social values and inappropriate cultural priorities.

Quality of school houses and choice of locations for them showed an under-developed appreciation of the merits of environments specifically suited to educational activity. In the first issue of the *Journal of Education and Agriculture* (1858), Forrester set out criteria for more appropriate sites for buildings and playgrounds.[27] In 1862, he still judged fewer than one-third of school houses acceptable.[28] Special government funding for poor school sections after 1864 did not alleviate the problem. Inspectors continued to chastise the population for unsuitable locations, playgrounds, and outhouses, and "deplorable" structures.[29] The Annual Report of 1866 considered only half the school houses in the province "in good repair;" 26% of the buildings were on unsuitable sites, and one third "without sufficient ventilation." Rev. D.O. Parker, the inspector for Queen's county, argued

409

neat [and] comfortable school houses are a demand of our nature [and buildings] repulsive in all their surroundings with a vitiated atmosphere within [were] poisoning the blood, stupefying the mind and blunting the moral sensibilities.[30]

Inspectors praised or criticized residents of some school sections for their willingness (or lack of it) to raise sufficient funds for the best trained teachers. The Normal School operated from 1855, but graduation from that institution was not required for teaching licenses. The shortage of teachers adequately trained in modern pedagogy was blamed on the "cheapness" of local school commissioners, who often hired those with the lowest level of license and least experience in order to reduce the budget. Although some inspectors praised the work of women teachers,[31] many believed the main reason for their growing predominance in the profession was financial. But commissioners were wrong in blaming trustees for this, since statutes authorized paying women 25–30% less (depending on classification) than male teachers holding the same license.[32] Some inspectors saw this as a future risk to stability in the profession.[33]

To inspectors, appointments of better teachers demonstrated the population's interest in the highest quality of education for their children. Financial difficulty, whether from crop failure or poor fishing, was no excuse.[34]

Properly trained teachers were of little value without the right textbooks and educational tools. The well-equipped school house needed maps, globes, blackboards, ball-frames, and other apparatus. Although such educational instruments were partially subsidized by the Education Department, many school sections still could not afford them. "Good wall maps," as they were categorized on inspection forms, were considered essential. If we divided the number of "good wall maps" by the number of schools in a given year, we arrive at a figure of 2.4 maps per school in 1867, improving to 3.1 per school in 1873. For every 3.7 schools, only one ball-frame could be found in 1867, and one thermometer for every 13.3 schools. Six years later, every 3.1 schools possessed a ball-frame and a thermometer could be found in only one of every eight schools.

Inspectors consistently complained that even when equipment was available, it was poorly used.

A teacher's appropriate use of educational apparatus might be equated with the skilled labourer's use of tools. Nova Scotia's *Journal of Education* compared the teacher to the blacksmith, tailor, and carpenter, "[no] better off for [their] knowledge, unless [they] ha[ve] [...] suitable tools to work with,"[35] Inspectors adopted this analogy to impress upon the rural public, who relied on acquired worklore and effective tools in their own occupations, that skilled and knowledgeable teachers could produce desired results efficiently if the effort were mediated by proper application of the best educational tools.

Blackboards had particular statistical importance in early inspectors' reports documenting total square footage of blackboards in all schools in a county and, from 1867, the annual average square footage of all schools in each county. As inspector McDonnell noted, a teacher properly trained to use the blackboard "adopts the more modern auxiliaries in the work of education."[36] Others reported some schools had good apparatus and blackboard space, but "a majority of the teachers are unable to use them advantageously."[37] Because blackboards could be locally made with painted boards or a mixture of paint, ashes, and oil (a recipe provided by Rand's "Commentary and Explanation" section of the Education Act), inspectors viewed them as an index of the quantity of voluntary labour given to education in the community.

Rev. Armstrong complained that the parents and trustees in his county were not convinced of the value of educational apparatus, and schools without it "remain almost stationary for weeks." Edmund Outram expressed exasperation that inappropriate and poorly made furniture was still in use in many poor sections' school houses, despite the carpentry skills of local people.

> This I consider to be inexcusable in the poor sections, as the people are able to make them for themselves, but the teachers do not seem to understand the utility of this simple apparatus, nor how much time might be gained by the appliance of it.[38]

The burden of providing essentials for the school—well-trained teachers, apparatus, the school building, volunteer labour—thus in great measure fell to local residents, even in school sections formally recognized by the state as needing extraordinary financial assistance. Inspectors worried about the quality and efficiency of the pedagogy used in the classroom,[393] but the underlying concern was for the "underdeveloped" attitude of parents and others to advanced pedagogy and its financial support.

Attendance: Schooling as a Rural Value

The 1861 census included a survey of reading and writing ability. About 43% of school-aged children (5–15) could not read, and 58% could not write. Figures for adults were 22% and 33% respectively.[40] Forrester and Rand repeatedly cited high levels of illiteracy as proof of the need for a more centrally organized system of education in the face of a predominantly rural, subsistence economy that required the unpaid labour of all family members, regardless of age.[41] For the state, the solution lay in compulsory school attendance.

Petitions for educational provision notwithstanding, significant numbers saw little immediate value in forfeiting their children's labour. Popular demand for schooling among the rural population should be interpreted as recognition of the value of such immediately useful knowledge as basic literacy and arithmetic skills. The distant, abstract benefits of schooling would not have been immediately apparent to many under the harsh conditions of Nova Scotian daily life. Inspectors (and others) had to convince the population that schooling was a viable means of social mobility. Popular demand for education was not an open-ended agreement for the state to require or even pressure families to send their children to school all day, five days a week, especially in seasons when their labour was considered crucial. Parents did not anticipate they would be subjected to questioning by an inspector or a teacher when their children were absent from school.

In order to increase attendance, inspectors promoted the class interests they served, equating ignorance with idleness, poverty, and crime, and education with wealth and social stability.[42] Inspector Calkin, for example, wrote of a question he had recently posed to an acquaintance in Boston:

> "You have a large immigration of the scum of all nations, what conservative element do you employ to save you from putrescence?"

"Our schools," he said, "our schools. Here we grind over the children of the vagabond and they come out to fill useful and honorable stations, and frequently they become our most worthy citizens."[43]

Inspectors took irregular attendance as proof that systematic education had yet to be accepted as either personally valuable or socially necessary.

"Dull times dispirit the working class," wrote A.S. Hunt, "and neglect of school is almost sure to follow." Children "thinly clad and poorly shod," especially in winter, publicly displayed their family's poverty—to them a sound excuse for non-attendance. Appropriate clothing and footwear for lengthy treks to and from school, and a presentable appearance of health, demonstrated a family's relative prosperity. The Inspector for Pictou County cited the logic of one citizen at a public meeting: "If you compel them to attend school you must clothe them to make them fit to come, and in some cases you must feed them too."[44]

Some inspectors suggested legislative force be tempered with an appreciation of the rural family's work requirements, R.B. Smith argued:

> There are seasons in the year when it is impossible for the poor man's child to attend school. However, in the summer term exempting two weeks at seed time; four at haying time and Harvest; and a week for potato digging, the remainder of the time might be made compulsory.[45]

Most inspectors reluctantly accepted poverty as an excuse for keeping children at home, whether or not to work. Whatever the demand for children's labour, it was viewed disparagingly as "frittering away their precious time in desultory employment."[46] Parents whose children might devote more time and energy to their crops, their cattle, or fish flakes, saw in them a concrete benefit. Although inspectors feared threatening the sanctity of parental rights,[47] the quality of such parenting was open to question and justified the state's legal authority to substitute as parent. One inspector wrote:

> Our schools are free to all, and if parents will not educate their children, the Government, who in many cases act as a parent, would only show a kindness and confer a

411

benefit by compelling every parent to send his children [to school].[48]

Calls for compulsory attendance grew throughout the 1860s, but it would not be legislated until 1883.

Diffusing the Inspectoral Function

Inspectors represented the state by enforcing the Education Acts, including assessment of community and family commitment to the progress of local schools. As paid agents of the state, teachers' work in the classroom included an important contribution to one of Dawson's original purposes of inspection: collecting educational information. The Superintendent of Education and his inspectors hoped to obtain accurate information consistently through a daily register covering a wide range of pedagogical and managerial categories. An official register was in use as early as 1850[49] and underwent many changes over the years. In 1859, Forrester argued that however necessary inspection might be to accurate statistical information, the first requirement was "the construction of a register that shall embrace the time of the admission and withdrawal of the scholars, their attendance and progress."[50] A more comprehensive register was required by the 1864 Act, and the Act of 1866 emphasized the register as a legal, not merely professional requirement. Teachers were

> To call the roll morning and afternoon and otherwise keep an accurate Register in the manner prescribed by the Council of Public Instruction, on pain of liability to forfeiture of the public grants; the Register to be at all times open to the inspections of the Trustees, Visitors, Examiners, Commissioners, Inspectors and Superintendent.[51]

The register became a feature of the widening intrusion of the state, and a tool to propagate the educational goals of the state and the value-orientation of the superior classes. Teachers' work was to go beyond merely recording attendance to accounting for absence and classifying reasons given for it.[52] Inspectors admonished teachers who "encouraged" absence or lateness as neglecting their right to demand explanations from the families. Inspector Upham, for example, reproached teachers for "carelessness" and "neglect" for failure "to search out and

record the causes of absence." Two years later, he reported the same problem, noting that this function was viewed by some teachers as "a mere vexation."

> But when it is considered what is implied by […] neglect [of the register], [he continued] we must cease to underrate its value, and conclude that he who neglects has not fully measured the extent and demands of his place.[53]

What exactly was neglected? The teacher's training and personal refinement; accuracy was important, but a neat and clean register more so. For Rev. Lawson, inspector for Lunenburg, registers "beautifully kept, reflect[ed] much credit on the care and taste of the teachers." Upham claimed want of neatness and tidiness revealed "a deficiency in early training or in natural taste."[54] The better-trained and higher classified teacher, presumably tidier and more professionally aware of the significance of the knowledge produced in the register, was more expensive to hire. For their part, teachers failed to see how such a simple instrument could overcome problems of uncommitted parents, penny-pinching local officials, and negligent visitors.

The properly kept register, it was argued, kept the school. Inspectors reproached county commissioners, clergy, and others for failure to visit schools regularly, review the register, and tackle problems of attendance and progress. D.M. Welton wrote that if the register were

> blotted, untidy and improperly kept, the school has been disorderly, poorly classified, and made little progress, and the converse [is true]. The use of the Register not only in keeping the attendance of the pupils, but also as a means of stimulating them in progress, in study and good deportment, is becoming better understood and more efficiently turned to account.[55]

In her analysis of registers in Scottish schools, Fiona Paterson[56] claims they were to make visible the efficiency of the teacher and the "institutional profiles" of individual students, and sees the register as one element in production of "a theory and practice of normality." Nova Scotian inspectors saw this educational "technology" as a means by which teachers and other community members could be evaluated on their commitments to the progress of education. The Shelburne County inspector wrote:

If no day were allowed to pass without a visit, the character of the school would soon become known, the ability or otherwise of the teacher apparent, the progress of the pupils exhibited, and an incitement given that would soon be evinced by greater diligence and more rapid improvement.[57]

The properly kept register as a knowledge-producing tool contributed much to educational intelligence in these first years of systematic inspection. But its equally important purpose was reduction of tensions by delegating inspectoral functions of information-gathering and "stimulation" to a broad range of people in the community. The well-kept register did indicate teacher competence in recording daily attendance, the neatness of the pupils, and their progress. But as vigilant and thorough recording progressed weekly, then semi-annually, then annually, cumulative evidence of success or weakness in pedagogy and in community involvement showed the inspector the degree of dedication of "Official Visitors" and others to school visitation, their presence at examinations, the policing of attendance, and the overall quality of school improvement. Inspectors thus diffused responsibility for promoting state interests as interests to be adopted by local populations.

Conclusion

Forrester's 1863 Report reviewed the growing requirements and authority of the state.

The state has a power which no society or church possesses, and is bound to use it; for her self-preservation is no longer believed to depend on the stolidity and ignorance of the industrial population, but on the enlightenment and morality of all classes. [...] What interference can there be with the liberty of the subject in demanding that parents educate their children so long as they are at liberty to send them to any teacher and bring them up in whatsoever religious belief they please? [58]

Inspection communicated changing social relations to all parts of the province and to all sectors of the population: broadly in terms of economic and political demands, more specifically in the normative prescriptions and expectations of everyday life. To much of the population schooling became something more than children learning the three Rs. As it was introduced, schooling came to mean interference with established patterns of work and family, and the necessity to re-structure everyday life in conformity to new and more powerful conventions determined elsewhere.

With increasing economic power and the corresponding legislative authority embodied in the state, the formation of the public system of education signalled its right to encroach upon local and familial terrains. The state's incursion through schooling and inspection was meant to produce positive attitudes to schooling, as valuable for individual development and for social progress. State action and the work of its local agents did not provoke organized resistance to schooling or to the scrutiny of everyday life, but they laid the ground for increased awareness of competing social interests and the relative powers behind them.

NOTES

1. *Journal of Education* 1 (September, 1866): 2. For a history of the early years of this publication, see *Journal of Education* 1, 1 (October, 1951): 5–16.
2. On Dawson's career, see P.R. Eakins and J. Sinnamon Eakins, "Sir John William Dawson" in *Dictionary of Canadian Biography*, vol. 12 (Toronto, University of Toronto Press, 1990), 230–37; Susan Sheets-Pyenson, *John William Dawson: Faith, Hope and Science* (Kingston-Montreal; McGill-Queen's University Press, 1996).
3. W. Dawson, Superintendent's Annual Report [hereafter, A.R.] (Nova Scotia, Dept. of Education, 1851), 13. Superintendent's Annual Reports from 1851 to 1864 were published in the Appendices of the Journal of the House of Assembly; from 1865 Reports were also printed separately and included county inspector's reports and statistical tables. Hereafter, references will name the inspector, county, year of Superintendent's report, and page numbers.
4. On Forrester's career, see Judith Fingard, "Alexander Forrester," *Dictionary of Canadian Biography*, vol 9 (Toronto: University of Toronto Press, 1976), 270–73.
5. A. Forrester, A.R., (1862), 2.
6. Bruce Curtis, *True Government by Choice Men?* (Toronto: University of Toronto Press, 1992), 19.

7. Bruce Curtis, "Policing pedagogical space "Voluntary" school reform and moral regulation," *Canadian Journal of Sociology* 13, 3, (1988): 283–304.

8. Industrial and related occupations accounted for about 15% of the labour force in 1861, and the professions about 2%. See, Census of Nova Scotia (Halifax, 1862); Census of Canada 1870–1871, vol. 1 (Ottawa, 1873), 427; Bryan D. Palmer, *Working Class Experience: Rethinking the History of Canadian Labour, 1800–1991*, 2nd ed. (Toronto: McClelland and Stewart, 1992), 84; R. T. Naylor, *Canada in the European Age, 1453–1919* (Vancouver: New Star Press, 1987), 298–301, 385.

9. Ibid., 48, 63.

10. Bruce Curtis, *Building the Educational State: Canada West, 1836–1871* (London: Falmer Press, 1988); Alison Prentice, *The School Promoters* (Toronto: McCelland and Stewart, 1977), 66–84.

11. Public Archives of Nova Scotia [PANS], RG5, Series P, vols. 75–8.

12. A. Forrester, "Address to the People of Nova Scotia on the Support of Common Schools," (n.p., 1860), 13,15.

13. Forrester, "Address …", 12, 15. On Ryerson, see Prentice, *The School Promoters,* 124–7.

14. Forrester, A.R. (1862), 3, 10, 17.

15. Forrester, A.R. (1857), 53; A.R (1859), 249.

16. The Superintendent's A.R. included statistics, but only a summary from the Chair of the City Board of School Commissioners; thus, far less information is available for Halifax schools.

17. Forrester, A.R. (1859), 258.

18. On Rand's life, see A. Laidlaw, "Theodore Harding Rand," *Journal of Education* (Nova Scotia), Part I (March, 1944): 207–18; Part II (April-May, 1944): 235–334; M. Conrad, "An Abiding Conviction of the Paramount Importance of Christian Education" in R.S. Wilson, ed., *An Abiding Conviction: Maritime Baptists and their World* (Saint John, N.B.: Acadia Divinity College), 155–95, and "Thomas Harding Rand," *Dictionary of Canadian Biography,* vol. 12 (Toronto: University of Toronto Press, 1990), 879–83.

19. Rand, A.R (1864), 1.

20. These figures were reached by averaging the number of schools open in the winter and summer terms, excluding schools in Halifax.

21. In the previous year salary was based on a percentage of the total county grant.

22. Beck, *Politics of Nova Scotia,* 158.

23. PANS, RG5, Series P, vol. 77, petitions numbered 97–104, 107–11, and 117–20.

24. The 1866 A.R. showed that the government had steadily increased grants in relation to "money raised by the people" since 1856. For every dollar raised by the people in 1856, the province contributed 40 cents; in 1866 the province contributed 81 cents.

25. Nova Scotia, An Act for the Better Encouragement of Education (28 Victoria, Cap.29) (Halifax, 1865), 83; Beck, *Politics of Nova Scotia,* 161.

26. J.B. Calkin, King's, A.R. (1865), 114.

27. "Choosing a Site," *Journal of Education* 1,1 (July. 1858): 4.

28. Forrester, A.R. (1862), 5.

29. Rev. J. Christie, Cumberland, A.R.(1865), 88. E. Outram, Cape Breton, A.R. (1866), 65, blamed local trustees: H.C. Upham, Colchester, A.R. (1867), 13, reporting on outhouses, did "not believe that any tribe of Indians would permit their children to be so exposed as they are at some schools …"; F.J. Farish, Yarmouth, A.R. (1873), 68–9, blamed parents for not voting sufficient funds, and wrote that he had seen little improvement in his nine years service as an inspector.

30. Rev. D.O. Parker, Queen's, A.R. (1867), 36.

31. H.C. Upham, Colchester, A.R. (1868), 52; Rev. W.H. Richan, Shelburne, A.R.(1870), 41; R. Somerville, King's, and D. McDonald, A.R. (1871), 10 and 20 respectively. See also *Journal of Education* 2, 1 (June, 1859), 10–11.

32. Nova Scotia, Act to Amend the Act for the Better Encouragement of Education (29 Victoria, Cap.30) (Halifax: Queen's Printer, 1866), 61.

33. S.R. Russell, Guysborough, A.R. (1867), 32; H.C. Upham, Colchester, A.R. (1868), 51–52; L.S. Morse, Annapolis, A.R. (1873), 17.

34. Several inspectors make references to these problems in the A.R.'s for 1867 and 1868.

35. T.J. Chapman, "School Apparatus," *Journal of Education* (Oct 1870): 518; see also A.S. Hunt, A.R. (1870), 36.

36. J. McDonnell, Inverness, A.R. (1865), 74; W. Eaton, King's, A.R. (1867), 33–4.

37. C. MacDonald, Victoria, A.R. (1865), 72.

38. Rev. G. Armstrong, Annapolis, A.R. (1866), 38–39; E. Outram, Cape Breton, A.R. (1869),41.

39. On the use of blackboards and other apparatus, see Alison Prentice, "From Household to Schoolhouse: The Emergence of the Teacher as a Servant of the State," *Material History Bulletin* 20 (Fall, 1984), 22.

40. A. Forrester, A.R.(1862), 4. The Census showed that nearly 52% of the population was under 20 years of age. The age commonly identified as school age (5–15 years) on inspection forms made up about 26% of the population; the age group 6–16 years, as reported in the 1871 Census, comprised 25% of the population.

41. D. Campbell and R. A. McLean's *Beyond the Atlantic Roar* (Toronto: McClelland and Stewart, 1974), 122.

42. H.C. Upham, Colchester, A.R. (1866), 15; T.H. Rand, A.R. (1867), xxii; Rev. W.H. Richan, Shelburne, A.R. (1868), 15 and (1871), 13; J.Y. Gunn, Inverness, A.R. (1869), 31, A.S. Hunt, A.R. (1873), xxiii.

43. J.B. Calkin, King's, A.R. (1865), 116.

44. A.S. Hunt, A.R (1874), x–xi; H.C. Upham, Colchester, A.R. (1866), 12–13; P.J. Fillieul, Digby, A.R. (1867), 43; D. McDonald, Pictou, A.R. (1870), 59.

45. R.B. Smith, Colchester, A.R. (1871), 53.

46. H. Condon, Halifax, A.R. (1873), 56; see also, D.M. Welton, Hants, A.R. (1866), 31; P.J. Fillieul, Digby, A.R (1867), 43; Rev. W.H. Richan, Shelburne, A.R.(1868), 15–16; E. Outram Cape Breton, A.R. (1869), 42; Rev. G. Armstrong Annapolis, A.R. (1870), 64.

47. E. Outram, Cape Breton, A.R. (1866), 65; T.H. Rand, A.R. and Rev. W.S. Darragh, Cumberland, A.R.

48. A. Munro, Victoria, A.R. (1873), 30; In the same year, inspector Lawson proposed "a small fine ... on parents of absentees." (45)

49. Campbell and MacLean, *Beyond the Atlantic Roar*, 140.

50. A. Forrester, A.R. (1859), 243–244.

51. "Explanations of the New Register," *Journal of Education* (September 1867): 144–46.

52. *Journal of Education* (Sept., 1867): 145–6.

53. H.C. Upham, Colchester, A.R. (1868), 52, and (1870), 99.

54. W.M.B. Lawson, Lunenburg, A.R. (1868), 19; H.C. Upham, Colchester, A.R. (1869), 35.

55. Rev. D.M. Welton, Hants, A.R. (1867), 25, and (1868), 10.

56. Fiona Paterson, "Measures of Schooling: registers, standards and the construction of the subject," *Journal of Historical Sociology* 1, 3 (1988): 278–300.

57. A.C.A. Doane, Shelburne, A.R. (1873), 33.

58. T.H. Rand, A.R. (1863), 5.

415

GENDER, RACE, AND SEXUALITY IN COLONIAL BRITISH COLUMBIA, 1849–1871

Lynne Marks
University of Victoria

GENDER, RACE, AND SEXUALITY IN COLONIAL BRITISH COLUMBIA, 1849–1871

Introduction by Lynne Marks

418

INTRODUCTION

Lynne Marks

British Columbia has sometimes been characterized as "The West beyond the West," a far and very different part of Canada. This module demonstrates that in the colonial period British Columbia's society was indeed quite different from that of the rest of Canada. However, as Adele Perry's work here suggests, it is not enough to examine British Columbia simply in the context of the rest of colonial British North America, soon to be Canada. Instead the colony needs to be studied in the broader context of the British Empire. Perry's work, which is part of a newer "transnational" focus among many historians, demonstrates that patterns of gender, race and sexuality in British Columbia were not that different from those in other far-flung parts of the British empire, and that like many other colonials, most British Columbians did not live up to British imperial ideals. The First Nations population remained in the majority for the colonial period and, given the nature of British Columbia as a resource frontier, particularly a gold mining frontier, among the non-Aboriginal population men dramatically outnumbered women. These demographic realities helped to create what respectable middle-class white colonists and British imperial observers alike saw as two major social problems: a rough male "homosocial" culture, in which men lived, worked, and socialized primarily with other men, and a high proportion of intermarriage between white men and First Nations women.

While both "rough" male culture and intermarriage were identified as problems by most middle- or upper-class white observers, people focused on different issues, demonstrating a range of attitudes on racial issues. Edmund Verney, a young upper-class naval officer posted in Victoria in the early 1860s, wrote very critically about the marriage of the governor of the colony, Sir James Douglas to Lady Amelia Douglas Connolly, whose mother was First Nations and father a fur trader. For Verney, such marriages set a bad example, and did not allow the governor to play the role in "refined" society that should be expected of him. Miss Sophia Cracroft, who visited the colony in 1861, was less overtly critical, but also clearly saw the Governor's wife and daughters as "different" because of their Aboriginal heritage. Cracroft was liberal in the context of her time, as seen in her critique of segregation by race within certain B.C. churches, but her strong Christian beliefs, which underlay her reformist views, also led her to be intolerant of Jewish concerns about religion in the schools.

The Rev. Matthew Macfie, while decrying the existence of any intermarriage between races, and supporting the segregation of European and African American worshippers within Christian churches, was willing to marry First Nations women and white men, as a way of trying to bring such marriages into what he saw as a more moral, Christian context. Macfie, while very fearful of what he saw as the dangers of "racial mixing" for the purity and superiority of the British "race," reserved his most scathing comments not for First Nations people, but for the "rough" white men who he felt treated First Nations people violently and unfairly, and introduced them to all of the vices of the white community. Macfie was also appalled by the lack of interest in Christianity among many new settlers in British Columbia. Macfie's attitudes were not that different from that of many clergy in British Columbia, who felt they had the right, and indeed the duty, to try to convert Aboriginal peoples to Christian beliefs, and to "civilize" them to European norms, but who reserved their most scathing attacks for the "near savage white man."

Many efforts were made to "civilize" the white man in British Columbia and to force him to adhere to dominant norms. The formation of temperance organizations intended

419

to reduce drinking, and the setting up of clubs and reading rooms to provide rational and respectable recreation, had only limited effectiveness in converting the rough miners of the period from their pleasure in gambling and drinking. While some of these miners enjoyed the freedom from religious and family strictures made possible in British Columbia, others felt differently. James Thomson's letters home reveal both his piety and his distress at leaving his family behind when he came to British Columbia. For Thomson, and probably many others, such separation could be justified only by the hope of "striking it rich" in the Gold Rush, or at least making enough money in other ways to improve life back home.

While various attempts were made to transform the behaviour of rough white men in British Columbia, probably the most well known were the active efforts by the colonial elite to bring white single women to British Columbia, primarily to become the wives of the white working-class men who were such a concern. White middle-class reformers believed that white wives would serve to "civilize" the rough working-class men of the province, end the "disgrace" of mixed marriages, and help to make British Columbia a fit part of the British empire. As a result, local groups of middle-class reformers organized in collaboration with the London Female Emigration Society in Britain to bring over single women in the 1860s. The first of these "bride ships," the *Tynemouth*, brought over 60 single or widowed women in 1862. As the article from the *British Colonist* of that period made clear, there was great excitement at the ship's arrival, suggesting that while the many of the rougher men may not have sought to be "civilized" through marriage to white women, they may have sought wives among the new arrivals.

While the organizers of these immigration schemes may have viewed the importation of British women primarily for their roles as future wives, middle- and upper-class women in British Columbia also hoped to find servants among the new immigrants. Sophia Cracroft felt that the ladies of the colony were the "most to be pitied" as they had no reliable supply of servants, and often had to do all of their own housework and childcare, something that would have been unthinkable in England.

Some scholars of other societies where white women have been in the minority, such as New France, have suggested that such demographic patterns could give women major advantages. In other work she has done, Perry does not agree with this rosy picture. In parts of *On the Edge of Empire* not excerpted here she suggests that the white women who came to colonial British Columbia, either on the "bride ships" or in other ways, did find it easier to get married than they might have in either Britain or eastern Canada. At the same time, however, they tended to be much younger than their husbands, exacerbating power imbalances that would have already existed between husbands and wives in the Victorian period. White women in British Columbia, being so much in the minority, could feel quite frightened and vulnerable among so many men. They often recorded feelings of loneliness, as their own racism made relationships with First Nations women difficult or unthinkable, while white women who could serve as friends and companions were usually few and far between. As well, while most of these women settled into heterosexual marriages, some women avoided marriage altogether, and found other, often less respectable ways of making a living, thus challenging the assumption that the importation of white women would solve British Columbia's "social problems" and make the colony a more fit member of the British empire.

QUESTIONS

1. Do Macfie, Verney, Cracroft, and Thomson's writings provide support for Perry's arguments, and, if so, in what ways? Do they illuminate any aspects of colonial B.C. society that Perry does not discuss? If so, what aspects?

420

2. According to Perry, what is wrong with the way historians have understood B.C. history in the past? What new approaches does she propose to use to deal with these problems? Did you find these approaches useful? Why or why not?

3. What does Perry see as the most significant demographic issues in colonial British Columbia? What impact did she think they had on the nature of B.C. society?

4. How does Perry view the homosocial male culture of colonial British Columbia? Were you convinced by her arguments? Why or why not?

5. Whose voices do we hear in Perry's work? Whose voices do we not hear, and why? Is this a problem?

6. Macfie argues that people tend to be more irreligious in the colony of British Columbia. Why does he think this was true, and why do you think this was the case?

FURTHER READINGS

Barman, Jean, *The West Beyond the West: A History of British Columbia* (University of Toronto Press, 2007).

Loo, Tina, *Making Law, Order and Authority in British Columbia, 1821–1871* (University of Toronto Press, 1994).

Lutz, John, *Makuk: New History of Aboriginal-White Relations*, (UBC Press, 2008).

Perry, Adele, *On the Edge of Empire: Gender, Race and the Making of British Columbia, 1849–1871* (University of Toronto Press, 2001).

Sandwell, Ruth, *Beyond the City Limits: Rural History in British Columbia*, (University of British Columbia Press, 1998).

▲ Document 1: Society in Vancouver Island and British Columbia

Matthew Macfie

Matthew Macfie was a British Congregational minister who served on Vancouver Island from 1859 to 1865. His racial attitudes may have been quite typical for the time. On the one hand, he challenged a fellow congregationalist minister who believed that African-Canadian and white settlers should not be segregated within the local Congregational church. As a result, Macfie started a segregated church for the white Americans who would not worship alongside African-Americans. On the other hand, he defended his right to marry Aboriginal women and white settler men, even if the women were not Christian, an attitude opposed by certain other clergy in the colony. He wrote The Far Western Frontier *to provide information about the colonies of Vancouver Island and British Columbia to prospective British immigrants.*

It was remarked by an intelligent shipmaster, whom I met in Victoria, that he had not found in any of the numerous ports he had visited during a long sea-faring career, so mixed a population as existed in that city. Though containing at present an average of only 5,000 or 6,000 inhabitants, one cannot pass along the principal thoroughfares without meeting representatives of almost every tribe and nationality under heaven. Within a limited space may be seen—of Europeans, Russians, Austrians, Poles, Hungarians, Italians, Danes, Swedes, French, Germans, Spaniards, Swiss, Scotch, English and Irish, of Africans, Negroes from the United States and the West Indies; of Asiatics, Lascars and Chinamen; of Americans, Indians, Mexicans, Chilanos, and citizens of the North American Republic; and of Polynesians, Malays from the Sandwich Islands [Hawaii].

Among the many remarkable matrimonial alliances to be met with, I have known Europeans married to pure squaws [common derogatory term for Aboriginal women], Indian half-breeds and Mulatto females respectively. One case has come under my observation of a negro married to a white woman, and another of a man descended from a Hindoo mother married to a wife of Indian extraction. A gentleman of large property, reported to be of Mulatto origin, is married to a half-breed Indian. From these heterogeneous unions, and from illicit commerce between the various races just enumerated, it is evident that our population cannot escape the infusion of a considerable hybrid offspring. [...]

It is to be feared that these varieties of humanity do not occupy our soil and multiply their kind, in every instance, without detriment to that type which we desire should preponderate. What is to be the effect, upon that section of posterity which will, in future centuries, inhabit the British North American shores of the Pacific, of this commingling of races so diverse in physiological psychological, intellectual, moral, religious, and political aspects? Circumstances of climate, scenery, race, and natural productions have combined to determine the particular mould in which the thought and life of other peoples, ancient and modern, have been cast. What then will be the resultant of the manifold and unequal forces operating in the formation of distinctive national characteristics in these colonies? This is an interesting and momentous problem which coming ages alone can solve.

Source: Matthew Macfie, *The Far Western Frontier: Vancouver Island and British Columbia, Their History, Resources and Prospects,* (Arno Press, New York, 1973, reprinted from 1865 edition) 378–81, 406–8, 414–17, 461–62, 471.

In description of resources Vancouver Island may resemble the parent country, and thus merit the proud title of 'the England of the Pacific.' But the peculiar elements composing the *nucleus* of the population render it physically impossible for that exact form of national character we have been accustomed to ascribe to Great Britain to be perpetuated in the island of the Far West. Does the presence, so largely, of inferior races forbode the fatal tainting of the young nation's blood and signal its premature decay, or will the vitality of the government race triumph over the contamination with which more primitive types threaten to impregnate it? This is the important enquiry that engrosses the attention of ethnological speculators in the nascent communities of the North Pacific.

It is gravely argued by some that to the Caucasian race has been assigned supremacy over the rest of mankind; that no new combination of distinct existing races can improve its towering excellence; that in proportion to the rapidity with which deleterious elements are introduced, must in course of time be the ratio of its degeneracy and final extinction. [...]

Single young men, many of them well connected and possessing a good education, form a large portion of the population. The habits of some indicate them to have been 'black sheep' in the domestic fold at home; others of good reputation are sometimes to be found, who fail in success for want of the tact, energy, and endurance requisite to conquer the difficulties peculiar to colonial life. Others are distinguished by an indomitable spirit that smilingly breasts the passing wave of misfortune; they never lose an affable and modest bearing, or a regard for integrity, under the most trying disappointments, but pursue their aims in the unfaltering assurance that victory, though delayed, will eventually reward their struggles. The beams of a prosperous future are reflected in the glance of such men, and the community instinctively makes way for their promotion.

If, however, there be any vulnerable point in the character of the young and inexperienced colonist, it is certain to be hit by the arrow of temptation. It is impossible for the imaginative youth, surrounded with the blandishments of fashionable English life, the associations of the Church, the proprieties of the debating club, or the restraints of fond relationship, to over-estimate the fiery trial that awaits him, when thrown like a fledged bird from the maternal nest into the society of strangers, for the most part selfish, and interested in the 'greenhorn' only as far as they can profit by the attentions they pay him. Should his concern for speedily entering a money-making career outweigh that better judgment which compasses its end by cautious measures and slow degrees, and looks out first for a right start, nothing is more probable than that he will be pounced upon by those disguised falcons that are ever on the watch for such a quarry. Once persuaded by their sophistry that under their counsel he is on the high-road to wealth, he will be induced, in his imagined shrewdness, to accommodate himself to their habits, under the impression that the flattering compliment he thus shows will have the effect of quickening their *disinterested* zeal in his behalf. He complacently argues within himself: 'These persons are evidently smart; but how fortunate I am to be smarter still, and able to manage them!' The speculation into which he has been lured, of course, bursts; his obliging friends (!) have got all they wanted out of him, and he is left to console himself as best he can under his losses. If of an excitable nature, he is likely to drown his sorrows in something stronger than water. It is, alas! the old and oft-told story.

But the picture has a reverse side. Should favourable prospects open up, exceeding, as sometimes happens, his most sanguine expectations, one of the nervous temperament just described might be tempted to find vent for his gratification in a *symposium*, graced by the presence of those 'jolly good fellows' that, like swallows, flutter around one in the sunshine of prosperity, but disappear when the winter of adversity approaches. Over the mortal remains of how many promising characters, wrecked on the shoals and reefs

423

against which friendly warning has been given above, have I been called to perform sad offices! Many still meet one's observation in the streets of Victoria, who, unless a merciful Providence interpose, are doomed to the drunkard's grave. Frequently have I been delighted to see the beneficial change effected by marriage, in arresting the progress of dissipation. It is only to be regretted that the paucity of respectable females in Vancouver Island and British Columbia limits so much the opportunities of single men who desire to cultivate domestic virtues, [...] Happy will it be, [...] for the comfort and morals of young men, when the 'shanty' life, involving the inconvenience of cooking with their own hands, and the restaurant, which fosters home feelings to even a smaller extent, are more generally displaced by lodging-houses, kept by private families, at moderate rates, and in the style familiar to clerks and warehousemen in England. [...]

Society in the interior is very depraved. In Yale, Douglas, Lytton, Lilloet, Forks of Quesnelle, and the mining towns, little trace of Sunday is at present visible, except in the resort of miners on that day to market for provisions, washing of dirty clothes, repairing machinery, gambling, and dissipation. Out of the 5,000 souls in Victoria, a few may be found who respect the ordinances of religion. But at the mines, adherents of religious bodies have hitherto been numbered by scores and units.

Up to the present there have been but two places of worship in Cariboo—one connected with the Church of England, and the other with the Wesleyan Methodists. Till the fall of 1863, when these were built, the services of public worship were conducted in a bar-room and billiard-saloon. At one end of the apartment was the clergyman, with his small congregation, and at the other were desperadoes, collected unblushingly around the *faro* or *pokah* table, staking the earnings of the preceding week.

Profane language is almost universal, and is employed with diabolical ingenuity. The names of 'Jesus Christ' and the 'Almighty' are introduced in most blasphemous connections. Going to church is known among many as 'the religious dodge,' which is said to be 'played out,' or, in other words, a superstition which has ceased to have any interest for enlightened members of society. A saloon-keeper, in one of the up-country towns, finding that business had been dull in his establishment during the previous week, and hearing the sound of the church-going bell one Sunday evening, was seized with an erratic wish to attend Divine service, under the impression that, possibly, the policy he had resolved upon might have the effect of improving his liquor traffic. Anxious for sympathy in the good work, he thus addressed a number of miners that were lounging on the premises: 'Come, boys; business has been flat this last week; we must try the religious dodge to-night; every man that's willing to go to church, come up to the bar and take a drink.' This novel and tempting premium had the result desired. [...]

Religious scepticism prevails to a remarkable extent, as it does in all new countries. I have known cases in which Christian pastors have been turned away from the bedside of the dying colonist, and forbidden by him either to offer prayer to Almighty God for his restoration to health, or administer the consolations of the Gospel. But I trust such cases of extreme obduracy are not common. [...]

The only occasions on which the extreme penalty of the law has been put in force since the advent of the whites in Vancouver Island have been in connection with Indian atrocities. In one case, a Songhish native was executed for the murder of a sailor belonging to one of Her Majesty's ships. This man, on his way from Victoria to Esquimalt, in a state of inebriation, one evening entered the dwelling of his destroyer, and attempted to take liberties with the squaw of the Siwash. The latter, stung by the insult, stabbed the sailor. Doubtless the verdict of the jury and the sentence of the Court were according to the evidence, but the provocation ought to have been accepted as in some degree palliative of the bloody deed. It is questionable whether, had the crime been committed by one white man against another under like circumstances, the claims of justice would have been exacted with so much rigour. Nine-tenths of the outrages perpetrated by natives upon the superior race, and supposed to be the result of insensate cruelty, can be traced to some wanton violation of the personal or domestic rights of the Indians on the part of the whites. This assertion receives melancholy verification on the other side of the American boundary, where inhuman 'rowdies' are known to esteem the life of a native as of no more consequence than that of a dog, and sometimes to shoot him down for the depraved gratification, as it has been expressed, of 'seeing him jump.' But even on British territory the principal and immediate effect of contact between the representatives of civilisation and the aborigines has been that 'fire-water,' debauchery, syphilitic disease, and augmented mortality have been introduced. Appalling as the anomaly may appear, it is nevertheless uniform that the nation which professes to bring into a virgin colony the blessings of the gospel in one hand, carries a moral Pandora box in the other; accomplishing the physical and moral ruin of the primitive inhabitants, whose interests, gratitude and respect should prompt it jealously to guard. [...]

Subsequently to the tide of immigration in '58, and until the removal of a bridge that formerly connected Victoria with the Indian encampment on the opposite side of the harbour, I have witnessed scenes after sunset calculated to shock even the bluntest sensibilities. The fires of Indian tents pitched upon the beach casting a lurid glare upon the water; the loud and discordant whoopings of the natives, several of whom were usually infuriated with bad liquor; the crowds of the more debased miners strewed in vicious concert with squaws on the public highway, presented a spectacle diabolical in the extreme. Even now [...] the extent to which the nefarious practices referred to are encouraged by the crews of Her Majesty's ships is a disgrace to the service they represent, and a scandal to the country. Hundreds of dissipated white men, moreover, live in open concubinage with these wretched creatures. [Aboriginal women, primarily those defined as slaves in First Nations communities]

▲ Document 2: For Friends at Home—Letters from the Cariboo Gold Rush, 1862

James Thomson

For Friends at Home is primarily a collection of the letters of James Thomson (1823-1895). He was born in Scotland, where he first worked as a baker's apprentice. He emigrated to Canada in 1844. In an effort to make money he went to the California gold fields in 1850—making more money from working as a baker and a lumberman than from gold—and came back to Canada with enough money to purchase a farm on the St. Lawrence River. In 1862 Thomson, who was not very prosperous in his farming, decided to try his luck in the goldfields again, this time in the Cariboo in British Columbia. This time, however, he had no success, and returned home to his wife and family no wealthier.

PROSPECTING IN
THE CARIBOO
To Mary Thompson 27 July 1862
Williams Lake, British Columbia.
July 27th 1862.
My Ever Dear Mary,

I have so much that I wish to say to you that I really hardly know where to commence. It is now two months and a week since I wrote to you from Victoria. Since that time till a week ago last night I have never been a week in one place. Part of the time 480 miles and am now 360 miles from a post office. An express messenger is expected to pass this place some time this week and I intend to embrace the opportunity of sending this by him. No doubt you will be looking anxiously for a letter before you receive this. But Oh Mary think of my feelings in that respect. Not a word have I heard from the loved ones at home since the morning of the 7th of April. Amidst all the toil and anxiety and privations experienced in this country that is hardest of all to bear. Would to God I knew how you all were. I expect to hear soon as I have made arrangements to have my letters forwarded from New Westminster to this place as I expect to remain here a few weeks.

By the mercy of a kind providence I have enjoyed uninterrupted good health and amidst the scarcity and high prices of provisions I have still had enough to eat. I suppose before this reaches you you will have heard of many a disappointed Canadian returning from this country with hard news from *Cariboo*. We too have had had our share of toil and disappointment, but in order to set your mind at ease concerning us I will now give you a short sketch of our travel since I last wrote to you from Victoria May 20th.

We left Victoria at noon on 20th May, reached the mouth of Frazer River at dark. On account of the high water and drift-wood floating down we anchored all night and ran up 15 miles to New Westminster next morning. There we changed Boats and had to wait till next day at noon for a steamer to Yale, distance 100 miles. The river is very rapid. We got to Emery Bar 5 miles below Yale on the morning of the 24th. Here the passengers and horses went ashore and walked to the town, while the boat, lightened of part of her load managed to stem the swift current with the freight. We got to town about noon. They were celebrating

Source: *For Friends at Home: A Scottish Emigrant's Letters From Canada, California, and the Cariboo 1844–1846*, Richard Arthur Preston, ed., (Queen's University Press, 1974). Reprinted with permission from the Estate of Richard Preston.

the Queens birthday by music and horse racing. We remained in Yale over Sunday. Rev Mr Browning preached twice. He called at our tent, after service and was very friendly.

Yale is at the head of steamboat navigation. Above it the river rushes at a rapid rate through a narrow channel of almost perpendicular rocks. The Trail of foot path winds along the mountain side sometimes at a fearful height above the river. We had 600 lbs of provisions on board the Boat, expecting to get it packed from Yale but when we got there the mules were all engaged. So we each took what we could carry, sold the balance and started on foot for a journey of 380 miles. We travelled 13 miles that afternoon and 22 miles the next day which brought us to Boston Bar. Here they had commenced work making a waggon road which is intended to run from Yale to the mines. As it was still early in the season to go to the mines the roads bad and provisions scarce and dear, we concluded it was better for some of us to remain. Accordingly Anson, James McIlmoyl, Irvine Raney and Smith from Mountain hired with the contractor for one month while Picken, Thos Harbottle and myself should go on to Cariboo and prospect.

I find that I have not paper enough to give you an account of my journey. Three weeks travel brought us to Forks of Quesnell (322 miles from Yale). We went 60 miles beyond the *Forks* to Antler and Williams Creek where some of the richest diggings are but did not succeed in finding any gold. We dug several holes, but like hundreds of others were unsuccessful. The ground is nearly all taken up and holes being dug but only a few claims are paying and they are very rich, which has given rise to the excitement about Cariboo. Every one seems to be convinced that this country has been greatly misrepresented both as an agricultural and a mining country. No doubt new discoveries will be made and much gold found but this season provisions will be so dear that very few will be able to stay long enough to prospect thoroughly When we were at Antler Creek, Flour, Beans, sugar, Salt & Rice were each one dollar per lb. Fresh Beef 50 cents & Bacon $1.25 6/3 and at Williams Creek a quarter of a dollar was added to the price of each. Just think of Two hundred & fifty dollars for a Barrel of Flour and everything else in proportion. We could not stand it long.

When we left the Boys the agreement was that at the end of a month they should come on after us and we would meet them at Forks of Quesnelle a month after we got there. Accordingly we returned to that place and found Anson & Irvine waiting for us. [...] When we met we concluded that it was no use trying to prospect any more at present, but go down where provisions were cheaper and work at any thing we could get to do. Accordingly we left the Forks a week past on Thursday and got here on Saturday night, staid over Sunday and on Monday morning took a job of building a clay oven for Mr Davidson proprietor of a Farm, Store & Tavern. He is newly settled here and is doing business in a large tent. Is now preparing to build a house and we will furnish the Lumber & Shingle. Here Flour is 60 cents 3/per lb milk 7/6 per gallon Beans 3/3 Bacon 4/ per lb.

[...] You can tell the friends of all my partners that they are well. The only sickness we have had in this country is some times an attack of Home sickness, and if we could only get some letters from home would be the best prescription for that disease. [...]

With heartfull respects for all I am ever,
Your Devoted Companion
James Thompson

Mary my Beloved Companion, I have written you quite a long letter, It may be that you will have to read some of it to enquiring friends. I would now wish to have a little talk between ourselves. Oh Mary were you by my side I have much that I would like to say. Mary I have thought of you more, prayed for you more, and if possible loved you more this summer than ever before. Volumes would not contain all the thoughts I have of Home and the loved ones there. Mary I often wish that I had more of your courage and energy and resignation to battle with the disappointments of life. I sometimes wonder how I ever came to leave a kind and affectionate wife and all that the heart of man could desire of a family to sojourn in this land. But then the thought comes up that we were poor, that you had to deny yourself many of the comforts of life that a little money would have secured, and then I think of my poor old Father toiling and labouring when he ought to be enjoying the evening of his days in ease and comfort. Then I pray God to strengthen my arm and encourage my heart and bless my exertions to procure the means to make you comfortable. Our prospects at present are rather poor for making much, yet I cannot say that I regret coming to this country for God has softened my heart and enabled me to see myself in the gospel glass as I never did before, and I never yet have been able to get over the conviction that God in His providence pointed it out as my duty to come. If so, good must come although it may not come just as we would wish. Mary continue praying for me, keep up your spirits, be cheerful and happy. We have much to be thankful for. May God enable us to be truly grateful.

Mary, I really hardly know what to think about this country I cannot make up my mind to remain long away from home and then to think of returning without making something, to be as poor as when I left and in debt besides, and it might be to be laughed at into the bargain is hard to think of. To think of bringing you to this country unless it were to Victoria, is out of the question, I cannot say much about Victoria, but for this upper country if it were nothing else than mosquitos and bad water I would never think of settling here to say nothing of bad roads and poor society. I sometimes think that I would like to go home, sell half my farm, build a little cottage for you to live in and stay with you and Minnie and the boys and let the world laugh and talk as they please. Then again I think if by staying here a little longer I would make enough to pay my debts and build the cottage it would be so much better. But I will not decide till I hear from you. I expect to go to Victoria in the Fall, when we can correspond regularly and I will be able to get your views on the subject.

What troubles me most is how you are to put in the long cold winter in that old house. Could you do anything by papering it to make it warmer? Could *Aunty* paper her house to keep out the wind some? I hope to be able to send you some money perhaps by Christmas to help you to rig up for winter. Try to get warm clothing for all.

I suppose the children have forgotten all about Pa. Tell them I have not forgotten them. I have got a Bible lesson for them to learn, I hope to hear them repeat it yet. Oh if God would enable one to return and hear Minnie repeat that verse I would be a happy man.[...]
J.T.

Mary, Although we take fits of homesickness, you must not think that we are always down-hearted. We are quite cheerful some times. I have not been half so lonesome since I met Anson and Joe at the Forks, and there we see so many that are worse off than ourselves that we cannot but be thankful. [...]

July 28th 1862
Mary, I have just got supper and am sitting on the smoke to keep away the mosquitos. We do our own cooking and sleep in our tent at the job we have now. We can make about six dollars a day each, but our provisions cost us about two dollars per day each.

Will have several weeks employment perhaps longer. [...] Great marchers are still passing down from the mines scarcety of provisions is their general cry.

[...] We all send our complements to every body [sic].
Good night
J.T.

▲ Document 3: Vancouver Island Letters of Edmund Hope Verney, 1862–65

Private
Not to be copied

> *Lieutenant Edmund Hope Verney, a young upper-class Englishman, was com-*
> *mander of the gunboat HMS Grappler on Vancouver Island between 1862 and*
> *1865. While on Vancouver Island he wrote regular letters to his father, Sir Harry*
> *Verney, a British MP, about many aspects of the early colony.*

H.M.S. Grappler, Esquimalt.
July. 20. 1862.
My dear Father,
I want to give you some idea of the necessity for a new Governor here, and drag-down-wards that the present Governor is. Yesterday there was a pic-nic in a bay on the harbour here, and I went thereto. [...] when he [the Governor] first came here, about a dozen years ago, he brought a niece with him to instruct him and his wife and daughters in the ways of the fashionable world, [...] she [...] at last married Mr. Young; in virtue of Mrs. Douglas being a half-breed, and her daughters quarter-breeds, Mrs. Young considers herself, and is considered by many, the leading lady in the island [...]

The governor's eldest daughter, a fine squaw, is married to the speaker of the House of Commons [Vancouver Island House of Assembly], Dr. Helmkin [Helmcken], an infidel, but the Governor and he have not spoken to each other for years: Mrs. Helmkin however, was there.

The governor's second [actually fourth] daughter eloped to Washington territory with Mr. Goode, a laddy-da government clerk; she is always correcting her sisters for not being sufficiently lady-like, but they can hardly be worse than herself: Mr. Goode was at the pic-nic, but not his wife.

The governors third daughter is perhaps the best of the lot, she is a fat squaw, but without any pretence to being anything else; very good-natured and affectionate, but not affected: she married a Mr. Bushy, who is, I think, Recorder of British Columbia [...]

Of the governor, I can only say that he is a wonderful man; considering that he has had no education, and knows nothing of the world, he deserves great credit for all he has done for the colony; he is thoroughly kind-hearted and pompous, but the colonies have now reached a stage so much beyond him, that he is a great drag on them: for instance, yesterday afternoon, he conversed chiefly with a man who is living in open adultery with an Australian woman, and who ought not to be admitted to decent society: this was all very well in the days of the Hudson's Bay company, when they encouraged their servants to co-habit with native women to keep up trade, but now it shocks refined people, and turns the balance the wrong way, with those who are not very decided.

Mrs. Douglas is a good creature, but utterly ignorant: she has no language, but jabbers French or English or Indian, as she is half Indian, half English, and a French Canadian by birth.

129

Have I not depicted a sad state of society? It would be a great stride for the colony to get a new governor, who might come out with enlightened feelings and ideas, and a lady for his wife, but Governor Douglas be removed with great kindness: it would not be right to hurt his feelings, for he has done much for the colonies: Colonel Moody is far from a perfect being, but he has done much towards raising the tone of British Columbia [the mainland colony, separate from Vancouver Island], which is much more English in feeling: New Westminster is but a small town of huts in a clearing of the forest, but I would far sooner live there than in Victoria, for there are more English feeling, more English Sabbath-observance, and less American democracy and equality: among that very small society reigns good-feeling, gentlemanly-kindness, and courtesy, and one can look up to such men as colonel Moody and his officers of Engineers. [...]

Although I feel competent to speak positively on few points, I do venture to say that the Governor is a great drag on the colony, and I can say this the more freely, because he is always extremely friendly to me, and is really a very good, kindhearted sort of man: with the democratic American feeling here, and the general immoral influence of the Hudson's Bay company, a refined English gentleman is sadly wanted at the head of affairs: a man who is perhaps living with a woman who is not his wife may be seen in intimate familiar conversation with the Governor, or even met at his table: then, really, for Mrs. Douglas and her daughters, the less said the better: I do not conceive that I can do any good by recounting instances of their ignorance & barbarism.

▲ Document 4: Lady Franklin Visits the Pacific Northwest, 1861

Lady Franklin was an upper-class British woman, the widow of well-known Arctic explorer Sir John Franklin. She was 68 at the time of her first visit to Vancouver Island. The letters are written by her husband's niece, Sophia Cracroft, who was 44 during her visit with Lady Franklin to Vancouver Island. Miss Cracroft was Lady Franklin's constant companion in those years, and shared her liberal Anglican views, as well as her sense of adventure.

Victoria

As might be supposed, one element in the motley population of Vancouver's Island, is the negro, or coloured class—the term "coloured" is not applied to the Indian, but only the negro race. You know that everywhere in America, they are treated as unworthy to be in contact with whites except as utterly inferior beings. They have separate churches & separate schools, & the mixture of races which is often pointed out to you in the American common schools never includes the negro. The same exclusive system was attempted to be introduced here in consequence of the American prejudice—the Americans threatened to withdraw their children from the schools if the coloured children remained. The Romanists yielded—so also the Independants—that is the home authorities of that body; upon which their minister resigned & another was sent out.

The same feud was excited in the Church [Church of England] schools, but the Bishop was not likely to give way upon such a point, and his firmness met with its reward—the threatened withdrawal of the other scholars never took place, and we saw the unmistakeable descendants of negros, in Mrs Woods' little school of 30, side by side with the English and American girls. This struggle has not been very long past, & at one time seemed serious. The Independants have since thought fit to revoke their former instructions, & their minister here now admits all alike.

Another difficulty the Bishop encountered, was with the Jews attending the schools. The basis of the teaching is essentially Christian, and no pupil is exempt from direct religious instruction from the Bible, but it is permitted to them to refrain from learning the Catechism if they desire it. This however did not satisfy the Jews who are pretty numerous here, and and after some passive opposition on the part of their children such as not bringing Bibles like the rest, & not answering the questions put, the parents threatened to remove them. The Bishop could not consent of course to deprive the schools of their distinctive *Christian* character, & again he gained all by firmness, for they were not removed—and now (Mr Woods reports) they are even forward in answering the questions he puts. [...]

We had a good many visitors & did not go out, being already engaged to dine out today with Mr & Mrs Dallas. He is a director of the Hudson Bay Company, resident here, at the head of the affairs of the Company in Vancouver's Isd; & he has married a daughter of the Governor. Mr. Douglas is the Governor (the first of course) who has been since a very

431

Source: *Lady Franklin Visits the Pacific Northwest: Being Extracts from the Letters of Miss Sophia Cracroft, Sir John Franklin's Niece, February to April 1861 and April to July 1870.* Victoria, British Columbia, Provincial Archives of British Columbia, Memoir No. XI, 1974. Edited, with an introduction and notes, by Dorothy Blakey Smith. Reprinted with permission from Royal BC Museum, BC Archives. Memoir No. XI, 1974.

young man, in the service of the Company through all its stages, & therefore thoroughly acquainted with the Upper Country of North America, from Canada, northward, and westward to the Pacific. His wife is a half caste Indian, and he has 6 children of whom Mrs Dallas is the 2nd.

Mrs Dallas is a very natural, lively & nice looking person, just 22—her face is exceedingly agreeable if not quite pretty, but the Indian type is remarkably plain, considering that she is two generations removed from it. She has a very bright complexion, pretty dark eyes & the other features very tolerable—but the great width & flatness of the face are remarkable, & even her intonation & voice are characteristic (as we now perceive) of the descent. We had a very pleasant evening, & like them both very much.

Thursday Feb. 28. We were engaged today to take luncheon with the Governor's wife Mrs Douglas, in place of paying her a formal visit. Have I explained that her mother was an Indian woman, & that she keeps very much (far too much) in the background; indeed it is only lately that she has been persuaded to see visitors, partly because she speaks English with some difficulty; the usual language being either the Indian, or Canadian French wh [sic] is a corrupt dialect. At the appointed time, Mrs Dallas came to introduce a younger sister Agnes, who was to take us to their house. She is a very fine girl, with far less of the Indian complexion & features than Mrs Dallas. Considering the little training of *any* kind these girls can have had, it is more wonderful they shd [illegible] be what they are, than that they should have defects of manner. They have never left Northern America, nor known any society but such as they now have—in fact they are only now, during the last 2 years since the colony began to encrease, within reach of any society at all beyond that of the usual few employés of the Hudson Bay Co attached to a fort.

The Governor's house is one of the oldest in the place—Mrs Douglas is not at all bad looking, with hardly as much of the Indian type in her face, as Mrs Dallas, & she looks young to have a daughter so old as Mrs Helmkin [Helmcken] the eldest, who is 26. Her figure is wholly without shape, as is already Mrs Helmkin's we hear, & even Mrs Dallas. She has a gentle, simple & kindly manner wh[illegible] is quite pleasing, but she takes no lead whatever in her family, & the luncheon arrangements & conduct, rested only with Agnes & Mr & Mrs Young, in the absence of the Governor. [...]

Hope *Sunday March 10*
We had promised to share the Pringles' early dinner, and adjourned therefore to their little dwelling with which we were much pleased, from the perfect order in which it is kept. Mrs Pringle has retained her English habits as far as possible, & the result is very evident. All the furniture & fittings are of the most ordinary kind, but the books were far more numerous than in other houses. She has 3 very nice little girls with a full share of the bloom which all the children get in this healthy country. She is just about to lose her only servant—a woman whom she brought from England, & made the great mistake of believing her the right person to engage, because the woman had already been in America! So the positions of mistress & servant have been for some time nearly reversed. Mrs Pringle finds her lying on the sofa in the little drawing room where she continues to take her ease, notwithstanding the entrance of her mistress! At another time she prefers the arm chair with a newspaper which she continues to read as long as it suits her! The other day she accused her mistress of telling "a lie" which was more than could be endured, so Mrs Pringle gave her notice to leave; & will replace her (?) by a young Indian girl from Mr Garrett's school if he can select one willing to go to Hope. You can imagine the task of training before her!

New Westminster

Tuesday. March 12. There is no steamer come as yet from Vancouver's Isd so we, as well as the Governor, are detained & likely to be so for some 2 or 3 days. Upon the pathway, Mrs Moody takes her 5 children day by day, & Mrs Grant her 2 little ones. Each lady has to be her own head nurse, if not *sole* nurse—but Mrs Moody is fortunate in having a young girl as a governess—just sufficient to teach her little ones (the eldest only 7) the beginnings of book learning. Miss Nagle of course shares whatever Mrs Moody has to do, as she wd [illegible] do in her own home; *all* the ladies here taking it for granted that they must do without servants or at least *may* have to do so. Mrs Moody & Mrs Grant each has her baby to carry, but are often relieved by a stray gentleman; & the babies are quite used to this. It is quite common to see gentlemen carrying the children, out of natural pity for the mothers!

   Tuesday. March 14. Mr Sheepshanks & Mr Knipe dined here today, as also Mr & Mrs Bacon who have lived a long time in California. She has no children & no servant of any kind—& her house is quoted as a very pattern of order & cleanliness. In the evens we had quite a party—of gentlemen only of course. We had been much amused at dinner, by the exclamations of wonder at seeing *4* ladies. We were assured that none of the party had seen such a thing before in New Westminster as 4 [white] ladies at a dinner party.

   Altogether this visit to Vancouver's Isd & British Columbia has been a very pleasant, as well as deeply interesting one, and we trust to see the colonies encrease in prosperity—the foundation of which must be laid in emigration from England, or at least from English colonies, so as to absorb (or at least outweigh) the American element. As for servants, they will obtain immense wages for a long time to come. The mistresses unfortunately will have to put up with a great deal, as they will be only too glad to get their services whether efficient or not.

   It is the ladies who are most to be pitied as they must absolutely & unreservedly devote themselves to the smallest cares of every day life—at any rate they must *expect* to have their hands so filled day by day & be prepared for the worst. But there is a set off to this in the fact that all are in the same predicament & there is not the least pretence to anything better. There is not a single lady in the colony who has a nurse, a cook, & a housemaid, so she has to be one of these, if not all three—this state of things saps mere conventionality at the very root—strong friendships are formed, and people are ready to help one another.

▲ Document 5: The British Colonist: The Arrival of the *Tynemouth*

Friday Morning, Sept. 19, 1862.

[...]

ARRIVAL OF THE "TYNEMOUTH."—This fine, iron steamship left San Francisco on the morning of the 12th and cast anchor in the mouth of Esquimalt harbour at 8 1/2 o'clock night before last. She [...] brings 242 passengers and 200 tons freight; and yesterday entered Esquimalt harbour, where the freight will be discharged. When the vessel left England there were 270 passengers on board—62 of whom were females. One of the latter (a widow named Elizabeth Buchanan) died two days before the vessel reached the Falkland Islands, where she was buried. She was of the number sent out under the auspices of the London Female Emigration Society. Thirty-four of the male passengers left the vessel at San Francisco—some of whom were accidentally left behind by the steamer. As a matter of course, we went aboard the steamer yesterday morning and had a good look at the lady passengers. They are mostly cleanly, well-built, pretty looking young women—ages varying from fourteen to an uncertain figure; a few are young widows who have seen better days. Most appear to have been well raised and generally they seem a superior lot to the women usually met with on emigrant vessels. Taken altogether, we are highly pleased with the appearance of the "invoice," and believe that they will give a good account of themselves in whatever station of life they may be called to fill—even if they marry lucky bachelor miners from Cariboo. They will be brought to Victoria and quartered in the Marine Barracks, James Bay, early this morning by the gunboat Forward. A large number of citizens visited Esquimalt yesterday and endeavoured to board the vessel, but were generally ordered off and returned from their fruitless errand with heavy hearts.

Source: Excerpts from *The British Colonist*, Friday Morning, September 19, 1862.

■ Article 1: On the Edge of Empire

Adele Perry

Introduction: Analysing Gender and Race on the Edge of Empire

Mid-nineteenth-century British Columbia hung precariously at the edge of Britain's literal and symbolic empire. A three- to six-month sea voyage separated the colony from its imperial headquarters, and a substantial portion of North America stood between British Columbia and its closest colonial cousins, Red River and the Canadas. The society that developed in this far-flung shore also hovered dangerously at the precipice of Victorian social norms and ideals. Racially plural, rough, and turbulent, British Columbia bore little resemblance to the orderly, respectable, white settler colony that imperial observers hoped it would become. [...]

Between 1849 and 1871 British Columbia's gender and racial character challenged normative standards of nineteenth-century, Anglo-American social life. First Nations people outnumbered whites dramatically, and within the small white community, males outnumbered females even more sharply. White male homosocial culture and mixed-race heterosexual relationships were common and persistent reminders that British Columbia fell short of Victorian standards. [...]

Rather than treat British Columbia as a wholly unique entity, this study emphasizes how it fits within a broader context of European colonialism.[1] British Columbia shared much with other British colonies like Australia and New Zealand that were economically and socially tied to resource extraction and politically committed to settlement. It had more common ground with the colonial societies of India and Africa than scholars have generally acknowledged. British Columbia's status as a white society may seem obvious in the late twentieth century, but it was not so in the nineteenth century. This supposed obviousness is also more an artefact of the success of imperialism than a sign of its absence.

Source: Selections from Adele Perry, *On the Edge of Empire: Gender, Race and the Making of British Columbia, 1849–1871* (University of Toronto Press, 2001). © University of Toronto Press Inc., 2001. Reprinted with permission of the publisher.

But to reckon with British Columbian history as colonial history goes against the grain of much popular and scholarly tradition. As Cole Harris had recently pointed out, white British Columbians are reluctant to recognize home-grown colonialism and instead 'associate colonialism with other places and other lives.'[2] Canadian historians as a whole are even less enthusiastic. In the 1930s, historian George Stanley did analyse colonization, albeit in whiggish and altogether laudatory terms—the unrelenting march of Western civilization, Stanley assures his readers, necessarily vanquished the 'primitive' Métis rebellions of 1869 and 1885.[3] Possibly in reaction to such celebratory accounts and certainly in response to a general postwar discomfort with colonialism, historians have largely abandoned discussions of imperialism in favour of analyses of settlement. Inasmuch as this term suggests that nobody was there, it subtly depoliticises the process whereby white people came to dominate First Nations territory. [...]

In the eventful years between 1849 and 1871, British Columbia went from a diverse, First Nations territory to a fur-trade colony, to a gold-rush society grafted on a fur-traded settlement, to a resource-oriented colony with an emergent settler society. People have lived and developed complex cultures on northern North America's Pacific coast at least since 12,000 BC. But British Columbia was born in the first half of the nineteenth century, the awkward and disappointing child of the fur trade and British imperial expansion. Explorers pushing the limits of European geographical reach visited the Pacific coast from 1778 onwards, travelling a path that would be followed by British, American, and Russian traders.[4] Their approach was matched by the arrival of the land-based fur trade in the first decades of the nineteenth century. Before 1849 no European power asserted a conclusive territorial claim, but Harris is correct to argue that the fur trade established a 'protocolonial' presence in the interests of profit.[5]

Based on the politics of fear and, after 1821, the strength of Hudson's Bay Company (HBC) monopoly, this protocolonial presence asserted itself in a territory that was both densely populated and culturally complex. While earlier estimates put the First Nations population at contact at roughly 100,000, scholars now estimate the population as hovering between 300,000 and 400,000.[6] Speaking over thirty-four distinct languages and possessing distinctive political, and economic structures, Aboriginal society in British Columbia defies broad generalizations.[7] The most salient division was probably between the large, highly structured, hierarchical, and rank-oriented cultures of the coast, and the smaller, egalitarian societies of the interior. Yet even this rudimentary distinction masks significant cultural, economic, political and historical differences.[8] While historians debate the impact of early contact and trade, it is safe to state that the fur trade reorganized First Nations trade patterns, cultural practices, and political alignments, and brought new diseases and intensified existing ones.

Formal colonial authority established on Vancouver Island in 1849 transformed a protocolonial presence to an overtly colonial one. But British Columbia remained firmly at empire's edge. As Jack Little notes, Britain colonized Vancouver Island because, in spite of declining interest in North America, it wanted a political foothold on the northern Pacific. Britain's desire for political presence was reconciled with fears of financial commitment when the old colonial system of the Caribbean was evoked and the HBC was granted proprietary rights to the island. Between 1849 and 1863 the colony slowly acquired all the constitutional trappings of settler colonies, namely, a governor and bicameral legislature.[9] While comprehensive white settlement of the island remained a vague goal, what Richard Mackie dubs 'a viable colony' did develop along local lines.[10]

The discovery of gold on the mainland's Fraser River profoundly shifted the trajectory of British Columbia's colonial project. Thousands of miners, chiefly American, arrived in the sparsely colonized and loosely organized colony in the spring of 1858. 'Never perhaps was there so large an immigration in so short a space of time into so small a place,'[11] opined one journalist. A transient, shifting gold-rush economy was thus awkwardly affixed to the existing fur-trade society. Politically, this simultaneously raised the possibility that British Columbia might be home to a white society and suggested that it might be neither British nor law-abiding. In response, the Colonial Office established a separate colony on the mainland and declared Vancouver Island Governor James Douglas governor of the new colony. It was not until 1863 that British Columbia would be granted a Legislative Council with a limited 'popular' element and a separate governor. In 1866 Vancouver Island was effectively absorbed by the mainland, the united colony retaining the name British Columbia but the island capital of Victoria. The colony joined Canada as a province in July 1871 and brought the colonial period to a close.[12]

These perambulations of the colonial state were motivated by the hope that an agricultural, white settler society akin to the Canadas or Australia would emerge in British Columbia. This chequered social and political history suggests how, despite these hopes, British Columbia remained on the edge of empire. Established during a low point of imperial expansion, the colony received limited financial, military, or political support from Britain. While it slowly acquired the administrative accoutrements of a British settler colony, settler colonies are fundamentally premised on the existence of a large and relatively stable settler population. Drawing and retaining such a white society to British Columbia proved a slow and profoundly difficult process.

The continued demographic dominance of First Nations people stands as the sharpest evidence of the local colonial project's fragility. In 1855 Douglas estimated Vancouver Island's white population at 774.[13] Numbers of non-Aboriginal people peaked during the Fraser River gold rush and again during the Cariboo gold rush of 1862–4. Yet it remained concentrated in a handful of colonial enclaves, most notably Victoria, New Westminster, Nanaimo, and in shifting interior towns on the Fraser River, throughout the Cariboo and along fur-trade routes. It never came close to rivalling the First Nations population. As late as 1871 observers estimated that the Aboriginal population on the mainland alone was roughly 45,000, while the 'settled' population of *both* the mainland and island was only 19,225.[14] Shifts in white–First Nations population ratios were caused not as much by natural growth or white immigration as they were by Aboriginal deaths. Disease, especially during the massive small-pox epidemic of 1862, took its toll: there were twice as many Aboriginal people on the eve of the Fraser River gold rush as there were in 1870.[15] Even aided by such population decline, the colonization of British Columbia occurred slowly. As Jean Barman argues, it was only in the fin de siècle that the 'fragile settler society on the frontier of the western world became a self-confident political and social entity.'[16]

The smallness of the setter population was matched by its diversity. Most colonists came from the United States and Britain, and smaller proportions hailed from Canada, Australia, and continental Europe. But colonization was never an all-white endeavour. Kanakas or Hawaiians settled in the wake of the fur trade, African-Americans clustered in Victoria and Saltspring Island, and the Chinese gravitated towards colonial centres or interior mining towns: in 1865 one observer put Quesnel's population at one hundred white men and one hundred Chinese.[17] This racial and ethnic heterogeneity was a characteristic that British Columbia shared with other settler societies.[18] Struggles to assert the whiteness were articulated not only in response to the Aboriginal population, but in relation to non-white and more especially non-British settlers.

Whatever their background, settlers worked in an unstable, resource-oriented economy centred around, but never entirely dominated by, the gold economy. The fur trade continued, and underground coal mining was initiated at Nanaimo and Fort Rupert. Commercial agriculture, attempted since early days of the HBC's Pacific trade, was stimulated by the demands of the trade in gold. Lumbering and fisheries employed a small workforce, but large-scale exploitation would not occur until the advent of new technology.[19] As the boom of the gold rushes faded, the economy diversified. In 1865, 72 per cent of the paid labour force was concentrated in the mining industry, while by 1870, 61 per cent of the waged labour force was in other occupations, about half of them in agriculture.[20]

British Columbia's emergent class structure reflected the significance of imperial ties, the importance of resource industries, and the continued influence of the fur trade. Three groups competed for the role of colonial elite. A tightly interwoven fur-trade cabal, with deep and often familial ties to Aboriginal society, maintained their significant political power throughout the colonial period. Led by men such as Douglas, Roderick Finlayson, W.H. Tolmie, and John Work, this faction of the bourgeoisie were also major landowners, especially around Victoria.[21] Their right to rule was constantly contested by a self-styled 'reform' group energetically if informally represented by journalist-politician Amor de Cosmos and his Victoria newspaper, the *British Colonist*. Frequently with Canadian, Maritime, or American roots, this aspiring elite had ties to the gold and merchant economy and a firm belief in the colony's potential as an agricultural, white settler society.[22] Anglican Bishop George Hills led a third elite. Connected to British missionary agencies

and with meaningful support from naval circles, they sometimes sided with the fur trade or reform party, and sometimes they used their considerable ideological muscle to challenge the legitimacy of both.

As traders, reformers, and clerics struggled for the upper echelon of colonial society, ordinary white men and women created the outlines of a working and middle class. A nascent, highly mobile, male, working-class culture was created as sailors, loggers, labourers, tradespeople, and especially gold miners combined independent commodity production with wage labour. In interior towns and urban enclaves—especially in the off-season—young, white, working men were a loud and sometimes disturbing presence. Their rough culture provided a convenient 'other' for the emergent middle class to construct itself in opposition to. Made up largely of shopkeepers, petty government officials, merchants, schoolteachers, and other 'middling' folk, this small middle class was centred in Victoria and, to a lesser extent, New Westminster. Through reform work, they were beginning to constitute themselves as a separate and identifiable class, although one that regularly spilled over into both working-class and elite society.

Settler society had a distinct gendered character as well as a racial and class one. British Columbia's settler society was overwhelmingly and persistently male. The resource industries that nurtured the colonial presence in British Columbia were gendered male here as elsewhere in the nineteenth-century Western world. Fur trading, gold mining, and the other trades that fed colonial British Columbia fundamentally depended on the back-breaking labour of men, especially young working-class ones, and it was young men that constituted the overwhelming bulk of migrants to this edge of empire. Colonial policies, while nominally devoted to securing a more gender-balanced settler population, did not counter the social patterns forged by economy and society. Contemporaries remarked regularly on the paucity of white women on both the mainland and the island, an impression that is reaffirmed by the available statistics. According to James Douglas's 1855 census, Vancouver Island was home to 150 white females over the age of fifteen compared with 338 males of the same age.[23] The female proportion of the mainland's settler population was considerably smaller. Women hovered at somewhere between 5 and 15 per cent of the white population on the mainland

437

between 1861 and 1865. Following the decline of the gold economy after the Cariboo rush and the incorporation of Vancouver Island into British Columbia, the percentage of women in the white population eventually rose, but only to the 1855 levels of about 30 per cent.

Most of the white female population was concentrated in Victoria and, to a lesser extent, New Westminster. An 1870 census recorded 1,645 white males and 1,197 white females in Victoria or roughly three women for every four men. In New Westminster there were 891 white males to 401 white females, or four women for every nine men.[24] In the colony's upper country, white women were truly a tiny minority. In the Cariboo in 1864, one observer estimated the white population at five hundred men and thirty-four women, or one woman to fifteen men.[25] There were four white women to twenty-seven white men in Lytton in 1861, while eight years later a colonial counter found 460 white males and 89 white females there.[26] That things were not substantially different in agricultural Vancouver Island is suggested by an 1864 census that found eight white women and forty-nine white men in the Comox Valley.[27]

The society that developed in colonial British Columbia was one that substantially departed from Victorian social norms and ideals. It was hard to reconcile an overwhelmingly male, racially diverse settler society living among a much larger First Nations population with mid-nineteenth-century dreams of sober, hard-working men, virtuous women, and respectable families. This social disruption was measured in numbers, but felt in everyday social interaction. Some white women complained of loneliness and social dislocation, while others remarked on the apparent maleness of social life. [...]

White male homosocial and mixed-race heterosexual relationships were the sharpest symbols of what happened to gender and race on this edge of empire.

Chapter 1

'Poor Creatures Are We without Our Wives': White Men and Homosocial Culture

In May 1862 a young Englishman named Charles Hayward sat in the Victoria home he shared with two male companions. 'We manage very well in our little Cabin,' he wrote. One man lit fires and prepared meals. The other two spent their days labouring in a building shop. But Hayward, who would later become mayor of Victoria, was uncomfortable doing his own marketing on Saturday nights, and more troubled still to be without his beloved female partner, Sally. 'Poor creatures are we without our wives,' he told his diary.[28] The combination of loneliness, competence, and mutuality that characterizes Hayward's experience says much about white men's relationship to race, gender, and the making of colonial society. In settler British Columbia, in the years between 1849 and 1871, customary gender relations were disrupted by the overwhelming demographic dominance of men. One result of this disruption was that white men developed a rough homosocial culture that existed side-by-side and occasionally overlapped with the mixed-race community. It did not challenge male power, but it did provide an alternative practice of racial and gendered identity.

The mid-nineteenth century witnessed the refashioning of dominant ideologies and practices of both masculinity and race throughout the English-speaking world. Middle-class masculinity especially was recast in the mould of the self-controlled, temperate, disciplined, and domestic patriarch. While this process was in many respects particular to the middle class, its implications were substantially broader. For the working classes, Wally Seccombe has persuasively argued, this ideal found expression in the male breadwinner norm, which mandated that men ought to earn sufficient wages to enable women and young children to live in uninterrupted domesticity.[29] Simultaneously, notions of racial difference hardened under the influence of imperial expansion and 'scientific' theories of race and racial hierarchy. Interracial sex was increasingly constructed as necessarily dangerous, and a vision of valiant imperial manhood circulated throughout popular culture.[30] The cumulative result was the creation of a dominant white masculine ideal in which European men were complete only when living in heterosexual, same-race, hierarchical unions.

The racially plural milieu and overwhelmingly male character of British Columbia's settler society rendered these ideals at best difficult to achieve. Alternatively, they encouraged and nourished a vibrant culture formed among and by white men. This homosocial culture was not entirely unique and had approximate equivalents in other cultur-ally diverse societies with resource-extractive econ-omies and heavily male populations like Australia, California, or Northern Ontario. Yet it was at heart a local phenomenon, with deep roots in the Fraser River gold rush of 1858 and the Cariboo gold rush of 1862–4. Some of its components reworked dominant gender norms and practices, while others recon-firmed them. Whether challenging or conforming to dominant norms, this homosocial culture was forged out of the everyday social relationships located in male households, friendships, and sexuality, and practices like labour, drinking, gambling, violence, and ideologies of racial solidarity and exclusion.

Reworking Masculinity: Male Households, Friendships, and Same-Sexuality

Male households were a key component of homo-social culture throughout colonial British Columbia. To create homes without white women was to chal-lenge increasingly hegemonic concepts of gender and domesticity. In what Mary Poovey has called the 'binary logic' of nineteenth-century gender sys-tems, women were assigned the domestic and moral spheres, while men weathered the capitalist economy and liberal polity. [...]

Popular literature routinely promoted male house-holds as an appropriate adaptation to the insurgen-cies of immigrant life. John Emmerson, a middle-aged British miner, suggested that groups of six, including one experienced miner, were ideal for Cariboo-bound immigrants. Others advised farmers to do the same.[31] Authors made clear that the goals of group immigra-tion were not simply economic since group living ensured among other things that the sick would be 'carefully tended.'[32]

Whatever the advice, white men joined together to create households both in and outside the cities. Probably because of the colony's imminent entry into Confederation, an Esquimalt police constable took a door-to-door census of Victoria in the spring of 1871. Recorded in dull pencil at the back of a note-book, this relatively untapped source found that over one-third of Victoria's homes contained no resident females whatsoever, even though Victoria's white female population was proportionately much larger than elsewhere. It also suggests important varia-tions in male households. Most housed a solitary white man, while a significant minority were group

households made up of two or more white men. Chinese and Black men displayed not entirely dis-similar residential patterns, while First Nations men were less likely to live alone. Men did not necessarily live in same-race groups: there were at least eleven mixed-race male group households.[33]

The form as well as membership of male house-holds varied. Most miners' homes in 1858 Victoria were reported to be 'simple tents,'[34] and canvas remained a common building material throughout the colonial period. In 1861 a magistrate found a few log cabins in the mining town of Antler, but reported that 'the rest of the miners were living in holes dug out of the snow.'[35] Other male households more closely conformed to conventional Anglo-American domestic space. Captain Phillip Hankin, between careers in the navy and colonial service, spent a month with five men 'in a very comfortable log cabin' in Barkerville. 'The house consisted of one fairly sized room, about 15 feet long, by 12 feet wide, with 5 bunks round like a large ship's cabin, and opposite the entrance door was a fire place with large logs on the ground, which were burning brightly, and a kettle hanging from a hook over the fire,' he wrote.[36]

While some male households were fairly stable, the membership of others was fluid. As Jock Phillips notes in his study of masculinity in frontier New Zea-land, 'mateship was a relationship of circumstance.'[37] The readiness of miners to share their homes with veritable strangers became proverbial. 'The gold miner is rather an enigmatical character, pecuniarily speaking he is generous to a fault, his purse and cabin are alike open to friend and stranger, countryman and cosmopolite,' wrote one commentator.[38] Such backwoods hospital led tired and hungry overland traveller R.H. Alexander to rethink his assumptions about dependence and mutuality. 'The people are very kind,' the Canadian wrote. 'It is not begging—you just tell them you are broke and hungry and of course you get a meal.'[39]

Bonds easily forged could be bonds easily broken. Miners followed the excitement from rush to rush, moving from California to the Cariboo to Aus-tralia to the Fraser and Thompson rivers. [...] Youth both reinforced and reflected this fluidity. Thirty-nine-year-old Canadian Jessie Wright was exceptionally old for a gold miner. In 1866, he told his fifty-one-year-old brother that he was too old for the Cariboo and its life of 'the pick and shovel, with hard fare and

439

harder knocks.' 'I am Known here by the cognoun of Old Man,' he wrote, 'what would be your position[?]'[40] [...]

Living without women necessitated reconfiguring the process whereby domestic duties were assigned and performed. A few relied heavily on wayside houses and saloons and a few employed servants, but most found ways of domestic survival that did not rely heavily on the market. Some men cared only for themselves, others assigned an unemployed member domestic responsibility, while still others devised schemes whereby work could be performed collectively. These arrangements departed from traditions of institutional group lodging for working men found in Hudson's Bay Company (HBC) 'bachelor halls' and military barracks which were maintained by employers, subject to employer discipline, and reliant on paid staff for domestic services.

Recreating the domestic required white men to come to grips with skills and labours that were often radically unfamiliar to them. Cooking was particularly trying, especially in the upper country where provisions were scarce, limited, and expensive. Besides hard physical labour with little return, wrote disillusioned gold miner Charles Major, 'you go home to your shanty at night, tired and wet, and have to cook your beans before you can eat them.'[41] Some men never adjusted. One Comox farmer's meat, fish, and potatoes were poor, but 'his bread was the crowning atrocity.'[42] Other men adjusted and took pride in their culinary knowledge and accomplishments, treating small victories with a bravado that betrayed their inexperience. 'Last evening we had the pleasure of hearing some very intellectual discourses by some of the residents of this thinly populated district of Goldstream,' wrote one in 1865, including 'an animated discussion on bush cookery, and a number of valuable hints were thrown out.'[43] 'I was cook,' wrote future Indian Agent Henry Guillod, 'which I confess took up nearly the whole of my time.' He produced a competent but overly dry apple pudding, but was particularly proud of his talent at 'throwing a fritter or "slap jack" in firstrate style.' He promised to show his mother how to cook backwoods specialities on his return.[44] Such gendered renegotiations around the cook-fire led one female commentator to speculate that, in British Columbia's backwoods at least, the best cooks were frequently men.[45]

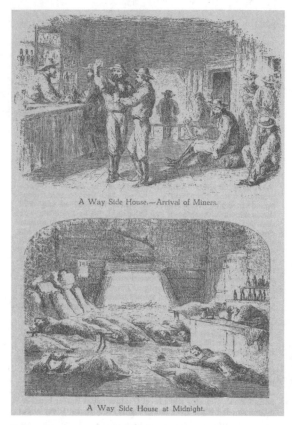

A Way Side House.—Arrival of Miners.

A Way Side House at Midnight.

● An evening at a wayside house.

Source: Walter B. Cheadle, *Cheadles' Journal of a Trip across Canada, 1862–1863* (Edmonton, M.G. Hurtig, 1971). Dr. Cheadle's Own Sketches, by Jean Redfern, 1931, page 206.

Without white women to clean and maintain households, men became inventive. The Norwegian who shared his Saltspring Island home with Blair and his brother Bill for the winter of 1863-4 'thought himself Very Clean but never used a Dish Scloth but his Briti[sh] flag.'[46] Emmerson's party washed their clothes in rivers and dried them by hanging them off their backs.[47] Housekeeping supplies were valued articles, sometimes carried from place to place across the backwoods. When a road-making crew found Duncan Munro's starved body between Williams Creek and Antler, they found no provisions or papers, but they did notice that the 'deceased had plenty of thread, pins and needles.'[48]

● Male household in the backwoods. Leech River, 1865.

Source: Image A-04468, courtesy of Royal BC Museum, BC Archives.

Like cooking, housework could be time-consuming. Chores dominated Richfield's Anglican missionary R.C. Lundin Brown's day, filling it with 'the lighting of the fire, fetching water from the spring, preparing breakfast, not to speak of sweeping the floor with an improvised broom, and sundry other little jobs.'[49] He was not alone. Missionaries argued that domestic responsibilities interfered with men's ability to perform their religious ones. Weekday services were impossible in Antler as 'directly the men were off work they had their suppers to prepare, and found themselves fit only to turn in and sleep after the meal was over.'[50] The Sabbath in Lytton was not a day of faith, but instead 'the grand account-settling, clothes-washing and mending, marketing and drinking day.'[51] Miners themselves inverted such critiques by appropriating the language of Christianity to describe the necessity of performing domestic tasks on Sunday. 'The Fourth Commandment' of the widely reprinted 'Miners' Ten Commandments' went

'Six days thou mayest dig or pick all that the body can stand under; but the other day is Sunday, when thou shalt wash all thy dirty shirts, darn all thy stockings, tap all thy boots, mend all thy clothing, chop thy whole week's firewood, make and bake thy bread and boil thy pork and beans.'[52]

Hardships aside, some represented their encounters with male households positively or even romantically. Lord called living in the bush an 'art' and could think of no other way of achieving 'a more perfect independence.'[53] R.H. Pidcock, a British minister's son who became a Comox farmer, fondly remembered living rough with his mate in 1862. 'I and Fred took to it at once and notwithstanding all we had been through never felt so happy and well as when we had nothing but our bed of branches and our blankets to lay on.'[54]

The tough reality of household maintenance convinced others that domestic patriarchy was a better bargain than they had previously estimated.

'Coming in from work, hungry and tried—firewood to provide and prepare—the fire to make on— supper to cook—the things to wash up—the floor to sweep—shirts, towels, stockings, &c., to wash and mend, and all the paraphernalia connected with housekeeping to attend to, there was not much comfort belonging to it,' wrote Emmerson about the Victoria house he shared with another man. 'I had by this time made a grand discovery,' he declared. 'It was simply this: "I had found out the real value of a good wife and home comforts."'[55] Hayward had a similar epiphany. 'Have been reading to the boys an account of Belashazzors feast and it teaches The influence of women. We realize their value now.'[56]

Others lamented the loss of female company and the bonds of kin, reflecting a dominant culture that increasingly associated the emotive and the caring with the presence of white women and the domestic space of family. James Thompson wrote many sad letters to his wife Mary in Canada West, regretting his decision to ever leave her and their children for the dubious charms of Williams Creek. [...] While Emerson waxed romantic about his male comrades, he was frequently suicidal and haunted by dreams of his wife and seven children, whom he missed terribly.[57] Hayward also deeply regretted his decision to leave his wife Sally in Britain and mourned her absence constantly, especially on Sundays.[58] Like the California miners studied by Andrew J. Rotter, these men found homosocial culture empty and isolating.[59]

Households were not the sole arena of white male homosocial culture. British Columbia created a broader male culture that fostered same-sex social, emotional, and sometimes sexual bonds. Nicknames symbolized the ties of men to each other and their membership in a distinct social world. In his private journal, Anglican Bishop George Hills noted that 'The appellation of all miners is "boy." Their chief is "Cap." All are called Dick, Tom, or Harry. Men are not known by their real names.'[60] Such language denoted affinity and occupational solidarity, but sometimes spoke of deeper ties. Illness and death made these bonds explicit. The sick and ailing of the Cariboo, thought the local press, were often 'tended with all the care and kindness they would have received in the bosom of their own families.'[61] A missionary noted the care an ailing miner received from his mates, describing the large attendance at his funeral as 'a good instance of the great sympathy and cordiality that exists even among these rough men.'[62]

The dissolution of male friendships could cause considerable torment. The parting scene was painful when Emmerson's group separated at Williams Lake. His mate William Mark wrote that 'we had shared the troubles and dangers together, for ten thousand miles, and here we part, in a strange, wild country, perhaps never to see each other again!'[63] Robert Stevenson, a miner who spent his old age in Kamloops writing virulent defences of his companion, 'Cariboo' Cameron, left a business diary containing affectionate, formulaic poetry and addresses of male companions. One read: 'Forget me not I only ask / This simple boon of thee / And let it be a Simple task / To sometimes think of me.'[64] One miner reputedly committed suicide after the death of his partner.[65]

White men could be many things to each other. Together, they constructed new versions of traditionally heterosocial activities. Some parties, like a Comox one, cancelled the dancing 'owing to the absence of crinoline.'[66] Others were more inventive in the face of gender's disruption. At a dance in Yale in 1858, 'The few ladies present had no lack of partners, while most of the men were forced to dance with each other.'[67] Travel writer R. Byron Johnson recalled meeting an old miner, Jake, who told of a winter ball on Williams Creek. When Johnson asked about ladies, Jake replied that they had none except for an African American washerwoman, a French madam, and the blacksmith's wife. 'But we danced some, I tell yu! It were stag dancin' of course, fur a hundred an' fifty men was too many fur three females, but it all came off gay.'[68] A largely male milieu was also no barrier to the performance of Anglo-American theatre. Journalist Edgar Fawcett remembered being cajoled into female roles in Victoria's Amateur Dramatic Club since 'female talent was scarce.'[69] One visitor speculated that actors must have shaved permanently for such roles.[70]

This homosocial culture was not necessarily a poor imitation of allegedly real, natural, or legitimate gender organization. While white men's desire for white women was often assumed, the lives of many of backwoods British Columbian men—lived in lifelong bachelorhood, with no apparent quest for formal marriage—suggests that same-race, heterosexual desires were not universal. One miner wrote that 'generally gold diggers are not marrying men. They work, spend their money in drink, and work again.'[71] Naval officer Richard Charles Mayne argued that gold miners' 'hard, wild life' ultimately 'unfit them for domestic existence.'[72] Historian of American masculinity Anthony Rotundo agrees on the importance of same-sex bonds, but argues that men's romantic friendships were a product of a distinct phase of the life cycle—youth. This explanation seems insufficient for explaining male bonds in colonial British Columbia. Steven Maynard suggests that the backwoods provided an environment where men could have their primary social and emotional bonds with other men. In much the same way that historians have persuasively argued that all-female institutions like settlement houses and female colleges offered a social space where early twentieth-century women could live a female-centred life, so the backwoods of British Columbia allowed men to create and maintain a social life revolving around same-sex ties and practices.[73]

Some members of this homosocial culture seem simply disinterested in conventional gender and familial organization, while others were actively fleeing from it. Mid-nineteenth-century British Columbia provided a useful haven for men on the lam from the unwanted encumbrances of wives and families. One local politician commented that three letters went up to the Cariboo for every one that went down.[74] Some of those unanswered letters were pleading ones in search of errant kin or their support. Ann Scott, living at the Alms House [poorhouse] of Blackwell's Island, New York, wrote to local clergy about her husband who was reputedly living in Victoria. She particularly wanted to know if he had another family, and told the cleric: 'You will understand my feelings, and agree with me, that it is best for me to know the truth, one way or other.'[75] Inquiries from wives and families overseas were frequent enough to prompt the Colonial Office to ask Victoria to clarify their responsibility on the matter.[76] As Scott feared, some men did flee their families only to form new ones. An act requiring the registration of births, marriages, and deaths was supported on the grounds that it would assist in the prosecution of bigamy cases.[77] New York divorce lawyers saw a market in this mobile world and advertised their services in the Cariboo press.[78]

Not all members of this homosocial culture showed interest in recreating conventional family relationships. In poem and prose, some white men celebrated their distance from the world of white women and the nineteenth-century discursive corollaries of religion and 'the social.' They represented their world as rough and masculine and made clear that these were admirable attributes. 'The man in the mines and the same man at home, with the influence of a loving mother, a wife, or virtuous sisters around him—bear no analogy to each other,' wrote one miner.[79] Sometimes the line between celebrating the maleness of the backwoods and misogyny blurred. Women at home, one wrote, would hardly recognize men at the mines since so rough and ready were the former fine gentlemen. 'There is no denying it, gold is all powerful and is the true mistress of destiny.'[80]

No clear line definitively and irreparably divided the homosocial from the homosexual. Historians of sexuality argue that before the widespread dissemination of a homosexual *identity* in the late nineteenth-century, homoerotic behaviour and desire was usually conceived as an 'act' rather than a persona, and subject to various levels of social regulation.[81] One letter writer announced that 'murderers, sodomites, and burglars have few sympathizers in Victoria,'[82] but the social history of the regulation of male homoerotic behaviour reveals a more complex history. D.W. Higgins's stories suggest how colonial British Columbia's homosocial culture could challenge conventional sexuality as well as gender. One grapples with the male narrator's ambivalence about his attraction to a young man named Henry Collins. 'I could not understand my feelings. Why should I be attracted towards him more than to any other young man? [...] Were the mysterious forces of Nature making themselves heard and felt?'[83] Higgins—a journalist and future speaker of the British Columbia provincial legislature—resolves the potential subversion of homosexuality by having Collins turn out to be a passing woman. But real life did not always end so tidily. Between 1849 and 1871 at least four men were charged with sodomy or buggery in three separate trials.[84]

Read for broadly social rather than narrowly legal evidence, the case of John Butts especially indicates the relative importance of homosexual behaviour and demonstrates how its regulation was shaped by the context of colonial British Columbia. Butts was simultaneously central and marginal to Victoria society in the 1850s and 1860s, a famous outcast who performed tricksterlike functions in local society. Of English extraction and Australian birth, Butts moved

443

to Victoria in 1858 after a sojourn in San Francisco. He was initially employed as the town crier and bell ringer. But, when the magistrate was out of earshot, Butts reportedly changed his proclamation to '"God Save (a pause of a few seconds) John Butt."' For this act of disloyalty he was deposed as town crier, and became a garbage collector until officially barred from the trade for charging customers for hauling the same rubbish back and forth across town.[85] Butts then became the most celebrated habitué of Victoria's police court, chain gang, and jail. In the early 1860s he was arrested for, among other things, stealing a keg of porter, selling a stolen goose, 'rowdyish and disorderly conduct,' and for being a rogue and a vagabond.[86] [...]

This daily routine of mockery and casual violence served as a backdrop for the prosecution of Butts's same-sex activity. In January 1860 he was charged for 'an abominable offence on the person of a little English boy, employed at the Union Hotel.'[87] The state marshalled an impressive amount of evidence about Butts's sexual relationships with the illiterate William Williams, described in the local press as 'a rather good looking youth of about sixteen years of age.'[88] That Williams himself was initially held in gaol on charges of 'buggery' suggests that he was initially seen as a participant rather than a victim. Yet he was released after a couple of weeks and eventually served as the Crown's star witness,[89] testifying that he met Butts at a hotel, and that the older man offered him work and a place to stay. 'I went there, and went to bed with him, he had connection with me, and ever since I have been in great pain,' said Williams.[90] Other residents of Butts's household confirmed Williams story, and in doing so, inadvertently revealed an intimate, crowded, and exclusively male world.[91]

This was not the first time Butts had propositioned young working-class boys who depended on older men for employment or shelter. A butcher recalled overhearing Butts make advances to a lad known as Ginger.[92] Ginger, or Francis Jackson, testified that Butts had approached him on three separate occasions, offering the homeless boy a job and a bed in exchange for sex. 'He told me he wished he had me in bed with him, and he put his hands on his privates and said if he had me in bed with him he would give me that,' Jackson testified. He spurned Butts by likening homosexual and interracial heterosexual sex. 'I told him if he wanted to fuck anything to get a squaw and he could do as much as he wanted.'[93] For Jackson, the 'squaw' or dangerous Aboriginal woman was presumed to be sexually available to all white men and an illicit enough object of desire to serve as a workable analogy to homosexual sex. These fraught connections between sexual identity, respectability, and race were also raised when the butcher chastised Butts not for suggesting sex to another man, but for doing so within earshot of what he called 'a lady'[94]—undoubtably a white woman. For him, Butts's language or behaviour were not inherently indecent, but merely not suitable for white women's ears.

It is not surprising that Butts's trial was a controversial one. The state mounted a serious case against which the poor and isolated Butts was unable to defend himself effectively. When tried by the attorney general in February 1860, Butts faced the court alone, without legal representation or even witnesses. Butts tried to turn these disadvantages to his favour with a elegantly pitiful self-representation, asking the court for mercy and explaining that 'the men I expected as witnesses have gone up the river and I am left without any.'[95] At nine o'clock in the evening after the trial, the jury announced that they could not agree on a verdict; the judge responded by locking them up until the following morning. After requesting 'instructions,' the jury declared that it was 'impossible for them to agree.' The judge dismissed them and impanelled a new jury.

The new jury, if nothing else, was efficient. they met for a mere five minutes before acquitting.[96] Butts, for one, had always maintained his innocence, testifying: 'All I have got to say is that this case is got up to extort money from me'[97]—an unlikely explanation given his obvious and indeed infamous poverty. [...]

The Butts case raises important connections between homosocial culture and homosexual behaviours. Witness testimony divulges a tightly woven homosocial milieu anchored in young white men's shared domestic and social ties. In Butts's crowded house, women only existed as infrequently invoked symbols of either propriety or danger. Homosexual acts seem to have been a relatively regular part of this homosocial milieu. Butts was known to proposition other men, and this behaviour does not seem to have been considered inherently problematic as much as it was inappropriate in certain circumstances—such as when white women were within earshot. Young men's testimonies reveal that they were easily fluent with language specifically describing homosexual sex.

That colonial British Columbia was a society that tolerated a certain amount of male same-sexuality is reaffirmed by other cases, as is the tendency of certain men to be singled out for their same-sex practices. In British Columbia as elsewhere, there was a special connection between seamen and same-sex practice. In 1866 Matti Rasid, a Greek sailor belonging to the HBC's *Princess Royal*, was found guilty of sodomy in a case that initially indicted Rasid and another sailor for a series of sexual acts committed with four boys over at least a three-week period and inadvertently revealed a working-class shipboard culture where sex between men was not uncommon.[98] In 1870 or 1873 a popular sailor named John Kingswell was found guilty of having attempted sodomy with another sailor at the Ship's Sun, an Esquimalt pub.[99]

No surviving records from the years between 1849 and 1871 indicate that any men were prosecuted for male homosexual sex in up-country British Columbia, including the overwhelmingly male mining towns. In large part, this reflects the limited reaches of the colonial state in British Columbia which, as Tina Loo has shown, was never able to establish conclusive legal authority over the backwoods.[100] Yet it also mirrors a particular pattern of sexual regulation that developed in colonial contexts. Historian Ronald Hyam explains male same-sexual practice in colonial settings as a situational response that was 'almost entirely opportunistic or the product of circumstance, and without prejudice to relationships with women.'[101] Others challenge this simplistic heterosexism. In *Colonial Desire: Hybridity in Theory, Culture and Race,* postcolonial theorist Robert Young suggests that fears of miscegenation could eclipse fears of homosexuality in imperial contexts. Same-sex sex, he writes, 'posed no threat because it produced no children; its advantage was that it remained silent, covert, and unmarked.'[102] Colonies could foster an environment of passive tolerance towards same-sex erotic practice because, however threatening, it did not create the boundless brown bodies whose very existence challenged racialized boundaries of rule. Such comparative tolerance would also have been fostered by the existence of a colonial community where men's social and emotional attachments to each other were nourished and reinforced by a wider homosocial culture.

Reconfirming Gender: Labour, Drink, Gambling, Violence, and White Identity

Some of the most compelling symbols of the homosocial culture of British Columbia's backwoods were those that reworked or challenged conventional gender organization. But much of the daily practice of this culture was not dissimilar from that of working-class men throughout the Anglo-American world. [...]

Drink [...] was indelibly marked on British Columbia's homosocial culture. It was something of a colonial pastime. In 1853 Douglas called drunkenness 'the crying and prevalent sin of this Colony,' and not much changed in the following years.[103] Drink, rather than the church or the domestic, seemed to sit at the centre of colonial society. HBC servant Robert Melrose, whose 1853 diary enumerated the days he and his friends were one-quarter, one-half, or fully drunk, argued that drink was symptomatic of Vancouver Island's colonial condition. 'Here we are settled on this Island, just lying as Nature finished it, among a band of untutored Indians, here we have no Church to go to, no tailor to make our cloths, not a shoemaker to sole a shoe for us; but thither that accursed Grog has found its way, and a temple of Bacchus erected.' The 'god of wine,' he concluded, was truly 'revered in the north-west of America.'[104]

Drinking was the special preserve of the colony's settlers and men. Aboriginal people were legally denied the right to imbibe by statute in 1854 and thereafter the 'Indian liquor trade' was policed by gunboat.[105] The justice of denying First Nations people legal drink was occasionally debated, but the white community seems to have usually enjoyed its monopoly on lawful liquor.[106] Access to liquor was a significant enough citizenship right that non-white settlers fought to defend it, as when Victoria's Black community challenged white barkeepers for denying them drink at least twice in 1862.[107] Like citizenship, drinking was gendered as well as raced. 'It is considered a heinous offence against public morals that a lady should be anything but a teetotaller,' opined Johnson.[108]

Among white men, sailors and gold miners were especially famed for their enthusiasm for drink. So much did sailors love their liquor, the *Victoria Press* commented, that 'it is likely they would be equally as contented and happy in jail as on board ship if they could get their daily allowance of grog.'[109]

445

Drink was the main focus of sociability in mining towns where there were few enough other options. That saloons and wayside houses were often the sole public meeting places in the upcountry is suggested by how frequently missionaries held services in them.[110] Regulated by the necessity of ritual 'treating,' drinking in these places was an intensely social activity. Aristocratic travellers Viscount Milton and W.B. Cheadle described the protocol at wayside houses, those combination saloon, restaurant, and hotel that were dotted along the colony's back roads. After the men unloaded their packs, a drink was proposed by 'some one of the party less "hard up" than his friends, and the rest of the company present are generally invited to join in.'[111] Men who refused ritual drinks, like German mathematician Carl Friesach, were treated with disdain.[112]

Drinking took place all year and in all locales, but the winter and the town held a special place in British Columbia's political economy of partying. Miners and other seasonal workers who moved back in forth between city and woods converged on Victoria for the slack season. 'Miners spent money lavishly—chiefly in public houses and dance houses and extravagance in general,' remembered John Helmcken.[113] Dance houses primarily provided places where white men and First Nations women could socialize, but also, according to their defenders, were a necessary space for miners' seasonal binges. Admitting that his kind were 'a little gayer than ordinary,' one miner argued that long periods of deprivation gave miners a natural 'desire to spree a little.'[114]

Opponents of dance houses challenged the idea that they were needed and comfortable spaces for working-class sociability. Instead, they presented them as hotbeds of mixed-race immorality superintended by shrewd and devious profiteers. Dance houses, attested Methodist missionary Ephraim Evans, really catered to 'tangle leg manufacturers, illicit traders in small wares with the Indians, receivers of goods from parties whose possecorry [*sic*] rights are not too strictly scrutinized, light-fingered gentry who are not scrupulous as to the means of acquisition; and kindred characters, are not to be confounded with an honest and industrial population.'[115] Yet others defended drink as a potent and appropriate symbol of the homosocial culture of the backwoods. 'The Bard of the Lowhee' wrote a 'A Reminiscence of Cariboo Life,' which began, 'Oh, I love to snore/On a bar-room floor/And sleep a drunk away!' adding pearls like 'I love the barley bree!' and 'I love the jolly spree!'[116]

Whether it occurred in a saloon, wayside house, or dance house, drinking often went hand in hand with gambling, another activity associated with British Columbia's homosocial culture. In British Columbia gambling was constructed as equivalent or endemic to mining, a product of its privileging of chance and easy gain above hard work, ambition, and obedience.[117] Gaming was sometimes superintended by the shrewd and prominent professionals that troubled mining towns, vying for power and influence with local colonial officials, yet it was generally a casual affair intermeshed with other forms of sociability. Men played for drink more often than money, and gaming often went hand in hand with music, drinking, and bare-fisted prizefighting.[118] Like drinking, gambling could both link white men together as well as divide them. As Gunther Peck points out in his study of the Comstock Lode, gambling and other risk-taking activities 'strengthened rather than weakened miners' commitment to a working-class moral economy that celebrated maleness, mutuality, whiteness, and the power of chance.'[119]

Violence was another keynote of this homosocial culture. An October 1866 prizefight between George Wilson, 'the Cariboo Champion,' and George Baker, 'the Canadian Pet,' prompted the local press to comment that 'Cariboo has never witnessed the assemblage of so many people since the white man came to work this "illihe" [land].'[120] Violence was not isolated to the spectacular and ritual. As in the Oregon context analysed by David Peterson del Mar, the settlement process gave white men an 'intimate knowledge' of violence and normalized the use of force to control others.[121] While Justice Matthew Begbie worked hard to construct the British Columbian frontier as uniquely peaceful,[122] it was hard to ignore the barroom and back-alley brawls. 'As you may imagine where there is so much young blood & no female population,' wrote British surveyor and diarist Charles Wilson about Victoria in 1858, 'there are sometimes fierce scenes enacted & the bowie knife & revolver which every man wears are in constant requisition.'[123]

Violence regulated relations within the white male community and reinforced its authority over both women and non-white peoples. The threat of violence could solidify male community: one author advised group emigration as a means to 'resist aggression.'[124] But solidarity could also encourage the use of force when mates came to each others' defence. The *Cariboo Sentinel* remarked: 'Every man has his friends, and it is not unlikely that some of these fights may end in a general row between the friends of the combatants, and where the strong and the weak fight in a mining camp serious consequences are sure to follow.'[125] Women and Aboriginal peoples were also targets of white men's violence. Such violence was often but not only sexual and conjugal. 'The white men kick the Indians about like dogs,' commented one observer.[126]

This suggests how white male homosocial culture was rooted not simply in identification as men, but in its members' tendency to identify as *white* men. The oft-remarked ethnic and racial plurality of backwoods British Columbia could challenge homogeneity and hierarchy. But it should not blind us to the centrality of whiteness to homosocial culture. The racial plurality of some gold-mining milieus could intensify rather than modify the significance of whiteness, as white men worked to assert their racial solvency in a context where it was cast into doubt. Immigrants carried racial ideologies premised on the distinctiveness of the Anglo-Saxon race and its dual superiority to and responsibility for all others with them from their home societies to British Columbia. There, notions of white supremacy were reinforced and reformulated against both the ethnic diversity of the settler population and the large Aboriginal population.

[...]

Prescribed gender organization was profoundly disrupted in colonial British Columbia. Among the results of this disruption is the complex homosocial culture forged among white men in the colony, which coexisted and sometimes overlapped with the mixed-race community. In the backwoods and urban enclaves, white men reconstructed domestic space without white women, creating their own structures of household life. They formed social, emotional, and sometimes sexual relationships with each other. In reconstructing these bonds, white men in British Columbia embraced same-sex relations at the same time heterosocial modes of sociability and domesticity were becoming hegemonic in middle-class Anglo-American culture and shaping expectations of working-class life. Similarly, white men drank, gambled, and fought, elevating these acts to social prominence and value at the very moment that metropolitan, middle-class visions of self-controlled, self-contained, and temperate manhood were constructed as both normative and necessary. When these pastimes held on in the working-class taverns and streets of metropolitan communities, British Columbians claimed them as prominent cultural practices and values.

Through daily practice and self-representation, this culture constructed a particular if fragmented vision of what it meant to be white and male. Whether it was reworking or reconfirming dominant practices of masculinity, this vision of white manhood did not reject, but rather reinforced, the power accorded white men in a colonial and patriarchal society. A shared white identity was celebrated, and men's authority over both women and First Nations people was reinforced through myriad daily practices. As much as the particular alignment of race and gender in colonial British Columbia gave birth to a homosocial white male culture, it also fostered intimate relationships between settler men and First Nations women.

Chapter 2

'The Prevailing Vice': Mixed-Race Relationships

In 1870 Anglican missionary R.C. Lundin Brown urged the English public to support his evangelical efforts in Lillooet, British Columbia. In a little wooden church among the mountains, he annually preached a sermon, usually in the week of Lent, against what he dubbed 'the prevailing vice, concubinage with native women.' Brown went on to speak of 'troops of young Indian girls' who annually migrated to Lillooet to live with white men in 'tumble-down cabins.' Such relationships, more than damaging Aboriginal women, imperilled the morality of their white partners. None, pondered Brown, 'could live intimately with persons of low tone and habits without sinking to their level.'[127] Brown's tirade was born out of his deep discomfort with the widespread practice of mixed-race relationships in British Columbia between 1849 and 1871. Sex lay at the heart of both British Columbia's colonial project and critiques of it. On this edge of empire, gender was organized

447

in different and challenging ways, and heterosexual unions forged between settler men and Aboriginal women were among the sharpest reminders of this.

In colonial British Columbia, cultural contact was literally gendered insofar as the political economy of the colonial project tended to bring settler men into contact with Aboriginal women. Prevailing patterns of European migration and a resource extractive economy meant that men made up an overwhelming percentage of the white population, while simultaneously the imperatives of the local labour market and sexual economy meant that women were overrepresented in urban First Nations communities. An 1868 census, for instance, recorded almost twice as many Aboriginal women as Aboriginal men in Victoria.[128] That social and discursive space literary scholar Mary Louise Pratt calls the 'contact zone'[129] was, in British Columbia, explicitly gendered, bringing together men and women rather than ungendered racial subjects.

Cultural contact was also highly sexualized. The topic of mixed-race relationships in colonial British Columbia, however, is as slippery and charged as it is important. The limited resources available to nineteenth-century historians relying primarily on written sources necessarily impose restrictions on the extent to which any scholar, particularly a non-Aboriginal one like me, can deduce (let alone 'speak for') First Nations experiences. Even white perspectives on mixed-race relationships can be difficult to read. Few authors commenting on mixed-race relationships were themselves members of white-Aboriginal unions, and those that were rarely admit it. Discussions of mixed-race relationships come chiefly from missionaries and journalists, authors whose adherence to specific literary norms often leads to sensational portrayals of colonial life. Missionaries were especially empowered by their social position to comment on aspects of others' lives that most nineteenth-century people felt honour-bound to ignore, at least in print. Their discursive access to the sexual and domestic lives of others renders missionary records unusually revealing sources for social history, but also deeply colours both their form and content.

The laden character of available source material renders it impossible to construct a tidy division between the experience and representation of mixed-race relationships, a complexity this analysis tries to respect. Yet this source material does indicate that,

for many, these unions amounted to even more evidence in colonial British Columbia that gender and race were lived in different and perhaps dangerous ways. Premised on the construction of First Nations women as sexually dangerous, this discourse represented mixed-race relationships and their children as inimical to the establishment of a respectable white settler colony in British Columbia.

Construction of First Nations Women

Beliefs about the dangerous character of First Nations women were the bedrock upon which constructions of mixed-race relationships were built. Ranya Green suggests that Europeans saw North American women through a powerful dualistic lens: the 'squaw' was lustful and threatening to white men, while 'Pocahontas' was pure and helpful, a cultural mediator, who, like her namesake, protected white interests. A related discourse represented the squaw as overworked and abused, the firmest evidence of Aboriginal savagism.[130] In mid-nineteenth century British Columbia, as in the prairie context recently studied by Sarah Carter in *Capturing Women: The Manipulation of Cultural Imagery in Canada's Prairie West,* the image of the squaw predominated.[131] Aboriginal women were constructed as lascivious, shameless, unmaternal, prostitutes, ugly, and incapable of high sentiment or manners—the dark, mirror image to the idealized nineteenth-century visions of white women.

First Nations women were represented as overtly sexual, physical, and base. White men were simultaneously attracted and alarmed by what they saw as Aboriginal women's sexual availability, signified most powerfully by their dress. James Bell, a draper visiting Victoria, found that 'among the Females there is a *painful* and *provoking* scarcity of petticoats.'[132] Others were unsettled by different politics of physical space. One found Northern women's curiosity about men's bodies 'frightfully disgusting' for 'a man of healthful proclivities.'[133] Thomas Bushby, a young middle-class British emigrant, saw the same physicality but interpreted it positively. He was deeply enamoured by his future wife, Governor James Douglas's mixed-blood teenage daughter, Agnes, especially with what he saw as her darkness and her willingness to engage in rough, physical play. He wrote that 'they say she looks with no savage eye on me—& true she is a stunning girl, black eye & hair & larky like the devil.'[134]

[....] White men's perception of First Nations women as sexually available was justified by the contention that Aboriginal cultures, especially North-Coast ones, did not promote chastity. While interior nations valued female chastity, reported naturalist John Keast Lord, 'among the fish-eaters of the northwest coast it has no meaning, or if it has it appears to be utterly disregarded.'[135]

[....] Discourses of prostitution were especially handy tools for defining respectable and unrespectable femininity in British Columbia as in Red River.[136] A convenient shorthand for signifying the immorality of First Nations womanhood was the suggestion that Aboriginal women were, by definition, prostitutes. The magistrate of Lillooet referred to 'the wholesale prostitution of the young women and even small children.'[137] Communities located around the city of Victoria received the lion's share of this scorn, reflecting the belief that Aboriginal people were necessarily degraded by cultural contact. In 1870 colonial official Joseph Trutch wrote that 'prostitution is another acknowledged evil prevailing to an almost unlimited extent among the Indian women in the neighbourhood of Victoria.'[138] Cultural rhetoric justified the intimate connection between Aboriginal women and prostitution. The sex trade was associated with First Nations gift-giving ceremonies, seasonal migration, social organization, and gender norms. Navy surgeon Edward Bogg wrote that 'the open practice of habitual Prostitution is not considered as a disgrace, but as a highly legitimate and very lucrative calling, nor does the Indian warrior consider it as in any way derogatory to his manhood to subsist in the earnings of his Squaws at this shameful trade.'[139]

[...] First Nations women were critiqued for 'native' hygiene, dress, and habits and also mocked for adopting the conventions of white femininity. In Victoria the local press derided 'Mary, Sunox, Carol, Kate, Emelie, and Mush, squaws belonging to the northern tribes,' for wearing hoop skirts at court.[140] Remembering a Quesnel dance, naval and colonial official Phillip Hankin found women's refusal to dance with men to whom they had not been introduced truly ironic. 'I recollect,' he wrote, 'asking one of the Kitty's in Chinook to dance with me and she drew herself up in a very dignified manner, and said "Halo introduce" [no introduction] which signified I had not been introduced to Her! and I couldn't help laughing which made her very angry.'[141] Incorporating the manners and clothing of European femininity did not guarantee Aboriginal women the respect accorded to ladies.

The logical extension of the representation of First Nations women as the mirror image to white women was the exclusion of Aboriginal women from the category of 'woman' altogether. In British Columbia the category 'woman' was given racial contours in both casual and formal acts. Local officials responded to queries about their gaol facilities by commenting that 'no woman had been imprisoned' and that 'drunken squaws have [...] been locked up until sobered.'[142] Hankin's reminiscences mention dancing with First Nations women and not being 'fit to sit down at table with Ladies' in one passage.[143] Just as the jail's 'squaws' were not women, Hankin's ladies could not be of the First Nations.

This image of Aboriginal women was a homespun, localized construct, as cultural historian Carrol Smith-Rosenberg suggests, based on the settlers' need 'to refute the positive representations of indigenous Americans found within British imperial discourse.'[144] The construction of First Nations women in colonial discourse bore little relationship to actual women's lives. Yet the image was an enduring one that continues to shape First Nations women's experience. Janice Acoose/Misko-Kisikàwihkwè (Red Sky Woman) powerfully demonstrates how the image of the 'easy squaw' legitimates violence against Aboriginal women, like the brutal 1971 rape and murder of Helen Betty Osborne in small-town Manitoba.[145] In colonial British Columbia, the construction of First Nations women as the dark and dangerous opposite of white women was given addition meaning by a related discourse on white-Aboriginal relationships. Colonial discourse built upon its representation of First Nations women as dangerous by constructing mixed-race relationships as an active threat to white men's fragile moral and racial selves.

Constructions of Mixed-Race Relationships

Secular and religious observers alike were compelled to notice the existence of heterosexual relationships between settler men and First Nations women throughout British Columbia. They especially associated them with the colony's fur-trade community that both Sylvia Van Kirk and Jennifer Brown have documented.[146] Even if mixed-relationships were losing

● **Embracing the latest Victorian fashions rarely convinced white observers that First Nations women were respectable. Lekwammen (Songhees) people in 1867–68.**

Source: J.C. Eastcott; p. 147, N. 91, City of Vancouver Archives.

their widespread acceptance among the higher echelons of the fur trade, wage earners remained deeply enmeshed in conjugal relationships with Aboriginal women. In 1861 an experienced Orkney servant reported that 'the custom of living with Indian women was universal in the Hudson's Bay Company (HBC) service.'[147]

Yet mixed-race relationships were not confined to the fur trade. Disillusioned miner John Emmerson wrote that only one unmarried man in the interior mining town of Douglas had failed to take an Aboriginal partner.[148] White male homosocial culture and mixed-race sociability overlapped: mining towns like Douglas were not as much without women as they were without white women. George Grant, secretary of Sandford Flemming's surveying party, noted that around Kamloops, 'most of the settlers live with squaws, or Klootchman as they are called on the Pacific.'[149] Methodist missionary Ebenezer Robson, visiting Salt Spring Island's north settlement,

despaired that of nine men '5 are living with Indian women in a state of adultery.'[150]

Mixed-race relationships were a part of city as well as bush, country, and mining life. The census of Victoria enumerated a total of 581 family households by race in the spring of 1871. In excluding the Lekwammen (Songhees) settlement and deeming people of mixed heritage like James Douglas's family and a plethora of lesser-known individuals as white, the census taker employed a definition of whiteness that was unusually expansive by nineteenth-century British Columbian standards. Yet it still found that sixty households or over 10 per cent of all family households contained an adult First Nations female and white man, thirty-one of which had resident children. These families were clustered in the poorer districts lying at the city's outskirts [...][151]

Mixed-race relationships frequently departed from the conventions of European marriage. Missionaries described encountering couples who had lived together for years without the benefit of white ceremony. It was usually the event of marriage, rather than the relationship itself, that occasioned notice. Crosby remembered that five mixed-race couples with children were married in one missionary visit to Chilliwack.[152] Some mixed-race couples challenged missionary sensibilities by explaining that their relationships were unchurched by choice. Anglican Bishop George Hills wrote about one Fort Rupert couple who had lived together for thirteen years. The white man 'objected to marriage because if she knew he was legally bound to her she would probably fall back into her old habits & perhaps cohabit with Indian men & expect him to be home to keep notwithstanding, he said this had happened in several cases when men had married.' Yet when Hills asked this man if 'he intended life long fidelity,' he replied, 'Yes,'[153] Another missionary wrote that white men blamed 'their Klootchmen' for refusing legal marriage.[154]

Other mixed-race couples conformed to the conventions and ceremonies of European marriage. In doing so, they revealed something about the character of their relationships. Sifting through the incomplete information included in the marriage registers of five Anglican churches St Paul's of Nanaimo, St John's of Victoria, St Mary's the Virgin of Sapperton, St John the Divine of Yale, and Christ Church of Hope it is possible to identify sixteen mixed-race marriages out of 126. These marriages are marked by significant age differences between the men and women, differences that probably exacerbated racial and gendered difference. Of the twelve couples for whom ages were given, the men were on average 31.25 years old, while the women were an average of 21.6 years of age. These were hardly extreme examples. Qwa-Wail-Yah or Madeline Williams, a Halkomelem woman from the Musquem village, remembered becoming the second wife of 'Gassy' Jack Dieghton when she was only twelve.[155] These marriage records also confirm mixed-race relationships were not confined to the fur trade. Except for the three men who married daughters of the fur-trade elite, all the grooms had working-class occupations characteristic of a coastal, resource economy: they were sailors, miners, and building, industrial and retail workers. All the women hailed from British Columbia, and most were members of Coast Salish nations whose territories abutted white settlements like the Lekwammen (Songhees), Halkomelem, and Sechelt.[156]

Aboriginal custom probably served more often than did the Christian ceremony. In 1866 Bishop Hills described a union of a white man and a Tsimshian woman: 'Married that is not of course with Xian rites or in legal union but as Indians marry, & as I suppose would satisfy the essentials of marriage, as for instance in Scotland.'[157] In the 1930s an influential Halkomelem elder from Musqueam, August Jack Khahtsahlano, described nineteenth-century marriage ceremonies to Vancouver archivist Major J.S. Matthews:

> Major Matthews:—I was talking to Mrs Walker […] and she told me that her father married an Indian girl at Musqueam, and that it was done with much ceremony; that Old Kiapilano took 'Portuguese Joe' by the arm, and another chief took the Indian girl by her arm, and put them together, and said they were going to be man and wife, and then gave them a lot of blankets, and then put all the blankets in a big canoe, and sat Joe and his wife on top, and they set out for Gastown. What do you think of it?
>
> August:—That's the way all Indians Marry. S'pose I've got a son, and he wants to marry. I go to you and say, 'My son want to marry your girl.' And he says, 'Alright, come on Tuesday,' or someday like that. And, they tell all their friends and each one of them come with his blanket; and the boy come with his blanket; and that's the way the Indian get married.[158]

Khatsalano describes a ceremony where the only evidence of Europe lies in the trade blanket given and, sometimes, the European bridegrooms.

Where Khatsalano saw 'the way all Indians Marry,' many Europeans saw casual and temporary relationships. Naval officer Richard Mayne wrote, 'Whenever a white man takes up his residence among them they will always supply him with a wife; and if he quits the place and leaves her there, she is not the least disgraced in the eyes of her tribe.'[159] Despite Mayne's equation of short relationships and Aboriginal tradition, fleeting unions were also a part of European culture. For some white men, casual connections with Aboriginal women were part of the travel experience. Canadian R.H. Alexander's journal of his 1862 overland trip from Canada to British Columbia includes mundane mention of his interaction with Aboriginal women. Passing through Fort Garry, he wrote that 'we went through the bush after some Indian girls and had some great fun.'[160]

Notions of the transiency of mixed-race relationships probably legitimated the ease with which some white men abandoned their Aboriginal partners. In 1861 a white man in Nanaimo fought with, and subsequently replaced, his First Nations wife. In response, the first wife hung herself. This led one letter writer to note that 'surely Indian life is held cheap here.'[161] Burrard Inlet sawmill owner S.P. Moody abandoned his Aboriginal family when his white wife joined him from Victoria, as did Okanagan rancher John Hall Allison.[162] Even if cherished by their partners, Aboriginal women could be rejected by their white in-laws. Qwa-Wail-Yah was denied the money intended for her and her son by her partner's family, and Khatsahloano's sister Louisa was evicted from her home after her husband's death. 'But that's the way they do with Indian woman who marries whiteman,' Khatsahlano argued, 'when their husbands die, they kick the woman out—because she's "just a squaw."'[163]

These experiences confirmed white observers' fears that mixed-race relationships were necessarily degraded ones. That Aboriginal women were 'used as slaves, and turned off at will' and that white men 'pursued a system of debauchery and vice, in their keeping Indian women, and exchanging or abandoning them at their pleasure' became key points in melodramatic and paternalistic missionary discourse.[164] The excesses of this rhetoric should not blind us to the presence of coercion and violence in intimate relations between white men and Aboriginal women. The regional historiography is replete with happy stories among which the long marriage of James Douglas and Amelia Connolly is probably the most famous. These stories are a necessary corrective insofar as they challenge that nineteenth-century discourse that predicted doom for all relationships forged across racial lines. Yet we also need to be wary of how stories of love and affection across racial lines can obscure both coercive details and the larger brutality of colonialism. [...]

Violence in mixed-race relationships belied such transracial love plots. The *British Colonist* reported that 'fights between squaws and squaw men' were a daily occurrence.[165] A Nanaimo missionary reported that one white settler beat his First Nations partner constantly and was reputed to have caused his childrens' deaths. 'His poor woman is constantly in a state of fear,' he wrote, 'he has beaten her so severely three times in the last nine weeks, each time the poor thing has taken to the woods only returning when driven to it by starvation she is now suffering from her last ill-treatment having had her head severely cut by a broken bottle.'[166] While this abuse was similar to that meted out in same-race relationships, the connections between conquering land and conquering women, explored by Anne McClintock in *Imperial Leather: Race, Gender and Sexuality in the Colonial Contest,* reinforced the bonds between heterosexual violence and the colonial project.[167] Judge W.H. Franklyn, referring to the many First Nations women 'persuaded to live with the white men,' argued that such relationships caused' an ill feeling against the whites.'[168] Scientist Robert Brown thought that 'the causes of nearly every quarrel between whites and Indians on this coast may be summed up in three lines,' the first of which was 'White men taking liberties with their women.'[169]

[...] While sex and domesticity across all racial lines was considered a threat, in British Columbia white-Aboriginal relationships were constructed as especially dangerous for white men, whose appropriate behaviour and identity would guarantee an orderly settler colony. White men who wedded First Nations women were said, first, to be on a fast road to moral turpitude. Such connections could even imperil public officials. In the late 1840s critics evoked the HBC's seeming acceptance of mixed marriages to challenge their ability to serve as proprietorial rulers of the new colony of Vancouver Island. While company defenders argued that officers were 'exerting themselves to check vice, and encourage morality and religion,'[170] the connection between the HBC and white-Aboriginal relationships persisted as a key rhetorical plank in anti-company discourse. Governor Douglas's mixed-blood family was used as a causal explanation for what critics saw as his poor government and the fur-trade elite's inherent corruption.[171] But fur traders were not the only public officials thought to be imperilled by their mixed-race attachments. One letter attacked magistrates who formed relationships with First Nations women. 'Sorrowful has it been to mark many of the victims of this deadly

452

453

● British Columbia's much-lauded and much-criticized mixed-race bourgeoisie. Sir James Douglas, ca 1860s, and Lady Amelia Connolly Douglas, 1862.

Source: Images A-01229 and H-04909, courtesy of Royal BC Museum, BC Archives.

gangrene,' it went, 'who once were men of mark for amiability and respectability—now how fallen!'[172]

Other men were also said to be imperilled by mixed-race attachments. Pemberton worried that local youth were 'demoralized' by First Nations women who led them to steal.[173] One impassioned letter writer wrote to the *British Columbian* that white men who lived with First Nations women were almost inevitably stripped of their manhood:

Almost without an exception those men who have sunk so low as to live with native women are degraded below the dignity of manhood. For instance, look at that creature, long-haired, badly dressed, dirty faced, redolent of salmon, who may be seen lounging at the door of almost every log cabin in the country, and tell me can that be a man? Enter any up-country dancing house; can that half-inebriated sot, who whispers obscene love speeches into the ear of yonder unfortunate squaw bedizened in all the finery which his bad taste and wasted money can supply, be a man? [...] Surely not, or we have indeed cause to be ashamed of our species.[174]

White men who married First Nations women were thus seen as dangerously flirting with relinquishing their place among the responsible gender and, more profoundly, the civilized race. They were in other words, in danger of being deracinated. [...]

These fears and judgments were based on the assumption that white men who lived with First

Nations women became more savage, rather than did their partners more civilized. Some personal narratives did tell of white men 'elevating' their First Nations partners to intelligence and cleanliness.[175] But most envisioned an opposite process. Civilization was thus constructed as a fragile state that might easily be undone by the more powerful force of savagery. Vancouver Island's first 'independent' settler, Walter Colquhoun Grant, wrote that 'though several White men have intermarried with the women of the various tribes, the result has always been that the white man has lowered himself to the standard of the wife, instead of the savage becoming at all elevated herself by the connexion.'[176]

[...] 'It is your ignorant, slothful, unpolished subject,' argued the *Cariboo Sentinel*, 'who digs about a few acres, hunts and goes fishing, and then after having done just sufficient to satisfy the typical wolf at the door, sits down in front of his log shanty and smokes his dodder with his aboriginal companion of the softer sex.'[177] Colonial backwardness, class, and rurality were encapsulated in mixed-race relationships. The *Mainland Guardian* argued that 'men living away in the interior, isolated from the centres of population, are fain to console themselves with companions, that too often, render them regardless of the future, and rob them of all energy and ambition.'[178]

[...] White men who engaged in mixed-race relationships ceased to be white and became nearly and sometimes entirely Aboriginal. [...]

More than an individual process, deracination was a palpable threat to the entire white society. Racial mixing, obviously, compromised specific colonial policies that depended on the self-evident character of racial identity and separation. When white married Aboriginal they threatened the reserve system by disrupting the process of racial identification and land allocation; they challenged the suppression of the liquor trade when Aboriginal wives drank their husbands' legal booze.[179] Aboriginal people's presence in white settlements compromised their status as imperial bastions. [...]

More profoundly, white men who cleaved themselves too closely to Aboriginal women violated white notions of racial distance and superiority. When mixed marriages took place, 'you make any *true* relation between the aboriginal people and the settlers an impossibility,' said Samuel Wilberforce, the Bishop of Oxford, at a London meeting of the Columbia Mission.[180]

[...] In these discussions, mixed-race relationships function as a symbol of imperialism gone awry. They speak of an explicitly white working-class vision of colonialism based on rough, racially plural sociability, one that differed sharply from models of imperialism rooted in racial distance and difference [...]

This discourse did not, of course, reflect social practice. The lives of mixed-race couples, like Aboriginal women, persisted and persistently defied those seeking to caricature, classify, or denigrate them. A handful of critics built on this resistance by explicitly and purposefully defending both the respectability of First Nations women and mixed-race relationships. Bogg argued that not only were Nanaimo's Aboriginal women decent wives and housekeepers, but that their domestic talents outstripped those of their white counterparts. 'It is worthy of remark that those miners who have *English* wives generally have their houses in a dirty, slatternly condition, while, on the other hand, those among the miners who have *married* Hydah or Tsimshian women have their houses kept [in] patterns of cleanliness, neatness, and comfort,'[181] he wrote. A Nanaimo resident admitted 'that there are a great many white men living with Indian women,' but denied the charge that their lives were ones of 'debauchery and vice.' Their moral character, indeed, was equivalent to that of their attackers.[182]

Yet these discursive disruptions were infrequent challenges to the construction of mixed-race relationships as deeply dangerous. [...] Aboriginal women were rarely the primary objects of concern. Rather, writers feared that mixed-race relationships imperilled white men's morality, manliness, and ultimately their claim to racial distinction and superiority. Since an orderly, large, and industrious population was key to the creation of a respectable white settler society, the tendency of mixed-race relationships to deracinate white men compromised British Columbia's colonial project. So too did the simple existence of mixed-race people. These people were constructed as inherently inferior, physically and morally weak, and a threat to the colony's political stability.

Constructions of Mixed-Blood Peoples

If sexual, domestic, and emotional relations between First Nations women and white men disturbed Victorian gender and race systems, the offspring of these unions also deeply troubled the imaginations of white British Columbians. In this sense, their fears were explicitly heterosexual one, premised not so much on a fear of sex, but on a fear of reproduction. This tendency was reinforced by the fact that the mid-nineteenth-century was a watershed in the development of 'scientific' racist thought, particularly as it related to reproduction.[183] While metropolitan in origin, these developments were not lost on this edge of empire. The invention of the word miscegenation in 1864 was duly noted by the Victoria press.[184] Hills owned a book that classified racial types and advised him on how to categorize any humans one might encounter.[185] The onset of a sustained and major white settlement in British Columbia thus occurred simultaneously with the increasing dissemination of theories of 'scientific' racism. The intensification of white settlement in British Columbia was surely enabled and encouraged by changes in racial thinking, but they did not cause it. The rise of racism and settlement were not so much causally connected as they were inextricably and largely accidentally bound by chronology.

This combination meant that race and reproduction were not solely intellectual issues for colonial British Columbians. As Homi Bhabha suggests, the hybrid, mixed-blood subject was both deeply symbolic of and troubling to colonial enterprises.[186] Certainly for many white observers, the simple existence of mixed-race people was confusing and often disturbing. Mayne wrote, 'You frequently see children quite white, and looking in every respect like English children, at an Indian village, and a very distressing sight it is.'[187] Charles Gardiner expressed a similar unease with the mixed-race community he encountered at a Fort Langley. 'There were the English, Scotch, French and Kanackas present,' he commented 'and all so thoroughly mixed with the native Indian blood, that it would take a well-versed Zoologist to decide what class of people they were, and what relation they had to each other.'[188] Such discomfort suggests how racial mixing challenged ideals of racial separation. The absence of clear markers separating 'the pure Indian to the comparative civilization of the race of partly white and partly red blood, and thence upwards to the pure white' thwarted attempts to develop race-based legislation.[189]

Many white observers were more than confused. Influenced by prevailing theories of race and reproduction, they constructed mixed-blood people as a unique and particular kind. A minority thought this specificity positive. Navy surgeon Bogg made a detailed argument about the physical fitness, reproductive prowess, and political reliability of British Columbia's 'half-breed' population: 'The offspring of intermarriage between the white and aboriginal races are generally of medium height, well-formed, and muscular, having a very light olive complexion, and high cheek-bones, while, to the intelligence of the Father, they add the quickness of observation and restless activity of the Savage. They are prolific, and are calculated to become a fine and intelligent race of people. Their antipathy to the Aborigines is very violent and intense, and should any serious difficulty arise with the natives, the Half-Breeds will afford valuable assistance in quelling the disturbance.'[190] Canadian politician Malcolm Cameron agreed. After visiting British Columbia, he told Montreal's Young Men's Christian Association that 'it is a mixed race which produces a great people, a powerful nation.'[191] But most settlers utilized notions of mixed-race specificity to an opposite end.

They evoked ideas of mixed-race degradation not in scientific jargon, but in everyday, commonsense language. Often, commentators repeated the trope that mixed-race people combined the worst of both races. To 'Indian abandonment to vice and utter want of self-control,' thought Mayne, there 'appears to be added that boldness and daring in evil which he inherits from his white parent.'[192]

Such ideas rested on the assumption that sex across racial boundaries was necessarily pathological. One commonly observed pathology was 'half-breed's' supposed physical weakness and inability to reproduce. [...]

The inferiority of mixed-blood people was thought to manifest itself in political and social terms as well, threatening British Columbia's colonial development. Congregationalist minister Matthew Macfie elevated the widely held fear of hybridity's political ramification to new levels of rhetorical excess. He traced the existence of twenty-three kinds of racial 'crosses' which, he feared, imperiled British Columbia's colonial future.[193] [..] 'The result of union between American Indians with all sections of the Aryan race,' Macfie wrote, 'is uniformly unsatisfactory, for in the *cross* that incapacity for improvement, which is the marked peculiarity of the Indian, is retained.'[194]

455

Other observers shared the fear that British Columbia's social institutions were unable to cope with a large mixed-blood population. Hills worried about how to educate these people, whose impulses for disorder were apparently so strong.[195] Fear of the potential political power of mixed-blood peoples intensified after the Red River Resistance of 1869.[196] In 1871 the Chief Commissioner of Lands and Works, B.W. Pearse, argued that only an intense state-driven reform program could compensate for mixed-blood people's ill-fated origins. Even with the establishment of a system of common schooling, he wrote, the colony's 'race of half-castes' would 'prove a curse to the Country in the next generation,' since 'the important part of the education necessary to make a good citizen will still be wanting in these young half castes, who can never have the tender care and virtuous teaching of a Christian mother, and who, being so neglected, will be too apt to copy the vices without emulating the virtues of the white man.'[197]

These related discourses about First Nations women, white-Aboriginal relationships, and mixed-race children never determined the course of peoples' lives. Yet they did set some significant parameters. Whatever their character, mixed-race relationships were lived against a discursive backdrop which, especially after the early 1860s, constructed them as dangerous both to individuals and to colonial development. At root, these ideas were premised on the representations of First Nations women as the dark, dangerous opposite to idealized images of white women. If white men cleaved themselves to their racial inferiors, they would be rendered immoral, unmanly, and, above all, deracinated; if children were born to the union, they would painfully bear the marks of their shoddy beginnings. When Brown preached his annual sermon about 'the prevailing vice' in Lillooet's little church, he was speaking to widely held concerns.

NOTES

1. Where to locate British Columbia is an old historiographic problem. See Allan Smith, 'The Writing of British Columbia History,' and Barry M. Gough, 'The Character of the British Columbia Frontier,' in W. Peter Ward and Robert A.J. McDonald, eds., *British Columbia: Historical Rendings* (Vancouver: Douglas and McIntyre, 1981).

2. Cole Harris, *The Resettlement of British Columbia: Essays on Colonialism and Geographical Change* (Vancouver: UBC Press, 1997) xi.

3. George F.G. Stanley, *The Birth of Western Canada: A History of the Riel Rebellions* (Toronto: University of Toronto Press, 1960 [1936]).

4. See Robin Fisher, 'Contact and Trade, 1774–1849,' in Hugh J.M. Johnson, ed., *The Pacific Province* (Vancouver: Douglas and McIntyre: 1996).

5. Cole Harris, 'Towards a Geography of White Power in the Cordilleran Fur Trade,' *Canadian Geographer* 39-2 (1995) 132.

6. Tennant, *Aboriginal Peoples and Politics,* 3. For a discussion of the earlier estimate, see Wilson Duff, *The Indian History of British Columbia,* vol. 1, *The Impact of the White Man* (Victoria: Province of British Columbia, 1969) 38.

7. Jean Barman, *The West beyond the West: A History of British Columbia* (Toronto: University of Toronto Press: 1991) 38.

8. Tennant, *Aboriginal Peoples and Politics*, 6–9; Fisher, 'Contact and Trade,' 48–9.

9. Jack Little, 'The Foundations of Government,' in Johnson, ed., *Pacific Province*, 68; James E. Hendrickson, 'The Constitutional Development of Colonial Vancouver Island and British Columbia,' in Ward and McDonald, eds., *British Columbia: Historical Readings,* 246.

10. Richard Mackie, 'The Colonization of Vancouver Island, 1849–1858,' *BC Studies* 96 (Winter 1992–3) 40.

11. Alfred Waddington, *The Fraser Mines Vindicated, or, the History of Four Months* (Victoria: De Cosmos, 1858) 16.

12. Little, 'The Foundations of Government,' in Johnson, ed., *Pacific Province,* 73-4.

13. In W. Kaye Lamb, ed., 'The Census of Vancouver Island, 1855,' *British Columbia Historical Quarterly* 4:1 (1940) 52.

14. The 'settled' population also included urban Aboriginal people. See Edward Mallandaine: *First Victoria Directory: Third [Fourth] Issue, and British Columbia Guide* (Victoria: Mallandaine, 1871) 94–5.

15. Sharon Meen, 'Colonial Society and Economy,' in Johnson, ed., *The Pacific Province*, 113. Also see Duff, *The Indian History,* 42.

16. Barman, *The West beyond the West,* 129. Also see Robert Galois and Cole Harris, 'Recalibrating Society: The Population Geography of British

Columbia in 1881,' *Canadian Geographer* 38:1 (1994) 37–53.

17. 'Letter From the Mouth of the Quesnelle,' *British Colonist*, 9 Nov. 1865.

18. Daiva Stasiulis and Nira Yuval-Davis, 'Introduction: Beyond Dichotomies-Gender, Race, Ethnicity and Class in Settler Societies,' in Daiva Stasiulis and Nira Yuval-Davis, eds., *Unsettling Settler Societies: Articulations of Gender, Race, Ethnicity and Class* (London: Sage, 1995) 21.

19. See Paul A. Phillips, 'Confederation and the Economy of British Columbia,' in W. George Shelton, ed., *British Columbia and Confederation* (Victoria: University of Victoria: 1967) 57.

20. Meen, 'Colonial Society and Economy,' 111.

21. See Mackie, 'The Colonization of Vancouver Island'; Sylvia Van Kirk, 'Tracing the Fortunes of Five Founding Families of Victoria,' *BC Studies*, 115/116 (Autumn/Winter 1997–8) 148–79.

22. Their critique of the HBC 'family compact,' was not new. See Loo, *Making Law, Order and Authority,* chapter 2.

23. See Lamb, ed., 'The Census of Vancouver Island, 1855,' 54–5. On the taking of this census, see James Douglas to John Russel, 21 Aug. 1855, Colonial Office, Vancouver Island Original Correspondence, CO 305/6, University of British Columbia Library (hereafter UBCL) Reel R288: 4.

24. See 'British Columbia—Blue Books of Statistics &c 1870,' 135–6. See Mallandaine, *First Victoria Directory*, 95 for what seems to be a breakdown of these figures.

25. 'Later from Cariboo,' *British Columbian*, 6 Jan. 1864.

26. Great Britain, Colonial Office, 'British Columbia—Blue Books of Statistics, 1861–1870,' BCA, CO 64/1, Reel 626A.

27. James Robb to Colonial Secretary, 2 March 1865, 'Colonial Correspondence,' BCA, CR 1372, Reel B-1361.

28. Charles Hayward, 'Diary 1862,' British Columbia Archives (hereafter BCA), Reel A-741.

29. Leonore Davidoff and Catherine Hall, *Family Fortunes: Men and Women of the English Middle Class, 1780–1850* (Chicago: University of Chicago Press: 1987); Anthony E. Rotundo, 'Body and Soul: Changing Ideals of American Middle-Class Manhood,' *Journal of Social History* 16:4 (1983) 23–38; Wally Seccombe, 'Patriarchy Stabilized: The Construction of the Male Breadwinner Wage Norm in Nineteenth-Century Britain,' *Social History* 2:1 (Jan. 1986) 53–76.

30. Robert J.C. Young, *Colonial Desire: Hybridity in Theory, Culture and Race* (London: Rougledge, 1995) chapter 4: Graham Dawson, *Soldier Heroes: British Adventure, Empire, and the Imagining of Masculinities* (London: Routledge, 1994); Mrinalini Sinha, *Colonial Masculinity: The 'Manly Englishman' and the 'Effeminate Bengali' in the Late Nineteenth Century* (Manchester: Manchester University Press, 1995).

31. John Emmerson, *Voyages, Travels, and Adventures by John Emmerson of Wolsingham* (Durham, England: Wm. Ainsley, 1865) 150; Anonymous, *The Handbook of British Columbia and Emigrant's Guide to the Gold Fields* (London: W. Oliver [1862]) 70.

32. Capt C.E. Barrett-Lennard, *Travels in British Columbia: With the Narrative of a Yacht Voyage Round Vancouver's Island* (London: Hurst and Blackett, 1862) 170.

33. Vancouver Island, Police and Prisons Department, Esquimalt, 'Charge Book 1862–1866,' BCA, GR 0428.

34. Beta Mikron [William Coutts Keppel, Earl of Albermarle], 'British Columbia and Vancouver's Island,' *Fraser's Magazine* 63 [1858] 499.

35. Phillip Nind to Colonial Secretary, in James Douglas to Duke of Newcastle, 2 May 1861, Great Britain, Colonial Office, British Columbia Original Correspondence (hereafter CO), National Archives of Canada (hereafter NAC), MG 11, CO 60/10, Reel B-84.

36. Captain P. Hankin, 'Memoirs' (Transcript), BCA, Add Mss E/B/H19A, 41.

37. Jock Phillips, *A Man's Country? The Image of the Pakeha Male: A History* (Auckland: Penguin, 1987) 27.

38. 'A Glimpse of Cariboo,' *British Colonist*, 24 Aug. 1866.

39. 'Diary of R.H. Alexander Commencing Tuesday, April 29th, 1862' (Transcript), City of Vancouver Archives (hereafter CVA) Add Mss 246, File 4, 50.

40. J.R. Wright to Amos Wright, 23 Sept. 1866, 'Correspondence of Jessie Hassard Wright,' BCA, Add Mss 1976.

41. E.E. Delavault and Isabel McInnes, ed. and trans., 'Letter from Charles Major, dated Fort Hope, Sept. 20, 1859,' in 'Two Narratives of the Fraser River Gold Rush,' in *British Columbia Historical Quarterly* (hereafter *BCHQ*) 1 (July 1941) 230.

457

42. Eric Duncan, *From Shetland to Vancouver Island: Recollections of Seventy-Five Years* (Edinburgh: Oliver and Boyd, 1937) 138–9.

43. Mirabile Dictu, 'Bush Life,' *British Colonist*, 27 Mar. 1865.

44. Dorothy Blakey Smith, ed., 'Henry Guillod's Journal of a Trip to Cariboo, 1862,' *BCHQ* 19 (July–Oct. 1955) 206.

45. Vera Angier, 'Are Men the Best Cooks?' *The Beaver* 290 (Autumn 1959) 52–3.

46. Blair, 'Diary,' 126.

47. Emmerson, *Voyages, Travels, and Adventures*, 39.

48. William G. Cox to Colonial Secretary, 9 April 1864, in Frederick Seymour to Duke of Newcastle 10 June 1864, NAC, MG 11, CO 60/18, Reel B-911.

49. R.C. Lundin Brown, *Klatsassan, And Other Reminiscences of Missionary Life In British Columbia* (London: Society for Promoting Christian Knowledge, 1873) 185.

50. R.J. Dundas, in J.J. Halcombe, *The Emigrant and the Heathen, or, Sketches of Missionary Life* (London: Society for Promoting Christian Knowledge [1870?]) 215.

51. Rev. William Burton Crickmer to Anonymous, 1 July 1860, 'Letters' (Transcript from original held at BCA), Anglican Church of Canada, Archives of the Diocese of New Westminster / Ecclesiastical Province of British Columbia, Vancouver School of Theology, University of British Columbia (hereafter ADNW/EPBC), PSA 50, File 3, 9.

52. 'The Miners Ten Commandments,' *Cariboo Sentinel*, 8 Sept. 1866. This originated in California in 1853.

53. Lord, *At Home in the Wilderness*, 1.

54. R.H. Pidcock, 'Adventures in Vancouver Island 1862' (Transcript), BCA, Add Mss 728, vol. 4a, 10.

55. Emmerson, *Voyages, Travels, and Adventures*, 80.

56. Hayward, 'Diary,' np.

57. See Emmerson, *Voyages, Travels, and Adventures*, 64.

58. Hayward, 'Diary,' n.p.

59. Andrew J. Rotter, '"Matilda for Gods Sake Write": Women and Families on the Argonaut Mind,' *California History* 63:2 (Summer 1979) 128-41.

60. George Hills, 'Journal 1836-1861' (Transcript), ADNM/EPBC, MS 65a, PSA 57, 411.

61. 'The Cariboo Hospital,' *Cariboo Sentinel*, 21 May 1866.

62. Dundas in Halcombe, *The Emigrant and the Heathen,* 205.

63. William Mark, *Cariboo: A True and Correct Narrative to the Cariboo Gold Diggings, British Columbia* (Stockton: W.M. Wright, 1863) 29; Emmerson, *Voyages, Travels, and Adventures,* 56.

64. Robert Stevenson, 'Diary' and 'Miscellaneous Materials relating to,' BCA, Add Mss 315.

65. Louis LeBourdais, 'Billy Barker of Barkerville,' *BCHQ* 1:1 (1937) 167.

66. Nobody, 'Letter from Comox—Progress of the Settlement,' *British Colonist,* 4 Oct. 1867.

67. D.W. Higgins, *The Mystic Spring and Other Tales of Western Life* (Toronto: William Briggs, 1904) 56.

68. R. Byron Johnson, *Very Far West Indeed: A Few Rough Experiences on the North-West Pacific Coast* (n.p: 1985 [London: Sampson Low, Marston, Low & Searle, 1872]) 14.

69. Edgar Fawcett, *Some Reminiscences of Old Victoria* (Toronto: William Biggs, 1912) 20–1.

70. Dorothy Blakey Smith ed., *Lady Franklin Visits the Pacific Northwest: Being Extracts from the Letters of Miss Sophia Craycroft, Sir John Franklin's Niece, Feb. to April 1861 and April to July 1870* (Victoria: Provincial Archives of British Columbia Memoir No. XI, 1979) 71.

71. A Returned Digger, *The Newly Discovered Gold Fields of British Columbia,* 8th ed. (London: Darton and Hodge, 1862) 8.

72. Richard Charles Mayne, *Four Years in British Columbia and Vancouver Island* (London: John Murray, 1862; reprint, Toronto: S.R. Publishers, 1969) 350.

73. E. Anthony Rotundo, 'Romantic Friendship: Male Intimacy and Middle-Class Youth in the Northern United States, 1800–1900,' *Journal of Social History* 23:1 (Fall 1989) 1; Steven Maynard, 'Rough Work and Rugged Men: The Social Construction of Masculinity in Working-Class History,' *Labour / Le Travail* 23 (Spring 1989) 159–69; Carroll Smith-Rosenberg, 'The New Woman as Androgyne: Social Disorder and Gender Crisis, 1870–1929,' in *Disorderly Conduct: Visions of Gender in Victorian America* (New York: Oxford University Press, 1985).

74. 'Legislative Council Proceedings,' *British Colonist*, 20 Mar. 1867.

75. Ann B. Scott to Edward Cridge, 1 June 1871, 'Edward Cridge, Correspondence Inward,' BCA, Add Mss 320, Box 1, File 4.

76. See correspondent re Hannah Jarman to Edward Cardwell, 28 July 1865, NAC, MG 11, CO 305/27, Reel B-249.

77. 'Registration of Births, Deaths, and Marriages,' *British Colonist*, 16 Jan. 1863.

78. 'Divorces,' *Cariboo Sentinel*, 25 Feb. 1871.

79. C. Sharp, 'A Glimpse of Cariboo,' *British Colonist*, 24 Aug. 1866.

80. 'Letter from Williams Creek,' *British Colonist*, 25 June 1863.

81. See Jeffrey Weeks, 'Discourse, Desire and Sexual Deviance: Some Problems in a History of Homosexuality,' in *Against Nature: Essays on History, Sexuality and Identity* (London: Rivers Oram, 1991).

82. Watchman, '"Twaddling Sensations of Anonymous Writers,"' *British Colonist*, 2 Mar. 1866.

83. Higgins, *The Mystic Spring*, 35–6. Also see D.W. Higgins, *The Passing of a Race and More Tales of Western Life* (Toronto: William Briggs, 1905), esp. 'The Pork Pie Hat.'

84. A.F. Pemberton to Acting Colonial Secretary, 25 Feb. 1865, 'Colonial Correspondence,' BCA, GR 1372, Reel B-1394.

85. See Higgins, *The Passing of a Race*, 116; Edward Mallandaine, *First Victoria Directory; Comprising General Directory* (Victoria: Mallandaine, 1860) 26; 'Distinguished Arrival,' *Weekly Victoria Gazette*, 1 June 1859.

86. 'John Butts Again,' *Vancouver Times*, 30 Mar. 1861; 'Police Court,' *Vancouver Times*, 17 Jan. 1865; 'Lodgings for the Remainder of the Season,' *Vancouver Times*, 4 Feb. 1865; 'Butts Again in Trouble' *Victoria Press*, 9 Apr. 1861; 'Street Cleaning,' *Victoria Press*, 9 Oct. 1861; 'Improving,' *Victoria Press*, 19 Oct. 1861; 'John Butts Once More,' *British Colonist*, 8 Apr. 1861; '"Necessity the Mother of Invention,"' *Victoria Press*, 3 June 1862; 'John Butts,' *Victoria Press*, 22 Aug. 1862.

87. 'Sodomy,' *British Colonist*, 31 Jan. 1860; 'Police Court,' *British Colonist*, 2 Feb. 1860.

88. 'Trial of John Butts,' *British Colonist*, 18 Feb. 1860.

89. See gaol records included in Aug. F. Pemberton to William A.G. Young, 7 Feb. 1860 and Aug. F. Pemberton to William A.G. Young, 13 Feb. 1860, BCA; 'colonial Correspondence,' GR 1372, Reel B-1356.

90. Deposition of William Williams, 30 Jan. 1860, 'Minutes of Evidence, Police Court,' *R v. John Butts*, 31 Jan. 1860, in British Columbia, Attorney General, 'Documents 1857–1966' (hereafter 'Attorney General Documents') BCA, GR 419, Box 1, File 1860/23.

91. Evidence of Thomas Cooper, 1 Feb. 1860; Evidence of Andrew Coyle, 2 Feb. 1860, 'Attorney General Documents,' BCA, GR 419, Box 1, File 1860/23.

92. Deposition of William M Dunham, 31 Jan. 1860, 'Attorney General Documents,' BCA, GR 419, Box 1, File 1860/23. On sex between men and working-class boys, see Steven Maynard, "Horrible Temptations": Sex, Men, and Working-Class Male Youth in Urban Ontario, 1890–1935,' *Canadian Historical Review* 78 (June 1997) 191–235.

93. Deposition of Francis Jackson, 31 Jan. 1860; 'Attorney General Documents, BCA, GR 419, Box 1, File 1860/23.

94. Dunham, 'Attorney General Documents,' BCA, GR 419, Box 1, File 1860/23.

95. 'Trial of John Butts,' *British Colonist*, 18 Feb. 1860.

96. 'Trial of John Butts,' *British Colonist*, 18 Feb. 1860; Untitled, *British Colonist*, 18 Feb. 1860.

97. Testimony of John Butts, 9 Feb. 1860, BCA, GR 419, Box 1, File 1860/23. The press reported that Butts said 'The whole charge is a conspiracy to get my house and lot from me.' See 'Trial of John Butts,' *British Colonist*, 18 Feb. 1860.

98. See Joseph Needham to Colonial Secretary, 1 Mar. 1866, 'Colonial Correspondence,' BCA, GR 1372, Reel B-1350; *R v Matthew Rusid*, 'Attorney General Documents,' BCA, GR 419, Box 5, File 1866/11; 'Assizes,' *British Colonist*, 22 Mar. 1865.

99. *R v Kingswell*, 'Attorney General Documents,' BCA, GR 419, Box 9, File 1870/24. This case is included in the '1870' file and case name, but the court documents included in this file are dated 1873.

100. Tina Loo, *Making Law, Order and Authority in British Columbia, 1821–1871* (Toronto: University of Toronto Press, 1993) esp. Chapters 3 and 6.

101. Ronald Hyam, *Empire and Sexuality: The British Experience* (Manchester: Manchester University Press, 1990) 212.

102. Robert J.C. Young, *Colonial Desire: Hybridity in Theory, Culture and Race* (London: Routledge, 1995) 25–6.

103. James Douglas to John Packington, 11 Nov. 1852, University of British Columbia Library (hereafter UBCL), CO 305/3, Reel R288:1.

104. Robert Melrose, 'Diary, Aug. 1852–July 1857' (photostat), BCA Add Mss, E/B/M49.1A, 18.

105. James E. Hendrickson, ed., *Journals of the Colonial Legislatures of the Colonies of Vancouver Island and British Columbia, 1851–1871*, vol. 1, *Journals of the Council, Executive Council, and Legislative Council of Vancouver Island, 1851–1866* (Victoria: Provincial Archives of British Columbia, 1980) 14–15.

459

106. 'Debating Class,' *British Colonist,* 1 Dec. 1866.

107. 'The License Question,' *Victoria Press*, 4 July 1862; Irene Genevieve Marie Zaffaroni, 'The Great Chain of Being: Racism and Imperialism in Colonial Victoria, 1858–1871,' MA Thesis, University of Victoria, 1987, 129–30.

108. Johnson, *Very Far West Indeed*, 142.

109. 'Lighthearted Prisoners,' *Victoria Press,* 6 May 1861.

110. *Report of the Columbia Mission, 1860,* 67.

111. Viscount Milton and W.B. Cheadle, *The North-West Passage by Land: Being the Narrative of an Expedition from the Atlantic to the Pacific* (London: Cassell, Petter, and Galpin, 1865) 359.

112. Carl Friesach, 'Extracts from *Ein Ausflug nach Britisch-Columbien im Jahre 1858*,' in Delevault and McInnes, 'Two Narratives,' 221–31.

113. In Dorothy Blakey Smith, ed. *The Reminiscences of Doctor John Sebastian Helmcken* (Vancouver: University of British Columbia Press, 1975) 208.

114. Pro Bono Publico, 'The Dance House,' *British Colonist*, 23 Dec. 1861.

115. Ephraim Evans, 'Rev. Dr. Evans on the Dance Houses,' *British Colonist*, 25 Dec. 1861.

116. Bard of the Lowhee, 'A Reminiscence of Cariboo Life,' *Cariboo Sentinel*, 14 Nov. 1868.

117. 'Gambling in British Columbia,' *Weekly Victoria Gazette*, 1 June 1859.

118. *Report of the Columbia Mission 1860*, 45; Higgins, *The Passing of a Race*, 257–8.

119. Gunther Peck, 'Manly Gambles: The Politics of Risk on the Comstock Lode,' *Journal of Social History* 26:4 (Summer 1993) 714.

120. 'The Prize Fight,' *Cariboo Sentinel*, 25 Oct. 1866.

121. David Peterson del Mar, *What Trouble I Have Seen: A History of Violence against Wives* (Cambridge: Harvard University Press, 1996) 21–3.

122. Matthew B. Begbie, 'Journey into the Interior of British Columbia, Communicated by the Duke of Newcastle, read Dec. 12 1859,' (np: nd) 247.

123. In George F.G. Stanley, ed., *Mapping the Frontier: Charles Wilson's Diary of the Survey of the 49th Parallel, 1858–1862, while Secretary of the British Boundary Commissions* (Toronto: Macmillian, 1970) 24.

124. Barrett-Lennard, *Travels in British Columbia*, 170.

125. Untitled, *Cariboo Sentinel*, 15 Dec. 1866.

126. Quoted in Capt. Fenton Aylmer, ed., *A Cruise in the Pacific: From the Log of a Naval Officer*, vol. 2 (London: Hurst and Blackett, 1860) 89.

127. R.C. Lundin Brown, British Columbia. *The Indians and Settlers at Lillooet, Appeal for Missionaries* (London: R. Clay: Sons, and Taylor, 1870) 6, 7.

128. 'Census,' *British Colonist*, 10 June 1868.

129. Mary Louise Pratt, *Imperial Eyes: Travel Writing and Transculturation* (London: Routledge, 1992) 4.

130. Ranya Green, 'The Pocahontas Perplex: The Image of Indian Women in American Culture,' in Ellen Carol DuBois and Vicki L. Ruiz, eds, *Unequal Sisters: A Multi-Cultural Reader in U.S. Women's History* (New York: Routledge, 1990); David D. Smits, 'The "Squaw Drudge": A Prime Index of Savagism,' *Ethnohistory* 29:4 (1982) 281–306.

131. Sarah Carter, *Capturing Women: The Manipulation of Cultural Imagery in Canada's Prairie West* (Montreal and Kingston: McGill-Queen's University Press, 1997) Chapter 5.

132. Willard E. Ireland, ed., 'Gold-Rush Days in Victoria, 1858–1859,' by James Bell, *British Columbia Historical Quarterly* (hereafter *BCHQ*) 12 (July 1948) 237. Emphasis in original.

133. 'Notes From the Northwest,' *British Colonist*, 30 Oct. 1863.

134. Dorothy Blakey Smith, ed., 'The Journal of Arthur Thomas Bushby, 1858–1859,' in *BCHQ* 21 (1957-8) 122.

135. John Keast, Lord, *The Naturalist in Vancouver Island and British Columbia* (London: Richard Bentley, 1866) vol. 1, 233.

136. Erica Smith, '"Gentlemen, This Is No Ordinary Trial": Sexual Narratives in the Trial of the Reverend Corbett, Red River, 1863,' in Jennifer S.H. Brown and Elizabeth Vibert, eds, *Reading beyond Works: Contexts for Native History* (Peterborough, ON: Broadview Press, 1966)

137. T.F. Elliot to Arthur Birch, 9 Nov. 1866, in Frederick Seymour to the Earl of Carnarvon, 11 Jan. 1867, Great Britain, Colonial Office, British Columbia Original Correspondence (hereafter CO) BCA, GR 1486, CP 60/27, Reel B-1439.

138. Joseph W. Trutch, 'Memo,' 13 Jan. 1870, in A. Musgrave to Earl of Granville, 29 Jan. 1870, BCA, GR 1486, CO 60/38, Reel B-1448.

139. Dr Edward B. Bogg, 'Journal of Her Majesty's Hired Surveying Vessel, Beaver, 1863,' Public Records Office (hereafter PRO), ADM 101/276, 16-16a.

140. 'Arrest of Street Walkers,' *British Colonist*, 8 May 1860.

141. Phillip Hankin, 'Memoirs' (Transcript), BCA, Add Mss E/B/H19A, 54. Translation mine.

142. See Frederick Seymour to Edward Cardwell, 1 May 1865, BCA, GR 1486, CO 60/21, Reel B-1435.

143. Hankin, 'Memoirs,' 54.

144. Carroll Smith-Rosenberg, 'Captured Subjects/Savage Others: Violently Engendering the New American,' *Gender and History* 5:2 (Summer 1993) 178.

145. Janice Acoose/Misko-Kisikāwihkwè (Red Sky Woman): *Iskwewak—Kalt'KiYaw Ni Wahkomakanak: Neither Indian Princesses Nor Easy Squaws* (Toronto: Women's Press, 1995) 85.

146. Sylvia Van Kirk, *Many Tender Ties': Women in Fur Trade Society in Western Canada, 1670–1870* (Winnipeg: Watson and Dwyer, 1980); Jennifer S.H. Brown, *Strangers in Blood: Fur Trade Company Families in Indian Country* (Vancouver: University of British Columbia Press, 1980).

147. George Hills, 'Journal 1836–1861' (Transcript), Archives of the Diocese of New Westminster/Ecclesiastical Province of British Columbia (hereafter ADNW/EPBC) MS 65a, PSA 57, 370.

148. John Emmerson, *Voyages, Travels, and Adventures by John Emmerson of Wolsingham* (Durham: Wm. Ainsley, 1865) 37.

149. George M. Grant, *Ocean to Ocean: Sandford Fleming's Expedition through Canada in 1872* (Toronto: James Cambell, 1873) 273.

150. Ebenezer Robson, 'Diary,' BCA, Reel 17A, np. Emphasis original.

151. Vancouver Island, Police and Prisons Department, 'Esquimalt Charge Book 1862–1866.' BCA, GR 0428.

152. Crosby, *Among the An-ko-me-nums*, 180.

153. George Hills, 'Journal 1 Jan-10 June 1863' (Transcript), ANDW/EPBC, 29.

154. Brown, *British Columbia*, 7.

155. J.S. Matthews, 'Memo of conversation with Mrs Madeline Williams, aged Indian woman, also known as Gassy Jack's wife, living with her granddaughter, Nita Williams, in a small cottage at the west end of the Indian Reserve, North Vancouver, 13 June 1940,' 'Indian Wives of White Men,' City of Vancouver Archives (hereafter CVA), Add Mss 54, vol. 13, File 06612.

156. 'Register of Baptisms and Marriages, 1860–1881, St Paul's Nanaimo,' ADBCA, Text 30, Box 8; 'Parochial Register of Baptisms and Marriages for district of St. John's Victoria 1860–1871.' ADBCA, Text 202, Box 6; 'Holy Trinity Cathedral Marriage Register,' CVA, Add Mss 603, vol. 1, Reel m-21; 'Christ Church Hope Marriage Register 1862–1872,' ADNW/EPBC,

RG4.0.34; 'St John the Divine Yale Marriage Register,' ADNW/EPBC.

157. George Hills, 'Hills Journal 1866' (Transcript), ADNW/EPBC, 65.

158. 'Memorandum of conversation of Aug. Jack Khahatsahlano, who called at the City Archives,' 31 Oct. 1938, 'Indian Wives of White Men,' CVA, Add Mss 54, vol. 13, File 06612. Mrs Walker would be the daughter of the white bridegroom, Joe Silvey, aka 'Portuguese Joe.' His bride was a high-born Squamish woman, Khaltinat.

159. Mayne, *Four Years in British Columbia and Vancouver Island*, 248.

160. 'Diary of R.H. Alexander Commencing Tuesday, Apr. 29th, 1862' (Transcript) CVA, Add Mss 246, File 48, 8.

161. N.P., 'Nanaimo,' *Victoria Press,* 27 June 1861.

162. 'Memo of conversation (over the phone) with Miss Muriel Crakanthorp,' in Matthews, 'Indian Wives of White Men,' CVA, Add Mss 54, vol. 13, File 06612, 2; Jean Barman, 'Lost Okanagan: In Search of the First Settler Families,' *Okanagan History* (1996) 9–20.

163. J.S. Matthews, 'Memo of Conversation with Mrs James Walker, 721 Cambie Street … [who] kindly called at the City Archives, 27 May 1940'; Memorandum of conversation of Aug. Jack Khahtsahlano, who called at the City Archives,' 31 Oct. 1838, in Matthews, 'Indian Wives of White Men,' CVA, Add Mss 54, vol. 13, File 06612, 2.

164. *Third Report of the Columbia Mission with List of Contributions, 1861* (London: Rivingtons [1862]) 26; Robin Hood, 'From Nanaimo,' Victoria Press, 28 June 1861.

165. 'A Disorderly Neighbourhood,' *British Colonist*, 14 Oct. 1861.

166. J.C.B. Cave to Captain Franklyn, 5 Dec. 1864, in W.H. Franklyn to Colonial Secretary, 5 Dec. 1864, BCA, 'Colonial Correspondence,' GR 1372, Reel B-1329.

167. Anne McClintock, *Imperial Leather: Race, Gender and Sexuality in the Colonial Contest* (New York: Routledge, 1995) 30.

168. W.H. Franklyn to Henry Wakeford, 13 July 1864, 'Colonial Correspondence,' BCA, GR 1372, Reel B-1329.

169. 'Extract of letter from Mr Robert Brown, Commander of Exploring Expedition 1864, dated 1st June 1865,' in Arthur Kennedy to Edward Cardwell, 3 Sept. 1866, Great Britain, Colonial Office, Vancouver Island Original Correspondence (hereafter

CO), National Archives of Canada (hereafter NAC), MG 11, CO 305/29, Reel B-250.

170. 'Extract from Lieutenant Wilkes Narrative of the United States Exploring Expedition'; in 'Testimony in Favour of the Hudson's Bay Company,' 1848, Great Britain, Colonial Office, Vancouver Island Original Correspondence, University of British Columbia Library, CO 305/I, Reel R288:1.

171. See, e.g., Edmund Hope Verney to Harry Verney, 15 May 1862; Edmund Hope Verney to Harry Verney, 16 Aug. 1862, in Allan Pritchard, ed., *Vancouver Island Letters of Edmund Hope Verney, 1862–1865* (Vancouver: University of British Columbia Press, 1996) 74–7, 84.

172. Lux, 'Magisterial Morality: A Voice from the Mountains,' *British Columbian,* 14 Nov. 1861.

173. A.F. Pemberton to Colonial Secretary, 2 Mar. 1870, BCA, 'Colonial Correspondence,' GR 1372, Reel BB-1357.

174. I.D.C., '"A Man's a Man for a' That,"' *British Columbian,* 4 June 1862.

175. See Emmerson, *Travels, Voyages, and Adventures,* 48–9.

176. Walter Colquohoun Grant to Brodie, 8 Aug. 1851, in James E. Hendrickson ed., 'Two Letters from Walter Colquhoun Grant,' *BC Studies* 26 (Jan.–Apr. 1978) 13.

177. 'Profits of Agriculture,' *Cariboo Sentinel,* 24 July 1869.

178. 'Immigration,' *Mainland Guardian,* 9 Feb. 1871.

179. 'The Indian Reserve Question,' *British Columbian,* 131 Nov. 1867; Settler, 'Our Indian Liquor Traffic Act,' *Nanaimo Gazette,* 18 Sept. 1865; 'The Ravine,' *Victoria Press,* 29 Sept. 1862.

180. In *Annual Report of the Columbia Mission 1860,* 51. Emphasis added.

181. Bogg, 'Journal of Her Majesty's Hired Surveying Vessel, Beaver, 1863,' PRO, ADM 101/276, 16. Emphasis in original.

182. C.S., 'Vice at Nanaimo,' *Victoria Press,* 24 July 1861.

183. Robert J.C. Young, *Colonial Desire: Hybridity in Theory, Culture, and Race* (London: Routledge, 1995) 9.

184. 'Miscegenation,' *Victoria Daily Chronicle,* 20 Mar. 1864.

185. *A Manual of Ethnological Inquiry Being a Series of Questions Concerning the Human Race, Prepared by a Sub-Committee of the British Association for the Advancement of Science … Adapted for the Use of Travellers and Others, in Studying the Varieties of Man* (London: Taylor and Francis, 1852) in ADNW/ EPBC, PSA 41, File 3, 'Documents.'

186. Homi Bhabha, 'Of Mimicry and Man: The Ambivalence of Colonial Discourse,' Oct. 28 (Spring 1984) 125–34.

187. Mayne, *Four Years,* 248.

188. In Robie L. Reid, ed., C.C. Gardiner, 'To the Fraser River Mines in 1858,' *British Columbia Historical Quarterly,* 1:1 (Oct. 1937) 248.

189. Henry Pellew Crease to William Duncan, 9 Nov. 1867, 'Colonial Correspondence,' BCA, GR 1372, Reel B-1326, File 498/19.

190. Bogg, 'Journal of Her Majesty's Hired Surveying Vessel, Beaver, 1863,' PRO, ADM 101/276, 16.

191. *Lecture Delivered by the Hon. Malcolm Cameron to the Young Men's Mutual Improvement Association* (Quebec: G.E. Desbartes, 1865) 21.

192. Mayne, *Four Years,* 277.

193. Macfie, 379, 381.

194. See Matthew Macfie, The *Impending Contact of the Aryan & Turanian Races, With Special Reference to Recent Chinese Migrations* (London: Sunday Lecture Society, 1878) 17.

195. Hills, 'Journal 1862,' 29.'

196. 'The Revolt and its Lessons,' *British Colonist,* 3 Dec. 1869.

197. B.W. Pearse, 'Memo on the Letter of the Bishop of Columbia to the Right Honourable Earl of Kimberley,' nd, in British Columbia, Attorney General, 'Documents,' BCA, GR 419, Box 10, 'Indian Improvement—aid to missionary societies,' File 1871/23, 11–12.

FIRST NATIONS AND THE NEW EMPIRE

Elizabeth Jane Errington
Queen's University
Royal Military College

FIRST NATIONS AND THE NEW EMPIRE

● INTRODUCTION

Elizabeth Jane Errington

European travellers to North America were usually eager (although at the same time, often a little apprehensive) to meet "real Indians." For hundreds of years, the Aboriginal population had been portrayed as fierce, demonic, wild, savage, noble, exotic creatures of the wilderness. What travellers found instead, according to their accounts, was a people who were poor, weak, and prone to drunkenness and disorder. Some visitors noted that there were still "wild" Indians in the north and the west; in the settled parts of the colonies, however, "civilization" had transformed these once-noble inhabitants into a population that was doomed to extinction. In the meantime, travellers reported, the Indians gave settlers little trouble. For the First Nations of British America, the seeming march of the British Empire across the northern half of the continent in the nineteenth century was certainly disruptive and, for many, seemed to place the very integrity of their cultures in jeopardy. The dramatic increase in the number of white settlers, with their axes and plow and sheep and cattle, threatened traditional economies; and from the Maritimes to the new European settlements on the Pacific coast, the imposition of British government and laws, together with the increasingly paternalistic attitudes of colonial and imperial officials, put increasing pressure on Aboriginal social and political organizations. And yet, although by mid-century First Nations peoples often felt under siege, they were to the amazement and often consternation of white society still very much a part of the British North American colonial world. The story of First Nations-European relations in the nineteenth century is not, as many traditional histories of the period concluded, one of passive victimization and tragic but inevitable disappearance. There is no question that thousands of Aboriginal people lost their lands, and their traditional livelihood. Europeans also brought disease; throughout the nineteenth-century, smallpox, scarlet fever, and other epidemics swept through Aboriginal villages and often decimated local populations. And Christian missionaries who were determined to "civilize and save" the Aboriginal people challenged traditional beliefs and practices. But the impact of these potentially devastating forces varied enormously from one region of the continent to another. It depended on local circumstances, the changing policies of colonial and imperial governments and. of course, on the responses of the First Nations people themselves. As the two articles in this module illustrate, the First Nations population developed numerous strategies to try to deal with imperial and colonial outsiders. They actively sought to maintain the cultural and economic integrity of their communities. Often they selectively appropriated Western ideas and beliefs and incorporated them into their own cultures and social and economic practices. They made representations to imperial and colonial authorities demanding recognition and their own place in the empire. Some, like the Beothuck of Newfoundland did, in the end, "disappear"; many others did not. The basic British policy toward Aboriginal populations in North America in the nineteenth century was a combination of segregation and protection, civilization, and eventual assimilation. Throughout the eighteenth century and into the early part of the nineteenth century, the British had needed the First Nations and, as valuable military and economic allies, the Mohawk and others had considerable leverage with officials in London and in the colonies. By the mid-eighteenth century, however, Britain had come to believe that the indigenous population also needed protecting from land-hungry settlers and colonial governments. The Proclamation of 1763, issued soon after New France was ceded to the British Crown, officially protected Aboriginal territories in the west from encroachment by white settlers and dictated that only the imperial government could purchase and obtain title to Indian lands. Twenty years later, when the British government began to open up the interior colony of Upper Canada to settlers, it negotiated treaties with local First Nations to gain title to the land; however, as the records now attest, many of these were signed under duress or were signed with representatives who could not speak for their communities. And as the First Nations people quickly discovered, British authorities often failed to live up to their treaty obligations. After 1815, Aboriginal communities were subject to increasing pressure not only to relinquish large portions of their land but also to accept in their midst missionaries who would teach them both the word of God and how to become "white." Communities of Ojibwa living along the Great Lakes, for example, were encouraged to give up the hunt, move to villages on reserves, and become farmers. Methodist missionaries opened village schools and performed Christian marriages that reinforced the importance of the nuclear family instead of the traditional extended-kin networks and clan associations. By mid-century, First Nations peoples living in the older settler societies in the Maritimes and the Canadas found themselves increasingly marginalized by white society. Native responses to these pressures varied. Without reserves and a dwindling population, the Mi'kmaq and other First Nations living in the Maritime colonies were forced to rely on seasonal work as guides in the bush or a labourers for local settlers, or on subsidies from the white community. Many of the Aboriginal peoples in the Canadas, even those already on reserves, continued to hunt; they also farmed (often collectively) and they traded with white neighbours. First Nations also continued to engage imperial and colonial authorities on their own terms. They sent petitions to local legislatures, to governors, and even to the Queen, demanding that the government meet its treaty obligations; and they made alliances with other Aboriginal communities, with white neighbours and other supporters, to help press their claims. By 1850, when the Robinson Treaties were signed, alienating much of Indian territory bordering the upper Great Lakes, it was clear that their leaders had learned a good deal about negotiating and about how best to secure their own future. Overtly rejecting assimilation, some First Nations people actively pursued a policy of segregation and reserves became a vehicle not of civilization but of cultural survival. Others sought a form of limited accommodation with white society. What all First Nations communities, in the Maritimes and the Canadas sought, however, was the means to maintain the economic viability of their communities and thus assure their cultural integrity. The situation in the western part of the continent was quite different. Until almost the time of Confederation, the demands of the fur trade determined the relationship between First Nations and Europeans. The Hudson's Bay Company, which until mid-century was the only European authority in Rupert's Land, depended on the Aboriginal population for its economic viability; it was in the HBC's interest not to restrict or to try to "civilize" local populations. For their part, First Nations peoples quickly integrated the rhythms of the fur trade into their own communities. Certainly, the dynamics of this interdependence between Europeans and First Nations changed throughout the nineteenth century. The development of the Red River settlement in what would become Manitoba brought white settlers and missionaries to the region in the 1820s. Thirty years later, the decision to make Fort Victoria a retirement settlement for HBC servants and their often Aboriginal families altered relations in the far West. In British Columbia, white miners, settlers, and missionaries wanted Aboriginal lands and souls. Until well after Confederation, the First Nations peoples outnumbered the white settlers, however, and in British Columbia, at least, their economies did not depend solely on extensive hunting grounds but, for most, on the rich fishing fields. As John Lutz illustrates in "After the Fur Trade," First Nations peoples were an essential part of the workforce that developed British Columbia.

Early histories of the settlement and development of British North America/Canada in the nineteenth century were remarkably silent about the history of the First Nations and about their relationships with white society. Most accounts told of the triumphal march of white settlement across the continent, of Euro-Canadians' battles with the wilderness, and of the creation of a "civilized" and modern nation that stretched from sea to sea. First Nations appeared only briefly, if at all—for example, in discussions about the Hudson's Bay Company and the western fur trade, or when First Nations and Métis resisted the encroachment of white settlers and government policies, as at Red River in 1869 or in 1885 with Riel in the North West. Like nineteenth-century travellers, many of these histories assumed that "Indians" were a sad lot, victims of their own inability to adjust to modern society, or they were often written out of the story altogether. In the last 40 or so years, however, scholars have begun to radically revise their understanding and appreciation of the history of First Nations in nineteenth-century British North America and to explore the rich and diverse relationships between settlers, governments, and Aboriginal populations. In part, this is as a result of the determination of First Nations peoples themselves to be heard and to assert their claims to traditional lands and hunting and fishing rights that had been guaranteed in eighteenth- and nineteenth-century treaties. At about the same time, scholars began to unravel the rich complexities of nineteenth century society in British North America. As the two articles here illustrate, scholars now use the tools of ethnohistory, which draws on insights from anthropology, archaeology, and ethnography, as well as traditional written sources, to explore the experiences and expectations of particular Aboriginal communities and nations in their encounters with white settlers and governments. Unlike those who are trying to recover First Nations voices in the sixteenth and seventeenth centuries, scholars of the late colonial period also have access to a wealth of government documentation, the commentary of numerous travellers and settlers, and written accounts and petitions of Aboriginal people themselves. Ethnohistorians also have photographs and, perhaps most important, vibrant oral evidence. This is particularly true for historians who examine the First Nations peoples in the West and in British Columbia, as is clear in Susan Neylan's study of how the Tsimshian received the Christian message. But as Janet Chute illustrates in her article, such evidence is also vital to uncovering how First Nations people in early Ontario coped with imperial and colonial authorities; at the same time, it offers a window into the complex thinking and actions of Native leaders themselves.

The politics of Singwaukonse and the British Sault seem a long way from the spiritual world of the Tsimshian of British Columbia. The two communities were not only divided by space but also had very different social structures and cultures, and they faced quite different challenges from their white neighbours. Each community coped with the pressures imposed by the British Empire in its own way and within the context of its understanding of the world. In so doing, each managed to maintain an identity that was both separate from and part of the colonial whole.

QUESTIONS

1. How have using the tools and perspectives of ethnohistory allowed scholars to reconsider the story of First Nations–European relationships in the nineteenth century?

2. Many historians understand First Nation's–European interaction in the nineteenth century as a clash and conflict of cultures. Was this always the case?

3. Different sources offer the scholar different and often conflicting understandings of relationships between First Nations peoples and white society. How, or can these be reconciled?

4. One of the conclusions many historians draw is that, by 1850, First Nations had been marginalized by the British Empire and colonial society in British North America. Is this what is reflected in First Nations' accounts? What alternative conclusions might you draw, and what is the basis of your conclusions?

5. How are the situations that the Ojibwa and the Tsimshian found themselves in different and similar, and what "tools" did each use to cope with their respective situations?

FURTHER READINGS

Kerry Abel, *Drum Songs: Glimpses of Dene History* (Montreal & Kingston: McGill-Queen's University Press, 1993).

Theodore Binnema, *Common and Contested Ground: A Human and Environmental History of the Northwestern Plains* (Toronto: University of Toronto Press, 2001).

Janet E. Chute, *The Legacy of Shingwaukonse: A Century of Native Leadership* (Toronto: University of Toronto Press, 1998).

Olive Patricia Dickason, *Canada's First Nations: A History of Founding Peoples from Earliest Times*, 2nd Edition (Toronto: Oxford University Press, 1997).

Jo-Anne Fiske, Susan Sleeper Smith, and William Wicken, eds. *New Faces of the Fur Trade: Selected Papers of the Seventh North American Fur Trade Conference, Halifax, Nova Scotia, 1995* (East Lansing: Michigan State University, 1998).

RM. Galois, "Colonial Encounters: The Worlds of Arthur Wellington Clah, 1855–1881" *BC Studies* No. 115/116, Autumn/Winter 1997/98.

John Lutz, "After the Fur Trade: The Aboriginal Labouring Class of British Columbia, 1849–1890" *Journal of the Canadian Historical Association* New Series, 3 (1992).

Susan Neylan, *The Heavens Are Changing: Nineteenth-Century Protestant Missions and Tsimshian Christianity* (Montreal & Kingston: McGill-Queen's University Press, 2003).

Edward S. Rogers and Donald B. Smith. ed. *Aboriginal Ontario: Historical Perspectives on the First Peoples* (Toronto: Dundurn Press, 1994).

Donald B. Smith, *Sacred Feathers: The Reverend Peter Jones (Kahkewaquonaby) and the Mississauga Indians* (Toronto: University of Toronto Press, 1987).

Sylvia Van Kirk, *"Many Tender ties": Women in Fur Trade Society, 1670–1870* (Winnipeg: Watson & Dwyer, 1980).

William Wicken, *The Colonization of Mi'Kmaw Memory and History, 1794–1828: The King v Gilbert Sylliboy* (Toronto: University of Toronto Press, 2012).

▲ Document 1: Chiefs from the Six Nations Reserve in Brantford Reading Wampum Belts, 1870s

● The Six Nations Reserve was established after the American Revolution, when, as military allies of the British, the Mohawk and many other members of the Iroquois Confederacy could no longer return home to New York State. Although by the time of Confederation the community on the Grand River resembled other settlements in Upper Canada (Ontario), residents continued to identify themselves as members of the Six Nations and to honour the wampum belt, the traditional tool of communicating with other nations and communities. What are some of the changes and the continuities of Mohawk culture that are represented in this photograph?

Source: *"Chiefs from the Six Nations Reserve in Brantford Reading Wampum belts,"* c. 1870s. Library and Archives of Canada/Library of Parliament Collection/Credit: C-085137.

470

▲ Document 2: Wikwemikong Indian Reserve, Manitoulin Island, 1856

● Wikwemikong was established in 1836 as part of Lieutenant-Governor Sir Francis Bond Head's decision to remove Native populations from white society. Hundreds of Aboriginal people were resettled on Manitoulin Island, in Georgian Bay. On the basis of this watercolour by William Armstrong, how had contact with white society influenced life on the reserve?

Source: "Wikwemikong Indian Reserve, Manitoulin Island, 1856." Metropolitan Toronto Reference Library, J. Ross Robertson Collection, T.16028.

▲ Document 3: Population of British Columbia, 1870

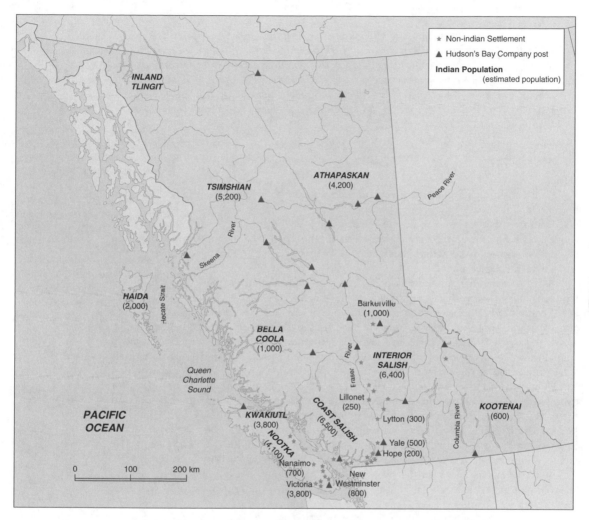

Legend:
★ Non-indian Settlement
▲ Hudson's Bay Company post
Indian Population
(estimated population)

INLAND TLINGIT

TSIMSHIAN (5,200)

ATHAPASKAN (4,200)

Peace River

Skeena River

HAIDA (2,000)

Hecate Strait

Barkerville (1,000)

BELLA COOLA (1,000)

INTERIOR SALISH (6,400)

Queen Charlotte Sound

Fraser River

PACIFIC OCEAN

Lillonet (250)

KWAKIUTL (3,800)

COAST SALISH (6,500)

Lytton (300)

KOOTENAI (600)

Columbia River

NOOTKA (4,100)

Yale (500)
Hope (200)

Nanaimo (700)

New Westminster (800)

Victoria (3,800)

0   100   200 km

● Population of the colony of British Columbia, 1870. Unlike in the older, settled colonies of British America, in 1870, Aboriginals in British Columbia were not yet marginalized by the "march of civilization" and white settlement. Indeed, British settlers in the colony were substantially outnumbered by the Aboriginal population throughout the nineteenth century. It was only in a few communities, like Victoria, that settlers could maintain the semblance of living in a "British" colony. At the Hudson's Bay posts dotted throughout the colony and in the other few small settlements, the local economy and often the rhythm of life was determined by that of Aboriginal neighbours.

Source: Data from Finlay & Sprague, *The Structure of Canadian History*, 2e; Scarborough: Prentice Hall, 1984: p. 195.

▲ Document 4: Petition of Paussamigh Pemmeenauweet to Queen Victoria, 25 January 1841

By the 1820s, the situation of the Mi'kmaq in the Maritimes was becoming increasingly dire. The population was declining. The province had not set aside lands for the First Nations people and many of the small communities relied on low-paying seasonal employment or government largess to survive. Paussamigh Pemmeenauweet's petition, which was sent directly to Queen Victoria in 1841, drew an immediate response from London. It took the Nova Scotian government some time to even begin to address the issue.

To the Queen

Madam,

I am Paussamigh Pemmeenauweet, and am called by the White Man Louis Benjamin Porninout.

I am the Chief of my People the Micmac Tribe of Indians in your Province of Nova Scotia and I was recognized and declared to be the Chief by òur good Friend Sir John Cope Sherbrooke in the White Man's fashion Twenty Fire [sic] Years ago; I have yet the Paper which he gave me.

Sorry to hear that the King is dead. Am glad to hear that we have a good Queen whose Father I saw in this Country. He loved the Indians.

I cannot cross the great Lake to talk to you for my Canoe is too small, and I am old and weak. I cannot look upon you for my eyes not see so far. You cannot hear my voice across the Great Waters. I therefore send this Wampum and Paper talk to tell the Queen I am in trouble. My people are in trouble. I have seen upwards of a Thousand moons. When I was young I had plenty: now I am old, poor and sickly too. My people are poor. No Hunting Grounds—No Beaver—no Otter—no nothing. Indians are poor—poor for ever. No Store—no Chest—no Clothes. All these Woods once ours. Our Fathers possessed them all. Now we cannot cut a Tree to warm our Wigwam in Winter unless the White Man please. The Micmacs now receive no presents, but one small Blanket for a whole family. The Governor is a good man but he cannot help us now. We look to you the Queen. The White Wampum tell that we hope in you. Pity your poor Indians in Nova Scotia.

White Man has taken all that was ours. He has plenty of everything here. But we are told that the White Man has sent to you for more. No wonder that I should speak for myself and my people.

The man that takes this talk over the great Water will tell you what we want to be done for us. Let us not perish. Your Indian Children love you, and will fight for you against all your enemies.

My Head and my Heart shall go to One above for you.

Pausauhmigh Pemmeenauweet, Chief of the Micmac Tribe of Indians in Nova Scotia.
His mark †

Source: Petition of Paussamigh Pemmeenauweet to Queen Victoria, 25 January 1841. From Penny Petrone, ed. *First People, First Voices* (Toronto: University of Toronto Press, 1983).

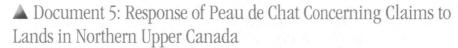

▲ Document 5: Response of Peau de Chat Concerning Claims to Lands in Northern Upper Canada

In 1850, the Government of the Canadas decided that it had to gain access to lands around Lake Superior. Copper had been discovered in the region four years earlier, and Ojibwa inhabitants of the region were incensed that not only had their occupancy of the land not been recognized, but also they were receiving no benefit from the lease that had been given to the mining companies. Peau de Chat's statement, recorded by agent T. G. Anderson, was given in response to the question as to how the local Aboriginal population could claim the land.

Father

You ask how we possess this land. Now it is well known that 4000 Years ago when we first were created all spoke one language. Since that a change has taken place, and we speak different languages. You white people well know, and we Red Skins know how we came in possession of this land—it was the Great Spirit who gave it to us—from the time my ancestors came upon this earth it has been considered ours—after a time the Whites living on the other side of the Great Salt Lake, found this part of the world inhabited by the Red Skins—the Whites asked us Indians, when there were many animals here—would you not sell the Skins of these various animals for the goods I bring—our old ancestors said Yes. I will bring your goods, they the whites did not say any thing more, nor did the Indian say any thing. I did not know that he said come I will buy your land, every thing that is on it under it &c &c he the White said nothing about that to me—and this is the reason why I believe that we possess this land up to this day. When at last the Whites came to this Country where now they are numerous—He the English did not say I will after a time get your land, or give me your land, he said indeed to our forefathers, when he fought with the French and conquered them come on our Side and fight them, and be our children, they did so, and every time you wanted to fight the Big knives you said to the Indians wont you assist me, Yes! We will help you this Man (pointing to Shinguaconse) was there and he was in much misery—the English were very strong when we gave our assistance. When the war was over the English did not say I will have Your land, nor did we say you may have it—and this father You know, this is how we are in possession of this Land—It will be known every where if the Whites get it from us.

Father

You ask in what instances the Whites prevent our Farming, there are bad people among us who are continually saying to us dont Farm, live as Indians always did, You will be unhappy if you cultivate the Land, take your Gun go and hunt, bring the Skins to me, and leave off tilling the Soil—and the Queen says to me become Christian my children. Yes I say we will become Christians but when this bad man (the Trader) sees me he says leave it alone do as you formerly did, and this is the way he destroys my religion and farming this is the way I explain the question you have now asked me.

Source: Public Archives of Canada, RG1 E5 Vol. 8, ECO file 1157 of 1848.

473

Father

The miners burn the land and drive away the animals destroying the land Game &c much timber is destroyed—and I am very sorry for it—When they find mineral they cover it once with Clay so that the Indians may not see it and I now begin to think that the White man wishes to take away and to steal my land, I will let it go, and perhaps I will accomplish it. I wish to let the Governor have both land and Mineral, I expect him to ask me for it, and this is what would be for our good. I do not wish to pass any reflections on the conduct of the whites—ask me then, send some one to ask for my land my Mineral &c. I wont be unwilling to let it go to the Government shall have it if they give us good pay. I do not regret a word I have said—You Father You are a White Man make Yourself an Indian, take an Indians heart come assist me to root out the evil that has been among us and I will be glad answer me is there any thing that requires explanation.

Father

The Indians are uneasy seeing their lands occupied by the Whites, taking away the mineral and they wish that our Great Father would at once settle the matter. Come and ask me for my land and mineral that there be no bad feelings left, I am Sorry, my heart is troubled. I dont know what would be good for us, it will not do for me an Indian to say to the Governor come buy my land, yet this is what I think would be very good, Yes very good for my people, then the White man the miner and trader could do what he liked with the land and so could the Indian on that part which we would like to reserve, when we give our land up we will reserve a piece for ourselves and we, with our families will live happily on it we will do as we please with it. There (pointing to Fort William) I will find out a place for my self. Perhaps you will come and arrange Matters it would be well if you could, and if an officer cannot come this autumn to settle our affairs I will look out for one in the Spring to do it for me and this is nearly all I have to say, tell the Governor at Montreal to send a letter and let us know what he will do and what our land is worth in the mean time I will converse with my tribe on the subject. When I am going to sell my land I will speak again and Settle Matters.

A great deal of our Mineral has been taken away I must have something for it. I reflect upon it, as well as upon that which still remains.

Certified

T.G. Anderson, V.S.I.A.

▲ Document 6: Letters from James Douglas, 1849–1851

James Douglas became chief factor for the Hudson's Bay Company in 1839. He wrote these letters around the time of his appointment as governor of the young colony on Vancouver Island. His letters and reports to HBC directors based in London, England, illustrate his concerns for his community and have been an invaluable source for historians.

Fort Victoria, 22 December 1850

Archibald Barclay Esquire

Sir

[...] In pursuance of the Committee's plans, I have selected a farm site, as Cadboro Bay, on lots No 4 and 12, I will have buildings erected there for the Bailiff and farm Servants expected from England by next ship. I gave the preference to that place, in consequence of it being well supplied with fresh water and containing the largest extent of level cultivable land in this neightbourhood [sic]. It is moreover surrounded by a large tract of very fine woodland, which besides supplying timber for building and fences, will when cleared of trees and brush, form a valuable addition to the farm.

I am sorry to inform you that the Sanitch and Cowetchin Tribes, have lately manifested an unusual degree of ill feeling, towards the Colony, in consequence of the Seizure of a run-away slave, a Cowetchin by birth, who is accused of being an accomplice in the murder of the three seamen, who were so cruelly put to death last Summer by the Indians of "Neweete". He was apprehended at this place, under a warrant from the Governor and lately sent in irons to Fort Rupert for identification. I have heard from a trusty Agent who enjoys the confidence of these tribes, that the Sanitch Chief who is also related to the slave in question, made two journeys to the Cowetchin Camp for the purpose of inducing them to unite with his people in an attack upon the Whites. His plan was to attack and drive in our dairy people and stockherds who are scattered over the plains, and afterwards to slaughter the stock. The Cowetchins however would not join in the confederacy and the plan has been for the present laid aside. The Sanitch Chief has not visited the Fort lately; but I shall take the first opportunity of speaking to him on the subject.

Though that storm has passed over without injury to the settlement [sic] we may not always be so fortunate, sound policy would suggest the necessity of unwearied vigilance, in watching the Conduct and movements of our savage neighbour, who though friendly and respectful in their deportment, are the mere creatures of impulse, and may be easily driven by real or imaginary wrongs into the commission of the wildest excesses. By knowing their designs in time, serious disturbances may often be prevented, by good advice alone, a course more consistent with the dictates of humanity and more conducive to the best interests of the Colony, than appeals to the sword by which the Company would moreover be involved in an endless train of expenses.

Governor Blanshard thinks that twenty men would be sufficient to settle any hostile difference with the Indians of Vancouvers [sic] Island: but my opinion on that subject is very different, and I need only refer to the example of the Cayuse War, undertaken by the provisional Government of Oregon, against tribes of Indians much more domesticated

475

Source: Excerpts of letters from James Douglas to the Governor, Deputy Governor and Committee of the Hon. Hudson's Bay Company, (Toronto: University of Toronto Press, 1983), 53–54.

than those of Vancouvers [sic] Island, and without the same advantages of a mountainous country, as a proof of the uncertain issue of such contest.

They had 500 Men in the field and the expense of one campaign came to about Four Hundred Thousand Dollars, yet not one object for which the war had been undertaken was gained. The punishment of the murderers was afterwards accomplished by negotiation alone. For my own part I am decidedly opposed to Indians wars, as desperate remedies which should never be resorted to, until all other means of settlement have been tried in vain.

As a precautionary measure, which circumstances will sooner or later render indispensable, I would strongly recommend to the Governor and Committee, that several small settlements should be formed on the borders of the Fur Trade Reserve as a protection against the depredations of Indians and to keep the Cattle from straying into the forest and becoming unmanageably wild. Six of these settlements consisting of ten men each, would for the present suffice for those purposes. [...]

I have the honor to be Sir

Your Most Obedt. Servt.
James Douglas

Fort Victoria, Vancouver's Island,
31 October 1851

To the Right Honble Earl Grey
Her Majesty's Principal Secretary of State
For the Colonial Department

My Lord

I have the honor to acknowledge the receipt of your Lordships communication of the 19th May 1851, transmitting a Commission under the Great Seal of the United Kingdom, appointing me to be Governor and Commander in Cheif [sic] in and over the Island of Vancouver, and its dependencies, together with instructions, under the Royal sign Manual and signet for my guidance in the administration of the Government thereof, and also a Commission under the Seal of the High Court of Admiralty, appointing me to be Vice Admiral of that Island and of its dependencies, all which Instruments were duly received by me on the 30th Instant.

I beg through your Lordship to convey to Her Most Gracious Majesty, my humble thanks for those distinguished marks of confidence, which, it shall be my endeavour to prove, are not misplaced. The Royal Instructions, will be faithfully executed and in the exercise of the powers and authority vested in me by the Royal Commission, it shall be my study to promote to the utmost of my ability the honor and advantage of the Crown, as well as the interests of her Majestys Subjects in this Colony.

I am happy to inform your Lordship that nothing has occurred to disturb the tranquility of the settlements on this Island, since the departure of the late Governor Blanchard by her Majestys Ship *Daphne* on the 1st September last. The Natives generally profess the most friendly disposition, and prove their sincerity by the character of their daily intercourse with the Settlers.

The late operations of Her Majestys Ship *Daphne* acting under instructions from Governor Blanchard against the Neweete Tribe, inhabiting the north end of Vancouver's Island,

476

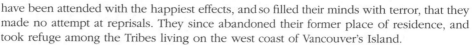

have been attended with the happiest effects, and so filled their minds with terror, that they made no attempt at reprisals. They since abandoned their former place of residence, and took refuge among the Tribes living on the west coast of Vancouver's Island.

To that point as soon as their retreat was discovered a party of friendly Indians were dispatched by Mr. George Blenkinsop the Hudsons Bay Compys. Officer in command of Fort Rupert with a message from this Government proffering peace to the Tribe at large, on condition of the delivery of the three Indians concerned in the murder.

Those terms were at once accepted by the Neweeti Chiefs, but before the proposed seizure could be effected the murderers received notice of their danger, and fled from the camp. They were however chased into the woods, and put to death by their own people after making desperate resistance, in which one of the assailants was severely wounded.

The mangled remains of the criminals were taken to Fort Rupert and after being identified by the Chiefs of the Quakeolth Tribe, were interred near the Fort, so that there is no doubt as to their having met with the fate they so justly merited.

The war with that nation may now be considered as virtually at an end, and I beg to express to your Lordship, how greatly I feel indebted to Mr. George Blenkinsop for his able and active aid in bringing it to a satisfactory and honourable close.

I propose in a short time to visit that part of Vancouver's Island for the purpose of establishing amicable relations with that, and other Tribes of Indians whose friendship will greatly conduce to the well being of the Colony. [...]

The Natives generally are turning their attention to the cultivation of the Potatoe, and to other useful arts, such as the manufacture of Shingles and Laths which are becoming popular among them.

I shall probably take the liberty of calling your Lordship's attention hereafter to the best means of improving the condition of the aborigines of this Island, who are in many respects a highly interesting people, and I conceive worthy of attention. They will become under proper management of service to the Colony and form a valuable auxiliary force, in the event of war with any foreign power.—From my long experience of Indian character and of the tribes on this coast in particular, I am led to regret that the Missionary Societies of Britain, who are sending Teachers to so many other parts of the world have not turned their attention to the natives of Vancouver's Island; as, by the aid of those Societies, schools might be established for the moral training and instruction of the Aborigines, to the manifest advantage of this Colony.

I have further to inform your Lordship that the natives have discovered Gold in Englefield Bay on the west coast of Queen Charlotte's Island. One of the Hudson's Bay Company's vessels visited the spot, in the month of July last, and succeeded in procuring about 60 oz. of Gold, principally by barter from the Indians. One lump of nearly pure Gold weighing 1 lb. 11 oz. was seen in the possession of one native, who demanded a price beyond its value so that it was not purchased. The Gold is associated with white Quartz rock similar to that of the auriferous deposites in California, it is yet found in small quantities, but I am of opinion that it exists abundantly in that and other parts of the Island.

The report of that discovery having become known in this country I am informed that several American vessels, are fitting out in the Columbia, for Queen Charlottes Island, for the purpose of digging Gold, a circumstance to which I would request your Lordship's attention, as it may be the desire of Government to exclude foreign vessels from that part of the Coast. [...]

477

I shall do myself the honor of addressing your Lordship from time to time, on the affairs of Vancouver's Island, as circumstances occur, deserving of your notice.

I have the honor to be your Lordship's

Most obt. Servant
James Douglas
Governor Vancouvers Island

Fort Victoria, 16 December 1851

To the Right Honble. Earl Grey
Her Majestys principal Secretary of State.
For the Colonial Department.

My Lord,

I have the honor to transmit herewith duplicate of my letter of the 31st Octr.

There is nothing of importance to communicate respecting the Colony since that date; the Native Tribes continue their friendly intercourse with the Settlements, and in return they are protected in their rights; and we endeavour by every possible means to conciliate their good will, as it is a matter of vast importance to acquire their confidence, and to lead them to appeal for redress in all cases of wrongs, to the law of the land, instead of having recourse to lawless retaliation.

A difficulty of some weight has lately occurred to me, in the settlement of dispute between the Colonists & Indians; which I will take the liberty of briefly submitting to your Lordship, for unless obviated in some way, it may prove dangerous to the peace of the Colony.

The question was forced upon my attention some days ago, on the occasion of a complaint made by Tenasman, Chief of the Soke Tribe, against Thomas Hall a white settler, who was charged with having forcibly dispossed the Plaintiff of a double barrelled fowling peice [sic], leaving the Plaintiff a much inferior Gun, in return. The Plaintiff had no evidence to support the charge except the testimony of one of his own countrymen who not being a Christian, could not be duly sworn. I nevertheless admitted the evidence of the Plaintiffs witness, which however failed in proving the fact of force being used by the defendant in obtaining the Plaintiffs gun; while it was on the contrary, proved by the defendant that the exchange was effected without force being used, and by the mutual consent of the parties. It appeared however that Plaintiff on being better informed as to the relative value of the two guns, wished to recover his own. The case was necessarily decided in favour of defendant, and against the Plaintiff, who nevertheless has evidently been duped in the transaction, and I therefore prevailed upon the defendant, not by order of Course but as a matter of justice to give the Plaintiff some further compensation.

The question arising out of that simple case on which I would request your Lordship's instructions is this; How far the testimony of Indians is to be admitted as evidence in the Law Courts of this Colony?

It is not in my opinion advisable to receive Indian testimony in adjudging the disputes of white men, but in the case of disputes between the white man, and Indians, I do not see how we can with justice reject the only species to testimony the latter may have to offer, and when offences against life or property are committed by Indians, the only testimony against the offenders may be that of their own countrymen. On that subject I

478

would take the liberty of remarking to your Lordship, how very important it is, to the peace and security of the settlements, that instant attention should be paid to the complaints of Indians, and their wrongs receive speedy redress, as nothing will tend more to inspire confidence in the governing power, and to teach them that justice may be obtained by a less dangerous and more certain method than their own hasty and precipitite acts of private revenge. [...]

Since I had last the honor of addressing your Lordship, two vessels from the American ports in Puget Sound, bound to Queen Charlottes Island, have touched at this Port. They had collectively about 64 passengers on board, who were going thither for the purpose of digging Gold. It is also currently reported that several vessels filled with passengers, have sailed from the Columbia and California for the same quarter. Their presince [sic] on the coast will I fear be productive of much evil, and lead to serious difficulties with the Native Tribes. [...]

I have the honor to be Your Lordship's

Most obedient Servt.
James Douglas
Governor Vancouvers Island

Article 1: A Unifying Vision: Shingwaukonse's Plan for the Future of the Great Lakes Ojibwa

Janet Chute

As Janet Chute argues in her article, the historiographical debate over Native "agency" or victim often misreads how men like Shingwaukonse represented his community and tried to secure its economic future. Susan Neylan's examination of the Tsimshian's response to Protestant missionaries illustrates the strength and complexity of many First Nation's attitudes toward Christianity.

The ideas and actions of Shingwaukonse, or Little Pine (1773–1854),[1] an enterprising Ojibwa leader who resided during his later years at Garden River, east of Sault Ste. Marie, set precedents which profoundly affected the course of Canadian Indian policy. Between 1820 and 1840 the chief directed

Source: Janet Chute, "A Unifying Vision: Shingwaukonse's Plan for the Future of the Great Lakes Ojibwa" *Journal of the CHA*, 1996, New Series, Vol. 7, pp. 55–80.

his energies principally towards establishing linkages to missionary organisations and government agencies, [...] by which he endeavoured to gain access to the corridors of metropolitan power. By earning both sympathy and respect from dynamic individuals deeply involved in the process of Canadian nation building, he endeavoured to develop an environment where cherished Ojibwa values and organisational structures might survive in a rapidly changing world. And after 1840, he shouldered an even more challenging task: to devise new strategies by which local band governments might progressively assume a degree of proprietorship over resources on Aboriginal lands. His speeches during this period furnish some of the most eloquent testimonials to the principle of Aboriginal right to be expressed during the nineteenth century.

These goals required that Shingwaukonse be a forceful and insightful policy maker. But could a nineteenth-century Aboriginal leader devise principled policies worthy of standing the test of time? Evidence from both oral and documentary sources indicate that the chief did indeed formulate policy. Yet prevailing ethnohistorical models provide few avenues to investigate such innovative decision making in a constructive way, a failing which has given rise to controversy concerning the role of Native peoples in Canadian historiography.

Recently Canadian historians have been compelled to review the ramifications of placing Native actors centre stage, or espousing what has been referred to as "Native agency"— a concept which derives from a specific western perspective on the nature of power relationships. As an analytical tool, the "Native agency" approach contrasts the concept of "agency" with the notion of "victimhood." Some social scientists, particularly cultural anthropologists and transactional analysts, have been able to sidestep this debate altogether in their examinations of Native decision making by contending that northeastern Algonquian views on power relations bear little resemblance to Western political conceptions. It is arguable, too, that the idea of "agency," when divorced from the agent/victim dichotomy of which it forms an integral part, is rendered semantically nebulous. In isolation, "Native agency" at best constitutes a blunt analytical tool, since it has been used to denote such a wide range of Native behaviours; among them fur-trade negotiating dexterity, calculated compliance in fighting in intercolonial wars, willingness to invite missionaries to reside in Native villages and, during the settlement era, sporadic protest against political encapsulation. Yet the penchant to view Native peoples as efficacious agents in support of their own interests has met with a certain amount of "backlash." Advocates of this approach have been centred out as unwittingly construing alibis for oppressive state regimes which perversely may be likened to necessary catalytic stimulants, gauged to spur Native groups into achieving heightened political awareness. Yet to the degree the controversy has forced historians to define what "Native agency" actually is, the debate has been deemed worthwhile.[2]

As this paper endeavours to demonstrate,[3] a study of Shingwaukonse's ideas and actions not only falls within the parameters of the "Native agency" approach, but ultimately extends such parameters by compelling the definition of "Native agency" to embrace the potential for devising and instrumenting sound policies.[4] Individuals belonging to non-Western cultures, even when encapsulated and marginalised within Western societies, do not operate in isolation, and this was particularly true for Shingwaukonse and his followers. This chief carefully scrutinised every alien ideology and technology presented to him. At the author's request, storytellers at Garden River tapped into their wealth of oral traditions relating to

the manner in which Shingwaukonse met challenges posed by new and unfamiliar ideas, and it was from such sources that the author acquired her first knowledge of how the chief elicited the information he needed to devise his schemes. Educated Métis, government agents, missionaries, merchants and lawyers,[5] whose education and status suggested they might be repositories of valuable knowledge, were singled out by him and subjected to intensive questioning. For Shingwaukonse this process of learning was invaluable, and he was willing to reward those who helped him handsomely with usufructuary rights to hunting-grounds, sugar-maple groves, fisheries, mines and timber locations which he considered to lie under his protective aegis. Concern for the future of his people and their culture fired his determination. Changing times continuously prompted this gifted leader to seek new strategies for preserving what to his people had become a cherished way of life.

SHINGWAUKONSE AND THE UPPER GREAT LAKES NATIVE COMMUNITY

The Great Lakes milieu into which Shingwaukonse was born not only allowed for an ease of intercommunication among diverse frontier agencies, but also held out opportunities for ambitious Native individuals which their successors would have difficulty emulating. Certain chiefs developed into influential political personages under the combined auspices of indirect colonialism and the fur trade. With the growth of territorialism, fostered by the availability of firearms and increasingly efficient technologies for local resource exploitation, these leaders came to exercise regulatory and protective jurisdiction over vast tracts used as hunting and fishing grounds. In consequence, a balance of power in the Upper Great Lakes area became mandatory, and this in turn compelled leaders to travel widely. Partly, this was engendered by traditional Ojibwa perceptions of power, which was viewed not as a possession but as a gift intimately linked to responsibility for others.[6] But there were also other benefits, for through their abilities at negotiation and exchange, leaders grew wealthy in terms of their potential to accumulate material assets,[7] and, during the War of 1812, gained additional prestige by acting as allies of the British Crown.

The necessity to adapt to radical social and political changes constituted a primary fact of

Shingwaukonse's life. Born either at the Sault or Mackinac in 1774 and raised on Grand Island, Michigan,[8] he assumed many roles before becoming a head chief in 1836, at 63 years of age. Acting as a trading chief, he guided brigades throughout the northwest, regularly travelling as far as the Red River and the headwaters of the Mississippi.[9] He gained notoriety fighting against the Dakota,[10] opposed the Shawnee Prophet's resistance campaign despite many other chiefs' involvement in it, and by 1809 became an *oskabewis* or spokesperson.[11] His attachment to John Askin Jr., the Métis son of a prominent British merchant at Mackinac and Detroit, strengthened his resolve to uphold the British interest during the War of 1812. He fought in many engagements on the British side, including the Detroit campaign, Queenston Heights and Moraviantown. In the role of a *kekedowenine*, or a peacekeeper,[12] he resolved a dispute between an official party of United States military personnel and a local Sault subchief at a treaty-making ceremony in 1820.[13] Although after this date he remained aloof from American treaty negotiations, the above event brought him to the attention of Henry Rowe Schoolcraft, who from then on became a principal recorder of his activities and accomplishments.

Shingwaukonse traced his lineage "from the old Crane band" at Sault Ste. Marie whose members regarded an eighteenth-century patriarch, Gitcheokanojeed, or Great Crane, as their common ancestor.[14] A celebrated war leader, orator, member of the *midewiwin*[15] and *wabano* medicine societies, and a *djiski* or shaking-tent conjuror, Shingwaukonse elicited respect from Native and non-Native alike. However, he did not possess the Crane *totem*, the bird symbol employed as a designating mark by most other Sault leaders, particularly in the council forum. A *totem* was both a personal and a group identifier, transferred between generations in the male line.[16] Linked to the local band through his mother and having either a French or French Métis father,[17] he initially lacked a totem. He had formally declared his autonomy from the United States in the spring of 1836,[18] but it was not until late in 1836, following the death of a Crane leader, Kaygayosh, who had been his mentor in the *midewiwin*,[19] that Shingwaukonse assumed both the rank of a traditional head chief and the plover *totem*, obtained through vision sanction.[20] From then on, he would exercise territorial jurisdiction over lands on the British shore—a right which, he would repeat

in future years, had been recognised in 1814 by John Askin Jr. and in 1833 by Lieutenant-Governor Sir John Colborne.[21]

During the 1830s, the British Sault was still very much a frontier community. Intermarriages had taken place between the local Ojibwa, French, British and Métis, yet the First Nation community still remained spatially and occupationally distinct from its white and Métis neighbours.[22] It conformed poorly to frontier social models, for it fitted neither the image of an exclusively fur-trading, hunter-gatherer society, nor the mould of a cohesive multiethnic community similar to those found at an earlier date in the Ohio River Valley region.[23] The best one can say is that it comprised an Aboriginal society in transition,[24] with leaders who could remember when their people once had been integral to events, and who expected to be consulted and heard during the birth pangs of the emerging social order in much the same way as they had been at the height of the fur trade or during the major intercolonial wars.

That Shingwaukonse's group rarely suffered economic shortages despite the declining fur-trade, contributed to its autonomy *vis-à-vis* both British and Americans. By contrast to the situation where fur trade monopoly conditions prevailed, Sault residents had access to independent trading establishments, as well as Hudson's Bay Company posts.[25] Local whitefish and trout fisheries had sustained a thriving Native enterprise since the early French era.[26] Individual Ojibwa families maintained their winter hunting limits in the interior, in keeping with the family hunting territory system. In the spring they made maple sugar, planted corn, beans and squash, and tended European-introduced crops such as potatoes in clearings near the coast. Each season elicited its own special economic endeavours, and provided a small surplus to tide over the beginning of the next.

Shingwaukonse recognised the importance of protecting his people's diversified economy as the key to their continued independence. By regulating membership in his band, he indirectly reduced pressure on group resources, and opposed encroachments on his territorial prerogatives. [...] In return, he received recommendations and advice from family heads, who also constituted the principal members of his council.

Yet even though a respected chief, Shingwaukonse often chose to assume the more humble role of a *mishiniway*, or data collector.[27] He constantly sought and processed new information on subjects he thought to be of importance to his people. While unable to read or write, and unlike several of his closest Ojibwa and Métis companions, incapable of speaking either French or English,[28] he proved to be a precise student of events, careful to check facts, and recorded his findings using mnemonic devices, some of which may have had their origin in *mide-wiwin* practices.[29] This enabled him to pursue his studies systematically, even when news threatened to be of a disturbing, or even shocking nature.[30] He tried to examine issues from all sides. In keeping with traditional Ojibwa beliefs regarding power, he judged an idea mainly by its effectiveness, and saw little utility in amassing stores of untried wisdom. He spoke with missionaries of many different Christian denominations, but chose baptism in the Anglican faith after his son Buhkwujjenene was healed of a severe nasal haemorrhage following a prayer session.[31] Aware of the strides in agriculture made by Ojibwa residing near the Credit River,[32] he called for government assistance to help his people achieve the same results near Sault Ste. Marie.[33]

In 1833 Lieutenant-Governer Colborne promised to provide Shingwaukonse's people with a farming instructor, schoolteacher, carpenter and sufficient funds to build 20 houses.[34] When no aid actually materialised, the chief sought a broader audience. To sustain his group's economy from encroachment by outsiders, he entered into a joint agreement with the Hudson's Bay Company in 1834 and 1835 to protect Native fisheries along the north shores of Lakes Huron and Superior against exploitation by American free traders.[35] He also ceased to subscribe exclusively to Anglicanism. He allowed his sons and daughters to exercise their own judgement in forming denominational attachments, and invited Roman Catholics as well as Anglicans to his council when deliberating upon the feasibility of granting land for an Anglican church.[36] To Shingwaukonse, missionaries of all faiths comprised potentially valuable mediators between his people and metropolitan society at large, to whom he directed numerous appeals for public assistance in building houses, schools and sawmills. Shingwaukonse evidently retained his sense of balance and perspective within a sea of ideological diversity by retaining much of his faith in his traditional beliefs, while gradually adding to the range of his religious knowledge by adoptions from Christianity. That his

views on Christianity never fully supplanted his Ojibwa thought system is evident in one of his son's statements that Shingwaukonse destroyed his *mide-wiwin* paraphernalia only shortly before his death.[37]

When his efforts to attain houses, a school, tools and sawmill machinery through missionary auspices proved no more efficacious than his earlier appeal to the Lieutenant-Governor, Shingwaukonse and his council embarked on a new policy. Many Métis individuals, whose prospects for permanent employment had faded in the climate of retrenchment surrounding the merger of the Hudson's Bay Company and the Northwest Company in 1821, had chosen to settle on the British side of the rapids. By inviting the Métis to come, join his group, and share their carpentry and other technical skills, the Garden River band were soon able to erect wooden houses, as well as to engage in boat building and numerous other occupations previously unfamiliar to them. For their part, the Métis who exercised this option, most of whom had kin ties to the local Ojibwa, gained a valuable ally and spokesperson.

Shingwaukonse's public announcement at a government present distribution to the Native nations on the western frontier in 1837 shocked Indian Affairs officials who, under policy directives from Colborne's successor, Sir Francis Bond Head, had anticipated removing the Ojibwa to an isolated mission station at Manitowaning on Manitoulin Island in northern Lake Huron.[38] Years later, when the Canadian government sought to reduce the number of claimants to annuities under the Robinson treaties, Shingwaukonse's actions in this regard would come under trenchant criticism. A posthumous charge was laid that he displayed a Machiavellian penchant to shift identities whenever he desired to amass a multiethnic following large enough to accomplish some self-interested goal, usually at government expense.[39] Yet the preponderance of historic evidence suggests that he perpetually judged his own competence by his effectiveness in attaining group goals, not his own. Although claiming Métis ancestry, he remained Ojibwa in cultural orientation and showed his determination to preserve cherished Ojibwa values to the degree that most Métis later stated that in 1837 they had rejected his offer, complaining they "were Indian enough without binding themselves to be under an Indian chief."[40]

It was not long before the chief was called to confront a new challenge. Between 1837 and 1853 the American government seriously considered removing the southwestern Ojibwa to lands beyond the Mississippi.[41] Suddenly, delegations sent by Native leaders began to visit Garden River from as far away as interior Minnesota.[42] Determined to aid Ojibwa groups who appealed to him for assistance and refuge, Shingwaukonse redoubled his efforts to enhance his community's economic base so that it could sustain a potentially large influx of Native immigrants from south of the border. Under the stress of this new mandate, he evidenced less shifting of roles by appointing one of his sons, Buhkwujjenene, or Wild Man, as his group's *kekedowenine*; another of his sons, Augustine Shingwauk, as his *mishiniway* and John Bell and Louis Cadotte as his interpreters. Then, rejecting British and American Indian policy as inadequate to protect his people against the dangers of encapsulation, he hurled a provocative challenge at the Anglican and Roman Catholic missionaries residing on Manitoulin Island in 1841, declaring:

> You are two Black Coats, now I want to know if our Saviour marked in the Bible, that the whites would journey towards the setting sun until they found a large Island in which there were many Indians living in rich country—that they should rob the natives of their animals, furs and land, after which the English and Americans should draw a line, from one to the other end of the Island and each take his share and do what he pleases with the Natives, I ask if that's written in the Bible?[43]

From this point onwards, he bypassed the Manitoulin Island missions as primary avenues of communication and sought to develop as direct and as personal linkages as possible to metropolitan governmental and other agencies.

CHAMPION OF THE UNRETREATING FRONTIER

In 1845 the Legislative Assembly of the United Canadas extended its jurisdiction to the Sault and, with a blatant disregard for issue of Native right, the following spring sent a provincial land surveyor by the name of Alexander Vidal to mark off allotments near the rapids. Incensed by such activity, Shingwaukonse asked Vidal to quit the area.[44] The chief further complained that Joseph Wilson, the newly appointed land agent, interfered with his people's logging activities. "[When] Mr. Wilson sells our wood & acts with us as he does, I feel as if he entered into my house and took without my leave what he might find therein," he explained.[45] In response to his grievances, he was informed that he could expect no assistance, not even an audience with a government official, until he and the 126 individuals belonging to his band moved to Manitoulin Island.[46] Shingwaukonse initially refused to be upset by this turn of events. In a petition to the Governor General, Baron Metcalfe of Fern Hill,[47] he inquired by what authority mining prospectors had been allowed to stake mineral locations in the Sault vicinity.[48] He then cordially invited Metcalfe to meet with him in Montreal, so they could discuss arrangements relating to mineral proprietorship, royalties and dues. As for the directive to move to Manitoulin Island, the chief viewed it as unworthy of notice. "I want always to live and plant at Garden River," he emphasised, and expect "a share of what is found on my lands."[49]

When Indian Affairs contacted him, however, warning him not to proceed to Montreal, but to move at once to Manitoulin Island, the chief suddenly realised that he faced a threat unlike any he had confronted before. "Already has the white man licked clean up from our lands the whole means of our subsistence, and now they commence to make us worse off. I call God to witness in the beginning and do so now again and say that it was false that the land is not ours, it is ours," he contended.[50] One large mining location took in the whole area of the Garden River village.[51] Since the chief had never negotiated in any way with the location's claimants he felt justified in driving exploring parties off the site.[52]

The ideological sides had been drawn. The chief would act far differently from the stereotypical image of the politically defenceless Indian. By drawing on a pool of new allies, both Native and non-Native, he soon attracted the notice of the press, and within three years his Native claim had escalated into an international issue. Aspects of this contest have stubbornly defied easy historical analysis. Scholars dealing with the subject have come to different conclusions regarding the nature of forces behind events.[53] Unfortunately, uncritical appraisal of the sensational metropolitan press reports, which emerged in 1849 and 1850 as a result of Shingwaukonse's and his allies' Native campaign, have coloured some

483

otherwise excellent accounts, for at no time did the Ojibwa ever resort to the use of force in gaining their goals. All scholars have agreed, however, that the contest arose as frontier resistance to metropolitan control. And yet, it constituted a form of protest which evidenced none of the flamboyant, tumultuous characteristics of cult-induced movements, such as the Shawnee uprising in the Ohio River Valley region in 1807–1808. Overall, it presented a principled show of opposition, basically moderate and non-violent. This study argues that the tendency of factors motivating this Native movement to elude simple historical analysis arises from the fact that they, as often as not, have drawn upon and complemented, rather than challenged, mid-nineteenth-century Western aspirations and goals.

Tired of waiting for replies to written appeals, in the spring of 1848 Shingwaukonse and a small party of Native supporters proceeded to Montreal to lay their claim in person before Metcalfe's successor, Lord Elgin. While in the metropolis, the chief directed a barrage of complaints against certain miners who, he argued, trespassed on his territory, blasted rock and set fires which drove away game. At the same time, he maintained that agents of mining companies prevented the Ojibwa from cutting timber, even though conditions of sale for the mine sites had not been fulfilled.[54]

To ascertain the validity of these grievances, Lord Elgin sent Thomas G. Anderson, Visiting Superintendent of Indian Affairs from Cobourg, to the Sault in the summer of investigate the matter. During his interviews with Shingwaukonse and Peau de Chat (one of Shingwaukonse's allies from Fort William), Anderson challenged the Ojibwa leaders to clarify by what authority they claimed the land and its resources.[55] Visibly taken aback, Shingwaukonse declared that copper had been placed in his people's lands as a gift from the Creator. He considered it part of an emerging plan by which the Ojibwa would be granted new sources of revenue by no less than Divine mandate. To give his statements additional bite, the chief requested Louis Cadotte to send a translation of his speech to Anderson to an American newspaper.

Anderson's favouring of agricultural over other industrial pursuits for the Ojibwa tended, unfortunately, to blind him to the Native population's range of economic potentials. Rather than evidencing docile conformity either to Anderson's or to broader government wishes, Shingwaukonse's press release demanded implementation of a system offering Ojibwa compensation of injuries to a resource base they unquestionably saw as being under their own proprietorship and protection. They also expected mining revenues to be translated into future income for their communities:

> The Great Spirit, we think, placed these rich mines on our lands, for the benefit of his red children, so that their rising generation might get support from them when the animals of the woods should have grown too scarce for our subsistence. We will carry out, therefore the good object of our Father, the Great Spirit. We will sell you lands, if you will give us what is right and at the same time, we want pay for every pound of mineral that has been taken off our lands, as well as for that which may hereafter be carried away.[56]

Copper had been viewed traditionally by the Ojibwa as a preserve of formidable spiritual agencies, and its unsanctioned extraction and use seen as detrimental to the cosmological foundations of the universe. Outcroppings were considered to be guarded by *Buhkwujjenenesug*, little wild people who resided in cliffs. Since he still subscribed, at least in part, to this cosmological order, Shingwaukonse would have been under the same ideological constraints regarding copper as other chiefs, but equipped with new knowledge about Western culture and what he had learned of Christianity he apparently felt confident enough to tackle the challenge of making mining a paying proposition for his people. This constituted a stance in which he firmly believed and from which he refused to deviate until his death. The chief hoped it would restore the Ojibwa to an integral place in the economy of the developing nation, and would have broad regional repercussions. Peau de Chat of Fort William, Totomenai of Michipicoten, and Keokonse and Noquagabo of Thessalon stood behind him. Southwestern Ojibwa leaders, among them such notable figures as Eshkebugecooshe of Leech Lake, Minnesota, and Gitche Besheke of Lapointe region, Wisconsin, sent delegations to Garden River to learn more concerning his plan.

Ultimately, Shingwaukonse's most advantageous linkages lay through his association with a new frontier element: a small number of well-educated non-Native individuals interested in independently prospecting for copper north of Lakes Huron and Superior. The foremost member of this group was Allan Macdonell, a lawyer and mining prospector from Toronto,[57] who understood something of Ojibwa society because of past family fur-trade connections. But, even more importantly, Macdonell maintained relations with Toronto's rising legal and business community, the metropolitan press and the corridors of political power.

A former shareholder in the Quebec and Lake Superior Association, which operated copper mines near Michipicoten, Macdonell surveyed a mineral location north of the Sault and entered into a long-term lease regarding it with Shingwaukonse and another chief named Nebenagoching. By this lease's terms, in 1848, still pending government approval, the Ojibwa would receive a royalty of 2 per cent on all mining proceeds, and the site in question would be returned to the band if not worked within five years.[58] Macdonell's arrangement, moreover, comprised only one of several systems introduced to the Ojibwa designed to capture and distribute potential mineral revenues to the Native peoples. John William Keating, a former Indian agent from Amherstburg, recommended that leases of mineral locations near Michipicoten be based on the model operating in Cornwall, "where the Lord of the Manor always retains the Royalty, tho' his returns vary with the profit of the mine."[59]

In the fall of 1848, according to Thomas G. Anderson's son, ... the Anglican missionary at Garden River, Shingwaukonse had re-extended his earlier invitation to Métis families to join the Garden River community, if they so desired.[60] By this time the chief had grown so impatient with government inactivity on the claims issue that he had prevailed upon Allan Macdonell to use his legal training to represent the Ojibwa's position, to which the lawyer immediately responded by warning the mining companies against cutting any more timber on band property.[61] Anderson and other government officials thus found themselves pitted against a formidable duo on the issue of Aboriginal right.

The following spring, during yet another visit to Lord Elgin in Montreal, the chief, accompanied by Macdonell, Ogista, Nebenagoching and Cadotte, made it clear that Anderson's scepticism regarding the foundations of Aboriginal right constituted

an insult not only to himself but to all persons of Native descent. In an eloquent speech, which was later translated and published in the *Montreal Gazette*, Shingwaukonse appealed to the government to forego its former lethargy and instead participate actively in helping the Ojibwa secure what was theirs by the will of the Creator. "Assist us, then, to reap that benefit intended for us," he proposed. "Enable us to do this, and our hearts will be great within, for we will feel that we are again a nation."[62] Instead of offering aid, the government stiffened its opposition to the Ojibwa's position, a response which drew a veiled warning from the chief. Even "the most cowardly of animals though they feel destruction sure, will turn upon the hunter," he cautioned.[63] But he also made it clear that any form of coercion would only be a last resort.

Shingwaukonse's importunity prompted a second government inquiry in September of 1849. This time, Indian Affairs dispatched two commissioners to the Upper Great Lakes region: Thomas G. Anderson, who had headed the investigation the previous year, and Alexander Vidal whose surveying operations had been disrupted in 1847. Both were instructed simply to gain an estimate of the amount of compensation the Ojibwa would accept for their lands, but to discuss nothing more. A map drawn by these two commissioners of the entire north shore of Lake Superior demonstrated a remarkable thing: the boundaries of tracts, claimed by the bands along the coastline, lay flush against one another— no land remained outside of the Ojibwa's territorial aegis.[64] The Native peoples had appropriated some of the richest mining country in Canada West as their inheritance. Since 1845, they had been instrumental in revealing outcroppings of copper, iron, gold and silver to the white prospectors, and now they expected to glean the rewards of the prerogatives their leaders so forcefully upheld over these sites. For Shingwaukonse to have spoken in 1848 and 1849 on behalf of most of the bands along the north shore of Lake Superior testifies to the degree of faith his Native constituents vested in his abilities as a power-holder. And he and his close Native allies in the resource business, Peau de Chat and Totomenai, had certainly gained attention. Public sympathy elicited by excerpts of Shingwaukonse's speeches in the Montreal press alarmed the Montreal-based mining interests, who feared that a treaty recognising Native right to resources other than fur might endanger their title to their mineral locations.

Aware of the miners' mounting fears during the course of his inquires at the Sault, Vidal drew up a policy statement which negated the Ojibwa's prerogatives even over their land use. Any forthcoming treaty transaction, he argued, should not be viewed as "a purchase or surrender of territory but as the purchase of the right of hunting in and occupation [of the land]."[65] During meetings with the Ojibwa, Vidal interpreted Native impassivity to his ideas not as a show of defiance, as it actually may have been, but as the consequence of manipulations by "designing whites." This led the commissioner to portray the Ojibwa leaders as ignorant and incompetent. Native irresoluteness, he held, required the imposition of an "ultimatum of the government" upon the bands north of Lakes Huron and Superior.[66]

On 15 October, when Vidal trenchantly demanded that Shingwaukonse place an evaluation on his "occupancy rights," the chief abruptly terminated the discussion by stressing his unfamiliarity with the terms Vidal proposed. Before answering, he would have to consult with his people, he concluded. When the council again assembled, the next day, Shingwaukonse immediately broached the subject of Macdonell's claim and the Hudson's Bay Company's rights, which at the Sault were founded on a treaty made with the Crane band in 1798. In response, Vidal declared that the government owned all the land and that all tracts allotted by the Native peoples in the past "were of no value to their holders." At this, Macdonell arose and challenged the government to defend its position in the courts. He knew the Ojibwa could not be considered "minors in law," he parried, for he had "good legal advice on the subject." Their right to the soil and its resources would be vindicated; he would personally see to it.[67]

Shingwaukonse, on being asked whether he joined with Macdonell in espousing this position, replied: "Hear him for us—you do not understand what we say, you understand one another; we will not make replies—talk to Macdonell." When the commissioners continued to ignore the lawyer, the chief charged that the government would cast the Ojibwa aside if they disregarded Macdonell, for the latter acted as the spokesman for Native views, not his own. He then turned to Macdonell and said, "Come, my friend, get up and speak."[68]

Vidal still would have nothing to do with the lawyer. The meeting was not a court of law, he retorted. There was no judge present. Vidal's denial of Aboriginal right and the chief's support of the opposite position only made a clash of perspectives inevitable. The prospect of being engaged in an argument in which the Ojibwa might be shown to have grounds for a legal case was not inviting. Rising, Vidal departed, leaving Anderson to listen to Macdonell's final speech and then close the council.

The chief's eventual response to what he felt to be a colossal affront to his people's rights, intelligence and aspirations was characteristic of him; it was deliberate and well planned.[69] Late in the autumn of 1849, Shingwaukonse, Allan Macdonell, Macdonell's brother Angus, another lawyer from Toronto named Wharton Metcalfe, Chief Nebenagoching, three Métis leaders—two brothers, Pierre and Eustace Lesage, and Charles Boyer—and about 25 other Native individuals[70] journeyed northwards up the Lake Superior coast by boat, and on the night of 14 November peaceably dispossessed the Quebec and Montreal Mining Association of its holdings at Mica Bay, not far from Michipicoten. The company manager shipped the residents of the Mica Bay community by schooner to the Sault and the Native party and their legal assistants held the mine site until the spring of 1850. Troops were sent to the Sault, although no violence ensued. Shingwaukonse and his closest Native supporters surrendered themselves voluntarily to justices of the peace, and then proceeded under escort to Toronto. Once in the city, they were placed in jail, and were released a few days later by the Chief justice, Sir John Beverley Robinson, a relative through marriage to Macdonell,[71] who argued that the party had been arrested illegally.[72] After continued government vacillation about what course to pursue, the group received an official pardon in 1851.[73]

John Bonner, the mine manager, who presided over the evacuation of the mining company's employees and their families, charged that Macdonell desired to use his position as an intermediary with the Ojibwa to secure leases which would be profitable only to himself.[74] From other sources, however, it appears that Macdonell may have been quite disinterested. The Hudson's Bay Company factor, William MacTavish, noted that Macdonell had stated repeatedly that if the Ojibwa could obtain better terms from others, he would have "great pleasure" in relinquishing his interest in his own claim.[75] In a letter written to the Superintendent-General of Indian Affairs on 23 December 1849, Macdonell described his role with regard to the Ojibwa in patron–client terms, yet implicit in his statements lay indications of a reciprocal relationship between himself and the chiefs of a different order than that which usually obtained between a lawyer and those whom he represented.[76] With an intensity of purpose, evidently imbued with a dynamism derived from Shingwaukonse's own vision for the future, Macdonell set out to formulate a case for Aboriginal right which he eventually anticipated testing in the courts.[77]

Viewed against a background of longer-term events, the Mica Bay mine takeover emerges as an act of protest against government insensitivity towards Native hopes for the future. From this perspective, the dispossession of the mine constitutes a brief incident in what was, on the whole, a well-organized Native claims compaign. At no time were Shingwaukonse and his allies against resource exploration and development; they simply wanted their fair share. They hoped to preserve an environment in which their community structures could evolve gradually to meet new economic and political challenges. They demanded a say in the regulation of local logging, fishing and mining activities directly affecting their lives. They also wanted to conserve the potentialities of their highly diversified resource base. In Macdonell, they found a champion for these interests, for the lawyer's political proclivities led him to oppose domination of the hinterland by powerful monopolising metropolitan interests, and he genuinely sympathised with the Ojibwa's struggle to preserve their rights to the land and its resources.

Macdonell was connected by marriage both to Sir John Beverley Robinson and to William B. Robinson, the Attorney-General's brother, who was selected by the government to preside over the signing of the Robinson treaties at Sault Ste. Marie on 7 and 9 September 1850. Macdonell's personal connections probably cast a moderating influence over events subsequent to the Mica Bay affair, and may even have helped to bring about the pardon. But one also cannot ignore the fact that the Reform government, owing to its tardiness in responding to the Native claim, would have found itself in an acutely embarrassing position if it had not acted quickly to draw attention away from the claims issue. The arrival of the Native party in Toronto had caused considerable public excitement, and the fact that Shingwaukonse had fought in the War of 1812 as a British ally and was now on trial by the Canadian government circulated in American as well as Canadian newspapers.[78] Not surprisingly, the government seriously searched for an approach which would silence the Ojibwa's demands once and for all.

Neither the Lieutenant-Governor nor the officials present at the signing of the Robinson treaties accorded any recognition whatsoever to Native demands or aspirations. When informed that the Hudson's Bay Company fully backed the government's position, Ojibwa bands residing further to the northwest along the Lake Superior coast distanced themselves from the Robinson treaty negotiations, or else simply lapsed into a state of passive defiance. Treaty terms provided bands with a lump-sum payment, small annuities, a reserve system based on the same model as that already established in southern Ontario[79] and stipulated that the Ojibwa could continue hunting and fishing on ceded lands not yet sold or leased by the Crown. Also incorporated was a promise that individuals would receive an annuity of £1, or more, per capita should revenue from the surrendered tracts enable the government, without loss, to increase payments. Yet by serving to deprive Native leadership of its traditional prerogatives over lands and resources, the terms had rendered bands susceptible to encroachment from many quarters.

Surveys disregarded treaty descriptions of reserves to the extent that several mineral locations originally recognised as lying on band property, afterwards lay outside reserve boundaries.[80] Meanwhile, claimants to locations still considered to lie on reserve land pillaged both mineral and timber without paying fees or dues, and then abandoned the denuded sites. These men often prevented the Ojibwa from cutting wood even for personal use, and challenged band members' rights to local fisheries which Native peoples had frequented for generations.

Initially unaware of this new lack of protection for their interests, Shingwaukonse and Macdonell entered into negotiations with a local merchant to begin a Native lumbering business.[81] To make their transaction legal, they apprised Indian Affairs of their plan and requested assistance in purchasing machinery for a sawmill. A final, decisive blow to their venture, however, fell when the Legislative Assembly introduced a bill which made "inciting Indians or half-breeds" an offence punishable by up to five years' incarceration in the provincial penitentiary. Wryly branded by the Ojibwa's legal counsellor as "an Act to procure the conviction of Allan Macdonell,"[82] the bill, which passed into law in June, 1853,[83] not only effectively terminated Macdonell's association with his former Native clients, but also prohibited the Ojibwa from seeking legal counsel in the future.

His petition regarding a sawmill ignored, Shingwaukonse prepared yet another direct personal appeal, this time to Queen Victoria. He knew that the southwestern chiefs, some from as far away as the upper reaches of the Mississippi River, had come to trust his ideas. Now many of these leaders were preparing to relocate northwards to Canada, along with two thousand of their people.[84] For him not to act in an effective manner was probably a fate the chief refused even to contemplate.[85] So upon learning that the government adamantly refused to allow any Ojibwa immigrants from the United States to settle at Garden River,[86] Shingwaukonse, with a local merchant's help, headed up a fund-raising campaign in 1853 for an expedition to England.[87] Although afflicted with gangrene in his back and "not expected to live,"[88] the old warrior roused himself sufficiently to set off towards Toronto in early June. Unfortunately, the 80-year-old chief travelled only as far as Penetanguishene; in September he and his party were forced to turn back owing to the chief's declining health. He died in the late fall.[89]

The outcome of the Robinson treaties had imbued Shingwaukonse with a restlessness. He had sought to do everything he could to restore his people some measure of their independence within the nation state, and before his death had transmitted this intensity of purpose to his sons. In the fall of 1854, his son and successor as chief, Augustine, led another brief attack on mining property, which involved firing some shots past employees working for the Quebec and Lake Superior Mining Association holdings on Michipicoten Island,[90] but the time for such activities had passed. Augustine soon modified his behaviour, and sought other, less volatile ways to forward his people's interests.

A LEADERSHIP LEGACY

Augustine and those who succeeded him confronted far more obstacles than had their predecessors. Canadian Ojibwa faced a future residing on small reserves with little control over local resources. With the passing of Aboriginal lands from Native to government control, revenue from mining and logging operations on reserves irrevocably was lost or fell into trust funds which were frittered away on surveys or the building of colonisation roads primarily to benefit white settlement. Native fisheries were alienated, gravel extracted without remuneration,[91] timber was taken without band permission, and the earlier system of cutting wood on individual family lots was replaced by block cutting which denuded the reserve's landscape. Local political lobbying compelled the band to cede their best farming areas in the late 1850s. Then, in the early twentieth century when reserves in the Sault vicinity became too small to support their growing populations, bands had to purchase lands from the tracts earlier taken away. An elective system, unilaterally imposed on the Garden River band in 1891 following Augustine's death,[92] not only structurally marginalised chiefs and councils away from the political mainstream, but subjected them to insidious external campaigns to render them almost wholly powerless insofar as local resource issues were concerned. In 1916, this fact became all too evident when one active and educated chief, George Kabaosa, after leading a campaign to gain a measure of community control over his reserve's gravel and timber reserves, found himself suddenly deprived of his status by government fiat, despite the protests of those who had elected him.[93]

In conclusion, then, what do these events say about the nature of leadership evidenced by Shingwaukonse? That, ultimately, it was weak and ineffectual? Or, though constrained by the workings of a restrictive legal system enshrined in successive legislation concerning First Nation peoples, it displayed a surprising resilience despite formidable odds? Did it respond merely to crises situations, or did it leave a more lasting legacy? Were Shingwaukonse and his successors, if considered in the light of the agent/victim dichotomy, unfortunate participants in a struggle where ultimately they could not win? This author debates this last interpretation. There is an air of awful finality to any dichotomous situation, where one side defines the other. Moreover, both the terms "Native agent" and "Native victim" denote stereotypes, not living, breathing individuals, so at best they apply to a temporary state of affairs. One may be a victim of an unjust law, but in Canadian society one hopes that such laws eventually may be changed. Victimhood cannot in any way properly characterise Shingwaukonse's career. He proved shrewd and calculating as well as far-sighted. And on reviewing the evidence, it appears that Garden River leaders have consistently exhibited faithfulness to his vision of the future, as well as to traditional group norms and values.

Owing to the fact that Shingwaukonse felt his vision to be a unifying, inclusive one, he encouraged non-Natives such as McMurray and Macdonell, as well as Natives such as Nebenagoching, to forward sophisticated ideas and philosophies in his name, thereby showing a willingness to shoulder the burden for their ultimate success or failure.[94] This confident stand entailed risks, but given the odds arrayed against him, his judgement proved uncannily sound. To the Ojibwa, the true measure of a leader is the ability to act in efficacious ways on behalf of those for whom one is responsible.[95] Shingwaukonse was making plans and projections, but, even more important, he was doing so wisely according to the strictures of his culture.

NOTES

The author wishes to acknowledge the invaluable assistance to the development of the ideas presented in this paper generously offered during the 1980s and early 1990s by Ronald Boissoneau, George Agawa, Charles Andrews, John Biron, Irene Boissoneau, Joseph Boissoneau Sr., Angeline Clark, Betty Graburger, Ernest Jones, Norman Jones, Eva Kabaosa, Abe Lesage, Oliver Lesage, Lawrence McCoy, Dan Pine Sr., Fred Pine Sr., Mark Pine Sr., Bertha Sayers and Jerome Syrette. Thanks also are extended to the many other individuals of the Garden River, Batchewana and Bay Mills First Nations who made the author's visits to their communities personally enjoyable as well as academically rewarding.

1. Shingwaukonse's birth and death dates are only approximate. At the time of the chief's conversion to Anglicanism in 1833, his age was given as 60, which meant he would have been born in 1773. However, an article appearing in the *British Colonist* on 14 December 1849 states the chief was 78 in that year, which would place his birth some time in 1771. His death date is also uncertain. The date cited in several unpublished sources at Garden River, in lieu of available church records, is 1854. Yet according to documentary evidence taken from Indian Affairs records in the National Archives, he died late in 1853. Canada, National Archives (NA), RG 10, Indian Affairs Records, Vol. 222: 131771–72, S. Y. Chesley to George Ironside, 30 January 1856. See also NA, RG 10, Vol. 201, Pt. 2: 119397.

2. Response made by J. R. Miller to "Desperately Seeking Absolution: Responses and a Reply," *Canadian Historical Review* 76 (December 1995): 635–39.

3. The present paper has a companion article entitled "Shingwaukonse: A Nineteenth-Century Innovative Ojibwa Leader," which also reviews Shingwaukonse's career, but focuses specifically on traditional Ojibwa leadership behaviour, not on an examination of historical evidence in the light of the agent/victim dichotomy. This second article will appear in a forthcoming issue of *Ethnohistory*.

4. The author recognises that this statement touches on another debate, as to whether or not academics should be proactive on the subject of Native political positions. Yet to examine this second controversy is not the goal of this particular paper, and besides, she has dealt with the subject elsewhere. Janet E. Chute, "Review of Edward J. Hedican, *Applied Anthropology in Canada, Understanding Aboriginal Issues* (Toronto, 1995)," in *Social Sciences and Humanities Aboriginal Research Exchange* 4 (1): 10–14.

5. Educated Métis found themselves a primary target for Shingwaukonse's investigations. In 1853, Allan Macdonell, a Toronto lawyer and friend of George Brown of the *Globe*, railed against metropolitan society's attempts to depreciate the Sault Métis on the grounds that Native peoples were mostly uneducated. At the height of the Native rights campaign at the Sault in the early 1850s, Macdonell went so far as to attack Robert Baldwin politically by stating that many Métis, including the "Birons, La Fonds, La Batt, Le Blanc, Fontaine, Jolineaux [and other families at Garden River and the Sault], had been educated in Montreal and elsewhere, and among them] . . . may be found men superior to Mr. Atty. Genl. in education as well as intellect." Macdonell's political denunciations give an idea of the degree of vehemence with which some of Shingwaukonse's non-Native supporters, when fired by Shingwaukonse's own determination to succeed at his goals, could attack those who attempted to

denigrate Native agency. Ontario Archives (AO), MS 9, George Brown Papers, Correspondence, Pkg. 11, Allan Macdonell to George Brown, 30 April 1853.

6. Mary Black-Rogers, "The Ojibwa Power Belief System," in *The Anthropology of Power*, R. D. Fogelson and R. N. Adams, eds. (New York, 1977), 141–51.

7. Kohl, a German visitor to Garden River in the mid-1850s, learned that Shingwaukonse himself had given another *midewiwin* practitioner, Kaygayosh, a great number of beaver packs, worth collectively over $30,000 American, for the latter's assistance in teaching him medicine ritual. J. G. Kohl, *Kitchi-Gami, Wanderings Around Lake Superior* (Minneapolis, 1856), 380–82.

8. Ibid., 374–77.

9. Shingwaukonse himself told of these travels, especially during the 1830s when he was meeting with chiefs and collecting data in the capacity of a "data collector, or *mishiniway*. His name appears in Vincent Roy's fur-trade account book from Vermilion Lake, present-day Minnesota, in the mid-1830s. George Fulford, "The Pictographic Account Book of an Ojibwa Fur Trader," in *Papers of the Twenty-Third Algonquian Conference*, William Cowan, ed. (Ottawa, 1992), 190–233.

10. One such expedition involving Shingwaukonse occurred in 1810. NA, RG 10, Vol. 27: 16, 70, John Askin [Jr.] to William Claus, 8 May 1810.

11. Dr. Oronhyatekha, a Mohawk, learned that the Ojibwa held a council at Mackinac in 1809 regarding which side to join, the British or the American, and the gathering found itself split as to its allegiances. A wampum belt was made to commemorate the event and Shingwaukonse became its keeper. F. Barlow Cumberland, *Catalogue and Notes on the Oronhyatekha Historical Collection* (Toronto, n.d. [1910?]), 26.

12. The role of *kekedowenine* is discussed in Frederick Frost, *Sketches of Indian Life* (Toronto, 1904), 143.

13. Even though he had a disposition to side with those hostile to the Americans, Shingwaukonse was expected to subordinate personal self-interest to band considerations. Henry Rowe Schoolcraft, *Summary Narrative*, Mentor L. Williams, ed. (New York, 1973), 77.

14. Henry Rowe Schoolcraft, *Personal Memoirs of a Residence of Thirty Years with the Indian Tribes on the American Frontier, A.D. 1812 to A.D. 1842* (New York, 1975), 570.

15. Shingwaukonse was a leading member of the *midewiwin*, or Grand Medicine Society, where traditional power-holders congregated for several days to perform rites which stressed revitalisation both on the personal and community level, and undoubtedly his reputation as a noted medicine practitioner enhanced his political stature.

16. All those bearing the same totemic mark treated each other as siblings. While totemic group exogamy prevailed, band and village exogamy did not, so that large bands became composite over time as individuals joined them through marriage. In 1850, each Ojibwa person at Garden River possessed one of the four local totemic designations: Plover, Crane, Sturgeon, Hawk and Plover.

17. J. G. Kohl states that Shingwaukonse's father was a British officer stationed in Detroit. However, this assertion, which had not been obtained from the chief directly, may just as easily have referred to the chief's attachment to John Askin Sr. Kohl, *Kitchi-Gami*, 374–77. There are many other clues of the depth of the chief's regard for Askin. Ex-councillor Dan Pine Sr., who the author interviewed at Garden River, was actually the son of one of Shingwaukonse's own sons named "John Askin." Interview with ex-councillor Daniel E. Pine Sr., 13 June 1983. Other oral traditions point to Jean Baptiste Barthe, a trader at the American Sault, or else Lavoine Barthe who, according to Jean Baptiste Barthe's account book in the Burton Historical Collection in the Detroit Public Library, moved to the Wisconsin portage in 1778. Janet E. Chute, "A Century of Native Leadership: Shingwaukonse and His Heirs," PhD thesis, McMaster University, 1986, 93–95.

18. Henry Rowe Schoolcraft, *Historical and Statistical Information*, 8 (Philadelphia, 1851), 112; Schoolcraft, *Personal Memoirs*, 549.

19. Kohl, *Gitchi-Gami*, 380–82.

20. Interview with ex-councillor Danial E. Pine Sr., 20 August 1982. According to Dan, the Ojibwa word for "plover" is *chueskweskewa*. Although Lewis Henry Morgan ascribed the meaning "snipe" to *chueskweskewa*, at Garden River "snipe" is *muhno menekashe*. Lewis Henry Morgan, *Ancient Society* (Chicago, 1877), 166.

21. NA, RG 10, Vol. 416: 5942, "Petition of William Shinguaconce [Shingwaukonse], Henry Shinguaconce [Buhkwujjenene], Thomas Shinguaconce [Augustine], Joseph Nebenagoshing [Nebenagoching],

Nawquagabo, Francis Kewahkunce [Keokonse], Charles Pahyabetahsun [Piabetasung], John Kabaoosa [Kabaosa], James Ahbatahkezhik and George Mahgahsahsuhqua," 20 August 1846; NA, RG 10, Vol. 157: 40407, Shingwaukonse to George Ironside, 20 February 1846.

22. Waubejejauk or White Crane, a leading chief of the Sault band who had been killed during the War of 1812, had married a daughter of a French trader, Perrault. His son, Nebenagoching, became a chief at the British Sault.

23. Richard White, *The Middle Ground: Indians, Empires and Republics in the Great Lakes Region, 1650–1815* (Cambridge, 1991).

24. It could not be called a composite society similar to several other transitional period settlements in the Ohio River Valley, since only one nation, the Ojibwa, represented by one totemic group, the Cranes, characterized Sault Aboriginal society—traits which superficially made it appear quite homogeneous. The Ojibwa would assimilate into their bands only Métis who adopted Ojibwa customs and mores. For a description of a late eighteenth-century Ohio River Valley composite society, The Glaize, see Helen Hornbeck Tanner, "The Glaize in 1792: A Composite Indian Community," *Ethnohistory* 25, 1 (1978): 15–39.

25. These Hudson's Bay Company posts were located at Michipicoten, Sault Ste. Marie and LaCloche.

26. E. H. Blair, ed., *The Indian Tribes of the Upper Mississippi Valley and Region of the Great lakes*, 1 (Cleveland, 1911), 309–10.

27. Thomas L. McKenney, *Sketches of a Tour to the Lakes* (Minneapolis, 1972), 235.

28. This was certainly true of Nebenagoching, the head chief at the British Sault.

29. Information used in *midewiwin* ritual was recorded by the use of mnemonic symbols inscribed on wooden boards or birch-bark scrolls.

30. For instance, when a zealous frontier preacher declared the end of the world was at hand and provided the chief with a firm date for the event, Shingwaukonse simply cut notches in his pipe-stem until the designated day arrived and, after watching the sky carefully, decided the whole affair was a hoax. AO, MH 25, Strachan Papers, "Report of the Reverend F. A. O'Meara," 19 December 1843.

31. "The Venerable Archdeacon McMurray," *Algoma Missionary News*, Sault Ste. Marie (January, 1833).

32. Charles Elliott, *Indian Missionary Reminiscences* (New York, 1837), 159.

33. *Third Annual Report of the Society for Converting and Civilizing the Indians &c* (York, Canada West, 1833).

34. *Fourth Annual Report of the Society for Converting and Civilizing Indians &c* (York, Canada West, 1834).

35. Incidents of such joint cooperation may be found in the Hudson's Bay Company correspondence books and post journals for 1834 and 1835. Microfilm copies of records of the Hudson's Bay Company Archives (HBCA) Winnipeg, NA, MG 20. "Correspondence Books, Sault Ste. Marie," B/194/b/9/1834–5; B/194/b/10/1835–6. NA, MG 20. "Post Journal, Sault Ste. Marie," B/194/a/8/1834–5.

36. Metropolitan Toronto Reference Library, Baldwin Room, Thomas G. Anderson Papers, S29, Folder C, No. 49, "Indenture Contract of a Gift of Land from Indians to the Rev. G. Anderson," 1849. Shingwaukonse, at the request of his son Tegoosh, granted land for a Roman Catholic Church in 1852. Sault Ste. Marie, Anglican Heritage Collection, Bishophurst, Reverend Canon Colloton Papers, "Copy of original statement of grant," 1852.

37. Kohl, *Kitchi-Gami*, 384.

38. Ontario. Metropolitan Toronto Reference Library, Baldwin Room, James Givens Papers. "First Speech of Chinquakous—Young Pine," 1837. In the fall of 1835, Sir Francis Bond Head succeeded Sir John Colborne as Lieutenant-Governor. After a tour of Indian missions in Upper Canada, Bond Head declared that the idea of establishing yet another government-supported settlement at Sault Ste. Marie would result in a costly and probably fruitless endeavour, and suggested removing the entire Garden River band to Manitoulin Island. Shingwaukonse was perturbed that Bond Head did not visit the Sault mission, however. At this time there were government plans to remove the Sault Métis to St. Joseph's Island in northern Lake Huron. The opposition of Britain's Protestant missionary societies to Bond Head's removal scheme led to a return to the former civilisation programme initiated by Sir John Colborne. As a result, Bond Head's successor, Sir George Arthur, directed that axes and other tools be sent to Garden River as a token of the government's good faith in the community. NA, RG 1, E5, ECO File 1157, Vol. 8: 1848, "Extract from

491

a letter from Sir George Arthur, Lieu. Governor, to Chief Shinquackouce, dated Govt. House, York," 19 September, 1839.

39. AO, Aemelius Irving Papers, MU 1465, 27/32/09, "Report of E. B. Borron relative to Annuities payable to Indians in terms of the Robinson Treaties," 31 December 1892.

40. AO, Aemelius Irving Papers, MU 1465, 27/32/10, "Statement of Joshua Biron. Made to John Driver and sworn to him. Testimonies enclosed with a letter from John Driver to E. B. Borron," 8 June 1893.

41. The author is indebted to Bruce White for providing her with a copy of his report "The Regional Context of the Removal Order," which he prepared in 1993 for the Mille Lacs Band of Ojibwa. White traces events leading up to and surrounding the American Removal Order of 1850. See also James A. Clifton, "Wisconsin Death March: Explaining the Extremes of Old Northwest Indian Removal," *Transactions of the Wisconsin Academy of Sciences, Arts and Letters* 75: 1–39.

42. Detroit, Detroit Public Library, Burton Historical Collection, George Johnston Papers, The Reverend William McMurray to George Johnston, 7 May 1833.

43. Metropolitan Toronto Reference Library, Baldwin Room, Thomas G. Anderson Papers, S 29, "Statement translated by John Bell," 1841.

44. AO, RG 1, Series A-1-6: 21675, "Letters received, General Land Commissioner," Alexander Vidal to D. B. Papineau, 17 April 1846; AO, RG 1, Series A-1-6: 21678, MS 563, Microfilm Reel 22, "Reply to communication of Alexander Vidal."

45. NA, RG 10, Vol. 157: 40407, "Shingwaukonse to George Ironside, 20 February 1846.

46. NA, RG 10, Vol. 612: 100–01, "J. M. Higginson to George Ironside," 11 May 1846.

47. Metcalfe had recently been raised to the peerage.

48. Native individuals had originally assisted the miners to locate the copper, iron, silver and lead deposits, and wished to retain a degree of proprietary right to these resources.

49. NA, RG 10, Vol. 612, "Petition of Chief Chingwauk (Petition No. 156)," 10 June 1846.

50. NA, RG 10, Vol. 416: 5942, "Petition of William Shingwaukonse [et al]," 20 August 1846.

51. In November 1846, the Executive Council had authorised the sale of approximately 30 large mining locations along the north shore of Lakes Huron and Superior in keeping with the terms of an order in council passed earlier in May. Each location had to conform in size to 6,400 acres to accord with a government standard set to discourage speculation and prevent minor entrepreneurial interests from competing with powerful Montreal-controlled mining companies. A copy of the order in council was sent to Joseph Wilson, the land agent and Indian agent at the Sault. NA, RG 10, Vol. 159: 91442–43.

52. George Desbarats to Major Campbell, 10 May 1847 [Indian Affairs Records]. A copy of the letter is in the Indian File at the Bruce Mines Museum, Bruce Mines, Ontario.

53. Olive Patricia Dickason, *Canada's First Nations: A History of Founding Peoples from Earliest Times* (Toronto, 1993), 253; Alan Knight, "Allan Macdonell and the Pointe au Mines–Mica Bay Affair," research paper, York University, 1981; Douglas Leighton, "The Historical Significance of the Robinson Treaties of 1850," paper presented at the Canadian Historical Association Conference, Carleton University, Ottawa, 9 June 1982; Douglas Owram, *Promise of Eden: The Canadian Expansionist Movement and the Idea of the West, 1856–1900* (Toronto, 1980), 39–40; Boyce Richardson, "Kind Hearts or Forked Tongues?" *The Beaver*, Outfit 67, 1 (1987), 16–41; Edward S. Rogers, "The Algonquian Farmers of Southern Ontario," *Aboriginal Ontario: Historical Perspectives on the First Nations*, Edward S. Rogers and Donald B. Smith, eds. (Toronto, 1994), 149; Rhonda Telford, "A History of Aboriginal Mineral Resources in Ontario," PhD thesis, University of Toronto, 1995; Nancy M. Wrightman and W. Robert Wrightman, "The Mica Bay Affair: Conflict in the Upper-Lakes Mining Frontier, 1840–1850," *Ontario History* 83 (1991): 193–208.

54. NA, RG 10, Vol. 173: 100434, T. G. Anderson to Major Campbell, 9 October 1849.

55. NA, RG 1, E5, ECO File 1157, Vol. 8, "Minutes of a Council led by T. G. Anderson, V.S.I.A., at Sault Ste. Marie on Friday the 18th day of August, 1848."

56. Anderson included the press release in a letter to his superior. NA, RG 10, Vol. 173: 100434–46, T. G. Anderson to Major Campbell, 9 October 1849.

57. It has been held that Allan Macdonell did not practise law from 1837 to 1858. Donald Swainson, "Allan Macdonell," *Dictionary of Canadian Biography*, Vol. 11 (Toronto, 1982), 552–55. Macdonell, however, informally assisted the Ojibwa legally from 1849 to 1853, and even afterwards.

58. AO. Aemelius Irving Papers, MU 1464, 26/31/04, "Report of Commissioners A. Vidal and Thomas G. Anderson on a visit to Indians on North Shore Lake Huron & Superior for purpose of investigating their claims to territory bordering on these Lakes, Appendix," October 1849.

59. NA, RG 10, Vol. 207: 122406–25, John William Keating, "Report," 1853.

60. The local Anglican missionary noted on 23 January 1849, "Chief Shingwaukonse gave them leave to settle here" at Garden River. Metropolitan Toronto Reference Library, Baldwin Room, Thomas G. Anderson Papers, S 29, Folder B, "Diary of the Reverend Gustavus Anderson, August 26, 1848, to May 23, 1849."

61. NA, RG 10, Vol. 173: 100434–36, T. G. Anderson to Major Campbell, 9 October 1849.

62. *Montreal Gazette*, 7 July 1849.

63. Ibid.

64. AO. Aemelius Irving Papers, MU 1464, 26/31/04, "Map of band hunting territories along the north shore of Lake Superior, Crown Lands Department, Surveyor's Office," August 1849.

65. Regional Collections, University of Western Ontario, London, Vidal Papers, CA 90N, VID 33, "Alexander Vidal, Memorandum of Indian Mission," 1849. See also *A Journal of proceedings on my mission to the Indians—Lake Superior and Huron, 1849, by Alexander Vidal.* Transcribed by George Smith with historical notes by M. Elizabeth Arthur (Bright's Cove, Ontario, 1974).

66. AO. Aemelius Irving Papers, MU 1464, 26/31/04, "Report of Commissioners A. Vidal and Thomas G. Anderson on a visit to Indians on North Shore Lake Huron & Superior for purpose of investigating their claims to territory bordering on these Lakes. Extracts from the notes Taken at the Conference with the Indians at the Sault Ste. Marie—October 15th and 16th, 1849," 1849, 7.

67. Ibid.

68. Ibid.

69. William MacTavish, the Hudson's Bay Company factor at the Sault, stated that the Mica Bay expedition had been in its planning stages for a long time, although there had been some dispute as to whether Michipicoten or Mica Bay would be the destination. NA, RG 20, B/194/b/15/1849–1850. "Sault Ste. Marie Post, Correspondence Book," William MacTavish to A. H. Campbell, 11 November 1849.

70. According to the Hudson's Bay Company factor, the expedition included the Macdonell brothers, another lawyer named Wharton Metcalfe, three American Ojibwa [one of whom was the head chief Oshawano, also named Cassaquadung], five American Métis, twelve Canadian Ojibwa, thirteen Canadian Métis and one French Canadian. NA., RG 20, B/194/b/15/1849–1850, "Sault St. Marie Post, Correspondence Book," William MacTavish to A. H. Campbell, 16 November 1849.

71. AO, MU 1778, Alexander Macdonell Estate Papers, Biographical Information; NA, Macdonell of Collochie Papers, MG 24 1 8, Finding Aid 99, Biographical Notes.

72. NA, RG 10, Vol. 179: 109890, Allan Macdonell to R. Bruce, 21 December 1849.

73. NA, RG 10, Vol. 188: 109891, "Attorney General of Canada West Recommends that Indians be pardoned," 22 May 1851.

74. *British Colonist* (Toronto), 7 February 1850.

75. NA, MG 20, B/194/b/15/1849–1850, William MacTavish to George Simpson, 17 October 1849.

76. NA, RG 10, Vol. 179: 103884. Macdonell, who spoke the Ojibwa language, wrote of this relationship: "I have lived among the Indians some little time and am received among them as one of their own people. The chiefs of the different bands upon the Lake have reposed a trust and confidence in me which I deem worthy of attention." Allan Macdonell to R. Bruce, 23 December 1849.

77. *The Patriot* (Toronto), 19 December 1849.

78. See, for example, articles in the *Detroit Free Press*, 22 December 1849, and the *Commercial Advertiser* (New York), 5 December 1849.

79. Robert J. Surtees, "Land Cessions, 1763–1830," in Rogers and Smith, eds., *Aboriginal Ontario*, 92–121.

80. Reserve boundaries delineated on a survey plan prepared in 1853 by J. S. Dennis do not conform with the description of the boundaries of the Garden River Reserve as set out in the Robinson Huron treaty of 1850. One explanation for the discrepancy is that the survey plan of 1853 releases the Clark location from the burden of Native title, by isolating it beyond the reserve's "revised" western boundary. Peterborough, Ontario, Ministry of Natural Resources, "Survey Records, Plan #14, K19, #2484 by J. S. Dennis," 14 May 1853.

81. The Ojibwa promised to keep Philetus Church's establishment "supplied with logs for sawing" for

493

10 years, while the merchant would pay £25 annually to Shingwaukonse for the privilege of having the timber protected from exploitation by other commercial agencies. The Ojibwa would be paid for logs they wished to sell, and Church promised to saw a certain quota of the timber hauled to his mill for the band's own use, free of charge. The local Anglican missionary felt the contract to be a good one because Church had dealt honestly with the band for many years. Unfortunately, the merchant resided on Sugar Island, just offshore of the reserve, but on the American side of the border. NA, RG 10, Vol. 191: 11383–84, "Agreement between Shingwaukonse and his Band and P. S. Church," July 1851. After 1851, a young and energetic Methodist missionary, the Reverend George MacDougall, renewed the band's interest in farming, and assisted with the building of houses and barns in the community.

82. AO, MS 91, Pkg. 11, George Brown Papers. Correspondence, Allan Macdonell to George Brown, 20 April 1853.

83. The law was entitled *An Act to Make Better Provision for the Administration of Justice in the Unorganized Tracts of the Country in Upper Canada* (16 Vict. Cap. 176).

84. NA, RG 10, Vol, 198, Pt. 1: 116289, "Petition of Ashkepogegosh of Leech Lake and other American Indians," 1853.

85. A recent article traces the effects of humiliation of such a kind on another chief, in this instance, Loon's Foot of Fond du Lac, Minnesota, who was the brother-in-law of Charles Oakes Ermatinger. Rebecca Krugel, "Religion Mixed with Politics: The 1836 Conversion of Mang'osid of Fond du Lac," *Ethnohistory* 37 (2): 127–57.

86. NA, RG 10, Vol. 198, Pt. 1: 116289, "Petition of Ashkepogegosh of Leech Lake and other American Indians," 1853.

87. The Garden River band raised £200 for the expedition and Church gave £70. NA, RG 10, Vol. 201, Pt. 2: 119396–97, Joseph Wilson to George Ironside, 21 March 1853.

88. Ibid.

89. Shingwaukonse's grave site lay on the west bank of the Garden River. Kohl, *Kitchi-Gami*, 373. It has since been destroyed by water erosion, but the Anglican church, which lay nearby, is sometimes regarded as a symbolic marker to his burial site.

90. *Lake Superior Journal* (Sault Ste. Marie), 4 November 1854: 2.

91. Four gravel pits, which constituted the source of the high-grade stone used by Ontario in 1909 in the construction of the Sault Ste. Marie to Sudbury trunk road, were expropriated by the CPR under the Railway Act of 1879, despite a major protest movement launched against their alienation by the Garden River band between 1897 and 1913. "Correspondence on the gravel pits," 1897–1914, NA, RG 10, Vol. 2068, File 10, 307, Pt. 2.

92. NA, RG 10, Vol. 2552, File 112, 279, William Van Abbott to Indian Affairs, 9 January 1891. Included with "Notice of Death of A. Shingwauk."

93. George Kabaosa was forced to step down as elected chief shortly after he had won office in March of 1916. AO, MS 216 (5), Sault Ste. Marie Agency Records, 4 March 1916. His campaigns to gain prerogatives over timber on the reserve were taken up by Chief Amable Boissoneau in the 1930s.

94. Shingwaukonse's unique vision militated against what may otherwise have been a fairly self-interested scheme on the part of Macdonell who, in his later writings, as an Expansionist and debunker of the Hudson's Bay Company's monopoly, still paid high regard to the political and economic potential of Native groups. Though by the late-1850s Macdonell no longer portrayed the Ojibwa as he once did, as proud proprietors of lands and resources, he praised the way in which the Ojibwa sought new opportunities despite the strictures set by oppressive legislation. AO, Aemelius Irving Papers, MU 1474/18/7, Allan Macdonell, "Report of the Committee Appointed to Receive and Collect Evidence to the Rights of the HBC Under Their Charter, 1857."

95. Black-Rogers, "The Ojibwa Power Belief System," 146.

494

Article 2: Longhouses, Schoolrooms and Workers' Cottages: Nineteenth Century Protestant Mission to the Tsimshian and the Transformation of Class Through Religion[1]

Susan Neylan

Christianity is an integral aspect of Native history, not simply an external force acting upon it. Nineteenth-century Aboriginal women and men frequently took the initiative and assumed roles of leadership in mission activities and within the churches themselves. While they never entirely directed or controlled their own Christianization, the identities they assumed as part of this process illuminate the extent to which conversion entailed negotiation. The relationship forged between Native and Euro-Canadian missionary was a dialogue of sorts, although not necessarily a mutually beneficial one. One of the pre-eminent themes in this dialogue on Protestant mission work among the Tsimshian of British Columbia's North Pacific Coast in the late nineteenth century revolved around class.

This paper explores the blurring of boundaries among spiritual expressions and identities in Protestant missions to the Tsimshian. It highlights several ways in which the class implications of work and religious association had profoundly different meanings in Native and non-Native milieus. Pre-existing indigenous understanding on class and spiritual transformation informed Native reception to Christianity. The Tsimshian and their immediate neighbours, the Nisga'a and Gitksan, were socially stratified by ranked class-based systems. When Native peoples participated in the missions, they did not entirely forsake this history. A number of religious forms with industrial working-class associations, such as the Salvation Army, the Church Army, and other evangelical forms of Methodism and Anglicanism, flourished in Tsimshian territories, yet those communities were neither working-class nor urban. In fact, several Tsimshian missions were pioneered by chiefly and noble families who firmly rejected the "working class" identity that some missionaries sought to impose upon them. ... [I]t is also readily apparent that others sought empowerment by using these new forms of spirituality in order to bolster existing social positions, as demands for literacy, Euro-Canadian education, and new styles of village architecture (especially housing) will aptly demonstrate.

CLASS AND SPIRITUAL IDENTITIES IN THE TSIMSHIAN CONTEXT

Defining Tsimshian notions of class is a complex matter because of the intersection between class and other important delineations of power, status, and family. Tsimshianic societies were hierarchical and ranked, organized into four matrilineal exogamous clans in a system they shared with their immediate neighbours, the Haida and Tlingit. Among the Coast Tsimshian, these clans were represented by two sets of crests (*pteex*), each with reciprocal obligations to the other in the pair: Killerwhale or Blackfish (*Gispuwudwada*) paired with Wolf (*Laxgibuu*), and Raven (*Ganhada*) linked with Eagle (*Laxsgiik*). Although clan members were responsible for mutual assistance and protection, because they were scattered over large territories, in practice, the main social grouping was the *walp* or *waap* (house).

The house was the core "family unit" for the Tsimshian.[2] The *walp* was a matrilineage that resided in a single or cluster of longhouses.[3] Symbolically, it was a box or container filled with food, wealth, and "real" people. Indeed, social and spiritual divisions within the elite membership in Tsimshian society were based on the degree to which individuals were more or less "real" and constantly striving to become more than human. These characteristics made comprehension of the missionary message of the possible transformation through the saving grace of Christ much easier because of its similarity to these existing notions. The ranked names were the *walp*, not the individuals who filled them. Therefore becoming more than human or a "real person" depended upon participation in the Tsimshian potlatch system.[4] The collection of immortal names is passed through the matriline and the house chief assumes the leading name. This social system remains in place today. ...

Source: Susan Neylan, "Longhouses, Schoolrooms and Workers' Cottages: Nineteenth Century Protestant Mission to the Tsimshian and the Transformation of Class through Religion," *Journal of the Canadian Historical Association/Revue de la SHC*, 2000 , New Series, Vol. 11, pp. 51–86.

Intersecting the clan and *walp* systems were broad categories of class: royals (*smgigyet* or "real people," who constituted the chiefly class) who held considerable economic, political, and spiritual power (this elite class also encompassed the nobles or *'alg-yagask* who belonged to the chiefs' lineages); the majority of the people or commoners (*liksgiget*) who supported the "real people" economically and morally; and slaves who, along with marginalized individuals who had lost their status, were considered *'wa'aayin* or unhealed, and thus, literally, outside society.[5] Hence, not all people residing in the longhouse were considered family members.[6] Furthermore, members of each class were also discreetly ranked within their category. The most prestigious crests were associated with the class of royals who maintained the house system by filling names and powers. Subsidiary crests within the four main ones were likewise ranked through the classes.[7] Competitive potlatches, known as *maxłye'tsü*, allowed for the re-ordering of social rank within the classes, something that occurred more frequently in the nineteenth century because of the influx of new sources of wealth following the entry of European traders into Tsimshian homelands. However, the convention itself predates contact.[8] This practice of facilitating social mobility would come to utilize Protestant missions and all they entailed in ways that both continued and challenged this custom.

Another ancient concept related to class, which would have a lasting impact on how mission Christianity was received in the nineteenth century, was the relationship between Tsimshian social classes and spiritual power. Guardian helpers were important to Tsimshian culture and were accessed by individuals to assist them in any and all aspects of their daily lives. All free persons thus saw power acquisition and spirit protection as essential.[9] However, aside from shamanic encounters and vision quests, most powers were obtained or consulted through a much more formalized structure in which hereditary sources and class were paramount.[10] Formalized spiritual leadership in Tsimshian culture could be wielded by chiefs (*smhalaayt*) and shamans (*swansk halaayt*). Membership of all high-ranking Tsimshian in one of the four dancing or secret societies (*wut'aahalaayt*) was socially mandatory and was partly related to power acquisition. These three arenas of superhuman power constitute the backbone of the more

formalized of Tsimshian religious practices. While shamans could come from royalty, nobility, or the commoner class, chiefly prerogatives were owned and inherited through one's house. Spiritual power acquired through initiation into the dancing societies, with membership in two groups reserved for the chiefs and nobles, meant that many powers were available only to Tsimshian social elites.[11] In other words, social standing played an important role for holding and exercising spiritual power. The most renowned shamans among the Tsimshian were not of the chiefly class but had acquired considerable status through their use of superhuman skills.[12] While affiliation in lineage and clan with other shamans was an advantage, it was not a requirement. In contrast, the empowerment of chiefs (when *smhalaayt*) and those they initiated in special ceremonies or in the secret societies was contingent upon which gifts of power they were entitled to receive from their house or lineage, or because of their social rank. In this respect, spiritual leadership and expertise were closely connected to class, and specifically to the higher classes (royals and nobles).

The implications for the reception of Christian power within this complex religious system are far-reaching. Conversion to Christianity extended the possibilities of transformative experience to more people, who were neither shamans nor chiefs. Paradoxically, it allowed the empowered shamans and chiefs another potential mode of retaining their roles of religious leadership and specialization, something that historically was true more for chiefs than for shamans. Consequently, the Tsimshian reception of Christianity was informed by this existing culture of spirituality, while it simultaneously created new social identities.

TSIMSHIAN AND MISSIONARIES IN CONTACT

The missionaries to the First Nations of coastal British Columbia were not the first Europeans to interact with Native societies there. Indeed, it was a half-century after sustained contact with non-Native peoples before mission work even received any serious interest. What had brought most newcomers into the area concerned material, not spiritual matters. In an age of exploration and mercantilism, the same forces that had sent wave after wave of

European ships to the Americas also drove them into the Pacific realm. By the beginning of the nineteenth century, the secular interests of fur traders operating in the interior of British Columbia (New Caledonia) brought Christian beliefs and instructors into the region in a sustained way. ... Yet this early period of sustained trading contact laid important groundwork for the nature of Native/non-Native interaction for the region. It was within this context that the Tsimshian acquired a utility for these visitors, and in part, accounts for the enduring material attraction of Christian missions.

The first coastal post, Fort Simpson, was established initially on the Nass River in 1831 but moved shortly thereafter in 1834 to its current position where it ensured better trading opportunities not only for the Nass River, but along the coast and the Skeena River to the south. Following the move, the Gispaxlo'ots tribe of Coast Tsimshian established a permanent winter village (*Lax'Kw'alaams*) close to the fort at a site that formerly had been a camping place for Coast Tsimshian groups travelling to the spring fishery on the Nass River. Both voluntarily and involuntarily, several other Native villages were amalgamated or moved to locations more beneficial for trading with the newcomers. In particular, the new sites permitted the inhabitants to hold a middleman position, trading European goods with other First Nations. Epidemics continued to be an adverse consequence of sustained contact with non-Natives, and this too altered social structures as villages joined together, unable to sustain a viable existence alone after massive depopulation.[13] This spatial clustering of Aboriginal populations at fewer sites throughout the region facilitated the dissemination of Christianity. However, conversion to this new Christian religion could act to bolster, as well as challenge the existing frameworks of class, status, and power in this period of social reconfiguration.

Christian missions appeared on the coast formally in 1857, when William Duncan, a lay preacher sponsored by the Church Missionary Society (CMS), established the first Anglican mission among the Tsimshian at the Hudson's Bay Company's Fort Simpson; he later founded perhaps British Columbia's most famous mission, Metlakatla. Both Metlakatla and Fort Simpson (Port Simpson after 1880), served as epicentres for Protestant mission work in the region. Other missionaries followed Duncan, and by the late nineteenth century, four versions of Christianity were available to the four Tsimshianic speaking groups: Roman Catholicism (generally in the Upper Skeena River region only), Anglicanism, Methodism, and the Salvation Army. Interestingly, the dominance of four variants of Christianity was very compatible with the "traditional" Tsimshian philosophy that conceived their culture in divisions of four. ...

Metlakatla was founded in 1862, when Duncan moved from Fort Simpson to the recently abandoned village site, with the explicit intention of isolating Native Christians not only from their "traditional" culture, but from the negative influences of Euro-Canadian settlements. From 1862 until 1887, Metlakatla grew from an original group of 50 converts to over 900 Tsimshian Christians and other First Nations from the region. Although Tsimshian chiefs, notably among them, Paul Ligeex, perceived their membership in the mission based on existing social and political criteria, Metlakatla encouraged nothing short of a sweeping reformation of Tsimshian society. As an industrial undertaking, it was designed to promote Victorian "progress" and the merits of European civilization, including work habits and discipline appropriate to a worker class in an industrial, capitalist system. Victorian-style homes patterned upon British workers' cottages, gardens, schoolhouse, library, weaving house, blacksmith's shop, cannery, carpentry shop, and sawmill, all attempted to convert Tsimshian space as well as souls.[14] Metlakatla lay at the heart of Anglican activity for the region, both as a model of practice, Episcopal See (of the Diocese of Caledonia after 1878), and as a physical base from which to launch new missionary endeavours and regular itinerant circuits. ...

Other Protestant groups found acceptance among the Tsimshian and, likewise, expanded mission work throughout the entire North Coast region. For the Tsimshian, the maintenance of authority and power had long depended on extensive systems of trade, exchange, and redistribution of material resources. The opportunity to gain access to new sources of both material and spiritual resources was likely one of the strongest appeals of Protestant missions, certainly for the Tsimshian classes who aimed to bolster their existing place in the social order, but also for those who wished to circumvent "traditional" routes for gaining status. Scholars must take into account historical Aboriginal viewpoints not only on conversion, but on their class positions in mission Christianity. One clear example is the role of Christian chiefs. In this region there is ample evidence to suggest that ordinary people tended to follow the example of their chiefs. In some locations, such as Port Simpson, conversion was literally a "top-down" phenomenon, which substantiates the idea of conversion as a shift in religious affiliation for an entire group, not merely the spiritual turning of individuals. ...

The presence of the Roman Catholics in Gitksan-Wet'suwet'en territory presented competition for Protestant missions who worked on the Upper Skeena River, but there were no Catholic missions within Coast Tsimshian homelands. Among the Protestant churches, there was much inter- and intrarivalry. There was a wide variety of denominations competing for Tsimshian souls. And within each mission, variation gave the Tsimshian a choice in Christian form: the Anglican church had a Church Army and Red and White Cross groups, and the Methodists had Epworth Leagues and Bands of Christian Workers. This variation gave the Tsimshian greater ability to retain those aspects of their pre-Christian cultures that they felt were vital, notions of class among them.

CHRISTIAN CHIEFS

One can make the argument that Christianity introduced new forms of power and authority among the Tsimshian. Here, I do not deny that Native individuals gained prestige and status through mission work in ways that circumvented their class positions under the ancient system. Yet the decline of deference to hereditary chiefs was not an immediate or necessary outcome of Christianization, as an examination of Chief Ligeex's role in the founding of Metlakatla will illustrate. The name-title of "Ligeex" was hereditary and several Tsimshian chiefs successively took the name in the late eighteenth and nineteenth centuries.[15] Ligeex ... was a chiefly title of the Gispaxlo'ots Tsimshian and of the Eagle clan (*Laxsgiik*). By the time missionaries entered the colony at mid-century, Ligeex was also an important priest-chief (*smhalaayt*) of the *Nułim* ("Dog-eater") secret society. Unravelling the distinctive histories of the many Ligeex name-holders is challenging for the ethnohistorian. ... For example, it is likely that it was a single Ligeex who was responsible for solidifying an Eagle clan trading monopoly along the Skeena River from the 1790s

to 1835, adding considerable wealth to his house through extensive trade with Europeans.[16] When the Hudson's Bay Company moved its fort to the present-day location (Port Simpson) in 1834, this Ligeex moved his entire village from Metlakatla to Wild Rose Point to be closer to the fort. However, it was a different individual leading the Gispaxlo'ots when William Duncan arrived on the North Coast in 1857, who became the first of several Christianized Ligeex title-holders. A number of missionaries and Euro-Canadian writers described him as a "fierce barbarian" and a "proud" and "powerful" chief who, nonetheless, still struggled to maintain his status among the other eight Tsimshian village-groups that lived in the area. ...[17] When Ligeex finally converted to Christianity after defying for several years the missionary's efforts, Euro–Canadian recorders framed it as a great sacrifice and rejection of his past wealth, status, and livelihood:

> This brutal murderer, who boasted of the number of lives he had taken—was at length humbled and led like a lamb. He had once ... attempted to assassinate Mr. Duncan, and had never ceased to persecute and harass him and his followers, until now, like Saul when stricken, he was transformed into a faithful disciple of him whom he had bitterly reviled, and had mercilessly pursued. Likewise, as Saul, when baptized he chose the name Paul. He became a simple citizen of Metlakahtla, an industrious carpenter and cabinet-maker, a truly exemplary Christian.[18]

Adopting the namesake of a disciple of Christ and a trade with a special appeal to Christians, Ligeex was ultimately transformed, both by faith and apparently through a replacement of class.

From the missionary's standpoint, Ligeex was an ideal candidate for conversion to Christianity with the added benefit that he was a highly influential figure among his people.[19] For the Tsimshian chief, Duncan was a significant addition to the Eagle clan.[20] But did Ligeex, in fact, forsake entirely his title and position after his conversion and move to Metlakatla? Biographer Michael Robinson suggested Ligeex "wanted umbrellas and admission to the Anglican church—not out of a desire to acculturate, but rather to gain the spiritual power of the whites to complement the powers he already controlled."[21] The umbrella was used on state occasions by several British Columbia First Nations as a symbol of power. Some Tsimshian oral traditions record that an umbrella was offered by Ligeex as a supernatural object owned by the *Nuɫim* (Dog-eaters) society.[22] It is logical that Ligeex wanted to continue his role as a spiritually empowered leader through his personal association with Christianity. Certainly, many individuals and families who had held politically and economically important positions in the pre-Christian community continued to do so, to some extent even within Metlakatla. ... Indeed, the chiefs who relocated to Metlakatla benefited in terms of their political and economic power through holding the only permanent positions on the village council, participation in the maintenance of civil justice, and until 1865, receiving half of the village taxes.[23] Although Ligeex resided at Metlakatla by 1868, "his title was still called at Fort Simpson feasts as if he were there, and he was represented by his headman, who spoke for him and received gifts intended for him."[24] He still maintained a home at Port Simpson, with a plaque inscribed: "Legaic, my crest is the Eagle, the King of the Birds, February 27, 1858."[25]

Furthermore, there is evidence against missionary claims that Ligeex had given up his title, wealth, and membership in the *Nuɫim* society. In fact, Paul Ligeex continued many "traditional" Tsimshian practices appropriate for a man of his position as chief of Gispaxlo'ots after his conversion and baptism (in 1863) as a Christian. For example, he continued his participation as a spiritual leader in the initiation of new members into the secret societies, and most remarkably, in 1866 he raised an Eagle pole in the mission village. Chiefs from Tsimshian and neighbouring nations throughout the region attended the pole-raising potlatch, and Ligeex distributed a considerable amount of wealth and property among his guests, including slaves for the most honoured among them.[26] Thus, while the Euro-Canadian missionary's descriptions of this man emphasized persecution, sacrifice, and replacement of old allegiances, ... in the case of Paul Ligeex, there is evidence to suggest that the outcome idealized by the missionary was nowhere near the historical reality. ...

Self-proselytizing preceding formal denominational involvement seems to have been the rule rather than the exception on the North Coast. Missions at Port Simpson, Kitamaat, Kitkatla, and China Hat were "founded" by First Nations and several were in fact, staffed in their formative years by Native missionaries and teachers. Missionaries preferred to see themselves as the impetus behind mission establishment, and their narratives reflect this egocentric view of the process whereby Native initiative always has its origins in their evangelistic work or through revivals led by Euro-Canadians in Victoria. The missionary version of how the Tsimshian Dudoward family established the Methodist mission at Fort Simpson is one such story. A chiefly Tsimshian woman, Elizabeth "Diex" Lawson who was living in Victoria, converted to Methodism in the dramatic revival meetings that took place in the early 1870s in a former bar-room. According to the Methodist literature, she convinced her son and daughter-in-law, Alfred and Kate Dudoward, to convert to Christianity. Instead of the cargo of whiskey they had travelled to Victoria to obtain in 1872, the Dudowards returned northward with their canoes laden with bibles, and once there, tirelessly lobbied the Methodist church for an "official" mission for their community.[27] However, when one considers the Dudowards' actions in light of their social class, they provide another instance of how missions were used by the Tsimshian to carry out chiefly responsibilities.

Native oral traditions of the event provide contrasting evidence and points of detail.[28] Both Alfred and Kate were converts to Christianity long before their alleged conversion in Victoria. Kate was the daughter of a Tsimshian mother and a non-Native customs officer named Holmes, although apparently her parents had parted company. Her mother was employed as a domestic servant and for a time Kate lived in Victoria. In 1870, her mother was called back to Fort Simpson to assume a title and rank in her family and Kate was left behind in the care of Roman Catholic nuns. However, after her mother and her travelling companions were killed *en route*, fourteen-year-old Kate was installed as chief instead, as there was no clear male heir. Kate began teaching other Tsimshian (particularly her kinswomen and slaves) what she knew of Christianity. She married Alfred Dudoward in 1871.

Alfred, like his wife, had a mixed Native and European heritage, but was born into the Tsimshian elite social class by virtue of his matriline. Alfred, too, had lived for a while in Victoria while his mother was employed as a domestic. He assumed a chieftainship

499

necessitating his return to the North Coast, while his mother remained in Victoria. He also had prior exposure to mission Christianity as a young man. Duncan's school registry for Fort Simpson in 1857 listed an Alfred Dudoire as one of his pupils.[29]

Clearly, Kate and Alfred Dudoward had been exposed to Christianity as children, and had their own agendas behind their interest in Methodism in adulthood. The couple continued to increase their familiarity with Christian teachings and with the Methodist denomination during their ten-month stay in Victoria when their supposed "conversion" occurred. Over the next year, Kate organized and led classes in Christian instruction, in addition to conducting worship services every Sunday.[30] However, an "urgent" invitation was sent to the Methodists to request formal missionary involvement only after a rival Tsimshian group, composed of those who had converted to Anglicanism, had left to live in Metlakatla. Kate's evangelism then sparked widespread interest.[31] According to ethnographer and ranked Tsimshian William Beynon, Alfred Dudoward had been expelled from the mission because he was initiated in the Human-Eating Dancers' Society (*Xgyedmhalaayt*), sometimes erroneously called Cannibals. Therefore, to maintain his prestige, but also in retaliation for the expulsion, Alfred may have had an additional motivation behind his encouraging the Methodists to come to Fort Simpson.[32] These sudden and mass conversions of entire communities do not come as a surprise when "traditional" Tsimshian methods of power acquisition are taken into account. The realization of one's superhuman potential through spiritual transformation commonly belonged within the framework of lineage organization, and new powers could always be added to the ones already owned by the house, even one of foreign origins.[33]

Moreover, beyond maintaining existing roles appropriate to one's class and rank, the case of Kate and Alfred Dudoward demonstrates how Tsimshian chiefs sought to augment their positions through continued involvement in daily mission life. Because both Dudowards were from high-ranking families in the community and both were designated chiefs, they already held a socially powerful position. Both would remain active in the Methodist church throughout their lifetimes. Kate worked for decades as an interpreter, teacher, and preacher for the Methodist

mission there, and indeed, as "official translator" for several other denominations.[34] Alfred sat on the village council and both of them were class leaders for weekly study meetings in the early 1870s. However, over the next several decades, the Methodist church would not always recognize the Christian status of these chiefs. The politics of missions was played out through the constant inclusion and removal of both Kate and Alfred from the membership rolls in the 1880s and 1890s, at the very height of their most active involvement in mission work.[35] Thus, although missionaries wanted a specific code of conduct from Native converts, even the most active and motivated Tsimshian Christians altered, challenged, and defied these expectations. "Traditional" chiefs who became Christians were rivals to Euro-Canadian missionaries, a role that perpetuated the Tsimshian's class-based systems of authority, but also a role that the missionaries were not prepared to accept. Furthermore, Christian chiefs exemplify Tsimshian defiance of missionaries' attempts to impose a Christian ideal of a class-less society, or rather, more practically, a working-class identity for Native peoples.

...

"THE INDIANS MUST BE TAUGHT. SIMPLY BEING GOOD WAS NOT ENOUGH; THEY MUST BE GOOD FOR SOMETHING."[36]

The Victorian ethos which valued hard work, orderliness, thrift, punctuality, "common sense," and perseverance undoubtedly influenced the Euro-Canadian missionary's vision of how mission work should proceed.[37] William Duncan was a prime example of a man who improved his social standing through self-education and moral betterment. Duncan's own journals reveal the arduous self-improvement and moral strengthening of a working-class man.[38] Duncan firmly applied an evangelical agenda which replicated and reinforced the earthly social order of the mainstream culture while preparing converts for Christian eternity through a strict system of rules and regulations.[39]

From the present-day vantage point, the public missionary discussion about First Nations seems remarkably patronizing, prejudiced, and static; in the nineteenth and early twentieth centuries, it was unremarkable in its adherence to the common stereotypes and tropes that extended across nearly all colonial literature. Missionaries saw their Native catechists as recently divorced from an "uncivilized" (by European definitions) past, and yet never entirely removed from it. These images were informed by the general perception of the "missionary's Indian" as warlike, superstitious, cruel, inhumane, devilish, drunken, slavers, debased, and heathen.[40] Like cultural evolutionists, Victorian missionaries conceptualized history as a hierarchy of stages in human development.[41] In general, mission discourse simultaneously emphasized the "savagery" and the humanity of potential converts.[42] After all, if First Nations were so irredeemable, the project of missionization would have been pointless. Hence, missionary accounts of the Northwest Coast temper negative descriptions of indigenous cultures with portrayals of admirable customs, work habits, cleanliness, respect for elders, and other characteristics which frequently allowed the missionaries to decry the decline of such values in their own societies. Ducan's first reports on the Tsimshian are an excellent example. While he includes some very negative and wildly exaggerated descriptions of Tsimshian rituals, these account for only a small portion of his extended ethnographic portrait of everyday Native life, which was generally quite positive.[43]

Metlakatla was an industrial village designed to promote Victorian "progress" and the merits of European civilization. Anglo-Canadian traditions were imposed through a number of public buildings that included a reading room and museum, the mission houses, a jail, boarding and day schools, and a guest-house for visitors to Duncan's "utopia." Duncan designed Metlakatla to be economically self-sustaining, and he established a number of commercial enterprises to this end, including a sawmill, soap factory, furniture factory, weaving shop, blacksmith shop, trading post, and salmon cannery. Here, as in other missions, First Nations partly financed many of these projects. They paid for and built the church of St. Paul's, reputedly the largest church west of Chicago and north of San Francisco and capable of seating over a thousand.[44] The prestige that communities attached to their churches recalled the "traditional" importance placed on a village's ability to display wealth and property.

Euro-Canadian education was one of the key tools in the missionary repertoire. In the first generation of missionization on the North Coast, the Protestant denominations introduced day and Sunday schools to achieve their goals of conversion, and in these schools incorporated industrial training and curriculum designed to forward the "civilizing" agenda. Eventually the system of residential schools developed from this base, a system which has, among other things, been responsible for a dark and enduring legacy of cultural genocide among Canada's First Peoples. Education throughout nineteenth-century Canada was very much influenced by evangelical Christianity. The potential improvement of each individual through Christian salvation could be achieved on a social level through discipline regulation, and the development of the higher faculties (moral and intellectual).[45]

Within the first week of his arrival on the North Coast, William Duncan wrote from Fort Simpson to his superior at the Church Missionary Society on how ripe the Tsimshian were for industrial pursuits: "They are a very fine—robust & exceedingly intelligent race. I have already seen specimens of their skill in both the useful & fine arts which would not shame European skills to have produced. The superior industry is universally acknowledged by those who know them."[46] Missionaries hoped that technical training in schools and through cottage and industrial projects in Metlakatla and nearby missions would instill not only a healthy work ethic, but provide Native peoples with employment on site so they would not be attracted by wage labour opportunities elsewhere.[47]

The Department of Indian Affairs was pleased with the industrial initiatives at Metlakatla, and anticipated that further development would be facilitated through westernized education. I.W. Powell, Indian Superintendent for British Columbia, reported: "As industrial pursuits, however, are the foundation of civilization in every Christian and progressive community, the mission which has the necessary arrangements, zeal, and ability, to inculcate and foster them in connection with the day school, will be successful in every respect, and certainly most deserving of much consideration and substantial assistance from the Government."[48] At the nearby Methodist mission at Fort Simpson, the Reverend Thomas Crosby also nurtured what he saw as natural mechanical aptitude among the Tsimshian by sponsoring an Industrial Fair with the explicit purpose of promoting "industry, thrift, and self-reliance."[49] Moreover, mission education was designed to prepare students for their future roles as workers and Christians by instilling Victorian work habits through the routines, discipline, and control maintained in the classroom.[50] As other historians have observed, vocational education in mission schools reveals the extent to which First Nations were perceived by colonial society as belonging to the lowest class in the socio-economic order, to be trained accordingly as a working class.

In their studies on British Columbian Native economies, Rolf Knight, Dianne Newell, and John Lutz have explored the class dimension of the wage labour system as it pertained to Native men, women, and families, a process contemporary with the emergence of industrial missions like Metlakatla.[51] Work habits and technical skills acquired through mission schools were translatable into marketable commodities in the wage labour economy. First Nations worked for wages in such jobs as hop-picking, farm labour, coal mining, sawmill work, and in the industrial salmon fisheries, to name a few. But more than merely a labouring class, Native peoples were also important consumers in the colony and province, a characteristic administrators and missionaries alike viewed as something to be further nurtured through the mission environment. "Even as they are," remarked Powell in 1876, "the Indians of this Province are its best consumers, and contribute much more to its wealth and vital resources than we have any idea of; but under the expanding and beneficent influence of civilization how much greater their value would be to us as inhabitants, I believe can scarcely be imagined."[52]

While the integration into the Euro-Canadian capitalist economy meant the configuration of a new social order, ... ancient social structures and classes did not simply vanish under the influences of capitalistic individualism. Chiefly powers and the Tsimshian corporate identity remained significant in the new industrial age. For example, the first salmon cannery appeared in the region in 1875, and the industry expanded rapidly over the following decades, always heavily reliant on Aboriginal labour. Once again, Tsimshian class structures had a bearing on the nature of this work. The most successful fishers tended to be high-ranking chiefs, as they could afford the costly equipment and support large crews. Miller points out that chiefs frequently distributed a salmon catch among the members of the community, thus maintaining a chiefly tradition of generosity.[53] Class and social rank also influenced how canneries secured both fishers and plant workers, as Newell explains, and the role played by high-ranking chiefs (typically men) as employment recruiters for this industry cannot be underestimated.[54] The Indian agent confirmed that, decades later, the Tsimshian nation appeared "to earn more money in proportion to their numbers than any other Indians.[55] One of the benefits of mission life was a Euro-Canadian education that facilitated entry into this wage labour market.

MISSION SCHOOLS AND CHIEFLY PREROGATIVE

While missionaries envisioned filling their converts' heads with Euro-Canadian values, industrial skills, and Christian beliefs, Native Christians saw a chance to gain a tool that would be useful in their struggle to retain control over their own political and economic autonomy: literacy in English. The Coast Tsimshian (*Sm'algyax*) verb "to read" is *littsx*, meaning also "to count," suggesting the significance of the fur trade in establishing a baseline for the explanation of the propose of writing. "To learn" was literally to store up food for the winter (*luudisk*). Their word for "book" was similar in definition: *sa'awünsk*, related to the verb *sa'awan*, meant "to put into a box, to put more into a box, or to shake down and make settle in a box" (dependng on the dialect).[56] These words draw heavily upon the container motif that permeates Tsimshian society and language, explaining texts as something with which one fills the bodily container. Once again, this concept reinforces the idea that certain mission ideas were added to existing social systems, not simply replacing them. Duncan's first pupils were the sons of chiefs and high-ranking heirs, and as such, the Tsimshian expected them "to learn about changing conditions and use this knowledge to benefit their constituents.[57] The advantages of attending school may have been that it added to the wealth of the house (filling the *walp*). After decades of sustained contact with European traders in their immediate territory, many Tsimshian, like Natives elsewhere, probably viewed the acquisition of the English language as a practical tool for success in the surrounding wage labour economy. Because mission residential schools also performed what they saw as a "rescue" role for disadvantaged children, there were, among the boarding school student body, low-ranking individuals and perhaps even former slaves who were elevated by virtue of their association with a new religion and training. Yet in the early days of mission schools, Western-style education was also actively sought out as a chiefly attribute.

The general consensus among First Nations people today is that the churches and their education system are largely responsible for the loss of Native languages. ... Literacy programs among Anglo or Canadian working classes aimed at creating good and orderly citizens, whereas among First Nations cultures they became effective tools of assimilation and marginalization. The legacy of Indian residential schools in Canada is a truly shameful one. While residential school at Port Simpson (Crosby's schools for girls and boys), Metlakatla (girls' boarding house), and Kitamaat (orphanage) originated during the missionary period focused on here, the Native role of *student* in missionization has been more thoroughly and effectively explored by scholars who give this topic the breadth it deserves. ...[58]

However, at Metlakatla, religious instruction still dominated school curriculum.[59] Converts sought out and submitted to Euro-Canadian-style education in preparation for baptism and to learn catechisms, gaining fluency in English for a better appreciation of religious texts. After they had obtained a new missionary, day schools were one of the first Tsimshian demands. While many of the schools were run by Euro-Canadian teachers (particularly young women, as was typical in the elementary school system in late nineteenth-century Canada), Native teachers were able to take some initiatives within the system.[60] This was particularly true in the case of religious instruction, where class meetings, Sunday school, and less formalized bible meetings were largely conducted by Native catechists and exhorters.[61] For the Tsimshian, there may have been a natural association between schools and chiefly prerogative because of the "traditional" connection between the upper class and spiritual leadership. At Fort Simpson, Duncan accepted the offer to use Ligeex's house as his first schoolroom, which thereby secured him an auspicious sponsor. ...[62]

Nor were schools or indeed Euro-Canadian teachers accepted uncritically by Tsimshian. For example, Arthur Wellington Clah (a remarkable Tsimshian Christian and self-styled evangelist) recounts how the Greenville Nisga'a refused to accept the teacher sent to them by the Methodist church because he did not have the prestige and authority of an ordained minister.[63] Aboriginal people evaluated the quality of education in direct proportion to the status and influence of the teacher as a recognizably spiritually powerful individual, clearly reflecting Tsimshian association of spiritual power and chiefly class. Missionaries may have constantly fretted over inconsistent school attendance by students, but the Tsimshian were equally critical about the level of commitment of their resident missionaries to teaching. ...

CHRISTIAN HOUSES, COLONIAL SPACES, AND CLASS

One of the most distinctive recurring visual and rhetorical images that permeates the missionary literature is the dichotomy of "before and after conversion." Conversion frequently appeared in the Euro-Canadian literature in literal or figurative portraits of outwardly changed Native individuals. The same principle also applied to the village space and, like assumptions about schooling, reflects something of the class position of those who applied it. Crosby discussed this phenomenon as "Christian street" versus "Heathen Street."[64] "Christian street" was characterized by the church, mission buildings, school, neat rows of Euro-Canadian-style single-family dwellings, perhaps guest house for visitors (as was the case in Metlakatla), streetlights, sidewalks and all other signifiers of "proper" Victorian urban life. In contrast, "Heathen street" was Native longhouses along the beach, spatially ranked to reflect the "traditional" social order, totem poles, smokehouses, and anything else the missionaries identified with Aboriginal material culture. In the minds of non-Native missionaries, like Crosby, "everything of heathenism, is of the devil."[65] As with the material version of the "before and after conversion" portraits of individuals, missionaries took the physical transformation of an entire village as proof of the community's acceptance of Christianity and Western modes of civilization. ...

The establishment of Christian missions in Tsimshian villages meant the further introduction of colonial spaces, a process that had been underway since first contact with Europeans. One has only to look

503

at any photographic record of the Christian towns to see the imposing and dominating character of church structures. Equally as important as a signifier of "Christian" (or as it may have been termed in the ethnocentric terminology of the nineteenth century, "civilization") was the presence of Euro-Canadian style architecture in all buildings and the absence of all "traditional" Native ones. As Crosby declared, "there is no better teaching than the object lesson of a good and well-ordered Christian home." Through direct instruction on Euro-Canadian building techniques, he continued, "this is the only way to win the savage from his lazy habits, sim, and misery … to get them out of the wretched squalor and dirt of their old lodges and sweat houses into better homes."[66]

For First Nations, the distinction between Christian and non-Christian was sometimes made through architecture, but never in ways as clear-cut as the missionaries viewed it. For instance, Clah refused to go to Metlakatla with Duncan, choosing instead to remain in Fort Simpson, a location which never aspired to become an exclusively Christian place, and to prove that not just "heathens" lived in Fort Simpson, Clah helped to organize the building of a bridge from Rose Island to the mainland. From the missionary perspective, the bridge project might have signified a symbolic and physical link between the mission space and the supposedly "heathen village" space. Yet Clah and his fellow villagers likely saw the bridge as a way to maintain communal unity and coherence in keeping with the expansion and modernization of the town.[67]

Missionaries frequently measured their success based on outward signs of Victorian "civilazation." Beyond industrial and commercial development, the appearance of single-family dwellings was certainly an important marker by which all missionaries sought to measure their progress. Indeed, a common refrain in the mission propaganda was the description of how "the old heathen lodges have given place to neat, comfortable homes."[68] For the Euro-Canadian missionaries, a house was a building where a nuclear family lived, ideally headed by the husband or father. In contrast to Tsimshian customs regarding inheritance of the property and wealth of each house passed down through the matrilineal group, a Christian house was private property whose title resided with an individual and to which widowed spouses and children had some claim upon

the principal owner's death. But was the adoption of Euro-Canadian style housing a sign of conversion and acceptance of non-Native values?

As described earlier, the central social unit in Tsimshian culture was the house (*walp/waap*). …Longhouses within each *walp* belonged to the matrilineage, as inalienable possessions controlled by Tsimshian individuals who had inherited the name and position of house chief.[69] The winter village site was spatially organized to reflect the status and wealth of each house and its chiefs. In this respect, the chiefs's physical house was a communal asset of the lineage group, and reflected its wealth, prestige, and authority. A chief's house simply could not be a worker's cottage in the eyes of the Tsimshian.

There is no denying the impact of Euro-Canadian architectural style and materials upon the physical space of Tsimshian villages. New ideas regarding house construction, including both interior and exterior design, were readily encouraged by missionaries who saw housing as a means to separate the nuclear family from its larger lineage group within a single-family dwelling home. Indeed, for Christian villages like Metlakatla and Port Simpson, "traditional" plankhouse construction had virtually disappeared soon after Christianization. However, it would be a mistake to interpret this transformation as solely attributable to Christian influence. Seventeen years after missionization, 72 percent of Metlakatlans still lived in lineage or extended-family households.[70] While the movement towards single-family dwellings occurred more rapidly in neighbouring Port Simpson, … the principal property-holding group remained the matrilineage, not the nuclear family.[71] Put another way, in 1857 Duncan estimated the Native population at Port Simpson to be 2,300 persons divided into 140 houses. In 1935, William Beynon listed 106 occupied houses at that location.[72] This data would suggest that given the massive population reductions (especially following the devastating smallpox epidemics of 1836 and 1862), the actual number of dwellings did not change as much as the missionaries would have liked.[73] Many buildings remained spatially consistent with class-based and ranked social geography, and house members resided in contiguous sites.[74] […]

Yet just as with other cultural forms deemed central to Tsimshian survival, Natives also adapted Christian structures to serve their needs. For example, the patterns of reciprocity, gift-distribution, and communal labour were channelled into Christian activities. When Port Simpson Christians opted to build a new church, labour and financial contributions were donated according to potlatch custom. As Viola Garfield explains, the church itself was much larger than the village required, "but the natives have the same attitude toward it as towards their own chief's house, it must be as ostentatious as possible. Pledges of funds were in the hands of a committee of chiefs and the donations made public in the manner of potlatch contributions."[75] Visitors to Christian villages remarked upon the degree to which church buildings reflected upon the community: "They are very proud of their churches and spend large sums of money upon them, either in building new ones or in decorations, &c."[76]

The force of Canadian laws would eventually have a considerable impact on (physical) property ownership and inheritance rights in a way that highlights the clash between the older matrilineal Tsimshian system and Canadian property statutes that favoured patrilineal and patriarchal rights. While the commoner class was the first to embrace individual-family home styles, conflict came over succession rights to the homes, of whatever architectural design. Furthermore, chiefs increasingly financed the construction of their own homes and thus insisted they had the right to sell, transfer, or will the property to whomever they wanted (although with considerable reluctance to anyone outside the tribe).[77] In addition to introducing a competing legal sysyem with a different concept of inheritance and property title, the missionaries contributed to the decline of co-operative building among members of the same lineage through their prohibitions on the potlatch and emphasis on single nuclear family dwellings and personal ownership.

CHANGE AND CONTINUITY

The prohibition against the potlatch was an attack on Tsimshian class that was not exclusively aimed at the eradication of the ranked system *per se*, but was rather a general attack on Tsimshian culture and values. ... Generally, the potlatch in British Columbia became a key issue around which government, missionaries, settlers, and Native peoples vied for control. Persistent condemnation and lobbying by church administrators and missionaries contributed greatly to the

ban, enacted in 1884 as an amendment to the Indian Act. In addition to legal prohibitions, missionaries employed moral suasion to discourage the potlatch, which they regarded as wasteful, unhealthy, and counter to the Protestant work ethic. They believed it promoted neglect, fostered a communal rather than individualistic identity, and took Native peoples "away" from the influence of the church. Many Native Christians fell in the middle of the debate. Some, like the anti-potlatch petitioners from the North Coast in the early 1880s, associated the potlatch with a past that they felt publicly obliged to denounce as they redefined themselves as Christians. Other "traditionalists" could not see their society, economy, or political structures functioning without it. As a "traditionalist" chief told Thomas Crosby on his first visit to the Nass River in the spring of 1875: "God gave you the Bible, but He gave us the dance and the potlatch [sic], and we don't want you here."[78] Caught between the two poles, the common plea of many Natives, Christian and non-Christian alike, was the desire to first pay off their own debts before the potlatch was discontinued. The dialogue over class had heated up to an outright debate. According to one missionary, by the 1890s, the internal divisions between pro-potlatch and anti-potlatch advocates had produced "one seething mass of disaffection and discontent" throughout the area.[79] Yet as I have demonstrated throughout this paper, the shifting alliances and definitions of identity were fluid, and not surprisingly, Christians frequently engaged in the potlatch, despite revisions to the Indian Act and promises of more stringent enforcement of the regulations against it.

As Frederick Cooper and Ann Stoler so aptly phrased it, "the question of knowledge and rule is always a political one. Such struggles are not just part of the wider battle, but a conflict over the nature of the battlefield itself."[80] If one examines Tsimshianic conceptions of power acquisition in "traditional" culture, the introduction of Christianity from external sources represents no great break from the past or a radical departure from the typical way new religious perspectives had previously been incorporated into Tsimshian class and society. Mythically and historically, the Tsimshian's transformative power was bestowed or activated through external donors. In essence, the Tsimshian had a tradition of obtaining new religious practices, rituals, and ideas from sources outside their territories or culture. This pattern continued for certain European resources, and hence offers one explanation as to why Christianity may have been sought after as a power, even though "traditional" sources were also available.

Protestant missions provided Tsimshian access to the spiritual power of the Euro-Canadian culture as well as economic, political, and social links. Thus, status derived from those who demonstrated initiative and leadership in the Christian church signified more than merely religious authority. The embrace of mission schooling with its promise of industrial training or literacy, or the adoption of new architectural home styles speaks volumes about the ongoing negotiation of Tsimshian and Christian identities. Missionaries like William Duncan saw themselves as much more than religious instructors; their self-appointed duty was to uplift and create self-supporting replicas of Victorian social order among their charges. And it was this very evangelical emphasis on Christian transformation, moral uplift, and self-reliance which ensured that Tsimshian converts, catechists, and evangelists would play a central role in the process of missionization. In so doing, social elites might retain "traditional" roles. On one level, chiefs who converted to the new religion, high-ranking individuals who became evangelists and missionaries themselves, and those Tsimshian who conducted class meetings and Sunday schools received additional social status and power. Thus, it is likely some used their roles as Christians to circumvent "traditional" methods of acquiring this status. Yet others, like the holders of the name-title Ligeex or the Dudowards, claimed conversion as a further validation of their existing class and rank. Christian power was added to further their potential of becoming more than human and to the wealth of their houses. Broadly speaking, however, Aboriginal people from all classes, ranks, and levels of society added Christianity to their identities as Tsimshian. The potential for the transformation of class through religion was apparent to missionary and convert alike; by their actions, it is certain that the Tsimshian had more in mind than merely becoming a Christianized worker class.

NOTES

These notes have been edited and some deleted. For full text and references, please see the original article.

1. This paper draws upon some of my doctoral research: Susan Neylan, "'The Heavens are Changing': Nineteenth Century Protestant Missionization on the North Pacific Coast" (PhD thesis, University of British Columbia, 1999) and my book, *"The Heavens are Changing": Nineteenth Century Protestant Missions and Tsimshian Christianity* (McGill-Queen's University Press, 2001). Thanks to Christopher Roth for his assistance on the intricacies of Tsimshian orthography; any errors in spelling reproduced here remain mine alone.

2. For a more extensive discussion of how missionization influenced concepts of the family among the Tsimshian, please see Susan Neylan, "Contested Family: Navigating Kin and Culture in Protestant Missions to the Tsimshian, 1857–1896," in *Households of Faith: Family, Religion, and Community in Canada, 1730–1969*, ed. Nancy Christie (Montreal and Kingston: McGill-Queen's University Press, 2002).

3. In the Coast Tsimshian language (*Sm'algyax*), the same word *walp* (called *waap* in southern villages) used for family also means house or dwelling. John Asher Dunn, *Sm'algyax: A Reference Dictionary and Grammar for the Coast Tsimshian Language* (Seattle and London: University of Washington Press and Sealaska Heritage Foundation, 1995), s.v. "family", "house" …

4. Margaret Seguin, "Lest There Be No Salmon: Symbols in Traditional Tsimshian Potlatch," in *The Tsimshian: Images of the Past, Views for the Present*, ed. Margaret Seguin (Vancouver: University of British Columbia Press, 1984), 111.

5. Garfield, *Tsimshian Clan and Society*, 177–78; John Cove, *Shattered Images: Dialogues and Meditations on Tsimshian Narratives* (Ottawa: Carleton University Press, 1987), 243–45.

6. Slaves, for example, existed outside the social structure except as property or labour within a particular lineage.

7. Jay Miller, *Tsimshian Culture: A Light Through the Ages* (Lincoln and London: University of Nebraska Press, 1997), 11; and Jay Miller, "Tsimshian Ethno-Ethnohistory: A "Real" Indigenous Chronology," *Ethnohistory* 45/4 (Fall 1998): 661.

8. Jay Miller, "Feasting with the Southern Tsimshian," in *The Tsimshian: Images of the Past; Views for the Present*, ed. Margaret Seguin [Anderson] (Vancouver: University of British Columbia Press, 1993), 29–30.

9. Viola E. Garfield, "The Tsimshian and Their Neighbors," in *The Tsimshian Indians and Their Arts*, by Viola Garfield and Paul S. Wingert (Seattle: University of Washington Press, 1966), 39.

10. I have employed the term "formalized" in reference to Tsimshian spirituality, although this is an artificial designation. Supernatural and human domains were not separate in Tsimshian worldview and therefore spiritual power was accessible to nearly everyone. However, there were certain "formal" (frequently seasonal) accesses to supernatural powers prominent in performances, rituals, and displays that also had important social functions. Spiritual practitioners who specialized in communication with the non-human and superhuman aspects of the universe, particularly in the context of healing, and who were trained and/or developed their skills over the course of a lifetime likewise merit the categorization of their religious practices as "formal" rather than informal.

11. Collectively known as *Wut'aahalaayt*, the four societies were *Mitaa* (Dancers), *Nulim* (Dogeaters), *Ludzista* (Destroyers), and *Xgyedmhalaayt* (Human-eaters), with membership in the last two reserved for only chiefs and nobles. *Xgyedmhalaayt* is frequently translated as Cannibal Dancers, which is incorrect. The biting and eating of human flesh that characterized some *Xgyedmhalaayt* performances was done by non-human spirits who used humans merely as vessels (i.e., the vessels were not the eaters, and never digested human flesh).

12. Garfield, "The Tsimshian and Their Neighbors," 47–48.

13. Robert Boyd, "Demographic History, 1774–1874," in *Handbook of North America Indians: Northwest Coast*, Vol. 7, ed. Wayne Suttles (Washington, DC: Smithsonian Institution, 1990), 135–48.

14. In the summer of 1879 on his first formal tour of the North Coast of the province, Indian Superintendent for British Columbia I. W. Powell was impressed with the scope and variety of industry at Metlakatla. I. W. Powell, Department of the Interior, *Annual Report of the Indian Branch*, 26, August 1879 (Ottawa: MacLean, Roger, and Co., Queen's Printer, 1880), 118.

15. Renowned anthropologist Franz Boas postulated there were at least six Ligeex title-holders in the 150 years prior to 1888. Interestingly, it has become a surname among the descendants of the first Christian Ligeex (spelled Legaic). The last chief to hold it did so in the first half of the twentieth century, but apparently by then it had passed through the female line to the Haisla nation at Kitamaat.

Most scholars and many of the Tsimshian agree that the Gispaxlo'ots Eagle House led by Ligeex was the most powerful group among the Coast Tsimshian during the contact and fur trade period. Miller, *Tsimshian Culture*, 134, 168–69 n. 4; Michael P. Robinson, *Sea Otter Chiefs* (n.p.: Friendly Cove Press, 1978), 8; and I.V.B. Johnson, "Paul Legaic," in *Dictionary of Canadian Biography, Vol. 12: 1891–1900*, ed. Frances G. Halpenny (Toronto: University of Toronto Press, 1990), 552.

16. With the marriage of one of his daughters (Sudaat) to a European trader (John Frederick Kennedy), Ligeex formed a powerful alliance with the Hudson's Bay Company at Fort Simpson (Nass River). Johnson, "Paul Legaic," 551.

17. Henry S. Wellcome, *The Story of Metlakahtla* (New York: Saxon and Co., 1887), 39.

18. Ibid., 39–40.

19. Jay Miller makes the argument that in hindsight, Duncan may have been so successful among the Tsimshian because he was able to assume the role of "high chief," replacing Ligeex in this capacity. Jay Miller, *Tsimshian Culture*, 6.

20. Johnson, "Paul Legaic," 551.

21. Robinson, *Sea Otter Chiefs*, 8.

22. In one narrative about Ligeex raiding the Upper Skeena village of Kispiox, Ligeex presents an umbrella as a new power possessed by the *Nulim* society in order to deceive local residents and draw them out of hiding to permit his attack and subsequent destruction of the village. Ibid., 84.

23. Madeleine MacIvor, "Science and Technology Education in a Civilizing Mission" (MA thesis, University of British Columbia, 1993), 129.

24. Robinson, *Sea Otter Chiefs*, 72.

25. Johnson, "Paul Legaic," 552; and Robinson, *Sea Otter Chiefs*, 72.

26. Johnson, "Paul Legaic," 552.

27. This narrative is a staple of the Methodist missionary literature (both published and unpublished) on their British Columbia missions to First Nations. See, for example, Thomas Crosby, *Up and Down the North Pacific Coast by Canoe and Mission Ship* (Toronto: Methodist Mission Rooms for the Missionary Society of the Methodist Church, The Young People's Forward Movement, 1914); Rev. C. M. Tate, *Our Mission in British Columbia* (Toronto: The Young People's Forward Movement, Methodist Mission Rooms, [1900]); C.M. Tate, "Reminiscences, 1852–1933,"

507

typescript, Tate Family Collection, British Columbia Archives Add. MSS. 303,Box 1, File 2, p.11.

28. Archibald Greenaway's graduate thesis on the Port Simpson mission gives a little more background on Kate Dudoward, based on the oral history of the Dudoward family. Archibald McDonald Greenway, "The Challenge of Port Simpson" (B.Div. thesis, Vancouver School of Theology, 1955), 24–26.

29. Alfred was the son of HBC employee (Fort Simpson) Felix Dudoire. R.M. Galois, "Colonial Encounters: The Worlds of Arthur Wellington Clah, 1855–1881," *BC Studies* 115/116 (Autumn/Winter 1991/98): 141, n. 133.

30. Greenaway, "Challenge of Port Simpson," 26.

31. Ibid., 28.

32. William Beynon, "The Tsimshians of Metlakatla, Alaska," *American Anthropologist* 43 (1941): 86.

33. Marie-Francoise Guédon,, "An Introduction to Tsimshian Worldview and Its Practitioners," in *The Tsimshian: Images of the Past, Views for the Present*, ed. Margaret Seguin (Vancouver: University of British Columbia Press, 1984), 143.

34. Oliver R. Howard, "Fire in the Belly: A brief introduction to a few of the Methodist Men and Women who presented the Gospel of Jesus Christ to the Natives of British Columbia," *Papers of the Canadian Methodist Historical Society* 8 (1990): 237.

35. Methodist Church of Canada, British Columbia Conference, Port Simpson District, Port Simpson Church Register, 1874–96, United Church of Canada Archives, BC Conference, Vancouver, BC; Greenaway, "Challenge of Port Simpson," 60, 75; and Bolt, *Thomas Crosby*, 48.

36. Mrs. Frederick C. Stephenson, *One Hundred Years of Canadian Methodist Missions, 1824–1924*, Vol. 1 (Toronto: Missionary Society of the Methodist Church for the Young People's Forward Movement, 1925), 140–41.

37. Jean Usher, *William Duncan of Metlakatla: A Victorian Missionary in British Columbia*, Publications in History No. 5 (Ottawa: National Museum of Man, 1974), 5.

38. Ibid., Chapter 1, 3–10.

39. William Duncan, "A Plan for Conducting Christianizing and Civilizing Missions on the North Pacific Coast: By Mr. William Duncan, based on his own experience, March 3, 1887," in *The Story of Metlakahtla*, by Henry S. Wellcome (New York: Saxon and Co., 1887), App., 379–80.

40. Stephenson, *Canadian Methodist Missions*, 140–41.

41. Usher, *William Duncan*, 33–38.

42. Thomas, "Colonial Conversions," 374.

43. William Duncan, "First Report from Fort Simpson," February 1858, Church Missionary Society Papers, C.2/0. App. C., #A–105; and [William Duncan] *Metlakatlah: Ten Years Work Among the Tsimsheean Indians* (London, Salisbury Square: Church Missionary House, 1869), 16–17.

44. William Henry Collison, *In the Wake of the War Canoe: A stirring record of forty years successful labour, peril and adventure among the savage Indian tribes of the Pacific coast, and the piratical head-hunting Haida of the Queen Charlotte Islands, British Columbia [1951]*, ed. Charles Lillard (Victoria: Sono Nis Press, 1981), 8, and the illustration of church between pp. 98–99.

45. Alison Prentice, *The School Promoters: Education and Social Class in Mid-Nineteenth Century Upper Canada* (Toronto: McClelland and Steward, 1977), passim.

46. William Duncan to Henry Venn, 6 October 1857, Church Missionary Society Papers, C.2/O. App.C., #A–105.

47. MacIvor, "Science and Technology Education," 107, 146.

48. I. W. Powell, Indian Superintendent for British Columbia, Department of the Interior, Indian Branch, *Annual Report 1877* (Ottawa: Queen's Printer, 1878), 49.

49. Crosby, *Up and Down the North Coast*, 74–75.

50. MacIvor, "Science and Technology Education," 145.

51. Rolf Knight, *Indians at Work: An Informal History of Native Labour in British Columbia, 1858–1930*, 2nd ed. (Vancouver: New Star Books, 1996); Dianne Newell, *Tangled Webs of History: Indians and the Law in Canada's Pacific Coast Fisheries* (Toronto: University of Toronto Press, 1993); John Lutz, "After the Fur Trade: The Aboriginal Labouring Class of British Columbia, 1849–1890, " *Journal of the Canadian Historical Association*, ns 3 (1992): 69–93.

52. I. W. Powell, Indian Superintendent for British Columbia, Department of the Interior, Indian Branch, *Annual Report 1876* (Ottawa: Queen's Printer, 1877), 33.

53. Jay Miller, *Tsimshian Culture*, 133–34.

54. Newell, *Tangled Webs*, 78–79

55. G. Todd, Indian Agent, North-West Coast Agency, Department of Indian Affairs, *Annual Report 1889* (Ottawa: Queen's Printer, 1890), 118.

508

56. Dunn, *Sm'algyax*, s. v. "read," "learn," "book."

57. Jay Miller, *Tsimshian Culture*, 138.

58. J. R. Miller, *Shingwauk's Vision: A History of Native Residential Schools* (Toronto: University of Toronto Press, 1996); Elizabeth Furniss, *Victims of Benevolence: The Dark Legacy of the Williams Lake Residential School*, 2nd ed. (Vancouver: Arsenal Pulp Press, 1995); Celia Haig-Brown, *Resistance and Renewal: Surviving the Indian Residential School* (Vancouver: Tillacum Library, 1988); and Jean Barman, Yvonne Hébert, and Don McCaskill, eds., *Indian Education in Canada, Vol. 1: The Legacy* (Vancouver: Nakoda Institute and University of British Columbia Press, 1986).

59. Usher, *William Duncan*, 92.

60. In 1874 and 1875 Kate and Alfred Dudoward were both listed as teachers whose salaries were partly or wholly paid by the Indian Branch of the Ministry of the Interior. Other Tsimshian were likewise paid by the federal government as school-teachers. For example, daughter of Ligeex, Sarah Legaic [Ligeex] in 1881 and 1882, and Duncan's protégé. David Leask, in 1880 and 1883. Canada, Department of the Interior, Indian Branch and/or Department of Indian Affairs, *Annual Report 1874, 1875, 1878–1883* (Ottawa: Queen's Printer, 1875–1876, 1879–1884), Tabular Data: School Returns.

61. [Eugene Stock], *Metlakahtla and the North Pacific Mission of the Church Missionary Society* (London: Church Missionary House and Seeley, Jackson, and Halliday, 1881), 69.

62. Jay Miller, *Tsimshian Culture*, 138.

63. Clah wrote that the Nisga'a "wanted no teacher. they wants high Priest to take charge them. they do not want Small man, to teach them. But good wise Priest to teache them…." Arthur Wellington Clah, Journals, Saturday 7 November 1891, National Archives of Canada (NAC) MG 40 F11, #A-1713.

64. Grant, *Moon of Wintertime*, 136.

65. Thomas Crosby, *Among the An-ko-me-nums, or Flathead Tribes of Indians of the Pacific Coast* (Toronto: William Briggs, 1907), 104.

66. Crosby, *Up and Down the North Coast*, 74.

67. Wellington Clah (Tamks), "How Tamks Saved William Ducan's Life," Recorded by William Beynon, 1950, in *Tsimshian Narratives 2: Trade and Warfare, collected by Marius Barbeau and William Beynon*, Mercury Series 3, ed. George F. MacDonald and John J. Cove (Ottawa: National Museums of Canada, 1987), no. 58, 212. In a recent article, Peggy Brock also capitalized on the symbolism behind the Rose Island bridge as one representing a new understanding and community cohesion. Peggy Brock, "Building Bridges: Politics and Religion in a First Nations Community," *Canadian Historical Review* 81/1 (March 2000): 67–96.

68. Thomas Crosby, "Letter to Dr. Winthrow, dated Oct. 1st, 1897, Victoria," in *Up and Down the North Coast by Canoe and Mission Ship*, by Thomas Crosby (Toronto: Methodist Mission Rooms for the Missionary Society of the Methodist Church, the Young People's Forward Movement, 1914), 402.

69. The building might be unoccupied or even permanently vacated, but no other lineage could use the structure without the owner's express permission, an important requirement when every house had several locations depending on the season and resource territory. Garfield, *Tsimshian Clan and Society*, 290.

70. Based on 1881 and 1891 census data as interpreted by Carol Ann Copper, "'To Be Free on Our Lands': Coast Tsimshian and Nisga'a Societies in Historical Perspective, 1830–1900" (PhD thesis, University of Waterloo, 1993), 313.

71. Ibid., 314.

72. Garfield, *Tsimshian Clan and Society*, 333.

73. Garfield described how "many of the older frame buildings still in use [in Port Simpson in the 1930s] are very large, two storey affairs containing from eight to twenty rooms and housing family groups resembling the old lineages." Ibid., 280.

74. Cooper, "To Be Free," 314; and Neylan, *The Heavens are Changing*, chapter 10.

75. Garfield, *Tsimshian Clan and Society*, 319.

76. A. W. Vowell, Indian Superintendent for British Columbia, Department of Indian Affairs, *Annual Report 1900* (Ottawa: Queen's Printer, 1901), 297.

77. Susman, Garfield, and Beynon, "Process of Change," 8; and Jay Miller, *Tsimshian Culture*, 49.

78. Crosby, *Up and Down the North Coast*, 197.

79. Rev. J. B. McCullagh to Vowell, Letter dated 1 February 1896, Department of Indian Affairs, Vol. 3628, f. 6244-1; as quoted in Douglas Cole and Ira Chaikin, *An Iron Hand Upon the People: The Law Against the Potlatch on the Northwest Coast* (Vancouver: Douglas and McIntyre, 1990), 46.

80. Fredrick Cooper and Ann L. Stoler, "Introduction: Tensions of Empire: Colonial Control and Visions of Rule," *American Ethnologist* 16/4 (November 1989): 612.

509

CONFEDERATION

What Kind of Country Are We to Have?

P. E. Bryden
University of Victoria

CONFEDERATION: WHAT KIND OF COUNTRY ARE WE TO HAVE?

Introduction by P. E. Bryden

INTRODUCTION

P. E. Bryden

By the 1860s, the British North American colonies of Canada (later to be split into Ontario and Quebec), New Brunswick, Nova Scotia, Prince Edward Island, and Newfoundland were facing a number of threats—both internal and external—that gave leaders in each of the colonies reasons to consider alternative political arrangements.

In Canada, where the *Act of Union*, 1840, had combined the predominantly English Upper Canada with the predominantly French Lower Canada, political progress was increasingly difficult to achieve. Partly, this was because of the convention that recognized the bilingual and bicultural nature of the colony. Leadership of the Canadas was shared between one representative of each half, and legislation, in order to pass, had to secure a majority of support from Canada East and a majority of support from Canada West. The system was known as the double majority, and while it was an effective way of recognizing the demographic reality of the united province, it was a difficult way to govern. The advent of responsible government in 1848, whereby the prime minister and cabinet were obliged to resign if a bill failed to secure majority support in the legislature, ironically made governing even more complicated. With the practice of double majority in place majorities were hard to come by, and by the 1860s the Canadas seemed trapped in a cycle of almost perpetual elections. Clearly, the system had become untenable.

Economic concerns plagued all of the colonies. The free trade agreement that the colonies had entered into with the United States in 1854, known as the Reciprocity Agreement, was not likely to be renewed. Not only had the producers of New England become increasingly vocal in their opposition to allowing Canadian raw materials into the United States duty-free, but also the Civil War had turned sentiment in the northern part of the United States against Britain and her colonies. British North America bore the brunt of that resentment, which had been fuelled by a sense that Britain, officially a neutral observer to the war that was ripping apart America between 1861 and 1865, actually supported the South. The completion of a British ship-building contract that produced the Southern warship the *Chesapeake* was the most convincing evidence supporting Union fears that Britain sided with the Confederacy, but there were other issues as well. Britain's colonies in North America—particularly those in the Maritimes—seemed to develop a strain of anti-Yankee, or anti-Northern, sentiment over the course of the war, and Canada East had proven to be the launching point for a Confederate raid on the Vermont town of St. Alban's in 1864. While the evidence that Britain, and therefore British North America, was actively supporting the Confederacy was scant, it was nevertheless sufficient to raise suspicions and to virtually ensure that the Reciprocity Treaty would be cancelled when its term ran out in 1864. That left the British North American colonies without a clear trading partner, and since all of them relied heavily on external trade, this potentially spelled disaster.

The financial situation in each of the colonies was also such as to make them particularly vulnerable to any fluctuations in international trade. In the Maritime provinces, for example, efforts to complete intercolonial railway projects had left each of the colonies heavily in debt; similar state undertakings in the united provinces of Canada, while not quite so debilitating financially, nevertheless meant that ensuring economic security for the future was imperative.

Defence issues had also begun to concern the tiny British North American colonies. Not only was there a possibility—or, at least, worried colonists believed there was a possibility—that the victorious Union army, the largest standing army the world had yet seen, would turn its attention toward attacking British North America, but there were also fears—and these turned out to be correct—that Irish Americans, or Fenians, would attack British North America to draw British attention to the issue of Irish independence. Moreover, there were also worries about the security of the west. British Columbia, already a colony in the empire, was unlikely to be threatened by American expansion, but the same could not be said for the vast expanse of prairie. American settlers were rapidly filling their own West, and thought that covetous eyes would be cast northward gave British North Americans cause for concern. While Britain was ostensibly responsible for protecting its colonies in North America, the cost of maintaining such an expansive empire was beginning to weigh heavily on them. If there was a way for the colonies to protect themselves, then that would be preferable to the British.

Such was the situation in the British North American colonies in the 1860s. While a confederation of the existing colonies—or at least some of them—was hardly the only solution to the problems each of them faced individually, it was the one solution that seemed most palatable to the most number of colonies. Meeting first in Charlottetown in September 1864, representatives from each of the colonial legislatures began to discuss the possibility of a broader union; they continued the conversation in a more formal way in Quebec City the following month, where the real shape of the potential confederation was debated. The resulting Quebec Resolutions, which are included here, formed the basis for the *British North America Act* that was passed by the British Parliament in 1867, establishing Canada as a new country on 1 July. Examined carefully, the Quebec Resolutions provide some interesting insights into what the men who negotiated the confederation deal thought was important, and what they wanted to protect about their existing system. So too do the excerpts from the debates that occurred in each of the colonies between 1864 and 1867. The comments included here pay particular attention to the institutional shape that the new country would take, and why a federal structure was desirable—or not, as the case may be.

This is a question taken up by the first article included here. Constitutional scholar Peter Russell begins his article "Confederation" by providing a more detailed exploration of the series of events that led to the creation of Canada and discussing the ways in which the colonial legislatures participated in the constitutional process. But having decided that unity would provide a solution to political deadlock, economic uncertainty, and defence concerns, the crafters of the Confederation deal were faced with stickier questions: What shape would this new nation take? How could the structure be massaged in such a way as to serve the needs of the most number of people? How could the shape of Confederation reflect not only British desire to see Canada follow a more independent course, but also concerns in the province of Canada East (later Quebec) that there be clear protection somewhere in the constitution for their language and way of life, and concerns in the Maritimes that the debt incurred over the railway be addressed by the new union? Russell tries to answer some of these questions by examining the contours of the agreement.

P.B. Waite's influential book on the period, *The Life and Times of Confederation,* remains an important study of the events in the colonies in the 1860s. In "Confederation and the Federal Principle," he examines the newspaper articles that reported on the federal nature of the deal that was being hammered out by delegates from the various colonies. In particular, he looks at the response that resulted from the publication of the Quebec Resolutions. Although Confederation was a deal struck among elites, it nevertheless attracted the interest of people across the British North American colonies, who greedily consumed the newspaper reports as they were made available. Christopher Moore also examines the meaning of the deal that was discussed first in Charlottetown, then in Quebec City, and finally with the Colonial Office in London. In his piece "Nation and Crown," he explores the relative power of Britain, the new federal government, and the provincial governments, as well as what the participants understood this new nationality to mean.

While there was much for the people of British North America, as well as for subsequent generations of historians, to discuss about the deal that was worked out, including questions of where sovereignty lay (which all three authors address in their articles), or about what was meant by national identity (as explained by Moore), or about how responsible government or the Senate would work in practice, there has also always been a great deal of debate about the meaning of federalism. It is certainly the aspect of the Confederation agreement that has attracted the most attention from scholars in the twentieth and twenty-first centuries. As a concept borrowed from the United States, the nineteenth-century commentators sometimes expressed hesitation in adapting the structure for Canadian purposes, despite the urging of those supporters that it was a system that would best protect the various interests of all colonies and regions in British North America. The views of both contemporary participants and scholarly commentators are included here, illustrating the differences of opinion that were voiced in the debates surrounding Confederation, the depth of feeling that this supposedly dry political agreement elicited amongst people in the British North American colonies, and the continued vigour of the debate over federalism and the shape of Canadian Confederation.

QUESTIONS

1. In what ways was the process of reaching agreement on a union of British North American colonies in the 1860s different from the way that we would undertake constitutional change now? In what ways was it the same?
2. What were some of the arguments used by Tupper, Tilley and Brown in favour of Confederation? What about the arguments used by people such as John Bourinot of Nova Scotia and Robert Thompson of New Brunswick?
3. Where did the people of British North America see power residing in this new nation of Canada?
4. What evidence can you find in the Quebec Resolutions that the participants at the Quebec Conference were eager to craft a highly centralized form of government? Is there evidence that suggests they were keen to protect the independence of the individual colonies?
5. What evidence would you use to show that Confederation was a compromise? Whose arguments would you use?

FURTHER READINGS

Creighton, Donald, *The Road to Confederation: The Emergence of Canada, 1863–1867,* (Toronto: Macmillan of Canada, 1964).

Martin, Ged, *Britain and the Origins of Canadian Confederation, 1837–67,* (Vancouver: UBC Press, 1995).

Martin, Ged, ed., *The Causes of Canadian Confederation,* (Fredericton: Acadiensis Press, 1990).

Romney, Paul, *Getting It Wrong: How Canadians Forgot Their Past and Imperilled Confederation,* (Toronto: University of Toronto Press, 1999), esp. chapters 6–9.

Saywell, John T, *The Lawmakers: Judicial Power and the Shaping of Canadian Federalism,* (Toronto: University of Toronto Press, 2002), esp, chapter 1.

515

▲ Document 1: The Quebec Conference, 1864

When representatives of the British North American colonies met in Quebec City in October 1864, they devised a series of resolutions that would form the basis for the creation of the new government of Canada. Below are the 72 resolutions which identify, among other things, the British roots of the constitutional framework, a federal structure, and ways of dealing with some, if not all, of the concerns of the regions. Very few changes were made to the 72 resolutions from the time they were hammered out in Quebec to their appearance in the BNA Act, 1867.

Report

Of Resolutions adopted at a Conference of Delegates from the Provinces of Canada, Nova Scotia and New Brunswick, and the Colonies of Newfoundland and Prince Edward Island, held at the City of Quebec, 10th October, 1864, as the Basis of a proposed Confederation of those Provinces and Colonies.

1. The best interests and present and future prosperity of British North America will be promoted by a Federal Union under the Crown of Great Britain, provided such Union can be effected on principles just to the several Provinces.
2. In the Federation of the British North American Provinces the System of Government best adapted under existing circumstances to protect the diversified interests of the several Provinces and secure efficiency, harmony and permanency in the working of the Union,—would be a general Government charged with matters of common interest to the whole Country, and Local Governments for each of the Canadas and for the provinces of Nova Scotia, New Brunswick and Prince Edward Island, charged with the control of local matters in their respective sections.—Provision being made for the admission into the Union on equitable terms of Newfoundland, the North-West Territory, British Columbia and Vancouver. [British Columbia was the mainland colony, and Vancouver a separate colony composed of Vancouver Island and the Gulf Islands; the two united in 1866 to form British Columbia.]
3. In framing a Constitution for the General Government, the Conference, with a view to the perpetuation of our connection with the Mother Country, and to the promotion of the best interests of the people of these Provinces, desire to follow the model of the British Constitution, so far as our circumstances will permit.
4. The Executive Authority or Government shall be vested in the Sovereign of the United Kingdom of Great Britain and Ireland, and be administered according to the well understood principles of the British Constitution by the Sovereign personally or by the Representative of the Sovereign duly authorized.
5. The Sovereign or Representative of the Sovereign shall be Commander-in-Chief of the Land and Naval Militia Forces.
6. There shall be a General Legislature or Parliament for the Federated Provinces, composed of a Legislative Council and a House of Commons. [The Legislative Council became known as the Senate.]
7. For the purpose of forming the Legislative Council, the Federated Provinces shall be considered as consisting of three divisions:—

Source: *Documents on the Confederation of British North America: A Compilation Based on Sir Joseph Pope's Confederation Documents Supplemented by Other Official Material,* edited and with an introduction by G.P. Browne. (Toronto: McClelland and Stewart, 1969).

1st, Upper Canada; 2nd, Lower Canada; 3rd, Nova Scotia, New Brunswick and Prince Edward Island, each division with an equal representation in the Legislative Council.

8. Upper Canada shall be represented in the Legislative Council by 24 Members, Lower Canada by 24 Members, and the three Maritime Provinces by 24 Members, of which Nova Scotia shall have Ten, New Brunswick, Ten, and Prince Edward Island, Four Members.

9. The Colony of Newfoundland shall be entitled to enter the proposed Union, with a representation in the Legislative Council of four members.

10. The North-West Territory, British Columbia and Vancouver shall be admitted into the Union on such terms and conditions as the Parliament of the Federated Provinces shall deem equitable, and as shall receive the assent of Her Majesty; and in the case of the Province of British Columbia or Vancouver, as shall be agreed to by the Legislature of such Province.

11. The Members of the Legislative Council shall be appointed by the Crown under the Great Seal of the General Government and shall hold Office during Life; if any Legislative Councillor shall, for two consecutive sessions of Parliament, fail to give his attendance in the said Council, his seat shall thereby become vacant.

12. The Members of the Legislative Council shall be British Subjects by Birth or Naturalization, of the full age of Thirty Years, shall possess a continuous real property qualification of four thousand dollars over and above all incumbrances, and shall be and continue worth that sum over and above their debts and liabilities, but in the case of Newfoundland and Prince Edward Island, the property may be either real or personal.

13. If any question shall arise as to the qualification of a Legislative Councillor, the same shall be determined by the Council.

14. The first selection of the Members of the Legislative Council shall be made, except as regards Prince Edward Island, from the Legislative Councils of the various Provinces, so far as a sufficient number be found qualified and willing to serve; such Members shall be appointed by the Crown at the recommendation of the General Executive Government, upon the nomination of the respective Local Governments, and in such nomination due regard shall be had to the claims of the Members of the Legislative Council of the Opposition in each Province, so that all political parties may as nearly as possible be fairly represented.

15. The Speaker of the Legislative Council (unless otherwise provided by Parliament) shall be appointed by the Crown from among the members of the Legislative Council, and shall hold office during pleasure, and shall only be entitled to a casting vote on an equality of votes.

16. Each of the twenty-four Legislative Councillors representing Lower Canada in the Legislative Council of the General Legislature, shall be appointed to represent one of the twenty-four Electoral Divisions mentioned in Schedule A of Chapter first of the Consolidated Statutes of Canada, and such Councillor shall reside, or possess his qualification in the Division he is appointed to represent.

17. The basis of Representation in the House of Commons shall be Population, as determined by the Official Census every ten years; and the number of Members at first shall be 194, distributed as follows:

Upper Canada	82
Lower Canada	65
Nova Scotia	19
New Brunswick	15
Newfoundland	8
and Prince Edward Island	5

517

18. Until the Official Census of 1871 has been made up there shall be no change in the number of Representatives from the several sections.

19. Immediately after the completion of the Census of 1871 and immediately after every Decennial Census thereafter, the Representation from each section in the House of Commons shall be re-adjusted on the basis of Population.

20. For the purpose of such re-adjustments, Lower Canada shall always be assigned sixty-five members, and each of the other sections shall at each re-adjustment receive, for the ten years then next succeeding, the number of members to which it will be entitled on the same ratio of representation to population as Lower Canada will enjoy according to the Census last taken by having sixty-five members.

21. No reduction shall be made in the number of Members returned by any section, unless its population shall have decreased relatively to the population of the whole Union, to the extent of five per centum.

22. In computing at each decennial period, the number of Members to which each section is entitled, no fractional parts shall be considered, unless when exceeding one half the number entitling to a Member, in which case a member shall be given for each such fractional part.

23. The Legislature of each Province shall divide such Province into the proper number of constituencies, and define the boundaries of each of them.

24. The Local Legislature of each Province may from time to time alter the Electoral Districts for the purposes of Representation in the House of Commons, and distribute the representatives to which the Province is entitled in any manner such Legislature may think fit.

25. The number of Members may at any time be increased by the General Parliament,—regard being had to the proportionate rights then existing.

26. Until provisions are made by the General Parliament, all the Laws which, at the date of the proclamation constituting the Union, are in force in the Provinces respectively, relating to the qualification and disqualification of any person to be elected or to sit or vote as a member of the Assembly in the said Provinces respectively—and relating to the qualification or disqualification of voters, and to the oaths to be taken by voters, and to Returning Officers and their powers and duties,—and relating to the proceedings at Elections,—and to the period during which such Elections may be continued, and relating to the Trial of Controverted Elections, and the proceedings incident thereto, and relating to the vacating of seats of Members and to the issuing and execution of new Writs in case of any seat being vacated otherwise than by a dissolution,—shall respectively apply to elections of Members to serve in the House of Commons, for places situate in those Provinces respectively.

27. Every House of Commons shall continue for five years from the day of the return of the writs choosing the same, and no longer, subject, nevertheless, to be sooner prorogued or dissolved by the Governor.

28. There shall be a Session of the General Parliament once at least in every year, so that a period of twelve calendar months shall not intervene between the last sitting of the General Parliament in one Session and the first sitting thereof in the next session.

29. [Section 29, with its various subsections, laid out the powers that would be held by the federal government. In later versions of the *British North America Act*, it would be renumbered section 91.] The General Parliament shall have power to make Laws for the peace, welfare and good Government of the Federated Provinces (saving the Sovereignty of England), and especially Laws respecting the following subjects:—

    1. The Public Debt and Property.

    2. The Regulation of Trade and Commerce.

3. The imposition or regulation of Duties of Customs on Imports and Exports, except on Exports of Timber, Logs, Masts, Spars, Deals and Sawn Lumber, and of Coal and other Minerals.

4. The imposition or regulation of Excise Duties.

5. The raising of money by all or any other modes or systems of Taxation.

6. The Borrowing of Money on the Public Credit.

7. Postal Service.

8. Lines of Steam or other Ships, Railways, Canals and other works, connecting any two or more of the Provinces together or extending beyond the limits of any Province.

9. Lines of Steamships between the Federated Provinces and other Countries.

10. Telegraphic Communication and the incorporation of Telegraph Companies.

11. All such works as shall, although lying wholly within any Province, be specially declared by the Acts authorizing them to be for the general advantage.

12. The Census.

13. Militia—Military and Naval Service and Defence.

14. Beacons, Buoys and Lighthouses.

15. Navigation and Shipping.

16. Quarantine.

17. Sea Coast and Inland Fisheries.

18. Ferries between any Province and a Foreign Country, or between any two Provinces.

19. Currency and Coinage.

20. Banking, Incorporation of Banks, and the issue of paper money.

21. Savings Banks.

22. Weights and Measures

23. Bills of Exchange and Promissory Notes.

24. Interest.

25. Legal Tender.

26. Bankruptcy and Insolvency.

27. Patents of Invention and Discovery.

28. Copy Rights.

29. Indians and Lands reserved for the Indians.

30. Naturalization and Aliens.

31. Marriage and Divorce.

32. The Criminal Law, excepting the Constitution of Courts of Criminal Jurisdiction, but including the procedure in Criminal matters.

33. Rendering uniform all or any of the laws relative to property and civil rights in Upper Canada, Nova Scotia, New Brunswick, Newfoundland and Prince Edward Island, and rendering uniform the procedure of all or any of the Courts in these Provinces; but any Statute for this purpose shall have no force or authority in any Province until sanctioned by the Legislature thereof.

34. The Establishment of a General Court of Appeal for the Federated Provinces.

35. Immigration.

36. Agriculture.

37. And Generally respecting all matters of a general character, not specially and exclusively reserved for the Local Governments and Legislatures.

30. The General Government and Parliament shall have all powers necessary or proper for performing and obligations of the Federated Provinces, as part of the British

519

Empire, to Foreign Countries, arising under Treaties between Great Britain and such Countries.

31. The General Parliament may also, from time to time, establish additional Courts, and the General Government may appoint Judges and Officers thereof, when the same shall appear necessary or for the public advantage, in order to the due execution of the laws of Parliament.

32. All Courts, Judges and Officers of the several Provinces shall aid, assist and obey the General Government in the exercise of its rights and powers, and for such purposes shall be held to be Courts, Judges and Officers of the General Government.

33. The General Government shall appoint and pay the Judges of the Superior Courts in each Province, and of the County Courts in Upper Canada, and Parliament shall fix their salaries.

34. Until the Consolidation of the Laws of Upper Canada, New Brunswick, Nova Scotia, Newfoundland and Prince Edward Island, the Judges of these Provinces appointed by the General Government, shall be selected from their respective Bars.

35. The Judges of the Courts of Lower Canada shall be selected from the Bar of Lower Canada.

36. The Judges of the Court of Admiralty now receiving salaries shall be paid by the General Government.

37. The Judges of the Superior Courts shall hold their offices during good behaviour, and shall be removable only on the Address of both Houses of Parliament.

Local Government

38. For each of the Provinces there shall be an Executive Officer, styled the Lieutenant-Governor, who shall be appointed by the Governor-General in Council, under the Great Seal of the Federated Provinces, during pleasure: such pleasure not to be exercised before the expiration of the first five years, except for cause: such cause to be communicated in writing to the Lieutenant-Governor immediately after the exercise of the pleasure as aforesaid, and also by message to both Houses of Parliament, within the first week of the first Session afterwards.

39. The Lieutenant-Governor of each Province shall be paid by the General Government.

40. In undertaking to pay the salaries of the Lieutenant-Governors, the Conference does not desire to prejudice the claim of Prince Edward Island upon the Imperial Government for the amount now paid for the salary of the Lieutenant-Governor thereof.

41. The Local Government and Legislature of each Province shall be constructed in such manner as the existing Legislature of such Province shall provide.

42. The Local Legislatures shall have power to alter or amend their constitution from time to time.

43. The Local Legislatures shall have power to make Laws respecting the following subjects:—

    1. Direct Taxation and the imposition of Duties on the Export of Timber, Logs, Masts, Spars, Deals and Sawn Lumber, and of Coals and other Minerals.
    2. Borrowing Money on the credit of the Province.
    3. The establishment and tenure of local Offices, and the appointment and payment of local Officers.
    4. Agriculture.
    5. Immigration.
    6. Education; saving the rights and privileges which the Protestant or Catholic minority in both Canadas may possess as to their Denominational Schools, at the time when the Union goes into operation.

520

7. The sale and management of Public Lands, excepting Lands belonging to the General Government.
8. Sea coast and Inland Fisheries.
9. The establishment, maintenance and management of Penitentiaries, and of Public and Reformatory Prisons.
10. The establishment, maintenance and management of Hospitals, Asylums, Charities and Eleemosynary Institutions.
11. Municipal Institutions.
12. Shop, Saloon, Tavern, Auctioneer and other licenses.
13. Local Works.
14. The Incorporation of private or local Companies, except such as relate to matters assigned to the General Parliament.
15. Property and civil rights, excepting those portions thereof assigned to the General Parliament.
16. Inflicting punishment by fine, penalties, imprisonment or otherwise for the breach of laws passed in relation to any subject within their jurisdiction.
17. The Administration of Justice, including the Constitution, maintenance and organization of the Courts, both of Civil and Criminal Jurisdiction, and including also the Procedure in Civil Matters.
18. And generally all matters of a private or local nature, not assigned to the General Parliament.
44. The power of respiting, reprieving and pardoning Prisoners convicted of crimes, and of commuting and remitting of sentences in whole or in part, which belongs of right to the Crown, shall be administered by the Lieutenant-Governor of each Province in Council, subject to any instructions he may from time to time receive from the General Government, and subject to any provisions that may be made in this behalf by the General Parliament.

Miscellaneous.

45. In regard to all subjects over which jurisdiction belongs to both the General and Local Legislatures, the laws of the General Parliament shall control and supersede those made by the Local Legislature, and the latter shall be void so far as they are repugnant to or inconsistent with the former.
46. Both the English and French languages may be employed in the General Parliament and in its proceedings, and in the Local Legislature of Lower Canada, and also in the Federal Courts and in the Courts of Lower Canada.
47. No lands or property belonging to the General or Local Governments shall be liable to taxation.
48. All Bills for appropriating any part of the Public Revenue, or for imposing any new Tax or Impost, shall originate in the House of Commons or House of Assembly, as the case may be.
49. The House of Commons or House of Assembly shall not originate or pass any Vote, Resolution, Address or Bill for the appropriation of any part of the Public Revenue, or of any Tax or Impost to any purpose, not first recommended by Message of the Governor-General, or the Lieutenant-Governor, as the case may be, during the Session in which such Vote, Resolution, Address or Bill is passed.
50. Any Bill of the General Parliament may be reserved in the usual manner for Her Majesty's Assent, and any Bill of the Local Legislatures may in like manner be reserved for the consideration of the Governor-General.

521

51. Any Bill passed by the General Parliament shall be subject to disallowance by Her Majesty within two years, as in the case of Bills passed by the Legislatures of the said Provinces hitherto, and in like manner any Bill passed by a Local Legislature shall be subject to disallowance by the Governor-General within one year after the passing thereof.

52. The Seat of Government of the Federated Provinces shall be Ottawa, subject to the Royal Prerogative.

53. Subject to any future action of the respective Local Governments, the Seat of the Local Government in Upper Canada shall be Toronto; of Lower Canada, Quebec; and the Seats of the Local Governments in the other Provinces shall be as at present.

Property and Liabilities.

54. All Stocks, Cash, Bankers' Balances and Securities for money belonging to each Province, at the time of the Union, except as hereinafter mentioned, shall belong to the General Government.

55. The following Public Works and Property of each Province shall belong to the General Government, to wit:—
    1. Canals;
    2. Public Harbours;
    3. Light Houses and Piers;
    4. Steamboats, Dredges and Public Vessels;
    5. River and Lake Improvements;
    6. Railway and Railway Stocks, Mortgages and other Debts due by Railway Companies;
    7. Military Roads;
    8. Custom Houses, Post Offices and other Public Buildings, except such as may be set aside by the General Government for the use of the Local Legislatures and Governments;
    9. Property transferred by the Imperial Government and known as Ordnance Property;
    10. Armouries, Drill Sheds, Military Clothing and Munitions of War; and
    11. Lands set apart for Public Purposes.

56. All lands, mines, minerals and royalties vested in Her Majesty in the Provinces of Upper Canada, Lower Canada, Nova Scotia, New Brunswick and Prince Edward Island, for the use of such Provinces, shall belong to the Local Government of the territory in which the same are so situate; subject to any trusts that may exist in respect to any of such lands or to any interest of other persons in respect of the same.

57. All sums due from purchasers or lessees of such lands, mines or minerals at the time of the Union, shall also belong to the Local Governments.

58. All assets connected with such portions of the public debt of any Province as are assumed by the Local Governments, shall also belong to those Governments respectively.

59. The several Provinces shall retain all other Public Property therein, subject to the right of the General Government to assume any Lands or Public Property required for Fortifications or the Defence of the Country.

60. The General Government shall assume all the Debts and Liabilities of each Province.

61. The Debt of Canada not specially assumed by Upper and Lower Canada respectively, shall not exceed at the time of the Union $62,500,000
    Nova Scotia shall enter the Union with a debt not exceeding $8,000,000
    And New Brunswick, with a debt not exceeding $7,000,000

62. In case Nova Scotia or New Brunswick do not incur liabilities beyond those for which their Governments are now bound and which shall make their debts at the date

of Union less than $8,000,000 and $7,000,000 respectively, they shall be entitled to interest at 5 per cent on the amount not so incurred, in like manner as is hereinafter provided for Newfoundland and Prince Edward Island: the foregoing resolution being in no respect intended to limit the powers given to the respective Governments of those Provinces by Legislative authority, but only to limit the maximum amount of charge to be assumed by the General Government; provided always that the powers so conferred by the respective Legislatures shall be exercised within five years from this date or the same shall then lapse.

63. Newfoundland and Prince Edward Island, not having incurred Debts equal to those of the other Provinces, shall be entitled to receive by half-yearly payments in advance from the General Government the Interest at five per cent. on the difference between the actual amount of their respective Debts at the time of the Union, and the average amount of indebtedness per head of the Population of Canada, Nova Scotia and New Brunswick.

64. In consideration of the transfer to the General Parliament of the powers of Taxation, an annual grant in aid of each Province shall be made, equal to 80 cents per head of the Population as established by the Census of 1861, the population of Newfoundland being estimated at 130,000. Such aid shall be in full settlement of all future demands upon the General Government for local purposes, and shall be paid half-yearly in advance to each Province.

65. The position of New Brunswick being such as to entail large immediate charges upon her local revenues, it is agreed that for the period of ten years from the time when the Union takes effect, an additional allowance of $63,000 per annum shall be made to that Province. But that so long as the liability of that Province remains under $7,000,000, a deduction equal to the interest on such deficiency shall be made from the $63,000.

66. In consideration of the surrender to the General Government by Newfoundland of all its rights in Mines and Minerals, and of all the ungranted and unoccupied Lands of the Crown, it is agreed that the sum of $150,000 shall each year be paid to that Province by semi-annual payments; provided that that Colony shall retain the right of opening, constructing and controlling Roads and Bridges through any of the said Lands, subject to any Laws which the General Parliament may pass in respect of the same.

67. All engagements that may, before the Union, be entered into with the Imperial Government for the Defence of the Country shall be assumed by the General Government.

68. The General Government shall secure, without delay, the completion of the Intercolonial Railway from Rivière-du-Loup through New Brunswick to Truro, in Nova Scotia.

69. The communications with the North-Western Territory, and the improvements required for the development of the Trade of the Great West with the Seaboard, are regarded by this Conference as subjects of the highest importance to the Federated Provinces, and shall be prosecuted at the earliest possible period that the state of the Finances will permit.

70. The Sanction of the Imperial and Local Parliaments shall be sought for the Union of the Provinces, on the principles adopted by the Conference.

71. That Her Majesty the Queen be solicited to determine the rank and name of the Federated Provinces.

72. The proceedings of the Conference shall be authenticated by the signatures of the Delegates, and submitted by each Delegation to its own Government, and the Chairman is authorized to submit a copy to the Governor-General for transmission to the Secretary of State for the Colonies.

▲ Document 2: Federal Union Debates

Once the form of unions was agreed upon by the political elites who met in Charlottetown and Quebec City, it was discussed in greater detail in the legislative assemblies of the various colonies. These debates were as close as the document got to any widespread public consideration.

Nova Scotia House of Assembly, 1865

[Charles Tupper and John Bourinot were both Conservative politicians from Nova Scotia, although only the former participated in the conferences in Charlottetown and Quebec City.]

Charles Tupper: I need not tell the house that a great deal of discussion has taken place in times past as to whether a legislative or federal union would be the best mode by which these provinces could be united, and I believe that I will be able to show this house that whilst a legislative union was really not practically before us—for there were difficulties lying in its path such as to render its adoption impossible—yet the union which was devised by the Quebec Conference possessed all the advantages of both without the disadvantages that attended each separately. No person who is acquainted with the character of legislative union but knows, when it is proposed for a country with the area and extent of territory that British America possesses, its realization is attended with great difficulties, if not with insuperable obstacles. No person who is acquainted with what has taken place in the imperial parliament but knows that great as that country has become under a legislative union, yet the difficulties connected with the union are such as at this moment to be occupying the attention of the foremost statesmen of Great Britain.

The difficulties in the way of a legislative union are that the legislature has not only to be occupied with the discussion of the great and leading questions which touch the vital interests of every section of the country, but to give its attention largely to matters of merely local concern. At present, the [British] parliament is obliged to take up and consider from five to six hundred local bills. When we consider that this body of six hundred men—the most influential and important assemblage of statesmen in the world, are called upon to give their attention upon some five hundred bills, which are not of general but of purely local concern, you can imagine the difficulty of carrying on the legislation of such a country. It is not strange that under such circumstances the parliament is obliged to sit eight out of twelve months in order to accomplish the legislation required at their hands.

If a legislative union were devised for British North America, the people occupying the different sections would not have the guarantee that they have under the scheme devised that matters of a local character would occupy the attention of the local legislatures, whilst those of a general nature would be entrusted to the general legislature. Therefore the scheme that was devised gave centralization and consolidation and unity that it was absolutely indispensable should be given. On the other hand, instead of having copied the defects of the federal constitution—instead of having the inherent weakness that must always attend a system where the local legislatures only impart certain powers to the government of the country—quite a different course was pursued and it was decided to define

Source: Ajzenstat, K., et al. (2003), *Canada's Founding Debates*, pp. 262–65, 269–70, 271–73, 285–90, 295–96, 300–302. © University of Toronto Press Inc., 2003. Reprinted with permission of the publisher.

the questions that should be reserved for local legislatures, and those great subjects that should be entrusted to the general parliament. Therefore, whilst the unity and consolidation connected with legislative union was obtained on the one hand, due care and attention to local matters interesting to each province were provided for by the preservation of local parliaments, and these powers were so arranged as to prevent any conflict or struggle which might lead to any difficulty between the several sections …

It was proposed … that all the questions of leading general importance should be entrusted to the general government … To the local governments were reserved powers of an important character, though of a local interest, which could be exercised without any interference whatever with the unity and strength of the central government … The local governments would not interfere with the powers of the general government, or weaken its strength and unity of action, but would be able to deal with such questions as touch the local interests of the country—the construction of roads and bridges, public works, civil jurisdiction, etc. …

Was our representation in the Commons the only guarantee that our rights would not be trampled upon? It is ample security, but I am ready to show the house the most extravagant demand that could enter into the mind of any man was conceded in the scheme of government for these provinces. I need not tell this house of the potent influence that is exercised in legislation by the Legislative Council. We have seen several striking examples of questions on which three-fourths of this body concurred, and yet this house did not succeed in attaining its object because it did not meet with the concurrence of the upper branch. It requires two to make a bargain and pass a law. I ask you, then, if you wish for a guarantee that the security of the people of the Maritime provinces will never be ignored, could you have a stronger one than that 600,000 people in these Maritime provinces should have obtained, under such a constitution, the same representation in the upper branch as was given to Upper Canada with 1,400,000 and to Lower Canada with 1,100,000? This we have for all time to come, although Upper Canada may increase to millions of people. Then I would ask the intelligent people of this country if the parties who devised the constitution did not give us all the security that our rights and interests could demand.

—*House of Assembly, April 10, 1865*

John Bourinot: [The scheme] provides for a federal union of these provinces. I have no hesitation in saying that if the conference had devised a legislative union, it would have been preferable. Everyone knows what the local legislatures will be under this scheme—very insignificant bodies. Another portion of the scheme provides that the lieutenant governors shall be selected by the governor general at Ottawa. What class of men shall we, then, have for our local governors? These very men who formed the convention. But how would they be looked upon? The position of lieutenant governor would become a mockery in the estimation of the public.…

It has never yet been fully explained why we have been given local legislatures in this scheme. It might be satisfactory to the Lower Canadians, but it would never do for these other provinces. The municipal system that is in full operation in Canada West, or the very system of county sessions that exists here now, might have done the work assigned to the local legislatures. If the Lower Canadians would not agree to legislative union, an arrangement might have been made so as to give them the control of those matters in which they felt especial interest without interfering with the rest of the provinces. I am glad, however, that some gentlemen who formed part of the conference had some respect for that section of Canada which has been so trampled upon by the western Canadians for years past. It is known to many that Upper Canada has long been endeavouring to deprive Lower Canada of many of those institutions and rights which they value—the very principle upon which the union was formed it has been attempted to destroy. Just in that way would the Upper Canadians, in case of a confederation, endeavour to override the interests and rights of these Maritime provinces …

—House of Assembly, April 17, 1865

New Brunswick House of Assembly, 1865 and 1866

Robert Thomson: By adopting this scheme we surrender our independence and become dependent upon Canada, for this federal government will have the veto power upon our legislation. The 51st section of the scheme says: "Any Bill passed by the General Parliament shall be subject to disallowance by Her Majesty within two years, as in the case of bills passed by the Legislatures of the said Provinces hitherto; in like manner any Bill passed by a local Legislature shall be subject to disallowance by the Governor General within one year after the passing thereof." Here is a written constitution with certain rights given and accorded to the local legislatures, and certain rights are given to the general government. Suppose there is a conflict between the two governments, where is the appeal? In the United States they have an appeal to the judges of the land; but here the general government has an arbitrary veto and we have to submit. I think this is a very serious defect in the constitution.

—House of Assembly, June 1, 1865.

Abner McClellan: Another objection taken was, the bills framed by the local legislatures would be liable to be disallowed by the general government. I do not see the point of this objection, as our local bills may now be disallowed by a power farther off, and whereas in the general government we should have representatives to explain and support them, in England we have none at all.

—House of Assembly, June 2, 1865

Albert J. Smith: Delegates … have probably taken the idea [for representation by population] from the plan adopted by the constitution of the United States. There they have representation by population in the House of Representatives. But in the Senate it is provided that every state alike send two senators. And it must be remembered that the Senate of the United States has executive as well as legislative functions; it has power even to veto many of the acts of the president. What he does must have their approval and consent. They have a check on the House of Representatives. But under the provisions of this scheme, the people's house will be the all-important and all-powerful branch, for they will be able even to overturn the executive of the country. It is not so in the United States. While the framers of this scheme have copied this provision from the United States, have they given us the same checks as are provided there? Not at all. There every state, large and small, sends one [sic] representative to the Senate.

Thus Canada is not only to have the great majority in the lower house, but in the Legislative Council she is to be represented by forty-eight members, whilst all the lower provinces will only have twenty-four [. . .] It may be asked why we should have an equal number with them in the second branch? I say because they have full power and control in the lower house … In the United States the senators are elected by the people, and not for life, but one-third of their numbers every two years. But here they acknowledge no sway from the people, and with all this Canada is to have a two-thirds majority in that house …

Now how are differences and controversies on this subject to be settled? Have they a superior court to which the matter can be carried as in the United States, where differences between states and the general government can be carried and settled? No, there is nothing of the kind provided. It is not important that there should be some tribunal where disputes of this nature may be settled; and I ask the attorney general to look into the matter and provide for some means of appeal. But even then there is the other power they possess of vetoing any action of the local legislatures. Should we submit that Canada should have the power to abrogate and nullify all or any of our legislation, with no power to which to appeal? They have also left us the power of managing our own private or local affairs, but the question may be raised what is private and local, and then who is to determine?

S. L. Tilley: The honourable member [Smith] stated that it was probable our local legislature would be left without any powers and dwindle down so low that its action would be a mere farce. Now, whatever may be the opinion of the honourable member with regard to this legislature, or of Mr. Brown in reference to the local government of Upper Canada, I believe that our constitution will remain just as it is. It is a fact that out of the whole number of bills passed by this legislature in 1864, all but seven would have come before us in Confederation, and all but three during the last session. No, the work to be performed will not dwindle down to insignificance.

—House of Assembly, June 27, 1866

[Tilley had a long political career in both New Brunswick and Canadian politics, but as premier of the province he was defeated over Confederation in 1865, and then reelected in 1866 in time to bring New Brunswick into Confederation the following year.]

Tilley: He [Smith] says we have not a sufficient number of representatives in the upper branch of the legislature. There might be some concessions made to us in this. When the arrangement was made, and representation by population was conceded, it was considered that there was a great protection given to the Maritime provinces, for New Brunswick was to have one representative for every 25,000 of her population, Lower Canada one to every 50,000, and Upper Canada one to every 75,000 … In every case the interests of the Maritime provinces are nearly identical, and there is scarcely an important question that can come up in which Lower Canada would not be with us … Again there is a protection in the fact that the number of representatives in the upper branch cannot be increased by the crown.

—House of Assembly, June 28, 1866

United Canada's Legislative Assembly, 1865

[Brown was a Reformer, founding editor of the Toronto *Globe*, and one of the original supporters of the federal solution to the problems of governing Canada East and Canada West.]

George Brown: I cannot help feeling that the struggle of half a lifetime for constitutional reform—the agitations in the country and the fierce contests in this chamber—the strife and the discord and the abuse of many years—are all compensated by the great scheme of reform which is now in your hands. (Cheers.) The attorney general for Upper Canada [Macdonald], as well as the attorney general for Lower Canada [Cartier], in addressing the house last night, were anxious to have it understood that this scheme for uniting British America under one government is something different from "representation by population"—is something different from "joint authority"—but is in fact the very scheme of the government of which they were members in 1858 … For myself, sir, I care not who gets the credit of this scheme—I believe it contains the best features of all the suggestions that have been made in the last ten years for the settlement of our troubles. The whole feeling in my mind now is one of joy and thankfulness that there were found men of position and influence in Canada who, at a moment of serious crisis, had nerve and patriotism enough to cast aside political partisanship, to banish personal considerations, and unite for the accomplishment of a measure so fraught with advantage to their common country. (Cheers.) … But seven short months have passed away since the coalition government was formed, yet already are we submitting a scheme well weighed and matured, for the erection of a future empire, a scheme which has been received at home and abroad with almost universal approval …

The constitutional system of Canada cannot remain as it is now. (Loud cries of hear, hear.) Something must be done. We cannot stand still. We cannot go back to chronic, sectional hostility and discord—to a state of perpetual ministerial crises. The events of the last eight months cannot be obliterated; the solemn admissions of men of all parties cannot be erased. The claims of Upper Canada for justice must be met, and met now. I say, then, that everyone who raises his voice in hostility to this measure is bound to keep before him, when he speaks, all the perilous consequences of its rejection …

The very essence of our compact is that the union shall be federal and not legislative. Our Lower Canada friends have agreed to give us representation by population in the lower house, on the express condition that they shall have equality in the upper house. On no other condition could we have advanced a step; and, for my part, I am quite willing that they should have it. In maintaining the existing sectional boundaries and handing over the control of local matters to local bodies, we recognize, to a certain extent, a diversity of interests; and it was quite natural that the protection for those interests, by equality in the upper chamber, should be demanded by the less numerous provinces. Honourable gentlemen may say that it will erect a barrier in the upper house against the just influence that Upper Canada will exercise, by her numbers, in the lower house over the general legislation of the country. That may be true, to a certain extent, but honourable gentlemen will bear in mind that that barrier, be it more or less, will not affect money bills. (Hear, hear.)

Hitherto we have been paying a vast proportion of the taxes, with little or no control over the expenditure. But, under this plan, by our just influence in the lower chamber, we shall hold the purse strings. If, from this concession of equality in the upper chamber, we are restrained from forcing through measures which our friends of Lower Canada may consider injurious to their interests, we shall, at any rate, have power, which we never had before, to prevent them from forcing through whatever we may deem unjust to us …

For myself, sir, I unhesitatingly say that the complete justice which this measure secures to the people of Upper Canada in the vital matter of parliamentary representation alone renders all the blemishes averred against it utterly contemptible in the balance. (Continued cheers.) But, Mr. Speaker, the second feature of this scheme as a remedial measure is that it removes, to a large extent, the injustice of which Upper Canada has complained in financial matters. We in Upper Canada have complained that though we paid into the public treasury more than three-fourths of the whole revenue, we had less control over the system of taxation and the expenditure of the public monies than the people of Lower Canada. Well, sir, the scheme in your hand remedies that. The absurd line of separation between the provinces is swept away for general matters; we are to have seventeen additional members in the house that holds the purse; and the taxpayers of the country, wherever they reside, will have their just share of influence over revenue and expenditure. (Hear, hear.)

We have also complained that immense sums of public money have been systematic-ally taken from the public chest for local purposes of Lower Canada, in which the people of Upper Canada had no interest whatever, though compelled to contribute three-fourths of the cash. Well, sir, this scheme remedies that. All local matters are to be banished from the general legislature; local governments are to have control over local affairs, and if our friends in Lower Canada choose to be extravagant, they will have to bear the burden of it themselves. (Hear, hear.) …

But, Mr. Speaker, there is another great evil in our existing system that this scheme remedies: it secures to the people of each province full control over the administration of their own internal affairs. We in Upper Canada have complained that the minority of our representatives, the party defeated at the polls of Upper Canada, have been, year after year, kept in office by Lower Canada votes, and that all the local patronage of our section has been dispensed by those who did not possess the confidence of the people. Well, sir, this scheme remedies that. The local patronage will be under local control, and the wishes of the majority in each section will be carried out in all local matters. (Hear, hear.)

We have complained that the land system was not according to the views of our western people; that free lands for actual settlers was the right policy for us—that the price of a piece of land squeezed out of an immigrant was no consideration in comparison with the settlement among us of a hardy and industrious family; and that the colonization road system was far from satisfactory. Well, sir, this scheme remedies that. Each province is to have control over its own crown lands, crown timber, and crown minerals—and will be free to take such steps for developing them as each deems best. (Hear, hear.)

We have complained that local works of various kinds—roads, bridges and landing piers, court houses, gaols, and other structures—have been erected in an inequitable and improvident manner. Well, sir, this scheme remedies that; all local works are to be con-structed by the localities and defrayed from local funds. And so on through the whole extensive details of internal local administration will this reform extend …

But, Mr. Speaker, I am further in favour of this scheme because it will bring to an end the sectional discord between Upper and Lower Canada. It sweeps away the boundary line between the provinces so far as regards matters common to the whole people—it places all on an equal level—and the members of the federal legislature will meet at last as citizens of a common country. The questions that used to excite the most hostile feelings among us have been taken away from the general legislature and placed under the control of the local bodies. No man need hereafter be debarred from success in public life because his views, however popular in his own section, are unpopular in the other—for he will not have to deal with sectional questions; and the temptation to the government of the day to make capital out of local prejudices will be greatly lessened, if not altogether at an end … a most happy day will it be for Canada when this bill goes into effect, and all these subjects of discord are swept from the discussion of our legislature. (Hear.)

We had either to take a federal union or drop the negotiation. Not only were our friends from Lower Canada against it, but so were most of the delegates from the Maritime provinces. There was but one choice open to us—federal union or nothing. But in truth the scheme now before us has all the advantages of a legislative union and a federal one as well. We have thrown over on the localities all the questions which experience has shown lead directly to local jealousy and discord, and we have retained in the hands of the general government all the powers necessary to secure a strong and efficient admin-istration of public affairs. (Hear, hear.) By placing the appointment of the judges in the hands of the general government, and the establishment of a central court of appeal, we have secured uniformity of justice over the whole land. (Hear, hear.) By vesting the

529

appointment of the lieutenant governors in the general government, and giving a veto for all local measures, we have secured that no injustice shall be done without appeal in local legislation. (Hear, hear.) For all dealings with the imperial government and foreign countries, we have clothed the general government with the most ample powers. And, finally, all matters of trade and commerce, banking and currency, and all questions common to the whole people we have vested fully and unrestrictedly in the general government. The measure, in fact, shuns the faults of the federal and legislative systems and adopts the best parts of both, and I am well persuaded it will work efficiently and satisfactorily. (Hear, hear.)

—Legislative Assembly, February 8, 1865

[A Liberal from the Quebec half of the colony of Canada, Dorion was the first to propose a limited federal association between the two parts of the colony. That did not mean, however, that he supported the extension of federalism any further.]

A.-A. Dorion: The Confederation I advocated was a real confederation, giving the largest powers to the local governments, and merely a delegated authority to the general government—in that respect differing in toto from the one now proposed which gives all the powers to the central government and reserves for the local governments the smallest possible amount of freedom of action. There is nothing besides in what I have ever written or said that can be interpreted as favouring a confederation of all the provinces. This I always opposed …

Now, sir, when I look into the provisions of this scheme, I find another most objectionable one. It is that which gives the general government control over all the acts of the local legislatures. What difficulties may not arise under this system? Now, knowing that the general government will be party in its character, may it not for party purposes reject laws passed by the local legislatures and demanded by a majority of the people of that locality? This power conferred upon the general government has been compared to the veto power that exists in England in respect to our legislation; but we know that the statesmen of England are not actuated by the local feelings and prejudices, and do not partake of the local jealousies that prevail in the colonies. The local governments have therefore confidence in them and respect for their decisions; and generally, when a law adopted by a colonial legislature is sent to them, if it does not clash with the policy of the empire at large, it is not disallowed, and more especially of late it has been the policy of the imperial government to do whatever the colonies desire in this respect, when their wishes are constitutionally expressed …

But how different will be the result in this case, when the general government exercises the veto power over the acts of local legislatures. Do you not see that it is quite possible for a majority in a local government to be opposed to the general government, and in such a case the minority would call upon the general government to disallow the laws enacted by the majority? The men who shall compose the general government will be dependent for their support upon their political friends in the local legislatures, and it may so happen that, in order to secure this support, or in order to serve their own purposes or that of their supporters, they will veto laws which the majority of a local legislature find necessary and good. (Hear, hear.) We know how high party feeling runs sometimes upon local matters even of trivial importance, and we may find parties so hotly opposed to each other in the local legislatures that the whole power of the minority may be brought to bear upon their friends who have a majority in the general legislature, for the purpose of preventing the passage of some law objectionable to them, but desired by the majority of their own section. What will be the result of such a state of things but bitterness of feeling, strong political acrimony, and dangerous agitation? (Hear, hear.)

—*Legislative Assembly, February 16, 1865.*

[Mackenzie would become the first Liberal prime minister in 1872, but in the years leading up to Confederation he was a reform politician in Canada West and a supporter of George Brown.]

Alexander Mackenzie: Some honourable gentlemen have asserted, and truly asserted, that this measure is not as perfect as it might have been—and that it is not as complete as some of us might have desired it to be … But, where there are two great parties in a nation—as there have been with us—it is quite clear that, when they agree to effect a settlement of the constitutional difficulties which have separated them, this can only be accomplished by mutual compromise to a greater or less extent. And the true question to be determined in this discussion, and by the vote at the close of this debate, is this— whether this is a fair compromise or not. I am prepared to say it is perhaps as fair as could reasonably be expected, and I have therefore no hesitation in giving it all the support in my power. (Hear, hear.) In its main features it is the very scheme which was proposed by the Toronto convention—only carried to a greater extent than the convention thought advisable or possible at the time. The speeches which were delivered at that convention, as well as the resolutions which were passed, showed clearly that it was the opinion of the delegates there present that a Confederation of the whole provinces would be desirable, if it were possible to attain it as speedily as they expected they could obtain a federation of the two provinces of Canada …

Personally, I have always been in favour of a legislative union where it can be advantageously worked. If it could be adapted to our circumstances in these colonies, I would at this moment be in favour of a legislative union as the best system of government. I believe that is the general opinion of the people in the west. But it is the duty of every public man to shape his course … according to the circumstances which may prevail locally. And it is quite clear that, if the legislative union could not be worked well with Upper and Lower Canada, it would work still worse with the other provinces brought in. There remained, therefore, in my opinion, no other alternative than to adopt the federal principle, or to dissolve entirely the connection which exists between Upper and Lower Canada at the present moment; and that I would look upon as one of the greatest calamities which could befall us. Even if this scheme were more objectionable than it is … I would without hesitation accept Confederation rather than dissolution. (Hear, hear.) …

It is reasonable and just to insert a provision in the scheme that will put it out of the power of any party to act unjustly. If the power that the central authority is to have—of vetoing the doings of the local legislature—is used, it will be ample, I think, to prevent anything of that kind. But the veto itself is objected to … Well, sir, under the British Constitution, in all British colonies, and in Great Britain itself, there is a certain elasticity to be presumed. Everything is not provided for, because a great deal is trusted to the common sense of the people. I think it is quite fair and safe to assert that there is not the slightest danger that the federal parliament will perpetrate any injustice upon the local legislatures, because it would cause such a reaction as to compass the destruction of the power thus exercised. The veto power is necessary in order that the general government may have a control over the proceedings of the local legislatures to a certain extent. The want of this power was the great source of weakness in the United States. So long as each state considered itself sovereign, whose acts and laws could not be called in question, it was quite

531

clear that the central authority was destitute of power to compel obedience to general laws. If each province were able to enact such laws as it pleased, everybody would be at the mercy of the local legislatures, and the general legislature would become of little importance. It is contended that the power of the general legislature should be held in check by a veto power … resident in the local legislatures, respecting the application of general laws to their jurisdiction. All power, they say, comes from the people and ascends through them to their representatives, and through the representatives to the crown. But it would never do to set the local above the general government. The central parliament and government must, of necessity, exercise the supreme power, and the local governments will have the exercise of power corresponding to the duties they have to perform. The system is a new and untried one, and may not work so harmoniously as we now anticipate, but there will always be power in the British parliament and our own to remedy any defects that may be discovered after the system is in operation.

—*Legislative Assembly, February 23, 1865*

▲ Document 3: Maps of Canada, 1849 and 1867

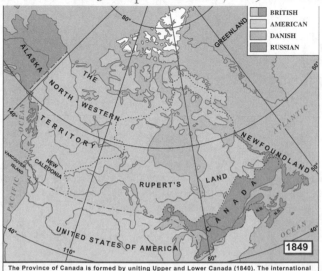

The Province of Canada is formed by uniting Upper and Lower Canada (1840). The international boundary from the Rocky Mountains to the Pacific is described by the Oregon Treaty (1846). The northern portion of the Oregon Territory is called New Caledonia, a name used by Simon Fraser in 1806. The Hudson's Bay Co. is granted Vancouver's Island to develop a colony (1849).

- In mid-19th century North America, British possessions were extended across all of present-day Canada, although only small portions of the territory were actually organized into colonies. These included Vancouver Island on the West Coast, and Canada, New Brunswick, Nova Scotia, Prince Edward Island, and Newfoundland on the East Coast.

533

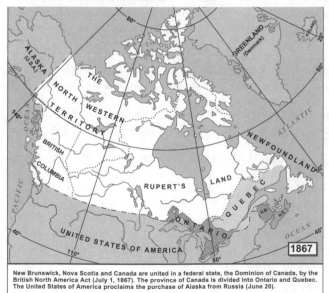

New Brunswick, Nova Scotia and Canada are united in a federal state, the Dominion of Canada, by the British North America Act (July 1, 1867). The province of Canada is divided into Ontario and Quebec. The United States of America proclaims the purchase of Alaska from Russia (June 20).

- Confederation in 1867 redrew some of the boundaries, and established four new provinces—Ontario, Quebec, New Brunswick, and Nova Scotia. Can you see why geography had a great deal to do with the decision to adopt a federal system?

Source: Maps from 1849 and 1867, http://www.collectionscanada.gc.ca/confederation/023001–5000–e.html.

Article 1: Confederation

Peter Russell

By the early 1860s Canadian politics had reached a point of deadlock between two sectional alliances: the alliance of John A. Macdonald's Conservatives and George-Etienne Cartier's *Bleus*, with a clear majority in Canada East, was almost evenly matched by the combination of George Brown's Reformers, a growing force in Canada West, and Antoine Dorion's anticlerical *Rouges* in Canada East. English Canadians who had readily accepted equality for the two sections of Canada at the beginning of the union period, when Canada East was considerably larger than Canada West, began to embrace a different principle of political justice once the population ratios were reversed. When Canada West's population came to surpass Canada East's in the 1850s, Brown's cause of 'rep by pop' (representation by population) became increasingly popular with English Canadians and increasingly threatening to French Canadians, who, though still a majority in the eastern section of the province, were now just a third of the Canadian population. Anyone who contemplates a binational, double majority system as the solution to Canada's present discontents should consider the frustrations and animosities generated by such a scheme during the union period.

Much ink has been spilled on whether Confederation was a compact. The compact theory, as we shall see, developed after Confederation.[1] Provincial premiers would base their claim that the Constitution could not be changed without their consent on the argument that Confederation was a contract or treaty between the founding provinces. Defenders of Quebec's right to a constitutional veto would argue that Confederation was based on a compact between the English and the French, Canada's 'two founding peoples.' Historians have had no difficulty in showing that, in a strict legal sense, Confederation could not have been a contract because, in 1867, neither the original provinces nor their people had

sovereign legal power. That power rested entirely with the imperial Parliament. But this debunking of the compact theory tends to miss the point that Confederation was based on a political agreement—a deal—first between English and French political elites in the Canadas and then between those Canadians and their Maritime counterparts.

The first stage of this deal occurred in June 1864 when George Brown and his Upper Canadian Clear Grits agreed to participate in a coalition government with their bitter opponents, John A. Macdonald, George-Etienne Cartier, and their Liberal-Conservative followers.[2] Since March 1864 Brown had chaired a parliamentary committee examining various approaches to constitutional reform. This committee … had at best lukewarm support from the various parties. Macdonald, Cartier, and Galt, as well as some of the Reform leaders, voted against its establishment. Nonetheless, the committee completed its work and, on 14 June 1864, reported that a federal system (for the two Canadas or for all of British North America) was strongly favoured as the solution to Canada's constitutional impasse. A few hours later the Macdonald-Taché coalition was defeated on a vote of confidence. Instead of forcing a dissolution of Parliament and yet another election, Brown, together with some other key Upper Canadian Reformers—to the total amazement of the political pundits of the day—agreed to join Macdonald and Cartier in a Great Coalition solely for the purpose of achieving a constitutional solution along the lines recommended by Brown's committee.

The Great Coalition represented something much more significant than a temporary agreement to set aside partisan differences. At its core was a recognition that if English Canadians and French Canadians were to continue to share a single state, the English majority could control the general or common government so long as the French were a majority in a province with exclusive jurisdiction over those matters essential to their distinct culture. This constitutional agreement was indeed a compromise. For many English Canadians (certainly for John A. Macdonald), federalism was an American abomination, a clear second choice to a unitary state. Not many English Canadians were committed to the long-term survival of French Canadians as a distinct collectivity. On the other side, many French Canadians, including the *rouge* leaders, saw the proposed federation as

Source: Russell, P. (2004), "Confederation" from *Constitutional Odyssey: Can Canadians Become a Sovereign People?* Third Edition, pp. 17–33. © University of Toronto Press Inc., 2004. Reprinted with permission from the publisher.

a sell-out, the latest in a long line of attempts to bring about the 'annihilation of the French race in Canada.'[3] Nonetheless, acceptance of a federal solution was the only possible basis on which leaders from the two sections of Canada could work together on a constitutional accord.

Brown's committee left open the question whether a federation of the two Canadas or of British North America as a whole should be the priority. Brown himself was so anxious to obtain justice for Upper Canada that he preferred the smaller project, since it would be easier to attain. But Macdonald and the Conservatives in the coalition had their eyes set on the larger vision and insisted that it be immediately pursued. An opportunity to do just that was at hand—a forthcoming conference of Maritime leaders to discuss Maritime union. And so the stage was set for the second part of the Confederation deal when Lord Monck, the Canadian governor general, on 30 June 1864 wrote to the lieutenant-governors or administrators of the Maritime provinces asking permission for a delegation from Canada to attend the conference on Maritime union.

Constitutional politics in the Maritimes had been moving in advance of events in Canada. On 28 March 1864 the Legislative Assembly of Nova Scotia adopted Charles Tupper's motion to appoint up to five delegates to meet with representatives of New Brunswick and Prince Edward Island 'for the purpose of arranging a preliminary plan for the union of the three provinces under one government and legislature.'[4] In April, similar motions were passed by the New Brunswick and Prince Edward Island assemblies. The idea of holding a conference on Maritime union did not arise from a ground swell of public opinion. As Creighton summarized the situation, 'It had been strongly resisted in one province, and accepted without any enthusiasm and with a good deal of sceptical indifference in the other two.'[5] Its most enthusiastic supporters were a few business-oriented politicians, who thought it would improve the prospects of an intercolonial rail link, and some imperial officials, who hoped it might be the first step to a larger union of the North American colonies.

Confederation would probably not have occurred without the pushing and prodding of the British Colonial Office and its field officers, the colonial governors. At this stage in the evolution of the British Empire, imperial policy-makers had come to the sensible conclusion that Britain's interests in the North American hemisphere could be more efficiently secured if its scattered colonies were brought together in a more self-reliant political union. Even though the imperial government possessed a full and uncontested legal sovereignty over the colonies, it was no longer willing to use this power in a coercive manner. The Duke of Newcastle, colonial secretary during these critical years, articulated the constitutional convention of the day: 'The initiative in all important internal changes in the colonies must lie with the colonists themselves.'[6] The colonial governors could encourage and throw the formidable weight of their office behind politicians whose ideas were in line with imperial policy; they could manipulate, but they would not dictate. Still, without the coaching, prodding, and fixing of imperial officials, Confederation would probably not have occurred. In the constitutional politics of our own time, for better or for worse, there is really no legitimate counterpart of this imperial steering force.

Through the summer of 1864 the eight members of the Canadian coalition cabinet hammered out a plan for a federal union of British North America. This was the plan they would present at the conference on Maritime union, scheduled for Charlottetown in September. As it turned out, this plan contained the basic elements of the constitution of the new Canada that would come into existence three years hence.

While the politicians were debating and drafting behind the closed doors of the cabinet room, the numerous and lively newspapers of the day carried on a spirited constitutional debate.[7] Among newspapers generally supportive of federation, the fundamental question concerned the division of powers. Today's Canadians will say, Was it not always so? The politicians then, like those of today, were not above using newspaper opinion to bolster their position in constitutional bargaining. Thus, we find George Brown's *Globe* insisting that in the federal system being planned, 'the local governments shall be delegated governments and ... the "sovereign" power shall be vested in the general or federal government.'[8] On the other hand, *La Minerve* was typical of French-Canadian *bleu* papers supporting Cartier and Taché in claiming that under the new federal arrangements, 'Il [le Bas-Canada] aura son gouvernement particulier dont l'autorité s'étendra à tous les objets qui suivent

535

le cours ordinaire des affaires, intéressant de la vie, la liberté et la prosperité des citoyens ... il sera maître chez lui en tout ce qui regarde son économie sociale, civile et religieuse.'[9]

At this crucial stage in constitution making, the coalition cabinet members were not prepared to disclose how they were balancing these conflicting outlooks on the structure of the new federation. They did not want to risk a public row over the details of their constitutional plan. Elite accommodation, the mechanism of consociational democracy, was the order of the day.

At the public level, an attempt was made to forge stronger social links between Canadians and Maritimers. At the very time that the coalition cabinet was hammering out its proposals in the Quebec cabinet room, a delegation of about a hundred Canadians—politicians, journalists, and interested citizens—was travelling through New Brunswick and Nova Scotia. With D'Arcy McGee as their chief troubadour, the Canadians served as Confederation missionaries, mixing with Maritimers at scores of picnics, dinners, and oratorical concerts. They did not debate the constitutional details of the Confederation scheme but endeavoured to kindle Maritimers' interest in becoming part of a larger political community. In this, they clearly had some success. When the *Queen Victoria* sailed into Charlottetown's harbour on 1 September 1864 with eight members of the Canadian Coalition cabinet on board, Maritime interest in the approaching constitutional conference was beginning to match Canada's.

As an instrument for constitution making, the Charlottetown Conference was somewhere between a first ministers' meeting and a constituent assembly of the kind proposed by populist critics in the post-Meech era. This was not a conference of ordinary citizens. All the delegates were politicians—indeed, most were experienced politicians. Included in their ranks were the first ministers or leaders of the largest party and, with the one exception of the Lower Canadian *Rouges*, 'the principal leaders on both sides of politics.'[10] That indeed was a key to success: co-opting political opponents into the negotiating process reduced the political vulnerability of the constitutional proposals that emerged from the conference.

At this stage in their negotiations, the twenty-three delegates (five each from New Brunswick, Nova Scotia, and Prince Edward Island, plus the eight Canadians) did not expose their deliberations to public scrutiny. For five days they met behind the closed doors of Prince Edward Island's Legislative Council chamber. From the outset the Canadians dominated the conference. Brown, Cartier, Macdonald, and the other coalition ministers laid out their plan for a federal union during the first four days. The plan had three basic elements: first, a division of legislative powers that reversed the American system, with the residual power (those powers not explicitly mentioned) assigned to the general (central) legislature; second, a two-chamber federal parliament, with an elected lower house based on rep by pop and an appointed upper house based on sectional (regional) equality, where Canada's two sections and the Maritimes each counted as a section; and, third, a central government that would take over the debts and some of the assets of the provinces.

By the fifth and final day of the Charlottetown Conference it was clear that the second part of the Confederation deal was nearly consummated. While the Maritimers had not accepted all the details of the Canadians' scheme, they did agree to set aside the Maritime union project and to make a federal union of British North America their constitutional priority. On 10 September 1864, three days after the close of the conference, the delegates assembled again in Halifax, where they decided to hold another conference in October at Quebec. At this next meeting they would focus on the confederation of British North America, and invite a delegation from Newfoundland.

The Quebec Conference was structured along the same lines as the meeting at Charlottetown. Again the delegations included both government and opposition leaders. An exception was Newfoundland, whose two delegates, F.B.T. Carter and Ambrose Shea, were not government members—a fact that did not help the prospects of confederation in Newfoundland. The delegations varied in size: Nova Scotia had five members, New Brunswick and Prince Edward island each had seven, and the Canadians were now represented by all twelve members of the coalition cabinet. Each delegation had a vote, except for Canada, which had two. So, in principle, the Atlantic colonies could outvote the Canadians two to one. The thirty-three politicians squeezed into the reading room of Quebec's Legislative Council, where once again the entire discussion took place behind closed doors.

In that stuffy chamber in Québec City over a two-week period in October 1864, details of the new Canadian federation's Constitution were worked out in the form of seventy-two resolutions. The Quebec Resolutions cover nearly all of what was to be contained in the BNA Act. Little was added or changed in the subsequent negotiations and enactment in London.

Most of the constitutional debate at Quebec— and indeed in Canada ever since—concerned the federal aspects of the Constitution. Here is where the British North Americans had to be creative. They were departing from Britain's unitary system and, with the United States in the throes of civil war, the only federal system they knew, the American, seemed thoroughly flawed. Their earlier decision to give the residual power to the central rather than the local legislatures aimed at reversing what many regarded as the most dangerously decentralizing feature of the American Constitution. At Quebec they now spelled out in detailed lists the 'exclusive' legislative powers of both the provinces and the new Canadian Parliament. This may well have muddied the waters, for even though the list of federal legislative powers was simply to be illustrative of the federal Parliament's power 'to make Laws for the Peace, Order, and good Government of Canada, in relation to all Matters not coming within the Classes of Subjects … assigned exclusively to the Legislatures of the provinces,' the listed powers would come under judicial interpretation to overshadow the general power. Among the explicit federal powers were many of what were then considered the main functions of government: defence, criminal law, trade and commerce, banking, currency, shipping, and interprovincial transportation. But the legislative powers assigned exclusively to the provinces were by no means negligible. They included 'Property and Civil Rights in the Province,' a phrase meant to cover the components of Quebec's civil law (most of the private, commercial, and family law), as well as education, hospitals, and other social welfare activities. The provinces were also given ownership of their lands and natural resources. Two areas, agriculture and immigration, were designated as concurrent fields of legislation, with federal law prevailing in the event of a conflict.

Other features of the structure gave the new federal government a paramount role. Under the fiscal arrangements, the federal government would have access to all modes of taxation while the provinces were confined to 'direct taxation,' licence fees, and royalties. The provinces could not levy customs and excise duties, which at the time constituted 83 per cent of the colonies' revenues.[11] The constitution-makers never conceived of direct taxes on personal and corporate income becoming the milch cow of public finance. The fiscal dependency of the provinces was underlined by building in a complex set of federal subsidies 'in full settlement of all future demands on Canada'—words that should make the Fathers of Confederation blush a little in their graves.

The judicial system was also federally dominated. The key courts for the new federation would be the existing superior, district, and county courts of the provinces, but the judges of these courts would be appointed, paid, and subject to removal by the federal government and Parliament. As for a supreme court, the colonial politicians were happy to carry on with the highest court in the empire, the Judicial Committee of the Privy Council, as Canada's final court of appeal, but if and when a general court of appeal was established for Canada, it would be created by the federal Parliament.

Considerably more contentious was the importation of an element of imperial structure into the federal plan. Just as the British government appointed the Canadian governor general, the federal government would appoint the provincial lieutenant governors. The lieutenant-governor (in parallel with the governor general's power over federal legislation) could reserve legislation passed by provincial legislatures for consideration by the federal government. Further, just as the British government retained the power to disallow (veto) legislation passed by the federal Parliament, the federal government could disallow provincial legislation. The federal powers of reservation and disallowance were surely the sharpest deviation from the federal principle of government. Their inclusion in the Constitution is a clear indication that many of the constitutional architects, and none more than John A. Macdonald, preferred unitary to federal government.

The point of federal structure that proved most troublesome and took the most time to resolve was the federal Senate. Prince Edward Island and the United Province of Canada had recently shifted from the British tradition of an appointed upper house to an elected second chamber. Some delegates now

537

pressed for a Senate that was directly elected or, as the American Senate then was, elected by the provincial legislatures. The balance of power within all the delegations lay with those who favoured the British parliamentary structure, and the Senate provided for in the Quebec Resolutions was a body appointed for life by the federal government, with full legislative powers except for the introduction of money bills. Even more contentious was the distribution of Senate seats among the provinces. With Newfoundland at the table, the Atlantic delegates now argued that their four provinces should have thirty-two senators—six more than Ontario's and Quebec's twenty-four. In the end, the principle of sectional equality was maintained by a resolution giving twenty-four each to Ontario, Quebec, and the three Maritime provinces (ten each for New Brunswick and Nova Scotia, and four for Prince Edward Island), with a vague promise of 'additional representatives' for Newfoundland.[12] The need for Senate reform was built into the very foundations of Confederation.

While the Constitution drafted at Quebec covered the new federal system in detail, it was relatively silent on other matters that have become of great importance to Canadian constitutionalists. The Fathers of Confederation expressed absolutely no interest in a bill of abstract natural rights. They were prepared, however, to afford constitutional protection to rights or interests that experience had shown were necessary for the peaceable coexistence of two distinct cultural communities. First, the English were assured of the right to use their language in the legislative and judicial institutions of Quebec, where they would be a minority, and the French were given a reciprocal right to use their language in the federal legislature and courts.[13] Second, the denominational schools of the Protestant minority in Quebec and the Catholic minority in Ontario would continue to function on the basis already provided for in law.[14] These two provisions for minority rights were not the only manifestations of cultural dualism in the new Constitution. Another dimension of dualism was the differential treatment of Quebec. Quebec, with its distinctive civil law, was exempt from a clause that envisaged the common law provinces eventually permitting the federal Parliament to take over their jurisdiction over property and civil rights.[15] Special provisions also governed the qualifications of Quebec judges and the appointment of Quebec

senators.[16] Quebec, however, was not the only province to have differential treatment. New Brunswick received a special subsidy over and beyond those provided for the other provinces.[17] The Fathers of Confederation were not strict believers in the principle of provincial equality.

The constitution drafters saw no need to spell out the vital democratic principle that government be directed by ministers who have the confidence of the elected branch of the legislature. Formally, all executive power in both levels of government would 'be vested in the Queen'—a system that has persisted to the present day.[18] The principle of responsible government would continue to depend on unwritten constitutional convention. The only hint of responsible government in the final constitutional text is the reference in the preamble to the BNA Act to a 'Constitution similar in Principle to that of the United Kingdom.'[19]

Aside from some minor changes which each level of government could make on its own, the new Constitution was totally silent on the question of amendment. This void was to be expected. … [T]he Fathers of Confederation assumed throughout that Canada's Constitution would take the form of an imperial statute and, as such, would be formally amended by the British Parliament. Philosophically, this arrangement did not trouble them, nor did they see it as posing any practical problems. Canada's founding fathers suffered even more than the usual hubris that afflicts constitution-makers. As John A. Macdonald was later to explain to Canada's Legislative Assembly, the constitutional drafting was so thorough and detailed that 'we have avoided all conflict of jurisdiction and authority.'[20] Again, posthumous blushes are in order.

With the signing of the Quebec Resolutions on 27 October 1864, substantive constitution making was nearly complete. There were still, however, important political and legal steps to be taken before the Constitution could be put into effect. The seventieth resolution stated that 'the sanction of the imperial and local parliaments shall be sought for the Union of the Provinces on the principles adopted by the Conference.'[21] Enactment of the Constitution by the imperial Parliament was the essential, final legal step. Approval by the colonial legislatures was a political, not a legal imperative. Still, for politicians living under the constraints of responsible government, it was important to secure legislative support for their constitutional plan.

538

For some commentators of the day, approval by the legislature was not a strong enough measure of popular support. While there were no calls for a referendum or a directly elected constituent assembly, a number of newspapers in Canada West and New Brunswick insisted that sweeping constitutional changes should not be made until they had been tested in a general election.[22] The leading politicians in Canada, including Reform leader George Brown, brushed these demands aside: 'A general election on such an issue, they argued, would be nothing more or less than a plebiscite; and a plebiscite was a dreadful republican heresy, French or American in origin, which would violate all the principles of parliamentary government, without the slightest beneficial result.'[23]

The seventy-two resolutions were debated in both houses of the Canadian legislature. The debate extended over a period of six weeks, from early February to mid March 1865. It was, by any standard, a brilliant debate—by far the best record of the hopes, dreams, and fears of those who supported and those who opposed Confederation. In the end, the supporters of Confederation carried the day, but only after withstanding searing criticism of flaws and inconsistencies in the constitutional plan, especially from the *Rouges* who, as French Canadians, viewed support of the scheme as amounting to treason. The Quebec Resolutions (like the Meech Lake Accord many years later) was a carefully negotiated package deal, so no amendments were allowed. The overall majority in favour of the resolutions was 91 to 33,[24] but support was much stronger among members from Canada West, who favoured Confederation 56 to 6, as compared with members from Canada East, who voted 37 to 25 in favour. Among French-Canadian members the vote was even closer, with 27 for and 21 opposed—a clear majority, but hardly a ringing endorsement from the French component of the political elite.

New Brunswick was the only colony in which Confederation was submitted to the people in an election. Indeed, New Brunswickers went to the polls twice to decide contests between confederates and anti-confederates. In each case it was New Brunswick's mercurial lieutenant-governor, Arthur Gordon, not the politicians, who forced the appeal to the people. Gordon did not like the confederation plan because it did not go far enough in giving absolute paramountcy to the federal government. He threatened to dismiss the pro-Confederation administration headed by Samuel Tilley and appoint other ministers, unless Tilley agreed to hold an election before submitting the Quebec Resolutions to the legislature. Tilley agreed to a dissolution. In the ensuing election, which was conducted at the very time the Canadian legislature was debating Confederation, Tilley and his confederate colleagues were defeated, winning only eleven of forty-one seats. Just over a year later, Gordon, now under strict instructions from the Colonial Office to have Confederation submitted to the legislature, forced the resignation of anti-confederate ministers and dissolved the legislature. This time, the case for a stronger British North American union was bolstered by the massing of Fenians along New Brunswick's border, and the confederates triumphed, taking all but eight of the forty-one seats. Even so, the Quebec Resolutions, although approved by New Brunswick's appointed Legislative Council, were never submitted to its elected assembly.

While Confederation was limping to victory in New Brunswick, it was being pushed off the political agenda in the two island colonies, Prince Edward Island and Newfoundland. On the last day of March 1865 Prince Edward Island's Legislative Assembly, by a vote of 23 to 5, passed a motion rejecting the Quebec Resolutions. The motion had been moved by the premier, J.C. Pope, who had not attended the Quebec Conference.[25] Earlier in that same month, Newfoundland's Legislative Assembly adopted Premier Hugh Hoyles's motion to postpone a decision on Confederation until after the next general election. Although many of the pro-confederation politicians were returned in the election held later in the year, they were considerably outnumbered by those who were opposed or doubtful.[26] Despite considerable pressure from the Colonial Office and the St John's newspapers, Newfoundland's coalition government was not prepared to proceed with Confederation.

In Newfoundland and Prince Edward Island, the politics of Confederation were worked out in a relatively democratic fashion—albeit with a negative outcome. This was not so in Nova Scotia, where opposition to Confederation was, if anything, more intense and articulate than in either of the island colonies. Opposition in Nova Scotia was not to the general idea of a British North American union. Indeed, for that idea, with particular emphasis on the *British* nature of such a union, there was considerable support. Criticism focused on the Quebec Resolutions and especially on the alleged weaknesses of any system of federal government.[27] The anticonfederates found an eminent spokesman in Joseph Howe, a former premier and major force in Nova Scotian politics for over thirty years, who at the time of Confederation was serving as an imperial fisheries officer. Criticism of the Quebec Resolutions dominated a lengthy legislative debate in the Nova Scotia legislature in the early spring of 1865. But the premier, Charles Tupper, was able to avoid a direct test of the Confederation scheme by seeking approval only for Maritime union. A year later, when the Confederation issue was forced by the opposition, with imperial connivance, he managed to corral enough support to win approval not for the Quebec Resolutions but for sending delegates 'to arrange with the imperial government a scheme of union which will effectually ensure just provision for the rights and interests of this Province.'[28]

The Quebec Resolutions were never approved by the Nova Scotia legislature. Indeed, the first time Nova Scotians had an opportunity to give a popular verdict on Confederation they left no doubt about where they stood. In September 1867 in the first Canadian general election, the anti-confederates took eighteen out of nineteen Nova Scotia seats and, in the provincial election, thirty-six out of thirty-eight seats in the Nova Scotia assembly. By then, however, Confederation was a fait accompli.

The implication of Tupper's motion that a new basis for British North American union could be negotiated from scratch had no basis for reality. Macdonald, Cartier, and the other members of the Canadian coalition had no intention of touching their delicate constitutional compromise. If there was any suggestion that the Quebec Resolutions were open to significant amendment, French Canada, in Creighton's words, 'would undoubtedly rise in violent protest.'[29] At the same time, the Canadian politicians did not dare admit publicly that the Quebec scheme was a sealed compact for fear of undermining the cause of Confederation in the Maritimes, which in both Nova Scotia and New Brunswick depended on the credibility of negotiating a different basis for union. The lack of consensus within the Confederation movement was therefore papered over by the political elites.

In December 1866 sixteen of these leaders (six from the Canadas, five each from New Brunswick

and Nova Scotia) met for the third Confederation conference in a London hotel room close by the Westminster Parliament. The object of this meeting was not to renegotiate the Quebec Resolutions but to consider some minor modifications and tidying up of loose ends. The only change in the division of powers was to give the federal Parliament, rather than the provinces, jurisdiction over 'Sea Coast and Inland Fisheries.' The Maritime provinces gained a modest increase in their per capita subsidies. Religious minorities in all the provinces were given the right to appeal to the federal government against provincial laws affecting their denominational school rights. A final push by Ontario reformers for an elected Senate was of no avail. The only change made in the structure of the federal upper house was to provide for the appointment of extra senators to break a deadlock between the two houses—a constitutional provision that most Canadians did not realize existed until it was used for the first time in 1990.[30]

With the conclusion of the London conference, the constitution was entirely in imperial hands. Only one further significant change was made—the formal name of the new country. The Fathers of Confederation had favoured the title Kingdom of Canada, but left the final choice to Queen Victoria. It was the Americans who effectively vetoed the monarchical title of kingdom. In their ignorance of the principles of constitutional monarchy they objected to the founding of anything so blatantly non-republican on their border. The Queen then chose the British Americans' second choice: Dominion of Canada. Although this title held out the expansive promise of the Seventy-second Psalm's 'He shall have dominion also from sea to sea,' it struck the British prime minister, Lord Derby, as 'rather absurd.'[31]

In February 1867 the Canadian Constitution, in the form of the British North America Act, was introduced in the House of Lords by the colonial secretary, Lord Carnarvon. The attention of British politicians at the time was fastened on a major development in Britain's constitutional politics, the Second Reform Bill. There was a desultory debate as a handful of Canadian politicians watched the BNA Act go through the two Houses of Parliament. The most vigorous attack came from the few parliamentarians moved by Joseph Howe's petition (supposedly bearing thirty thousand signatures) to postpone further action on the Canadian Constitution until it had been submitted to the people of Nova Scotia in the approaching general election. On 8 March 1867 the BNA Act passed third reading in the House of Commons. It received royal assent on 29 March and was proclaimed in effect on 1 July 1867.

The Dominion of Canada was born, but the constitutional process that brought it into existence provided a thin and uncertain foundation for the birth of a people. True, elected politicians played the leading role in putting the Constitution together, but they were elected on a restricted franchise that excluded unpropertied males and all women.[32] Further, the dominant members, both English and French, showed not the slightest intention of submitting their constitutional handiwork to the people. At the elite level, the process of Confederation produced a wide-based and practical, though not philosophical accord; at the popular level, however, it did not produce a political community with a clear sense of itself. In the language of political science, Canada in 1867 'must be viewed essentially as a political unit that had become amalgamated without necessarily achieving integration.'[33]

For the aboriginal peoples affected by Confederation, the new Constitution was entirely an imperial imposition. There was no thought among the constitution-makers of consulting with the native peoples living on the territory encompassed by the BNA Act, nor did any of the legislative bodies that dealt with the Constitution represent these peoples. The Royal Proclamation of 1763, British North America's first constitution, enacted that the native peoples 'should not be molested or disturbed' on their hunting grounds in the territory reserved to them until the Crown purchased 'their' lands by a treaty of cession. This fundamental aboriginal right was recognized in the subsequent treaties between the British Crown and the aboriginal nations. Although the Royal Proclamation continued as part of Canadian law, the rights it recognized were not explicitly included in the BNA Act.[34] In the 1867 constitution, 'Indians, and Lands reserved for the Indians' were mentioned only as a subject of federal jurisdiction.[35] Aboriginal peoples were treated as subjects, not citizens, of the new dominion.

Not even among the small cadre of politicians who pushed through the Confederation plan was there a clear and common conception of the new nation they were building. As Eugene Forsey was tireless in pointing out, they all recognized they were establishing a new nation-state.[36] Their Constitution provided for the completion of a continental state stretching from Newfoundland to British Columbia,[37] and the lure of performing in this larger political arena was part of their shared vision. But while the Fathers of Confederation thought of themselves as nation-builders, they did not share a common vision of the essential nature of the nation they were building. A few like Cartier espoused the idea, daring in that day, of forming a new 'political nationality' based on deep 'racial' diversity—a society in which "British and French Canadians alike could appreciate and understand their position relative to each other … placed like great families beside each other.'[38] As we have seen, there were marks of this dualistic view of Canada in the new Constitution. But there were just as many Fathers of Confederation, especially in English Canada, who did not share Cartier's ideal of a culturally pluralist nation and who still harboured Lord Durham's dream of building a British North American nation. These Fathers of Confederation could empathize with George Brown, who, writing to his wife at the end of the Quebec Conference, exclaimed: 'Is it not wonderful? French Canadianism entirely extinguished!'[39]

In 1867 there was no need to agree on the fundamental nature of the new Canadian nation because the final custodian of its Constitution was not the Canadian political community but the imperial Parliament. Imperial stewardship of Canada's constitutional politics made it relatively easy to inaugurate Confederation. A new country could be founded without having to risk finding out if its politically active citizens agreed to the principles on which its Constitution was to be based. But if this was a gift, it was a tainted gift. The Confederation compromise was sheltered from the strain of a full public review in all sections of the country, but at the cost of not forming a political community with a clear sense of its constituent and controlling elements. Thus, at Canada's founding, its people were not sovereign, and there was not even a sense that a constituent sovereign people would have to be invented.

NOTES

1. For a discussion of the compact theory and its current relevance see Robert C. Vipond, 'Whatever

Became of the Compact Theory? Meech Lake and the New Politics of Constitutional Amendment in Canada,' Queen's Quarterly, 96 (1989): 793.

2. For a detailed account of the events leading to Confederation see Creighton, *Road to Confederation* (Toronto: Macmillan of Canada, 1964).

3. The words are from the newspaper, *Le Pays*, and are quoted in A.I. Silver (Toronto: University of Toronto Press 1982), 38.

4. Creighton, *Road to Confederation*, 32.

5. Ibid., 35.

6. Ibid., 20.

7. For an account of newspaper coverage of Confederation see P.B. Waite, *The Life and Times of Confederation, 1864–1867: Politics, Newspapers, and the Union of British North America*, 2nd ed. (Toronto: University of Toronto Press 1962).

8. Creighton, *Road to Confederation*, 98.

9. Waite, *Life and Times of Confederation*, 139.

10. Creighton, *Road to Confederation*, 188.

11. R. MacGregor Dawson, *The Government of Canada*, 4th ed., revised by Norman Ward (Toronto: University of Toronto Press 1966), 105.

12. Creighton, *Road to Confederation*, 152.

13. Section 133 of the BNA Act.

14. Section 93 of the BNA Act.

15. Section 94 of the BNA Act.

16. Sections 98 and 22 of the BNA Act.

17. Section 119 of the BNA Act. That section is now spent.

18. Section 9 of the Constitution Act, 1867 (the new title of the BNA Act) states that 'the Executive Government and Authority of and over Canada is hereby declared to continue and be vested in the Queen.'

19. Besides responsible government, the other principle incorporated in this phrase is the independence of the judiciary.

20. P.B. Waite, ed., *The Confederation Debates in the Province of Canada, 1865* (Toronto: McClelland and Stewart 1963), 44.

21. Creighton, *Road to Confederation*, 187.

22. Waite, *Life and Times of Confederation*, 122.

23. Creighton, *Road to Confederation*, 189–90.

24. For an analysis see Waite, ed., *Confederation Debates*, xviii.

25. His older brother, W.H. Pope, had attended the Quebec Conference, but in the legislature went no further than proposing that the Island put off its decision until the terms of union had been submitted to the people in a general election.

26. Waite, Life and Times of Confederation, 173.

27. For an analysis see 'The Opposition to Confederation in Nova Scotia, 1864–1868,' in Ged Martin, *The Causes of Confederation* (Fredericton: Acadiensis Press 1990), 114–29.

28. Creighton, *Road to Confederation*, 366.

29. Ibid., 381.

30. The original section 26 provided that the Queen, on the advice of the governor general, could appoint three or six senators (representing equally the three Senate divisions, Ontario, Quebec, and the Maritimes). This was amended in 1915 to provide for four or eight extra senators to accommodate a fourth Senate division consisting of the four western provinces. The Mulroney government used the provision, for the first time ever, in 1990 to ensure passage of its Goods and Services Tax Bill.

31. Creighton, *Road to Confederation*, 424.

32. The first federal election following Confederation was based on the provincial election laws. It is estimated that, on average, about 15 per cent of the population of the four original provinces was eligible to vote. See Reginald Whitaker, 'Democracy and the Canadian Constitution,' in Keith Banting and Richard Simeon, eds., *And No One Cheered: Federalism, Democracy and the Constitution Act* (Toronto: Methuen 1983), 245.

33. Ralph C. Nelson, Walter C. Soderlund, Ronald H. Wagenberg, and E. Donald Briggs, 'Canadian Confederation as a Case Study in Community Formation,' in Ged Martin, ed., *Causes of Confederation*, 85.

34. For an account of the Proclamation and its continuing relevancy in Canada's constitutional system see Bruce Clark, *Native Liberty, Crown Sovereignty: The Existing Aboriginal Right to Self-Government in Canada* (Montreal and Kingston: McGill-Queen's University Press 1990).

35. Section 91(24) of the BNA Act.

36. See, especially, Eugene Forsey, *A Life on the Fringe: The Memoirs of Eugene Forsey* (Toronto: Oxford University Press 1990), chap. 11.

37. Section 146 of the BNA Act.

38. These words are from his contribution to the Confederation Debates. Waite, ed., *Confederation Debates*, 50–1.

39. J.M.S. Careless, *Brown of the Globe* (Toronto: Macmillan 1963), vol. 2, 171.

■ Article 2: Confederation and the Federal Principle

P. B. Waite

Confederation was to be a reality in 1865. Before all else was the determination of the leaders of the movement—Brown, Cartier, Macdonald, Tupper, Tilley, Gray—to strike while the iron was hot. Every delegation to the [Quebec] Conference had represented the two major parties in each colony, and while no one was very sure of Prince Edward Island, Carter and Shea from Newfoundland seemed optimistic and Tupper of Nova Scotia and Tilley of New Brunswick had some cause to be. In Nova Scotia and New Brunswick there seemed no reason why the combined power of the two parties should not be effective. The expiry of the life of the New Brunswick legislature in June, 1865, and that of the Newfoundland legislature in October, 1865, was inconvenient; elections would come too soon to be sure of public opinion. But Tilley and Shea were sanguine of success, and Tupper was, if anything, more so. All was to be in readiness by the spring. Then, Tilley assumed, Confederation would be "a fixed fact."[1] The timetable was breathtaking: Brown was to go at once to England; Galt (and perhaps Brydges) were to go to the Maritimes to discuss the Intercolonial in relation to the existing railway assets of Nova Scotia and New Brunswick.[2] [Alexander Galt was another "father of confederation," a Conservative from Canada East, and C. J. Brydges was the manager of the Grand Trunk railway.] Moreover, the imperial government's enthusiastic approval of the scheme, soon to be forthcoming, was warrant that the full power of the Colonial Office would be placed at the disposal of Confederation. The imperial government would, if requested, legislate the provinces into union in the summer of 1865.[3] "The time is short," wrote Cardwell to MacDonnell, on December 8, 1864. [Edward Cardwell, 1st Viscount Cardwell, was a British politician who, between 1864 and 1866, was Secretary of State for the Colonies in the Colonial

Office in London. He was replaced in 1866 by the 4th Earl of Carnarvon; Sir Richard Graves MacDonell was the lieutenant-governor of Nova Scotia.] His despatch was the reflection of lengthy and recent conversations with George Brown. "The time is short, since those who have undertaken this great measure desire to bring it forward during the ensuing session for the decision of the Imperial Parliament:—and it is impossible to say what evil consequences might not follow the unnecessary interposition of a year's delay...."[4] There was to be no delay. It "only wants the Lower Provinces to say aye, and it is done."[5] "Rarely, if ever," wrote MacDonnell, "has there occurred in history so remarkable and fortunate a concurrence of circumstances to enable distinct Provinces to frame equitable conditions of a Union."[6] There were to be none of the hesitations and fumbling that had characterized so many intercolonial arrangements in the past; the process of joining the colonies together was to be short, swift, and sure.

The Quebec Resolutions were first published on November 8, 1864, little more than a week after the end of the Conference, in *Le Journal de Québec*. Two days later, from another source, they appeared in the Charlottetown *Monitor*.[7] From these two sources they soon spread over all five eastern provinces.[8] Almost every paper published them, in full more often than in part; even a paper as remote from the scene of events as the *Standard*, of Harbour Grace, Newfoundland, took space to print them.[9] They excited much comment. Information had been made public during both Conferences, but except for the brief semi-official report on the Charlottetown Conference, there had been nothing official until Cartier's speech in Montreal on October 29, and Brown's more revealing one in Toronto on November 3. Even these were no more than informative outlines. The battle for Confederation was thus begun long before the legislatures of the several provinces met, and its course was determined, at this critical stage, not by resolutions of legislatures, but by public opinion. In the Maritimes the newspapers, issue after issue, were filled with editorials, letters to the editor, and reports of meetings. Prince Edward Island was the most lively of all. The Saint John *Telegraph* said that the Island papers "come to us completely filled with Confederation. The little Island is determined to assert the truism that small people sometimes make the greatest fuss in the world."[10] But New Brunswick

Source: P.B. Waite, *The Life and Times of Confederation*, Robin Brass Studios, pp. 104–116. Reprinted with permission of the publisher.

543

papers were little different. Even in the small towns along the north shore of New Brunswick, Confederation became "the subject matter at the corner of the streets, and at 'a thousand and one firesides.'"[11] When the Newcastle Debating Club invited Peter Mitchell and the Attorney General, J.M. Johnson, to publicly discuss Confederation, Newcastle Temperance Hall was filled to overflowing. The crowds at the meetings in Charlottetown, Moncton, Saint John, Truro, and Halifax, testify how powerful—even explosive—an issue Confederation had become. This public discussion continued for many months to come, and crowded every other issue into insignificance.

The Quebec Resolutions, once published, had to be expounded and explained, to be clothed with institutional and political meaning. Tilley and Gray began this process in New Brunswick, a bare week after they had returned from Quebec, and shortly after the Quebec Resolutions had appeared in the Saint John papers. The first meeting, held in Saint John on November 17, was by all accounts not a success since neither Gray nor Tilley seemed to have the broad grasp of the subject necessary to give it coherence. Tilley in particular failed to give any general financial structure for Confederation or to indicate by what means the proposed central government could sustain its admittedly large commitments.[12] One of Tilley's characteristics—his capacity for understatement—showed here to his disadvantage. Tilley lacked the "extraordinary facility of statement which on such subjects distinguishes Mr. Galt. ..."[13]

It was Galt, in fact, who gave the best exposition of any of the delegates. He was the first Canadian minister to give a thoroughly comprehensive analysis of the financial and legal basis for Confederation. His speech at Sherbrooke on November 23 was given before 300 people and took over three hours. It was, despite its length, well received and became at once a textbook for the supporters of Confederation. Widely circulated in all of British North America, it became, as the Saint John *Telegraph* predicted it would, December 19, 1864, "a storehouse from which arms and ammunition may be drawn without limit to defend the holy cause of Confederation. [. . .]" Galt, never one to hide his light under a bushel, mailed off numerous copies of his speech to cohorts in the Maritimes. Tupper wrote, "many thanks for your speech—by far the ablest exposition of the Confederation scheme altho' a little too much from the Canadian point of view to suit this meridian." Whelan thanked Galt for several copies and for "the immense service you have done to the cause of Confederation. ..."[14] [Edward Whelan was a journalist and one of Prince Edward Island's delegates to the Quebec conference.]

The financial aspect of Galt's analysis is well known and it would be redundant to give it again.[15] But his legal and constitutional analysis was also sound and serves to introduce the British North American reaction to this interesting and complex subject. The proposal is, Galt said, "to go back to the fountainhead, from which all our Legislative powers were derived—the Imperial Parliament—and seek at their hands a measure. ..."[16] The sovereign authority of Westminster simplified wonderfully the task of uniting British North America. All that was necessary was an address to the Queen from each of the colonial legislatures, praying that an act be passed to unite them. There were no ratifying conventions, no elections to decide who should compose them, both of which had made the passing of the American constitution an uncertain, tortuous, even unscrupulous business. The British Parliament had merely to pass an act. Some were, indeed, disturbed by this sovereignty, "one and indivisible," from which all power flowed.[17] A considerable issue was to arise in 1866 in French Canada under this head; it was feared that changes would be silently introduced into an imperial act by delegates in London, against which there could be no recourse.[18]

Some Bleu newspapers recognized that imperial sovereignty could usefully define the powers of the central and local governments and be the guarantor of the constitutional boundaries so established. Such was the clear-headed and sensible view of *Le Courier de St. Hyacinthe,* October 28, 1864:

> Le fait est que les pouvoirs du gouvernement fédéral, comme ceux des corps locaux émaneront également du parlement impérial, qui seul a le droit de les déléguer. Chacun de ces gouvernements sera investi de pouvoirs absolus pour les questions de son ressort et sera également souverain dans sa sphère d'action. ...

Le Courrier du Canada of Quebec expressed similar, though less well-defined, views.

Imperial sovereignty certainly simplified constitutional changes, but even for those with a clear-cut theory of federation, the role of the new central government was rather novel. An intermediate government, between Great Britain and British colonies, so to speak, had never been created before. The London *Times* said that the proposed changes "violate the Constitution of the whole empire."[19] When responsible government had been established in 1848, Britain and the self-governing colonies divided the sphere of government between them. No systematic division was then attempted and Canada had found the omission convenient for pre-empting more for her share as time went on. Nevertheless, the division was not less real for being unsystematic. However, a third government might have seemed rather anomalous. The Montreal *True Witness*, a shrewd judge, said (July 8, 1864) that a central government in British North America would inevitably "encroach upon the legitimate functions either of the Imperial or of the Provincial Government."

Remarks such as this were rare. There were, perhaps, few critics acute enough to recognize the problem. A more convincing explanation is that British North Americans never thought of their central government in quite these terms. The new central government for the Dominion of Canada was simply an expansion of the government of the old Province of Canada. The central government would not be "interposed" between the imperial government and the provincial governments: it would be the provincial governments of old, rolled into one. The really new governments would be the "local" governments, called local and meant to be what they were called, half-municipal bodies, the remnants of the old provincial governments. Galt said as much in Sherbrooke.[20] No great difficulty was therefore anticipated with the new constitutional arrangements. The central government at Ottawa would take over most of the existing functions of the old provincial governments, leaving them with such limited powers and responsibilities that they could be appropriately called "local" rather than "provincial." "The theory will be," said the Montreal *Herald*, June 22, 1864, "that the Federal Government is the fountain of power. ..." The Montreal *True Witness* was afraid this would happen:

We oppose the proposed plan of *Colonial* Federation, since no matter in what terms it may be conceived, it proposes to saddle us with a sovereign central government which in our actual position must derive its authority, not from within, or from the States over which it is to bear rule, but *ab extra*, and from an Imperial Government with which our connection must cease ere many years be past; and to which, and to the plenitude of whose authority, the said central government would then inevitably succeed. Our position would then be that of a subject Province, not that of a State or independent member of a Confederation. (September 23, 1864.)

The French-Canadian Liberals (Rouges) unquestionably sympathized with such a view, but it is safe to say that the prospect intimidated only a few others.

There was thus a general division of opinion in British North America about the kind of government the new colonial union ought to be. Some wanted a federal system in the present-day meaning of the word "federal": that is, a clear recognition of what would now be called "co-ordinate sovereignty,"[21] with the provinces and the central government each having clearly defined powers and protected against encroachment by the other. But this was not a widely held view, nor was it characteristic of those men who created the Quebec Resolutions. The word "federal" was used to describe the Quebec plan, not because it defined the proposed relation between the central and the provincial governments, but because it was the word the public was most familiar with. "It is astonishing," noted the Kingston *British American*, "the looseness with which the term 'federal' is used in these discussions, indicating but an indifferent acquaintance with the actual meaning of the word. . . ."[22] The French Canadians and the Prince Edward Islanders insisted that the constitution be federal, and the constitution was certainly called federal; what it was really intended to be was another matter. The Montreal *Gazette* was not far off the mark when it suggested that the constitution would be a "legislative union with a constitutional recognition of a federal principle."[23] In Britain, Goldwin Smith amplified the point, early in 1865.

They intend to create not a federation, but a kingdom, and practically to extinguish the independent existence of the several provinces. ... They hope, no doubt, that the course of events will practically decide the ambiguity in favor of the incorporating union.[24]

The *Westminster Review* said much the same.[25] This was undoubtedly true of Macdonald, who wanted elbow room for the central power. Tupper of Nova Scotia frankly preferred legislative union. So did Galt. Brown, for the moment at least, was largely satisfied with "rep. by pop." Cartier, like Sir Etienne Taché, was confident, perhaps too confident, that French-Canadian privileges could be defended better by French-Canadian ministers in a central government than by a local legislature.

The members of the Canadian Coalition had originally agreed to address themselves to negotiations "for a confederation of all the British North American provinces."[26] Should this fail to be realized, then the federal principle would be applied to Canada alone. This seemed, on the face of it, simple enough. The question was, what was the federal principle? Macdonald said that under Confederation local matters would be committed to local bodies, and matters common to all to a general legislature. He then went on to say that the general legislature would be constituted on "the well understood principles of federal government." A revealing debate took place on this very point and it was for the government, particularly the French-Canadian members of it, rather embarrassing.[27] What it revealed was that most of the members of the Canadian Coalition government thought of federation largely in terms of the composition of the central legislature. In the lower house there would be "rep. by pop."; in the upper house there would be representation by territory, "equal" representation as the Canadians described it. What could be simpler? Of course local powers would be given to local bodies, but that was taken as a matter presenting little difficulty. The basis of the federal principle lay in the central legislature and in the balance between the House of Commons on the one hand and the Senate on the other. Of the constitution of the House of Commons there could be no doubt, and the constitution of the Senate became of critical importance.

The Charlottetown, Quebec, and London Conferences laboured hard on this very point. It was considered the heart of the system. At the same time, the local governments were apt to be regarded merely as conveniences for dissipating sectional prejudices or absorbing sectional difficulties. Consequently, the division of powers between the central and the local governments which bulks so large in any modern analysis of federation was not a particular difficulty. It never really became so, even when the Maritime delegates appeared on the scene. The general effect was unmistakable. It gave the central legislature and its institutions a preponderant role; it is also the answer to the puzzle of everyone's preoccupation with the Senate. The same problem had existed at Philadelphia seventy-seven years before, and the result was not dissimilar. The Senates of both Canada and the United States caused enormous difficulties, and the division of powers seemed relatively easy. One explanation is that government was neither so pervasive nor so complex in the nineteenth century as in the twentieth. Jurisdictional problems were anticipated by Dunkin and others, but the "difficulties of divided jurisdiction," to use the title of Professor Corry's work,[28] were not very apparent. That the division of powers is the heart of the federal system is a modern proposition, not a nineteenth-century one.

On this point the Quebec Resolutions themselves were enigmatic. No definition of federal was given; perhaps one was not intended. The formal symmetry of the American constitution was probably not even considered desirable. There is much in the argument that Confederation was a practical answer to a political difficulty. "Rarely indeed," said the London *Times*, November 24, 1864, "has constitutional legislation been conducted in so practical and unpretending a style." Macdonald himself has been described as a "natural empiricist in action."[29] Empiricism can be emotional as well as practical and the reference of British Americans to their British political inheritance was both. The Quebec Resolutions remained a working outline; their purpose was practical, their ideas empirical, and their solutions sometimes circumstantial. The Conference had not believed in putting its assumptions into ordered prose; these assumptions remained to be discovered, some implied within the seventy-two resolutions that were the blueprint of the system, others not.

Not without reason did the *Times* of London remark on December 13, 1864, that it was "exceedingly difficult" to construe the clauses on the division of powers. The *Edinburgh Review* said that "the distinction attempted to be drawn between general and local matters is in some respects scarcely traceable. [...]"[30] The Halifax *Morning Chronicle* referred to this question as the "binomial theorem of government."[31] The Montreal *True Witness*, January 13, 1865, cunningly observed that the unintelligibility of the resolutions on the division of powers was inevitable; the Quebec Conference was "attempting to 'define the powers' of a government intentionally armed with indefinite power." That was the matter in a nutshell.

Most British American newspapers fought shy of these thorny problems of political theory, and when analysis of the federal principle was attempted, many newspapers, and not a few politicians, simply bogged down. Ambrose Shea's explanations to the Newfoundland Assembly in February, 1865, were barely comprehensible.[32] The debate in the Canadian Assembly on the "well-understood principles of federal government" largely indicated that they were not well understood at all. Christopher Dunkin's brilliant and devastating analysis in the Canadian Confederation debates was one of the few successful attempts of its kind.[33] Numerous other examples can be given of the difficulty that Canadians and others had in interpreting the division of powers, and, in a more general sense, in understanding the federal principle at all. It was so often referred to in a manner thick with prejudice. The following is from the *Canadian Quarterly Review and Family Magazine* of April, 1865.

The federation and confederation system is the adoption of the principle that *each* member of the *"body politic"* shall, while apparently under the control of a supreme head [,] at the same time possess a separate and independent mind or controlling power, each capable of working, like a *false* rule in arithmetic to the injury of all the other rules or members of the "body politic." [...] A sound system of government requires no *checks* and *guarantees*, for its head is supreme; so all true principles possess internal evidence to prove that they are sound, *immutable* and *ultimate*.

To many sovereignty must reside somewhere and it ought to be at the centre where it belonged. It could be said of the Maritime provinces that their traditions of responsible government made their prejudice against the federal system understandable, but this explanation is less satisfactory for Canada.

Canadians had been familiar with forms of double legislation, with "the Federal principle recognized in the Union Act [of 1840]," as Galt put it.[34] The extension of these devices had grown with the years; by 1864 it had gone so far that the province of Canada was ready to separate into its two halves. Certainly federation had been thought of before as a solution for Canadian difficulties. But after four years of civil war in the United States, fought, it would appear, because of the federal principle, the principle itself was suspect. Indeed the most conspicuous single feature of British North American discussion of Confederation was the prevalent fear of what might now be considered its basic principle. There were exceptions and important ones, particularly the French Canadians, but many Canadians, including a preponderant majority of the English, found the federal principle a wind which, once sown, would reap the whirlwind of civil strife. As the Mount Forest *Examiner* put it,

... will the application of the federal principle heal the sectional difficulties under which we labor? On this point we may refer to the experience of our neighbours across the lines, where under the fostering care of this same "Federal principle," the sectional difficulty has grown, in one generation, to proportions so gigantic as to astonish the world by the "irrepressible conflict" waged in its interest.[35]

Or the Ottawa *Union*, September 8, 1864,

It is not a little singular ... how the federation idea should be taken up in British America at the very time that war, ruin, and demoralization are its effects in the American republic. ... A war of secession in the future ... must flow from copying the errors in statesmanship of our republican neighbours.

The Hamilton *City Enterprise*, October 22, 1864, though more optimistic, was entirely characteristic:

We do not say nor do we wish to believe the popular cry of today that the federation of the Provinces will bring trouble upon

548

us if consummated. We would rather trust that our case will prove an exception to the many instances ...

The general proposition was, appropriately, stated by the *Halifax Citizen*, November 19, 1864, "a sectional legislature under a general congress is only a nursery of sectional feeling, a fruitful factory for local jealousies, grievances and deadlocks to progress." Federation was like a drug: efficacious it might be, in small quantities for relieving the pain of the patient, but it was dangerous when used indiscriminately. This quantitative view of federation was a significant feature of Canadian discussion of the subject. "Canadians and Acadians alike will infuse as little of the federal principle into their union ... as will suffice to meet the absolute necessities of the case." Thus the Montreal *Gazette* on August 24. The *Globe*, October 15, was not dissimilar: "Federation is, in a large degrees, but an extension of our political system, and is sustained by precisely the same reasoning as are municipal institutions." This last was too much for the Montreal *True Witness*, and on October 28 it read both papers a lesson in political theory. Federation was not a quantity. It was not analogous to municipal institutions. It differed from a legislative union "not in degree but in kind." There was a "formal and essential difference" between legislative and federal union.

This was a lesson that few British North American newspapers and politicians learned, and their ignorance was indisputably part of their conception of Confederation. With some significant exceptions, they did not believe that federation meant the fundamental recognition of the sovereignty of both central and local governments. They would have regarded with suspicion a principle that would establish such governments in a way that would make each "coordinate and independent."[36] If that was the federal principle, they did not want it. Most, however, never fully understood the principle that they were opposing.

It is worth noting a popular and perhaps influential pamphlet published between the Charlottetown and Quebec Conferences, called *A Northern Kingdom*.[37] It was one of many published in 1864, and afterward, on Confederation, part of a considerable body of literature whose uneven merits still remain to be assessed. *A Northern Kingdom* summed

up in eighteen pages much of the current wisdom of British North Americans. Its views on federation were repeated again and again.

Federation! Have we not seen enough of federations with their cumbrous machinery of government, well enough in fair weather, but breaking up with the least strain—with treble taxation—with staffs of state functionaries, and of supreme functionaries, and with harassing disputes of various jurisdictions? Shall we not draw wisdom from the errors of others? Must we steer our bark on that rock on which the neighbouring magnificent union has split? . . . The main problems of government have been solved for us. The problem of a federal union has been worked out—a failure. The problem of a Legislative union has been worked out—a success.[38]

The ministerial paper in Quebec, the *Morning Chronicle*, published this extract as the leading editorial, on October 17, while the Quebec Conference was sitting. The Saint John *Evening Globe*, which was to become the foremost advocate of legislative union in New Brunswick, cited it as well on September 26. The pamphlet was quoted and commented upon by many newspapers, and probably achieved a wider currency than any other published at the time.[39] That it did so was as much a tribute to its views as to the succinctness with which they were expressed.

Canadian Confederation was a native creation. There was no intention of imitating the United States. On the contrary, in legislative union, many believed, lay the unequivocal, sovereign design of political excellence. A compromise with the realities of British American political circumstances was necessary, but it was not to be allowed to weaken the structure of the whole. Federation was essential, but it was federation in a unique, and to some at the present time a strange and twisted, form embodied not so much in the relation between the general and the local governments as in that between the House of Commons and the Senate. The great compromise between representation by areas and by population that lay at the heart of the American Congress was understood to be the basis of the federal principle and so accepted; but even here the Senate of Canada was not intended to be similar to its American counterpart. The Canadian Senate was peculiar in its use of regional, as opposed to state, representation. It is conspicuous that no attempts were made in the Quebec Conference, and few outside to develop the American view. Thus, while it is fair to say that the federal principle in its application to the central legislature reflected the American example, it is also probable that American ideas did not, in any sense more specific than this, determine the character of Confederation. The immediate character of Confederation was determined by British North American political experience and political traditions. And it may well be asked if Macdonald did not suspect that the principle of cabinet government might weaken fatally the Senate in its federal capacity, and thus its principal *raison d'être*. Christopher Dunkin was to suggest that the federalization of the Cabinet was inevitable. It is impossible to believe that Macdonald, and perhaps others, were not shrewd enough to see the gist of this point: that a responsible Cabinet would suck in, with silent, inexorable, vertiginous force, the whole regional character of the Senate and with it all the strength that lay in the Senate's regional identities. In circumstances such as these, the question of whether Confederation really was a federation or not was perhaps irrelevant. The French Bleus thought it was, but for a powerful majority of others confederation was an attempt to put aside the insidious federal contrivances that had grown up within the Union of Canada, to relegate the questions that had caused them to the care of subordinate, local legislatures, and to establish at Ottawa a strong, cohesive, sovereign, central government.

NOTES

1. Shanly Papers, Tilley to Shanly, Dec. 20, 1864. Cf. Lord Monck, who opened the Canadian parliament in January, 1865 with the hope that it would be the last Canadian provincial parliament ever to assemble. (Monck Papers, Monck to his son, Henry, Jan. 20, 1865.) Cf. also *Sarnia Observer*, June 28, 1867: "in 1864 the universal expectation of the country was that the Federation, either of all the Provinces together, or of the two Canadas together . . . would be carried in about a year from 1864. . . ."

2. P. B. Waite, "A Chapter in the History of the Intercolonial Railway, 1864," *Canadian Historical Review,* XXXII, 4 (Dec. 1951), 356–69.

3. Note the following from the independent *London* [C.W.] *Evening Advertiser*, Jan. 28, 1865: "It is thought desirable, too, that the subject should pass the several Provincial legislatures in time to lay it before the Imperial Parliament during the ensuing summer, and that all may be prepared for a general election by the end of the year . . . ."

4. Nova Scotia, Lieutenant Governor, Despatches Received, Cardwell to MacDonnell, Dec. 8, 1864. This dispatch had a curious fate. MacDonnell had part of the dispatch (including the quotation above) withdrawn from the regular series and made a Separate. The reason seems to have been that Cardwell's answers to MacDonnell's allegations of personal motives on the part of Tupper and others could hardly fail to be embarrassing if published.

5. Halifax *Morning Chronicle*, Feb. 4, 1865.

6. MacDonnell to Monck, Jan. 9, 1865 (confidential), enclosure in C.O. 42, Monck to Cardwell, Jan. 20, 1865 (confidential).

7. The source of the *Monitor's* information was almost certainly Edward Palmer. W. M. Whitelaw, *The Maritimes and Canada before Confederation* (Toronto, 1934), 265 analyses the differences in the documents printed in Canada and the Maritimes.

8. Halifax Citizen, Nov. 17, 1864; Chatham Gleaner, Nov. 19, 1864; Newfoundland Express, Newfoundlander, St. John's Daily News, Dec. 1, 1864.

9. Harbour Grace *Standard*, Dec. 14, 1864.

10. Saint John *Weekly Telegraph,* Dec. 14, 1864.

11. *Ibid.,* Jan. 11, 1865, letter from "Veni, Vidi," Dec. 31, 1864, from Miramichi.

12. Saint John *Morning Telegraph*, Nov. 19, 1864. See also *infra,* 236.

13. Montreal *Gazette*, Oct. 28, 1864.

14. Tupper to Galt, Dec. 13, 1864; Whelan to Galt, Dec. 17, 1864, in W. G. Ormsby, "Letters to Galt Concerning the Maritime Provinces and Confederation," *Canadian Historical Review*, XXXIV, 2 (June, 1953), 167–8.

15. R. G. Trotter quotes Galt's tables fully in his *Canadian Federation* (Toronto, 1924), 120–2. D. G. Creighton's "British North America at Confederation," an Appendix to the Rowell-Sirois Report uses Galt's work with discernment.

16. Galt's Sherbrooke speech was widely printed. The Toronto *Globe* published it in 12 columns of fine print, Nov. 28, 1864. Extensive extracts appeared in the Saint John *Morning Telegraph*, Dec. 5; Halifax *Morning Chronicle*, Dec. 1; Charlottetown *Examiner*, Dec. 12; St. John's *Courier*, Dec. 21, 1864, to give a few examples. Galt published it himself as *Speech on the Proposed Union of the*

British American Provinces (Montreal, 1864). The above quotation is from page 8 of this edition.

17. *Montreal Herald*, Jan. 18, 1867. E. G. Penny, the editor, published his views in a pamphlet, *The Proposed British North American Confederation: Why It Should Not Be Imposed upon the Colonies by Imperial Legislation* (Montreal, 1867).

18. *Infra,* 276–7.

19. London *Times*, July 21, 1864. Despite these remarks the *Times*, by the end of 1864, was a strong supporter of Confederation.

20. Galt, *Speech on the Proposed Union*, 15.

21. K. C. Wheare, *Federal Government* (London, 1953), 11.

22. Kingston *Daily British American*, Dec. 19, 1864.

23. Montreal *Gazette*, Sept. 9, 1864. Cf. Monck's remark: "So far from the word 'Federal' being an apt designation . . . its general meaning conveys an idea the direct contrary of . . . the intent of the Quebec plan." Monck to Cardwell, Sept. 7, 1866 (confidential), in W. M. Whitelaw, "Lord Monck and the Canadian Constitution," *Canadian Historical Review*, XXI, 3 (Sept., 1940), 301.

24. Goldwin Smith, "The Proposed Constitution for British North America," *MacMillan's Magazine*, March, 1865, 408.

25. "The Canadian Confederacy," *Westminster Review*, April, 1865, 259: "It is impossible to mistake the direction in which these [centralizing] provisions point, and they are calculated to raise the question whether there exists the most perfect conformity and good faith between the semblance and the essence of the yielding to local interests in the name of federation."

26. Toronto *Globe*, June 23, 1864. Also J. Pope, *Memoirs of the Right Honourable Sir John Alexander Macdonald* (Toronto, [1930]), Appendix V.

27. This debate is discussed briefly in P. B. Waite, "The Quebec Resolutions and *Le Courrier du Canada*, 1864–1865," *Canadian Historical Review*, XL, 4 (Dec., 1959), 296.

28. J. Corry, "Difficulties of Divided Jurisdiction," Appendix to Rowell-Sirois Report, 1940.

29. T. W. L. Macdermot, "The Political Ideas of John A. Macdonald," *Canadian Historical Review*, XIV, 3 (Sept., 1933), 264

30. "The British American Federation," *Edinburgh Review*, Jan., 1865, 191.

31. Halifax *Morning Chronicle*, Oct. 16, 1865. Discussed *infra*, 218.

32. St. John's *Newfoundlander*, March 16, 1865. See *infra*, chapter xi.

33. *Infra,* 153–4.

34. Galt, *Speech on the Proposed Union*, 4.

35. Mount Forest *Examiner* (Conservative) quoted in the Toronto *Leader*, July 2, 1864.

36. Wheare, Federal Government, 11.

37. It was written by S. E. Dawson of Dawson & Co., Montreal, publishers. Published anonymously by "A Colonist" (Montreal, Dawson, 1864). S. E. Dawson (1833–1916) was the son of the Rev. Benajmin Dawson, born in Halifax and who came to Montreal with his father in 1847. S. E. Dawson later became owner of the firm.

38. *Ibid.,* 13.

39. E.g., Charlottetown *Examiner,* Oct. 3, 1864; Halifax *Acadian Recorder* Sept. 28, 1864; Saint John *New Brunswick Courier*, Oct. 1, 1864.

■ Article 3: Nation and Crown

Christopher Moore

Thomas D'Arcy McGee, who turned forty in 1865, was a small, ugly, charming Irish-Catholic journalist with a complicated past. He had been an Irish rebel who recanted, a patriotic American who grew disillusioned, an anti-clerical who had made his peace with the Catholic Church, a reformer who had gone over to John A. Macdonald, and a teetotaller given to alcoholic binges. (Macdonald once instructed him he would have to quit drinking; the cabinet did not have room for two drunks.) In 1857 he had settled in Montreal, launched a newspaper, and got himself into the legislature. His constituents, Montreal's Irish, were a narrow and not always secure power base, but McGee was funny, quick-witted, and a natural orator. He soon became popular in the House, and a prominent, more than a powerful, figure in Canadian affairs.

McGee was barely off the train from Boston in 1857 when he began advocating federal union, westward expansion, and the nurturing of a national literature for Canada. "A new nationality" became his platform and slogan. McGee had good reason to seek a nation. He despaired of Ireland, was an alien in Britain, and resented American intolerance of foreigners and Catholics. He was also a journalist, but unlike George Brown, the millionaire publisher of the *Globe*, or Edward Whelan, who was at least solidly established in his Charlottetown newspaper, McGee always scrambled to make a living. The national vision became a valuable stock in trade.

McGee travelled widely in British North America. With help from railway barons who had their own reasons to encourage such visions, he organized intercolonial good-will trips for politicians and public figures. By 1865, he had been to Atlantic Canada seven or eight times, when many Canadians were still asking him, "What kind of people are they?" Though he had never gone west of Canada West, McGee even outlined a plan for a separate province to be set aside for the native nations on the plains of the far North-West. He had begun to imagine a new country where none existed.

It was a vision upon which he launched many articles and speeches. Amid the tension of the confederation debate in the Parliament of the united Canadas early in 1865, McGee was the first speaker to make the House laugh. It was a feat he achieved consistently in that speech and throughout his public career, but he was just as adept at rolling, patriotic oratory. "I see in the not remote distance," he declared in 1860, when there was no serious prospect of British North American union, "one great nationality bound, like the shield of Achilles, by the blue rim of ocean. ... I see within the ground of that shield the peaks of the western mountains and the crests of the eastern waves." In the confederation debate, he celebrated the beauty of the Canadian land, rejoiced that confederation would elevate "the provincial mind" to nobler contests, and welcomed the advent of "a new and vigorous nationality."[1]

McGee's passionate Canadianism—"not French-Canadian, not British-Canadian, not Irish-Canadian; patriotism rejects the prefix"—disquieted listeners for whom the prefixes defined patriotism. But "a new nationality" had gone into the language. McGee modestly disclaimed sole credit for the phrase (It's always the same, he told the House: "Two people hit upon the same thought, but Shakespeare made use of it first"), but it popped up in many celebratory speeches during the 1860s. Anticipation of a "new nationality" was even written into the Throne Speech that Governor General Lord Monck read to the legislature at Quebec on the eve of the great debate on the Quebec resolutions—inspiring the *rouges*' clever amendment, proclaiming that they were too loyal to want such a thing.

Bleu supporters of the coalition defeated Dorion's amendment, and their unanimity was an early indication that they would not be swayed by attacks on the Quebec resolutions, but they did not much like doing it. McGee defended his phrase, and Macdonald made a point of using "the expression which was sneered at the other evening." But George-Étienne Cartier was careful to say that confederation would create "a political nationality," and he went on to stress that "the idea of unity of races was utopian—it was impossible. Distinctions of this kind would always appear. [. . .] In our own federation we should have Catholic and Protestant, French, English, Irish and Scotch, and each by his efforts and his success would increase the prosperity and glory of the new confederacy."[2]

Cartier was glad to escape from awkward questions of nationality to the safer ground of monarchy. He celebrated the benefits of monarchical rule and French Canada's love of monarchy. "If they had their institutions, their language, and their religion intact today, it was precisely because of their adherence to the British Crown," he said. Confederation had been made, he said, "with a view of perpetuating the monarchical element. [. . .] the monarchical principle would form the leading feature." In the Nova Scotia legislature, Charles Tupper said something similar, covering his declaration that the colonies should "advance to a more national position" with assurances that confederation would bind the new nation to the British Crown "by a more indissoluble tie than ever before existed."[3]

McGee, for all his celebration of the Canadian land and the Canadian nationality, took the same stand. "We need in these provinces, we can bear, a large infusion of authority," he said, and he wound up his speech in direct address to Queen Victoria: "Whatsoever charter, in the wisdom of Your Majesty and of your Parliament you give us, we shall loyally obey and fulfill it as long as it is the pleasure of Your Majesty and your successors to maintain the connection between Great Britain and these colonies." Such frankly deferential talk was as common in confederation speeches as talk of the new nationality.[4]

It too had its pitfalls. Confronted with it, Dorion smoothly shifted his line of attack to declare that confederation's advocates were reactionary tories, who "think the hands of the Crown should be strengthened and the influence of the people, if possible, diminished, and this constitution is a specimen of their handiwork." A Halifax newspaper put the same thought more vividly after the Charlottetown conference. When the delegates let their secrets out of the bag, said the *Acadian Recorder*, their constitution would prove to be "a real sleek constitutional, monarchical, unrepublican, aristocratic cat."[5]

This view of confederation—something imposed on cringing colonial Canadians by the reactionary local agents of Imperial dictate—became part of the late-twentieth-century consensus, much more than the confederation-makers' talk of a new nationality. The political scientist Peter Russell opened his survey of Canadian constitutional history, *Constitutional*

Odyssey, by quoting a piously deferential Canadian declaration that confederation would "not profess to be derived from the people but would be the constitution provided by the imperial parliament." Taking the statement at face value, Russell identified the 1867 constitution as an Imperial and monarchical imposition. It could not be considered a legitimate beginning for a sovereign community, Russell concluded. Like many theorists and politicians, he declared this failing made the work of the original constitution-makers irrelevant, deserving of the neglect lavished upon it.[6]

Walter Bagehot, who sometimes enjoyed playing the plain journalist taking the mickey out of rarefied theorists, might have enjoyed seizing on lines like these. In parliamentary government, Bagehot had insisted, monarchy was always part of the "dignified," that is, ceremonial side of the constitution. Beneath the trappings of monarchy and aristocracy, which could mislead even the wisest scholars, political power in mid-nineteenth-century Britain, and even more in British North America, was securely in the hands of the representatives of the people. The confederation-makers knew that worshipful addresses to Victoria lent dignity to their business, but they also knew power lay elsewhere. Britain and British North America were disguised republics—in disguise certainly, but certainly republics, if republic meant a government derived from the people.

Bagehot understood as soon as he looked at the Quebec resolutions that the Senate and the governor general were going to be largely powerless in the new Canadian confederation. Dignified for ceremonial purposes they might be, but real power would rest securely in a Canadian House of Commons, elected to represent the Canadian people on a franchise as wide as any then existing in the world. The role of the monarchy was even more illusory. Bagehot did not take seriously the confederation-makers' florid assertions of loyalty and devotion.

In *The English Constitution*, Bagehot had argued that, although the monarchy was integral to British society and tradition, it was not essential to parliamentary government itself. In his confederation editorials, which welcomed the rise of an independent nationality in Canada, he doubted whether Canada needed a monarchy at all. He even suggested that the confederation-makers were not entirely sincere in proposing one. "We are not quite certain this extra

552

and, so to speak, ostentatious display of loyalty was not intended to remove objections which might have been entertained at home," he said of the monarchical clauses of the Quebec resolutions.[7]

Bagehot was wrong to suspect the confederation-makers were insincere about the monarchy. But he would certainly have been right to mock the idea that confederation had been made by Imperial dictate. As late as 1841, Britain had imposed a made-in-London constitution on the mostly unwilling colonists of Upper and Lower Canada. But in 1862, with responsible government firmly established, the colonial minister informed the colonies that, if they worked out a plan of union, Parliament would pass it. When the colonies took up the offer in 1864, the constitution that emerged was indeed what McGee called it: "a scheme not suggested by others, or imposed upon us, but one the work of ourselves, the creation of our intellect and of our own free, unbiased, and untrammelled will." By "us," he meant the legislatures representing the people of British North America.[8]

The confederation deal hammered out by the British North Americans in conference had appalled most of the British colonial officials involved with it. Lacking parliamentary experience, lieutenant-governors like Gordon of New Brunswick and MacDonell of Nova Scotia never fully grasped the compromises that had produced the Quebec resolutions. When the Colonial Office requested clause-by-clause comments on the resolutions, they responded with contemptuous disapproval, demanding an assertion of central power on virtually every point. Officials in London were frequently just as obtuse about the political realities that made federal union a necessity. Expecting deference, not direction, from colonials, they largely ignored the elaborate division of powers worked out in the Quebec resolutions when they began to draft a text for the British North America bill.[9]

Fortunately, British politicians were more realistic. Colonial Office functionaries could still imagine they were administering an empire in North America, but British politicians understood that trying to intervene in Canadian domestic politics meant responsibility without power. Even on a constitutional measure that required action by the British Parliament, they avoided any policy commitment that was not endorsed by the colonial legislatures themselves. The British government formally accepted the

Quebec plan for confederation, not merely as advice, but as "the deliberate judgment of those best qualified to decide upon the subject." Bagehot approved. "It is not, that we know of, the duty of Parliament to see that its colonial allies choose constitutions such as Englishmen approve," he said of the Quebec resolutions (though in this case, he did approve and thought Parliament also would).[10]

When Britain's Liberal government collapsed in mid-1866, the outgoing colonial minister, Edward Cardwell, left two questions for his successor, First, could they draft a confederation bill that would get through Parliament quietly, without partisan division? More important, if the staff could draft such a bill, would the provinces accept the text? "This is of cardinal importance," emphasized Cardwell about the second point. His Conservative successor, the thirty-five-year-old aristocrat Lord Carnarvon, agreed. Like his officials, he thought power in the new state ought to be centralized at Ottawa as much as possible. But he understood changes in that direction were possible "only with the acquiescence of the delegates . . . this must depend upon them." Both ministers overruled their advisers to endorse the colonials' choices. When Governor MacDonell of Nova Scotia proved intransigent, he was transferred to Hong Kong, glad to be off to a colony where he could actually wield power. Gordon of New Brunswick held his job only by shelving his doubts about confederation.[11]

George Brown, who went to Britain after the Quebec conference to sound out British reaction, wrote back to John A. Macdonald that the British government might criticize a few details of the seventy-two resolutions, but only for the sake of appearances. "I do not doubt that if we insist on it, they will put through the scheme just as we ask it." Canadian politicians of the 1860s may have been more polite than Pierre Trudeau, who suggested that, since his patriation package had been ratified in Canada, the British Parliament should hold its nose and pass it. But British and Canadian politicians agreed in the 1860s that the political relationship was much the same.[12]

The bill drafted early in 1867 sailed through the Lords and Commons. Britain had been looking forward to British North American union for years, and there was no party division over its terms. This proved fortunate, since the British government was about to collapse in bitter debates about expanding the franchise, and no contentious measure could

553

have passed. Lord Carnarvon, indeed, resigned from cabinet early in March 1867 to protest a bill that would give British men voting rights approaching those long enjoyed by men in British North America, but a new minister shepherded his confederation bill through to the final vote on March 12. Queen Victoria granted the royal assent to the British North America Act on March 29, 1867.

The confederation bill passed so speedily that some of its makers were discomfited. They noticed that even a measure concerning dog licences, introduced in the Commons after second reading of the British North America Act, provoked livelier debate. Macdonald later complained that confederation was treated like "a private bill uniting two or three English parishes," but he would not have tolerated changes to his bill, and British MPs were unlikely to waste time simply dignifying the passage of a bill when their only function was to approve it.[13]

[…] British leaders accepted that they would be obliged to protect British North America if it were threatened, but they were ready to consider granting Canada outright independence if the colonists insisted on it. The confederation-makers, however, were so absolutely sincere in desiring both a monarchy and continued ties to Britain that British observers were struck by the "excessive timidity" with which British North America advanced toward its inevitable independence. Political independence and the "new nationality" somehow lived in harmony with monarchical deference.

They did so because the politicians who negotiated the Quebec resolutions were determined to preserve the pomp and dignity of a constitution modelled on Britain's—and equally determined that having one would not fetter their actions. Bagehot's distinction between the dignified and efficient aspects of parliamentary government had not entered the vocabulary of politics in 1864, but the concept was no mystery to the seasoned parliamentarians who gathered at Quebec. Once they established that the efficient (that is, the power-wielding) parts of confederation were securely in parliamentary hands, they could see nothing but benefits in the dignified aspects Britain could provide in abundance. They were eager to remain loyal subjects of Queen Victoria's Empire, even when there was no pressure on them to remain, even when some in Britain thought they should be striking out on their own.

The confederation-makers of the 1860s had many reasons to avoid challenging the new nation's place in the old Empire, and also one hard, realistic, positive reason to embrace the Empire. In the 1860s, Canada needed Britain, needed it much more than Britain needed Canada. Canadian development depended on British capital, often supported by British government guarantees. Canadian exports depended on access to British markets, assisted by Britain's maternal attitude. Above all, Canada was a small nation sharing a large continent with a huge neighbour, and that meant it needed to shelter under both the military force and the diplomatic influence that only Britain could provide.

D'Arcy McGee caught this sense in his confederation speech. There had always been a desire among the Americans for expansion, he said, "and the inexorable law of democratic existence" in the United States seemed to require appeasing that desire. "They coveted Florida, and seized it; they coveted Louisiana, and purchased it; they coveted Texas, and stole it, and then they picked a quarrel with Mexico, which ended by their getting California. They sometimes pretend to despise these colonies as prizes beneath their ambition; but had we not had the strong arm of England over us, we should not now have had a separate existence." If you seek reasons for confederation under the Crown, he had said earlier, look to the embattled valleys of Virginia, "and you will find reasons as thick as blackberries."[14]

[…] If Canada had somehow been cut loose from Britain's Empire in 1867, it might indeed have survived. With good fortune and American restraint, it might even have achieved its westward expansion. Bagehot breezily concluded in 1867 that, if Canada became wholly independent, merely twenty years of growth would render it able to stand on its own feet, impervious to any American military threat. With or without British support, capital would have come, export markets would have been found. Canada would have developed foreign policies, armed forces, and other attributes of sovereignty merely at a more accelerated pace than it actually did.

But Canadian leaders had to contemplate those twenty years. No Canadian leader was willing to ask Britain to cut ties that would have been cut upon request. In the 1860s, Canada wanted the symbols of monarchy and Empire not least because it urgently needed the benefits of alliance with the most powerful state in the world. In 1864, when he was arguing that the colonies must united to defend themselves better, George-Étienne Cartier said it was a good question whether Britain would fight to help Canada, and a few years later a British statesman doubted whether the colonials would ever fight for Britain in a European war. In fact, the British did accept that, if Canada needed protection, national honour would compel a British response, even at the risk of a nightmare war with the United States. By 1918, sixty thousand Canadian war graves proved the commitment cut both ways, but in the 1860s, Canada needed that alliance far more than Britain did.

There was no debate about monarchy and Empire in the 1860s, because there were almost no voices arguing against them. Financially, economically, politically, culturally, militarily, London was the capital of the world in the mid-nineteenth century, even more than Washington and New York were in the late twentieth. Even Antoine-Aimé Dorion and George-Étienne Cartier could speak unselfconsciously of "home" when they spoke of England. Joseph Howe in his anti-confederate phase did his best to suggest Nova Scotians were choosing between "London under the dominion of John Bull" and "Ottawa under the dominion of Jack Frost," but the confederation-makers assiduously avoided forcing such a choice. Instead, Charles Tupper cited the Maritime provinces' chronic lack of influence in London to prove that "if these comparatively small countries are to have any future whatever in connection with the Crown of England, it must be found in a consolidation of all British North America."[15]

The alliance with Britain, so tangible, so "efficient," in the 1860s, had by the mid-twentieth century dwindled to nothing but dignified traditions. There had been a moment around 1900 when English-Canadian "Imperial federationists" aspired to share in running the British Empire, but Britain's long decline from Imperial might gradually took away most of the benefits the Imperial alliance had offered Canada in 1860 or 1900. Canada and Britain had clearly grown into foreign countries. Incorporating another country's monarchy in its constitution was vastly more anomalous in the 1990s than it had been in the 1860s.

As Walter Bagehot grasped, and the experience of many nations has shown, parliamentary democracy thrives without monarchy. In Canada, an elected governor general, holding the same limited powers as

the appointed one, would be more legitimate both in the exercise of those powers in a constitutional emergency and as a Canadian symbol around which the meaning of Canadian nationality could continue to be debated. The inability of modern constitutional negotiators to discuss the head of state surely indicated their inability to respond to Canada's actual situation. A constitutional process that imitated the 1860s by including representatives of all shades of political opinion and by giving them time to debate the issues would surely find that issue arising, among many others. A constitutional process that debated such issues would gain legitimacy whatever it decided.

The monarchy helped the confederation-makers to bypass potentially awkward issues of the "nationality" of the societies being joined by the British North America Act. Nationalism was one of the defining concepts of the nineteenth century, but allegiance to monarchy allowed McGee to boast of a nation even as Cartier and Langevin emphasized that confederation did not require a single tribal nationality. Allegiance, however, was sharply separated from the exercise of sovereign power. Before and after 1867, the confederation-makers consistently identified the legislatures elected by the people as the legitimate source of political authority. Cartier carefully called that "political nationality," and no threat to the French-Canadian nation he represented, but McGee could still frame the question of national allegiance in terms that resonated with men from whom "manliness" was always a vital touchstone. "For what do good men fight?" he asked the legislature. "When I hear our young men say as proudly 'our federation' or 'our country' or 'our kingdom,' as the young men of other countries do, speaking of their own, then I shall have less apprehension for the result of whatever trials the future may have in store for us."[16]

On the eve of July 1st, 1867, George Brown sat in the *Globe* offices in Toronto, back in his favourite role, writing for the newspaper. They were finishing the Dominion Day edition, and Brown wanted the front page for a long article. Maurice Careless captured the scene in his biography. He evoked Brown scribbling relentlessly through the hot night, sweating and gulping down pitchers of water and steadily handing out pages for the typesetters. He continued to write as the harassed night foreman warned that the mail train that would deliver the paper to eastern Ontario would soon be leaving. But the deadline

555

for the eastern mail was missed, and then for the western mail, too. Then "Mr. Brown, all the mails are lost," but Brown kept demanding a little more time. He ignored the pealing church bells at midnight, and he ignored the roar of artillery at dawn. Early in the morning, celebrating crowds gathered on King Street for a copy of the historic edition, and Brown was still writing. Finally, about seven in the morning, Brown declared, "There's the last of it." He handed over the final sheet of a nine-thousand-word history of confederation and went home to bed.[17]

Careless's evocation of the article's creation is wonderful, but Brown's article was really rather dull. Loaded down with a conventional recital of history back to John Cabot, and with reams of unlikely economic statistics, this account by one of the insiders said almost nothing about the way confederation was actually made. Even in its time, it must have been neglected in favour of the *Globe*'s descriptions of how Toronto would celebrate July first: the fireworks, the bonfires, the parades, the boat excursions, the roasting on Church Street of an immense ox purchased by public subscription from a Yorkville farmer, "the new farce 'Dominion Day'" opening at the Royal Lyceum, even the grand balloon ascension hoped for at Queen's Park ("if arrangements can be consummated with parties in New York"). Brown's only really vivid line in the whole historical article was his opening, in which he offered that stirring and ambiguous phrase, "WE hail the birthday of a new nationality."

Brown's true voice, the roar of the passionate politician, ran out more truly in the accompanying editorial. With the first federal election to be held later than summer, he warned with ungrammatical passion that "the only danger that threatens us is les the same men who have so long misgoverned us, should continue to misgovern us still."

These same men were just about to remove Brown from active politics. A year before, he had left the coalition government he had helped create in 1864. Brown had plunged back into partisan politics, intending to make his Ontario reformers the core of a pan-Canadian Liberal Party to sweep John A. Macdonald permanently from office. Macdonald, however, had already drawn many of Brown's natural allies into his own coalition. Brown was no longer exactly "the impossible man," but John A. Macdonald was making it impossible for him to hold on to political power. The Liberals would be badly defeated

in the summer elections of 1867, and Brown himself would lose to a Conservative, Thomas Gibbs, who drew many reform votes to the confederation candidate. Brown never sat in the Canadian House of Commons he had done so much to bring into being. He would only go to Ottawa when a later Liberal leader appointed him to the Senate, which Brown helped to ensure would never wield serious political power.

Brown was not too sorry to be out. He preferred journalism to politics and crusades over intrigues. If political success required honing the political adroitness that John A. Macdonald had, it was a price Brown was not willing, and probably unable, to pay.

When Brown and Macdonald were both dead, a wrangle continued among their partisans as to which was the true father of confederation. "Some inspired historians of Canada insist on referring to Macdonald as the father of confederation. He, who tried to prevent it until the lat ring of the bell. To George Brown and to George Brown alone belongs the title," insisted W.T.R. Preston, Oliver Mowat's indispensable "Hug-the-Machine," in his 1927 memoir *My General of Politicians and Politics.*"[18]

The "inspired" historian who provoked Preston to sarcasm may have been Macdonald's first biographer, Sir. Joseph Pope. As a ten-year-old, Pope had watched his father, William Henry Pope, organizing the Charlottetown conference. He grew up to be John A.'s personal secretary and keeper of the Macdonald flame. In *The Memoirs of John A. Macdonald*, which he published upon Macdonald's death, Pope dismissed Brown as a merely sectional leader. Smugly, he quoted Macdonald's patronizing view of his rival: "He deserves the credit of joining me; he and his party gave be that assistance in Parliament that enabled us to carry confederation."[19]

This battle to identify a single hero in the confederation wars was renewed by two Toronto history professors in the 1950s. Donald Creighton relentlessly championed John A. Macdonald ("The day was his, if it was anybody's," was Creighton's take on July 1, 1867) and Maurice Careless insisted there was also a place for George Brown, "the real initiator of confederation." Later, there were ghostly echoes of the search for a father in the debates of the 1980s that set "the Trudeau constitution" against "the Mulroney deal."

Concerning the 1860s, however, the quest for a father has always been misguided. The brilliance of the 1860s process was the way it permitted a George

Brown to make a fundamental contribution to constitution-making, even as it kept him from executive authority. The confederation process let Brown, and much-less-prominent delegates, and even ordinary representatives like those who changed their minds in Nova Scotia and New Brunswick, assert their aims and contribute their ideas without ever achieving unrivalled power. This was the success of a parliamentary process rather than a leader-driven, quasi-presidential one.

A clue to the success of the confederation-makers was inadvertently given in 1865 by one of their most incisive critics. Tearing the Quebec resolutions apart in the legislature at Quebec, Christopher Dunkin seized on some damaging statement made in New Brunswick by George Hatheway, "one of the gentlemen who took part in the negotiations."

"Mr. Hatheway was not here at all," shouted D'Arcy McGee across the floor.

Dunkin was unabashed. "I acknowledge I have not burdened by memory with an exact list of the thirty-three gentlemen who took part in the conference," he said.[20]

Far from being an insult to them or a comment on Canadians amnesiac attitude to history, the anonymity, even in their own time, of most of the makers of confederation suggests a critical ingredient of the constitutional achievement of the 1860s. The constitution-making of the 1860s drew in relatively minor figures from almost every political faction, several of whom dissented from the agreement their meetings reached. Their agreement was then reviewed by rather independent legislatures—four out of five of which at first declined to endorse it. The confederation-makers would have done well to have been more broadly representative, and their confederation might have been received more warmly had they seated even more political factions around the table. Still, their achievement should not be minimized.

In the 1990s, it was impossible for a regional or sectional representative, whether from the West, from Quebec, or from any class or ethnic bloc, to influence constitutional matters without becoming a first minister—or perhaps head of a separate state. Yet a constitution for the twenty-first century would probably require, not eleven first ministers, but several times the thirty-six delegates of the 1860s in order to match the degree of inclusiveness they achieved. The efficient secret of Canada's parliamentary government in the 1860s was its ability to incorporate in constitution-making even those it kept from power. It was an idea the 1860s were lucky to have and the 1990s desperately needed.

NOTES

1. Canada, *Parliamentary Debates on Confederation of the British North American Provinces* (Quebec: 1865), p. 125–46.
2. *Confederation Debates*, p. 60.
3. *Confederation Debates*, p. 59; Nova Scotia, *Debates and Proceedings of the House of Assembly 1865* (Halifax: 1865), p. 207–10.
4. *Confederation Debates*, p. 146.
5. Dorion: *Confederation Debates*, p. 255; *Acadian Recorder* (Halifax), September 12, 1864, quoted in Phillip Buckner, "The Maritimes and Confederation: A Reassessment," in *Canadian Historical Review* 61 #1 (March 1990), p. 25.
6. Peter Russell, *Constitutional Odyssey: Can Canadians Be a Sovereign People?* 2nd edition (Toronto: University of Toronto Press, 1993) p. 3.
7. *Economist*, Vol. 2, October 15, 1864, p. 1279.
8. *Confederation Debates,* p. 146.
9. G. P. Browne, ed., *Documents on Confederation of British North America* (Toronto: McClelland & Stewart, 1969), pp. 185–9, Observations and Notes on the Quebec Resolutions, July 24, 1866; pp. 247–62, initial draft of the BNA Act, January 23, 1867.
10. Browne, ed., *Documents*, p. 169; *Economist*, Vol. 22, November 26, 1864, p. 1455.
11. Browne, ed., *Documents*, p. 180.
12. Joseph Pope, *The Memoirs of Sir John A. Macdonald* (Toronto: Musson, 1927), p. 289.
13. The quotation and much of the detail here are from Ged Martin, *Britain and the Origins of Canadian Confederation, 1837–67* (Vancouver: UBC Press), pp. 284–90.
14. *Confederation Debates,* p. 132; Peter Waite, *The Life and Times of Confederation* (Toronto: University of Toronto Press, 1962), p. 28.
15. Waite, *Life and Times of Confederation*, p. 194; Nova Scotia *Debates* 1865, p. 211.
16. *Confederation Debates*, p. 145.
17. *Globe*, July 1, 1867; Careless, *Brown of the Globe* Vol. II, p. 251–53.
18. W.T.R. Preston, *My Generation of Politicians and Politics* (Toronto: Rose Publishing, 1917), p. 18.
19. Pope, *Memoirs of Sir John A. Macdonald*, p. 274.
20. *Confederation Debates*, p. 541.